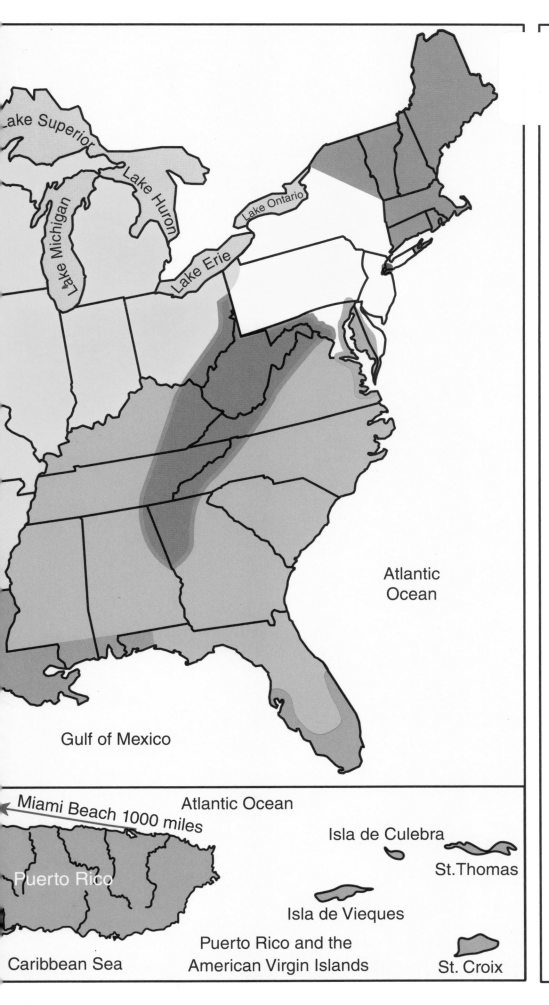

Lake Superior

Lake Huron

Lake Michigan

Lake Ontario

Lake Erie

Atlantic
Ocean

Gulf of Mexico

Miami Beach 1000 miles

Atlantic Ocean

Isla de Culebra

St. Thomas

Puerto Rico

Isla de Vieques

Puerto Rico and the
American Virgin Islands

St. Croix

Caribbean Sea

☐ Mid-Atlantic

☐ Chesapeake Bay Shore

☐ Louisiana

☐ Mexican Border

☐ Appalachian South

☐ Central Farmlands
   and Cities

☐ Western Ranchlands

☐ Rocky Mountains
   and Great Basin

☐ Anglo-Asian California

☐ Pacific Northwest

☐ Hawai'i

☐ South Florida,
   Puerto Rico,
   and Virgin Islands

☐ New York City

american regional cuisines
food culture and cooking

LOU SACKETT

DAVID HAYNES

PEARSON

Boston   Columbus   Indianapolis   New York   San Francisco   Upper Saddle River
Amsterdam   Cape Town   Dubai   London   Madrid   Milan   Munich   Paris   Montreal   Toronto
Delhi   Mexico City   São Paulo   Sydney   Hong Kong   Seoul   Singapore   Taipei   Tokyo

Editorial Director: Vernon Anthony
Senior Acquisitions Editor: William Lawrensen
Editorial Assistant: Lara Dimmick
Director of Marketing: David Gesell
Senior Marketing Manager: Thomas Hayward
Marketing Assistant: Les Roberts
Associate Managing Editor: Alexandrina Benedicto Wolf
Project Manager: Kris Roach
Senior Operations Supervisor: Pat Tonneman

Operations Specialist: Deidra Skahill
Senior Art Director: Diane Y. Ernsberger
Text and Cover Designer: Candace Rowley
Cover Art: Jim Smith
Media Editor: Michelle Churma
Full-Service Project Management: WordCraft, LLC
Composition: S4Carlisle Publishing Services
Printer/Binder: Courier/Kendallville
Cover Printer: Phoenix Color
Text Font: Avenir-Book

Credits and acknowledgments borrowed from other sources and reproduced, with permission, in this textbook appear on appropriate page within text.

Photography, unless otherwise indicated, is by Jim Smith/owned and copyrighted by Pearson.

Library of Congress Cataloging-in-Publication Data
Sackett, Lou.
    American regional cuisines : food culture and cooking / Lou Sackett, David Haynes.
      p. cm.
    ISBN-13: 978-0-13-110936-0
    ISBN-10: 0-13-110936-7
  1. Cooking, American.   2. Cooking—United States—History.   3. Food habits—United States—History.   4. Cookbooks.   I. Haynes, David-   II. Title.
    TX715.S1325 2012
    394.1'20973—dc23   2011016148

10 9 8 7 6 5 4 3 2 1
ISBN 10:   0-13-110936-7
ISBN 13: 978-0-13-110936-0

This book is dedicated to Ms. Chris Haynes, our beloved Muggy.

You planted the seeds:
When other kids were eating canned ravioli and TV dinners,
you fed your family tagliatelle Bolognese and cassoulet.

You fostered the dreams:
When others said no, you said—why not?

You remain a guiding force:
When the road gets rough or foggy,
your insight, discernment, and keen sense of justice show us the way.

And you never asked, When will it be done?

contents

Preface   xiii
Advice to Students   xxiii
About the Authors   xxvi

CHAPTER ONE
KEYS TO UNDERSTANDING REGIONAL CUISINES   2

Introduction to Food Culture and Cuisine   4
History Creates Cuisine   4

Elements of Food Culture and Cuisine   5
Ingredients   6
Cooking Methods   6
Attitudes about Food, Cooking, and Eating   7

The Making of a Melting Pot   8
Understanding Regional Cuisines   9
America's Fifteen Culinary Regions   9
Five Factors in the Development of a Regional Cuisine   10
Factor 1: The Characteristics of the Land   11
Factor 2: The Food Culture of the Indigenous People   15
Factor 3: The Food Culture of the First Settlers   18
Factor 4: Foods and Cooking Techniques Brought by Immigrants   19
Factor 5: Economic Viability   19

America's Microcuisines   20
Foreign Cuisines in America   20
America's National Cuisine   21
On the Road to Discovery   21
Study Questions   22

CHAPTER TWO
THE PLANTATION SOUTH   24

An Agricultural Paradise   27
Gentle Terrain and Rich Soil   27
A Mild and Moist Climate   28

Native Americans of the Plantation South   28
A Migratory Lifestyle   29
Hunting and Gathering   29
Native American Agriculture   30
Native Food Preservation   31
Plantation South Native American Cuisine   31

Colonial Cuisine of the Plantation South   36
English Settlement   36
Culinary Conservatives Gain a Liberal Outlook   37
Women in the Kitchen   37
Colonists Embrace Indigenous Foods   37
English Cooking Methods   38
English Ingredients   39
Hybrid Foods Complete Colonial Cuisine   40

Unwilling Settlers: The Plantation System and Slavery   41

Traditional Plantation South Cuisine   43
Dining in the Big House: Planter Cuisine   43
Slave Cooks Add African Sizzle and Spice   43
Southern Hospitality and Entertaining   44
Eating in the Quarters: Slave Cooking   44
Middle-Class Cooking   44

The Civil War and Beyond   45
Southern Barbeque   45
Southern Desserts   45

Contemporary Plantation South Cuisine   46
The Future of the Cuisine   46
The Lowcountry Microcuisine   46
The Soul Food Microcuisine   47
Plantation South Defining Dishes   47
Study Questions   51
Recipes of the Plantation South   52
Plantation South Regional Ingredients   80

CHAPTER THREE
NEW ENGLAND   84

A Challenging Land   87
Mountain, Forest, and Sea   87
A Climate of Extremes   87

New England Native Americans   88
New England Native Agriculture   89
Fishing, Hunting, and Foraging   89
Sweetness from Trees   89
A Lasting Native Legacy   90

Pilgrims and Puritans   91
   In Search of Religious Freedom   91
   Embracing the Native Diet   92
New England Colonial Cuisine   92
   Old World Foods and Dishes   92
   Preserved Foods   93
   Caribbean Imports   94
   Colonial Hybrids   94
   Conservative Culture Creates Conservative
   Foodways   95
Yankee Culture and Traditional New England
Cuisine   95
Foods from the Sea   96
   King Cod   96
   Cold-Water Lobster   97
   Quahogs and Steamers   97
   Oysters   97
   Scallops   97
   Mussels   98
   New England Chowder   98
   Clambake   98
Foods from the Land   98
   Maple Syrup and Maple Sugar   98
   Native Berries   98
   Fruits and Vegetables   99
   New England Dairy Products   99
   Smoked Meats   100
   New England Desserts   100
Dining Out in New England   100
   Boston Dining   100
   Contemporary New England Dining   101
Immigrant Cooking in New England   101
   Portuguese Cuisine in New England   101
   Italian-American Cuisine in New England   102
   Irish Influence   102
The Future of New England Cuisine   102
New England Defining Dishes   103
The Acadian-American Microcuisine   107
Study Questions   108
Recipes from New England   109
New England Regional Ingredients   138

CHAPTER FOUR
THE MID-ATLANTIC   146

Middle Ground   149
Topographical Diversity   149

Native Americans of the Mid-Atlantic   150
   Native American Agriculture and Cuisine   150
European Settlement   151
   The Dutch and the Swedes   151
   English Rule and Agricultural Economy   151
New York Food Products   152
New Jersey Farming and Fishing   152
Pennsylvania Agriculture   152
Traditional Mid-Atlantic Cuisine   153
   Mid-Atlantic Attitudes   153
English Cooking of the Mid-Atlantic   154
   Philadelphia Cuisine   154
   The Many Cuisines of Washington, D.C.   156
   Long Island Cuisine   156
   Upstate New York and Hudson Valley Cuisines   156
   New Jersey and Coastal Delaware Cuisines   156
Pennsylvania Dutch Cooking of the Mid-Atlantic   157
Industrial Food Production   157
Mid-Atlantic Cuisine Today and Tomorrow   157
Mid-Atlantic Defining Dishes   158
Study Questions   160
Recipes of the Mid-Atlantic   161
Mid-Atlantic Regional Ingredients   190

CHAPTER FIVE
THE CHESAPEAKE BAY SHORE   192

The Chesapeake Bay   195
   A Drowned River   195
   A Region Divided   195
   Plants and Animals of Bay and Shore   197
Native Americans of the Chesapeake Bay Shore   197
Foundations of Chesapeake Cuisine   198
   Indigenous Land Foods   198
   Indigenous Seafood   199
   Colonial Domesticates   201
Chesapeake Bay Culture and Cuisine   201
   Chesapeake Watermen   201
   Traditional Chesapeake Bay Shore Cooking   204
Restaurant Cuisine of the Chesapeake Bay Shore
Region   205
   Baltimore Cuisine   205
The Decline and Rebirth of the Bay   206
Chesapeake Cuisine in the 21st Century   206
Chesapeake Defining Dishes   207
Study Questions   209

Recipes of the Chesapeake Bay
Shore   210
Chesapeake Regional Ingredients   231

CHAPTER SIX
LOUISIANA   234

The Land the River Built   237
Louisiana Native Americans   238
French Settlement   239
Traditional Louisiana Cuisine   240
The French Foundation (Root #1)   240
Native American Influence (Root #3)   242
The African Element (Root #2)   243
Foods from the Plantation South (Root #3)   243
Caribbean Ingredients (Root #4)   244
German Settlers (Root #7)   244
Spanish Rule (Root #6)   245
American Louisiana (Root #3)   245
Italian Immigrants (Root #5)   246
Creole Cuisine   247
Sophisticated City Cuisine   247
Gumbo   248
Étouffée, Courtbouillon, Creole, and
Piquante   250
Red Beans 'n' Rice   250
Creole Restaurants   250
Cajun Cuisine   250
Country Cooking   252
Dishes That "Stretch"   252
Flavor-Building Techniques   252
Cajun Charcuterie   252
Eatin' Swamp Critters   253
Cajun Restaurants   253
Characteristics of Louisiana
Cuisine   253
Complex Cooking   253
Individualism   253
Showcasing Louisiana Seafood   254
New Orleans Food Culture and Cuisine   254
Mardi Gras   255
Katrina and Rita   255
The Macondo Blowout   256
The Future of Louisiana Cuisine   256
Louisiana Defining Dishes   257
Study Questions   262
Recipes of Louisiana   263
Louisiana Regional Ingredients   296

CHAPTER SEVEN
THE MEXICAN BORDER   300

American Southwestern Cuisine   303
The Southwestern High Desert   303
Native Americans of the Southwest   304
Spanish/Mexican Colonial Cuisine   309
Traditional Southwestern Cuisine   312
Contemporary Southwestern Cuisine   314
Mexican-American Cuisine   315
Mexican-American Convenience Foods   316
Mexican-American Restaurant Fare   317
Contemporary Mexican Border Cuisine   317
The Southwestern Native American
Microcuisine   318
Mexican Border Defining Dishes   319
Study Questions   323
Recipes of the Mexican Border   324
Mexican Border Regional Ingredients   351

CHAPTER EIGHT
THE APPALACHIAN SOUTH   358

In Search of Appalachia   361
Terrain Shapes Cuisine   361
Elderly Mountains   361
Mountain Climate   362
Native Hunting Grounds   362
The Cherokees   362
Into the Appalachians   364
America's First Pioneers   364
Pioneers from Great Britain   364
Pioneers from the American Colonies   365
Pioneers from the Rhineland   365
Appalachian Farming   365
Appalachian South Cuisine   366
Roots of Appalachian South Cuisine   367
Homegrown and Homemade   370
Railroads, Industry, and Exploitation   372
Bringing the Past into the Future   372
Appalachian South Defining Dishes   373
Study Questions   376
Recipes of the Appalachian South   377
Ingredients of the Appalachian South   402
Appalachian South Regional
Ingredients   402

CHAPTER NINE
THE CENTRAL FARMLANDS AND CITIES   404

A Flat and Fertile Land   407
  A Network of Lakes and Rivers   407
  Flatlands, Plains, and Plateau   408

Native Americans of Woodland and Plain   410
  Wild Rice   410
  Indigenous Fish and Game   411

European Influence   412

America Pushes West   412

Midwest Agriculture   412
  Pioneer Farmers   412
  Early Farming   413
  Technology Revolutionizes Farming   414
  Midwestern Grain   415
  Dairy and Cheese   415
  The Downside of Industrial Agriculture   415

Traditional Farmlands Cuisine   416
  Farmlands Favorite Foods   416
  Farmlands Baking   417
  Eastern European Influence   418

The Central Cities   418
  Meat Production and Packing   418
  Industrial Food Production   419
  City Cuisine   419

Future Cuisine of the Central Farmlands and Cities   421

Microcuisines of the Central Farmlands and Cities   422

Central Farmlands Defining Dishes   423

Study Questions   426

Recipes of the Central Farmlands and Cities   427

Central Farmlands Regional Ingredients   456

CHAPTER TEN
THE WESTERN AND CENTRAL RANCHLANDS   458

The Western Plateau   461
  Shortgrass Prairie   461
  A Climate of Extremes   461
  River Valley Oases   462
  Prairie Wildlife   462

Native Americans of the Western Plateau   462
  Plains Equestrians   463

Western Ranching   464
  Ranchers and Cattle Barons   465
  The Cattle Boom Goes Bust   466

Traditional Ranchlands Cooking   467
  Cooking with Provisions   467
  A Diet Based on Beef   468
  Cooking by Professionals   468
  Chuck Wagon Grub   468
  Sourdough   469
  The Mexican Connection   470
  German Influence   471
  Barbeque Goes West   471

Alternative and Specialty Ranching   471
  Alternative Ranching   472

Ranchlands Tourism   472

Contemporary Ranchlands Cuisine   472

Western and Central Ranchlands Defining Dishes   473

Study Questions   475

Recipes of the Western and Central Ranchlands   476

Western and Central Ranchlands Regional Ingredients   502

CHAPTER ELEVEN
THE ROCKY MOUNTAINS AND GREAT BASIN   504

The Rocky Mountains   507
  Mountain Climates and Varied Vegetation   507
  Mountain Wildlife   508

The Great Basin   508

Native Americans of the Mountains and Basin   509

Pioneer Cooking   509
  Cooking on the Wagon Trails   510
  Good Eating at the Forts   510

Early Rocky Mountain Cooking   511
  Transcontinental Travel and Transport   512
  International Dining in Denver   512

The Cuisine of Basque Immigrants   512
  Basque Flavors and Ingredients   513

Mormon Cuisine in the Great Basin   514

Traditional Rocky Mountain and Great Basin Cuisines   515
  Hunting Lodge Dining   515
  Casino Dining   515

Modern Rocky Mountain Cuisine   516

Rocky Mountains and Great Basin Defining Dishes   517

Study Questions   518

Recipes of the Rocky Mountains
and Great Basin   519

Rocky Mountains and Great Basin Regional
Ingredients   536

CHAPTER TWELVE
ANGLO-ASIAN CALIFORNIA   538

A Slice of the Pacific Rim   541
Wealth and Danger in the Ground   542
Climatic Diversity   543

California's Native Americans:
The Missing Multitude   545

Spanish and Mexican California   545

American California   547

Pioneer Cooking of the Gold Rush   547
Mining Camp Cooking   547
Gold Rush San Francisco   548

San Francisco Cuisine   549
San Francisco's Continental Cuisine   549
Good Eating in Ethnic Enclaves   549

California Agriculture   551
Watering the West   551
California Citrus   551
Horticultural Advances   552
California Agro-Industry   552
Specialty Produce   553

California Seafood   555

California Wines   556

Traditional California Cuisine   557
Asian Influence   557
Salad Eaters   558
Fruit First   559
Grilled Foods   559
Burgers, Car Culture, and the Drive-In   559
Dining in Glamorous Hollywood   560

The Birth of Modern Anglo-Asian California
Cuisine   560
Counterculture Ideas   560
World Cuisines Influences   562
Alice Waters and Chez Panisse   562
Celebrity Chef Wolfgang Puck   563
Three Pillars of Contemporary California Cuisine   563

Contemporary Anglo-Asian California Cuisine
Today   563

The Future of California Cuisine   564

The Chinese-American Microcuisine   564
Anglo-Asian California Defining Dishes   565
Study Questions   569
Recipes of Anglo-Asian California   570
Anglo-Asian California Regional Ingredients   594

CHAPTER THIRTEEN
THE PACIFIC NORTHWEST   600

A Land of Contrasts   603
Varied Topography   603
Climatic Diversity   604

Pacific Northwest Native Americans   605
Tribes of the Lower Pacific Northwest   606
Native American Legacy Foods   607
Native American Influence on Modern Northwest
Cuisine   609
Subarctic Native Americans and the Inuit   609

European and American Settlement   610
English Traders and Russian Farmers   610
American Pioneers   612

Traditional Cooking in the Pacific Northwest   612
First Settler Foods   612
Immigrants' Influence   613
Northern Gold Creates European-Style
Opulence   613
Food Production Anchors an Emerging Cuisine   614

Modern Pacific Northwest Cuisine   616
Pacific Northwest Wine Making   616
Chef-Driven Cuisine   616

Alaskan Cooking   617
Alaska's Farms and Fisheries   618
Traditional Alaskan Cooking   618

Pacific Northwest Defining Dishes   619

Study Questions   621

Recipes of the Pacific Northwest   622

Pacific Northwest Regional Ingredients   641

CHAPTER FOURTEEN
HAWAI'I   646

A Unique and Isolated Land   649

First Hawai'ians   650
Early Polynesians   651
First Hawai'ian Agriculture   652
First Hawai'ian Fishing   654
Seaweed   656

The Cuisine of the First Hawai'ians   656
  Pit Roasting in the Imu   656
  Roots and Tubers   657
  Preserved Foods   658
  Fresh Fish Dishes   658
  The *Lu'au*   658
  A Lasting Food Legacy   659
Europeans and Americans in Hawai'i   659
  Traders, Planters, and Ranchers   659
Traditional Hawai'ian Cuisine   661
Hawai'i's Immigrant Cuisines   662
  The Portuguese   662
  The Chinese   662
  The Japanese   663
  The Koreans   663
  The Filipinos   664
World War II and Postwar Development   664
Local Food   665
  The Plate Lunch   667
  Hawai'ian Barbeque   667
  Pupu   667
  Snack Foods   668
Hawai'i Regional Cuisine   668
The Future of Hawai'i's Cuisines   669
Hawai'i Cuisines Defining Dishes   671
Study Questions   674
Recipes of Hawai'i   675
Hawai'i Regional Ingredients   708

CHAPTER FIFTEEN
SOUTH FLORIDA
AND PUERTO RICO   718

A Balmy Peninsula   721
  A Tropical Climate   721
  Varied Topography   722
  Unusual Wildlife   723
South Florida Native Americans   723
  Foodways of the Four Original Tribes   723
  Foodways of the Seminoles   725
  A Limited Legacy   725
European Exploration and Settlement   726
  Keys Culture and Cuisine   726
American Settlement   727
  Florida Crackers   727
  Florida Citrus   728
Cubans in Florida   729

The Development of Modern South Florida   729
  Railroads Span the Peninsula   729
  Changing the Face of South Florida   730
  Ups and Downs in the 20th Century   731
Traditional South Florida Cuisine   732
Jamaican-American Cooking   734
  Jerk   734
New South Florida Cuisine   734
  The Mango Gang   734
  Characteristics of New South Florida Cuisine   735
The Future of South Florida's Cuisines   736
The Cuban-American Microcuisine   737
South Florida Defining Dishes   737
Puerto Rican Cuisine   739
  Roots of Puerto Rican Cuisine   740
  Characteristics of Puerto Rican Cuisine   741
  Puerto Rican Cooking on the Mainland   742
Puerto Rico Defining Dishes   742
Study Questions   744
Recipes of South Florida and Puerto Rico   745
South Florida and Puerto Rico Regional
Ingredients   780

CHAPTER SIXTEEN
NEW YORK CITY   786

Islands of Rock   789
Native Americans and Colonists   790
  Colonial Cooking   791
Delmonico's Sets the Standard   791
New York Restaurants of the Gilded Age   792
  The First French Invasion   792
  Lobster Palaces   792
  New York Steakhouses   792
  New York Seafood Houses   792
  New Restaurants for a New Century   793
Immigrants Fill the Melting Pot   794
  The Irish: Politics and Pubs   794
  The Germans: *Hofbraus* and *Rathskellers*   794
  The Italians: Produce and Pasta   795
  The Jews: Bagels and Deli   795
  The Chinese and Other Asians   796
  African-Americans: The Arts and Soul Food   796
  The Greeks: Coffee Shops and Diners   797
World Cuisines at the World's Fair   797
The Second French Invasion   797
The Four Seasons   798

Nouvelle Cuisine: The Third French Invasion 799

American Cooking in New York City 799

New York City Food Markets 801

Late-20th-Century Immigrants 802

New York Haute Ethnic 804

The New York City Melting Pot in the 21st Century 805

The Italian-American and Jewish-American Microcuisines 805

New York City Defining Dishes 807

Study Questions 810

Recipes of New York City 811

New York City Regional Ingredients 844

CHAPTER SEVENTEEN
AMERICA'S NATIONAL CUISINE

GLOSSARY 849

RECIPE INDEX 857

SUBJECT INDEX 877

preface

When you open this book, you begin a journey of the mind, in your imagination traveling both across space and through time. In these pages you'll traverse the breadth and length of America in search of authentic regional dishes and the ingredients and cooking methods used to create them. You'll also time-travel, going back into the past to understand the food history of America's culinary regions and to discover how cultural developments and political events shaped their cuisines. Along the way, you'll experience new and exciting flavors and acquire valuable technical skills.

■□■
OUR GOALS

American Regional Cuisines is written primarily **for students attending culinary schools** in the United States. Just as American studies has become an important field in academics, the topic of American cooking is now at the forefront of culinary arts education. Having mastered the basics of professional cooking, as an intermediate-level culinary student you can confidently progress to American cuisine, discovering its many facets through guided study of America's fifteen culinary regions. Learning the information presented in this book gives you a sound foundation of knowledge about America's regional cuisines that you can later refine and expand through independent study. Mastering this book's recipes affords you a basic repertoire of authentic American regional dishes that you'll use throughout your career.

For the chef instructor, *American Regional Cuisines* is designed as a powerful and versatile teaching tool that makes learning easy and fun. Using this book's many special pedagogical features, both the experienced culinary educator and the chef new to teaching will be able to effectively transmit essential information in theory classes and plan rewarding hands-on laboratory classes. Instructors managing production classes or teaching in student-run restaurants will find this book's professional recipe format expressly tailored for both catering and à la carte service.

These same features make *American Regional Cuisines* useful **for working chefs** cooking in restaurants and other foodservice operations. Today the American dining public understands and appreciates American cuisine as never before. Customers' growing level of sophistication challenges the chef to present an ever-changing repertoire of authentic dishes. *American Regional Cuisines* offers a wealth of restaurant-ready recipes, plus historical, cultural, and ingredient information that will help you create new dishes faithful to the spirit of each region.

Although it is a professional textbook, *American Regional Cuisines* has great appeal **for the amateur cooking enthusiast** who is searching for deeper understanding of America's culinary heritage and is eager to experience real American food. This book's lively text presents America's culinary history as a clear and easily readable story. Although written in the professional format, the recipes are thoroughly accessible and appropriate for the home kitchen.

The ultimate goal of *American Regional Cuisines* is helping chefs and cooks become fluent in the American regional cuisines of their choosing. Culinary fluency involves a variety of skills and attributes. Achieving fluency requires well-practiced mastery of specialized cooking methods and techniques particular to the region. It involves long familiarity with the region's ingredients. It requires deep understanding of the culture and customs of the region's people including, but not limited to, their attitudes about food and their culinary sensibilities and preferences. Once fluent in a regional cuisine, the chef or dedicated home cook is able to work freely within the parameters of the style, duplicating established dishes from memory and creating new dishes that are true to the region's sensibilities and traditions. For each of America's fifteen culinary regions, *American Regional Cuisines* provides a foundation of knowledge, skill, and taste recognition intended to start you on the path to further discovery.

■□■
ORGANIZATION

American Regional Cuisines is organized in a logical, linear progression: it begins with foundation material, then progresses through fifteen regional cuisine chapters presented roughly in order of settlement. To conclude your study, an overview of America's national cuisine is presented as a bonus chapter on the book's companion website.

■□■
THE FOUNDATION: KEYS TO UNDERSTANDING

Chapter 1, Keys to Understanding Regional Cuisines, is a food studies toolkit that contains instruments of understanding. After reading this chapter you'll be familiar with **fundamental food studies concepts** on which today's culinary analysts and food historians base their research. You'll know and be able to correctly use **food studies terminology** essential to understanding these concepts and expressing your ideas about them.

A most valuable tool you'll acquire is an evaluation device called the **five factors in the development of a regional cuisine**. Applying each of the five factors—the land, its indigenous inhabitants, first settlers, immigrants, and economic viability—to the regional cuisine you are studying enables you to understand its development from prehistory to modern times. The factors also provide a framework with which one region may be compared to another. Chapter 1 introduces the five factors and helps you understand how to use them.

■ □ ■

REGIONAL CHAPTERS

The identification of **fifteen American culinary regions** is the groundbreaking premise of *American Regional Cuisines*. This book identifies a regional cuisine using three essential criteria: geography, food culture, and defining dishes. Thus, we reject the old model based on geopolitical borders and culinary generalizations. The land, the people, and their cooking are the elements used to determine whether an area qualifies as having a discrete regional cuisine. For example, using these criteria, the American South—in most other texts covered as a single region—is divided into the Plantation South, the Appalachian South, the Chesapeake Bay Shore, Louisiana, and South Florida. Although these areas share many ingredients and cooking methods, each has strikingly different climate and topography, each is home to a culturally different population having its own particular history and foodways, and each produces markedly different dishes. Thus, each deserves independent recognition and study in its own right.

In *American Regional Cuisines,* each of America's fifteen culinary regions is discussed in its own comprehensive chapter. Regions are introduced in chronological order of culinary development, beginning with the Plantation South, which was the first permanently settled agricultural area to become part of the United States and, thus, is home to America's first regional cuisine. To ensure full understanding of indigenous and colonial cuisines, readers and instructors are advised to follow the table of contents at least through Chapter 4, The Mid-Atlantic. To experience the unfolding of America's food history as it occurred, we recommend following the general chapter order throughout your course of study. However, you can plan your culinary journey to suit your individual interests and class schedule, if desired omitting some regions and spending more time on others. Regional coverage concludes with Chapter 16, New York City, saving America's greatest ethnic melting pot for last.

The organization of regional chapters is based primarily on the **five factors** introduced above. Each regional chapter begins with the region's (1) **land characteristics** and resulting agricultural capabilities. Superior to minimal coverage in other texts, *American Regional Cuisines* emphasizes the (2) **Native American cuisine** of those regions in which indigenous foodways played a significant role. Analysis of hybrid (3) **first-settler cuisine** is supported by information on the Old World cuisine style and food imports brought to the Americas by each particular settler group. The impact of (4) **immigrant foodways** is emphasized. Finally, each chapter correlates the development of a mature regional cuisine with the achievement of (5) **economic viability**.

A number of American culinary regions are home to microcuisines, less prominent yet noteworthy cooking styles often similar to, but in crucial ways different from, the host region's cuisine. Unlike other texts, *American Regional Cuisines* **recognizes microcuisines**, which are discussed in special sections on the companion website.

After the text, each regional chapter lists the region's defining dishes, presented in convenient table format. Study questions help you assess your comprehension and retention of the chapter material. Recipes for appetizers, complete main dishes, and desserts follow. Finally, information on the region's signature ingredients appears in table format.

■ □ ■

AMERICA'S NATIONAL CUISINE

Your study of American regional cuisines would be incomplete if, at the end of the journey, you forgot to take a look at the big picture. Chapter 17, America's National Cuisine, appears on this book's companion website as a highly recommended conclusion to your American regional cuisine course. This chapter documents the rise of a pan-national cooking style that emerged in the late 1800s as a result of industrialization, and that continues evolving today. Unlike other texts, *American Regional Cuisines* recognizes the discrete nature of this national cuisine and makes clear the difference between it and the regional cooking styles that are the main focus of this book. Comparing **the evolution of America's national cuisine** to the development of our regional cuisines gives you a clear understanding of the difference between an artificially established and promoted cooking style and styles that developed organically.

■ □ ■

SPECIAL FEATURES

American Regional Cuisines abounds with special features that make it easy to read and study. Among them are distinctive learning tools developed exclusively for this book.

Differentiated Learning Objectives— Exclusive!

Each chapter of *American Regional Cuisines* begins with a list of **learning objectives** that alerts you to important concepts to understand and skills to master. Unique to this book, many of the learning objectives are linked to the **five factors** evaluation tool described above. This connection helps you correlate the concept to its cause and enables you to compare and contrast the concepts presented in one chapter with those in another. You're encouraged to keep the learning objectives in mind not only when reading and studying the chapter, but also when working on the recipes in the laboratory or production kitchen, or when practicing at home.

AFTER STUDYING THIS CHAPTER YOU SHOULD BE ABLE TO:

- describe the topography and climate of California (Factor 1) and explain how they affected the region's food production and cuisine
- explain why the contributions of California's first-settler group (Factor 3) rightfully belong to another American culinary region
- discuss the region's international second-settler group (Factor 4), identify the two main food cultures it comprises, and describe the culinary contributions of each
- list the major event that initiated the region's initial economic viability (Factor 5) and describe subsequent events that added to it
- describe traditional California cuisine and list its most important defining dishes
- describe contemporary California cuisine and list its primary elements
- discuss the history of Chinese-American cuisine and list its most important defining dishes
- identify and work with a variety of California ingredients and seasonings
- prepare authentic Anglo-Asian California cuisine dishes and Chinese-American dishes

---

Factor Icons—Exclusive!

Factor icons located next to corresponding text alert you to important information in the text that relates to one of the five factors. Factor icons are accompanied by a caption summarizing the text. In addition to alerting you to facts you should know, factor icons make it easier to find information when you need it.

---

consumption these squashes were boiled, steamed, and pit-baked. Maple syrup was the preferred seasoning for squash, a taste preference handed down to modern cooks. Today in most New England homes, a casserole of winter squash seasoned with maple syrup is a favored side dish and is indispensable on the Thanksgiving table.

FACTOR 2

Indigenous Three Sisters crops are foundation foods of the cuisine.

Factor icons highlight important information in text.

Website Information

For many topics we offer additional information for in-depth study on this book's companion website. Also, we provide additional regional recipes and basic recipes on the web. Whenever you see the magenta-colored type, you can access more information by going to www.pearsonhighered.com/Sackett.

---

deemed the land suitable only for grazing. However, under this arid land lies the **Ogallala Aquifer,** the nation's largest concentration of underground water (Figure 9.4). The presence of this important water resource explains why the land could eventually be farmed and, thus, why the western plateau is included in the Farmlands culinary region. Water from the aquifer made it possible to grow certain crops in a land that otherwise could not sustain agriculture. More information about the Ogallala Aquifer can be found on this book's companion website.

Magenta-colored type indicates more information on the website.

Key Terms

Knowing and correctly using culinary and food history terminology are essential to communicating about regional cuisines. Throughout the text, **key terms are indicated in boldface**. Key terms are also listed and defined in the **glossary**.

Food historians believe that the ancestors of American Southwestern pueblo tribes learned desert agriculture, including corn cultivation, from the ancient civilizations of central Mexico. The Aztecs, Mayas, and other ancient people of the area are collectively called **Meso-Americans.**

Key terms appear in boldface type.

Elements Boxes—Exclusive!

Although cooking styles are varied and complex, virtually any cuisine can be reduced to a profile of basic elements. These elements comprise foundation foods, favored seasonings, principal cooking media, primary cooking methods, and food attitudes. To reinforce information learned in the text, each regional chapter includes a review of basic cuisine elements, boxed for easy recognition. In addition, an **elements box** is provided when the text references a regional or world cuisine not previously covered.

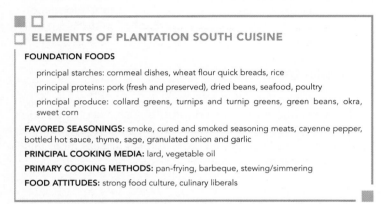

◼️ ◻️
◻️ ELEMENTS OF PLANTATION SOUTH CUISINE

FOUNDATION FOODS

principal starches: cornmeal dishes, wheat flour quick breads, rice

principal proteins: pork (fresh and preserved), dried beans, seafood, poultry

principal produce: collard greens, turnips and turnip greens, green beans, okra, sweet corn

FAVORED SEASONINGS: smoke, cured and smoked seasoning meats, cayenne pepper, bottled hot sauce, thyme, sage, granulated onion and garlic

PRINCIPAL COOKING MEDIA: lard, vegetable oil

PRIMARY COOKING METHODS: pan-frying, barbeque, stewing/simmering

FOOD ATTITUDES: strong food culture, culinary liberals

Elements boxes summarize important food culture information.

Custom Maps

To understand the cuisine of a particular region, you must be familiar with its geography. *American Regional Cuisines* includes a variety of **custom maps** developed to enhance your understanding. Our maps illustrate topographical features, climatic conditions, patterns of settlement, agricultural usage, and many other key concepts.

FIGURE 9.5
Midwestern Native American Settlement, circa 1750
(Before Displacement of East Coast Tribes)

Maps enhance understanding.

Regional Cuisine Graphic Organizers— Exclusive!

Because many students are visual learners, graphic organizers, such as charts and wheels, are proven learning tools. To enhance your understanding, each regional chapter includes a **regional cuisine graphic organizer** that visually represents the contributions of various food cultures to the region's cuisine. Viewing these tree-style organizers helps you understand the development of a particular regional cuisine through a concrete representation of culinary relationships and chronology.

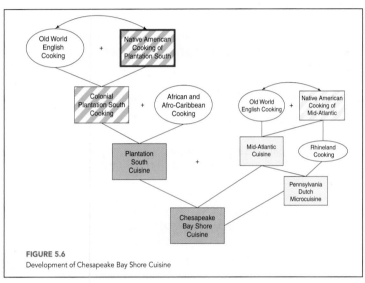

FIGURE 5.6
Development of Chesapeake Bay Shore Cuisine

Graphic organizers visually represent concepts and relationships.

Ingredients Tables

An essential key to understanding any cuisine is knowing its ingredients. Each regional chapter of *American Regional Cuisines* includes a table listing the cuisine's special ingredients, along with background information such as preparation methods, storage, and seasonal availability. Each **ingredients table** functions both as a learning tool and a purchasing guide.

◻️ **TABLE 14.2 HAWAI'I REGIONAL INGREDIENTS** *(continued)*

ITEM	MARKET FORMS	USES	SEASONALITY	OTHER	STORAGE
CHINESE SPRING ROLL WRAPPERS/ FILIPINO LUMPIA WRAPPERS	Very thin, almost translucent squares or rounds of wheat-flour dough are used to wrap a variety of fillings before deep-frying. They are sold frozen in packages of 10 to 20 wrappers.	Spring roll skins must be thoroughly defrosted before using and, once the package is opened, kept tightly sealed or under a damp towel to prevent drying. The 7" × 7" squares may be used whole to make large spring rolls or cut in quarters to make miniature spring rolls.	N/A	Do not substitute the thicker, pastalike Chinese egg roll wrappers.	Store frozen. Thaw overnight in the refrigerator before using.
JAPANESE GYOZA WRAPPERS/ CHINESE DUMPLING WRAPPERS	Thin, 3" round discs of wheat-flour dough are sold frozen in packages of 40 to 50. Gyoza wrappers are typically thinner, whereas dumpling wrappers are thicker.	These wrappers are used to make a variety of Japanese, Korean, and Chinese dumplings, which are steamed, boiled, or pan-braised.	N/A	Wonton wrappers are square rather than round.	Store frozen. Thaw overnight in the refrigerator before using.

Defining Dishes Tables—Exclusive!

Some regional cuisines have a long culinary history and a wide repertoire of traditional dishes. Other, newer cuisines have a number of chef-invented dishes recently prominent or, alternatively, ingredients combinations and flavor profiles signature to them. Creations such as these are known as defining dishes, prepared foods that represent a particular cuisine through widespread use and recognition. Each regional chapter in *American Regional Cuisines* includes a **defining dishes table** listing the region's best known dishes and giving background information on them.

□ TABLE 13.1 PACIFIC NORTHWEST DEFINING DISHES			
ITEM NAME	**HISTORY**	**DOMINANT INGREDIENTS AND METHOD**	**OTHER**
TILLAMOOK CHEDDAR SOUP WITH ALE	This smooth, rich soup was popularized in the region's brew pubs.	A velouté soup based on poultry stock and fresh microbrew ale is enriched with artisanal Tillamook Cheddar cheese.	The soup may be garnished with minced fresh herbs, crumbled bacon, or croutons.
PACIFIC NORTHWEST SEAFOOD CHOWDER	Transplanted New Englanders prepared chowders similar to those of home but using local seafood.	These cream-based soups include potatoes and a preserved pork product. They feature razor or Pacific littleneck clams, scallops, local fish, or Dungeness crab.	Pacific Northwest chowder is accompanied by crackers or sourdough bread.

■ □ ■

THE RECIPES

American Regional Cuisines presents more than three hundred original recipes for appetizers, entrées, and desserts. Moreover, most recipes include one or more variations that suggest ways to modify the recipe into a new and different dish.

In choosing recipes for this book, the authors strove to achieve a balance between time-honored traditional dishes and newer, chef-created contemporary dishes. While remaining true to original flavors and textures, recipes for traditional dishes are updated to make them suitable for à la carte restaurant service and to meet customer expectations for attractive, contemporary presentations. All entrées include regionally appropriate starch and vegetable accompaniments to create a complete plate.

Written in the Professional Recipe Format

Because *American Regional Cuisines* is written primarily for culinary students aspiring to become restaurant chefs, our recipes are written for use in à la carte restaurant service in a style we call the **professional recipe format**. Even if you're not cooking in a restaurant, but rather preparing these recipes in your laboratory class or practicing at home, working in this format will help you cook—and think about cooking—like a professional.

Restaurant cooking is divided into two phases: preparation and service turnout. Preparation is all the work that can be done to a particular dish ahead of time without compromising its quality. Preparation includes both fabrication of raw materials and precooking of components such as sauces and accompaniments. Service turnout is the work done to a dish after the customer order is placed. Between those two phases, components of the prepared dish must be correctly held, or stored. In our professional-format recipes, the **procedure directions reflect the actual processes of restaurant cooking**, giving you instruction on how to prepare and hold the components of the dish, and how to turn out the dish once it's ordered.

Dishes conceived and presented in the professional style are complex creations comprising many elements. For example, even a relatively simple appetizer typically includes the main item, a sauce, and a garnish. Contemporary entrées usually comprise a main protein item, its sauce, a starch accompaniment, one or more vegetable accompaniments, and a garnish. Often, these individual elements are dishes in their own right, requiring recipes. Modern plated desserts also include several elements. For the sake of efficiency, an element of one dish may be used in another. Thus, professional cooking is modular. Reflecting the way professionals cook in restaurants, *American Regional Cuisines* features **modular recipes**.

For each complete, finished dish—whether appetizer, entrée, or dessert—you'll first encounter a **master recipe** that instructs you how to turn out the finished dish. Reflecting the processes of a modern à la carte restaurant, the master turnout recipe is written in a yield of one portion because customer orders typically come in one at a time. If two customers at the same table order the same dish, the line cook simply doubles the recipe, making two dishes—and so forth, depending on how many orders are needed at one time. When turning out your master recipe, you'll follow the restaurant model, either turning out one serving at a time for practice or turning out four servings for your entire class to taste.

Buckwheat Rolls
with Country Ham, Asparagus, and Herbed Fresh Cheese

yield: 1 (4-oz.) appetizer serving
(multiply × 4 for classroom turnout; adjust equipment sizes accordingly)
🕐 Requires 3 days advance preparation.

MASTER RECIPE

production		costing only
1 Tbsp.	melted butter	1/2 fl. oz.
2	Buckwheat Pancake Rolls	1/4 recipe
1/2 c.	Cheddar Cheese Sauce, hot in steam table	1/4 recipe
1 Tbsp.	thin-sliced scallion	1/8 bunch a.p.

service turnout:
1. Brush a sizzle plate with a thin coat of butter, place the Buckwheat Pancake Rolls on the sizzle plate, and brush the rolls with the remaining butter.
2. Bake at 400°F about 10 minutes, until heated through.
3. Plate the dish:
   a. Place one roll on a hot 10" plate positioned diagonally from 2 o'clock to 8 o'clock.
   b. Prop the remaining roll on top of the first, positioned on a diagonal from 11 o'clock to 5 o'clock.
   c. Nap the Cheddar Cheese Sauce across the center of the rolls, allowing much of the sauce to pool in the center.
   d. Sprinkle a line of scallion across the sauce.

Before you can turn out a finished dish, however, you must first prepare its component elements. Usually, **component recipes follow the master recipe**. Occasionally you'll be directed to another chapter to find a component recipe or, for basic preparations such as stocks or pastry doughs, to download the component recipe from the companion website. Most component recipes are written in a yield of four portions because, through testing, we've determined that four portions is just enough food to provide a class of twenty students an adequate tasting.

COMPONENT RECIPE
BUCKWHEAT PANCAKE ROLLS

yield: 8 (2-oz.) rolls

production		costing only
8	Sourdough Buckwheat Cakes	1 recipe
1 c.	Herbed Fresh Cheese	1 recipe
2 oz.	julienne country ham	2 oz.
16	thin asparagus spears, peeled, blanched and refreshed, and blotted dry	8 oz. a.p.

preparation:
1. Place a Sourdough Buckwheat Cake on the work surface, browned side down.
2. Spread with a thin, even layer (2 Tbsp.) of Herbed Fresh Cheese.
3. Sprinkle with 1/4 oz. ham.
4. Place 2 asparagus spears on the cake and roll up tight.
5. Repeat with the remaining ingredients to make 8 Buckwheat Pancake Rolls.

holding: refrigerate, covered with a clean, damp towel and plastic film, up to 2 days

---

Focused on Plate Presentation

In today's top-level restaurants, artful presentation is as important as good cooking. In addition to conveying the authentic flavors and textures of regional dishes, *American Regional Cuisines* also emphasizes plating skills. Our **professional-format recipes teach contemporary plate presentation** by giving you detailed directions for placing the various elements of a dish on the plate in a predetermined design, in the correct order, and using the proper tools. Presentation styles are chosen to reflect the spirit of the cuisine, ranging from rustic to elegant and from traditional to avant-garde.

Many of the master recipe finished dishes in *American Regional Cuisines* feature full-color photographs that illustrate proper plating. **All finished-dish photos accurately reflect the plating instructions.** Thus, if you prepare the food elements correctly and follow the plating directions faithfully, your dishes will look exactly like the photographs.

b. Place the 2 standard sushi roll cylinders on the left side of the plate at 8 o'clock and 10 o'clock. Stack one of the slanted sushi roll cylinders on top of the 10 o'clock cylinder, and then arrange the remaining slanted cylinders next to the stack, in a row.

c. Quickly arrange the pickled ginger slices on the work surface in an overlapping row and roll them up into a loose cylinder. Fan the tops to create a rose. Place the ginger rose on the plate, front center, against the sushi roll cylinders.

d. Make a bouquet of the radish sprouts and stick it upright in the center of the sushi roll cylinders.

e. Squeeze a dot of Wasabi Sauce onto the shoyu sauce at 4 o'clock.

Observant of Safety and Sanitation Practices

In the culinary school laboratory, as in the restaurant kitchen, accidents must be prevented before they occur, and sanitary food preparation is a must. Thus, each recipe in *American Regional Cuisines* is written with both safety and sanitation in mind.

In our professional recipe format, the procedure directions include a special warning symbol ⚠ that identifies problems or dangers you may encounter when preparing your recipe. While some warnings are intended to prevent food disasters, many identify physically harmful results if a particular procedure is not performed correctly. These warning symbols alert you to be careful, helping you to maintain a safe learning or working environment.

The recipes in *American Regional Cuisines* follow the latest sanitation guidelines as outlined in the ServSafe® food safety program and the 2009 United States Food and Drug Administration Food Code Supplement. Procedure directions observe accepted time-temperature guidelines and stress the importance of keeping foods out of the temperature danger zone (TDZ). Individualized holding instructions expressly specify essential procedures such as sanitizing of containers, open-pan cooling, and use of nonreactive vessels for acidic foods. For each component recipe, the length of safe refrigerated holding time is specified. Sanitation-safe ingredients, such as pasteurized eggs and certified meats, are specified for preparations requiring them.

> **holding:** store the duck breasts individually wrapped, refrigerated, up to 3 days; open-pan cool the braised duck legs and immediately refrigerate in a freshly sanitized, covered container up to 5 days

Holding instructions emphasize proper sanitation.

The modular nature of our professional recipe format enables you to seamlessly integrate the recipes presented in *American Regional Cuisines* into your existing Hazard Analysis and Critical Control Points (HACCP) plan, or to easily develop a new HACCP plan using them. Because this book's master recipes are already broken down into modular component recipes having their own sanitation-savvy holding specifications, much of the work is already done for you.

Ready for Costing and Pricing

All recipes featured in *American Regional Cuisines* are ready for costing. The amount of each recipe ingredient is listed two ways: to the left of the ingredient name is a kitchen-appropriate unit of measurement for use when cooking; to the right, the same *ingredient amount is expressed in a costing-ready, as-purchased unit of measurement*. For example, on the left side of the ingredients column, the volume amount of minced onions is expressed in cups, while on the right side the weight amount of as-purchased (AP), uncut and unpeeled onion is given in ounces. Because this book will be of interest primarily to Americans, ingredient amounts are expressed in U.S. Standard units of measurement.

production		costing only
3 Tbsp.	butter	1 1/2 oz.
3/4 c.	minced yellow onion	3 oz. a.p.
1/4 c.	peeled, minced celery	1/20 head a.p.
1/2 c.	peeled, minced carrot	2 1/2 oz. a.p.
1/2 c.	peeled, chopped tart apple	3 oz. a.p.
3 c.+	Poultry Stock	1/4 recipe
1 c.	peeled, medium-chopped russet potatoes	6 oz. a.p.
1	bay leaf	1/16 oz.
1 sprig	fresh thyme	1/20 bunch a.p.
tt	kosher salt	1/20 oz.
tt	fresh lemon juice	1/8 [90 ct.] lemon
1 c.	grated extra-sharp Vermont Cheddar cheese	4 oz.

Each component recipe includes an accurate yield amount expressed in the most practical unit, whether weight or volume. Many recipes supply both. As previously noted, most component recipes are written in the proper yield to make four servings.

> ### COMPONENT RECIPE
> BEER-BRAISED BEEF SHORT RIBS
>
> **yield:** 4 (12-oz.) bone-in entrée servings plus 3 c. sauce

Once the cost of each component recipe is calculated, you can easily determine per-serving costs and transfer them to the master turnout recipe. Adding these costs along with any remaining ingredient costs gives you the total food cost for the dish.

Because master recipes are written in a yield of one serving, you can quickly and easily calculate the desired menu price. Simply divide the food cost of the dish by the desired food cost percentage (expressed in decimal form).

Student-Tested Recipes

All recipes in *American Regional Cuisines* were developed by the authors, both of whom are culinary educators currently teaching students of varying abilities at a variety of skill levels. Our recipes were first **tested by culinary professionals** and then **retested by culinary students**. Therefore you can be confident that, if you have a solid foundation in basic culinary skills and if you follow the directions carefully, you'll be able to prepare a successful dish. We recommend that you read the section entitled "Advice to Students" that follows the Preface.

■ □ ■

ACKNOWLEDGMENTS

Producing a book the size and scope of *American Regional Cuisines* has been a large and lengthy project that benefited from the efforts of many talented professionals. From composing the first draft of the manuscript to proofing the final pages, this book has been a team effort.

The idea of writing *American Regional Cuisines* began more than ten years ago when David was teaching at the California Culinary Academy. There he was inspired by a dynamic Food of the Americas class taught by Chef Clyde Serda. Chef Serda's knowledge of and passionate approach to Native American cuisines sparked David's interest in our nation's indigenous foods and cooking styles, and resulted in the book's comprehensive coverage of this fundamental topic. David also thanks Chef Suzie Moffett for her support while he was developing the American regional cuisines curriculum that eventually blossomed into this book. Both Lou and David appreciate Chef Michael Kalanty's constant encouragement and enthusiasm, as well as his valuable and discerning criticism.

We're both deeply indebted to Chef Jackie Pestka, culinary program director of Channels Food Rescue in Harrisburg, Pennsylvania, for countless hours of work and lots of good advice. Jackie tirelessly managed student recipe testing in countless laboratory classes and, through the years, featured many of the recipes on her restaurant menus. She stepped in and saved the day when illness threatened a photo shoot, styling plates with contemporary flair. Her culinary expertise was invaluable, particularly when writing, testing, and sourcing products for Mexican Border recipes.

During recipe development, "the home team" at Larchwood Farm pitched in to prep, record, and taste hundreds of dishes. Thanks particularly to Stewart Watson, Diana Hochner, Travis Haynes, and Obert Chulu for lots of prep and cleanup, and to Liz Johnson for both prep and dessert development.

The beautiful plated-dish photos in *American Regional Cuisines* are the work of photographer Jim Smith. Beyond his expertise with the camera, Jim's stylistic sense and broad understanding of food cultures enabled him to choose plates, place settings, and props that both enhance the dish and convey the spirit of the region. Jim remained focused on our project during a difficult time, and always walked onto the set with enthusiasm and a smile. Many thanks to Jim and his support team, Jeremy Grubard and Mike Vasiliauskas.

Photographing plated dishes requires a well-equipped kitchen and a skilled culinary staff. The food photos for *American Regional Cuisines* were created in photo shoots at three locations: York, Pennsylvania; Falls Church, Virginia; and Gettysburg, Pennsylvania.

Thanks to Jean Parks for facilitating our shoot at York County School of Technology in York, Pennsylvania. There Chef Gus Gianapoulos graciously opened his kitchen to our crew and organized our student help. Special thanks to student Catherine Dillard, who gave up a family vacation to help us find our way around. Despite partial incapacitation due to deep-frying in the dark during photo selection, Chef Jillian Weisenreider nonetheless created meticulously crafted garnishes. Chef Dani Sanders of the Red Brick Bakery faithfully reproduced several key desserts for this shoot.

Chef Mitch Watford welcomed us to Stratford University in Falls Church, Virginia, where we were assisted by a group of talented culinary students, including outstanding helper Casey McGrory. We thank Chef Mitch for his hard work, expertise, and hospitality.

Program Director Jim Cramer of Gettysburg Area School District–Adams County Tech Prep made possible our final shoot on David's home turf in Gettysburg, Pennsylvania. There, student helpers Victor Kendelhart, Danielle McMullen, and Lu Webster exhibited skills and professionalism far beyond their years. The team received additional prep help, as well as prop assistance, from Holly and Heidi Hart. Again, special thanks to Jackie Pestka for a long day of styling.

Many of the distinctive plates, bowls, and serving vessels featured in the photos were supplied by Heidi Hart of Wrightsville, Pennsylvania. The commercial food smoker used in recipe development and for photo shoot preparation was contributed by Cookshack, Inc. Thanks to Taylor Shellfish Farm for shipping Olympia Oysters across the country, and to Anson Mills for supplying stone-ground grits.

Not all of our acknowledgments involve foodservice professionals. We'd like to thank the countless photographers, archivists, and history buffs who contributed the historical and cultural photographs that illustrate the text. Thanks also to Bob Shepherd, IP attorney and master of the road trip.

We'd like to thank the editorial, production, and marketing teams at Pearson Education. Vernon Anthony began this book with us and remained a guiding force throughout. Senior Acquisitions Editor William Lawrensen took over and gave the project new life. Thanks to Development Editor Sonya Kottcamp, who saw the manuscript through to completion, as well as to Editorial Assistant Lara Dimmick and copyeditor Amy Schneider. Alex Wolf and Kris Roach oversaw the various aspects of photo research and permissions, scheduling, and production; and Deidra Skahill managed the manufacturing and costing aspects of the book's production. Michelle Churma headed up the efforts to establish a website and supervised the production of the various media ancillaries. Thanks also to Linda Zuk of WordCraft LLC for supervising the transition from manuscript through page proofs and to final files for printing. Senior Marketing Manager Thomas Hayward and Marketing Assistant Les Roberts handled the marketing plan and implementation.

Most important, we'd like to thank the many culinary students we've worked with throughout our teaching careers. Many of them were directly involved in the preparation of this book. Others helped us indirectly by asking questions, making mistakes, and thinking outside the box—in general, challenging us to become better teachers. Because of our students, we're able to approach the subject of American regional cuisines from the student's point of view, making it accessible, interesting, and fun.

We hope that reading *American Regional Cuisines* will be as rewarding and enjoyable for you as writing it was for us. We wish you success in preparing the recipes, and enjoyment in savoring the delicious food of America's fifteen culinary regions.

Thanks to Our Reviewers

From the beginning of the project through the final draft, a group of knowledgeable and experienced chef-instructors contributed valuable feedback in the form of peer reviews. Their constructive criticism helped us refine the text down to the essentials and present the information clearly. By sharing their requirements for a classroom teaching tool and their preferences regarding recipes, they enabled us to write a textbook that suits the demands of the market. Thanks to:

Susan E. Adams, La Salle University
Leonard G. Bailey II, Mountain State University
Michael Baldwin, Bellingham Technical College
John Bandman, Art Institute of New York City
Brian Bergquist, University of Wisconsin-Stout
Madonna Berry, Newbury College
Andree Burton, Faulkner State College
Michael Carmel, The Illinois Institute of Art
Chris Crostwaite, Lane Community College

Greg Forte, Utah Valley State College

Klaus Friedenreich, Art Institute of Ft. Lauderdale

Wendy Gordon, SUNY Rockland Community College

Edward Hamilton, City College of San Francisco

G. Michael Harris, Jr., Mohave Community College

Brian Hay, Austin Community College

Virginia Scott Jenkins, Chesapeake College

Michael Kalanty, Red Seal Books

Pamela Lewis, University of Southern Mississippi-Gulf Coast

Dean Louie, Maui Community College

Brian McDonald, Bellingham Technical College

Paul Mendoza, Galveston College

Michael Nenes, Art Institute of Houston

Michael Palmer, Western Culinary Institute

James Paul, Art Institute of Atlanta

Robert Reid, Palomar College

Urbano Salvati, Le Cordon Bleu

Arno Schmidt, Culinary Institute of America

Jim Switzenberg, Harrisburg Area Community College

Daniel Traster, Stratford University

Mitchell Watford, Stratford University

William Woys Weaver, Drexel University

Richard Webb, El Paso Community College, Culinary Arts and Related Sciences Program

Mark Wright, Erie Community College

advice to students

We hope you enjoy your American regional cuisines course and encourage you to give it your very best effort. Having taught this interesting and rewarding subject to many classes of students, we'd like to offer some advice that we believe will help you learn the information more fully and retain it longer. We also want to help you adjust to the professional recipe format if you've never worked with it. Finally, we have some suggestions we hope will make your preparation and turnout of American regional dishes more successful.

■□■ LEARNING ABOUT REGIONAL CUISINES

Understanding the food culture and cooking of a particular culinary region requires studying its geography; history; sociology; and, to a lesser extent, its politics and economics. It also requires hands-on experience cooking the region's most representative dishes, as well as thoughtful tasting and critique of the finished products. Many culinary schools guide your learning experience by scheduling a lecture/discussion/demonstration session we'll call a theory class, followed by a hands-on cooking class structured as a laboratory or production class. The following twelve-step study method is applied before, during, and after your classes. This method has helped many of our students succeed in learning and retaining the information in this book.

TWELVE-STEP STUDY PLAN

BEFORE each regional cuisine theory class and cooking class, familiarize yourself with the corresponding chapter material:

Step 1. Look at the culinary region map presented at the beginning of the regional chapter. Become familiar with the states it comprises. Compare this regional map to the U.S. culinary map presented on the book's endpapers to ensure that you know which culinary regions border the one you're studying. Also know the region's general location within (or in relation to) the U.S. landmass.

Step 2. Read the list of learning objectives that open the chapter you're studying. Pay special attention to the objectives linked to the five factors. Keep the chapter's learning objectives in mind as you read the chapter and participate in your cooking class.

Step 3. Look over the menu box located at the beginning of the chapter. The menu box lists the recipes presented at the end of the chapter and on the companion website. These dishes are representative of the region's cuisine; many are defining dishes. Also look over the defining dishes table. Consider whether you've ever experienced any of these dishes and, if so, call to mind their flavors, textures, and presentation styles. As you read the chapter, look for references to these representative dishes in the text.

Step 4. Read the chapter text through for the first time from start to finish, as if you were reading a story. Pay special attention to text having a factor symbol in the margin next to it.

Step 5. Look over the recipes, paying special attention to the cooking methods and techniques used. If necessary, refer to a comprehensive culinary text to refresh your memory of how they're done. Also note special ingredients used. Refer to the ingredients table to learn about ingredients particular to the region. If your instructor has preassigned the recipe(s) you'll be preparing in your cooking class, study them carefully.

DURING your theory class:

Step 6. Take notes, especially relating to extra information your instructor adds to the information presented in the textbook. Ask questions about any material you don't understand.

DURING your cooking class:

Step 7. Try to benefit from other students' work as well as your own.

- While focusing on your own work, try also to be aware of what's going on around you. If you have any down time, watch other students as they work.
- Taste every dish to experience the cuisine as fully as possible.
- Pay close attention to your instructor's critique, not only of your own dish(es) but also of the other dishes.

TWELVE-STEP STUDY PLAN *(continued)*

AFTER your classes, reinforce your grasp of the material by studying:

Step 8. Reread the chapter slowly and carefully, adding to your class notes or highlighting the most important points, including those marked with factor symbols. To learn the chapter's key terms, write each in your notebook and, later, with the book closed, define it in your own words.

Step 9. Without referencing your notes or the chapter, to the best of your ability write answers to the study questions. *Don't be tempted to answer the study questions as you are reading the chapter*: that defeats their purpose. The study questions are provided so you can evaluate how much of the chapter information you've retained *after* reading it.

Step 10. Complete and/or correct your study question answers and key terms definitions by referring to your notes and the chapter.

Step 11. Meet with fellow classmates to review the information. Quiz each other on facts and ingredient identification. Talk over various topics related to the region's history and food culture.

Step 12. (Optional). Go to this book's website for supplementary information. Use the bibliography to find additional resource materials and read them for more in-depth study.

■ □ ■ WORKING WITH THE RECIPES

The professional recipe format featured in *American Regional Cuisines* is designed to help you cook like a professional. It will help you think about the processes of à la carte cooking in a professional manner, as well.

In the recipes, ingredients amounts are listed two ways: working amounts on the left and costing amounts on the right. When preparing the recipes **you must use the ingredient amounts listed on the left.** Amounts listed on the right side of the ingredient names are for costing purposes only. Although in most cases the volume and weight amounts are essentially the same, for items used in tiny amounts (such as spices), weights given are approximate. Measuring these ingredients by weight could result in an unsuccessful dish.

When you begin preparing the recipes in *American Regional Cuisines*, we suggest you observe the following guidelines in the order presented.

RECIPE GUIDELINES

To save time, complete steps 1 through 4 before class.

1. Read through the master recipe and, if applicable, look at the finished-dish photo. If your recipe has no photo, carefully read the plating directions and visualize how the finished dish should look. Sketch a plating diagram that corresponds to the recipe's plating directions.
2. Read through all the master recipe's component recipes, including those presented elsewhere in the book. Make sure to download any website recipes needed.
3. If you're using a recipe variation, or scaling a recipe up or down to make a larger or smaller portion, you'll avoid confusion by rewriting the recipe with the new ingredients and/or amounts.
4. Write a prep list, deciding which component recipe should be prepared first, second, and so on.
5. Assemble your equipment and serviceware mise-en-place as well as your ingredients mise-en-place. Be sure to store your food at the proper temperature during preparation. Check with your instructor to find out whether substitutions are necessary. *Refer to the box at the bottom of page xxv for notes on basic ingredients.*
6. When you begin preparation, avoid confusion by using a separate prep tray for each component recipe. Remember to *use the amounts listed on the left.*
7. Note the holding time for each of your component recipes. Keep in mind that holding instructions and times are designed primarily for use in à la carte restaurant cooking and may not apply to the laboratory kitchen. In other words: you *can* hold the food as directed, but in the laboratory kitchen *you may not need to.* Use your judgment and knowledge of food safety procedures to determine how to hold. When in doubt, ask your instructor.
8. When preparation is complete, double-check that all component recipes and other master recipe ingredients are finished and ready to go.
9. Prior to turnout, reread the master recipe directions and make sure you understand how to finish and plate the dish. Look at the plated-dish photo or refer to your plating diagram.

10. Keep in mind your instructor's specified turnout time. The master turnout recipes in *American Regional Cuisines* are designed with a turnout time of fifteen minutes or fewer. Therefore, you should *begin the master recipe fifteen to twenty minutes before turnout time.* If you're properly prepped and you understand the procedures, you should be right on time. If you begin turning out most dishes too far ahead of time, you'll end up with cold, "tired" food.

11. If you're turning out in a laboratory class, you'll probably be plating four servings of your dish. You can turn out four separate plates or create one plate presentation for critique and serve the remaining portions on a platter for student tasting. Ask your instructor which he/she prefers.

12. Do everything within your capabilities to ensure serving attractive, well-seasoned food at the appropriate temperature:
    a. Have serviceware properly warmed or cooled.
    b. Finish the food quickly, using the proper tools. When appropriate, wear fresh foodservice gloves.
    c. Using proper sanitation techniques, check every element of your dish to make sure it is:
       - at the designated doneness (feel)
       - properly seasoned (taste)
       - and at the correct temperature (taste or thermometer).
    d. Make sure sauces are of the proper consistency (test on spoon or plate).
    e. Plate neatly, using the proper tools and keeping food and your fingers off the plate rims. If you have drips, smears, or fingerprints on the plate rims or on empty spaces in the plate well, wipe them away with the corner of a clean kitchen towel dampened with very hot water.
    f. Be prepared to add garnish(es) quickly and as directed in the recipe.
    g. Get your plate(s) to the turnout area quickly and on time.

BASIC INGREDIENTS

Salt: Most recipes specify kosher salt because of its mild, neutral flavor; low cost; and coarse texture that makes it easily controllable. For best control, always use your fingers to add salt rather than shaking it from the box or using a spoon. Most recipes specify salt to taste, leaving the amount up to the cook. Use salt with judgment; it's best to salt lightly at the beginning and correct with more toward the end of the procedure. Recipes for baked goods usually give specific amounts of salt. These and some other preparations require fine-ground salt; sea salt or noniodized table salt is recommended.

Herbs: The recipe ingredients list typically specifies either the fresh or dried form of the herb. Parsley, chervil, and cilantro (coriander leaf) are always used in fresh form. Do not attempt to replace a fresh herb with its dried form; if the fresh herb is unavailable, it's usually best to leave it out or replace it with another fresh herb. Ask your instructor's advice before making a substitution. Don't chop or mince fresh herbs too far ahead of time, especially if they are to be used as a garnish.

Spices: The recipe ingredients list specifies whole or ground spices, except for those available only in ground form. If possible, use ground spices prepared by grinding whole spices just prior to use. Black pepper ground fresh from the mill is recommended.

Flour: Unless a particular type of flour is specified, use all-purpose flour. Unbleached flour is recommended.

Sugar: Unless a particular type of sugar is specified, use plain granulated sugar.

Butter: In traditional American regional cuisines, most butter is salted. For savory dishes, you may use either salted or unsalted butter, adjusting the amount of additional salt as appropriate. For table use, serve salted butter. For baking and desserts, use unsalted butter.

Tomatoes: Vine-ripened tomatoes are recommended. The recipe ingredients list specifies several forms:
- tomato filet or tomato flesh is tomatoes that have been blanched a few seconds only, immediately refreshed in ice water, peeled, and seeded (by squeezing out most of the seeds)
- tomato concassée is tomato filet or tomato flesh fabricated coarse to medium chop
- tomato coulis is tomatoes prepared as concassée but then chopped to a smooth paste or forced through a food mill; avoid puréeing in a food processor as this creates too much froth
- pressed tomatoes are whole tomatoes that have been blanched a few seconds only, immediately refreshed in ice water, peeled, sliced thick, and then left to drain between layers of paper towels

Peeled celery: Has had strings removed with a swivel peeler

Peeled peppers: Raw bell peppers cut into sections along their contours and then skinned with a swivel peeler

Roasted peppers: Bell peppers that have had skins lightly charred over a gas or charcoal grill, under a broiler, or over a gas flame; the peppers are then encased in a loose wrapping of aluminum foil or placed in a closed container to steam in their own heat just until they collapse; the peppers are peeled by scraping off the blackened skins and cleaned by removing their stems, seeds, and veins; do not rinse roasted peppers under water; chiles for stuffing are prepared the same way, but they are left whole with stems intact and seeds and membranes removed

about the authors

Lou Sackett is a food writer, culinary educator, and chef with more than thirty years' experience in food-related fields. After working in her family's restaurant, she studied English literature at the University of Pennsylvania and then refined her culinary skills as an apprentice at a Michelin three-star-rated restaurant in France. A career as executive chef and restaurateur in Philadelphia led to a chef instructor position at The Restaurant School (now at Walnut Hill College), freelance food styling, and writing for local and national publications. Relocating to south-central Pennsylvania, Lou gained education experience teaching culinary arts at both the postsecondary and secondary levels. Her writing credits include a culinary textbook on garde manger. Lou is the food stylist and primary writer of *American Regional Cuisines*.

David Haynes earned his BA in political science and American history at Boston University and then began a foodservice career after graduating from The Restaurant School. As an executive chef and restaurateur, David led the kitchens of fine-dining restaurants in Fredericksburg, Virginia. As a culinary educator, David taught at Stratford University in Falls Church, Virginia, and at the California Culinary Academy in San Francisco. Now based in south-central Pennsylvania, David currently teaches secondary school culinary arts. He is the book's lead researcher and mapmaker.

american regional cuisines

food culture and cooking

■□■ chapter one
Keys to Understanding Regional Cuisines

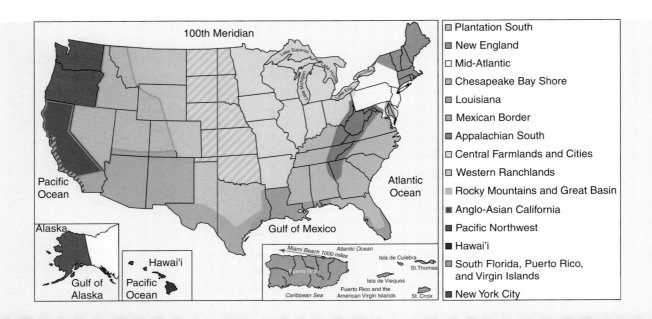

■ Plantation South
■ New England
□ Mid-Atlantic
■ Chesapeake Bay Shore
■ Louisiana
■ Mexican Border
■ Appalachian South
□ Central Farmlands and Cities
□ Western Ranchlands
■ Rocky Mountains and Great Basin
■ Anglo-Asian California
■ Pacific Northwest
■ Hawai'i
■ South Florida, Puerto Rico, and Virgin Islands
■ New York City

IN THE 21ST CENTURY America is now, more than ever before, the focus of world interest. Through films, television, and mass marketing, American culture is exported around the globe. However, most of the world has experienced our cuisine only superficially. Today when many people think of American food, the images that come to mind are hamburgers, hot dogs, and other fast-food items globally recognized because of advertising. Luxury dishes such as grilled steaks and steamed lobsters demonstrate our wealth. But there is much more to our cuisine than these well-known foods.

People throughout the world—and even in the United States—are unaware of the many dishes American cuisine has to offer. In fact, most Americans have not yet discovered the richness of their own culinary heritage. They don't realize that there is not just one American cuisine, but many.

The United States is home to fifteen distinctive regional cuisines. Each cooking style is unique, with its own ingredients, techniques, and flavor combinations, reflecting the skill, creativity, and ingenuity of American cooks and the bounty of America's food resources.

Many of America's regional cuisines trace their origins to the earliest days of our nation. In fact, much of America's regional cooking predates the birth of our national cuisine and is the foundation on which our national cuisine is based. Thus, in-depth knowledge of America's regional cuisines is key to understanding modern American cooking.

AFTER STUDYING THIS CHAPTER YOU SHOULD BE ABLE TO:

- trace the typical stages of regional settlement
- list the three basic elements of a food culture and its cuisine
- list the three characteristics that define a culinary region
- identify America's fifteen culinary regions on a map of the United States
- list and explain five factors in the development of a regional cuisine
- explain the concept of a microcuisine
- explain the concept of a national cuisine
- use correct terminology to discuss food cultures and cuisines

■ INTRODUCTION TO
☐ FOOD CULTURE
■ AND CUISINE

Each of America's regional cuisines developed from a unique combination of factors involving geography, history, and culture. *Geography* is the foundation of all regional cuisines because topography, soil type, and climate dictate the type of foods a region can produce. A region's *history* influences its cooking because historical events affect different groups of people over an extended period of time and for many reasons. Knowing the history of a region enables us to understand its people and their food cultures. Food *culture* includes taste preferences, cooking technology, and beliefs and attitudes about food. Thus, learning about a region's geography, history, and food culture enables us to understand its cuisine.

History Creates Cuisine

Let's start by examining the way most culinary regions are settled, typically in three stages (Figure 1.1): (1) indigenous people, (2) first settlers (colonists or pioneers), and (3) second settlers (immigrants). We'll use the American model to help us learn how history affects the way people cook and eat. Along the way you'll learn some important terms used throughout this book.

The population of the United States comprises people whose origins span the globe. No matter how many new ethnic groups are added to our cultural mix, we eventually embrace them and, over time, they become Americans. Thus, it's no surprise that America is described as a **melting pot,** a vessel in which various metals are heated together to become one cohesive, molten mass. America is a figurative melting pot because we're a nation of immigrants. Let's examine what that means.

An immigrant is a person who leaves his or her homeland and resettles in another place. Except for people of pure Native American heritage, all Americans can be considered immigrants (or the descendants of immigrants). From the first Jamestown colonists to the last person passing through customs this very day, we all came to America from somewhere else. Even Native Americans originally came to the North American continent from Asia during prehistoric times. However, Native Americans have been here so long that they're considered America's indigenous people. The term *indigenous* is derived from Latin words meaning "inborn"

FIGURE 1.1
Three Stages of Regional Settlement

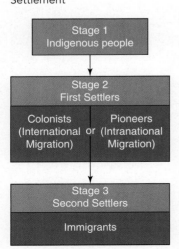

or "original." Thus, an **indigenous** group comprises the descendants of a land's original inhabitants.

Today, few places on earth are inhabited solely by indigenous people. Since ancient times, groups of humans have abandoned their original homes and resettled in other places. When this happens, they encounter the indigenous people of the place to which they have traveled. This is how the mixing of cultures begins.

In ancient times human resettlement was spontaneous and usually not generated by governments. However, by the early 1600s some European nations sought to relocate some of their citizenry to other parts of the world in order to create *colonies* in Asia, Africa, Australia, South America, and North America. **Colonists** are people sponsored by a sovereign nation to travel to a new, unclaimed land and create permanent settlements under the control of that nation. Colonists transplant the culture of one nation to another. Thus, *the migration of colonists is international.*

By the late 1700s, several new nations had been created from former colonies. These vast new nations had large tracts of unsettled land, and they encouraged exploration and resettlement into unsettled areas. **Pioneers** are citizens of a sovereign nation who travel into the wilderness and create permanent settlements in previously unsettled areas of that nation. Like colonists, pioneers also bring their culture to their new homes. Because they resettle from one area of a nation to another, *the migration of pioneers is considered intranational.*

In this book, both colonists and pioneers are called **first settlers** because they are the earliest nonindigenous people to arrive in a particular region. Soon after arrival, the first settlers of a region meet the indigenous people living there, a crucial point called **first contact,** At first contact, one of two things can happen: a positive interaction that leads to the exchange of goods and ideas, or a negative interaction that results in estrangement or even violence. *Positive interaction between indigenous groups and first settlers typically leads to a blending of cultures, and thus a blending of cuisines.* As indigenous people and first settlers begin to use each other's ingredients and cooking methods, and eventually blend them together, they create hybrid dishes and eventually develop a new, **hybrid cuisine.**

Once a region's first settlers are established, the stage is set for other groups to arrive. Some groups arrive unwillingly. For example, many European convicts and all African slaves were forced to *emigrate,* or leave their homelands. However, most emigrants leave of their own accord to escape persecution or to find economic opportunity. In the mid-1800s, more people began leaving their homelands to resettle in other parts of the globe. Many came to America. Because of this, the period from 1850 to 1930 is often called the *Age of Immigration.* By the mid-1800s, however, many of the world's regions had already been settled by colonists or pioneers. Settlers arriving after that date can be called **second settlers.** In this book, second settlers are frequently called **immigrants,** although colonists and pioneers are technically immigrants as well.

When immigrants arrive in a region, they add yet another element to the cultural mix, making an already blended culture more complex. Some regions experience several, or many, successive waves of immigration. In fact, unless a nation closes its borders to new immigrants, immigration remains an ongoing phenomenon.

Now that you understand how new people arrive in a particular region and know the specific terms used for the various settlement groups, we can go on to discuss how these various groups create a regional cuisine. But first, we'll present some basic information on food culture and cuisine. Knowing about these topics will help you think about and discuss the regional cuisines that you'll soon encounter.

■ ELEMENTS OF FOOD
□ CULTURE AND CUISINE
■

The word *culture* has many meanings. Its root is the Latin word *cultura*, "to grow." When used in reference to human beings, *culture* refers to a group's patterns of behavior, including thought, belief systems, language, action, and the production of goods, artifacts, and art. In other words, *culture* refers to the ways in which people, as a group, think and act. Thus, the term **food culture** describes the ways in which a particular group of humans thinks about food and how they cook and eat that food. The cooking and dining practices of a particular food culture are collectively called its **foodways.**

Culture is considered part of civilization. *Civilization* refers to a group's relative state of advancement, typically measured by achievements in science, technology, art, government, and

spirituality. Civilizations that have progressed slowly and relatively little (usually in regard to science and technology) are called *primitive civilizations.*

Primitive civilizations typically lack the technology to have achieved a stable and abundant food supply. They spend most of their time searching for food, and when they obtain food, it is prepared quickly, simply, and without much thought. The act of preparing food in this way is generally referred to as *cooking.*

One marker of an advanced civilization is that it has achieved a stable and reliable food supply, and specialization of labor has progressed to the point that some of its members have leisure time and wealth. Leisure gives people the opportunity to spend time thinking about food and cooking and to care about how their food tastes. They have time to cook more complex dishes and experiment with seasonings and flavor combinations. They practice preparing these dishes and try to make them better each time. In this situation one group member's cooking style will be fundamentally similar to that of the others because all use the same basic ingredients and share ideas. The group keeps records of its cooking, either orally or as written recipes, and thus passes its knowledge and techniques along to new generations. Wealth allows people to purchase fine ingredients, to travel in search of new ingredients, and to pay professional cooks to create a repertoire of culinary masterpieces. At this point, cooking becomes cuisine. Thus, **cuisine** can be defined as skilled, thoughtful, refined cooking belonging to a particular style.

Food cultures and their resulting cuisines are based on three elements: *ingredients, cooking methods,* and *attitudes* about food, cooking, and eating (Figure 1.2).

FIGURE 1.2
Three Elements of Food Culture and Cuisine

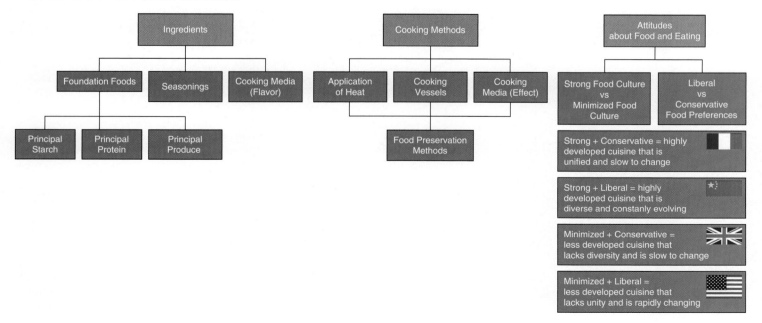

Ingredients

Ingredients are the basic components of a cuisine, and they strongly influence the development of a food culture. We classify ingredients into three categories: foundation foods, seasonings, and cooking media.

Foundation Foods

Foundation foods comprise a food culture's principal starch(es), principal protein food(s), and principal produce items (vegetables and fruits). Starchy foods—most frequently grains—are a cuisine's most important foundation food because in most civilizations they form the bulk of the human diet. Refer to Figure 1.3 to review cultivation areas of the world's foundation starches.

Seasonings

Seasonings include herbs, spices, and condiments.

Cooking Media

Cooking media include fats for frying and liquids used for poaching and stewing. Cooking media contribute flavor and, in part, determine which cooking methods are used.

Cooking Methods

Although ingredients are the foundation of any cuisine, the way in which they are fabricated and cooked greatly affects the outcome of any dish. Thus, cooking methods are another important element in any cuisine.

Application of Heat

How heat is applied to a particular food largely determines its color and texture, and can affect its flavor. Until recently, the sole method of generating heat for cooking was to create fire. Fire technology began with burning wood, then coal, and then finally various gases. The only real variation was in how the fire's heat

FIGURE 1.3
Areas of Foundation Grain/Starch Cultivation, circa 1600 C.E.

Corn
Barley, Rye, Wheat
Millet
Rice

was applied. Now we have electricity and microwave technology to supply heat as well. A good way to begin evaluating the cooking techniques of a particular food culture is to examine the heat technology it has developed.

Cooking Vessels

Without vessels, such as pots and pans, cooks are largely limited to grilling, pit roasting, and other primitive methods. The earliest food cultures used natural materials such as skin bags, animal stomachs, leaf wrappings, and flat stones as cooking vessels. Over time humans learned to make earthenware vessels for simmering and stewing. In many cuisines earthenware vessels are still used for certain dishes because they impart a special flavor to food cooked in them. Metal vessels were a significant technological advance because they conduct heat more safely and efficiently, withstand higher heat, and are less breakable. Sturdy, conductive metal vessels allow a wider repertoire of cooking methods, including boiling and steaming. Beginning with copper and progressing through bronze, iron, steel, aluminum, and stainless steel, technology has developed many materials for cooking vessels. When studying cooking methods you should take cooking vessels into consideration because the type used affects both heat conduction and flavor.

Cooking Media

Some cooking methods depend on ingredients as well as vessel technology. For example, frying methods require frying fats as well as metal pots or pans. Food cultures that don't use fats (because of either preference or lack of available fats) thus do not fry their foods.

Food Preservation Methods

Food preservation is an essential element of many cuisines. Traditional food preservation methods include drying, curing with salt, preserving with sugar, smoking, and sealing from air. When you study the early food history of a particular region, pay attention to the food preservation methods used because they can strongly affect the modern cuisine.

Attitudes about Food, Cooking, and Eating

The attitudes of the members of a particular food culture are instrumental in shaping its cuisine. People's attitudes about food fundamentally determine which ingredients and cooking methods are accepted and favored. Beliefs and attitudes about food influence the amount of time, money, and attention that a person or group is willing to spend on food and cooking. In fact, attitudes are even more important than ingredients. A prime example is the vast difference between the cuisines of the Plantation South and New England, two food cultures that began with many of the same food products. Later you'll learn how these two cuisines were primarily shaped by the different attitudes of their colonist groups.

Attitudes about food and eating can be subtle, complex, and difficult to understand. In many cases, these thoughts and feelings are subconscious. In other words, people frequently hold beliefs and attitudes about food without knowing why. Food preferences and taboos are frequently linked to social practices and to ethical and spiritual beliefs that are deeply rooted in the group's culture. Thus, to fully understand a food culture, you must learn about the history, culture, and religion of the group. This is true for indigenous people as well as for first settlers and immigrants. Each regional cuisine chapter includes information to help you identify the attitudes and beliefs of the group you are studying.

- **Strong Food Cultures.** Strong food cultures have positive attitudes about food and eating. Such people enjoy food and love to eat. They see no harm in indulging in the physical pleasure of eating and consider food and cooking to be occupations worthy of their time. Strong food cultures typically produce highly developed cuisines. Refer to the box above for indicators of a strong food culture.

- **Minimized Food Cultures.** *Minimized food cultures* are groups conditioned by their belief systems to care very little about food. In these cultures, food is considered merely fuel for the body. People in these cultures pay little attention to cooking and dining, instead focusing their energies on other pursuits. In some minimized food cultures, food and eating have negative connotations. This attitude is often associated with thrift, self-denial, and the suppression of physical pleasure. It is also associated with the quest for a particular standard of physical beauty. Minimized food cultures rarely produce highly developed cuisines.

A group's level of general culture and the strength of its food culture are not necessarily related. Advanced civilizations typically have sophisticated cultures; however, this does not necessarily mean having a strong food culture. Some highly advanced civilizations have minimized food cultures; although they have the technology and leisure time necessary to create a highly developed cuisine, for one reason or another, they choose not to do so.

Another element to consider is whether the members of a food culture are conservative or liberal in their food preferences. Although the terms *conservative* and *liberal* are frequently used when discussing politics, in this context we use the words in a

TEN INDICATORS OF A STRONG FOOD CULTURE

People who have a strong food culture typically:

1. spend time thinking about and talking about food.
2. carefully plan menus for ordinary meals as well as for special occasions.
3. spend a high proportion of their income on food.
4. eat sitting down, with others.
5. eat slowly and mindfully.
6. eat foods in season.
7. prefer locally produced foods and traditional dishes.
8. develop a large repertoire of recipes and maintain oral and written records of them.
9. accord high status to people who grow and cook food.
10. include food images in visual art and include descriptions of food in literature.

more general sense: *liberal* meaning open to change, and *conservative* meaning disposed to preserving existing conditions.

■ A **culinary liberal** may be defined as a person willing to try a wide variety of foods and to adopt new foods and culinary ideas. Culinary liberals tend to be adventurous about other aspects of life as well.

■ A **culinary conservative** may be defined as a person unwilling to experiment with new foods and who regards new foods and culinary ideas with suspicion. Culinary conservatives strongly prefer to eat familiar foods and believe that foods of their own food culture are superior to all others. They are often cautious about other aspects of life.

In each regional cuisine chapter, look for boxes outlining the basic elements of the cuisine under discussion. These elements boxes present an overview of the cuisine's foundation foods (principal starch, protein foods, produce items), favored seasonings, principal cooking media, primary cooking methods, and food attitudes.

■ THE MAKING OF
▢
■ A MELTING POT

We've used the model of American cuisine to explain some basic food culture concepts. Let's continue using this model to further illustrate how cuisines develop. We'll use some American cuisine dishes as examples, starting with turkey, corn on the cob, roast beef, apple pie, and cornbread. Let's look at the origins of these familiar dishes and use them to exemplify some important terms.

The cooking style of a region's indigenous people is called its **indigenous cuisine.** An indigenous cuisine comprises **indigenous foods,** or ingredients that are native to a particular land. Indigenous foods may be wild or cultivated. In American cuisine, turkey and corn are indigenous foods. Both turkeys (wild) and corn (cultivated) existed on the North American continent before European settlers arrived. Precontact Native Americans had the cooking technology to spit-roast a turkey and boil corn. Thus, roast turkey and boiled corn on the cob are **indigenous dishes,** or dishes primarily made with indigenous foods and indigenous cooking techniques.

The point in history at which an indigenous group of people first makes contact with another culture is typically a crucial turning point in their way of life and thus also in their food culture. We call the indigenous cooking style prevalent before this point **precontact cuisine** and the style that develops after this point **postcontact cuisine.** When studying the modern cooking of indigenous groups, it's important to distinguish between precontact and postcontact cuisines. For example, Native American griddle-baked corn tortillas are a precontact dish, but wheat flour fry bread is a postcontact dish.

The first settlers to arrive in a particular region are either colonists or pioneers. American colonists primarily came from Europe. To them, the American continents constituted a "new world," whereas Europe was the "old world." Thus, the homeland cooking styles of America's European colonists are collectively called **Old World cuisines.** Colonists traveling to a new land try to bring along familiar foods and raise them in their new homes. Food plants and animals that settlers bring from home and establish in the new land are called **colonial domesticates.** Colonists also bring previously developed cooking technology to their new homes. Roast beef and apple pie are considered Old World dishes because beef, apples, and the wheat used to make the flour for the piecrust were brought from Europe by European settlers, and because oven roasting and baking is European cooking technology. Dishes made primarily with colonial domesticates and European cooking technology are called **Old World dishes.**

> indigenous cuisine + Old World cuisine = colonial cuisine

When the Old World cuisine of a colonist group is blended with indigenous cuisine, the resulting hybrid cooking style is called **colonial cuisine.** Thus, a **colonial dish** is made with a mixture of indigenous foods and colonial domesticates and may use both indigenous and European cooking technology. New England–style cornbread is a good example of a colonial dish; it is made from Old World wheat flour blended with indigenous American cornmeal and baked in an oven using Old World cooking technology. If the Thanksgiving turkey is stuffed with a wheat bread dressing and roasted in an oven, it becomes a colonial dish as well.

As colonial cuisine becomes established, cooks develop a repertoire of colonial dishes that become the foundation of the region's cuisine. When first-settler colonists become pioneers, they take their cooking style on the road and transplant it to the new lands where they settle. En route, and until their farms or ranches become established, pioneers achieve only a rough version of their original colonial cuisine. They may need to borrow new ingredients and cooking techniques from the new indigenous groups they encounter, creating another hybrid cooking style known as **pioneer cuisine.** Thus, **pioneer dishes** combine previously adopted indigenous ingredients, Old World ingredients, and newly discovered indigenous ingredients from a new area. They may combine European cooking technology with several types of indigenous technology. Pies made from chokecherries and other wild fruits indigenous to the Midwest are examples of pioneer dishes.

Both colonial cuisine and pioneer cuisine are first-settler cooking styles. Sooner or later, though, first-settler cuisines are altered and enriched by the food products and techniques brought by immigrants.

Today some of America's favorite ingredients are immigrant foods. **Immigrant foods** are items added to the ingredients of an established regional cuisine by groups who arrive later in the area's history. Olive oil, pasta, soy sauce, and tofu are examples of immigrant foods that have been embraced across America.

When immigrant cooks prepare versions of their homeland cuisines using American ingredients—blending immigrant foods with colonial foods, Old World foods, indigenous foods, or any mixture thereof—the resulting creations are called **immigrant dishes.** In many

> colonial cuisine + indigenous cuisine of a new territory = pioneer cuisine

first settler cuisine + immigrant cuisine = modern cuisine

regions, immigrant dishes substantially enriched the region's modern cuisine.

When immigrant cooks create a broad, recognizable repertoire of immigrant dishes, these dishes become the foundation of yet another type of hybrid cuisine. In the United States, these hybrid cooking styles are called *ethnic-American cuisines* (defined on p. 20) and are typically given hyphenated names. The well-known dish spaghetti and meatballs is part of Italian-American cuisine; chop suey belongs to Chinese-American cuisine. Both of these dishes are purely American creations and cannot be found in Italy or China.

America is a cultural melting pot, and America's regional cuisines were created by the mixing of food cultures. Each of America's regional cuisines can be compared to a simmering stewpot in which many different ingredients have been blended to make something new, complex, and delicious.

This culinary blending is not unique to America. Anthropologists and food historians recognize that nearly all of the world's modern cuisines are a mixture of indigenous, settler, and immigrant cooking styles. They also acknowledge the fact that the world's cuisines are fundamentally regional, or specific to small, homogenous localities. Let's now explore the meaning of the term *regional cuisine* and introduce additional key terms you'll need to know.

■
□ UNDERSTANDING
■ REGIONAL CUISINES

A **regional cuisine** is a unified style of cooking common to most of the people living in a culinary region. But what do we mean by *culinary region*, or even *region*? When a country creates large subdivisions according to climate and topography, those subdivisions are called regions. The land of a particular region typically has a relatively uniform topography and climate. For most purposes, regions are defined following these geographical guidelines. However, when studying food and cooking, we must add elements to our subdivision guidelines. In doing so, we create and define **culinary regions** using three criteria: geography, homogenous food culture, and defining dishes that are unique and noteworthy (Figure 1.4).

FIGURE 1.4

Three Criteria That Define a Culinary Region

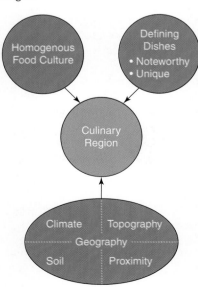

Culinary regions are fundamentally defined by their *geography*: having uniform topography, climate, and soil, and sharing proximity to other regions. However, another important characteristic must be considered.

For a particular area to be considered a culinary region, the food culture of its inhabitants must be *homogenous*, or uniform. As new foods and culinary ideas enter the region, they must be widely accepted and adopted, so that the food culture remains primarily homogenous even through a succession of changes.

Finally, the repertoire of *dishes* produced in the region must be unique and noteworthy, singular enough to be readily distinguished from the dishes of all other regions. Recipes that unmistakably represent a particular region are called its **defining dishes.**

■
□ AMERICA'S FIFTEEN
■ CULINARY REGIONS

Using the parameters of geography, homogenous food culture, and defining dishes, we identify fifteen American culinary regions:

> The Plantation South
> New England
> The Mid-Atlantic
> The Chesapeake Bay Shore
> Louisiana
> The Mexican Border
> The Appalachian South
> The Central Farmlands and Cities
> The Western and Central Ranchlands
> The Rocky Mountains and Great Basin
> Anglo-Asian California
> The Pacific Northwest
> Hawai'i
> South Florida and Puerto Rico
> New York City

This list of American culinary regions may differ from others you've seen. Geographers divide the United States into New England, the Mid-Atlantic, the South, the Midwest, the Southwest, and the West. In the past, culinary regions were modeled after these geographic regions, with boundaries drawn along state lines. However, there has long been inaccuracy and oversimplification in defining American culinary regions.

Many of the six formerly recognized American culinary regions encompass areas that deserve the distinction of regionhood in their own right. For example, it's an extreme oversimplification to speak of "Southern" cuisine. The American South encompasses five distinct regional cuisines: the Plantation South, the Chesapeake Bay Shore, Louisiana, the Appalachian South, and South Florida. Although they are all Southern and share some of the same ingredients, each developed a cooking style significantly different from the others. Thus, we recognize five separate culinary regions within the traditionally defined American South.

Some culinary regions span recognized regional borders. For example, New England cooking can be found south of the

New York State border as well as on northern Long Island. Thus, culinary New England has different boundaries from geopolitical New England.

One of America's traditionally defined culinary regions, the Midwest, encompasses two different food cultures within its boundaries. However, in this case the area cannot be simply divided into two separate culinary regions. In the Midwest, two distinct types of cooking developed side by side, formed by the two different occupations that coexisted there. Farming is the primary occupation in the Great Lakes states and the Mississippi corridor, and is practiced in the plains states, as well. Farm wives traditionally cooked straightforward, hearty dishes featuring pork and chicken, homegrown vegetables, pickles and preserves, and wheat flour baked goods. We call this culinary style "Farmlands cooking." The Great Plains area is known for ranching. Ranchers ate simpler but equally hearty meals based on beef and beans and used cornmeal as often as wheat flour. This cuisine style is called "Ranchlands cooking." Although farming tended toward the north and east, and ranching toward the south and west, in many areas, such as Kansas and Nebraska, one can find Farmlands cooking and Ranchlands cooking in the same county. Thus, the Midwest encompasses two unique culinary regions that have indistinct and overlapping boundaries.

Instead of fewer regions listed in other books, we recognize and celebrate fifteen discrete American culinary regions. These fifteen regions are not defined by conventional geopolitical boundary lines but by a combination of factors, including climate and topography, food culture, ingredients, cooking methods, and defining dishes. Refer to the map on p. 2 and the endpapers to see how these culinary regions sometimes overlap, and sometimes exist within, standard geopolitical boundaries. They reflect our nation's diverse culinary heritage as expressed by the cooks and chefs of today.

We'll explore our fifteen culinary regions roughly in the order of settlement. Thus, we begin with the Plantation South, the site of America's first culinarily influential settlement at Jamestown, Virginia. New England is next, settled not long after at Plymouth, Massachusetts. As we progress westward, the exact order of settlement becomes less clear, so the order in which you encounter the various regions is planned to make the most sense in a food history context. To understand how the chapters are ordered, see Figure 1.5.

◼◻◼ FIVE FACTORS IN THE DEVELOPMENT OF A REGIONAL CUISINE

Suppose you had the time and money to take a tour of America's fifteen culinary regions. As you traveled around the country watching people cook and sampling each region's defining dishes, you would notice similarities and differences between the various regional cooking styles and begin comparing the re-

gions to one another. You'd wonder how and why the various regional cuisines developed. Questions would arise. For example: Why is the cuisine of New England so different from the cuisine of the Plantation South when both were colonized by the English, at virtually the same time, and both shared the same indigenous foods and colonial domesticates?

Fortunately, in this book you have the advantage of a built-in set of tools that will help you answer such questions. Your toolbox consists of the basic factors illustrated in the box on this page. These five factors apply to regional cuisines not only in America but also throughout the world. No matter which regional cuisine is singled out for study, these five factors almost always come into play.

As you read the American regional cuisine chapters in this book, look for the factor icons in the page margins. These symbols indicate information in the text that relates to one of the five factors. As you notice factor information in the text, stop and evaluate its importance. Note how early or how late in the region's history that factor came into play. Observe how one factor affects the other factors. In doing so, you'll get some valuable clues.

In many ways, applying the five factors to the history and food culture of an American culinary region is like reading a mystery story. To arrive at the solution to a mystery, the detective looks deeply into past events, asks the right questions, and critically evaluates the answers. Following the same process enables you, as a student of American regional cuisines, to ask important questions whose answers lead to a sound understanding of the region's food culture and cuisine.

After you've studied several regions, you can also use the factors to compare and contrast one region with another. For example, apply Factor 4 to the cuisines of the Plantation South and New England to discover why today the two cuisines are so different.

In order to apply the five factors to America's fifteen culinary regions, you must understand the concepts behind each factor and know some key terms used in discussing it. Let's look at the factors in greater detail.

FIVE FACTORS IN THE DEVELOPMENT OF A REGIONAL CUISINE

The Characteristics of the Land

FACTOR 1

The Food Culture of the Indigenous People

FACTOR 2

The Food Culture of the First Settlers

FACTOR 3

Foods and Cooking Techniques Brought by Immigrants

FACTOR 4

Economic Viability

FACTOR 5

	1492	Columbus discovers the Americas
Plantation South	1600	Jamestown, VA, settled 1607; colonial cuisine established
New England		Plymouth, MA, settled 1621; colonial cuisine established
		Manhattan Island settled 1624; no real cuisine
		Mexican Border missions begin 1609; cuisine not yet developed
	1675	
Mid-Atlantic		Pennsylvania colony settled late 1680s; colonial cuisine established
		Chesapeake emerges as a separate culinary region circa 1700; traditional cuisine
Chesapeake Bay Shore	1700	established
Louisiana		Louisiana colony settled 1718; colonial cuisine established
	1725	
Mexican Border	1750	Mexican Border colonial cuisine established by 1750
		French and Indian War 1756–1763
Appalachian South		Appalachian Mountain settlement begins 1760s; pioneer cuisine established
	1775	American Revolution 1775–1783
Central Farmlands		Major settlement of the Mid-West by farmers begins 1780s, pioneer cuisine
and Cities		established
	1800	Louisiana Purchase–July 14, 1803; doubled the size of the U.S.
		First Steamboat to run the Ohio and Mississippi Rivers–1811
		War of 1812 (to 1815)
	1825	1825–Erie Canal opens linking the east coast with the Central Farmland
		War of Texas Independence 1836
		Mormon settlement of Great Basin begins 1847; hardships preclude cuisine
		Mexican-American War 1846–1848
Anglo-Asian California	1850	California Gold Rush begins 1849; pioneer cuisine established
		US Civil War 1861–1865
		Trans continental Railroad completed at Promontory, Utah, May 10, 1869
Western and Central	1875	Settlement of western ranchlands begins 1870s; pioneer cuisine established
Ranchlands		Gradual settlement of Rocky Mountains begins mid-1800s; pioneer cuisine
Rocky Mountains		established
and Great Basin		Pacific Northwest settled mid-1800s; pioneer cuisine established
Pacific Northwest		Late 1800–early 1900s; Industrial revolution has great impact on food
		production, processing, transportation and refrigerated storage
Hawai'i		Although Hawaiian first settlers make contact with Europeans late 1700s, traditional
		cuisine established late 1800s
		Spanish– American War 1898
South Florida and the	1900	
American Caribbean		World War I 1914–1918
New York City		Development begins in early 1900s with completion of Florida East Coast
		Railroad; traditional cuisine established
		New York City becomes center for immigrant cuisines in the early 1900s
	1925	
		World War II 1939–1945; veterans experience European and Asian cuisines
	1950	
		Korean War 1950–1953
		Julia Child's TV show *The French Chef* debuts 1963
		1964 New York World's Fair kindles American interest in world cuisines
		New York City emerges as an international restaurant center circa 1965
	1975	
		Vietnam War ends 1975
		Easing of Asian immigration restrictions in the 1980s adds new Asian cuisine influence
	2000	

FIGURE 1.5
American Regional Cuisines Timeline

Factor 1: The Characteristics of the Land

Land is the first factor to consider when studying a regional cuisine because food is a product of the land. When we speak of the land, we refer not only to the earth and its soil, but also to climate, elevation, bodies of water, and proximity, or the position of the land in respect to geographical bodies and to other regions. All of these elements combine to form a unique regional environment. The environment of a region largely determines whether agriculture will be successful.

Agriculture is the practice of growing plants and raising animals, primarily for food. A more commonly used term for agriculture is *farming*. To understand a region's farmland and its capacity to produce food crops, we'll focus on three main environmental elements: soil, climate, and topography.

Soil

One of the most important elements in the success of a food crop is the quality of the soil (see Figure 1.6). Much more than just dirt, soil is a mixture of mineral and organic components containing the nutrients that enable food crops to grow. Soil with a high proportion of organic matter and a good balance of plant nutrient minerals is called *rich soil*. Soil with little organic matter and/or unbalanced mineral content is considered *poor soil*.

Even if a region's soil is rich, there has to be enough of it to make large-scale farming possible. Deep soil is essential for many food crops, and large fields are necessary for mechanized agriculture. In prehistoric ice ages, glaciers repeatedly pushed their way south from the Arctic and then receded during warm periods. As they traveled, glaciers scraped away soil from some places in America and deposited it in others. Areas that received glacial deposits have thick soil; areas that lost soil because of glacial scouring have thin soil. Mountainous areas also lose soil to **erosion,** the removal of soil by the action of wind or water. Regions with large expanses of deep, rich soil are more likely to produce plentiful and superior food crops. Regions with poor and shallow soil, or good soil found in only in scattered areas, are not likely to produce food crops on a sufficient scale to feed a growing population.

Deep, rich soil remains fertile only if a region's inhabitants use good farming practices. Even good soil can quickly become depleted of nutrients. When soil is planted with food crops, the crops use the nutrients in the soil to promote growth and reproduction. After several plantings of food crops, most crops deplete the soil of certain key nutrients. In order to continue growing plants in the soil, farmers must fertilize it.

Fertilization is the process of nourishing the land by replenishing essential nutrients. In nature, ongoing fertilization occurs via decomposition of fallen leaves, dead plants, animal waste, and animal carcasses. Farmers can replenish soil nutrients by

FIGURE 1.6
Soil Depth in America

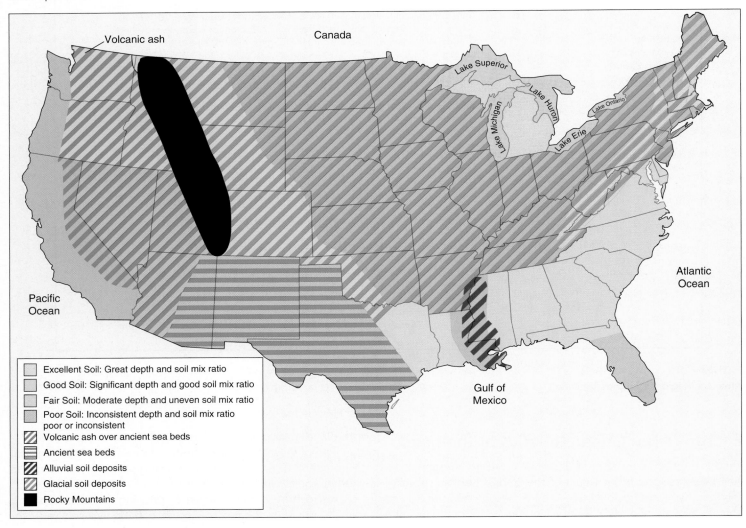

Excellent Soil: Great depth and soil mix ratio
Good Soil: Significant depth and good soil mix ratio
Fair Soil: Moderate depth and uneven soil mix ratio
Poor Soil: Inconsistent depth and soil mix ratio poor or inconsistent
Volcanic ash over ancient sea beds
Ancient sea beds
Alluvial soil deposits
Glacial soil deposits
Rocky Mountains

THE TASTE OF THE SOIL

Naturally fertile soil gives the food that grows in it a distinctive, localized flavor. Chefs have long recognized this fact and have coined a name for it. The original French expression, *le goût de terroir*, literally means "the taste of the soil." American chefs frequently shorten this expression to simply *terroir*.

Terroir (tair-WAH) refers to the flavor imparted to a food product by the soil in which it grows. Each region has a unique combination of minerals and organics in its soil and water that affects the flavor of its fruits, vegetables, and even food animals grazed on the grasses that grow in it. Unless the soil has been excessively modified by the use of chemical fertilizers, pesticides, and herbicides, that unique local flavor is instantly recognizable to a sensitive and educated palate. Georgia peaches, New Jersey tomatoes, and Colorado lamb are good examples of food products that have a distinctive regional flavor due to the soil where they are raised.

fertilizing it with *compost*, a natural mixture of manure and shredded plant material, or with industrially produced chemical fertilizers.

In addition to fertilizing, farmers can take other steps to preserve soil quality. By planting a different crop in a particular field each season, a practice called **crop rotation,** farmers avoid depletion of certain plant nutrients. **Cover crops** are plants that produce needed nutrients; they are grown to semimaturity and then tilled back into the soil. Cover crops also prevent erosion and weed growth.

Natural fertilization, crop rotation, and the use of cover crops are important steps in producing successful harvests year after year. Farming that uses these practices is called **sustainable agriculture.** If sustainable agricultural practices are not followed, after a period of years existing fields play out, or lose fertility. In regions where farmers practice sustainable agriculture, farmland remains consistently productive. In addition, sustainable agricultural practices produce food that is both nutritious and delicious to eat.

Climate

Climate refers to the average weather patterns of a particular area over a period of years. The climate of a culinary region is even more crucial than the soil in determining the success of agriculture because humans can improve the soil but cannot intentionally change the climate. A region's climate typically determines which food plants will thrive, which will struggle, and which will fail. When evaluating a region's climate, temperature and the availability of water are the two most important considerations.

The average temperature of a particular region is fundamentally determined by its **latitude,** a system of expressing location ranging from 0 degrees at the equator to 90 degrees (north or south) at the poles. The climate at the equator is hot; the climate at the North and South Poles is very cold. Thus, a lower latitude usually corresponds to a warmer climate, whereas a higher latitude usually means a cooler climate. However, other factors come into play when determining the average temperature of a region.

Each type of plant has specific temperature requirements in order for it to germinate, grow, and reach maturity. If a foreign food plant is introduced into a climate much different from that in which it was originally developed, the plant may not thrive—and may not even survive. In the mid-1900s, horticulturists began to develop plant *cultivars*, or specifically bred plant types, that can adapt to inhospitable climates. However, during the founding and development of most of America's culinary regions, such horticultural advances were unknown.

Water is equally important to plant growth. Some food plants, such as standard rice cultivars, require enormous amounts of fresh water, whereas others, such as field corn, require relatively little; most fall somewhere in between. And, of course, food animals need water to drink. The most obvious source of fresh water is rainfall. The amount and seasonal distribution of rainfall determines the type of crop or livestock that the land can support. For example, coastal areas of the Plantation South are blessed with substantial and consistent rain and thus were perfect for the cultivation of paddy rice and other high-water-demand produce. America's western plains receive limited amounts of seasonal rain and therefore can sustain only specialized crops and certain animal breeds. See Figure 1.7.

Water also flows in creeks and rivers and exists in *aquifers*, or underground lakes and channels. Diverting aboveground water to agricultural fields requires the creation of irrigation systems; reaching underground water requires digging wells. Before irrigation and well-drilling technology were developed, many lands, such as the American Southwest and California's arid interior valleys, were useless for large-scale farming. Wells and irrigation turned them into valuable farmland. Because water is crucial to farming, it determines how early in history an area will be settled—or whether it will be settled at all.

Topography

Topography refers to the physical features of the land and its elevation: whether the land is flat, rolling, or steeply sloped; and whether the land is at sea level or at a higher altitude. Topography includes the presence of nearby bodies of water, mountains, or other geological elements that influence the region's environment.

Topography affects agriculture in several ways (see Figure 1.8). Where the land is flat or gently rolling, such as in the American Midwest, farming is relatively easy and large-scale agriculture develops. In places where land is mountainous, such as in New England, the Appalachian South, and the far Western Ranchlands regions, farming is difficult. In mountainous terrain, mechanized farming is frequently impossible because the steep slopes don't permit the use of large agricultural machinery. Extremely low-lying land, such as in the Carolina Lowcountry, is frequently wet and marshy, which also precludes the use of

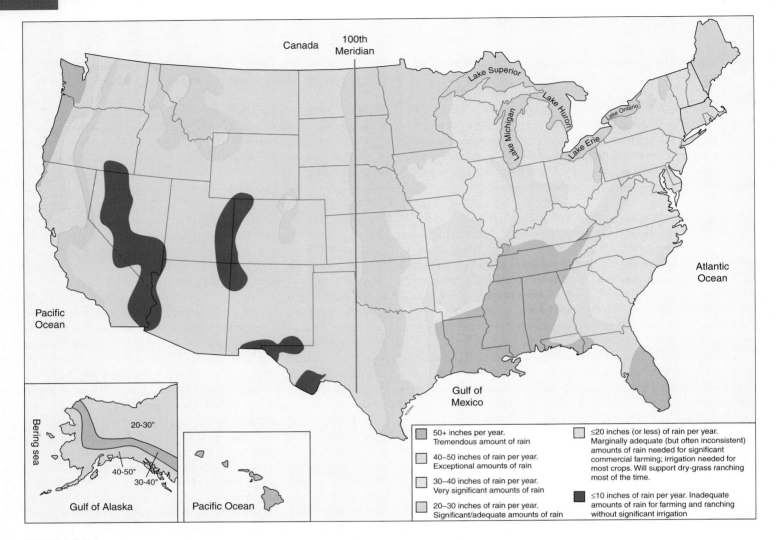

FIGURE 1.7
Annual Rainfall in America

machinery. In such areas, large-scale farming is not practical, and the people of these regions typically look to other resources for their livelihoods.

Topography affects climate, and thus agriculture, largely because of the effects of altitude. **Altitude** is land elevation expressed as the number of feet above sea level. Regions closer to the equator typically have warmer weather than regions farther away from it. However, altitude can drastically alter that formula. Land at a high elevation has significantly cooler weather than land at sea level. In fact, altitude can trump latitude as far as climate is concerned. Hawai'i is a good example; although the Hawai'ian Islands have a subtropical climate at sea level, many of Hawai'i's mountain peaks are covered with snow year-round.

Proximity to water also influences climate. Areas near large bodies of water typically enjoy milder and more consistent weather because air passing over water picks up moisture and retains solar heat more efficiently.

Northern California is a good example of a *maritime*, or water-influenced, climate. Although California's Napa Valley lies at a latitude of 38.5 degrees N, its altitude is 89 feet above sea level, and it is located near the Pacific Ocean. As a result, the Napa Valley's climate is consistently mild and warm, rarely experiencing blazing hot or freezing cold weather. Compare the Napa Valley to Santa Fe, New Mexico, at a similar latitude of 36 degrees N but at an altitude of 7,000 feet and landlocked. A summer day in Santa Fe can reach 120°F, whereas a Santa Fe winter night can easily reach 0°F and is often far colder.

Topography is also an important element in the discovery and settlement of a region because it typically determines how quickly and in what direction settlement can expand (see Figure 1.9). Groups of settlers usually arrive in a new land from a common starting point. Before air transportation, these starting points were typically seacoasts. From the coast, settlers gradually fan out into interior lands. Where the terrain is flat and relatively

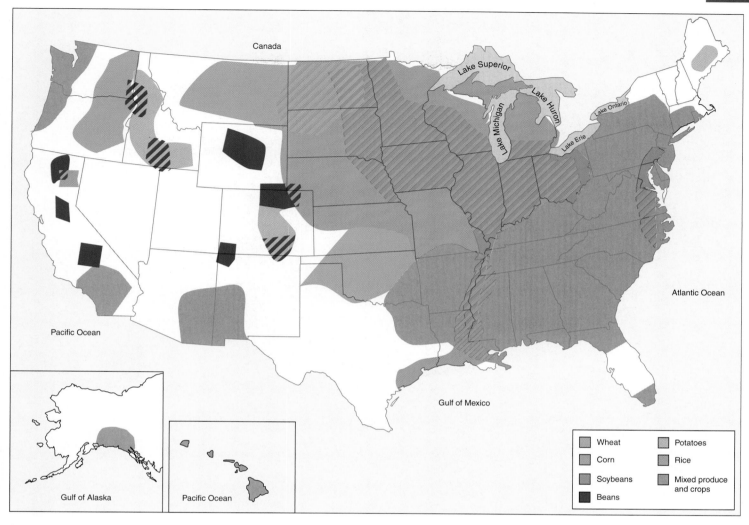

FIGURE 1.8
Crop Cultivation in America

clear, penetration into the interior happens quickly and evenly. However, mountains, forests, marshlands, and other hard-to-cross terrains typically block travel and deter settlement. Conversely, navigable waterways speed settlement because water transportation is fast and efficient in most terrains. For settlers, bodies of water are also important sources of food in the form of fish, shellfish, and waterfowl.

Proximity to Other Regions

The position of a particular region in regard to other vital regions can greatly affect its cuisine. Just as neighbors tend to swap recipes and borrow a cup of sugar from each other, neighboring regions adopt each other's cooking methods and food products. For example, Mid-Atlantic cuisine was enhanced by nearby Chesapeake fish and shellfish and adopted many of the special techniques used to prepare them. Similarly, southern California,

the Ranchlands, and the Mexican Border states were heavily influenced by their proximity to Mexico.

Factor 2: The Food Culture of the Indigenous People

The next factor to consider when studying a regional cuisine is the contributions of its indigenous food culture. In many American culinary regions, the indigenous food culture is an important foundation element of the modern regional cuisine. For these regions, it's important to know and understand the precontact indigenous cuisine.

Let's use the American model again to learn how to apply Factor 2 in evaluating a culinary region. Using Native American food culture as an example has the additional benefit of giving you base-level information that applies to most of the Native

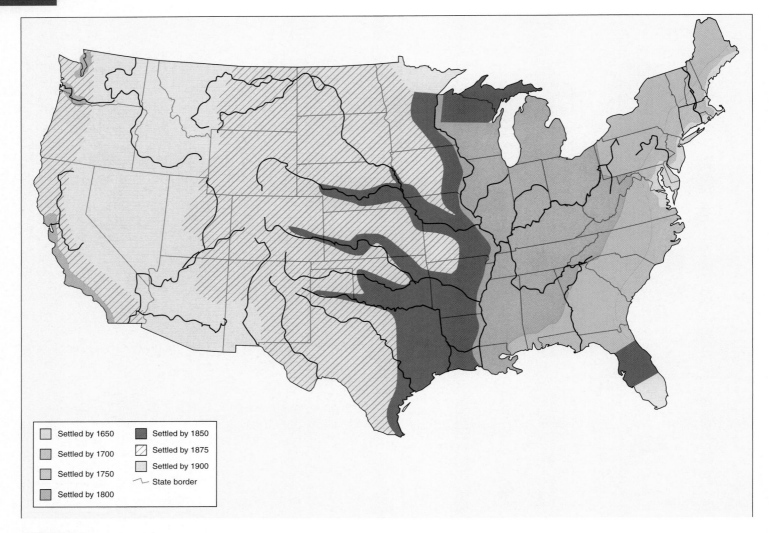

FIGURE 1.9
Patterns of American Settlement

Legend:
- Settled by 1650
- Settled by 1700
- Settled by 1750
- Settled by 1800
- Settled by 1850
- Settled by 1875
- Settled by 1900
- State border

American cultures you'll encounter when studying individual American culinary regions.

Elements of Indigenous Cuisines

To understand any cuisine you must first focus on its three basic elements: ingredients, cooking methods, and attitudes about food, cooking, and eating.

Indigenous Ingredients

Most Native American groups had the same foundation foods. For most, the principal grain food was corn, more specifically known as *maize* (see Figure 1.10). (Read the box on p. 17 to understand the origin of these two words.) When we refer to "corn" as a Native American foundation food, we mean dried field corn, the kind that is ground into cornmeal and other dry, flourlike substances. Although Native Americans ate immature or "green" corn fresh in season, for most of the year they did not have access to corn as a vegetable. Sweet corn, the vegetable as we know it, did not exist until the late 1800s.

Although for many groups protein foods traditionally are secondary to grains in importance, they add vital nutrients to the diet and reveal much about the flavor profile of the cuisine. Most Native American groups had ample access to game meats and fish, and for some these foods constituted the bulk of the diet. However, for many other groups the most reliable protein food consisted of dried beans of various types. Although most Native Americans grew and gathered a number of different vegetables and fruits, various squashes were the mainstay vegetables of the diet. Thus, for the Native American model we can designate wild game, corn, beans, and squash as foundation foods. Because they are both essential and interrelated, the trio of corn, beans, and squash are known to Native Americans

FIGURE 1.10
Dried corn, or maize, America's foundation grain. Shutterstock

CORN OR MAIZE?

Throughout most of the English-speaking world, the word *corn* is a generic term for any type of grain. The original meaning of the word *corn* was "a round, hard core," later signifying "a grainlike object." (That's why we refer to the round seeds of black pepper as *peppercorns*.) In Great Britain, wheat, oats, and barley are all considered types of corn, meaning grain.

When Europeans discovered *Zea mais*, or maize, they frequently called it *Indian corn*. After time, American colonists began using the generic term *corn* to refer solely to their staple crop, maize, identifying all other grains by their specific names. However, the rest of the English-speaking world did not follow suit. Only in America is the word *corn* used specifically to refer to maize.

as **the Three Sisters.** You'll learn much more about Three Sisters foods in subsequent chapters.

Once you have ascertained the foundation foods of a particular group, the next step is to identify its adjunct foods, cooking media, and seasonings. In our Native American model, these elements vary from group to group and help identify the differences between Native American cuisines.

Indigenous Cooking Methods

When you begin to identify and evaluate the cooking methods used by a particular food culture, you must first consider the technology available to its members. In our American model, precontact indigenous Americans had fire technology but not oven-building skills. For cooking vessels they had only stone, skin, and earthenware. They had no domesticated animals to provide fat, and no source of easily extractable vegetable oil. Therefore, Native American cooking methods included stone griddle baking, pit-roasting, and stewing. Precontact Native Americans did not widely use frying methods because they did not have the required technology or ingredients.

Food preservation methods are the key to survival in most early food cultures. Precontact Native American groups had surprisingly sophisticated food preservation technology, often equal to that of more advanced European civilizations of the time. Among the food preservation methods they used were drying, salt curing, and smoking.

Indigenous Attitudes about Food, Cooking, and Eating

Attitudes about food, cooking, and eating are varied and complex. The importance of cooking and eating to a group of people, and thus their attitudes about food, are a result of many different factors. One vital factor is need. The difficulty involved in obtaining food and the effort required to prepare it correspond to its importance within a culture. Indigenous people typically have a close relationship to food through hunting, foraging, and farming and thus value food highly. This was the case with virtually all precontact Native Americans.

Another factor is spirituality. Most indigenous food cultures attribute a mystical or religious aspect to growing and eating food.

For example, Native Americans hold food to be sacred in general and revere corn in particular. Food is used both symbolically and physically in Native American worship practices. Indigenous people typically link the sacredness of food to the importance of resource conservation and sustainability and include sustainable practices as part of their ethical and religious conduct.

Yet another element in a group's attitude about food involves wealth and leisure. People who have wealth in the form of currency or resources can afford the best ingredients and have time to be creative with them. In our Native American model, some groups enjoyed relative wealth and had an abundance of resources; these groups boasted strong food cultures and highly developed cuisines. The precontact Native Americans of the Mexican Border region, the Pacific Northwest, and the Plantation South were among the most highly developed food cultures of the North American continent.

Indigenous Influence in the Modern Cuisine

As you apply Factor 2 to each regional cuisine, evaluate its importance by searching for indigenous ingredients and cooking techniques in the modern cuisine. Figure 1.11 shows the degree of Native American influence in American culinary regions. Some regional cuisines have many indigenous elements, and others have few or none. You may wonder why this is so.

Modern cuisines that have many indigenous elements are said to have strong indigenous roots. Such cuisines typically develop where and when the indigenous people have a highly developed civilization: in other words, where they're well nourished, healthy, and strong; where they have reasonably advanced technology; and where they have organized themselves into large and powerful groups. (In most cases the development of cooperative agriculture is a marker of a highly developed civilization.) In such civilizations food culture and cooking typically flourish. Even when powerful invaders overwhelm such natives, their strong food culture usually reemerges after a time.

Other modern regional cuisines exhibit virtually no trace of the indigenous food culture. Such regional cuisines are said to have few or no indigenous roots. This occurs for several reasons. Sometimes the indigenous people have a less highly developed civilization, and thus more primitive cooking techniques, than subsequent settler groups. In some cases indigenous foods are fewer and less palatable than new foods brought by colonists or pioneers. In these situations the indigenous people typically prefer the new foods that colonists or pioneers introduce. In time they abandon their own foods in favor of colonial domesticates or pioneer foods.

The survival of an indigenous food culture also depends on the situation of the colonists or pioneers. When newcomers are few and poorly provisioned, they become dependent on indigenous foods and frequently grow to like them. Thus native foods survive. When a region is settled by large groups that are powerful and well provisioned, the settlers do not need indigenous foods and, especially if they are culinary conservatives, have no desire to try them. In this case the native people are frequently placed in a powerless position by the more powerful

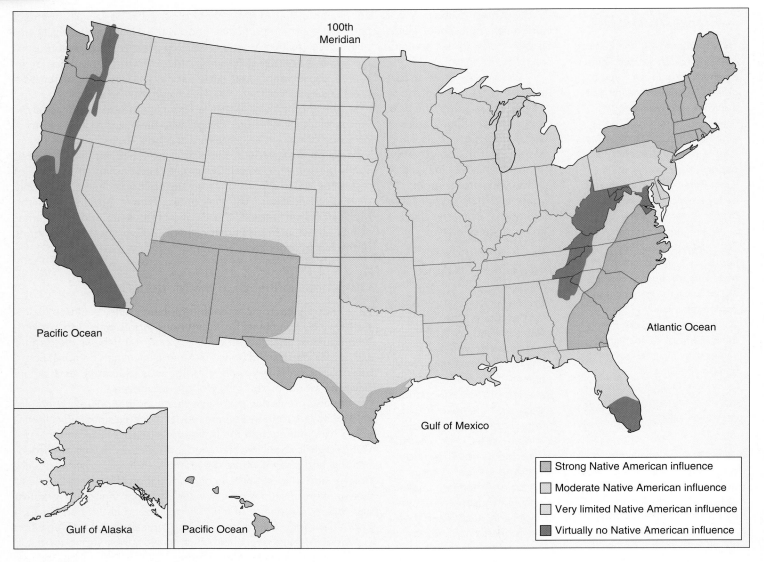

100th
Meridian

Pacific Ocean

Atlantic Ocean

Gulf of Mexico

Gulf of Alaska

Pacific Ocean

■ Strong Native American influence

□ Moderate Native American influence

□ Very limited Native American influence

■ Virtually no Native American influence

FIGURE 1.11
Areas of Native American Culinary Influence

newcomers. The demoralized native population loses respect for its indigenous dishes and abandons them. In this way, indigenous foods and cooking techniques disappear.

Sadly, yet another reason for the disappearance of indigenous cuisines is the early and complete destruction of the indigenous population. This was the case in several American culinary regions. Such regional cuisines have no indigenous roots.

Neither civilization nor food culture is static. In other words, both are constantly changing. However, the rate of change depends on the circumstances. Before contact with more advanced civilizations, the civilization and food culture of an indigenous people tend to develop slowly over many centuries. By the time Europeans reached them, the civilizations of America's various native groups had widely differing levels of advancement. Although some Native Americans were still hunter-gatherers, others were accomplished agriculturalists with complex technologies, social

systems, and governments. However, all Native American cultures changed rapidly and dramatically after European contact.

Factor 3: The Food Culture of the First Settlers

The next factor to consider when studying the development of a regional cuisine is the food culture of the first settlers. First-settler food culture comprises two elements: the cuisine of their original homeland and the hybrid cuisine created by intermingling the homeland cuisine with indigenous ingredients and cooking methods.

The Homeland Cuisine

First settlers initially bring with them the ingredients and cooking methods of their homeland. Colonists bring Old World cuisine to the new colony, and pioneers bring colonial cuisine to the new territory. Thus, to understand first-settler cuisine you must become familiar with all elements of the first settlers' homeland cuisine: its foundation foods, favored seasonings, principal cooking media, primary cooking methods, and food attitudes.

The Hybrid Cuisine

Once you understand the homeland cuisine of a settler group, you can determine how much of the indigenous cuisine they adopted. Technology and preparedness typically determine whether first settlers must depend on indigenous foods. The earliest settlers to a region cannot rely solely on the provisions brought with them. Their supplies inevitably run out long before their seeds grow to harvest or their food animals bear young. They must find and use indigenous food plants and animals. How well they do so—and for how long—depends on the strength of their food culture and their level of culinary liberalism. When indigenous ingredients and techniques are adopted with skill and enthusiasm, the result is a repertoire of interesting hybrid dishes and a vibrant first-settler cuisine.

Later arrivals are usually better prepared and provisioned. Often they can rely on the colonial domesticates established by their predecessors. If they are culinary liberals, they may adopt indigenous ingredients and create a cuisine with strong indigenous roots. If, on the other hand, they are culinary conservatives, they typically ignore indigenous foods, and the cuisine they create has few or no indigenous roots.

In our American model, some European colonists and American pioneers were well provisioned and adequately prepared to survive in a rugged new land, but others were not. Some had strong food cultures, whereas the food cultures of others were minimized. Some were culinary liberals, and others were conservatives. Applying Factor 3 to a region will help you understand the beginnings of its hybrid cuisine.

Factor 4: Foods and Cooking Techniques Brought by Immigrants

A region's colonial or pioneer cuisine combines indigenous foods and cooking techniques with those of the region's first settlers. Usually, a region's early colonial or pioneer period is a time of relative ethnic uniformity. In other words, shortly after first contact a region is primarily populated by an ethnically homogenous first-settler group along with the existing indigenous inhabitants. However, sooner or later secondary settlers, or immigrants, begin to arrive.

Although first-settler cooking is the cornerstone of most regional cuisines, often secondary settlers, or immigrants, add the spice to the stew. Just as new bloodlines improve the gene pool and make a biological species stronger, the fresh infusion of ingredients, cooking methods, and attitudes brought by immigrants reinvigorates the existing cuisine.

The timing of secondary settlement varies from one region to another. Immigration typically occurs in waves, one cultural group following another. Each significant wave of immigration leaves a mark on the cuisine of the region—if the immigrants' food culture is strong enough to generate attention and the existing food culture is liberal enough to welcome new tastes, techniques, and ideas.

The ingredients and cooking methods introduced by immigrants are often more exciting and complex than those of the existing regional cuisine. Their culinary impact often changes the course of the area's culinary destiny. Consider the early cooking of the Plantation South and New England. Both were colonies in which English first-settler cooks adopted the same Native American products and techniques; the only real difference between them was the South's agricultural advantage. But the Plantation South received tremendous early influence from the powerfully seasoned, highly sensual cooking of second-wave Africans and Caribbean-Africans, whereas New England benefited from second-wave Portuguese and Italian culinary influence much later and to a lesser degree. Thus, the question posed on p. 10—why is the cuisine of New England so different from the cuisine of the Plantation South?—is answered by applying Factor 4.

The culinary contributions of successive waves of immigrants are a vital element in the establishment of a regional cooking style. But the final factor unites many disparate culinary elements into a distinctive, sophisticated, unified regional cuisine.

Factor 5: Economic Viability

It takes wealth to produce truly fine food. Farmers must have land, equipment, and labor to produce the best ingredients, and consumers must be willing and able to pay a fair price for them. Home cooks must have the leisure to spend time on complex food preparations, and professional chefs must be paid high salaries to create culinary masterpieces. Diners must be experienced and educated to a level where they recognize and appreciate the best dishes and must have the disposable income to dine out in expensive restaurants.

In order for all of these things to occur, a region must achieve **economic viability,** the point at which a region has fully utilized its resources and can support its own population with the revenues from its goods and services. Another marker of economic viability is that most of its population has moved from subsistence (just getting by) to affluence (having enough money to be comfortable). Once a region has established itself economically, it will have a sizable upper class with plenty of disposable income and the desire to spend that income on the pleasures of the table.

During the development of Europe's and Asia's most respected regional cuisines, the finest cooking took place in the palaces of the aristocracy, or ruling class. Although America has no formal aristocracy, a largely self-made economic aristocracy emerged along with each region's economic viability. The owners of the great Southern plantations, the railroad barons of the Mid-Atlantic, the financiers of New York City, and the Gold Rush millionaires of California all flaunted their newfound money by setting grand tables. They employed the finest local cooks and offered extravagant salaries to lure chefs from Europe. They built heated greenhouses so they could enjoy fresh produce year-round. They imported seasonings and other ingredients from all over the world. In an era of one-upmanship, they vied to outdo each other's extravagances. In their kitchens, and later in the fine restaurants they patronized, American haute cuisine was born.

However, in regions with solid economic viability, not only the aristocracy but also the middle class and even the working class benefited from the resulting culinary advances. When times are good, the middle class concentrates on the refinements of the table. Cookbooks, cooking appliances, and cooking classes all raise culinary awareness. People with discretionary income frequently dine out, expanding their knowledge and appreciation of cuisine. When restaurants thrive, the working class gains employment in their kitchens. This allows workers to learn about fine cuisine and to acquire more money to spend on food.

Economic viability also generates travel and trade, which bring new ingredients into a region's culinary repertoire. Travel to foreign countries or other regions introduces people to new foods and cooking techniques. Returning home with these new items and ideas, they not only broaden their own palates and cooking repertoires, but also become more receptive to new ideas and dishes brought back by others. Where there is demand, trade follows. Once people establish a need for a particular food product or cooking implement, the market opens for others. The resulting food import trade generates money and further increases economic viability.

Finally, economic viability establishes a regional cuisine so that it's recognized and understood by people outside the region. When viability is reached later rather than sooner, the cuisine often remains undefined and unsung, known only within its region. For example, it took the economic impetus of 20th-century tourism to push Hawai'i's cooks and chefs into acknowledging the value of Hawai'i's regional cooking style.

If a region's economic viability is lost, the region runs the risk of losing its established culinary traditions. After the Civil War the economy of the Plantation South was in ruins, and Southern cooking went into serious decline. Only the tenacity and resilience of a few traditional Southern cooks kept Plantation South cuisine alive until the post–World War II economic revival of the 1960s.

■ AMERICA'S □ MICROCUISINES

In order to qualify as a separate culinary region, an area must have a homogenous food culture as well as uniform climate and topography. However, some regions include people and places that dare to be culinarily different. In other words, some small groups of people with their own, unique food culture live and cook together within the boundaries of a larger culinary region. Although their cooking style is often closely related to that of the larger region, it is dissimilar in several important ways and thus can be recognized as separate and different. We call these unique, narrowly practiced, lesser-known cooking styles **microcuisines.**

Although American microcuisines are quite diverse, microcuisine groups have several things in common:

- Microcuisine groups typically have a shared cultural heritage; many are immigrant groups. Microcuisines founded by immigrant groups are additionally classified as ethnic-American cuisines, defined below.
- Microcuisines are often site-specific. In other words, to experience some of America's microcuisines you must travel to a certain county, town, or neighborhood.
- Microcuisines are selectively practiced; not every family within that county or town knows and practices the area's particular microcuisine.
- Microcuisines are often well-kept secrets. Few people outside the group are familiar with their defining dishes. Unfortunately, because they are little known, some microcuisines are in danger of being forgotten.

A good example of a little known microcuisine is Acadian-American cuisine, practiced in the New England culinary region and explored in this book's website. Few Americans are familiar with this cooking style, and for a number of reasons, it's in danger of dying out. Other microcuisines were spread widely throughout the United States by events of history and are now nationally known. Soul Food, the African-American cuisine of the Plantation South discussed in the website, is a good example of a well-known and widespread microcuisine.

Many of America's microcuisines were developed by immigrants blending their homeland cuisines with the regional ingredients and techniques of their new homes. These immigrant-based, hybrid microcuisines are called **ethnic-American cuisines.** Today these cooking styles have become thoroughly American; their defining dishes are unknown in the immigrants' homeland cuisines. For example, Chinese-American dishes such as egg rolls, chop suey, and fortune cookies are unknown in China. Italian-American dishes such as spaghetti and meatballs can't be found in Italy—at least in the form to which Americans are accustomed.

■ FOREIGN CUISINES □ IN AMERICA

As you progress in your study of American regional cuisines, you may wonder why some foreign-sounding dishes are included in this book but others are not. To answer this question, let's distinguish between ethnic-American cuisines and foreign cuisines practiced in America.

A **foreign cuisine** is simply a national or regional cuisine practiced outside its homeland. A foreign cuisine retains its original ingredients, techniques, and flavors, with little or no modification. In other words, it remains virtually unchanged. To exemplify the concept of a foreign cuisine, we'll once again use the American model.

The United States welcomes immigrants from all over the world. Today, in the American homes of most first-generation immigrants, and in American foreign-cuisine restaurants, it's possible to eat foreign dishes that are virtually identical to those prepared in the country of their origin. The ability to prepare authentic foreign dishes largely depends on access to authentic ingredients.

Early immigrants had difficulty obtaining authentic homeland ingredients and were forced to make substitutions that led to the development of new, hybrid cuisines. Because of better transportation, immigrant groups arriving in America after 1970 could import virtually every ingredient and cooking implement necessary to reproduce the authentic cuisines of their homelands. For example, today immigrants from countries such as India, Thailand, and Korea can easily acquire the ingredients necessary to prepare a pure form of their native cuisine. They have no need to hybridize. For this reason we have not yet seen the development of distinct and separate Indian-American, Thai-American, or Korean-American cuisines.

In our coverage of American cuisine we've made an important distinction between ethnic-American dishes and foreign-cuisine dishes. Because our mission in this book is to present *American* cuisine, the recipes you'll find here were created in America, using American ingredients, to suit American palates. Therefore, you won't find recipes for authentic foreign dishes such as Italian pesto alla Genovese and Mexican mole poblano, even though they are both popular and delicious. Instead, you'll find ethnic-American dishes, such as spaghetti and meatballs and chili—because as hybrids, they are truly American. Only in the few cases in which most of a culinary region's cooks have embraced a foreign dish have we included it in our recipe list.

AMERICA'S NATIONAL CUISINE

A nation's culinary development begins with regional cuisines. Typically these cuisines spring up independently, born of the land's indigenous food products, and evolve at their own pace according to the currents of history. However, for all nations, some or all of these disparate regional cuisine styles eventually synthesize into a recognizable national cuisine. We'll use the American model to examine how and why this occurs.

A **national cuisine** is a unified style of cooking common to most of a country's population. Although today its repertoire of dishes is well known, America's national cuisine actually has not existed for very long.

America began as a group of unrelated colonies belonging to various European nations. Moreover, even before the first European set foot in the New World, indigenous Native American groups were disunited; they lived in separate tribal groups and had different cultures, languages, and cooking styles. After the American colonies were politically bound into a single nation, there was still very little exchange of ingredients or cooking techniques between, say, Virginia and Massachusetts. Thus, their cuisines remained quite dissimilar.

As America expanded westward, distances became vast and culture and cooking became even more diverse. People living on the prairie raised and ate very different foods than people living on the East Coast or in Louisiana. As America grew larger, it comprised a number of geographical regions, each having its own climate, topography, history, and culture—and, as a result, its own cooking style. For nearly three hundred years, from the first European settlements in the early 1600s until the Industrial Revolution in the late 1800s, there were distinct and separate American regional cuisines, but no American national cuisine.

Only after the far-flung corners of America were connected by railroads could a national cuisine begin to emerge. Nationally published newspapers and magazines promoted it. The exchange of ingredients and ideas resulting from advanced technology made it possible. When it first emerged, American national cuisine comprised the most popular dishes from America's most influential regions, for the first time shared by cooks across the nation. New England's roast turkey and the Plantation South's fried chicken became standards of American national cuisine. As time went by and new regions were settled, new dishes were added to the national cuisine. Ranchlands chili and California roll sushi are now enjoyed across the nation. Like all cuisines, America's national cuisine is ever evolving. A bonus chapter on America's national cuisine is included on this book's website.

ON THE ROAD TO DISCOVERY

You've now learned the basics of food culture and cuisine. You've learned how a culinary region is defined, and you've identified America's fifteen unique culinary regions. You've become familiar with the five factors in the development of a regional cuisine and learned how they're used to analyze a particular region or to compare one region to another. In addition, you've become familiar with key terms and important concepts used in subsequent chapters.

Armed with the understanding gained by studying this chapter, you're now ready for an in-depth exploration of America's fifteen regional cuisines. You have an exciting culinary journey ahead of you. Let's begin.

■ □ ■   STUDY QUESTIONS

1. List the three stages of regional settlement and discuss the manner in which these stages occur. Include in your discussion the difference between colonists and pioneers.

2. Explain the difference between cooking and cuisine.

3. List the three elements of a food culture and its cuisine. Briefly explain each element and its components.

4. List the three categories of ingredients basic to all cuisines.

5. Contrast the eating attitudes and behaviors of a strong food culture with those of a minimized food culture.

6. Explain the term *melting pot* as it applies to food culture and cuisine. Include in your explanation the ways in which patterns of successive settlement change and enrich an existing cuisine. Give examples from the American model.

7. List the three characteristics that define a culinary region.

8. Explain the effects of soil, climate, topography, and proximity (Factor 1) on the development of a regional cuisine.

9. Briefly discuss Native American cuisine, including indigenous ingredients, cooking methods, and attitudes about food, cooking, and eating (Factor 2).

10. Explain the effects of first settlers (Factor 3) and immigrants (Factor 4) on the development of a regional cuisine.

11. Explain the effect of economic viability (Factor 5) on the development of a regional cuisine.

12. Draw a map of the United States and sketch in the fifteen culinary regions.

13. Define the term *microcuisine*. Give an example of an American microcuisine.

14. Explain the difference between an ethnic-American cuisine and a foreign cuisine practiced in America. Give examples.

15. When did America's national cuisine develop? What historical events were responsible for its emergence?

■□■ chapter two

The Plantation South

eastern and central Virginia, eastern and central North Carolina, eastern and central South Carolina, eastern and central Georgia, northern Florida, Alabama, Mississippi, central and western Tennessee, central and western Kentucky

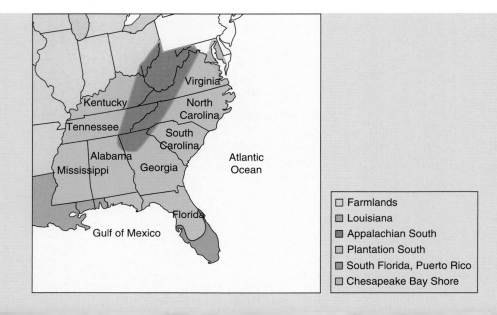

☐ Farmlands
☐ Louisiana
■ Appalachian South
☐ Plantation South
■ South Florida, Puerto Rico
☐ Chesapeake Bay Shore

WHY USE THE TERM *PLANTATION* to name a modern American culinary region? The era of plantations is long gone, faded into history. Nonetheless, the plantation culture that thrived throughout much of the American South from the mid-1600s through the mid-1800s gave birth to a unique and noteworthy regional cuisine. No other word so aptly describes this cooking style and, thus, it best defines the culinary region you're about to explore.

We use this term in full knowledge of its connotations. The bitter legacy of slavery in America is still with us, and the resulting issues are still unresolved. The descendants of white slave owners and black slaves have achieved only an uneasy peace. However, this combination of European master and African slave resulted in one of America's most complex and varied regional cuisines. White planters founded the cuisine, bringing European food crops to the new land and spending their wealth on good eating. But the skills and sensibilities of African-American slave cooks transformed the planters' cooking into cuisine, creating world-class dishes that are still prepared and enjoyed today. Thus, we use the prefix *Plantation* to signify a special kind of Southern cooking—one that stands apart from all other American Southern cuisines.

AFTER STUDYING THIS CHAPTER YOU SHOULD BE ABLE TO:

- explain how land characteristics (Factor 1) led to the region's economic viability (Factor 5)
- list the Native American ingredients and cooking methods that contributed to Plantation South cuisine (Factor 2)
- briefly describe the Old World cuisine of English planters (Factor 3) and discuss their food attitudes
- describe the colonial cooking of the Plantation South (Factor 2 and Factor 3)
- list African ingredients, cooking methods, and taste preferences that became important features of Plantation South cuisine (Factor 4)
- list the foundation foods, favored seasonings, principal cooking media, primary cooking methods, and food attitudes of Plantation South cuisine
- discuss the effects of the Civil War on the Plantation South economy (Factor 5) and the resulting effects on Plantation South cuisine
- recount the development of the Lowcountry microcuisine, featured on the website; describe its ingredients and cooking methods; and list its defining dishes
- recount the development of the soul food microcuisine, featured on the website; describe its ingredients and cooking methods; and list its defining dishes
- prepare authentic Plantation South dishes, Lowcountry dishes, and soul food dishes

APPETIZERS

Charleston She-Crab Soup with Buttermilk Biscuit

Georgia Peanut Soup with Southern Brittle Bread

Shrimp 'n' Grits

Chickasaw Bean Cake with Sunflower Salad

Granddaddy's Corncakes with Country Ham and Crab

Kentucky Limestone Salad with Clemson Blue Cheese, Cornbread Croutons, and Candied Pecans

Cheese Grits Soufflé with Frizzled Ham

Fried Green Tomatoes with Fresh Tomato Sauce and Bacon

ENTRÉES

Lowcountry Shrimp Perloo with Sugar Snap Peas

Calabash Fish Fry with Hush Puppies and Southern Coleslaw

Pan-Fried Catfish with Tartar Sauce, Southern Potato Salad, and Home-Style Sliced Tomatoes

Southern Fried Chicken with Mashed Potatoes, Cream Gravy, and Down-Home Green Beans

Country Captain with Pan-Steamed Rice and Fried Okra

Quail with Oyster Pilau Dressing, Pumpkin Purée, and Sautéed Spinach

Peachy Duck with Mashed Potatoes and Turnips 'n' Turnip Greens

Grilled Dove or Squab with Candied Sweet Potatoes and Bacon-Pecan Wilted Watercress

Smoked Spareribs with North Carolina Barbeque Sauce, Fancy Hoppin' John, and Collard Greens

Country-Style Pork Ribs with Spicy Vidalia Onion Ketchup, Creasy Greens, Butter Beans, and Cornbread

Country Ham with Pineapple, Fresh Corn Spoon Bread, and Braised Tender Greens

Pork Tenderloin in Bourbon Sauce with Stuffed Vidalia Onion and Stewed Okra

DESSERTS

Old-Fashioned Biscuit Strawberry Shortcake

Dixie Peach Cobbler

Still Master's Pecan Pie

Choctaw Persimmon Pudding with Custard Sauce

Sky-High Coconut Cake

Ambrosia

WEBSITE EXTRAS

Breakfasts   Sandwiches   Hors d'Oeuvres   Thanksgiving Menu

AN AGRICULTURAL PARADISE

The Plantation South culinary region begins just south of the Mason-Dixon Line in north central Maryland, where it's bounded on the east by the Chesapeake Bay Shore region and on the west by the Appalachian South region. It encompasses much of Virginia and the eastern Carolinas, then sweeps southwestward along America's coastal plain. The Plantation South also encompasses parts of the states running northward along the eastern bank of the Mississippi River from Louisiana to the Indiana border. Although the Appalachian Mountains thrust themselves through the heart of the Plantation South region, they are culturally and culinarily separate from it. The map on page 24 illustrates the region's scope.

Certain areas within the Plantation South culinary region are distinguished as subregions. The region's southernmost tier of states—Georgia, Alabama, Mississippi, and northern Florida—are known as the **Deep South.** Coastal South Carolina is known as the Lowcountry, home to a microcuisine covered on this book's companion website.

FIGURE 2.1
Plantation South Topographical Zones

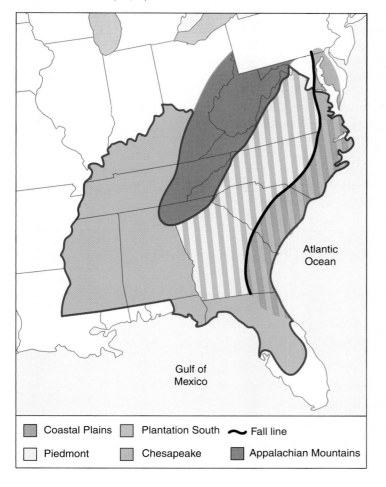

Atlantic Ocean

Gulf of Mexico

▨ Coastal Plains	▨ Plantation South	∿ Fall line
☐ Piedmont	▨ Chesapeake	▨ Appalachian Mountains

Although early European explorers didn't find gold and spices in the Plantation South, they were impressed by the superiority of its soil and climate. In an era when most of the world's economy was based on farming, the Plantation South was an agricultural paradise.

Gentle Terrain and Rich Soil

The geological story of the Plantation South begins in the Appalachians; these ancient mountains are the source of the region's deep and fertile soil. Geologists believe that sixty million years ago, the Appalachian Mountains were about twenty times their present height. However, erosion gradually decomposed the mountain rock, breaking it down into mineral-rich soil. During the ice ages, glaciers leveled the mountain peaks, carved out valleys, and pushed soil downhill. In warmer periods, the glaciers receded and forests grew on the slopes. Fallen leaves added organic matter to the soil. Melting ice created rushing rivers that carried soil farther downhill. When the water slowed in the foothills and the flatlands below, it released the soil, forming thick deposits covering the underlying subsoil by many feet. Thus, the Appalachians' lost soil became a valuable resource for the Plantation South region that surrounds them.

The Appalachians were eventually worn down into a long chain of low, rounded mountains. Below them the terrain gradually flattens, becoming **piedmont**—literally "foot of the mountain," an area of rolling hills at a mountain's base. Plantation South piedmont hilltops have adequate amounts of nutrient-rich soil, with only the occasional rocky outcrop. Southern piedmont valleys are protected from mountain winds and have thick soil and few rocks. Fast-flowing creeks and rivers provide water.

Below the piedmont lies the Southern **coastal plain,** a flat band of land bordering an ocean, in this case the Atlantic and the Gulf of Mexico. From the Delaware Bay to Georgia, the Appalachians' eastern piedmont is separated from the coastal plain by the **fall line,** a rocky shelf over which the region's rivers plummet in a series of low waterfalls. In the Plantation South, the fall line became an important line of demarcation, both agriculturally and socially. Land above the fall line is suitable for light farming and, especially, grazing. Below it, the Southern coastal plain stretches broad and flat, with deep and richly fertile soil, for many miles until it reaches the sea. Europeans recognized the Southern coastal plain's potential as an agricultural powerhouse capable of producing cash crops on a massive scale. Moreover, below the fall line the region's rivers flow slowly, deep, and wide, forming safe harbors for trading vessels at their mouths. This land gave rise to plantation society.

FACTOR 1

Flat land and deep, rich soil made the region ideal for large-scale agriculture.

Today much of the region's terrain is visible as open land. However, when Europeans first arrived in the early 1600s, both the Southern piedmont and coastal plain were covered with deciduous forest. The dense canopy of trees further enriched the region's soil with layers of fallen leaves that gradually decomposed into superb organic fertilizer.

FACTOR 1

Ample rainfall and numerous creeks and rivers ensure water for growing food crops.

A Mild and Moist Climate

The Plantation South enjoys a mild climate with ample moisture as rainfall and humidity because of its weather-moderating proximity to the Atlantic Ocean. The Appalachian Mountains help shield lands to the east from harsh westerly weather while funneling warm, moist Gulf of Mexico weather northward. Thus, lowland Maryland, Virginia, and the Carolinas have climates suitable for virtually all types of European food plants. Proximity to the Gulf substantially warms the Deep South. There, a total of more than three hundred frost-free days makes the cultivation of subtropical plants possible and allows two separate growing seasons for many temperate-climate crops.

In the Plantation South, average precipitation ranges from 30 to more than 60 inches per year. In much of the region, cool weather is moist and summers are thickly humid. Water concentrates on the ground in many places. The Southern coastal plain was once covered with thousands of acres of wetlands, and many remain even after extensive drainage projects. Despite cyclical droughts, the Plantation South has ample water for irrigation thanks to its many streams and rivers. Only in the past few decades has overdevelopment and the drought cycle made water scarcity an issue.

In the Plantation South, the mild weather, ample moisture, flat terrain, and thick, rock-free, fertile soil set the stage for agricultural success. The only obstacle to achieving this success was millions of trees. As any gardener knows, food crops need sunlight to thrive. The region's Native Americans developed an ingenious way of dealing with the dense Southern woodland.

NATIVE AMERICANS OF THE PLANTATION SOUTH

Many anthropologists believe that the first humans on the North American continent entered from the west by crossing the **Beringan land bridge,** a strip of land joining Asia and Alaska that emerged during an ice age and then disappeared. Some suggest that Asian people also arrived later by boat on the Pacific shore. Over thousands of years, America's native people gradually filtered eastward across the continent and into the Plantation South. As their cultures developed, early natives banded into groups, until scores of culturally and linguistically disparate tribes were scattered across the land. By the late 1500s Catawbas, Cherokees, Creeks, Chickasaws, Tuskegees, and Powhatans were among the indigenous people found throughout the Plantation South. Figure 2.2 shows where these tribes settled.

The hunting and foraging methods, agricultural methods, and cooking meth-

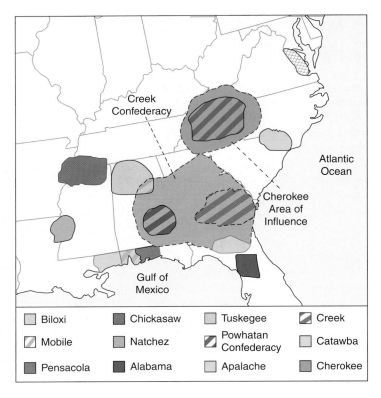

Creek Confederacy

Atlantic Ocean

Cherokee Area of Influence

Gulf of Mexico

Biloxi	Chickasaw	Tuskegee	Creek
Mobile	Natchez	Powhatan Confederacy	Catawba
Pensacola	Alabama	Apalache	Cherokee

FIGURE 2.2

Native American Settlement in the Plantation South

ods of Plantation South Native American tribes are presented here in depth because Plantation South Native American foodways serve as a model for most East Coast native groups. Before and during early European contact, the Native Americans of New England, the Mid-Atlantic, the Chesapeake Bay Shore, and Louisiana acquired and prepared their food in much the same manner as the Plantation South tribes, used the same basic indigenous ingredients and cooking methods, and had similar attitudes about food, cooking, and eating. However, the favorable climate and topography of the Plantation South made its native groups the most successful farmers of the Eastern tribes.

ELEMENTS OF PLANTATION SOUTH NATIVE AMERICAN CUISINE

FOUNDATION FOODS

principal starch: dried corn (maize)

principal proteins: fish, large and small game, dried beans

principal produce: squashes, pumpkins, sunflower root, wild greens

FAVORED SEASONINGS: wild herbs, wild fruits, wild onions and garlic

PRINCIPAL COOKING MEDIA: water, bear fat

PRIMARY COOKING METHODS: grilling, roasting, boiling, poaching, stewing

FOOD ATTITUDES: strong food culture, culinary liberals

A Migratory Lifestyle

During the spring planting season and the late-summer harvest, Plantation South Native Americans lived in large, lowland villages. The typical native settlement consisted of pole-and-bark structures clustered in a woodland clearing surrounded by agricultural plots. Figure 2.3 is a contemporary European artist's depiction of a Virginia Algonquian village. These villages were considered semipermanent because of their inhabitants' frequent need to move.

Although they were excellent farmers, Native Americans of the Plantation South did not practice fertilization and thus could not farm their fields for extended periods. After eight or ten years, when the local soil had been depleted of nutrients, Southern tribes simply moved to a new location. Sometimes they began fresh with virgin land; other times they returned to older villages where fields had been cultivated, abandoned, and

FIGURE 2.3

This watercolor of a Virginia Algonquian village illustrates the East Coast Native American building style. Peter Dennis © Dorling Kindersley

regenerated naturally. Archaeological digs reveal signs of repeated building and rebuilding on many village sites. This practice is called **cyclical land use,** an ongoing pattern in which farmland is used, abandoned, and used again.

The East Coast native practice of cyclical land use underscores an important traditional Native American belief: Land is a common resource to be shared by all, owned by none. This philosophy opposed the prevailing European concept of land as owned property to be held and protected, bought and sold. Knowing about this fundamental difference of opinion is key to understanding how relations between Native Americans and European settlers deteriorated during the colonial period.

In the spring planting season, women worked the crops while men hunted for small game and fished in local rivers and creeks. Around midsummer, once crops were established, villagers split up into extended family groups and traveled inland to hunt and forage in the mountains. They returned to the village for the late-summer harvest, then traveled upland again for large-scale winter hunting. Stated in anthropological terms, they practiced **human seasonal migration,** moving from place to place throughout the year to obtain food. In doing so, they spent roughly half the year involved in agriculture, and the other half hunting and gathering.

Hunting and Gathering

Before European settlement the Plantation South woodlands provided habitat for a wide variety of animals, most of which were used by Native Americans for food. Virtually every part of the animal was used; in addition to meat, game animals provided skins, fur, or feathers for clothing and bones for making tools. The primary large game animal in the Plantation South region was the whitetail deer; thus, venison was an important Native American foundation food. Bears were hunted not only for their meat but also for their fat; bear fat was virtually the only cooking fat available to Native Americans. Small game abounded, with raccoon, opossum, squirrel, and rabbit among the most frequently harvested. Wildfowl, including teal duck, pintail duck, mallard duck, grouse, pheasants, wild geese, and wild turkeys, were important elements of the diet. In western areas near the Mississippi River, herds of bison occasionally appeared; Southern natives hunted them using methods similar to those of precontact Plains tribes. (p. 463). Eastern woodland bison were relatively abundant into the 1700s, but extinct by 1825.

For coastal tribes, seafood was a major part of the diet. Each season brought its particular species. In the spring anadromous fish such as shad and herring swam upriver in great numbers. Throughout the summer and fall, native fishermen harvested weakfish (speckled sea trout), mullet, flounder, grouper, red snapper, red drum, ocean

FACTOR 2

Native American agriculture was based on cyclical land use with no use of fertilizer.

FACTOR 2

Venison was a Plantation South Native American foundation food, and bear fat was virtually their only frying medium.

perch, pompano, bluefish, Spanish mackerel, and porgies. Shell-fish included blue crabs, oysters, clams, and shrimp. Inland tribes fished for catfish, freshwater trout, spots, bluegills, sunfish, craw-fish, turtles, and frogs. Many of these remain important seafood items in the modern cuisine.

Native American women were expert foragers knowing the use and location of indigenous plants for both food and medi-cine. Wild foods added nutrition and variety to the Native American diet, especially in spring and early summer before the corn crop matured. Though most Southern tribes relied mainly on cul-tivated foods, if crops failed because of drought or plant disease they could survive on foraged wild foods year-round.

For coastal tribes the staple wild starch was tuckahoe root; in western and upland areas foragers relied on acorns processed by shelling, grinding, and then soaking to remove bitter tannins. Other wild foods included hickory nuts and filberts (hazelnuts); wild strawberries, raspberries, blackberries, blueberries, huckle-berries, plums, persimmons, and crabapples; wild mushrooms; wild onions; and a wide variety of greens including purslane, cresses, dock, dandelion, ramps, and poke weed (p. 368).

Native American Agriculture

FACTOR 2

Native American land-clearing methods were effective in the Southern woodlands.

Although hunting and fishing provided protein, and foraged fruits and vegetables afforded dietary vari-ety, for Plantation South Native Americans as for many others, the cultivation of food plants was cen-tral to domestic life and culture. Plantation South tribes were among the most successful native farm-ers because of the region's superior resources. Tree cover was their only obstacle to farming. In re-sponse, Plantation South Native Americans and other East Coast tribes developed ingenious meth-ods of clearing and working farmland.

Until contact with Europeans, Native Americans did not have metal tools or domesticated animals other than dogs. Working in small groups with primitive tools and no draft ani-mals, Native Americans could not cut down hundreds of trees and pull out their stumps and roots as in standard European farming. Instead, Native Americans developed a unique farming method called **swidden agriculture,** in which crops are grown in small plots amid standing tree trunks.

The first step in this method involves killing trees by a process called **girdling,** in which trees are destroyed by starving them of water and nutrients. Native American women selected a promising site for farming, typically one with access to a stream for irrigation. The men then used stone hatchets to chop away a gir-dle, or wide band, of bark around the trunks of all the larger trees. Girdling exposes the trees' tender interiors, stopping the flow of water and nutrients from the roots to the leaves. Within months af-ter girdling, the trees were dead, standing devoid of leaves. The following spring, when the men chopped down any remaining saplings and then burned the undergrowth, the resulting ashes further enriched the soil. After loosening the soil with stone hoes, the women planted their crops in clusters spaced around the standing tree trunks. The leafless trees did not shade the ground

around them, and thus plenty of sun reached the plants growing among the trunks. Swidden agriculture is still used today in parts of Africa and Latin America.

Three Sisters Crops

Corn, beans, and squash thrive under swidden agriculture for several reasons. Because all three plants have shallow root systems and grow well in clumps, they don't require deep plowing in long, straight rows as do European grains. Corn, beans, and squash are ideal **companion plants**—in other words, they grow well when planted together. When beans and corn are planted in hills or mounds of soil, the beans' climbing vines grow up the corn stalks and support them in windy weather. While corn uses up the ni-trogen in the soil, beans return nitrogen to it. Squash plants grow well in the spaces between the hills. Their large, spreading leaves act as living mulch, keeping down weeds and holding in moisture. Figure 2.4 shows companion plants corn, beans, and squash growing together.

FACTOR 2

Three Sisters crops thrive under swidden agriculture.

FIGURE 2.4

Companion planting: bean vines climb the cornstalk and support it; squash plants shade the soil and prevent moisture loss.

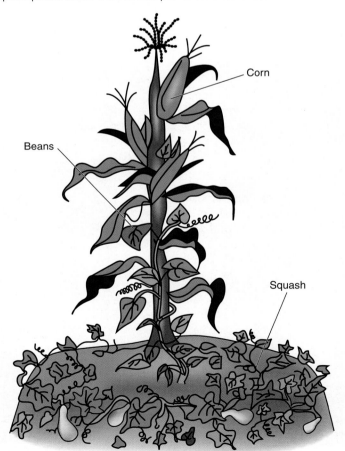

Corn

Beans

Squash

THE THREE SISTERS

Why are the Native American foundation foods, corn, beans, and squash, called the Three Sisters? One reason is that, like most sisters, they're good companions. When planted together, they support and shelter one another. Like sisters, they share: Corn needs nitrogen to grow, and beans supply nitrogen to the soil. As sisters do, they work well together. As you'll learn in Chapter 7, the nutrients each food provides to the human diet combine to create a nearly perfect balance. Why sisters and not brothers? In the Native American worldview the female of the species is revered as a life-giver; these life-sustaining crops are, therefore, feminine.

As you learned in Chapter 1, Native American corn was of the field corn variety. Although it was eaten "green," or fresh, near the end of its growing season, most was dried and used as a grain. Corn was the most valued of all Native American crops. In precontact Native American society it was considered a **high status food,** prepared for important guests and used as a valuable item of trade. In addition, corn had great religious significance. Figure 2.5 illustrates the origin and spread of corn culture in the Americas. In Chapter 7 we'll discuss this topic in greater depth.

The beans grown by precontact Native Americans were not modern string beans but shell beans ranging from red, kidney-type beans to speckled beans and white beans. In early summer, tender young bean pods were eaten in their fresh, immature state much as we eat string beans today. Shelled mature beans were also eaten fresh in season. However, most beans were dried on the vine and then removed from the pods.

Native squash varieties were of the hard-shelled, winter type. Both the sweet flesh and crunchy seeds were used as food. During the growing season, squash blossoms were selectively harvested and cooked, considered a delicacy. Mature squash and pumpkins could be stored for long periods, often kept underground in cool caves or in hand-dug pits.

Sunflowers

Native Americans cultivated indigenous sunflower plants and harvested two separate food products from them. The shelled seeds of mature sunflowers were used as a snack food and as a cooking ingredient. Sunflower roots, today known as Jerusalem artichokes and marketed as sunchokes, were boiled as a vegetable.

Tobacco

The tobacco plant, indigenous to the American South, was carefully cultivated by Native Americans. Dried tobacco leaves were smoked in hand-carved wooden pipes for both recreational and ceremonial purposes. Tobacco was an important trade item because it was highly valued by tribes living in other regions where it grew less well. Trade in tobacco was at least partly responsible for the wealth and power of the Powhatan Confederation (p. 36). As you'll learn later in this chapter, tobacco became a major source of wealth for plantation owners and the foundation of the region's economic viability.

Native Food Preservation

Even in the gentle climate of the Plantation South, winter brought food scarcity. Except in the Deep South, during the cold months most food plants died or became dormant. The migratory cycles of fish and shellfish took many out of reach during the winter. Game animals grew thin and scarce. Harsh weather made it more difficult to search for food. In preparation for winter, Plantation South Native Americans spent much of the spring, summer, and autumn harvesting large amounts of food and preserving it.

Hunted and foraged foods were preserved in hunting camps before transport to settlements. Nuts were stored in baskets or fiber bags. Berries were spread in the sun to dry. Men caught hundreds of pounds of fish, and women salted and air-dried it, as illustrated in Figure 2.6. In fall, salted game meats were air-dried or suspended over low fires to dry and preserve them in smoke. Smoked meats are one of the most important legacies of Plantation Southern Native Americans. Indeed, the taste of wood-smoked meats is a defining flavor of Plantation South cuisine.

Agricultural products were also preserved. Corn was handled in several ways. After the mature ears dried in the early autumn sun, they were harvested and husked. Dried corn was temporarily stored on the cob in large baskets. As time permitted, the dry kernels were removed from the cobs and stored in waterproof pottery containers. Plantation South Native Americans also prepared parched corn (p. 35). Mature beans were dried on the vine and shelled before storage. Pottery vessels full of dried corn or dried beans were buried underground to keep them safe from foraging animals and hidden from other humans. Mature squashes were sliced into rings, threaded onto plant fiber cords, and hung in the sun to dry.

Plantation South Native American Cuisine

Plantation South Native Americans used a combination of hunting, gathering, and agriculture to obtain their foundation foods. Before we discuss their most important dishes, let's look at the cooking methods used to create them.

Native Cooking Methods

Cooking methods can be as important as ingredients in defining a cuisine. In most Native American groups, cooking was the responsibility of women. For everyday meals native women typically cooked in individual family groups, with all adult women and older girls sharing the work. For meals involving an entire village, such as during a festival or after a group hunt, they cooked communally.

Natives of the Plantation South had only open-fire technology and, before European contact, did not possess metal utensils or cooking vessels. They overcame these limitations by using

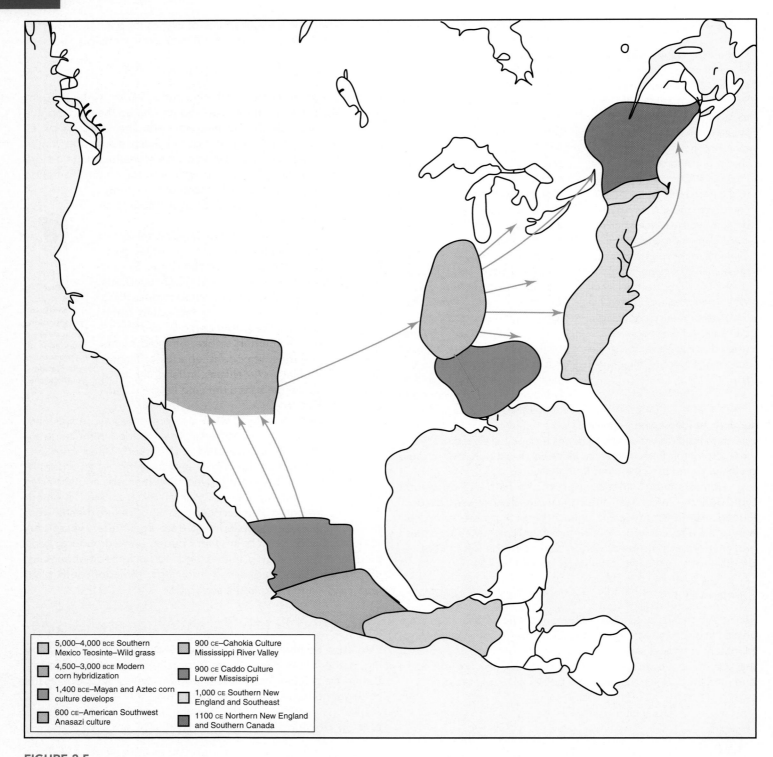

FIGURE 2.5
The Origin and Spread of Corn Culture in the Americas

FIGURE 2.6
Native Americans of the Plantation South preserved game by salting and smoking it. Picture Desk, Inc./Kobal Collection

available technology in creative ways. Following are the six most important precontact Native American cooking methods.

- *Hot stone griddling* is one of the most ancient cooking methods. A large, flat, smooth slab of rock is placed on the hot embers of a campfire to absorb its heat. A variety of foods can be cooked on a hot stone, as on a modern steel griddle. Native cooks sometimes lubricated the stone with bear grease to prevent sticking.
- *Spit roasting* is used for meats and large fish. Carcasses are impaled and lashed onto a sturdy greenwood pole suspended over a fire. The pole is turned to rotate the carcass and ensure even roasting. Today this method is called *rotisserie*. Smaller items are impaled on sticks and propped up with stones so they hang over the fire in the same way you toast a marshmallow.
- *Smoke roasting* is used for tougher cuts of meat. A low framework of slender greenwood poles is suspended over hot embers, and seasoned meat is placed on it. The meat is basted frequently with a flavorful liquid, creating steam. This method is the precursor to modern barbeque.
- *Pit roasting* is an efficient way to feed a large group. A pit, or deep hole, is dug in the ground and a fire is built in it. When the fire dies down to hot embers, the pit is lined with stones that absorb the heat. A layer of damp leaves or seaweed is placed on top of the stones, and seasoned food items are added. The food is covered with more leaves, and sometimes additional stones heated in a separate fire are added. Finally, the pit is filled in with the earth or sand previously removed from it. The food slowly steam-roasts over a period of time, after which it is dug out and eaten. In New England this method is used for shellfish and is called a *clambake* (pp. 91 and 98).
- *Sling bag simmering* uses a leather bag filled with liquid and suspended over low-burning embers. Heated stones are added to the bag as an additional source of heat.

Because leather is flammable, only low heat can be used. This was a primary cooking method for plains natives (p. 464).

- *Clay pot cooking* requires the technology to make heat-resistant pottery. Earthenware vessels filled with liquid ingredients are suspended over hot embers supported on a ring of stones. Fired clay pots make it possible to poach, stew, and boil. Minerals transferred from the clay into the food impart a special flavor and can enhance nutrition.

FACTOR 2

Native American smoke roasting is the precursor to modern barbeque, an important Plantation South cooking method.

Plantation South tribes were skilled at making pottery from the region's abundant clay soil. Most tribes made many kinds of heat-treated vessels, including pots with capacity up to ninety gallons. The combination of clay and smoke from a wood fire imparts a flavor that is highly prized by native people of North America and Mexico. That's one reason why traditional clay vessels are still used by Native Americans for campfire cooking at festivals and religious ceremonies. However, clay cooking was not embraced by European first settlers or African immigrants and is not an important part of modern Plantation South cuisine.

To fully use their foundation starch, dried corn, as well as seeds, wild grain, and dried tuckahoe root, Plantation South native cooks developed adequate, if not superlative, grinding technology. To create a mortar, a native craftsman hollowed out a section of a large hardwood tree trunk using a combination of burning and carving. He carved a slender log into a pestle. To grind dried corn or other ingredients, native women placed the item in the mortar and pounded it with the pestle, often working in teams as shown in Figure 2.7. Wooden mortars and pestles enabled them to pulverize dried corn kernels into coarse and medium-grind cornmeal.

Cooking with Corn

Native Americans of the Plantation South and throughout the East Coast prepared their foundation starch in many different ways. Some of these preparations have evolved into important dishes in the modern cuisine.

European settlers confronted with complex Native American corn cuisine were hopelessly confused when attempting to identify products and dishes made from corn. This confusion remains today. Throughout modern America, different corn products and dishes are known by names that vary from one culinary region to another, and even within regions. Moreover, some Native American corn products and dishes no longer exist, at least in the realm of commercially available products. Although it may conflict with some regional and historic nomenclature, the following section identifies corn products by names that are most technically correct.

Native American corn dishes can be grouped into four categories:

- ground unprocessed dried corn
- processed dried corn, whole or ground
- green corn
- parched corn

FIGURE 2.7
Native American women pounded dried corn into meal using wooden mortars made from tree trunks. Library and Archives of Canada website, www .collectionscanada.ca

A corn kernel comprises three elements: a starchy center called the *endosperm*; the flavorful, oil-rich *germ*; and the thick, fibrous *hull* (see Figure 2.8). The hull consists almost entirely of *cellulose*, an indigestible substance that has a coarse mouthfeel and that causes doughs made from whole corn to lack cohesion. For this reason, Native American and modern dried-corn dishes are made from corn treated to either pulverize or remove the hull. Both yellow and white corn varieties are used.

- **Ground unprocessed dried corn** begins as whole dried field corn kernels. Products in this category are made by physical means only, with no chemical treatment. Both yellow and white corn varieties are used. Ground corn products are subcategorized by texture: coarse- and fine-ground meal; and flour.
- **Processed dried corn** refers to dried corn kernels with the hulls removed, traditionally by soaking in alkalized water or by a modern steaming method. This results in large, chewy, irregularly shaped morsels containing endosperm and

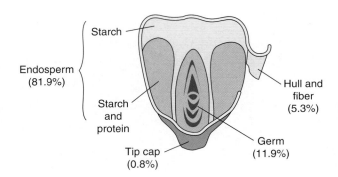

FIGURE 2.8
Composition of the Corn Kernel

germ only. (In Mexican cuisine and modern Mexican Border cuisine, processed corn is handled differently, as you'll learn on this book's companion website and in Chapter 7.)

Native Americans of the Plantation South and other East Coast natives practiced **traditional alkaline processing,** a method that makes dried corn more palatable, easier to digest, and more nutritionally valuable. This method involves soaking or cooking dried corn in alkalized water in order to soften it, remove its hulls, and improve its nutritive qualities. As you'll learn in Chapter 7, traditional alkaline processing was developed by early civilizations living in what is now Mexico. The method gradually spread northward to native groups of the Mexican Border region and, over centuries, eventually reached the American East Coast. However, the Mexican method of alkalizing corn-cooking water uses a different alkali.

Natives of the Plantation South and other East Coast groups alkalized water by filtering it through ashes from hardwood cooking fires, creating a weak lye solution. They soaked corn kernels in this water until the hulls loosened and then removed the hulls by beating the drained corn with flexible wooden implements and rinsing the hulls away with fresh water.

English colonists mistook the Native American word *rockahominie* (see p. 35) to mean alkaline-processed corn. They soon shortened the word to *hominy*, the name used in this book for corn kernels softened and hulled by any process. Thus, **hominy** is dried corn processed to soften its starchy endosperm and remove its hull.

East Coast Native Americans handled hominy in several ways. The soft, hulled whole kernels could be further simmered in water to a chewy-tender texture. Whole hominy was added to soups and stews or sweetened with berries (and maple syrup in the north). Alternatively, fresh processed hominy was dried in the sun to preserve it. Dried whole hominy was reconstituted and cooked whole, or pulverized to make hominy grits.

Traditional alkaline processing of corn results in distinctive flavor and significant nutritional benefits. As explained in detail in Chapter 7, alkaline processing makes available certain proteins that, in combination with proteins found in legumes, create a

FACTOR 2

Traditional alkaline processing of corn was a noteworthy, yet not essential, part of East Coast Native American cooking.

UNPROCESSED CORN AND PLANTATION SOUTH DISHES MADE FROM IT

Whole-grain grits is medium-grind dried corn. (Refer to the website for history and grammatical construction relating to the word *grits*.) This product is produced in traditional stone mills at cool temperatures and contains all parts of the corn kernel. Containing a high proportion of pulverized hull, whole-grain grits is high in fiber and has a coarse, rustic texture when cooked. When simmered in water, the larger grits particles soften into chewy bits while the starch released by the smaller particles gelatinizes, thickening the cooking liquid. Depending on the amount of water used, cooked whole-grain grits can have a loose, porridgelike consistency or a thicker, pilaflike texture. Because it contains the germ, whole-grain grits is flavorful but perishable and should be stored frozen.

Quick grits is the best-known name for modern refined grits. Whole corn kernels are ground to a medium texture in industrial steel roller mills that produce heat. A significant proportion of the coarse hull particles is removed by screening. To increase the product's shelf life, the perishable germ is removed. Heating and removing the germ also removes much of the flavor. Because it consists mainly of starchy endosperm, when cooked, quick grits become a pasty mass. A precooked form of this product is called *instant grits*.

The following dishes may be made from whole-grain grits or quick grits:

Cooked grits is served as a side dish, most frequently at breakfast, or as a starch accompaniment.
Cheese grits is a modern dish in which grated sharp Cheddar cheese is added to the grits at the end of cooking.
Fried grits or **grits cakes** consist of cold, solidified cooked grits cut into slices or formed into patties and then reheated by frying in bacon
   drippings or butter.

Cornmeal is fine-grind whole corn kernels. It is typically obtained by sifting out larger particles during grinding. Stone-ground cornmeal produced at low temperatures is more flavorful but also more perishable. Industrial steel-roller-produced cornmeal has a longer shelf life but lacks flavor and texture.

Following are the most popular dishes made from cornmeal:

Cornmeal mush is a soft porridge made by simmering cornmeal with water or milk.
Corn pone is made with cornmeal moistened with enough water to make a stiff dough formed into a flat cake and then griddle-baked. In
   the Algonquian language such corn cakes were called *apone*, meaning "baked." Colonists later shortened the word to *pone* and called
   the cakes *corn pones*.
Shuck bread is cornmeal dough wrapped in cornhusks and then boiled or steamed. This Native American dish can be considered a
   simplified tamal (p. 23).
Pure Southern cornbread is a baked good made from batter bound and leavened with eggs; it contains no wheat flour.

Corn flour is whole-grain dried corn ground extremely fine by modern processes. It is used in baking and for breading foods before frying. (Do not confuse corn flour with "cornflour," the UK term for cornstarch.)

---

protein source nearly as valuable as the proteins found in meat. We call this the **corn-bean synergy.** Combining corn and beans was crucial for Native Americans of the Mexican Border region, who had little access to meat proteins. However, for natives of the American East Coast the corn-bean synergy was not essential because they had ample game meat and fish. This helps explain why they never developed a sophisticated repertoire of alkaline-processed corn dough breads, such as tortillas and tamales, that are a feature of Mexican and Mexican Border cuisines.

- **Green corn** is fresh, slightly immature field corn. Native Americans pit-roasted green corn in the husk or boiled the husked ears in the same way modern cooks prepare corn on the cob. Kernels of green corn were simmered in water and served as a side vegetable or added to soups and stews, or pounded into a paste and simmered to make smooth corn soup or corn pudding. Alternatively, the paste was wrapped in cornhusks and steamed to make green corn shuck bread.
- **Parched corn** is green corn kernels removed from the cob and dry-roasted until most of the moisture evaporates. Native Americans parched corn on stone griddles. Modern

parched corn is prepared in dehydrators. Today this product is a feature of Mid-Atlantic cuisine. Plantation South natives ground dried parched corn in mortars to make *rockahominie*.

Cooking Meats, Fish, and Vegetables

After a successful hunting or fishing expedition, when large quantities of fresh game meats or fish were available, natives cooked it by the roasting methods previously discussed. Meats were seasoned with wild herbs, berry juices, and precious salt evaporated from seawater or dug out of mineral salt outcroppings.

However, most Plantation South Native American meals consisted of slow-simmered, one-pot dishes in which smaller amounts of meat or fish were simmered in water with beans, vegetables, or fruits. Often such a soup/stew was thickened with cornmeal. Alternatively, a brothy stew was complemented by a corn-dough product such as a pone, dumpling, or shuck bread. Various leafy greens were eaten both raw and cooked, in spring considered a digestive tonic much needed after a winter diet of preserved foods.

PROCESSED CORN AND PLANTATION SOUTH DISHES MADE FROM IT

Traditional alkaline-processed hominy consists of dried corn kernels cooked in alkalized water to soften the interior and remove the tough hull. The alkaline process gives this product a distinctive flavor. Today this type of traditional alkaline-processed hominy is not commercially available; however, it is still prepared by Native American cooks and colonial period reenactors. (A different type of alkaline-processed corn, known by a different name, is commercially produced in Mexico and in the Mexican Border culinary region.)

Steam-processed hominy is made without alkali. In this modern process the kernels' hulls are loosened by high-pressure steaming. It is often called *pearl hominy* because the dark-colored tip cap of the kernel is removed during processing, resulting in a pale color and spherical shape. This product has a full corn flavor but lacks the distinctive taste produced by alkaline processing. Canned after processing, it is available packed in water or in thick, gelatinized cooking liquid. Steam-processed hominy is featured in the cuisines of the Plantation South, Louisiana, and the Chesapeake Bay Shore.

These are modern dishes made from steam-processed hominy:

> **Hominy side dish** is heated canned hominy dressed with butter and seasoned with salt and pepper. Modern cooks add chopped fresh herbs or sautéed onions and peppers.
>
> **Hominy casserole** is a savory baked custard made of canned hominy, milk, and eggs. It is sometimes topped with Cheddar-type cheese.
>
> **Sweet hominy** is warm canned hominy dressed with cream and sugar like oatmeal.

The only sweeteners available to most pre-contact Plantation South Native Americans came from wild fruits and berries that were actually more tart than sweet. Most Southern native cooks had no access to maple syrup because maple trees grow no farther south than upland Virginia and Maryland. Honey was not available because honeybees are not indigenous to the Americas. The resulting lack of sweetening ingredients created a taste preference in sharp contrast to that of New England natives, who extensively used maple sap and syrup in both sweet and savory dishes. Not until the arrival of second-settler Afro-Caribbean slaves would sugar and a taste for sweet-savory dishes enter the cuisine.

Native American Attitudes about Food

Precontact Plantation South Native Americans were successful agriculturalists and expert hunters. They had ample indigenous resources and cooked with a broad palette of ingredients. They had the technology to support several effective cooking methods. They spent most of their time seeking and preparing food and included food in their religious observations. Thus, Plantation South Native Americans had a strong food culture and were culinary liberals. These strong indigenous roots are the foundation of one of America's most complex and interesting cuisines.

■
□ COLONIAL CUISINE OF
■ THE PLANTATION SOUTH

In the first decade of the 1600s, East Coast Native Americans faced the beginning of an unstoppable invasion. In Europe, political unrest and advances in navigation instigated growing colonial expansion aimed primarily at the Americas. France, the Netherlands, Sweden, Portugal, and England joined Spain in the quest to explore and colonize the New World. England's initial target was North America's flat, fertile, and temperate southern Atlantic coast.

English Settlement

In the spring of 1607 one hundred Englishmen aboard three ships reached the Chesapeake Bay and sailed into a waterway they named the James River. They landed near the river's mouth and began building a settlement called Jamestown. The territory surrounding their settlement became an English colony named Virginia, after Elizabeth I, "the virgin queen."

Forty miles upstream at the fall line stood a large Native American village that formed the seat of the powerful Powhatan Confederacy, an organized group of tribes led by a chief called Powhatan. The chief's scouts were immediately aware of the presence of strangers downriver. Powhatan, seeing the newcomers as possible allies against tribes outside his control, sent emissaries to make contact, and a tentative relationship was established. Powhatan initially supplied the colony with gifts of corn, game meats, and other foodstuffs.

However, the men of Jamestown had little interest in cooking. The site had been chosen for military reasons, primarily because it was easily defendable. Certainly no farmer would have settled such a low and marshy spot, but these first colonists were too busy thinking about finding treasure to worry about growing or cooking food. Surrounded by standing water, the site proved to be a breeding ground for mosquitoes, and malaria soon became rampant. When Powhatan's supplies ran out, they subsisted on ship's rations such as salt pork, ship's biscuits, and ale only occasionally supplemented with game meat and seafood. With limited rations and no women to cook for them, the men lacked proper nutrition and easily succumbed to disease. By September forty-six colonists had died.

During the winter of 1608 twenty-one more colonists perished. Only the arrival of another ship bearing additional

FIGURE 2.9
Pocahontas saves the life of
captain John Smith.
LOC, LC-USZC4-3368

colonists and a new leader, Captain John Smith, prevented the colony's demise. The story is well known: the now-disputed kidnapping of John Smith by Powhatan (Figure 2.9), the marriage of Pocahontas and John Rolfe, and the meaningless crowning of Powhatan as "the Indian king." The Jamestown settlement endured further deprivations due to weather and disease. However, renewed support from England finally resulted in success. By 1616 the Virginia colony boasted 350 citizens and thousands of acres claimed by the English crown. Regularly arriving ships brought new colonists and food supplies as well as seeds, plants, and breeding stock to establish European-style agriculture.

Finally, under Smith, the Virginia colonists began to work seriously at farming, raising both indigenous food crops and colonial domesticates. Thus, the Virginia colony became America's first permanent agricultural settlement. Following Virginia's success, the English Crown claimed additional tracts of land and established the Maryland and Carolina colonies. Members of the English aristocracy were given huge land grants, and middle-class citizens applied for smaller tracts. Throughout the colonies, women began cooking with both indigenous foods and colonial domesticates, blending them in innovative ways and creating new dishes. Additional lands were claimed and cleared, eventually creating the productive plantations that lend their name to both the region and its cuisine.

Today the Jamestown site and its surrounding countryside are considered part of the Chesapeake Bay Shore culinary region, home of a cooking style that developed later in history. However, during early colonial times this area was the birthplace of the new, hybrid cooking style that would eventually become Plantation South cuisine.

Culinary Conservatives Gain a Liberal Outlook

A colonial cuisine is a hybrid cooking style formed by blending indigenous ingredients and cooking methods with Old World ingredients and cooking methods. The depth and character of a colonial cuisine depends largely on the acceptance of indigenous foods by first settlers. Acceptance of new foods may be generated by a liberal culinary outlook or forced by necessity.

Early Jamestown settlers cooked and ate Native American foods simply to survive. However, most English people who settled the Virginia, Maryland, and Carolina colonies continued to prepare and enjoy indigenous foods by choice. Why they did so—while colonists and pioneers in other regions did not—can be discovered by examining who these colonists were, where they came from, and why they became colonists in the first place.

In the 1600s English emigration to America crossed all social and economic classes. However, emigration typically occurred in groups from a particular area. Most people who initially came to the Southern colonies hailed from the rural west of England and were members of the government-sanctioned Protestant Anglican Church. However, most were not overly religious and tended to be free thinkers. Whether rich or poor, they came to the New World in search of economic opportunity.

In general, England does not have a strong food culture, and mainstream English foodways include a conservative attitude about food. However, those individuals willing to cross the Atlantic and settle the Southern colonies were the exception. As a result of their adventurous mindset, most Plantation South colonists quickly became culinary liberals; after arriving in the New World they were willing to try new foods and experiment in their cooking. This liberal element, combined with the fact that they did not have a strong food culture to overcome, set the stage for the creation of a lively and rapidly evolving hybrid cuisine.

A significant element in the development of Plantation South cuisine was the continued Native American presence in the region through colonial times and into the plantation era. Although in some areas the native population disappeared rather quickly, in other places tribes such as the Cherokees remained influential to cuisine well into the 1800s. Continued contact enriched both colonial and native cooking.

Women in the Kitchen

The great land grants that became Southern plantations were given primarily to younger sons of the English aristocracy. Although some arrived as bachelors, many more brought their families. However, neither the planters nor their wives or children performed any of the labor on the plantation. In the early years of plantation settlement they primarily used indentured servants from the British Isles, as explained on this book's companion website. Many of these indentured servants were women who worked as cooks or kitchen servants. Middle-class settlers arrived in the Plantation South as small farmers, craftsmen, and overseers, or agricultural managers. In these households the wife was the primary cook, although she typically retained at least one woman or older girl indentured servant as a kitchen helper. Thus, the early cooking of the Plantation South was the domain of women—typically young, white, middle- or lower-class women from England.

Colonists Embrace Indigenous Foods

Early Southern colonists were forced to eat whatever indigenous foods they could find. Most hailed from rural areas and had previous experience hunting and fishing. Small game, including rabbit and wildfowl, were favored protein foods for middle-class colonists and, later, for aristocratic landowners. Anyone with a hook, skill, and luck could enjoy a fish dinner. From colonial times to this day, wild game and fish are sought-after foods frequently enjoyed.

Taught by local Native Americans, early English colonists practiced swidden cultivation of corn, beans, and squash. They learned to grind dried corn into meal and to cook the meal into a satisfying porridge they called *samp*. Like the natives, they mixed cornmeal and water into a firm dough and formed it into cakes. Instead of baking their corn cakes on a hot stone, the colonists used metal pans. Farmers working outdoors allegedly cooked corn dough on metal hoe blades heated over a fire to make *hoe cakes*. Native cooks showed the colonists how to boil corn kernels with alkalized water to make hominy, which became a staple starch eaten for breakfast, added to soups and stews, and served as a side dish with game meats.

For early colonists, a pot of indigenous beans became the fallback protein food when game meat was not available. Although some consider this poverty fare, a dish of slow-simmered beans remains a favored comfort food in the Plantation South. Squashes of many kinds were served as a side vegetable and, when sweetened with sugar or honey, replaced European fruits in desserts.

FACTOR 2 **FACTOR 3**

Indigenous foods sustained English colonists.

Although colonists throughout the Plantation South came to appreciate and enjoy indigenous foods, as soon as it became possible to import European foods and equipment they also began preparing the familiar foods of their homeland, using European cooking technology. This pattern was followed throughout the English-settled colonies. Therefore, the information in this section pertains not only to the Plantation South, but also to New England, the Mid-Atlantic, and the Chesapeake Bay Shore.

English Cooking Methods

From the mid-1600s through the 1700s, the immigrant English housewife brought with her the tools she had previously used in her Old World kitchen. As soon as a permanent house was constructed, she applied the same cooking methods (Figure 2.10).

English colonists used both open-flame and oven technology. In the typical early colonial house, the main room served as both kitchen and living area. Its focus was a huge fireplace built into a stone sidewall. Most cooking took place on the open **hearth,** or fireplace floor (Figure 2.10). Open-hearth cooking uses the hot embers of a wood fire as the heat source. The fireplace is equipped with specialized equipment, such as a rotating spit and hinged arms from which cauldrons are suspended. Other important hearth cooking equipment includes the following:

- A *reflector* oven placed on the hearth in front of the fire (Figure 2.11) captures heat and reflects it back onto small cuts of meat or roasting fowl turned on a self-contained spit.
- A *Dutch oven* is a heavy casserole used for hearth baking or braising (Figure 2.12); set directly in the embers, it has a concave lid so that additional embers can be placed on top for even heating. Some have legs.
- A *spider* is a frying pan with four legs, designed to sit evenly in the coals and also equipped with a concave lid for embers.

FIGURE 2.10

The hearth was the focus of the colonial house and the site of virtually all of the family's cooking. John S. Sfondilias/Shutterstock

FIGURE 2.11

A reflector oven captures heat from the fire. Image supplied by Kathy Ring, made by Larry Ring, Cobb Creek Merchants

FACTOR 3

Colonial cast-iron cooking remains a signature method in Plantation South and other Southern cuisines.

Most colonial cooking vessels and tools were made of cast iron, a metal that is heavy, is prone to rusting, and reacts with certain foods. When lighter, rustproof, nonreactive cookware became available, most Americans abandoned their cast iron in favor of it. However, in the Plantation South and several other culinary regions, cast-iron cooking remains in use for cooking certain traditional dishes, such as fried chicken, chili, and gumbo (p. 321). The benefits and drawbacks of cast-iron cooking are explained on p. 39.

CAST-IRON COOKING

Cast-iron skillets give fried foods and cornbread a distinctive thick, crunchy crust that can't be duplicated using a vessel made of any other material. Soups and stews simmered in cast iron cook slowly and evenly and rarely scorch. Many cooks maintain that the iron gives food a special flavor as well, likely the result of a chemical reaction between the food and the metal.

Traditional cooks from many American regions swear by their cast-iron cookware even though it requires special care. To remain smooth and rust-free, a cast-iron pan must undergo a special seasoning process outlined on this book's companion website. A properly seasoned pan must be pampered: used carefully, cleaned in a special way, and stored properly. In a traditional Southern family, cast-iron skillets and cauldrons are considered family heirlooms to be handed down to the most worthy cook of the next generation.

FIGURE 2.12
A Dutch oven is placed directly in the embers and topped with hot coals. Courtesy Lee Raine, www.cowboyshowcase.com

Oven technology was an important element of Old World English cooking. In well-equipped colonial kitchens a small oven was built into the wall next to the fireplace, connected by a flue to receive its heat. Breads, pies, and cakes were baked in this oven.

Colonial cooking entailed considerable hard work and discomfort. Although in fair weather some cooking could be done outdoors, most foods and all bread products were prepared indoors. Colonial kitchens were smoky and stuffy in the winter and unbearably hot in the summer. The physical work of cooking required handling heavy cast-iron pots that, when filled with food, could easily weigh 30 pounds. Moreover, the colonial cook had to split wood, build the cooking fire, carry water, and often slaughter animals before the actual cooking could begin.

English Ingredients

Colonial Plantation South cuisine mirrored the Old World English cookery of the time: simple and straightforward, but not totally plain. Refer to the box on the right to learn this cuisine's defining elements. Middle-class colonial housewives and early plantation cooks used an assortment of spices such as black pepper, cloves, cinnamon, mace, nutmeg, and ginger. Herbs such as parsley, sage, lovage, savory, and thyme grew in well-tended kitchen gardens that, in much of the South, grew year-round.

Within a few years of settlement, food animals imported on English ships multiplied. Chickens provided eggs for baking and poultry for the pot. Although beef was the English people's foundation protein food and by far their favorite meat, in most of the Plantation South the climate was not healthful for English beef breeds. Planters and small farmers raised a limited number of dairy cattle and slaughtered them for meat only when they were no longer productive. Thus, Southern beef was both lean and tough. Similarly, in most of the South sheep were raised for wool production and slaughtered only when far past their prime. Therefore, neither beef nor mutton were considered high-status foods and were eaten only out of necessity. Even today, beef and lamb are not frequently prepared meats in Southern cuisines. Conversely, chicken was universally enjoyed and appreciated. However, chickens were more valuable for their eggs than for meat. Although old hens ended up in the stewpot, young layers were slaughtered only for special occasions. But the hog had one use only: to provide a large amount of succulent meat and essential frying fat, fed only on kitchen scraps and what it could forage. For this reason the hog

---

ELEMENTS OF OLD WORLD ENGLISH CUISINE

FOUNDATION FOODS

principal starch: wheat bread

principal proteins: beef, cheese

principal produce: cabbages, root vegetables, apples

FAVORED SEASONINGS: parsley, thyme, sage, pepper, cinnamon, nutmeg, ginger, onions

PRINCIPAL COOKING MEDIA: water, butter, beef suet

PRIMARY COOKING METHODS: open-hearth cooking, including roasting, boiling, stewing; baking

FOOD ATTITUDES: minimized food culture, culinary conservatives

FACTOR 3

Pork became the foundation meat of the Plantation South.

was—and still is—the most important food animal in the Plantation South.

From colonial times well into the 20th century, pork was the everyday meat of the Plantation South. All of a slaughtered hog was used: The liver, kidneys, and loin were eaten fresh; meat scraps and trimmings were ground with additional fat and encased in the hog's intestines to make sausage; the remaining fat was rendered into lard (see right). However, most of the carcass, including the shoulders and hams, was preserved for future use by curing and smoking.

The defining flavor of the Plantation South results from the marriage of smoke and hog. Native Americans preserved game meat by salting it and then suspending it over smoky wood fires

FACTOR 2   FACTOR 3

The marriage of native smoking techniques with the European hog created the Plantation South's signature flavor: smoked pork.

to dry. Because their game meat was lean and their seasonings simple, native smoked meats were palatable, but not delectable. However, when the same technique is applied to well-marbled pork enhanced with a wide palette of seasonings, the result is a culinary masterpiece.

The colonists' fat hogs smoked up rich and succulent. When cured not only with salt but also with sugar and spices, smoked pork develops a deep, complex flavor. Smoked pork shoulders, hams, and bacon became main-course meats (see Figure 2.13). In addition, a hog carcass provided smoked ham hocks and neck bones, ham scraps, and bacon ends—collectively called **seasoning meats.** These are

simmered in water to make broth for soups and to flavor beans and greens. **Bacon drippings**, the fat released when bacon is fried, are a signature frying medium of the region. Today, one way to recognize a traditional Southern cook is by his or her pot of carefully reserved bacon drippings.

Although bacon drippings are frequently used to fry potatoes, vegetables, and eggs, the universal Southern frying medium is pure pork lard. To make lard, artisan producers **render,** or melt, diced fresh pork fat over low heat with a little water to prevent scorching. As the fat melts, its fluid component is released from the solid component. This clear liquid is **lard,** a fluid fat when hot that becomes a firm, white substance when chilled. The solid component that remains after lard is rendered out is called **cracklings.** Fried or baked crisp, cracklings are a favorite snack and can be used on salads in place of croutons.

The flavor of pork lard is one of the essential elements of traditional Plantation South cooking. Used as a fat for frying, lard gives a golden, crunchy crust and a meaty flavor to a variety of foods. Used in baking, lard gives biscuits and pastry a long flake and crisp texture. Unless there are overarching medical or cultural reasons not to use it, traditionally rendered, nonhydrogenated lard is the recommended fat for most Southern dishes. A recipe for rendering lard appears on this book's companion website.

Hybrid Foods Complete Colonial Cuisine

Adventurous cooks in the Plantation South quickly began combining indigenous foods with colonial domesticates to create a new, hybrid cuisine. Imported European millstones (and later, millstones quarried in rocky New England) soon replaced primitive log mortars and pestles, enabling colonists to grind corn not only into grits, but also into meal and flour (see Figure 2.14). The same stones ground Southern wheat into flour. Combining abundant corn with expensive flour created a wider range of baked goods, such as corn griddlecakes and spoonbread. Adding eggs and dairy products made these baked goods taste better,

FACTOR 3

Pork lard and bacon drippings are the region's signature frying media.

FIGURE 2.13

Artisan producer Tom Calhoun displays country hams and bacon.

Courtesy of Calhoun's Country Hams, Culpeper, VA, www.calhounhams.com

FIGURE 2.14

Water power drives this grist mill, where whole grains are ground into grist, or grits. Francesca Yorke

© Dorling Kindersley

FACTOR 3

In the Plantation South, biscuits and cornbread frequently take the place of yeast-leavened breads.

gave them a lighter texture, and allowed them to be kept for a longer time before staling.

The strains of wheat that can grow in the South primarily produced "soft," low-protein flours, not the best choice for making yeast-leavened breads. Moreover, the region's hot, humid weather made yeast difficult to control. Thus, the colonial Southern housewife or servant cook didn't make many yeast-leavened breads. For everyday meals early Southern bakers made cornbread leavened with beaten eggs and soft flour biscuits, called *beaten biscuits*, made light by pounding the dough. Yeast breads made with expensive imported English wheat flour were reserved for special occasions.

Thus far we've discussed the development of early colonial Plantation South cuisine, a cooking style based on the region's indigenous Native American cooking blended with the colonial domesticates and Old World cooking of English colonist first settlers. Much of the information you've learned thus far on Native American and English colonial cooking also applies to the other East Coast regions. We're now poised at the point in history where subsequent developments in agriculture and commerce brought about a dramatic new influence on Plantation South colonial cuisine.

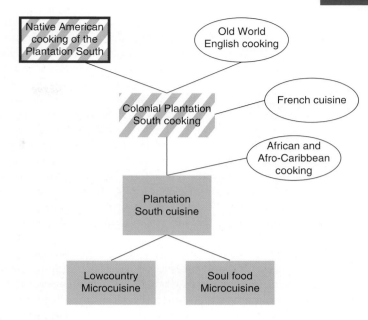

FIGURE 2.15
The Development of Plantation South Cuisine

UNWILLING SETTLERS: THE PLANTATION SYSTEM AND SLAVERY

Within fifty years of the settlement of Jamestown, most of the arable land in the Virginia, Maryland, and Carolina coastal plain had been granted. Although a number of smaller inland grants went to middle-class farmers and completed indentures, most prime coastal land had been distributed in vast tracts to wealthy merchants and aristocrats, primarily from England, but also from France and other European nations. These large parcels of land were called **plantations,** and the owners were called *planters.*

The English government expected Southern plantations to become successful business enterprises producing agricultural commodities for export, thereby generating large tax revenues. Large-scale commercial agriculture requires large fields cleared of trees, with tree stumps and rocks removed from the ground and crops planted in long rows. When attempts at forcing Native Americans to work at European-style agriculture failed, early planters had only indentured servants to clear the woodland covering their properties. Once fields were laboriously cleared and planted, both indigenous and colonial domesticate food crops thrived. Among the most important early food crops, dried corn (called *Indian corn*) was shipped to Africa and the Caribbean, where it was used to feed both animals and slaves. In Europe, cornmeal became a cheap starch food for the lower classes.

BISCUITS: BEATEN AND BUTTERMILK

In early colonial times chemical leaveners such as baking soda and baking powder did not yet exist. Southern cooks leavened beaten biscuits by physical means; dough made of soft Southern wheat flour, water, and pure pork lard was pounded with a wooden mallet to incorporate air.

Baking soda, or sodium bicarbonate, became available in the 1800s. This alkaline substance reacts with an acidic liquid to produce CO_2 gas for leavening. The acidic liquid most frequently used for baking was buttermilk, the watery substance remaining after butterfat is separated from cream, resulting in butter. In the Southern heat, buttermilk quickly fermented, becoming thick and tangy. Because of its acidity, buttermilk was a perfect moistener for baking soda–leavened baked goods. Buttermilk biscuits soon became the daily bread of the Plantation South.

Biscuits were served at virtually every meal and even became a dessert component. Because it was easier to handle than flaky pastry, biscuit dough often replaced piecrusts. Cobbler—fruit filling baked under dollops of biscuit dough—is a classic Southern dessert.

FACTOR 2   FACTOR 5

Tobacco becomes a vital cash crop, creating economic viability.

Although corn provided substantial revenue, tobacco soon became the region's most valuable crop. After early colonists learned to smoke tobacco from natives, they shipped samples back to England. By the mid-1600s pipe smoking was the rage all across Western Europe, creating huge demand for American tobacco. Tobacco became the first cash crop of North America, so valuable that it was used in place of money. Although not a food, tobacco was instrumental to the development of Plantation South cuisine because the wealth produced by tobacco created the opulent planter lifestyle that made possible the development of a complex, world-class cuisine.

To achieve financial success, early Southern planters needed to grow more and more product. Their business plan lacked only one element: cheap labor. Native Americans resisted plantation work, many preferring to die rather than face a lifetime of hard labor. Indentured servants were costly to import and expensive to maintain in conditions acceptable by European standards. Moreover, they were a poor long-term investment. By the time an indentured servant was fully trained in a particular craft or skill, his term of indenture was over and he had to be released. Planters quickly recognized that they needed a cheaper source of long-term labor. The obvious answer to this problem was slavery.

French and Spanish planters had been using African slaves in the Caribbean since the early 1600s and had amassed great fortunes. Following their example, Southern planters began acquiring slaves from the Caribbean and then from Africa. Between 1700 and 1776, almost 225,000 slaves were imported to the Southern colonies. Although they were unwilling immigrants, this large number of African and Afro-Caribbean slaves comprised an important second-settler group that had a dramatic impact on Plantation South cuisine. The techniques, ingredients, and taste preferences of African-American slave cooks transformed colonial Southern cooking, bringing it to a new level of complexity and creating one of America's most spirited and delectable cuisines.

Using cheap slave labor, plantation owners cleared large tracts of land and cultivated a wide variety of crops. Cash crops were shipped out on small merchant ships that arrived several times a year. In addition to cash crops for export, plantations produced nearly everything their inhabitants needed and thus were virtually self-sufficient. Nonetheless, the typical planter's family imported numerous luxury goods, such as furniture, books, and fabrics, as well as expensive foodstuffs, such as spices, condiments, and wines and spirits, which enriched the cuisine.

FACTOR 5

Wealthy planters imported foodstuffs, creating a broad palette of ingredients.

The typical plantation employed hundreds of slaves, most for fieldwork but others as skilled craftspersons such as blacksmiths and carpenters. The social status of plantation slaves was based on the type of work they performed. Well-trained slaves who prepared and served the planters'

food were among the highest-ranking and often enjoyed special privileges.

On Southern plantations the kitchen building was always separated from the mansion house to minimize heat, odor, and risk of fire (see Figure 2.16). The typical plantation kitchen was equipped with the latest in European cooking technology: a huge open hearth, several ovens, and a battery of tools and equipment for virtually every purpose. The plantation's head cook, usually a woman slave, might supervise a dozen cooks, kitchen maids, porters, and scullery maids. A slave butler, typically an older man, oversaw slave servers as they transported the family's food from kitchen to dining room, often via a covered walkway, carrying scores of covered dishes.

Eating well was a primary source of pleasure for planters and their families. Entertaining guests at table was not only a social activity but also a duty. Because there were few towns with accommodations for travelers, plantations were expected to extend hospitality to both friends and strangers. Unexpected guests could arrive at all hours of the day or night, and invited guests came often. Setting a lavish table became an important status symbol; a plantation's reputation depended as much on its cuisine as on its agricultural success. Thus, the planter class developed a strong food culture that would pervade all levels of Southern society.

FACTOR 4

African and Afro-Caribbean slave cooks transformed colonial cooking into traditional Plantation South cuisine.

Between the late 1700s and mid-1800s, the Plantation South produced excellent domestic food products, had access to imported ingredients, enjoyed unlimited cheap labor, and developed a strong food culture based on a liberal outlook—all of the elements necessary to create a world-class cuisine. Most food historians agree that the cooking of the Plantation South reached its highest level during this time period.

FIGURE 2.16

This colonial-era watercolor depicts the layout of a typical plantation, showing the planter's mansion on a hill, workshops, slave quarters, the overseer's house, and the warehouse and river dock. Handmade oil painting reproduction of The Plantation 1825, a painting by anonymous artist

TRADITIONAL PLANTATION SOUTH CUISINE

ELEMENTS OF WEST AFRICAN CUISINE

FOUNDATION FOODS

principal starches: true yams, millet, rice, (later) cornmeal

principal proteins: game meats, goat, fish, black-eyed peas

principal produce: okra, groundnuts, eggplant, leafy greens

FAVORED SEASONINGS: onions, garlic, dried and fresh chiles, sesame seeds

PRINCIPAL COOKING MEDIA: palm oil, vegetable oil

PRIMARY COOKING METHODS: spit-roasting, frying, boiling, stewing

FOOD ATTITUDES: strong food culture, culinary liberals

In studying traditional Plantation South cooking you'll discover several facets of the same cuisine: planter cooking, slave cooking, and the cooking of the region's middle class. Planters, their families, and their guests enjoyed a complex cuisine based on expensive foodstuffs and unlimited labor. Slaves subsisted on scraps, trimmings, and foraged foods assembled in haste. Both cooking styles evolved in the hands of the plantation's slave cooks, who prepared their own food with the same skill and verve as the food they cooked for their masters. Middle-class Southerners strove to emulate planter cuisine but often ate fare more closely resembling slave cooking.

Dining in the Big House: Planter Cuisine

The everyday diet of Southern planter families was varied, substantial, and rich. They typically ate large amounts of protein foods: their meals typically focused on meat, poultry, game, or seafood.

Plantations produced chickens that were roasted, stewed, fricasseed or, most famously, fried. Cows produced milk that was primarily processed into butter, buttermilk, and a Cheddarlike type of cheese. Hogs provided most of the South's meat. The best cuts went to the planters' tables; pork chops and pork roasts, country hams, and bacon were everyday fare. Planters used much of their ample leisure time for hunting, typically bagging small game animals and wildfowl for the table.

FACTOR 3
Planters' protein-based diets included colonial domesticate meats, wild game, and seafood.

Because most plantations were located on the water, fish and shellfish frequently appeared on the plantation table. Throughout the region shrimp, crab, and oysters were among the most favored foods, whether caught along the property shore or brought by boat to plantations farther inland. Both freshwater and saltwater fish were frequently served.

Although plantation kitchens had the ingredients, equipment, and labor to produce fine wheat flour baked goods, wealthy planters retained the colonial taste preference for cornbread and other cornmeal dishes, and plantation menus featured them often. Abundant corn was also used for making mellow Bourbon whiskey.

FACTOR 2
Indigenous game meats, fish, and corn remain important in traditional Plantation South cuisine.

Plantations produced a wide variety of vegetables and fruits. Because many seeds, bulbs, and cuttings shipped from England and continental Europe thrived in the Southern soil and climate, plantation gardens and orchards yielded a wider selection of colonial domesticates than those of other regions. The mild climate even allowed the cultivation of Mediterranean food plants such as artichokes and figs.

In addition to wines, spirits, cheeses, and seasonings imported from Europe, planters also imported Caribbean ingredients, including rum, cane sugar, cane syrup, molasses, and tropical fruits. Spices worked their way through the trade routes from Asia and across the Atlantic to planters' tables.

European influence on Plantation South cooking wasn't confined to ingredients. Planters' wives and daughters learned "domestic management" as part of their education. Using handwritten heirloom recipes as well as French and English cookbooks, they planned menus as lavish and sophisticated as those of their European counterparts. However, their role was to advise and direct rather than actually cook.

Slave Cooks Add African Sizzle and Spice

Although planters' wives planned the menus, slaves did the cooking. In the early days of slavery, women fresh from Africa or the Caribbean learned English cooking from indentured servant cooks. Later they learned from one another; experienced older cooks taught the younger ones who would eventually replace them. Because slaves were not permitted to learn to read, generations of slave cooks acquired large repertoires of elaborate recipes simply by watching and memorizing. Some plantation owners, such as Thomas Jefferson, hired European chefs to give their slave cooks instruction in French cuisine.

FACTOR 4
African and Caribbean flavors transformed Plantation South cuisine.

Although technically skilled at European cooking, few slave cooks embraced the subtle seasoning of European cuisine, finding English dishes, in particular, bland and boring. In response, slave cooks applied their own African and Caribbean taste preferences to Plantation South cuisine. Using a free hand with spices and seasonings, they made European and colonial dishes livelier. They introduced African cooking techniques, such as pounding starches into purées and using ground peanuts to thicken soups and sauces. Fond of frying, they used indigenous cornmeal to make fritters and coat fried fish. Slave cooks banished dreary English-style boiled vegetables from the Southern repertoire, replacing them with fried and sautéed ones. Afro-Caribbean slaves added their barbeque techniques and knowledge of tropical produce such as bananas, mirlitons, and coconuts. Caribbean chiles were ground into fiery table sauces.

Many vegetables now associated with Southern cuisine arrived via Africa and the Caribbean. According to legend, captured Africans hid the seeds of okra in their hair so that they could grow it when they reached their unknown destinations in the New World. Black-eyed peas and sesame seeds, first introduced to Africa by the Arabs, also traveled to the Americas with African slaves. Both peanuts and South American chiles recrossed the Atlantic on slave ships to become staples of the evolving Plantation South cuisine. Slaves brought rice culture and cooking to the Carolina Lowcountry, a unique microcuisine area discussed on this book's companion website.

Although sweet potatoes are indigenous to southern Mexico, they had arrived in the Caribbean and Deep South by the time of European contact. African slaves found the sweet potato similar to the true yam and called it by the same African name, *nyam* (nyahm). Thus, in the Plantation South sweet potatoes are frequently called "yams," although the term is technically incorrect. Candied "yams" and sweet potato pie are dishes favored by Southerners both black and white.

The influence of African and Afro-Caribbean slave cooks on Plantation South cuisine simply can't be overestimated. They contributed an important foundation starch, new produce items, new seasonings and ways of using existing seasonings, and new cooking techniques. Thus, the Plantation South's African-American second-settler group profoundly enriched its cuisine, making Plantation South cooking substantially different from other English-based regional cooking styles.

Southern Hospitality and Entertaining

Planters entertained often and based their reputations at least partially on the quality of their hospitality. For special occasions the plantation kitchen went into high gear, often producing food for hundreds of guests. The plantation's head cook, with dozens of assistants, turned out a magnificent array of sumptuous dishes for a variety of occasions ranging from hunt breakfasts to formal dinners to grand buffets.

Warm Southern weather gave rise to a variety of outdoor feasts. In the summer hundreds of guests might be invited to a fish fry down by the river, where huge cast-iron cauldrons of pork lard heated over wood fires awaited the sizzle of breaded fish fillets. Early autumn brought oyster roasts, at which bushels of oysters were set to steam and pop on wire racks over glowing coals. The warm season's most anticipated event was the plantation barbeque, to which guests came from miles around to feast on succulent pork slow-cooked in smoky pits and steaming with droplets of spicy mopping sauce. The head cook of every plantation had his or her own special barbeque recipe, and guests argued about the merits of each plantation's signature style.

Eating in the Quarters: Slave Cooking

Creative cooking was not confined solely to the big house. Women slaves lower in the plantation hierarchy labored long days in workshops or fields only to come home afterward and begin preparing meals for their families. In order to prepare nourishing and enjoyable meals, they had to use both ingenuity and imagination because their ingredients were both poor and severely limited.

FACTOR 4

Slave cooks made nutritious, satisfying meals with ingenuity and limited ingredients.

Slave rations doled out by the plantation manager consisted of little more than cornmeal, dried beans, lard, and salt. In what little free time they were allowed, slaves grew okra, black-eyed peas, peanuts, chiles, collards, and other greens in tiny garden plots behind their cabins. These starches and vegetables formed the foundation of the slave diet; protein foods were used primarily for seasoning. Ham rinds and smoked neck bones flavored slow-simmered beans and greens. When a hog was butchered, slaves received the ribs, neck bones, ears, tails, and feet. Thus, using odds and ends, discards, and seasonings "borrowed" from the plantation kitchen, ingenious slave cooks prepared nutritious and tasty meals, making something delicious out of virtually nothing.

Even more important than the food was the fellowship of dining. A few precious minutes sitting around the dinner table accounted for virtually the only time a slave family could spend together. No wonder that, for modern African-Americans, food remains a strong expression of tradition, family, and cultural solidarity.

The cooking of plantation slaves and, later, free African-Americans evolved into a distinctive microcuisine called soul food. While similar to Plantation South cuisine, in many ways it's different and unique. The soul food microcuisine is discussed on this book's website.

> "For over two hundred years we were told where to live and where to work. We were given husbands, and we made children, and all these things could be taken away from us. The only real comfort came at the end of the day, when we took either the food we were given, or the food we raised, or the food we had caught, and we put it in the pot, and we sat with our own kind and talked and sang and ate."
>
> —Ruth Gaskins, Alexandria, Virginia, from Betty Fussell's *I Hear America Cooking*

Middle-Class Cooking

Not all white people in the Plantation South lived the lavish lives of the planter aristocracy. Many white farmers, including former indentured servants and their descendants, worked their own fields and cooked their own food. Middle- and lower-class whites and, later, free blacks practiced a scaled-down version of planter cuisine.

As in planter families, proteins were favored, high-status foods. However, ordinary folks couldn't eat them every day. Although just about everyone hunted and fished and could afford to feed a few chickens and a hog, protein foods were typically reserved for Sundays and holidays. Like the slaves, ordinary white folks lived primarily on starches and vegetables flavored with seasoning meat. Corn in all its forms—from cornbread to hominy soup—was the staff of life. Because even the smallest farm had room for a garden, ordinary Southerners enjoyed a variety of vegetables such as collard and turnip greens, sweet potatoes, turnips, cabbage, green corn, black-eyed peas, pole beans, butter beans, and okra. Housewives made jams and jellies from local fruit and dried and pickled their garden produce.

THE CIVIL WAR AND BEYOND

The plantation system ended when the South lost the Civil War in 1865. During the war agriculture had come to a standstill. Land, buildings, equipment, and goods were destroyed. The abolition of slavery removed the inexpensive labor that fueled the Southern economy. Formerly wealthy planter families were now penniless, and much of the middle class was jobless. For the poorest Southerners, poverty led to a diet based almost entirely on cornmeal dishes, causing a devastating nutritional-deficiency disease called *pellagra,* discussed on the book's companion website. Economic conditions in the American South remained bleak for more than a hundred years, and traditional Plantation Southern cooking was in danger of being lost.

Fortunately, the cuisine was kept alive both by African-American cooks and the "genteel poor," descendants of the planter aristocracy who maintained a gracious lifestyle despite having little money. Through two world wars and the Great Depression, struggling Southern families prepared heirloom recipes using homegrown vegetables and foods obtained by farming, hunting, fishing, and foraging.

Although economic viability is normally essential to the development of fine cuisine, through the mid-1900s the depressed economy of the Plantation South helped preserve the cuisine. While more prosperous parts of America suffered a culinary decline in the 1950s and 1960s (America's national cuisine, website), of necessity Southern cooks kept traditional cooking alive. When other Americans were turning to industrially processed convenience foods, Southern cooking still featured homegrown, home-canned, and home-raised food—partly because it was affordable, but mainly out of preference. Sunday dinner, depicted in Figure 2.17, was the highest expression of Plantation South home cooking.

Although most of the Plantation South's defining dishes were created during the plantation era, two major elements of the cuisine were developed during the post–Civil War period: barbeque and Southern desserts.

Southern Barbeque

After the Civil War, barbeque moved from the plantation to the roadside, becoming a true American culinary art form. Today traditional Southern barbeque can be found at country crossroads and on city street corners throughout the region.

FIGURE 2.17

A Southern Sunday dinner. Barnabas Kindersley © Dorling Kindersley

Traditional barbeque is cooked outdoors. The modern barbeque pit is a low rectangle built of cinder blocks. A hickory wood fire built in the pit burns down to embers, and a metal grate is placed on top. Tough, fatty cuts of pork, typically shoulder and spareribs, are seasoned with spice rub. The meat is placed on the grate and periodically basted with a bucket of vinegar-based mopping sauce—actually applied with a clean, new string mop. Like the Native American and plantation versions, modern barbeque is bathed in fragrant smoke. It alternately steams in the mop sauce vapors and crisps over dry heat.

City barbeque happens indoors in specially constructed wood ovens. Although the heat technology is different, in expert hands the result is the same: moist, tender, succulent meat with crisp edges and a spicy, tangy flavor.

Some barbeque lovers prefer their meat sauceless; others enjoy adding a splash of sweet or tart barbeque sauce. The consistency, spiciness, and acidity of barbeque sauces vary from place to place within the region.

For an in-depth look at Plantation South barbeque, as well as the barbeque of other culinary regions, refer to the barbeque section of this book's companion website.

Southern Desserts

Home-style baking is a Southern tradition that reached its peak after the Civil War, when baking powder became widely available. Of all Americans, only the Pennsylvania Dutch surpass Southerners in their love of sweet baked goods. Whether at breakfast, afternoon teatime, or the end of a meal, Southern folks just have to have a little something sweet. Today Southern home bakers still compete for prizes at state and county fairs. At church or school bake sales, jealous eyes watch to see whose cake, pie, or cookie tray sells first. Per Southern hospitality, no guest is ever received without being offered a little taste of homemade baked goods.

Among the many signature Plantation Southern desserts are tall layer cakes frosted with fluffy boiled icing. Old-fashioned biscuit shortcake is filled with fresh fruit and topped with whipped cream. Pecans are featured in cakes, cookies, and pecan pie, typically spiked with a little Bourbon whiskey.

Near the end of the 20th century, Southern towns and cities finally began to prosper when economic incentives brought service and telecommunications jobs to the region. The 1970s and 1980s saw an influx of new Southerners eager to explore the cuisine of their adopted home. At the same time, established Southerners began rediscovering traditional cuisine, seeking out local artisan products and reviving old-fashioned cooking methods. Heirloom ingredients, such as stone-ground grits and Carolina Gold rice (website), are making a comeback as home cooks and restaurant chefs showcase the fine products of days gone by.

FACTOR 5

In the 1980s, the return of economic viability revitalized Southern cuisine.

> ### ■□ ELEMENTS OF PLANTATION SOUTH CUISINE
>
> **FOUNDATION FOODS**
>
> principal starches: cornmeal dishes, wheat flour quick breads, rice
>
> principal proteins: pork (fresh and preserved), dried beans, seafood, poultry
>
> principal produce: collard greens, turnips and turnip greens, green beans, okra, sweet corn
>
> **FAVORED SEASONINGS:** smoke, cured and smoked seasoning meats, cayenne pepper, bottled hot sauce, thyme, sage, granulated onion and garlic
>
> **PRINCIPAL COOKING MEDIA:** lard, vegetable oil
>
> **PRIMARY COOKING METHODS:** pan-frying, barbeque, stewing/simmering
>
> **FOOD ATTITUDES:** strong food culture, culinary liberals

■□ CONTEMPORARY ■ PLANTATION SOUTH CUISINE

Until the end of the 20th century, Plantation South cooking meant home cooking. Although good Southern food could be found at barbeque shacks, old-fashioned luncheonettes, and family-style restaurants, white-tablecloth operations featuring authentic Plantation South cuisine were few. In the South, fine restaurant dining usually meant French or Continental cuisine (p. 791).

In the 1980s, chefs and cookbook authors began exploring and celebrating regional American cuisines. Restaurants featuring Southern food sprang up in urban areas nationwide, and entrepreneurs founded national chain restaurants featuring barbeque. Chefs in the Plantation South returned to their roots and devoted their energies to interpreting Southern cooking as a restaurant cuisine. Now Southern chefs are refining traditional Southern cooking, applying European techniques and devising elegant presentations to bring their traditional dishes into the forefront of American dining. Refer to this book's companion website for noteworthy Plantation South cuisine restaurants.

■□ THE FUTURE ■ OF THE CUISINE

Although no cuisine is static, the regional cuisine of the Plantation South is, perhaps, changing faster than any other. Through the turn of the 21st century, growing economic migration to the South, by both Americans and immigrants from around the world, is swelling the populations of Southern cities. These new arrivals will surely add a thick overlay of new foodways to the established cuisine, changing it in unpredictable ways.

At the same time, modern health concerns threaten some of the Plantation South's most venerable ingredients. Today's sedentary lifestyle makes frequent use of fundamental elements of the cuisine, such as pork lard and frying, problematic. Cultural preferences among many African-Americans and immigrants are reducing the use of pork as the region's preferred meat. Global climate change is threatening Southern agriculture, evidenced in recent regional droughts. Though cooks and chefs across the nation have discovered many of the region's traditional ingredients, such as stone-ground grits and heirloom bean and rice varieties, limited production is not keeping up with demand.

Finally, the fast pace of modern life means that home cooks, the standard-bearers of traditional Plantation South cuisine, are spending less time at the stove. As this trend continues, the future of the cuisine now lies in the hands of professional chefs. Your challenge as a chef is to understand the cuisine and faithfully interpret it for future audiences.

■□ THE LOWCOUNTRY ■ MICROCUISINE

The Carolina coastal plain from Charleston to Savannah, Georgia, is an area of flat land bordered on the east by saltwater marshes protected from the Atlantic Ocean by the Sea Islands.

This topographically unique area was settled by a more diverse group of European planters who imported the South's largest concentration of African slaves to plant and tend vast tracts of paddy rice. The rice trade brought incredible wealth to the area, engendering a thriving maritime trade and an opulent lifestyle that included a highly developed food culture and cuisine. From rice, abundant seafood, and an international palette of ingredients, African-American plantation cooks created a Lowcountry haute cuisine world famous in its time. African slaves and their descendants developed Gullah cooking, a spicier, more rustic cuisine. Two faces of the same coin, these cooking styles make up Lowcountry cooking. Go to this book's companion website for in-depth information about Lowcountry cuisine.

■ THE SOUL FOOD □ ■ MICROCUISINE

During the plantation era, African-American slave cooks developed their own distinctive cuisine using indigenous cornmeal,

hunted and foraged foods, garden produce, and scraps from the masters' larders. After Emancipation, Southern slaves began a great diaspora, migrating first to Mid-Atlantic and Midwestern cities and then across America. Wherever they went, African-American cooks took with them the comfort foods of home, such as cornbread, collard greens, black-eyed peas, and barbeque. In the 1960s, the civil rights movement brought a new spirit of cultural pride to the African-American community. At this time the traditional cooking of black Americans became known as *soul food.* Although born in the Plantation South, soul food is now a microcuisine that transcends its origins, found throughout America. The companion website offers more information about this lively cuisine.

Visit this book's companion website at ***www.pearsonhigh ered.com/sackett*** to learn more about the Carolina Lowcountry and Soul Food microcuisines. Following are some photos relating to these two microcuisines.

☐ TABLE 2.1 PLANTATION SOUTH DEFINING DISHES

ITEM NAME	HISTORY	DOMINANT INGREDIENTS AND METHOD	OTHER
PEANUT SOUP	A significant part of Southern cuisine by the early 20th century.	Poultry stock flavored, thickened, and enriched with ground peanuts.	Some versions are subtle and creamy; others are bright and spicy, showing the influence of African cuisine.
DEVILED EGGS	In the South no picnic, church supper, or holiday dinner is complete without a platter of these tasty treats.	Hard-cooked eggs are cut in half and the yolks puréed with mayonnaise, yellow mustard, a dash of hot sauce, and something sweet.	Modern versions add ingredients such as chopped shrimp or crabmeat, deviled ham, minced fresh herbs.
SOUTHERN PICKLES	Pickling was originally done for preservation, now done for flavor.	Cucumbers, watermelon rind, okra, peaches, and green beans are preserved in vinegar with sugar and seasonings.	Southern-style pickles tend to be on the sweet side, with "bread-and-butter" cucumber pickles a favorite.
SOUTHERN FRIED CHICKEN	Once a dish seasonal to spring and early summer, fried chicken remains the centerpiece of the traditional Sunday dinner throughout the South.	Fried chicken is always cooked from a raw state, fried at a low-to-moderate temperature that allows the meat to cook moist and juicy while the exterior coating becomes crisp and golden.	The dense legs and thighs are cooked longer than the breasts and wings.
FRIED SEAFOOD AND HUSH PUPPIES	This treat is essential at a Southern outdoor fish fry. Deep-frying is the most effective method of frying for a crowd; many Southerners prefer the crunchy texture of breaded fish pan-fried in a black cast-iron skillet.	Fish, shrimp, and shucked oysters are dipped into seasoned cornmeal or corn flour and fried crisp and golden in vegetable oil, traditionally flavored with a little lard. Deep-fried fish is incomplete without hush puppies.	Hush puppies are light, round, relatively greaseless, golden-brown cornmeal fritters. Fish is always served with tartar sauce; shrimp is teamed with a ketchup-based cocktail sauce; oysters go either way.
SMOTHERED FOODS	Called "smothered" because the main ingredient is cooked in a thick, dense sauce.	Items are browned in lard or bacon drippings; then flour is added to the pan and cooked into a light brown roux that is simmered with flavorful stock to make a thick, substantial sauce.	Pork chops and chicken are the usual candidates for smothering, but turkey legs, elderly game birds, tough cuts of venison, or any lean meat can be smothered. Smothered foods are normally served over rice or with biscuits.

(continued)

☐ TABLE 2.1 PLANTATION SOUTH DEFINING DISHES (continued)

ITEM NAME	HISTORY	DOMINANT INGREDIENTS AND METHOD	OTHER
COUNTRY HAM	Dry, dense, and salty, with a deep, complex flavor, a Southern country ham is similar to European cured hams. It is served in small portions. Baked ham, glazed with brown sugar, studded with cloves, and sometimes garnished with pineapple, is the ultimate centerpiece of a Southern buffet.	The ham is first scrubbed to remove the mold that develops during aging, soaked for several days in several changes of water to remove some of the salt, then poached in a sweet and slightly acidic liquid: wine, apple cider, or even Coca-Cola. The ham is cooked through to 160°F, cooled, glazed, decorated, and then finished in the oven.	Ham is served with fried eggs, grits, and redeye gravy, a sauce made by deglazing the pan with strong black coffee. "Ham, biscuits, and gravy" is the quintessential Southern breakfast. Hot biscuits are split and filled with thin-sliced country ham and topped with creamy pan gravy. Mini-biscuits filled with ham are a popular Southern hors d'oeuvre.
SOUTHERN QUICK BREADS: BISCUITS AND CORNBREAD	The earliest and most famous of biscuits could be called "quick" only in the culinary sense of having no yeast. For beaten biscuits, the dough was literally pounded with a heavy object, such as a mallet or the flat of an ax head, until it became glossy and blistered with air bubbles. Beaten biscuits bake up crisp and unusually light.	Baking powder biscuits and buttermilk biscuits are made from soft flour with milk or buttermilk and lard. Eaten at breakfast with butter and honey or cane syrup. Classic with thin-sliced country ham and cream gravy. Accompany any lunch or dinner entrée.	Traditional Southerners prefer a pure, unsweetened cornbread made from corn-meal, eggs, baking powder, baking soda, and buttermilk. The batter is poured into a hot cast-iron skillet greased with bacon drippings to develop a tasty, well-browned crust. Given body and protein from white wheat flour, this batter be-comes the basis for fritters, muffins, corn-sticks, and griddlecakes.
GRITS	Artisanally produced, whole-grain, stone-ground grits are the original; worth finding for their superior texture and deep corn flavor.	Simmered in salted water. Cooled, so-lidified grits are sliced or formed into cakes and fried.	Grits are the staple starch of Southern breakfasts. They are also used as a side starch to accompany sauced entrées. Commercially produced grits cook up quickly but lack texture and flavor.
GREENS	No food is more representative of old-fashioned Southern cooking than a dish of greens long-cooked with smoked meat in a savory broth called "pot liquor" or "pot likker."	Collard greens are the best-known choice, but kale, cabbage, chard, dan-delion, spinach, cress, mustard greens, and turnip greens are also simmered in water with seasoning meat.	A frugal supper, greens are served with cornbread or corn dodger dumplings and a glass of fresh buttermilk. At Sunday din-ner or other festive meals, they are an in-dispensable side dish.
VEGETABLES COOKED WITH SEASONING MEAT	Early vegetable cultivars required longer cooking, simmered until tender with salty, smoky seasoning meat and tasty pot liquor.	String beans, shell beans, squashes, turnips, kohlrabi, cabbage, and many other vegetables are cooked this way. Chunks of potato may be added to thicken the broth. Alternatively, corn-meal dumplings are poached in the pot liquor.	Despite long cooking times, vitamins and minerals are recaptured when the pot liquor is consumed, as all good Southern-ers love to do.
FIELD PEAS, DRIED BEANS AND SHELL BEANS	Called *field peas*, to distinguish them from English or garden peas, black-eyed peas, cowpeas, and crowder peas are not peas at all, but actually beans. Small, round, and beige with a single black-brown spot, to some Southerners black-eyed peas represent all the soldiers, black and white, who served in the Civil War.	Simmered with smoked pork and aro-matic vegetables.	Dried beans are a traditional comfort food in the South. Shell beans are bean seeds eaten in fresh form. *Butter beans* is a term for several members of the lima bean family, ranging from the tiny seiva ("sivvy") bean to large, mature yellow lima beans.
PORK, FIELD PEAS 'N' GREENS: THE SOUTHERN TRINITY	Served on New Year's Day, this meal is so uni-versal that many stores completely sell out of greens and black-eyed peas several days be-fore the holiday. Pork symbolizes health and luck, black-eyed peas represent coins, and greens represent paper money.	Prepared separately, this trinity of in-gredients comes together on the plate.	Not reserved for New Year's only, the trin-ity appears in many dishes such as spareribs with Hoppin' John and collards, country ham with black-eyed pea cakes and wilted salad, or a tasty pot of black-eyed pea soup simmered with neck bones and cabbage.
OKRA: SAUTÉED, SIMMERED, OR FRIED	West African slaves brought with them not only the seeds of okra, but also its African name, *gombo*, which has mutated into *gumbo*, now the name of an entire group of defining dishes found in both the Lowcountry and Louisiana.	Okra thickens stews and gumbos; it is served as a side dish sautéed in bacon drippings or simmered in a fresh tomato sauce and as an appetizer or side dish when floured and deep-fried.	Pickled okra appears on Southern relish trays.

☐ TABLE 2.1 PLANTATION SOUTH DEFINING DISHES *(continued)*

ITEM NAME	HISTORY	DOMINANT INGREDIENTS AND METHOD	OTHER
FRIED GREEN TOMATOES	Green tomatoes are an autumn staple. Picked at the last minute before the first hard frost, they keep well in the cold cellar for weeks or even months. Many cooks pick tomatoes green all summer.	Dipped in flour, egg, and cornmeal, then fried crunchy-brown in bacon drippings.	Fried green tomatoes are traditionally served as a side dish or casual supper entrée; in a restaurant the dish works well as an appetizer or brunch entrée.
CANDIED "YAMS"	Adopted by the rest of America as a Thanksgiving favorite, candied yams are a regular feature on the Southern table.	Sweet potatoes are peeled, boiled, and then baked with butter and brown sugar to acquire a sweet, golden glaze.	The orange-fleshed variety are the best choice for candying; their firmer texture stands up to the double cooking.
FORAGED FOODS	Inspired by their deep-rooted love of the land (and necessitated by a century of hardship), quite a few Southerners maintain the vanishing tradition of American foraging.	Preparation varies.	Foraged items include: mushrooms, wild fruits, wild vegetables, and greens (see pp. 368–369).
GAME, WILD AND FARMED	Southern hunters regularly stock their freezers with wild game such as venison, bear, 'coon (raccoon), 'possum (opossum), groundhog, rabbit, squirrel, wild turkey, duck, grouse, dove, and quail.	Young, tender game is roasted, sautéed, or pan-fried. Older, tougher game is braised, stewed, or made into soups.	Game farming has become an important agricultural activity, especially in the Carolinas, where excellent quail are raised to be shipped to fine restaurants throughout the country and overseas.
SOUTHERN PIES	Pies reflect the Plantation South's English heritage, although many feature New World ingredients.	Southern pie crust includes lard for a rich flavor and flaky crust. Selections include pecan pie, sweet potato pie, peanut butter pie, chess pie (dairy-free clear custard flavored with lemon or chocolate), black bottom pie (chocolate bottom, bourbon chess top), and preaching pies/fried pies (half-moon-shaped, fruit-filled fried pastries).	Pie was not an everyday dish in the South, but usually heralded a special occasion. Pies were especially popular around the winter holidays. Southern cookbooks record thousands of recipes for pies, many only slight variations of others.
FRUIT COBBLERS	Because hot, humid Southern weather made rolling piecrust a difficult task, Southern cooks turned to the easier, more forgiving cobbler as their everyday dessert. Seasonal fruit, such as peaches and cherries in summer and apples and pears in fall, are used.	The fruit is placed in a baking dish, sugared, dotted with butter, seasoned with spice, and then topped with a soft, biscuit-like dough, sometimes rolled out thick to cover the fruit, but most often punched out with a biscuit cutter or simply dolloped on top so the fruit shows through.	Served hot from the oven, the fruit virtually swims in sweet, syrupy juice, and the golden pastry on top stays crispy. Cobblers may be topped with whipped cream or ice cream.
BISCUIT SHORTCAKE	Classic Southern shortcake is composed not of spongecake but rather old-fashioned flaky biscuits sweetened with sugar.	Large, sweetened biscuits are split in three layers, slathered with soft whipped cream, and filled with sliced fruits.	
SOUTHERN CAKES	In the early South, *cake* meant traditional English poundcake, so named because the recipe called for a pound of butter, a pound of sugar, a pound of eggs, and a pound of flour, leavened only by the air incorporated by vigorous and prolonged beating, done by hand with a wooden spoon.	Southern cakes include coconut cake (with boiled icing), three-layer yellow cake (often with chocolate fudge icing), black walnut pound cake, burnt sugar cake/caramel cake, jam cake (with fruit preserves added to the batter), Lane cake (white cake with boiled icing and a filling of pecans, coconut, and candied fruits), and Lady Baltimore cake (similar to a Lane cake, but with nut and raisin filling).	With the advent of baking powder in the late 1800s, Southern bakers went into a frenzy of creativity, developing elaborate multilayer cakes often standing eight inches tall. Many began to prefer a light, airy cake layer with a large crumb. Nuts, fruit, and jam were added between layers, often with rich, custard fillings. The favored frosting was a light, white boiled icing or Italian buttercream icing that could be decorated with coconut, chopped nuts, candied fruits, or sugared flower petals.

(continued)

☐ TABLE 2.1 PLANTATION SOUTH DEFINING DISHES *(continued)*

ITEM NAME	HISTORY	DOMINANT INGREDIENTS AND METHOD	OTHER
FRUIT DESSERTS AND GELATINS	Gelatins based on fruit juice and sweet wines became popular desserts once refrigeration became widely available in the South.	Preparations vary.	Ambrosia is the favored dessert of Southern church suppers and potluck dinners. Fresh or syrup-poached fruit is layered with whipped cream and shredded coconut. Mixed with custards or ice creams, sparking gelatins add color to the dessert table.
PUDDINGS AND CONFECTIONS	Trifles and bread puddings were traditionally made to use up stale bread or cake. Often spiked with Caribbean rum and/or Bourbon whiskey, they offered an opportunity for "proper" ladies to indulge in a taste of spirits.	Banana pudding, made with sliced bananas, vanilla wafer cookies, and cooked custard, is favored in the deep South. Spirits also find their way into bourbon balls and rum balls, both popular homemade confections.	Nut brittles, pralines, macaroons, kisses, divinity, and benne wafers are only a few of the South's many confections.
ICE CREAMS	When Thomas Jefferson returned from France, he brought a "cream machine for ice" to Monticello and is reputed to have made the first ice cream in America. Food historians argue that ice cream was made in Charleston and on the Ashley River plantations some twenty years earlier.	A sweet custard base is churned over salted ice until frozen. Hand-cranked churns were replaced by electrically powered and cooled machines.	In 1835, the first shipment of block ice made its way to Savannah, and the era of the ice cream garden was born.

Pre–Civil War mansions line the Charleston waterfront. Matty Symons/Shutterstock

Locally caught shrimp are sold fresh and head-on in Lowcountry markets. Dave King © Dorling Kindersley

Soul food restaurants brought Plantation South African-American home cooking to a mainstream dining audience. Demetrio Carrasco © Dorling Kindersley

■ □ ■ STUDY QUESTIONS

1. Describe the topography and climate of the Plantation South and explain how they influenced the region's economy and cuisine.

2. Describe the agricultural method used by Plantation South and other East Coast Native American groups. List the three main indigenous food plants that formed the basis of the Native American diet and describe their cultivation.

3. Discuss Native American influence on the cuisine of the Plantation South. Which Native American dishes and cooking methods survive today?

4. Who were the Plantation South's first settlers? List the elements of their Old World cuisine. Explain how their attitudes and eating habits changed after they arrived in the Plantation South.

5. Who were the Plantation South's second settlers and why did they arrive? List the elements of their Old World cuisine. How did their ingredients and cooking methods alter the existing cuisine?

6. What is the Plantation South's fundamental protein food? List and describe three preserved products made from this food and explain two ways each of these products is used in cooking.

7. Describe the effect of the Civil War on the economy and cuisine of the Plantation South.

8. For what specialized, signature cooking method is the Plantation South most famous? Explain the Native American origin of this technique. What was the most important European contribution to this technique? Describe some of the interregional variations of this technique as presented on this book's website.

9. List and describe five defining dishes of Plantation South cuisine.

10. Discuss the Carolina Lowcountry microcuisine: Recount its origin and development; list its foundation starch and protein foods; list three of its defining dishes.

11. Discuss the Soul Food microcuisine: Explain the origin of the name; compare and contrast it with mainstream Plantation South cuisine.

12. Using the information learned in this chapter and your imagination, create a four-course special-event dinner menu featuring Plantation South cuisine.

Charleston She-Crab Soup

with Buttermilk Biscuits

yield: 1 (8-fl.-oz.) appetizer serving
(multiply × 4 for classroom turnout; adjust equipment sizes accordingly)

MASTER RECIPE

production		costing only
1 c.	She-Crab Soup Base	1/4 recipe
as needed	water	n/c
1/4 c.	crabmeat (from She-Crab Soup Base recipe)	n/c
1 1/2 tsp.	minced parsley	1/40 bunch a.p.
1 Tbsp.	crab roe (from She-Crab Soup Base recipe)	n/c
2	6" doilies	2 each
2	Buttermilk Biscuits	1/8 recipe

service turnout:
1. Heat the She-Crab Soup Base just to the boil, thinning with water if necessary.
2. Plate the dish:
   a. Place the crabmeat in a hot 10-fl.-oz. soup cup.
   b. Pour in the soup base.
   c. Sprinkle with parsley and float the crab roe on top.
   d. Place a 6" doily on an 8" underliner plate and place the soup cup on top.
   e. Place the biscuits on another doily-lined plate.

COMPONENT RECIPE

SHE-CRAB SOUP BASE

yield: 2 pt.

production		costing only
as needed	water	n/c
8	large, live female crabs	8 each
1 Tbsp.	Chesapeake seasoning	1/8 oz.
2	bay leaves	1/16 oz.
1	clove	1/16 oz.
1/4 tsp.	dried thyme	1/16 oz.
4 Tbsp.	butter	2 oz.
1/2 c.	minced yellow onion	2 1/2 oz. a.p.
1/4 c.	peeled, minced celery	1/20 head a.p.
3 Tbsp.	long-grain white rice (not parboiled)	1 3/4 oz.
2 tsp.	tomato paste	1/8 oz.
1/2 c.	half-and-half	4 fl. oz.
tt	kosher salt	1/16 oz.
1/4 tsp.	fine-ground white pepper	1/16 oz.
1/4 c.	dry sherry	2 fl. oz.

preparation:
1. Steam the crabs:
   a. Place 1/2" water in a large pot and bring to the boil.
   b. Alternately add the crabs and the Chesapeake seasoning to the pot, quickly cover the pot, and steam the crabs for 15 minutes.
   c. Remove the crabs to a hotel pan and cool. Reserve the liquid in the pot.
2. Prepare the crabmeat and stock shells:
   a. Open the crabs and discard the hard, red back carapaces and aprons. Remove and discard the gills.
   b. Pick the crabmeat and place it in a small, freshly sanitized plastic container. Refrigerate.
   c. Discard the hard claw shells but reserve all of the soft body shells and leg shells.
   d. Crumble the red crab roe into a small ramekin and refrigerate.
3. Prepare the crab stock:
   a. Place the remaining soft-textured crab shells in a saucepan and pack them down. Pour 1 c. crab cooking liquid over the crab shells in the saucepan and add 4 c. water. Add the bay leaves, clove, and thyme. Simmer 30 minutes.
   b. Strain the stock, pushing down on the solids to extract as much liquid as possible. You should have about 1 qt. crab stock.
4. Rinse out the stock saucepan and add the butter, onion, and celery. Sweat until soft.
5. Add the hot crab stock and the rice. Cover and simmer 40 minutes, stirring occasionally, until the rice is very soft.
6. Strain the soup and return the solids to the pot.
7a. Add 1 c. soup broth back to the pot and purée the mixture with an immersion blender. Whisk the remaining soup broth.
   —or—
7b. Place the solids and 1 c. soup broth in a blender and purée until smooth, then add the remaining soup broth through the feed tube. Pour the soup back into the saucepan.
8. Whisk in the tomato paste and half-and-half and heat to just under the boil.
9. Season the soup base with salt, white pepper, and sherry.

holding: open-pan cool in an ice bain-marie; refrigerate in a freshly sanitized, covered plastic container up to 3 days; hold the crabmeat and crab roe refrigerated up to 3 days

RECIPE VARIATION

Mock She-Crab Soup (using male crabs)
Omit the crab roe. Mash together equal parts hard-cooked egg yolk and red tobiko caviar; use this mixture to garnish the soup.

Georgia Peanut Soup

with Southern Brittle Bread

yield: 1 (8 fl.-oz.) appetizer serving (multiply × 4 for classroom turnout; adjust equipment sizes accordingly)

MASTER RECIPE

production		costing only
1 c.	Peanut Soup Base	1/4 recipe
as needed	water	n/c
1 Tbsp.	roasted chopped peanuts	1/8 oz.
1 Tbsp.	fine diagonal-sliced scallion	1/16 bunch a.p.
1 Tbsp.	brunoise-cut red bell pepper	1/4 oz. a.p.
1	6" doily or cocktail napkin	1 each
1 piece	Southern Brittle Bread	1/8 recipe
1	lemon wedge	1/8 [90 ct.] lemon

service turnout:

1. Heat the Peanut Soup Base just to the boil in a small saucepan, thinning with water if necessary.
2. Plate the dish:
   a. Pour the soup base into a hot 10-fl.-oz. soup cup.
   b. Add the peanuts and sprinkle with the scallion and red bell pepper.
   c. Place the doily on an 8" underliner plate and place the soup cup on top.
   d. Break the Brittle Bread into pieces and arrange on the underliner plate.
   e. Place the lemon wedge on the underliner plate.

COMPONENT RECIPE

PEANUT SOUP BASE

yield: 1 qt.

production		costing only
1/2 c.	minced yellow onion	2 1/2 oz. a.p.
1/2 c.	peeled, minced celery	1/10 head a.p.
1/3 c.	peeled, minced carrot	1 oz. a.p.
6 Tbsp.	butter	3 oz.
1 tsp.	minced garlic	1/8 oz. a.p.
1/2 tsp.	crushed dried red pepper	1/16 oz
2 Tbsp.	flour	1/16 oz.
5 c.	hot Poultry Stock	5/8 recipe
1/2 c.	peanut butter	5 oz.
1 tsp.	sugar	1/16 oz.
1 sprig	fresh thyme	1/16 bunch a.p.
tt	kosher salt	
1/2 c.	peeled, seeded tomatoes, cut in 1/4'' dice	6 oz. a.p.
1/2 c.	half-and-half	4 fl. oz.

preparation:

1. In a heavy 2 1/2-qt. saucepan, sweat the onion, celery, and carrot in the butter until soft. Add the garlic and dried red pepper and sweat 1 minute more.
2. Stir in the flour and cook to a blond roux.
3. Whisk in half of the Poultry Stock.
4. Whisk the remaining stock into the peanut butter, then pour the mixture into the soup. Add the sugar, thyme, and a little salt. Simmer about 15 minutes, until lightly thickened. Thin with water or more stock if necessary.
5. Add the tomatoes and simmer 5 minutes more.
6. Remove the thyme sprig stem, add the half-and-half, and bring the soup just to the boil.
7. Correct the salt and sugar.

holding: open-pan cool and immediately refrigerate in a freshly sanitized, covered container up to 5 days; may be frozen up to 3 months, but may separate and require reemulsification using a blender or immersion blender

---

RECIPE VARIATION

Gullah Chicken in Spicy Peanut Sauce
Fabricate 4 (12-oz.) chicken legs as directed in the Country Captain recipe (p. 63). Brown the chicken in peanut oil and drain excess fat. Prepare the Peanut Soup Base through step 4 and pour it over the chicken. Cover the pan and simmer the legs 20 minutes, until cooked through. Add the tomatoes as directed, but omit the half-and-half. Serve over Pan-Steamed White Rice with Braised Tender Greens.

Shrimp 'n' Grits

yield: 1 appetizer serving: 3 1/2 oz. shrimp plus sauce and grits (multiply × 4 for classroom turnout; adjust equipment sizes accordingly)

MASTER RECIPE

production		costing only
3/4 c.	Shrimp Sauce for Grits	1/4 recipe
3	(21–25 ct.) white shrimp, peeled and tails removed, deveined	2 oz. a.p.
as needed	water, in squeeze bottle	n/c
3/4 c.	hot Stone-Ground Grits	1/4 recipe
1	Scallion "brush," p. 276	1/4 recipe

service turnout:

1. Heat the Shrimp Sauce for Grits in an 8" sauté pan. Add the shrimp, cover, and cook about 30 seconds, until just cooked through. Thin the sauce with water as necessary.
2. Plate the dish:
   a. Mound the Stone-Ground Grits in the center of a hot 10" plate. Make a well in the center.
   b. Spoon in the shrimp and sauce.
   c. Stick the Scallion brush upright out of the back of the grits.

COMPONENT RECIPE
SHRIMP SAUCE FOR GRITS

yield: 3 c.

production		costing only
3 Tbsp.	bacon drippings or pork lard	1 1/2 oz.
2 Tbsp.	flour	1/8 oz.
1/2 c.	fine-chopped green bell pepper	4 oz. a.p.
1/2 c.	fine-chopped yellow onion	2 1/2 oz. a.p.
1/4 c.	fine-chopped peeled celery	1/20 head a.p.
1 tsp.	minced garlic	1/8 oz. a.p.
1/2 c.	tomato concassée	6 oz. a.p.
3 c.	hot Shellfish Stock 24 fl. oz.	
tt	kosher salt	1/16 oz.
tt	bottled hot sauce (Crystal brand or other acidic hot sauce)	1/16 oz.

preparation:

1. In a 10" sauté pan, make a light brown roux with the bacon drippings and flour.
2. Add the green bell pepper, onion, and celery. Cook, stirring, until the vegetables are soft.
3. Add the garlic and tomato and cook until dry.
4. Whisk the hot Shellfish Stock into the hot roux mixture. Cook at a brisk simmer about 15 minutes, stirring occasionally, until the sauce reduces to a thick nappé consistency.
5. Season with salt and hot sauce.

holding: open-pan cool and immediately refrigerate in a freshly sanitized, covered plastic container up to 4 days

---

RECIPE VARIATION
Shrimp 'n' Grits with Brown Gravy
Omit the tomatoes from the Shrimp Sauce for Grits recipe and increase the flour in the roux to 3 Tbsp. Add a small sprig of fresh thyme as the sauce simmers. Add fresh-ground black pepper at the end of cooking.

Chickasaw Bean Cake
with Sunflower Salad

yield: 1 appetizer serving: 3 oz. cake plus sauce and accompaniment (multiply × 4 for classroom turnout; adjust equipment sizes accordingly)

MASTER RECIPE

production		costing only
2 Tbsp.	bacon drippings	n/c
2 fl. oz.	Bean Cake Batter	1/6 recipe
1/2 c.	Fresh Tomato Sauce	1/8 recipe
3/4 c.	Sunflower Salad	1/4 recipe
1 sprig	fresh flat-leaf parsley	1/20 bunch

service turnout:
1. Heat a 6" sauté pan, add the bacon drippings, and heat until medium-hot.
2. Using a 2-fl. oz. portion scoop, place Bean Cake Batter in the pan, flatten it, and fry the bean cake about 2 minutes, until the bottom is golden brown. Flip the cake and fry another 2 minutes, until browned on both sides. Remove and drain on a rack set over a sheet tray.
3. Spoon the Fresh Tomato Sauce into the same pan and heat just until warm.
4. Plate the dish:
   a. Place the bean cake in the center of a warm 10" plate.
   b. Pool the tomato sauce on the front right of the plate.
   c. Spoon the Sunflower Salad on the back left.
   d. Stick the parsley sprig upright from the back of the bean cake.

COMPONENT RECIPE
BEAN CAKE BATTER

yield: 1 1/2 c.

production		costing only
1/4 c.	stone-ground yellow cornmeal	1 1/4 oz.
1/4 c.	flour	1 1/2 oz.
1/4 tsp.	baking powder	1/16 oz.
tt	kosher salt	1/16 oz.
1/2	egg, beaten	1 fl. oz.
1/4 c.	half-and-half	2 fl. oz.
1 c.	cooked, drained black-eyed peas	8 fl. oz.
2 Tbsp.	minced scallion	1/10 bunch a.p.
tt	fresh-ground black pepper	1/16 oz.

preparation:
1. In a medium stainless bowl, stir together the cornmeal, flour, baking powder and salt. Make a well in the center.
2. Add the egg and half-and-half in the well and begin stirring the dry ingredients into the wet to make a smooth batter.
3. Mash the black-eyed peas into a very rough purée and mix them into the batter along with the scallion and pepper.
4. Refrigerate at least 30 minutes.

holding: refrigerate up to 6 hours; after that time, if baking powder loses strength, add another 1/4 tsp. in a 1 Tbsp. water slurry. (Alternatively, prefry the cakes and cool on a rack; refry to order with some loss of quality.)

COMPONENT RECIPE
SUNFLOWER SALAD

yield: approx. 3 c.

production		costing only
3 c.	peeled, 1/8"-sliced sunchokes (Jerusalem artichokes)	3/4 lb. a.p.
tt	kosher salt	1/16 oz.
as needed	water	n/c
1/4 c.	corn oil	2 fl. oz.
3 Tbsp.	minced shallot	1 1/2 oz. a.p.
1/2 tsp.	yellow mustard seeds	1/16 oz.
1/4 tsp.	crushed dried red pepper	1/16 oz.
1 Tbsp.	pure maple syrup	1/2 fl. oz.
tt	kosher salt	1/16 oz.
3 Tbsp.	cider vinegar	1 1/2 fl. oz.
tt	fresh-ground black pepper	1/16 oz.
1/4 c.	fine-julienne red bell pepper	2 oz. a.p.
1/4 c.	fine diagonal-sliced scallion	1/5 bunch a.p.
3 Tbsp.	toasted sunflower seeds	3/4 oz.

preparation:
1. Blanch the sunchokes in salted boiling water until crisp-tender. Refresh and blot dry.
2. Place the oil and the shallot in an 8" sauté pan. Cook over low heat until the shallot begins to brown. Add the mustard seeds and dried red pepper and cook a few seconds more until the seeds swell and the dried red pepper is fragrant. ⚠ Do not allow the spices to brown. Immediately scrape the oil and seasonings into a bowl and cool to room temperature.
3. Whisk the syrup, salt, vinegar, and black pepper into the oil mixture and correct the seasoning. Fold in the sunchokes, red bell pepper, scallion, and sunflower seeds.

holding: refrigerate in a freshly sanitized, covered plastic container up to 2 days

---

RECIPE VARIATIONS
Chickasaw Bean Cake with Kohlrabi Salad
Replace the sunchokes with tender young kohlrabi. Replace the sunflower seeds with toasted pecan pieces.

Chickasaw Bean Cake with Sprout Salad
Replace the sunchokes with a mixture of raw sprouts, such as mung bean sprouts, radish sprouts, alfalfa sprouts, and so on.

Kentucky Limestone Salad

with Clemson Blue Cheese, Cornbread Croutons, and Candied Pecans

yield: 1 appetizer serving: approx. 2 oz. lettuce plus garnishes (multiply × 4 for classroom turnout; adjust equipment sizes accordingly)

MASTER RECIPE

production		costing only
1/2 head	cleaned and dried Bibb lettuce, pulled into bite-size pieces	1/2 head a.p.
3 Tbsp.	Basic Vinaigrette	1/4 recipe
3 Tbsp.	crumbled Clemson Blue cheese	1/2 oz.
1/2 c.	Cornbread Croutons	1/4 recipe
1/4 c.	Candied Pecans	1/4 recipe

service turnout:
1. In a small bowl, toss the lettuce with the Basic Vinaigrette.
2. Plate the dish:
   a. Mound the salad on a cool 10" plate.
   b. Sprinkle with the cheese, Cornbread Croutons, and Candied Pecans.

COMPONENT RECIPE
CORNBREAD CROUTONS

yield: 2 c.

production		costing only
1/4 recipe	day-old Pure Southern Cornbread	1/4 recipe
3 Tbsp.	melted butter	1 1/2 oz.

preparation:
1. Preheat an oven to 400°F.
2. Cut the Pure Southern Cornbread into 1/2" cubes.
3. Toss the cornbread cubes with the butter and place on a half-sheet tray.
4. Bake in the center of the oven 5 to 8 minutes, until crisp and lightly browned.
5. Cool to room temperature.

holding: store in a freshly sanitized, tightly covered plastic container at room temperature up to 3 days

COMPONENT RECIPE
CANDIED PECANS

yield: 1 c.

production		costing only
1 c.	small pecan halves	2 3/4 oz.
2 tsp.	softened butter, optional	1/4 oz.
3/4 c.	sugar	4 1/2 oz.
1/4 c.	water	n/c
1/2 tsp.	fine salt	1/16 oz.
1/2 tsp.	pure vanilla extract	1/12 fl. oz.

preparation:
1. Preheat an oven to 400°F.
2. Spread the pecans on a half-sheet tray and toast in the center of the oven 3 to 5 minutes, until crisp. Remove and cool.
3. Place a silicone mat or buttered pan liner on the cooled half-sheet tray.
4. In a heavy 1-qt. saucepot, bring the sugar, water, and salt to the boil without stirring. Cook at a rapid boil to the soft-ball stage, 238°F. Add the vanilla.
5. Immediately stir the pecans into the syrup, then pour the mixture out onto the lined sheet tray. Using two forks, pull apart the pecans.
6. Cool to room temperature.

holding: store at room temperature in a tightly sealed plastic container up to 2 weeks

---

RECIPE VARIATION
Kentucky Limestone Salad with Frizzled Country Ham, Cornbread Croutons, and Candied Pecans
Replace the Clemson Blue cheese with 1/2 oz. julienne country ham sautéed in a little butter until almost crisp.

Fried Green Tomatoes
with Fresh Tomato Sauce and Bacon

yield: 1 appetizer serving: approx. 4 oz. tomatoes plus sauce and garnishes
(multiply × 4 for classroom turnout; adjust equipment sizes accordingly)

MASTER RECIPE

production		costing only
1/2 c.	Fresh Tomato Sauce	1/4 recipe
1 Tbsp.	butter	1/2 oz.
1 thick slice	smoked bacon, cooked crisp, cut in half	3/4 oz. a.p.
4 Tbsp.	bacon drippings	n/c
1/2 large	green tomato, cut in 3 even slices	3 oz. a.p.
1/2 tsp.	Southern Seasoning for Poultry	1/16 oz.
1/2 c.	corn flour	2 1/4 oz.
4 Tbsp.	egg wash	1 egg plus water
2 tsp.	chopped flat-leaf parsley	1/20 bunch a.p.
1 sprig	fresh flat-leaf parsley	1/20 bunch a.p.

service turnout:

1. In an 8" sauté pan, heat the Fresh Tomato Sauce, work in the butter, and hold warm.
2. Heat the bacon in a 350°F oven or in the microwave and hold warm.
3. Fry the tomatoes:
   a. Heat another 8" sauté pan and heat the bacon drippings over medium-low heat.
   b. Season the tomato slices on both sides with Southern Seasoning for Poultry. Dip them in the corn flour, then in the egg wash, and then in the corn flour again.
   c. Fry the slices about 2 minutes on each side, until golden brown.
   d. Drain on a rack set over a hotel pan.
4. Plate the dish:
   a. Arrange the tomatoes in an overlapping circle in the center of a hot 10" plate.
   b. Spoon the tomato sauce around the edge of the plate well.
   c. Sprinkle a diagonal stripe of chopped parsley across the tomato slices.
   d. Arrange the bacon in an X on top of the tomato slices.
   e. Place the parsley sprig in the center of the bacon X.

RECIPE VARIATIONS

Vegetarian Fried Green Tomatoes
Omit the bacon and replace the bacon drippings with equal amounts corn oil and butter.

Fried Summer Squash with Fresh Tomato Sauce and Bacon
Replace the green tomatoes with 5 slices large, firm zucchini or yellow squash, or 3 slices pattypan squash, cut 1/2" thick.

Lowcountry Shrimp Perloo
with Sugar Snap Peas

yield: 1 main-course serving: approx. 8 oz. plus accompaniment (multiply × 4 for classroom turnout; adjust equipment sizes accordingly)

MASTER RECIPE

production		costing only
1/2 c.	Shellfish Stock	1/32 recipe
2 c.	Shrimp Perloo Base	1/4 recipe
6	(21–25 ct.) white shrimp, peeled and deveined, shells reserved for stock	5 oz. a.p.
as needed	boiling water	n/c
3 oz.	sugar snap peas, stringed, blanched, and refreshed	3 oz. a.p.
tt	kosher salt	1/16 oz.
1 Tbsp.	butter	1/2 oz.
1 Tbsp.	cooked crumbled bacon (from Shrimp Perloo Base recipe)	n/c
1 Tbsp.	chopped flat-leaf parsley	1/20 bunch a.p.

service turnout:
1. Place the Shellfish Stock in a 10" sauté pan and bring it to the simmer. Add the Shrimp Perloo Base, cover, and cook over medium heat about 3 minutes, stirring occasionally with a rubber scraper to break up lumps and separate the rice grains, until heated through.
2. Add the shrimp, stir well, cover, and simmer 3 minutes more, stirring occasionally, until the shrimp are cooked through and the rice is separate and fluffy. Add boiling water as necessary to make the rice moist but not wet.
3. Reheat the sugar snap peas by microwaving, steaming, or pan-steaming. Season with salt.
4. Using a rubber spatula, work the butter and half of the parsley into the perloo.
5. Plate the dish:
   a. Mound the perloo slightly at front left on a hot 12" pasta plate, making sure that a few shrimp show on the surface.
   b. Arrange the snap peas at the back right of the plate.
   c. Sprinkle the perloo with bacon and the remaining parsley.

COMPONENT RECIPE
SHRIMP PERLOO BASE

yield: 8 c.

production		costing only
2 thick slices	smoked bacon, cut in 1/2" pieces	1 1/2 oz.
1 1/4 c.	fine-chopped yellow onion	6 oz. a.p.
1/2 tsp.	crushed dried red pepper	1/16 oz.
2 c.	long-grain white rice, preferably Carolina Gold variety (not parboiled)	14 oz.
1 c.	vine-ripe tomato, coarse concassée	12 oz. a.p.
3 c.	Shellfish Stock	3/16 recipe
tt	kosher salt	1/16 oz.

preparation:
1. Preheat an oven to 300°F.
2. Cook the bacon and render the bacon drippings:
   a. Heat a heavy 2 1/2-qt. saucepan with a tight-fitting lid.
   b. Add the bacon and sauté until crisp.
   c. With a slotted spoon, lift the bacon bits into a small container, allowing all of the drippings to remain in the pan. Reserve the bacon for service turnout.
   d. If necessary, add more drippings or butter to total 4 Tbsp. in the pan.
3. Prepare the rice perloo base:
   a. Reheat the bacon drippings and sweat the onion and dried red pepper in it over low heat until translucent.
   b. Add the rice and cook, stirring, about 1 minute, until the grains become opaque and are well coated with fat.
   c. Add the tomato and cook a few seconds more.
   d. Add the Shellfish Stock. Bring it to the simmer, add salt, and cover the pot. Simmer 15 minutes.
   e. Quickly peek under the lid; the stock should have absorbed into the rice.
   f. Transfer the pot to the oven and bake 10 minutes.
   g. Immediately turn the rice out into a hotel pan, fluff it with a fork, and spread it out to cool, covered with a damp towel.

holding: refrigerate in a freshly sanitized, covered plastic container up to 3 days

RECIPE VARIATIONS

Seafood Perloo
For each serving use 5 oz. total of the following mixture: cooked crabmeat, shucked oysters, diced fish fillets, small peeled shrimp.

Chicken Perloo
Replace the Shellfish Stock with Poultry Stock. Replace the shrimp in each serving with 1 c. (3/4"-diced) chicken breast cubes, browned but still raw in the center.

Pan-Fried Catfish
with Tartar Sauce, Southern Potato Salad, and Home-Style Sliced Tomatoes

yield: 1 main-course serving: approx. 6 oz. catfish plus accompaniments
(multiply × 4 for classroom turnout; adjust equipment sizes accordingly)

MASTER RECIPE

production		costing only
1/2	vine-ripened tomato	2 1/2 oz. a.p.
2 tsp.	cider vinegar, in squeeze bottle	1/3 fl. oz.
tt	kosher salt	1/16 oz.
tt	sugar	1/16 oz.
1/2 c.	corn oil	4 fl. oz.
1/4 c.	pork lard	2 oz.
1	6 oz. skinned, pinned, trimmed catfish fillet	7 oz. a.p.
1/4 c.	Corn Flour Breading for Seafood	1/4 recipe
4 Tbsp.	egg wash	1 egg plus water
1 c.	Southern Potato Salad	1/6 recipe
3 Tbsp.	Tartar Sauce	1/4 recipe
dash	paprika	1/16 oz.
1 sprig	fresh flat-leaf parsley	1/20 bunch a.p.
1	lemon wedge	1/6 [90 ct.] lemon

preparation:

1. Prepare the tomato slices:
   a. Cut the tomato into 3 thick slices.
   b. Remove excess moisture by pressing the slices gently between paper towels.
   c. Place on a work plate and sprinkle with half of the vinegar, salt, and sugar. Turn the slices over and season the other side.
2. Fry the fish:
   a. Heat an 8" black cast-iron skillet or heavy sauté pan over medium-low heat. Add the oil and lard. Heat the fats to about 325°F.
   b. Roll the fish fillet in the Corn Flour Breading for Seafood, then dip it in the egg wash, then roll it in the breading again to make a thick, even coating. Shake off any excess breading.
   c. Pan-fry the fish about 2 minutes on each side, until crisp and golden. Drain on a rack.
3. Plate the dish:
   a. Scoop the Southern Potato Salad onto the back center of a warm 12" plate.
   b. Place the fish fillet slightly left of center front, propped against the potato salad.
   c. Arrange the tomato slices on the right side of the plate in an overlapping arc, propped against the fish and potato salad.
   d. Spoon the Tartar Sauce into a 2-fl.-oz. ramekin or butter pot and place on the back left of the plate.
   e. Sprinkle the potato salad with a dash of paprika.
   f. Stick the parsley sprig upright between the fish and the potato salad.
   g. Place the lemon wedge at 10 o'clock.

COMPONENT RECIPE
CORN FLOUR BREADING FOR SEAFOOD

yield: 1 c.

production		costing only
1 c.	corn flour	4 1/2 oz.
1 Tbsp.	Chesapeake seasoning (pp. 199, 226)	1/8 oz.
tt	fine-ground salt	1/16 oz.

preparation:
1. Thoroughly mix the corn flour with the Chesapeake seasoning and enough salt to make the mixture highly seasoned. (Salt amount depends on salt content of seasoning blend.)

holding: store at room temperature in a tightly sealed container up to 2 weeks

COMPONENT RECIPE
SOUTHERN POTATO SALAD

yield: 6 c.

production		costing only
1 1/2 lb.	new potatoes	1 1/2 lb. a.p.
as needed	water	n/c
1/2 c.	mayonnaise	4 fl. oz.
1/4 c.	sour cream	2 fl. oz.
2 tsp.	brown mustard	1/3 fl. oz.
1 Tbsp.	bread-and-butter pickle juice	n/c
dash	bottled hot sauce (Crystal brand or other acidic hot sauce)	1/16 oz.
tt	kosher salt	1/16 oz.
tt	fresh-ground white pepper	1/16 oz.
1/8 c.	fine-diced peeled celery	1/40 head a.p.
1/8 c.	fine diagonal-sliced scallion	1/10 bunch a.p.
1/8 c.	fine-diced red bell pepper	1 oz. a.p.
1/8 c.	fine-diced bread-and-butter pickles	1 fl. oz.
2 Tbsp.	chopped flat-leaf parsley	1/20 bunch a.p.
as needed	mayonnaise	1 fl. oz.

preparation:
1. Boil the potatoes in their skins in water to cover by 1" until fork-tender. Drain and spread out in a hotel pan to cool slightly.
2. In a large bowl, mix together the mayonnaise, sour cream, mustard, pickle juice, and hot sauce. Season liberally with salt and white pepper.
3. When the potatoes are just cool enough to handle, peel them and cut into 1/2" chunks.
4. Fold the potatoes into the dressing along with the celery, scallion, red bell pepper, pickles, and parsley. Mash a few potato chunks and continue to fold until the potatoes are well coated with dressing.
5. Rest at room temperature 30 minutes.
6. If necessary, correct the seasoning and correct the texture with more mayonnaise.

holding: refrigerate in a freshly sanitized, covered plastic container up to 3 days

RECIPE VARIATIONS

Egg Potato Salad
Reduce the amount of potatoes to 1 1/4 lb. Add 2 hard-cooked eggs, 3/8" diced.

Potato Salad with Boiled Dressing
Substitute Boiled Dressing for the mayonnaise and sour cream.

COMPONENT RECIPE
TARTAR SAUCE

yield: 6 fl. oz.

production		costing only
1	hard-cooked egg	1 each
2 Tbsp.	minced scallion	1/5 bunch a.p.
1 tsp.	minced lemon zest	n/c
1 Tbsp.	sweet pickle relish	1/2 fl. oz.
1 Tbsp.	minced flat-leaf parsley	1/40 bunch a.p.
6 Tbsp.	mayonnaise	3 fl. oz.
1 tsp.	sugar	1/8 oz.
1 tsp.	fresh lemon juice	1/16 [90 ct.] lemon
tt	kosher salt	1/16 oz.
tt	fresh-ground white pepper	1/16 oz.

preparation:
1. Separate the egg white from the yolk and discard half of the white. Mince the remaining egg white. Place the yolk in a small bowl and mash with a fork.
2. Mix in the remaining ingredients.
3. Rest at room temperature 15 minutes.
4. Correct the seasoning.

holding: refrigerate in a freshly sanitized, covered container up to 3 days

RECIPE VARIATIONS

Pan-Fried Brook Trout or Ocean Fish
Replace the catfish fillet with other fish (whole, butterflied trout or ocean fish fillets). Adjust the breading and egg wash amounts accordingly.

Pan-Fried Soft-Shell Crabs
Replace the catfish fillet with 2 cleaned soft-shell crabs.

Pan-Fried Shrimp
Replace the catfish fillets with 6 (21–25 ct.) white shrimp, peeled with tails on, butterflied and flattened. Replace the Tartar Sauce with Cocktail Sauce (p. 206).

Southern Fried Chicken

with Mashed Potatoes, Cream Gravy, and Down-Home Green Beans

yield: 1 main-course serving, 1 1/4 lb. bone-in chicken plus accompaniments (multiply × 4 for classroom turnout; adjust equipment sizes accordingly)

🕐 Requires 24 hours advance preparation.

MASTER RECIPE

production		costing only
1/2 c.	corn oil	4 fl. oz.
1/2 c.	pork lard	4 oz.
1/2	Buttermilk-Marinated Frying Chicken	1/4 recipe
1 Tbsp.	Southern Seasoning for Poultry	1/8 oz.
as needed	flour for dredging	1 oz.
2 Tbsp.	flour	3/4 oz.
1/2 c.	hot Poultry Stock	1/32 recipe
1/2 c.	half-and-half	4 fl. oz.
tt	kosher salt	1/16 oz.
tt	fresh-ground white pepper	1/16 oz.
1 c.	Classic Mashed Potatoes, hot in steam table	1/4 recipe
1 c.	Down-Home Green Beans	1/4 recipe

service turnout:

1. Preheat an oven to 200°F. Place a rack on a half-sheet tray.
2. Heat a heavy 10" cast-iron skillet over medium heat. Add the oil and lard, turn down the heat, and heat the fat to about 300°F.
3. Fry the chicken:
   a. Remove the Buttermilk-Marinated Frying Chicken pieces from the buttermilk, selecting one thigh, one drumstick, one winged breast quarter, and one wingless breast quarter for each serving. Sprinkle evenly with Southern Seasoning for Poultry.
   b. Dredge the chicken heavily in flour and then tap off any excess.
   c. Place the chicken pieces, skin side down, in the skillet; the fat should come halfway up the sides of the chicken. Reduce the heat to low and pan-fry 4 to 5 minutes, until a few beads of red liquid form on the top of the chicken pieces.
   d. Increase the heat to high and turn the chicken pieces. Fry 30 seconds.
   e. Reduce the heat to low and pan-fry 4 to 5 minutes more.
   f. At this point, all of the chicken pieces should be golden brown and cooked through. Check a thigh by cutting into it; it should be no more than very slightly pink at the bone.
   g. Remove the chicken to the rack and place in the oven.
4. Make the gravy:
   a. Pour off all but 2 Tbsp. fat from the skillet, leaving the deep brown pan glaze in the bottom of the skillet.
   b. Add 2 Tbsp. flour and stir over low heat for a few seconds to make a light brown roux.
   c. Stir in the Poultry Stock and then the half-and-half to make a smooth gravy.
   d. Increase the heat to medium and simmer briskly until the sauce reduces to nappé consistency.
   e. Season with salt and white pepper.
5. Plate the dish:
   a. Spoon the Classic Mashed Potatoes onto the back right of a hot 12" plate. Make a well in the center.
   b. Arrange the chicken pieces stacked together at the front of the plate.
   c. Spoon the Down-Home Green Beans into a ramekin or monkey dish and place on the back left of the plate.
   d. Ladle the gravy into the well in the mashed potatoes.

RECIPE VARIATIONS

Southern-Fried Chicken with Giblet Gravy
Poach the chicken gizzards in seasoned water for 30 minutes or until tender. Drain and chop fine. Sear the livers in corn oil or bacon drippings until browned outside, medium-rare inside. Cool. Cut into very fine dice. Add the gizzards and livers to the cream gravy just before serving.

Spicy, Extra-Crispy Southern-Fried Chicken
Prepare a triple amount of Southern Seasoning for Poultry, adding as much additional cayenne as desired. Remove the chicken pieces from the buttermilk and pat dry. Season the chicken pieces with half of the Southern Seasoning and mix the remaining seasoning with 2/3 c. flour. Dredge the pieces in the flour, then coat with egg wash, then dredge again in flour. Pan-fry according to the recipe.

Southern-Fried Chicken Picnic-Style
Serve the chicken at room temperature accompanied by Southern Potato Salad (p. 60), Home-Style Sliced Tomatoes (p. 59), Cucumber Salad (p. 219), and Deviled Eggs.

Spicy Fried Chicken Tidbits
Cut boneless, skinless chicken breast into 1" cubes and prepare as for Spicy, Extra-Crispy Southern-Fried Chicken. Pan-fry at 375°F. Serve as an hors d'oeuvre speared with cocktail picks.

Fried Chicken Salad
Prepare an iceberg and/or Romaine salad with Buttermilk Ranch Dressing (p. 477) and cucumbers, peppers, radishes, Vidalia onions, and so on. Top with Spicy Fried Chicken Tidbits.

COMPONENT RECIPE
BUTTERMILK-MARINATED FRYING CHICKEN

yield: 4 (1 1/4-lb. half-chicken) main-course servings

production		costing only
2	2 1/2-lb. young fryer/broiler chickens (no larger)	5 lb. a.p.
tt	kosher salt	1/16 oz.
1 qt.	buttermilk	32 fl. oz.

preparation:
1. Fabricate the chickens without removing the bones or skin from the pieces:
   a. Remove the legs from the carcasses and cut each leg into thigh and drumstick. Chop the knuckles off the drumsticks.
   b. Remove the backbones from the carcasses and split the breasts in half without removing the wings.
   c. Cut each breast half into two pieces, one slightly smaller with the wing attached, the other slightly larger with no wing.
   d. Reserve the knuckles, backbones, and giblets for stock.
2. Marinate the chicken pieces:
   a. Season the chicken pieces with salt.
   b. Place in a freshly sanitized nonreactive container just big enough to hold the pieces snugly.
   c. Pour the buttermilk over the chicken, cover the container, and refrigerate at least 24 hours and up to 2 days.

holding: refrigerate; after 2 days, drain the chicken of buttermilk; may be refrigerated up to 1 day longer

> **CHEF'S NOTE:**
> The success of this recipe depends on using small fryer/broiler chickens. If larger chickens are used, the specified frying times will be too short, and the chicken will not cook through. Longer frying of larger pieces typically results in a too-dark crust. If only larger chickens are available, chop them into smaller bone-in pieces.

COMPONENT RECIPE
DOWN-HOME GREEN BEANS

yield: 1 qt.

production		costing only
1 c.	water	n/c
1/4 c.	fine-diced country ham	1 oz. a.p.
2 Tbsp.	bacon drippings	n/c
1/2 c.	minced yellow onion	2 1/2 oz. a.p.
1 1/4 lb.	pole beans or green beans, trimmed and stringed, cut into 2" lengths	1 1/2 lb. a.p.
tt	kosher salt	1/16 oz.
tt	fresh-ground black pepper	1/16 oz.

preparation:
1. Place the water, ham, bacon drippings, and onion in a 2-qt. saucepan. Cover, bring to the simmer, and cook 10 minutes.
2. Add the beans, cover, and simmer briskly, stirring occasionally, 15 minutes, or until the beans are tender.
3. Remove the beans from the pan and bring the cooking liquid to a boil. Reduce to 1/2 c.
4. Return the beans to the pan and toss to coat with the cooking liquid.
5. Correct the salt and season with pepper.

holding: open-pan cool and immediately refrigerate in a freshly sanitized, covered container up to 5 days

MASALA FOR COUNTRY CAPTAIN

4 tsp. cumin seeds
4 tsp. coriander seeds
1" cinnamon stick
8 cloves
8 cardamom pods, hulled
2 tsp. black peppercorns
2 tsp. ground turmeric
2 tsp. cayenne powder (or to taste)

1. Separately toast the cumin, coriander, cinnamon, cloves, cardamom, and peppercorns in a small, dry sauté pan. As each spice is finished toasting, transfer to a mortar or spice mill.
2. Grind the spices together.
3. Mix in the turmeric and cayenne.

Country Captain
with Pan-Steamed Rice and Fried Okra

yield: 1 main-course serving: approx. 10 oz. bone-in chicken plus sauce and accompaniments (multiply × 4 for classroom turnout; adjust equipment sizes accordingly)

MASTER RECIPE

production		costing only
1/4 recipe	Country Captain Chicken (1 chicken leg + 8 fl. oz. sauce)	1/4 recipe
as needed	water, in squeeze bottle	n/c
1 c.	corn oil	8 fl. oz. (may be reused)
3 oz.	trimmed, 3/8"-sliced fresh okra, soaked in ice-cold water	4 oz. a.p.
1/4 c.	corn flour	1 1/4 oz.
tt	fine salt	1/16 oz.
1 1/2 c.	Pan-Steamed White Rice preferably Carolina Gold variety	1/4 recipe
2 Tbsp.	fine diagonal-sliced scallion	1/10 bunch a.p.
2 Tbsp.	toasted slivered almonds	1/4 oz.
2 Tbsp.	toasted, sweetened, shredded coconut	1/4 oz.

service turnout:

1. Heat the Country Captain Chicken and its sauce in a covered 10" sauté pan until heated through, adding a little water if necessary.
2. Fry the okra:
   a. Heat an 8" sauté pan, add the oil, and heat to about 400°F. Line a half-size hotel pan with paper towels.
   b. Drain the okra and shake it dry.
   c. Toss the okra with the corn flour.
   d. Fry the okra, turning the pieces with a slotted spoon, about 1 minute, until browned and crisp.
   e. Drain in the hotel pan and season with salt.
3. Plate the dish:
   a. Spoon the Pan-Steamed White Rice onto a hot 12" plate, leaving a little extra space at the back right. Make a well in the rice.
   b. Place the chicken leg in the well and nap the sauce over it, allowing the sauce to pool into the well.
   c. Arrange an arc of okra on the back right of the plate.
   d. Sprinkle the chicken with the scallion, almonds, and coconut.

COMPONENT RECIPE
COUNTRY CAPTAIN CHICKEN

yield: 4 (10-oz.) cooked chicken legs plus 1 qt. sauce

production		costing only
4	12 oz. chicken legs	3 lb. a.p.
tt	kosher salt	1/16 oz.
1 Tbsp.	Madras curry powder	1/8 oz.
2 Tbsp.	corn oil	1 fl. oz.
2 Tbsp.	bacon drippings	n/c
1 c.	minced yellow onion	5 oz. a.p.
1/2 c.	fine-chopped green bell pepper	4 oz. a.p.
1/2 c.	peeled, minced celery	1/10 head a.p.
2 Tbsp.	peeled, minced fresh ginger	3/4 oz. a.p.
2 tsp.	minced garlic	1/8 oz. a.p.
1 Tbsp.	Madras curry powder	1/4 oz.
1 Tbsp.	flour	1/16 oz.
3 c.	vine-ripe tomato concassée	2 1/4 lb. a.p.
1 c.	Poultry Stock	1/16 recipe
1 Tbsp.	light brown sugar	1/3 oz.
2	bay leaves	1/16 oz.
2 Tbsp.	currants	1/4 oz.
tt	kosher salt	1/16 oz.

preparation:

1. Fabricate and season the chicken:
   a. Skin the chicken legs and trim off excess fat.
   b. Chop off the knuckles, leaving a clean-cut bone.
   c. Slit open the thigh from underneath and remove the thigh bone.
   d. Rub the legs with salt and 1 Tbsp. curry powder.
2. Heat a 14" sauté pan and heat the oil and bacon drippings. Add the chicken legs and brown them on both sides. Remove.
3. Add the onion, green bell pepper, celery, and ginger. Cover and sweat over medium heat until translucent.
4. Add the garlic and 1 Tbsp. curry powder, sauté 1 minute more, then add the flour and make a light roux.
5. Add the tomato and cook, stirring, until the liquid is reduced but the tomatoes are still moist.
6. Add the Poultry Stock, sugar, bay leaves, currants, and salt. Bring to the simmer.
7. Return the chicken legs to the pan, baste with the sauce, cover the pan, and simmer 15 to 20 minutes, until the chicken legs are just done. Add a little water if the sauce becomes too thick.
8. Uncover and correct the seasoning.

holding: open-pan cool and immediately refrigerate the chicken legs, in their sauce, in a freshly sanitized, covered, nonreactive container up to 5 days

CHEF'S NOTES
The unique, authentic flavor of this dish depends on the use of fresh, high-quality Indian curry powder, preferably a South Indian blend as specified. If unavailable, prepare the Country Captain with Fresh Spice Masala recipe variation.

RECIPE VARIATIONS

Country Captain with Boneless Chicken
Prepare the sauce. Fabricate raw boneless chicken breasts or thighs into 1" chunks. Sear in oil or clarified butter and simmer in the sauce until just cooked through.

Country Captain with Fresh Spice Masala
Replace the Madras curry powder with the masala spice mix in the sidebar on p. 62.

ENTREES

63

Quail with Oyster Pilau Dressing,
Pumpkin Purée, and Sautéed Spinach

yield: 1 main-course serving: 2 (3-oz.) semiboneless quail plus accompaniments
(multiply × 4 for classroom turnout; adjust equipment sizes accordingly)

MASTER RECIPE

production		costing only
1 Tbsp.	corn oil	1/2 fl. oz.
2	Pilau-Stuffed Quail	1/4 recipe
tt	kosher salt	1/16 oz.
tt	fresh-ground black pepper	1/16 oz.
1/4 c.	Demi-Glace	1/16 recipe
1/2 c.	Poultry Stock	1/32 recipe
as needed	water, in squeeze bottle	n/c
1 Tbsp.	Madeira	1/2 fl. oz.
1 Tbsp.	butter	1/2 oz.
tt	lemon juice	1/8 [90 ct.] lemon
1 Tbsp.	butter	1/2 oz.
6 oz.	baby spinach	6 oz. a.p.
tt	kosher salt	1/16 oz.
tt	fresh-ground black pepper	1/16 oz.
3/4 c.	Pumpkin Purée, hot in steam table*	1/4 recipe
1 sprig	fresh thyme	1/12 bunch a.p.
1 sprig	fresh sage	1/10 bunch a.p.
1 sprig	fresh flat-leaf parsley	1/20 bunch a.p.

service turnout:

1. Cook the quail:
   a. Heat an 8" sauté pan until very hot, heat the oil, and sear the Pilau-Stuffed Quail on all sides. Season with salt and pepper.
   b. Place the quail on a sizzle pan and finish in a 425°F oven, about 5 minutes.
2. Make the sauce:
   a. Pour out any remaining oil from the pan and add the Demi-Glace and Poultry Stock. Reduce to a light nappé consistency. Thin with water if the sauce overreduces.
   b. Add the Madeira and remove from the heat.
   c. Work in 1 Tbsp. butter to make an emulsion.
   d. Season with salt and balance with lemon juice.
3. Prepare the vegetables:
   a. Heat a 10" sauté pan, add 1 Tbsp. butter, and sauté the spinach just until wilted. Season with salt and pepper.
   b. Spoon the hot Pumpkin Purée into a pastry bag fitted with a large star tip.
4. Plate the dish:
   a. Pipe the pumpkin purée in a large rosette at the back of a hot 12" plate.
   b. Remove the trussing strings from the quail and arrange them on the front of the plate propped against the purée.
   c. Place a mound of spinach on either side of the quail.
   d. Nap the quail with the sauce, allowing it to pool in the plate well.
   e. Make a bouquet of the herb sprigs and stick it upright between the quail legs.

*If a plastic star tip is available, the pumpkin purée may be held in the pastry bag and microwaved until hot before each plating.

COMPONENT RECIPE
OYSTER PILAU

yield: 3 c.

production		costing only
3 Tbsp.	butter	1 1/2 oz.
1/2 c.	minced yellow onion	2 1/2 oz. a.p.
1/4 c.	peeled, minced celery	1/20 head a.p.
2/3 c.	long-grain white rice, preferably Carolina Gold variety (not parboiled)	5 3/4 oz.
3/4 c.	oyster liquor (from Pilau-Stuffed Quail recipe)	n/c
1/2 c.	Poultry Stock	4 fl. oz.
tt	kosher salt	1/16 oz.
1 tsp.	fresh thyme leaves	1/20 bunch a.p.
1 tsp.	minced fresh sage	1/20 bunch a.p.
tt	fresh-ground white pepper	1/16 oz.

preparation:
1. Preheat an oven to 200°F.
2. Place the butter, onion, and celery in a heavy 1-qt. saucepan with a tight-fitting lid. Cover and sweat over low heat until translucent.
3. Add the rice and stir over medium heat until the rice grains are opaque in color and well coated with butter.
4. Add the oyster liquor and Poultry Stock to the rice and season with salt. Add the thyme, sage, and white pepper, stir once, cover, and bring to the boil. Immediately reduce the heat to the lowest setting and simmer 10 to 12 minutes.
5. Quickly peek under the lid; the liquid should be absorbed into the rice. Transfer the pot to the oven and bake 15 minutes.
6. Uncover the pot and, using a fork, fluff the rice into a half-size hotel pan. Cover with a clean, damp towel and cool to room temperature.
7. Refrigerate until cold.

holding: cover the pan and refrigerate no longer than 24 hours; may be frozen up to 1 month

COMPONENT RECIPE
PILAU-STUFFED QUAIL

yield: 8 stuffed quail

production		costing only
8	3 1/2-oz. semiboneless quail, cold*	8 each or 1 3/4 lb.
tt	kosher salt	1/16 oz.
1/2 pt. (8 pc.)	select shucked oysters, drained, liquor reserved for Oyster Pilau, cold	1/2 pt.
3 c.	cold Oyster Pilau	1 recipe

preparation:
1. Stuff the quail:
   a. If the quail are held flat with wire supports, remove and discard them.
   b. Wipe the quail dry with paper towels inside and out, and season the insides with salt.
   c. Stuff each quail with 1 oyster and slightly less than 1/2 c. of the Oyster Pilau. Sew the quail shut with fine kitchen string and a trussing needle.
2. Truss each quail:
   a. Tuck the wing tips under the breasts.
   b. Make a slip knot at the end of a 12" length of string.
   c. Pull the legs together, place the loop of the slip knot around the legs, and pull tight. Bring the remaining string around the front of the quail between the breast and the wings and then back up to the legs. Tie the ends of the string together, pulling gently to plump the breast and hold the quail together securely.
   d. Brush off any rice grains or vegetables clinging to the outside of the quail.

*If semiboneless quail are unavailable, remove the backbones of bone-in quail, and then gently remove the breastbones and ribs. Sew the quail partially closed to form a cavity, then fill and sew shut.

holding: refrigerate in a freshly sanitized, covered container up to 12 hours

---

RECIPE VARIATIONS

Quail with Pecan Rice Dressing
Alter the Oyster Pilau dressing as follows: Omit the oysters and oyster liquor and use 1 1/2 c. Poultry Stock. Replace the long-grain white rice with "pecan" rice (p. 296). Add 1/2 c. toasted, chopped pecans to the rice after cooling.

Quail with Sausage Dressing
Alter the Oyster Pilau dressing as follows: Omit the oysters and oyster liquor and use 1 1/2 c. Poultry Stock. Fry 6 oz. mild sage breakfast sausage until cooked through and the fat has rendered. Drain and crumble the sausage. Replace the butter with sausage drippings. Add the sausage to the cooled rice.

COMPONENT RECIPE
PUMPKIN PURÉE

yield: 3 c.

production		costing only
1 1/4 lb.	peeled, seeded, 1"-diced cooking pumpkin*	2 lb. a.p.
tt	kosher salt	1/16 oz.
1 sprig	fresh sage	1/10 bunch a.p.
as needed	water	n/c
1/3 c.	heavy cream	2 2/3 fl. oz.
3 Tbsp.	butter	1 1/2 oz.
tt	fresh-ground white pepper	1/16 oz.

preparation:

1. Place the pumpkin, salt, and sage in a 2-qt. saucepan and add water to cover by 1". Bring to the boil and simmer briskly about 10 minutes, until the pumpkin is very tender.
2. Drain off the cooking water and discard the sage sprig.
3a. While still hot, run the pumpkin through a food mill or potato ricer.
  —or—
3b. Purée the pumpkin with an immersion blender and force it through a strainer.
4. Return the pumpkin purée to the saucepot, place over low heat, and add the cream. Reduce over medium heat, stirring constantly, until the purée is thick enough to hold its shape when piped from a pastry bag.
5. Work in the butter, add the white pepper, and correct the salt.

*Do not attempt to make Pumpkin Purée with a decorative jack-o'-lantern pumpkin; the resulting product will be thin, stringy, and tasteless. Cooking pumpkins are available from specialty produce dealers and in Caribbean and Spanish markets in the fall and winter seasons.

holding: open-pan cool, then immediately refrigerate in a freshly sanitized, covered container up to 3 days

Quail with Oyster Pilau Dressing, Winter Squash Purée, and Sautéed Spinach
Substitute acorn or butternut squash for the pumpkin. (AP/EP yields may vary.)

ENTREES

Peachy Duck
with Mashed Potatoes and Turnips 'n' Turnip Greens

yield: 1 main-course serving: 1 (approx. 5-oz.) bone-in cooked duck leg and 4-oz. duck breast plus accompaniments (multiply × 4 for classroom turnout; adjust equipment sizes accordingly)

MASTER RECIPE

production		costing only
1	Duck Setup	1/4 recipe
	(1 raw breast half, 1 braised duck leg, 3/4 c. sauce)	
as needed	water, in squeeze bottle	n/c
1 Tbsp.	corn oil	1/2 fl. oz.
tt	kosher salt	1/16 oz.
tt	fresh-ground black pepper	1/16 oz.
1 Tbsp.	peach preserves	1/2 fl. oz.
1	Spice-Baked Peach half	1/4 recipe
1 c.	Turnips 'n' Turnip Greens	1/4 recipe
1 c.	Classic Mashed Potatoes*, hot in steam table	1/4 recipe

service turnout:

1. Place the duck leg and its sauce in an 8" sauté pan and add a little water. Cover and heat over low heat.
2. Heat an 8" sauté pan, heat the oil, and sear the duck breast about 30 seconds on each side, until very rare. Season it with salt and pepper.
3. Place the seared breast on a sizzle plate, skin side up, and brush it with the peach preserves. Add the Spice-Baked Peach half to the sizzle plate.
4. Heat the Turnips 'n' Turnip Greens in a covered sauté pan or in the microwave.
5. Place the sizzle pan in the oven and bake at 425°F just until hot, about 2 minutes.
6. Plate the dish:
   a. Spoon the Classic Mashed Potatoes into a pastry bag fitted with a large star tip; pipe a rosette of potatoes onto the center back of a hot 12" plate.
   b. Place a bed of turnips and greens in the remainder of the plate well.
   c. Rest the duck leg against the potatoes, presentation side up, with the drumstick bone at the top.
   d. Nap the duck leg with its sauce.
   e. Place the Spice-Baked Peach half at 10 o'clock.
   f. Slice the duck breast thin across the grain on the diagonal.
   g. Fan the slices against the duck leg.

*If a plastic star tip is available, the potatoes may be held in the pastry bag and microwaved until hot for each serving.

ENTREES

RECIPE VARIATION

Braised Country Spareribs with Turnips 'n' Turnip Greens
Use 8 (4-oz.) country-style spareribs in place of the Duck Setups. Braise the spareribs in Poultry Stock in the same manner as the duck legs, but simmer as long as 45 minutes, until the spareribs are tender.

COMPONENT RECIPE
DUCK SETUPS

yield: 4 raw duck breasts, 4 braised duck legs, 3 c. sauce

production		costing only
2	4-lb. Long Island ducks	8 lb. a.p.
1 1/2 qt.	Poultry Stock	3/8 recipe
as needed	water	n/c
2 Tbsp.	corn oil	1 fl. oz.
1/4 c.	minced shallot	2 oz. a.p.
2 Tbsp.	flour	3/4 oz.
tt	kosher salt	1/16 oz.
2 Tbsp.	high-quality red Port wine	1 fl. oz.
tt	fresh-ground black pepper	1/16 oz.
tt	fresh lemon juice	1/8 [90 ct.] lemon

preparation:
1. Fabricate the ducks:
   a. Remove the duck giblets from the cavities and place in a half-size hotel pan. Reserve the livers for another use. Remove the fat pads and discard.
   b. Remove and skin the legs:
      (1) Slit the skin between the duck legs and breasts. Bend back the legs of each duck until the joints pop out of the sockets. Cut through the joints to remove the duck legs from the carcasses.
      (2) Chop off the knuckles of the drumsticks, making a clean, even cut.
      (3) Remove the skin from the duck legs and trim away excess fat.
   c. Remove the breasts from each duck:
      (1) Using a sharp, flexible boning knife, cut off the excess skin at the neck cavity.
      (2) Make a slit on one side of the breastbone, running the blade from the neck cavity back to the tail cavity.
      (3) Slide the blade between the breast meat and the rib cage and cut/scrape the breast meat off the bones, leaving the skin intact on the breast meat.
      (4) Repeat with the remaining breast meat to make 4 boneless breast halves.
   d. Trim and score the breast halves:
      (1) Trim off the excess skin from around the edges of the boneless breast halves.
      (2) Remove the vertical strand of cartilage from the breast tenders, if possible keeping the tenders attached to the breast meat.
      (3) Remove the thick silverskin from the rounded end of each breast half.
      (4) Score the skin of each breast half in a fine, even 3/8" crosshatch.
2. Prepare double duck stock:
   a. Preheat an oven to 425°F.
   b. Remove all possible fat from the duck carcass and chop it into small pieces.
   c. Place the carcass and knuckles in the hotel pan with the gizzards and rinse with cold water. Drain well.
   d. Brown the carcass pieces, knucklebones, neck bones, and gizzards in the oven.
   e. Pour off the fat from the duck roasting pan and transfer the browned bones into a 4-qt. saucepan. Add the Poultry Stock.
   f. Deglaze the roasting pan with a little water and add the deglazings to the pan.
   g. Simmer 40 minutes to make 1 qt. double stock.
   h. Strain, defat the surface of the stock and hold warm.
3. Braise the duck legs:
   a. Heat a 12" sauté pan and add the oil. Brown the duck legs on both sides and remove.
   b. Add the shallot to the pan, stir, and then add the flour. Stir over low heat to make a light brown roux.
   c. Whisk in the double stock and bring to the boil. Reduce to the simmer, skim, and add the duck legs. Season with salt, cover the pan, and braise about 35 minutes, turning the legs once, until the duck legs are tender.
   d. Remove the duck legs and reduce the braising liquid to 3 c. nappé consistency sauce.
   e. Add the Port and pepper, season with lemon juice, and correct the salt.
   f. Return the duck legs to the sauce.

holding: store the duck breasts individually wrapped, refrigerated, up to 3 days; open-pan cool the braised duck legs and immediately refrigerate in a freshly sanitized, covered container up to 5 days

COMPONENT RECIPE
SPICE-BAKED PEACHES

yield: 4 peach halves

production		costing only
2	small, firm-ripe freestone peaches	6 oz. a.p.
as needed	water	n/c
2 Tbsp.	butter	1 oz.
1 tsp.	minced lemon zest	n/c
2 tsp.	fresh lemon juice	1/8 [90 ct.] lemon
1/2 tsp.	ground cinnamon	1/16 oz.
1/8 tsp.	ground cloves	1/16 oz.
1/8 tsp.	fresh-grated nutmeg	1/16 oz.
1/2 tsp.	light brown sugar	1/16 oz.
tt	kosher salt	1/16 oz.

preparation:
1. Blanch the peaches in boiling water for a few seconds and immediately refresh in ice water.
2. Peel the peaches and cut in half. Remove and discard the pits.
3. Make a composed butter by mixing together the remaining ingredients.
4. Top each peach half with 1/4 of the composed butter.

holding: refrigerate in a covered, freshly sanitized container up to 3 days

COMPONENT RECIPE
TURNIPS 'N' TURNIP GREENS

yield: 1 qt.

production		costing only
3 lb.	fresh turnip greens	3 lb.
6 Tbsp.	rendered duck fat or bacon drippings	n/c
2 c.	peeled, 1/2"-diced young white turnips	1 lb. a.p.
3/4 c.	fine-chopped yellow onion	4 oz. a.p.
1/4 c.	minced country ham	1 oz. a.p.
1 tsp.	minced garlic	1/8 oz. a.p.
tt	kosher salt	1/16 oz.
3 c.	water	n/c
2 tsp.	cider vinegar	1/3 fl. oz.
tt	fresh-ground black pepper	1/16 oz.

preparation:
1. Fabricate the greens:
   a. Remove the thick veins from the turnip greens.
   b. Cut the greens into 1 1/2" rough square pieces.
   c. Wash the greens thoroughly in several changes of cool water.
   d. Drain in a colander.
2. Braise the vegetables:
   a. Heat a 6-qt. brazier, heat the fat, and add the turnips. Sauté about 3 minutes, until the edges begin to brown.
   b. Add the onion and ham and sauté 1 minute more.
   c. Add the garlic, greens, a little salt, and the water. Stir to mix well, cover the pan, and braise over medium heat about 30 minutes, stirring occasionally, until the turnips and greens are tender. ⚠ Watch the pan liquid and add water if necessary; do not allow the vegetables to scorch.
   d. When the vegetables are tender, use a perforated spoon to transfer them to a bowl.
   e. Reduce the cooking liquid over high heat, stirring occasionally and adding juices accumulated around the vegetables, until the cooking liquid becomes a light glaze.
   f. Add the vinegar to the glaze and toss the vegetables back into it.
   g. Correct the salt and season liberally with pepper.

holding: open-pan cool and immediately refrigerate in a freshly sanitized, covered, nonreactive container up to 5 days

ENTREES

Smoked Spareribs

with North Carolina Barbeque Sauce,
Fancy Hoppin' John, and Collard Greens

yield: 1 main-course serving: approx. 14 oz. cooked, bone-in meat
plus accompaniments
(multiply × 4 for classroom turnout; adjust equipment sizes
accordingly)

🕐 Requires advance preparation; please read the barbeque
section on this book's companion website.

MASTER RECIPE

production		costing only
1/4 rack	Smoked Spareribs	1/4 recipe
1/2 c.	North Carolina Barbeque Sauce	1/4 recipe
1 1/4 c.	Fancy Hoppin' John	1/4 recipe
as needed	water, in squeeze bottle	n/c
1 c.	Collard Greens with Pot Liquor	1/4 recipe
2 Tbsp.	chopped scallion	1/10 bunch a.p.
1 Tbsp.	brunoise-cut red bell pepper	1/2 oz. a.p.
tt	bottled hot sauce (Crystal brand or other acidic hot sauce)	1/8 fl. oz.

service turnout:

1. Grill the Smoked Spareribs over medium heat, basting with
   about half of the North Carolina Barbeque Sauce, about
   5 minutes, until heated through.
2. Heat the Hoppin' John with a little water in a covered sauté
   pan or in the microwave.
3. Heat the Collard Greens with Pot Liquor in a covered sauté
   pan or in the microwave.
4. Plate the dish:
   a. Spoon a mound of Hoppin' John on the back right of a
      hot 12" plate.
   b. Ladle the collard greens into a ramekin or monkey dish
      and place at the back left. Arrange the ribs upright at
      front of the plate leaning against the Hoppin' John.
   c. Nap the ribs with the remaining sauce.
   d. Sprinkle the Hoppin' John with scallion and red bell
      pepper.
   e. Serve the bottled hot sauce on the side.

ENTREES

COMPONENT RECIPE

SMOKED SPARERIBS

yield: 1 (3 1/2 to 4-lb.) rack

production		costing only
1	4 1/2-lb. pork sparerib rack	4 1/2 lb.
1/2 c.	Carolina Rub	2/3 recipe
as needed	hickory for smoking, type per smoker manufacturer's specification	% of pkg.
2 c.	Carolina Mop	1 recipe

first day preparation:
1. Fabricate and rub the rack:
   a. Trim off excess fat from the sparerib rack.
   b. Using a paring knife, loosen the membrane at the narrow end of the back of the ribs. Grasp the membrane with a paper towel and peel it off.
   c. If necessary, cut the rack in half to fit into the smoker.
   d. Coat the ribs with the Carolina Rub and massage it into the meat.
   e. Place the ribs in a freshly sanitized, covered, nonreactive container and refrigerate 1 to 2 days.
2. If necessary, soak the hickory wood overnight in cold water.

second or third day preparation:
3. Prepare the smoker:
   a. Set the smoker to operate at 180°F.
   b. Place a drip pan on the lowest rack.
   c. Add half of the soaked wood and close the smoker.
   d. When heated enough to produce strong smoke, place the ribs in the smoker. Smoke, adding more wet chips as necessary, about 3 hours, turning and brushing with Carolina Mop every 20 minutes. When the ribs are done, the mopping sauce should be used up.
4. Open-pan cool the rib racks to room temperature.
5. Cut the rack into individual ribs and divide the ribs into 4 portions, allotting to each portion some thick and some thin ribs. Wrap each portion in a plastic bag and refrigerate immediately.

holding: refrigerate up to 5 days

Clockwise from left: country-style rib, baby back ribs, rib tips, standard spare ribs, St. Louis ribs, baby back ribs with membrane removed

ENTREES

RECIPE VARIATIONS

Grilled Baby Back Ribs with North Carolina Barbeque Sauce, Fancy Hoppin' John, and Collard Greens
Replace the spareribs with 2 racks of baby back ribs. Rub the ribs and cure as described. Instead of cooking the ribs in a smoker, grill the ribs, covered, over medium heat, with 2 c. soaked fruitwood chips on the heat source, for 30 minutes, basting with the mopping sauce. Cut each slab in half. Finish the ribs on the grill over medium heat, basting with barbeque sauce as described. Serve the slab halves intact on an oval plate and provide a steak knife.

Barbeque Pork Shoulder for Pulled or Chopped Pork
Replace the spareribs with a 4 1/2-lb. boneless pork butt. Open the butt by slicing it lengthwise almost in half. Rub, cure, and smoke as described, except raise the heat to 200°F and smoke for 6 to 8 hours. Pull the cooked pork into shreds or chop into 1/2" chunks. Reheat in a covered sauté pan with a little barbeque sauce and water. See the barbeque section of this book's companion website.

COMPONENT RECIPE
FANCY HOPPIN' JOHN

yield: 5 c.

production		costing only
2/3 c.	dried black-eyed peas	5 1/2 oz.
6 c.	water	n/c
3 oz.	smoked pork neck bones	3 oz.
1/2 c.	fine-chopped yellow onion	2 1/2 oz. a.p.
1	small dried red chile	1/16 oz.
2 Tbsp.	bacon drippings	n/c
2 Tbsp.	brunoise-cut red bell pepper	1 oz. a.p.
1 c.	long-grain white rice (not parboiled)	7 oz.
tt	kosher salt	1/16 oz.
2 Tbsp.	chopped scallion	1/10 bunch a.p.

preparation:
1. Pick over the peas and remove any stones or other foreign matter.
2. Place the peas in a heavy 1 1/2-qt. saucepan with a tight-fitting lid. Rinse them under cold running water and then pour the water out. Add 6 c. fresh water and place the pan on the stove.
3. Bring the water to a brisk simmer and skim off the foam.
4. Add the neck bones, onion, and chile to the pan. Cover and simmer about 1 hour, until the peas are tender and the water is reduced to about 2 c.
5. Preheat an oven to 350°F.
6. Strain the peas, reserving the cooking liquid. Remove and discard the neck bones and dried chile. Measure 1 3/4 c. cooking liquid, adding water if needed.
7. Rinse out the pot and add the bacon drippings and the red bell pepper. Sweat the red bell pepper over low heat for a few seconds, then add the rice. Sauté until the grains are opaque and well coated with fat, about 30 seconds.
8. Add the peas and the measured cooking liquid, stir once, add a little salt, cover the pan, and bring to the boil. Immediately reduce the heat to the lowest setting and cook 8 to 10 minutes.
9. Quickly peek under the lid; the liquid should be absorbed. Transfer the pot to the oven and bake 10 minutes.
10. Transfer the Hoppin' John to a half-size hotel pan and fluff it with a fork. For prolonged holding, cover with a clean, damp cloth.

holding: open-pan cool and refrigerate, covered, in a freshly sanitized container up to 5 days; may be frozen up to 3 months

COMPONENT RECIPE
COLLARD GREENS WITH POT LIQUOR

yield: 1 qt.

production		costing only
6 oz.	smoked pork neck bones	6 oz. a.p.
—or—		
1	(5 oz.) smoked ham hock, sawed in 3 pieces	5 oz. a.p.
1 c.	fine-chopped yellow onion	5 oz. a.p.
1 Tbsp.	minced garlic	1/4 oz. a.p.
2	small dried red chiles	1/16 oz.
1 qt.	water	n/c
2 1/2 lb.	fresh collard greens	2 1/2 lb.
tt	cider vinegar	1/2 oz.
tt	kosher salt	1/16 oz.
tt	sugar, optional (used in Soul Food–style greens)	1/8 oz.

preparation:
1. Place the smoked pork, onion, garlic, and chiles in a 6-qt. saucepot and add the water. Cover the pot and simmer 45 minutes, until the pork is tender and the broth is flavorful.
2. Remove the stems and thick veins from the collard greens. Cut into 1 1/2" rough square pieces.
3. Wash the greens in several changes of cold water and drain in a colander.
4. Add the greens to the pot, stirring and pushing down into the broth. Cover the pot and simmer briskly about 30 minutes for young, tender greens; cook longer for mature greens. Cook until the greens are tender but not mushy.
5. Use a perforated spoon or spider to remove the greens and meat to a freshly sanitized plastic container.
6. Reduce the broth to about 1 c. of flavorful pot liquor, adding juices that accumulate around the greens to the reduction.
7. Pick the meat from the smoked pork bones and discard the bones.
8. Return the greens and meat to the pot liquor and stir well.
9. Add the vinegar, correct the salt, and season with pepper. (For Soul Food–style greens, season additionally with sugar.)
10. Return the greens to the container and open-pan cool to room temperature.

holding: immediately cover and refrigerate up to 5 days; may be frozen up to 3 months

Pork Tenderloin in Bourbon Sauce
with Stuffed Vidalia Onion and Stewed Okra

yield: 1 main-course serving: approx. 6 oz. pork plus accompaniments
(multiply × 4 for classroom turnout; adjust equipment sizes accordingly)

MASTER RECIPE

production		costing only
1	Stuffed Vidalia Onion	1/4 recipe
1 1/4 c.	Stewed Okra	1/4 recipe
as needed	water, in squeeze bottle	n/c
1 Tbsp.	clarified butter	3/4 fl. oz. a.p.
6 oz.	trimmed pork tenderloin	6 oz. a.p.
tt	kosher salt	1/16 oz.
tt	fresh-ground black pepper	1/16 oz.
2 Tbsp.	Bourbon whiskey	1 fl. oz.
1 Tbsp.	minced shallot	1/2 oz. a.p.
1 tsp.	Dijon mustard	1/6 fl. oz.
1/2 c.	Demi-Glace	1/8 recipe
2 Tbsp.	butter	1 oz.
1 sprig	fresh thyme	1/12 bunch a.p.
1 sprig	fresh sage	1/10 bunch a.p.
1 sprig	fresh flat-leaf parsley	1/20 bunch a.p.

service turnout:

1. Place the Stuffed Onion on a sizzle pan and bake 12 minutes at 425°F, until heated through and browned on top.
2. Heat the Stewed Okra in an 8" covered sauté pan or in a microwave, adding a little water if necessary, but keeping the tomato sauce tight, not runny.
3. Cook the pork:
   a. Heat an 8" sauté pan, then heat the clarified butter.
   b. Season the pork with salt and pepper, then sear on all sides.
   c. Remove the pan from the heat, cool slightly, then pour the Bourbon over the pork. Return the pan to the heat, tilt it to ignite the liquor, and flambé.
   d. When the flame dies, remove the pork to the sizzle pan along with the stuffed onion and finish in the oven for 5 minutes to a medium doneness.
   e. Hold warm.
4. Make the sauce:
   a. Add the shallot, mustard, and Demi-Glace to the pan and bring to the simmer, adding a little water if the sauce becomes too thick.
   b. Work in the butter and season with salt and pepper.
5. Plate the dish:
   a. Place the Stuffed Onion on the back left of a hot 12" plate.
   b. Arrange the okra on the right side of the plate, points facing inward.
   c. Pool the sauce in the plate well.
   d. Slice the pork on the diagonal and fan the slices across the front of the plate, leaning against the onion.
   e. Make a bouquet of the herb sprigs and stick it upright in the middle of the plate.

RECIPE VARIATION

Medallions of Pork in Bourbon Sauce
Replace the pork tenderloin with 3 (1 1/2-oz.) medallions cut from a pork loin. Pan-sear the medallions.

COMPONENT RECIPE
STUFFED VIDALIA ONIONS

yield: 4 (3") onions

production		costing only
4	3"-diameter Vidalia onions	1 1/4 lb. a.p.
1 Tbsp.	melted, cooled butter	1/2 oz.
tt	kosher salt	1/16 oz.
3 c.	Cornbread Dressing	1 recipe

preparation:
1. Prepare a stovetop steamer or prime a commercial steamer.
2. Fabricate the onions:
   a. Cut off the top third (stem end) of each onion and reserve for another use.
   b. Peel the onions without cutting away too much of the root end.
   c. Using a Parisienne scoop, hollow out each onion, leaving a 1/2" shell. Reserve the onion flesh for another use, such as the Cornbread Dressing.
3. Place the onions, upside down, on the stovetop steamer rack and steam about 5 minutes, or in the commercial steamer about 15 seconds. Cool to room temperature.
4. Brush the outside of the onions with melted butter and season with salt.
5. Stuff each onion with 3/4 c. Cornbread Dressing.

holding: refrigerate in one layer in a covered, freshly sanitized container up to 3 days

COMPONENT RECIPE
CORNBREAD DRESSING

yield: approx. 3 c.

production		costing only
3 Tbsp.	butter	1 1/2 oz.
1/3 c.	fine-chopped Vidalia onion (from shells)	n/c
1/3 c.	peeled, fine-chopped celery	1/16 head a.p.
1 Tbsp.	chopped fresh sage leaves	1/12 bunch a.p.
1 tsp.	fresh thyme leaves	1/20 bunch a.p.
2 c.	crumbled Pure Southern Cornbread	1/3 recipe
±1/4 c.	warm Poultry Stock	1/64 recipe
1 Tbsp.	chopped flat-leaf parsley	1/20 bunch a.p.
tt	kosher salt	1/16 oz.
tt	fresh-ground black pepper	1/16 oz.

preparation:
1. Heat an 8" sauté pan, heat the butter, and sweat the onion and celery over low heat until soft. Add the sage and thyme, stir to blend, and then remove from the heat.
2. Place the Pure Southern Cornbread in a bowl. Pour the butter-onion mixture over the cornbread and toss. Add the Poultry Stock in a thin stream, continuing to toss, until the dressing is evenly moistened. (Use just enough stock to make the dressing hold together but not enough to make it soggy.)
3. Allow the dressing to stand 15 minutes, then correct the texture with more stock if needed.
4. Mix in the parsley and season with salt and pepper.

holding: open-pan cool and immediately refrigerate in a covered, freshly sanitized container up to 3 days

COMPONENT RECIPE
STEWED OKRA

yield: 5 c.

production		costing only
1 lb.	small, young okra pods	1 lb.
2 Tbsp.	bacon drippings	n/c
tt	kosher salt	1/16 oz.
tt	fresh-ground black pepper	1/16 oz.
2 c.	Fresh Tomato Sauce	1/2 recipe
±1 c.	water	n/c

preparation:
1. Wash the okra well and blot it dry.
2. Trim away the outer skin of the okra pods' conical tops.
3. Heat a 12" sauté pan, heat the bacon drippings, and sauté the okra pods over medium heat until their color brightens and they begin to brown a little on their ridges. Season with salt and pepper.
4. Add the Fresh Tomato Sauce and a little water, stir to combine, and cover the pan. Cook at a brisk simmer about 3 minutes, until the okra is tender. Check occasionally to make sure the sauce does not cook dry; add water as necessary.
5. Uncover the pan and adjust the consistency of the sauce by reduction so that it is thick enough to cling lightly to the okra.

holding: open-pan cool and immediately refrigerate in a covered, freshly sanitized, nonreactive container up to 3 days

Old-Fashioned Biscuit Strawberry Shortcake

yield: 1 dessert serving
(multiply × 4 for classroom turnout)

MASTER RECIPE

production		costing only
1	3" Sweet Shortcake Biscuit (variation)	1/4 recipe
3/4 c.	Soft Vanilla Bean Whipped Cream	1/4 recipe
1 c.	Sugared Berries	1/4 recipe
1	perfect berry with green hull intact	1/20 pt. a.p.

service turnout:
1. Using a serrated knife, slice the Sweet Shortcake Biscuit in half horizontally.
2. Plate the dish:
   a. Place the bottom biscuit slice on a cool 8" plate.
   b. Spoon half of the Soft Vanilla Bean Whipped Cream onto the biscuit and then spoon half of the Sugared Berries on top.
   c. Press the top biscuit slice onto the stack.
   d. Spoon the remaining berries onto the shortcake, allowing some berries to fall onto the plate.
   e. Dollop the remaining whipped cream onto the shortcake.
   f. Place the perfect berry on top.

COMPONENT RECIPE
SOFT VANILLA BEAN WHIPPED CREAM

yield: approx. 3 c.

production		costing only
2 c.	cold heavy cream	16 fl. oz.
1/3 c.	confectioner's sugar	1 oz.
2"	vanilla bean	1/3 bean

preparation:
1. Place the cream in a large stainless bowl set in an ice bain-marie and add the sugar.
2. Slit open the vanilla bean and scrape the seeds into the cream. (Reserve the pod to make vanilla extract or vanilla sugar.)
3. Whip the cream until it is just thick enough to pour in voluptuous dollops.

holding: refrigerate in a freshly sanitized, covered plastic container up to 8 hours

COMPONENT RECIPE
SUGARED BERRIES

yield: approx. 4 c.

production		costing only
2 pt.	fresh strawberries	2 pt.
±1/2 c.	sugar	±4 oz.

preparation:
1. Wash the berries and drain in a colander.
2. Blot the berries dry between kitchen towels.
3. Using a tomato shark or small Parisienne scoop, remove the hulls.
4. Slice the berries and place in a bowl.
5. Toss with the sugar, using less or more according to the sweetness of the berries.

holding: refrigerate in a covered, freshly sanitized, nonreactive container up to 8 hours; leftover berries may be puréed and frozen up to 3 months

---

RECIPE VARIATIONS

Peach Shortcake
Replace the strawberries with peeled, sliced peaches.

Fourth of July Shortcake
Replace the strawberries with equal parts raspberries and blueberries.

Dixie Peach Cobbler

yield: 1 dessert serving
(multiply × 4 for classroom turnout)

MASTER RECIPE

production		costing only
1	Individual Peach Cobbler	1/4 recipe
1	a cocktail napkin or doily	1 each

service turnout:
1. Heat the Individual Peach Cobbler in a 400°F oven 5 to 8 minutes, until warm.
2. Plate the dish:
   a. Line a 10" oval plate with the cocktail napkin and place the cobbler on top.

COMPONENT RECIPE
INDIVIDUAL PEACH COBBLERS

yield: 4 dessert servings

production		costing only
1 Tbsp.	cornstarch	1/8 oz.
1 tsp.	flour	1/16 oz.
1/2 tsp.	ground cinnamon	1/16 oz.
1/4 c.	granulated sugar	2 oz.
1 qt.	peeled, 3/4"-diced ripe peaches	1 1/3 lb. a.p.
1 Tbsp.	fresh lemon juice	1/4 [90 ct.] lemon
2 tsp.	minced or grated lemon zest	n/c
2 oz.	melted butter	2 oz.
7 oz.	flour	7 oz.
2 oz.	granulated sugar	2 oz.
1/2 tsp.	baking soda	1/16 oz.
1/4 tsp.	fine salt	1/16 oz.
3 oz.	cold unsalted butter, 1/2" cubes	3 oz.
1/2 c.+	buttermilk	4 fl. oz.+
2 Tbsp.	sanding sugar or coarse-grain raw sugar	1 oz.

preparation:
1. Mise en place:
   a. Preheat an oven to 400°F.
   b. Have ready 4 (10-oz.) gratin dishes on a half-sheet tray with pan liner.
2. Prepare the fruit:
   a. Sift together the cornstarch, flour, and cinnamon.
   b. Mix in 1/4 c. granulated sugar.
   c. Place the peaches in a bowl and stir in the sugar mixture, lemon juice, and lemon zest.
   d. Divide the peach mixture among the gratin dishes and pack down.
   e. Drizzle an equal amount of melted butter over each.
3. Mix the dough:
   a. Sift the flour, 2 oz. granulated sugar, baking soda, and salt together onto the work surface.
   b. Using a bench scraper, cut the butter into the flour until the butter bits are the size of peas.
   c. Scrape the mixture into a bowl.
   d. Using a fork, blend in the buttermilk to make a shaggy, sticky dough.
4. Top the cobblers:
   a. Using a #60 portion scoop or two teaspoons, cover the surface of the peaches with small dollops of dough.
   b. Press down lightly to help the topping adhere to the peaches.
   c. Sprinkle the tops with sanding sugar.
5. Bake the cobblers:
   a. Immediately place the cobblers in the center of the oven and bake about 35 minutes, until golden brown.
   b. If necessary, run the cobblers under a broiler or use a foodservice torch to achieve a rich, golden-brown color.
6. Remove the cobblers from the oven and cool to warm service temperature or room temperature.

holding: best served warm from the oven; for restaurant service hold at room temperature covered with a kitchen towel up to 3 hours; after 3 hours refrigerate, loosely covered with plastic wrap, up to 2 days

---

RECIPE VARIATIONS
Cherry, Blueberry, Apple, or Other Fruit Cobbler
Replace the peaches with another fruit, suitably fabricated. Increase or decrease the cornstarch, flour, and sugar in accordance with the moisture content and sweetness of the fruit.

DESSERTS

Still Master's Pecan Pie

yield: 1 dessert serving
(multiply × 4 for classroom turnout)

MASTER RECIPE

production		costing only
1 slice	Bourbon Pecan Pie	1/8 recipe
1/4 c.	Sweetened Whipped Cream in pastry bag with star tip	1/4 recipe

service turnout:
1. Plate the dish:
   a. Place the Bourbon Pecan Pie on a cool 8" plate.
   b. Pipe a rosette of Sweetened Whipped Cream on the plate next to the pie.

COMPONENT RECIPE

BOURBON PECAN PIE

yield: 1 (9") pie

production		costing only
as needed	flour for dusting	
8 oz.	American Flaky Pie Pastry	1 recipe
2 Tbsp.	room-temperature unsalted butter	1 oz.
1/8 c.	sugar	1 oz.
3 Tbsp.	flour	1 1/4 oz.
3/4 tsp.	fine salt	1/16 oz.
3	eggs	3 each
2 Tbsp.	Bourbon whiskey	1 fl. oz.
1/2 tsp.	pure vanilla extract	1/12 fl. oz.
1 1/3 c.	dark corn syrup	10 2/3 fl. oz.
1 1/2 c.	pecan pieces	8 oz.
55–60 pc.	small pecan halves	approx. 6 oz.

preparation:
1. Prepare the pie shell:
   a. Lightly flour the work surface and roll out the American Flaky Pie Pastry to fit a 9" pie pan.
   b. Place the pastry in the pan and trim the edges to 3/4" around. Turn the edges under and flute the rim.
   c. Dock the bottom of the pastry.
   d. Refrigerate at least 20 minutes.
2. Preheat an oven to 400°F.
3. Blind-bake the shell:
   a. Place a 10" circle of pan liner into the pastry shell and fill the shell with dried beans or other pie weights.
   b. Bake 10 minutes, until lightly set.
   c. Remove the shell from the oven and remove the pie weights and the pan liner.
4. Reduce the oven temperature to 325°F.
5. Prepare the filling:
   a. In a large bowl, whisk together the butter, sugar, flour, and salt.
   b. Add the eggs and beat to blend well.
   c. Stir in the Bourbon, vanilla, and corn syrup.
   d. Mix in the pecan pieces.
6. Assemble the pie:
   a. Pour the pecan custard into the pie shell.
   b. Arrange concentric circles of pecan halves on top of the custard and press gently.
7. Place the pie on a half-sheet tray and bake about 45 minutes, until set.
8. Remove the pie from the oven and cool on a rack to room temperature.

holding: best served the same day; hold at cool room temperature covered with a towel up to 3 hours; may be refrigerated under a cake dome up to 2 days

---

RECIPE VARIATION

New England Maple-Walnut Pie
Replace the corn syrup with pure maple syrup, replace the Bourbon with dark rum, and replace the pecans with walnuts.

Sky-High Coconut Cake

yield: 1 dessert serving
(multiply × 4 for classroom turnout)

MASTER RECIPE

production		costing only
1 slice	Coconut Cake	1/12 recipe
1	edible flower	1 each

service turnout:
1. Plate the dish:
   a. Place the Coconut Cake slice upright on a cool 8" plate.
   b. Garnish with the edible flower.

COMPONENT RECIPE
COCONUT CAKE

yield: 1 (9") 3-layer cake

production		costing only
3	Coconut Cake Layers	1 recipe
1	9" round cake board	1 each
2 c.	Coconut Buttercream	1 recipe
1 1/2 qt.	Boiled Icing	1 recipe
3 c.	sweetened shredded coconut	6 oz.

preparation:
1. Remove the pan liner from the Coconut Cake Layers.
2. Place one cake layer on the cake board. Spread the top with half of the Coconut Buttercream.
3. Place a second cake layer on top and press gently. Spread with the remaining buttercream.
4. Place the third cake layer on top and press gently to secure all layers together and make the top level.
5. Frost the sides and top of the cake with Boiled Icing.
6. Fluff up the coconut and press it evenly all over the cake.

holding: best served the same day; refrigerate under a cake dome up to 3 days

COMPONENT RECIPE
COCONUT CAKE LAYERS

yield: 3 (9" round) cake layers

production		costing only
as needed	baker's pan coating spray	% of container
14 oz.	cake flour	14 oz.
2 Tbsp.	baking powder	1/8 oz.
3/4 tsp.	fine salt	1/8 oz.
12 oz.	room-temperature unsalted butter	12 oz.
22 oz.	sugar	22 oz.
6	room-temperature egg yolks	6 each
1 tsp.	pure vanilla extract	1/6 fl. oz.
1 1/2 c.	fine-chopped sweetened flaked coconut	approx. 3 oz.
12 fl. oz.	unsweetened coconut milk	12 fl. oz.
6	room-temperature egg whites	n/c

preparation:
1. Mise en place:
   a. Preheat an oven to 375°F.
   b. Prepare 3 (9" round) cake pans: spray the bottoms and sides with pan coating, place a 9" circle of pan liner in the bottom of each, and then spray again.
2. Sift together the cake flour, baking powder, and salt.
3. Begin mixing the batter:
   a. Using the paddle attachment of a mixer, cream the butter and sugar until light and fluffy.
   b. Beat in the egg yolks one at a time.
   c. Add the vanilla and chopped coconut.
   d. Pulsing on low speed, alternately add the flour mixture and the coconut milk to make a smooth batter.
4. In a large, clean, dry bowl, beat the egg whites just below firm peaks.
5. Fold 1/4 of the egg whites into the batter, then fold the batter into the remaining egg whites.
6. Pan the batter:
   a. Evenly divide the batter among the cake pans.
   b. Run the batter up the sides of the pans, making a slight depression in the centers.
7. Bake the layers:
   a. Immediately place the pans on the center rack of the oven and bake 20 minutes.
   b. Rotate the pans and bake 10 minutes more, until the layers are risen and golden in color and a tester inserted in the center comes out clean.
8. Cool the pans on a rack 5 minutes.
9. Turn the layers out of the pans and cool to room temperature.

holding: wrap in plastic film and store at cool room temperature up to 24 hours; store frozen up to 3 months

---

RECIPE VARIATION
Coconut Cake with Raspberry Filling
Replace the Coconut Buttercream with seedless raspberry preserves.

COMPONENT RECIPE
COCONUT BUTTERCREAM

yield: approx. 2 c.

production		costing only
4	egg yolks	4 each or 2 3/4 oz.
6 fl. oz.	sweetened canned coconut milk	6 fl. oz.
1 tsp.	fresh lemon juice	1/16 [90 ct.] lemon
8 oz.	room-temperature unsalted butter	8 oz.

preparation:
1. Using the whip attachment of a mixer, beat the egg yolks until very pale yellow and fluffy.
2. Bring the coconut milk to the boil and pour it in a thin stream into the beating egg yolks. Continue to beat the yolks until they cool to room temperature.
3. Add the lemon juice.
4. Reduce the speed to medium and add the butter a little at a time to make a smooth icing.

holding: store covered at room temperature no longer than 1 hour until ready to fill the cake; hold refrigerated up to 5 days; frozen up to 3 months (refrigerated or frozen buttercream must be brought to cool room temperature and rewhipped before using)

COMPONENT RECIPE
BOILED ICING

yield: 1 1/2 qt.

🕐 Assemble the cake before preparing the Boiled Icing.

production		costing only
12 oz.	sugar	12 oz.
1/2 c.	water	n/c
6	room-temperature egg whites	6 each or 6 oz.
1/4 tsp.	fine salt	1/16 oz.
1/4 tsp.	cream of tartar	1/16 oz.
1 Tbsp.	pure vanilla extract	1/2 fl. oz.

preparation:
1. Prepare the syrup:
   a. Place the sugar and water in a saucepan set over high heat. Stir only until the sugar dissolves.
   b. Cover the pan and boil about 2 minutes, until the pan has a full head of steam and any sugar crystals have dissolved off the sides of the pan.
   c. Remove the lid and boil to 225°F. Hold over low heat.
2. Using the whip attachment of a mixer, beat the egg whites, salt, and cream of tartar on high speed just under soft peaks.
3. Bring the syrup back to the boil and cook to 238°F.
4. With the mixer on high speed, pour the 238°F syrup into the egg whites in a thin stream.
5. Continue beating until the icing is fluffy and has cooled to room temperature.
6. Beat in the vanilla.
7. Use immediately.

☐ TABLE 2.2 PLANTATION SOUTH REGIONAL INGREDIENTS

ITEM	MARKET FORMS	USES	SEASONALITY	OTHER	STORAGE
CORNMEAL	Industrially produced or natural stone ground white or yellow cornmeal is sold by the pound.	Used in baking corn-based quick breads; as a coarse, crunchy breading for fried foods.	Stone-ground variety is freshest in fall and winter.	For true Southern flavor and texture, use artisan-produced stone-ground variety.	Store at cool room temperature or freeze for long-term storage.
CORN FLOUR	Milled from yellow corn.	In the South used primarily as a breading for fried foods.	N/A	Results in a more adherent, lighter coating than coarser cornmeal.	Store at cool room temperature or freeze for extended storage.
STANDARD AND QUICK GRITS	Both are sold in pound containers and in bulk.	Served for breakfast in ordinary homes, restaurants, and diners.	N/A	Standard grits cook in about 35 minutes and have more texture; quick grits cook in about 15 minutes and are smoother.	Store at cool room temperature or freeze for extended storage.
STONE-GROUND GRITS	Yellow corn or white corn grits are sold by the pound by specialty producers.	The proper type for shrimp and grits, cheese grits, or grits cakes. A bed or side dish for any dish with sauce.	Freshest in fall and winter.	Require long, careful cooking with lots of stirring.	Store at cool room temperature or freeze for extended storage.
PEARL HOMINY	Canned in gelatinous broth or water-packed in 13.5-oz. and #10 cans.	Side dish, breakfast dish with milk and sugar, soup or casserole ingredient.	N/A	Do not confuse with Mexican hominy (posole), a different product.	Store at cool room temperature.
SOFT SOUTHERN WHEAT FLOUR	Standard or self-rising (baking powder and salt added). White Lily, Martha White are popular brands.	Biscuits and other quick breads.	N/A		Store at cool room temperature or freeze for extended storage.
RICE	Long-grain natural rice is widely available by the pound. Do not use par-boiled or converted rice.	Boiled and pan-steamed plain rice is a bed or side dish for stews, smothered foods, and gumbos. Perloo (pilaf method) is a main dish.	N/A	Southern rice should be fluffy with intact, separate grains. Wash rice in several changes of water to remove surface starch. Rice:liquid ratio varies per brand.	Store at cool room temperature or freeze for extended storage.
CAROLINA GOLD RICE	Produced in limited quantity by artisanal growers/mills.	Used in Lowcountry cooking See website for side dishes, perloos, fritters, and puddings.	Harvested in November and sells out quickly.	Mail order directly from heirloom producers.	Frozen.
COUNTRY HAM	Whole hams, ham slices, ham bits. Sometimes available cooked and glazed.	Sliced paper-thin as an appetizer; sliced thin and fried as a breakfast meat; used to flavor greens, beans, and other dishes.	N/A	Smithfield is a proprietary name that applies only to hams produced by a patented process in the county surrounding Smithfield, VA.	Dry store while intact; refrigerated after opening.
SMOKED SLAB BACON	Unsliced whole slab; thick or thin sliced; ends for seasoning.	Sliced thick, fried crisp, and served as breakfast meat; used for barding; diced or chopped, fried, and used as seasoning meat in greens, beans, and other dishes.	N/A	Bacon drippings, liquid fat rendered from frying bacon, are used as a frying medium for other foods.	Refrigerated.

☐ TABLE 2.2 PLANTATION SOUTH REGIONAL INGREDIENTS *(continued)*

ITEM	MARKET FORMS	USES	SEASONALITY	OTHER	STORAGE
SALT PORK (SALT PORK BELLY AND STREAK O' LEAN)	Salt pork belly: cryovac 8 oz. to 1 lb. chunks. Streak o' Lean: whole slab or slices.	Diced and fried for use as a seasoning meat; drippings are used as a frying medium.	N/A	Salt pork belly is pure fat with no meat; streak o' lean is the same cut as bacon, salt-cured but not smoked.	Refrigerate.
SMOKED HAM HOCKS AND SMOKED PORK NECK BONES	Purchased by the pound.	Simmered in water with herbs and spices to make a flavorful ham broth used as a base for soup or to cook vegetables.	N/A	The bone, skin, and gristle are discarded and the smoked meat is pulled into shreds and returned to the dish.	Refrigerate.
SMOKED TURKEY BUTTS AND WINGS	Purchased by the pound.	Used in place of smoked ham hocks and smoked pork neck bones.	N/A	Popular in Muslim Soul Food cooking.	Refrigerate.
PORK LARD	Industrially processed lard has a milder taste and is partially hydrogenated. Pure artisan lard has fuller flavor.	Used as a frying medium or a solid fat for pastry.	N/A	A recipe for artisan lard appears in the companion website.	Refrigerate or freeze.
SOUTHERN SAUSAGE	Fresh sausage encased, formed into patties, or bulk; encased smoked sausage; turkey sausage fresh or smoked.	Served as a breakfast meat or used in stuffings and gravies. Smoked sausage is used as a seasoning meat for beans and gumbos.	N/A	Turkey sausage is featured in Muslim Soul Food.	Refrigerate or freeze.
FRESH PORK	Whole loin, loin chops, rib chops, medallions, tenderloin, backbone, shoulder (butt), spare ribs, baby back ribs, country-style ribs.	Pork shoulder and country-style ribs are used for stewing, braising, or barbeque; spareribs are barbequed; baby back ribs are barbequed or grilled; loin is roasted; chops grilled or pan-fried; medallions sautéed.	Formerly seasonal to late fall and winter; now available year round.	Pork leg, or fresh ham, is rarely eaten in the South; it is usually reserved for curing and smoking.	Refrigerate or freeze.
SOUTHERN FISH AND SEAFOOD	Sea trout (weakfish), red snapper, porgy and grouper, shrimp, oysters, crabs, and scallops are from the coast; Carolina dry-pack and diver scallops are a special delicacy; Southern fish are widely available throughout the United States.	Traditional cooking features breaded or battered, pan-fried or deep fried. Modern cooks sauté, grill, and roast.	N/A	Farming freshwater catfish has become big business in the South. Crayfish and softshell crabs are also farmed.	Refrigerate or freeze.
SOUTHERN SYRUPS	Cane syrup is processed from sugarcane; sorghum syrup (golden syrup) is processed from sorghum, a cornlike plant also used for animal feed. Both are availale in cans and jars.	Used as a table syrup on pancakes, cornbread, and biscuits. Also used in baking.	N/A		Dry store.

(continued)

☐ **TABLE 2.2 PLANTATION SOUTH REGIONAL INGREDIENTS** *(continued)*

ITEM	MARKET FORMS	USES	SEASONALITY	OTHER	STORAGE
PEANUTS	Roasted and salted in shell; roasted, salted, shelled; roasted, un-salted, shelled; peanut butter (sweetened or unsweetened, smooth or chunky). Fresh, raw peanuts are a regional specialty.	Most are roasted for eating out of hand; used in cooking and baking.	N/A	Raw peanuts are boiled in salted water and eaten as a snack accompanied by a cola beverage.	Dry-stored or frozen for extended storage.
SESAME SEEDS/ BENNE SEEDS	White sesame seeds are preferred.	Used as a bread topping and garnish. Lowcountry cooks make sweet and savory wafers.	N/A	A favorite with Southern black cooks; called *bennes*, their name in an African dialect.	Dry store or freeze for extended storage.
PECANS (puh-KAHNS)	Whole in shell; shelled halves of varying sizes and pieces.	Used in candies, baked goods, and savory dishes. Pecan-crusted fried foods emerged in the 1980s.	N/A	Because of high demand, pecans are now relatively expensive.	Pecans have a high oil content and are quite perishable; should be frozen for extended storage.
OKRA	Fresh, whole pods; frozen whole pods and slices. Pickled okra is sold in jars.	Fried as an appetizer or side dish; sliced and simmered in side dish stews or to thicken gumbos. Pickled okra is served as an hors d'oeuvre.	Summer; best picked when the pods are still small and tender.	Okra contains a mucilaginous substance many find objectionable; cooking okra pods whole minimizes this substance.	Refrigerate or freeze.
SWEET POTATOES	Mealy white-fleshed sweet potatoes and waxy, sweeter, orange-fleshed sweet potatoes. Fresh are best. Canned sweet potatoes have a mushy texture and off flavor. Frozen sweet potato fries are a relatively new product.	Baked, mashed/puréed, candied, French fried, in salads.	Late summer/fall	African slaves began calling sweet potatoes *yams* after the tropical tuber that is the staple starch of sub-Saharan Africa.	Room temperature in a cool, dark place.
VIDALIA ONIONS	Purchased fresh by the pound.	Eaten raw in salads and on sandwiches; cooked Vidalias are sweeter still, their high sugar content making them perfect for caramelization.	May through November	Grown in Vidalia, Georgia, and 18 surrounding counties; flat yellow onions have a sweet, taste and tender, juicy, white flesh.	Room temperature, in a cool dark place.
JERUSALEM ARTICHOKES/ SUNCHOKES	Purchased fresh by the pound.	Sliced thin and served raw in salads and as a crudité; boiled or steamed as a side dish; Lowcountry cooks use them to make "artichoke" pickles.	Fall/early winter	Marketers popularized the name *sunchoke*.	Refrigerate.
BLACK-EYED PEAS	Fresh black-eyed peas may be available in season from specialty growers. Dried black-eyed peas are sold by the pound.	Cooked with seasoning meat as a side dish and component of Hoppin' John. Simmered in soups.	Fresh—summer; dried—year round.	Need no soaking before cooking.	Fresh—refrigerate; dried—dry store.
BUTTER BEANS	Fresh in season; sold by the pound in pod. Dried butter beans are sold by the pound.	Simmered with seasoning meat in soups and as a side dish.	Fresh—summer; dried—year round		Fresh—refrigerate; dried—dry store.

☐ **TABLE 2.2 PLANTATION SOUTH REGIONAL INGREDIENTS** *(continued)*

ITEM	MARKET FORMS	USES	SEASONALITY	OTHER	STORAGE
MUSCADINE AND SCUPPERNONG GRAPES	Available fresh in season from foragers and backyard growers in limited amounts. Jelly sold in jars.	Juice and jelly are used in desserts, baked goods, and sweet-savory sauces.	Late summer/early fall.	Indigenous to the Deep South, these grapes were cultivated for making wine as early as the 1500s.	Refrigerate.
AMERICAN PERSIMMONS	Fresh in season from foragers, backyard growers, and some specialty purveyors. Sweetened pulp is available in cans.	Pulp is used to make puddings, ice cream, dessert sauces, and sweet-savory sauces.	Late summer/early fall.	Must be ripened until soft and almost mushy; then run through a food mill.	Refrigerate; pulp can be frozen.

■ □ ■ chapter three
New England

Maine, Vermont, Massachusetts, Rhode Island, New Hampshire, Connecticut, upstate New York, northern Long Island

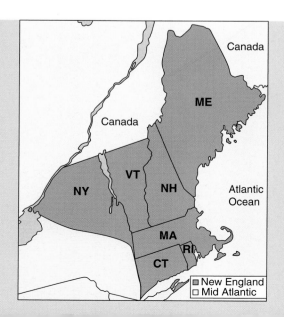

THE NORTHEASTERN ARM of America was named "New England" by its first settlers, English men and women who arrived on its rocky shore with the hope of creating a colony and culture modeled after the homeland they left behind. When the region was first named it was, indeed, new—a land virtually untouched by humankind, both a wilderness and a forbidding frontier.

Today New England is no longer new. Second in length of settlement only to the coastal Plantation South, New England is one of the longest-inhabited parts of America. Over many years the New England wilderness was transformed by the hard work of its inhabitants. The modern traveler experiences New England as a most civilized place, with historic cities, tidy villages, and small, stone-walled family farms.

New England's history as the linchpin of the American Revolution and the birthplace of America's Industrial Revolution is well known because it is, in fact, the early history of our nation. Less well known is its food history, one of Puritan austerity, Yankee thrift, and a long-standing relationship with the sea. In this chapter you'll discover the straightforward, elemental cooking of New England, a style that strongly influenced many other regional cuisines and became a foundation of America's national cuisine.

AFTER STUDYING THIS CHAPTER YOU SHOULD BE ABLE TO:

- list the ways in which New England's climate and topography (Factor 1) shaped the agricultural and economic development of the region
- explain why New England cuisine exhibits a greater Native American influence (Factor 2) than many other regions
- describe the effect of the early colonists' religious beliefs on their cooking and on modern New England cuisine (Factor 3)
- explain the importance of both commercial fishing and maritime trade (Factor 5) to the New England economy and cuisine
- explain why there was no real second settler/immigrant influence (Factor 4) in New England cuisine, and how this affected its development
- compare and contrast New England's food history and cuisine with that of the Plantation South
- list and describe the ingredients, cooking methods, and flavor profiles of New England cuisine
- describe Acadian-American cuisine featured on the website; recount its history, and list some of its defining dishes
- prepare authentic New England and Acadian-American dishes

APPETIZERS

New England Clam Chowder with Pilot Crackers

Vermont Cheddar Cheese Soup with New England Soda Bread

Crispy Fried Clam Bellies with Lemon Wedges

Salt Cod Cakes with Homemade Ketchup and Pepper Slaw

Petite Tourtière with Pickled Beets

Watercress and Boston Lettuce Salad with Maple Vinaigrette, Cranberries, and Walnut-Crusted Cheddar Croutons

Creamy Fiddlehead Ferns and Morels in Pastry Coffer

Tarragon Lobster Salad in Lobster Shell

Chilled Lobster with Beet Carpaccio, Mâche, and White Truffle Oil

ENTRÉES

Halibut Poached in Hard Cider with Apples and Parsnips, Served with Sautéed Kale and Potato Croquettes

Broiled Scrod in Lemon Butter Sauce with Parsley Potatoes, Broiled Tomato, and Summer Succotash

Fourth-of-July Grilled Salmon with Dill Sauce, Fresh Peas, and New Potatoes

Portuguese Mussel Stew with Potatoes and Peppers

Turkey Roulade with Bread Stuffing, Mashed Potatoes, Giblet Gravy, Brussels Sprouts, and Cranberry Sauce

Boston Baked Beans with Salt Pork and Fresh Pork, Served with Brown Bread and Piccalilli

Acadian Garlic Rôti of Pork with Rapée Potatoes, Tomato Crown, and Haricots Verts

Wampanoag Maple-Glazed Roast Rack of Venison with Winter Succotash and Broccoli Florets in Baby Pumpkin

Newport Roast Ribeye for Two with Yorkshire Pudding, Creamed Onions, Glazed Baby Carrots, and Pan-Steamed Spinach

Yankee Pot Roast with Braised Vegetables and Ginger-Pear Chutney

New England Corned Beef Boiled Dinner with Three Sauces

DESSERTS

Apple Pie with Vermont Cheddar

Boston Cream Pie

Blueberry Crisp with Vanilla Ice Cream

Acadian Maple-Walnut Tart

Pumpkin Pie with Whipped Cream

Spice Trade Gingerbread with Cranberry Ice Cream

WEBSITE EXTRAS

Breakfasts   Sandwiches   Hors d'Oeuvres   Thanksgiving Menu

■ A CHALLENGING
□ LAND

Largely because of geographical restrictions, the New England culinary region is virtually identical to geopolitical New England. To the east and southeast, the Atlantic Ocean forms a definitive border. To the north and northeast lies Canada, whose East Coast culinary regions share elements of the New England style. In most of New England, these restrictions constrained the cuisine within the region's generally accepted borders. New England cooking oversteps geopolitical lines only in the west, into upstate New York, and along its southern coast to the northern tip of Long Island.

Similarly, New England's ability to produce its own food was restricted by geographical barriers. New England's arable coastal plain is narrow, squeezed between the mountains and the sea. The region's foothills are steep and farming valleys small. For culinary regions geography is destiny, and this is amply true for New England. Let's look at the geographical elements that shaped the cuisine.

Mountain, Forest, and Sea

Sweeping diagonally northward, the Appalachian Mountains become a narrow, rocky spine as they run through Connecticut, Massachusetts, New Hampshire, Vermont, and Maine, dominating the New England landscape. Although Rhode Island and the eastern coastal plain of Connecticut and Massachusetts have areas of low, flat land, in most of central New England only a small strip of level ground separates mountains and coast. In the far north, the foothills drop down to the sea, and in many places ocean waves crash directly onto rocky cliffs.

Erosion gradually wore down the Appalachian Mountains and created the soil of the foothill regions. Enriched by organic matter from decaying forest debris, in New England this soil has adequate plant nutrients; however, there's not much of it. Most of New England's soil is deposited in narrow river valleys and small basins between mountain ridges. In the foothills, shallow plots of soil are interspersed with areas of loose shale and bare granite. In some places hillside soil is only 2 inches deep. Thus, New England's tracts of commercially viable farmland are small—rarely more than 250 acres—and widely scattered.

Before European settlement, most of New England was tree-covered. Dense forests of pine, spruce, and fir crowned the mountains; at lower altitudes, oak, chestnut, maple, birch, and beech thrived. In the early 1600s this majestic northeastern forest stretched from the Atlantic Ocean to the Arctic Circle, broken only by small clearings caused by fire or Native American swidden agriculture (p. 30).

In New England, heavy forest combined with steep terrain hindered Native American farmers and, later, English colonial agriculture. Because of mountainous topography New England's rivers are navigable only a short distance inland, which made exploration slow and dangerous (Figure 3.1). These daunting conditions were only made worse by the New England climate.

A Climate of Extremes

FACTOR 1
Climatic extremes make agriculture risky.

Located about halfway between the equator and the North Pole, the New England culinary region spreads across seemingly temperate latitudes. In fact, the latitude of central New England is approximately the same as that of the northern Mediterranean. However, New England's topography and location make its weather patterns extremely changeable and unpredictable.

New England lies in a treacherous crossroads of westerly frontal movement across North America and variable weather

FACTOR 1
Mountainous topography restricted early exploration and agriculture.

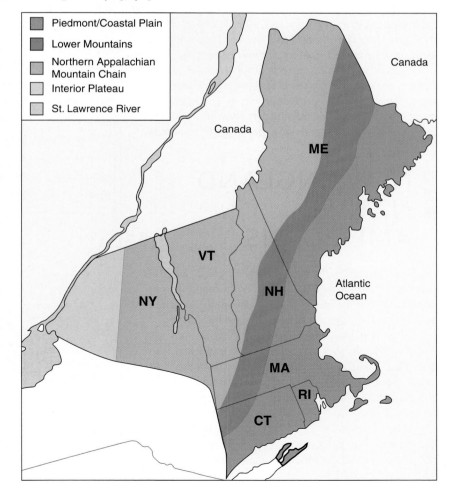

FIGURE 3.1
New England Topography

Legend:
- Piedmont/Coastal Plain
- Lower Mountains
- Northern Appalachian Mountain Chain
- Interior Plateau
- St. Lawrence River

Canada
Canada
ME
VT
NH
NY
Atlantic Ocean
MA
RI
CT

patterns in the Atlantic. Depending on the interaction of these two entities, New England is sometimes under the influence of southern weather cells bringing in warm, moist Caribbean air, and at other times under the force of northern cells that blow in cold, dry air from the Arctic. This makes the region a climatic battleground where fronts collide and extreme weather changes occur quickly. In a matter of minutes, bright, sunny skies fill with ominous black clouds bringing hair-raising thunderstorms that blow over just as quickly as they came. New England's temperatures are equally varied. The region may experience 40°F nights in August and 70°F afternoons in January. New Englanders often say to tourists, "Don't like the weather? Wait a minute, it'll change."

No matter where its weather patterns originate, New England's proximity to the Atlantic Ocean frequently causes large amounts of moisture to collect in the air. This moisture often falls to earth in tremendous downpours, or in heavy snow measured in feet rather than inches. A unique New England weather event occurs when low barometric pressure off the coast draws powerful wind and heavy precipitation northward and eastward along the New England coast. Called a **nor'easter,** this type of storm brings hurricane-like wind and rain in summer and blizzard conditions in winter.

New England also suffers from a short growing season. Although Connecticut is relatively temperate with an average of 120 frost-free days, as one moves northward the growing season becomes progressively shorter, with as few as 80 frost-free days in Maine. Moreover, parts of New England have occasionally recorded frost in all twelve months.

New England's unpredictable and frequently damaging weather makes crop farming a risky business. Such weather, combined with its short growing season and sparse soil, resulted in New England having little chance of becoming a major agricultural area.

NEW ENGLAND NATIVE AMERICANS

Anthropologists believe that New England was the last part of America to be settled by humans. The inhospitable climate and rugged terrain may have been at least partially responsible for its late habitation.

The region's earliest Native Americans most likely arrived from the west, moving eastward from the Great Lakes area or northeastward from the Plantation South. By the time of the European incursion, the region was home to Native Americans of two language groups.

New England's coastal tribes were primarily Algonquian, with languages, religious practices, and foodways similar to those of Plantation South and Mid-Atlantic natives. The Massachusetts, Narra-

gansetts, and Nausets are tribes recognizable as modern place names. Other important coastal tribes include the Wampanoags, Pequots, and Abenaki. These groups were likely the first Native Americans to have contact with Europeans, possibly as early as 1000 C.E., when Viking ships are thought to have explored the New England coast. During the Age of Exploration they experienced frequent contact with Europeans even before English settlement of the region. Later, as a result of European diseases, English aggression, and assimilation, many of these tribes would virtually disappear until achieving a cultural resurgence in the late 20th century. Some left only their names as places on the map and their foodways as the foundation of the region's cuisine.

Tribes in the Iroquoian language group ruled the mountains and eventually formed a powerful confederacy called the Iroquois League. Typically tall, strong, and warlike, the Iroquoian people eventually dominated not only interior New England but also much of the northern Mid-Atlantic, the Great Lakes region, and the Ohio Valley.

Before European settlement, New England Native Americans were seminomadic, practicing human seasonal migration similar to that of Plantation South natives. During the spring planting season and the early fall harvest season, Algonquians lived in coastal villages and the Iroquois inhabited river valley settlements in the foothills (see Figure 3.2). Both groups typically traveled to higher ground during the summer, and again in the late-autumn and winter hunting seasons. Unlike the many large,

FIGURE 3.2
New England Native American Settlement

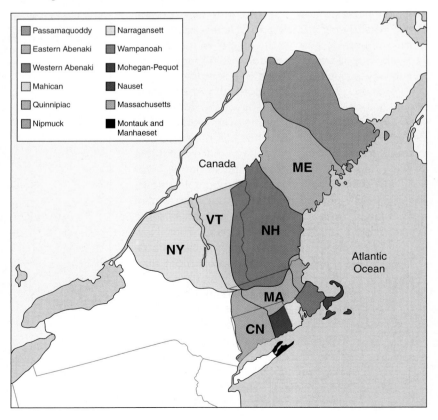

■ Passamaquoddy	□ Narragansett
■ Eastern Abenaki	■ Wampanoah
■ Western Abenaki	■ Mohegan-Pequot
□ Mahican	■ Nauset
■ Quinnipiac	■ Massachusetts
■ Nipmuck	■ Montauk and Manhaeset

Canada

ME

VT

NH

NY

Atlantic Ocean

MA

CN

organized Southern native groups, Native Americans of New England tended to live in small, independent tribal groups and had varying customs and beliefs.

New England Native Agriculture

With little arable land and a short growing season, New England natives were forced to rely less on agriculture than the Southern tribes. In harsh New England conditions, native farmers struggled to produce food crops and, in doing so, developed methods unique to the region. New England native farmers—almost exclusively women—developed corn cultivars capable of reaching maturity in the short New England growing season. New England natives were among few Native Americans known to use fertilizer, typically adding decomposed fish or marine waste into the soil of their swidden plots. Despite these advances, northern native farmers were far less successful than their southern counterparts, and New England tribes rarely had surplus crops. Often they produced less food than necessary to sustain the tribe through the winter and had to rely heavily on hunted and foraged foods.

It's human nature to value things that are scarce. Thus, for New England Native Americans, Three Sisters crops were extremely high-status foods. Dishes made with corn, beans, and squash were typically reserved for the most special occasions and served to the most honored guests. In years of good harvest, these products were also important trade commodities. Corn was held in highest esteem and was considered sacred, as in most other Native American cultures.

By the time of European contact, New England natives had developed agricultural techniques as good as or better than those of other American native groups. However, the growing conditions in New England made farming almost a sideline compared to fishing, hunting, and foraging.

Fishing, Hunting, and Foraging

Hunting and fishing were the primary occupation for the men and boys of any New England native group, occupying most of their time. Spring brought large schools of migrating fish up the rivers and creeks of the coast. Harvested in simple nets, and sometimes even by hand, these fish were preserved with sea salt and eaten throughout the cold season. Coastal tribes relied heavily on abundant North Atlantic shellfish, such as mussels, clams, oysters, and cold-water lobsters. Winter hunting in the mountains yielded beaver, venison, bear, moose, and small game.

Foraged foods were part of the yearly cycle of cooking and food preservation. Several wild foods were, and still are, specialties of the region. **Fiddleheads** are shoots of the ostrich fern plant, so named because they're shaped like the scroll of a violin (see Figure 3.3). Fiddleheads are a springtime delicacy. In midsummer New England natives feasted on tiny wild blueberries and also dried them for winter use. Late summer brought beach plums and wild cranberries that were pounded with venison and bear fat to make *pemmican*, a highly nutritious travel provision. Wild mushrooms grew on the forest floor from late spring to the first frost. However, the indigenous food that would prove most important to modern New England cuisine is the sap of the maple tree.

FIGURE 3.3

Fiddlehead Fern Kelly MacDonald/ Shutterstock

Sweetness from Trees

Anthropologists believe that New England natives first discovered the sweetness of maple by tasting icicles of sap suspended from broken maple branches. Native cooks recognized the sweet sap as a nutrition source and discovered how to create a delicious and long-keeping food product from it.

Each year in early spring, New England natives waited for a stretch of warm, sunny days with frosty nights, conditions that indicated the annual rising of the maple sap. Using stone hatchets, they cut V-shaped incisions in the trees and inserted hollow reeds to channel the sap into buckets made from birch bark. During the season natives drank the sap as a refreshing beverage. However, most of it was transformed into syrup.

As it comes from the tree maple sap is a thin, pale liquid with no more than a hint of sweetness. However, natives learned to concentrate the sugar in the sap by boiling away the water, changing the thin sap into a thick, sweet, distinctively flavored syrup. Before the arrival of European metal cookware, native women reduced the sap using sling bag simmering (p. 33), a slow and laborious process. With the introduction of English metal tools and cauldrons, the production of maple syrup became much more efficient (see Figure 3.4).

FIGURE 3.4

Metal buckets and cauldrons introduced by colonists enabled Native Americans to make maple syrup more efficiently. Courtesy of the Minnesota Historical Society

ELEMENTS OF NEW ENGLAND NATIVE AMERICAN CUISINE

FOUNDATION FOODS

principal starch: dried corn (maize)

principal proteins: fish, game meats, dried beans

principal produce: squashes, pumpkins, wild fruits, wild greens

FAVORED SEASONINGS: maple syrup, wild herbs, wild fruits

PRINCIPAL COOKING MEDIA: water, bear fat

PRIMARY COOKING METHODS: pit-roasting, sling bag simmering, poaching, stewing, boiling

FOOD ATTITUDES: strong food culture, culinary liberals

A Lasting Native Legacy

New England is one of few American culinary regions in which Native American cooking is still directly represented in the modern cuisine. This influence shows in native-derived taste preferences and the survival of many native dishes in virtually unchanged form.

FACTOR 2

The American taste preference for sweet-savory flavors is a direct legacy of New England Native American cuisine.

The Sweet-Savory New England Palate

Although coastal New England natives had access to salt from seawater, inland tribes had few sources of mineral salt and reserved most of what they obtained for curing meats. Instead of salt, they typically used maple syrup and dried wild fruits to season their foods, substituting sweetness for saltiness. This practice, embraced by English settlers, is evident today in many New England dishes such as baked beans and brown bread. In fact, old-time New Englanders typically blur the distinction between sweet and savory foods, traditionally serving sweetened porridges or fruit pies as main dishes at supper and topping apple pie with sharp Cheddar cheese. As New Englanders migrated westward in the 1800s, they carried this sweet-savory taste preference with them throughout the continent. Today it is an element of the American national cuisine and a well-recognized characteristic of the American palate.

New England's Indigenous Dishes

In modern New England cuisine, diners encounter traditional dishes virtually identical to those found in precontact Native American cooking.

A Bounty of Squash

New England natives grew a wide variety of squashes, from small, gourdlike specimens to large pumpkin types. For immediate consumption these squashes were boiled, steamed, and pit-baked. Maple syrup was the preferred seasoning for squash, a taste preference handed down to modern cooks. Today in most New England homes, a casserole of winter squash seasoned with maple syrup is a favored side dish and is indispensable on the Thanksgiving table.

FACTOR 2

Indigenous Three Sisters crops are foundation foods of the cuisine.

Dishes Made from Cornmeal

New England natives prepared virtually all of the corn dishes made by their counterparts in the Plantation South (see pp. 33–35). Although they were familiar with traditional alkaline processing and prepared hominy, New England natives were far less dependent on alkaline-processed corn because their diet was largely based on wild-caught protein foods. For New England natives, corn-based dishes were special-occasion delicacies, and nutrition was not the main point when preparing them. However, for starving English settlers—and, later, for thrifty New Englanders—corn dishes acquired a much greater significance. Filling, warming, and cheap dishes such as cornmeal mush and corn pone were a good antidote to the cold, damp, New England winters. Though New England colonists transformed corn foods into hybrid colonial dishes, they continued to prepare corn-based dishes in the native manner, without wheat flour. Rhode Island Jonnycakes and cornmeal mush are well-known examples of dishes that are a direct native legacy.

Baked Beans

Several varieties of shell beans, from red to white to speckled, grew in New England native cornfields. Although the immature pods and mature bean seeds were eaten fresh in season, most native beans were dried and shelled. New England natives perfected a unique method of slowly cooking their dried beans until succulent and tender. After briefly boiling the beans in a narrow-necked clay pot with maple syrup and water, native cooks then sealed the pot and buried it in a hole lined with the glowing embers of a wood fire. After hours of slow steam-baking, the beans emerged thick, bubbling, and smoky-sweet. This Native American dish was the precursor of New England's famous signature dish, baked beans.

English colonists used additional Old World ingredients, such as salt pork and spices, in their baked beans. Although ovens later replaced holes in the ground, for special occasions New Englanders still make "beans in a hole" in the traditional native manner.

Succotash

New England natives frequently cooked corn and beans together in the same pot. Even without traditional alkaline processing, the

FIGURE 3.5
A legacy of Native Americans, at a clambake seafood is cooked in stone-lined pits. Courtesy Ipswich Fish Market, www.ipswichfishmarket.com

corn-bean synergy creates a nutritious dish rich in protein. Moreover, the flavors of the two vegetables perfectly complement each other. New England Native Americans named this dish *msickquatash*, called **succotash** by English colonists. Though traditional Native American succotash is made with dried corn and beans, today a summer version made from fresh sweet corn and fresh lima beans is more prevalent.

Clambake

Coastal tribes used holes in the ground to cook seafood as well as beans. In warm weather they spent much time on the region's beaches, where it was cooler, relatively insect-free, and also easy to dig. To prepare a seafood feast, they built a driftwood fire in the bottom of a deep pit; when it burned to bright embers, they placed ocean-polished stones on top. Once the stones became white-hot, native cooks threw in a thick bed of moist seaweed and added layers of in-husk green corn, hundreds of clams, scores of cleaned whole fish, and as many lobsters as they could catch. The food was then covered with another layer of seaweed and the hole refilled with sand. After several hours they opened the pit to reveal delicious food cooked to perfection in the salty, smoky steam (see Figure 3.5). This Native American cooking technique eventually became known as a New England clambake, described on p. 98.

■ PILGRIMS
▢ AND PURITANS
■

The European settlement of New England was similar in many ways to that of the Plantation South. Both settler groups were English, and both were determined to conquer the new land and prosper in colonies modeled after their English homelands. However, they were fundamentally different in motivation and temperament.

In Search of Religious Freedom

The English people who settled New England came primarily from East Anglia, a relatively urbanized area. Most were middle- and upper-middle-class townspeople who enjoyed financial security in their homelands. They emigrated not for financial reasons but, rather, for cultural ones—based primarily on religious beliefs.

In England, the early 1600s was a time of forced conformity. The Protestant Church of England had been named the nation's official religion, and citizens who did not belong to it, particularly Catholics and separatist Protestant groups, were being persecuted by the government. The leaders of these groups were becoming uncomfortable about their members' future in England. After a brief stay in Holland, the first group—the Pilgrims—sailed for the New World seeking religious freedom. The Pilgrims believed they were heading for the colony of Virginia, by then a known territory reputed to be good for farming.

The Pilgrims' journey was fraught with dangers and discomforts. Frigid weather, crowding, poor rations, and illness combined with powerful North Atlantic storms made the passage a nightmare. Hundreds of miles off course, they finally sighted the coast of Cape Cod and landed in the New World, near Plymouth, Massachusetts, on December 11, 1620—less than two weeks before the beginning of winter.

No American settler group ever arrived at a worse place at a worse time. Most other early colonist groups carefully planned their voyages so as to arrive in the spring. Such timing allowed them months of good weather in which to build shelters, plant crops, explore their surroundings, and generally acclimate themselves before bad weather set in. Not the Pilgrims. Although the winter they experienced was mild by New England standards, it devastated the fledgling colony.

A larger problem for the Pilgrims was their lack of wilderness training. Most members of the Pilgrim group were artisans and merchants by trade. As town dwellers, they had no experience with foraging or hunting and little knowledge of farming. Moreover, the Pilgrims, like other separatist Protestant groups, were highly conservative in general and thus were culinary conservatives as well. They were unwilling to try strange foods, such as local fish, shellfish, and indigenous plants, which were the only sustenance available. They discovered a cache of Native American dried corn in an abandoned village. In desperation they cooked and ate it. This store of corn was virtually their only food until local natives supplied them with game meat and beans. However, native generosity was short-lived, probably because the English settlers did not reciprocate with gifts in return. Less than adequate hunters, and unwilling to eat seafood, the Pilgrims suffered both hunger and disease through the winter of 1620–1621, known as "the starving time." Of the 102 Pilgrims who arrived in New England, half survived.

The tiny Pilgrim presence at Plymouth was soon overshadowed by a larger, more organized migration of another separatist Protestant sect, the Puritans, that would soon become the dominant force in New England. They founded the Massachusetts Bay Colony, a large tract of land centered on the port of Boston. Between 1629 and 1640 approximately 21,000 English citizens immigrated to New England, almost all of them from England's eastern counties. Virtually all were culinary conservatives with a minimized food culture.

In the 1600s the most important foundation foods of the English middle classes were wheat bread and beef (p. 39). To the colonists' dismay, wheat refused to mature in New England's short growing season. The few cattle brought from England by ship were needed for milk production and draft purposes and were slaughtered only near death. A diet based on bread and beef was not an option. Thus, early New Englanders were deprived of their two most basic foods.

Embracing the Native Diet

Initially, New England's English settlers had no choice but adopt the Native American diet. Local natives taught them to grow indigenous crops and to cook indigenous foods using native techniques and seasonings. Corn products replaced wheat flour, becoming the colonists' staple starch. Dried-bean dishes were everyday fare, often replacing meat. Squashes of various types were eaten year-round. These Three Sisters foods became the foundation of New England cuisine.

With corn for a staple starch, only one important element was missing: meat. Unlike the natives, early English settlers rarely ate game because most had little skill at hunting. A few men were successful at wildfowling. However, on the rare occasions when they ate venison, they had usually received it as a gift from Native Americans. Only later would game become a significant element of the New England diet.

Because harvesting the region's abundant seafood required little expertise, fish and shellfish became the early colonists' main source of protein. However, seafood had not been a preferred food in England, and it became even less favored when it was the only food available. Written accounts of the time repeatedly complain about the monotony of a diet consisting of nothing but fresh fish, clams, and lobster.

■ NEW ENGLAND
□ COLONIAL CUISINE
■

By the mid-1600s English settlement in New England was well established. The Massachusetts Bay Colony fared far better than the Pilgrims. Arriving in greater numbers and with more supplies, they soon prospered. Among the Puritan colonists were experienced farmers with the determination to clear and cultivate their own patch of New England wilderness.

New England farms were small enterprises operated by a single farmer and his family, with little or no hired help. These small farms did not require the massive labor that made slavery so necessary in the Plantation South. Moreover, slaves from equatorial Africa frequently sickened and died in the cold New England climate. Although a significant number of colonial New Englanders owned slaves, African-Americans were not brought to New England in large numbers.

Even after cold-tolerant grain cultivars were discovered, large-scale production of European grain crops was not practical in New England because of the small size of arable land tracts and the

FACTOR 1
New England's topography and climate made large-scale slavery unnecessary.

short growing season. Similarly, small pastures were not cost-effective for raising beef cattle, although they supported dairy operations of limited size. Because of the climate, New England did not readily accommodate many European crops. Thus, colonial New England's principal food products were dairy foods, tree fruits, and indigenous corn. Farmers raised hogs and chickens primarily for their own use, offering only a few for sale. Fish and shellfish remained the most readily available protein foods. Though New England's food production eventually sustained its population, the lack of certain foods radically changed the diet of early colonists. Even after the region reached economic viability, most Old World ingredients remained expensive luxuries.

Old World Foods and Dishes

As trade and commerce developed, New England cooks began importing limited amounts of European ingredients. English dishes made with imported foods were served for special occasions. Old World foods that became successful colonial domesticates were used more freely and became everyday fare.

Wheat Flour Yeast Breads and Quick Breads

As soon as they could, New England colonists imported English wheat—but at a high cost. Because wheat was bulky and heavy and had to be kept perfectly dry, transporting it across the ocean was expensive. Millstones crafted from the region's abundant granite were used to grind both English wheat and New England–grown corn. Although the flour bin was a fixture in every New England pantry, New England cooks used wheat flour in small quantities, typically reserving it for pastry making and to lighten doughs made of other grains. Even after agriculture in the Mid-Atlantic colonies was established enough to export domestic wheat to New England, flour remained more expensive than locally grown grains and was used sparingly by thrifty New Englanders.

FACTOR 3
English colonists brought Old World foods and introduced colonial domesticates.

Special occasions brought out the flour bin for the preparation of English-style yeast breads. The region's cooler weather was conducive to yeast dough production, and early colonists made a variety of yeasted wheat flour products. When industrially produced chemical leaveners became available in the mid-1800s, New England bakers embraced them with enthusiasm. Biscuits, scones, muffins, and popovers are among the most favored New England quick breads.

Apples: Fresh, Dried, and Liquid

Although many European food crops didn't grow well in New England, apple trees thrived. By the mid-1600s the apple had become the most important fruit in the colonists' diets.

Fresh apples were baked whole and in pies, fried as a side dish, and simmered into applesauce. Stored properly, apples kept for a long time. In late summer and fall, newly harvested

FIGURE 3.6

In the cider house, apples were pressed into a nutritious beverage drunk fresh or fermented into hard cider. Courtesy of Jersey City Free Public Library

apples were packed in barrels and stored in cellars to last well into winter. For longer storage—to make them last an entire year until the next harvest—apples were peeled, cored, sliced into thin rings, and dried. When needed, the dried apples were reconstituted in water and used in many of the same dishes as fresh apples. However, apples kept even better in liquid form.

Most apples grown in colonial New England were made into cider, a tart, crisp, and highly nutritious beverage when drunk fresh. However, most cider was allowed to ferment into **hard cider,** a fizzy, dry (not sweet) beverage with modest alcohol content. New England hard cider replaced expensive English ale as the colonists' beverage of choice. Every large New England farmstead had a cider mill and cider press (see Figure 3.6). Smallholders without cider presses used community equipment for a small fee.

European Root Vegetables and Cabbages

Although fresh vegetables were enjoyed throughout the short summer and in early fall, for most of the year New Englanders made do with storage vegetables: sturdy roots and head cabbages held for long periods of time at moderately cool temperatures. New England farmers grew large quantities of these cold-tolerant root vegetables and cabbages and, after harvest, carefully buried them in deep pits layered with sand. Throughout the winter, the vegetables remained at a constant cool temperature and didn't freeze because they were buried below the frost line. Carrots, onions, turnips, rutabagas, beets, salsify, and especially parsnips made up the majority of the New England diet. White and green cabbages were stored in the same manner. To this day, these vegetables are an important part of New England cuisine.

Preserved Foods

As a seafaring nation, 17th-century England needed foods that would last throughout yearlong ocean voyages. In response, the English became experts at processing preserved foods. In New England, these foods were important on land as well. Traditional New England cooking remains dependent on a limited number of these English-origin food products, most of them preserved in some way.

FACTOR 3
English preserved foods become staples of the cuisine.

Salt Meat and Salt Fish

Before refrigeration, one of the best-known and most reliable methods of preserving protein foods was salt curing. Both meats and fish can be made to keep under virtually any conditions if heavily permeated with salt. Some forms of salt preservation include drying and/or smoking; others use a **brine,** a solution of salt and water that was a favored preservation agent for New England colonists.

Every colonial New England cellar boasted a barrel of **salt pork.** When a hog was slaughtered, chunks of pork fat and pork belly (p. 81) were packed in wooden barrels and submerged in a heavy brine. Used as a seasoning meat—or in hard times as a main protein in its own right—salt pork appeared in virtually every New England colonial recipe, including seafood dishes and even some desserts. The satisfying crunch and salty savor of crisp-fried salt pork adds richness and textural interest to many a heavy, starchy, or bland New England dish.

Tough cuts of beef, such as brisket, were also cured in brine. This product was called **corned beef,** a name that requires explanation. Remember that in Britain the word *corn* means "grain." Just as Americans refer to a grain of salt, English colonists used the phrase "a corn of salt." Over time beef preserved with corns of salt became *corned beef.* Corned beef is the basis of New England boiled dinner (p. 105), red flannel hash, and the Irish-American dish corned beef and cabbage.

Although seafood was abundant, in bad weather coastal New Englanders couldn't risk ocean fishing. Thus, there might be long stretches of time during which no fresh seafood was available. To ensure a reliable protein source, New Englanders used salt to preserve fish in the same manner as Native Americans (p. 31) and Southern colonists. As settlement grew, inland colonists purchased salt fish and used it as a staple protein as well. In fact, many traditional New Englanders prefer salt fish to the fresh variety. Eventually, fish preserved in salt—especially salt cod—would become an important New England trade good shipped around the world.

Crackers

One of England's earliest commercially processed foods was developed to satisfy the needs of seafarers. On sailing ships, moist fresh bread quickly became moldy. However, dough products dehydrated by baking them completely hard and dry lasted for months if packed in airtight tin containers. Called *ship's biscuits* or *sea biscuits*, these hard, dry crackers were eaten in place of bread and eventually became an ingredient in many colonial New England dishes. Pounded into crumbs (traditionally with a hammer), they can be used to make stuffings and toppings. Topped with cheese and baked, they become a tooth-challenging toasted cheese sandwich. Broken up and simmered in broth with meat, poultry, or fish, they absorb the cooking liquid, soften to a dumplinglike consistency, and thicken the broth; this dish is called **brewis** (pronounced "brews"). Today New Englanders enjoy similar biscuits, called **common crackers** or **pilot crackers,** that are very crunchy but not as hard as traditional ship's biscuits.

Caribbean Imports

Thrifty New Englanders knew that import goods from the Caribbean were less expensive than those shipped from Europe. When the port of Boston became a regular stop on the Triangle of Trade the cost of these goods dropped even lower.

Molasses

Molasses is an inexpensive by-product of Caribbean sugar production. This dark, thick, bittersweet syrup is a signature New England flavor, used in cooking and baking and as a topping for biscuits and doughnuts. In a well-provisioned colonial New England household, the molasses barrel stood in the cellar next to the salt pork and apple barrels.

Rum

Far less expensive than English or Scotch whiskey or French brandy, Caribbean rum soon became the spirit of choice in New England. Though the Puritans disapproved of overindulgence in alcohol, strong drink taken in moderation had its place for men and women enduring New England's harsh climate and frequent hardships. Rum was used as medicine for the ill or injured and as a beverage to boost flagging morale. It was served straight from the bottle or mixed with milk and/or eggs. Hot buttered rum was flavored with cinnamon sticks and other whole spices.

Colonial Hybrids

New England's colonial dishes are some of the most creative in the cuisine. Blending Old World ingredients into dishes based on indigenous foods, New England cooks created delicious, satisfying hybrid dishes. The following dishes are pure Native American–English hybrids that have survived virtually unaltered.

Colonial Baked Beans

As learned from Native American cooks, early New Englanders simmered dried beans with sweet maple syrup in an earthenware pot. However, Old World ingredients transformed the indigenous bean dish into a more sumptuous colonial hybrid. Fatty English-style salt pork gives it a creamy mouthfeel and rich flavor and contributes meat protein. Added savor comes from sea salt, an onion stuck with a clove, and a jolt of piquant English mustard. Later, when molasses became plentiful, it often replaced maple syrup, although northern New Englanders continue to prefer the flavor of maple in their beans. Tomato is never added to true New England baked beans.

In colonial times beans were baked in an outdoor pit, native style, or simmered in the glowing embers of the hearth. Later, they were baked in ovens. Because they are prepared ahead of time, baked beans became the universal Sabbath dish for Puritans, who did no work from sundown on Saturday to sundown on Sunday. The Puritan housewife prepared a large batch of beans on Saturday morning, baked them all day, and then served them up hot on Saturday night after the Sabbath began at sunset. The cooled beans were then eaten once again for Sunday's midday dinner after church. Although rules forbidding work on the Sabbath had been relaxed by the 1800s, traditional New Englanders continue to eat baked beans on Saturday nights, typically accompanied by steamed brown bread and a tart, piquant accompaniment such as pickles or coleslaw.

Wild Turkey and the Thanksgiving Bird

The Thanksgiving turkey is a national signature dish. According to legend, the practice of serving roast turkey for celebratory meals was handed down by the Pilgrims. If the roasted birds served at the first Thanksgiving were, indeed, turkeys, they would have been indigenous wild turkeys, very different fowl from the plump, tender, domestic turkey we know today. The American wild turkey is lean with dark meat and a rich, gamey flavor. Following English custom, the birds would have been bled, drawn, and hung at least overnight to tenderize them and develop depth of flavor. After plucking, the turkeys might have been stuffed with a dressing made from cornpone highly seasoned with wild onions, wild herbs, and possibly mace or some other sweet spice. In the early days turkeys were spit-roasted in the hearth or over an outdoor fire.

Pies, Sweet and Savory

Although we frequently hear the phrase *as American as apple pie*, the apple is an Old World import, and pie making originated in Europe. New England colonists applied their Old World pie-making expertise not only to apples and other colonial domesticate fruits, but also to indigenous ingredients. Native pumpkin was baked and mashed; mixed with maple syrup, milk, and eggs; and then baked in a flaky shell to become pumpkin pie. In traditional New England homes, fruit pies and custard pies are served for breakfast and often reappear for supper.

Savory pies are also popular in New England cooking. In early days these were prepared with leftovers or less desirable foods. For example, stringy old chickens and tough cuts of meat or game were chopped, highly seasoned, and baked into meat pies. The abundant seafood that was fundamentally disliked by the early colonists could be disguised and "improved" by becoming clam, fish, or lobster pie. Today savory pies with tender, flaky crusts and luscious fillings are considered special-occasion foods.

Hybrid Cornmeal Dishes

When they tired of native-style corn dishes, English colonists blended cornmeal with Old World ingredients to make hybrid colonial dishes. Refer to the table beginning on p. 138 to learn about Indian pudding, New England cornbread, rye 'n' Injun, Boston brown bread, and boiled puddings.

Conservative Culture Creates Conservative Foodways

Thus far the culinary history of New England is quite similar to that of the Plantation South. In both regions colonists arrived in the New World unprepared, at about the same time, and were forced to subsist on similar indigenous foods. Both groups eventually learned to grow colonial domesticates—although with less success in New England—or imported them. Both combined indigenous ingredients with colonial domesticates to create a hybrid colonial cooking style. Further, both regions achieved economic viability at roughly the same time, although by different means.

However, from this point onward New England cuisine developed in a drastically different manner from that of the Plantation South. Factor 1, the land, partially explains the dissimilarity. The geography of the two regions and their respective resources are quite different. New England could never hope to produce foods as varied or abundant as the Plantation South eventually enjoyed. A lavish and expansive cuisine can't develop without excellent and abundant domestic ingredients. Another reason involves Factor 4: No large and significant immigrant group influenced New England cuisine. But the primary reason for the great difference between the two cuisines stems from the vastly different sensibilities of the two English settler groups.

Unlike the freewheeling, multicultural Southern colonists, New England Puritans were a homogenous group that adhered to a rigid set of social norms. Their brand of Protestantism required a serious and cautious attitude about all aspects of life, including food. The proper Puritan was expected to think of God first, community second, family third, and personal happiness last—if at all. Pleasure was not part of the equation. Food was considered merely sustenance; spending unnecessary time and money on its preparation was considered frivolous. So much more important was religion than gastronomy that precooked dishes, such as baked beans, were created to avoid doing even minimal cooking on the Sabbath. The many cook-ahead stews, soups, and casseroles in New England cuisine exemplify the New England culinary ideal of food as a no-fuss fuel.

This attitude about food shows that early New Englanders had a minimized food culture. Moreover, Puritan-influenced New Englanders were culinary conservatives. Although early New England settlers had been forced to eat indigenous foods, after several generations these foods eventually became ingrained in the colonists' diet and became foundations of the colonial cuisine. New Englanders gradually embraced indigenous seafood as well. However, in New England exploration of new foods never

FACTOR 3
Puritan characteristics of thrift and self-denial resulted in a conservative food culture.

progressed much further. The conservative Puritan attitude seamlessly evolved into the simple, thrifty lifestyle of the New England Yankee.

■ YANKEE CULTURE ▫ AND TRADITIONAL ■ NEW ENGLAND CUISINE

In the 150 years following the Pilgrims' landing, the Massachusetts Bay Colony grew rapidly. From the colony's founding through the American Revolution, the population of New England doubled each generation.

Unlike the Plantation South, New England could not rely on agriculture for economic viability. By the early 1700s, New England was feeding its growing population but had little surplus. Rather than exporting agricultural products, New England sold lumber, salt cod, and manufactured goods to Europe, the Caribbean, and the South. Many New England merchants participated in the infamous Triangle of Trade that brought slaves from Africa to the New World.

In the late 1800s New England led America's Industrial Revolution, specializing in textiles, lumber milling, and light manufacturing, and led the world in industrial food production. In addition to producing trade goods, New England was renowned for shipbuilding, which created thousands of jobs. Swift New England ships, called *Yankee clippers*, sailed the globe dealing in all manner of goods.

Through the 1800s the region's largest source of income was the New England fishing industry. Hardy fishermen braved the treacherous North Atlantic in search of codfish, salmon, and other food fish. Whales were sought for the oil extracted from their blubber, a liquid wax used in 19th-century lamps and to make candles. By far the most important fishery was cod, discussed on p. 96.

By the mid-1800s New England had amassed great wealth. However, this wealth was distributed far differently than that of the Southern colonies. New England had few aristocratic landowners with hundreds of servants and lavish lifestyles. Instead, most New England families lived comfortable lives in snug homes eating bountiful yet simple meals. Even wealthy Boston manufacturers and merchants lived modestly by New York City or Charleston standards. The thrifty, sober Puritan sensibility continued to drive the New England lifestyle for many generations. New Englanders were known for hard work, plain speech, and, above all, frugality. These qualities are embodied by the term **Yankee.** They're also evident in traditional New England cuisine, often referred to as "Yankee cooking."

Unlike the Plantation South, where the spicy cooking of African slaves transformed colonial cooking into a vastly different modern cuisine, New England cooking remains close to its colonial

FACTOR 5
New England's role in the Industrial Revolution ensured continuing economic viability.

ELEMENTS OF NEW ENGLAND CUISINE

FOUNDATION FOODS

principal starches: dried corn dishes, yeasted wheat breads, crackers

principal proteins: fish and shellfish, cheese, preserved pork, dried beans

principal produce: root vegetables, cabbages, apples, other fruits

FAVORED SEASONINGS: maple syrup, molasses, parsley, bay leaf, thyme, sage

PRINCIPAL COOKING MEDIA: water, butter, lard

PRIMARY COOKING METHODS: roasting, boiling, poaching, braising, stewing

FOOD ATTITUDES: minimized food culture, culinary conservatives

roots. Many dishes in modern New England cuisine would not look out of place on a 17th-century table. Economic viability did little to enrich the cuisine. Although world trade resulted in virtually every spice and seasoning on the globe passing through New England's warehouses, these exotic ingredients did not enter the cuisine to any significant extent.

In general, traditional New England cooking is simple, straightforward, and plainly seasoned. With the exception of seafood, which became scarce and costly only in the mid-20th century, New England cuisine is inexpensive to prepare. Most traditional New England dishes are substantial, satisfying comfort food. Because preparations and seasonings are simple, success in preparing New England cuisine depends on fine ingredients.

■ FOODS FROM
■ THE SEA

New England has always looked to the sea for sustenance. Early colonists forced to eat seafood out of necessity developed numerous recipes for it. These old recipes typically specify overlong cooking times and heavy sauces and seasonings that mask the flavor of the seafood to a degree unacceptable today. However, once they overcame early prejudice against seafood, New Englanders developed a distinctive regional seafood cuisine. Their treatment of fine local seafood is typically simple and straightforward, featuring a few carefully chosen, complementary ingredients—and today, much shorter cooking times—that bring out its innate goodness.

King Cod

Of all the many varieties of seafood caught off the New England coast, none was as important as the abundant cod. By 1700, cod had become the mainstay of New England fishery and was used in many ways.

Fresh cod is a signature dish of Yankee cooking, typically dressed with butter, vinegar or lemon, and bread crumbs, then baked golden brown. Small, young cod is marketed as **Boston scrod,** prized for its finegrained texture and mild flavor. Connoisseurs prefer skin-on scrod fillets broiled with butter until the skin is crisp and blistered.

Although fresh cod is a regional specialty, salt cod filled both New England's larder and her pocketbook. As early as the 1700s, New England salt cod was an essential provision for ships of all nations. Transported to Europe, Africa, and the Caribbean, New England salt cod challenged Scandinavian and Portuguese salt cod in the European market. Salt cod was also used as an inexpensive food for captive Africans on their way to the New World.

Revenues from the salt cod trade created enormous wealth for many New England families, resulting in a powerful merchant elite called the "codfish aristocracy." So important was cod to the economy of Massachusetts that a 6-foot wooden sculpture was hung in the Massachusetts State House; still there today, it's nicknamed "The Sacred Cod" (see Figure 3.7).

Although it was an important export, much of New England's salt cod stayed home, served as an inexpensive protein food. To prepare salt cod, the hard slabs of fish are rinsed and then soaked in several changes of water for up to 48 hours, depending on the amount of salt used in processing. (Modern salt cod is salted much more lightly than the colonial product and usually needs only overnight soaking.) The fish is then simmered in a flavorful liquid

> "The codfish was to us what wool was to England or tobacco to Virginia: the great staple which became the basis of power and wealth."
>
> —Samuel Adams

FIGURE 3.7

"The Sacred Cod," a 6-foot wooden sculpture of a codfish, hangs in the Massachusetts State House. Linda Whitwam © Dorling Kindersley, Courtesy of the Massachusetts State House, Boston

until tender. The taste and texture of soaked and poached salt cod is quite different from that of fresh cod. Although it can be an acquired taste, for New Englanders who grew up eating salt cod dishes it's pure comfort food. Poached salt cod fillet may be served with a rich sauce to enhance its leanness. Cooked salt cod is pulled into shreds, mixed with mashed potatoes, and formed into patties to make **codfish cakes,** affectionately called **coddies.** Coddies fried crisp in bacon drippings are served for breakfast or supper, traditionally accompanied by ketchup.

Cold-Water Lobster

A New England icon and the state symbol of Maine, the Atlantic cold-water lobster is among the most prized of all sea products. *Homarus americanus*, the large-clawed lobster found all along the East Coast from Belle Isle, Canada, to South Carolina, is arguably one of the world's finest foods.

New England lobsters are in season almost year round; they are unavailable only when the weather is too bad for the lobster boats to venture out to sea. Although local consumption of New England lobsters is highest during the summer tourist season, lobsters are actually at their best in the cooler months. As the name implies, the colder the water, the better the lobster.

Today New England lobsters are growing scarce because of water pollution and overfishing. In addition, lobstering is one of the most dangerous professions; each year fewer young people are willing to become lobstermen. For these reasons New England lobsters are considered a luxury food, demanding a high price.

One of the pleasures of a New England summer is a trip to the lobster pound. (The term *pound* is short for *impoundment,* meaning "enclosure.") A **lobster pound** is a saltwater tank where freshly caught lobsters are held before they're sold or cooked. At most New England lobster pounds you can buy lobsters to take home and cook, or order a shore dinner to eat on the spot, usually at a picnic table in a screened porch under revolving fans. A classic New England **shore dinner** begins with a pot of steamers (described shortly) and then proceeds to steamed lobster, corn on the cob, and a side of coleslaw. Dessert requires a trip to the custard stand for frozen custard (p. 100).

Quahogs and Steamers

The New England coast produces two different types of clams: hard-shell and soft-shell. Both are regional delicacies.

Hard-shell clams range almost the entire East Coast of North America and are familiar to most cooks. Hard-shells are round with thick, solid shells that remain tightly closed when the clams are alive. English colonists adopted a variation of these clams' Narragansett name, calling this type a **quahog** (KO-hog). Old-time New Englanders still call all sizes of hard-shell clams quahogs, although in modern practice only the largest are commonly called so. Hard-shell clams served raw on the half shell is one of New England's favorite appetizers. Smaller hard-shells are also served steamed.

The Atlantic **soft-shell clam** is a pale-gray, oval bivalve with a loosely hinged shell and a protruding neck, or siphon, covered with thick, black skin. Live soft-shell clams may have open shells, but the shells draw closed when the clam is touched or jostled. The body of a soft-shell clam has two distinct textures. The "belly" meat is soft and tender; the meat of the neck, or siphon, is firm and chewy. (The shells of these clams are not really soft; a better name would be "brittle-shell" clam, as their shells are thinner and more easily broken than those of the quahog.) Because the coast near Ipswich, Massachusetts, is a prime source of soft-shell clams, they are sometimes referred to as *Ipswich clams.*

In New England, soft-shell clams are commonly called **steamers** because they are usually served steamed. A bucket of steamers is a seaside treat. To eat them, diners pull the meat from the shell, strip off the black skin from the neck, and then use the neck as a handle to dip the clam first into hot clam broth to wash off grit and then into lemon-flavored drawn (melted) butter.

Fried clams are a New England specialty. The best are made with freshly shucked soft-shell clams and are distinguished by the name **fried clam bellies.** The clams are shucked, dipped in a seasoned batter, and deep-fried golden brown. Eaten immediately, with only salt and a squeeze of lemon as accompaniments, they are a regional specialty that is becoming difficult to find. Today many New England restaurants serve only frozen breaded clam strips.

New Englanders know that the best place to eat clams is at a **clam shack,** a seaside, open-air stand offering clams on the half shell, steamers, fried clams, and broth-based clam chowder.

Oysters

Many connoisseurs believe that oysters harvested off the New England coast surpass those of the Chesapeake and the northern Pacific coast, and even the finest of Europe. The Wellfleet oysters of Cape Cod are among the best known, although Bourne and Cotuit oysters are also superb. These fine, expensive oysters are typically enjoyed raw on the half shell. (In-depth information on oysters is presented in Chapter 5 on pp. 194 and 225.)

Scallops

New England waters supply much of the American sea scallop harvest, as well as a limited number of prized cold-water bay scallops. Sea scallops are fished in water up to 800 feet deep off the northern New England coast; most of the scallop fleet sails out of Maine. New England bay scallops are caught in shallow water around Cape Cod and along the Rhode Island and Connecticut coasts. Refer to the chart on p. 145 for information on scallop market forms by harvest type.

Because the scallop cannot clamp its shell completely shut, it is highly perishable once removed from the water. For this reason few scallops are sold in the shell; most are cleaned and packed on scallop boats. Typically only the prominent round muscle mass is retained and the remainder of the scallop discarded. However, the crescent-shaped coral roe is a delicacy in Europe and elsewhere and is gaining popularity among American connoisseurs. Thus, in-shell scallops are becoming more widely available.

Mussels

The Atlantic blue mussel thrives along the New England coast, clinging underwater to rocks and boulders along the shoreline. Although New England Native Americans enjoyed mussels, these tasty bivalves were disdained and neglected until Portuguese and Italian immigrants arrived. Not until the 1980s did Americans, and New Englanders in particular, embrace this delectable, versatile seafood item. In response, New England developed a thriving business in mussel aquaculture, discussed on this book's companion website.

In New England mussels are most frequently served in Italian restaurants, where they're typically steamed with white wine and garlic or marinara sauce. Portuguese-American cooks (p. 102) combine mussels with sausages, such as linguiça.

New England Chowder

Chowder is a hearty American soup that always includes diced potatoes and a preserved pork product. The English term *chowder* is derived from the French-Canadian word *chaudière*, or "cast-iron cauldron." This French term illustrates the close bond between New England and Canadian cooking. On both sides of the border French and English colonists followed the European tradition of cooking rustic soups and stews in huge iron pots. They simply named the dish after its cooking vessel.

Per definition, two ingredients are necessary to produce an authentic chowder: diced potatoes and a preserved pork product. In the past, salt pork was the meat of choice for chowders. Today bacon is more commonly used. Eastern white potatoes, nationally known as Maine potatoes, give chowders substance and body. Russet potatoes are an acceptable substitute.

The best-known chowders are based on seafood, such as fish, clams, or lobster, and include seafood stock. New England cooks also make vegetable chowders, in particular one prepared with corn. Most New England chowders contain milk or cream, although some coastal clam shacks serve a clear, broth-based chowder. The thickness of a particular chowder depends on personal taste and local tradition. In Boston and southern New England, chowders may contain roux and are thick and full-bodied. Maine chowders are lighter in consistency, often topped with dabs of raw butter that melt into golden pools. Renegade Rhode Island adds a hint of tomato, making their version a pink chowder.

Clambake

A modern New England clambake is an affair for a crowd. Although some families still throw individual clambakes on unrestricted beaches, today most clambakes are held as fund-raisers for local fire companies and other community organizations. Based on the Native American clambake described on p. 91, the modern **clambake** features softshell or hardshell clams, lobsters, fish, and corn on the cob steamed in a pit between layers of seaweed. A modern clambake includes new potatoes and may include chicken and smoked sausage. Melted butter and lemon wedges accompany the food—and lots of beer washes it down.

The best community clambakes serve a variety of homemade baked goods as the grand finale.

■□ FOODS FROM
■ THE LAND

Although the foundation of modern New England cuisine is seafood, much traditional New England cooking is based on the products of its inland farms. Unlike other regions, where industrial agriculture became the norm, New England's farming has always been small-scale, concentrating on quality rather than quantity. In addition to raising traditional products, many regional farmers are experimenting with specialty items such as aquaculture freshwater fish, pastured poultry, and microgreens.

Maple Syrup and Maple Sugar

Pure New England maple syrup is renowned as a regional delicacy. Traditionally served on pancakes and waffles, in the region maple syrup also tops cornbread and jonnycakes and is used in baked beans, squash and pumpkin casseroles, and pie fillings. Refer to this book's companion website to learn about the history of maple syrup production.

Maple syrup begins as maple sap, a thin, clear liquid collected from taps drilled into the trees using buckets or through a modern tap-and-tube system (see Figure 3.8). Back at the sugarhouse, the sap is boiled to evaporate much of its water content. As much as 43 gallons of sap is needed to make 1 gallon of maple syrup. Maple syrup is graded by color and flavor.

Maple sugar is a light-brown granular sugar made by boiling maple syrup until it crystallizes. New Englanders sprinkle it on hot and cold cereals and use it in baked goods.

Native Berries

All types of European berries are now grown on New England farms. However, native blueberries and cranberries are most associated with New England regional cuisine.

Cranberries

Although New England's production of cranberries has been surpassed by that of New Jersey and Wisconsin, the tart red berries were first cultivated in the region and are so closely associated with its cooking that

FIGURE 3.8
Maple sap runs through a network of nonreactive tubing to a central collection tank. Chiyacat/Shutterstock

FIGURE 3.9
New England cranberries float in a flooded bog, awaiting harvest.
Courtesy of Cape Cod Cranberry Growers' Association

we discuss cranberry culture and lore in this chapter rather than in the Farmlands or Mid-Atlantic chapters.

Rambling, low-growing cranberry vines prefer a base of damp, loamy soil covered by a layer of sand—the conditions of New England's coastal sand dunes. Native wild cranberries thrive on Cape Cod and in other wild places along the coast. However, most of the cranberries produced for commercial sale in New England are cultivated (see Figure 3.9).

Cranberry cultivation began in 1816 when a Cape Cod farmer began to experiment with "sanding," or applying a layer of sand over the wild cranberry vines on his oceanfront property. This first experiment led to nearly two hundred years of development, from hybridizing native cranberry cultivars to building specialized machinery for harvesting, cleaning, and processing the berries.

Most cranberry producers flood their bogs and pick their berries with gas-powered "egg beater" harvesters that churn up the water and knock the berries off the vines. The floating berries are swept from the surface of the water with a boomlike arm and "corralled" in floats.

Though most Americans eat cranberries only at Thanksgiving, New Englanders appreciate them year round. Cranberries are used in relishes and chutneys, dressings for meats and poultry, and baked goods such as cranberry bread.

Low-Bush Blueberries

Like cranberries, blueberries underwent cultivation and domestication in the 1800s. Because their low growing habit made them difficult to pick, wild blueberries were bred for height, resulting in the cultivated high-bush blueberry. This type is most common on the commercial market and is used for blueberry muffins, blueberry pancakes, and the New England desserts listed on p. 106. New England was once the nation's largest pro-

ducer of cultivated blueberries; however, New Jersey production now far surpasses that of New England.

Demand is growing for the more flavorful original blueberry, and the state of Maine leads in its production. "Wild" or low-bush blueberries are an expensive specialty item because they require hand harvesting with old-fashioned metal rakes. These tiny, dark-purple berries are far less sweet than the plump, pale-blue cultivated berries. Their acidic tang and distinctive flavor make them excellent in baked goods, jams, jellies, and preserves.

Fruits and Vegetables

Because New England farming is widely diversified, few crops stand out as major specialties. Tree fruits abound in many areas, and apples are the most widely grown. Many producers offer heirloom varieties. Aroostook County, Maine, is known for round, white, all-purpose potatoes marketed nationwide.

New England Dairy Products

Though too steep and stony for growing crops, the hillsides of New England were acceptable grazing land for dairy cattle, and New England farmers were willing to do the hard work of dairying. However, to remain viable New England's dairy industry has had to change with the times, adapting its methods and products. Some of the dairy products listed here are traditional legacies from colonial times, but others are new.

New England Cheddar

New England cheeses are famous nationwide for their high quality. From the colonial period through the mid-1800s, New England dairies produced much of America's cheese. However, westward expansion soon made the Ohio Valley and the Midwest states more profitable for grazing.

The best-known New England cheese is unquestionably Cheddar, particularly types made in Vermont. True Cheddar cheese is an English product. Settlers arriving in New England brought their cheese-making skills to the New World and copied the cheddaring process to make a colonial version of the Cheddar they knew at home.

New Englanders prefer white Cheddar, made without yellow annatto coloring. They also like their Cheddars sharp and tangy, although mild Cheddars are available. Today most of New England's Cheddar and other cheeses are factory made. The best are produced by co-op factories owned and operated by farm families. New England is also home to scores of artisan cheese makers, many of whom produce single-herd cheeses made by hand on the farm. Some have gone beyond Cheddar to produce sophisticated, European-style soft-ripening cow's-milk cheeses as well as goat's- and sheep's-milk cheeses. Refer to this book's companion website for a list of noteworthy New England cheese makers.

Ice Creams

In the late 1700s New Englanders joined the postcolonial craze for ice cream, and the hand-cranked ice cream churn became a front-porch fixture during the summer months. In the 1800s dairies began producing ice cream on a commercial scale. Early ice cream production was of the Philadelphia style (p. 149), without egg. For this reason New Englanders still refer to ice creams made with egg yolks as **frozen custard,** a term used primarily for soft-serve ice cream.

New England dairy farms are known for the richness and high fat content of their milk, and the region's farmers were in the forefront of the 1980s super-premium ice cream trend. **Super-premium ice creams** have higher butterfat content than standard ice creams, usually measured between 10 and 16 percent. In addition, these rich products are denser than regular ice creams, by USDA regulation having a lower *overrun,* or air content percentage. Super-premiums are typically flavored with expensive and unusual ingredients. New England boasts the nationally known super-premium brand Ben & Jerry's, as well as lesser-known regional brands that offer artisan-quality ice creams to discerning local customers. Refer to this book's companion website for a list of noteworthy New England ice cream makers.

Smoked Meats

When many Americans think of hams and bacon, the Plantation South comes to mind. However, the tradition of curing and smoking pork products is just as venerable in New England, although production is on a smaller scale. The flavors of New England smoked goods are distinctly different from those of the South because of the use of different cures and smoking woods. New England producers use local maple sugar in their cures and maple wood for their smoking fires. Corncobs are another fuel that lends a special flavor. Maple-cured hams and bacon smoked with corncobs are New England specialties enjoyed locally and shipped nationwide.

Canadian bacon is a smoked product unique to New England, believed to be a legacy of Irish immigrants. Unlike American-style bacon made from pork belly, **Canadian bacon** is cured and smoked pork loin and is almost totally lean. Lightly cured and smoked to ensure a moist mouthfeel, this tasty product is served as a breakfast meat and as a lunch or dinner entrée. Refer to this book's companion website for a list of noteworthy New England smokehouses.

New England Desserts

The best-known and most popular New England dessert is pie. In the 1800s a New England farmwife typically made pies by the dozen. New England pie making follows a seasonal cycle of fresh fruit fillings: rhubarb and strawberries in the spring, blueberries and cherries in the summer, and apples and pumpkin in the fall. When pressed for time, New England bakers top fruit fillings with biscuit dough for cobbler, or with streusel-like mixtures to make crisps or crumbles. Winter brings pies made from preserved fruits, nuts, and custards. Traditional New England pie crusts were made with lard, and beef suet enriched mincemeat fillings.

Served for breakfast or dessert, New England cider doughnuts are sweetened with apple cider and coated with a translucent sugar glaze. Fresh cider is the indispensable accompaniment.

Steamed puddings are an English legacy still featured in New England cuisine, although today many classic formulas are baked. Indian pudding is made from cornmeal bound with eggs and milk and flavored with cinnamon and molasses. It's always served with vanilla ice cream.

Boston cream pie is not a pie at all, but spongecake layers filled with vanilla custard and coated with chocolate glaze. Beyond this classic, New England is not well known for cakes. Dense, moist gingerbread is the exception.

■ DINING OUT IN
□
NEW ENGLAND
■

Unlike the large and sparsely populated Plantation South, New England became a region of towns and villages surrounded by small farms and connected by a network of roads. Every town had at least one inn and several taverns serving travelers and locals alike.

From colonial times through the Civil War, eating establishments offered only one set meal served at a predetermined time. In the late 1800s, restaurants offered à la carte menus similar to those used today. Early New England restaurant food was simple, inexpensive, and served in large portions. Locally made hard cider and British ale were the most commonly served beverages; in better establishments imported wines were available to those who could afford them.

Boston Dining

As the capital of the Massachusetts Bay Colony and later the region's premier city, Boston traditionally led New England in commerce and culture as well as fine dining. Boston cooking has been known since colonial times for plentiful, straightforward food of the best quality. Until the 20th century, most of Boston's food goods passed through the Faneuil Hall Market (FAN-yull), originally an indoor-outdoor marketplace and meeting hall, today restored with upscale food stalls, shops, and restaurants (see Figure 3.10).

FIGURE 3.10
Faneuil Hall was Boston's original food market. Mary Lane/Shutterstock

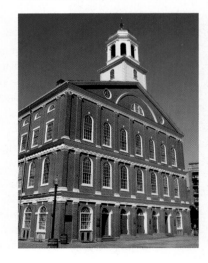

FIGURE 3.11
Parker House rolls are a Boston tradition. Courtesy Leila Milner Parker

Until recently, Boston was not a center of fine cuisine. Instead, Boston's dining establishments were known for serving satisfying, nourishing foods such as baked beans and codfish cakes, in ample portions. Boston restaurants specialized in seafood, serving it fresh and cooking it simply. As one of the world's busiest ports through the 1800s, Boston received food goods from around the globe but used spices and other foreign seasonings sparingly.

The Parker House Hotel

In 1854, a Boston foodservice entrepreneur named Harvey Parker built an ornate five-story hotel on the corner of Tremont and School Streets. The Parker House was one of America's first full-service hotels, offering affluent guests private rooms, à la carte dining, and other services unheard of in lodging houses or inns of the time. For more than 150 years, the Parker House has welcomed the cream of society, including luminaries in the fields of music, art, theater, and letters, as well as American political leaders from Ulysses S. Grant to the Kennedys to Bill Clinton. Parker House chefs created several of New England's best-known defining dishes, including Parker House rolls (Figure 3.11) and modern Boston Cream Pie (p. 100).

Contemporary New England Dining

By the early 1980s, New England chefs were rediscovering their culinary roots along with the rest of America. Many began their training in the venerable old-style restaurants of Boston; others were transplanted from other regions but embraced New England's cuisine as their own.

"New" New England cuisine features traditional ingredients and flavors but expands on them with a broader seasoning palette and modern presentation. As in traditional New England cuisine, seafood stars. Some New England chefs look to colonial cuisine for inspiration, creating new interpretations of English settler and Native American dishes. Refer to this book's companion website for listings of traditional and contemporary New England restaurants.

■□■ IMMIGRANT COOKING IN NEW ENGLAND

Unlike the Plantation South, where second-settler slaves had a huge impact on the cuisine, New England didn't benefit from African-American foodways. Although colonial New England

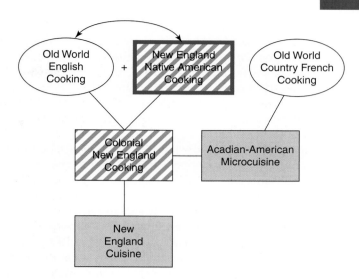

FIGURE 3.12
The Development of New England Cuisine

had a small slave population, abolitionist sentiment grew quickly and slavery ended early. Although this was a positive cultural factor, it had a negative effect on cuisine. Largely spared the evils of slavery, New England unfortunately also missed out on the lively culinary influence of Africa and the Caribbean.

No great second wave of settlement enriched New England cuisine. The region's population remained homogenous until late in history. Well into the 1800s, most of New England's citizens were of British ancestry. Moreover, New England's culinary conservatism created resistance to new foodways. The arrival of scattered groups of later immigrants—even those with vibrant food cultures—did little to change the solidly English-based cuisine of the region.

Portuguese Cuisine in New England

In the mid-1800s, many Portuguese fishermen who initially came to try their luck in the waters off New England decided to remain in the region. Portuguese immigrants established coastal communities in and around Cape Cod, on Nantucket and Martha's Vineyard, and along the Massachusetts and Rhode Island coasts. Arriving from the Azores and later from Cape Verde, the Portuguese brought with them a lively, Latin-influenced cuisine.

Most Portuguese dishes begin with a flavor base of aromatics including onions, garlic, tomatoes, bay leaves, marjoram or oregano, and mild paprika, all sautéed together in olive oil. Favored garnishes include tangy black olives and sliced or chopped hard-cooked eggs. Wine and wine vinegar provide important flavors, and olive oil is used at the table as well as in cooking.

The primary catch of Portuguese fishermen was cod. In New England as in Portugal, salt cod, or *bacalhau*, was one of their most important foods. Simmered in tomato sauce or formed into fritters, salt cod may be served several times a week in Portuguese-American homes. Portuguese-Americans soon began to reproduce the sausage products of their homeland; chouriço and linguiça have become popular ethnic foods across the region. Portuguese soups are warming and sustaining in the cold New England winters. *Caldo verde*, literally "green broth," is a smooth purée of potatoes and Portuguese kale. A signature flavor of Portuguese cooking is the combination of pork and shellfish in a single dish, as in the classic cataplana of pork and clams.

Although Portuguese cuisine is popular with mainstream New Englanders, Portuguese cooking did little to change New England's conservative English-based cuisine. Moreover, there was virtually no reverse influence. The signature dishes of Portuguese cooking were transplanted to America at a late date and with few changes. In seaport New England the imported herbs, spices, olives, and olive oil needed to prepare authentic Portuguese cuisine were readily available, and pork and seafood were already regional specialties. Because there was no need to substitute or improvise, Portuguese cooking in New England remained thoroughly Portuguese. Therefore, a Portuguese-American microcuisine did not develop.

Italian-American Cuisine in New England

During the Age of Immigration in the late 1800s and early 1900s, New England welcomed its share of immigrants, mostly from Europe. Thousands of Italians who arrived in southern New England around the turn of the 20th century brought with them the foodways of their largely southern Italian origins. Many came to New England after living in New York City. In New England as in other American regions, Italian immigrants opened restaurants, pizzerias, and sandwich shops. Variations on the Italian sandwich are popular foods in New England, and are listed on the book's companion website. Having a strong food culture, Italian-Americans also excelled at home cooking.

As you'll learn in Chapter 16, American ingredients significantly altered how Italian immigrants prepared their traditional dishes and gave rise to the Italian-American microcuisine. However, Italian-American ingredients and techniques remained separate, not entering the New England regional cuisine in any meaningful way.

Irish Influence

Fleeing a series of famines, hundreds of thousands of people emigrated from Ireland to the United States in the 1800s. Many Irish entered New England, some through the port of Boston and many more moving northward from New York City. In New England, and particularly in Boston, they became a major social and political force but not a great contributor to cuisine. The best explanation for this fact is that the Irish historically have a minimized food culture and, because of years of famine, they had little experience with all but the simplest forms of cooking. In addition, their Irish cooking style was little different from the established English-based cuisine.

Only a few New England dishes are the result of Irish influence. New England Canadian bacon is modeled after Irish bacon. However, Canadian bacon was an expensive food produced by inland farmers and was not readily available to low-income, city-dwelling Irish immigrants.

Ingenious Irish immigrants substituted Yankee corned beef for Irish bacon, creating a totally new Irish-American dish. Corned beef and cabbage, served across America on St. Patrick's Day, is unlike any dish found in Ireland.

FACTOR 4

Because they are similar to English foods, a limited number of Irish dishes were accepted into New England cuisine.

■ THE FUTURE OF NEW □ ENGLAND CUISINE ■

In its four-hundred-year history, New England cuisine has changed relatively little. Mainstream New Englanders remain culinary conservatives, enjoying the region's signature dishes and seeing little reason to change them. Although the region welcomes various immigrant groups, New Englanders typically enjoy their foreign cuisines in restaurants but rarely add immigrant ingredients to their home cooking.

The double threat of water pollution and overfishing continues to affect the New England fishing industry. Fewer young people are willing to endure the hardships of fishing and lobstering. If measures are not taken to reverse this trend, many of New England's foundation seafoods may disappear from the market.

The recapturing of cultural identity by New England's Native American groups may usher in a renaissance of New England Native American cuisine. Restaurants in Native American–owned casinos boast menus featuring Native American–inspired dishes, and New Englanders are learning about the Native American roots of their own regional cuisine.

◻ TABLE 3.1 NEW ENGLAND DEFINING DISHES

ITEM NAME	HISTORY	DOMINANT INGREDIENTS AND METHOD	OTHER
NEW ENGLAND CHOWDER	The creation of chowder is attributed to 17th-century French-Canadian fishermen. The word "chowder" is derived from *chaudière*, French for *cauldron*. Early chowders were made by layering diced or sliced onions, salt pork, seafood, and ship's biscuits in a cauldron, covering them with water, and simmering them in the fireplace.	Chowders must contain potatoes and a preserved pork product, traditionally salt pork. Modern chowders may contain bacon or ham. Most New England chowders include milk or cream; Rhode Island chowder is tinted pink by a touch of tomato. Seafood chowders are best known, although corn chowder is a summer favorite.	No longer thickened with ship's biscuits, modern chowder is usually thickened with roux. Chowder is traditionally served with oyster crackers.
STEAMER CLAMS (SOFT-SHELL CLAMS)	The quintessential New England appetizer, a pot of steamers begins almost every meal at seaside lobster pounds and clam shacks.	Clams are steamed in the shell and served hot, with steaming liquid, melted butter, and lemon wedges. Strip the membrane off the clams' necks and dip them in the broth to remove grit. Some diners drink the broth as a chaser, avoiding the layer of sediment in the bottom.	Soft-shell clams from Ipswich are the most prized.
FRIED CLAMS	Authentic New England-style fried clams are virtually unknown outside New England. Most other regions serve breaded strips cut from large hard-shell clams.	Soft-shell clams are opened and cleaned, then dredged in a mixture of seasoned flour and cornmeal, dipped in milk-based egg wash, dredged again, and then deep-fried until crisp.	May be served with American-style tartar sauce or simply with lemon wedges.
FRIED CLAM STRIPS	At Howard Johnson's restaurant chain in the 1950s, fried clam strips became a national favorite. These restaurants dotted the newly built interstate highway system.	Large hard-shelled clams are opened and cut into strips, then prepared as fried soft-shell clams.	Prebreaded, frozen clam strips are inferior to the freshly made dish. Outside New England they are the most recognized form of fried clams.
CLAM PIE	A traditional supper dish and relic of the days when hard-shell clams were cheap and plentiful.	Shucked, chopped clams are layered in a casserole with cracker crumbs and creamy clam velouté sauce, topped with pastry, and then baked.	Updated clam pie topped with puff pastry makes an elegant appetizer.
NEW HAVEN WHITE CLAM PIZZA	A specialty of Pepe's, a venerable brick-oven pizzeria in New Haven, Connecticut, this pizza variation is popular throughout New England.	Thin pizza dough is topped with chopped hard-shell clams, dried oregano, olive oil, and grated pecorino romano cheese.	Baked in a very hot oven, the pizza emerges crackly crisp, slightly scorched on the edges, chewy in the center, and full of the briny-sweet flavor of the clams.
OYSTERS ON THE HALF SHELL	Refer to p. 197.	Oysters are traditionally served freshly opened, raw, on the half shell with lemon and cocktail sauce.	In New England oysters are accompanied by oyster crackers or pilot crackers.
SCALLOPED OYSTERS	A classic Boston dish often served for Sunday supper, scalloped oysters was at one time a cheap family meal.	Shucked oysters are seasoned with herbs and dry sherry, enriched with cream, and baked between layers of cracker crumbs.	Today this dish is usually served as an appetizer because of its high cost.
SALT COD CAKES, OR CODDIES	A classic New England breakfast or supper dish, salt cod cakes were served at least once a week in traditional homes.	Salt cod is soaked and poached, shredded, mixed with mashed potatoes, and formed into patties, then fried in bacon drippings or lard.	The cakes are served with eggs at breakfast or with ketchup and coleslaw at supper. Crispy strips of bacon are an optional accompaniment.
CAPE COD "TURKEY"	A fancy preparation of lowly salt cod was humorously labeled "turkey" in an attempt to make a cheap and common food more desirable.	Salt cod is soaked and poached in a court bouillon, drained, napped with a Béchamel sauce enriched with chopped hard-cooked egg, and garnished with parsley and crisp-fried bits of salt pork.	This dish is traditionally accompanied by boiled potatoes, carrots, and beets.

(continued)

☐ TABLE 3.1 NEW ENGLAND DEFINING DISHES (continued)

ITEM NAME	HISTORY	DOMINANT INGREDIENTS AND METHOD	OTHER
FOURTH-OF-JULY SALMON	In New England this seasonal dish was the standard Fourth-of-July holiday meal long before the advent of burgers and hot dogs.	Atlantic salmon is poached in a flavorful court bouillon that is used to make a creamy velouté sauce with chopped boiled egg and fresh dill.	Essential accompaniments are fresh peas pan-steamed with tiny pearl onions and lightly steamed new potatoes.
BOSTON SCROD	A marketing term popularized at the Parker House, "scrod" refers to young codfish or haddock weighing less than 2 pounds.	Scrod fillets are basted with butter and lemon juice, topped with a coating of fresh bread crumbs, and broiled.	Parsleyed potatoes and a green vegetable complete the plate.
NEW ENGLAND SHORE DINNER	New England's most prized summer meal, the "shore dinner" is a restaurant adaptation of the clambake.	A first course of steamer clams is followed by a steamed lobster, corn on the cob, creamy coleslaw, and boiled or French-fried potatoes.	Other than a warm sea breeze and the smell of the ocean, lemon wedges and melted butter are the only accompaniments needed.
BAKED STUFFED LOBSTER	Lobsters were once considered trash fish; a law was passed forbidding daily feeding of lobsters to occupants of New England's prisons and jails as "cruel and inhumane."	A live lobster is split or butterflied, then cleaned; the arms are slit open and the top of the claws removed. Buttered bread crumbs are mixed with the reserved roe and tomalley, lemon zest, and parsley, then packed on top of the lobster flesh. The stuffed lobster is baked until just cooked and crusty-golden on top.	Baked stuffed lobster is served with lemon wedges and melted butter.
CLAMBAKE	Whether done traditionally in a pit on the beach or cooked in a kettle, this collation of seafood and vegetables is a summertime treat.	Purists insist on nothing more than steamer clams, corn on the cob, and new potatoes. A modern clambake may include boiling onions, chicken, fish, and lobster. Melted butter and lemon wedges are the only seasoning.	The operative seasoning comes from the seaweed in which the food is steamed; rockweed, with its many small, moisture-filled nodes, provides both flavor and moisture.
PORTUGUESE SEAFOOD STEW	The classic Portuguese caldeirada shows its Mediterranean origins, with olive oil as both a frying and flavoring medium and the pungent seasoning of tomato, garlic, and Mediterranean herbs.	May feature a selection of fish, like bouillabaisse, or one or more shellfish, as in cioppino. A favorite of New England's Portuguese community is a fish stew based on salt cod.	All versions are accompanied with whole boiled potatoes added just before serving.
BAKED BEANS	A variation of an Algonquian Native American dish of beans and maple syrup cooked in clay pots has become the quintessential New England dish. A crock of baked beans is more than just a side dish.	Dried beans are simmered in a wide-bottomed, earthenware vessel with salt pork, dry mustard, molasses, and/or maple syrup, then baked for hours, producing a sweet-savory pot of creamy beans with a thick sauce.	Unlike the canned beans, classic New England baked beans use no tomato products. Served with brown bread and relish, pickles, or coleslaw, baked beans are the traditional Saturday night supper of the region.
HASH	Named after the verb "to hash," or cut a food into small pieces, hash was made from leftover meat and potatoes. Hash is a diner staple throughout America. New Englanders make it a specialty, devising many different recipes.	Variations include hash made from roasted, braised or corned beef. Add diced red beets for red flannel hash. Chicken, turkey, or clam hash is enriched with cream and/or leftover stuffing. The only constants are diced boiled potatoes and rendered bacon—and a crispy crust resulting from slow cooking in a black cast-iron skillet.	Hash is eaten for supper, accompanied by bread and a salad. At breakfast it's topped with poached or fried eggs.
YANKEE POT ROAST	From the New England hearth cooking tradition; a tough cut of beef is braised in a cast iron casserole on the hearth.	Beef chuck is trussed, browned, and simmered with beef broth until nearly tender; parsnips, turnips, carrots, boiling onions, and round white potatoes are added and cooked until tender.	The jus can be served as is or thickened with a flour slurry. Today's Yankee pot roast is usually oven-cooked, and arrowroot may take the place of flour as thickener.

◻ **TABLE 3.1 NEW ENGLAND DEFINING DISHES** *(continued)*

ITEM NAME	HISTORY	DOMINANT INGREDIENTS AND METHOD	OTHER
NEW ENGLAND BOILED DINNER	Not actually boiled, this dish is a colonial adaptation of English Boiled Beef.	Corned beef brisket and vegetables are simmered in water, resulting in tasty broth. In Irish-American corned beef, the vegetables may include cabbage wedges, carrots, potatoes, and boiling onions. To be considered a real New England boiled dinner, it must also have beets and parsnips.	Boiled dinner is served with condiments such as grated horseradish, brown mustard, horseradish cream, or herbed mayonnaise. Sharp, tangy mustard pickles are a favored accompaniment.
HARVARD BEETS	The bright-red appearance of this classic side dish reminded New England sports fans of Harvard's team color. Yale beets add a touch of orange juice or orange marmalade for a bittersweet citrus note.	Cooked beets are diced and tossed in a sweet-and-sour sauce made from cider vinegar spiced with cloves, sweetened with sugar, thickened with cornstarch, and enriched with butter.	Although the beets were traditionally boiled for the dish, roasted beets better retain both color and flavor.
SUCCOTASH	One of the first foods introduced to settlers by New England Native Americans, the original succotash was a combination of dried corn and dried beans stewed together. Today's succotash is prepared in two versions.	Summer succotash combines fresh sweet corn and lima beans, and often string beans. Pan-steamed to a crisp-tender texture, summer succotash is finished with butter or cream, salt, and pepper. Some recipes add brunoise-cut ham.	Winter succotash is closer to the Native American dish. Dried sweet corn (see p. 184) is simmered with presoaked dried lima or cranberry beans. Bacon or salt pork adds richness and flavor. Finished with cream, the dish develops a rich, custard-like texture and a deep, complex flavor.
FIDDLEHEAD FERNS	Also known as ostrich ferns, fiddleheads are a foraged springtime specialty served in many ways.	After an initial boiling and refreshing, fiddleheads may be sautéed in butter, creamed, or teamed with morel mushrooms.	Contemporary chefs combine them with other spring vegetables in composed salads.
PARSNIPS	In colonial New England, root vegetables were essential for winter survival, and parsnips were particularly popular.	Braised with bacon drippings, then puréed with potatoes, parsnips are seasoned with fresh-ground black pepper to complement their bitter-sweet flavor.	New Englanders consume more parsnips than any other United States region.
PUMPKIN	A traditional Native American food; in New England, pumpkin is not just enjoyed as a pie filling but also as a frequently served vegetable.	Pumpkin soup, baked pumpkin wedges, and pumpkin purée grace the fall and winter table.	In addition to large jack-o'-lantern pumpkins, local markets stock cooking pumpkins throughout New England.
CRANBERRY SAUCE	Seventeenth-century English cooks served fruit sauces with roasted and boiled meats. Cranberry sauce is a colonial adaptation traditionally served with roast turkey.	Fresh cranberries are simmered with sugar until they soften and burst, then cooled to make a chunky, lightly gelled sauce. For jellied cranberry sauce, the mixture is forced through a sieve and the clear sauce is poured into a mold; natural pectins in the berries cause the sauce to set.	Whole-berry cranberry sauce is made by puncturing each berry with a needle before cooking. Berries remain whole and are suspended in a clear, lightly gelled sauce. Uncooked cranberry sauces are made from ground raw berries mixed with other ingredients.
QUICK BREADS	Beginning in the mid-1800s chemically leavened bread products were a staple of all American cooks; no region had more varieties than New England.	Popular quick breads include muffins, soda bread, biscuits, and cornbread. Unlike Plantation South cornbread, New England cornbread includes wheat flour and sugar.	Lesser known New England quick breads include Rye 'n' Injun (made with rye flour and cornmeal) and Boston Brown Bread (made with wheat flour, rye flour, and cornmeal; steamed in a metal mold, such as a coffee can).
JONNYCAKES	The term *jonnycake* is derived from "journey cake," so called because these flat, chewy corn pancakes remained fresh and tender when packed for traveling.	Fine-ground white cornmeal is hydrated with boiling water, which softens and precooks the meal. Traditional jonnycakes are unleavened and seasoned only with salt.	Jonnycakes are served with butter and maple syrup or molasses.

(continued)

☐ **TABLE 3.1 NEW ENGLAND DEFINING DISHES** *(continued)*

ITEM NAME	HISTORY	DOMINANT INGREDIENTS AND METHOD	OTHER
NEW ENGLAND PICKLES AND PRESERVES	The starchy, fatty winter diet of New Englanders required something sharp, crisp, and vegetal to add much-needed vitamins. Fruit-based jams and jellies provided nutrients and color.	New England favorites include home-made tomato ketchup, dilly beans, mustard pickle/chowchow, low-bush blueberry jam/jelly, and beach plum jelly.	Beach plums are uniquely native to coastal New England and are difficult to find fresh, especially outside the region.
PIE	Pie making is a legacy of British foodways. No American region eats as much pie as New England or makes more varieties.	Classic pies include apple pie with sharp Cheddar cheese, blueberry pie, mincemeat pie, pumpkin pie, maple chiffon pie, and maple-walnut pie.	In New England pie is served for breakfast and supper as well as for dessert.
INDIAN PUDDING	This dark, moist dessert is a direct descendant of colonial hasty pudding, itself descended from English boiled puddings. The word *Indian* in the dish's name is a relic of the colonists' name "Indian meal" or "Indian corn" for maize products.	Cornmeal is simmered with milk or cream, enriched with butter, and seasoned with sugar, molasses, and spices. The mixture is water-bath baked or steamed in a mold and served warm.	Indian Pudding is topped with whipped cream or served with vanilla ice cream.
GINGERBREAD/ GINGER COOKIES	New England merchants brought exotic Asian spices to the kitchens of New England. Housewives put these spices to good use replicating the traditional spiced cakes and cookies of Europe, making their products even darker and moister with thick, black Caribbean molasses.	Gingered baked goods range from chemically leavened cakes to soft, chewy cookies to crisp wafers.	New England gingerbread and ginger cookies are fall and winter favorites, often accompanied by a mug of hot apple cider.
FRUIT DESSERTS	New England cooks pioneered the repertoire of homey, homely desserts based on fruit and chemically leavened wheat flour dough that flooded the national cuisine by the end of the 19th century. Common characteristics are ease of preparation and somewhat silly, nonsensical names that attempt to describe the finished dish.	Among the best known: *Cobbler:* topped with dollops of biscuit dough; when baked, looks like the rough cobblestones of colonial streets. *Crisp:* topped with a streusel mixture of flour, sugar, and butter cut together. *Pandowdy:* topped with a sheet of biscuit dough and baked; the browned dough is then broken up and pushed into the juices underneath to absorb and soften.	*Brown Betty/Crunch:* sweetened fruit is layered with buttered bread crumbs and baked golden brown. *Buckle:* fruits are layered in coffeecake batter and covered with streusel topping; as it bakes and rises, the layers tilt and buckle. *Slump/Flummery:* sweetened fruit is simmered until juicy, and wheat flour dumplings are poached in the juice.
SUGAR-IN-SNOW	This sweet treat was served at parties during the early spring sugaring season.	Maple syrup is boiled to between 230°F and 232°F, then drizzled onto plates full of fresh snow. The syrup hardens into spirals of chewy maple candy.	Sugar-in-Snow maple candy is often served with cake doughnuts and/or sour pickles.
MAPLE DESSERTS	Desserts made with maple were originally considered poor people's food. Today they are considered luxurious because now maple syrup and maple sugar are expensive artisanally produced foods.	Maple syrup or maple sugar replaces standard sugar in many desserts and baked goods. Examples include maple cream pie, maple chiffon pie, and maple bread pudding.	Desserts flavored with maple are seasonal to spring but may be served year round.
BOSTON CREAM PIE	This signature New England dessert is a cake, not a pie. Some food historians believe the name arose because many New England Kitchens did not have cake pans, so the batter was baked in pie pans.	Yellow sponge cake layers are filled with vanilla custard and frosted with dark chocolate glaze.	Masking with toasted almonds is optional.

THE ACADIAN-AMERICAN MICROCUISINE

While English colonists were settling the Atlantic coast, French explorers penetrated the area north of New England via the St. Lawrence River and claimed it for France. French settlers followed, establishing lumbering operations, fur tradeposts, and small farms. This area became known as *Acadia*. In the Canadian wilderness Acadian settlers built a unique culture and created a distinctive cuisine. Acadian cooking is based on Canadian indigenous ingredients and native cooking methods—virtually the same as in New England—blended with the imported ingredients and cooking methods of 18th-century country French cuisine.

In the mid-1800s France was forced to cede its Canadian holdings to Great Britain. Acadians unwilling to become British citizens were forcibly expelled. Although many were deported to overseas destinations, some Acadians crossed the border into northern New England. There they developed yet another hybrid cuisine: Acadian-American cooking is a little-known cooking style that combines Acadian cooking with dishes developed by British heritage New England colonists. Go to this book's companion website at www.pearsonhighered.com/sackett for in-depth information on the Acadian-American microcuisine.

FIGURE 3.13

At an Acadian-American festival, cooks prepare a giant ploye, or large buckwheat pancake. Courtesy St. John Valley Times

■ ◻ ■ # STUDY QUESTIONS

1. Describe New England's climate and topography. How did these Factor 1 characteristics affect the region's settlement? How did they affect its agriculture?

2. Why did Native American cooking so greatly influence New England cuisine? List and describe five of New England's defining dishes that are direct descendants of Native American dishes.

3. Recount the history of New England maple syrup production, beginning with Native American methods and on through the 21st century.

4. List the elements of the first settlers' Old World English cuisine. What New World foods replaced them? List and describe at least three hybrid colonial dishes created by New England colonists.

5. Describe Puritan religious beliefs and list three ways in which these beliefs affected New England cuisine.

6. Why were preserved foods so important in colonial New England cooking? Why did they remain in use well into the 20th century? List and describe three New England dishes that feature preserved foods.

7. Discuss the two ways in which New England profited from the sea. How did these sea-related activities affect New England cuisine?

8. What family of fish sustained New England's economy and features prominently in its cuisine? In what form was this fish used as a trade good and to whom was it sold? List and describe three dishes made from this fish.

9. Compare and contrast the modern Thanksgiving meal with the first Thanksgiving meal.

10. Compare and contrast the cuisines of New England and the Plantation South. Although both resulted from the same foundation of Native American and English cooking, why did they develop so differently?

11. Tell the story of the Acadian diaspora as it relates to New England Acadian-Americans. Describe their foodways and defining dishes. Compare and contrast the Acadian-American microcuisine with New England cuisine.

12. Using the information learned in this chapter and your imagination, plan a four-course special-occasion dinner menu featuring New England cuisine.

New England Clam Chowder

with Pilot Crackers

yield: 1 (8-fl.-oz.) appetizer serving plus accompaniment (multiply × 4 for classroom turnout; adjust equipment sizes accordingly)

MASTER RECIPE

production		costing only
1 c.	New England Clam Chowder	1/4 recipe
1	cocktail napkin or 6" doily	1 each
dash	sweet Hungarian paprika	1/16 oz.
tt	fresh-ground white pepper	1/16 oz.
2 tsp.	chopped flat-leaf parsley	1/40 bunch
1 tsp.	cold butter, cut into a thin, square pat	1/6 oz.
3	Pilot Crackers	1/6 recipe

service turnout:

1. Stir the New England Clam Chowder well and ladle it into a 1-qt. saucepan. Heat just to the boil.
2. Plate the dish:
   a. Ladle the soup into a hot 10-fl.-oz. soup cup.
   b. Place the cup slightly to the left on an 8" plate lined with a cocktail napkin.
   c. Sprinkle the soup with paprika, white pepper, and parsley.
   d. Float the pat of butter on the soup's surface.
   e. Place the Pilot Crackers on the plate to the right of the soup cup.

COMPONENT RECIPE

NEW ENGLAND CLAM CHOWDER

yield: 1 qt.

production		costing only
1 dz.	chowder clams, scrubbed and soaked in cold water for 1 hour	1 dz.
1/4 c.	water	n/c
2 slices	lemon	1/6 [90 ct.] lemon
1 oz.	smoked slab bacon or salt pork, rind removed, brunoise-cut	1 1/4 oz. a.p.
2 Tbsp.	butter	1 oz.
1/2 c.	minced yellow onion	2 1/2 oz. a.p.
1/4 c.	peeled, minced celery	1/20 head a.p.
2 Tbsp.	flour	2/3 oz.
as needed	boiling water	n/c
1 sprig	fresh thyme	1/40 bunch a.p.
2 c.	peeled, 3/8"-diced russet potatoes	12 oz. a.p.
1/3 c.	heavy cream	2 3/4 fl. oz.
tt	kosher salt, optional	1/16 oz.

preparation:

1. Prepare the clams:
   a. Place the clams in a heavy 4-qt. saucepan with 1/4 c. water and the lemon slices. Cover the pan and steam over high heat for a minute or two, just until the clams open enough to get a knife inside.
   b. Pour the clams and their liquid into a bowl and cool to room temperature.
   c. Open the clams over the bowl to catch the liquid, and discard the shells.
   d. Rinse the clam meat under cool running water to remove any grit.
   e. Place the clam meat on a cutting board set in a sheet tray, and chop it coarse. Add any liquid that collects on the board and in the tray to the bowl of clam liquid.
   f. Strain the clam liquid through a fine sieve and measure it.
2. Fry the bacon in a 1 1/2-qt. saucepan over low heat about 1 minute, until the drippings render out and the meat is beginning to crisp at the edges. Remove with a slotted spoon and reserve.
3. Add the butter, onion, and celery to the pan and sweat the onion and celery until soft.
4. Add the flour and stir over low heat to make a light blond roux.
5. Add enough boiling water to the clam liquid to total 3 c., and then whisk the liquid into the roux. Add the thyme and potatoes, and then bring the mixture to the simmer.
6. Add the clams and bacon to the soup. Simmer, partially covered, about 20 minutes, until the potatoes and clams are tender.
7. Stir in the cream and add salt only if needed.

holding: open-pan cool and immediately refrigerate in a freshly sanitized, covered, nonreactive container up to 3 days

---

RECIPE VARIATIONS

Summertime Corn and Clam Chowder
Reduce the amount of potatoes to 1 1/2 c. Add 1 c. fresh raw corn kernels in step 6.

New England Lobster Chowder
Omit the clams. Replace the clam liquor/water with 3 1/2 c. lobster stock. Add 1/4 c. cooked, 3/8"-diced lobster meat to each portion at service turnout.

Vermont Cheddar Cheese Soup
with New England Soda Bread

yield: 1 (8-fl.-oz.) appetizer serving plus accompaniment (multiply × 4 for classroom turnout; adjust equipment sizes accordingly)

MASTER RECIPE

production		costing only
1 c.	Vermont Cheddar Cheese Soup	1/4 recipe
1	6" doily or cocktail napkin	1 each
1 tsp.	minced parsley	1/20 bunch a.p.
1 Tbsp.	brunoise-cut red apple	1/4 oz. a.p.
1 wedge	New England Soda Bread	1/10 recipe

service turnout:
1. Stir the Vermont Cheddar Cheese Soup well and ladle it into a 1-qt. saucepan. Heat to just under the boil.
2. Plate the dish:
   a. Ladle the soup into a hot 10-fl.-oz. soup cup.
   b. Place the cup slightly to the left of an 8" plate lined with a 6" doily.
   c. Sprinkle the soup with the parsley and apple.
   d. Place the New England Soda Bread wedge to the right of the soup cup.

COMPONENT RECIPE
VERMONT CHEDDAR CHEESE SOUP

yield: 1 qt.

production		costing only
3 Tbsp.	butter	1 1/2 oz.
3/4 c.	minced yellow onion	3 oz. a.p.
1/4 c.	peeled, minced celery	1/20 head a.p.
1/2 c.	peeled, minced carrot	2 1/2 oz. a.p.
1/2 c.	peeled, chopped tart apple	3 oz. a.p.
3 c.+	Poultry Stock	1/4 recipe
1 c.	peeled, medium-chopped russet potatoes	6 oz. a.p.
1	bay leaf	1/16 oz.
1 sprig	fresh thyme	1/20 bunch a.p.
tt	kosher salt	1/20 oz.
tt	fresh lemon juice	1/8 [90 ct.] lemon
1 c.	grated extra-sharp Vermont Cheddar cheese	4 oz.

preparation:
1. Melt the butter in a 1 1/2-qt. saucepan and sweat the onion, celery, carrot, and apple until soft.
2. Add 3 c. Poultry Stock and the potatoes, bay leaf, thyme, and a little salt. Cover the pan and simmer for about 20 minutes, until the vegetables are very soft.
3a. Remove and discard the herbs and purée the soup with an immersion blender.
   —or—
3b. If an immersion blender is not available:
   a. Remove the herbs and transfer the solids to a blender or food processor.
   b. Add a little of the liquid and purée the solids smooth.
   c. Return the purée to the pan and whisk in the remaining liquid.
   d. Return the soup to the simmer over low heat.
4. Thin with additional stock if necessary.
5. Add a few drops of lemon juice and then whisk in the cheese. Correct the seasoning, adding salt and more lemon juice to taste. Once the cheese has been added, do not heat the soup to a temperature higher than 160°F.

holding: open-pan cool and immediately refrigerate in a freshly sanitized, covered, nonreactive container up to 3 days

---

RECIPE VARIATION

Wisconsin Beer and Cheddar Soup
Replace 1 c. of the stock with lager beer. Replace the Vermont Cheddar with extra-sharp yellow Wisconsin Cheddar. Omit the apple and increase the celery to 1/2 c. Garnish with parsley, paprika, and optional wild rice, boiled or popped in the same manner as popping corn.

Salt Cod Cakes
with Ketchup and Pepper Slaw

yield: 1 (3-oz.) appetizer serving plus accompaniments (multiply × 4 for classroom turnout; adjust equipment sizes accordingly)

🕐 Requires 24 hours advance preparation.

MASTER RECIPE

production		costing only
2 Tbsp.	bacon drippings	n/c
2	Salt Cod Cakes	1/4 recipe
1 leaf	Boston lettuce	1/12 head a.p.
1/2 c.	Pepper Slaw, drained	1/4 recipe
2 Tbsp.	Homemade Tomato Ketchup, in squeeze bottle	1/8 recipe

service turnout:

1. Place an 8" nonstick sauté pan over medium heat, add the bacon drippings, and fry the Salt Cod Cakes about 1 minute on each side, until golden.
2. Plate the dish:
   a. Place the lettuce leaf on the back left of a warm 10" plate.
   b. Fill the leaf with the Pepper Slaw.
   c. Arrange the Salt Cod Cakes overlapping on the front right of the plate.
   d. Drizzle with the Homemade Tomato Ketchup.

COMPONENT RECIPE

SALT COD CAKES

yield: 8 (1 1/2-oz.) cakes

(requires 24 hours advance preparation)

production		costing only
6 oz.	best-quality imported salt cod	6 oz.
1/2 c.	fine-chopped yellow onion	2 1/2 oz.
1/4 c.	fine-chopped peeled celery	1/20 head a.p.
1/4 c.	fine-chopped peeled carrot	3/4 oz. a.p.
1	bay leaf	1/20 oz.
as needed	water	n/c
2 c.	peeled, 1/2"-diced russet potatoes	10 oz. a.p.
tt	kosher salt	1/20 oz.
2 Tbsp.	room-temperature butter	1 oz.
tt	fresh-ground white pepper	1/20 oz.
pinch	ground ginger	1/20 oz.
1/4 c.	chopped scallion	1/4 bunch a.p.
±1	egg, beaten	±1 each or 2 oz.

first day preparation:

1. Rinse the salt cod thoroughly, then soak it in cold water 4 hours.
2. Change the water and soak 4 hours longer.
3. Repeat, changing the water at 4-hour intervals as practical, with longer soaking overnight.

second day preparation:

4. Poach the cod:
   a. Drain the cod and place it in a small saucepan with the onion, celery, carrot, and bay leaf.
   b. Cover with cold water, bring to the simmer, and cook at a gentle simmer 20 minutes, until the fish flakes easily. Top up the water level with boiling water if necessary to keep the cod covered.
   c. Cool the cod in the liquid.
5. Prepare the potato binder:
   a. Boil the potatoes in lightly salted water until tender.
   b. Drain the potatoes and, while still hot, push them through a ricer or coarse sieve.
   c. Stir in the butter, white pepper, and ginger. Cool to room temperature.
6. Drain the salt cod and tear it into fine shreds, leaving any bits of mirepoix that remain on the fish. Discard the bay leaf and poaching liquid.
7. Mix together the potatoes, salt cod, and scallion. Work in enough egg to bind the mixture. Correct the seasoning.
8. Form the mixture into 8 flat cakes about 1/2" thick.

holding: refrigerate with pan liner between layers in a covered nonreactive container up to 4 days; may be frozen up to 1 month

COMPONENT RECIPE
PEPPER SLAW

yield: 2 c.

production		costing only
2 1/2 c.	fine-chopped Savoy or other tender cabbage	3/4 lb. a.p.
1 c.	water	n/c
1/2 c.	cider vinegar	4 fl. oz.
1 Tbsp.	kosher salt	1/2 oz.
2 Tbsp.	sugar	1 oz.
1/4 c.	1/4"-diced red bell pepper	2 oz. a.p.
1/4 c.	1/4"-diced green bell pepper	2 oz. a.p.
1/4 c.	fine-chopped yellow onion	1 1/4 oz. a.p.
1/4 tsp.	celery seeds	1/16 oz.
tt	fresh-ground black pepper	1 oz.
1 Tbsp.	corn oil	1/2 fl. oz.

preparation:
1. Wilt and season the cabbage:
   a. Place the cabbage in a stainless bowl and have a colander ready in a sink.
   b. Bring the water, vinegar, salt, and sugar to the boil in a nonreactive saucepan and simmer a few seconds, until the salt and sugar are dissolved.
   c. Immediately pour the hot liquid over the cabbage and toss well. Let stand 2 to 3 minutes, tossing occasionally, until the cabbage is slightly wilted.
   d. Pour the cabbage into the colander and squeeze out all excess moisture.
   e. Return the cabbage to the bowl and cool to room temperature.
2. Toss in the remaining ingredients and correct the seasoning.

holding: refrigerate in a freshly sanitized, covered nonreactive container up to 3 days (if holding, omit the onion; cut and add just before service)

RECIPE VARIATION
Salmon Cakes with Ketchup and Pepper Slaw
Replace the cooked, flaked salt cod with 6 oz. flaked poached salmon.

APPETIZERS

Petite Tourtière
with Pickled Beets

yield: 1 (6-oz.) appetizer serving plus accompaniment (multiply ✕ 4 for classroom turnout)

🕐 Accompaniment requires 2 days advance preparation.

MASTER RECIPE

production		costing only
1	Petite Tourtière	1/4 recipe
1 bouquet	watercress	1/6 bunch
1/2 c.	Pickled Beets, p. 431 (prepared without eggs, batonnet-cut)	1/4 recipe

service turnout:
1. Place the Petite Tourtière on a sizzle plate and bake in a 400°F oven about 10 minutes, until hot through and crisp.
2. Plate the dish:
   a. Place the watercress on the back right of a warm 10" plate.
   b. Unmold the tourtière and place it on the plate slightly left of center.
   c. Drain the Pickled Beets well and mound on the watercress stems next to the tourtière.

COMPONENT RECIPE
PETITE TOURTIÈRES

yield: 4 (4 1/2") individual tourtières, about 6 oz. each

production		costing only
4 Tbsp.	bacon drippings	n/c
2 c.	fine-chopped yellow onion	10 oz. a.p.
2 tsp.	minced garlic	1/4 oz. a.p.
1 tsp.	ground dried sage	1/16 oz.
1 tsp.	granulated onion	1/16 oz.
1/2 tsp.	ground allspice	1/16 oz.
1/2 tsp.	dried thyme	1/16 oz.
1/2 tsp.	dried savory	1/16 oz.
1 lb.	ground pork shoulder	1 lb.
1/2 lb.	ground chuck	1/2 lb.
tt	kosher salt	1/6 oz.
4 Tbsp.	flour	1 1/3 oz.
1 c.	diced canned tomatoes in juice	8 fl. oz.
1/2 c.	dried bread crumbs	1 1/2 oz.
2 Tbsp.	chopped flat-leaf parsley	1/10 bunch
3/4	egg, beaten	1 each or 1 1/2 oz.
tt	fresh-ground black pepper	
18 oz.	American Flaky Pastry	1 1/2 recipe
4 Tbsp.	dried bread crumbs	3/4 oz.
as needed	water	n/c
1/4	egg, beaten with a few drops of water	n/c or 1/2 oz.

preparation:
1. Prepare the filling:
   a. Heat the bacon drippings in a sauté pan, add the onion, and sauté over medium heat until soft.
   b. Add the garlic, sage, granulated onion, allspice, thyme, and savory and sauté a few seconds longer.
   c. Add the ground pork and ground chuck and a little salt. Cook over low heat, stirring to break up the lumps, about 30 seconds, until the meat has just lost its red color.
   d. Push the meat to the side, tilt the pan, and allow the fat to pool in the low end. Spoon off all but 4 Tbsp. fat.
   e. Stir in the flour and make a white roux, and then stir the meat into it.
   f. Add the tomatoes and cook, stirring, about 3 minutes, until the liquids in the pan thicken and reduce to almost dry.
   g. Season with salt.
   h. Cool to room temperature and then refrigerate until cold.
   i. Mix 1/2 c. bread crumbs, the parsley, the 3/4 beaten egg, and a generous amount of pepper into the cold meat filling.
2. Preheat an oven to 400°F.
3. Make up the tourtières:
   a. Roll out the American Flaky Pastry to an even 3/8" thickness.
   b. Cut out 4 (7 1/2") circles and 4 (5 1/4") circles.
   c. Line 4 (4 3/8" ✕ 1 3/16") round disposable aluminum pie pans with the larger dough circles, but do not flute the edges.
   d. Refrigerate the lined pans and additional circles at least 20 minutes.
   e. Sprinkle 1 Tbsp. bread crumbs into the bottom of each pastry shell.
   f. Divide the meat filling into the shells and press to firm.
   g. Moisten the edges of the pastry with a little water and place the smaller dough circles on top. Roll the edges under and flute.
   h. Cut decorative slashes in the pastry tops.
   i. Brush the tops with egg wash.
4. Place the tourtières on a half sheet tray and bake about 25 minutes, until the pastry is golden brown.
5. Remove the Tourtières to a rack and cool to room temperature.

holding: refrigerate, loosely covered with plastic wrap up to 4 days

---

RECIPE VARIATION

Petite Tourtière with Homemade Ketchup and Creamy Coleslaw
Replace the Pickled Beets and watercress with 3 Tbsp. Homemade Ketchup and Coleslaw.

Watercress and Boston Lettuce Salad

with Maple Vinaigrette, Cranberries, and Walnut-Crusted Cheddar Crouton

yield: 1 (5-oz.) appetizer serving (multiply × 4 for classroom turnout)

MASTER RECIPE

production		costing only
1	Walnut-Crusted Cheddar Crouton	1/4 recipe
1/2 head	Boston lettuce, washed, dried, and pulled into bite-size pieces	1/3 head a.p.
1/3 bunch	watercress, largest stems removed	1/3 bunch a.p.
4 Tbsp.	Maple Vinaigrette	1/4 recipe
1 Tbsp.	Rehydrated Cranberries	1/4 recipe

service turnout:
1. Place the Walnut-Crusted Cheddar Crouton on a sizzle pan and bake at 400°F about 3 minutes, until heated through.
2. In a small bowl, toss the lettuce and watercress with the Maple Vinaigrette.
3. Plate the dish:
   a. Mound the salad on a cool 10" plate.
   b. Place the crouton on top of the salad.
   c. Scatter the Rehydrated Cranberries over the salad.

COMPONENT RECIPE

WALNUT-CRUSTED CHEDDAR CROUTONS

yield: 4 croutons

production		costing only
2 Tbsp.	butter	1 oz.
4 slices	3 1/2"-diameter French or Italian baguette, cut 3/8" thick	% of bread
3/4 c.	grated extra-sharp Vermont Cheddar cheese	3 oz.
1/2	egg, beaten with 1 Tbsp. water	1 each or 1 oz.
1/2 c.	medium-chopped walnuts	3 oz.

preparation:
1. Begin preparing the croutons:
   a. Heat an 8" nonstick sauté pan, melt the butter over medium heat and add the bread slices.
   b. Remove the pan from the heat and press 1/4 of the cheese in an even layer on each slice.
   c. Cover the pan and return it to low heat. Heat about 1 minute, until the bottoms of the croutons are light brown and the cheese has melted slightly.
   d. Cool the croutons on a rack.
2. Brush the top and sides of each crouton with egg wash, then press the walnuts onto it.
3. Return the croutons to the rack and refrigerate uncovered 1 hour.

holding: refrigerate with pan liner between layers in a covered nonreactive container up to 4 days

COMPONENT RECIPE

MAPLE VINAIGRETTE

yield: 1 c.

production		costing only
3 Tbsp.	pure maple syrup	1 1/2 fl. oz.
1 tsp.	kosher salt	1/16 oz.
2 tsp.	Dijon mustard	1/3 fl. oz.
1 Tbsp.	minced shallot	1/2 oz. a.p.
5 Tbsp.	cider vinegar	2 1/2 fl. oz.
2/3 c.	corn oil	5 1/3 fl. oz.

preparation:
1a. Prepare the vinaigrette by hand:
   a. In a small bowl, whisk together the syrup, salt, mustard, shallot, and vinegar.
   b. Whisk in the oil in a thin stream to create an emulsified vinaigrette.
   c. Correct the seasoning.
   —or—
1b. Prepare the vinaigrette in a blender or with an immersion blender.

holding: store in a freshly sanitized, covered nonreactive container at room temperature up to 24 hours; refrigerate up to 1 month; will separate; re-emulsify in a blender or with an immersion blender

COMPONENT RECIPE

RE-HYDRATED CRANBERRIES

yield: 4 Tbsp.

production		costing only
3 Tbsp.	dried cranberries	3/4 oz.
1/2 c.	water	n/c
1 Tbsp.	light rum	1/2 fl. oz.

preparation:
1. Place the cranberries in a very small bowl or ramekin.
2. Bring the water and rum to the simmer in a small sauté pan, then pour the mixture over the cranberries.
3. Steep 15 minutes, until the cranberries are plump and the liquid absorbed.

holding: refrigerate in a freshly sanitized, covered, nonreactive container up to 1 month

---

RECIPE VARIATION

Watercress and Boston Lettuce Salad with Mustard Vinaigrette, Grape Tomatoes, and Walnut-Crusted Goat Cheese Crouton
Replace the Maple Vinaigrette with Basic Vinaigrette made with additional mustard. Replace the Vermont Cheddar with New England goat cheese. Replace the Rehydrated Cranberries with grape tomatoes.

Tarragon Lobster Salad in Lobster Shell

yield: 1 (5-oz.) appetizer serving (multiply × 4 for classroom turnout)

MASTER RECIPE

production		costing only
1 c.	Tarragon Lobster Salad and Lobster Half Shell	1/4 recipe
1 Tbsp.	peeled, brunoise-cut seedless cucumber	1 oz. a.p.
1 Tbsp.	brunoise-cut ripe tomato (from tomatoes sliced later in the recipe)	n/c
2 tsp.	chopped scallion	1/20 bunch a.p.
2 tsp.	chopped fresh tarragon leaves	1/20 bunch a.p.
1 large sprig	fresh tarragon	1/8 bunch a.p.
3 slices	miniature tomato, preferably cut from multicolored tomatoes	approx. 1 oz. a.p.

service turnout:

1. Toss the Tarragon Lobster Salad with the cucumber, brunoise-cut tomato, scallion, and chopped tarragon.
2. Fill the Lobster Half Shell with the salad.
3. Plate the dish:
   a. Place the filled lobster shell on a 10" rectangular or oval plate.
   b. Arrange the tarragon sprig behind it.
   c. Arrange the tomato slices on the front left of the plate.

COMPONENT RECIPE

TARRAGON LOBSTER SALAD AND LOBSTER HALF SHELLS

yield: 1 qt. (approx. 20 oz.) plus 4 half shells

production		costing only
as needed	water	n/c
2	1 1/2-lb. live cold-water lobsters	3 lb.
1 c.	Shellfish Stock	1/16 recipe
1 Tbsp.	minced lemon zest	n/c
2 Tbsp.	fresh lemon juice	1/4 [90 ct.] lemon
2 Tbsp.	minced shallot	1 oz. a.p.
1/2 c.	mayonnaise	4 fl. oz.
1/4 c.	sour cream	2 fl. oz.
as available	lobster tomalley and minced roe from step #2c	n/c
2 Tbsp.	chopped tarragon leaves	1/6 bunch a.p.
as needed	kosher salt	1/16 oz.
tt	fine-ground white pepper	1/16 oz.
tt	sugar	1/16 oz.

preparation:

1. Cook the lobsters:
   a. Place 1" of water in a 7-qt. saucepot with a tight-fitting lid. Bring to the boil.
   b. Add the lobsters and cover the pot. Steam 18 to 20 minutes, checking toward the end of the cooking time to make sure that the water does not run dry.
   c. Remove the lobsters and cool to room temperature.
2. Fabricate the lobsters, working on a cutting board placed inside a sheet tray to catch the juices:
   a. Twist off the lobster forearms and claws and reserve them.
   b. Using a sharp, heavy chef knife, split each lobster exactly in half lengthwise. Be careful not to detach the tails from the body sections.
   c. Remove and reserve the green tomalley and red roe, if any. Remove and discard the gills. Remove the tail meat from the lobster halves.
   d. Crack the lobster claws and remove the meat. Slit open the forearms and remove the meat.
   e. Cut all the lobster meat into 3/4" dice.
3. Prepare the Lobster Half Shells:
   a. Working carefully to keep the red exterior shells intact, remove the soft inner cartilage from the lobster bodies. Pick out the backfin meat from the cartilage and add it to the diced meat. (Reserve the cartilage and juices remaining in the tray for making shellfish stock.)
   b. Clean out all of the remaining debris from the half shells and rinse them well. Blot the half shells dry, seal individually in plastic bags, and immediately refrigerate.
4. Place the Shellfish Stock in an 8" sauté pan and carefully reduce to about 2 Tbsp. of glaze. Cool.
5. Mix the shellfish glaze, lemon zest, lemon juice, shallot, mayonnaise, sour cream, tomalley, roe, and tarragon. Taste and then season with salt if needed, white pepper, and a little sugar.
6. Mix the dressing and the lobster meat.

holding: refrigerate in a freshly sanitized, covered, nonreactive container up to 3 days

---

RECIPE VARIATION

Dilled Lobster Salad in Lobster Shell
Replace the tarragon with dill.

Halibut Poached in Hard Cider

with Apples and Parsnips, Served with Sautéed Kale and Potato Croquettes

yield: 1 (7-oz.) entrée serving plus accompaniments (multiply × 4 for classroom turnout; adjust equipment sizes accordingly)

MASTER RECIPE

production		costing only
3/4 c.	hard apple cider	6 fl. oz.
3/4 c.	Fish Stock	1/20 recipe
1 Tbsp.	minced shallot	1/4 oz. a.p.
1 sprig	fresh thyme	1/12 bunch a.p.
tt	kosher salt	1/16 oz.
1	7-oz. Atlantic halibut fillet	7 oz.
1 c.	peeled, 3/4"-diced Granny Smith apple, stored in acidulated water	6 oz. a.p.
3/4 c.	peeled, 2" batonnet-cut parsnip, blanched al dente, refreshed	7 oz. a.p.
1/4 c.	peeled, julienne carrot	1 oz. a.p.
2 Tbsp.	butter	1 oz.
3 c.	cleaned, deveined, chiffonade-cut kale	6 oz. a.p.
2	Potato Croquettes	1/4 recipe
as needed	frying compound or corn oil	% used
1 tsp.	arrowroot, dissolved in 2 tsp. water	1/16 oz.
1 tsp.	minced flat-leaf parsley	1/20 bunch a.p.

service turnout:
1. Poach the fish:
   a. Place the cider, Fish Stock, shallot, thyme, and a little salt in an 8" sauté pan and bring to the boil.
   b. Add the halibut, apple, parsnip, and carrot. Cover and simmer about 3 minutes.
   c. Turn the fish over, cover, and simmer 3 minutes longer, until the fish is almost done.
   d. Remove the halibut and vegetables and hold hot.
   e. Boil the poaching liquid until reduced by about half.
2. Heat a 10" sauté pan and add the butter, kale, and a little salt. Sauté until wilted.
3. Deep-fry the Potato Croquettes at 375°F about 1 minute, until golden and heated through. Drain on absorbent paper.
4. Plate the dish:
   a. Mound the kale on the back left center of a hot 12" plate.
   b. Place the halibut on the front of the plate, propped against the kale.
   c. Mound the vegetables to the right of the kale.
   d. Stir up the arrowroot slurry and, with the cooking liquid at a simmer, whisk in enough slurry to thicken the sauce to a nappé consistency.
   e. Spoon the sauce over the halibut.
   f. Arrange the croquettes behind the vegetables.
   g. Sprinkle the vegetables with the parsley.

COMPONENT RECIPE
POTATO CROQUETTES

yield: 8 croquettes

production		costing only
4 c.	peeled, 1/2"-diced russet potatoes	1 1/2 lb. a.p.
as needed	water	n/c
tt	kosher salt	1/16 oz.
2 Tbsp.	softened butter	1 oz.
1/4 c.	sour cream	2 fl. oz.
tt	fine-ground white pepper	1/16 oz.
1	egg, beaten	1 each or 2 oz.
1 Tbsp.	minced flat-leaf parsley	1/20 bunch a.p.
as needed	flour	1/2 oz.
1 c.	fine dried bread crumbs	2 oz.

preparation:
1. Prepare the potato mixture:
   a. Boil the potatoes in salted water until tender.
   b. Drain the potatoes and, while still hot, push them through a ricer or coarse sieve.
   c. Stir in the butter, sour cream, and white pepper.
   d. Season with salt and cool to room temperature.
   e. Stir in half of the egg and the parsley, then cover and refrigerate 1 hour.
2. Beat 1 Tbsp. water into the remaining egg and reserve this egg wash.
3. Fabricate the croquettes:
   a. With floured hands, form the potato mixture into 8 football-shaped croquettes.
   b. Dredge each croquette in the flour, coat with egg wash, and then roll firmly in the bread crumbs.
   c. Place the croquettes on a rack set over a sheet tray and refrigerate, uncovered, 1 hour longer.

holding: refrigerate in one layer in a freshly sanitized, covered, nonreactive container up to 5 days

---

RECIPE VARIATION
Codfish Cheeks Poached in Hard Cider with Apples and Parsnips, Served with Sautéed Kale and Potato Croquettes
Replace the halibut with 7 (1-oz.) codfish cheeks.

Broiled Scrod in Lemon Butter Sauce

with Parsley Potatoes, Broiled Tomato, and Summer Succotash

yield: 1 (7-oz.) entrée serving plus accompaniments (multiply × 4 for classroom turnout; adjust equipment sizes accordingly)

MASTER RECIPE

production		costing only
1 1/2 c.	Summer Succotash, with cooking liquid	1/4 recipe
3	small, new Maine white potatoes, boiled and peeled	4 oz. a.p.
2 Tbsp.	clarified butter	1 1/2 oz. a.p.
1	7-oz. scrod fillet, trimmed and pinned	8 oz. a.p.
1	Tomato Crown	1/4 recipe
tt	kosher salt	1/16 oz.
tt	fine-ground white pepper	1/16 oz.
1/4 c.	Butter-Toasted Bread Crumbs	1/8 recipe
dash	sweet Hungarian paprika	1/16 oz.
1 Tbsp.	butter	1/2 oz.
2 Tbsp.	chopped flat-leaf parsley	1/10 bunch a.p.
1/4 c.	Fish Stock	1/64 recipe
1 Tbsp.	fresh lemon juice	1/4 [90 ct.] lemon
6 Tbsp.	butter	3 oz.
1 sprig	flat-leaf parsley	1/20 bunch a.p.

service turnout:

1. Place the Summer Succotash and potatoes in a 10" sauté pan, cover, and heat over medium heat.

2. Cook the fish:
   a. Heat an 8" nonstick sauté pan until very hot and add 2 tsp. clarified butter.
   b. Add the scrod fillet, skin side down, along with the Tomato Crown placed upright.
   c. Season both the tomato and the scrod with salt and white pepper and brush with the remaining clarified butter.
   d. Place under a broiler about 2 minutes, until almost done.
   e. Sprinkle the scrod and tomato with the Butter-Toasted Bread Crumbs and paprika.
   f. Finish in a 400°F oven about 2 minutes, until the crumbs are golden brown.

3. Finish and plate the dish:
   a. Spoon the succotash onto the back left of a hot 12" plate, retaining the potatoes in the pan.
   b. Place the pan over low heat, add 1 Tbsp. butter, season the potatoes with salt, and toss with the parsley.
   c. Using a wide offset spatula, transfer the scrod to the front left of the plate extending from 10 to 5 o'clock. Place the tomato crown at 12 o'clock.
   d. Arrange the potatoes on the back right of the plate.
   e. Add the Fish Stock, lemon juice, and a little salt to the pan. Bring to the boil and work in the remaining butter to form an emulsion.
   f. Nap the scrod and vegetables with the sauce.
   g. Stick the parsley sprig upright between the scrod and the potatoes.

COMPONENT RECIPE

SUMMER SUCCOTASH

yield: 6 c.

production		costing only
2 Tbsp.	butter	1 oz.
1/2 c.	minced yellow onion	2 1/2 oz. a.p.
1/2 c.	brunoise-cut smoked ham	1 1/2 oz. a.p.
2 c.	shelled lima beans	2 lb. a.p.
±1 c.	water	n/c
2 c.	fresh corn kernels	2 lg. ears a.p.
tt	kosher salt	1/16 oz.
2 Tbsp.	butter	1 oz.
10 oz.	3/4" diagonal-cut green beans, blanched, refreshed	3/4 lb. a.p.

preparation:

1. Place 2 Tbsp. butter and the onion and ham in a 10" nonstick sauté pan. Cover and sweat over very low heat about 1 minute.
2. Add the lima beans and water to the pan, mix with the vegetables and ham, cover the pan, and simmer briskly about 3 minutes, until the lima beans are almost tender.
3. Add the corn, cover, and continue to simmer about 2 minutes longer, until the corn is just cooked through.
4. Uncover and increase the heat. Boil, tossing, until only about 1/4 c. liquid remains in the pan. Correct the salt and work in the remaining butter.
5. Open-pan cool to room temperature, then toss in the green beans.

holding: refrigerate in a freshly sanitized, covered, nonreactive container up to 5 days

---

RECIPE VARIATION

Broiled Cod in Lemon Butter Sauce with Parsley Potatoes, Broiled Tomato, and Summer Succotash
Replace the scrod fillet with cod fillet.

Fourth-of-July Grilled Salmon

with Dill Sauce, Fresh Peas, and New Potatoes

yield: 1 (7-oz.) entrée serving plus accompaniments (multiply × 4 for classroom turnout; adjust equipment sizes accordingly)

MASTER RECIPE

production		costing only
1	Marinated Salmon Pinwheel	1/4 recipe
1/4 c.	water	n/c
5 to 7	new or fingerling potatoes, scrubbed, boiled	4 oz. a.p.
1 c.	shelled fresh peas	1 lb. a.p.
tt	kosher salt	1/16 oz.
2 Tbsp.	butter	1 oz.
tt	fine-ground white pepper	1/16 oz.
1/4 c.	Dilled Sour Cream Sauce	1/4 recipe
2 tsp.	chopped fresh dill	1/40 bunch a.p.

service turnout:

1. Grill the salmon:
   a. Mark the Marinated Salmon Pinwheel on a hot char-grill.
   b. Rotate 90 degrees and grill a total of 2 1/2 minutes.
   c. Turn and grill about 2 minutes longer, until the salmon is medium rare.
   d. Hold hot.
2. Cook the vegetables:
   a. Place the water, potatoes, peas, and a little salt in an 8" sauté pan. Cover and heat over medium heat about 3 minutes, until the potatoes are hot and the peas just cooked.
   b. Uncover and work in the butter to form an emulsion.
   c. Season with salt and white pepper.
3. Plate the dish:
   a. Spoon the peas onto a hot 12" plate and make a well in the center.
   b. Place the salmon in the center and remove the cocktail pick.
   c. Arrange the potatoes around the salmon.
   d. Spoon a diagonal line of Dilled Sour Cream Sauce across the salmon from 10 o'clock to 4 o'clock.
   e. Sprinkle a line of dill on the sauce.

COMPONENT RECIPE

MARINATED SALMON PINWHEELS

yield: 4 (7-oz.) pinwheels

production		costing only
4	9-oz., 1"-thick center-cut salmon steaks	2 1/4 lb. a.p.
1 c.	New England Salmon Marinade	1 recipe

preparation:

1. Remove the skin from each salmon steak in one piece. Wash the skin, blot dry, and reserve.
2. Using a sharp, flexible knife, remove the salmon fillet strips from either side of the center bones. Keeping the fillets in pairs, trim away any membrane and remove any pin bones.
3. Assemble the pinwheels:
   a. Choosing one pair of fillets, lay one of the pieces on the work surface on its side.
   b. Place the thin end of the other fillet piece on its side against the thick end of the first fillet.
   c. Roll the fillets together into a pinwheel shape.
   d. Wrap a strip of skin around the rim of the pinwheel and secure the pinwheel and skin together with a cocktail pick.
   e. Repeat with the remaining fillet pairs to make 4 pinwheels.
4. Place the pinwheels in a freshly sanitized nonreactive container just large enough to hold them in one layer.
5. Pour the New England Salmon Marinade over the fillets. Cover and refrigerate 1 hour.
6. Turn the pinwheels over and refrigerate 1 hour longer.

holding: after 2 hours, drain off the marinade; hold refrigerated up to 24 hours

NEW ENGLAND SALMON MARINADE

yield: 1 c.

production		costing only
2 Tbsp.	fresh lemon juice	1/4 [90 ct.] lemon
2 Tbsp.	minced lemon zest	n/c
2 Tbsp.	minced shallot	1 oz. a.p.
2 Tbsp.	Dijon mustard	1 fl. oz.
1 Tbsp.	prepared horseradish	1/2 fl. oz.
1 Tbsp.	pure maple syrup	1/2 fl. oz.
tt	fresh-ground black pepper	1/16 oz.
2 tsp.	kosher salt	1/16 oz.
1/2 c.	corn oil	4 oz.

preparation:
1. Mix together all ingredients except the oil.
2. Whisk in the oil in a thin stream to create an emulsion.

holding: refrigerate in a freshly sanitized, covered, nonreactive container up to 1 week; bring to room temperature before using; re-emulsify in a blender or with an immersion blender

DILLED SOUR CREAM SAUCE

yield: 1 c.

production		costing only
2 Tbsp.	minced shallot	1 oz. a.p.
1 Tbsp.	minced lemon zest	n/c
1 Tbsp.	Dijon mustard	1/2 fl. oz.
2 Tbsp.	minced dill	1/16 bunch a.p.
1 tsp.	pure maple syrup	1/6 fl. oz.
1/4 c.	mayonnaise	2 fl. oz.
1/2 c.	sour cream	4 fl. oz.
tt	kosher salt	1/16 oz.
tt	fine-ground white pepper	1/16 oz.
±2 Tbsp.	half-and-half	±1 fl. oz.

preparation:
1. Mix together all ingredients except the half-and-half.
2. Whisk in enough half-and-half to make the sauce thick yet spoonable.
3. Taste and correct the seasoning.

holding: refrigerate in a freshly sanitized, covered, nonreactive container up to 5 days

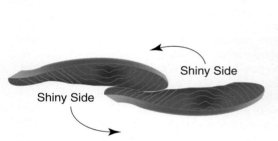

1 Place the thin end of one fillet piece on its side against the thick end of another fillet.

2 Roll the fillets together into a pinwheel shape.

ENTREES

RECIPE VARIATIONS

Early-Spring Grilled Salmon with Chervil Sauce, Asparagus, and New Potatoes
Replace the dill with chervil. Replace the peas with peeled, 1" diagonal-cut asparagus.

Late-Summer Grilled Salmon with Dill Sauce, Poached Cucumbers, and New Potatoes
Replace the peas with peeled, seeded cucumbers cut into lozenge shapes.

Portuguese Mussel Stew
with Potatoes and Peppers

yield: 1 (7-oz.) e.p. entrée serving (multiply × 4 for classroom turnout; adjust equipment sizes accordingly)

MASTER RECIPE

production		costing only
1	whole Maine potato, boiled and peeled	4 oz. a.p.
1 lb.	farm-raised mussels, scrubbed, soaked, debearded	1 lb.
1/4 c.	white wine	2 fl. oz.
6 Tbsp.	pure golden olive oil	3 fl. oz.
1/2 c.	peeled, julienne red bell pepper	4 oz. a.p.
1/4 c.	peeled, julienne yellow bell pepper	2 oz. a.p.
1/2 c.	peeled, julienne green bell pepper	4 oz. a.p.
tt	kosher salt	1/16 oz.
1/2 c.	medium-sliced yellow onion	2 1/2 oz. a.p.
1 Tbsp.	minced garlic	1/3 oz. a.p.
2	bay leaves	1/16 oz.
pinch	dried oregano	1/16 oz.
1 sprig	fresh thyme	1/8 bunch a.p.
1 c.	vine-ripe tomato concassée	12 oz. a.p.
1 c.	Fish Stock, hot in steam table	1/16 recipe
tt	fresh-ground black pepper	1/16 oz.
1 Tbsp.	chopped flat-leaf parsley	1/20 bunch a.p.
1 Tbsp.	chopped pitted brine-cured black olives	1/2 oz. a.p.

service turnout:

1. Have ready a small colander set over a bowl, and a fine-mesh strainer.
2. Heat the potato in a steamer or microwave oven.
3. Place the mussels and wine in a 10" sauté pan, cover, and pan-steam over high heat about 1 minute, until the shells begin to open.
4. Pour the mussels and their pan juices into the colander.
5. Rinse out the pan, place over high heat, and add about 1 Tbsp. oil. Sauté the bell peppers with a little salt until al dente and place them on top of the mussels.
6. Add the remaining oil and sauté the onion, garlic, bay leaves, oregano, and thyme over high heat for a few seconds. Add the tomatoes and sauté until dry.
7. Add the Fish Stock and bring to the boil, then add the mussels and bell peppers. Strain the mussel juices into the pan. Cover the pan and heat the mussels, keeping on the heat no longer than 1 minute.
8. Plate the dish:
   a. Spoon the mussels into a hot 12" pasta plate. Remove and discard the bay leaves.
   b. Press the potato down into the mussels in the center of the plate.
   c. Spoon the pan juices over the mussels and potato.
   d. Grind black pepper over the top.
   e. Sprinkle with parsley and chopped olives.

RECIPE VARIATIONS

Portuguese Fisherman's Stew with Potatoes and Peppers
Replace 2/3 of the mussels with a 4-oz. halibut fillet, 6 littleneck or steamer clams, and 3 trimmed sea scallops. Increase the Fish Stock to 2 c.

Portuguese Sausage and Clams with Potatoes and Peppers
Replace the mussels with 2 dz. littleneck clams or 1 1/4 lb. steamer clams. Add 2 oz. poached, sliced Portuguese linguiça sausage to the onions in step 1; replace the fish stock with clam broth; omit the olives.

Turkey Roulade

with Bread Stuffing, Mashed Potatoes,
Giblet Gravy, Brussels Sprouts,
and Cranberry Sauce

yield: 1 (8-oz.) entrée serving plus accompaniments (multiply × 4 for classroom turnout; adjust equipment sizes accordingly)

MASTER RECIPE

production		costing only
1 Tbsp.	clarified butter	3/4 oz. a.p.
1	Turkey Roulade	1/4 recipe
tt	kosher salt	1/16 oz.
1/4 c.	Poultry Stock	1/64 recipe
1 Tbsp.	clarified butter	3/4 oz. a.p.
1 1/4 c.	Brussels sprouts, trimmed, boiled tender, refreshed, squeezed dry	1/2 pt. a.p.
tt	fresh lemon juice	1/6 [90 ct.] lemon
1 c.	Turkey Giblet Gravy, hot in steam table	1/4 recipe
as needed	water, in squeeze bottle	n/c
1 1/2 c.	Classic Mashed Potatoes, hot in steam table	1/4 recipe
1	small leaf green kale	1/20 head a.p.
1/3 c.	Cranberry Sauce	1/4 recipe

service turnout:

1. Cook the Turkey Roulade:
    a. Heat an 8" sauté pan, heat 1 Tbsp. clarified butter, and brown the roulade on all sides.
    b. Season with salt and pour the Poultry Stock into the pan.
    c. Finish in a 400°F oven about 10 minutes, until heated through.
2. Heat another 8" sauté pan, heat 1 Tbsp. clarified butter, and sauté the Brussels sprouts about 1 minute, until heated through and beginning to brown. Season with salt and lemon juice.
3. Finish and plate the dish:
    a. Remove the roulade to a cutting board and remove the string.
    b. Ladle the Turkey Giblet Gravy into the roulade pan and deglaze it, adding a little water as necessary to achieve a nappé consistency.
    c. Spoon the Classic Mashed Potatoes onto the back center of a hot 12" plate and make a well in the center.
    d. Arrange the Brussels sprouts in a mound to the left of the potatoes.
    e. Cut the roulade into 5 or 6 even slices.
    f. Lean the last slice against the right front of the potatoes and fan the remaining slices in an arc around the potatoes.
    g. Place the kale leaf at 2 o'clock and mound the Cranberry Sauce on it.
    h. Pour the gravy into the well in the potatoes, allowing some to flow over the roulade slices and into the plate well.

COMPONENT RECIPE
TURKEY ROULADES

yield: 4 (8-oz.) entrée servings plus turkey for another use

production		costing only
1/2	small young turkey breast half	approx. 4 lb. a.p.
tt	kosher salt	1/16 oz.
tt	fine-ground white pepper	1/8 oz.
1 qt.	very cold Bread Stuffing	1 recipe

preparation:
1. Skin the turkey breast and remove the meat from the rib cage in one piece. Reserve the tender for another use.
2. Trim away all membranes and fat from the turkey breast.
3. Cut the breast meat across the grain into 4 (1/2"-thick) cutlets approximately 3" × 6". Reserve the remaining meat for another use.
4. Butterfly the cutlets and open them out.
5. Place the turkey slices on one side of a piece of pan liner and fold the other side of the pan liner over the top. Using the flat side of a meat mallet or cleaver, gently pound the cutlets into large, evenly thick escalopes.
6. Fabricate the roulades:
   a. Season one of the escalopes with salt and white pepper.
   b. Wearing foodservice gloves, squeeze 1/4 of the Bread Stuffing into a cylinder and place it at the wider end of the escalope.
   c. Roll up the escalope to enclose the stuffing, tucking in the sides to completely encase it.
   d. Tie the roulade with kitchen string to secure it.
   e. Repeat to make 4 roulades.
   f. Wrap the roulades individually in plastic film and immediately refrigerate.

holding: prepare just enough for the day's service; hold refrigerated up to 12 hours only

COMPONENT RECIPE
BREAD STUFFING

yield: 1 qt.

production		costing only
1/2 c.	butter	4 oz.
1 c.	peeled, 3/8"-diced celery	1/5 head a.p.
1 1/2 c.	medium-chopped yellow onion	7 oz. a.p.
2 Tbsp.	chopped fresh sage leaves	1/6 bunch a.p.
tt	kosher salt	1/16 oz.
tt	fresh-ground black pepper	1/16 oz.
tt	fresh lemon juice	1/6 [90 ct.] lemon
1 qt.	1/2" cubes stale, crustless, firm white bread	12 oz. a.p.
1	egg, beaten	1 each
1/2 c.+	Poultry Stock	1/32 recipe
2 Tbsp.	chopped flat-leaf parsley	1/20 bunch a.p.

preparation:
1. Melt the butter in a 10" sauté pan, add the celery and onion, and sweat over low heat, covered, about 5 minutes, until soft.
2. Add the sage to the onion mixture and season highly with salt, pepper, and lemon juice.
3. Toss the celery mixture with the bread cubes.
4. Mix the egg with the Poultry Stock and toss with the bread cubes. (The mixture should hold together in a loose ball when lightly squeezed; if not, add more stock.)
5. Correct the salt.
6. Open-pan cool to room temperature and then stir in the parsley.

holding: refrigerate in a freshly sanitized, covered, nonreactive container up to 2 days

Butterfly the cutlet: use a sharp, thin-bladed knife to slice the cutlet horizontally almost in half.

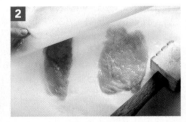

Place the cutlet between sheets of pan liner and gently pound into a large, even escalope.

Roll the filled escalope into a roulade, tucking in the sides to completely encase the stuffing.

Tie the roulade with kitchen string.

COMPONENT RECIPE
TURKEY GIBLET GRAVY

yield: 1 qt.

production		costing only
1 Tbsp.	clarified butter	1 1/2 oz. a.p.
1	skinned turkey neck,* chopped into 2" pieces	n/c
1	turkey gizzard,* trimmed	n/c
2 Tbsp.	butter	1 oz.
3 Tbsp.	fat from Poultry Stock	n/c
5 Tbsp.	flour	2 oz.
5 c.	Poultry Stock	1/3 recipe
tt	kosher salt	1/16 oz.
as needed	water, in squeeze bottle	n/c
tt	fine-ground white pepper	1/16 oz.
1 Tbsp.	clarified butter	3/4 oz. a.p.
1	turkey liver,* trimmed	n/c

preparation:
1. Heat an 8" sauté pan, heat 1 Tbsp. clarified butter, then sauté the turkey neck and gizzard until well browned. Cool.
2. In a 6-qt. saucepan, heat the butter and poultry fat. Add the flour and make a blond roux, then whisk in the Poultry Stock to make the gravy. Add the turkey neck. Bring to the simmer, skim, and season with a little salt.
3. Remove the gizzard from the pan and chop fine. Add to the gravy.
4. Deglaze the pan with a little water and add to the gravy.
5. Simmer the gravy about 30 minutes, adding water if necessary, until nappé and full-flavored.
6. Remove and discard the turkey neck pieces.
7. Correct the salt and season with white pepper.
8. Open-pan cool to room temperature.
9. Heat a 6" sauté pan until very hot, add 1 Tbsp. clarified butter, and sear the turkey liver on both sides until medium rare inside. Cool to room temperature.
10. Chop the liver coarse and stir into the cooled gravy.

*If parts from a whole turkey carcass are not available, substitute a chicken drumstick or wing for the turkey neck and gizzard, and 2 chicken livers for the turkey liver.

holding: refrigerate in a freshly sanitized, covered, nonreactive container up to 2 days

COMPONENT RECIPE
CRANBERRY SAUCE

yield: approx. 1 1/2 c.

production		costing only
3/4 c.	water	n/c
3/4 c.	sugar	6 oz.
2 c.	cranberries, picked over	6 oz. a.p.
1 Tbsp.	minced orange zest	1/2 [88 ct.] orange

preparation:
1. Bring the water and sugar to a boil in a 3-qt. nonreactive saucepan. Boil 3 minutes.
2. Add the cranberries and simmer about 4 minutes, skimming often, until the berries are tender and translucent.
3. Add the orange zest.
4. Pour into a freshly sanitized nonreactive container and refrigerate, uncovered, until cold and lightly set.

holding: refrigerate, covered, up to 7 days

RECIPE VARIATION

Southern Turkey Roulade with Cornbread Dressing, Mashed Potatoes, Giblet Gravy, Braised Tender Greens, and Pickled Peach
Replace the Bread Stuffing with Cornbread Dressing (p. 74). Replace the Brussels sprouts with Braised Tender Greens. Replace the Cranberry sauce with a Spice-Baked Peach half (p. 69).

Boston Baked Beans

with Salt Pork and Fresh Pork, Served with Brown Bread and Piccalilli

yield: 5 oz. pork loin and approx. 6 oz. beans, plus accompaniments (multiply × 4 for classroom turnout; adjust equipment sizes accordingly)

🕐 Requires 24 hours advance preparation.

MASTER RECIPE

production		costing only
1 crock	Boston Baked Beans with Salt Pork	1/4 recipe
1 Tbsp.	clarified butter	3/4 oz. a.p.
1/4 recipe	Mustard-Cured Pork Tenderloin	1/4 recipe
1 Tbsp.	Dijon mustard	1/2 fl. oz.
1	cocktail napkin	1 each
2 slices	Boston Brown Bread	1/4 recipe
2 Tbsp.	softened butter, in a pastry bag fitted with a large star tip	1 oz.
1	small Boston lettuce leaf	1/12 head a.p.
1/2 c.	Piccalilli	1/4 recipe

service turnout:

1. Microwave the crock of Boston Baked Beans with Salt Pork until heated through and then finish in the top of a 400°F oven, about 5 minutes.
2. Heat an 8" sauté pan, heat the clarified butter, and sear the Mustard-Cured Pork Tenderloin on all sides. Brush with the mustard and place in the top of the oven. Roast about 8 minutes, to a medium doneness.
3. Plate the dish:
   a. Place the crock of beans on a 6" plate lined with a cocktail napkin.
   b. Slice the pork tenderloin on the diagonal and arrange in an overlapping arc across the front of a warm 12" plate.
   c. Overlap the Boston Brown Bread slices at the back left and pipe a rosette of butter onto each.
   d. Place the lettuce leaf at the back center and spoon in the Piccalilli. (Leave a space in the center for the beans.)
4. Present the crock of beans on the side and spoon some of the beans into the vacant space on the plate.

COMPONENT RECIPE
BOSTON BAKED BEANS WITH SALT PORK

yield: 4 (12-fl.-oz.) crocks, approx. 6 oz. cooked beans

🕐 Requires 24 hours advance preparation.

production		costing only
2 c.	dried yellow-eye beans or Great Northern beans*	12 oz.
as needed	water	n/c
1	4" × 4" × 1" piece salt pork with rind	8 oz.
1 c.	fine-chopped yellow onion	10 oz. a.p.
2	bay leaves	1/16 oz.
1 tsp.	dried savory	1/16 oz.
1/4 c.	pure dark maple syrup	2 fl. oz.
1/4 c.	light molasses	2 fl. oz.
1 Tbsp.	dry mustard	1/4 oz.
1 Tbsp.	kosher salt	1/2 oz.
1 tsp.	fresh-ground black pepper	1/16 oz.
4	boiling onions	2 oz. a.p.
4	cloves	1/16 oz.
1/4 c.	cider vinegar	2 fl. oz.
1/2 c.	water	n/c

first day preparation:

1. Soak the beans in 2 qt. cool water for 24 hours.

second day preparation:

2. Drain the beans, rinse, and place in a 4-qt. saucepan. Add fresh water to cover by 1/2". Bring to the simmer and skim off the foam.
3. Cut the salt pork through the rind into 4 even-size cubes. Score each cube almost to the rind in a cross-hatch pattern.
4. Add the scored salt pork cubes, onion, bay leaves, and savory to the beans, and then simmer very gently 30 to 40 minutes, until the beans are al dente. (Add water as necessary to keep the beans covered.)
5. Preheat an oven to 275°F.
6. Mix together the maple syrup, molasses, mustard, salt, and pepper. Pour the bean liquid off the beans, measure it, and if necessary add water to equal 3 c. Whisk the bean liquid into the maple syrup mixture and correct for salt-sweet balance.
7. Assemble the crocks:
   a. Divide the beans among 4 (12-fl.-oz.) soup crocks, removing the bay leaves. Divide the seasoned bean liquid among them.
   b. Peel the boiling onions, cut an X into the root ends, and stick each one with a clove. Bury an onion in the beans in each crock.
   c. Press a salt pork cube, scored side up, into each crock so that the top of the salt pork cube is level with the top of the beans.
8. Bake the crocks in the top of the oven about 1 hour.
9. Bring the vinegar and water to the boil, divide the mixture among the crocks, and continue to bake about 40 minutes longer, checking periodically and adding more boiling water only if necessary to keep the beans barely covered.
10. When the beans are tender and the liquid reduced into a thick sauce, remove from the oven. If they will be held for service, cool to room temperature on a rack. Use a thermometer to ensure that the interior beans reach 70°F before wrapping.

*This recipe was developed with New England yellow-eye beans; if Great Northern or other dried beans are used, liquid ingredient amounts and cooking times may vary.

holding: refrigerate the crocks, covered with plastic wrap, up to 1 week

ENTREES

COMPONENT RECIPE
MUSTARD-CURED PORK TENDERLOIN

yield: 4 (5-oz.) servings

🕐 Requires 24 hours advance preparation.

production		costing only
3 Tbsp.	dry mustard	1/3 oz.
1 Tbsp.	brown sugar	1/3 oz.
2 tsp.	granulated onion	1/16 oz.
1/2 tsp.	ground dried sage	1/16 oz.
1/2 tsp.	dried thyme	1/16 oz.
2 tsp.	kosher salt	1/3 oz.
1 tsp.	fresh-ground black pepper	1/16 oz.
2	10-oz. pork tenderloins, trimmed	1 1/4 lb. a.p.

preparation:
1. Mix together the mustard, sugar, onion, sage, thyme, salt, and pepper.
2. Cut each pork tenderloin roughly in half into 2 (5-oz.) servings.
3. Blot each piece dry and rub each with the seasoning mix.
4. Wrap individually in plastic film. Refrigerate at least 24 hours.

holding: refrigerate up to 4 days

COMPONENT RECIPE
BOSTON BROWN BREAD

yield: 8 (1/2") slices

production		costing only
as needed	water	n/c
1 Tbsp.	softened butter	1/2 oz.
1/2 c.	rye flour	2 1/2 oz.
1/2 c.	whole-wheat flour	2 1/2 oz.
1/2 c.	yellow cornmeal	2 oz.
2 tsp.	fine salt	1/16 oz.
1 1/4 tsp.	baking soda	1/16 oz.
6 Tbsp.	molasses	3 fl. oz.
1 c.+	buttermilk	8 fl. oz.+

preparation:
1. Prepare a tall 10-qt. stockpot with a round cake rack set in the bottom. Have ready a kettle of boiling water.
2. Prepare the pan:
    a. Heavily butter the inside of a clean 1-lb. coffee can.
    b. Cut a round of pan liner to fit the bottom of the can. Butter it and fit it down into the bottom of the can, butter side up.
    c. Prepare a large square of aluminum foil folded into fourths (making a 6" square of quadrupled foil) and heavily buttered on one side.
    d. Have ready a piece of kitchen string.
3. Mix and pan the batter:
    a. In a medium bowl, mix together the flours, cornmeal, salt, and baking soda and make a well in the center.
    b. Pour the molasses and buttermilk into the well and stir in the dry ingredients to make a thick batter.
    c. Scrape the batter into the prepared can.
    d. Place the foil square, buttered side down, on the top of the can and tie it on with the kitchen string.
4. Steam the batter:
    a. Place the can on the cake rack inside the pot, foil-covered side up.
    b. Fill the pot with boiling water to a level halfway up the sides of the can.
    c. Turn on the burner to achieve a lively simmer.
    d. Cover the pot and steam the bread 1 1/2 hours, adding boiling water as necessary to keep the water level halfway up the sides of the can.
5. Remove the can from the pot and cool on a rack for 1 hour.
6. Run a knife around the sides of the can and release the bread. Peel off the pan liner.
7. If not serving right away, wrap the bread in damp cheesecloth.

holding: wrap the cheesecloth-wrapped bread in plastic film and store at cool room temperature up to 2 days

COMPONENT RECIPE
PICCALILLI

yield: approx. 2 c.

🕐 Requires 24 hours advance preparation.

production		costing only
1/12 head	cauliflower, very small florets	1/12 head
1/2 c.	3/8" lengths green beans	2 oz. a.p.
1/2 c.	peeled, seeded, 1/2"-diced cucumber	1/3 each
1/2 c.	seeded, 1/2"-diced zucchini	3 oz. a.p.
1/4 c.	3/8"-diced green bell pepper	1 oz. a.p.
1/4 c.	3/8"-diced red bell pepper	1 oz. a.p.
1/4 c.	kosher salt	2 oz.
2 Tbsp.	brown sugar	1/6 oz.
1 tsp.	dry mustard	1/16 oz.
1 tsp.	ground dry ginger	1/16 oz.
1/2 tsp.	turmeric	1/16 oz.
1 tsp.	cracked black peppercorns	1/16 oz.
1/4 tsp.	celery seeds	1/16 oz.
1 Tbsp.	flour	3/4 oz.
1 c.	cider vinegar	8 fl. oz.
1/2 c.	water	n/c
1/4 c.	bottled cocktail onions, drained	2 oz.

first day preparation:
1. Place the cauliflower, beans, cucumber, zucchini, and bell peppers in a nonreactive bowl and mix with the salt. Weight the vegetables down with a plate and allow to stand at cool room temperature for 24 hours. Mix occasionally.

second day preparation:
2. Dump the vegetables into a colander set in a food prep sink, rinse them, and blot them dry.
3. Place the sugar, mustard, ginger, turmeric, peppercorns, and flour in a 4-qt. nonreactive saucepan. In a thin stream, whisk in the vinegar and water to make a smooth, lump-free liquid. Bring to the simmer and mix in the vegetables. Cover and cook, stirring occasionally, for 10 minutes.
4. Add the onions and correct the salt-sugar-vinegar balance.
5. Open-pan cool and refrigerate in a covered, nonreactive container at least 24 hours (better after 1 week).

holding: refrigerate in a freshly sanitized, covered, nonreactive container up to 1 month

---

RECIPE VARIATION

All-American Baked Beans with Bacon, Frankfurters, and Cole Slaw
Omit the salt pork. Cut 6 oz. rindless smoked slab bacon into 1/2" × 3/8" lardons. Sauté over low heat until the fat is rendered and the bacon is browned. Add the bacon and drippings to the beans in step 3. Replace the maple syrup with ketchup. In step 7, top each crock with a thick half-slice of raw bacon. Serve with grilled frankfurters and any of the regional slaws (see recipe index).

Wampanoag Maple-Glazed Roast Rack of Venison

with Winter Succotash and Broccoli Florets in Baby Pumpkin

yield: 1 (6-oz.) entrée serving plus accompaniments (multiply × 4 for classroom turnout; adjust equipment sizes accordingly)

MASTER RECIPE

production		costing only
1 Tbsp.	corn oil	1 fl. oz.
1	3-rib young venison rack, trimmed and frenched	10 oz. a.p.
tt	kosher salt	1/16 oz.
tt	fresh-ground black pepper	1/16 oz.
1 slice	thin bacon, halved widthwise	1/3 oz.
1	Steamed Baby Pumpkin	1/4 recipe
1/4 c.	Maple Glaze	1/4 recipe
1 c.	broccoli florets, blanched and refreshed	3 oz. a.p.
as needed	water, in squeeze bottle	n/c
1 Tbsp.	butter	1/2 oz.
3/4 c.	Red Wine Venison Demi-Glace	1/4 recipe
1 1/4 c.	Winter Succotash, hot in steam table	1/4 recipe
1 tsp.	minced parsley	1/20 bunch a.p.
1 Tbsp.	butter	1/2 oz.

service turnout:

1. Roast the rack:
   a. Heat an 8" sauté pan, heat the oil, and sear the venison rack on all sides.
   b. Season with salt and pepper, turn so the meaty side is up, and then lay the bacon strips across the meat.
   c. Roast in a 400°F oven about 6 minutes.

2. Place the Steamed Baby Pumpkin on a sizzle plate and place in the oven. Bake 10 to 12 minutes, until hot and beginning to brown at the edges.

3. Remove the bacon strips from the venison and discard them. Brush the venison rack with the Maple Glaze. Return it to the top of the same oven and continue to roast to desired doneness (rare recommended, about 5 minutes longer).

4. Heat the broccoli in a microwave, steamer, or covered 8" sauté pan with a little water. Season with salt and 1 Tbsp. butter.

5. Finish and plate the dish:
   a. Remove the venison rack to a cutting board and pour any fat out of its sauté pan.
   b. Add the Red Wine Venison Demi-Glace to the pan and deglaze it over medium heat, adding a little water if necessary.
   c. Fill the pumpkin with the hot broccoli florets, arranging them attractively on top.
   d. Place the pumpkin on the back left of a hot 12" plate.
   e. Slice the venison into 3 chops and place them in the center of the plate, rib bones propped up against the front of the pumpkin.
   f. Spoon the Winter Succotash onto the right side of the plate and sprinkle it with parsley.
   g. Work the remaining butter into the demi-glace and nap over the venison.
   h. Prop the pumpkin lid against the left side of the pumpkin.

COMPONENT RECIPE
MAPLE GLAZE

yield: 1 c.

production		costing only
2 Tbsp.	applejack	1 fl. oz.
6 Tbsp.	Dijon mustard	3 fl. oz.
1/2 c.	pure maple syrup	4 fl. oz.
1 tsp.	kosher salt	1/8 oz.

preparation:
1. Mix thoroughly.

holding: refrigerate in a freshly sanitized, covered, nonreactive container up to 1 month

COMPONENT RECIPE
RED WINE VENISON DEMI-GLACE

yield: 3 c.

production		costing only
1 Tbsp.	corn oil	1/2 fl. oz.
1	12-oz.venison shank, sawed into 1" pieces	12 oz.
1/2 c.	medium-diced yellow onion	2 1/2 oz. a.p.
1/4 c.	unpeeled medium-diced carrot	1 1/2 oz. a.p.
1/4 c.	medium-diced celery	1/20 head a.p.
3 c.	water	n/c
3 c.	Demi-Glace	3/4 recipe
2	bay leaves	1/16 oz.
2 tsp.	juniper berries	1/16 oz.
2 sprigs	fresh thyme	1/10 bunch a.p.
1 tsp.	black peppercorns	1/16 oz.
1/2 c.	red wine	4 fl. oz.
tt	kosher salt	1/16 oz.

preparation:
1. Heat a 10" sauté pan until very hot, add the oil, and sear the venison shank pieces on all sides. Add the onion, carrot, and celery and continue to sauté until they begin to brown.
2. Transfer the venison and mirepoix to a 2 1/2-qt. saucepan. Deglaze the sauté pan with some of the water and pour it over the venison. Add the remaining water and Demi-Glace, bring to the simmer, and skim. Add the bay leaves, juniper berries, thyme, and peppercorns and simmer 2 hours, adding water as necessary to keep the venison covered.
3. Place the wine in a 6" sauté pan and reduce it by half over very low heat.
4. Strain the demi-glace into a fresh saucepan, pushing firmly on the solids. Add the wine and, if necessary, reduce to a nappé consistency. Correct the salt.

holding: open-pan cool and immediately refrigerate in a freshly sanitized, covered, nonreactive container up to 1 week

COMPONENT RECIPE
WINTER SUCCOTASH

yield: 5 c.

production		costing only
2 1/2 c.	toasted dried sweet corn, such as Cope's brand	10 oz.
1 tsp.	kosher salt	1/6 oz.
2 c.	boiling water	n/c
1 1/2 c.	dried baby lima beans	5 1/2 oz.
as needed	water	n/c
1 Tbsp.	butter	1/2 oz.
2 Tbsp.	bacon drippings	n/c
1/2 c.	minced yellow onion	2 1/2 oz. a.p.
1/2 c.	brunoise-cut smoked ham	3 oz. a.p.
pinch	dried savory	1/16 oz.
1/4 c.	heavy cream	2 fl. oz.
tt	fresh-ground white pepper	1/16 oz.

1. Place the dried corn, salt, and water in a small saucepan, bring to the boil, remove from the heat, and quick-soak at least 1 hour.
2. Rinse the lima beans, place them in a small saucepan, add water to cover by 1", bring to the boil, remove from the heat, and quick-soak at least 1 hour.
3. Place the butter and bacon drippings in a 3-qt. saucepan; add the onion, ham, and savory, and sweat over low heat about 3 minutes, until the onions are soft.
4. Drain the lima beans and add to the seasonings saucepan along with water just to cover. Bring to the simmer, partially cover the pan, and cook about 20 minutes, until the lima beans are beginning to soften.
5. Add the corn and its soaking liquid. Return to the simmer, partially cover the pan, and continue to cook, stirring often and adding water only as necessary to keep the vegetables from scorching.
6. When the corn and limas are tender and the broth is reduced almost to a glaze, stir in the cream.
7. Correct the salt and season with white pepper.

holding: open-pan cool and immediately refrigerate in a freshly sanitized, covered, nonreactive container up to 5 days

---

RECIPE VARIATION
Wampanoag Maple-Glazed Roast Pork Chop with Winter Succotash and Broccoli Florets in Baby Pumpkin
Replace the venison rack with a 10-oz. center-cut double pork chop.
Replace the Red Wine Venison Demi-Glace with Red Wine Demi-Glace.

New England Corned Beef Boiled Dinner
with Three Sauces

yield: 1 (6-oz.) entrée serving plus accompaniments (multiply × 4 for classroom turnout; adjust equipment sizes accordingly)

🕐 Best with 24 hour advance preparation.

MASTER RECIPE

production		costing only
6 oz.	Cooked Corned Beef, sliced across the grain in 1/2" slices, with 1 set Boiled Dinner Vegetables	1/4 recipe
2 c.	Poultry Stock	1/8 recipe
1 (2 1/2 oz.)	roasted red beet, peeled, cut almost through from the top into 6 wedges attached at the bottom	3 oz. a.p.
tt	kosher salt	1/16 oz.
1 Tbsp.	butter	1/2 oz.
as needed	water	n/c
1/4 c.	Horseradish Cream	1/4 recipe
1/4 c.	Mustard Pickle Relish	1/4 recipe
1/4 c.	Herbed Mayonnaise	1/4 recipe
1	8" doily or cocktail napkin	1 each
1 Tbsp.	chopped flat-leaf parsley	1/40 bunch a.p.
1	flat-leaf parsley bouquet	1/20 bunch a.p.

service turnout:

1. Place the Cooked Corned Beef and Boiled Dinner Vegetables in a 10" sauté pan along with the Poultry Stock. Cover and simmer until all are heated through.
2. Season the beet with salt, place the butter between the wedges, and heat in a microwave or by pan-steaming with just a little water.
3. Plate the dish:
   a. Spoon each of the three sauces into a 2 1/2-oz. ramekin and place the ramekins on a 9" plate lined with an 8" doily.
   b. Mound the vegetables and beet in an attractive pattern on the back and center of a hot 12" soup plate.
   c. Overlap the corned beef slices across the front.
   d. Moisten all with about 3/4 c. of the stock.
   e. Sprinkle the chopped parsley across the vegetables.
   f. Stick the bouquet of parsley upright at 2 o'clock.

COMPONENT RECIPE
COOKED CORNED BEEF AND BOILED DINNER VEGETABLES

yield: 4 (6-oz.) entrée servings plus 1 1/2 lb. cooked meat for another use

production		costing only
1	4-lb. corned beef brisket	4 lb.
as needed	water	n/c
3	bay leaves	1/8 oz.
4 sprigs	fresh thyme	1/5 bunch a.p.
2	cloves	1/16 oz.
1 tsp.	coriander seeds	1/16 oz.
1 Tbsp.	black peppercorns	1/8 oz.
1 tsp.	celery seeds	1/16 oz.
4	small carrots	12 oz. a.p.
4	medium parsnips	10 oz. a.p.
4	small turnips	10 oz. a.p.
12	boiling onions	12 oz. a.p.
4	Red Bliss potatoes	12 oz. a.p.
1/2 head	2-lb. Savoy cabbage	1 lb. a.p.
4	4" bamboo skewers	4 each

preparation:

1. Cook the brisket:
   a. Remove the corned beef from its packaging and rinse it well.
   b. Place it in a braising pan just large enough to hold it, and add water to cover.
   c. Bring the water to the simmer and skim thoroughly every few minutes until the meat stops producing scum.
   d. Add the bay leaves, thyme, cloves, coriander, peppercorns, and celery seeds. Partially cover the pan and simmer about 2 hours, until the meat is fork tender.
2. Prepare the vegetables:
   a. Peel the carrots and parsnips and trim to create attractive, rounded stem ends. Leave these vegetables whole; do not cut them into pieces.
   b. Peel the turnips and leave them whole.
   c. Blanch the onions in boiling water for about 10 seconds, refresh them, peel them, and cut an X into the root end.
   d. Wash the potatoes. Using a swivel peeler, trim a band of skin around the middle of each potato.
   e. Trim the core from the cabbage and discard it. Cut the cabbage into 4 even-sized wedges. Secure the layers of the wedges together with bamboo skewers.
3. When the corned beef is done, remove it to a cutting board or, if preparing ahead, to a deep half-size hotel pan. If preparing ahead, open-pan cool the brisket to room temperature.
4. Add the vegetables to the pan and cook at a brisk simmer until each individual vegetable is just tender when pierced with a sharp knife. As each type reaches doneness, carefully remove it to the hotel pan and, if preparing ahead, cool to room temperature.
5. If preparing ahead, open-pan cool the poaching liquid and pour it over the cooled corned beef. Cover the hotel pan with plastic wrap and immediately refrigerate 24 hours.
6. Slice the corned beef across the grain into thin, even slices.
7. If preparing ahead, individually package 4 servings (6 oz. corned beef plus equal portions of vegetables) in freshly sanitized containers and cover with the poaching liquid.

holding: refrigerate up to 4 days

COMPONENT RECIPE
HORSERADISH CREAM

yield: 1 c.

production		costing only
2 Tbsp.	minced shallot	1 oz. a.p.
4 Tbsp.	prepared horseradish	2 fl. oz.
2 tsp.	sugar	1/6 oz.
tt	fine-ground white pepper	1/16 oz.
tt	kosher salt	1/16 oz.
5 fl. oz.	sour cream	5 fl. oz.

preparation:
1. Mix thoroughly.
2. Taste and balance the seasonings.

holding: refrigerate in a freshly sanitized, covered, nonreactive container up to 1 week

COMPONENT RECIPE
MUSTARD RELISH

yield: 1 c.

🕐 Best if prepared at least 1 day in advance.

production		costing only
8	unwaxed pickling cucumbers, such as Kirbys	12 oz. a.p.
2 Tbsp.	kosher salt	1 oz.
1 c.	distilled water	8 fl. oz.
1/2 c.	brunoise-cut red bell pepper	2 1/2 oz. a.p.
1/2 c.	fine-chopped yellow onion	2 1/2 oz. a.p.
2 Tbsp.	flour	3/4 oz.
1/2 tsp.	ground turmeric	1/16 oz.
1 Tbsp.	dry mustard	1/4 oz.
1/2 tsp.	celery seeds	1/16 oz.
pinch	ground cloves	1/16 oz.
pinch	ground allspice	1/16 oz.
3 Tbsp.	brown sugar	1 oz.
3/4 c.	cider vinegar	6 fl. oz.

preparation:
1. Scrub the cucumbers, halve them lengthwise, and scrape out the seeds. Fabricate into brunoise cuts.
2. In a nonreactive container, dissolve the salt in the distilled water to make a brine, then add the cucumbers, red bell pepper, and onion. Refrigerate at least 3 hours.
3. Place the flour, turmeric, mustard, celery seeds, cloves, allspice, and sugar in a 1 1/2-qt. nonreactive saucepan and mix until smooth. Whisk in the vinegar.
4. Pour the vegetables and their brine into a 1 1/2-qt. stainless saucepan and bring to the boil. Immediately pour into a strainer set over a bowl to separate the vegetables from the brine.
5. Whisk the hot brine into the flour-vinegar mixture and bring to the simmer. Taste and balance the seasonings to achieve a sweet-sour-salty taste with a sharp mustard bite.
6. Add the vegetables to the pickling sauce and bring to the boil.
7. Immediately ladle the relish into a freshly sanitized, nonreactive container. Open-pan cool to room temperature.

holding: refrigerate in the covered container up to 2 weeks

COMPONENT RECIPE
HERBED MAYONNAISE

yield: 1 c.

production		costing only
1 Tbsp.	minced shallot	1/2 oz. a.p.
2 tsp.	minced lemon zest	n/c
1 Tbsp.	minced flat-leaf parsley	1/20 bunch a.p.
1 Tbsp.	minced fresh dill	1/40 bunch a.p.
1 Tbsp.	minced fresh tarragon	1/20 bunch a.p.
1 tsp.	minced fresh thyme leaves	1/40 bunch a.p.
1 Tbsp.	minced fresh chives	1/20 bunch a.p.
5 fl. oz.	mayonnaise	5 fl. oz.
tt	kosher salt	1/16 oz.
tt	fine-ground white pepper	1/16 oz.
tt	fresh lemon juice	1/8 [90 ct.] lemon

preparation:
1. Mix thoroughly.

holding: refrigerate in a freshly sanitized, covered container up to 1 week

---

RECIPE VARIATION
Cape Cod Boiled Dinner with Egg Sauce
Replace the corned beef with salt cod, prepared as on p. 111 but left in whole fillet form. Replace the Poultry Stock with strained Court Bouillon. Omit the three cold sauces. Serve the poached cod with a light Béchamel sauce enriched with chopped hard-cooked egg. Garnish with sliced hard-cooked egg, sweet paprika, and parsley.

ENTREES

Boston Cream Pie

yield: 1 dessert serving (multiply × 4 for classroom turnout)

MASTER RECIPE

production		costing only
1 slice	Assembled Boston Cream Pie	1/10 cake

service turnout:
1. Place the cake slice in the center of a cool 8" plate.

COMPONENT RECIPE
ASSEMBLED BOSTON CREAM PIE

yield: 1 (10" round) cake

production		costing only
1 c.	sliced almonds	4 oz.
1	Boston Spongecake Layer	1 recipe
1/2 c.	Rum Syrup, in squeeze bottle	1 recipe
2 c.	Pastry Cream Filling	2/3 recipe
2 c.	Chocolate Glaze	1 recipe

preparation:
1. Preheat an oven to 400°F.
2. Spread the almonds on a sheet tray and toast them in the oven about 5 minutes, until golden brown. Cool to room temperature.
3. Using a long serrated knife, split the Boston Spongecake Layer in half. Place the top layer on a piece of pan liner, crumb side up.
4. Squeeze the Rum Syrup onto the cake layers, moistening them evenly.
5. Spread the bottom layer with the Pastry Cream Filling.
6. Press the top layer onto the filling, crumb side down.
7. Place the cake on a rack set over a piece of pan liner. Pour the warm Chocolate Glaze onto the cake and spread it evenly over the top and sides.
8. Refrigerate the cake for about 10 minutes to allow the glaze to begin to set up.
9. Wearing foodservice gloves, mask the sides of the cake with the toasted almonds by picking up the cake and pressing the almonds onto its sides with the palm of your hand.

holding: refrigerate under a cake dome in a dessert refrigerator up to 3 days; after cutting, cover cut surfaces directly with plastic wrap

COMPONENT RECIPE
BOSTON SPONGECAKE LAYER

yield: 1 (10" round) cake layer

production		costing only
as needed	baker's pan coating spray	% of container
6	eggs	6 each or 12 oz.
8 oz.	sugar	8 oz.
pinch	fine salt	1/16 oz.
5 oz.	flour, placed in sifter	5 oz.
1 tsp.	pure vanilla extract	1/6 fl. oz.
1	10" round cake board	1 each

preparation:
1. Preheat an oven to 350°F.
2. Prepare a 10" × 2" round cake pan:
   a. Cut a circle of pan liner to fit the bottom of the cake pan.
   b. Spray the interior of the pan with pan coating.
   c. Press the pan liner into the cake pan.
   d. Spray the pan liner.
3. Mix the batter:
   a. Break the eggs into a large stainless bowl and whisk in the sugar and salt.
   b. Use an oven mitt to hold the bowl over very low heat and whisk until the mixture reaches 100°F. ⚠ Do not overheat.
   c. Using the whip attachment of a mixer, beat the egg mixture on high speed until the mixture is doubled in volume and pale yellow and has the consistency of whipped cream.
   d. Sift the flour over the mixture while folding it in. Fold in the vanilla.
4. Pour the batter into the prepared pan.
5. Immediately place the pan in the center of the oven and bake about 35 minutes, until risen, light golden in color, and springy to the touch.
6. Place the cake pan on a rack and cool 15 minutes.
7. Turn the cake out onto a 10" round cake board, return it to the rack, and cool to room temperature.

holding: wrap tight in plastic film and hold at cool room temperature up to 3 days; may be frozen up to 1 month

COMPONENT RECIPE
RUM SYRUP

yield: 1/2 c.

production		costing only
2 oz.	sugar	2 oz.
1/4 c.	water	n/c
1 Tbsp.	light rum	1/2 fl. oz.

preparation:
1. Combine the sugar and water in a small saucepan, bring to the boil, and boil 1 minute. Cool to room temperature.
2. Mix in the rum.
3. Pour into a freshly sanitized squeeze bottle.

holding: refrigerate up to 1 week

COMPONENT RECIPE
PASTRY CREAM FILLING

yield: approx. 3 c.

production		costing only
1 pt.	milk	16 fl. oz.
3/4 c.	sugar	6 oz.
2	egg yolks	2 each or 1 1/3 oz.
1	egg	1 each or 2 oz.
6 Tbsp.	cornstarch	1 1/2 oz.
2 Tbsp.	room-temperature unsalted butter	1 oz.
2 tsp.	pure vanilla extract	1/3 fl. oz.

preparation:
1. Fill a large bowl with equal parts ice and water and place it near the stove.
2. Place the milk in a saucepan and whisk in 1/4 c. of the sugar. Scald the milk over medium heat just until bubbles form around the edge of the pan.
3. Place the egg yolks, egg, remaining sugar, and cornstarch in a heavy 6-qt. stainless bowl and whip until pale yellow and fluffy.
4. Temper the egg mixture by whisking the hot milk into it in a thin stream.
5. Use an oven mitt to hold the bowl over low heat and whisk constantly, rotating the bowl, for about 3 minutes until the mixture begins to foam. Increase the heat to medium and continue whisking constantly, rotating the bowl, watching carefully to avoid scorching or scrambling, and removing the bowl from the heat as necessary, until the mixture becomes very thick and forms two or three large bubbles. Whisk over low heat for 1 minute longer.
6. Immediately place the bowl in the ice water and whisk until the pastry cream cools to about 110°F.
7. Whisk in the butter and vanilla.
8. Continue whisking occasionally until the pastry cream is thoroughly cold.

holding: refrigerate in a freshly sanitized, covered, nonreactive container up to 3 days

COMPONENT RECIPE
CHOCOLATE GLAZE

yield: 2 c.

production		costing only
2 oz.	unsweetened chocolate	2 oz.
2 oz.	bittersweet chocolate	2 oz.
2 Tbsp.	light corn syrup	1 fl. oz.
8 oz.	confectioner's sugar	8 oz.
4 Tbsp.	light rum	2 fl. oz.
2 tsp.	pure vanilla extract	1/3 fl. oz.

preparation:
1. If necessary, chop the chocolate into small, even-size pieces.
2. Place the chocolate in a clean, dry stainless bowl of the appropriate size to fit into a saucepan filled with about 1" of hot water. (The bottom of the bowl should not touch the water.)
3. Place the saucepan over low heat and melt the chocolate, stirring constantly with a clean, dry rubber spatula.
4. Stir in the corn syrup, sugar, rum, and vanilla.
5. Hold over hot water until needed, stirring occasionally.

holding: hold over hot water up to 1 hour

RECIPE VARIATION
Home-Style Boston Cream Pie
Omit the Rum Syrup, Chocolate Glaze, and toasted almonds. Sift a light dusting of confectioner's sugar over the assembled cake.

Blueberry Crisp
with Vanilla Ice Cream

yield: 1 dessert serving (multiply × 4 for classroom turnout)

MASTER RECIPE

production		costing only
1	Blueberry Crisp	1/4 recipe
1	6" doily or cocktail napkin	1
1	3-fl.-oz. scoop Vanilla Ice Cream or New England super-premium brand	3 fl. oz.

service turnout:
1. Heat the Blueberry Crisp in a 400°F oven about 8 minutes, until very warm.
2. Plate the dish:
   a. Place the crisp on an 8" round plate lined with a 6" doily.
   b. Scoop the Vanilla Ice Cream on top and serve immediately.

COMPONENT RECIPE
BLUEBERRY CRISPS

yield: 4 (8-fl.-oz.) gratins

production		costing only
1 Tbsp.	butter	1/2 oz.
1/2 c.	quick-cooking oatmeal	2 1/2 oz.
1/2 c.	flour	2 1/2 oz.
1/2 c.	brown sugar	2 3/4 oz.
1/2 tsp.	salt	1/12 oz.
4 Tbsp.	cold butter	2 oz.
4 c.	blueberries, preferably low-bush variety, fresh or frozen (do not thaw)	approx. 1 1/4 lb.
3/4 c.	granulated sugar	6 oz.
1 Tbsp.	flour	1/3 oz.
1 Tbsp.	cornstarch	1/2 oz.
1/2 tsp.	ground cinnamon	1/16 oz.
2 tsp.	minced lemon zest	n/c

preparation:
1. Mise en place:
   a. Preheat an oven to 400°F.
   b. Use 1 Tbsp. butter to heavily coat 4 (8-fl.-oz.) gratin dishes. Place them on a sheet tray with pan liner.
2. Make the topping:
   a. Combine the oatmeal, flour, brown sugar, salt, and cold butter on a sanitized work surface.
   b. Use a pastry scraper to cut the topping ingredients together, chopping fine as for streusel.
3. Prepare the fruit:
   a. If using fresh berries, pick them over and discard stems and underripe berries.
   b. Mix the berries with the granulated sugar, flour, cornstarch, cinnamon, and lemon zest.
4. Assemble the gratins:
   a. Divide the berries among the 4 gratin dishes and press to firm.
   b. Cover the surface with the topping and press to firm.
5. Bake in the center of the oven about 25 minutes, until the berries are bubbling and the topping is golden brown.

holding: best served the same day; if not serving immediately, cool on a rack, cover with a kitchen towel, and hold at room temperature up to 3 hours; if necessary, cover with plastic film and refrigerate up to 4 days

---

RECIPE VARIATIONS

Apple Crisp with Vanilla Ice Cream
Replace the blueberries with peeled, cored, and diced tart cooking apples.

Strawberry Crisp with Vanilla Ice Cream
Replace the blueberries with hulled, halved or quartered strawberries; increase the cornstarch to 2 Tbsp.

Rhubarb Crisp with Vanilla Ice Cream
Replace the blueberries with diced rhubarb; increase the sugar to 1 c.

Pumpkin Pie
with Whipped Cream

yield: 1 dessert serving (multiply × 4 for classroom turnout)

MASTER RECIPE

production		costing only
1 slice	Pumpkin Pie	1/8 recipe
1/4 c.	Sweetened Whipped Cream, in a pastry bag fitted with a large star tip	1/4 recipe
3	Sugar-Coated Cranberries	1/4 recipe
1 sprig	fresh mint	1/12 bunch a.p.

service turnout:

1. Plate the dish:
   a. Place the Pumpkin Pie slice slightly left of center on a cool 8" plate.
   b. Pipe a rosette of Sweetened Whipped Cream next to the slice.
   c. Arrange the Sugar-Coated Cranberries in a cluster in front of the rosette.
   d. Stick the mint sprig upright out of the rosette.

COMPONENT RECIPE
PUMPKIN PIE

yield: 1 (10") pie

production		costing only
12 oz.	American Flaky Pastry	1 recipe
as needed	dry beans or other pie weights	n/c
4	eggs	4 each or 8 oz.
3/4 c.	brown sugar	4 oz.
1/2 c.	granulated sugar	3 oz.
2 3/4 c.	canned, unsweetened pumpkin purée	22 fl. oz.
1/2 tsp.	fine salt	1/16 oz.
1 tsp.	ground cinnamon	1/16 oz.
1/4 tsp.	ground cloves	1/16 oz.
1/4 tsp.	ground nutmeg	1/16 oz.
1/4 tsp.	ground allspice	1/16 oz.
2 1/2 c.	half-and-half	20 fl. oz.

preparation:

1. Prepare the pie shell:
   a. Roll out the American Flaky Pastry and fit it into a 10" pie pan.
   b. Trim the edges 1/2" larger than the lip of the pan.
   c. Roll under the dough edges and flute the rim.
   d. Refrigerate at least 20 minutes.
2. Preheat an oven to 400°F.
3. Blind-bake the pie shell to partial doneness:
   a. Line the pie shell with a circle of pan liner and fill it with pie weights.
   b. Place the pie shell on a half-sheet tray with pan liner.
   c. Bake the shell in the center of the oven about 10 minutes, until the dough is set but not crisp or golden.
   d. Remove from the oven, remove the pie weights and pan liner, and cool on a rack.
   e. Reduce the oven temperature to 300°F.
4. Mix the custard:
   a. Place the eggs in a large bowl and use a whip to beat the eggs until well combined.
   b. Whisk in the sugars until smooth.
   c. Use the whip to stir in the pumpkin.
   d. When smooth, stir the salt, cinnamon, cloves, nutmeg, allspice, and half-and-half.
5. Pour the pumpkin custard into the pie shell.
6. Bake the pie about 40 minutes, until almost set but still just a little wobbly in the center.
7. Cool to room temperature on a rack.
8. Place in a dessert refrigerator under a cake dome about 1 hour, until cold.

holding: best served the same day; if necessary, refrigerate up to 3 days

SUGAR-COATED CRANBERRIES

yield: 12 perfect berries

production		costing only
1/2 c.	sugar	4 oz.
1/8 c.	water	n/c
16 to 20	cranberries	1 1/2 oz.
2 Tbsp.	pasteurized egg whites	1 oz.
1/2 c.	sugar	4 oz.

preparation:

1. Poach the cranberries:
    a. Bring 1/2 c. sugar and the water to the boil in a small, nonreactive saucepan. Boil 2 minutes.
    b. Add the cranberries to the syrup and poach over low heat until just tender but still intact.
    c. Remove the berries from the syrup, place on a plate or sheet tray, and cool to room temperature.
2. Coat the cranberries:
    a. Beat the egg whites until foamy.
    b. Place 1/2 c. sugar in a small, flat container.
    c. Blot the cranberries dry on paper towels.
    d. Dip each cranberry in the egg whites and then roll in the sugar.

holding: store in the sugar, loosely covered with plastic film, at cool room temperature and low humidity up to 3 days

DESSERTS

RECIPE VARIATION

Pecan Pumpkin Pie

Omit the Sugar-Coated Cranberry garnish. Reduce the amount of pumpkin filling ingredients by half. Prepare a half recipe of Pecan Pie filling, p. 77. Half-fill the pie shell with the Pecan Pie filling and bake about 20 minutes, until just beginning to set. Carefully pour the pumpkin pie filling on top and continue to bake per the recipe directions.

Spice Trade Gingerbread
with Cranberry Ice Cream

yield: 1 dessert serving (multiply × 4 for classroom turnout)

🕐 Ice cream requires 24 hours advance preparation.

MASTER RECIPE

production		costing only
1 slice	Spice Trade Gingerbread	1/8 recipe
1	4-fl.-oz. scoop Cranberry Ice Cream	1/6 recipe
1 sprig	fresh mint	1/12 bunch a.p.

service turnout:

1. Plate the dish:
   a. Place the Spice Trade Gingerbread wedge toward the back of a cool 10" plate resting on its rounded edge with the point of the slice upright.
   b. Place the scoop of Cranberry Ice Cream in front of the gingerbread.
   c. Place the mint sprig between the ice cream and the gingerbread.

COMPONENT RECIPE

SPICE TRADE GINGERBREAD

yield: 1 (9") cake

production		costing only
as needed	baker's pan coating spray	% of container
10 oz.	flour	10 oz.
2 tsp.	baking soda	1/16 oz.
1 Tbsp.	ground ginger	1/8 oz.
1 tsp.	ground cinnamon	1/16 oz.
3/4 tsp.	ground mace	1/16 oz.
1/2 tsp.	ground cloves	1/16 oz.
1/2 tsp.	salt	1/16 oz.
4 oz.	room-temperature butter	4 oz.
3 oz.	dark brown sugar	3 oz.
2	eggs	2 each or 4 oz.
4 fl. oz.	molasses	4 fl. oz.
4 fl. oz.	pure maple syrup	4 fl. oz.
1 1/2 oz.	fine-chopped crystallized ginger	1 1/2 oz.
1/8 c.	minced orange zest	n/c
2 fl. oz.	orange juice	1 [100 ct.] orange
4 fl. oz.	sour cream	4 oz.
1	9" round cake board	1 each

preparation:

1. Preheat an oven to 350°F.
2. Prepare a 9" × 2" round cake pan:
   a. Cut a circle of pan liner to fit the bottom of the cake pan.
   b. Spray the interior of the pan with pan coating.
   c. Press the pan liner into the cake pan.
   d. Spray the pan liner.
3. Sift together the flour, baking soda, ground ginger, cinnamon, mace, cloves, and salt, and then sift again.
4. Mix the batter:
   a. Using the paddle attachment of a mixer, cream the butter and sugar on high speed until fluffy.
   b. On medium speed, beat in the eggs, one at a time.
   c. Add the molasses, syrup, crystallized ginger, and orange zest.
   d. On low speed, alternately stir in the flour with the orange juice and sour cream.
5. Pan the batter, smoothing the surface and making the center a little lower than the edges.
6. Bake in the middle of the oven about 45 minutes, until risen and a tester inserted in the center emerges with large, moist crumbs clinging to it.
7. Cool on a rack for 15 minutes.
8. Turn out of the pan onto the cake board and cool on the rack to room temperature.

holding: best served the same day; hold wrapped in plastic film at cool room temperature up to 3 days; may be frozen up to 1 month

COMPONENT RECIPE
CRANBERRY ICE CREAM

yield: approx. 1 qt.

(requires 24 hours advance preparation)

production		costing only
1/2 lb.	fresh or frozen cranberries	1/2 lb.
1 c.	sugar	8 oz.
1 c.	water	n/c
3 c.	Philadelphia-Style Ice Cream, base only, prepared one day ahead	3/4 recipe

preparation:
1. Prepare a large bowl filled with equal parts ice and water and place it near the stove.
2. Make the cranberry purée:
   a. Place the cranberries, sugar, and water in a 2-qt. nonreactive saucepan and bring to the boil. Simmer briskly 15 minutes, until the cranberries are very tender.
   b. Force the cranberry mixture through a food mill or sieve into a clean saucepan.
   c. Place the saucepan over high heat and, stirring often, reduce the cranberry purée to 1 c.
   d. Place the saucepan in the ice bath and chill the purée until cold.
3. Whisk the cold cranberry purée into the ice cream base.
4. Place in a prepared ice cream freezer and freeze according to the manufacturer's instructions.
5. Transfer the ice cream to a freshly sanitized container. Cover the surface directly with plastic film, then cover with the lid.
6. Place in a freezer at least 1 hour to harden.

holding: store frozen up to 3 days; before serving, temper at 30 degrees for at least 1 hr.

RECIPE VARIATION
Spice Trade Gingerbread with Vanilla Custard Sauce
Present the gingerbread flat on the plate. Replace the Cranberry Ice Cream with 1/2 c. Vanilla Custard Sauce spooned onto the plate.

☐ **TABLE 3.2 NEW ENGLAND REGIONAL INGREDIENTS**

ITEM	MARKET FORMS	USES	SEASONALITY	OTHER	STORAGE
WHOLE-WHEAT FLOUR OR GRAHAM FLOUR	Flour made from the entire wheat kernel, including the perishable germ.	Used for making yeast breads and hybrid quick breads. Graham flour may be used for pie crusts and crackers.	N/A	Graham flour is a combination of fine-milled wheat endosperm (white flour) and coarse-ground bran and germ.	Store at cool room temperature or freeze for extended storage.
RYE FLOUR	Light rye flour is rye endosperm only. Medium rye flour includes a lesser amount of bran and germ; dark rye flour has more.	Rye flour is used in New England Rye 'n' Injun, p. 105.	N/A		Store at cool room temperature or freeze for extended storage.
JONNYCAKE MEAL	Rhode Island cooks insist on locally grown, fine stone-ground whitecap flint corn. Mail order it through Internet sources.	Used primarily for jonnycakes.	N/A		Store at cool room temperature or freeze for extended storage.
GRAHAM CRACKERS AND GRAHAM CRACKER CRUMBS	Graham crackers and crumbs are available for foodservice use in 10-lb. boxes.	The slightly sweet, crisp biscuits are used in crumb form to make pie crusts and crumb toppings.	N/A	These products were popularized in the late 19th century by Sylvester Graham, promoting the health benefits of whole-wheat flour.	Store at cool room temperature or freeze for extended storage.
CRACKERS	Purchase in consumer size or 10-lb. foodservice packs.	Crackers accompany soups, dips, and cheeses. Crushed crackers or cracker meal is a favored breading and topping ingredient and may be used to thicken casseroles.	N/A	*Vermont Common Crackers:* these lozenge-shaped, unsalted crackers are perforated lengthwise to easily split in half. *Oyster Crackers:* these small, round and hard, unsalted crackers accompany raw clams and oysters.	Store tightly sealed at cool room temperature.
LEGUMES	Dried beans, peas, and lentils are available in 1-lb. packs and 10-lb. boxes. Some types are available cooked in 15-oz. and #10 cans.	Used in soups, salads, casseroles, and dips.	N/A		Store at room temperature.
HEIRLOOM BEANS	Available dried, heirloom beans may be purchased from specialty growers or mail ordered from Internet sources.	These special products elevate ordinary soups, salads, and casseroles. In fresh form they are served as a special side dish and in salads.	In season from July to September, fresh local heirloom beans may be found at farm stands and farmer's markets in the region.	Types include yellow-eyed beans, soldier beans, tongues of fire beans, and Jacob's cattle beans.	Refrigerate fresh beans and use immediately. Store dried beans at room temperature.
PURE MAPLE SYRUP	Four standard grades are available: Grade A Light Amber, Grade A Medium Amber, Grade A Dark Amber, and Grade B. Some producers designate their best and lightest-colored product as AA.	For table use, the light and medium A grades are generally preferred and demand correspondingly higher prices. Grade B goes primarily to food processors.	Though available year round, maple syrup dishes are featured in early spring when maple products are made.	When substituting maple syrup for sugar in cooking, as in glazes and puddings, the general rule is to use 3/4 c. syrup to 1 c. sugar. Adjust liquids when used in baking.	Once opened. store under refrigeration.

☐ TABLE 3.2 NEW ENGLAND REGIONAL INGREDIENTS *(continued)*

ITEM	MARKET FORMS	USES	SEASONALITY	OTHER	STORAGE
MAPLE SUGAR	This sweet, fine-grained sugar is sold by the pound by maple syrup producers and specialty purveyors in granular and block forms.	Sprinkle on hot or cold cereals. Replace granulated sugar in almost any recipe; because it is sweeter, use 3/4 c. maple sugar for 1 c. granulated sugar.	N/A		Store in a tightly sealed container at cool room temperature.
MAPLE CREAM OR MAPLE BUTTER	Maple cream is sold in small jars or tubs by maple syrup producers or specialty purveyors.	Used primarily as a spread for toast or other breakfast pastries, maple cream can also be used as a frosting.	N/A	This smooth, sweet paste is made by rapidly cooling boiled maple syrup while at the same time beating it to prevent the formation of large-grained crystals. The name refers to its texture; the product contains no dairy products.	Store in a tightly sealed container at cool room temperature.
MOLASSES	For foodservice, molasses is sold by the gallon. Light or "first" molasses is the result of the first processing of the cane, while dark or "second" molasses comes from the second boiling and has a stronger, slightly bitter flavor. True blackstrap molasses comes from the third processing and is used primarily in animal feed.	In the past, molasses was used as a table sweetener. Today it is used primarily in baked goods. Molasses adds sweetness and dark color to sauces.	N/A	Molasses is less sweet than sugar; when replacing sugar with molasses, use 1 c. molasses to every 3/4 c. of sugar and reduce the liquids in the recipe by 5 Tbsp. Molasses is highly acidic; if a chemical leavener is used, add 1/2 tsp. baking soda per cup of molasses and decrease the amount of baking powder accordingly.	Store in a tightly sealed container at cool room temperature.
BELL'S SEASONING	This blend of powdered herbs is similar to other poultry seasoning mixes. It is sold in 1-oz. consumer packages.	As was Bell's intention, it is used to flavor a wide variety of New England dishes ranging from turkey stuffing to stuffed clams.	N/A	Concocted in the 1860s by William Bell of Boston, this seasoning mix with the distinctive turkey on the label can today be found in virtually every New England pantry.	Store in a tightly sealed container at cool room temperature.
DRY MUSTARD	One of the colonists' favorite seasonings, pungent dry mustard is found in glass jars and cans.	Used in baked beans, cheese dishes, egg dishes and a wide variety of sauces, rubs, and marinades.	N/A		Store in a tightly sealed container at cool room temperature.
PREPARED MUSTARD	A "hot" English-style prepared mustard is the type that would have been used by early New Englanders. Sharp, full-flavored Dijon style mustards are today more readily available and make a good substitute. Mustard is sold in jars and tubs of varying sizes.	Mustard is used in baked beans, cheese dishes, egg dishes and a wide variety of sauces, rubs, and marinades.	N/A		Store in a tightly sealed container at cool room temperature.
DRIED POWDERED GINGER	Ginger is sold by the pound. To ensure freshness, purchase ginger from a spice dealer rather than from a general purveyor.	Ginger is widely used in both sweet and savory New England dishes.	N/A		Store in a tightly sealed container away from sunlight. Discard after 1 year.

(continued)

☐ **TABLE 3.2 NEW ENGLAND REGIONAL INGREDIENTS** *(continued)*

ITEM	MARKET FORMS	USES	SEASONALITY	OTHER	STORAGE
NUTMEG AND MACE	Whole nutmegs and fresh-ground mace are best purchased by the pound from a spice dealer.	Used primarily in baked goods and sweet beverages such as eggnog, these spices are used in New England cooking to add a hint of exotic flavor to cheese dishes, cream sauces, and baked or boiled squash.	N/A		For optimum freshness, purchase nutmeg in whole seed form, store it frozen, and grate it as needed. Store powdered mace in the freezer.
SAGE	Sage is one of the most frequently used herbs in New England cooking. Dried sage is available powdered (ground into a fine dust) or "rubbed" into coarse flakes. Both forms are sold by the ounce or pound. Fresh sage is sold by the bunch.	Sage is particularly associated with pork dishes and is a major flavor in poultry seasoning and Bell's seasoning.	N/A		Keep dried sage in a tightly sealed container away from sunlight. Store bunches of fresh sage in water like cut flowers.
THYME	Dried thyme is sold by the ounce or pound in leaf and ground form. Fresh thyme is sold by the bunch.	Thyme flavors a variety of savory new England dishes.	N/A		Keep dried thyme in a tightly sealed container away from sunlight. Store bunches of fresh thyme in water like cut flowers.
WALNUTS	Walnuts are available for foodservice use in halves of various sizes, in pieces, and ground into flour, with larger specimens commanding higher prices.	Walnuts are widely used in New England baking and confectionery. They may be used in savory stuffings and as a coating for sauteed foods.	N/A	Like all nuts, walnuts can turn rancid over time and actually produce toxins. Walnut halves are less perishable than pieces or flour.	Store at cool room temperature; for extended storage, refrigerate or freeze.
BLACK WALNUTS	See p. 402.				
HEIRLOOM APPLES	Fresh heirloom apple varieties include the Baldwin, Rhode Island Greening, Blue Pearmai, Ginger Gold, and Honey Crisp.	The staple fruit of New England, apples are used in both sweet and savory dishes. Fried apples are a breakfast specialty and may be used as a side dish with savory foods.	Late summer and fall.		Refrigerate.
DRIED APPLES	See p. 402.				
BLUEBERRIES	Large, sweet domestic blueberries are sold fresh in season in flats of 12 pints or 8 quarts. IQF (individual quick-frozen) blueberries are sold to foodservice operations in packs of various sizes.	Fresh and frozen berries are used in pies, cobblers, and muffins, as well as for toppings and in fresh fruit salalds.	New England blueberries are in season from July into August. Blueberries from other sources are available year round.		Store fresh blueberries in the refrigerator in their original carton. Invert cartons to take pressure off the bottom berries. Keep IQF blueberries frozen until needed.

☐ TABLE 3.2 NEW ENGLAND REGIONAL INGREDIENTS *(continued)*

ITEM	MARKET FORMS	USES	SEASONALITY	OTHER	STORAGE
LOW-BUSH OR "WILD" BLUEBERRIES	Fresh New England low-bush blueberries are sold in flats of twelve pints. Individually quick-frozen low-bush blueberries are also available in packs of various sizes. Canned low-bush blueberries are inferior in texture and are usually sweetened by the processor.	Low-bush blueberries give a distinctive New England flavor to pies, cobblers, and muffins, as well as to toppings and fresh fruits salads.	The New England low-bush season is short, usually only a few weeks in July. Canadian berries may be harvested into October.	Low-bush "wild" blueberries are a Maine and Canada specialty crop. Smaller, more tart, and with thicker skins, they have a distinctive flavor that is worth the higher price.	Store fresh blueberries in the refrigerator in their original carton. Invert carton to take pressure off the bottom berries. Keep IQF blueberries frozen until needed.
CRANBERRIES AND CRANBERRY JUICE	Fresh cranberries are marketed in 1-lb. cello packs. Bottled cranberry juice and frozen cranberry juice concentrate are also available.	In addition to Thanksgiving cranberry sauce, cranberries are used in baked goods, salads, sauces, relishes, and compotes. Cranberry juice is usually used for beverages, but it is also useful for sauces and dessert preparations.	Fresh cranberries are sold from October through December; individually quick-frozen cranberries are available year round.	Cello packs of fresh cranberries may be frozen with no prior processing.	Refrigerate fresh cranberries up to 2 months or freeze. Keep frozen until needed.
PUMPKIN, FRESH AND CANNED	It is essential, when purchasing fresh pumpkin, to choose a cooking variety rather than a decorative, jack-o-lantern cultivar. Heirloom field pumpkins and varieties with names that emphasize eating qualities, such as sugar pumpkins, are appropriate for cooking. Choose from American, Latin American, and Asian cultivars. Not all cooking pumpkins are orange: green, white, and blue-green varieties are available. Very small decorative cultivars are called baby pumpkins. Canned, unsweetened pumpkin is sold in 15-oz., 29-oz., and #10 cans.	New England cooks use pumpkin throughout the winter season as a side dish; in sauces; and, of course, for sweet pies, puddings, soufflés and other desserts. Baby pumpkins are used for presentation of soups, soufflés, and vegetable side dishes.	New England pumpkins are available from late summer through the first frost. Latin American and Asian pumpkins are sold year round.	For pies and other desserts, many chefs believe that canned, unsweetened pumpkin purée makes a more consistent product; compared to fresh pumpkin, the labor cost is significantly lower.	Store fresh pumpkins in a cool, dark, well-ventilated area, preferably on racks for good air circulation. Check occasionally for mold and soft spots. Store canned pumpkin at room temperature.
FIDDLEHEAD FERNS	The unfurled fronds of the ostrich fern, fiddleheads are a foraged food found in wooded areas throughout the American northeast and in the Appalachian Mountains. Fresh fiddleheads are sold in season by specialty purveyors. Individually quick-frozen fiddleheads are sold year round but may go out of stock due to limited production.	Fiddlehead ferns are traditionally served as a seasonal side dish dressed with butter and lemon. They may be used as a salad ingredient.	The short season begins during the first warm days of early spring and lasts only until the fronds mature and open. Mid-Atlantic fiddleheads may emerge as early as March; the New England and Canadian season may begin in April and extend into early May.	To prepare fiddleheads for cooking, remove the dry and slightly fibrous stem ends. Remove any brown frond tips by rubbing between the palms while the fiddleheads are submerged in a sink full of water. If picked young and shipped very fresh, fiddleheads may be pan-steamed crisp tender. However, most purchased fiddleheads need a more thorough cooking because they are more mature and can dry out during transport. These specimens must be boiled tender and refreshed.	Store fresh fiddleheads refrigerated in their carton or in a paper bag for several days only. They may be cleaned, blanched, refreshed, and frozen for a few weeks only.

(continued)

▢ TABLE 3.2 NEW ENGLAND REGIONAL INGREDIENTS *(continued)*

ITEM	MARKET FORMS	USES	SEASONALITY	OTHER	STORAGE
PORTUGUESE SAUSAGES: LINGUIÇA AND CHOURIÇO	Fresh and frozen Portuguese sausages are available by the pound from the producer or from specialty purveyors, usually in 10-lb. boxes. In the region they are also sold in supermarkets.	Linguiça is usually grilled or pan-roasted to be served sliced as an appetizer or served in a Portuguese sandwich roll, often topped with sautéed onions and peppers. Chouriço is simmered into soups and stews and used as a seasoning meat for vegetables.	N/A	To make linguiça, ground pork and pork fat are seasoned with wine or wine vinegar, salt, paprika, and granulated garlic, forced into casings, then lightly smoked. Chouriço is slightly leaner and is spiked with cayenne powder.	Refrigerate fresh sausages up to 2 weeks, vacuum-packed sausages up to 1 month. Both may be frozen up to 2 months.
HERITAGE-BREED POULTRY	Heritage-breed poultry is sold fresh or frozen by the producer or through specialty purveyors. Whole birds are most common, although some producers offer parts. Both are sold by the pound. New England chickens include the Rhode Island Red and the Cornish Rock. The Narragansett turkey is New England's foundation breed, although other North American heritage turkeys are available.	Replace factory-produced poultry with heritage breeds in high-end operations where customers are willing to pay for quality and sustainability.	Available year round.	Heritage breed poultry is raised by small-scale breeders with the support of Slow Foods USA. The New England Heritage Breeds Conservancy in Richmond, Massachusetts, fosters the continuation of traditional American poultry breeds. Access their website to find sources.	Refrigerate fresh poultry in a self-draining, iced storage container; keep frozen poultry no longer than 3 months.
COD AND SCROD	Whole codfish ranges from 3 to 12 lb. dressed weight, although larger fish are sometimes available. Most cod is sold as skinless fillets, both fresh and frozen. Young or baby cod less than 3 lbs. is marketed as scrod at higher prices. Scrod is sold whole or as skinless fillets.	Cod and scrod are traditionally baked or broiled with lemon and butter, sometimes topped with buttered breadcrumbs.	Available year round.	Mainstream customers appreciate cod for its lean, white flesh and mild flavor. Scrod is little known outside the region and may need in-house marketing to sell for its higher price.	Refrigerate fresh fish in plastic bags in a self-draining, iced storage container; keep frozen fish no longer than 1 month.
MONKFISH	Monkfish tail is sold as 1- to 3-lb. skinless fillets.	Monkfish fillets are covered with a thick membrane that must be thoroughly removed before cooking. The firm, gelatinous meat is well suited to moist cooking methods and holds up well in seafood soups and stews.	Available year round.	In the 1980s monkfish was popularized as "poor man's lobster."	Refrigerate fresh fish in plastic bags in a self-draining, iced storage container; keep frozen fish no longer than 1 month.
SALT COD	For foodservice, salt cod is sold by the side, either skinned or skinless, packed in 10-lb. boxes. Small, wooden 1-lb. crates are sold to retail markets.	Salt cod is soaked in several changes of water, after which it swells to approximately double its original size and weight. Old-time New Englanders poach soaked salt cod fillets and eat them with lemon and butter or egg sauce. Today most recipes use shredded salt cod. Fritters, cod cakes, and codfish dips and spreads are typical uses.	N/A	Although a small amount of salt cod is still produced in New England, most of the product available in the United States is imported from Canada.	Best stored in the refrigerator; keeps for extended periods, up to 1 year.

☐ TABLE 3.2 NEW ENGLAND REGIONAL INGREDIENTS (continued)

ITEM	MARKET FORMS	USES	SEASONALITY	OTHER	STORAGE
SMOKED AND PRESERVED FISH	Best known among New-England-produced preserved fish products is smoked salmon, sold by the pound in various grades and cure types in vacuum packaging. Finnan Haddie is cured, smoked haddock. Kippers are smoked herring available both vacuum packed and canned. Sardines are small fish of the herring family that are salted and canned. Eels are most commonly sold in the smoked form, in vacuum packaging or canned.	Smoked and preserved fish are typically served as appetizers or snacks. They may be used in chowders and other soups, as well as to flavor dips and sauces.	N/A	New England still makes a significant amount of America's preserved ocean fish products.	Store refrigerated intact in vacuum packaging to manufacturer's expiration date. Once opened, refrigerate a few days only. Store canned products at cool room temperature.
ATLANTIC COLDWATER LOBSTER	Whole live lobsters are sold by the pound and graded by weight per unit: 1 1/4 lb. is called a *chicken lobster*; 1 1/4 to 1 1/2 lb. is called a *quarter*; 1 1/2 to 2 lb. is called a *select*; 2 to 2 1/2 lb. is called a *deuce*; 2 1/2 to 3 lb. is called a *small jumbo*; 3+ lb. is called a *jumbo*. Cooked coldwater lobster meat and tails are available frozen by the pound.	Whole lobsters are traditionally steamed and served with melted butter and lemon. Lobster meat is mixed with mayonnaise for loster cocktail or as a filling for lobster roll sandwiches.	Prices are highest when the weather is at its worst, from January through April. Price/value ratio is highest in May and September, when the lobsters are hard shelled and full of meat yet the price remains low.	The best lobster is sold live, packed in seaweed, to restaurants, wholesalers, and retailers.	Seaweed-packed live lobsters must be cooked within a day or two of their arrival because they deteriorate quickly once removed from the water. Restaurants specializing in lobster invest in a salt water holding tank. Dead lobsters must be discarded.
ATLANTIC HARD-SHELL CLAMS	Round, gray, hard-shell clams are sold both live and processed. Live clams are packed in net bags or "bushel" boxes of varied counts. Clams 1 1/2" or less in diameter are called *littlenecks*; clams 1 1/2" to 2 1/2" in diameter are called *topnecks*; clams from 2 1/2" to 3" in diameter are called *cherrystones*; clams over 3" in diameter are called *chowder clams* or *quahogs*. Clams may be processed into canned or pasteurized chopped clams or frozen clam strips.	Clams served raw on the half shell and accompanied by lemon wedges and cocktail sauce are a New England specialty. Half-shell clams may be covered with various toppings and baked or broiled. Chopped clams are used in chowders, fritters, and dips. Clam strips are breaded and fried.	Available year-round, hard-shell clams reach premium prices during the winter months, particularly in bad weather.		Refrigerate live clams layered with seaweed or wet newspaper in a self-draining container up to 5 days. Cull, or pick over, frequently, to remove dead specimens. Store processed clam products according to package specifications.

(continued)

☐ TABLE 3.2 NEW ENGLAND REGIONAL INGREDIENTS *(continued)*

ITEM	MARKET FORMS	USES	SEASONALITY	OTHER	STORAGE
ATLANTIC SOFTSHELL CLAMS	Most New England soft-shell clams are pale gray, oval clams with open shells and long siphon "necks." They are some-times called *steamer clams* or *Ipswich clams.* Standard pack for live softshell clams is the 40- to 45-lb. bushel carton. In the region, fresh shucked clam bellies are sold in pints, quarts, and gallons. Elongated At-lantic razor clams are a specialty item.	Softshell clams are traditionally steamed and served with melted butter and lemon. A cup of steaming broth is used for dunking to wash off grit. Clam bellies are breaded and deep-fried and served with lemon and tartar sauce.	Available from spring through fall, softshell clams are very perishable and are not sold by many inland purveyors.		Store softshell clams in the same manner as hard-shell clams but use within 2 to 3 days.
ATLANTIC BLUE MUSSELS	Most blue mussels in to-day's market are culti-vated, or farm-raised, and are consistent in size at about 20 mussels to the pound. Farmed mus-sels have far less waste than wild. Foodservice mussels are packed loose in 40 to 45-lb. bushel cartons or in 2-lb. retail bags. Steamed vacuum-packed whole mussels are available in 2-lb. sleeves. Slightly inferior in texture than fresh, they offer convenience and the advantage of no dead loss.	Mussels are steamed in white wine with garlic or in a tomato-based broth with Italian season-ings. They may be accompanied by crusty bread or tossed with pasta. Chilled steamed mussels are used in salads. Mussels on the half shell are covered with a topping and baked.	Farmed mussels are available year round.	Except among Por-tuguese-Americans and Italian-Americans, mussels did not become popular in the United States until the 1980s.	Store live mussels in the same manner as softshell clams; re-move mussels from bags for longer stor-age and easier culling.
NEW ENGLAND OYSTERS	For general information on oysters, see p. 225.	Wellfleets and other Cape Cod oysters are considered among America's finest. They are most often served raw on the half shell to highlight their fine fla-vor and texture.	September through March.		

☐ TABLE 3.2 NEW ENGLAND REGIONAL INGREDIENTS *(continued)*

ITEM	MARKET FORMS	USES	SEASONALITY	OTHER	STORAGE
ATLANTIC SCALLOPS	Most scallops are sold shucked and priced by the pound. (See size grades at right.) Sea scallops are 1" or more in diameter. Bay scallops are 1/2" to 3/4" in diameter. Shucked scallops may be water packed with preservatives to retain size and prevent drying; they exude water when cooked and have an inferior flavor. Superior dry-pack scallops are harvested by day boat and rushed to market; they have a sticky feel. The best dry-pack scallops are called diver scallops because they are hand harvested by scuba divers. Live, in-shell scallops are a specialty item.	Shucked scallops are sauteed, broiled, or breaded and deep-fried. They may be gratinéed in a velouté sauce, often presented in a scallop shell. Chilled poached scallops are used in salads. Live scallops contain both meat and roe. They are steamed or broiled on the half shell.	Available year round.	Sea scallops are graded by count/pound: *colossal* fewer than 10 per pound; *jumbo* 10 to 20 per pound; *large* 20 to 30 per pound *medium* 30 to 40 per pound. Bay scallops count 50 to 80 per pound and 80 to 120 per pound. Calico scallops are the smallest, at 150 to 250 per pound.	Refrigerate shucked scallops in their original container bedded in ice 1 to 2 days only. Store highly perishable fresh scallops in the same manner as soft-shell clams.

■□■ chapter four
The Mid-Atlantic

Pennsylvania; north-central Maryland; Delaware; New Jersey; southern and central New York State; Washington, D.C.

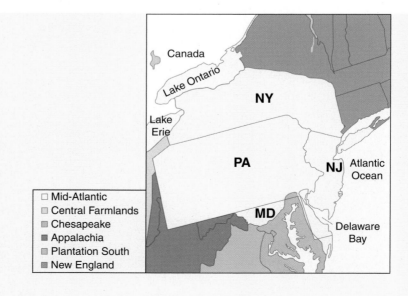

□ Mid-Atlantic
□ Central Farmlands
■ Chesapeake
■ Appalachia
■ Plantation South
■ New England

THE GEOPOLITICAL REGION that encompasses Pennsylvania, Delaware, New Jersey, and New York is called the Mid-Atlantic. When the term was first coined, *Mid-Atlantic* described this region's central position within the group of thirteen colonies that stretched along America's Atlantic seaboard. Lying between two venerable and distinctive American regions, New England and the Plantation South, the Mid-Atlantic acted as a buffer between the two. From colonial times to the American Revolution, the Mid-Atlantic was truly "in the middle," not only geographically but also culturally and politically. Today it remains a region known for moderation expressed in several ways.

The Mid-Atlantic region enjoys moderate weather, spared the climatic extremes of New England and the South. Most of its topography is moderate as well. Its temperate climate and agriculture-friendly land encourage cultivation of a wide variety of food crops rather than a single monoculture as in some other regions.

Mid-Atlantic cuisine is moderate, too—in the best sense of the word. Lacking the spice and sizzle of Plantation South cooking, yet richer and more expansive than New England cuisine, Mid-Atlantic cooking is solid, unpretentious, and ingredient-driven. Blessed with some of the world's richest soil and home to many of the nation's best farmers, the Mid-Atlantic produces a bounty of fine food products that are the foundation of both its traditional and modern cuisines.

AFTER STUDYING THIS CHAPTER YOU SHOULD BE ABLE TO:

- list the ways in which the Mid-Atlantic region's climate and topography (Factor 1) affected its agriculture and cuisine
- discuss the minimal influence of Native American cooking (Factor 2) on Mid-Atlantic cooking, and explain why the region had no true colonial cuisine period
- describe the effects of the Mid-Atlantic's varied first-settler groups (Factor 3), and the resulting mixture of Old World cuisine influences, on the development of the region's early cuisine
- describe the effect of the region's early-arriving second-settler group (Factor 4) and the resulting development of two discrete subregional styles of Mid-Atlantic cooking
- discuss the food products and cooking styles of the Mid-Atlantic's two major cuisine cities (Factor 5) and three main "English" cuisine areas
- recount the history and development of the Pennsylvania Dutch microcuisine and list its defining dishes
- list and describe the ingredients, cooking methods, and flavor profiles of traditional Mid-Atlantic cuisine
- prepare authentic Mid-Atlantic and Pennsylvania Dutch dishes

APPETIZERS

U.S. Senate Bean Soup with Butter Crackers

Pennsylvania Dutch Chicken Corn Soup with Rivels and Cloverleaf Roll

Spinach, Mushroom, and Bacon Salad with Poppy Seed Dressing

Kennett Square Stuffed Mushroom Medley

Shad Roe in Brown Butter with Bacon and Asparagus

Corn Zephyrs with Fresh Tomato Sauce

Chilled New York State Foie Gras in Sauternes Gelée with Cranberry Compote

ENTRÉES

Baked Stuffed Shad in Mushroom Cream with Dried Corn Pudding and String Beans

Lenape Smoke-Roasted Bluefish with Cranberry-Maple Velouté, Corn Cake, and Watercress

Pan-Seared "Snapper" Bluefish on Potato Cake with Jersey Tomato Sauce and Tricolor Peppers

Pennsylvania Dutch Chicken Bot Boi with Saffron Noodles

Roast Long Island Duckling in Port Wine Demi-Glace with North-Shore Cauliflower Gratin and Arugula

Pennsylvania Dutch Sausage Trio with Sauerkraut and New Potatoes

Pan-Roasted Veal Chop in Apple-Mushroom Cream with Handmade Noodles and Brussels Sprouts

Lancaster County Roast Lamb in Minted Pan Gravy with Peas 'n' Pearl Onions in Potato Basket and Carrot Purée

DESSERTS

Shoofly Pie with Whipped Cream

Hershey Brownie Sundae with Philadelphia-Style Ice Cream and Hot Fudge Sauce

Pumpkin Roll with Cranberry Coulis

Allegheny Mountain Apple Dumpling with Vanilla Custard Sauce

WEBSITE EXTRAS

Breakfasts   Sandwiches   Hors d'Oeuvres   Thanksgiving Menu

MIDDLE GROUND

The Mid-Atlantic's culinary map roughly parallels its geopolitical boundaries, although some of its border areas reach into neighboring culinary regions. Much of upstate New York and the northern tip of Long Island are part of culinary New England. Similarly, extreme western New York State near Lake Erie, and western Pennsylvania beyond the Allegheny Mountains, merge into the Central Farmlands culinary region. A small crescent of south-central Pennsylvania belongs to the Chesapeake Bay Shore region. Finally, in this book New York City is considered its own, separate culinary region, although geographically it's located within the Mid-Atlantic. New York City cuisine is covered in Chapter 16.

The Mid-Atlantic culinary region oversteps its geopolitical borders in two areas. In southern Pennsylvania, Mid-Atlantic cooking crosses the Mason-Dixon Line and claims part of northern Maryland roughly from Westminster to the Appalachian Mountains. The Mid-Atlantic culinary region also claims Washington, D.C., a city that is not geographically connected to it. We'll discuss the development of D.C. cooking, and why it's classified as Mid-Atlantic cuisine, later in this chapter.

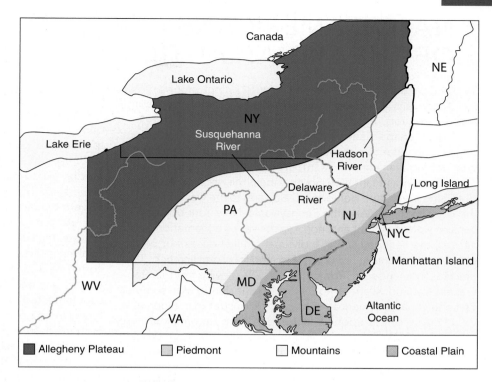

FIGURE 4.1
Mid-Atlantic Topography

TOPOGRAPHICAL DIVERSITY

The Mid-Atlantic's topography is dominated by three great rivers: the Susquehanna, the Delaware, and the Hudson. Each of these rivers and its valley were created by fast-flowing water during the recession of the last ice age.

The region's coastal topography changes as one moves northward from the mouth of the Chesapeake Bay. Along the flat, sandy Delaware and New Jersey shores, a system of low barrier islands and tidal inlets is an extension of Plantation South coastal topography. Just north of New Jersey, foothills meet sea in a series of rocky cliffs. Here the Hudson River flows southeast through granite walls to meet the Atlantic at Manhattan, an island formed of solid bedrock. Figure 4.1 shows the Mid-Atlantic's varied topography.

The region's inland topography is equally varied. In central Pennsylvania and south-central New York, the coastal plain rises to piedmont and then climbs to form part of the Appalachian chain. Both plain and piedmont are covered with deep, fertile glacial soil; they once were covered with beech, hemlock, and oak trees but now are mostly clear farmland. Farther west, Pennsylvania's Allegheny Mountains are gentle and rounded, covered

with deciduous trees. The region's mountains become higher and more forbidding as one travels north into New York, where the steep Adirondacks are mantled with deep forests of evergreen trees. West of the Appalachians the land flattens out to meet Lakes Erie and Ontario and slopes gently downward to become the eastern Ohio River Valley.

The Mid-Atlantic region lacks the crushing heat of Plantation South summers and the extreme weather of New England. Coastal and southeastern areas enjoy the weather-moderating effects of ocean and bay. Although the growing season is shorter in the north and in the mountains, most of the region has ample frost-free days to accommodate European food plants. Combined with the region's rich soil and gentle topography, the temperate climate paved the way for successful agriculture.

A variety of agricultural products are produced throughout the region. Certain areas are known for the quality of a specific product. Upstate New York is dairy country, producing milk for the region and cheeses distributed nationwide. The Hudson River Valley and New York Finger Lakes areas are known for fine fruits and vegetables and wine production. New Jersey is known as the Garden State, shipping produce across the nation and famous for the tomatoes and blueberries that thrive in its sandy soil. Delaware produces much of the nation's poultry. In Pennsylvania, Lancaster County is world famous for Pennsylvania Dutch farm products, and the Kennett Square area is known for cultivated mushrooms.

FACTOR 1

Varied topography and temperate climate allow diversified agriculture.

■
□ NATIVE AMERICANS
■ OF THE MID-ATLANTIC

By the time of European settlement two distinct groups of Native Americans inhabited the Mid-Atlantic region: the Lenape and the Iroquois.

The Lenape (len-AH-pay) were the Mid-Atlantic region's original inhabitants, numbering around twenty thousand at the time of European contact. Members of the same Algonquian language group as Plantation South tribes, they settled a territory stretching from Cape Henlopen, Delaware, to the western bank of the Hudson River along the Pennsylvania–New York border. The Lenape were peaceful and nonaggressive. Like Plantation South natives, the Lenape lived in individual family houses but participated in communal hunting, farming, and food preservation. They practiced human seasonal migration (p. 29), moving from semipermanent lowland villages into the mountains during high summer. Precontact native American settlement is illustrated in Figure 4.2.

People of the Iroquois language group entered northern areas of the Mid-Atlantic region in the early 1400s. By the late 1500s they had formed a confederation of five distinct tribes: the Mohawks, Cayugas, Oneidas, Onondagas, and Senecas. Their territory, divided longitudinally into five separate, locally controlled districts, stretched across present-day New York State from the Hudson River to the Great Lakes. Their inland location resulted in later contact with Europeans and, at first, protected them from European diseases. The Iroquois lived in large wooden longhouses, some of which sheltered as many as forty families. Hunting and farming were also communal. More aggressive and warlike than the Lenape, the Iroquois frequently fought among themselves as well as against other tribes.

Native American Agriculture and Cuisine

The agricultural practices and foodways of both Lenape and Iroquois Native Americans were similar to those of Plantation South tribes. Both practiced seasonal human migration and cyclical land use. Sharing the worldview of other Native American groups, Mid-Atlantic tribes had no concept of personal land ownership. Though territorial rights were recognized and observed, the land was considered a shared resource.

As the group coming into earlier contact with European settlers, the Lenape had far more influence on early Mid-Atlantic cooking than the Iroquois. Successfully raising Three Sisters corn, beans, and squash, they taught the region's first colonists to cook and enjoy these foods. Like other agricultural tribes, they supplemented agricultural produce with hunted and foraged foods. In spring they caught migratory shad in nets and feasted on both the flesh and the **roe,** or fish eggs. Today shad is a seasonal Mid-Atlantic specialty fish, and shad roe is a much-anticipated springtime treat. Because of its rich, oily flesh, shad is particularly suited to curing and smoking.

Foraged fruits, nuts, green plants, and root vegetables were a valued addition to the Three Sisters diet. Coastal Lenapes foraged for tuckahoe root, a starchy tuber that also sustained early European settlers in time of crop failure. This wild food remains a part of traditional Mid-Atlantic Native American cooking but has not entered the mainstream cuisine.

The inland and more northerly Iroquois had little positive contact with early European settlers. By the time the well-provisioned Holland Dutch were establishing farms in the Hudson Valley, relations with local Native Americans were already strained, and the Iroquois were headed westward. Thus, the cooking of the upper Mid-Atlantic exhibits virtually no Native American influence.

Although adopted by early colonists, Native American foods and food preservation techniques became less important in Mid-Atlantic cuisine once European food crops were established. Arriving later in history and better prepared than earlier first settlers, Mid-Atlantic colonists quickly grew wheat and raised food animals and temperate-climate crops. Though corn, beans, and squash remained part of the Mid-Atlantic diet, they were not as frequently served or as nutritionally important as in New England, the Chesapeake Bay Shore, the Plantation South, or the Appalachian South. Of all European settler groups, the Pennsylvania Dutch (p. 157) embraced cornmeal dishes most fully, and primarily continued to prepare them as everyday foods. In fact, until the rediscovery of America's Native American

FIGURE 4.2
Native American Settlement in the Mid-Atlantic

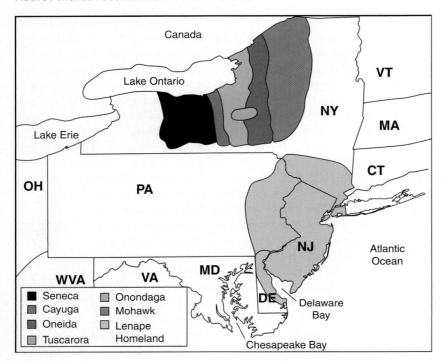

Seneca
Cayuga
Oneida
Tuscarora
Onondaga
Mohawk
Lenape Homeland

FACTOR 2

Native American foods influenced early cooking but are largely absent in modern cuisine.

food heritage in the 1990s, mainstream Mid-Atlantic cooking exhibited virtually no Native American influence.

■ EUROPEAN
□ SETTLEMENT

Throughout the 1600s various European powers vied with each other to reap the riches of the New World. By the middle of the century England had claimed and settled the Plantation South, the Chesapeake Bay Shore, and New England. However, the Mid-Atlantic—a large stretch of prime land between New England and the Chesapeake Bay—remained unclaimed and unoccupied by Europeans. The Mid-Atlantic region was easily accessible, had fertile soil and a moderate climate, and was populated by generally hospitable natives. It has never been explained why the English ignored such a choice territory for such a long time. However, the vacuum would soon be filled, albeit temporarily, by two other nations.

The Dutch and the Swedes

Both Holland Dutch and Swedish sailing ships were exploring the Delaware River as early as the 1620s. Unlike England, where overpopulation and social unrest drove emigration, these nations enjoyed prosperous economies and had comfortable middle classes with homogenous beliefs. Thus, Dutch and Swedish motives for gaining a foothold in the Americas were different from England's. Rather than establishing permanent colonies in which to resettle dissidents and the poor, they were interested in trading with Native Americans for furs and tobacco and cutting timber for export to Europe. Represented by the Dutch West India Company and the New Sweden Company, these two nations attempted to slip into the void between the English colonies to the north and south.

Having a merchant mentality, and no doubt wishing to avoid the violence that had occurred in other regions, the Swedes and Holland Dutch took a different approach to New World settlement. Upon arriving in several Mid-Atlantic locations, they proceeded to barter with the native inhabitants for land tracts on which to settle. Although the concept of individual land ownership was foreign to them, the Lenape universally accepted these land transactions.

Swedes were the first Europeans to settle in the Mid-Atlantic, establishing a small colony at the site of present-day Philadelphia. However, the Swedish presence was minimal, and Swedes had no significant impact on the region's cuisine. Although the Swedish people have a strong food culture, Swedish settlers in the Delaware Valley were primarily woodsmen who were more interested in logging and trading with the Lenape than in farming and cooking. Although today a small group of people living in the area still celebrate Swedish culinary heritage, Scandinavian cooking actually made little mark on Mid-Atlantic cuisine.

Dutch colonists from Holland settled Manhattan Island, Long Island, and the Hudson River Valley. Unlike the Swedes, the Holland Dutch arrived in search of farmland and soon began growing the familiar food crops of Western Europe. Buckwheat, a northern European staple, grew well in the cool upstate New York climate, and buckwheat dishes became a staple starch. However, New York Holland Dutch farmers eventually succeeded in growing wheat, as well as barley and hops. Thus, Mid-Atlantic colonists were the first in America to "grow" their own bread and beer. Preferring wheat to corn, and pork to game, Holland Dutch settlers began a tradition of Mid-Atlantic cooking that minimized native foods. Even after the region was ceded to the English, the baked goods, cheeses, hearty main dishes, and refined beers of Holland could be found throughout New York State. Additionally, the Hudson Valley Holland Dutch established St. Nicholas as the provider of Christmas gifts and instituted the Dutch custom of making and serving *kookjies* (cookies).

FACTOR 3
Dutch settlers in New York State grew wheat for bread and beer.

English Rule and Agricultural Economy

The foreign presence separating the New England and Plantation South colonies proved intolerable to the English government. In 1651, the English began a political and military campaign that would eventually wrest control of the Mid-Atlantic from the Holland Dutch and Swedes. Through armed conflict and the imposition of English settlers in Philadelphia and New York, the English finally prevailed. Soon Delaware, Pennsylvania, New York, and New Jersey became English colonies.

Contrary to Holland Dutch and Swedish policies, English governance included plans to remove Native Americans from the land to make way for English farmers. Through displacement, disease, and violence, the Mid-Atlantic was virtually emptied of its native population within a generation of English rule.

■ □
□ **ELEMENTS OF OLD WORLD HOLLAND DUTCH CUISINE**

FOUNDATION FOODS

    principal starches: wheat breads (potatoes)

    principal proteins: pork, dairy products, seafood

    principal produce: root vegetables, cabbages, tree fruits

FAVORED SEASONINGS: minimal

PRIMARY COOKING MEDIUM: butter

PRIMARY COOKING METHODS: stewing, poaching

FOOD ATTITUDES: strong food culture, culinary conservatives

Once the English controlled the entire eastern seaboard, a thriving food trade developed between the Mid-Atlantic and England's northern and southern colonies. Having the proper terrain and climate for growing colonial domesticates, the Mid-Atlantic became America's first breadbasket, providing wheat and other food crops to a hungry colonial market.

NEW YORK FOOD PRODUCTS

In the Hudson Valley, both long-established Holland Dutch farm families and newly arrived English and Scots-Irish farmers expanded arable lands and began to grow wheat on a larger scale. Central New York State shipped its wheat and other grain products to a growing New England market. Dairy farms expanded. Tree fruits, berries, and garden produce were also important products.

In response to the urbanization of colonial New York City, eastern Long Island became the market garden of Manhattan. Long Island provided the city with fruits and vegetables, especially cauliflowers, cucumbers, potatoes, buckwheat, and native pumpkins and corn. Long Island farmers raised chickens and ducks, among them a small, tender crossbred Peking type that became known as the Long Island duck. The island was also an important breeding ground for sheep, cattle, hogs, and other domestic animals.

Long Islanders early recognized their limited space. Thus, Long Island farmers understood the need for land management much earlier than their counterparts on the mainland. Among few colonists of their time to use fertilizer, Long Island farmers had a ready source: New York City shipped the manure from its draft horses to Long Island. By the time other areas of New York State were facing soil nutrient depletion caused by poor agricultural practices, eastern Long Island was producing record crop yields.

Long Island soon became the center of a booming regional fishing industry. During early colonial days, Sheepshead Bay was home to one of the world's largest fishing fleets. The shallows surrounding the island were teeming natural oyster beds; Long Island oysters were considered America's finest, fetching high prices at Manhattan's Fulton Fish Market. In addition, Long Island fishing fleets were willing to venture out across the continental shelf and into deep water in search of ocean fish.

FACTOR 5
The Mid-Atlantic grew colonial domesticate cash crops for export to the Plantation South and New England.

Today the prefix *Long Island* added to the name of oysters or any other seafood automatically raises the price. Long Island bay scallops are hand-harvested and sold fresh, making them far superior to mechanically shucked, treated scallops. Lobsters caught off Long Island rival those of New England.

Today farming and fishing are threatened by Long Island's appeal as a beach resort. Both state and local governments seek to protect Long Island farmland by creating agricultural districts, buying up development rights, and extending tax breaks to working farms. To maximize land values, many Long Island truck farmers have turned to high-labor, high-profit specialty items such as microgreens, baby vegetables, heirloom tomatoes, and Asian vegetables.

Wine grapes are a Long Island specialty crop. Because of the mild climate and sandy soil, Long Island growers established European vinifera vines and today produce high-quality, European-style table wines.

NEW JERSEY FARMING AND FISHING

Soon to be called the Garden State, New Jersey was not far behind Long Island in both truck farming and fishing. Here the flat terrain, temperate climate, and sand-loam soil composition made market gardening easy and profitable. All manner of European and American fruits and vegetables were grown for sale in New York City, Philadelphia, and smaller cities and towns. By the mid-1800s New Jersey had become famous for both sweet corn and tomatoes. Because New Jersey produced food in excess, in the late 1800s it became the site of some of America's earliest food-processing plants.

Today much of northern New Jersey has become industrial, and much of central New Jersey is covered with suburban housing tracts. However, South Jersey still comprises mile after mile of cultivated land. Flat, sandy fields near the coast are well suited for crops such as blueberries and tomatoes. The Jersey tomato is renowned for its meaty texture, sweet and tangy flavor, and hefty size. Jersey sweet corn is a summertime specialty, the fresh ears picked and packed at dawn to be shipped to Philadelphia and New York City markets for same-day service. Spinach, broccoli rabe, zucchini, and bell peppers are important crops as well.

New Jersey's commercial fishing fleet brings in a variety of seafood, such as flounder, fluke, bluefish, weakfish, tuna, sea bass, drum, and shad as well as clams, mussels, scallops, lobsters, and squid. Sport fishermen venture into the Atlantic for striped bass, swordfish, and tuna, and individual anglers cruise the bays and inlets for smaller catch, with young "snapper" bluefish a favorite for summer eating.

PENNSYLVANIA AGRICULTURE

The Pennsylvania colony's original name was Penn's Sylvania—literally "Penn's Woods"—so called because the land was covered with deciduous woodland. Founded by William Penn as a haven for members of the Society of Friends, commonly called Quakers, Pennsylvania became known the world over as a beacon of religious tolerance. Penn's colony equally welcomed second-settler immigrants of all faiths and became an ideal destination for Europe's separatist religious groups.

The largest second-settler group to arrive in Pennsylvania consisted of German-speaking people from the **Rhineland,** an area that borders the Rhine River from the Swiss Alps along the French/German border through Germany and the Netherlands to the North Sea. This group comprised members of several separatist Protestant sects. Primarily farmers, they migrated west from Philadelphia into south-central Pennsylvania's Lancaster County, an area they made nationally famous for fine produce, dairy products, and meats. Following the custom of the day, English-speaking colonists called these former Rhinelanders "Dutch," soon to be known as **Pennsylvania Dutch.** This second-wave settler group arrived directly after the original English settlers, and almost instantly began affecting the region's cuisine.

Pennsylvania Dutch settlers blended their traditional Germanic cooking with New World products to create the unique American microcuisine discussed on this book's companion website. Additionally, their cooking style and fine food products strongly influenced mainstream Mid-Atlantic cooking. Generations of "English" cooks relied on Pennsylvania Dutch farm markets (Figure 4.3) for the best Mid-Atlantic ingredients.

Once its trees had been cleared for farming, Pennsylvania had the largest amount of arable land of any Mid-Atlantic colony. Pennsylvania Dutch farmers grew much of the colonies' wheat and produced a wide variety of other food crops. Even today, agriculture is Pennsylvania's largest industry. Although wheat production eventually moved to the Midwest, Pennsylvania remains an important producer of corn, soybeans, and other commodity crops. Pennsylvania is the nation's fourth-largest dairy producer and leads in mushroom production. In the 21st century Pennsylvania farmers have begun growing specialty products such as microgreens, wine and table grapes, free-range lamb, game animals, and Christmas trees.

FACTOR 4
Pennsylvania Dutch settlers established prosperous farms.

FIGURE 4.3

Amish farmers sell produce at Lancaster's Central Market. Courtesy Pennsylvania Dutch Convention and Visitors Bureau

■ TRADITIONAL MID-
■ ATLANTIC CUISINE

Because the Mid-Atlantic is located between New England and the Plantation South and was founded by the same first-settler group, you might expect its cuisine to be similar to that of one or both of these neighbors. Although Mid-Atlantic cooking is somewhat influenced by its neighbors and shares the same foundation cuisine, it's quite different from both.

Like its neighboring cuisines, Mid-Atlantic cooking is based on the Old World English cooking introduced in Chapters 2 and 3. However, much Mid-Atlantic cooking is based on the foodways of a different group of second settlers. Even more important, the cuisine's development was affected by different philosophies about growing food and eating it.

Mid-Atlantic Attitudes

As agricultural centers, the colonial Mid-Atlantic and the colonial Plantation South shared many similarities: large expanses of good soil, easily tillable terrain, and temperate weather. Nonetheless, these two regions had different ideas about farming that shaped their cuisines in profoundly different ways. Unlike aristocratic Southern planters with huge land grants, most Mid-Atlantic farmers were small landowners who chose to grow food crops for their own use and for domestic sale rather than raise labor-intensive cash crops for international trade. Mid-Atlantic farmers typically worked their own properties using the help of large extended families that included many children. Therefore, the use of slaves did not suit their farming practices. Moreover, highly influential Pennsylvania Quakers strongly opposed slavery in that state. Thus, slavery did not contribute to the region's development, economically or culinarily. Although the Mid-Atlantic was largely spared the social evils of slavery, its traditional cooking was not enriched by the culinary influence of African and African-Caribbean slaves. Mid-Atlantic cooking remains mild and moderate, lacking the bold flavors, strong seasoning, and signature ingredients that African-American foodways lent to America's Southern cuisines.

Though Mid-Atlantic cuisine lacks the sizzle and spice of Plantation Southern cooking, it also rejects the Puritan austerity of New England cooking. Although both were English and highly religious, Mid-Atlantic Quakers and New England Puritans had fundamentally different worldviews. Therefore, they had different attitudes about food and eating.

As you've learned, the English food culture on which most American colonial cooking is based is classified as minimized—and Puritans discouraged focusing on food. However, the immediate arrival of second settlers affected the Mid-Atlantic's food attitudes early on. Both Holland Dutch colonists in New York and settlers from other Rhineland areas in Pennsylvania brought a stronger and more expansive food culture to the area. The bounteous dining habits of Holland Dutch farmers made the New York countryside famous for the abundance of its tables. These Rhineland settlers shared a strong Germanic food culture and loved to eat. Although

TWO STYLES OF MID-ATLANTIC COOKING

"English" Mid-Atlantic cuisine is primarily based on the Old World cooking of English and other British Isles settlers, with limited influence from Pennsylvania Dutch cooking.

Pennsylvania Dutch Mid-Atlantic cuisine is based on Old World Germanic Rhineland cooking, with limited adoption of Native American foods and cooking methods and slight influence of Old World "English" cuisine.

However much they liked to eat, most Mid-Atlantic settlers were culinary conservatives and rarely experimented with native foods. Although the Pennsylvania Dutch adopted a limited number of New World corn dishes and some indigenous foraged foods, Mid-Atlantic cuisine is mostly based on European colonial domesticates and has not embraced many external influences from later immigrant groups.

In summary, Mid-Atlantic cuisine blended Old World English cooking and Old World Rhineland cooking, primarily using colonial domesticates as ingredients. Because the region's first settlers made little use of indigenous ingredients and cooking methods, the Mid-Atlantic lacked a lengthy colonial cuisine period. Instead, the region progressed almost immediately to traditional Mid-Atlantic cuisine based on English and Rhineland foodways. As it evolved, Mid-Atlantic cuisine developed two distinctive subregional cooking styles: "English" and Pennsylvania Dutch (Figure 4.4).

FIGURE 4.4
Development of Mid-Atlantic Cuisine

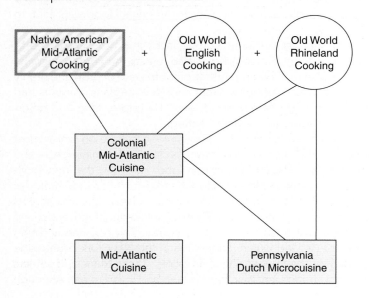

they valued moderation, first-settler English Quakers looked kindly on the pleasures of the table and tolerated excess in others. This stands in sharp contrast to Puritan New England, where gluttony was considered a major sin. In short: New Englanders ate to live, but much of the Mid-Atlantic lived to eat. Large portions of well-marbled meats, rich sauces, steaming bowls of potatoes and handmade noodles, fresh vegetables dripping with butter, and sideboards laden with homemade desserts are representative of Mid-Atlantic cuisine.

As you'll learn later in this chapter on p. 157, the Pennsylvania Dutch are a large and unique American minority community. You'll explore the Pennsylvania Dutch microcuisine on the website. First, though, let's learn about the "English" style.

ENGLISH COOKING OF THE MID-ATLANTIC

The Pennsylvania Dutch typically refer to people not of Rhineland extraction as *English*, no matter what their ancestry may be. For the purposes of this book, the term *English* is helpful in distinguishing the Mid-Atlantic cuisine style practiced by non–Pennsylvania Dutch cooks.

The Mid-Atlantic's English cooking originally comprised English, Scots-Irish, and Holland Dutch foodways, later to be enriched by Irish and Welsh influences and, especially in port cities, French cooking techniques and selected Caribbean imports. Despite these varied influences, note that most are of British Isles origin, and virtually all are European.

The English style of Mid-Atlantic cooking prevailed throughout New York State, New Jersey, Delaware, and most large towns and cities. However, Pennsylvania Dutch cooking significantly influenced the English style in the Dutch homeland areas.

In the 1700s and 1800s the English-style cooking of Wilmington, Philadelphia, New Jersey, and the Hudson Valley was famous throughout the Americas and in Europe. Travelers to the Mid-Atlantic wrote of sumptuous meals and overflowing markets. Their praises were divided between American-grown European cultivars, such as asparagus, celery, and tree fruits, and native foods such as sweet corn and pumpkins. The quality of American pork and beef surpassed that of English-raised meat; moreover, meats from the Mid-Atlantic were considered the best in America. Mid-Atlantic seafood was extolled for its quality and abundance. Fishermen harvested striped bass, bluefish, weakfish, flounder, and fluke as well as blue crabs, oysters, and lobsters. The spring shad run brought thousands of the plump, silvery fish struggling upriver to spawn. People simply caught them in nets and baskets, seeking not only the fish itself but also the succulent roe.

FACTOR 3

The Mid-Atlantic's English cuisine style is based on first-settler cooking.

Philadelphia Cuisine

From colonial times to the early years of independence, Philadelphia was America's largest, most sophisticated city. Philadelphia cooks blended Mid-Atlantic English cooking with products from all over the globe. An important seaport, Philadelphia welcomed rum, sugar, molasses, ginger, allspice, and tropical fruits arriving daily from the Caribbean. Eastern spices, such as peppercorns, cloves, nutmeg, mace, saffron, cardamom, and cinnamon, arrived from Asia. Cheeses, olive oil, condiments, and fine wines were shipped from France, Italy, and Spain. The bounty of the Pennsylvania countryside rolled in from the west

FACTOR 5
Philadelphia boasted European-trained cooks and ingredients from around the world.

on Conestoga wagons, while New Jersey farm products floated eastward across the Delaware on barges. Philadelphia's outdoor food market was more than half a mile long and featured not only local products but the best of the imports as well.

As a center of commerce, education, and the arts—and also the nation's first capital—Philadelphia offered fine cuisine in private homes and in scores of inns and public eating houses such as the City Tavern, still in operation today. George Washington, Thomas Jefferson, and other political luminaries frequented Philadelphia's taverns and maintained households in the city. Ever the epicure, Jefferson shipped produce from his Monticello estate and imported French food products. The finest Philadelphia cooks supplemented plain English cooking with French techniques, featuring rich cream sauces, egg emulsion sauces, and aspic gelées. Vegetables were given pride of place on Philadelphia tables, with dishes such as asparagus mimosa, breaded fried Jerusalem artichokes, and creamed salsify.

Terrapin, or turtle, was a specialty that appeared on important Mid-Atlantic menus from colonial days through the late 1800s. Turtle soup, made from the prized diamondback terrapin, was often the subject of discussion and controversy, with regional recipes hotly debated.

Surrounded by lush pastureland, Philadelphia enjoyed an abundance of dairy products. French confectioners operating candy shops in the city soon took advantage of plentiful Pennsylvania and New Jersey milk and cream to produce ice cream of superb quality. Original Philadelphia-style ice cream is made with milk, cream, sugar, and natural flavorings only, with no egg yolks or other thickeners. In post-Revolutionary days, the most favored flavors were vanilla and lemon. Today certain Philadelphia ice cream companies such as Bassett's still make Philadelphia-style ice cream the traditional way. To distinguish between their local product and others, modern Philadelphians sometimes refer to egg-based ice cream as *frozen custard*.

As America transitioned from tavern food to restaurant cuisine in the late 1800s, Philadelphia led the trend. Seafood houses such as Bookbinder's offered diners the best of New Jersey, Long Island, and Chesapeake fish and shellfish. The large, elegant luncheon room of Wanamaker's department store offered ladies the opportunity to dine together without a male escort, while men continued to dine sumptuously in urban business clubs. Country clubs in Philadelphia's affluent Main Line suburbs offered fine family dining and catered events.

In the mid-1800s railroads revolutionized food transport. In Philadelphia and other cities, food markets were linked to rail lines. Home cooks and restaurant chefs frequented the Reading Terminal Market, a grand food hall located in what was then the city's primary railway station (see Figure 4.5). New Jersey and Pennsylvania Dutch farmers shipped their finest produce to the market situated just below the elevated terminal, while live cattle arrived by rail car to be slaughtered and fabricated in the sub-basement. Spices, groceries, preserved products, and cooked foods were available to urban residents and businessmen commuting to suburban

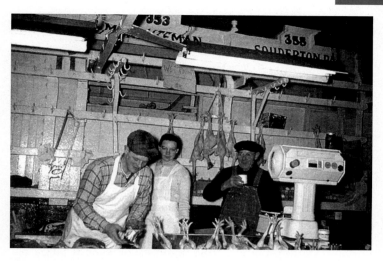

FIGURE 4.5

Halteman's Poultry sells Pennsylvania Dutch–raised chickens and turkeys in Philadelphia's Reading Terminal Market. Courtesy of the Reading Terminal Market

homes along the railroad's Main Line. By the late 1800s a rail spur running to South Philadelphia supplied the bustling outdoor Italian Market on 9th Street (Figure 4.6), offering pungent imported cheeses, cured meats, and olive oils, as well as an array of fresh meats, seafood, and produce.

The Great Depression, World War II, and postwar urban blight all took their toll on Philadelphia and other big cities. By the middle of the 20th century Philadelphia cuisine was in decline, and the city offered few serious dining experiences. The Reading Terminal Market had become dilapidated and stood virtually empty. However, in the 1970s renewed interest in cuisine revitalized the Philadelphia food scene and led to the Philadelphia restaurant renaissance. Today Philadelphia is once again recognized nationwide as a great food town.

FIGURE 4.6

In 1939 Di Bruno Bros. in Philadelphia's 9th Street Italian Market specialized in cheeses, cured meats, and groceries imported from Italy. The business remains in the family today. Courtesy of Di Bruno Bros.

FACTOR 5
Washington, D.C., boasts many fine American regional and world-cuisine restaurants.

The Many Cuisines of Washington, D.C.

In 1790 Washington, D.C., was carved out of two Southern states—Maryland and Virginia—to become our nation's capital. At its founding, D.C. welcomed congressmen previously posted in Philadelphia, the former capital, and their largely Mid-Atlantic staffs. Thus, the early cooking of Washington, D.C., was roughly equal parts Mid-Atlantic and Plantation South. Having excellent rail service early on, D.C. had access to prime ingredients from the eastern seaboard and the international port of Baltimore. Thanks to the nearby Chesapeake Bay, D.C. was and still is famous for serving fine seafood. However, as the influence of northern states grew, D.C.'s Southern flavor waned. Today, although Southern touches still exist in D.C. cooking, its traditional cuisine is primarily Mid-Atlantic.

In addition to its status as a Mid-Atlantic cuisine city, Washington, D.C., has been instrumental in defining America's national cuisine because the White House historically sets the standard for American dining. White House cuisine is discussed on this book's companion website.

Today Washington, D.C., welcomes an international community of embassy staff and world-traveled professionals. In response, hundreds of restaurants offer a variety of world cuisines. Although all major cuisines are well represented in D.C., its real treasures are the many tiny, authentic ethnic spots serving little-known world cuisines.

Long Island Cuisine

Long Island cuisine is primarily ingredient-driven. Although much of Long Island's fine produce and seafood is shipped to New York City and throughout the country, a significant amount stays on the island to become the basis of innovative dishes made by creative and free-thinking chefs.

The island reached economic viability early in its history; today its central and eastern parts are one of America's most exclusive and affluent areas. Wealthy vacationers in the Hamptons and other fashionable resort towns patronize Long Island farm stands, paying top dollar for sparkling-fresh local produce. Both amateur cooks and the personal chefs of the wealthy prepare seasonal meals featuring Long Island ingredients. High-end catering companies serve cutting-edge menus for the summer season's many parties.

The shore areas of central and eastern Long Island boast scores of luxury restaurants, many of them seasonal outposts of Manhattan hot spots. A number of Long Island restaurant chefs use primarily local products and serve only Long Island–produced wines.

As you travel eastward toward Montauk on the tip of the island, you leave the culinary Mid-Atlantic and enter the New England culinary region. Here traditional cooking features seafood prepared in the New England style.

Upstate New York and Hudson Valley Cuisines

The Hudson Valley and the Finger Lakes are known for exceptional dairy products, tree fruits, specialty produce, and fine wines. Originally settled by the Holland Dutch, the Hudson Valley retains the richness and abundance of their foodways but features few traditional Dutch dishes. Here the Mid-Atlantic "English" style is most purely English. Lacking the multicultural influences of more coastal areas, Hudson Valley and upstate New York cooking has always been farm-based and ingredient-driven.

Hudson Valley farmers were among America's first to specialize in high-quality **niche market products,** specialty items grown for a specific group of consumers. Organic dairy products, specialty produce, and free-range poultry and game are among the Hudson Valley's notable offerings. Hudson Valley duck **foie gras,** or fattened liver, rivals the goose foie gras of France. In the 1980s, when Hudson Valley winemakers began producing award-winning vinifera table wines and affluent New Yorkers joined artists and writers buying summer homes in the Woodstock area, many fine restaurants opened to national acclaim.

New Jersey and Coastal Delaware Cuisines

Vacationers and summer-home owners from across the southern Mid-Atlantic go "down the shore" to enjoy New Jersey's and Delaware's beaches and great fishing. Nonfishing summer residents and unlucky anglers rely on local seafood shops for fresh-caught local fish and shellfish.

Traditional Jersey Shore and coastal Delaware seafood restaurants typically serve simple fried and broiled dishes; however, fine-dining restaurants in shore towns such as Cape May, Stone Harbor, Margate, and Loveladies cater to a more sophisticated clientele and offer more imaginative presentations. Atlantic City's top casino restaurants cater to high rollers with the same types of buffets and restaurants seen in Las Vegas, discussed on p. 515.

North Jersey is home to a small but vibrant Portuguese community and a significant number of authentic Portuguese-cuisine restaurants (see pp. 101 and 102).

At roughly the same time, Henry John Heinz began bottling prepared horseradish in Pittsburgh, Pennsylvania. By 1890 Heinz boasted "57 Varieties" of products, tomato ketchup the best seller. Today Heinz produces more than half of the world's ketchup.

In 1894, Milton Hershey founded a small candy company in the heart of Pennsylvania Dutch dairy country. After experimenting with various formulas, Hershey developed a milk chocolate candy bar that took America by storm in 1900. Today Hershey is the largest confectionery company in the world, and the town of Hershey, Pennsylvania is known as "Chocolate Town, U.S.A."

PENNSYLVANIA DUTCH COOKING OF THE MID-ATLANTIC

In the Pennsylvania Dutch homeland areas of central Pennsylvania, south-central New York, and north-central Maryland, home cooking strongly reflects the Germanic heritage of the region's Rhineland immigrants. People of Pennsylvania Dutch heritage and their "English" neighbors prepare hearty dishes based on fresh pork, beef, and chicken, as well as preserved meats such as hams, sausages, and meat puddings. These protein foods are accompanied by Rhineland favorites such as braised cabbage and sauerkraut; many kinds of wheat flour noodles and dumplings; various potato dishes; and an array of pickles, jams, and preserves. Pennsylvania Dutch baked goods, including wheat and rye breads, sweet rolls, cakes, pies, and cookies, are renowned.

Pennsylvania Dutch cooks developed one of America's most distinctive—and commercially misrepresented—microcuisines.

INDUSTRIAL FOOD PRODUCTION

The Mid-Atlantic gave birth to some of America's earliest food technology. Shortly after the Civil War, the Anderson and Campbell Preserve Company of Camden, New Jersey, first began canning locally grown produce. The introduction of canned condensed soups made both the Campbell's name and the distinctive red-and-white label into American icons. Located near the tomato fields of southern New Jersey, the Campbell company made canned tomato soup a staple item in virtually every American kitchen.

MID-ATLANTIC CUISINE TODAY AND TOMORROW

Today's Mid-Atlantic cooking remains close to the traditional cuisine, blending both "English" and Pennsylvania Dutch foodways. Mid-Atlantic chefs champion locally produced food products and create new dishes faithful to the traditional style. A few chefs have researched the region's Native American cuisine heritage and create new dishes based on indigenous flavors and techniques. Mid-Atlantic dishes prepared by traditional methods are frequently brought up-to-date with modern plate presentations.

As in other highly populated areas, the Mid-Atlantic faces loss of agricultural land due to suburbanization. In addition, adverse market forces are driving Mid-Atlantic farmers off the land. Recent decreases in the price of milk are causing farmers to abandon dairying. Increases in the price of corn due to ethanol fuel production have led Mid-Atlantic farmers to grow more corn and less hay. The resulting high cost of both feeds makes small-scale meat production less profitable. For a cuisine based on fine local products, these trends are not encouraging.

In the late 1900s new immigrant groups settled in the Mid-Atlantic region. Mexicans were among the earliest, arriving in the 1960s to work in Southeastern Pennsylvania's mushroom houses and fruit orchards. Immigrants from India and Southeast Asia are also prominent in the region. However, their cuisines and foodways have remained separate. Although world-cuisines restaurants can be found in the region's urban areas and in some small towns, Mid-Atlantic regional cuisine has not been significantly altered. It remains moderate and ingredient-driven, reflecting its "English" and Pennsylvania Dutch roots.

Visit this book's companion website at www.pearsonhighered.com/sackett to learn more about the Pennsylvania Dutch microcuisine. Following are some photos relating to this microcuisine.

An Amish barn raising provides an occasion for hearty feasting. City of Toronto Archives, Fonds 1568, item 177

Pennsylvania Dutch farmers still use horse-drawn farm equipment. Jana Shea/Shutterstock

☐ TABLE 4.1 MID-ATLANTIC DEFINING DISHES

ITEM NAME	HISTORY	DOMINANT INGREDIENTS AND METHOD	MORE
US Senate Bean Soup	The presence of this dish on the menus of all eleven Capitol dining rooms is credited to Representative Joseph Cannon (US Speaker of the House 1903–1911) who loudly complained when it was not available, "Thunderation, I had my mouth set for bean soup! From now on, hot or cold, rain, snow or shine, I want it on the menu every day."	Small, white Navy beans are simmered in ham broth with aromatic vegetables.	This soup has both a Senate variation (thickened with potato) and a House variation (lightly thickened with crushed beans).
Philadelphia Pepperpot	According to legend, this soup was created during the harsh winter at Valley Forge when George Washington asked his cook to prepare something hearty and nourishing to raise the morale of his cold, hungry soldiers. In actuality, soups of this type were regularly prepared throughout the Mid-Atlantic colonies long before the Revolution.	Beef tripe, aromatic vegetables, and potatoes are slowly simmered in beef broth to achieve a thick, gelatinous texture. The soup is spiked with lots of ground black pepper.	Formerly a best-seller among Campbell's 21 original soups, in the late 1900s Pepperpot lost popularity due to changing tastes.
Spinach, Mushroom, and Bacon Salad	Originally made with standard curly spinach and local Kennett Square mushrooms, this signature dish of the 1970s Philadelphia restaurant renaissance pioneered the use of raw spinach and raw mushrooms.	Raw baby spinach is tossed with a sweet and tangy poppyseed vinaigrette and garnished with sliced raw mushrooms, red onions, crumbled cooked bacon, cherry tomatoes, and hard-cooked eggs.	Only fresh, firm, unblemished mushrooms should be used for this salad.
Oyster Stew	In the late 1800s and early 20th century, upper-class households often served this dish for supper on the cook's day off because it could be prepared at table in a chafing dish.	Shucked oysters are heated in their liquor (juices) with dry sherry, minced celery and onion, and cream. The dish is topped with pats of butter and a sprinkling of paprika, then served with toast.	The oysters must be heated a few seconds only, until they "ruffle."
Buffalo Wings	Now nationally popular, this dish was created in 1964 at the Original Anchor Bar in Buffalo, New York, when regular customers wanted something new for a bar snack.	Disjointed chicken wings are deep-fried crisp and then tossed with a combination of bottled hot pepper sauce, vinegar, and melted butter. Celery sticks and creamy blue cheese dip are served on the side.	Original style wings are called "naked." Today breaded and fried wings are also prepared and served Buffalo style.

☐ TABLE 4.1 MID-ATLANTIC DEFINING DISHES (continued)

ITEM NAME	HISTORY	DOMINANT INGREDIENTS AND METHOD	MORE
Baked Shad	A whole baked shad was the traditional center-piece of springtime feasts in the Mid-Atlantic region.	Professionally butchered boneless shad sides are baked just until the flesh is firm and opaque. The pocket resulting from boning may be stuffed before baking. Lemon juice, white wine, tomatoes, or other acidic ingredients contrast with shad's rich mouthfeel and full flavor.	Because of its complex structure of tiny pin bones hidden within the fillets, formerly shad was subjected to lengthy cooking times that dissolved the pin bones.
Shad Roe	The roe, or egg sacs, of the female shad are another spring delicacy.	Roe sacs are lightly precooked by poaching. The trimmed roe sacs are sautéed in bacon drippings or basted with butter and broiled. Shad roe is typically seasoned with lemon juice and garnished with crisp bacon.	Shad roe soufflé is an interesting variation.
Bluefish/ Snapper Bluefish	Dark-fleshed, oily bluefish are a traditional summer specialty in shore towns along the Mid-Atlantic coast and in the region's cities and towns. Freshness is key to good flavor and texture.	Bluefish from 3 to 15 pounds are filleted and portioned. Grilled and broiled fillets are basted with lemon juice, white wine, or other acidic ingredients. Baby "snapper blues" under 3 pounds are often grilled whole.	In New Jersey bluefish is often served with fresh tomato sauce.
Chicken 'n' Waffles	Mid-Atlantic cooks have used waffles as a starch base for saucy, savory dishes since colonial times.	A hot waffle is topped with a creamy chicken stew with fresh peas and diced carrots.	In colonial Philadelphia waffles were topped with a creamy catfish stew.
Stuffed Mushrooms	Kennet Square mushroom producers promoted stuffed mushroom recipes in the late 1960s.	Large, firm mushroom caps are filled with ingredients bound with breadcrumbs and then baked. Popular fillings include spinach and cheese, sausage, and crabmeat mixtures.	A very large portabella mushroom with a meatless filling makes a good vegetarian entrée.
Brownie Sundae	According to urban legend, this dish was created in the 1970s when a Philadelpia restaurant needed a quick, easy dessert because the pastry chef walked out.	A chocolate brownie is topped with a scoop of vanilla Philadelphia-style ice cream and drizzled with Hershey's chocolate sauce.	Hot fudge may replace the Hershey's chocolate syrup.

■ □ ■ STUDY QUESTIONS

1. Describe the climate and topography of the Mid-Atlantic region. Contrast Mid-Atlantic climate and topography with those of New England and the Plantation South.

2. Explain the lack of Native American influence in traditional Mid-Atlantic cuisine.

3. Discuss the differences between Mid-Atlantic agricultural philosophies and practices and those of the Plantation South.

4. Describe the "English" style of Mid-Atlantic cooking. In addition to the English, what other groups contributed to the cuisine? Give three examples of their culinary contributions.

5. Discuss the food history and modern cuisines of the following Mid-Atlantic areas:

    a. Philadelphia
    b. Washington, D.C.
    c. Long Island
    d. the Hudson Valley and upstate New York
    e. the New Jersey and Delaware shores

6. Relate the history of the Pennsylvania Dutch, beginning with their European origin and including early settlement and the Pennsylvania Dutch diaspora.

7. Describe Pennsylvania Dutch cuisine. List and describe three Pennsylvania Dutch defining dishes.

8. List and describe five defining dishes of the Mid-Atlantic culinary region.

9. Using the information in this chapter and your imagination, plan a four-course special-occasion dinner menu featuring Mid-Atlantic cuisine.

U.S. Senate Bean Soup
with Butter Crackers

yield: 1 (8-fl.oz.) appetizer serving
(multiply × 4 for classroom turnout; adjust equipment sizes accordingly)

MASTER RECIPE

production		costing only
1 c.	U.S. Senate Bean Soup, hot in steam table	1/4 recipe
1	6" doily or cocktail napkin	1 each
tt	fresh-ground black pepper	1/16 oz.
1 tsp.	chopped flat-leaf parsley	1/40 bunch a.p.
3	Butter Crackers	1/8 recipe

service turnout:
1. Plate the dish:
   a. Stir the U.S. Senate Bean Soup well and ladle it into a hot 10-fl.-oz. soup cup.
   b. Place the cup slightly to the left on an 8" plate lined with a 6" doily.
   c. Grind pepper onto the soup and sprinkle it with parsley.
   d. Arrange the Butter Crackers on the plate to the right of the soup cup.

COMPONENT RECIPE
U.S. SENATE BEAN SOUP

yield: 1 qt.

production		costing only
1 c.	Navy beans or white pea beans	6 oz.
1	smoked ham hock, sawed crosswise into 4 pieces	7 oz.
6 c.	water	n/c
1	clove	1/16 oz.
1/4	small yellow onion	1 1/2 oz. a.p.
1	bay leaf	1/16 oz.
1 sprig	fresh thyme	1/20 bunch a.p.
1	peeled russet potato, in one piece	2 1/4 oz. a.p.
2 Tbsp.	butter	1 oz.
1 c.	fine-chopped yellow onion	5 oz. a.p.
1/2 c.	peeled, fine-chopped celery	1/10 head a.p.
1 tsp.	minced garlic	1/9; oz. a.p.
tt	kosher salt	1/16 oz.

preparation:
1. Quick-soak the beans:
   a. Place the beans in a 2-qt. saucepan, cover with water to twice their depth, and bring to the boil.
   b. Immediately remove from the heat and allow to soak for 1 hour.
2. Prepare the ham broth:
   a. Place the ham hock in a 3-qt. saucepan and add 6 c. water. Bring to the simmer and skim off the foam.
   b. Stick the clove into the onion.
   c. Add the onion, bay leaf, thyme, and potato to the ham broth. Cover the pan and simmer 30 minutes.
   d. Remove the potato, which should be quite soft. Place in a small bowl and reserve at room temperature.
3. Drain and rinse the beans. Add them to the ham broth and simmer 30 minutes.
4. In a 10" sauté pan, melt the butter and sweat the onion, celery, and garlic until soft.
5. Scrape the vegetables into the soup and continue to simmer 30 minutes, until the beans are tender and the flavors melded.
6. Remove the ham hocks, onion and clove, bay leaf, and thyme stem from the soup.
7. Cool the hock, then pick the meat from it. Tear the meat into small pieces and return it to the soup.
8. Thicken the soup:
   a. Ladle a little of the soup broth into the bowl with the potato.
   b. Mash the potato into a smooth purée.
   c. Stir enough purée back into the soup to thicken it lightly.
9. Taste the soup and season with salt if needed.

holding: open-pan cool and immediately refrigerate in a freshly sanitized, covered container up to 5 days; freeze up to 3 months

---

RECIPE VARIATION

U.S. House of Representatives Bean Soup
Omit the potato. Lightly thicken the soup at the end of cooking by crushing some of the white beans.

Pennsylvania Dutch Chicken Corn Soup
with Rivels and Cloverleaf Roll

yield: 1 (8-fl.-oz.) appetizer serving
(multiply × 4 for classroom turnout; adjust equipment sizes accordingly)

MASTER RECIPE

production		costing only
1 c.	Chicken Corn Soup	1/4 recipe
1	6" doily or cocktail napkin	1 each
1 Tbsp.	chopped hard-cooked egg	1/4 each
2 tsp.	chopped celery leaves	n/c
1 tsp.	chopped flat-leaf parsley	1/40 bunch a.p.
1	Cloverleaf Roll	1/8 recipe
1 Tbsp.	chilled butter rosette	1/2 oz.
1	small lettuce leaf	1/12 head a.p.

service turnout:
1. Stir the Chicken Corn Soup well and ladle it into a 1-qt. saucepan. Heat just to the boil.
2. Plate the dish:
   a. Ladle the soup into a hot 10-fl.-oz. soup plate.
   b. Place the soup plate on a 10" plate lined with a 6" doily.
   c. Sprinkle the soup with the egg, celery, and parsley.
   d. Place the Cloverleaf Roll on a side plate with the butter rosette on the leaf.

COMPONENT RECIPE

CHICKEN CORN SOUP

yield: 1 qt.

production		costing only
1	chicken leg	8 oz. a.p.
4 c.	Poultry Stock	1/4 recipe
1 sprig	fresh thyme	1/20 bunch a.p.
1 sprig	fresh sage	1/10 bunch a.p.
2 Tbsp.	butter	1 oz.
1/2 c.	minced yellow onion	2 1/2 oz.
1/4 c.	peeled, minced celery	1/20 head a.p.
3 ears	fresh corn on the cob	3 ears a.p.
1/2 tsp.	crushed saffron threads	0.01 oz. or 0.35 g
tt	kosher salt	1/16 oz.
1/2 c.	Rivels	1 recipe
tt	sugar, optional	1/16 oz.

preparation:
1. Fabricate and cook the chicken:
   a. Skin the chicken leg and trim it of all fat.
   b. Chop the leg through the bone into 4 pieces.
   c. Place the chicken pieces in a 6-qt. saucepan and add the Poultry Stock.
   d. Bring the stock to the simmer, skim, add the thyme and sage, and simmer 30 minutes, until the chicken is tender.
2. Melt the butter in an 8" sauté pan and sweat the onion and celery until soft.
3. Fabricate the corn:
   a. Husk the corn and remove all silk.
   b. Cut one ear of corn in half and reserve 1/2 ear for whole kernels.
   c. Using the tip of a sharp knife, and holding the remaining ears upright in a large bowl, slit each row of kernels lengthwise. Using the back of the knife, scrape out the corn pulp.
   d. Cut the whole kernels off the reserved 1/2 ear.
4. Remove the chicken pieces and herb sprigs from the stock.
5. Cool the chicken pieces and cut the meat into 3/8" dice. Reserve.
6. Scrape the onion and celery into the stock. Add the corn pulp and kernels and the saffron. Season with salt and bring to a lively simmer.
7. Add the Rivels, cover the pan, and simmer about 20 minutes until the rivels are al dente and the flavors melded.
8. Return the chicken to the soup, correct the salt, and balance the flavor with a little sugar if the corn is not naturally sweet.

holding: open-pan cool and immediately refrigerate in a freshly sanitized, covered container up to 3 days

COMPONENT RECIPE
RIVELS

yield: 1/2 c.

production		costing only
1/2 c.	flour	2 1/2 oz.
±1/2	beaten egg	±1/2 each or 1 oz.

preparation:
1. Mix the dough:
   a. Place the flour on the work surface and make a well in the center.
   b. Add the egg and mix to make a stiff dough.
   c. Knead about 3 minutes.
2. Fabricate the rivels:
   a. Hold a box grater over a half-sheet tray and grate the dough through the large holes, pushing hard to make large nuggets.
   b. Cover the tray with a kitchen towel.

holding: store covered with a towel at cool room temperature up to 3 hours; may be individually frozen on the tray, transferred to a plastic bag, and frozen up to 3 months

---

RECIPE VARIATIONS

Winter Chicken Corn Soup with Rivels
Replace the fresh corn with 2 c. canned creamed corn.

Egg-Drop Chicken Corn Soup
Omit the Rivels. Heat the soup to order and, just before serving, stir in 2 Tbsp. beaten egg to form soft strands. Omit the chopped-egg garnish.

Spinach, Mushroom, and Bacon Salad
with Poppy Seed Dressing

yield: 1 (4-oz.) appetizer serving
(multiply × 4 for classroom turnout)

MASTER RECIPE

production		costing only
3 oz.	precleaned baby spinach	3 oz.
3	small, very fresh white mushrooms, wiped clean and sliced thin	1 1/2 oz. a.p.
3 Tbsp.	Poppy Seed Dressing, in squeeze bottle	1/5 recipe
2 thin slices	small peeled red onion	1/2 oz. a.p.
1/2 c.	Onion Croutons	1/4 recipe
1/4 c.	crumbled crisp-cooked bacon	1 oz. a.p.
3	cherry tomatoes, halved	1/8 pt. a.p.

service turnout:
1. Place the spinach and mushrooms in a bowl, shake the Poppy Seed Dressing well, and squeeze about 2 Tbsp. of the dressing onto them. Toss to lightly coat.
2. Plate the dish:
   a. Mound the spinach and mushrooms on a cool 10" plate.
   b. Break the onion into rings and arrange them on top of the spinach.
   c. Scatter the Onion Croutons and bacon on the salad.
   d. Arrange the tomatoes around the edge of the salad greens.
   e. Drizzle with the remaining dressing.

COMPONENT RECIPE
POPPY SEED DRESSING

yield: 1 c.

production		costing only
1 Tbsp.	minced shallot	1/2 oz. a.p.
1 Tbsp.	honey	1/2 fl. oz.
2 tsp.	kosher salt	1/3 oz.
1 tsp.	fine-ground white pepper	1/16 oz.
1 tsp.	dry mustard	1/16 oz.
2 Tbsp.	black poppy seeds	1/2 oz.
1/4 c.	raspberry vinegar	2 fl. oz.
1 Tbsp.	fresh lemon juice	1/5 [90 ct.] lemon
1/2 c.	canola or safflower oil	4 fl. oz.

preparation:
1. Have all ingredients at room temperature.
2. Place all ingredients except the oil in a bowl.
3. Whisk in the oil in a thin stream to form an emulsion.
4. Correct the seasoning to make a slightly sweet, tart dressing.

holding: store in a freshly sanitized squeeze bottle at cool room temperature up to 3 hours; refrigerate up to 2 weeks; bring to room temperature before using

COMPONENT RECIPE
ONION CROUTONS

yield: 2 c.

production		costing only
2 c.	3/8" cubes crustless American White Bread	1/6 recipe
1/4 c.	melted butter	2 fl. oz.
tt	fine salt	1/16 oz.
1 tsp.	granulated onion	1/16 oz.

preparation:
1. Preheat an oven to 400°F.
2. Toss the bread cubes with the butter and place them on a half-sheet tray.
3. Bake in the center of the oven 8 to 10 minutes, until crisp and lightly browned.
4. While still warm, toss with the salt and onion.

holding: open-pan cool and store in a freshly sanitized, covered container at cool room temperature up to 3 days

---

RECIPE VARIATION

Spinach, Mushroom, and Bacon Salad with Creamy Blue Cheese Dressing
Replace the Poppy Seed Dressing with a dressing made by blending 1/3 c. crumbled blue cheese with 1/3 c. mayonnaise, 1/3 c. sour cream, 1 Tbsp. minced shallot, and sugar and cider vinegar to taste.

Kennett Square Stuffed Mushroom Medley

yield: 1 (5-oz.) appetizer serving
(multiply × 4 for classroom turnout)

MASTER RECIPE

production		costing only
1	Spinach-Stuffed Mushroom	1/4 recipe
1	Sausage-Stuffed Mushroom	1/4 recipe
1	Crab-Stuffed Mushroom	1/4 recipe
1/4 c.	Aurora Cream Sauce, in squeeze bottle, held in steam table	1/4 recipe
1/4 c.	Emerald Cream Sauce, in squeeze bottle, held in steam table	1/4 recipe
1 sprig	flat-leaf parsley	1/20 bunch a.p.

service turnout:

1. Place the Stuffed Mushrooms on a sizzle plate and bake in a 400°F oven about 12 minutes, until heated through and beginning to brown on top.
2. Plate the dish:
   a. Squeeze an arc of Aurora Cream Sauce on the right side of a hot 10" plate.
   b. Squeeze a similar arc of Emerald Cream Sauce on the left.
   c. Arrange the mushrooms in the center.
   d. Stick the parsley sprig upright in the center of the mushrooms.

COMPONENT RECIPE
SPINACH-STUFFED MUSHROOMS

yield: 4 mushrooms

production		costing only
4	3" stuffing-size domestic mushrooms	8 oz. a.p.
1 Tbsp.	corn oil	1/2 fl. oz.
12 oz.	cleaned, stemmed, deveined spinach	12 oz.
2 Tbsp.	butter	1 oz.
1 Tbsp.	minced shallot	1/2 oz. a.p.
1 tsp.	minced garlic	1/9 oz. a.p.
tt	kosher salt	1/16 oz.
tt	ground nutmeg	1/16 oz.
1/2 c.	Butter-Toasted Bread Crumbs*	1/4 recipe

preparation:

1. Fabricate and par-cook the mushrooms*:
   a. Wipe the mushrooms clean with damp paper towels.
   b. Trim away any dry, brown stem ends and then pull the stems out of the caps.
   c. Chop the stems fine.
   d. Heat a 10" sauté pan until very hot. Add the oil, then add the mushroom caps, concave side up. Sear a few seconds until browned on the bottom, then turn the mushrooms over and sear a second or two longer.
   e. Place the mushrooms concave side down on a half-sheet tray and cool to room temperature.
   f. Reserve any liquid that collects around the mushrooms.
2. Prepare the stuffing:
   a. Blanch the spinach in rapidly boiling water 5 seconds, refresh it in cold water 10 seconds, then squeeze it very dry.
   b. Chop the spinach fine.
   c. Heat an 8" sauté pan, add the butter, and sauté the chopped mushroom stems, shallot, and garlic until soft.
   d. Add the mushroom liquid and the spinach, and sauté until well coated with butter.
   e. Season the mixture with salt and nutmeg, then mix in the Butter-Toasted Bread Crumbs.
   f. Cool to room temperature.
3. Stuff the mushrooms with the spinach filling.

holding: refrigerate in a freshly sanitized, covered container, with pan liner between layers, up to 3 days

*If preparing three types of stuffed mushrooms for the Kennett Square Stuffed Mushroom Medley, parcook all mushrooms at the same time. Prepare enough Butter-Toasted Bread Crumbs for all three stuffings.

COMPONENT RECIPE
SAUSAGE-STUFFED MUSHROOMS

yield: 4 mushrooms

production		costing only
4	3" stuffing-size domestic mushrooms	8 oz. a.p.
1 Tbsp.	corn oil	1/2 fl. oz.
6 oz.	bulk sweet Italian sausage	6 oz.
1/2 c.	Butter-Toasted Bread Crumbs	1/4 recipe
2 Tbsp.	brunoise-cut red bell pepper	1 oz. a.p.

preparation:
1. Prepare the mushrooms as directed in step 1 of Spinach-Stuffed Mushrooms, p. 165.
2. Prepare the stuffing:
   a. Place the sausage in an 8" sauté pan and cook over medium heat, breaking up the lumps, until the sausage is cooked through.
   b. Remove the sausage with a slotted spoon and drain on paper towels.
   c. Pour off all but 1 Tbsp. sausage drippings.
   d. Add the mushroom stems to the pan and sauté until soft.
   e. Mix in the sausage and Butter-Toasted Bread Crumbs.
   f. Cool to room temperature.
3. Stuff the mushrooms with the sausage mixture.
4. Press 1/4 of the red bell pepper on top of each mushroom.

holding: refrigerate in a freshly sanitized, covered container, with pan liner between layers, up to 3 days

COMPONENT RECIPE
CRAB-STUFFED MUSHROOMS

yield: 4 mushrooms

production		costing only
4	3" stuffing-size domestic mushrooms	8 oz. a.p.
1 Tbsp.	corn oil	1/2 fl. oz.
2 Tbsp.	butter	1 oz.
1 Tbsp.	minced shallot	1/4 oz. a.p.
tt	kosher salt	1/16 oz.
2/3 c.	backfin crabmeat, picked over for shell fragments	4 oz. a.p.
2 Tbsp.	mayonnaise	1 fl. oz.
pinch	Chesapeake seasoning	1/16 oz.
2 tsp.	minced lemon zest	n/c
1 tsp.	fresh lemon juice	1/16 [90 ct.] lemon
1 Tbsp.	minced flat-leaf parsley	1/20 bunch a.p.
1/4 c.	Butter-Toasted Bread Crumbs	1/8 recipe

preparation:
1. Prepare the mushrooms as directed in step 1 of Spinach-Stuffed Mushrooms, p. 165.
2. Prepare the stuffing:
   a. Heat an 8" sauté pan, heat the butter, and sauté the mushroom stems and shallot until soft.
   b. Season with salt and cool to room temperature.
   c. Mix the chopped mushrooms with the crabmeat, mayonnaise, Chesapeake seasoning, lemon zest, lemon juice, parsley, and any liquid that accumulated around the mushroom caps.
   d. Correct the seasoning.
3. Stuff the mushrooms with the crab filling and press the Butter-Toasted Bread Crumbs on top.

holding: refrigerate in a freshly sanitized, covered container, with pan liner between layers, up to 3 days

COMPONENT RECIPE
AURORA CREAM SAUCE

yield: 1 c.

production		costing only
1 Tbsp.	minced shallot	1/4 oz. a.p.
1 Tbsp.	canned tomato purée	1/2 fl. oz.
1 1/2 c.	heavy cream	12 fl. oz.
tt	kosher salt	1/16 oz.

preparation:
1. Place the shallot, tomato purée, and cream in an 8" sauté pan and bring to the boil.
2. Reduce the sauce to a nappé consistency.
3. Force the sauce through a fine-mesh strainer.
4. Season with salt.

holding: refrigerate in a freshly sanitized, covered, nonreactive container up to 5 days; correct consistency before using

COMPONENT RECIPE
EMERALD CREAM SAUCE

yield: 1 c.

production		costing only
1/4 c.	flat-leaf parsley leaves	1/8 bunch a.p.
1/4 c.	fresh chives, cut in 1" lengths	1/6 bunch a.p.
1 1/2 c.	heavy cream	12 fl. oz.
1 Tbsp.	minced shallot	1/4 oz. a.p.
tt	kosher salt	1/16 oz.

preparation:
1. Prepare the herbs:
   a. Blanch the parsley and chives in rapidly boiling water for 2 seconds then immediately refresh in ice water.
   b. Drain the herbs and squeeze them dry.
   c. Chop the herbs.
2. Place the cream and shallot in an 8" sauté pan and bring to the boil.
3. Reduce to a nappé consistency.
4. Season with salt and cool to room temperature.
5. Place the herbs and cream sauce in a blender and purée smooth.
6. Force the sauce through a fine-mesh strainer.
7. Correct the seasoning.

holding: refrigerated in a freshly sanitized squeeze bottle up to 2 days; correct thickness before using

---

RECIPE VARIATIONS

Spinach-Stuffed Mushrooms with Aurora Cream Sauce
Prepare 3 Spinach-Stuffed Mushrooms per serving. Pool 4 fl. oz. Aurora Cream Sauce on a hot 10" plate and arrange the mushrooms on top. Garnish with a parsley sprig.

Crab-Stuffed Mushrooms with Chive Hollandaise
Prepare 3 Crab-Stuffed Mushrooms per serving. Add 1 Tbsp. minced chives to 4 fl. oz. warm Hollandaise sauce and spoon it onto a warm 10" plate. Arrange the mushrooms on top. Garnish with a chive bouquet.

Sausage-Stuffed Mushrooms Marinara
Prepare 3 Sausage-Stuffed Mushrooms per serving, adding some grated Parmesan cheese to the filling. Pool 4 fl. oz. thin Marinara Sauce on a hot 10" plate and arrange the mushrooms on it. Sprinkle the mushrooms with additional cheese and garnish with a parsley sprig.

Shad Roe
in Brown Butter
with Bacon and Asparagus

yield: 1 (5-oz.) appetizer serving
(multiply × 4 for classroom turnout; adjust equipment sizes
accordingly)

MASTER RECIPE

production		costing only
1	3/8"-thick, crustless slice American White Bread, cut into a 3" × 3" square	1/20 recipe
1/2	shad roe pair, trimmed of all membrane	3 oz. a.p.
as needed	boiling water	n/c
1 Tbsp.	clarified butter	3/4 oz. a.p.
as needed	flour	1 oz.
tt	kosher salt	1/16 oz.
6	asparagus spears, peeled, blanched, and refreshed	3 oz. a.p.
6 Tbsp.	butter	3 oz.
as needed	water, in squeeze bottle	n/c
2 Tbsp.	fresh lemon juice	3/8 [90 ct.] lemon
2 tsp.	minced lemon zest	n/c
2 slices	thin-sliced bacon, fried crisp	3/4 oz. a.p.
1 Tbsp.	minced flat-leaf parsley	1/20 bunch a.p.

service turnout:
1. Toast the bread square crisp on both sides.
2. Cook the shad roe:
   a. Place the roe in an 8" nonstick sauté pan and pour in enough boiling water to cover it.
   b. Immediately pour off the water, then gently tip the roe onto a paper towel and blot dry.
   c. Wipe out the pan and reheat it over medium heat.
   d. Add the clarified butter to the pan, dredge the roe in the flour, and sauté it on both sides, about 3 minutes total, until golden brown. ⚠ Watch out for popping roe that can spatter and burn.
   e. Season the roe with salt.
   f. Remove the roe to a sizzle plate and hold warm.
3. Heat the asparagus in a steamer or in a microwave.
4. Prepare the brown butter sauce:
   a. Wipe out the sauté pan and add the butter.
   b. Place the pan over medium heat and melt the butter. Continue heating the butter, swirling it in the pan, until it is a rich brown color.
   c. Immediately stop the cooking with a squeeze of water and the lemon juice. Add the lemon zest and season with salt.
5. Plate the dish:
   a. Arrange the bacon slices in an X pattern in the center of a hot 10" plate.
   b. Place the toast square on top of the bacon.
   c. Arrange the asparagus spears on the toast.
   d. Place the roe on the asparagus.
   e. Pour the sauce over the roe.
   f. Sprinkle the plate with parsley.

RECIPE VARIATION
Salmon in Brown Butter with Bacon and Asparagus
Replace the shad roe with a 3-oz. skinless salmon fillet. Do not blanch the salmon in water; sauté only.

Corn Zephyrs
with Fresh Tomato Sauce

yield: 1 (5-oz.) appetizer serving
(multiply × 4 for classroom turnout; adjust equipment sizes accordingly)

production		costing only
3/4 c.	Fresh Tomato Sauce	1/6 recipe
1/2 c.	corn oil	4 fl. oz.
1	egg white	1 each or 1 oz.
1 c.	Corn Zephyr Base	1/4 recipe
1/4 tsp.	baking powder	1/16 oz.
3 Tbsp.	grated sharp white Cheddar cheese	3/4 oz.
1 sprig	flat-leaf parsley	1/40 bunch a.p.

service turnout:

1. Heat the Fresh Tomato Sauce in an 8" sauté pan or in a microwave.
2. Fry the zephyrs:
   a. Heat an 8" sauté pan, add the oil, and heat it over medium heat to approximately 325°F.
   b. In a clean, dry stainless bowl beat the egg white just below firm peaks.
   c. Spoon the Corn Zephyr Base into the side of the egg white bowl and stir the baking powder into it. Fold the Zephyr base and beaten egg white together.
   d. Place 3 individual heaping Tbsp. zephyr batter into the hot corn oil.
   e. Immediately place 1 Tbsp. cheese on top of each zephyr.
   f. Immediately top each with the remaining zephyr batter to make 3 cheese-filled fritters.
   g. In a few seconds, when the bottoms are browned, turn the zephyrs over and continue to fry until the new bottoms are browned, the zephyrs are puffed, and the cheese inside is melted, about 45 seconds longer.
3. Plate the dish:
   a. Spoon the tomato sauce onto a hot 10" plate.
   b. Blot the zephyrs on paper towels, then arrange them on the sauce in a spoke pattern.
   c. Place the parsley sprig in the center.

COMPONENT RECIPE
CORN ZEPHYR BASE

yield: 1 qt.

production		costing only
4 c.	fresh corn kernels, cut from the cob	4 ears a.p.
2 Tbsp.	butter	1 oz.
1/4 c.	minced yellow onion	1 3/4 oz. a.p.
tt	kosher salt	1/16 oz.
±1/2 c.	water	n/c
6 Tbsp.	flour	1 3/4 oz.
2	egg yolks	2 each or 1 1/3 oz.

preparation:

1. Place 3 c. of the corn in a blender or food processor and grind it to a rough purée.
2. Heat an 8" sauté pan; heat the butter and sweat the onion until soft.
3. Add the remaining corn kernels, a little salt, and the water. Cook at a brisk simmer, stirring constantly, until the corn is tender and the water has reduced away. Cool to room temperature.
4. Whisk together the flour and egg yolks, then whisk in the corn purée.
5. Stir in the corn kernel mixture and season with salt.

holding: refrigerate in a freshly sanitized, covered container up to 2 days

---

RECIPE VARIATIONS

Shrimp and Corn Zephyrs
Add 1/4 c. poached, peeled, chopped shrimp and a pinch of Chesapeake seasoning to the Corn Zephyr Base in step 1. Omit the cheese. Garnish with a grilled or poached shrimp in the center of the plate along with the parsley sprig.

Corn and Ham Zephyrs
Add 2 Tbsp. brunoise-cut smoked ham to the Corn Zephyr Base in step 1.

APPETIZERS

Baked Stuffed Shad in Mushroom Cream

with Dried Corn Pudding and String Beans

yield: 1 (7-oz.) entrée serving plus accompaniments
(multiply × 4 for classroom turnout; adjust equipment sizes
accordingly)

MASTER RECIPE

production		costing only
1 tsp.	melted butter	1/6 fl. oz.
1	Stuffed Shad Fillet	1/4 recipe
2 strips	thin-sliced smoked bacon, fried soft to render out fat	3/4 oz.
1	Dried Corn Pudding	1/4 recipe
1 Tbsp.	butter	1/2 oz.
2	small domestic mushrooms, cleaned and sliced thin	1 oz. a.p.
1 Tbsp.	thin-sliced shallot	1/2 oz. a.p.
1/4 c.	white wine	2 fl. oz.
1 tsp.	minced lemon zest	n/c
3/4 c.	Fish Stock	1/20 recipe
1/3 c.	heavy cream	2 1/3 fl. oz.
tt	kosher salt	1/16 oz.
tt	fine-ground white pepper	1/16 oz.
3 1/2 oz.	whole green beans, trimmed, blanched, and refreshed	4 oz. a.p.
2 tsp.	chopped flat-leaf parsley	1/40 bunch a.p.
1 Tbsp.	chopped celery leaves	n/c

service turnout:

1. Bake the shad:
   a. Brush a sizzle plate with melted butter, place the Stuffed Shad Fillet on it, and arrange the bacon on top in an X pattern.
   b. Bake the shad in a 425°F oven for 12 to 15 minutes.
2. Place the Dried Corn Pudding in the oven and heat through.
3. Prepare the sauce:
   a. Heat an 8" sauté pan, heat the butter, and sauté the mushrooms and shallot until wilted.
   b. Add the wine, lemon zest, and fish stock; reduce to about 1/3 c.
   c. Add the cream and reduce to a nappé consistency.
   d. Season with salt and white pepper.
4. Heat the beans in a steamer or in a microwave.
5. Plate the dish:
   a. Unmold the pudding onto a wide spatula and remove the pan liner circle.
   b. Place the pudding on the back center of a hot 12" plate, browned side up.
   c. Arrange the beans on either side of the Pudding with the tips at 10 o'clock and 2 o'clock and the ends in the center.
   d. Pour any juices accumulated around the shad into the cream sauce.
   e. Place the shad horizontally across the plate, resting against the pudding and on the ends of the beans.
   f. Heat the sauce and spoon it around the shad.
   g. Sprinkle the shad with the parsley and celery leaves.

COMPONENT RECIPE
STUFFED SHAD FILLETS

yield: 4 (7-oz.) servings

production		costing only
2 Tbsp.	clarified butter	1 1/4 oz. a.p.
2 c.	cleaned and minced domestic mushrooms	6 oz. a.p.
tt	kosher salt	1/16 oz.
tt	fresh lemon juice	1/6 [115 ct.] lemon
2 Tbsp.	butter	1 oz.
1/2 c.	peeled, fine-chopped celery	1/10 head a.p.
1/2 c.	fine-chopped yellow onion	2 1/2 oz. a.p.
1/2 c.	Fish Stock	1/32 recipe
2 c.	Butter-Toasted Bread Crumbs	1 recipe
1 Tbsp.	minced lemon zest	n/c
1 Tbsp.	minced tarragon leaves	1/8 bunch a.p.
1 Tbsp.	minced flat-leaf parsley	1/20 bunch a.p.
tt	fine-ground white pepper	1/16 oz.
1	egg, beaten	1 each or 2 oz.
2	14-oz. professionally boned shad sides	28 oz. a.p.

preparation:
1. Prepare the stuffing:
   a. Heat a 10" sauté pan, heat the clarified butter, and sear the mushrooms until dry. Season with salt and lemon juice. Remove to a bowl and cool.
   b. Heat the butter in the same pan and sweat the celery and onion until softened.
   c. Add the fish stock and a pinch of salt; reduce until almost dry.
   d. Scrape the celery mixture into the bowl with the mushrooms and cool to room temperature.
   e. Add the Butter-Toasted Bread Crumbs, lemon zest, tarragon, parsley, and white pepper to the bowl and mix well.
   f. Taste and correct the seasoning, then mix in 3/4 of the beaten egg.
   g. Refrigerate until completely cold.
2. Fabricate and stuff the shad:
   a. Rinse the shad sides under cold water and pat dry, particularly inside the flaps.
   b. Cut each side in half to make 2 servings.
   c. Open the flaps and brush the interior flesh with the remaining egg.
   d. Divide the stuffing evenly among the fillets, and press to firm the stuffing and ensure that it adheres to the fish. Close the flaps.
   e. Season the exterior of the fillets with salt and a little lemon juice.

holding: refrigerate in a covered plastic container with pan liner for 24 hours only

---

RECIPE VARIATION
Baked Stuffed Salmon with Mushroom Cream, Dried Corn Pudding, and String Beans
Replace each shad fillet portion with a thick 6-oz. salmon fillet, skinned, trimmed, and pinned. Butterfly each fillet open from the top to create a pocket as in a professionally boned shad fillet.

COMPONENT RECIPE
DRIED CORN PUDDING

yield: 4 (6-fl.-oz.) ramekins

production		costing only
1 1/2 c.	half-and-half	12 fl. oz.
1 c.	toasted dried sweet corn, such as Cope's brand	4 oz.
2 Tbsp.	butter	1 oz.
tt	kosher salt	1/16 oz.
1 Tbsp.	sugar	1/2 oz.
as needed	butter	1/2 oz.
2	eggs	2 each or 4 oz.

preparation:
1. Preheat an oven to 325°F.
2. Place the half-and-half in a 1-qt. saucepan and scald it over high heat.
3. Remove the half-and-half from the heat; add the corn, 2 Tbsp. butter, a little salt, and the sugar. Allow to steep at room temperature for 1 hour.
4. Prepare the ramekins:
   a. Heavily butter 4 (8-oz.) ramekins.
   b. Cut 4 circles of pan liner to fit the bottoms of the ramekins.
   c. Place the circles in the bottoms of the ramekins and turn them over, buttered side up.
   d. Place the ramekins in a half-size hotel pan lined with a clean, damp towel.
   e. Cut out 4 circles of aluminum foil 1/2" larger than the diameter of the ramekins.
5. In a small bowl, beat the eggs until frothy. Stir in the corn mixture and season the mixture with more salt if needed.
6. Pour the corn pudding into the ramekins and cover each with a foil circle.
7. Fill the hotel pan with very hot water 3/4 of the way up the sides of the ramekins.
8. Bake the puddings in the center of the oven about 30 minutes, until set.
9. If preparing ahead, cool on a rack to room temperature.

holding: wrap the individual cooled puddings in plastic film and refrigerate up to 5 days

ENTREES

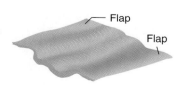

Open the flaps created when the side bones were removed.

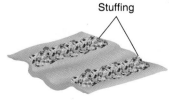

Gently pack the stuffing into the opening.

Lenape Smoke-Roasted Bluefish

with Cranberry-Maple Velouté, Corn Cake, and Watercress

yield: 1 (7-oz.) entrée serving plus accompaniments (multiply × 4 for classroom turnout; adjust equipment sizes accordingly)

MASTER RECIPE

production		costing only
1 c.	hickory chips, soaked 6 hours	% of package
1 Tbsp.	corn oil	1/2 fl. oz.
1 Tbsp.	butter	1/2 oz.
1	Lenape Corn Cake	1/4 recipe
3/4 c.	Cranberry-Maple Velouté	1/4 recipe
4 sprigs	fresh thyme	1/10 bunch a.p.
1	scallion	1/8 bunch a.p.
1	Lenape Marinated Bluefish Fillet	1/4 recipe
1 bouquet	watercress	1/6 bunch

service turnout:

1. Drain the hickory chips and drop them through the rack of a hot gas grill onto the briquets or burner assembly shield in a neat, flat pile.
2. Fry the Lenape Corn Cake:
   a. Heat a 6" nonstick sauté pan, heat the oil and butter, and fry the corn cake over low heat about 5 minutes, until the bottom browns.
   b. Flip the cake and continue to fry about 5 minutes longer, until the new bottom is browned.
3. Stir the Cranberry-Maple Velouté well and ladle it into an 8" sauté pan. Heat over medium heat.
4. Smoke-roast the Lenape Marinated Bluefish Fillet:
   a. Drop the thyme sprigs and scallion through the grill rack on top of the smoking chips.
   b. Place the bluefish on the grill, shiny side up, over the smoking chips and cover it with a dome lid. Smoke-roast the fish about 3 minutes.
   c. Uncover the bluefish and turn it over. Spoon a little of the liquid part of the velouté over the fish, replace the lid, and smoke-roast 3 to 4 minutes longer, until the fish is just cooked through.
5. Plate the dish:
   a. Place the corn cake on the back of a warm 12" plate.
   b. Place the bluefish on the front of the plate, propped against the corn cake.
   c. Separate the watercress into 2 bouquets and tuck them on either side of the corn cake with the stems under the fish.
   d. Nap the fish with the velouté, arranging a few of the whole cranberries on top of the fish.

COMPONENT RECIPE
LENAPE CORN CAKES

yield: 4 (3-oz.) cakes

production		costing only
as needed	pan coating spray	% of container
1 Tbsp.	butter	1/2 oz.
1 1/4 c.	half-and-half	10 fl. oz.
1 c.	water	n/c
1 tsp.	minced garlic	1/6 oz. a.p.
2 sprigs	fresh thyme	1/10 bunch a.p.
tt	kosher salt	1/16 oz.
1/3 c.	instant polenta	2 oz.
1 c.	cooked corn kernels, fresh or frozen	1 ear a.p. or 6 oz.

preparation:

1. Prepare the forms:
   a. Line a half-sheet tray with pan liner and spray it with pan coating.
   b. Heavily butter the insides of 4 (3 1/2" × 1 1/2") entremet rings. Place the rings on the tray.
2. Prepare the corn cake batter:
   a. Place the half-and-half, water, garlic, thyme, and salt in a 3-qt. saucepan. Bring to the boil, then sprinkle in the polenta, stirring constantly, to achieve a lump-free mixture.
   b. Reduce the heat to medium and cook, stirring often, for 10 minutes, until the polenta becomes very thick and begins to pull away from the sides of the pan. Remove the thyme sprigs and correct the salt.
   c. Stir in the corn.
3. Pack the polenta into the entremet rings and smooth the tops.
4. Cool to room temperature and immediately refrigerate until cold and firm.
5. Remove the corn cakes from the entremet rings and wrap each individually in plastic film.

holding: refrigerate up to 5 days

COMPONENT RECIPE
CRANBERRY-MAPLE VELOUTÉ

yield: 3 c.

production		costing only
1 1/2 c.	cranberries, picked over	10 oz.
2 c.	water	n/c
3 Tbsp.	butter	1 1/2 oz.
3 Tbsp.	flour	1 oz.
3 c.	hot Poultry Stock	1/5 recipe
1 c.	hot Fish Stock	1/16 recipe
6	crushed juniper berries	1/6 oz.
tt	pure maple syrup	1/2 oz.
tt	kosher salt	1/16 oz.
tt	fine-ground white pepper	1/16 oz.

preparation:
1. Place the cranberries and water in a 2-qt. nonreactive saucepan and simmer about 10 minutes, until the berries are almost tender.
2. Prepare the sauce:
   a. In a 2-qt. saucepan heat the butter, add the flour, and make a blond roux. Remove from heat.
   b. Whisk in the hot stocks and bring to the simmer. Add the juniper berries and a little salt; cook over medium heat about 20 minutes.
   c. Drain the cranberries, discarding the cooking liquid.
   d. Add half of the cooked cranberries to the sauce and simmer 10 minutes longer, until the cranberries are soft.
   e. Run the sauce through a food mill into a clean saucepan.
   f. Add the remaining cranberries to the sauce.
   g. Season the sauce with maple syrup, salt, and white pepper to achieve a tangy, slightly sweet flavor.

holding: open-pan cool and refrigerate in a freshly sanitized, covered, nonreactive container up to 3 days

COMPONENT RECIPE
LENAPE MARINATED BLUEFISH FILLETS

yield: 4 (7-oz.) fish fillets

production		costing only
2 sprigs	thyme	1/10 bunch a.p.
6	juniper berries	1/6 oz.
10	black peppercorns	1/6 oz.
1/2 c.	thin-sliced yellow onion	2 1/2 oz. a.p.
2	crushed garlic cloves	2/3 oz. a.p.
tt	kosher salt	1/16 oz.
1 Tbsp.	cider vinegar	1/2 fl. oz.
1/2 c.	corn oil	4 fl. oz.
4	7-oz. bluefish fillets, skinned, pinned	2 lb. a.p.

preparation:
1. Prepare the marinade:
   a. Place the thyme, juniper berries, peppercorns, onion, garlic, and salt in a mortar or small, heavy bowl.
   b. Using the pestle or improvising with a mallet or the end of a French rolling pin, pound the ingredients until they break up and release juices.
   c. Whisk in the vinegar and oil.
2. Rinse the bluefish fillets under cold water and pat them dry with paper towels.
3. Place the fillets in a freshly sanitized, nonreactive container just large enough to hold them.
4. Pour the marinade over the fish and turn it to coat all pieces well.
5. Cover and refrigerate at least 2 hours.

holding: refrigerate in the marinade up to 6 hours longer; drain off the marinade and hold 24 hours only

---

RECIPE VARIATION

Lenape Grilled Fish with Cranberry-Maple Sauce, Corn Cake, and Watercress
Use any sturdy fish steak or fillet. Marinate and grill to desired doneness.

Pan-Seared "Snapper" Bluefish on Potato Cake

with Jersey Tomato Sauce and Tricolor Peppers

yield: 1 (7-oz.) entrée serving plus accompaniments
(multiply × 4 for classroom turnout; adjust equipment sizes accordingly)

MASTER RECIPE

production		costing only
1 Tbsp.	corn oil	1/2 fl. oz.
1	Straw Potato Cake	1/4 recipe
1 Tbsp.	golden-color pure olive oil	1/2 fl. oz.
1 Tbsp.	butter	1/2 oz.
1 c.	large-julienne yellow bell peppers	5 oz. a.p.
1 c.	large-julienne red bell peppers	5 oz. a.p.
1 c.	large-julienne green bell peppers	5 oz. a.p.
tt	kosher salt	1/16 oz.
tt	fresh-ground black pepper	1/16 oz.
1 Tbsp.	corn oil	1/2 fl. oz.
1	7-oz. "snapper" (young, small) bluefish fillet, skinned and pinned	8 oz. a.p.
1 c.	Fresh Tomato Sauce	1/4 recipe
1 Tbsp.	extra-virgin olive oil	1/2 fl. oz.
2 Tbsp.	chiffonade fresh basil	1/20 bunch a.p.

service turnout:
1. Heat an 8" sauté pan, heat 1 Tbsp. corn oil, and fry the Straw Potato Cake about 2 minutes on each side, until crisp. Transfer to a sizzle pan and hold in a low oven, about 250°.
2. Add the pure olive oil and butter to the pan, sauté the bell peppers until crisp-tender, and season with salt and pepper. Place on the sizzle pan along with the potato cake and return the pan to the oven.
3. Heat the sauté pan until very hot, add 1 Tbsp. corn oil, and pan-sear the bluefish fillet on both sides about 3 minutes total, until just cooked through. Pour off any excess oil and season with salt and pepper.
4. Heat the Fresh Tomato Sauce in an 8" sauté pan.
5. Plate the dish:
   a. Place the potato cake slightly back center of a hot 12" plate.
   b. Mound the bell peppers on the potato cake.
   c. Place the bluefish fillet on the front of the plate propped against the potato cake and bell peppers.
   d. Whisk the extra-virgin olive oil into the tomato sauce and immediately nap the sauce diagonally across the bluefish from 10 o'clock to 4 o'clock.
   e. Scatter the basil across the bluefish fillet.

COMPONENT RECIPE

STRAW POTATO CAKES

yield: 4 (6") cakes

production		costing only
2 lb.	russet potatoes	2 lb. a.p.
tt	kosher salt	1/4 oz.
6 Tbsp.	corn oil, preferably in squeeze bottle	3 fl. oz.

preparation:
1. Fabricate the potatoes:
   a. Peel the potatoes, placing them in a bowl of cold water as you work.
   b. Set up a mandoline or food processor fitted with a julienne blade.
   c. Pat each potato dry with a towel and julienne it.
   d. Immediately spread the julienne potatoes on kitchen towels, roll up the towels, and squeeze the rolls firmly to remove excess moisture.
   e. Toss the potatoes with salt.
2. Immediately fry the potato cakes:
   a. Heat 2 (8") nonstick sauté pans, add 1 Tbsp. corn oil to each, and pack 1/4 of the potatoes into each pan.
   b. Cover the pans and cook over medium heat, about 3 minutes, until the bottoms are light golden brown.
   c. Uncover the pans, flip the potato cakes over, and add a little more corn oil around the edges of each cake. Continue to cook, uncovered, about 3 minutes longer, until the new bottoms are golden and the potatoes are cooked through.
   d. Remove the cakes to a cooling rack set over a sheet tray.
   e. Repeat with the remaining potatoes, making a total of 4 potato cakes.

holding: when completely cool, refrigerate in a covered container, with pan liner under and between layers, up to 5 days

---

RECIPE VARIATIONS

Pan-Seared Swordfish on Potato Cake with Jersey Tomato Sauce and Tricolor Peppers
Replace the bluefish with a swordfish steak. Sear to medium-rare only.

Grilled Whole Baby Snapper Bluefish on Potato Cake with Jersey Tomato Sauce and Tricolor Peppers
Replace the bluefish fillet with a whole 14-oz. baby "snapper" bluefish (scaled, gilled and gutted, and soaked for 4 hours in white wine). Pat the fish dry, slash the sides, coat with pure olive oil, and char-grill.

ENTREES

Pennsylvania Dutch Chicken Bot Boi
with Saffron Noodles

yield: 1 entrée serving: approx. 8 oz. bone-in chicken plus noodles and vegetables
(multiply × 4 for classroom turnout; adjust equipment sizes accordingly)

MASTER RECIPE

production		costing only
2 c.	Chicken Bot Boi sauce	1/4 recipe
1/4 c.	water	n/c
2 1/2 oz.	Saffron Bot Boi Noodles	1/4 recipe
approx. 6 oz.	Chicken Bot Boi portioned chicken pieces	1/4 recipe
1 1/2 c.	Bot Boi Vegetables	1/4 recipe
tt	kosher salt	1/4 oz.
1 tsp.	chopped flat-leaf parsley	1/40 bunch a.p.
1 tsp.	minced fresh marjoram leaves	1/20 bunch a.p.
1 sprig	flat-leaf parsley	1/40 bunch a.p.
1 sprig	celery leaves	n/c
1 sprig	fresh marjoram	1/20 bunch a.p.

service turnout:

1. Assemble and heat the Chicken Bot Boi:
   a. Bring the bot boi sauce and the water to the boil in a 10" sauté pan. Add the Saffron Noodles, cover the pan, and cook at a brisk simmer about 3 minutes, until the noodles are just al dente.
   b. Add the chicken bot boi portioned chicken pieces, cover the pan, and heat 2 minutes longer.
   c. Add the Bot Boi Vegetables, cover, and heat 1 minute longer until the dish is heated through.
   d. Correct the salt.
2. Plate the dish:
   a. Spoon the bot boi into a hot 12" pasta plate.
   b. Rearrange the ingredients so that the chicken pieces are prominent and some colorful vegetables are on top.
   c. Sprinkle with the chopped parsley and marjoram.
   d. Make a bouquet of the herb sprigs and stick it upright behind the chicken.

COMPONENT RECIPE
CHICKEN BOT BOI

yield: 4 entrée servings: 2 qt. sauce plus approx. 24 oz. cooked bone-in chicken

production		costing only
1	5-lb. stewing fowl	5 lb.
2 qt.	Poultry Stock	1/2 recipe
1 c.	peeled, medium-chopped celery	1/5 head a.p.
1/2 c.	peeled, medium-chopped carrot	2 oz. a.p.
1/2 c.	peeled, medium-chopped rutabaga (use scraps from Bot Boi Vegetables)	n/c
2 sprigs	fresh marjoram	1/10 bunch a.p.
2 sprigs	flat-leaf parsley	1/20 bunch a.p.
2 sprigs	fresh thyme	1/20 bunch a.p.
1/2 c.	butter	4 oz.
1/2 c.	flour	2 1/2 oz.
1 1/2 c.	cleaned, 1/4"-sliced leeks, white and pale parts only	1/2 bunch a.p.
8	pitted prunes	2 1/2 oz.
tt	kosher salt	1/16 oz.

preparation:
1. Fabricate the chicken:
   a. Disjoint the stewing fowl to yield 2 drumsticks, 2 thighs, 2 boneless breast halves, and 2 wings.
   b. Remove and discard the skin from all chicken pieces.
   c. Chop off the drumstick knuckles and reserve them.
   d. Cut each breast half in half again.
   e. Separate the drumettes from the middle sections of the wings by cutting through the joint.
   f. Clean out any blood or bits of liver from the chicken back, remove and discard the tail, and chop the back into 2 or 3 pieces.
2. Prepare the broth:
   a. Place the Poultry Stock in an 8-qt. saucepan. Add the back pieces, knuckles, neck, gizzard, and wing middle sections with tips. Bring the stock to the simmer and skim off the resulting foam.
   b. Add the celery, carrot, rutabaga, marjoram, parsley, and thyme. Partially cover the pan and simmer 1 hour.
   c. Strain the broth, pressing hard on the solids before discarding them.
3. Finish the bot boi:
   a. Rinse out the saucepan, add the butter and flour, and stir them over low heat to make a blond roux. Remove from heat.
   b. Whisk in the hot broth and bring it to the simmer.
   c. Add the drumsticks and thighs to the broth and simmer 20 minutes.
   d. Add the drumettes, breast pieces, and leeks and simmer 20 minutes longer.
   e. Add the prunes and simmer 5 minutes longer.

4. If preparing ahead, portion the bot boi*:
   a. Carefully remove the chicken pieces and prunes from the sauce. Arrange them in a freshly sanitized shallow container grouped into 2 servings consisting of 1 thigh, 1 breast piece, some leeks, and 2 prunes, and 2 servings consisting of 1 drumstick, 1 drumette, 1 breast piece, some leeks, and 2 prunes.
   b. Season the sauce with salt and spoon a little of it over the chicken pieces to keep them moist.

holding: store the cooled sauce in a freshly sanitized, covered container; store the portioned chicken in the covered container; refrigerate both up to 5 days

*If plating immediately, follow step #4a for portioning directions.

COMPONENT RECIPE
SAFFRON BOT BOI NOODLES

yield: approx. 10 oz.

production		costing only
1	room-temperature egg	1 each or 2 oz.
1	room-temperature egg yolk	1 each or 2/3 oz.
1/2 tsp.	ground saffron	0.01 oz. or 0.35 g
±1 1/4 c.	flour	±7 oz.

preparation:
1. Mix the dough:
   a. Beat together the egg, egg yolk, and saffron.
   b. Place 1 c. flour on a sanitized work surface and make a well in it.
   c. Pour the egg mixture into the well.
   d. Using a fork, begin stirring the flour into the eggs, a little at a time, to make a smooth dough.
   e. When the dough forms a workable mass, use a pastry scraper to scrape the work surface clean. Dust the surface with flour and knead the dough vigorously for 3 minutes, adding additional flour only if needed. (The dough should be soft but not sticky and very elastic, and it will begin to form blisters.)
   f. Dust the dough with flour, wrap it in plastic film, and let it rest at room temperature for 20 minutes.
2. Roll out the dough:
   a. With a rolling pin or pasta machine, roll and stretch the dough into a sheet a little thicker than 1/16".
   b. Lay the rolled dough out on kitchen towels and allow it to dry for 5 to 10 minutes, turning it once.
3. Cut the dough into bot boi noodles:
   a. Using a fluted pastry wheel, cut the dough into 1 1/2" squares.
   b. Line a plastic container with a clean, dry kitchen towel and lay out the noodles in a single layer. If making a large batch, place additional towels between layers.

holding: refrigerate up to 8 hours; freeze up to 3 months

COMPONENT RECIPE
BOT BOI VEGETABLES

yield: 4 servings

production		costing only
12	peeled baby carrots	6 oz. a.p.
12 lg. pc.	batonnet-cut rutabaga	8 oz. a.p.
2	large celery ribs, peeled, cut diagonally into 12 (1 1/2") lengths	1/10 head a.p.
12	boiling onions, peeled, with an X cut in the root end	9 oz. a.p.

preparation:

1. Separately boil and refresh each type of vegetable to a tender texture.
2. Drain the vegetables and blot them dry on clean towels.
3. Divide the vegetables into 4 portions, each portion consisting of 3 pieces of each type.

holding: store each portion refrigerated in a plastic bag up to 5 days

---

RECIPE VARIATION

Pennsylvania Dutch Chicken Pie
Omit the noodles. Double the amount of roux. Bone the cooked chicken and cut it into large chunks. At turnout, heat one portion each of the chicken and vegetables in the sauce and pour it into a 30-fl.-oz. ovenproof crock. Egg-wash the edges of a puff pastry round and place it over the crock. Slash pastry in a decorative pattern and bake at 400°F until the pastry is golden.

Roast Long Island Duckling in Port Wine Demi-Glace

with North-Shore Cauliflower Gratin and Arugula

yield: 1 (9-oz.) entrée serving plus accompaniments (multiply × 4 for classroom turnout; adjust equipment sizes accordingly)

MASTER RECIPE

production		costing only
1 tsp.	melted butter	1/6 oz.
1	Port-Glazed Roast Duck Half	1/4 recipe
1	Cauliflower Gratin Disc	1/4 recipe
1 Tbsp.	minced shallot	1/2 oz. a.p.
1 c.	Poultry Stock preferably made with a duck carcass	1/16 recipe
1 tsp.	minced lemon zest	n/c
1 tsp.	minced orange zest	n/c
1/2 c.	Demi-Glace	1/8 recipe
3 Tbsp.	New York State Port wine	1 1/2 fl. oz.
tt	kosher salt	1/16 oz.
tt	fine-ground white pepper	1/16 oz.
1 bouquet	arugula, stemmed, washed, and dried well	1 oz. a.p.
1 cluster	Red Flame grapes, washed and dried	1 oz. a.p.

service turnout:

1. Brush a large sizzle pan with melted butter. Place the Port-Glazed Roast Duck Half and the Cauliflower Gratin Disc on it and bake in the top of a 400°F oven for 15 minutes, until heated through.
2. Prepare the sauce:
   a. Place the shallot, Poultry Stock, lemon and orange zest, and Demi-Glace in an 8" sauté pan and reduce to nappé consistency.
   b. Add the Port and season with salt and white pepper.
   c. Hold hot.
3. Plate the dish:
   a. Place the cauliflower disc on the back center of a warm 12" plate.
   b. Arrange the duck horizontally across the plate propped against the cauliflower disc.
   c. Stick the arugula bouquet upright behind the duck to the right of the cauliflower disc.
   d. Place the grape cluster to the left of the cauliflower disc.
   e. Nap the duck with the sauce.

COMPONENT RECIPE

PORT-GLAZED ROAST DUCK HALVES

yield: 4 entrée servings: 1 duck half

production		costing only
2	4 1/2-lb. Long Island ducks	9 lb. a.p.
tt	kosher salt	1/16 oz.
tt	fresh-ground black pepper	1/16 oz.
1/2 c.	New York State Port wine	4 fl. oz.
2 Tbsp.	honey	1 fl. oz.

preparation:

1. Preheat an oven to 425°F.
2. Fabricate each duck:
   a. Disjoint each of the duck wings between the drumette and the lower wing section.
   b. Remove the backbones and open the duck carcass out flat.
   c. Split each duck down the breastbone into 2 halves.
   d. From each duck half, remove the thigh bones, rib bones, and any other small bones, leaving only the drumstick bones, drumette wing bones, and breastbones intact.
   e. With the heel of a sharp chef knife or cleaver, chop the knuckles off the drumsticks in a clean cut.
   f. Reserve the bones, gizzard, and trimmings for stock and the livers for another use.
   g. Gently tap the duck thighs and drumsticks with a meat mallet to flatten them slightly.
   h. Season the duck halves with salt and pepper.
3. Par-roast the duck halves:
   a. Place the duck halves, skin side up, on a rack set over a roasting pan with 1/2" water in the bottom.
   b. Place the ducks in the middle of the oven and roast them about 25 minutes, until the duck reaches an internal temperature of 120°F at the thickest part of the breast.
   c. Remove the ducks from the oven and cool them to room temperature on a rack set over a half-sheet tray.
   d. As soon as the ducks reach room temperature, refrigerate them, uncovered, until they are cold.
4. Glaze the duck halves:
   a. Combine the Port and honey in a 6" sauté pan and reduce, stirring constantly with a heatproof rubber scraper, to a glaze.
   b. Brush the glaze onto the duck halves and immediately return them to the refrigerator, uncovered, until the glaze is set.

holding: refrigerate in one layer, in a covered container with pan liner, up to 3 days

ENTREES

COMPONENT RECIPE
CAULIFLOWER GRATIN DISCS

yield: 4 (3 1/2") discs, plus scraps for another use

production		costing only
as needed	butter	1/2 oz.
4 c.	large cauliflower florets	1/2 [12 ct.] head a.p.
1	small russet potato	7 oz. a.p.
1 Tbsp.	minced shallot	1/4 oz. a.p.
1 tsp.	minced garlic	1/9 oz. a.p.
tt	kosher salt	1/16 oz.
1 1/2 c.	half-and-half	12 fl. oz.

preparation:
1. Prepare the oven and pan:
   a. Preheat an oven to 425°F.
   b. Butter an 8" round or square cake pan.
   c. Cut 2 pieces of pan liner to fit both the bottom and the top of the cake pan.
   d. Place the bottom sheet in the pan and turn it over so the buttered side is up.
   e. Place the cake pan on a sheet tray with pan liner.
   f. Butter one side of the remaining pan liner.
2. Assemble the gratin:
   a. Cut the cauliflower florets into 1/4" slices, reserving the crumbs.
   b. Peel the potato, rinse it under cool water, blot dry, and cut into very thin slices.
   c. Layer the cauliflower slices, cauliflower crumbs, and potato slices in the cake pan, scattering the shallot, garlic, and salt between the layers.
   d. Pour the half-and-half over the vegetables.
   e. Place the remaining piece of pan liner, buttered side down, on top of the vegetables. Press firmly.
3. Bake the gratin in the center of the oven about 30 minutes, until the vegetables are tender and the half-and-half has absorbed.
4. Cool to room temperature and immediately refrigerate until cold.
5. Fabricate the discs:
   a. Run a knife around the edge of the cake pan to loosen the gratin.
   b. Invert the pan onto a sanitized work surface and peel off the top piece of pan liner.
   c. Using a 3 3/4" round cutter, punch out 4 discs and remove the scraps. (The scraps may be used to thicken and enrich a puréed soup.)
   d. Use a wide spatula to remove the discs from the bottom pan liner.

holding: refrigerate in a container with pan liner under and between layers, covered, up to 5 days

---

RECIPE VARIATION

Pan-Seared Long Island Duck Breast in Port Wine Demi-Glace with North-Shore Cauliflower Gratin and Arugula
Replace the Port-Glazed Roast Duck Half with a boneless duck breast, its skin scored in a tight crosshatch. Pan-sear, brush with glaze, and finish the duck breast in a hot oven to a rare doneness. Slice the breast on a sharp diagonal and fan the slices across the front of the plate.

Pan-Roasted Veal Chop in Apple-Mushroom Cream

with Handmade Noodles and Brussels Sprouts

yield: 1 (12-oz. bone-in) entrée serving plus accompaniments (multiply × 4 for classroom turnout; adjust equipment sizes accordingly)

MASTER RECIPE

production		costing only
1 Tbsp.	corn oil	1/2 fl. oz.
1	(12 oz.) frenched milk-fed rib veal chop	12 oz. a.p.
tt	kosher salt	1/16 oz.
tt	fine-ground white pepper	1/16 oz.
1 Tbsp.	clarified butter	3/4 oz. a.p.
3	1/4"-sliced domestic mushrooms	2 oz. a.p.
1/4	tart cooking apple, peeled, cored, soaked in acidulated water	1 1/4 oz. a.p.
3/4 c.	Apple-Mushroom Cream Velouté	1/4 recipe
as needed	water, in squeeze bottle	n/c
5 to 7	Brussels sprouts, trimmed, boiled, refreshed, squeezed dry	1/3 pt. a.p.
1 Tbsp.	butter	1 oz.
3 oz.	Fresh Pasta rolled 1/16" thick and cut into 1/2" × 2" noodles	1/5 recipe
1 Tbsp.	softened butter	1/2 oz.
1 Tbsp.	chopped flat-leaf parsley	1/40 bunch

service turnout:

1. Have ready a pot of salted boiling water and a spider or strainer and tongs. Place a stainless steel bowl in a hot place near the stove.
2. Cook the veal chop:
   a. Heat an 8" sauté pan, heat the oil, and sear the veal chop on both sides.
   b. Season the chop with salt and white pepper.
   c. Place the chop on a sizzle pan and finish in a 400°F oven for about 8 minutes, until it reaches medium doneness.
3. Finish the sauce:
   a. Heat the same sauté pan, heat the clarified butter, add the mushrooms and a little salt, and sauté for a few seconds.
   b. Quickly slice the peeled apple thin and add to the mushrooms.
   c. Sauté the mushrooms and apple together for a few moments until they begin to brown.
   d. Add the Apple-Mushroom Cream Velouté and a little water, heat to the simmer, and hold hot.
4. In a covered 8" sauté pan or in a microwave, heat the Brussels sprouts with the butter and a little salt.
5. Cook the Fresh Pasta:
   a. Drop the pasta into the boiling water and cook 1 minute or less, until al dente.
   b. Lift the pasta out to the hot bowl and toss it with softened butter, salt, and white pepper.
6. Plate the dish:
   a. Mound the pasta on the back left of a hot 12" plate.
   b. Mound the Brussels sprouts on the back right.
   c. Prop the veal chop upright against the pasta and Brussels sprouts.
   d. Nap the chop with the sauce, spooning most of the mushrooms and apples in front of the chop.
   e. Sprinkle the pasta and veal chop with a diagonal line of chopped parsley.

COMPONENT RECIPE
APPLE-MUSHROOM CREAM VELOUTÉ

yield: 3 c.

production		costing only
1/4 oz.	dried boletus (porcini) mushrooms	1/4 oz.
1/2 c.	white wine	4 fl. oz.
1/2 c.	apple cider	4 fl. oz.
2 Tbsp.	butter	1 oz.
1 c.	minced mushroom stems and trimmings (or domestic mushrooms)	n/c or 4 oz. a.p.
tt	kosher salt	1/16 oz.
2 Tbsp.	minced shallot	1 oz. a.p.
1 c.	chopped, peeled, and cored tart cooking apple	5 oz. a.p.
1 Tbsp.	flour	1/3 oz.
2 c.	hot Poultry Stock	1/8 recipe
1 c.	heavy cream	8 fl. oz.
tt	fine-ground white pepper	1/16 oz.

preparation:
1. Rehydrate the dried mushrooms:
   a. Place the dried mushrooms in a small bowl.
   b. Combine the wine and cider in a saucepan, heat them to a bare simmer, and pour the liquid over the mushrooms. Weight the mushrooms with another small bowl to keep them submerged. Steep for 15 minutes.
2. Make the sauce:
   a. Place the butter, minced mushrooms, and a little salt in a 2-qt. saucepan over low heat. Sweat about 5 minutes, until softened.
   b. Pour the mushroom-soaking liquid through cheesecloth into a bowl to remove any grit.
   c. Rinse the rehydrated mushrooms under cool running water. Squeeze dry and chop them fine.
   d. Add the shallot, apple, and flour to the mushrooms and stir over low heat for a few seconds.
   e. Whisk in the Poultry Stock and mushroom liquid. Cover and simmer over medium heat about 20 minutes, until the solids are very tender and have released their flavors.
   f. Force the sauce through a strainer into a clean saucepan.
   g. If necessary, reduce to a consistency slightly thicker than nappé.
   h. Add the cream to the sauce, bring it to the simmer, season with white pepper, and correct the salt.

holding: open-pan cool and immediately refrigerate in a freshly sanitized, covered container up to 5 days

RECIPE VARIATION
Pan-Roasted Pork Chop in Apple-Mushroom Cream with Handmade Noodles and Brussels Sprouts
Replace the veal chop with a center-cut rib pork chop.

Lancaster County Roast Lamb in Minted Pan Gravy

with Peas 'n' Pearl Onions in Potato Basket and Carrot Purée

yield: 1 (6-oz.) entrée serving plus accompaniments (multiply × 4 for classroom turnout; adjust equipment sizes accordingly)

ENTREES

MASTER RECIPE

production		costing
1 Tbsp.	corn oil	1/2 fl. oz.
1	6 oz. piece trimmed and seamed-out lamb leg (single muscle)	12 oz. a.p.
tt	kosher salt	1/16 oz.
tt	fresh-ground black pepper	1/16 oz.
2 Tbsp.	thin-sliced shallot	1 oz. a.p.
1/2 c.	Brown Stock	1/32 recipe
1 c.	shelled fresh young peas	1 lb. a.p.
1/3 c.	pearl onions, peeled, boiled, refreshed	2 oz. a.p.
1/2 c.	water, in squeeze bottle	n/c
1 Tbsp.	butter	1/2 oz.
as needed	frying compound or corn oil	% used
1	Individual Potato Basket	1/4 recipe
1/2 c.	Demi-Glace	1/8 recipe
1 Tbsp.	butter	1/2 oz.
1 c.	Carrot Purée, hot, in steam table	1/4 recipe
1 Tbsp.	chopped fresh mint	1/12 bunch a.p.
1 sprig	fresh mint	1/12 bunch a.p.

service turnout:

1. Cook the lamb:
   a. Heat an 8" sauté pan, heat the oil, and sear the lamb on all sides.
   b. Pour off any excess fat, season with salt and pepper, scatter the shallot around the lamb, and add the Brown Stock to the pan.
   c. Roast the lamb in the sauté pan in a 400°F oven for 8 to 12 minutes, depending on the doneness desired. (Test with an instant-read meat thermometer; rare recommended.)
2. Cook the peas:
   a. Place the peas, pearl onions, water, and salt in a covered 8" sauté pan and pan-steam a minute or two.
   b. Uncover, reduce the liquid to 1 Tbsp., and work in 1 Tbsp. butter.
3. Fry the Individual Potato Basket in 400°F oil until crisp and golden. Drain on paper towels and season with salt.
4. Make the sauce:
   a. Remove the lamb from the oven and place it on a cutting board.
   b. Add the Demi-Glace to the reduced pan juices, season it with salt and pepper, and work in 1 Tbsp. butter to create an emulsion.
5. Plate the dish:
   a. Fill the potato basket with the peas and onions and place it on the back left of a hot 12" plate.
   b. Scoop the Carrot Purée into a pastry bag fitted with a star tip and pipe a rosette of purée on the back right of the plate.
   c. Slice the lamb against the grain and fan it across the front of the plate. (Pour any accumulated juices into the sauce.)
   d. Add the chopped mint to the sauce and spoon it over the lamb.
   e. Stick the mint sprig upright between the lamb and the vegetables.

COMPONENT RECIPE
INDIVIDUAL POTATO BASKETS

yield: 4 (4") potato baskets

production		costing only
as needed	frying compound or corn oil	% used
1 lb.	russet potatoes	1 lb. a.p.
tt	fine-ground salt	1/16 oz.

preparation:
1. Preheat the frying oil to 375°F. Drop the fryer basket(s) into the oil. Place a hotel pan lined with paper towels near the fryer.
2. Fabricate the potatoes:
   a. Peel the potatoes and immerse them in a bowl of cold water.
   b. Set up a mandoline or food processor with a julienne blade.
   c. Blot each potato dry and julienne it.
   d. Immediately spread the julienne potatoes on a clean, dry kitchen towel, roll it up, and squeeze firmly until the potatoes lose their excess moisture.
3. Fry the potato baskets:
   a. Open a 4" *nid de pommes* (potato nest) form and dip it in the oil for a few seconds until it becomes hot and coated with oil.
   b. Remove the form from the oil and line it with 1/4 of the potatoes spread in an even layer.
   c. Close the top of the form and lower it into the oil, allowing the form to rest on the bottom of the fryer basket. Fry about 1 minute, until the potatoes are cooked through and light golden.
   d. Open the form and release the potato basket upside-down on the paper towels.
   e. As soon as it can be handled, turn the basket upright and gently press the bottom flat so that it sits level.
   f. Season the basket with salt.
   g. Repeat with the remaining potatoes to make a total of 4 potato baskets.
   h. If preparing ahead, cool all baskets completely.

holding: refrigerate in one layer in a paper-towel-lined, covered container up to 5 days

COMPONENT RECIPE
CARROT PURÉE

yield: 1 qt.

production		costing only
5 c.	peeled, chopped carrots	1 1/4 lb. a.p.
as needed	water	n/c
tt	kosher salt	1/16 oz.
2 tsp.	fresh lemon juice	1/8 [90 ct.] lemon
1/2 c.	heavy cream	4 fl. oz.
3 Tbsp.	room-temperature butter	1 1/2 oz.
tt	fine-ground white pepper	1/16 oz.

preparation:
1. Place the carrots in a 2-qt. saucepan and add enough water to cover by 1/2". Add a little salt. Bring to the boil and cook briskly until the carrots are very soft.
2. Drain the carrots, reserving the cooking liquid.
3. Purée the carrots with an immersion blender or in a food processor, adding only enough of the cooking liquid to release the blades.
4. If necessary, scrape the carrot purée back into the saucepan. Add the lemon juice and the remaining cooking water. Cook over high heat, stirring constantly with a heatproof rubber spatula, about 2 minutes, until the liquid reduces/absorbs and the purée is thick and tight.
5. Add the cream and cook, stirring, until the purée is thick enough to hold a shape when piped from a pastry bag.
6. Remove from the heat, work in the butter, and season with salt and white pepper.

holding: open-pan cool and refrigerate in a freshly sanitized, covered container up to 5 days

---

RECIPE VARIATION

Lancaster County Roast Lamb in Minted Pan Gravy with Peas 'n' Pearl Onions in Baked Potato Shell and Carrot Purée
Omit the Individual Potato Baskets. For each serving, bake and cool a russet potato. Cut off the top 1/3 of each potato and hollow it out, leaving a 3/8" shell. Deep-fry the potato shell, drain, and fill with the peas and onions.

Shoofly Pie
with Whipped Cream

yield: 1 dessert serving
(multiply × 4 for classroom turnout)

MASTER RECIPE

production		costing only
1 slice	Shoofly Pie	1/8 recipe
1/4 c.	Sweetened Whipped Cream, whipped soft	1/4 recipe

service turnout:
1. Plate the dish:
   a. Place the Shoofly Pie slice on a cool 8" plate.
   b. Spoon a dollop of Sweetened Whipped Cream next to the pie.

COMPONENT RECIPE
SHOOFLY PIE

yield: 1 (9") pie

production		costing only
as needed	flour	1 oz.
10 oz.	American Flaky Pastry	1 recipe
1 1/2 c.	flour	7 1/2 oz.
1 tsp.	ground cinnamon	1/16 oz.
1/2 tsp.	ground mace	1/16 oz.
1/4 tsp.	ground cloves	1/16 oz.
1/2 tsp.	fine salt	1/16 oz.
2/3 c.	brown sugar	3 2/3 oz.
1/2 c.	cold butter, 1/2" cubes	4 oz.
1/2 tsp.	baking soda	1/16 oz.
1/2 c.	warm water	n/c
2	eggs	2 each or 4 oz.
1/4 tsp.	fine salt	1/16 oz.
3/4 c.	molasses	6 fl. oz.

preparation:
1. Preheat an oven to 400°F.
2. Make up the pie shell:
   a. Lightly flour the work surface and roll out the American Flaky Pastry to fit a 9" pie pan.
   b. Place the pastry in the pan and trim the edges to a 3/4" overhang.
   c. Turn the edges under and crimp to make a fluted rim.
   d. Dock the bottom of the pastry.
   e. Place the pie shell on a sheet tray with pan liner and refrigerate at least 20 minutes.
3. Blind-bake the shell:
   a. Place a 10" circle of pan liner into the pastry shell and fill the shell with pie weights.
   b. Bake the shell 10 minutes, until lightly set.
   c. Remove from the oven and remove the pie weights and the pan liner circle.

4. Prepare the crumb mixture:
   a. Sift together the flour, cinnamon, mace, cloves, and 1/2 tsp. salt directly onto a sanitized work surface.
   b. Mix in the sugar.
   c. Using a pastry scraper, cut in the butter until the mixture has the texture of coarse crumbs.
5. Mix the molasses custard:
   a. Dissolve the baking soda in the warm water.
   b. Beat the eggs, then beat in 1/4 tsp. salt, the molasses, and the baking soda mixture.
6. Pour the molasses custard into the pie shell.
7. Top with the crumb mixture, sprinkling it out to the edge of the pie shell in an even layer.
8. Bake the pie:
   a. Place the pie in the center of the oven and bake 15 minutes.
   b. Reduce the oven temperature to 325°F and bake 35 to 40 minutes longer, until the center is set.
9. Remove the pie from the oven and cool on a rack to room temperature.

holding: best served the same day; may be refrigerated under a cake dome up to 2 days

---

RECIPE VARIATIONS

Wet-Bottom Shoofly Pie
Omit the eggs. Double the crumb mixture and stir half into the molasses mixture before putting it into the shell.

Pennsylvania Dutch Stack Pie
Double the ingredients and prepare 3 Shoofly Pies in 3 (9") fluted tart pans with removable bottoms. Chill the pies, remove from the pans, and stack them on top of each other. Frost the stack with Boiled Icing, p. 79.

DESSERTS

Hershey Brownie Sundae

with Philadelphia-Style Ice Cream and Hot Fudge Sauce

yield: 1 dessert serving
(multiply × 4 for classroom turnout)

MASTER RECIPE

production		costing only
1	3" × 3" square Classic Brownie or Walnut Brownie	1/15 recipe
1	5-fl.-oz. scoop Philadelphia-Style Ice Cream	1/6 recipe
1/2 c.	Hot Fudge Sauce, hot in steam table	1/4 recipe
1 Tbsp.	white chocolate shavings	1/4 oz.
1 tsp.	multicolor décor sprinkles	1/8 oz.

service turnout:
1. Plate the dish:
   a. Place the Classic Brownie in the center of a cool footed compote dish or 10" plate.
   b. Top with the Philadelphia-Style Ice Cream scoop.
   c. Nap the ice cream with Hot Fudge Sauce.
   d. Scatter the white chocolate shavings and décor sprinkles on top.

COMPONENT RECIPE
CLASSIC BROWNIES

yield: 1 half-sheet tray

production		costing only
as needed	baker's pan coating spray	% of container
8 oz.	unsweetened chocolate	8 oz.
8 oz.	room-temperature unsalted butter	8 oz.
8	room-temperature eggs	8 each or 1 lb.
2 lb.	sugar	2 lb.
1/4 tsp	fine salt	1/16 oz.
1 tsp.	pure vanilla extract	1/6 fl. oz.
12 oz.	flour	12 oz.

preparation:
1. Preheat an oven to 350°F.
2. Spray a half-sheet tray with pan coating, place a piece of pan liner on it, and spray the pan liner.
3. If the chocolate is in block form, chop it into small, even pieces.
4. Combine the butter and chocolate in the top of a double boiler and melt them over low heat, stirring occasionally with a clean, dry rubber spatula. Cool to room temperature.
5. Using the paddle attachment of a mixer, beat the eggs on medium speed just until foamy. Reduce the speed to low and stir in the sugar in a thin stream.
6. Stir in the salt and vanilla.
7. Turn off the mixer, add the flour, and mix by pulsing the machine on and off a few times, mixing only until the flour is incorporated. Pulse in the chocolate mixture. Scrape down the bowl and beater as needed.
8. Pour the batter into the prepared pan and spread it evenly. Make the corners a little thicker than the rest of the pan to prevent burning. (If using a deck oven, double-pan the brownies by placing another half-sheet tray under their tray.)
9. Bake the brownies 35 to 40 minutes, until set but still very moist in the center.
10. Cool to room temperature on a rack.
11. Cut away the hard edges of the brownies, then use a ruler or adjustable rolling cutter to cut the brownies to even portions of the size desired. (Standard brownies are 2" × 2". Brownies for Brownie Sundae are 3" × 3".)

holding: store at cool room temperature on a tight-wrapped tray or in a sealed container with pan liner between layers; alternatively, wrap each brownie individually in plastic film

RECIPE VARIATIONS
Walnut Brownies
Add 1 c. chopped walnuts after step 7.
Cheesecake Brownies
Scale the formula down by 1/4 (multiply all formula amounts × 0.75). After panning the batter, swirl in 1/4 recipe New York Cheese Cake batter.

COMPONENT RECIPE
HOT FUDGE SAUCE

yield: approx. 2 c.

production		costing only
4 oz.	unsweetened chocolate	4 oz.
2 Tbsp.	butter	1 oz.
2/3 c.	boiling water	n/c
1 lb.	sugar	1 lb.
4 Tbsp.	light corn syrup	2 fl. oz.
2 Tbsp.	dark rum	1 fl. oz.

preparation:
1. If necessary, chop the chocolate and place it in a saucepan along with the butter. Melt the chocolate over very low heat, stirring occasionally with a rubber scraper, until the mixture is smooth.
2. Stir in the boiling water, sugar, and corn syrup; cover the pan; and boil the sauce 3 minutes.
3. Remove the lid and continue to boil 3 to 4 minutes. Do not stir.
4. Remove from heat and stir in the rum.
5. Transfer to a steam table and hold at 180°F.

holding: best prepared for each service; open-pan cool leftovers and refrigerate in a freshly sanitized, covered container up to 5 days; reheat gently, preferably in a hot-water bath, working with a rubber scraper to smooth out lumps; may require thinning with boiling water

RECIPE VARIATIONS

Triple-Threat Brownie Ice Cream Sundae
Replace the vanilla ice cream with dark chocolate ice cream.

Brownie Ice Cream Sandwich
Use a 3" round cutter to punch out discs of brownie. Allow the ice cream to soften in a refrigerator about 45 minutes, place it in a heavy pastry bag fitted with a large star tip, and pipe a 3/4" layer of ice cream on half the brownie discs. Make "sandwiches" by placing the remaining brownie discs on top and pressing gently. Freeze until the ice cream firms. Roll the edges in miniature chocolate chips.

Waffle Ice Cream Sundae
Replace the brownie with a 4 1/2" vanilla-flavored Belgian waffle.

Pumpkin Roll
with Cranberry Coulis

yield: 1 dessert serving

MASTER RECIPE

production		costing only
1	1" slice Pumpkin Roll	1/16 recipe
1/3 c.	Sweet Cranberry Coulis, in squeeze bottle	1/4 recipe
1 sprig	fresh mint	1/20 bunch a.p.

service turnout:
1. Place the Pumpkin Roll slice slightly left of center on a cool 8" round plate.
2. Squeeze a pool of Sweet Cranberry Coulis on the plate to the right of the slice.
3. Place the mint sprig on the coulis against the slice.

COMPONENT RECIPE
PUMPKIN ROLL

yield: 12 dessert servings: 1 (16" long × 4" diameter) roulade

production		costing
as needed	confectioner's sugar	1 oz.
1	Pumpkin Spongecake Sheet, rolled as in step 7	1 recipe
1 qt.	Cream Cheese Frosting, p. 452, softened to spreadable consistency	1 recipe

preparation:
1. Unroll the Pumpkin Spongecake Sheet and trim off about 1/2" of the thick edges.
2. Spread an even layer of Cream Cheese Frosting on the sheet.
3. Starting from a longer end, roll up the sheet into a tight, even, cylindrical roulade.
4. Wrap the pan liner around the pumpkin roll and carefully lift it onto a half-sheet tray.
5. Refrigerate the pumpkin roll until firm.
6a. To serve in platter presentation, place the roulade on a 16" × 4" rectangular cake board and trim the ends. Sift confectioner's sugar over it.
   —or—
6b. For plate presentation, freeze the pumpkin roll solid. Trim the ends and then cut the roulade into 16 (1") slices. Place the slices on a sheet tray with pan liner. Refrigerate until thawed.

holding: wrap in plastic film and refrigerate up to 3 days or freeze up to 1 month

COMPONENT RECIPE
PUMPKIN SPONGECAKE SHEET

yield: 1 half-sheet

production		costing only
as needed	baker's pan coating spray	% of container
1 2/3 c.	flour	9 oz.
3/4 tsp.	ground nutmeg	1/16 oz.
2 tsp.	ground cinnamon	1/8 oz.
1 1/2 tsp.	ground ginger	1/16 oz.
1 Tbsp.	baking powder	1/4 oz.
1/4 tsp.	fine salt	1/16 oz.
18 oz.	granulated sugar	18 oz.
6	room-temperature eggs	6 each or 12 oz.
11 oz.	canned unsweetened pumpkin	11 oz.
as needed	confectioner's sugar	1 oz.

preparation:
1. Preheat an oven to 375°F.
2. Spray a half-sheet tray with pan coating, place pan liner on it, and spray again.
3. Mix the batter:
   a. Sift together the flour, nutmeg, cinnamon, ginger, baking powder, and salt, then sift again to ensure thorough mixing.
   b. Using the paddle attachment of a mixer, beat the granulated sugar into the eggs on medium speed.
   c. Add the pumpkin and beat on medium speed until smooth.
   d. Stop the machine and add 1/3 of the flour mixture. Pulse the machine on and off until the flour is almost incorporated.
   e. Repeat twice until all flour is incorporated.
4. Pour the batter into the prepared pan and smooth it.
5. Bake about 15 minutes, until set and springy.
6. Cool on a rack 10 minutes and then turn it out of the pan or immediately proceed to step 7.
7. If the spongecake sheet is to be a roulade:
   a. Sift an even layer of confectioner's sugar on a sheet of pan liner.
   b. Run a spatula around the edge of the cake to release it from the pan.
   c. Turn the cake out of the pan onto the confectioner's-sugar-dusted pan liner.
   d. Peel the pan liner off the top of the cake and discard it.
   e. Starting at a longer end, loosely roll the cake in the paper and leave it to rest, seam side down, about 20 minutes, until completely cool.

holding: best used within a few hours; for longer storage, wrap loosely in plastic film and hold at room temperature up to 2 days, frozen up to 1 month

---

RECIPE VARIATION
Pumpkin Roll with Whipped Cream
Replace the Cream Cheese Frosting with Sweetened Whipped Cream

COMPONENT RECIPE
SWEET CRANBERRY COULIS

yield: approx. 1 1/3 c.

production		costing only
1 c.	fresh or frozen cranberries	3 1/3 oz.
1 1/2 c.	sugar	12 oz.
1 1/2 c.	water	n/c

preparation:
1. Combine the cranberries, sugar, and water in a 3-qt. nonreactive saucepan.
2. Bring the mixture to the simmer and cook about 20 minutes, until the berries have burst.
3. Force the sauce through a strainer.
4. Rinse out the pan, return the sauce to it, and reduce to a light nappé consistency.
5. Cool to room temperature.

holding: refrigerate in a freshly sanitized, covered container up to 5 days

Allegheny Mountain Apple Dumpling
with Vanilla Custard Sauce

yield: 1 dessert serving
(multiply × 4 for classroom turnout)

MASTER RECIPE

production		costing only
1	Apple Dumpling	1/4 recipe
3/4 c.	Vanilla Custard Sauce	1/3 recipe

service turnout:
1. Place the Apple Dumpling on a sizzle plate and warm it in a moderate oven, about 325°F, about 8 minutes.
2. Plate the dish:
   a. Ladle the Vanilla Custard Sauce into a 10" pasta plate.
   b. Place the dumpling in the center of the plate.

COMPONENT RECIPE
APPLE DUMPLINGS

yield: 4 dessert servings

production		costing only
20 oz.	American Flaky Pastry formed into 5 discs and refrigerated 20 minutes	2 recipes
as needed	flour	1 oz.
1/4 c.	brown sugar	1 1/3 oz.
1/4 c.	granulated sugar	2 oz.
1/2 tsp.	ground cinnamon	1/16 oz.
pinch	fine salt	1/16 oz.
1 Tbsp.	granulated sugar	1/2 oz.
1/4 tsp.	ground cinnamon	1/16 oz.
4	small (4-oz.) cooking apples	1 lb. a.p.
1 Tbsp.	fresh lemon juice	1/4 [90 ct.] lemon
1/2 c.	vanilla cake crumbs or cookie crumbs	2 oz.
4 Tbsp.	cold butter, cut in 4 pieces	2 oz.
5 Tbsp.	egg wash (1 egg + 1 Tbsp. water)	1 each or 2 oz.

preparation:
1. Preheat a standard oven to 400°F.
2. Roll out the American Flaky Pastry dough on a sanitized work surface:
   a. Flour the work surface and rolling pin, then roll out each pastry disc into a circle 1/8" thick.
   b. Place on a sheet tray and refrigerate at least 20 minutes.
3. Mix together 1/4 c. brown sugar, 1/4 c. granulated sugar, 1/2 tsp. cinnamon, and salt for the filling.
4. Mix together 1 Tbsp. granulated sugar and 1/4 tsp. cinnamon for sprinkling.

5. Peel and core the apples. Coat each apple with lemon juice.
6. Make up the décor:
   a. Place the least perfect rolled-out pastry circle on the work surface.
   b. Using a leaf cutter, or freehand with a knife, cut out 12 (1 1/2") leaf-shaped cutouts.
   c. Using the back of a paring knife, score the cutouts with veins to look like leaves.
   d. Refrigerate until needed.
7. Make up the dumplings:
   a. Place another pastry circle on the work surface and mound 1/4 of the cake crumbs in the center.
   b. Place an apple on the crumbs and spoon 1/4 of the brown sugar filling into it.
   c. Press a piece of butter on top of the apple.
   d. Bring up the edges of the pastry circle to evenly encase the apple, cutting away excess dough where pleats form, and sealing the dough together with egg wash.
   e. Brush the top of the dumpling with egg wash and arrange 3 pastry "leaves" on top.
   f. Use a plain pastry tip to punch a small, round vent in the very top of the dumpling.
   g. Place the dumpling on a half-sheet tray with pan liner.
   h. Sprinkle the dumpling with 1/4 of the cinnamon sugar.
   i. Repeat with the remaining ingredients to make 4 dumplings.
8. Bake the dumplings:
   a. Place the tray of dumplings in the center of the oven and bake 10 minutes.
   b. Reduce the oven temperature to 350°F and bake about 30 minutes longer, until the apples are tender and the crust is golden brown. (If the crust becomes brown too fast, shield the dumplings with foil and reduce the heat 25°F.)
9. Place the dumpling tray on a rack and cool to room temperature.

holding: cover with a clean, dry kitchen towel and store at room temperature up to 8 hours; best made for each service; may be refrigerated for 24 hours and then recrisped in a moderate oven

---

RECIPE VARIATIONS
Raisin-Walnut Apple Dumplings with Vanilla Custard Sauce
Reduce the brown sugar in the filling to 3 Tbsp. Add 2 Tbsp. raisins soaked in 1 Tbsp. dark rum and 2 Tbsp. chopped walnuts.

Amaretti Peach Dumplings with Vanilla Custard Sauce
Replace the apples with firm, slightly underripe peaches, peeled, halved, pitted, and pressed back together with crushed Amaretti cookie crumbs inside.

☐ TABLE 4.2 MID-ATLANTIC REGIONAL INGREDIENTS

ITEM	MARKET FORMS	USES	SEASON	OTHER	STORAGE
DRIED SWEET CORN	Available from John Cope's Food Products, Inc., Rheems, Pennsylvania.	Reconstituted in boiling water or scalded milk, it lends a special flavor to puddings, soufflés, and creamed corn.	N/A	Yellow sweet corn is lightly toasted and air-dried; the small, tender kernels shrivel up into tiny flakes with a concentrated, almost caramelized sweetness.	Store at room temperature, tightly sealed.
SPELT	Available in whole grain form or as flour. Purchase from health food stores or specialty purveyors.	Spelt flour is used in the same manner as wheat flour. Whole-grain spelt can be cooked by the pilaf method and served as a savory side dish, or sweetened and served with milk for breakfast.	N/A	An ancient cultivated grain, spelt is higher in nutrition and easier to digest than wheat.	Store at room temperature or frozen for longer storage.
BUCKWHEAT	See p. 402.				
FRESH SAUERKRAUT	Available in 1 lb. refrigerated packages or in refrigerated quarts from artisan producers.	Simmer with a preserved pork product and serve as a side dish with pork, sausages, duck, or turkey. Use in casseroles and fillings. Use as a garnish on hot and cold sandwiches. Serve cold in salads.	Late fall through winter. Supplies dwindle in spring.	Shreds of fresh sauerkraut are crisp and opaque in color as opposed to the limp, translucent strands of processed sauerkraut.	Refrigerate 3 to 4 weeks; freeze for prolonged storage.
HORSERADISH	Fresh horseradish root is available as a produce item. Prepared horseradish (grated and mixed with vinegar and salt) is sold fresh or pasteurized in refrigerated jars.	Used as a table condiment, in sauces and dressings, and on sandwiches.	Local horseradish root is harvested in early autumn. Imported root is widely available in spring for Passover.	The best horseradish is the freshest horseradish. Once prepared, this pungent root loses potency very quickly.	Store fresh root in a box or bin covered with a damp towel. Refrigerate prepared horseradish 1 month. Discard when discolored brown.
SAFFRON	Whole dried saffron threads are purest and most flavorful. Dried ground saffron is less costly. For best price purchase from Indian or Pakistani grocers or wholesale spice purveyors.	Lends a rich yellow color and aromatic flavor to broths, soups, stews, noodles, rice dishes, and baked goods.	N/A	Famed as the world's most expensive spice, saffron is the stigma of the flower *Crocus sativus*.	Room temperature, tightly sealed.
SHAD	Available fresh as: whole gutted fish; unfabricated sides; boneless sides (with pocket for stuffing). Females are larger and fattier; males are smaller and leaner.	Shad is cooked by dry methods, such as baking, grilling, and broiling.	Seasonal to early spring; the main run occurs in March and April.	Shad is best flavored with sharp, tangy seasonings such as vinegar, citrus or tomato.	Refrigerate on ice 1 or 2 days only. Soft-fleshed and oily, shad is very perishable and must be served extremely fresh. It does not freeze well.
SHAD ROE	Tiny beige to pink eggs in two connected crescent-shaped sacs are referred to as a pair or set. Jumbo sets weigh about 8 oz., large sets weigh 6 to 7 oz., and medium sets weigh about 5 oz.	After cleaning and soaking, shad roe is briefly poached to firm its texture. Whole or half sets are sautéed, breaded and fried, or broiled, and served with bacon or butter sauces.	Spring	Shad roe is typically accented with lemon.	Extremely perishable, shad roe should be stored refrigerated in a plastic bag on ice, and used within 24–36 hours.

☐ TABLE 4.2 MID-ATLANTIC REGIONAL INGREDIENTS *(continued)*

ITEM	MARKET FORMS	USES	SEASON	OTHER	STORAGE
BLUEFISH	Whole 3 to 15 lb. fresh bluefish are sold gutted. Bluefish sides and portioned fillets are usually cut from fish between 3 and 10 lb. weight. Fresh baby or snapper bluefish under 3 lb. are sold whole. Smoked bluefish is available from specialty purveyors.	Bluefish fillets are baked, grilled, or broiled, usually skin-on. Smoked bluefish is served as an appetizer or used in dips and spreads.	Summer and fall.	For milder flavor, remove dark flesh at the fillet's center line.	Extremely perishable due to soft flesh and high oil content. Store refrigerated on ice 24–36 hours only.
FRESH DUCK FOIE GRAS	Fresh foie gras is sold in vacuum sealed packages. One to 2 lb. Grade A livers are perfectly shaped and have few interior veins. Grade B livers weigh 1–1 1/2 lb., may be irregular in shape, and have more interior veining. Small Grade C livers are irregular in shape, have more veins, and may have discolored areas.	Rich, expensive foie gras is served in small portions as an appetizer. Grade A foie gras is poached and served cold. Grades A or B are sliced and seared medium-rare. Grade C is cut into pieces and used in pâtés, stuffings, and sauces.	Supply is greater and prices lower in late spring and summer.	Foie gras is produced by force-feeding ducks or geese to enlarge and fatten their livers. Practices used in producing foie gras are under scrutiny by food ethicists.	Refrigerate in a plastic bag on ice up to 2 weeks.
CULTIVATED MUSHROOMS	For foodservice fresh mushrooms are sold in 10-lb. cartons or plastic lugs; also available in smaller consumer packs. Varieties include: white, creamer, brown, cremini, portabella, shiitake, enoke, and oyster.	Many uses.	N/A	Kennett Square, Pennsylvania, is the birthplace of America's mushroom industry.	Refrigerate in the original cardboard carton up to 1 week. Cover open lugs with damp kitchen towels to prevent surface drying.

■□■ chapter 5

The Chesapeake Bay Shore

the Bay Shore areas of Maryland, Virginia, and Delaware and extreme south-central Pennsylvania

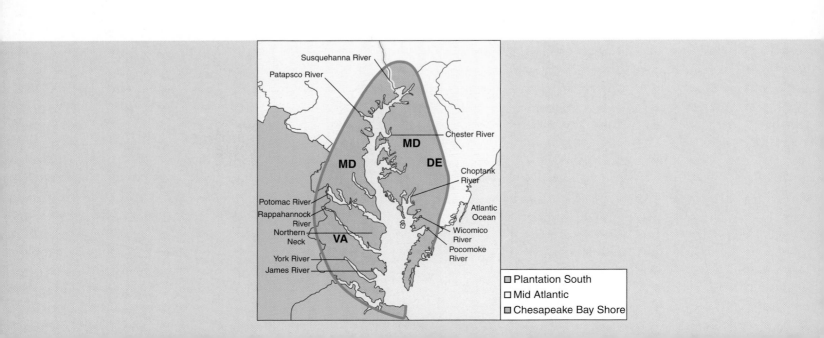

CHESAPEAKE, WHICH MEANS "great shellfish bay" in the Algonquian language, describes an estuary that once teemed with oysters and crabs and today yields some of the nation's finest seafood. Although much of the Chesapeake's bounty is shipped to food stores and restaurants around the country, the people who live along its shores are also avid consumers of local fish and shellfish. For more than a century they've developed a distinctive cuisine built around the products of the bay. Indeed, no other American body of water has had such a profound effect on the cuisine of the surrounding land.

The Chesapeake Bay Shore began its history as the earliest-settled part of the Plantation South culinary region. However, by the early 1800s the Chesapeake area's cooking began to diverge from the Plantation South style. Commercial activity on and around the bay, and the middle-class fishing and artisan families who engaged in it, initiated the development of a new regional cuisine.

Traditional Chesapeake Bay cooking is influenced by the Plantation South cuisine of Maryland and Virginia to the west, the Pennsylvania Dutch cooking of York and Lancaster counties to the north, and the "English" Mid-Atlantic cooking of Delaware and Philadelphia to the east. However, the bay's fine local fish and shellfish remain the foundation of the cuisine, enhanced by the distinctive cooking methods and seasonings applied to it by people who live and work on the water.

AFTER STUDYING THIS CHAPTER YOU SHOULD BE ABLE TO:

- describe the unique ecosystem of the Chesapeake Bay and the climate and topography of the land around it
- outline the life cycle of the blue crab and explain how its life stages relate to crab cookery
- explain the importance of the oyster in Chesapeake economics and cuisine
- discuss the history and lifestyle of the Chesapeake watermen
- list the ways in which the cooking of the neighboring Plantation South and Mid-Atlantic regions have affected Chesapeake cuisine
- list and describe the important cooking techniques, ingredients, and flavor profiles of Chesapeake Bay cuisine
- list and describe the defining dishes of Chesapeake Bay cuisine
- prepare authentic Chesapeake Bay dishes, both traditional and modern

APPETIZERS

Creamy Corn and Crab Soup with Beaten Biscuit

Spicy Home-Style Crab Soup with Sweet Potato Roll

Chesapeake Fried Oysters with Fresh Tomato Cocktail Sauce

Oyster Fritters with Herbed Red Bell Pepper Mayonnaise

Deviled Crab

Tilghman Island Chicken Salad with Fried Oysters

ENTRÉES

Maryland-Style Crab Cakes with Smashed Redskin Potato Salad and Summer Garden Diced Vegetable Salad

Imperial Stuffed Flounder with Lemon Butter Sauce, Baby Spinach, and Sweet Potato Pearls

Sautéed Soft-Shell Crabs with Lemon Butter Sauce, Parsley Potatoes, and Summer Squash in Tomato Sauce

Grilled Rockfish on Grilled Vegetable Ratatouille with Sweet Potato Hay

DelMarVa Roadside Barbeque Chicken with Tidewater Kidney Bean Salad and Cucumber Salad

Chicken Virginia Stuffed with Ham and Collards in Creamy Mushroom Sauce,
Served with Pan-Steamed White Rice and Glazed Baby Carrots

DESSERTS

Lady Baltimore Cake

Hominy Custard with Glazed Strawberries and Black Walnut Crisps

WEBSITE EXTRAS

Crab Procedures   Breakfasts   Sandwiches   Hors d'Oeuvres   Thanksgiving Menu

■ THE CHESAPEAKE
□ BAY
■

FACTOR 1
The bay's unique ecosystem shaped the region's cuisine.

The Chesapeake Bay is North America's largest **estuary,** a body of water formed where a river meets the sea. The bay is nearly 200 miles long and as much as 30 miles wide. Its average depth is 30 feet with a central channel more than 100 feet deep. However, its many treacherous bars and shallows threaten the unwary sailor. At its northern reach, where the Susquehanna River flows into it, the bay's water is only lightly saline. **Salinity,** or the water's salt content, increases as one moves southward; the bay's mouth is highly saline seawater. These varied salinity levels provide habitat for a wide variety of fish and shellfish.

East of the bay the land is low and flat, with marshland meeting the water's edge. At the bay's northern head the Atlantic coastal plain slopes gently downward, funneling the waters of the Susquehanna River southward into the bay. The terrain of the Chesapeake's western shore is configured in a line of ridges carved out by five rivers that drop over the fall line (p. 27) and flow southeast to the bay.

The Chesapeake Bay drains a huge **watershed,** the land area whose streams, creeks, and rivers flow into it (Figure 5.1).

FIGURE 5.1
The Chesapeake Bay Watershed

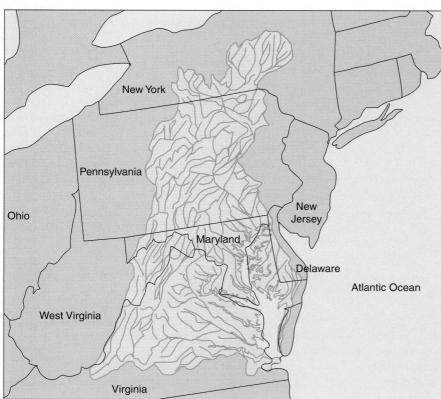

The Chesapeake watershed extends west to the spine of the Appalachian Mountains, encompassing virtually all of Maryland, central and northern Virginia, central Pennsylvania, and half of Delaware. It reaches as far north as the headwaters of the Susquehanna River in central New York—more than 64,000 square miles.

A Drowned River

This enormous bay was created by geological events that began about sixty million years ago. Volcanic activity had previously thrust the Appalachian Mountains upward, and erosion had already started wearing them down. Then, during the ice ages, advancing glaciers began carving valleys out of rock. Melting, receding glaciers caused extensive water runoff. In the southern Mid-Atlantic region, small rivers and creeks that resulted from rainwater and melting glaciers converged to become a powerful southward flowing river that dug a deep rift into the newly formed land. This ancient river, now called the Susquehanna, was originally a narrow waterway flowing between two wide plateaus and emptying directly into the Atlantic Ocean.

However, climatic changes eventually altered the appearance of the Susquehanna and its surrounding lands. When the ice ages ended, much of the world's glacial mass melted, and the resulting water flowed into the world's oceans. Ocean water levels rose, and the lower reaches of the Susquehanna River became submerged. The former riverbed and its banks were covered by the waters of a great estuary that one day would be called the Chesapeake Bay. The Susquehanna's ancient bed is still evident as the bay's deep central channel, now "drowned" under many feet of Chesapeake Bay water. For this reason the Chesapeake Bay is called a **drowned river.** Understanding the bay's unique topography, both under water and of the surrounding land, is key to understanding the fish and shellfish that are the foundation of the region's cuisine.

A Region Divided

The Chesapeake Bay divides its surrounding culinary region roughly in half, from north to south, creating two cultures and resulting in two subtly different subcuisines (Figure 5.2).

The Western Shore

The Chesapeake Bay's western shore extends from Havre de Grace, Maryland, in the north to Cape Henry, Virginia, in the south. The western shore is considered part of the Atlantic coastal plain because it lies below the fall line. However, its terrain is quite different from the coastal plain in the Carolinas and Georgia. In Maryland, the land slopes east from the fall line in waves of rolling hills. Moving south into an area called

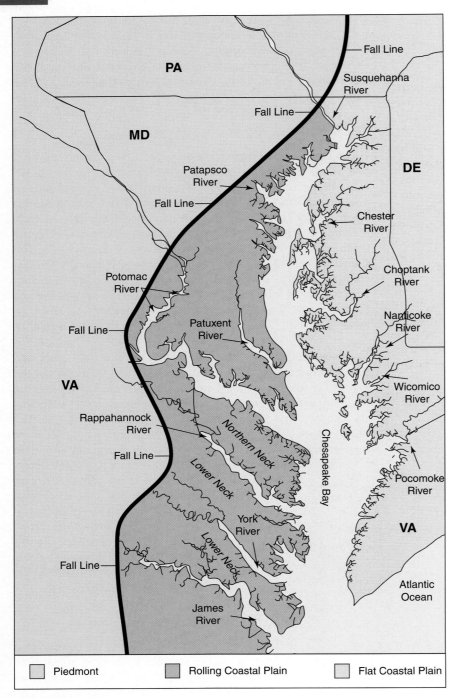

FIGURE 5.2

Topography of Chesapeake Bay's Western and Eastern Shores

[map labels: PA; MD; DE; VA; VA; Fall Line; Susquehanna River; Fall Line; Patapsco River; Fall Line; Potomac River; Fall Line; Patuxent River; Chester River; Choptank River; Nanticoke River; Wicomico River; Rappahannock River; Fall Line; Northern Neck; Lower Neck; Chesapeake Bay; Pocomoke River; York River; Lower Neck; Fall Line; James River; Atlantic Ocean]

Legend: Piedmont | Rolling Coastal Plain | Flat Coastal Plain

whose mouths and lower reaches accept a significant inflow of saline bay water at high tide and discharge the saline water back into the bay at low tide. For this reason the land around these rivers is referred to as a **tidewater area.** Many of the early Southern plantations were built along these rivers, and some of the most important events of American history occurred on their banks.

Because these five rivers were easily navigable, and because the soil along their banks was exceptionally fertile, the western shore of the Chesapeake Bay became populated and prosperous at an early date. This area is the birthplace of Plantation South cuisine. However, as time passed and settlement expanded, the cooking of the Chesapeake shore diverged from other Plantation South areas. Seafood-based Chesapeake cooking is lighter and uses less fat. The bay shore's cooler climate allows cultivation of a wider range of vegetables. The area's proximity to the Mid-Atlantic resulted in more wheat-based baking. The food attitudes and taste preferences of the Chesapeake watermen (p. 201) largely replaced those of African-American slave cooks. Thus the cuisine of Chesapeake Bay's western shore diverged from the Plantation tradition and emerged as a separate cooking style that eventually spread in a great arc all around the bay.

The Eastern Shore

On the eastern side of the Chesapeake Bay, the topography is quite different from that of the western shore. Here, between Chesapeake and Delaware Bays and the Atlantic Ocean, lies a teardrop-shaped expanse of land known as the **DelMarVa Peninsula,** so named because parts of it are claimed by the states of Delaware, Maryland, and Virginia.

All across the DelMarVa Peninsula the land stretches low and flat from bay to bay and out to the ocean. Its interior ground rises slightly, covered with a thick layer of fertile soil. The peninsula's Atlantic coast is lined with barrier islands similar to those of the Carolinas and New Jersey. On its western side six meandering tidal rivers, fed by creeks and marshy wetlands, flow slowly into Chesapeake Bay. Figure 5.4 shows topography typical of this area.

The western half of the DelMarVa Peninsula looks to the Chesapeake region both historically

tidewater Virginia, one encounters a row of low, parallel ridges ending at the bay, as shown in Figure 5.3. Seperated by rivers, these ridges create peninsulas called **necks.** The area's five historically important rivers are the Patuxent, the Potomac, the Rappahannock, the York, and the James. These are tidal rivers,

FIGURE 5.3

On the western shore of the Chesapeake Bay, at the mouth of the Potomac River, one of the region's many ridges meets the water as a sandy bluff. Courtesy Stratford Hall, Stratford, VA

and culinarily and is called the **Eastern Shore**. Go to this book's companion website to learn more about this place name. A group of large islands clustered midbay near the Maryland-Virginia border are considered part of the Eastern Shore as well. Although the Eastern Shore was also lined with plantations, in this area fishing became more important than agriculture. Thus, the Eastern Shore developed a different and unique culture, discussed later in this chapter.

Plants and Animals of Bay and Shore

When the ancient glaciers receded for the last time and the climate became warmer, an abundance of animal life began to flourish in the bay area. Oysters colonized the bay in great number, and crabs adapted to its semisaline waters. Anadromous fish, such as herring, shad, and sturgeon, entered the bay to spawn. Each spring migratory waterfowl arrived by the millions. Whitetail deer, black bears, rabbits, raccoons, muskrats, wild turkeys, squirrels, and opossums thrived on the shore along with turtles, snakes, and frogs.

At the same time, ice age timberlands on the western shore were replaced by forests of oak, maple, and hickory. Droughts and the accompanying fires created expanses of parklike woodland

FIGURE 5.4

The Chesapeake Bay's Eastern Shore is low, flat, and marshy. Courtesy of Robert A. Haynes, Ph.D.

and open, grassy spaces with a variety of bushes, berries, herbs, and other food plants. Eelgrass and cordgrass emerged in the salt marshes of the lower Eastern Shore, providing ideal habitat for the eastern blue crab, which would become both the region's signature dish and its enduring icon.

■□■ NATIVE AMERICANS OF THE CHESAPEAKE BAY SHORE

As prehistoric animals arrived, humans in search of game followed them into the region. By the time of European contact, the Native American people of the Chesapeake region had settled into semipermanent villages grouped into distinct tribal confederations. On the western shore, Powhatan (p. 36) had loosely unified most of the Algonquian-speaking tribes in his locality. This native group lived in relative peace and prosperity as agriculturalists, with gathering, hunting, and trade as important sidelines. On the Eastern Shore smaller Algonquian tribes such as the Choptanks, Nanticokes, Pocomokes, and Accomacs were less affluent and far less organized. These Eastern Shore natives engaged in subsistence farming, but relied more on gathering, hunting, and fishing. To the north were the Susquehannocks, "people of the muddy river," an aggressive, warlike tribe of the Iroquoian language group. Although they lived primarily along the banks of the Susquehanna River in Pennsylvania's York and Lancaster counties, the Susquehannocks made frequent forays along both shores of the bay for the purposes of hunting, fishing, and raiding coastal villages. Figure 5.5 shows patterns of Native American settlement in the Chesapeake Bay region.

All of these tribes followed the same East Coast Native American agricultural practices and culinary traditions you learned about in Chapter 2. Cornmeal and hominy, long-simmered dried beans, and various squashes made up the vegetable component of the native diet and remain as side dishes in traditional Chesapeake cuisine. The region's indigenous black walnuts (unrelated to the European walnut) were harvested and painstakingly shelled. However, fish and shellfish made up the bulk of their diet.

Chesapeake natives prized the blue crab above all other seafood and prepared crabs by steaming them much as modern Chesapeake cooks do. Native cooks picked the crab meat, mixed it with corn dough, and formed it into cakes that were baked on hot stones. These were the precursor to the Chesapeake region's most famous dish, crab cakes. Soft-shell crabs (p. 199) were a seasonal treat.

FACTOR 1
The bay's fish, shellfish, waterfowl, and land animals are the foundation of the cuisine.

FACTOR 2
Native American ways with bay seafood endure in the modern cuisine.

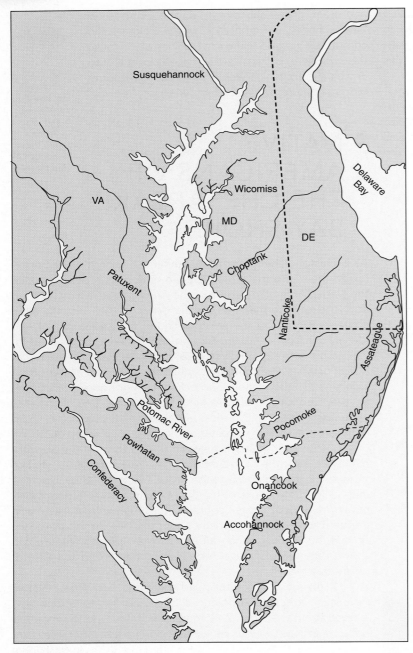

FIGURE 5.5
Chesapeake Native American Settlement

Native Americans traversed the bay and its tributary rivers in dugout canoes that are the prototype of the most famous Chesapeake fishing vessel, the skipjack. In fact, the art of boat building is the Chesapeake Native Americans' most lasting legacy, one that enabled the future harvest of the bay's vital seafood resources. Boats and water travel shaped the history, culture, and cuisine of the Chesapeake Bay region for generations. Not until the arrival of railroads in the late 1800s did land transportation rival water transportation in the region.

■ FOUNDATIONS
□ OF CHESAPEAKE
■ CUISINE

Chesapeake cuisine began with the cooking of the Plantation South, which in turn is based on Old World English cuisine combined with Native American ingredients and techniques. Southern cooking was further enriched by the contributions of African and Afro-Caribbean slave cooks. Thus, both Native American and African foodways figure in Chesapeake cuisine's roots. However, both of these influences waned as Chesapeake cooking diverged on its own course in the early 1800s. At that time Mid-Atlantic cuisine and its Pennsylvania Dutch microcuisine began to shape the cooking of the Chesapeake Bay Shore. Two major cultural and economic events caused Chesapeake cooking to diverge into a distinctly separate regional cuisine: the emergence of a middle class and the commercial distribution of bay seafood.

Though Plantation South cuisine is based on lavish ingredients and unlimited slave labor, traditional Chesapeake cuisine is largely middle-class cooking. Although the Chesapeake style is based on the plantation kitchen's ingredients and techniques, it was modified by women cooking at home and by fishermen cooking aboard their boats. The Chesapeake middle class largely comprised fishermen and the artisans and merchants who supported the fishing industry. Fishing supplied the raw materials essential for Chesapeake cooking and the money to buy adjunct ingredients.

Let's look more closely at the roots of Chesapeake Bay Shore cuisine.

Indigenous Land Foods

Of the many foraged plant foods used by the region's natives, only one remains in the Chesapeake Bay Shore cuisine. Early settlers used indigenous black walnuts in place of English walnuts in cakes and cookies. Today the unique taste of black walnuts is a signature flavor in many Chesapeake Bay desserts.

Three Sisters foods are most frequently served in the form of fresh vegetables. Sweet corn, green beans and lima beans, and summer squash are popular side dishes. Dishes made from dried corn and dried beans are considered home-style comfort foods. As in the rest of the Plantation South, Chesapeake settlers began preparing hominy without alkaline processing; today dried and canned steam-processed hominy remains a favorite ingredient, eaten as a side dish or breakfast food and even used in custard desserts.

FACTOR 1

Indigenous seafood is the foundation of Chesapeake cuisine.

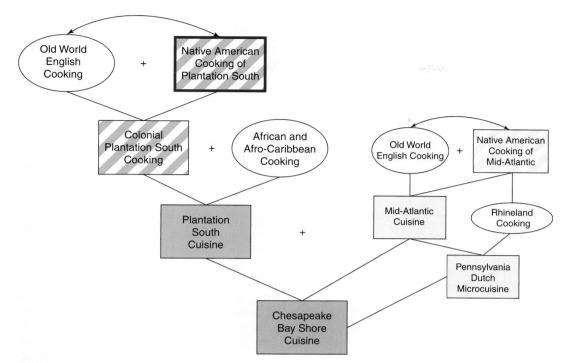

FIGURE 5.6
Development of Chesapeake Bay Shore Cuisine

Indigenous Seafood

Indigenous fish and shellfish are the foundation of Chesapeake cooking. Native American methods of cooking bay seafood, including steaming crabs, grilling fish, and making crab cakes, remain in the modern cuisine. Salt fish, once a necessity for winter survival, was a Chesapeake favorite that today is preferred as a breakfast food.

The Chesapeake Bay is home to numerous species of fish and shellfish.

Blue Crabs

The Atlantic blue crab is the iconic symbol of the Chesapeake Bay. The blue crab's Latin name, *Callinectes sapidus*, meaning "savory beautiful swimmer," aptly describes both its appearance and its flavor. Not actually blue, when alive these crabs are gray-green in color with sky-blue highlights (Figure 5.7). Females "paint their fingernails," meaning their claws have red tips. Fast and fierce, these crabs can escape most marine predators and, using formidable claws, put up a deadly fight with those they can't outswim.

FIGURE 5.7
The Atlantic blue crab is actually gray-green in color with blue highlights. Females have red tips on their claws. sbarabu © Shutterstock

Knowing about the blue crab's life cycle is key to understanding both its seasonality and its culinary uses. Mature blue crabs hibernate over winter buried in the bottom of the Atlantic Ocean or in the mouths of Atlantic estuaries. The warming water of early spring wakes the crabs, and they slowly drift upward and northward from their winter sleep, then migrate to shallower waters and feed among the aquatic plants in salt marshes and along the edges of estuaries. In spring and summer, the crabs grow and reproduce.

Soft-Shell Crabs

Crabs grow by molting, or shedding their shells, in late spring and early summer. Immediately after molting they're known as *soft-shell crabs*. However, those who catch and cook crabs use more specific terms for the additional stages in the crabs' unique growth process. When a crab is ready to molt, it takes in large quantities of water and forms a thin, rudimentary shell membrane between its flesh and outer shell. The outer shell then splits near the crab's swimming paddles. At this point the crab is variously called a **peeler, buster,** or **shedder.** In the wild, the crab normally hides deep within a dense cover of aquatic grasses to **molt,** or crawl out of its old shell, a process that takes about 2 hours. Once free of its shell, the crab is totally soft, having only a thin membrane covering its flesh. Now it takes in even more water, causing it to swell and grow in size. While soft, the crab is totally defenseless against predators. However, in about 2 hours, the crab's external membrane begins to harden into a new shell. The crab's outer membrane remains soft for only about 12 hours longer. During these few hours after molting the crab is called a **soft-shell crab,** recognized as a world-class delicacy. When a soft-shell crab is sautéed, pan-fried, or deep-fried, its outer membrane becomes crackling crisp in counterpoint to its soft and juicy interior.

Within 12 hours of molting the crab's exterior membrane acquires a leathery, fibrous texture, and the crab is then correctly called a **papershell.** At this point the crab's thicker back membrane becomes chewy and unpalatable and must be removed before cooking. In 2 to 3 days the crab's shell fully hardens, and the crab is once again encased in its protective armor. The former soft-shell is once again a **hard-shell crab,** or **hard crab.**

Obviously, the chances of a commercial fisherman catching a crab at the precise moment it crawls out of its shell are slim to none. For this reason, crabs that are caught at the peeler stage are sent to a **crab pound,** where they're kept in enclosed floats and watched carefully until they molt. As soon as they emerge from their shells, the new soft-shells are packed live in damp sea-weed and rushed to market. Although removing the crabs from the water helps slow the hardening of their membranes, rudimentary shells begin to develop. Thus, time is of the essence in delivering to market a fresh soft-shell that is truly soft. Moreover, fresh soft-shell crabs are delicate and perishable and, because of rapid bacterial growth, cannot be eaten after they have died. To avoid loss of product, producers typically clean and freeze most of their soft-shells immediately after harvesting. However, the taste and texture of a frozen soft-shell are inferior to that of a correctly handled fresh soft-shell.

Hard-Shell Crabs

Today most hard-shell Atlantic blue crabs are steamed and processed into crab meat. However, many are sold live to seafood dealers primarily in the Atlantic coastal region and across the Gulf Coast. Live hard crabs are traditionally sold by the bushel.

Chesapeake crab season extends from early spring through late fall, peaking in high summer. (Gulf crabs are usually available year round.) Because they're highly perishable, fresh raw crabs must be alive when cooked. Dead crabs not only are unpalatable, but also can harbor harmful microorganisms.

Hard-shell crabs are typically sprinkled with spicy Chesapeake seasoning (p. 205) and steamed. A half-dozen hard-shells is a delicious, messy feast that must be picked and eaten with the hands. Steamed crabs are best enjoyed outdoors on a paper-lined table with lots of beer to wash them down.

Most of the hard-shell crabs sold alive for steaming are males, considered meatier and, thus, worth the trouble to pick. Female crabs are necessary to make she-crab soup (p. 52) garnished with roe. Both females and males, shown in Figure 5.8, are used for commercially processed crab meat.

The story of the crab's life cycle continues with reproduction. During one of several springtime molts the female crab, or **sook,** begins the reproduction process. At that time a hard male crab, called a **jimmy,** cradles the soft sook gently in his legs while he fertilizes her. After her shell hardens, the eggs develop inside the female's body until the bright red roe, or **berries,** protrude from her **apron,** or undershell. Deposited in the shallows among the aquatic grasses, the eggs hatch into millions of tiny crablets that, like their parents, continue to feed and grow by molting un-

til fall. Those that survive their many predators then swim south to hibernate over the winter, and next season continue the cycle.

Atlantic Oysters

As crabs are to summer, so oysters are to winter. From late September through early spring, these bivalves are at their best—firm, briny, and succulent. Only one species of oyster, *Crassostrea virginica*, is found in the Chesapeake Bay as well as along the American East Coast and in the Gulf of Mexico. However, their taste, texture, and appearance vary widely depending on the area in which they live.

Oysters acquire their taste from the minute marine organisms that they eat. Because different areas provide different organisms, oysters from various locations have distinct flavors. As **filter feeders,** oysters take in their food along with copious amounts of water, and thus are susceptible to pollution and microbes. Salinity also affects flavor: Oysters from water with high salinity, such as those gathered off the Atlantic coast, have a saltier flavor, whereas those harvested in the bay are less salty. The texture of oysters is affected by the temperature of the water in which they live, as well as by the food they ingest. Cold-water oysters from New England have a firmer texture, whereas warm-water oysters from the Gulf tend to be softer. All oysters have better texture when harvested in the winter months.

Because of these factors, oysters are typically identified by locale (Figure 5.9). For example, Blue Point oysters are harvested from the waters off the town of Blue Point on Long Island, and Tangier oysters are from the environs of Tangier Island in the Chesapeake Bay. Generally speaking, the more specific the location, the better (and more expensive) the oyster. Less prized Gulf oysters are harvested from the Gulf of Mexico, usually along the Louisiana coast. Although all of these oysters are the same species, their appearance, texture, and taste are quite different.

FIGURE 5.9

Oysters are identified by the location where they were harvested. These are Rappahannock River oysters harvested on the Chesapeake Bay's western shore. Paul Shot © Shutterstock

FIGURE 5.8

Knowledge of Washington, D.C., architecture is helpful when sexing crabs: the female's apron (left) is shaped like the Capitol dome, and the male's apron tab (right) resembles the Washington monument.

FIGURE 5.10
The Atlantic striped bass, known locally as the Chesapeake rockfish, ranks among America's most prized food fish. Colin Newman © Dorling Kindersley

Oysters are also harvested along the northern Pacific coast; these are discussed in Chapter 13.

Striped Bass: The Chesapeake Rockfish

The Atlantic striped bass (Figure 5.10) is an anadromous roundfish, living in salt water but traveling to fresh water for spawning. Thus, these fish are traditionally harvested in fall and spring as they migrate. Although the Atlantic striped bass ranges from the Gulf of St. Lawrence in Canada to St. John's River in northern Florida, its two major breeding grounds are the Hudson River and the Chesapeake tributaries. The Chesapeake Bay's varying salinity levels make it an ideal breeding ground for striped bass and extend its harvest season, as well.

To residents of the Chesapeake Bay Shore the Atlantic striped bass, *Morone saxatilis*, is known as the **rockfish.** Most agree that this local name was bestowed during colonial times when the fish were so plentiful around Rock Hall, Maryland, that legend says they nearly jumped into the boats.

In the late 1800s, Chesapeake striped bass commonly weighed in at 60 or more pounds. However, by the middle of the 20th century, pollution and overharvesting had decimated the population. A 1980s ban on striped bass fishing helped restore the Chesapeake population. Today a wild Chesapeake striped bass generally weighs between 6 and 8 pounds. Although wild-caught striped bass are far superior, today most market specimens are produced by aquaculture.

Other Chesapeake Seafood

In addition to the all-important blue crabs and oysters, the Chesapeake Bay also yields clams, both hard-shell and soft-shell. As in New England, soft-shell clams are called *steamers*, but old-timers around the bay call them *manos*, short for the Algonquian name, *manninose*. Chesapeake fish include flounder, croakers, whiting, perch, bluefish, and weakfish. Anadromous herring and shad run the bay in spring.

Colonial Domesticates

Colonial domesticate foods are mainstays of Chesapeake cooking. Although hybrid cornmeal quick breads are occasionally served, wheat flour from the nearby Mid-Atlantic makes biscuits and yeast breads everyday foods. Noodles made from wheat flour are a legacy of the Pennsylvania Dutch. Scots-Irish settlers introduced potatoes to the region, and they remain a favored starch.

Cured and smoked pork products are a Plantation South legacy. Locally produced bacon and ham are used as seasoning meats in traditional Chesapeake cooking. Seafood dishes flavored with smoked pork are a signature regional taste combination.

■ CHESAPEAKE BAY
□ CULTURE AND CUISINE

So far you've learned about Chesapeake Bay Shore cuisine's roots and its early cooking. We've discussed the most important seafood products of the Chesapeake Bay. Now let's discover how local ingredients are transformed into traditional Chesapeake cuisine. We'll start by learning about the watermen who harvest the Chesapeake Bay's seafood bounty and the history of the Chesapeake fishing industry.

Chesapeake Watermen

In the late 1700s the towns and villages of the Chesapeake Bay Shore region became home to a unique second-settler group called Chesapeake watermen. Most early watermen and their families were of British Isles origin. Many were newly freed indentured servants or their descendants. Others were second sons of small landholders having no hope of acquiring farms of their own. Later, freed African-American slaves joined their ranks. All were fiercely independent entrepreneurs with the will to invest in their own vessels, shoulder the costs of equipment and bait, and bear the risks of fishing the treacherous waters of the bay.

Watermen adapted the Native American dugout log canoe into sleek sailing vessels such as the Chesapeake bugeye and skipjack, considered the best-designed working boats of their time. Watermen follow the seasonal life cycles of the sea creatures they catch. A typical waterman spends the winter oystering and the summer crabbing, with occasional runs for fish or clams (Figure 5.11).

Oysters were the bay's first commercially viable product because they could be shipped to market in the days before refrigeration. In-shell oysters were packed in barrels layered with

FIGURE 5.11
Hooper's Island watermen set crab traps at sunup. Courtesy Robert A. Haynes, Ph.D.

FIGURE 5.12

A Chesapeake waterman tongs for oysters in the traditional manner.
Courtesy National Oceanic and Atmospheric Administration, Dept. of Commerce

ice and insulating sawdust, which kept them cold during over-land and water transport.

The original method of harvesting Chesapeake oysters is called **tonging,** in which a man standing in a small, open boat lowers a set of joined iron rakes over the side, scoops up the oysters lying on the bay bottom, hefts the full tongs over the side of the boat, and dumps the oysters in the bottom (Figure 5.12). Today most commercially caught oysters are dredged (p. 203).

Then as now, crabs were caught in traditional wire traps baited with rotting fish. The crabber sets out a row of traps by lowering them over the side of his boat and marking their location with a buoy painted in his own, distinctive colors. A day or two later he returns, pulls up the traps, and harvests the crabs inside.

Chesapeake fish are typically trawler-caught in nets dragged behind boats. However, the finest specimens are line-caught. Because Chesapeake fishermen's range is small compared to that of ocean fishermen, most are day-boat fishermen. In other words, fresh Chesapeake seafood is brought to shore daily rather than being frozen on the boat.

Most Chesapeake watermen now have modern boats fitted out with the latest in navigational and fish-finding equipment. A few women have joined the watermen's ranks. But in many ways the work of the Chesapeake waterman is the same as that of his father and grandfather, braving sudden storms and dangerous shoals, working long hours in the cold and dark, enduing heavy physical labor, and risking injury and death. The decline of seafood populations described on p. 206, combined with competition from Asian and Latin American fisheries, makes Chesapeake fishing a financial risk as well. However, for traditional Chesapeake watermen there is no better life or livelihood.

Transportation Creates Prosperity

In the 1800s, advancements in transportation brought prosperity to the entire Chesapeake region. Steamships made travel and transport faster, safer, and more reliable. Baltimore became a bustling port city. The completion of the Chesapeake and Delaware Canal, a human-made waterway cut across the northern end of the DelMarVa Peninsula, enabled boats to transport goods directly from the Chesapeake Bay to the Delaware River and then north to Wilmington, Delaware, and Philadelphia (Figure 5.13). However, the real seafood boom began after the completion of railroad lines to Eastern Shore towns in the late 1800s. Now Chesapeake oysters could be shipped to Chicago, Pittsburgh, Philadelphia, Trenton, and New York.

Growing demand for oysters and a ready means to transport them led to rapid expansion of the Chesapeake fishing fleet. Newly emancipated African-Americans entered the industry, first as hired crew and later purchasing their own vessels to become watermen in their own right. Hundreds of new boats were built to meet the demand for more and more Chesapeake seafood. Refrigerated rail cars opened the market for the

FIGURE 5.13

The Chesapeake and Delaware Canal enabled seafood to be shipped by boat from the Chesapeake Bay to Wilmington and Philadelphia.

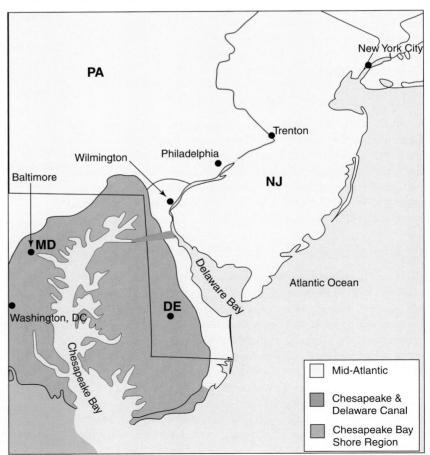

FIGURE 5.14
Dredging is an efficient but environmentally damaging method of harvesting oysters. Courtesy of Don Merritt, IAN Image Library (ian.umces.edu/imagelibrary)

summer crab harvest, formerly unmarketable because of the crabs' high perishability. Chesapeake fish and clams fetched high prices. But, without doubt, the oyster was king.

An Economy Built on Oysters

Unlike fish and crustaceans that continually move around the bay, oysters are sedentary, remaining in their established beds throughout their lives. Ownership of Chesapeake Bay oyster beds was traditionally associated with property rights in the nearest town or farmstead, and rights to harvest the beds were treated as property handed down from father to son. The richest oyster beds are located along Maryland's Eastern Shore, where oysters have remained prolific for generations. Marylanders believed these beds belonged to them, and thus encroachment by Virginia watermen was a source of early conflict.

By the late 1800s the traditional Chesapeake method of tonging was proving too slow and cumbersome to meet growing demand. Soon oystermen from New England entered the bay, bringing steel dredges to rake up hundreds of oysters at a time (Figure 5.14). Although this invasion by outsiders was strongly protested, the **oyster dredge** (or "drudge," in local dialect) was adopted by many Chesapeake watermen. Skipjacks were quickly fitted out with the new equipment, and large-scale dredging ensued.

Oyster dredging is problematic because dredges tear up the bay bottom, damaging the oysters' environment by loosening the shells from their beds, muddying the water, and disturbing young *spats*, or infant oysters. Dredging began a rapid decline of the Chesapeake oyster population.

At War Over Oysters

The feud over dredging escalated into all-out war between two groups of watermen. Tongers, already at a technological disadvantage, objected to the destruction caused by the dredges and protested strenuously against the dredgers. States' rights were also at issue, with Virginia watermen crossing into Maryland waters in hope of a better catch.

Eastern Shore watermen began building forts on stilts out in their oyster beds and took turns sleeping in them to keep watch for poachers. When physical presence was not enough to deter outsiders, they turned to violence. From the late 1800s into the 20th century, watermen waged a shooting war out on

CRAZY OVER OYSTERS

Today it seems irrational to have fought the oyster wars over a simple bivalve. But one should never underestimate the economic impact of a fad. Although oysters had been popular along the East Coast since colonial times, in the late 1800s they suddenly became the rage in big cities and small towns throughout the nation (Figure 5.15). In Boston; New York City; Philadelphia; Baltimore; and Washington, D.C., stand-up oyster bars opened on seemingly every street corner. Rail transportation made it possible to ship oysters to the Midwest, and soon diners in St. Louis, Kansas City, and Chicago were eating oysters. In restaurants, oyster bars, and private homes, millions of Chesapeake oysters were consumed raw on the half shell and in numerous cooked dishes. For quite a few Chesapeake watermen, the revenue derived from selling oysters was high enough to justify violence if their territory was invaded.

FIGURE 5.15
In the late 1800s and early 1900s Americans went crazy over oysters. These sisters were the winners of an oyster-eating contest. © Bettmann/CORBIS. All rights reserved

the bay. Historians call this period *the Chesapeake oyster wars* and estimate that more than seven thousand men participated in the hostilities, with frequent deaths.

Technology Opens Up the Market

The traditional method of shipping oysters in the shell was soon augmented with new forms of fabrication and packaging created by the latest technology. Hand-shucked oysters were packed in oyster liquor in sanitized metal tins and shipped on ice in refrigerated rail cars at reasonable prices. Technology developed for oysters was soon applied to other types of seafood. When refrigerated rail service reached Crisfield, Maryland, more than a hundred packing plants sprang up, most of them crab processors. Chesapeake blue crabs were steamed in huge vats and quickly chilled, and their meat was picked, sorted, and packed in tins.

East Coast restaurant chefs now had access to Chesapeake seafood in laborsaving market forms. Shucked oysters, chopped clams, and picked crab meat opened the door for the creation of America's best-known seafood dishes. Once high-labor regional specialties, dishes such as clam chowder, spaghetti and clams, oyster pie, oyster stew, and scalloped oysters could now be prepared for a larger dining audience. Seafood restaurants, such as New York's Grand Central Oyster Bar and Philadelphia's Bookbinder's, served vast quantities of Chesapeake product to eager diners. Chesapeake-style crab cakes, once unknown outside the region, became a signature menu item throughout the East Coast. But the dish that most captured the public's imagination was Crab imperial, the invention of an unknown Chesapeake cook who blended bell peppers, scallions, Chesapeake seasoning, and mayonnaise into lump crab meat and then baked the mixture in crab back shells. Deviled crab, a similar concoction made "devilishly spicy" with hot pepper sauce and/or mustard, debuted in the early 1900s. Crab imperial and deviled crab became so popular that packinghouses of the era routinely shipped a dozen crab shells with every pound of crab meat.

Traditional Chesapeake Bay Shore Cooking

Chesapeake Bay cooking is largely home cooking. Even regional restaurants aim to reproduce home-cooked dishes as made by the wives and mothers of traditional watermen. Chesapeake cooks recognize the high quality and impeccable freshness of their ingredients and see no reason to embellish them with unnecessary seasonings or accompaniments. Foods from outside the region are the exception, rather than the norm. Thus, Chesapeake cooks can be classified as culinary conservatives.

Around the Chesapeake Bay, home cooking extends outside the home to include boat galleys and the great outdoors. On board both commercial fishing vessels and pleasure boats, Chesapeake seafood is expertly cooked in cramped but well-organized floating kitchens. Roadside stands feature DelMarVa-style chicken barbeque cooked in concrete-lined pits. Churches and volunteer fire halls hold outdoor fish frys and pig roasts. In these venues men are often the primary cooks. Ladies' auxiliaries frequently hold bake sales. In the Chesapeake region virtually every important event is celebrated with food, and ordinary evenings find a home-cooked dinner on most tables. The importance accorded to cooking and eating proves that the Chesapeake region has a strong food culture.

A CHESAPEAKE CRAB FEAST

One of the great pleasures of a Chesapeake summer is eating steamed crabs. For a Chesapeake crab feast, live blue crabs are layered in a big pot with a few inches of flat beer and a heavy coating of spicy Chesapeake seasoning. In-husk corn on the cob may be added. The crabs are steamed until they turn brilliant red and are typically served in cut-down cardboard beer boxes with extra seasoning on the side. Diners sit at newspaper-lined picnic tables armed with wooden mallets and paring knives and spend hours tapping shells, picking crab meat, and munching on arguably the world's sweetest crab. Ice-cold beer is the beverage of choice.

Seafood Dishes

Until it became prohibitively expensive in the late 1900s, seafood was a staple of everyday cooking. Today its high cost makes seafood the focus of Sunday dinners and special-occasion meals. Watermen's families prepare fish simply—typically poached, baked, or broiled—and dress it with butter and lemon juice. In some homes, oysters and hard-shell clams are eaten raw on the half shell. More frequently, home cooks serve baked oysters and steamed clams, or shuck the bivalves to be baked into savory pies, puddings, or casseroles. Soft-shell crabs are a spring and early summer treat. Cleaned, seasoned, and dredged in flour, soft-shells are sautéed or pan-fried crisp and served with lemon or tartar sauce. One particular seafood preparation has become a regional signature dish, deserving of special mention.

Crab Cakes

Fresh-picked crab meat is the foundation of the region's best-known signature dish: the crab cake. Authentic Chesapeake crab cakes are virtually all crab, with just enough filler to hold them together and just enough moistener to bind them. Beyond crab meat and the indispensable Chesapeake seasoning, the remaining ingredients vary throughout the region. Some cooks use bread crumbs; others use cracker crumbs. Some bind with mayonnaise and others with beaten egg or even basic white sauce. Crab cakes may be sautéed, pan-fried, deep-fried, or broiled and are traditionally served with tartar sauce. Refer to the table on p. 207 for more information on Chesapeake crab cakes.

Meat, Fowl, and Local Produce

True to the region's Plantation South roots, in Chesapeake home cooking, pork is the favored meat. In addition to fresh pork dishes, ham and bacon are featured as breakfast foods and flavor vegetables and beans as seasoning meats. Lard and bacon drippings are used for frying meats, seafood, and vegetables. Chesapeake cuisine frequently pairs ham with seafood.

DelMarVa poultry is enjoyed locally as well as shipped throughout the nation. DelMarVa producers were the nation's first to market small, tender fryer chickens. In the region these are favored for frying, sautéing, and Chesapeake-style barbeque. Maryland-style fried chicken is similar to the Plantation South dish (p. 61) but includes spicy Chesapeake seasoning.

FACTOR 4
Plantation South cooking significantly influenced Chesapeake cuisine.

The Chesapeake Bay is part of the great eastern migratory flyway used by millions of birds winging southward for the winter and returning in spring. Thus, the Chesapeake Bay Shore is a favorite destination for wildfowl hunters. Wild ducks and geese, as well as land birds such as pheasants, doves, and quail, appear on Chesapeake tables throughout the fall and winter season.

Chesapeake vegetables are famous for both freshness and flavor. Truck farms lining the valley floors of the western shore's necks grow all types of produce, including excellent sweet corn. Sandy Eastern Shore soil produces wonderful tomatoes, rivaling those of New Jersey. The DelMarVa peninsula's mild climate frequently ripens summer melons earlier than neighboring regions. Most of the Chesapeake produce crop is sold locally in season, often traveling no farther than Baltimore, Philadelphia, and south-central Pennsylvania. Many Chesapeake families have gardens and prepare meals featuring home-grown vegetables throughout the season.

FACTOR 3
Pennsylvania Dutch and German immigrants added Rhineland ingredients and dishes.

Pennsylvania Dutch and German Dishes

As early as 1800, Pennsylvania Dutch farmers began expanding south of the Mason-Dixon line to farm the rolling upland plateau of central Maryland. In the late 1800s the port of Baltimore welcomed German immigrants arriving directly from Germany.

Germanic groups brought their hearty Rhineland style of cooking typified by sausages, scrapple, pickles and preserves, and especially sauerkraut. Throughout the region sauerkraut is a staple dish, accompanying not only pork and sausages but also roast turkey and chicken. In many Chesapeake homes sauerkraut is as indispensable on the Thanksgiving table as cranberry sauce. Chesapeake slippery dumplings in gravy (p. 208) is a version of Pennsylvania Dutch bot boi (p. 175).

Chesapeake Desserts

Pennsylvania Dutch–style apple butter, apple dumplings, strudels, and streusel-topped pies have become part of the Chesapeake repertoire of sweets. In addition, many Chesapeake desserts are Plantation creations, including cobblers, crisps, and puddings. Lady Baltimore Cake (p. 228) has become a signature dessert in both the region and the city bearing its name, although food historians have ascertained that it was created in Charleston, South Carolina.

RESTAURANT CUISINE OF THE CHESAPEAKE BAY SHORE REGION

From colonial days through the 1800s, most Chesapeake cooking was done at home. Except in Baltimore, taverns and small restaurants featured the same home-style dishes made in family kitchens. However, in the early 20th century railroads transporting seafood to East Coast and Midwest cities began bringing tourists to the region and created a thriving hospitality industry. City dwellers from New York; Philadelphia; Baltimore; Washington, D.C.; and Chicago were drawn to the bay's shoreline villages to enjoy recreational fishing, hunting, and sailing.

One of the earliest restaurant types in the region, the Chesapeake **dinner house** (Figure 5.16) offers local seafood and other traditional fare served family-style at long tables. In this casual format tourists and locals alike could enjoy Chesapeake seafood sold at reasonable prices. The Chesapeake crab shack is another dining institution. Often no more than open-air pavilions or sheds, crab shacks offer steamed seafood "in the rough," to be taken home or eaten at outdoor picnic tables. Country inns and small hotels accommodate more affluent tourists, offering traditional Chesapeake cuisine with elegant Southern-style service typically featuring fine tableware and white-gloved waiters.

FACTOR 5
Tourism created the Chesapeake hospitality industry.

FIGURE 5.16

Diners eating Chesapeake Bay crabs at The Crab Claw in St. Michael's, Maryland. Customers arrive on foot, by car, and by boat. Nick Hanna/Alamy

Baltimore Cuisine

Located at the head of the bay, Baltimore became a shipping hub for much of the Chesapeake region's bounty and one of the main consumers of it. The dining rooms of Baltimore's deluxe hotels featured Chesapeake seafood dishes in elegant surroundings. Men's dining clubs in Baltimore vied with those of Philadelphia for best terrapin soup or oyster stew. The Baltimore and Ohio Railroad was noted for the fine cuisine served in its luxurious dining cars.

FACTOR 4
African-American, German, and Italian immigrants influenced the Baltimore style.

After Emancipation, thousands of freed African-American slaves migrated northward to Baltimore, many becoming professional cooks in fine homes, clubs, and restaurants and on the railroads. Thus, the African-American love of spicy seasonings and complex, layered flavorings strongly influenced Baltimore cuisine. African-American cooks favored a bold mixture of ground spices and granulated aromatics that became known as **Chesapeake seasoning**, best known by the proprietary name Old Bay. Baltimore's African-American cooks prepared rich crab meat and oyster dishes spiked with spicy Chesapeake seasoning and slathered with butter or thick cream. Baltimore crab cakes are more heavily seasoned than those of the rural Chesapeake region and are typically fried crisp. Some of the nation's best soul food can be found in Baltimore's African-American neighborhoods as well.

German immigrants arrived in Baltimore in the late 1800s. In addition to opening breweries producing fine local beer, German immigrants brought fresh and smoked sausages and sour beef and dumplings, a version of sauerbraten. As in other areas of the Chesapeake region, sauerkraut is served with roast chicken and turkey, especially on Thanksgiving. Baltimore African-Americans eat sauerkraut and pig's tails on New Year's Day for good luck. Germans introduced coleslaw, today a favored accompaniment to fried Chesapeake seafood. Baltimore cooks combined German-processed prepared horseradish with newly available commercial ketchup to make cocktail sauce, today served with steamed shrimp, raw and fried oysters, and other types of seafood.

At roughly the same time, immigrants from southern Italy brought pasta, thick tomato "gravy", and a taste for mussels steamed in white wine and garlic. Mussels red or white is a Mediterranean dish adopted in Italian-American enclaves throughout the East Coast. Spaghetti and crabs is a messy but delicious Baltimore specialty created by southern Italian immigrants. This unique dish tops al dente spaghetti with steamed and quartered hard-shell crabs in marinara sauce; eating it involves forks, knives, fingers, mallets, and plenty of napkins.

> □ ■
> ⬜ □
> □ **ELEMENTS OF CHESAPEAKE BAY SHORE CUISINE**
>
> **FOUNDATION FOODS**
>
> principal starches: yeasted wheat breads, wheat quick breads, potatoes
>
> principal proteins: shellfish, fish, waterfowl, poultry
>
> principal produce: all types of European and indigenous fruits and vegetables
>
> **FAVORED SEASONINGS:** Chesapeake seasoning such as Old Bay, smoked seasoning meats, bay leaf, thyme, scallions
>
> **PRINCIPAL COOKING MEDIA:** butter, lard, bacon drippings
>
> **PRIMARY COOKING METHODS:** steaming, pan-frying, deep-frying, stewing/simmering, barbeque
>
> **FOOD ATTITUDES:** strong food culture, culinary conservatives

■ THE DECLINE AND
□ REBIRTH OF THE BAY
■

FACTOR 5
Prosperity led to over-development, overfishing, and a drastic decline of the bay's resources.

From the early 1800s until World War I, Chesapeake watermen harvested a staggering amount of seafood from the bay. Oysters were dredged in massive numbers. Hard-shell clams were sent to both local and Mid-Atlantic markets while soft-shell clams were shipped to New England to supplement the dwindling local catch. Blue crabs were taken by the millions.

Growing prosperity brought by the seafood industry led to burgeoning population. Cities on the western shore were expanding at an astounding rate. On the Eastern Shore a new and prosperous middle class was building houses, starting businesses, and expanding farms. Agribusiness took over much of the DelMarVa Peninsula, and western shore farms became larger and more industrialized. Untreated sewage and agricultural runoff, such as animal waste, pesticides, and chemical fertilizer residue, poured into the bay. Motorized commercial vessels and pleasure craft choked the bay with petrochemical contamination. The result of this unchecked development was ecological disaster for the bay.

After World War II, tourism became a major industry in the Chesapeake region. A destination for pleasure boaters and a haven for weekend and summer residents from the urban Northeast, the Chesapeake Bay slowly gained recognition as an important national resource and, finally, important steps were taken to save it. In 1967, a coalition of ecologists and concerned citizens formed the Chesapeake Bay Foundation (CBF), a nonprofit organization with a simple motto: "Save the Bay." Since then, the CBF has raised millions of dollars and launched numerous programs to protect the ecology, culture, and economic stability of the region.

Today, the Chesapeake region is in a phase of slow but steady recovery. Shellfish harvests are improving year to year, with aquaculture supplementing the yield. A 10-year ban on striped bass fishery enabled the population to stabilize to the point where harvest could begin once more, but under strict regulation.

■ CHESAPEAKE CUISINE
□ IN THE 21st CENTURY
■

Because the foundation of Chesapeake cuisine is bay seafood, its future depends on the success of federal and state governments and citizens in managing this valuable resource. Another factor is the high price of Chesapeake seafood. Today's watermen face growing operating costs and deserve proper compensation for their products. Low-cost seafood from Asia and South America is flooding the world market, making Chesapeake and other do-

FIGURE 5.17

The Inn at Perry Cabin in St. Michaels, Maryland, serves fine Chesapeake Bay cuisine in an elegant setting. Courtesy The Inn at Perry Cabin, St. Michaels, MD

mestic seafood unprofitable for many foodservice operations. Chefs working in fine-dining venues must be willing to buy these superior regional products, and their clientele must have the discernment to recognize quality and be willing to pay for it.

Today the Chesapeake Bay Shore culinary region boasts elegant restaurants (Figure 5.17) with innovative chefs whose mission is to present the best of bay seafood while working to ensure its sustainability. For a list of noteworthy Chesapeake Bay Shore cuisine restaurants, visit this book's companion website. Their dishes combine traditional flavors with contemporary presentations and add to the evolution of this distinctive regional cuisine.

☐ TABLE 5.1 CHESAPEAKE DEFINING DISHES

ITEM NAME	HISTORY	DOMINANT INGREDIENTS AND METHOD	OTHER
CRAB SOUP	From Native Americans to modern restaurant chefs, Chesapeake region cooks have always used the flexible, pale-colored shells, juices, and innards of crabs to make soups.	Elegant cream of crab soup is thickened with roux and enriched with heavy cream. Roe from "she crabs" is the traditional garnish. Spicy homestyle crab soup includes diced vegetables, tomatoes, and ham broth or beef stock.	Crab meat is added just before serving.
CRAB CAKES	Chesapeake Bay Shore Native Americans mixed crabmeat with cornmeal dough to make the first crab cakes. Modern cooks from the Eastern Shore, western shore, and Baltimore created intra-regional variations discussed on the website.	Crab cakes may be pan-fried, deep-fried, baked, or broiled.	Nouvelle-style crab cakes are bound with shrimp and scallop mousseline.
CRAB IMPERIAL	This popular dish was created in the late 1800s when commerical crabmeat became available. Served as an appetizer or main course, or used as a stuffing, crab imperial is featured on traditional restaurant menus throughout the Chesapeake region.	Lump or backfin crab meat is blended with mayonnaise, bell peppers, scallion, and Chesapeake seasoning. Although the mixture is traditionally baked in a crab shell, gratin dishes or large scallop shells may be used.	Crab imperial may be stuffed into butterflied jumbo shrimp or rolled up in flounder fillets.
DEVILED CRAB	"Deviled" dishes traditionally include hot and spicy seasonings.	Crabmeat is bound with a highly seasoned Béchamel sauce flavored with mustard, white pepper, hot pepper sauce, and sometimes horseradish and topped with hot paprika.	Use and presentation is the same as crab imperial.
CRAB SALAD/ CRAB COCKTAIL	In the 1920s during Prohibition, restaurateurs began serving chilled shrimp, shucked oysters, and crab salad in otherwise useless martini glasses, creating the seafood cocktail.	Chilled crab meat is lightly bound with mayonnaise-based dressing. For crab salad the mixture is served over greens and accented with tomatoes, cucumbers, and other crisp vegetable garnishes. For crab cocktail it is presented in a martini glass.	In these preparations, fresh jumbo lump crab meat is a must; sauce and seasonings should be subtle and minimal.
SPAGHETTI AND CRABS	A specialty of Baltimore's Italian-American community.	Crabs are cleaned live, quartered, and pan-steamed in white wine and garlicky marinara sauce, then tossed with hot spaghetti.	Forks and spoons, fingers, bibs, and wet wipes are in order when eating spaghetti and crabs.
SOFT-SHELL CRABS	High on the list of the world's most prized foods, soft-shell crabs are best prepared simply, so that their incomparable flavor and texture is not masked.	Most elegant preparation is à la meunière: dredged in flour, sautéed crisp in clarified butter, and served with a lemon butter emulsion sauce. Pan-fried soft-shells are dredged in a flour-egg-flour coating; deep-fried softshells may be coated in a beer batter.	Soft-shells are popular served on toasted hamburger buns or mini-kaiser rolls; they are dressed with lettuce, tomato, and tartar sauce. A soft crab sandwich has two decorative rows of little legs hanging out of the bun.
FRIED OYSTERS	Fried oysters are a specialty of the Chesapeake region's African-American cooks.	Breaded fried oysters are coated in a mixture of flour and cracker meal. Batter-fried oysters may be single dipped or fritters. Both are fried quickly and at high temperatures, and must be served immediately.	Fried oysters can be simply served with lemon wedges or paired with horseradish cream, tartar sauce, cocktail sauce, or mustard sauce.

(continued)

☐ TABLE 5.1 CHESAPEAKE DEFINING DISHES (continued)

ITEM NAME	HISTORY	DOMINANT INGREDIENTS AND METHOD	OTHER
ROASTED OYSTERS	Traditional Chesapeake oyster roasts are an outdoor event held in early autumn.	In-shell oysters are placed on wire racks suspended over coals. The oysters steam until they open just wide enough to spoon in melted butter and lemon juice. Alternatively, oysters may be roasted by spreading them on sheet trays lined with rock salt to hold them steady and baking them in a hot oven.	Hot sauce and cold beer are standard accompaniments.
CLAMS, STEAMED AND RAW	Soft-shell clams were formerly disdained by bay residents who used them for bait or shipped them to appreciative New Englanders.	Soft-shell clams and littleneck hard-shell clams are steamed and served with clam broth, melted butter, and lemon wedges. Cherrystones are served raw on the half shell with lemon and cocktail sauce or baked with various toppings. Topneck clams go either way.	
ROCKFISH/ STRIPED BASS	For a buffet or family-style dinner, a whole Chesapeake rockfish makes an elegant presentation.	Butterflied whole rockfish or rockfish fillets are grilled, broiled, or baked and served with melted butter and lemon.	Whole poached rockfish is served chilled with a mayonnaise sauce for cold buffets.
MARYLAND FRIED CHICKEN	This famous dish blends the chicken-frying of the Plantation South with the spicy seasoning of the Chesapeake region.	Hot pepper sauce and Chesapeake seasoning are added to both the buttermilk soak and the flour coating.	Traditional accompaniments are mashed potatoes, cream gravy, and greens. Picnic style calls for potato salad and sliced cucumbers and tomatoes.
DELMARVA BARBEQUE CHICKEN	This signature dish evolved as DelMarVa farmers began raising small, tender fryer/broiler chickens. Entrepreneurs set up roadside barbeque stands and community groups featured barbeque chicken as a fund-raiser.	Half chickens are slow-cooked over hot coals and basted with a thin and tangy mopping sauce. Home cooks often use cut-up pieces.	When food injectors became available, many cooks began injecting the mopping sauce into the birds' flesh as well as basting the exteriors.
WILD FOWL, ROASTED OR BRAISED	The Chesapeake Bay region is a stopover for millions of migratory fowl and provides abundant feed so the birds become fat and tasty. Hunters harvested fowl for their own table and earned extra income selling to restaurants.	Young birds, such as ducks dressing out under 2 lb. and geese under 5 lb. are usually roasted, often under a barding of smoked bacon. Older birds are braised.	Traditional Chesapeake flavorings include apples, chestnuts, sage, and thyme. Stuffings may include oysters.
ST. MARY'S COUNTY STUFFED HAM	A truly original dish, St. Mary's County Stuffed Ham is traditionally prepared for parties, community events, and fund-raisers.	A whole, fresh ham is brine cured or the ham is boned out, brine cured, rolled, and trussed. Parallel slits are made all over the ham's surface and then stuffed with highly seasoned, chopped greens, such as collards, wild cress, and kale. The ham is then wrapped in a cotton cloth, poached until tender, and chilled in its broth.	Served cool and sliced thin to show its attractive pattern of green veining, the succulent ham is served with country biscuits.
SLIPPERY DUMPLINGS IN GRAVY	Inspired by Pennsylvania Dutch bot boi (p. 169), slippery dumplings are not conventional dumplings, but actually squares of noodle dough.	Square noodles are poached in a thin, flavorful chicken gravy.	Often served as a side dish with country ham, "slipperies" also make a light supper entrée served with a green salad.
PEARL HOMINY	In the late 1800s industrial food processors devised a steam method to soften and hull dried corn kernels.	Pearl hominy is used as a side dish or breakfast food straight from the can, requiring only heating.	Pearl hominy may be teamed with tomatoes, squash, and Cheddar cheese in casseroles, or simmered with greens and a ham bone.
LADY BALTIMORE CAKE	Actually created in South Carolina, Lady Baltimore cake has become the Chesapeake region's most famous dessert.	A light white cake with a traditional Southern boiled icing; its filling of liquor-soaked raisins, nuts, and figs lends distinction.	Lord Baltimore cake, made yellow from egg yolks, is a lesser-known variation.
BLACK WALNUT CAKE OR PIE	Chesapeake cooks commonly used indigenous black walnuts in place of other nuts in classic recipes.	Basic English poundcake is flavored with them to become black walnut cake, and pecan pie is transformed into black walnut pie.	

■□■ STUDY QUESTIONS

1. Discuss the geological events that created the Chesapeake Bay. Include in your discussion the resulting topography of the Chesapeake Bay bottom and its Eastern and western shores.

2. List and describe the most important fish and shellfish of the Chesapeake Bay.

3. Explain the life cycle of the Atlantic blue crab. What food products result from harvesting crabs at two key stages in the cycle? How are crabs obtained at these stages?

4. At what point in history did Chesapeake Bay cuisine emerge as a separate entity? Which two American culinary regions significantly influenced it? List three of the foods and cooking techniques of each contributing region that are featured in traditional Chesapeake cuisine.

5. How did the development of rail transportation affect the Chesapeake Bay region? What effect did it have on the development of Eastern Shore waterfront communities and the seafood industry?

6. Give a brief account of the oyster wars and the factors that caused them. Include in your account a description of the late-19th-century oyster craze.

7. Discuss Baltimore cuisine in the 1800s and today. Describe the Baltimore style of Chesapeake cooking. Include in your discussion the effect of late-19th-century and early-20th-century immigrants on Baltimore cuisine, and list some of the unusual dishes and food combinations they created.

8. How does water quality affect oysters and other bivalves? What steps have been taken by the federal government and the Chesapeake Bay Foundation to ensure oyster quality and safety?

9. List and describe five defining dishes of the Chesapeake Bay Shore culinary region.

10. Using the information you learned in this chapter and your imagination, plan a four-course special-occasion dinner menu featuring Chesapeake Bay Shore cusine.

Creamy Corn and Crab Soup

with Beaten Biscuit

yield: 1 (8-fl.-oz.) appetizer serving
(multiply × 4 for classroom turnout; adjust equipment sizes accordingly)

MASTER RECIPE

production		costing only
1 c.	Creamy Corn and Crab Soup Base	1/4 recipe
1/4 c.	backfin crab meat, picked over for shell fragments	1 oz. a.p.
1 tsp.	minced flat-leaf parsley	1/40 bunch a.p.
1 Tbsp.	brunoise-cut tomato flesh	1/2 oz. a.p.
1	cocktail napkin or 6" doily	1 each
1	Beaten Biscuit	1/8 recipe

service turnout:
1. In a small saucepan, heat the Creamy Corn and Crab Soup Base to just under the boil.
2. Plate the dish:
   a. Place the crab meat in a hot 10-fl.-oz. soup cup.
   b. Pour in the soup base.
   c. Sprinkle with parsley and float the tomato on top.
   d. Place a cocktail napkin on an 8" underliner plate and place the soup cup on top.
   e. Place the Beaten Biscuit on the plate.

COMPONENT RECIPE
CREAMY CORN AND CRAB SOUP BASE

yield: 1 qt.

production		costing only
1/4 c.	butter	2 oz.
1/4 c.	minced yellow onion	2 1/2 oz. a.p.
1/4 c.	peeled, minced celery	1/20 head a.p.
3 Tbsp.	flour	1 oz.
1/2 tsp.	Chesapeake seasoning	1/16 oz.
1 qt.	hot Shellfish Stock, Crab Variation	1/4 recipe
1 c.	fresh or frozen corn kernels	1 ear a.p. or 6 oz.
1/2 c.	heavy cream	4 fl. oz.
tt	kosher salt	1/16 oz.
tt	fine-ground white pepper	1/16 oz.
1 Tbsp.	dry sherry	1/2 fl. oz.

preparation:
1. Heat a medium saucepan, heat the butter, and sweat the onion, celery, and Chesapeake seasoning about 3 minutes, until soft.
2. Add the flour and Chesapeake seasoning, and make a white roux.
3. Whisk in the Crab Stock and bring to the simmer.
4. Add the corn kernels and simmer 20 minutes, until light nappé in consistency.
5. Add the cream and heat to just under the boil.
6. Season with salt (if needed), white pepper, and sherry.

holding: open-pan cool and immediately refrigerate in a freshly sanitized, covered container up to 3 days

---

RECIPE VARIATIONS
Creamy Crab Soup
Omit the corn. Increase the crab meat by 1 Tbsp. per serving.
Creamy Crab, Corn, and Ham Soup
Add 1/4 c. brunoise-cut country ham in step 3.

APPETIZERS

210

Spicy Home-Style Crab Soup

with Sweet Potato Roll

yield: 1 (10-fl.-oz.) appetizer serving
(multiply × 4 for classroom turnout; adjust equipment sizes accordingly)

MASTER RECIPE

production		costing only
1 1/4 c.	Spicy Home-Style Crab Soup Base	1/5 recipe
1/4 c.	shredded claw crab meat	1 oz. a.p.
2 Tbsp.	Pan-Steamed White Rice, hot in steam table	1/48 recipe
1 tsp.	chopped flat-leaf parsley	1/40 bunch a.p.
1	6" doily or cocktail napkin	1 each
1	Sweet Potato Roll	1/8 recipe
2 tsp.	cool salted butter pat	1/3 oz.

service turnout:

1. Stir the Spicy Home-Style Crab Soup Base well, ladle it into a small saucepan, and heat it just to the boil.
2. Plate the dish:
   a. Place the crab meat and Pan-Steamed White Rice in a hot 12-fl.-oz. soup cup.
   b. Ladle in the soup base.
   c. Sprinkle with the parsley.
   d. Place a 6" doily on an 8" underliner plate and place the soup cup on the plate slightly right of center.
   e. Place the Sweet Potato Roll and butter pat on the left side of the plate.

COMPONENT RECIPE
SPICY HOME-STYLE CRAB SOUP BASE

yield: 6 c.

production		costing only
3 Tbsp.	bacon drippings	n/c
1/2 c.	fine-chopped yellow onion	2 1/2 oz. a.p.
1/2 c.	3/8"-diced carrot	3 oz. a.p.
1/2 c.	peeled, 3/8"-diced celery	1/10 head a.p.
6 Tbsp.	brunoise-cut country ham	1 oz.
1 tsp.	Chesapeake seasoning	1/16 oz.
tt	cayenne pepper	1/16 oz.
1 tsp.	minced garlic	1/9 oz. a.p.
3 c.	Shellfish Stock, Crab Variation	1/5 recipe
3 c.	Brown Beef Stock	1/5 recipe
1 sprig	fresh thyme	1/20 bunch a.p.
1/2 c.	sliced okra pods	3 oz. a.p.
1/3 c.	fresh or frozen corn kernels	1/3 ear a.p. or 2 oz.
1/3 c.	fresh or frozen shelled baby lima beans	3/4 oz. or 1/3 lb.
1/2 c.	tomato, coarse concassé	6 oz. a.p.
tt	kosher salt	1/16 oz.
tt	hot pepper sauce, such as Crystal brand	1/10 fl. oz.

preparation:

1. Heat a medium saucepan, heat the bacon drippings, and then sweat the onion, carrot, celery, ham, Chesapeake seasoning, cayenne pepper, and garlic about 3 minutes, until soft but not browned.
2. Add the Crab Stock, Brown Beef Stock, and thyme, then simmer 20 minutes.
3. Add the okra, corn kernels, lima beans, tomato, and salt. Simmer 15 minutes longer.
4. Add hot pepper sauce to taste and correct the salt.

holding: open-pan cool and immediately refrigerate in a freshly sanitized, covered container up to 3 days

---

RECIPE VARIATIONS

Home-Style Seafood-Only Crab Soup
Replace the bacon drippings with corn oil. Omit the ham. Replace the Beef Stock with more Crab Stock.

Wintertime Home-Style Crab Soup
Replace the okra, corn, and baby limas with winter vegetables such as turnips, cabbage, and precooked dried beans.

Chesapeake Fried Oysters
with Fresh Tomato Cocktail Sauce

yield: 1 (5-oz.) appetizer serving
(multiply × 4 for classroom turnout; adjust equipment sizes accordingly)

MASTER RECIPE

production		costing only
as needed	corn oil for pan-frying	approx. 6 fl. oz. (may be reused)
6 pc.	Chesapeake Breaded Oysters	1/4 recipe
tt	fine salt	1/16 oz.
1	8" greaseproof doily	1 each
3 Tbsp.	Fresh Tomato Cocktail Sauce	1/4 recipe
1 sprig	flat-leaf parsley	1/20 bunch a.p.
1	lemon wedge	1/8 [90 ct.] lemon

service turnout:
1. Pan-fry the oysters:
   a. Heat an 8" sauté pan and heat 1/2" oil to 400°F (just under the smoke point).
   b. Add the Chesapeake Breaded Oysters and fry about 10 seconds on each side.
   c. Drain briefly on a rack.
   d. Sprinkle with salt.
2. Plate the dish:
   a. Place an 8" doily on a 10" plate.
   b. Spoon the Fresh Tomato Cocktail Sauce into a 2-oz. ramekin or sauce cup and place it on the plate slightly back of center.
   c. Place the parsley sprig and lemon wedge to the right of the ramekin.
   d. Arrange the oysters in an arc around the left side of the ramekin.

COMPONENT RECIPE
CHESAPEAKE BREADED OYSTERS

yield: 20 pc.

production		costing only
2/3 c.	cracker meal or saltine cracker crumbs	3 oz. a.p.
1/2 c.	flour	2 1/2 oz.
1/2 tsp.	Chesapeake seasoning	1/16 oz.
24 pc.	extra-select shucked oysters	1 pt.

preparation:
1. Mix together the crumbs, flour, and Chesapeake seasoning.
2. Drain the oysters and reserve the oyster liquor for another use.
3. Dredge each oyster in the crumb-flour mixture and place on a rack set over a sheet tray.
4. Refrigerate uncovered 30 minutes. (If the coating becomes moist, dredge again before frying.)

holding: store in one layer, in a shallow container with pan liner, covered with a tight-fitting lid, refrigerated up to 24 hours

COMPONENT RECIPE
FRESH TOMATO COCKTAIL SAUCE

yield: 3/4 c.

production		costing only
1 Tbsp.	prepared horseradish	1/2 fl. oz.
2/3 c.	vine-ripe tomato coulis, drained	8 oz. a.p.
1 Tbsp.	corn oil	1/2 fl. oz.
2 tsp.	minced shallot	1/4 oz. a.p.
1 tsp.	sugar	1/6 oz.
1 tsp.	minced lemon zest	n/c
1/2 tsp.	fresh lemon juice	1/32 [90 ct.] lemon
1 tsp.	minced parsley	1/40 bunch a.p.
tt	kosher salt	1/16 oz.

preparation:
1. Squeeze the horseradish in cheesecloth or in the corner of a clean kitchen towel until it is very dry.
2. Place the horseradish and tomato coulis in a mortar (or sturdy bowl) and grind them with a pestle (or heavy spoon) to a rough paste.
3. Whisk in the oil and the remaining ingredients.
4. Refrigerate at least 30 minutes.

holding: prepare just enough for service; hold refrigerated in a freshly sanitized, covered container up to 8 hours

RECIPE VARIATION
Chesapeake Fried Oysters with Tartar Sauce
Replace the Fresh Tomato Cocktail Sauce with Tartar Sauce (p. 60).

Oyster Fritters
with Herbed Red Bell Pepper Mayonnaise

yield: 1 (5-oz.) appetizer serving
(multiply × 4 for classroom turnout; adjust equipment sizes accordingly)

MASTER RECIPE

production		costing only
as needed	frying compound or corn oil	% used
3/4 c.	Oyster Fritter Batter, on ice	1/4 recipe
9 pc.	standard shucked oysters, drained (reserve oyster liquor for Oyster Liquor Batter)	1/5 pt.
tt	fine salt	1/16 oz.
1	8" greaseproof doily	1 each
3 Tbsp.	Herbed Red Bell Pepper Mayonnaise	1/4 recipe
1 sprig	fresh tarragon	1/12 bunch a.p.
1	lemon wedge	1/6 [90 ct.] lemon

service turnout:
1. Fry the oysters:
   a. Set a deep fryer to 375°F. Lower the basket into the oil.
   b. Take up about 3/4 c. Oyster Fritter Batter in a 16-fl.-oz. ladle or small bowl.
   c. Using a slotted spoon, add the oysters to the ladle.
   d. Using a flatware tablespoon, stir the oysters into the batter.
   e. Holding the ladle over the fryer, spoon 3 fritters (each containing 3 oysters) into the hot oil.
   f. Deep-fry about 1 minute, basting with hot oil if necessary, until golden brown.
   g. Lift out and drain briefly on a rack.
   h. Season with salt.
2. Plate the dish:
   a. Place an 8" doily on a 10" plate.
   b. Spoon the Herbed Red Bell Pepper Mayonnaise into a 2-fl.-oz. ramekin or sauce cup and place it on the plate at 2 o'clock. Place the tarragon sprig and lemon wedge alongside the ramekin.
   c. Arrange the fritters at the front of the plate.

COMPONENT RECIPE
OYSTER FRITTER BATTER

yield: 3 c.

production		costing only
1 1/2 c.	flour	7 1/2 oz.
1 Tbsp.	baking powder	1/3 oz.
1 tsp.	fine salt	1/6 oz.
1 tsp.	Chesapeake seasoning	1/16 oz.
1	egg	1 each or 2 oz.
1	egg white	1 each or 1/2 oz.
±1/2 c.	oyster liquor (reserved from master recipe)	n/c
±1/2 c.	milk	±4 fl. oz.

preparation:
1. Sift together the flour, baking powder, salt, and Chesapeake seasoning and make a well in them.
2. Add the liquid ingredients:
   a. Place the egg and egg white into the well, whisk until well combined, and then begin to whisk in the flour mixture, drawing in from the sides to make a smooth, thick batter.
   b. Begin adding oyster liquor and continue whisking.
   c. Whisk in enough milk to make a smooth batter of a consistency a little thicker than pancake batter.

holding: prepare only the amount needed for service; hold on ice up to 6 hours. The batter will thicken as it stands; thin as necessary with milk or water.

COMPONENT RECIPE
HERBED RED BELL PEPPER MAYONNAISE

yield: 1 c.

production		costing only
1	red bell pepper	6 oz. a.p.
1/2 c.	mayonnaise	4 fl. oz.
2 tsp.	minced lemon zest	n/c
1 tsp.	fresh lemon juice	1/16 [90 ct.] lemon
1 Tbsp.	minced parsley	1/40 bunch a.p.
1 Tbsp.	minced tarragon	1/16 bunch a.p.
tt	kosher salt	1/16 oz.
tt	fine-ground white pepper	1/16 oz.
tt	sugar	1/16 oz.
as needed	water	n/c

preparation:
1. Roast and clean the red bell pepper:
   a. Place the pepper directly on a gas burner or on a gas grill, turning often, until blackened all over.
   b. Immediately wrap the pepper in foil and allow it to steam in its own heat until cool.
   c. Scrape off the blackened skin, remove the stem and core, and clean out the veins and seeds. (Do not wash the pepper.)
2. Place the pepper in a blender and purée until smooth.
3. Place the pepper purée in an 8" nonstick sauté pan and cook, stirring constantly with a heatproof rubber scraper, until dry. ⚠ Do not allow to scorch. Cool to room temperature.
4. Mix the roasted pepper purée with the remaining ingredients. If necessary, thin with water to a dipping consistency.
5. Correct the seasoning.

holding: refrigerate in a freshly sanitized, covered plastic container up to 5 days; if made with handmade mayonnaise, 24 hours only

---

RECIPE VARIATION
Clam Fritters with Herbed Red Bell Pepper Mayonnaise
Replace the oysters with diced cherrystone clams. Use the clam liquor in the batter.

APPETIZERS

Deviled Crab

yield: 1 (4-oz.) appetizer serving plus accompaniments (multiply × 4 for classroom turnout; adjust equipment sizes accordingly)

MASTER RECIPE

production		costing only
1	Deviled Crab in Shell	1/4 recipe
1/2 bunch	watercress	1/2 bunch a.p.
1 Tbsp.	Sweet Cider Vinaigrette, in squeeze bottle	1/16 recipe
dash	paprika	1/16 oz.
pinch	minced flat-leaf parsley	1/40 bunch a.p.
1	small lemon crown	1/2 [90 ct.] lemon

service turnout:

1. Place the Deviled Crab in Shell on a sizzle plate and bake in a 400°F oven about 8 minutes, until heated through.
2. Plate the dish:
   a. Remove the thick stems of the watercress and arrange the cress, stems at the center, around the well of a cool 10" plate.
   b. Shake the Sweet Cider Vinaigrette thoroughly and drizzle it on the watercress.
   c. Place the Deviled Crab in Shell in the center of the plate.
   d. Sprinkle the Deviled Crab with a dash of paprika.
   e. Place a dot of parsley in the center of the lemon crown and place the crown directly behind the Deviled Crab.

COMPONENT RECIPE
DEVILED CRAB IN SHELLS

yield: 4 (4-oz.) servings

production		costing only
3 Tbsp.	minced yellow onion	3/4 oz. a.p.
2 Tbsp.	butter	1 oz.
2 Tbsp.	flour	3/4 oz.
1/4 tsp.	cayenne powder	1/16 oz.
1 c.	hot Shellfish Stock, Crab Variation	1/16 recipe
1/2 c.	heavy cream	4 fl. oz.
1 Tbsp.	Dijon mustard	1/2 fl. oz.
1/2 tsp.	fine-ground white pepper	1/16 oz.
2 tsp.	fresh lemon juice	1/8 [90 ct.] lemon
tt	kosher salt	1/16 oz.
12 oz.	backfin crab meat, picked over for shell fragments	12 oz.
4	large crab shells (back carapace), cleaned and sterilized in boiling water (or use purchased scallop shells)	n/c or 1/3 dz.

preparation:

1. Prepare the sauce:
   a. Sweat the onion and butter in a medium saucepan until the onion is soft but not brown.
   b. Add the flour and cayenne pepper, make a white roux, and then whisk in the hot Crab Stock and cream.
   c. Simmer over low heat 15 minutes, stirring often, until the sauce becomes very thick.
   d. Add the mustard, white pepper, lemon juice, and salt if needed. Taste and correct the seasoning; the sauce should have a spicy "bite" but not be so hot as to overwhelm the crab.
   e. Cool the sauce to room temperature in an ice-water bath, then immediately proceed.
2. Gently mix the sauce into the crab meat, keeping the crab meat as fluffy and separate as possible.
3. Fill each crab shell with 1/4 of the deviled crab and press gently to firm it.

holding: refrigerate in one layer in a covered plastic container with pan liner up to 2 days

RECIPE VARIATION
Crab Imperial Appetizer
Replace the Deviled Crab mixture with Crab Imperial (p. 220).

Tilghman Island Chicken Salad
with Fried Oysters

yield: 1 (5-oz.) appetizer serving
(multiply × 4 for classroom turnout; adjust equipment sizes accordingly)

APPETIZERS

MASTER RECIPE

production		costing only
as needed	corn oil for frying	approx. 6 fl. oz. (may be reused)
3 pc.	Chesapeake Breaded Oysters, p. 206 (made with select oysters)	1/8 recipe
tt	fine salt	1/16 oz.
2 c.	washed, dried, torn leaf lettuce	1/6 head a.p.
1 Tbsp.	Sweet Cider Vinaigrette	1/16 recipe
2/3 c.	Tilghman Island Chicken Salad	1/4 recipe
3	grape tomatoes	1/12 pt.
2 tsp.	minced flat-leaf parsley	1/40 bunch a.p.
1	lemon wedge	1/8 [90 ct.] lemon

service turnout:
1. Fry the oysters:
   a. Heat an 8" sauté pan, add 1/2" oil, and heat to just under the smoke point.
   b. Pan-fry the oysters about 10 seconds on each side.
   c. Drain briefly on a rack.
   d. Season with salt.
2. Toss the lettuce with the Sweet Cider Vinaigrette.
3. Plate the dish:
   a. Mound the lettuce in the center of a cool 10" plate.
   b. Scoop the Tilghman Island Chicken Salad into the middle of the lettuce.
   c. Arrange the oysters and tomatoes alternately around the chicken salad.
   d. Sprinkle the chicken salad with the parsley.
   e. Place the lemon wedge against the chicken salad at 2 o'clock.

COMPONENT RECIPE
TILGHMAN ISLAND CHICKEN SALAD

yield: 2 3/4 c.

production		costing only
2 c.	Poultry Stock	1/8 recipe
1 Tbsp.	fresh lemon juice	1/6 [90 ct.] lemon
1	bay leaf	1/16 oz.
1 lb.	boneless chicken breast	1 lb.
as needed	boiling water	n/c
3 Tbsp.	brunoise-cut country ham	1 oz.
1/2 c.	mayonnaise	4 fl. oz.
2 Tbsp.	sour cream	1 fl. oz.
2 tsp.	Dijon mustard	1/3 fl. oz.
1 tsp.	minced lemon zest	n/c
1 tsp.	sugar	1/6 oz.
1/2 tsp.	Chesapeake seasoning	1/16 oz.
tt	fine-ground white pepper	1/16 oz.
1/3 c.	peeled, 3/8"-diced celery	1/20 bunch a.p.
1/4 c.	thin-sliced scallion	1/6 bunch a.p.
tt	fresh lemon juice	1/8 [90 ct.] lemon

preparation:
1. Poach the chicken breast:
   a. Bring the Poultry Stock, 1 Tbsp. lemon juice, and bay leaf to the boil in a 10" sauté pan.
   b. Add the chicken breast and add boiling water as necessary to cover.
   c. Poach at a bare simmer about 12 minutes, until just cooked through.
   d. Transfer the chicken and its poaching liquid to a small container and immerse the container in an ice-water bath until the chicken is cold.
2. Prepare the sauce:
   a. Return the chicken poaching liquid to the sauté pan and reduce it to about 1/4 c. of glaze. ⚠ Do not allow to scorch. Watch the pan carefully and stir/scrape with a rubber spatula.
   b. Place the ham in a bowl and pour the hot chicken glaze over the top. Cool to room temperature.
   c. Whisk in the mayonnaise, sour cream, mustard, lemon zest, sugar, Chesapeake seasoning, and white pepper.
3. Trim the chicken of fat and connective tissue, then fabricate it into 1/2" cubes.
4. Fold together the chicken, dressing, celery, and scallion.
5. Season with lemon juice.

holding: refrigerate in a freshly sanitized, covered plastic container up to 4 days; for best quality, hold out the scallions and add before each service; if made with handmade mayonnaise, hold 24 hours only

---

RECIPE VARIATION
Tilghman Island Seafood Salad with Fried Oysters
Replace the chicken with equal parts jumbo lump crab meat; poached, peeled 36–40 ct. shrimp; steamed, shucked mussels; poached scallops; and the like. Replace the chicken glaze with shellfish glaze. Omit the ham.

Maryland-Style Crab Cakes

with Smashed Redskin Potato Salad and Summer Garden Diced Vegetable Salad

yield: 1 (5-oz.) entrée serving plus accompaniments
(multiply × 4 for classroom turnout; adjust equipment sizes accordingly)

MASTER RECIPE

production		costing only
1/4 c.	corn oil	2 fl. oz.
1	Maryland Crab Cake	1/4 recipe
1 1/4 c.	Smashed Redskin Potato Salad	1/4 recipe
3 Tbsp.	Tartar Sauce, p. 60	1/4 recipe
1 leaf	Boston lettuce	1/12 head a.p.
1 1/4 c.	Summer Garden Diced Vegetable Salad	1/4 recipe
1 sprig	flat-leaf parsley sprig	1/20 bunch a.p.

service turnout:

1. Pan-fry the Maryland Crab Cake:
   a. Heat a 6" nonstick sauté pan, add the oil, and heat it over medium-low heat.
   b. Add the crab cake and pan-fry about 2 minutes on each side, until golden brown.
   c. Blot on paper towels.
2. If necessary, gently microwave the Smashed Redskin Potato Salad to room temperature.
3. Plate the dish:
   a. Spoon the Tartar Sauce into a 2-oz. ramekin or sauce cup and place it on the back left of a room-temperature 12" plate.
   b. Spoon the potato salad on the right side of the plate.
   c. Place the lettuce leaf on the back of the plate between the ramekin and the potato salad. Fill the leaf with Summer Garden Diced Vegetable Salad.
   d. Place the crab cake on the front of the plate propped against the ramekin and the potato salad.
   e. Stick the parsley sprig upright between the crab cake and the potato salad.

RECIPE VARIATIONS

Economy Crab Cakes
Replace the lump crab meat with 6 oz. claw crab meat and 6 oz. special crab meat, carefully picked over for shell fragments.

Eastern Shore Crab Cakes
Omit the mayonnaise and vegetables. Replace the mayonnaise with 1/3 c. room-temperature butter. Add a dash of Worcestershire sauce. Replace the cracker meal with soft, fine-ground fresh bread crumbs.

COMPONENT RECIPE

MARYLAND CRAB CAKES

yield: 4 (5-oz.) cakes or 8 (2 1/2-oz.) cakes

production		costing only
1	egg	1 each or 2 oz.
1/2 c.	mayonnaise	4 fl. oz.
1/3 c.	brunoise-cut red bell pepper	2 3/4 oz.
1/3 c.	peeled, brunoise-cut celery	1/20 bunch a.p.
1 Tbsp.	minced flat-leaf parsley	1/40 bunch a.p.
1/4 c.	chopped scallion	1/4 bunch a.p.
1 Tbsp.	minced lemon zest	n/c
2 tsp.	fresh lemon juice	1/8 [90 ct.] lemon
1/2 tsp.	Chesapeake seasoning	1/16 oz.
3/4 lb.	backfin crab meat	3/4 lb.
±3 c.	cracker meal or saltine cracker crumbs	5 oz. a.p.

preparation:

1. In a 4-qt. bowl beat the egg, then beat in the mayonnaise. Stir in the red bell pepper, celery, parsley, scallion, lemon zest and juice, and Chesapeake seasoning. (The mixture should be highly seasoned.)
2. Pick over the crab meat without breaking up the lumps.
3. Add the picked crab meat to the bowl with the mayonnaise mixture.
4. Wearing foodservice gloves and working lightly with fingertips, add just enough cracker meal (about 1 c.) to bind the mixture so that it holds a shape. Be careful to keep the crab meat lumps intact.
5. Fabricate the crab cakes:
   a. Divide into 4 or 8 even portions using a portion scale.
   b. Form one portion into a round disc and press it into the remaining crumbs to coat on all sides.
   c. Place the crab cake on a rack set over a half sheet tray.
   d. Repeat, making 4 or 8 cakes as desired.
   e. Refrigerate the crab cakes uncovered 1 hour, until firm.

holding: transfer to a covered container with pan liner under and between layers; best made for each service, but will hold refrigerated up to 2 days

COMPONENT RECIPE

SMASHED REDSKIN POTATO SALAD

yield: 5 c.

production		costing only
1 lb.	medium (size B) Red Bliss potatoes	1 lb.
1/3 c.	liquid from refrigerated-style dill pickles	n/c
1/2 c.	mayonnaise	4 fl. oz.
1/3 c.	fine diagonal-sliced scallion	1/6 bunch a.p.
1/3 c.	3/8"-diced refrigerated-style dill pickles	1 1/2 oz.
tt	kosher salt	1/6 oz.
tt	fresh-ground black pepper	1/16 oz.

preparation:
1. Scrub the potatoes thoroughly and rinse well.
2. Place the potatoes in a saucepan and add cold water to cover. Bring to the boil and cook until tender when pierced with a knife.
3. Drain the potatoes and spread them on a sheet tray to cool.
4. As soon as the potatoes can be handled, cut them into 3/4" dice.
5. Place the potatoes in a bowl. Add the pickle liquid and mix it into the potatoes, mashing them slightly.
6. Add the mayonnaise and mix it into the potatoes, stirring and mashing to make a chunky purée.
7. Add the scallion and pickles, then season with salt and pepper.

holding: best served immediately at room temperature. For restaurant service, refrigerate in a freshly sanitized, covered container up to 2 days; gently microwave to room temperature before serving

COMPONENT RECIPE

SUMMER GARDEN DICED VEGETABLE SALAD

yield: 5 c.

production		costing only
2 c.	peeled, seeded, 3/8"-diced cucumber	1 lb. a.p.
2 c.	peeled, seeded, 3/8"-diced vine-ripe tomato	1 1/4 lb. a.p.
1 c.	3/8"-diced sweet onion	5 oz. a.p.
1/2 c.	3/8"-diced radish	1/3 bunch or 3 oz. a.p.
tt	kosher salt	1/16 oz.
1/2 c.	Sweet Cider Vinaigrette	1/2 recipe
2 Tbsp.	1/8" sliced chives	1/10 bunch

preparation:
1. Toss together the cucumber, tomato, onion, and radish and a little salt.
2. Place the vegetables in a colander and drain 30 minutes, tossing lightly once or twice.
3. Turn the vegetables out onto a kitchen towel and blot gently.
4. Transfer to a bowl and toss with the Sweet Cider Vinaigrette and chives.

holding: prepare just before service; store refrigerated 5 to 6 hours only

---

RECIPE VARIATIONS

Dinner-House Crab Cake Platter
Replace the potato salad with 6 oz. Classic French Fries tossed with Chesapeake seasoning. Replace the vegetable salad with Southern Cole Slaw. Garnish with lemon wedges and tomato wedges.

Crab Cake Salad Appetizer
Serve a 2 1/2-oz. crab cake garnished with 2/3 c. Summer Garden Diced Vegetable Salad.

RECIPE VARIATION

Roasted-Toasted Smashed Redskin Potato Salad
Add 1/2 c. each diced roasted red bell peppers and caramelized red onions.

Imperial Stuffed Flounder

with Lemon Butter Sauce, Baby Spinach, and Sweet Potato Pearls

yield: 1 (7-oz.) entrée serving plus accompaniments
(multiply × 4 for classroom turnout; adjust equipment sizes
accordingly)

MASTER RECIPE

production		costing only
1 tsp.	melted butter	1/6 fl. oz.
1	Imperial Stuffed Flounder	1/4 recipe
2 Tbsp.	white wine	1 fl. oz.
1 Tbsp.	butter	1/2 oz.
1 1/4 c.	Sweet Potato Pearls	1/4 recipe
tt	kosher salt	1/16 oz.
tt	fine-ground white pepper	1/16 oz.
4 oz.	precleaned baby spinach	4 oz.
2 Tbsp.	fresh lemon juice	3/8 [90 ct.] lemon
2 tsp.	minced lemon zest	n/c
1 Tbsp.	minced shallot	1/2 oz. a.p.
1/4 c.	Shellfish Stock, optional	1/64 recipe
6 Tbsp.	cold butter, cut in small dice	3 oz.
3	thin lemon slices	1/4 [90 ct.] lemon
1 sprig	flat-leaf parsley	1/40 bunch a.p.

service turnout:

1. Bake the Imperial Stuffed Flounder:
   a. Brush a sizzle plate with melted butter. Place the floun-
      der on the sizzle plate and sprinkle it with white wine.
   b. Bake in a 400°F oven about 10 minutes, until lightly
      cooked through and browned on top. (Run under the
      broiler or glaze with a foodservice torch if necessary.)

2. Finish the vegetables:
   a. Heat a 10" nonstick sauté pan, add 1 Tbsp. butter, and
      then add the Sweet Potato Pearls. Sauté about a minute
      to reheat and glaze with the butter. Season with salt and
      white pepper.
   b. Push the sweet potato to one side and add the spinach.
      Toss the spinach until barely wilted.

3. Prepare the sauce:
   a. Remove the flounder from the oven and tip the sizzle pan
      over an 8" sauté pan to catch the juices. Hold the floun-
      der under warming lights or above the stove.
   b. Add the lemon juice and zest, shallot, and Shellfish Stock,
      if using, to the sauté pan and reduce to about 1/4 c.
   c. Work in the diced cold butter to make a tight emulsion.
   d. Correct the seasoning with lemon juice and/or salt.
   e. Pour any more juices that have accumulated around the
      flounder into the butter sauce.

4. Plate the dish:
   a. Place the flounder on the front of a hot 12" plate.
   b. Spoon the sweet potato behind the flounder at 2 o'clock.
   c. Mound the spinach behind the flounder at 10 o'clock.
   d. Nap the flounder with the butter sauce, allowing some to
      flow onto the spinach.
   e. Fan the lemon slices together and place them upright be-
      tween the flounder and the spinach.
   f. Stick the parsley sprig upright between the flounder and
      the lemon slices.

COMPONENT RECIPE

IMPERIAL STUFFED FLOUNDER

yield: 4 (7-oz.) entrée servings

production		costing only
4	4-oz. flounder fillets, pinned and trimmed	1 lb. a.p.
1/2	egg, beaten	1/2 each or 1 oz.
2 c.	Crab Imperial	1 recipe
4 dashes	paprika	1/16 oz.

preparation:
1. Place a flounder fillet on the work surface, shiny side up.
2. Brush the center of the fillet with beaten egg and fold in the two ends to make an even rectangle.
3. Flip the rectangle over.
4. Make a slit down the center line of the fillet and pull the edges open to make a pouch.
5. Brush the inside of the pouch with beaten egg and fill the pouch with 1/2 c. Crab Imperial.
6. Sprinkle the top with paprika.
7. Using a wide offset spatula, lift the stuffed flounder into a flat container with pan liner.
8. Repeat with the remaining ingredients to make a total of four flounder setups.

holding: cover and refrigerate up to 2 days

COMPONENT RECIPE

CRAB IMPERIAL

yield: 2 c.

production		costing only
2 Tbsp.	butter	1 oz.
1/8 c.	brunoise-cut red bell pepper	1 oz. a.p.
1/8 c.	brunoise-cut green bell pepper	1 oz. a.p.
2 Tbsp.	fine-chopped scallion	1/8 bunch a.p.
2 tsp.	minced lemon zest	n/c
1/2 c.	mayonnaise	4 fl. oz.
1 Tbsp.	heavy cream	1/2 fl. oz.
1 Tbsp.	Dijon mustard	1/2 fl. oz.
2 drops	Worcestershire sauce	1/10 oz.
dash	bottled hot sauce (such as Crystal brand)	1/6 oz.
1/2 tsp.	Chesapeake seasoning	1/16 oz.
tt	kosher salt	1/16 oz.
tt	fine-ground white pepper	1/16 oz.
12 oz.	backfin crab meat, picked over for shell fragments	12 oz. a.p.

preparation:
1. Heat the butter in a small sauté pan and sauté the bell peppers until softened. Cool.
2. In a small bowl, mix together the peppers and all remaining ingredients except the crab meat. Correct the seasoning.
3. Lightly toss in the crab meat until well blended. Keep the crab meat pieces as intact as possible and keep the mixture loose and fluffy.

holding: immediately refrigerate in a freshly sanitized, covered plastic container up to 2 days

COMPONENT RECIPE

SWEET POTATO PEARLS

yield: 5 c.

production		costing only
5	large, orange-fleshed sweet potatoes	3 3/4 lb. a.p.
1 tsp.	kosher salt	1/6 oz.
2 Tbsp.	butter	1 oz.

preparation:
1. Peel the sweet potatoes and place them in a container with cool water to cover.
2. Using the small end of a Parisienne scoop, scoop out small spheres or "pearls" of sweet potato and drop them immediately into a saucepan of cool water. (Return the sweet potato scraps to the container and reserve for a soup or purée.)
3. Pour off excess water from the sweet potato pan, leaving just enough to cover the pearls.
4. Add salt and butter to the pan and poach at the simmer about 8 minutes, until just cooked through. Drain.

holding: open-pan cool and immediately refrigerate in a covered, freshly sanitized plastic container up to 4 days

---

RECIPE VARIATIONS

Crab Imperial Appetizer
See variation on p. 209.

Dinner-House Imperial-Stuffed Flounder Platter
Serve the flounder with the accompaniments for the Dinner-House Crab Cake Platter variation (p. 212).

Sautéed Soft-Shell Crabs

with Lemon Butter Sauce, Parsley Potatoes, and Summer Squash in Tomato Sauce

yield: 1 (5- to 6-oz.) entrée serving plus accompaniments (multiply × 4 for classroom turnout; adjust equipment sizes accordingly)

MASTER RECIPE

production		costing only
5 pc.	small Red Bliss or fingerling potatoes, boiled and drained	4 oz. a.p.
as needed	water, in squeeze bottle	n/c
1 Tbsp.	butter	1/2 oz.
tt	kosher salt	1/16 oz.
tt	fine-ground white pepper	1/16 oz.
1 Tbsp.	corn oil	1/2 fl. oz.
3 oz.	seeded, batonnet-cut yellow summer squash	4 oz. a.p.
3 oz.	seeded, batonnet-cut zucchini	4 oz. a.p.
1/2 c.	Fresh Tomato Sauce	1/8 recipe
2 Tbsp.	corn oil	1 fl. oz.
2	prime or jumbo soft-shell crabs, cleaned	2 each
as needed	flour	1 oz.
2 Tbsp.	fresh lemon juice	3/8 [90 ct.] lemon
2 tsp.	minced lemon zest	n/c
2 tsp.	minced shallot	1/4 oz. a.p.
1/4 c.	Shellfish Stock	1/64 recipe
6 Tbsp.	cold butter, cut in small dice	3 oz.
1 Tbsp.	fine-chopped flat-leaf parsley	1/40 bunch a.p.
1 sprig	flat-leaf parsley	1/20 bunch a.p.

service turnout:

1. Finish the vegetables:
   a. Heat the potatoes with a little water, butter, and salt in a covered 8" sauté pan or in the microwave. Hold hot.
   b. Heat a 10" sauté pan, heat 1 Tbsp. oil, and sear the squash and zucchini. Season with salt and pepper and ladle in the Fresh Tomato Sauce. Toss until the sauce clings to the vegetables and then hold hot.
2. Sauté the soft-shells:
   a. Heat an 8" sauté pan, add 2 Tbsp. oil, and heat until very hot.
   b. Press the soft-shells gently between paper towels to force out excess liquid.
   c. Dredge the soft-shells in flour and add to the pan; sauté about 30 seconds on each side, until browned and crisp. ⚠ Take care: Soft-shells may spatter hot oil.
   d. Remove the soft-shells to a sizzle pan, season them with salt, and hold hot.
3. Prepare the sauce:
   a. Wipe out the pan and add a squeeze of water, the lemon juice and zest, the shallot, a little salt, and the Shellfish Stock. Reduce over high heat to half the original volume.
   b. Work in the cold butter to make a light emulsion.
4. Plate the dish:
   a. Toss the chopped parsley into the potatoes and spoon them onto the back left of a hot 12" plate.
   b. Spoon the squash in tomato sauce onto the back right of the plate.
   c. Overlap the crabs on the front of the plate and nap them with the butter sauce.
   d. Place the parsley sprig in the center of the plate.

ENTREES

RECIPE VARIATIONS

Dinner-House Fried Soft-Shell Crab Platter
After pressing the soft-shells to force out fluids, dredge them in flour mixed with Chesapeake seasoning, dip in beaten egg, then dredge again in flour. Pan-fry the soft-shells in corn oil. Serve with the same accompaniments as the Dinner-House Crab Cake Platter variation (p. 212).

Beer-Battered Soft-Shell Crab Appetizer
Prepare Calabash Batter, using all white flour and replacing the milk with flat beer. After pressing the soft-shells to force out fluids, dredge in flour mixed with Chesapeake seasoning, then dip in the batter and deep-fry. Serve with Tartar Sauce (p. 60) or Herbed Red Bell Pepper Mayonnaise (p. 208).

Grilled Rockfish on Grilled Vegetable Ratatouille

with Sweet Potato Hay

yield: 1 (7-oz.) entrée serving plus accompaniments
(multiply × 4 for classroom turnout; adjust equipment sizes
accordingly)

MASTER RECIPE

production		costing only
2 c.	Grilled Vegetable Ratatouille	1/4 recipe
1	7-oz. striped bass (rockfish) fillet, skinned, pinned, and trimmed	8 oz. a.p.
1/2 c.	Chesapeake Grill Baste	1/4 recipe
3 c.	loosely packed julienne sweet potato	10 oz. a.p.
1/4 c.	flour mixed with Chesapeake seasoning	2 oz. flour + 1/16 oz. seasoning
tt	fine salt	1/16 oz.
1 sprig	fresh thyme	1/20 bunch a.p.
1 sprig	fresh rosemary	1/10 bunch a.p.
1 sprig	fresh oregano	1/20 bunch a.p.

service turnout:

1. Set a deep-fryer to 400°F. Prepare a hotel pan lined with paper towels.
2. Heat the Grilled Vegetable Ratatouille in a covered 10" sauté pan and hold hot.
3. Brush the striped bass with some of the Chesapeake Grill Baste and char-grill it on both sides, about 5 minutes total, brushing often with the baste, leaving about 2 Tbsp. of the baste for plating.
4. Fry the sweet potato hay:
   a. Toss the sweet potato with the seasoned flour.
   b. Holding the fryer basket over a waste bowl, place the floured julienne sweet potato in the basket and shake off the excess flour.
   c. Deep-fry the sweet potatoes about 30 seconds, shaking the basket often, until crisp and golden.
   d. Drain on paper towels and season with salt.
5. Plate the dish:
   a. Make a bed of ratatouille on the front of a hot 12" plate.
   b. Place the striped bass fillet on top of the ratatouille.
   c. Mound the sweet potato hay on the back of the plate.
   d. Spoon the remaining baste onto the fish.
   e. Make a bouquet of the herb sprigs and stick it upright behind the fish.

COMPONENT RECIPE

GRILLED VEGETABLE RATATOUILLE

yield: 1 1/2 qt.

production		costing only
2	small eggplants, preferably the slender, lavender-color Chinese variety, trimmed and cut lengthwise into 3/8" planks	10 oz. a.p.
2	small zucchini, trimmed and cut lengthwise into 3/8" planks	12 oz. a.p.
2	red bell peppers, cleaned and cut into 3/8" rings	12 oz. a.p.
1	sweet onion, peeled and cut into 3/8" rings	6 oz. a.p.
3/4 c.	extra virgin olive oil	6 fl. oz.
3	fresh garlic cloves, peeled and crushed	1 oz. a.p.
tt	kosher salt	1/16 oz.
tt	fresh-ground black pepper	1/16 oz.
2 c.	cold Fresh Tomato Sauce	1/2 recipe

preparation:

1. Preheat a gas or charcoal grill to high heat.
2. Mix the eggplants, zucchini, red bell peppers, and onion with the oil, garlic, salt, and pepper. Allow the vegetables to absorb the oil about 20 minutes at room temperature, tossing occasionally.
3. Separately grill the vegetables over high heat, basting with the seasoned oil, until lightly charred and just cooked through.
4. Spread the vegetables on a sheet tray to cool.
5. Cut the vegetables into 1" pieces.
6. Mix the vegetables (and any oil left on the sheet tray) with the Fresh Tomato Sauce.

holding: refrigerate in a freshly sanitized, covered, nonreactive container up to 3 days

COMPONENT RECIPE
CHESAPEAKE GRILL BASTE

yield: 2 c.

production		costing only
1/4 c.	minced scallion	1/4 bunch a.p.
1 Tbsp.	minced fresh garlic	1/3 oz. a.p.
1 Tbsp.	minced lemon zest	n/c
2 Tbsp.	minced flat-leaf parsley	1/20 bunch a.p.
1 tsp.	kosher salt	1/9 oz.
1 tsp.	fresh-ground black pepper	1/16 oz.
1 tsp.	Chesapeake seasoning	1/16 oz.
1 drop	liquid smoke, optional	1/16 fl. oz.
1/2 c.	fresh lemon juice	1 1/2 [90 ct.] lemons
1/2 c.	golden-color pure olive oil	4 fl. oz.
1/2 c.	butter, melted and cooled	4 oz.

preparation:
1. Place the scallion, garlic, lemon zest, parsley, salt, pepper, Chesapeake seasoning, and liquid smoke, if using, in a mortar (or small, heavy bowl). With the pestle (or a heavy spoon), grind the mixture into a rough paste.
2. Whisk in the lemon juice, then whisk in the oil and butter to form an emulsion.

holding: best prepared just before service; if prepared ahead, hold refrigerated in a freshly sanitized, covered, nonreactive container up to 2 days; before service, bring to room temperature and whisk or blend to reemulsify

DelMarVa Roadside Barbeque Chicken
with Tidewater Kidney Bean Salad and Cucumber Salad

yield: 1 (12 -oz. bone-in) entrée serving plus accompaniments (multiply × 4 for classroom turnout; adjust equipment sizes accordingly)

MASTER RECIPE

production		costing only
1	DelMarVa Fryer Half	1/4 recipe
1/2 c.	DelMarVa Mop and Sauce, hot in steam table	1/8 recipe
1	Boston lettuce leaf	1/12 head a.p.
1 1/4 c.	Kidney Bean Salad	1/4 recipe
1 c.	Cucumber Salad, drained	1/4 recipe
1 Tbsp.	chopped flat-leaf parsley	1/40 bunch a.p.

service turnout:

1. Place the DelMarVa Fryer Half on a sizzle plate and finish it in a 400°F oven about 10 minutes. Spoon half of the DelMarVa Mop and Sauce over the top and finish 2 minutes longer.
2. Plate the dish:
   a. Place the lettuce leaf on the back left of a room-temperature 12" oval plate. Fill the leaf with Kidney Bean Salad.
   b. Mound the Cucumber Salad on the back right of the plate.
   c. Place the fryer half on the front of the plate, propped against the salads.
   d. Pour the juices from the sizzle plate over the fryer half, along with the remaining mop and sauce.
   e. Sprinkle the kidney bean salad with the parsley.

COMPONENT RECIPE
DELMARVA FRYER HALVES

yield: 4 (9-oz.) chicken halves

production		costing only
as needed	fruitwood chips/blocks, soaked in water per smoker manufacturer's specification	% of package
2	2 1/2-lb. fryer/broiler chickens*	5 lb. a.p.
2 c.	DelMarVa Mop and Sauce	1/2 recipe

preparation:

1. Prepare a smoker with fruitwood chips/blocks and set the heat control to 225°F. Alternatively, set up a char-grill or stovetop smoking setup.
2. Fabricate and marinate the chickens:
   a. Split each chicken into two halves by cutting out its backbone.
   b. Remove the thigh bones by severing the joint between the thigh and drumstick and cutting underneath the thigh bone to free it.
   c. Remove the rib bones by slicing underneath them and pulling them away from the breast bones.
   d. Using a food injector, inject about 1/4 c. DelMarVa Mop and Sauce into each chicken half in several places. (Reserve the remaining mop and sauce for turnout.)
3. Smoke-roast the chickens to an internal doneness of 145°F.
4. If preparing ahead, place the chickens on a sheet tray and immediately refrigerate, uncovered, until cold.

*All cooking times are based on 2 1/2-lb. chickens. If unavailable, use large Cornish hens and adjust cooking times accordingly.

holding: refrigerate in a freshly sanitized, covered container up to 3 days

COMPONENT RECIPE
TIDEWATER KIDNEY BEAN SALAD

yield: 5 c.

production		costing only
2/3 c.	seeded, 3/8"-diced vine-ripe tomatoes	4 oz. a.p.
tt	kosher salt	1/16 oz.
1/2 c.	mayonnaise	4 fl. oz.
1 tsp.	sugar	1/6 oz.
1/4 tsp.	dry mustard	1/16 oz.
tt	fine-ground white pepper	1/16 oz.
1 tsp.	cider vinegar	1/6 fl. oz.
4 c.	drained, cooked red kidney beans —or— 2 (14-oz.) cans	9 oz. (dried)
1/3 c.	peeled, 3/8"-diced celery	1/20 head a.p.
1/4 c.	3/8" diced green bell pepper	2 oz. a.p.
1/3 c.	medium-chopped red onion	1 1/2 oz. a.p.

preparation:
1. Toss the tomatoes with a little salt and drain them on paper towels 15 minutes.
2. Blend the mayonnaise with the sugar, mustard, white pepper, and vinegar.
3. Fold in the beans, celery, green bell pepper, and onion.
4. Correct the seasoning.
5. Fold in the tomatoes just before service.

holding: refrigerate (without the tomatoes) in a freshly sanitized, covered container up to 3 days

COMPONENT RECIPE
CUCUMBER SALAD

yield: 1 qt.

production		costing only
3	slender cucumbers	24 oz. a.p.
tt	kosher salt	1/6 oz.
1/2 c.	slivered sweet onion	2 1/2 oz. a.p.
2 Tbsp.	corn oil	1 fl. oz.
tt	sugar	1/6 oz.
tt	cider vinegar	1/2 oz.

preparation:
1. Fabricate the cucumbers:
   a. Peel the cucumbers and cut off the ends.
   b. Cut the cucumbers in half lengthwise and scrape out the seeds.
   c. Slice the cucumbers 1/8" thick.
   d. Toss the cucumber slices with a little salt.
   e. Spread the cucumber slices out on a clean kitchen towel, cover with another towel, and roll up. Squeeze gently and allow to drain at room temperature about 20 minutes.
2. Mix the salad:
   a. Transfer the cucumbers to a bowl and add the onion.
   b. Toss the cucumbers and onion with the oil and a little sugar.
   c. Toss in a little vinegar and taste for seasoning. Add more vinegar and/or sugar to make a dressing that is lightly sweet and slightly tart.

holding: prepare enough for one service only; hold refrigerated during service

---

RECIPE VARIATION

Smoke-Roasted Pork Loin with Tidewater Kidney Bean Salad and Cucumber Salad
Replace the chickens with a boneless pork loin; adjust cooking times accordingly.

Chicken Virginia

Stuffed with Ham and Collards
in Creamy Mushroom Sauce,
Served with Pan-Steamed White Rice
and Glazed Baby Carrots

yield: 1 (8-oz.) entrée serving plus accompaniments
(multiply × 4 for classroom turnout; adjust equipment sizes
accordingly)

MASTER RECIPE

production		costing only
4 Tbsp.	clarified butter	2 1/2 oz. a.p.
1	Chicken Virginia Roulade	1/4 recipe
1 1/4 c.	Glazed Baby Carrots	1/4 recipe
as needed	pan coating spray	% of container
1 1/2 c.	Pan-Steamed White Rice, hot in steam table	1/4 recipe
3/4 c.	Creamy Mushroom Sauce, hot in steam table	1/4 recipe
1 tsp.	minced flat-leaf parsley	1/40 bunch a.p.

service turnout:

1. Cook the Chicken Virginia Roulade:
   a. Heat an 8" sauté pan, then add the butter and heat it to medium heat.
   b. Add the roulade and pan-fry until golden on all sides.
   c. Remove the roulade to a sizzle pan and finish it in a 400°F oven about 10 minutes.
2. Heat the Glazed Baby Carrots in a covered sauté pan (add a little water) or in the microwave.
3. Plate the dish:
   a. Spray the inside of a 2 1/2" × 1 3/4" entremet ring with pan coating, place on the back center of a hot 12" plate, pack in the Pan-Steamed White Rice, and lift the ring.
   b. Arrange the carrots on the left of the rice.
   c. Remove the toothpick from the roulade and cut it on the diagonal into 4 slices.
   d. Lean a roulade slice against the right side of the rice, at 2 o'clock, and arrange the remaining slices in an overlapping arc across the front of the plate.
   e. Ladle the Creamy Mushroom Sauce into the space between the roulade slices and the rice, allowing it to flood the plate well.
   f. Place a dot of parsley in the center of the rice.

ENTREES

COMPONENT RECIPE
CHICKEN VIRGINIA ROULADES

yield: 4 (8-oz.) entrée portions

production		costing only
2	eggs	2 each or 4 oz.
1/4 c.	water	n/c
1 1/2 c.	Collard Greens, p. 72, pot liquor reduced to a glaze, cold	3/8 recipe
4	large, 1/8" slices smoked ham, such as tavern ham, trimmed of rind	4 oz.
4	6 oz. boneless, skinless chicken breast halves, trimmed	28 oz. a.p.
4	plain wooden toothpicks	4 each
±1/2 c.	flour	±2 1/2 oz.
tt	fine salt	1/16 oz.
tt	fine-ground white pepper	1/16 oz.
±2 c.	soft, fine-ground fresh bread crumbs	±5 oz. a.p.

preparation (wear foodservice gloves throughout; change to fresh gloves between steps):
1. Fabricate the stuffing rolls:
   a. Beat the eggs with the water to make egg wash.
   b. Chop the Collard Greens fine and check their seasoning. Mix 2 Tbsp. egg wash into the collards.
   c. Lay out a piece of ham on the work surface. Brush lightly with egg wash. Form 1/4 of the collards into a cylinder, place on one end of the ham, and roll up into a tight roll. Repeat to make four ham/collard rolls.
2. Fabricate the chicken breasts:
   a. Place a chicken breast half flat on the work surface. Insert a sharp boning knife in the side of the breast near the thickest end; keeping the opening as small as possible, run the knife around the inside of the breast, cutting out toward the thin end and back toward the thick end, to make a large pocket inside. Be careful not to pierce the top, bottom, or sides; try to keep the knife centered so that there is an even amount of meat top and bottom.
   b. Repeat with the remaining chicken breast halves.
3. Stuff the chicken breast halves:
   a. Brush the outside of a ham roll with egg wash and insert into one of the chicken breast halves. Secure shut with a toothpick.
   b. Repeat with the remaining ingredients to make 4 stuffed chicken breast roulades.
4. Coat the roulades with breading:
   a. Mix the flour with the salt and white pepper.
   b. Dredge each roulade in the seasoned flour, then dip it in the remaining egg wash, and then dredge it in the bread crumbs, pressing firmly so that the crumbs adhere well.
   c. Place the roulades on a rack set over a sheet tray and refrigerate, uncovered, at least 1 hour.

holding: refrigerate on the rack, loosely covered with plastic film, up to 3 days

COMPONENT RECIPE
GLAZED BABY CARROTS

yield: 1 qt.

production		costing only
1 lb.	peeled baby carrots	1 lb. a.p.
2 Tbsp.	light brown sugar	2/3 oz.
3 Tbsp.	butter	1 1/2 oz.
tt	kosher salt	1/16 oz.
as needed	boiling water	n/c

preparation:
1. Place all ingredients in a 10" nonstick sauté pan and add boiling water just to cover. Place a loose-fitting lid on the pan and bring to a brisk simmer.
2. Cook about 10 minutes, until the carrots are al dente.
3. Remove the lid and bring to the boil. Reduce the liquid to a glaze, stirring and scraping with a heatproof rubber spatula. ⚠ Watch carefully; do not allow to scorch.
4. Taste and correct the salt.

holding: open-pan cool and immediately refrigerate in a freshly sanitized, covered container up to 5 days

COMPONENT RECIPE
CREAMY MUSHROOM SAUCE

yield: 3 c.

production		costing only
2 Tbsp.	clarified butter	1 1/4 oz. a.p.
1 1/2 c.	cleaned, 3/8"-diced domestic white or cremini mushrooms	6 oz. a.p.
2 Tbsp.	butter	1 oz.
3 Tbsp.	flour	1 oz.
3 c.+	hot Poultry Stock	1/5 recipe
tt	kosher salt	1/16 oz.
1 sprig	fresh thyme	1/20 bunch a.p.
1/4 c.	heavy cream	2 fl. oz.
1 tsp.	minced lemon zest	n/c
tt	fine-ground white pepper	1/16 oz.

preparation:
1. Heat a heavy 2-qt. saucepan, add the clarified butter, and sear the mushrooms until lightly browned. Remove the mushrooms and allow the pan to cool down a little.
2. Add 2 Tbsp. butter and the flour to the pan and make a blond roux. Whisk in the Poultry Stock and any mushroom liquid, then add the thyme and a little salt.
3. Simmer the sauce 20 minutes.
4. At this point the sauce should be a medium nappé consistency; if not, correct the texture by reducing it or thinning it with water or stock. Remove the thyme sprig.
5. Add the mushrooms, cream, and lemon zest. Heat to just under the boil.
6. Add the white pepper and correct the salt.

holding: open-pan cool and immediately refrigerate in a freshly sanitized, covered container up to 5 days

Lady Baltimore Cake

yield: 1 dessert serving
(multiply × 4 for classroom turnout)

MASTER RECIPE

production		costing only
1 slice	Lady Baltimore Cake	1/10 recipe
1	edible flower, optional	1 each or % of pkg.

service turnout:
1. Plate the dish:
   a. Place the Lady Baltimore Cake slice on a cool 8" plate.
   b. Place the edible flower, if using, on the plate to the right of the cake slice.

COMPONENT RECIPE
LADY BALTIMORE CAKE ASSEMBLY

yield: 1 (9") 2-layer cake

production		costing only
1/4 c.	cognac or brandy	2 fl. oz.
1/4 c.	water	n/c
2/3 c.	chopped golden raisins	4 oz.
2/3 c.	chopped dried figs	3 1/2 oz.
1 c.	toasted pecan pieces	3 oz.
1 qt.	Boiled Icing, p. 79, prepared just before assembly	1 recipe
1	White Cake Layer	1 recipe

preparation:
1. Prepare the filling:
   a. In a 1-qt. saucepan, heat the cognac and water to just under the boil.
   b. Stir in the raisins and figs.
   c. Remove from the heat and cool to room temperature, stirring occasionally.
   d. Drain the fruits and squeeze out all the liquid, reserving both liquid and fruits.
   e. Mix the fruits and pecan pieces with about 1 c. of the Boiled Icing.
2. Assemble the cake:
   a. Split the White Cake Layer in half horizontally; the half that remains on the cake board is the bottom layer.
   b. Moisten the crumb side of the layer halves with the liquid that resulted from soaking the fruits.
   c. Spread filling on the bottom cake layer.
   d. Place the top layer on the filling, crumb side down, and press to firm it.
   e. Frost the sides and top of the cake with the remaining icing.
   f. Decorate the cake with swirls and peaks by touching it with the tip of a spatula and then pulling the spatula away.

holding: refrigerate under a cake dome up to 2 days

RECIPE VARIATIONS
Lord Baltimore Cake
Replace the white cake layer with a yellow cake layer. Replace the pecans, figs, and raisins with a mixture of toasted almonds, toasted walnuts, crushed almond macaroon cookies, and chopped maraschino cherries.

COMPONENT RECIPE
WHITE CAKE LAYER

yield: 1 (9" round) cake layer

production		costing only
as needed	baker's pan coating spray	1/50 container
7 oz.	cake flour	7 oz.
2 tsp.	baking powder	1/16 oz.
1/4 tsp.	fine salt	1/16 oz.
4 oz.	room-temperature unsalted butter	4 oz.
8 oz.	sugar	8 oz.
1/2 c.	milk	4 fl. oz.
1/2 tsp.	pure vanilla extract	1/12 fl. oz.
1/4 tsp.	almond extract	1/24 fl. oz.
4	egg whites	4 each or 4 oz.
1	9" round cake board	1 each

preparation:
1. Mise en place:
   a. Preheat an oven to 375°.
   b. Prepare a 9" × 2" round cake pan: spray the bottom and sides with pan coating, place a 9" circle of pan liner in the bottom, and then spray again.
2. Sift together the cake flour, baking powder, and salt.
3. Mix the batter:
   a. Using the paddle attachment of a mixer, cream the butter and sugar until pale yellow and very fluffy.
   b. Mixing on low speed, alternately add the flour mixture and the milk to make a smooth batter. Add the extracts.
   c. In a large, clean, dry bowl, beat the egg whites just below firm peaks. Fold 1/4 of the egg whites into the batter, and then fold the batter into the remaining egg whites.
4. Place the batter in the pan and run it a little way up the sides of the pan to make a slight depression in the center.
5. Immediately place the pan on the center rack of the oven and bake 25 to 30 minutes, until the layer is risen and golden in color and a tester inserted in the center comes out clean.
6. Cool the pan on a rack 5 minutes.
7. Turn out the layer onto the cake board and allow to cool completely.

holding: wrap in plastic film and store at cool room temperature up to 24 hours; freeze up to 3 months

DESSERTS

Hominy Custard
with Glazed Strawberries and Black Walnut Crisps

yield: 1 dessert serving
(multiply × 4 for classroom turnout)

MASTER RECIPE

production		costing only
1	Strawberry-Topped Hominy Custard	1/5 recipe
1	6" doily or cocktail napkin	1 each
1 sprig	fresh mint	1/12 bunch a.p.
3	Black Walnut Crisps	1/10 recipe

service turnout:
1. Plate the dish:
   a. Place the Strawberry-Topped Hominy Custard slightly left of center on an 8" plate lined with a 6" doily.
   b. Place the mint sprig on the back right of the plate and arrange the Black Walnut Crisps in front of it.

COMPONENT RECIPE
STRAWBERRY-TOPPED HOMINY CUSTARDS

yield: 5 (8-fl.-oz.) dessert servings

production		costing only
2 c.	half-and-half	16 fl. oz.
2"	vanilla bean	1/3 bean
2	eggs	2 each or 4 oz.
1	egg yolk	1 each or 2/3 oz.
1/2 c.	sugar	4 oz.
pinch	fine salt	1/16 oz.
1 1/4 c.	canned pearl hominy (such as Manning's brand)	1/2 (20-oz.) can
1 pt.	small strawberries	1 pt.
3/4 c.	warm Strawberry Glaze	1 recipe

preparation:
1. Mise en place:
   a. Preheat an oven to 275°F.
   b. Place 5 (8-oz.) round gratin dishes in a hotel pan lined with a clean, damp kitchen towel.
   c. Prepare 5 (6") rounds of aluminum foil.
   d. Have boiling water ready at hand.
2. Prepare the custard:
   a. Measure the half-and-half into a saucepan.
   b. Slit open the vanilla bean and scrape the seeds into the milk. (Reserve the bean to make vanilla sugar, or drop it into the pan.)
   c. Scald the half-and-half over medium heat until steam rises from it.
   d. Beat the eggs and egg yolk, then beat in the sugar and salt.
   e. Add the hominy and break it apart with a spoon.
   f. Temper the egg-hominy mixture by whisking in the hot half-and-half in a thin stream.
   g. Remove the vanilla bean, if necessary.
3. Pan the custard:
   a. Using a slotted spoon, divide the hominy equally among the 5 gratin dishes.
   b. Pour the custard over the hominy to make equal portions.
   c. Cover each gratin with a foil square, folding the edges up so that the foil will not wick water up into the custard.
   d. Pour the boiling water into the hotel pan to make a water bath that reaches 3/4 up the sides of the gratins.
4. Place the pan in the center of the oven and bake about 25 minutes, until the custard is lightly set.
5. Cool the custards on a rack to room temperature and then refrigerate 1 hour, until cold.
6. Top the custards:
   a. Wash the strawberries and blot them dry on a clean towel.
   b. Hull the berries and cut them into thin slices.
   c. Arrange the berry slices, wide ends out, on the surface of the custards in attractive concentric circles.
   d. Brush the strawberries with warm Strawberry Glaze.
   e. Refrigerate 10 minutes, until the glaze is set.

holding: refrigerate up to 2 days

COMPONENT RECIPE
STRAWBERRY GLAZE

yield: 3/4 c.

production		costing only
3/4 c.	high-quality strawberry jam	6 fl. oz.
1/4 c.	water	n/c
1 Tbsp.	Chambord or strawberry liqueur	1/2 fl. oz.

preparation:
1. Place the jam and water in an 8" sauté pan. Melt together over low heat.
2. Strain the mixture.
3. Rinse out the pan and return the strained glaze to the sauté pan. Over medium heat, stirring constantly with a heatproof rubber scraper, reduce to a light glaze.
4. Remove from the heat and add the liqueur.

holding: refrigerate in a freshly sanitized, covered container up to 2 weeks

COMPONENT RECIPE
BLACK WALNUT CRISPS

yield: approx. 30 cookies

production		costing only
10 oz.	flour	10 oz.
2 tsp.	baking powder	1/16 oz.
1/4 tsp.	fine salt	1/16 oz.
1/2 tsp.	ground cinnamon	1/16 oz.
4 oz.	room-temperature butter	4 oz.
5 oz.	brown sugar	5 oz.
1	egg	1 each or 2 oz.
1 Tbsp.	egg white	1/2 oz.
1 c.	black walnut pieces	5 oz.
as needed	baker's pan coating spray	% of container

preparation:
1. Sift together the flour, baking powder, salt, and cinnamon.
2. Mix the dough:
   a. Using the paddle attachment of a mixer, cream together the butter and sugar on medium speed until light and fluffy.
   b. Beat in the egg and egg white. On low speed, pulse in the flour mixture and black walnut pieces.
3. Transfer the dough to a half sheet of pan liner and form it into a rectangular 1 1/2" × 1/2" × 10" slab. Wrap the slab and refrigerate it about 1 hour, until firm.
4. Mise en place:
   a. Preheat an oven to 400°F.
   b. Line a half-sheet tray with pan liner and apply a light spray of pan coating.
5. Slice the slab of dough into 3/16"-thick rectangles and place them close together on the tray.
6. Bake in the center of the oven about 8 minutes, until light brown.
7. Transfer to a rack and cool to room temperature.

holding: store at cool room temperature in a tightly sealed container up to 1 week; dough slab may be frozen up to 1 month

---

RECIPE VARIATIONS
Raisin-Spice Hominy Custard
Replace the vanilla bean with 1/2 tsp. pure vanilla extract. Add 1/2 c. raisins and a dash of cinnamon to the custard mixture. Omit the strawberries and Strawberry Glaze. May be served warm.

☐ TABLE 5.2 CHESAPEAKE REGIONAL INGREDIENTS

ITEM	MARKET FORMS	USES	SEASONALITY	OTHER	STORE
SHELL OYSTERS	Live, in-shell oysters are size graded by count per bushel: Bistro—45 dozen Buffet—30 dozen Standard—25 dozen Large—20 dozen Jumbo—15 dozen.	Usually served raw on the half shell, shell oysters are also barbequed and used in baked preparations.	Now available year round, fresh oysters are traditionally served in months with the letter "r," September through April.	Only freshly shucked, live oysters should be served raw.	Store covered with seaweed or damp newspaper between 36°F and 38°F, up to a week. Discard any open oysters.
SHUCKED OYSTERS	Shucked oysters are graded by count per gallon: Small—500+ ct. Standard—301–499 ct. Select—211–300 ct. Extra-select— 160–210 ct. Count—under 160 ct.	Use in soups, stews, and stuffings, and for frying.	Available year round.	The oyster liquor, or fluid in which shucked oysters are packed, is valuable for making soups and sauces.	Store at 33°F to 34°F 3 to 4 days. To avoid contamination, use a utensil, rather than hands, to remove oysters from the container.
IQF RAW OYSTERS	IQF half-shell oysters are available by count in cartons.	Use in topped and baked preparations, such as Oysters Rockefeller.	Available year round.	Popular because of their safety and convenience. Although freezing damages the texture of the oyster flesh, when it is cooked the altered texture is less noticeable. Frozen oysters should not be served raw.	Keep frozen until needed for service/prep.
LIVE BLUE CRABS	Bushel is the common foodservice pack: Colossal—4 to 5 dozen per bushel Jumbo—5 to 6 dozen per bushel Large—6 to 7 dozen per bushel Medium—7 to 8 dozen per bushel Small—8 to 9 dozen per bushel.	Live blue crabs are typically steamed for eating "in the rough."	In season from April through October.	There are usually only three grades: #1 Jimmies—largest males with the most firm flesh #2 Jimmies—smaller males, less meaty #3—mixed and unsized, often with some small females. Crabs, when steamed and picked, yield ±15 percent meat by weight.	Refrigeate as they come from the purveyor, usually in boxes or baskets covered with seaweed or damp newspaper.
IQF RAW CLEANED CRAB HALVES	Available in 2-lb. bags. The apron, back shell carapace, gills, and innards are removed before freezing.	Cleaned crabs are commonly used for spaghetti and crabs or for gumbos and seafood soups.	Available year round.	Frozen cleaned crabs are useful for making crab stock when live crabs aren't available.	Keep frozen until needed for service/prep.
CRAB MEAT	Foodservice crab meat is primarily sold in 1 lb. containers, both fresh and pasteurized. Crab meat is graded by its location in the crab and corresponding color and size: *jumbo lump*, large white nuggets from the front of the body; *lump*, smaller white pieces from the same area; *backfin*, flaky white body meat; *special*, shreds of white meat with some shell fragments; *claw meat*, dark, moist meat from the claws and arms; *cocktail claws*, the tip of the crab claw shell with a "lollipop" of crab meat attached.	Used primarily in salads, cocktails, and crab cakes.	Although crab meat is available year round, peak season for fresh crab meat is summer through early fall.	Specify the correct grade of crabmeat for the dish: cocktails and salads demand jumbo lump or lump; for crab cakes determine whether your customers will pay for a luxury cake made with lump and special meat or prefer economy cakes made with claw meat.	Unopened, plastic-packed fresh crab meat keeps refrigerated on ice up to 5 days. Unopened pasteurized crab meat keeps refrigerated up to 3 months. Once opened, use crabmeat within 2 days. Avoid freezing crab meat, as it loses significant taste and acquires a stringy texture.

(continued)

☐ **TABLE 5.2 CHESAPEAKE REGIONAL INGREDIENTS** *(continued)*

ITEM	MARKET FORMS	USES	SEASONALITY	OTHER	STORE
SOFT-SHELL CRABS	Available by count in trays of 24, fresh soft-shell crabs are graded by width of the back shell from tip to tip. Mediums: 3 1/2"–4" Hotels: 4"–4 1/2" Primes: 4 1/2"–5" Jumbos: 5"–5 1/2" Whales: 6"+. Frozen soft shells are also available.	Sautéed or fried soft-shells are served as an entrée (2 to 3) or as an appetizer (1). Fried soft-shell sand-wiches on a hamburger roll are garnished with lettuce, tomato, and mayonnaise or tartar sauce.	Live soft-shells are available May through August; frozen, year-round.	Soft-shells should be cleaned at the last minute before service and must be kept very cold, prefer-ably on ice, during ser-vice. Leftover soft-shells should be frozen at the end of service.	Store refrigerated in original tray under seaweed or damp newspaper. Dead crabs are unsafe to eat and must be dis-carded. Crabs that sur-vive being out of water for several days will begin to harden to the point where the back shell becomes unpalatable and must be removed before cooking.
CHESAPEAKE ROCKFISH/ STRIPED BASS	When purchasing, specify striped bass in order to dis-tinguish this fish from the en-tirely different Pacific rockfish. Wild-caught striped bass is superior to and more expensive than the farmed variety. Striped bass is avail-able as whole, gutted fish and fillets.	Striped bass fillets are pan-seared, sautéed, or broiled and dressed simply with lemon butter sauce. For buf-fets and banquets, an 8-lb. rockfish is presented whole, hot or cold.	Wild striped bass is in season from February through December; farmed striped bass is available year round.		Store whole gutted fish buried in self-draining ice up to 4 days; fillets and pieces should be in ice in a plastic bag or con-tainer up to 2 days.
CRAB BASE	Sold in 1-lb. containers and 5-lb. tubs, crab base varies widely in flavor and salt content.	Used to prepare crab stock for soups and sauces.	N/A	Fine dining restaurants prepare natural stock from crab shells and bodies. Crab base is used in midlevel and budget operations.	Refrigerated or frozen for storage longer than 3 months.
CANNED PEARL HOMINY	The dominant and prefer-able commercially available canned hominy is Manning's brand. Do not substitute Mexican posole.	Served as a side dish, in soups and casseroles, in desserts, and as a breakfast cereal.	N/A	Originating in Baltimore in the 1800s, Manning's brand is now processed in Lottsburg, Virginia.	Dry stored.
PREPARED HORSE-RADISH	Prepared horseradish is sold refrigerated in small jars and 1 lb. plastic containers.	Essential in tomato-based cocktail sauce, horseradish is featured in other dips and sauces for Chesapeake seafood, both fresh and smoked.	N/A	Baltimore is a center for horseradish production, with several packing plants marketing their spicy product nationwide. Quality brands are free of preservatives.	Store refrigerated about 1 month, after which the horseradish loses flavor and oxi-dizes to an unappeal-ing brown color.
CHESAPEAKE SEASONING	A number of proprietary blends are available, with Old Bay the most popular. For foodservice Chesapeake seasoning is sold in 1 lb. tins and in bulk.	Used in a wide range of re-gional dishes, including crab cakes, baked crab dishes, fried chicken, French fries, potato chips, and deviled eggs.	N/A	Ingredients include cayenne, paprika, white and/or black pepper, de-hydrated onion and gar-lic, dry mustard, mace, cloves, ginger, bay leaf, thyme, savory, and salt. Mix well before using.	Store at room temperature.

■□■ chapter six

Louisiana

Louisiana, the Mississippi and Alabama Gulf coasts, the western Florida panhandle, extreme eastern Texas

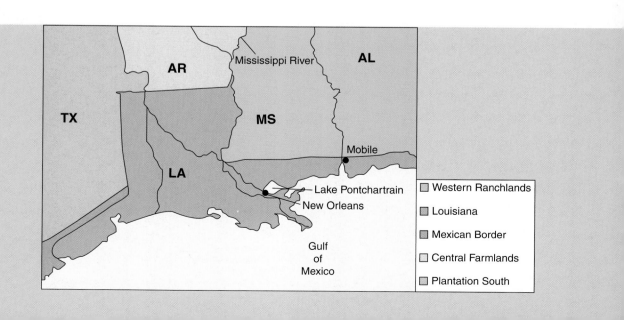

LOUISIANA IS MORE than just a state; it's a state of mind. Driving along the bayous or strolling French Quarter streets, you sometimes feel you're in another country. Even the language is different: French words punctuate the soft Louisiana drawl. There's a lazy, tropical feel that makes matters less urgent. The air is heavy, and it often smells of spicy cooking. Food is a constant topic of conversation. At breakfast, Louisianans wonder what's for lunch, and at lunch they're thinking about dinner. Although laid back about most other things, Louisianans are passionate about eating.

Although the culinary region you're about to discover is named for a single state, the scope of Louisiana's culinary influence is actually larger, extending along the Gulf of Mexico from Pensacola to Galveston. Around the delta, where Gulf and Mississippi River waters meet, indigenous seafood anchors the cuisine. Commerce on these important waterways engendered a rich overlay of seven strong food cultures beginning with Native American influence and first-settler French cooking, the region's foundation cuisine. Immigrants added African, Caribbean, German, Spanish, and Italian foodways. Because of this lively ethnic mix, Louisiana culture and cuisine can be compared to a bubbling pot of gumbo, the region's best-known dish. Made with a little of this and a little of that, assembled with skill and love, and combined with easy tolerance, both gumbo and Louisiana are complex creations much greater than the sum of their parts.

AFTER STUDYING THIS CHAPTER YOU SHOULD BE ABLE TO:

- describe the climate and topography of Louisiana and the surrounding Gulf Coast (Factor 1) and explain their impact on the region's agriculture and cuisine
- describe Louisiana's geographical location and explain the correlation between its location and its early economic viability (Factor 5)
- list the seven roots of Louisiana cuisine (Factors 2, 3, and 4)
- discuss the French food culture, cooking techniques, and ingredients that form the foundation of Louisiana cuisine (Factor 3)
- list Louisiana's primary food products, favored seasonings, and predominant cooking methods
- recount the history of Louisiana's Creole population (Factor 3) and describe Creole cuisine
- recount the history of Louisiana's Cajun population (Factor 3) and describe Cajun cuisine
- correctly and safely prepare Louisiana brown roux
- prepare authentic Creole, Cajun, and contemporary Louisiana dishes

APPETIZERS

Crawfish Bisque with Stuffed Crawfish Heads and Creole Baguette

Gumbo z'Herbes with Rice

Creole Shrimp Rémoulade

Frog Legs Sauce *Piquante*

Creole "Barbeque" Shrimp

Cajun Popcorn with Tabasco Dip

Oysters Rockefeller

Shrimp and Tasso–Stuffed Mirliton with Sauce Aurore

Cajun Boudin Blanc with Green Lentil Salad

ENTRÉES

Pompano en Papillote with Champagne Cream, Pecan Rice Pilaf, Parisienne Carrots, and Haricots Verts

Red Snapper *Courtbouillon* with Pan-Steamed Rice and Smothered Butter Beans

Blackened Redfish with Eggplant 'n' Shrimp Pirogue and Maquechoux

Shrimp Creole with Pan-Steamed Rice and Fried Okra

Duck, Andouille Sausage, and 'Gator Filé Gumbo

Shrimp and Crab Okra Gumbo

Crawfish Étouffée with Pan-Steamed Rice and Sauté Mirliton

Chicken, Shrimp, and Oyster Filé Gumbo

Creole Jambalaya with Pepper Medley

Pecan-Crusted Suprême of Chicken with Tasso Cream, Red Rice, and Sautéed Spinach

Red Beans 'n' Rice with Andouille Sausage and Collard Greens

Pork Backbone Stew with Pan-Steamed Rice and Tomato-Smothered Pattypan Squash

DESSERTS

Bananas Foster with Palmier

Chocolate Voodoo Torte with Raspberry Sauce

King's Cake with Queen's Sauce

Gâteau au Syrop

Creole Bread Pudding with Bourbon Sauce and Praline

WEBSITE EXTRAS

Basic Preparations   Breakfasts and Brunches   Sandwiches   Hors d'Oeuvres   Thanksgiving Menus

THE LAND THE RIVER BUILT

Millions of years ago successive geological upheavals raised the Appalachian Mountains in the east and then elevated the Rocky Mountains in the west. Between these two mountain ranges lies an expanse of lower land shaped like a funnel. On either side of this funnel the land slopes downward from the mountains, meeting at a vertical depression that roughly bisects the continent. Precipitation falling east of the Rockies' crest and west of the Appalachians' crest flows downhill, guided by this natural funnel, to become a wide and powerful river flowing south and emptying into the Gulf of Mexico. Native Americans called this vast waterway *Mississippi*, Algonquian for "big river" (Figure 6.1).

As the Mississippi and its tributaries flow downhill, they pick up billions of soil particles, carrying them suspended in the stream. Where the land flattens near sea level, at the mouth of the funnel, the water slows. Dissolved organic matter and suspended minerals precipitate out of the water and float to the bottom. Over time the soil particles pile up, raise the river bottom, and slow the flow of water even more. Eventually the river takes the path of least resistance and changes course, abandoning the former river bottom to become solid ground. Land created by sediment deposited at the mouth of a river, where it empties into a larger body of water such as a bay or a gulf, is called a **delta** because it's roughly triangular.

In this way the Mississippi dropped millions of tons of sediment as it met the Gulf of Mexico. Thus, southern Louisiana was created by the river, built up out of soil washed away from the American heartland. During the formation of southern Louisiana the river's relentless action, continually creating new land and carving out new waterways, changed the landscape many times. Over millennia, successive deposits extended the delta farther out into the Gulf. Although waves and tides wear away soil, working against delta formation, the Mississippi has prevailed. Geological studies prove that in only six hundred years, the river has added hundreds of square miles of land to Louisiana in the form of the modern "bird's-foot" delta that extends the river mouth far out into the Gulf (Figure 6.2).

Delta land is exceptionally fertile. Soil created by river deposits, called **alluvial soil,** is loose-textured, rock-free, and rich with minerals and organic material. From the coastal flatlands to the tip of the bird's-foot delta south of New Orleans, any Louisiana land solid enough for planting yields vegetables of superlative quality and is suitable for rice cultivation.

However, much of south Louisiana is not solid ground. The delta's dry land is only a foot or two above sea level and riddled with marshes connected by a maze of slow-moving, meandering

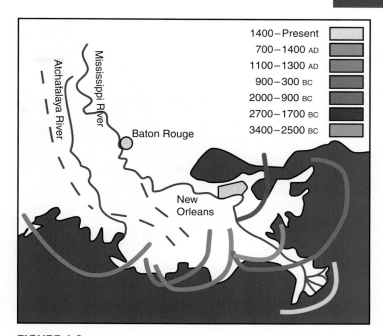

FIGURE 6.2

The Mississippi Delta

Map by Steve Dutch

Legend:
1400–Present
700–1400 AD
1100–1300 AD
900–300 BC
2000–900 BC
2700–1700 BC
3400–2500 BC

FACTOR 1

The delta's alluvial soil is exceptionally fertile.

FIGURE 6.1

The Mississippi Watershed

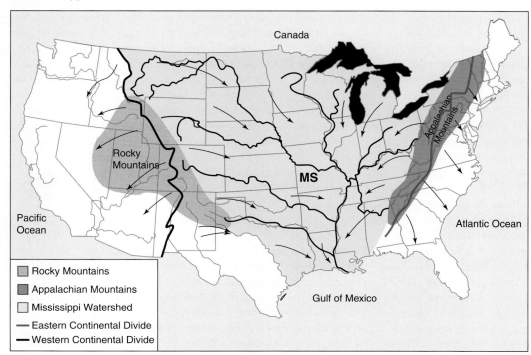

Legend:
- Rocky Mountains
- Appalachian Mountains
- Mississippi Watershed
- Eastern Continental Divide
- Western Continental Divide

FIGURE 6.3
South Louisiana is a maze of bayous and marshes that provide habitat for fish and shellfish. Paul S. Wolf © Shutterstock

waterways, called **bayous** (Figure 6.3). This type of topography can only be described as fluid. A strong storm surge may submerge a meadow, creating a swamp. Crashing waves wash away shorelines. In the delta, weather can change the landscape overnight.

South Louisiana's wetlands provide areas of variable salinity (p. 195) that support a variety of marine life. Brackish inland water provides habitat for frogs, turtles, crawfish (crayfish), and alligators. Gulf Coast waters support shellfish such as shrimp, blue crabs, and oysters as well as fish such as grouper, pompano, snapper, and red drum. (More information about Louisiana seafood begins on p. 254.) Because the Mississippi Delta is the terminus of the most important bird flyway in North America, Louisiana's wetlands are the winter home of wild ducks prized for the table. Woodlands shelter deer, bears, opossums, squirrels, and wild turkeys.

Because of its low latitude and proximity to the Gulf, southern Louisiana and the surrounding coastal areas have a subtropical climate. Summers are hot and humid, and winters are mild. The Mississippi Delta and Louisiana coastal plain boast annual average temperatures of 60°F to 70°F and up to 340 frost-free days per year, enabling food crops to be cultivated virtually year round. Combined with an average annual rainfall of 40 to 60 inches, the warm climate makes southern Louisiana ideal for growing subtropical food plants such as tomatoes, peppers, eggplant, okra, black-eyed peas, and sweet potatoes as well as Mediterranean-climate cultivars such as artichokes, peaches, melons, table grapes, and figs. However, the humid weather and moist alluvial soil are not appropriate for grain crops such as wheat, barley, or oats.

Inland and upland, northern Louisiana forms a transition zone between the Appalachian foothills and the semiarid Texas hill country. Before European settlement, prairie extended as far south as Shreveport, bringing occasional herds of bison into the region. Beneath the prairie vegetation lay deep deposits of fertile alluvial soil. These land characteristics, combined with sufficient rainfall and firm, relatively flat terrain, made northern Louisiana well suited to large-scale agriculture, including grain production. As in other areas you've studied, Native Americans were the region's first farmers.

FACTOR 1
The region's two climate and topography zones make possible a variety of agricultural products.

■ LOUISIANA NATIVE
□ AMERICANS
■

By the mid-1500s Louisiana was home to five Native American groups: the Chitimachas and Houmas in the delta area; the Natchez in central Louisiana; the Choctaws, primarily west of the Mississippi; and the Caddos in northwest Louisiana. Each of these groups had its own distinctive language, culture, and cuisine.

The delta tribes were expert watermen, piloting dugout canoes through the bayous for fishing and transportation. Seafood and waterfowl formed the protein foundation of their diet. Here foraging was of equal importance to Three Sisters farming. Many of the indigenous foods eaten by Plantation South Native Americans thrived in the delta as well. The dried, ground leaves of indigenous sassafras trees were a favored Louisiana Native American ingredient that would became a signature flavor of the region.

The foodways of inland groups differed from those of the delta area tribes. Western Choctaws and Caddos combined Three Sisters agriculture with plains-style hunting and foraging (p. 464). Of all Louisiana tribes, the Natchez had the most highly developed civilization. Their prehistoric ancestors built large burial mounds at various locations along the Mississippi. At the time of European contact the Natchez lived among these mounds in large, organized settlements resembling small cities and had a complex social structure that included a strict class hierarchy, trade organizations, and a central government. They enjoyed a diet that included river fish, woodland and prairie foraged foods, and cultivated crops.

Although Louisiana Native American groups had divergent foodways, all relied on corn as a primary starch. All of the region's tribes grew and cooked a variety of corn cultivars, preparing traditional alkaline-treated foods such as hominy as well as ground, whole-kernel corn dishes such as shuck bread and pones (p. 35). All venerated corn as the staff of life and engaged in corn-oriented religious practices. Corn became an important staple starch for early French settlers but survived in the modern cuisine only as an adjunct food of lesser importance.

In 1539 Spanish explorer Hernando de Soto landed on the west coast of Florida and began an expedition into the American South that led him to the Mississippi River in central Louisiana. In this area he first encountered the Natchez and was astonished by their advanced civilization. Although de Soto died en route, his company sailed south on the Mississippi and became the first Europeans to navigate the Mississippi Delta.

FACTOR 2
Initially important in early Louisiana cooking, in the modern cuisine corn has become an adjunct food.

The initial Spanish goal in the American South was exploration, not settlement. After de Soto, Louisiana Native Americans remained undisturbed by Europeans for more than 140 years. However, de Soto's passage left a mixed legacy. As in other regions, European diseases soon decimated native populations that made contact with his company. Violent encounters with de Soto's men created deep hostility toward Europeans. Later, this hostile attitude greatly affected French settlement. However, not all of the results of Spanish exploration were negative. Horses that escaped from the expedition became the foundation breeding stock of the American mustang, an animal that would later revolutionize the lives of many Native American groups (p. 463) and change their foodways. Swine left behind by de Soto's company multiplied and became the Southern **razorback hog.** These feral pigs roamed the Deep South and central and northern Florida, adding protein and fat to the Native American diet. Today the razorback is a coveted game animal for sport hunters and a delicious addition to the Deep South table. The presence of peach trees in the American South has been attributed to De Soto, although it's more likely they arrived from the Southwestern missions via trade.

FRENCH SETTLEMENT

French claim to Louisiana began about 140 years after de Soto with an expedition led by René-Robert Cavelier, known as La Salle. La Salle's initial exploration began in New France, in present-day southern Quebec. After exploring the Great Lakes area, his company paddled canoes down the Mississippi River, reaching the Gulf of Mexico in 1682 and claiming all lands on either side of the river for France. The new French territory was named *Louisiana* in honor of King Louis XIV.

The French government recognized the Mississippi's potential for transporting goods from the heartland to ships in the Gulf of Mexico. To solidify their claim, the French made plans to settle the entire Gulf Coast. In 1699 the French established Louisiana's first permanent settlement at Mobile, Alabama. Soon the colony of Louisiana extended from the Florida panhandle across Mississippi and into the delta, with Mobile its capital.

Local Native Americans made uneasy peace with the French and introduced them to indigenous foods. French settlers initially engaged in subsistence farming of Three Sisters crops. However, a rapid influx of colonists from Europe and the American colonies soon made other foods available. Although agriculture was successful, the main goal of French settlement was to control access to the Mississippi.

In 1718 the French founded a new settlement in the heart of the Mississippi Delta at a big bend in the river about 20 miles from the Gulf. Its founders believed the site was far enough inland to be safe from storms, yet with water deep enough for oceangoing vessels. Called *Nouvelle Orleans*, or New Orleans, the settlement became the gateway to the Mississippi River (Figure 6.4).

Before rail and motor transport, travel by water was the only way to efficiently move trade goods. Boats laden with furs and lumber—and later grain and hides—floated down the Mississippi to the Port of New Orleans, where these valuable goods were loaded onto ships and transported around the globe. By 1722 New Orleans had become Louisiana's capital city and the center of a rich and rapidly expanding colony. Thus, *Louisiana reached economic viability early in its history.*

Although New Orleans's location was economically advantageous, the geological foundation on which much of the city was built is less than ideal. Although the original crescent of land rises several feet above water level, the surrounding area was mostly marshland. As the city grew, its inhabitants built **levees,** or embankments, to hold back river water and drained the marshes to create new land for building. Thus, parts of New Orleans lie as much as 5 feet below sea level. The risks of building in such unstable conditions were partially understood by its founders and became clear to those who continued to develop New Orleans over a wider and lower area. Nonetheless, New Orleans continued growing into a major city and a center of world commerce.

With New Orleans as the hub, Louisiana settlement spread into the interior. French entrepreneurs established large plantations similar to those of the Carolinas and the Deep South. Rice

FACTOR 5
New Orleans's position at the mouth of the Mississippi made it a center of trade from its founding.

FIGURE 6.4

Built in a bend of the Mississippi River, New Orleans is called the Crescent City

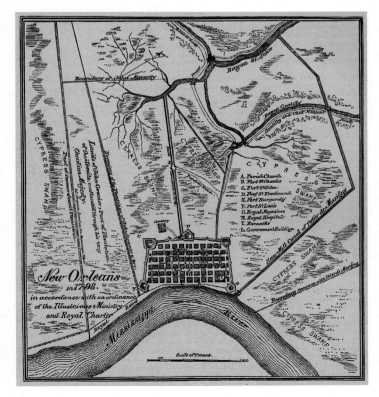

grew well in the moist delta soil. Soon plantations ringed Lake Pontchartrain and lined the bayous to the city's southwest. The plantation system depended on low-cost labor in the form of slavery, and Louisiana's plantations were no exception. Throughout the 1700s and early 1800s, massive numbers of slaves were imported to the region. Plantations supplied New Orleans and Mobile with fine food products, including pork, poultry, dairy, fruits, and vegetables, as well as shipping commodity crops to France and around the world. Most Louisiana planters owned a city residence as well as a plantation mansion and maintained slave house staffs in both locations. Louisiana attracted others of African heritage, called *free persons of color*, many of whom worked as professional cooks and chefs. Thus, African-Americans influenced Louisiana cooking almost from the beginning.

By the mid-1700s the Louisiana colony had all the elements necessary to create a distinctive regional cooking style. Let's discover how Louisiana cuisine developed.

■ TRADITIONAL
□ LOUISIANA CUISINE
■

In previous chapters we identified a formative period in each region's food history, beginning with the development of a Native American/first-settler hybrid cooking style, designated colonial or pioneer cooking. Then additional influences from second-settler immigrant groups slowly enrich the cuisine. However, in Louisiana, culinarily important second-settler groups immediately followed the first-settler French and influenced Louisiana cooking from its birth. Thus, although Louisiana was a colony, and remained one until it became part of the United States in 1803, it did not have a colonial cuisine in the same sense as other American culinary regions. Instead, Louisiana cooking developed into a complex, mature cuisine within only two or three generations of its founding. During that time, Louisiana welcomed and embraced six of the seven world cuisine influences that shaped its modern cuisine. Figure 6.5 illustrates them.

The French Foundation (Root #1)

With Spain pushing eastward from Texas and westward from northern Florida, and the English expanding the Plantation South, France needed to quickly establish a strong presence in this strategically crucial territory. The solution was to send just about anyone willing to go: decommissioned French soldiers, woodsmen transported from Canadian New France, working-class indentures, and prisoners from French jails. These would-be colonists had little farming experience. However, they did have experience eating.

Louisiana's French colonists were accustomed to relatively sophisticated food. Even the lowliest kitchen maid baked yeast breads and thickened sauces with roux. Even cooks with limited training prepared emulsion sauces such as mayonnaise and hollandaise and baked cakes and pastries. Louisiana's French settlers hailed from a strong food culture and thus were accustomed to a higher standard than the typical English colonist.

THE SEVEN ROOTS OF LOUISIANA CUISINE

Food historians recognize seven roots of Louisiana cuisine: France, Africa, North America, the Caribbean, Spain, Italy, and Germany. Figure 6.5 shows these seven roots nourishing a tree representing modern Louisiana cuisine and its two branches, the Creole and Cajun subcuisines, covered later in this chapter. In the figure, numbers signify each root's level of importance, with #1 (France) as most influential and #7 (Germany) as least influential. In the following sections, Louisiana roots are listed chronologically, but headings include importance-ranking numbers.

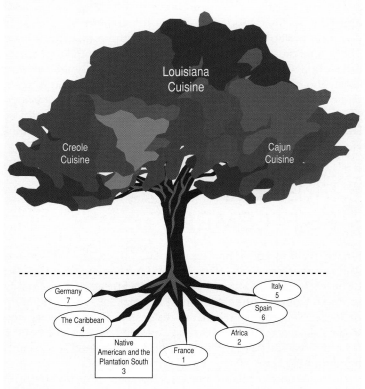

FIGURE 6.5
The Seven Roots of Louisiana Cuisine

Although generally the French are culinary conservatives, most French immigrants to Louisiana were not. Their adventurous mindset carried through to eating. They readily adopted Native American products and embraced virtually all second-settler foodways. A strong food culture combined with culinary liberalism results in a vibrant cuisine; from these first French settlers to the present day, Louisianans have perpetuated a food culture of strength and distinction (Figure 6.6).

Louisiana's Old World French cooking foundation is too complex to fully review in this text. Moreover, as a student of cuisine you already should be familiar with its flavor profiles and primary cooking methods. However, a number of French ingredients and techniques have become essential elements of Louisiana cuisine and merit discussion.

ELEMENTS OF OLD WORLD FRENCH CUISINE

FOUNDATION FOODS

principal starch: yeasted wheat breads

principal proteins: pork, poultry, cheese

principal produce: virtually all Western fruits and vegetables

FAVORED SEASONINGS: mirepoix, shallots, garlic, tarragon, thyme, parsley, bay leaf, black and white pepper, mustard

PRINCIPAL COOKING MEDIA: butter, olive oil, lard, stock

PRIMARY COOKING METHODS: sautéing, roasting, poaching, braising, stewing

FOOD ATTITUDES: strong food culture, culinary conservatives

FIGURE 6.6

French chefs man the stoves at Antoine's in the 1950s.

Courtesy New Orleans Public Library/Louisiana Division/City Archives

Mirepoix Becomes the Holy Trinity

One of the most important flavor elements of French cuisine is *mirepoix*, a rough-cut mixture of onions, celery, and carrots used as an aromatic base in stocks and simmered dishes. Because of soil and climate conditions, Louisiana cooks had to make substitutions: green bell peppers for carrots, and scallions or fresh onions (p. 242) for mature onions. Known as the **holy trinity,** a mixture of celery, green bell peppers, and fresh onions forms a distinctive flavor base for Louisiana soups, sauces, and composed dishes.

The Three Domains of Fat

Louisiana cuisine uses the three traditional cooking fats of France: butter, olive oil, and lard. In colonial Louisiana, imported olive oil was mainly used for salad dressings and mayonnaise, although today it's used for sautéing as well. Clarified butter was used for sautéing, whereas raw butter was preferred for sauces and table use. Lard or bacon drippings were the choice for bean dishes, pan-frying, and making brown roux (p. 249). These three fats remain essential in modern Louisiana cooking.

Roux of Many Colors

The predominant thickening method in classic French cuisine is the *roux*, a mixture of fat and flour cooked together. In the French fashion, virtually all Louisiana cooks used roux in making soups and sauces. However, they were not content with the French practice of making only white, blond, and brown roux. The Louisiana preference for strong, bold flavors led them to experiment when it came to browning the flour. Louisiana cooks began making roux in colors ranging from beige to almost black. We'll discuss roux browning at length on page 249.

Cast-Iron Cooking

Like their counterparts in other colonies, early Louisiana cooks relied on cast iron vessels for cooking most of their dishes. Like other Southerners, Louisianans continued using cast iron for frying and simmered dishes long after vessels made of other materials became available. Cast iron's gentle, even heat conduction enables cooks to gently coax a roux to a deep, dark-brown color with minimal risk of scorching. In cast iron, pan-fried foods cook evenly and develop a crunchy crust. Many Louisianans believe that cast iron imparts a distinctive flavor to food cooked in it.

Cooking with Wine

Although wine grapes would not grow in Louisiana's soil and climate, wine was so important to French food culture that it was regularly imported from France. Wine was not only the beverage of choice but also a cooking ingredient. In Louisiana cuisine, table wines are simmered into sauces, and fortified wines, such as Port and Madeira, flavor soups. In addition, liqueurs frequently flavor desserts.

French Bread, Served Hot

Although the earliest settlers relied on corn as a primary starch, Louisiana almost immediately enjoyed thriving trade with France and thus had access to imported flour early on. Skilled French cooks tended yeast starters, maintaining them even in the hottest weather. In Mobile, New Orleans, and other Louisiana towns, French bakers opened *boulangeries*, or bakeries, offering breads equal in quality to those found in France.

However, in the humid Gulf climate, breads tend to soften quickly and lose the crisp crust prized by the French. For this reason, Louisiana cooks typically recrisp French breads by heating them in the oven and—although never done in France—serve them hot.

Because French bread contains no fat or sugar, it stales quickly. To use up every scrap of their precious bread, Louisiana cooks frequently make bread crumb stuffings and toppings and serve croutons, rusks, bread puddings, and *pain perdu*, or French toast.

Fondness for Seafood

As a Catholic nation, France observed many religious fast days on which eating meat was forbidden. Though seafood was merely tolerated in Old World English cuisine, the French considered seafood meals a pleasure rather than a penance. When Louisiana's French settlers discovered many of their favorite seafood items in abundance, they cooked and ate them with enthusiasm. They learned to prepare indigenous shellfish and amphibians from local Native Americans and created new dishes with them. Unlike in New England, where it took several generations to appreciate indigenous seafood, Louisianans embraced seafood from the beginning, and it remains the region's most popular protein food.

Colonial Domesticates from France

In addition to growing rice as a cash crop, delta planters fared well at produce farming, although they had to adjust their choice of crops to the soil and climate. European root vegetables frequently rotted in southern Louisiana's wet soil and didn't store well in hot, humid weather. In response, growers often harvested onions at the immature stage. Green onions, or scallions, are the shoots of the onion plant, a universal aromatic vegetable and a favored garnish. Fully grown onions marketed fresh, before they develop dry, papery skins, are called **knob onions** or **fresh onions.** Though white potatoes were not successful in delta soil,

FACTOR 3
European colonial domesticates and Europeanized Old World ingredients expanded the cuisine.

sweet potatoes grew well. Mediterranean-climate food plants, such as chard, turnip greens, salad greens, and artichokes, flourished. In addition to French cultivars New World vegetables, such as tomatoes, eggplants, and chiles that had made their way from Meso-America to Europe, returned home to thrive in the hot, damp delta climate. European breeds of poultry and hogs became acclimated to the delta climate, and thus chicken, duck, and pork supplemented local seafood and game meats to provide a broad palette of ingredients for Louisiana cooks.

Native American Influence (Root #3)

It's difficult to gauge the impact of Native American cooking on Louisiana's French first-settler group because they had different levels of experience with New World foods. For example, settlers from (Canadian) New France or Acadia had been cooking and eating cornmeal products for generations. However, settlers from France likely had never even seen an ear of corn. Nonetheless, Native American influence, direct or indirect, is evident in Louisiana's cooking. To review elements of Plantation South Native American cuisine, refer to the box on p. 28.

As in other regions, delta natives taught settlers to grow Three Sisters crops and to harvest corn as a staple grain. Frenchwomen learned to pound corn kernels in wooden mortars to make cornmeal, which they then cooked with water to make porridge, or mush. They cooked parched corn kernels with fish and salt pork to make simple *chaudières*, or chowders (p. 98). However, such plain, bland food didn't satisfy French taste buds. Adventurous Louisiana colonists wished to liven up their diet, as in the frying pan revolt. In response, Louisiana cooks began experimenting with indigenous ingredients and seasonings early on.

Indigenous seafood and Native American farmed foods remain in the modern cuisine.

Local seafood posed culinary challenges as French cooks learned to shell crawfish and pick blue crabs. By far the most daunting seafood was the alligator (Figure 6.7). Although all of the alligator's flesh is edible, its thick, muscular tail offers mild-tasting white meat generally considered the best. Cleaning 'gator tail was a special skill learned from native cooks.

FIGURE 6.7
Farmed Alligators. Chet Mitchell © Shutterstock

'GATOR

The American alligator is found in brackish water along the coasts of South Carolina, Georgia, Florida, Alabama, Mississippi, and Louisiana. Alligator was an important food source for natives who hunted it with spear and bow and arrow. Natives tanned alligator skin to make leather and made ornaments and tools from the teeth. Europeans hunted alligators with firearms, drastically reducing their numbers. Throughout the 1800s the alligator population declined from not only hunting but also loss of habitat caused by development. By 1967 the American alligator was listed as an endangered species.

The popularization of Cajun cooking in the 1980s brought new demand for alligator meat at a time when the wild alligator population was just beginning to recover. Entrepreneurs responded with 'gator farming, a specialized form of aquaculture. Alligators were removed from the endangered list in 1987.

FIGURE 6.8

Sassafras leaves are dried and ground to make filé powder.

© Shutterstock

FACTOR 2

Filé, a Native American seasoning, is a signature flavor in Louisiana cuisine.

Native American cooks taught colonists to use ground, dried sassafras leaves, called **filé powder** (FEE-lay) by the French (Figure 6.8). The name *filé* is derived from the French word *filet*, meaning "string," and refers to the viscous, ropy texture that results when filé is used incorrectly. As an ingredient, filé has dual functions: As a seasoning, it adds a distinctive woodsy-spicy taste; as a thickener, it adds body to sauces. However, in order to achieve a pleasant texture, filé powder must be added to a sauce just before serving. If filé is subjected to prolonged heating, it acquires the unpleasant, stringy texture that inspired its name. For this reason filé is typically served as a table condiment, added to taste by the diner. Filé is primarily used in gumbos (p. 248).

The African Element (Root #2)

In 1719, one hundred years after the introduction of slaves to the Jamestown colony, two ships landed in Louisiana bearing 450 slaves of African origin. Their arrival marked the beginning of a massive forced immigration not only of Africans but also of Caribbean-Africans and African-Americans from the Plantation South. Slave labor made possible large-scale cultivation of cotton, indigo, sugar cane, and rice. Slaves changed the face of delta topography, transforming marshes into agricultural fields by constructing a complex system of levees and digging ditches to drain the land within them.

Slaves of African origin also changed Louisiana cuisine, adding ingredients, cooking methods, and taste preferences virtually from the beginning. Even the language of Louisiana cooking is replete with African words. To review elements of African cuisine, refer to the box on p. 43.

Rice Culture and Cuisine

As in the Carolina Lowcountry, Louisiana rice cultivation required a large labor force and specialized knowledge. Delta rice planters paid high prices for slaves from the Carolina rice islands. African-American slaves not only knew how to grow rice but were skilled at cooking it. Louisiana's black cooks knew how

FACTOR 4

African slaves contributed skill at rice cultivation and cooking.

to boil and then pan-steam plain rice so that each grain is separate and fluffy. In addition, they expanded the pilaf technique into an entire repertoire of braised rice dishes, of which jambalaya (p. 258) is best known. Rice overtook bread as the foundation starch of Louisiana cuisine. Traditional Louisiana cooking includes scores of rice dishes: soups, side dishes, main dishes, and even breads and desserts. As in the Lowcountry, in Louisiana rice is often served three meals a day.

Okra

Among all of the vegetables African slaves introduced to the American South, okra is possibly the most distinctive. In Louisiana as in the Plantation South, slender pods of young okra are dredged in corn flour or cornmeal and deep-fried crisp to make a tasty side dish or accompanied by a dipping sauce for a popular appetizer. Louisianans prize okra for its flavor and for the thickening power it lends when cut and simmered in a soup or stew. As you'll shortly learn, okra is an adjunct thickener for a particular type of Louisiana stew called gumbo, an important Louisiana defining dish.

Moussa and Coush-Coush

By 1700, North American cornmeal had become a staple food in most of sub-Saharan Africa. Although corn is indigenous to the Americas, African slaves previously had acquired a strong taste preference for corn dishes and, in Louisiana, were the primary consumers. *Moussa* is a savory version of cornmeal mush served as a starch accompaniment to stews and braised dishes. During the post–Civil War rice culture collapse, Louisianans ate their beloved gumbos with moussa instead of rice. *Coush-coush* is a soft cornmeal mush sweetened and served with cream for breakfast.

Strong Seasonings and Inventive Combinations

As in the Plantation South, in Louisiana African slaves did most of the cooking both in the cities and on the plantations. Free persons of color, both male and female, took jobs as cooks in private homes. Others staffed the kitchens of New Orleans restaurants. African-American women worked in the city's food markets, selling raw materials and prepared dishes. Thus, early Louisiana cooking was predominantly black cooking.

Louisiana's African-American cooks applied innovation and creativity to their work. With sailing ships loaded with spices and seasonings arriving daily, they combined ingredients from around the globe in interesting ways. Spice blends containing multiple ingredients and dishes mixing meats or poultry with seafood are typical of the cuisine. The exuberance of Louisiana's black culture was matched by that of its cooking.

Foods from the Plantation South (Root #3)

Louisiana's proximity to the Carolina colonies made them a cost-effective source of slaves. Among these slaves were thousands of cooks bringing recipes and techniques learned in Southern planters' kitchens. Thus, Louisiana cooking includes Plantation dishes such as fried chicken, cornmeal-crusted fried fish, vegetables cooked with seasoning meats, and barbeque.

Louisiana's best-known dish, gumbo, fundamentally belongs to the Carolina Lowcountry. Since the mid-1600s, Gullah cooks on Carolina's sea islands had been preparing okra-thickened seafood stews and serving them over rice. Written recipes for Carolina gumbo predate Louisiana's founding. Indeed, much of Louisiana's rice repertoire owes its heritage to Carolina cooking; in fact, jambalaya is a version of Lowcountry perloo (p. 58).

After the Civil War, many working-class white Southerners relocated to the Deep South and upland Louisiana in search of undeveloped land, and their taste preferences accompanied them. Many Louisiana dishes, such as neckbone stew and slow-simmered beans, reflect their cooking.

Despite many shared techniques and dishes, however, the two cuisines remain quite different. Plantation South cuisine lacks the fiery flavors and multi-layered complexity of Louisiana cooking. A comparison of the two regions' settler groups reveals why. Whereas English Plantation Southerners merely accepted Africa's flavor preferences, Louisiana's French and Spanish settlers embraced the bold and spicy cooking of their African and Afro-Caribbean cooks. Although as emigrants and adventurers both groups acquired liberal palates, the difference lies in the strength of the respective food cultures: English minimized, and both French and Spanish quite strong. Early on, Louisiana settlers were keenly interested in food and cooking, demanding complexity and variety in their meals. Given free rein in the kitchen and an eager, appreciative audience, African-American cooks in Louisiana experimented with a variety of herbs, spices, and seasonings. Therefore, Louisiana cuisine is richer, spicier, and more complex than Plantation South cuisine.

Caribbean Ingredients (Root #4)

FACTOR 4   FACTOR 5
Sugar culture from the Caribbean provided wealth as a trade good and sweetened Louisiana's cuisine.

A small but influential group of Louisiana settlers arrived from the French islands of the Caribbean, then called the West Indies. Shortly after the Revolutionary War, the West Indian sugar trade was in decline because of overproduction, unsustainable agricultural practices, and the war's economic impact on trade. Many French sugar-cane planters moved their operations, including slaves, to the new Louisiana colony. These Afro-Caribbean slaves had mastered the use of Caribbean ingredients, such as rum, molasses, and tropical fruits and vegetables, and were familiar with Caribbean barbeque. They had learned to roast and blend South Asian spices brought by indentured workers from India. These ingredients and techniques came to Louisiana along with Caribbean immigrants and became an important element in Louisiana cuisine. However, the most important contribution from the Caribbean, both culinarily and economically, was sugar.

Along with cotton and rice, sugarcane became a cash crop that fueled Louisiana's economy and sweetened its cooking. The ready availability of cane sugar allowed Louisianans to make sumptuous desserts and sweet beverages everyday fare. Caramelized sugar, in the form of praline candies, caramel frostings, and caramel sauces, is an important element in the Louisiana dessert repertoire. Cane syrup remains a popular topping for pancakes, crêpes, and *pain perdu*, or French toast.

Caribbean immigrants brought with them a strange-looking fruit known in Louisiana as the **mirliton,** a tropical squash also known as *chayote* or *christophene*. The pale, celery-green mirliton is shaped like a flattened pear and has an edible pit. Its pale-green flesh is often described as a cross between a cucumber and a squash, with a similarly delicate flavor.

Although most Louisiana cooks refer to them as *hot peppers*, chiles are an essential part of Louisiana cooking. The migration of chiles from and to the Caribbean is an interesting story related on this book's companion website. In the Caribbean, African slaves who already enjoyed hot-spicy foods discovered new chile varieties and cooking techniques. Louisiana cuisine uses chile in several forms. Cayenne powder is used in rubs and added to the roux of sauces and gumbos; crushed red pepper is used in marinades and sprinkled on sandwiches; fresh cayenne peppers and Italian green chiles are used raw and cooked; and, in the past few years, Mexican jalapeño and serrano chiles have entered the cuisine. Hot pepper sauce is a universal condiment. Although spicy-hot flavors are mainly associated with Cajun cooking, a little chile finds its way into the most elegant Creole dishes, adding a note of piquancy not found in their French counterparts.

Louisiana's proximity to the Caribbean ensured consistent trade between the two areas even after the French exit. In addition to the ingredients just discussed, Caribbean fruits such as bananas, pineapples, and coconuts are important in Louisiana desserts. Caribbean rum is used in Louisiana desserts, particularly Creole flambé specialties. Rum is also the liquor of choice in the region's specialty cocktails, made famous in New Orleans's French Quarter bars.

German Settlers (Root #7)

In 1721 the French government, recognizing the agricultural potential of Louisiana's uplands, authorized a venture company to settle persons of non-French origin in the colony. Most were German immigrants who brought their agricultural expertise and strong work ethic to the region. German farmers primarily settled a corridor of land on either side of the Mississippi, beginning about 25 miles north of New Orleans and reaching northward for 100 miles. This area became known as the *Côte des Allemandes* (coat days ahl-lay-MAHND), or the German Coast. Within only a few years they were producing food, including meat, dairy products, and much-needed wheat, for New Orleans.

Like all immigrant groups, Louisiana's German settlers brought their Old World taste preferences and cooking style with them. (To review elements of Germanic cuisine, go to the companion website.) However, German cooking didn't catch on in the region because its heavy, mildly seasoned dishes didn't suit Afro-French taste preferences. Instead, German farmers' food products enhanced the quality of the region's already established cuisine. In the 1800s German food artisans began opening businesses primarily selling breads, sausages, and beer.

Though Louisiana's foundation starch is described as French bread, most of the region's commercially produced loaves are actually made in bakeries founded by Louisianans of German ancestry. German bakers began producing breads modeled after the crisp-crusted, airy-crumbed *baguettes* and *boules* of France. A prominent characteristic of Louisiana French bread is its crackly crust that sets into a distinctive 'gator hide pattern as it cools.

Germans were the first Louisianans to produce sausages and preserved pork products for the commercial market. Louisiana-German-style smoked pork sausage is a favored ingredient in the defining dish red beans 'n' rice and is often included in gumbos and crawfish boils. Catering to the region's international population, German butchers soon expanded their offerings to include Spanish-style chorizo and French andouille. After Acadians arrived, they began making Cajun-style pork products such as tasso and boudin (Figure 6.9).

As in other American culinary regions, Louisiana's beer industry was founded by Germans. By the late 1800s New Orleans boasted more than twelve breweries producing a variety of local beers. Falstaff, Regal, Dixie, and Jax are legendary Louisiana brews.

FIGURE 6.9
Boudin Sausage
Courtesy of Sara Roahen,
Southern Foodways Alliance,
www.southernfoodways.com

Spanish Rule (Root #6)

In 1762, France lost the Seven Years' War. As part of war reparations, the Treaty of Fontainebleau removed Louisiana from France and gave it to Spain. For the next 40 years Louisiana was under Spanish rule. Although Spain banned the import of French trade goods, Louisianans simply obtained French food products and wines through other countries. Thus, Spanish rule didn't diminish Louisiana's strong French food culture. Rather, Louisiana cuisine was enriched with an infusion of new ingredients, techniques, and taste preferences from Spain.

The Spanish introduced tomatoes to Louisiana cooking. The New World tomato had traveled to Europe with returning Spanish conquistadores but found slow acceptance in most European countries because it was thought to be poisonous. Tomatoes caught on first in Mediterranean countries, particularly Italy and Spain. Soon Spanish cooks on both sides of the Atlantic were simmering tomato sauces and adding tomatoes to numerous recipes.

The Spanish also popularized eggplants and bell peppers, both often sautéed or stuffed and baked. Green bell peppers are an indispensable part of the "holy trinity" aromatic vegetable base. During Spanish rule, paprika entered the array of chile products used in Louisiana cooking, adding flavor and color to Louisiana dishes. Today paprika is dusted onto gratins and other composed dishes and is typically included in the seasoning mix for blackened dishes (p. 253).

The extent of Spanish influence on Louisiana cuisine is significant, considering the short duration of Spanish rule. After only 40 years, Spain ceded Louisiana back to the French, who then held it for less than a month. In 1803 Louisiana became a U.S. territory as part of the Louisiana Purchase.

American Louisiana (Root #3)

When Louisiana became part of the United States, the region entered a new stage of economic prosperity. Made possible by slavery, commercial agriculture continued to produce wealth for planters and merchants alike. Rice, sugar, and cotton were the cash crops fueling Louisiana's pre–Civil War economy. Both commerce and cuisine flourished.

But the Civil War took its toll on Louisiana as on the rest of the South. For all its wealth, the region had failed to develop an industrial base to complement its agriculture. At the beginning of the war, half of Louisiana's population consisted of enslaved African-Americans; after Emancipation, Louisiana's agriculture system totally broke down. Without slave labor, levees collapsed, thousands of acres of farmland were either flooded or neglected, and planters no longer could obtain bank loans without human property for collateral. Much of Louisiana's economy was in ruins—but not New Orleans's.

While the rest of Louisiana floundered, New Orleans held its ground. As a center of commerce far from the enemy North, New Orleans survived the war with culture and cuisine intact. The biggest blow to Louisiana cooking was the demise of rice cultivation; until the development of mechanized rice farming in northern Louisiana and eastern Texas, Louisianans had to eat expensive imported rice or make do with moussa. Louisiana greatly benefited from Reconstruction and soon regained economic viability through commercial fishing; diversified agriculture; and, in the mid-20th century, petrochemicals.

By the turn of the 20th century, Louisiana had become thoroughly American in its commerce, industry, and communications. However, Louisiana culture remained unique, its population largely retaining French folkways and foodways. Because of the region's strong food culture, Louisiana cuisine largely escaped the culinary decline of the 1950s, surviving the 20th century virtually intact. As you'll soon discover, however, Louisiana cuisine would face even greater challenges as the 21st century dawned.

Italian Immigrants (Root #5)

By the late 1800s, Louisiana cuisine exhibited all of the characteristics of a mature and fully developed regional cuisine. However, history would provide an additional element—like the Louisiana concept of lagniappe, just a little something extra to make a good thing better.

Part of the great wave of immigration that poured into the United States in the late 1800s, immigrants from the south of Italy were drawn to Louisiana's warm climate and economic opportunities. In New Orleans, Italian-American entrepreneurs opened grocery stores and sandwich shops, at first catering to other Italian immigrants but soon serving the city as a whole. Italians opened restaurants as well, at first offering only traditional southern Italian fare. Before long the inclusion of Louisiana's abundant seafood and other local ingredients and seasonings created a special Louisiana style of Italian-American cuisine that is richer, spicier, and more flamboyant than elsewhere. (Italian-American cuisine is discussed on the companion website.)

FACTOR 4
Italian immigrants added Parmesan cheese, pasta, vegetable dishes, and an array of sandwiches to the Louisiana repertoire.

Conversely, southern Italian cooking had a marked effect on Louisiana cuisine. The Louisiana repertoire began acquiring subtle southern Italian touches as Louisiana cooks embraced pungent Parmesan cheese, anchovies, Italian-style cured meats, and thicker, spicier tomato sauces. One of the most prominent Italian influences is the addition of pasta dishes to Louisiana cuisine.

At first Louisiana cooks began using southern Italian dried pastas, primarily spaghetti and macaroni. In the late 20th century, northern Italian fresh pasta entered the repertoire. As in Italian-American dining, Louisiana pasta dishes are served as entrées, or main-course items. Usually the pasta is combined with seafood, meats, or poultry plus

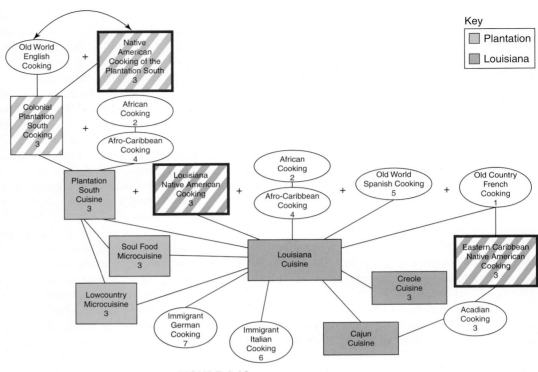

FIGURE 6.10
The Development of Louisiana Cuisine

vegetables to make a complete dish. However, modern restaurants often offer a meatless pasta dish for vegetarian customers. Contemporary Louisiana cuisine includes rich, substantial pasta dishes often bound with a thick, creamy béchamel sauce. Black pepper, white pepper, cayenne powder, and fresh chiles add a spicy kick.

Italians introduced Parmesan cheese to the Louisiana region, at first as a topping for tomato-sauced pastas. Soon Parmesan cheese was added to casseroles, savory crêpes, stuffed vegetables, and sauces. In Louisiana cuisine Parmesan is even added to seafood dishes, a practice unknown in traditional Italian cooking. Italian-style cheeses, such as Provolone, Asiago, and mozzarella, are featured in Louisiana sandwiches, many of which are Italian in origin. Refer to this book's companion website for a list of Louisiana signature sandwiches.

Although artichokes were used throughout Europe during the formation of Louisiana cuisine and are ingredients in both French and Spanish cooking, Italian immigrants made them an important part of 20th-century Louisiana cuisine. Two well-known Louisiana artichoke preparations are Italian legacies: crumb-stuffed baked artichokes and marinated artichoke hearts.

Italian immigrants, particularly Sicilians, brought their repertoire of stuffed vegetable dishes. Hailing from a hot, dry, economically disadvantaged area, Southern Italians of the 19th century survived on a largely vegetarian diet in which stuffed vegetables often took the place of meat or fish. In Catholic Louisiana, cheese- or seafood-stuffed vegetables were served on the many fast days. Louisiana vegetable stuffings are based on rice or bread crumbs and may contain meat, poultry, or seafood. Eggplant, artichokes, squashes, and tomatoes are only a few of the vegetables that may be hollowed and stuffed. A hollowed and stuffed baked eggplant is called a *pirogue* (PEE-rogh), named after the Louisiana dugout canoe it resembles.

Thus far we've examined the seven roots of Louisiana cuisine in depth. Now let's learn about its two branches: Creole cuisine and Cajun cuisine. These two branches of Louisiana cuisine are similar in many ways, but different in others. To compare them, refer to Figure 6.13.

■□ CREOLE
■ CUISINE

The word *Creole* is a Romance language term that originally described people of pure European ancestry born and raised in a colonial territory. In the Americas it usually applied to people of French, Spanish, or Portuguese descent born in the New World. Because of frequent racial intermingling, Louisiana recognized two separate Creole societies: white Creoles and Creoles of color. However, the modern, popularly accepted definition lists **Creole** as a person of mixed European-African race born in Louisiana, the Caribbean, or Latin America. Louisiana Creoles are typically urban or suburban, and of Catholic heritage. Creole history and culture are more fully explained on this book's companion website.

By the late 1700s, Louisiana's population was predominantly Creole, both white and of color. Wealthy Creole planters lived along the larger bayous, the Mississippi River, and Lake Pontchartrain. Though most planters were white Creoles, a significant number of plantation owners—and slave owners—were Creoles of color. Most planters maintained town homes in New Orleans and lived there during the social season. Plantation society moved from country to city with ease, traveling on the water to reach their chosen destinations.

Creole merchant families, including many Creoles of color, built opulent mansions and townhouses in New Orleans's French Quarter, filled them with French furnishings and European art, and kept slaves as house servants and cooks. New Orleans also fostered a large Creole middle class consisting of shopkeepers, artisans, and professionals. Along with free blacks, working-class Creoles supported the thriving New Orleans economy. No matter their social status, all Louisiana Creoles were dedicated to the pleasures of the table, spending time and money on good food. Whether they could afford to employ a cook or not, Creole women were expected to master the culinary arts, and many Creole men were accomplished cooks as well.

Sophisticated City Cuisine

Louisiana Creole cooks had access to virtually any ingredient they desired. Each day scores of oceangoing ships arrived in New Orleans from the Caribbean, South America, Europe, Africa, the Middle East, and Asia. French food products were most prevalent. Fine cheeses, hams and dried sausages, Dijon mustard, wine vinegars, confectionery supplies, Bordeaux and Burgundy wines, liquors, and liqueurs are only a few of the homeland products available to Louisiana's Creoles. After 1762 Spanish ingredients entered the mix. Saffron and paprika, olives, capers, pimentos, Spanish-style hams and dried sausages, salt cod, sherry vinegar, and Spanish wines and fortified wines arrived directly from Spain, and chiles, chocolate, vanilla, coffee, and tropical fruits came from Mexico and South America. Rum, allspice, coconuts, citrus, and other varieties of tropical fruit arrived from the nearby Caribbean. New Orleans received Chinese and Indian teas as well as a full spectrum of spices from Asia. Cosmopolitan Creole cooks blended these ingredients in new combinations, stopping only a tiny bit short of excess, to create a cuisine of depth, imagination, and sophistication.

Traditional Creole families follow the European style of multicourse dining, all but the most casual dinners having at least three courses. Special-occasion menus are planned on the formal French seven-course model: hors d'oeuvre, soup, fish course, meat course, salad, cheese, and dessert.

Creole meals include European-style beverages. A traditional Creole evening begins with *aperitifs*, or wine-based predinner drinks. Complementary wines accompany dinner. Cognac or cordials follow dessert, served after strong, chicory-laced Creole coffee. Creole cuisine also features alcohol-laced coffee drinks. Alcoholic beverages play an important role in Creole cooking as well. Table wines add acidity and complex flavor to many sauces, marinades, and desserts. Sauces are often finished with fortified wines such as sherry and Madeira. Showy flambé dishes, such as bananas Foster, require potent alcohol to create dramatic flames.

Creole cooks go to great lengths to present their food both attractively and dramatically. Whether the presentation is plate- or platter-style, Creole cooks have an artistic eye for color, texture, and the juxtaposition of elements. In restaurant and home cooking, garnishes are an important part of the ingredients list. Figure 6.11 shows an attractively presented Creole buffet.

Louisiana's Creole cooking was highly influenced by the classic cuisine period of French cooking. Creole dishes almost always include a sauce in the style of Escoffier. Béchamel sauce binds croquettes and casseroles. Smooth, light velouté sauce is used in fish and chicken dishes. Hollandaise and béarnaise are served with seafood, poultry, and egg dishes, and hollandaise accompanies asparagus and artichokes. Mayonnaise binds poultry and seafood salads, dresses po'boy sandwiches, and is the base of Creole rémoulade sauce (p. 266). In Louisiana, traditional Creole home cooks prepare these sauces almost as frequently as restaurant chefs. As mentioned earlier, Louisiana cooks use classic brown roux as a seasoning as well as a thickener. Brown roux is an indispensable ingredient in gumbo, a Louisiana signature dish popularized by Creoles of color.

emulsion. To do so, make sure the stock is hot and that you whisk the hot stock into the roux in a thin stream. If you pour cold stock into a hot roux and then try to stir them together, you'll end up with a greasy, broken sauce.

separately, to be added by the diner. This Native American–French type of gumbo, in which filé powder replaces okra, is called **filé gumbo.**

Thus, Louisiana cuisine recognizes two dis-

Gumbos may be rustic or elegant. Rustic gumbos are traditionally served as a substantial main course accompanied by plain, pan-steamed white rice. In the traditional entrée presentation, a rounded portion scoop of rice is placed in the center of a hot soup plate, the solid ingredients are mounded around the rice, and then the sauce is ladled in. Gumbo is never served *over* rice. Because rustic main-course gumbos often include bone-in poultry and in-shell seafood, eating them is a messy affair requiring side plates and wet wipes. Elegant gumbos are served as part of a formal meal, in smaller portions with only a tiny scoop of rice. In these gumbos, poultry is boneless and seafood shelled. When gumbo is served, bottled hot sauce is offered and, if the gumbo doesn't contain okra, a shaker of filé powder is placed on the table.

Étouffée, Courtbouillon, Creole, and Piquante

In addition to gumbo, Creole cuisine features four prominent dish categories having sauces thickened with Louisiana brown roux: *étouffées, courtbouillons, Creoles,* and *piquantes.*

Étouffée

The French term *étouffée* means "smothered." In a Louisiana **étouffée** (eh-too-FAY), food is cooked in a thick brown-roux sauce similar in consistency to gravy. "Holy trinity" vegetables and caramelized onions are frequent additions to étouffée sauce. Tomatoes are not included. Fish, seafood, poultry, and pork are typically étoufféed.

Courtbouillon

In classic French cuisine, seafood is frequently simmered in *courtbouillon,* a poaching liquid consisting of white wine, water, mirepoix, and bouquet garni. However, Creole cooks adapted this thin, mild broth to Louisiana tastes by replacing the mirepoix with "holy trinity" vegetables, replacing the water with fish stock, adding tomatoes, and thickening it with brown roux, transforming it into a hearty, brownish-red sauce redolent of wine and herbs. Creole **courtbouillon** (COO-bee-yong) teams the sauce with red snapper or Gulf redfish, whereas Cajuns typically prepare this sauce with crawfish.

Creole

Louisiana cuisine includes a category of dishes called *Creole,* of which shrimp Creole is best known. A true Creole consists of food cooked in a light-textured fresh tomato sauce subtly flavored with brown roux—similar to a classic French *sauce tomate* but not as smooth or as brown. Peppers, onions, and ham are traditional ingredients as well. (Outside the region, a dish called shrimp Creole is frequently prepared without the roux.)

Piquante

The French term *piquante* means "spicy-hot." Originally attributed to Creole cuisine, but enthusiastically adopted by Cajuns, a **piquante** (pee-KAHNT) is basically a Creole sauce with the addition of fresh or canned green chiles. In Southwest Louisiana, many cooks use a Texas product, Ro-Tel canned diced tomatoes with green chiles, to make *sauce piquante.*

Red Beans 'n' Rice

Though many of Creole cuisine's best-known recipes are complex creations made with expensive ingredients, possibly the most beloved New Orleans Creole dish is red beans 'n' rice. This venerable dish is traditionally served on Mondays, as explained on this book's companion website. Preparation begins by slowly simmering Louisiana red beans (similar to red kidney beans) with a ham bone or other seasoning meat. Each cook has his or her secret seasonings. Red wine adds color and flavor, and fresh parsley is said to counteract the beans' effects on digestion. The tender beans and their savory sauce are served over plain, pan-steamed white rice, often accompanied by andouille sausage or a pork chop.

Compare	
Complex flavors Sophisticated techniques Based on French cuisine Product of a strong food culture	
Creole Cuisine	Cajun Cuisine
City	Country
Rich	Poor
African-American	Caucasian
Mild	Spicy
Fancy	Plain
Contrast	

FIGURE 6.13
Creole and Cajun Cuisines Compare and Contrast Chart

Creole Restaurants

Although much of the finest Creole cooking was and still is practiced in the home, Creole cuisine is very much restaurant fare. New Orleans is the center of Creole restaurant dining, home to a venerable group of Creole restaurants listed on this book's companion website. Many oldtime New Orleans restaurants were situated in hotels. Just after the Civil War, a formal meal at a first-class New Orleans hotel might include oysters, turtle soup, broiled pompano, beef or game with two vegetables, a second entrée of duck or turkey, a soufflé, pastry, dessert, and coffee, all accompanied by appropriate wines. Such a meal would typically cost twenty dollars, a princely sum at the time.

Through the mid-1900s, New Orleans Creole restaurants specialized in serving the classic dishes of Creole cuisine, such as Creole Shrimp Rémoulade (p. 266), Crawfish Étouffée (p. 284), and Gâteau au Syrop. Many were located in fine old mansions, recreating the atmosphere of dining in a private home.

■ CAJUN
□ CUISINE

In Chapter 3 and on the website you learned about the Acadians, French colonists who settled in eastern Canada in the early 1700s, and the Acadian diaspora that occurred when the British took control of Canada (Figure 6.14). A few Acadians avoided deportation by crossing into New England, where they developed

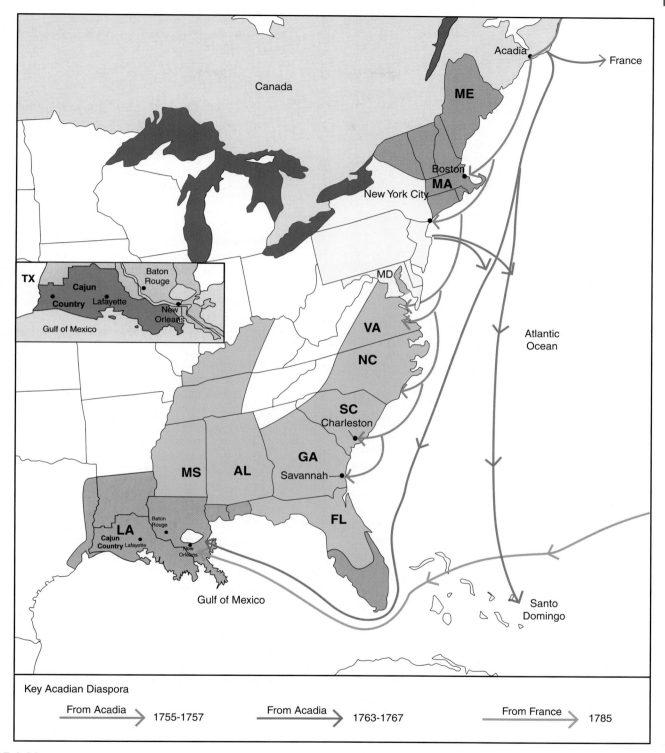

FIGURE 6.14
The Acadian Diaspora

the Acadian-American microcuisine. However, most Acadians were loaded onto ships—husbands separated from wives, children from parents—and sent away. Some landed in the American colonies, others in the Caribbean, and yet others back in a France they had never known. All yearned for a homeland of their own where they could be reunited with friends and family.

Wishing to build the population of their newly acquired Louisiana colony, the Spanish government offered to transport displaced Acadians to Louisiana. In 1785, seven ships delivered 1,600 Acadians to the port of New Orleans and, through subsequent decades, many more arrived. Each Acadian family was given a parcel of land and supplied with tools, seeds, and livestock. Most chose to settle in the undeveloped bayou country southwest of New Orleans.

Country Cooking

When Acadians arrived in southwest Louisiana, they adopted Native American dugout canoes and became experts at catching indigenous fish, shellfish, and game animals. They mingled with free African-Americans preparing both soul food–style Plantation South cooking and Creole cooking. Acadians embraced the region's ingredients and bold seasonings and took spicing to a higher level. However, authentic Cajun dishes are not fiery-hot. Over time their French language took on a lazy Southern drawl, and *Acadian* became *Cajun.* Thus, a **Cajun** is a person of Acadian ancestry born in Louisiana.

Although their cuisines are fundamentally similar, Cajuns cooked in a vastly different environment than often affluent, mostly urban Creole cooks. Cajuns were primarily fishermen, hunters, and subsistence farmers living in remote rural areas. As late as the 1940s the typical Cajun family raised and butchered hogs, grew and preserved vegetables, and relied on wild-caught fish, shellfish, and game for much of its protein. Only salt, wheat flour, sugar, spices, wine, and coffee came from the store. Nonetheless, Cajun cooks fed their families tasty, satisfying dishes made with skill and imagination.

Most Cajun dishes are made in large quantity to feed a crowd. Until only recently Cajun couples had many children, who in turn had many children of their own. Few left the Cajun homeland area and, even today, migration is minimal. Thus, a simple family get-together may include a hundred guests. Then and now, Cajun hospitality is spontaneous. Cajun visitors frequently arrive unannounced and often have no definite plans for leaving. For this reason Cajun cooks rarely plan precise food portions, preferring to make dishes that can be stretched with more sauce and more starch accompaniment if the need arises.

Dishes That "Stretch"

Cajuns readily adopted Creole gumbos, *courtbouillons,* and étouffées, transforming them into Cajun style with many personal variations. In such dishes the protein item is frequently considered secondary to the sauce. Long, slow cooking; deep browning; skillful thickening; and robust seasoning make Cajun sauces full-bodied and intensely flavorful. Such sauces make a little bit of meat, poultry, or seafood pack a lot of satisfaction.

As in Creole cuisine, plain pan-steamed white rice accompanies most Cajun dishes. However, dressings often replace or accompany it. The Cajun term **dressing** means "stuffing." Cajuns prepare dressings based on rice, wheat-flour breads, and cornbreads. These dressings are typically flavored with a small amount of protein food. For example, cornbread dressing may include diced tasso ham, and rice dressing may be flavored with chopped crawfish tails. Perhaps the most famous Cajun dressing is dirty rice, a pilaf flavored and colored with chopped chicken livers. Dressings are yet another way to "stretch" the expensive protein component of a meal: With a plate piled high with tasty dressing, you need only a little bit of meat. Although Cajun dressings are stuffings, they're also prepared separately and served as a side dish.

Flavor-Building Techniques

Because they traditionally had limited amounts of protein food and often serve large portions of bland starch accompaniments, Cajun cooks go the extra mile to develop flavor. As in Creole cooking, strong-tasting, full-bodied stocks are an essential element in Cajun soups, sauces, and composed dishes. Equally important are ingenious Cajun flavor-building techniques.

Browning

Browned is a signature flavor of Cajun cuisine. Both caramelization (the browning of sugar) and Maillard browning (the browning of proteins) are important elements of Cajun cooking. When sautéing "holy trinity" aromatics, Cajun cooks often allow the softened vegetables to caramelize slowly in the cooking fat and stick to the pan; liquid is then added and the resulting pan glaze is lifted by scraping. Often this process is repeated several times so the dish acquires a deep, bittersweet flavor. Vegetable dishes, such as smothered cabbage or corn maquechoux (p. 278), are subjected to the same treatment. Maillard browning occurs when roux is cooked through the various categories discussed on p. 249, and when meats are grilled, roasted, or sautéed deep brown. Maillard browning is combined with caramelization when syrups or fruit glazes are brushed onto roasting and barbequing meats to produce a sweet-savory, crusty exterior.

Layering and Staging

Cajun cooks use a variety of seasonings, including dried and fresh herbs, whole and ground spices, homemade or purchased condiments, shallots and scallions, and garlic and onions in both granulated and fresh form. In a Cajun method called **flavor layering,** the same basic ingredient is used in two or more forms to create a complex taste. For example, granulated garlic may be used in the rub for a rack of pork, whole peeled garlic cloves strewn around it to braise in the pan juices, and minced fresh garlic added to the sauce.

Another flavor-enhancing method called **ingredient staging** involves adding the same ingredient at different stages in the cooking process. For example, when making a gumbo a Cajun may add only half of the "holy trinity" vegetables to the roux at the beginning of cooking so they dissolve into the sauce, and then add the remaining half later in the cooking process to create texture.

Cajun Charcuterie

Like New England Acadians, Louisiana Cajuns are masters of **charcuterie,** the preparation of preserved pork products. In fall most traditional Cajun families hosted a **boucherie** (boo-shair-EE), or hog-processing party, in which home-raised hogs are butchered, fabricated, and then preserved in many ways. At a *boucherie* some of the pork is cooked on the spot and served to hungry participants. Much more is transformed into spicy Cajun-style hams, sausages, bacon, and other products listed in the table on p. 297. The hog's skin becomes *grattons* (grah-TAWN), or cracklings. The fat is rendered into lard, the Cajuns' most important cooking fat. The products prepared at their autumn *boucherie* were expected to last a Cajun family throughout the winter.

Today few individual families still hold annual *boucheries*. Instead, they purchase traditional Cajun pork products from small, artisan producers found throughout the homeland area.

Eatin' Swamp Critters

Hunting and fishing remain popular pastimes among Cajuns who enjoy the sport but primarily want the food. Delta marshlands are the last stop on America's central migratory flyway, where teal, pintail, and mallard ducks, and wild geese stop to rest before crossing the Gulf. Amphibians have a place of honor on the Cajun table. Turtle, called **cooter** as in the Plantation South and South Florida, is used in stews, soups, and gumbos and is baked in its own shell. Frog legs are fried crisp or simmered in spicy sauce. Alligator is prized for its firm, pale tail meat. Crawfish are a hallmark of Cajun cuisine. At a traditional crawfish boil (Figure 6.15), crawfish are steamed in a cauldron and are often served with new potatoes, knob onions, and corn on the cob. Cooked, peeled crawfish tails are finished in thick, spicy étouffée sauce, simmered in gumbos, or added to dressings. Although some of these swamp critters are enjoyed by many Louisianans and are part of Creole cuisine as well, they most properly belong in a discussion of Cajun cooking, as all come from Cajun country and are caught, processed, and sold primarily by people of Cajun origin.

Cajun Restaurants

Unlike Creole cuisine, until the 1980s Cajun cooking was not represented by large, well-known restaurants but was primarily a home cuisine. Outsiders experienced it only in local cafés and

FIGURE 6.15
Louisiana Crawfish Boil
Courtesy Lawrence O'Keefe, Paradise Project, Edmunds Middle School, Burlington, VT

roadhouses or at public events such as church picnics or community fund-raisers.

In the 1980s Cajun cuisine came to national prominence when Chef Paul Prudhomme took over the kitchen of the famous New Orleans Commander's Palace restaurant and added his own version of Cajun cooking to its predominantly Creole and Continental menu. There he created and popularized blackened redfish, a heavily spiced, pan-seared fish fillet that today is widely believed to be a traditional Cajun dish. Chef Prudhomme and his wife promoted Cajun-Creole fusion cuisine at their own restaurant, K-Paul's Louisiana Kitchen. Cajun cooking became a national pastime after Prudhomme published his first Cajun cookbook and began appearing on television. Soon Cajun seasonings filled supermarket shelves and household smoke alarms blared as amateur cooks attempted to reproduce Prudhomme's highly publicized "blackened" dishes.

Other chefs and food celebrities jumped on the Cajun bandwagon. Predating Paul Prudhomme by more than fifteen years, Cajun cookbook author and humorist Justin Wilson was rediscovered. Emeril Lagasse, actually a French-Canadian/Portuguese, became America's best-known Cajun-style chef. For a list of noteworthy Cajun restaurants, refer to this book's companion website.

■□■ CHARACTERISTICS OF LOUISIANA CUISINE

Throughout much of Louisiana's history, Creole cuisine and Cajun cuisine flourished side by side, sharing many of the same ingredients, techniques, and recipes. By the 20th century the dividing line between the two cooking styles had blurred as Cajuns adopted Creole dishes such as red beans 'n' rice and Creoles added Cajun flavor-building techniques to their repertoire. Today these two cuisines have much in common. Let's discover the overarching characteristics that define traditional Louisiana cuisine.

Complex Cooking

In a culture as complex as Louisiana's, it is no surprise that people prefer equally complex food. Louisianans, whether they live back in the bayous or in towns or cities, like their food highly seasoned, sauced, and interesting. Here, less is definitely not more. Why season a dish with only one herb or spice when you can use three? If oysters are good, wouldn't they be even better topped with shrimp and cream? Louisiana foods are often spice-rubbed or marinated before cooking, accompanied by or simmered in a sauce, enhanced with a tasty garnish, and served with several side dishes. Appetizers are the norm, and dessert is a must. The plain meat-and-potatoes diet of the American heartland would bore a Louisianan to tears.

Individualism

Louisiana cooks "do it their own way," each making his or her own statement when rendering a classic dish. Heated arguments about the proper technique or correct combination of ingredients are common. Thus, there's rarely one single, authentic recipe for any Louisiana dish.

Although this individualistic culinary philosophy results in interesting eating, it can also lead to frustration among students of Louisiana cuisine. When you begin researching Louisiana recipes you'll be faced with a bewildering repertoire of dishes, each with many variations. As soon as you grasp the fundamentals of a particular dish, you're likely to discover a contradictory version. Like New Orleans jazz music, Louisiana cooking is based on traditional themes interpreted differently by each individual player.

Showcasing Louisiana Seafood

Both the Creole and Cajun styles of Louisiana cuisine showcase the region's fine seafood.

Gulf Oysters

Although connoisseurs agree that the cooler waters of the Chesapeake Bay, the North Atlantic coast, and the Pacific Northwest produce better-quality oysters, the Louisiana Gulf Coast produces more oysters during a longer season. Gulf oysters are often the only ones available in summer months and are an important resource for theme restaurants featuring oysters on the menu year-round.

Though most of the Louisiana oyster harvest is dredged in the wild, a growing number of Louisiana's oysters are produced by aquaculture. Refer to p. 200 for a description of oyster harvesting methods and the website for information on oyster aquaculture.

Gulf Shrimp

The warm waters of the Gulf of Mexico are ideal habitat for shrimp, which are an essential part of Louisiana cuisine and an important source of revenue. Pink shrimp are a Louisiana specialty most abundant in the spring season. These small, tender shrimp are sold fresh, with heads on. They have thin, almost transparent shells; a delicate texture; and sweet flavor. White and brown Gulf shrimp are available year-round; most are deheaded and frozen for commercial sale.

Blue Crabs, Hard and Soft

Like Gulf oysters, Gulf blue crabs are considered inferior to those of the Chesapeake Bay. Nonetheless, Gulf crabs are more plentiful and larger, and their harvest is more dependable. Most Gulf crab is processed into pasteurized, packaged crab meat. Live crabs are sold locally and, in the winter, shipped to crab houses in the north.

At one time Louisiana surpassed the Chesapeake Bay in soft-shell crab production. However, after Hurricane Katrina destroyed the region's seafood pounds, more than one-third of the region's producers left the industry, which has yet to recover. Virtually all Louisiana soft-shells are sold cleaned and frozen.

Alligator Meat

Nationwide demand for alligator meat began in the 1980s with the promotion of Cajun cuisine. Although wild alligators were protected, 'gator farms provided a sustainable source. Today alligator tail meat is sold frozen for use in soups; gumbos; fried preparations; and marinated, grilled "gator-on-a-stick," popular at fairs and other outdoor events.

Crawfish

The small, lobsterlike creatures Louisianans call *crawfish* are correctly known as *crayfish* and are marketed under both names. In Louisiana these crustaceans are also affectionately called *crawdaddies* and *mudbugs*. Wild crawfish inhabit shallow, brackish water, living in ponds, estuaries, swamps, and even roadside ditches during the rainy spring season when they breed.

Through the 1970s crawfishing was a cottage industry. Live crawfish were a local specialty, rarely transported out of the region. Like alligator, in the 1980s crawfish became a hot item served in trendy restaurants throughout the country. In response, Louisiana rice farms began using rice impoundments to produce both rice and crawfish. The early success of these pioneer rice/crawfish farmers led to others exclusively farming crawfish.

Outside Louisiana it's still difficult to obtain live crawfish because they're highly perishable. Although frozen wholecooked crawfish are available, their best use is as a garnish. Cleaned cooked crawfish tails with fat are the most cost-effective frozen product, having no waste and needing only reheating before serving.

Gulf Finfish

Fishing fleets from Louisiana, Alabama, Mississippi, and eastern Texas range far out into deep water to harvest a variety of Gulf fish. Among the most popular are pompano, speckled trout/weakfish, whiting, king mackerel, Spanish mackerel, tuna, swordfish, shark, and Gulf redfish or red drum, an overfished species that is slowly recovering. More than twelve types of snapper and fourteen types of grouper lead the fishery. In addition, aquaculture of both saltwater and freshwater fish is an important industry. Of the many fish varieties farm raised in Louisiana, tilapia, hybrid striped bass, and catfish are most important.

■ NEW ORLEANS FOOD □ CULTURE AND CUISINE ■

Thus far we've discussed Louisiana cooking in general and the Creole and Cajun subcuisines in particular. Now let's look at the food culture and cooking of the region's premier city.

Well into the 1800s New Orleans food was Creole food. Although American governance brought Plantation South cuisine and late 19th century immigration added Italian touches to the city's cooking, the food in both homes and restaurants was largely prepared by Creole cooks. Indeed, many Creole signature dishes were created by restaurant chefs.

New Orleans has been a well-known restaurant town since 1791, when the Café des Émigrés opened to serve French refugees fleeing the Haitian slave revolts. Hundreds of bars, cafés, and restaurants opened in the following decades, serving both classic French and Creole cuisines. In the 1830s, after Louisiana became part of America, the newly constructed St. Charles and St. Louis Hotels were considered best in the nation for dining. In 1840 Antoine Alciatore opened Antoine's, the famous restaurant where Oysters Rockefeller (p. 257) and Pompano en Papillote (pp. 259, 272) were invented.

Food markets are among the most vivid expressions of a region's food culture and cuisine. New Orleans's French Market is no exception. A popular tourist attraction as well as a thriving commercial center, the French Market on Decatur Street is a fixture of New Orleans life. At the heart of today's French Market is the Café du Monde, world famous for its **café au lait,** strong chicory coffee with hot milk, and **beignets** (bane-YAY), or French doughnuts. The Farmer's Market offers a cornucopia of local, seasonal produce. Scores of shops selling meats, seafood, produce, and specialty groceries are frequented by local cooks and restaurant chefs. The Flea Market offers a wide range of trash and treasures, and the Cuisine Market features prepared foods such as hot sauces, sandwiches, and 'gator on a stick.

A must-try New Orleans specialty is the **po'boy** sandwich, a hollowed baguette filled with fried seafood, hot roast beef, meatballs, or Italian cold cuts. Italian meats and cheeses also fill the **muffaletta,** a round loaf garnished with olive salad. New Orleans sandwiches are listed and described on this book's companion website.

Louisianans are always ready to have a good time, and New Orleans is party central. In the city's famous French Quarter, hundreds of clubs, theaters, music halls, bars, and restaurants throb with excitement 24 hours a day, 365 days a year, catering not only to tourists but also to natives. In late winter New Orleans hosts the biggest party of all.

Mardi Gras

Mardi Gras—literally, "Fat Tuesday"—is the grand finale of Carnival, a monthlong festival that begins on January 6, the Christian holiday of Epiphany. For more information on the origin of Mardi Gras, refer to this book's companion website. Although other Louisiana towns and cities observe Mardi Gras and plan festivities, New Orleans is known for the largest and wildest season. During Carnival, New Orleans residents host and attend a lengthy round of formal and casual parties. New Orleans Mardi Gras organizations, called krewes, sponsor exclusive costume balls that include elaborate buffet suppers typically served at midnight (Figure 6.16). However, ordinary citizens host simpler, more casual parties in their homes.

Menus served during Carnival and on Mardi Gras vary from place to place and event to event, depending on the background of the host and the budget of the party. At a Mardi Gras

FIGURE 6.16

Members of a traditional New Orleans krewe ride elaborate floats and dance in the streets during a Mardi Gras parade. Natalia Bratslavsky © Shutterstock

ball you're as likely to be served red beans 'n' rice as an expensive seafood gumbo or pompano in champagne cream. One dish stands alone as the indispensable Mardi Gras food: the Louisiana king's cake appears at virtually every Mardi Gras dinner. Sweet, buttery brioche dough is baked in a ring shape, then decorated with colored sugar in the Mardi Gras colors: purple, green, and gold. Hidden inside the cake is a prize, traditionally a tiny ceramic figure or a dry bean. The diner who finds the prize in his or her slice is crowned king or queen of the party and must throw another party the next night.

Katrina and Rita

No treatment of Louisiana cuisine is complete without a discussion of the hurricanes that devastated southern Louisiana in 2005. Since its founding, New Orleans has been in a precarious position. As it expanded, levees created large neighborhoods situated below sea level, and New Orleans became more and more vulnerable to the effect of storms. Moreover, hundreds of dredging and drainage projects by the U.S. Army Corps of Engineers had interfered with the delta's natural renewal processes, compromising the wetlands and barrier islands that had previously protected the area.

It was only a matter of time before a large tropical storm struck New Orleans. On August 29, 2005, Hurricane Katrina made landfall on the Gulf Coast. Under pressure from rainwater and storm surge, several levees failed and New Orleans was inundated with water. Between Katrina and, less than a month later, Hurricane Rita, 80 percent of the city was flooded.

As a result of the hurricanes, more than 60 percent of New Orleans's residents fled. A high proportion were African-Americans, including most of the city's foodservice workers. Although the French Quarter and Garden District, where many of New Orleans's great restaurants are located, survived the hurricanes physically unscathed, most of the city's restaurants lost scores of valuable employees. Without professional cooks the future of New Orleans restaurants—the vanguard of Louisiana cuisine—looked bleak.

In addition to their human toll, the storms profoundly affected the Louisiana seafood industry by harming the region's ecology. The storm surge deposited enormous amounts of silt on the region's oyster beds, smothering the sedentary bivalves and destroying two-thirds of the 2005 oyster harvest. Boats, docks, packinghouses, and seafood impoundments were destroyed by high winds and crashing waves.

For the Louisiana seafood industry, the slow recovery is being hampered by reconstruction. For years the Mississippi Delta had been suffering continual loss of seafood breeding habitat due to agricultural and refinery pollution, and to erosion eating away at the wetlands at a rate of 15,000 acres per year. Hurricanes Katrina and Rita destroyed 70 additional square miles of this crucial spawning ground. However, the dredging and levee reconstruction necessary to rebuild New Orleans is working against nature, preventing the Mississippi from creating new land that could protect the wetlands and their marine inhabitants.

The Macondo Blowout

Only 5 years after hurricanes devastated southern Louisiana, yet another disaster injured the region's economy and may have long-term effects on its fishing industry. On April 20, 2010, the Deepwater Horizon drilling rig in the Gulf of Mexico, about 40 miles off the Louisiana coast, exploded due to a blowout of the Macondo underwater oil well. Crude oil gushed from the well for 3 months, contaminating much of the Gulf's water and the Louisiana shoreline and wetlands. Dispersants used in the cleanup effort constituted an additional contaminant.

The oil spill instigated temporary closure of Gulf fisheries, which reopened after testing deemed Gulf seafood safe for consumption. To date the effects of the Macondo blowout on the region's seafood and migratory fowl are unknown.

▪ THE FUTURE OF ▫ LOUISIANA CUISINE

Modern Louisiana cuisine began in the 1980s when Chef Paul Prudhomme and other contemporary chefs began creating new versions of classic Cajun dishes and fusing the Cajun and Creole styles. Dishes such as Blackened Redfish (p. 276) and Cajun popcorn crawfish (batter-fried crawfish tails) (p. 257) belong to this relatively new cuisine style.

▢ ELEMENTS OF LOUISIANA CUISINE

FOUNDATION FOODS

principal starches: rice, yeasted wheat breads

principal proteins: shellfish, fish, pork, poultry

principal produce: European and indigenous fruits and vegetables, okra, mirliton

FAVORED SEASONINGS: brown roux, "holy trinity," filé powder, smoked seasoning meats, cayenne powder, bottled hot sauce, all European herbs, many spices

PRINCIPAL COOKING MEDIA: lard, butter, olive oil, stock

PRIMARY COOKING METHODS: stewing, sautéing, pan-frying, braising

FOOD ATTITUDES: strong food culture, culinary liberals

After the Vietnam War, thousands of Vietnamese refugees settled in southwestern Louisiana, primarily to work in the seafood industry. During the next two decades many more followed. By the end of the 20th century, only two generations after arrival, the beginnings of a fusion cuisine emerged. Today southwestern Louisiana and Baton Rouge feature food shops and restaurants offering Chinese, Vietnamese, and Louisiana Cajun dishes on the same menu. Taking the obvious next step, Asian cooks began fusing the two cuisines, creating dishes such as crawfish spring rolls and "dirty" fried rice. As in other regions, in Louisiana the mixing of Asian and local regional cooking likely will continue to produce interesting dishes and may eventually give birth to a microcuisine.

FACTOR 4
Asian immigrants create Cajun-Asian fusion cuisine.

After Katrina, the reopening of New Orleans's foodservice operations happened much faster than many projected. Though it took several years for New Orleans fine-dining restaurants to reach pre-Katrina levels of staffing and sales, by 2007 more than half were back in business.

As a result of reconstruction, Louisiana is now welcoming yet another wave of immigrants with a strong food culture and a vibrant cuisine. The post-Katrina rebuilding of New Orleans attracted a large number of Mexican and South American workers. Initially employed in the building trades, many Hispanics moved on to work in newly reopening restaurants. Already young chefs are applying Latin American ingredients and techniques to traditional dishes. Because Louisianans are culinary liberals and welcome new influences, we're likely to see Latin-Louisiana fusion dishes on formal and casual menus.

Because the rebuilding of Gulf Coast communities has been slow and the area suffered a second setback after the Macondo oil spill, in many places the return to economic viability has not yet occurred. A thriving economy is typically required to push a cuisine forward. Thus, the continuing evolution of Louisiana cuisine awaits full recovery of the tourism and seafood industries. With a strong food culture and the collective will to succeed, the citizens of Louisiana will surely overcome their current challenges and, once again, focus their attention and creativity on food.

☐ TABLE 6.1 LOUISIANA DEFINING DISHES

ITEM NAME	HISTORY	DOMINANT INGREDIENTS AND METHOD	OTHER
CRAWFISH BISQUE WITH STUFFED HEADS	Creole cooks adapted the classic French *bisque d'ecrevisses* (bisk day-cray-VEECE) to the lustier taste buds of the New World.	Crawfish are simmered in classic French courtbouillon and the tail meat is removed and reserved. A few crawfish heads are reserved and the remaining shells are crushed and simmered in the courtbouillon to make a strong, sultry stock which is thickened with rice, puréed with most of the tail meat, and enriched with cream.	The reserved heads are stuffed with a spicy forcemeat of crawfish tails and bread crumbs and are floated in the soup as a garnish.
BAKED TOPPED OYSTERS	Best known of this genre, Oysters Rockefeller was created in 1899 by Jules Alciatore, chef/owner of Antoine's in New Orleans, who proclaimed it to be "rich as Rockefeller." Antoine's signature recipe is still a closely guarded secret.	Oysters on the half shell are napped with a thick sauce and baked until the sauce is bubbly and the oysters heated through. *Oysters Rockefeller* features a thick, bright green, anise-scented puréed herb topping; most recipes add spinach for its color. *Oysters Bienville* (bee-ahn-VEE) are topped with a thick, creamy seafood velouté with shallots, white wine, egg yolk liaison, and chopped shrimp *Oysters Roffignac* (row-feen-YAH) are topped with a thick red wine/tomato/mushroom seafood velouté. *Oysters Broussard* (brew-SAHR) are topped with a creamy mixture of chopped artichoke hearts, mushrooms, ham, and crab meat, and Parmesan.	Oysters are traditionally baked and presented on a bed of rock salt to prevent tipping and hold in heat.
SHRIMP RÉMOULADE	Creole cooks jazz up sauce rémoulade by adding spicy, grainy Creole mustard; cayenne powder, scallions; celery; and ketchup.	Poached, chilled, peeled Gulf shrimp are tossed with this robust sauce and served on a bed of shredded lettuce.	Shrimp rémoulade may be served in a steamed, hollowed, chilled artichoke or stuffed into a hollowed ripe tomato or avocado half.
OYSTERS AND ARTICHOKES	A classic Creole combination, gratin of oysters and artichokes was a specialty of Corinne Dunbar's restaurant in New Orleans.	Options include a creamy puréed soup; a cream-enriched, crumb-topped gratin; and a hot, cream sauce–based dip served with artichoke leaves.	May also be used in a cold, cream cheese–based spread for canapés or crackers.
CRAWFISH PIE	Along with jambalaya and filé gumbo, crawfish pie is celebrated in Hank Williams's classic song "Jambalaya (On the Bayou)."	Cooked crawfish tails and crawfish fat are bound in a thick, crawfish velouté with "holy trinity" vegetables and spicy Cajun seasonings, then baked in a deep dish under a flaky crust.	
CAJUN POPCORN	Created in the early 1980s when commercially processed frozen crawfish tails became widely available, these crunchy tidbits became wildly popular.	Cooked tails are coated in a thin batter spiked with hot sauce and deep-fried crisp, then served with various dipping sauces.	Creole rémoulade, mustard mayonnaise, and sauce *piquante* are favored accompaniments.
NATCHITOCHES MEAT PIES (NACK-uh-tow-chis)	Similar to empanadas, Jamaican patties, and Cornish pasties, these savory fried pies are a specialty of the town of Natchitoches in northern Louisiana.	Highly seasoned, cooked ground beef is folded into lard-enriched, half-moon-shaped pastries that are deep-fried golden brown.	Served warm or at room temperature, Natchitoches meat pies are sometimes accented with sweet-and-spicy red pepper jelly.
OKRA GUMBOS	The term *gumbo* is derived from *n'gombo*, meaning "okra" in several African languages. Soups and stews thickened with okra are the original gumbos brought to Louisiaina by slaves imported directly from Africa or via the Lowcountry.	*Seafood Okra Gumbo:* #4 roux, quartered in-shell crabs, shrimp, oysters, tomatoes, and optional tasso or ham. *Chicken and Shrimp Okra Gumbo:* #3 roux, chicken legs, tomatoes, shrimp, and optional tasso or ham. *Chicken and Tasso Okra Gumbo:* #3 roux, chicken legs, and tasso ham. *Duck and Oyster Okra Gumbo:* #3 roux, domestic or wild duck legs, and oysters.	Okra gumbo is never seasoned with filé.

(continued)

☐ TABLE 6.1 LOUISIANA DEFINING DISHES *(continued)*

ITEM NAME	HISTORY	DOMINANT INGREDIENTS AND METHOD	OTHER
FILÉ GUMBOS	When okra was not available, Louisiana cooks substituted filé, or ground dried sassafras leaves. Filé thickens similarly to okra and adds a distinctive flavor favored by Cajun cooks.	*Duck and Andouille Sausage Filé Gumbo:* #2 roux, wild or domestic duck legs, andouille sausage slices, and tomatoes. *Rabbit, Squirrel, and Crawfish Filé Gumbo:* #3 roux, rabbit pieces, squirrel pieces, whole crawfish, tomatoes, and optional tasso or ham. *Duck and Oyster Filé Gumbo:* #3 roux, wild or domestic duck, and oysters.	Filé must be added to gumbo at the last minute and should not cook. A dish or shaker of filé is placed on the table for diners to add according to taste.
MISCELLANEOUS GUMBOS	Some gumbos defy categorization.	*Fish and Dried Shrimp Gumbo:* #3 roux, reconstituted dried shrimp, and firm fillets of freshwater fish. *Gumbo z'Herbes:* a combination of seven or more greens and herbs simmered together; #3 roux or no roux; okra or filé; ham bone or meatless.	
ÉTOUFFÉE (ay-too-FAY)	From the French verb *étouffer*, meaning "to smother," étouffée is a dish in which food is cooked in a thick sauce.	A Louisiana étouffée is smothered in sauce thickened with brown roux. Foods commonly étoufféed include shrimp, crawfish, rabbit, frog legs, 'gator, pork, and chicken. Classic étouffée contains no tomato.	Étouffée is important in Cajun cuisine.
COURTBOUILLON (COO-be-yong)	Louisiana cooks transformed the French poaching liquid based on wine, water, and mirepoix into a hearty sauce.	Fish fillets, fish steaks, or whole fish are browned in lard and smothered in the thick, tomato-enriched brown sauce. Gulf redfish, red snapper, and red drum are popular choices.	*Courtbouillon* may be served over rice but is commonly accompanied by hot Creole French bread instead.
SAUCE *PIQUANTE* (pee-KAHNT)	Cajuns made Louisiana Creole sauce spicy-hot with fresh or dried chile and sometimes bottled hot sauce.	Foods prepared with sauce *piquante* include chicken, squirrel, and frog legs. Choice of chile includes fresh long green chiles, fresh Tabasco chiles, hot wax peppers, fresh red or green cayenne chiles, or cayenne pepper.	
SHRIMP CREOLE	With many interpretations, this dish has become a part of America's national cuisine.	Simple versions are nothing more than shrimp simmered in a thick, slightly sweet tomato sauce with "holy trinity" vegetables. More complex versions add diced bacon or tasso ham, chile in various guises, and even okra. Cajun cooks make a darker, more sultry sauce that begins with a medium-brown roux and gains flavor from shellfish stock, making it actually a form of étouffée or piquante. Creoles often omit the roux for a lighter, brighter fresh tomato taste.	Shrimp Creole is always served over plain steamed white rice.
CRAWFISH BOIL	Like the New England clambake, the Louisiana crawfish boil is a legacy of the region's Native Americans.	A proper boil includes new potatoes, boiling onions, corn on the cob, and sometimes links of smoked sausage. The foods are boiled in salt water flavored with whole garlic cloves, celery, lemon, and "seafood boil" (a mixture of bay leaves, whole spices, and dried chiles).	Some Cajuns dump ice into the boil when it is just finished to "drive the seasoning into the mudbugs." The crawfish are immediately drained before they get cold.
JAMBALAYA	True to its original French/African name, "jambon à la ya-ya" (ham in the style of rice), jambalaya must include a smoked pork product in rice cooked by the pilaf method. It is not a dish of rice topped with sauce, often found in restaurants outside the region, nor is jambalaya properly made by mixing sauced main ingredients with separately cooked white rice.	Long-grain white rice is sautéed in the fat rendered from bacon, ham, or sausage and simmered in stock with various other ingredients. The Louisiana "holy trinity" of aromatic vegetables is almost always present; tomatoes are popular but not always included. Jambalayas may feature a single main ingredient, as in chicken jambalaya, or a mixture of ingredients. Seafood jambalaya is made with ham, shrimp, crawfish tails, crab meat, and oysters. Meats, poultry, and seafood are commonly mixed together in the same jambalaya.	Turning out a perfect jambalaya for restaurant service is as difficult as turning out a perfect risotto, requiring proper preparation, skill, and timing.

TABLE 6.1 LOUISIANA DEFINING DISHES (continued)

ITEM NAME	HISTORY	DOMINANT INGREDIENTS AND METHOD	OTHER
POMPANO EN PAPILLOTE	Created at Antoine's, this take on the classic French papillote teams pompano fillets and crab meat with Creole seasonings and scallions.	Baked in a parchment pouch, the dish is presented all puffed and brown before the diner, opened by the server, and then napped with a champagne cream velouté.	
BLACKENED REDFISH	Not a traditional dish, but rather a 1980s creation of Chef Paul Prudhomme, "blackened" redfish was Prudhomme's attempt at reproducing in his restaurant the taste of his family's highly seasoned wood-fire cooking. Soon blackened dishes could be found on the menus of mainstream American restaurants. Today the craze for blackening has abated, but blackened foods continue to represent Cajun cooking in the minds of most Americans.	Prudhomme's blackening method involves heating a cast-iron skillet white-hot, seasoning the fish fillets with a dry spice mixture, dipping them in melted butter, and searing them almost black. The method then spread, first to other fish and then to chicken, pork, and steaks.	In the 1990s, a handful of New Orleans chefs were arrested and prosecuted by U.S. Fish and Wildlife officers for serving blackened redfish in their restaurants. Gulf redfish had been placed on the endangered species list and banned from harvest because of overfishing to meet the demand in restaurants throughout the United States.
FROG LEGS	Accustomed to eating frog legs in France, Louisiana colonists took advantage of the region's abundant supply of indigenous frogs.	Dredged in seasoned flour and deep-fried, frog legs may be accompanied by a Creole rémoulade or lemon wedges for a classic appetizer.	Sautéed and served in a parsley lemon butter sauce in the French manner, or braised in sauce *piquante*, they make an unusual entrée.
'GATOR	Alligator was a wild-caught subsistence food for Cajuns that had little following among modern Creole cooks until the 1970s, when Louisiana new-wave chefs embraced it as an ingredient with historic roots.	'Gator tail can be sliced into steaks, tenderized, and then grilled or pan-fried. Alternatively it may be cubed, breaded, and deep-fried, or simmered in a sauce.	Threaded onto skewers, cubed 'gator is marinated and grilled. Sold as "'gator on a stick," it is a favorite street food at fairs and other outdoor events.
CHICKEN ROCHAMBEAU (row-sham-BOW)	This elaborate dish is a classic example of Creole embellishment.	Holland rusks are napped with a thick, chicken stock–based mushroom velouté and then topped with a sautéed boneless chicken breast; the chicken is then napped with sauce béarnaise.	
GRILLADES 'N' GRITS	Despite the French name, Louisiana *grillades* are not grilled; they're braised. This dish is eaten for breakfast by Cajuns and brunch by Creoles.	Grillades simmers veal or baby beef cutlets in a spicy "holy trinity" tomato sauce. The meat and sauce are served on a bed of white or yellow grits.	Though traditional for morning, this dish is complex and substantial enough to stand as a dinner entrée accompanied by a salad or side vegetable.
RICE "DRESSINGS" OF MANY COLORS	In Louisiana, a dressing is a rice pilaf side dish that includes some form of meat, poultry, or seafood. Dressings are classified by color.	Red rice is flavored and colored with tomato sauce, green rice with fresh herbs, and yellow rice with saffron; dirty rice becomes beige with brown flecks because it is cooked with poultry livers and gizzards.	Rice dressings are often stuffed into vegetables or poultry.
STUFFED VEGETABLES/ PIROGUES (PEE-rowges)	As an appetizer, a fancy side dish, or the entrée of a thrifty meal, stuffed vegetables are part of Cajun, Creole, and Louisiana Italian cuisines.	Stuffings include rice dressings and bread crumb mixtures using white bread and/or cornbread. Flavorings include tasso ham, andouille, Italian sausage, seafood, cheese, "holy trinity" vegetables, and fresh herbs. A variety of sauces, such as tomato sauce, cream veloutés, or warm egg emulsions, may accompany stuffed vegetables.	Vegetables to be stuffed include artichokes, mirlitons, tomatoes, bell peppers, cabbage leaves, eggplants, and squashes. Cajuns call elongated-shaped stuffed vegetables, such as zucchini and eggplant, *pirogues* or "canoes."
MAQUECHOUX (MOCK-shoo)	Literally "fake cabbage," this summer-season corn dish uses the Cajun technique of repeated caramelization to produce a rich and creamy corn dish with a haunting, bittersweet taste.	Corn kernels, poultry stock, butter, Cajun seasonings, and "holy trinity" vegetables are simmered until dry and are allowed to stick lightly to the pan; deglazed several times with stock and finally finished with cream, this rich preparation makes a good side dish with grilled or roasted meats or poultry.	In winter months, Cajuns use the same technique with cabbage.

(continued)

☐ TABLE 6.1 LOUISIANA DEFINING DISHES *(continued)*

ITEM NAME	HISTORY	DOMINANT INGREDIENTS AND METHOD	OTHER
BOUCHERIE (boo-shair-EE) **DISHES**	*Boucherie* has several meanings: a hog-butchering party; a butcher shop that specializes in preserved pork products; and the entire spectrum of Cajun and Acadian preserved food dishes made from pork. *Boucherie* items may be homemade or commercial.	*Boudin (boo-DAN):* Louisiana boudin consists of pork meat and pork innards simmered in broth or water until they fall apart; mixed with cooked rice and seasoned with salt, black pepper, and cayenne pepper, the meat is packed into hog casings and poached. *Boudin Blanc (White Boudin):* Creamy chicken and/or veal mousseline is forced into casings and poached. *Boudin Rouge (Red Boudin):* Flavored with hog's blood, this homemade product is not sold commercially. Boudin fresh from the poaching kettle is eaten out of hand by squeezing the insides out of the tough casings. Boudin casings become palatable when fried crisp. *Fromage de Tête de Cochon* (fro-MAHG duh TETT duh ko-SHOWN): A Cajun variety of headcheese, it is made in the same basic manner as Pennsylvania Dutch headcheese, but Louisianans prefer the dish to be more highly seasoned and consisting of finely shredded meat solidified to a soft, lightly jellied spread. *Chaudin and Paunce Bourré* (show-DAN/pawns-boo-RAY): two names for Louisiana stuffed pig's stomach, like Scottish haggis without the oats. Some variations are smoked. *Pork Backbone Roast:* Rubbed with spicy seasoning and roasted, the tender meat, crispy fat, and succulent bones were the reward for a hard day's work. *Pork Backbone Stew:* Pork backbone and ribs are chopped into pieces, browned, and simmered with onions, garlic, aromatic vegetables, rich pork stock, and spicy seasonings and then served over rice.	
RED BEANS 'N' RICE	Traditional fare on Monday, New Orleans's traditional wash day, this simple bean dish simmered unattended while the housekeeper was busy doing laundry. Others say it's served on Mondays because the combination of starchy, protein-rich legumes and rich pork is good "hangover food," the perfect antidote for an excessive weekend.	Light red kidney beans are simmered with a variety of smoked pork products, almost always including andouille sausage. "Holy trinity" vegetables, bay leaf, thyme, dried and fresh chiles, and any manner of "secret seasonings" are added by each individual cook. Near the end of cooking, a splash of red wine adds depth, color, and acid balance; a handful of fresh parsley is said to counteract gas. The beans are served over pan-steamed white rice.	Red beans 'n' rice was so loved by Dixieland jazz pioneer Louis Armstrong that he signed his letters "Red beans and ricely yours, Louis."

ITEM NAME	HISTORY	DOMINANT INGREDIENTS AND METHOD	OTHER
SWEET FRIED PASTRIES	Louisiana cooking features many fried pastries, most enjoyed as breakfast foods.	*Beignets* (bane-YAY): Light, fluffy, diamond-shaped pillows of fried dough are dusted with confectioner's sugar and served with chicory-scented café au lait. *Croquesignoles* (croak-seen-YOLE): These cakelike, rectangular doughnuts served with confectioner's sugar or a sugar glaze, are a Cajun specialty. *Calas* (CALL-ah): Crisp round fritters are made from a sweetened, spiced wheat-flour batter blended with cooked rice. This popular breakfast item or afternoon snack is served with cane syrup, honey, or jam. *Oreilles de Cochon* (oh-RAY duh co-SHOWN), "pig's ears," are thin discs of dough, slit from edge to center. When fried they curl into the shape of a pig's ear. Dusted with confectioner's sugar, they accompany coffee. *Pain Perdu* (pan pear-DOO): "lost bread"; classic French toast saves stale Creole baguette by soaking it in egg and milk seasoned with sugar, brandy, and orange flower water, then frying it crisp in clarified butter. Served with cane syrup, jam, and/or clotted cream, *pain perdu* is a breakfast and brunch staple.	
CORNMEAL DISHES	Cornmeal mush, cornmeal simmered with water and salt, became an African, Caribbean, and African-American staple starch as early as 1600.	*Moussa* (MOOSE-uh) is the Louisiana term for savory cornmeal mush that often replaces rice as a bed for sauced dishes. *Coush-Coush* (KOOSH-koosh): Corrupted from *couscous*, the North African word for tiny wheat pasta pellets, Louisiana coush-coush is cornmeal mush "refried," or repeatedly browned and flipped in bacon drippings, lard, or butter. Served with milk and cane syrup or jam, coush-coush is a traditional Cajun breakfast or supper dish.	In addition, Louisiana cooks prepare all manner of cornmeal and corn-flour dishes, including pure or sweetened cornbread and corn-flour–breaded fried foods.
BANANAS FOSTER	Invented at Brennan's restaurant in honor of restaurant patron Dick Foster.	This tableside spectacle calls for halved bananas to be caramelized in brown sugar and butter and then flambéed with rum and banana liqueur. The hot bananas and sauce are served over vanilla ice cream.	It has become a popular tableside presentation throughout the United States.
CREOLE/CAJUN BREAD PUDDING	With perishable French-style breads a staple of the cuisine, Louisiana cooking is sure to feature bread pudding as a ubiquitous dessert.	Cajun and Creole cooks have various recipes. Some include raisins and/or pecans; some are made with white sugar and some with brown; some are served warm and others chilled.	Louisiana bread puddings are often teamed with a Bourbon whiskey sauce.
GÂTEAU DE SYROP (gah-toe duh see-ROW)	Louisiana cooks make many variations of this classic dessert.	Lightly spiced white cake is sweetened with cane syrup; the layers may have raisins and nuts incorporated into them or the layers may be split and filled with a raisin-nut icing.	Elaborate gâteaux are frosted with caramel icing; plain, tea-cake versions are simply dusted with confectioner's sugar or drizzled with a light vanilla glaze.
KING'S CAKE	A must for Carnival and Mardi Gras, this ring-shaped cake is decorated with colored sugar in the traditional colors of purple, green, and gold.	Often served plain, it also may be accompanied by a vanilla or liqueur-scented custard sauce.	A dry bean or tiny ceramic "baby Jesus" figurine is baked into the dough and found by a lucky diner, who is expected to throw a party the next night and serve another king's cake in order to perpetuate the progression of parties.
VOODOO CAKE	This dessert was popularized by New Orleans restaurants in the 1990s.	Dense, bittersweet chocolate cake is frosted with a chocolate-molasses glaze.	The "voodoo" element is added by sticking the cake with caramel "needles," a reference to voodoo practitioners' practice of sticking needles into dolls representing their victims.

■ ☐ ■ STUDY QUESTIONS

1. Describe the climate and topography of Louisiana's delta region and upland/inland area. Explain how Louisiana's delta area was formed. Explain how the agriculture of these two areas differs.

2. List the seven roots of Louisiana cuisine, and describe several ingredients and/or techniques contributed by each.

3. Discuss the impact of French food culture on Louisiana foodways.

4. Recount the history of Louisiana Creoles and describe their cuisine. Recount the history of Louisiana Cajuns and describe their cuisine. Compare and contrast Creole and Cajun cooking.

5. Compare and contrast the similarities and differences between Louisiana cooking and the cooking of the Plantation South; account for the differences.

6. List the four categories of Louisiana brown roux. Demonstrate your understanding of its use and preparation:

    a. What three characteristics does brown roux impart to the dish in which it is used?
    b. What criteria do Louisiana cooks use in deciding which category of brown roux to use in a dish?
    c. What qualities should you look for in a cooking vessel in which to prepare brown roux?
    d. How long should it take a person of beginning skill level to prepare brown roux? An experienced Creole or Cajun cook?
    e. When should you stop the cooking of a brown roux, and how is it done?

7. What is the "holy trinity" of Louisiana cooking? How does it differ from the French *mirepoix*? Why does it differ?

8. Explain flavor layering: How is it done and why? Explain ingredient staging: How is it done and why?

9. List and describe the two types of gumbo. List four characteristics that virtually all gumbos have in common.

10. List three types of fish or shellfish harvested along the Louisiana Gulf Coast. For each, describe a Louisiana cuisine dish made from it.

11. List three types of fish, shellfish, or amphibians harvested in Louisiana's swamps and bayous. For each, describe a Louisiana cuisine dish made from it.

12. Using the information in this chapter and your imagination, plan two four-course special-occasion menus: one in the Creole style and the other in the Cajun style.

Crawfish Bisque
with Stuffed Crawfish Heads and Creole Baguette

yield: 1 (8-fl.-oz.) appetizer serving
(multiply × 4 for classroom turnout; adjust equipment sizes accordingly)

MASTER RECIPE

production		costing only
3	Stuffed Crawfish Heads	1/4 recipe
1	3" length Creole Baguette	1/8 recipe
1 c.	Crawfish Bisque	1/4 recipe
1	cocktail napkin or 8" doily	1 each
1 small sprig	curly parsley	1/40 bunch a.p.

service turnout:
1. Place the Stuffed Crawfish Heads and the Creole Baguette section on a sizzle pan and heat for 3 to 4 minutes in a 400°F oven.
2. Ladle the Crawfish Bisque into a small saucepan and heat to just under the boil. Thin with water if necessary.
3. Plate the dish:
   a. Place a cocktail napkin on a 10" underliner plate.
   b. Ladle the bisque into a hot 8" soup plate and place it on the underliner plate.
   c. Float the stuffed crawfish heads* in a spoke pattern in the center of the soup.
   d. Pull the parsley into 4 tiny leaflets. Place one in the center of the heads and the rest between them.
   e. Serve the baguette in a napkin-lined basket or on a side plate.

*Depending on the depth of the soup plate, you may need to place a toasted bread crouton under the Stuffed Crawfish Heads so they remain visible.

COMPONENT RECIPE
CRAWFISH DRESSING

yield: 1 c.

production		costing only
1 Tbsp.	butter	1/2 oz.
1/8 c.	peeled, minced celery	1/40 head a.p.
1/8 c.	minced fresh knob onion or white part of scallion	3/4 oz. a.p.
1/8 c.	minced green bell pepper	1 oz. a.p.
1/2 tsp.	minced garlic	1/9 oz. a.p.
pinch	cayenne powder	1/16 oz.
pinch	fine-ground white pepper	1/16 oz.
1/2 c.	Butter-Toasted Bread Crumbs	1/10 recipe
1/2 c.	cooked crawfish tails (from Crawfish Bisque recipe)	n/c
tt	fresh lemon juice	1/8 [90 ct.] lemon
±1/4 c.	crawfish stock (from Crawfish Bisque recipe)	n/c
tt	fine salt, optional	1/16 oz.

preparation:
1. Heat the butter in a small sauté pan, then add the celery, onion, green bell peppers, garlic, cayenne, and white pepper. Sweat over low heat until the vegetables soften.
2. Chop the cooked crawfish tails fine.
3. Mix the Butter-Toasted Bread Crumbs and crawfish into the sweated vegetables. Season with lemon juice and moisten with enough stock to make a moist, but not wet dressing.
4. Taste and season with salt if needed.

holding: open-pan cool and immediately refrigerate in a freshly sanitized, covered container up to 3 days

Twisting the tail off the crawfish body.

COMPONENT RECIPE
STUFFED CRAWFISH HEADS

yield: 12 heads

production		costing only
12	cooked crawfish bodies (from Crawfish Bisque recipe)	n/c
1 c.	Crawfish Dressing	1 recipe

preparation:
1. Clean the crawfish bodies:
   a. Pull the legs and feelers off one of the crawfish bodies and discard them.
   b. Pry open the exterior body shell and remove the leg joints and inner cartilage.
   c. Use the small end of a Parisienne scoop to clean out the innards.
   d. Repeat with the remaining bodies to make 12 hollow crawfish "heads."
   e. Rinse the "heads" under cool water and blot them dry with paper towels, paying particular attention to the interiors.
2. Stuff the crawfish heads with Crawfish Dressing.

holding: refrigerate in a freshly sanitized, covered container up to 2 days; freeze up to 3 months

Emptying the crawfish body.

Cleaning out the innards with a scoop.

Stuffing the crawfish with dressing.

COMPONENT RECIPE

CRAWFISH BISQUE

yield: 2 pt.

production		costing only
2 lb.	large live crawfish or frozen whole crawfish	2 lb.
1 Tbsp.	whole-spice seafood boil, in cheesecloth sachet	1/8 oz.
1 c.	white wine	8 fl. oz.
3 c.	water	n/c
4 Tbsp.	butter	2 oz.
1/2 c.	minced yellow onion	2 1/2 oz. a.p.
1/4 c.	peeled, minced celery	1/20 bunch a.p.
3 Tbsp.	natural long-grain white rice	1 1/2 oz.
2 tsp.	tomato paste	1/3 fl. oz.
1/2 c.	half-and-half	4 fl. oz.
tt	kosher salt	1/16 oz.
tt	fine-ground white pepper	1/16 oz.
1/4 c.	Madeira	2 fl. oz.

preparation:

1. Cook the crawfish:
   a. Rinse the crawfish under cool running water.
   b. Place the seafood boil, white wine, and 1 1/2 c. water in a nonreactive saucepan and bring to the boil.
   c. Add the crawfish and cover the pan. Boil the crawfish 1 minute, stir, re-cover the pan, and boil 2 minutes longer. (If using frozen crawfish, boil 1 minute only.)
   d. Cool the crawfish in their liquid.
2. Shell the crawfish:
   a. Remove the crawfish from the cooking liquid and reserve the liquid in the pan.
   b. Working over a bowl to catch the juices, bend a crawfish backward and twist its tail until the tail and body separate.
   c. Pull the tail meat out of the shell and place it in another bowl.
   d. Repeat until all the crawfish are shelled.
   e. Reserve 12 of the best-looking crawfish bodies for the Stuffed Crawfish Heads, and reserve 1/2 c. cooked crawfish tails for the Crawfish Dressing.
   f. Refrigerate the remaining crawfish tails and retain the cooking liquid, crawfish juices, and crawfish fat.

3. Make crawfish stock:
   a. Place the crawfish shells in a food processor fitted with the metal blade and pulse them a few times to break them up. Return the broken shells to the cooking liquid.
   b. Add the reserved crawfish juices and fat to the cooking liquid along with 1 1/2 c. water. Press down on the shells to submerge them. Bring the mixture to the simmer, partially cover, and cook 20 minutes.
   c. Strain the stock, pushing down on the solids to extract as much liquid as possible. You should have a little more than 1 qt. crawfish stock.
   d. Reserve 1/2 c. crawfish stock for the Crawfish Dressing.
4. Make the bisque:
   a. Rinse out the saucepan and add the butter, onion, and celery. Sweat over low heat until soft.
   b. Add the remaining crawfish stock and the rice. Cover and simmer 40 minutes, stirring occasionally, until the rice is very soft.
   c. Strain the soup, retaining the liquid and placing the solids in a blender. Add 1 c. of the liquid to the blender along with the remaining cooked tail meat.
   d. Purée the mixture very smooth, adding more of the liquid if necessary.
   e. Scrape the purée back into the saucepan.
   f. Whirl the remaining liquid in the blender to clean out every last bit of purée. Add the liquid to the saucepan. (If the purée seems thin, reduce it by boiling, but don't allow the bottom to scorch.)
   g. Whisk the tomato paste and half-and-half into the crawfish purée. Heat to just under the boil.
   h. Season with salt, white pepper, and Madeira.
   i. If the bisque seems too thick, thin it with water or crawfish stock.

holding: open-pan cool and refrigerate in a freshly sanitized, covered container up to 3 days

---

RECIPE VARIATION

Crawfish Bisque with Herbed Crouton and Crawfish Tails
Omit the Stuffed Crawfish Heads. Toast 4 baguette croutons, cool, and spread each with 1 Tbsp. composed butter flavored with lemon and fresh herbs of choice. Float the crouton in the Crawfish Bisque and top it with three cooked crawfish tails.

Creole Shrimp Rémoulade

yield: 1 (3 1/2-oz.) appetizer serving
(multiply × 4 for classroom turnout)

MASTER RECIPE

production		costing only
3 oz.	Creole Poached Gulf Shrimp	1/4 recipe
1/4 c.	Creole Rémoulade Sauce	1/4 recipe
3	small Boston lettuce leaves, washed and dried	1/6 head a.p.
5	grape tomatoes	1/6 pt. a.p.
2 tsp.	chopped fresh tarragon	1/16 bunch a.p.

service turnout:

1. Thoroughly drain the Creole Poached Gulf Shrimp and blot them dry on paper towels.
2. Place the shrimp in a small bowl and toss them with the Creole Rémoulade Sauce.
3. Plate the dish:
   a. Arrange the lettuce leaves on a cool 10" plate to make a cup-shaped liner.
   b. Mound the shrimp rémoulade in the center of the cup.
   c. Arrange the grape tomatoes around the shrimp.
   d. Sprinkle the shrimp with the tarragon.

COMPONENT RECIPE
CREOLE POACHED GULF SHRIMP AND SHRIMP GLAZE

yield: 14 oz. shrimp + 1 fl. oz. glaze

production		costing only
2 Tbsp.	whole-spice seafood boil	1/4 oz.
1/2 c.	white wine	4 fl. oz.
2 c.	water	n/c
2 tsp.	kosher salt	1/3 oz.
1 slice	lemon	1/8 [90 ct.] lemon
1	bay leaf	1/16 oz.
dash	bottled hot sauce (Tabasco or Crystal brand)	1/8 fl. oz.
1 lb.	(51–60 ct.) white Gulf shrimp, shell on	1 lb.

preparation:

1. Prepare the poaching liquid and ice-water bath:
   a. Place all of the ingredients except the shrimp in a 4-qt. nonreactive saucepan. Cover and simmer 10 minutes.
   b. Prepare an ice-water bath large enough to hold the saucepan and place it next to the stove.
2. Cook the shrimp:
   a. Bring the poaching liquid to the boil, add the shrimp, and cover the pan.
   b. When the poaching liquid returns to a brisk simmer, uncover the pan, stir once, replace the cover, and remove the pan from the heat.
   c. Allow the shrimp to steep, covered, 2 minutes.
   d. Remove the lid, place the pan in the ice-water bath, and cool the shrimp to room temperature.
3. Shell and devein the shrimp:
   a. Lift the shrimp out of the poaching liquid.
   b. Shell the shrimp. As you work, return the shells to the poaching liquid.
   c. Devein the shrimp and pack them tightly in a freshly sanitized container just large enough to hold them.
   d. Strain just enough poaching liquid over the shrimp to submerge them.
   e. Cover the container and refrigerate the shrimp.
4. Make the shrimp glaze:
   a. Cover the poaching liquid pan and simmer the liquid and shells for 15 minutes.
   b. Strain the shrimp stock, pushing firmly on the shells and then discarding them.
   c. Return the shrimp stock to the pan and bring it to a brisk simmer. Reduce the stock to a glaze, stirring constantly with a heatproof rubber spatula when it becomes thick enough to stick and scorch.
   d. Scrape the glaze into a small, freshly-sanitized container. Cool, cover, and refrigerate.

holding: refrigerate up to 3 days; glaze may be frozen up to 3 months

COMPONENT RECIPE
CREOLE RÉMOULADE SAUCE

yield: approx. 1 c.

production		costing only
2 Tbsp.	minced scallion	1/10 bunch a.p.
2 Tbsp.	peeled, minced celery	1/40 head a.p.
1 tsp.	Creole or French whole-grain mustard	1/6 fl. oz.
1 tsp.	prepared horseradish	1/6 fl. oz.
2 tsp.	coarse-chopped capers	1/6 oz.
1 Tbsp.	minced flat-leaf parsley	1/40 bunch a.p.
2 tsp.	minced tarragon	1/16 bunch a.p.
1/2 c.	mayonnaise	4 fl. oz.
2 Tbsp.	Shrimp Glaze	1 recipe
tt	fresh lemon juice	1/6 [90 ct.] lemon
tt	sugar	1/4 oz.
tt	fine-ground white pepper	1/16 oz.
tt	bottled hot sauce (Tabasco or Crystal brand)	1/16 oz.

preparation:

1. Mix all of the ingredients.
2. Cover and allow the flavors to blend, about 30 minutes.
3. Taste and adjust the seasonings.

holding: refrigerate in a freshly sanitized, covered, nonreactive container: if made with commercial mayonnaise, up to 5 days; if made with handmade mayonnaise, 24 hours only

---

RECIPE VARIATION

Cajun Crawfish Rémoulade
Replace the shrimp with cooked crawfish tails and the Shrimp Glaze with Crawfish Glaze. Add minced garlic and cayenne to the rémoulade sauce.

APPETIZERS

Frog Legs Sauce *Piquante*

yield: 1 (4 1/2-oz.) appetizer serving
(multiply × 4 for classroom turnout; adjust equipment sizes accordingly)

MASTER RECIPE

production		costing only
1/2 c.	gold-color pure olive oil	4 fl. oz. (may be reused)
2 pairs	frog legs (16–18 ct.)	4 1/2 oz. a.p.
1 Tbsp.	egg wash (1 egg + 1 Tbsp. water for 4 servings)	1 each or 2 oz.
2 tsp.	Cajun Seasoning for Seafood	1/12 recipe
as needed	flour	1 oz.
tt	fine salt	1/16 oz.
3/4 c.	Sauce *Piquante*	1/4 recipe
as needed	water, in squeeze bottle	n/c
1 sprig	curly parsley	1/20 bunch a.p.

service turnout:
1. Fry the frog legs:
   a. Pour the oil into an 8" sauté pan and place it over medium heat.
   b. Dip the frog legs in the egg wash, sprinkle them with the Cajun Seasoning for Seafood, and then dredge them in the flour.
   c. Pan-fry the frog legs about 2 minutes on each side, until crisp and golden brown. Remove to a rack set over a sheet tray, season with salt, and hold hot.
2. Heat the Sauce *Piquante:*
   a. Place the sauce in another sauté pan and add a little water.
   b. Cover and bring to the simmer.
3. Plate the dish:
   a. Spoon the sauce into the well of a hot 10" plate.
   b. Place one pair of frog legs slightly left center on the plate, and prop the other pair against it on the right.
   c. Stick the parsley sprig upright behind the frog legs.

COMPONENT RECIPE
SAUCE PIQUANTE

yield: 3 c.

production		costing only
1/4 c.	gold-color pure olive oil	2 fl. oz.
1/2 c.	fine-chopped fresh knob onion or yellow onion	3 oz. a.p.
1/4 c.	fine-chopped green bell pepper	1 1/2 oz. a.p.
1/4 c.	peeled, minced celery	1/20 bunch a.p.
1 tsp.	minced garlic	1/6 oz. a.p.
1 1/2 tsp.	cayenne powder	1/8 oz.
1 c.	hot Poultry Stock	1/16 recipe
1 qt.	vine-ripe tomato concassée	3 lb. a.p.
1/4 c.	chopped scallion	1/5 bunch a.p.
2 tsp.	tomato paste	1/3 fl. oz.
tt	kosher salt	1/16 oz.
tt	sugar	1/4 oz.

preparation:
1. Place the oil, onion, green bell pepper, and celery in a wide, nonreactive saucepan and cook over moderate heat, stirring, about 1 minute, until the vegetables soften.
2. Add the garlic and cayenne and cook 1 minute longer.
3. Stir in the hot Poultry Stock, then add the tomato, scallion, tomato paste, salt, and a little sugar. Simmer briskly about 15 minutes, until the sauce reduces to a thick nappé consistency and the flavors meld.
4. Correct the salt and sugar balance to make a tangy, spicy-hot sauce with a hint of sweetness.

holding: open-pan cool and immediately refrigerate in a freshly sanitized, covered container up to 5 days.

RECIPE VARIATIONS
'Gator Sauce *Piquante*
Replace the frog legs with 4 oz. 'gator tail cut into 1" chunks.

Shrimp Sauce *Piquante*
Replace the frog legs with 4 (16–20 ct.) white Gulf shrimp peeled but with the tails on; replace the Poultry Stock with Shrimp Stock; add the sautéed shrimp to the sauce just before serving.

Serve any *piquante* dish as an entrée by increasing the portion size accordingly, increasing the sauce to 1 1/2 c., and serving over Pan-Steamed White Rice with a green vegetable or side salad.

Creole "Barbeque" Shrimp

yield: 1 (4-oz.) appetizer serving
(multiply × 4 for classroom turnout)

MASTER RECIPE

production		costing only
1	3" length Creole Baguette	1/8 recipe
1	Shrimp Skewer for Grilling	1/4 recipe
4 Tbsp.	butter	2 oz.
2 tsp.	minced garlic	1/6 oz. a.p.
2 tsp.	cracked black pepper	1/8 oz.
2 Tbsp.	white wine	1 fl. oz.
1 Tbsp.	water	n/c
few dashes	bottled hot sauce (Tabasco or Crystal brand)	1/4 fl. oz.
1 sprig	parsley	1/20 bunch a.p.

service turnout:
1. Heat the Creole Baguette in a 400°F oven about 3 minutes, until crisp.
2. Grill the Shrimp Skewer for Grilling over high heat until just cooked through. If necessary, hold hot on a sizzle plate.
3. Make the sauce:
   a. Place 1 Tbsp. butter in an 8" sauté pan, set the pan over low heat, and add the garlic and pepper. Sauté gently until the garlic is just beginning to turn golden. Do not allow the garlic to brown.
   b. Add the wine, water, and hot sauce to the pan and bring to the simmer.
   c. Work in the remaining butter to form an emulsion.
4. Plate the dish:
   a. Push the shrimp off the skewers into the sauce. Toss to coat them thoroughly.
   b. Mound the shrimp on the left side of a warm 9" oval plate and scrape the sauce over the top.
   c. Place the baguette on the right side of the plate.
   d. Place the parsley sprig in the center.

COMPONENT RECIPE
SHRIMP SKEWERS FOR GRILLING

yield: 4 (4-oz.) skewers

production		costing only
20 pc.	(16–20 ct.) white Gulf shrimp	approx. 1 lb.
1/4 c.	gold-color pure olive oil	2 fl. oz.
tt	kosher salt	1/8 oz.
8	5" bamboo skewers (or metal skewers)	% of pkg.

preparation:
1. Rinse the shrimp under cool water and blot them dry with paper towels.
2. Fabricate the shrimp:
   a. Insert the blade of a paring knife between the belly shell of a shrimp and the flesh.
   b. Grasp the shell with your thumb and pull upward with the knife to remove the belly shell without dislodging the back shell.
   c. Place the shrimp on the work surface, shell side down. Slit the shrimp flesh down to the shell, exposing the vein.
   d. Use your fingers, foodservice tweezers, or clean needlenose pliers to pull out the vein.
   e. Repeat with the remaining shrimp.
3. Toss the shrimp with the oil and salt.
4. Thread shrimp onto a doubled skewer to make 4 even-size portions.

holding: refrigerate in a freshly sanitized, covered container up to 2 days

(a) Inserting the knife into the belly shell.

(b) Removing the belly shell.

(c) Slitting the shrimp flesh down to the back shell.

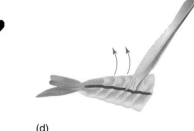

(d) Removing the vein.

RECIPE VARIATION
Traditional Baked Creole "Barbeque" Shrimp
Do not oil or skewer the shrimp. Place the shrimp in an individual gratin with all ingredients except the parsley and baguette. Bake at 400°F for 15 minutes, basting occasionally. Serve the gratin and baguette on an underplate lined with a doily or cocktail napkin and garnished with the parsley sprig.

Oysters Rockefeller

yield: 1 (5-pc.) appetizer serving
(multiply × 4 for classroom turnout)

MASTER RECIPE

production		costing only
1 1/2 c.	rock salt	% of pkg.
5	Gulf oysters	5 each
1/2 c.	Rockefeller Sauce	1/4 recipe
1	small plum tomato crown	2 oz. a.p.
1 sprig	curly parsley	1/16 bunch a.p.

service turnout:
1. Spread the rock salt evenly on an 8" round sizzle plate.
2. Open the oysters and discard the top shells. Slide the knife under the oyster meat to detach it from the bottom shells. (If you wish to reserve the oyster liquor for another use, open the oysters over a strainer set in a bowl.)
3. Press the oysters into the rock salt in a spoke pattern, leaving room for the tomato crown in the center.
4. Spoon the Rockefeller Sauce onto the oysters.
5. Bake in the top of a 400°F oven for about 5 minutes, until the sauce is hot and bubbling.
6. Plate the dish:
   a. Place a folded linen napkin on a 10" plate.
   b. Place the pan of oysters on the napkin-lined plate.
   c. Set the tomato crown in the middle of the oysters and place the parsley sprig on top.

COMPONENT RECIPE
ROCKEFELLER SAUCE

yield: 2 c.

production		costing only
10 oz.	fresh spinach leaves	10 oz.
3 oz.	scallion greens	1/3 bunch a.p.
6 sprigs	flat-leaf parsley	1/6 bunch a.p.
as needed	water	n/c
3 Tbsp.	butter	1 1/2 oz.
2 tsp.	minced garlic	1/4 oz. a.p.
1 Tbsp.	minced scallion whites	1/8 bunch a.p.
2 Tbsp.	flour	2/3 oz.
pinch	cayenne powder	1/16 oz.
1/2 c.	boiling water	n/c
1 c.	Fish Stock or Shellfish Stock	1/16 recipe
1 tsp.	anchovy paste	1/6 fl. oz.
2 tsp.	minced lemon zest	1/8 [90 ct.] lemon
tt	kosher salt	1/16 oz.
as needed	water	
1 tsp.	Pernod or anisette liqueur	1/6 fl. oz.
6 Tbsp.	butter	3 oz.
tt	fine-ground white pepper	1/16 oz.

preparation:
1. Prepare the greens purée:
   a. Devein the spinach.
   b. Wash and drain the spinach.
   c. Separately blanch, refresh, and drain the spinach, scallion greens, and parsley, immersing them in the boiling water only a second or two in order to wilt them.
   d. Squeeze the spinach dry.
   e. Blot the scallion greens and parsley dry on paper towels.
   f. Place the spinach, scallion greens, and parsley in a blender and process to a smooth purée. (If necessary, add a small amount of water to loosen the blades.)
2. Melt 3 Tbsp. butter in a small, nonreactive saucepan. Add the garlic and scallion whites, sauté a minute over low heat, then add the flour and cayenne. Cook to a blond roux over medium heat.
3. Whisk in the water and Fish Stock to make a smooth sauce. Simmer, stirring occasionally, about 10 minutes, until the sauce thickens.
4. Add the anchovy paste and lemon zest, then stir in the puréed greens and a little salt, if needed. Cook, stirring constantly, 1 to 2 minutes, until the flavors meld. This sauce should be very thick; add water only if necessary to prevent scorching.
5. Season with the Pernod and adjust the salt.
6. Remove the sauce from the heat and work in 6 Tbsp. butter to form an emulsion.
7. Season with white pepper.

holding: open-pan cool and immediately refrigerate in a freshly sanitized, covered container up to 2 days

---

RECIPE VARIATION

Oysters Rockefeller au Gratin
Place 1/4 c. Butter-Toasted Bread Crumbs in the bottom of a 6" gratin. Arrange 5 shucked oysters in the gratin and nap them with the Rockefeller Sauce. Bake 6 to 8 minutes.

Shrimp and Tasso–Stuffed Mirliton
with Sauce Aurore

yield: 1 (5-oz.) appetizer serving
(multiply × 4 for classroom turnout; adjust equipment sizes accordingly)

MASTER RECIPE

production		costing only
1 Tbsp.	melted butter	1/2 fl. oz.
1	Shrimp and Tasso–Stuffed Mirliton	1/4 recipe
4 fl. oz.	Seafood Sauce Aurore*	1/4 recipe
as needed	water, in squeeze bottle	n/c
1	Creole Poached Gulf Shrimp, p. 266	1/20 recipe
2 Tbsp.	smooth Fresh Tomato Sauce*, in squeeze bottle held in steam table	1/32 recipe

service turnout:

1. Bake the Shrimp and Tasso–Stuffed Mirliton:
   a. Brush a sizzle pan with half of the melted butter.
   b. Place the mirliton on the pan and brush the top with the remaining butter.
   c. Bake in a 400°F oven 15 minutes, until heated through and browned on top.
2. Ladle the Seafood Sauce Aurore into a small sauté pan, add a little water*, and reheat it.
3. Plate the dish:
   a. Spoon the Seafood Sauce Aurore onto a hot 10" plate.
   b. Squeeze evenly-spaced dots of Fresh Tomato Sauce on the Sauce Aurore about 1/2" in from the edge of the plate well.
   c. Drag the tip of a small knife or toothpick through the dots to create a "string of hearts" pattern.
   d. Place the mirliton in the center of the plate.
   e. Press the shrimp into the top of the mirliton.

*Make sure the two sauces are the same consistency.

COMPONENT RECIPE

SHRIMP AND TASSO–STUFFED MIRLITON

yield: 4 (5-oz.) appetizer servings

production		costing only
2 small	mirlitons	12 oz. a.p.
1 Tbsp.	butter	1/2 oz.
1/3 c.	medium-chopped red bell pepper	2 3/4 oz. a.p.
1/4 c.	fine-chopped tasso ham	1 oz.
tt	kosher salt	1/16 oz.
1/4 c.	fine-chopped scallion	1/5 bunch a.p.
1/2 c.	heavy cream	4 fl. oz.
1 c.	Butter-Toasted Bread Crumbs	1/4 recipe
6 oz.	coarse-chopped Creole Poached Gulf Shrimp, p. 266	1/2 recipe
1 Tbsp.	minced flat-leaf parsley	1/40 bunch a.p.
tt	fine-ground white pepper	1/16 oz.
1/2	egg, beaten	1/2 each or 1 oz.

preparation:

1. Cook and fabricate the mirlitons:
   a. Cut the mirlitons in half lengthwise through the narrow width so that they form a deep cup when hollowed.
   b. Place the mirlitons in a steamer pan, cut side down. Steam until tender (about 5 minutes in a pressure steamer, about 15 minutes in a stovetop steamer).
   c. Cool the mirlitons to room temperature.
   d. Remove the seeds from the mirliton halves and discard.
   e. Hollow out the mirlitons, leaving an even 3/8" shell. If necessary, cut a slice off the bottoms so that they sit upright on a flat surface.
   f. Squeeze the scooped-out mirliton flesh between paper towels to dry it, and then chop the flesh fine.
2. Make the stuffing:
   a. Heat the butter in a 10" nonstick sauté pan, add the red bell pepper and ham, and sauté over low heat about 1 minute, until softened.
   b. Add the mirliton flesh and a little salt, increase the heat to medium, and sauté until dry.
   c. Add the scallion and cream, bring to the boil, and reduce to nappé consistency.
   d. Cool the reduction to room temperature.
   e. Stir the Butter-Toasted Bread Crumbs, shrimp, and parsley into the reduction.
   f. Correct the salt and season with white pepper.
   g. Mix in enough egg to bind the stuffing.
3. Blot dry the inside of the mirliton cups and pack the stuffing into them, pressing gently to firm it. Smooth the tops into rounded mounds.

holding: refrigerate in one layer in a freshly sanitized, covered container up to 3 days

COMPONENT RECIPE
SEAFOOD SAUCE AURORE

yield: 2 c.

production		costing only
2 Tbsp.	butter	1 oz.
2 Tbsp.	minced scallion whites	1/8 bunch a.p.
pinch	cayenne pepper	1/16 oz.
1 Tbsp.	flour	1/3 oz.
1/4 c.	white wine	2 fl. oz.
3 c.	hot Shrimp Stock	3/16 recipe
1 c.	heavy cream	8 fl. oz.
2 Tbsp.	smooth Fresh Tomato Sauce	1/32 recipe
tt	kosher salt	1/16 oz.
tt	fine-ground white pepper	1/16 oz.

preparation:
1. Place the butter, scallion whites, and cayenne in a nonreactive saucepan and heat until the butter melts. Stir in the flour and make a blond roux.
2. Whisk in the wine and Shrimp Stock and simmer briskly about 10 minutes, until the sauce reaches a very light nappé consistency.
3. Add the cream and continue reducing until the sauce is a light nappé consistency once again.
4. Add enough Fresh Tomato Sauce to tint the sauce pale pink.
5. Season with salt and white pepper.
6. Strain through a fine-mesh sieve, pushing through as much solid matter as possible.

holding: open-pan cool and refrigerate in a freshly sanitized container up to 3 days

Stuffing the mirlitons.

RECIPE VARIATIONS

Shrimp and Tasso–Stuffed Squash with Sauce Aurore
Replace the mirlitons with pattypan squash or zucchini. Adjust steaming times accordingly.

Sausage-Stuffed Mirliton with Creole Tomato Sauce
Replace the shrimp and tasso with cooked, crumbled mild Italian sausage. Replace the Sauce Aurore with smooth Fresh Tomato Sauce seasoned with bottled hot sauce and brown sugar.

Pompano en Papillote

with Champagne Cream,
Pecan Rice Pilaf, Parisienne Carrots,
and Haricots Verts

yield: 1 (7-oz.) entrée serving plus accompaniments
(multiply × 4 for classroom turnout; adjust equipment sizes
accordingly)

MASTER RECIPE

production		costing only
1	Pompano Papillote	1/4 recipe
1 tsp.	melted butter	1/6 oz.
2 oz.	Parisienne-cut carrots, boiled and refreshed	4 oz. a.p.
2 oz.	haricots verts, trimmed, blanched and refreshed	2 1/4 oz. a.p.
1 Tbsp.	melted butter	1/2 oz.
tt	kosher salt	1/16 oz.
1 1/2 c.	Pecan Rice Pilaf, hot in steam table	1/4 recipe
1 bouquet	curly parsley	1/8 bunch a.p.

service turnout:

1. Place the Pompano Papillote on a sizzle pan and brush the parchment with 1 tsp. melted butter. Bake in a 400°F oven 12 minutes, until puffed and brown.
2. Place the carrots and haricots verts in a small serving dish, brush with 1 Tbsp. melted butter, season with salt, and re-heat in a microwave oven.
3. Set up for tableside service:
   a. Place the papillote on the front of a large warmed platter.
   b. Spoon the Pecan Rice Pilaf into a hot serving dish and place it on the platter behind the papillote.
   c. Place the dish of vegetables behind the papillote.
   d. Place the parsley bouquet between the vegetables and rice.
   e. Make sure the server is prepared with a hot 12" plate, a wide spatula, foodservice scissors or a sharp paring knife, and serving fork and spoon.
4. At tableside:
   a. Place the hot plate in front of the customer and present the platter.
   b. Lift the papillote onto the plate with the spatula, cut it open with the scissors or knife, and use the fork to fold open the paper.
   c. Use the fork and spoon to place the vegetables and rice in the open papillote next to the fish.

COMPONENT RECIPE
POMPANO PAPILLOTES

yield: 4 (7-oz.) entrée servings

production		costing only
1 Tbsp.	clarified butter	3/4 oz. a.p.
4	5-oz. pompano fillets, pinned and trimmed	1 1/4 lb. a.p.
1 Tbsp.	fresh lemon juice	1/6 [90 ct.] lemon
tt	kosher salt	1/16 oz.
1 Tbsp.	butter	1/2 oz.
1 Tbsp.	minced lemon zest	n/c
1 c.	backfin crab meat, picked over for shell fragments	6 oz.
2 c.	cold Champagne Cream	1 recipe
2 Tbsp.	thin diagonal-sliced scallion	1/8 bunch a.p.
12 pc.	(51–60 ct.) white Gulf shrimp, peeled	3 1/2 oz. a.p.

preparation:

1. Heat a 10" nonstick sauté pan, heat the clarified butter, and sear the pompano fillets very briefly on both sides so that the fish is still raw in the center. Season with lemon juice and salt, then immediately transfer to a half-sheet tray and refrigerate, uncovered, about 30 minutes, until cold.
2. Assemble the papillotes:
   a. Cut 2 sheets of pan liner in half to make 4 pieces of pan liner. Cut each into a heart shape.
   b. Fold a pan liner heart in half, then open it back up and coat it with butter.
   c. Place a cold pompano fillet off-center on one of the hearts with a long side of the fillet aligned with the fold.
   d. Sprinkle 1/4 of the lemon zest on the fillet, and then top with 1/4 of the crab meat, pressing gently to firm it.
   e. Nap the crab-topped fish with 1/4 of the Champagne Cream.
   f. Sprinkle the fish with 1/4 of the scallion, and then arrange 3 shrimp on top.
   g. Fold the top half of the heart over the fillet and, starting at the rounded end, pleat the heart shut with 3/4" folds. Finish by twisting the pointed end to make a "tail."
   h. Repeat with the remaining ingredients to make a total of 4 papillotes.

holding: refrigerate in one layer on a sheet tray for no longer than 12 hours

COMPONENT RECIPE
CHAMPAGNE CREAM

yield: 2 c.

production		costing only
5 Tbsp.	butter	2 1/2 oz.
2 Tbsp.	minced scallion whites	1/8 bunch a.p.
4 Tbsp.	flour	1 1/2 oz.
pinch	cayenne pepper	1/16 oz.
3 c.	hot Fish Stock	3/16 recipe
1/2 c.	Champagne or dry white sparkling wine	4 fl. oz.
tt	kosher salt	1/16 oz.
1/2 c.	heavy cream	4 fl. oz.
1 Tbsp.	minced lemon zest	1/6 [90 ct.] lemon
tt	fine-ground white pepper	1/16 oz.

preparation:
1. Heat the butter and scallion whites in a heavy, nonreactive saucepan. Stir in the flour and cayenne and make a blond roux.
2. Whisk in the Fish Stock and Champagne, add a little salt, and simmer briskly about 20 minutes, until the sauce is very thick.
3. Prepare an ice-water bath large enough to hold the saucepan.
4. Whisk the cream into the sauce and add the lemon zest. Simmer a minute or so to make a thick sauce.
5. Correct the salt and season with white pepper.
6. Place the saucepan in the ice-water bath and stir the sauce occasionally until cold.

holding: refrigerate in a freshly sanitized, covered container up to 3 days

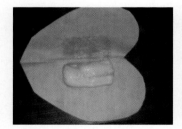

Example: Papillote with fish fillet.
Photos by Lou Sackett

Pleating the papillote.

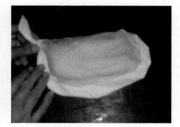

Twisting the papillote tail.

RECIPE VARIATION

Flounder en Papillote with Champagne Cream, Pecan Rice Pilaf, Parisienne Carrots, and Haricots Verts
Replace the pompano with flounder fillets.

Red Snapper *Courtbouillon*
with Pan-Steamed Rice and Smothered Butter Beans

yield: 1 (14-oz.) bone-in entrée serving plus accompaniments (multiply × 4 for classroom turnout; adjust equipment sizes accordingly)

MASTER RECIPE

production		costing only
2 Tbsp.	brunoise-cut tasso or country ham	1/2 oz. a.p.
1/4 c.	fine-chopped fresh knob onion or yellow onion	1 1/2 oz. a.p.
1 Tbsp.	butter	1/2 oz.
1 1/4 c.	shelled fresh butter beans or shelled lima beans	1 1/4 lb. a.p.
tt	kosher salt	1/16 oz.
1/2 c.	water	n/c
1/2 c.	pork lard	4 oz.
1/2 c.	flour	2 1/2 oz.
1 tsp.	fine salt	1/6 oz.
1/2 tsp.	cayenne pepper	1/8 oz.
1/2 tsp.	fresh-ground black pepper	1/8 oz.
1	whole red snapper, gilled, gutted, trimmed, washed, and blotted dry	1 lb. a.p.
2 c.	*Courtbouillon* Sauce	1/4 recipe
1 1/2 c.	Pan-Steamed White Rice, hot in steam table	1/4 recipe
as needed	water, in squeeze bottle	n/c
1 Tbsp.	butter	1/2 oz.
2 Tbsp.	chopped scallion	1/10 bunch a.p.
1	scallion "brush," soaked in ice water* (see illustrations)	1/8 bunch a.p.

service turnout:

1. Smother the butter beans:
   a. Place the ham, onion, and 1 Tbsp. butter in an 8" sauté pan and sauté for a few seconds, until soft but not brown.
   b. Add the butter beans, salt, and 1/2 c. water; cover the pan; and simmer briskly about 5 minutes, until the beans are tender.
   c. Uncover the lima beans and, if necessary, reduce the cooking liquid almost to a glaze. Cover and hold hot.
2. Braise the fish:
   a. Place the lard in a 12" nonstick sauté pan and heat over medium heat to about 325°F.
   b. Mix together the flour, fine salt, cayenne, and black pepper.
   c. Cut three diagonal slashes down to the bone on each side of the fish and pat it dry with paper towels.
   d. Dredge the fish in the flour mixture on both sides.
   e. Pan-fry the fish about 4 minutes on each side.
   f. Pour out the lard remaining in the fish pan and spoon the *Courtbouillon* Sauce over the fish. Bring the sauce to the boil over high heat.
   g. Transfer the pan to a 400°F oven and bake the fish about 5 minutes, or until the fish is just cooked through.
3. Plate the dish:
   a. Spoon the Pan-Steamed White Rice onto a hot 12" oval plate and make a horizontal well in the center.
   b. Using two wide spatulas, carefully lift the fish onto the rice.
   c. If the *Courtbouillon* sauce has over-reduced in the oven, thin it with water to a consistency thicker than nappé. Work in the butter to form an emulsion.
   d. Spoon a diagonal line of sauce across the fish from 2 o'clock to 7 o'clock.
   e. Sprinkle a line of chopped scallion on the sauce.
   f. Drain the scallion "brush" and shake it dry. Stick it upright out of the fish's gill cavity.
   g. Spoon the butter beans into a hot 4" vegetable dish.

*For best appearance, fabricate and soak the scallion "brush" before you prepare the component recipes.

Cut straight down through the scallion, roll it a quarter turn, cut again, and repeat, making four or more cuts.

Soak in ice water at least 30 minutes.

The scallion layers will open out into a "brush" shape.

COMPONENT RECIPE
COURTBOUILLON SAUCE

yield: 2 qt.

production		costing only
1/2 c.	pork lard	4 oz.
1/2 c.	flour	2 1/2 oz.
1 c.	fine-chopped fresh bulb onion or yellow onion	5 oz. a.p.
1/2 c.	fine-chopped green bell pepper	4 oz. a.p.
1/2 c.	peeled, minced celery	1/10 bunch a.p.
2 Tbsp.	seeded, minced Italian green chile	1 1/2 oz. a.p.
1/4 c.	chopped scallion	1/4 head a.p.
1 Tbsp.	minced garlic	1/2 oz. a.p.
1 tsp.	cayenne powder	1/8 oz.
3 c.	hot Fish Stock	1/5 recipe
3 c.	hot Poultry Stock	1/5 recipe
1 tsp.	dried tarragon	1/8 oz.
1/2 tsp.	dried thyme	1/16 oz.
2	bay leaves	1/16 oz.
tt	kosher salt	1/4 oz.
3/4 c.	red wine	6 fl. oz.
2 Tbsp.	clarified butter	1 1/2 oz. a.p.
1 c.	slivered fresh bulb onion or yellow onion	5 oz. a.p.
1 c.	thick-julienne green bell pepper, cleaned	8 oz. a.p.
2 c.	coarse tomato concassée	1 1/2 lb. a.p.
as needed	sugar	1/4 oz.

preparation:
1. Heat a small, heavy brazier or 12" cast-iron skillet, melt the lard, and stir in the flour. Cook, stirring, about 8 minutes, to make a category 3 (fudge brownie brown) roux.
2. Add the chopped onion, chopped green bell pepper, and celery. Cook, stirring, about 3 minutes, until the vegetables soften.
3. Stir in the chile, scallion, garlic, and cayenne.
4. Whisk in the Fish Stock and Poultry Stock and add the tarragon, thyme, bay leaves, and a little salt. Partially cover the pan and simmer briskly, stirring occasionally, about 15 minutes.
5. Place the wine in a small, nonreactive saucepan over low heat and reduce it by half.
6. Heat a 10" sauté pan, heat the clarified butter, and sauté the slivered onion and julienne green bell pepper with a pinch of salt about 30 seconds, until just tender. Cool.
7. Add the wine and tomato to the sauce and simmer, uncovered, about 10 minutes, until the sauce reduces to a thick nappé consistency.
8. Correct the salt and balance the flavor with sugar, if needed.
9. Stir in the sautéed onion and green bell pepper.

holding: open-pan cool and immediately refrigerate in a freshly sanitized, covered, nonreactive container up to 5 days

---

RECIPE VARIATIONS

Red Snapper Fillet *Courtbouillon* with Pan-Steamed Rice and Smothered Butter Beans
Replace the whole red snapper with an 8-oz. skin-on red snapper fillet. Reduce cooking times accordingly.

Red Snapper *Courtbouillon* with Creole Baguette and Green Salad
Prepare and present the fish and its sauce in a 10" black cast-iron pan placed on a serving tray lined with a linen napkin. Accompany with a hot Creole Baguette and a green salad with Basic Vinaigrette.

Redfish *Courtbouillon* with Pan-Steamed Rice and Smothered Butter Beans
Replace the snapper with red drum.

Blackened Redfish

with Eggplant 'n' Shrimp Pirogue and Maquechoux

yield: 1 (7-oz.) entrée serving plus accompaniments
(multiply × 4 for classroom turnout; adjust equipment sizes
accordingly)

MASTER RECIPE

production		costing only
1 tsp.	melted butter	1/6 fl. oz.
1	Eggplant 'n' Shrimp Pirogue	1/4 recipe
3/4 c.	Maquechoux Base	1/4 recipe
1/4 c.	water	n/c
1/4 c.	Maquechoux Liaison, in squeeze bottle	1/4 recipe
1	7-oz. Gulf redfish fillet, skinned and pinned	8 oz. a.p.
1 Tbsp.	Cajun Seasoning for Fish	1/10 recipe
3 Tbsp.	melted clarified butter, in an eighth-size hotel pan	2 oz. a.p.
1 oz.	cleaned baby spinach	1 oz.
1 tsp.	chopped flat-leaf parsley	1/40 bunch a.p.
1 Tbsp.	brunoise-cut red bell pepper	1/2 oz. a.p.

service turnout:

1. Place a well-seasoned 8" black cast-iron skillet over high heat. ⚠ Make sure the stovetop and kitchen are well ventilated.
2. Brush a sizzle pan with melted butter, place the Eggplant 'n' Shrimp Pirogue on it, and bake in a 400°F oven about 10 minutes, until heated through.
3. Finish the maquechoux:
   a. Place the Maquechoux Base and water in an 8" non-stick sauté pan, cover, and heat over low heat.
   b. Use a rubber spatula to stir the Maquechoux Liaison into the base in a thin stream, and cook the mixture over low heat, stirring constantly, about 1 minute, until the liaison thickens. ⚠ Do not allow to curdle.
   c. Hold hot.
4. Blacken the redfish:
   a. Dredge all surfaces of the redfish in the Cajun Seasoning for Fish, pressing firmly so it adheres.
   b. With sleeves rolled down, dip the fish into the clarified butter on both sides, and then immediately place it in the hot cast-iron skillet. The fish will spatter and smoke; work carefully to avoid burns and inhaling smoke. Sear approximately 30 seconds on each side, depending on the thickness of the fillet, until the fish is medium rare. (If the fillet is very thick, transfer it to a sizzle pan and finish in a 400°F oven.)
5. Plate the dish:
   a. Place the pirogue diagonally on a hot 12" plate with the tip at 2 o'clock and the rounded end at 7 o'clock.
   b. Spoon the maquechoux into a 3" side dish or ramekin and place it behind the pirogue.
   c. Place the blackened redfish on the front of the plate propped against the pirogue. Pour the blackened butter over the fish.
   d. Mound the spinach behind the pirogue.
   e. Sprinkle lines of parsley and red bell pepper across the blackened redfish.

ENTREES

COMPONENT RECIPE
EGGPLANT 'N' SHRIMP PIROGUES

yield: 4 side servings

production		costing only
4	4-oz. Asian or Italian eggplants, with stems	1 lb. a.p.
2 Tbsp.	gold-color pure olive oil	1 fl. oz.
tt	kosher salt	1/16 oz.
2 Tbsp.	butter	1 oz.
1/4 c.	fine-chopped fresh knob onion or yellow onion	1 1/4 oz. a.p.
1/8 c.	peeled, fine-chopped celery	1/20 head a.p.
1/8 c.	fine-chopped green bell pepper	1 oz. a.p.
pinch	cayenne powder	1/16 oz.
pinch	fresh-ground black pepper	1/16 oz.
pinch	fine-ground white pepper	1/16 oz.
1/2 c.	Shellfish Stock	1/32 recipe
1/2 c.	room-temperature Pan-Steamed White Rice	1/6 recipe
3 oz.	Creole Poached Gulf Shrimp, p. 266, chopped	1/5 recipe
1 Tbsp.	minced scallion	1/16 bunch a.p.
1/2 tsp.	minced fresh thyme leaves	1/20 bunch a.p.
1/2	egg, beaten	1/2 each or 1 oz.

preparation:
1. Fabricate and cook the eggplants:
   a. Prepare a pressure steamer or stovetop steamer.
   b. Place an eggplant on the work surface so that its flattest surface is on top and its rounded surface is on the bottom. Using a sharp, flexible knife, slice off the top 1/5 of the eggplant and reserve it.
   c. Using a small paring knife and a Parisienne scoop, hollow out the eggplant to resemble a pirogue, or canoe. Reserve the scooped-out flesh.
   d. Repeat to make a total of 4 pirogues.
   e. Use a swivel peeler to remove the skin from the eggplant tops.
   f. Combine the peeled tops and scooped-out flesh, and medium-chop them.
   g. Place the eggplant pirogues on a steamer rack, hollow side down. Steam until barely tender and still holding their shape, about 1 minute in a pressure steamer and about 5 minutes in a stovetop steamer.
   h. Cool the pirogues and drain upside down on paper towels.

2. Make the stuffing:
   a. Heat a 10" nonstick sauté pan, heat the oil, and sauté the chopped eggplant with a little salt until golden brown. Remove to a bowl.
   b. Add the butter, onion, celery, green bell pepper, cayenne pepper, black pepper, white pepper, and a little salt to the pan. Stir, cover, and sweat over low heat about 2 minutes, until the vegetables are soft.
   c. Return the chopped eggplant to the pan along with the Shellfish Stock. Cook, stirring constantly, over high heat about 2 minutes, until the mixture reduces to a very thick, almost dry pulp. Cool slightly.
   d. Mix in the Pan-Steamed White Rice, Creole Poached Gulf Shrimp, scallion, and thyme. Taste and correct the seasoning, then mix in the egg.

3. Blot the inside of the eggplant pirogues dry with paper towels and fill them with the stuffing. Press firmly, mounding the filling in the center and smoothing the tops.

holding: refrigerate in a single layer in a freshly sanitized, covered container up to 3 days

COMPONENT RECIPE
MAQUECHOUX BASE

yield: 3 c.

production		costing only
3 ears	fresh corn on the cob	3 ears a.p.
2 c.	water	n/c
1 c.	Poultry Stock	1/16 recipe
1/2 c.	butter	4 oz.
2/3 c.	fine-chopped yellow onion	3 1/3 oz. a.p.
2 tsp.	minced garlic	1/3 oz. a.p.
1/8 c.	medium-chopped green bell pepper	1 oz. a.p.
1/8 c.	medium-chopped red bell pepper	1 oz. a.p.
1 Tbsp.	seeded, minced Italian green chile	1/2 oz. a.p.
tt	fresh-ground black pepper	1/16 oz.
tt	fine-ground white pepper	1/16 oz.
tt	cayenne pepper	1/16 oz.
tt	kosher salt	1/16 oz.
tt	sugar	1/4 oz.
as needed	water	n/c

preparation:
1. Fabricate the corn:
   a. Husk the corn and remove all silk.
   b. Hold a cob of corn upright in a large bowl and, using a sharp, flexible boning knife, cut the kernels off the cob. Use the back of the knife to scrape the cut cob, releasing the milky juices from it. Discard the cob.
   c. Repeat with the remaining cobs.
2. Place the corn kernels, 2 c. water, Poultry Stock, butter, onion, garlic, bell peppers, chile, black pepper, white pepper, cayenne, salt, and sugar in a 10" nonstick sauté pan. Bring to a low simmer and cook, stirring occasionally, about 10 minutes, until the liquid is reduced and absorbed, and the corn is tender.
3. Continue to cook, monitoring the pan constantly and scraping with a heatproof rubber spatula, until the mixture begins to stick to the pan and slightly caramelize.
4. Add about 1/4 c. water and deglaze the pan.
5. Repeat steps 3 and 4 until the corn acquires a rich, complex flavor.
6. Taste and balance the sweetness with salt.

holding: open-pan cool and immediately refrigerate in a freshly sanitized, covered container up to 5 days

COMPONENT RECIPE
MAQUECHOUX LIAISON

yield: 1 c.

production		costing only
2	egg yolks	2 each or 1 1/3 oz.
3/4 c.	half-and-half	6 fl. oz.

preparation:
1. Mix well.
2. Pour into a freshly sanitized squeeze bottle.

holding: refrigerate up to 2 days

RECIPE VARIATION
Blackened Snapper with Eggplant 'n' Shrimp Pirogue and Maquechoux
Replace the Gulf redfish with red snapper.

Shrimp Creole
with Pan-Steamed Rice and Fried Okra

yield: 1 (5-oz.) entrée serving plus accompaniments
(multiply × 4 for classroom turnout; adjust equipment sizes
accordingly)

MASTER RECIPE

production		costing only
1/2 c.	pork lard	4 oz. (may be reused)
1/4 c.	corn oil	2 fl. oz. (may be reused)
1/4 c.	corn flour	1 oz.
1 Tbsp.	yellow cornmeal	1/4 oz.
1 tsp.	Cajun Seasoning for Meat	1/12 recipe
4 pc.	whole okra, trimmed, steamed al dente, refreshed	3 oz. a.p.
tt	fine salt	1/16 oz.
1 1/2 c.	Shrimp Creole Sauce	1/4 recipe
as needed	water, in squeeze bottle	n/c
5 oz.	(51–60 ct.) white Gulf shrimp, peeled and deveined	5 1/2 oz. a.p.
1 1/2 c.	Pan-Steamed White Rice, hot in steam table	1/4 recipe
1 Tbsp.	butter	1/2 oz.
1 Tbsp.	thin diagonal-sliced scallions	1/20 bunch a.p.
1	slender scallion, cleaned	1/8 bunch a.p.

service turnout:

1. Fry the okra:
   a. Heat an 8" sauté pan, add the lard and oil, and bring to about 350°F over medium heat.
   b. In a small bowl, mix together the corn flour, cornmeal, and Cajun Seasoning for Meat.
   c. Coat the okra with the corn flour mixture and let stand 5 minutes.
   d. Fry the okra on both sides until crusty and pale golden.
   e. Drain on a rack and season with salt.
2. Place the Shrimp Creole Sauce and a little water in an 8" sauté pan. Bring to the boil, stir in the shrimp, cover, and simmer about 1 minute, until the shrimp are just cooked through.
3. Plate the dish:
   a. Spoon the Pan-Steamed White Rice into a hot 12" pasta plate and make a well in the center.
   b. Work the butter into the Creole sauce.
   c. Spoon the shrimp and sauce into the well.
   d. Arrange the fried okra on the rice from 12 o'clock to 4 o'clock.
   e. Sprinkle the shrimp with sliced scallions and place the whole scallion across the plate in front of the okra.

RECIPE VARIATION

Seafood Creole with Pan-Steamed Rice and Fried Okra
Replace 4 oz. of the shrimp with 2 oz. lump crab meat and 3 shucked oysters.

COMPONENT RECIPE
SHRIMP CREOLE SAUCE

yield: 1 1/2 qt.

production		costing only
2 Tbsp.	bacon drippings	n/c
2 Tbsp.	butter	1 oz.
1 c.	minced fresh knob onion or yellow onion	5 oz. a.p.
1/2 c.	fine-chopped green bell pepper	4 oz. a.p.
1/2 c.	peeled, minced celery	1/10 head a.p.
1 Tbsp.	seeded, minced Italian green chile	3/4 oz. a.p.
1 tsp.	minced garlic	1/6 oz. a.p.
3 Tbsp.	flour	1 oz.
2 c.	Shellfish Stock	1/8 recipe
1 1/2 qt.	vine-ripe tomato concassée	4 1/2 lb. a.p.
1 c.	3/8"-sliced celery hearts	1/5 head a.p.
1 c.	3/8"-diced green bell pepper	5 oz. a.p.
1/3 c.	1/4"-diced tasso or other smoked ham	2 oz.
tt	kosher salt	
tt	bottled hot sauce (such as Tabasco brand)	1/4 fl. oz.
tt	sugar	1/4 oz.

preparation:

1. Place the bacon drippings, butter, onion, chopped green bell pepper, minced celery, chile, and garlic in a heavy, nonreactive saucepan. Cover and sweat over low heat, stirring occasionally, about 8 minutes, until the vegetables are soft but not brown.
2. Stir in the flour and make a category 2 (sticky bun brown) roux.
3. Whisk in the Shellfish Stock, bring to a lively simmer, and cook about 15 minutes until thickened and reduced by almost half.
4. Add the tomato, celery hearts, diced green bell pepper, ham, and a little salt. Increase the heat and simmer briskly, uncovered, about 10 minutes, to achieve a light nappé consistency.
5. Season with hot sauce, then balance the flavor with salt and sugar.

holding: open-pan cool and immediately refrigerate in a freshly sanitized, covered container up to 5 days; freeze up to 1 month

Duck, Andouille Sausage, and 'Gator Filé Gumbo

yield: 1 (7-oz.) entrée serving plus accompaniments
(multiply × 4 for classroom turnout; adjust equipment sizes
accordingly)

MASTER RECIPE

production		costing only
1 Tbsp.	corn oil	1/2 fl. oz.
2 oz.	cleaned and tenderized alligator tail meat, cut in 1" dice	2 oz. a.p.
tt	kosher salt	1/16 oz.
1/2 c.	water, in squeeze bottle	n/c
1/4 recipe	Duck and Andouille Sausage Gumbo Base, with 1 duck leg and 3 slices sausage	1/4 recipe
as needed	pan coating spray	% of container
1 1/2 c.	Pan-Steamed White Rice, hot in steam table	1/4 recipe
2 Tbsp.	fine diagonal-sliced scallion	1/10 bunch a.p.
1 Tbsp.	brunoise-cut red bell pepper	1/2 oz. a.p.
1 Tbsp.	brunoise-cut yellow bell pepper	1/2 oz. a.p.
tt	filé powder, in shaker or ramekin	1/8 oz.

service turnout:

1. Finish the gumbo:
   a. Heat a 10" sauté pan until very hot, add the oil, and sear the alligator meat with a little salt until browned.
   b. Add the water and simmer briskly about 5 minutes.
   c. Add the Duck and Andouille Sausage Gumbo Base, cover, and simmer about 5 minutes longer, until heated through.
2. Plate the dish:
   a. Spray the inside of a 12-fl.-oz. ladle with pan coating. Scoop up the Pan-Steamed White Rice, packing it firmly, and then turn it out in the back of a hot 12" pasta bowl.
   b. Prop the duck leg upright against the rice and arrange the sausage slices, alligator cubes, and gumbo vegetables in the bowl.
   c. Spoon the gumbo broth into the bowl over the meats but not over the rice.
   d. Sprinkle with the scallion and bell peppers.
   e. The diner sprinkles filé powder into the broth to taste.

COMPONENT RECIPE

DUCK AND ANDOUILLE SAUSAGE GUMBO BASE

yield: 2 qt. sauce plus 4 (5-oz.) entrée servings (combined duck meat and sausage)

production		costing only
4	8-oz. Long Island duck legs	2 lb.
1 c.	fine-chopped fresh knob onion or yellow onion	5 oz. a.p.
1/2 c.	fine-chopped green bell pepper	4 oz. a.p.
1/2 c.	peeled, minced celery	1/10 head a.p.
±1/4 c.	pork lard	±2 oz.
1/2 c.	flour	2 1/2 oz.
3 Tbsp.	seeded, minced Italian green chile	1 1/2 oz. a.p.
1/4 c.	minced scallion	1/4 bunch a.p.
1 Tbsp.	minced garlic	1/3 oz. a.p.
1 tsp.	cayenne pepper	
3 qt.	hot Brown Poultry Stock, made from duck carcasses	3/4 recipe
1/2 tsp.	dried thyme	1/16 oz.
4	bay leaves	1/8 oz.
tt	kosher salt	1/16 oz.
1/2 c.	3/8"-diced green bell pepper	3 oz. a.p.
1/2 c.	3/8"-diced red bell pepper	3 oz. a.p.
1/2 c.	peeled, 3/8"-diced celery	1/12 bunch a.p.
1/4 c.	coarse-chopped scallion	1/4 bunch a.p.
12	diagonal slices Louisiana andouille sausage or smoked kielbasa	6 oz.
tt	bottled hot sauce (Tabasco or Crystal brand)	1/4 fl. oz.

preparation:

1. Fabricate and brown the duck legs:
   a. Chop off the knuckles of the duck legs and trim away excess skin and fat.
   b. Heat a heavy, 12" sauté pan over medium heat. Add the duck legs, skin side down, and fry about 3 minutes, until golden brown.
   c. Turn and fry about 1 minute longer, and then remove.
   d. Measure the duck fat in the pan.
2. Make the gumbo:
   a. Mix together the fine-chopped onion, green bell pepper, and celery "holy trinity."
   b. Add enough lard to the duck fat in the pan to make a total of 1/2 c.
   c. Melt the lard and stir in the flour. Cook, stirring, about 8 minutes, to make a category 3 (fudge brownie brown) roux.
   d. Add half of the "holy trinity" and cook, stirring constantly, about 3 minutes longer, until the vegetables soften.
   e. Stir in the chile, minced scallion, garlic, and cayenne, then whisk in the Brown Poultry Stock to make a smooth sauce. Add the thyme, bay leaves, and a little salt. Simmer briskly, stirring occasionally, about 30 minutes.
   f. Add the remaining "holy trinity" and the duck legs, and simmer 20 minutes longer.
   g. Add the diced bell peppers, diced celery, chopped scallion, and andouille sausage, and simmer 10 minutes longer, until the duck is tender and the sauce reaches a light nappé consistency.
   h. Remove the bay leaves, season with hot sauce, and correct the salt.

holding: open-pan cool; optionally divide the sauce and solid ingredients into 4 equal portions; refrigerate in a freshly sanitized, covered container up to 5 days

---

RECIPE VARIATIONS

Duck, Andouille Sausage, and Oyster Filé Gumbo
Replace the water in the master recipe with oyster liquor, adding it to the heated sauce. In each serving, replace the alligator with 4 shucked, select-size oysters added just before plating.

Chicken, Andouille Sausage, and 'Gator Filé Gumbo
Replace the duck legs with chicken legs and prepare the Brown Poultry Stock with chicken carcasses.

Shrimp and Crab Okra Gumbo

yield: 1 (6-oz.) entrée serving plus accompaniments
(multiply × 4 for classroom turnout; adjust equipment sizes
accordingly)

MASTER RECIPE

production		costing only
2 c.	Seafood Gumbo Base	1/4 recipe
1/4 c.	water	n/c
6	Cleaned Raw Blue Crab Quarters or 6 frozen cleaned blue crab quarters	1 1/2 crabs or about 4 oz.
2/3 c.	trimmed, 3/8"-sliced okra	3 oz. a.p.
5	(21–25 ct.) white Gulf shrimp, peeled	3 1/2 oz. a.p.
as needed	pan coating spray	% of container
1 1/2 c.	Pan-Steamed White Rice, hot in steam table	1/4 recipe
1 Tbsp.	butter	1/2 oz.
1 Tbsp.	fine diagonal-sliced scallions	1/20 bunch a.p.

service turnout:

1. Finish the gumbo:
   a. Place the Seafood Gumbo Base and water in a 10" sauté pan, cover, and bring to the simmer.
   b. Add the Cleaned Raw Blue Crab Quarters and okra, cover, return to a lively simmer, and cook, covered, about 3 minutes.
   c. Add the shrimp, cover, and simmer 1 minute longer. Hold hot.
2. Plate the dish:
   a. Spray the inside of a 12-fl.-oz. ladle with pan coating. Scoop up the Pan Steamed White Rice, packing it firmly, then turn out on the back of a hot 12" pasta bowl.
   b. Arrange the crabs and shrimp in the bowl.
   c. Work the butter into the sauce to form an emulsion.
   d. Spoon the sauce and okra over the seafood, but not over the rice.
   e. Sprinkle with scallions.
   f. Make sure the server provides a seafood cracker, a pointed steak knife, a plate for shells, and a packaged moist towelette.

COMPONENT RECIPE
SEAFOOD GUMBO BASE

yield: 2 qt.

production		costing only
1/2 c.	pork lard	4 oz.
2/3 c.	flour	3 1/3 oz.
1 c.	fine-chopped fresh knob onion or yellow onion	5 oz. a.p.
1/2 c.	fine-chopped green bell pepper	4 oz. a.p.
1/2 c.	peeled, minced celery	1/10 head a.p.
2 Tbsp.	seeded, minced Italian green chile	1 oz. a.p.
1/2 c.	fine-chopped scallion	1/2 bunch a.p.
1 Tbsp.	minced garlic	1/3 oz. a.p.
1/2 tsp.	cayenne powder	1/8 oz.
1/2 c.	fine-chopped smoked ham, tasso or country	2 oz. a.p.
2 qt.	hot Shellfish Stock, made from shrimp and crab shells	1/2 recipe
1 qt.	water	n/c
1/4 tsp.	dried thyme	1/16 oz.
pinch	ground allspice	1/16 oz.
2	bay leaves	1/16 oz.
tt	kosher salt	1/16 oz.
1 c.	vine-ripe tomato, coarse concassée	12 oz. a.p.
tt	seeded, minced Scotch bonnet or habanero chile	1/4 oz. a.p.
1 Tbsp.	minced lemon zest	n/c
tt	fresh lemon juice	1/4 [90 ct.] lemon
tt	sugar	1/4 oz.

preparation:
1. Melt the lard in a heavy 4-qt. saucepan and stir in the flour. Cook, stirring, about 10 minutes, to make a category #4 (black coffee brown) roux. ⚠ Watch carefully; do not allow to scorch.
2. Add the onion, green bell pepper, and celery "holy trinity."
3. Cook, stirring, about 3 minutes longer, until the vegetables soften.
4. Stir in the Italian green chile, scallion, garlic, cayenne, and ham, then whisk in the Shellfish Stock and water to make a smooth sauce. Add the thyme, allspice, bay leaves, and a little salt. Simmer briskly, stirring occasionally, about 45 minutes.
5. Remove the bay leaves, and add the tomato and Scotch bonnet chile. Simmer 15 minutes longer.
6. Season with the lemon zest and juice, and then balance the flavor with salt and sugar.

holding: open-pan cool and refrigerate in a freshly sanitized, covered, nonreactive container up to 5 days

---

RECIPE VARIATION
Seafood Okra Gumbo
Reduce the number of crabs to 2 quarters. Reduce the shrimp to 3 pc. Add 3 shucked, select-count oysters, 3 (1-oz.) pc. firm fish fillet, and 5 cooked, peeled crawfish tails along with the shrimp.

Crawfish Étouffée

with Pan-Steamed Rice and Sauté Mirliton

yield: 1 (4-oz.) entrée serving plus accompaniments (multiply × 4 for classroom turnout; adjust equipment sizes accordingly)

MASTER RECIPE

production		costing only
1 1/2 c.	Seafood Étouffée Sauce	1/4 recipe
1/4 c.	water	n/c
4 oz.	cooked, shelled crawfish tails	4 oz. frozen or prepared from 1 lb. fresh crawfish
1 Tbsp.	clarified butter	3/4 oz. a.p.
1/2	steamed, peeled mirliton, cut into thin wedges	1/2 [24 ct.] mirliton
tt	fresh lemon juice	1/6 [90 ct.] lemon
tt	kosher salt	1/16 oz.
tt	fine-ground white pepper	1/16 oz.
1	whole boiled crawfish	1 oz. a.p.
as needed	pan coating spray	% of container
1 1/2 c.	Pan-Steamed White Rice, hot in steam table	1/4 recipe
1 Tbsp.	chopped flat-leaf parsley	1/20 bunch a.p.
1 large sprig	flat-leaf parsley	1/20 bunch a.p.

service turnout:
1. Place the Seafood Étouffée Sauce, water, and crawfish tails in an 8" sauté pan, cover, and bring to the simmer. Hold hot.
2. Sauté the mirliton:
   a. Heat a 10" sauté pan, heat the clarified butter, and sauté the mirliton wedges until heated through.
   b. Season with lemon juice, salt, and white pepper.
   c. Hold hot.
3. Heat the whole crawfish in a steamer or in simmering water.
4. Plate the dish:
   a. Spray the inside of a 12-oz. timbale mold or ramekin with pan coating. Pack in the Pan-Steamed White Rice, then turn it out onto the back of a hot 12" pasta plate.
   b. Spoon the étouffée onto the front of the plate.
   c. Arrange the mirliton wedges on either side of the molded rice timbale.
   d. Sprinkle the étouffée with chopped parsley.
   e. Stick the parsley sprig upright out of the back of the timbale.
   f. Blot the crawfish dry and place it on the timbale.

RECIPE VARIATIONS

Shrimp Étouffée with Pan-Steamed Rice and Sauté Mirliton
Replace the crawfish with peeled (51–60 ct.) white Gulf shrimp. Omit the crawfish garnish or replace it with a large cooked shrimp.

Chicken Étouffée with Pan-Steamed Rice and Sauté Mirliton
Replace the shrimp with an 8-oz. chicken leg, skinned and trimmed. Brown the chicken in lard and then simmer in the sauce 15 to 20 minutes, until cooked through. Replace the Shellfish Stock with Poultry Stock. Omit the crawfish garnish.

COMPONENT RECIPE
SEAFOOD ÉTOUFFÉE SAUCE

yield: 1 1/2 qt.

production		costing only
1/2 c.	pork lard	4 oz.
1/2 c.	flour	1 2/3 oz.
1 c.	fine-chopped fresh knob onion or yellow onion	5 oz. a.p.
1/2 c.	peeled, minced celery	1/10 head a.p.
1/2 c.	fine-chopped green bell pepper	4 oz. a.p.
2 Tbsp.	seeded, minced Italian green chile	1 1/2 oz. a.p.
2 tsp.	minced garlic	1/3 oz. a.p.
1/2 tsp.	cayenne pepper	1/8 oz.
2 qt.	hot Shellfish Stock	1/2 recipe
1 sprig	fresh thyme	1/12 bunch
2	bay leaves	1/16 oz.
tt	sugar	1/2 oz.
tt	kosher salt	1/16 oz.
tt	fresh lemon juice	1/4 [90 ct.] lemon
2 tsp.	minced lemon zest	n/c
1/4 c.	fine-chopped scallion	1/4 bunch a.p.

preparation:
1. Heat the lard in a heavy 4-qt. saucepot. Add the flour and cook, stirring, over medium heat about 8 minutes, to make a category 3 (fudge brownie brown) roux.
2. Add the onion, celery, and green bell peppers. Cook, stirring, about 3 minutes, until the vegetables are soft.
3. Add the chile, garlic, and cayenne. Cook a few seconds longer.
4. Whisk in the Shellfish Stock, bring it to the simmer, then add the thyme sprig, bay leaves, sugar, and salt. Simmer briskly about 30 minutes, until the flavors meld and the sauce is reduced to a full-bodied nappé consistency.
5. Remove the thyme sprig and bay leaves.
6. Add the lemon juice, lemon zest, and scallion, then correct the salt.

holding: open-pan cool and immediately refrigerate in a freshly sanitized, covered, nonreactive container up to 5 days

ENTREES

Creole Jambalaya
with Pepper Medley

yield: 1 entrée serving: 5 oz. protein plus rice
(multiply × 4 for classroom turnout; adjust equipment sizes
accordingly)

MASTER RECIPE

production		costing only
1 1/2 oz.	1"-diced boneless, skinless chicken thigh	1 1/2 oz.
1/2 tsp.	Louisiana Seasoning for Meat	1/48 recipe
2 Tbsp.	bacon drippings	n/c
±1/2 c.	water, in squeeze bottle	n/c
1 1/2 oz.	thick diagonal slices Louisiana andouille sausage or smoked kielbasa	1 1/2 oz.
1 1/2 oz.	(21–25 ct.) white Gulf shrimp, peeled and deveined	1 1/2 oz. a.p.
2 c.	Jambalaya Base	1/4 recipe
1/2 c.	peeled, seeded, 1/2"-diced tomato	5 oz. a.p.
1/2 oz.	lump crab meat, picked over for shell fragments	1/2 oz.
1 Tbsp.	soft butter	1/2 oz.
1 Tbsp.	gold-color pure olive oil	1/2 fl. oz.
1 oz.	thin-sliced red bell pepper	2 oz. a.p.
1/2 oz.	thin-sliced green bell pepper	1 oz. a.p.
1 oz.	thin-sliced yellow bell pepper	2 oz. a.p.
tt	kosher salt	1/16 oz.
1 Tbsp.	fine diagonal-sliced scallion	1/20 bunch a.p.
1 Tbsp.	chopped flat-leaf parsley	1/40 bunch a.p.

service turnout:
1. Finish the jambalaya:
   a. Sprinkle the chicken with Louisiana Seasoning for Meat.
   b. Heat a 10" nonstick sauté pan, heat the bacon drippings, and sauté the chicken for a few seconds until it browns.
   c. Add the water, sausage, and shrimp. Cook at a brisk simmer approximately 30 seconds.
   d. Add the Jambalaya Base and tomato. Use a heatproof rubber spatula to mix the base with the water, then cover the pan and heat over low heat, stirring occasionally, until the rice is heated through.
   e. Uncover the rice and fold in the crab meat and butter. Add a little more water if needed to make a moist, but not wet pilaf.
2. Heat a 10" sauté pan, add the oil, and sauté the bell peppers with a little salt until just tender. Hold warm.
3. Plate the dish:
   a. Mound the jambalaya into a hot 12" pasta bowl.
   b. Sprinkle the jambalaya with the scallion and parsley.
   c. Arrange the bell pepper medley around the jambalaya.

COMPONENT RECIPE
JAMBALAYA BASE

yield: 2 qt.

production		costing only
4 Tbsp.	bacon drippings	n/c
1 c.	fine-chopped fresh knob onion or yellow onion	4 oz. a.p.
1/2 c.	medium-chopped green bell pepper	4 oz. a.p.
2 c.	natural long-grain white rice	12 oz.
2 Tbsp.	seeded, fine-chopped Italian green chile	1 oz. a.p.
2 tsp.	minced garlic	1/4 oz. a.p.
1/2 tsp.	cayenne powder	1/16 oz.
1/4 tsp.	ground allspice	1/16 oz.
1/2 tsp.	celery seeds	1/8 oz.
2	bay leaves	1/16 oz.
2 sprigs	fresh thyme	1/10 bunch a.p.
1 Tbsp.	minced lemon zest	n/c
3 oz.	3/4"-diced smoked ham, preferably tasso	3 oz.
2 c.	Shellfish Stock	1/8 recipe
1 c.	Poultry Stock	1/16 recipe
tt	kosher salt	1/8 oz.

preparation:
1. Preheat an oven to 300°F.
2. Place the bacon drippings, onion, and green bell pepper in a heavy 2 1/2-qt. saucepot that has a tight-fitting lid. Sauté uncovered over medium heat about 1 minute, until softened but not browned.
3. Add the rice and cook, stirring, about 30 seconds, until the grains become opaque and are well-coated with fat.
4. Add the remaining ingredients, stir, bring to the simmer, and cover the pot. Simmer 15 minutes.
5. Quickly peek under the lid; the stocks should have absorbed into the rice.
6. Transfer the pot into the oven and bake 15 minutes longer.
7. Immediately turn the rice out into a freshly sanitized half-size hotel pan, fluff it with a fork, and spread it out to cool. Cover the surface with a clean, damp kitchen towel.

holding: refrigerate up to 3 days, covered with the towel and plastic film

---

RECIPE VARIATIONS
Jambalaya variations are countless: the only constant ingredients are ham (or other preserved pork products) and rice. Following are some ideas for jambalayas.

Chicken and Sausage Jambalaya

Andouille Sausage and Oyster Jambalaya

Chopped Beef and Cabbage Jambalaya

Summer Vegetable Jambalaya

Shrimp, Crab, and Oyster Jambalaya

Quail and Bacon Jambalaya

Crawfish Jambalaya

Pecan-Crusted
Suprême of Chicken
with Tasso Cream, Red Rice, and Sautéed Spinach

yield: 1 (7-oz.) entrée serving
(multiply × 4 for classroom turnout; adjust equipment sizes
accordingly)

MASTER RECIPE

production		costing only
1/4 c.	corn oil	2 fl. oz.
1	Pecan-Crusted Chicken Suprême	1/4 recipe
1 Tbsp.	minced shallot	1/4 oz. a.p.
1/4 c.	white wine	2 fl. oz.
pinch	cayenne pepper	1/16 oz.
1/2 c.	Poultry Stock	1/32 recipe
2 Tbsp.	brunoise-cut tasso ham	1/2 oz.
1 tsp.	minced lemon zest	1/16 [90 ct.] lemon
1/2 c.	heavy cream	4 fl. oz.
tt	kosher salt	1/16 oz.
tt	fine-ground white pepper	1/16 oz.
pinch	brown sugar	1/8 oz.
as needed	water, in squeeze bottle	n/c
1 Tbsp.	clarified butter	3/4 oz. a.p.
4 oz.	precleaned baby spinach	4 oz. a.p.
as needed	pan coating spray	% of container
1 1/4 c.	Red Rice, hot in steam table	1/4 recipe
1 Tbsp.	fine diagonal-sliced scallion	1/20 bunch a.p.
1 Tbsp.	brunoise-cut red bell pepper	1 oz. a.p.
1 large sprig	curly parsley	1/12 bunch a.p.

service turnout:

1. Cook the Pecan-Crusted Chicken Suprême:
   a. Heat the oil in an 8" nonstick sauté pan to about 400°F. Add the suprême and cook about 1 minute on each side, until the pecans are light golden.
   b. Remove to a sizzle pan and finish in a 400°F oven 5 to 8 minutes longer. Don't allow the pecans to over-brown.
2. Make the sauce:
   a. Pour the oil out of the pan, wipe out the pan, and add the shallot, wine, cayenne, Poultry Stock, ham, and lemon zest. Reduce to 1/4 c.
   b. Add the cream, bring to the boil, and cook very briefly until the sauce reaches a nappé consistency.
   c. Season with salt, white pepper, and a hint of brown sugar. Hold hot, thinning with water as necessary.
3. Sauté the spinach:
   a. Heat a 10" sauté pan very hot, add the clarified butter, and toss the spinach in it with a little salt until barely wilted.
4. Plate the dish:
   a. Spray the inside of a 10-oz. timbale or ramekin with pan coating, pack in the Red Rice, and turn it out on the back of a hot 12" plate.
   b. Mound the spinach on either side of the rice timbale.
   c. Spoon the sauce into the plate well.
   d. Prop the suprême against the rice.
   e. Sprinkle the suprême with a diagonal line of scallion and red bell pepper.
   f. Stick the parsley sprig upright out of the top of the rice timbale.

COMPONENT RECIPE
PECAN-CRUSTED CHICKEN SUPRÊMES

yield: 4 (7-oz.) entrée servings

production		costing only
4	6-oz. airline-fabricated boneless chicken breasts	1 1/2 lb.
1 tsp.	dry mustard	1/8 oz.
1/2 tsp.	cayenne pepper	1/16 oz.
1/2 tsp.	fresh-ground black powder	1/8 oz.
1/2 tsp.	dried tarragon	1/16 oz.
1 tsp.	sugar	1/6 oz.
1 tsp.	kosher salt	1/6 oz.
1/2 c.	flour	2 1/2 oz.
1	egg, beaten	1 each or 2 oz.
5 oz.	fine-chopped pecans	5 oz.

preparation:
1. Skin the chicken breasts, including the wingette area.
2. Chop off the knuckle of the wingette, making a clean cut, and french the bone.
3. Mix together the mustard, cayenne, black pepper, tarragon, sugar, and salt.
4. Rub the seasoning mixture onto the suprêmes.
5. Set a rack over a half-sheet tray.
6. Dredge the suprêmes in flour, dip them in egg, and coat them on all sides with the pecans, pressing to make the pecans adhere.
7. Place the suprêmes on the rack and refrigerate 1 hour uncovered.

holding: refrigerate on the rack, covered with a clean, dry kitchen towel, up to 48 hours

COMPONENT RECIPE
RED RICE

yield: 5 c.

production		costing only
3 Tbsp.	bacon drippings	n/c
3/4 c.	fine-chopped fresh knob onion or yellow onion	3/4 oz. a.p.
1/4 c.	fine-chopped green bell pepper	2 oz. a.p.
1/4 c.	peeled, minced celery	1/20 head a.p.
1 tsp.	minced garlic	1/6 oz. a.p.
pinch	cayenne powder	1/16 oz.
1 1/2 c.	natural long-grain white rice	9 oz.
1	bay leaf	1/16 oz.
1 c.	vine-ripe tomato concassée	8 oz. a.p.
1 1/4 c.	Poultry Stock	1/12 recipe
tt	kosher salt	1/16 oz.

preparation:
1. Preheat an oven to 350°F.
2. Place the bacon drippings, onion, green bell peppers, and celery in a heavy 2 1/2-qt. saucepan that has a tight-fitting lid. Sauté uncovered over medium heat about 1 minute until softened.
3. Add the garlic, cayenne, and rice. Cook, stirring constantly, about 30 seconds, until the rice grains become opaque and are well coated with fat.
4. Add the remaining ingredients, stir, bring to the simmer, and cover the pan. Simmer 15 minutes.
5. Quickly peek under the lid; the stock should have absorbed into the rice.
6. Transfer the pan into the oven and bake 15 minutes longer.
7. If not serving immediately, turn the rice out into a freshly sanitized half-size hotel pan, fluff it with a fork, and spread it out to cool. Cover with a clean, damp kitchen towel.

holding: refrigerate up to 3 days, covered with the towel and plastic film

---

RECIPE VARIATION

Pecan-Crusted Red Snapper with Tasso Cream, Red Rice, and Sautéed Spinach

Replace the chicken breasts with skinned and pinned 6-oz. red snapper fillets. Replace the Poultry Stock with Fish Stock.

Red Beans 'n' Rice

with Andouille Sausage and Collard Greens

yield: 1 entrée serving: 3 oz. andouille and 12 fl. oz. beans, plus accompaniments
(multiply × 4 for classroom turnout; adjust equipment sizes accordingly)

MASTER RECIPE

🕐 Best prepared 24 hours in advance.

production		costing only
3 oz.	Louisiana andouille sausage, sliced into 6 pieces on a sharp diagonal	3 oz.
1/2 c.	water	n/c
1 1/2 c.	New Orleans Red Beans	1/4 recipe
1 c.	Collard Greens with "Pot Likker," p. 72	1/4 recipe
1 1/2 c.	Pan-Steamed White Rice, hot in steam table	1/4 recipe
1 Tbsp.	chopped flat-leaf parsley	1/40 bunch a.p.
1 Tbsp.	fine diagonal-sliced scallion	1/16 bunch a.p.
2 Tbsp.	brunoise-cut red onion	3/4 oz. a.p.
as desired	bottled hot sauce (Tabasco or Crystal brand)	% of bottle
as desired	black pepper in a pepper mill	1/8 oz.

service turnout:

1. Finish the New Orleans Red Beans:
   a. Place the sausage slices and water in an 8" sauté pan, cover, and cook over medium heat about 1 minute, until the sausage is plumped and hot through.
   b. Add the red beans, stir, cover, and simmer about 5 minutes, until heated through.
2. Heat the Collard Greens with "Pot Likker" in a microwave or covered pan on the stove.
3. Plate the dish:
   a. Spoon the Pan-Steamed White Rice into a hot 12" pasta plate and make a well in the center.
   b. Spoon the red beans into the well. Pull up the sausage slices so they are visible on the top of the beans and arrange them attractively.
   c. Sprinkle the beans with the parsley, scallion, and onion.
   d. Spoon the collard greens into a hot 3" side dish.
   e. Provide hot sauce and a pepper mill.

RECIPE VARIATIONS

Red Beans 'n' Rice with Grilled Andouille and Collard Greens
Instead of warming sliced andouille in the beans, cook a length of andouille on a gas grill or charcoal grill and serve on top of the beans.

Red Beans 'n' Rice with Pork Chop
Replace the andouille sausage with a pork chop seasoned with Louisiana Seasoning for Meat and pan-fried or grilled.

Smoked Turkey Red Beans 'n' Rice
Replace the andouille sausage with smoked turkey sausage. Replace the ham hocks with smoked turkey butts or wings. Replace the bacon and bacon drippings with butter. Serve with collard greens prepared with smoked turkey in place of pork, or with a green salad dressed with vinaigrette on a side plate.

288

COMPONENT RECIPE

NEW ORLEANS RED BEANS

yield: 1 1/2 qt.

🕐 Best prepared 24 hours in advance.

production		costing only
2 c.	dried Louisiana red beans or dried light red kidney beans, picked over and soaked overnight or quick-soaked	11 oz.
2	4-oz. ham hocks	8 oz.
as needed	water	n/c
1 3/4 c.	fine-chopped fresh knob onion or yellow onion	9 oz. a.p.
1 Tbsp.	minced garlic	1/3 oz. a.p.
1/2 c.	fine-chopped green bell pepper	4 oz. a.p.
2 Tbsp.	seeded, minced Italian green chile	1 oz. a.p.
2	bay leaves	1/16 oz.
1/2 tsp.	dried thyme	1/16 oz.
1/2 tsp.	dried tarragon	1/16 oz.
1/2 tsp.	dried savory	1/16 oz.
1 tsp.	crushed dried red pepper	1/8 oz.
1/2 lb.	3/8"-diced rindless slab bacon	1/2 lb.
3/4 c.	red wine	6 fl. oz.
tt	kosher salt	1/8 oz.
1/2 c.	fine-chopped flat-leaf parsley	1/5 bunch a.p.

preparation:

1. Drain the beans, rinse them, and drain again.
2. Use a meat cleaver to split each ham hock in half, exposing the bone.
3. Place the beans in a heavy 4-qt. saucepan. Add the ham hocks and cool water to cover by 1". Bring to the simmer and skim away the foam.
4. Add the onion, garlic, green bell pepper, chile, bay leaves, thyme, tarragon, savory, and dried red pepper. Return to the simmer.
5. Place the bacon in a 10" sauté pan and fry it over low heat to render its fat. Continue frying until the bacon is almost crisp.
6. Pour the bacon and drippings into the beans and scrape in all the residue, deglazing the pan with a little water if necessary.
7. Continue simmering the beans over very low heat, stirring occasionally, and adding just enough water to keep the beans barely covered with liquid, about 45 minutes, until they are just tender.
8. In a small, nonreactive saucepan, heat the wine over very low heat about 5 minutes, until it is reduced by half. ⚠ Do not allow the wine to overreduce or scorch.
9. When the beans are tender and their cooking liquid has reduced to a thick nappé consistency, remove and discard the bay leaves. Remove the ham hocks and cool them to room temperature.
10. Stir the red wine into the beans and season them with salt. Simmer a few minutes longer.
11. Pick the meat off the ham hocks, pull it into shreds, and stir it into the beans along with the parsley.
12. If not serving immediately, open-pan cool the beans, place them in a freshly sanitized, nonreactive container, and refrigerate.

holding: refrigerate up to 5 days; may be frozen up to 3 months

ENTREES

Bananas Foster

with Palmier

yield: 1 dessert serving
(multiply × 4 for classroom turnout; adjust equipment sizes
accordingly)

MASTER RECIPE

production		costing only
1	4-fl.-oz. scoop Vanilla Ice Cream	1/8 recipe
2 Tbsp.	butter	1 oz.
1/4 c.	light brown sugar	1 1/3 oz.
1/4 tsp.	ground cinnamon	1/16 oz.
1	firm banana, peeled, halved widthwise, each half split lengthwise	10 oz.
as needed	water, in squeeze bottle	n/c
2 Tbsp.	banana liqueur	1 fl. oz.
1/4 c.	dark Caribbean rum	2 fl. oz.
1/2	lime	1/2 [63 ct.] lime
1	Miniature Palmier	1/12 recipe
1 sprig	fresh mint	1/12 bunch a.p.

service turnout:

1. Mise en place:
   a. Scoop the Vanilla Ice Cream onto the center of a chilled 10" plate and place the plate in the freezer.
   b. Arrange the remaining ingredients in appropriate serviceware on a service tray lined with a linen napkin. Provide small serving spoons, a fork, a large serving spoon, and tongs.
   c. Cover a service trolley with a tablecloth and set up a fueled butane burner and presentation sauté pan on it. Place the service tray on the trolley.
   d. Obtain a lid that completely covers the presentation pan and place it on the trolley's lower shelf.

2. At tableside, the chef or server proceeds as follows:
   a. Turn on the burner and place the presentation pan on it.
   b. Place the butter, brown sugar, and cinnamon in the pan and stir until the mixture bubbles.
   c. Add the banana pieces and turn them in the sauce until they begin to soften and caramelize. (If, at any time, the sauce gets too thick or threatens to scorch, thin it with water.)
   d. Send a food runner to the kitchen to bring the plate of ice cream.
   e. ⚠ *Holding the pan off the flame*, add the banana liqueur and rum to the pan.
   f. Return the pan to the flame and ignite by tipping the pan to bring the floating spirits in contact with the burner flame. Flambé, stirring and turning the bananas, until the flames begin to sputter and decrease. ⚠ If the flames get out of control, cover the pan with the lid and turn off the burner to extinguish them.
   g. Turn off the burner, then stick the fork into the lime half and squeeze the lime juice into the sauce.
   h. Arrange the bananas on the plate around the ice cream and pour the sauce on them. Stick the Miniature Palmier upright out of the back of the ice cream, then place the mint sprig in front of it.

COMPONENT RECIPE

MINIATURE PALMIERS

yield: 12 cookies

production		costing only
1	7" × 4 1/2" rectangle sheet puff pastry	% of pkg.
as needed	water	n/c
as needed	sanding sugar or granulated sugar	2 oz.

preparation:

1. Mise en place:
   a. Preheat an oven to 400°F.
   b. Prepare a half-sheet tray with pan liner.
2. Sugar the dough:
   a. Place the puff pastry sheet on the work surface with the 7" length perpendicular to you.
   b. If the puff pastry dough seems dry, brush it very lightly with water so the sugar will adhere.
   c. Sprinkle the dough with a heavy coating of sugar and gently press the sugar into the dough with a rolling pin.
   d. Turn the dough over and repeat.
3. Fold the dough:
   a. Fold the bottom edge of the dough up toward the center to make a 1" overlap.
   b. Fold the top edge down toward the center to make a 1" overlap.
   c. Sprinkle on a little more sugar.
   d. Again fold the bottom up and the top down so that they nearly meet in the center.
   e. Sprinkle on more sugar.
   f. Finally, fold the two double overlaps together to make one long, flat, 6-layer strip of dough.
   g. Place the dough on the sheet tray and refrigerate about 15 minutes, until the puff pastry becomes firm.
4. Make up the palmiers:
   a. Place the dough strip horizontally on a cutting board and, using a sharp chef's knife, cut it into 14 (3/8") slices. (The end slices will be imperfect.)
   b. Place the palmiers on the tray, well spaced apart to allow for expansion.
   c. Sprinkle the tops with sugar.
5. Bake the palmiers:
   a. Place the tray in the center of the oven and bake about 8 minutes, until the palmiers are puffed and light golden.
   b. Turn the palmiers over, sprinkle the tops with sugar, and return them to the oven.
   c. Bake about 4 minutes longer, until golden brown.
6. Cool to room temperature on a rack.

holding: in a tightly sealed container at cool room temperature up to 3 days

RECIPE VARIATION

Peaches Foster with Palmier
Replace the banana with a large, firm-ripe, peeled, pitted, and quartered peach

Chocolate Voodoo Torte

with Raspberry Sauce

yield: 1 dessert serving
(multiply × 4 for classroom turnout)

MASTER RECIPE

production		costing only
1 slice	Chocolate-Pecan Torte	1/8 recipe
1/2 c.	Raspberry Sauce*, in squeeze bottle	1/4 recipe
1 Tbsp.	Crema*, in squeeze bottle	1/16 recipe
5	Chocolate-Caramel "Needles"	1/10 recipe

service turnout:
1. Plate the dish:
   a. Place the Chocolate-Pecan Torte slice slightly back left of center on a cool 10" plate with the point at 7 o'clock.
   b. Squeeze a pool of Raspberry Sauce around the torte.
   c. Create a starburst on the raspberry sauce: Squeeze a 3/4"-diameter dot of Crema on the raspberry sauce, then squeeze a smaller dot of raspberry sauce on the crema dot, and finally squeeze a tiny dot of crema in the center. Drag the tip of a toothpick from the center out past the rim of the large dot; repeat several times to make the starburst.
   d. Stick the Chocolate-Caramel "Needles" out of the top of the torte.

*Make sure both sauces are the same consistency.

COMPONENT RECIPE

CHOCOLATE-PECAN TORTE

yield: 1 (9") glazed cake

production		costing only
1	Chocolate-Pecan Torte Layer	1 recipe
1	9" round cake board	1 each
2 1/4 c.	Chocolate Molasses Glaze, slightly warmer than room temperature	1 recipe

preparation:
1. Place the Chocolate-Pecan Torte Layer on the cake board and set it on a rack set over a half-sheet tray.
2. Pour the Chocolate Molasses Glaze over the cake, smoothing it with a thin, flexible metal spatula, nudging it over the edges and allowing it to run evenly down the sides of the cake. Smooth the edges to make an even, shiny coating.
3. Place the torte in a dessert refrigerator at least 1 hour to set the glaze.
4. Using a cake portioner or long metal spatula, score the cake into 8 even-size servings.

holding: under a plastic cake dome in a cool place up to 3 days; once the torte is sliced, cover the cut surfaces with plastic wrap

COMPONENT RECIPE
CHOCOLATE-PECAN TORTE LAYER

yield: 1 (9" round) cake layer

production		costing only
as needed	baker's pan coating spray	% of container
9 oz.	pecan flour (or pecan pieces)	9 oz.
8 oz.	butter, chopped into bits	8 oz.
7 oz.	bittersweet couverture chocolate, chopped if necessary	7 oz.
9	egg yolks	9 each or 6 oz.
8 oz.	sugar	8 oz.
6	room-temperature egg whites	n/c or 6 oz.
pinch	salt	1/16 oz.

preparation:
1. Mise en place:
   a. Preheat an oven to 325°F.
   b. Prepare a 9" × 2" round cake pan: Spray with pan coating, fit a circle of pan liner into the bottom, and spray again.
2. If necessary, prepare the pecan flour:
   a. Place the pecans in a food processor fitted with the metal blade and pulse them to a fine-chopped consistency. Be careful not to overprocess, or you'll extract the nut oil and end up with pecan butter.
   b. Place the chopped pecans in a coarse-mesh sifter set in a bowl. Sift the very fine pieces through the mesh, and return the coarser-chopped pecans still in the sifter to the processor bowl.
   c. Repeat steps 2a and 2b until the pecans are fine-chopped and light in texture, like dust.
3. Place the butter and chocolate in a small saucepan over very low heat. Stir constantly until melted. Cool to room temperature.
4. Mix the batter:
   a. Place the egg yolks and sugar in the bowl of a small mixer. Using the whip attachment, whip about 3 minutes on high speed, until light and fluffy.
   b. Reduce the speed to low and pulse in the chocolate. Do not overmix.
   c. Place the egg whites in a clean, dry bowl with a pinch of salt. Using a clean, dry whisk, beat the whites to just under firm peaks. Do not beat to stiff peaks or until crumbly. If the egg whites become overbeaten, discard them and start over.
   d. Immediately fold 1/4 of the whites into the chocolate-yolk mixture, then fold the chocolate-yolk mixture back into the whites, sprinkling in the pecan flour as you fold.
5. Pan the batter:
   a. Immediately pour the batter into the cake pan.
   b. Run the batter a little way up the sides of the pan, making a slight depression in the center.
6. Immediately place the pan on the center rack of the oven. Bake 40 or more minutes, until the cake is puffed and risen and a tester inserted in the center comes out with big moist crumbs, but not wet batter.
7. Cool the pan on a rack for 10 minutes.
8. Turn the cake out of its pan onto the rack and cool to room temperature.

holding: wrapped in plastic film at cool room temperature up to 24 hours; freeze up to 3 months

COMPONENT RECIPE
CHOCOLATE MOLASSES GLAZE

yield: approx. 2 1/4 c.

production		costing only
9 oz.	bittersweet couverture chocolate, chopped, if necessary	9 oz.
1 c.	heavy cream	8 fl. oz.
4 Tbsp.	butter	2 oz.
3 Tbsp.	molasses	1 1/2 fl. oz.

preparation:
1. Place the chocolate in a large bowl near the stove.
2. Mix the cream, butter, and molasses in a small, heavy saucepan. Bring to the boil and cook at a hard boil 1 minute.
3. Pour the cream mixture over the chocolate and stir with a rubber spatula until the chocolate is melted and smooth.
4. Cool almost to room temperature, stirring occasionally.

holding: do not hold; prepare just before glazing cake

COMPONENT RECIPE
CHOCOLATE-CARAMEL "NEEDLES"

yield: 40 needles to garnish 8 cake servings, plus extra for practice

production		costing only
2 c.	sugar	1 lb.
1/2 c.	water	n/c
1 fl. oz.	foodservice glucose or light corn syrup	1 fl. oz.
6 oz.	bittersweet couverture chocolate, chopped if necessary	6 oz.
as needed	a cake pan filled with sugar	may be re-used

preparation:

1. Make the caramel "needles":
   a. Place a full-sheet-size silicone mat on a full-sheet tray and set it near the stove.
   b. Place the sugar and water in a heavy saucepan and stir them together until the mixture resembles wet sand. Do not stir the mixture again. Add the glucose.
   c. Prepare an ice-water bath large enough to hold the sugar saucepan and place it near the stove.
   d. Place the sugar pan over moderate heat and heat the sugar, swirling the pan occasionally, until the sugar melts, bubbles, and begins to caramelize.
   e. Reduce the heat and swirl the pan constantly about 2 minutes, until the caramel acquires a light brown color. ⚠ Do not allow the sugar syrup to splash or spatter, and do not let the caramel burn.
   f. When the caramel reaches the correct color, stop the cooking by transferring the sugar pan to the ice-water bath. Swirl the pan occasionally and observe the consistency of the caramel. When the caramel reaches the consistency of molasses, remove it from the ice-water bath and wipe the bottom of the pan dry.
   g. Hold the pan over the silicone mat and dip up some of the caramel in a hotel spoon. Sweep the spoon back and forth over the mat, drizzling thin, straight strands of caramel from the tip of the spoon onto the mat.
   h. Allow the caramel strands to cool and harden into "needles."
2. Coat the "needles":
   a. Place the chocolate in the dry, clean top of a double boiler filled with 1" hot water. Place over low heat and melt the chocolate, stirring often with a rubber spatula.
   b. Wearing foodservice gloves, break the caramel strands into 4" lengths, or "needles." Discard the curved end pieces and scraps.
   c. Remove the smooth melted chocolate from the heat and cool it to room temperature, stirring occasionally.
   d. Place the pan of sugar on a sheet tray near you.
   e. Wearing foodservice gloves, dip each caramel "needle" into the chocolate, allow the excess chocolate to drip off, and then stick the coated "needle" upright into the pan of sugar.
   f. Transfer the pan of "needles" to the refrigerator and chill 30 minutes so that the chocolate hardens more quickly.

holding: on the tray, uncovered, at cool room temperature up to 1 week

DESSERTS

RECIPE VARIATION
Chocolate-Pecan Torte with Raspberry Sauce
Omit the "needles" and Crema décor.

King's Cake
with Queen's Sauce

yield: 1 dessert serving
(multiply × 4 for classroom turnout)

MASTER RECIPE

production		costing only
2/3 c.	Queen's Sauce	1/4 recipe
1	Individual King's Cake	1/4 recipe

service turnout:
1. Plate the dish:
   a. Ladle the Queen's Sauce onto a cool 10" plate.
   b. Place the King's Cake in the center of the plate.

COMPONENT RECIPE
INDIVIDUAL KING'S CAKES

yield: 4 dessert servings

production		costing only
1 Tbsp.	active dry yeast	1/4 oz.
1/4 c.	lukewarm water	n/c
pinch	sugar	1/18 oz.
2	egg yolks	2 each or 1 1/3 oz.
1/2 c.	room-temperature milk	4 fl. oz.
1/2 c.	granulated sugar	4 oz.
1/2 tsp.	fine salt	1/12 oz.
1 Tbsp.	minced lemon zest	1/4 [90 ct.] lemon
1 Tbsp.	minced orange zest	1/6 [100 ct.] orange
±10 oz.	flour	±10 oz.
1/4 c.	softened butter	2 oz.
as needed	flour for dusting	1 oz.
as needed	baker's pan coating spray	% of container
6 oz.	fine-chopped pecans	6 oz.
1/2	egg, beaten	1/2 each or 1 oz.
2 oz.	brown sugar	2 oz.
pinch	fine salt	1/16 oz.
1/2 tsp.	pure vanilla extract	1/12 fl oz.
1/2 tsp.	cinnamon	1/8 oz.
1/4 tsp.	ground allspice	1/16 oz.
1/2	egg, beaten with 2 tsp. water to make egg wash	1/2 each or 1 oz.
1/2 c.	Royal Icing	1/2 recipe
as needed	golden yellow decorating sugar	1/8 oz.
as needed	green decorating sugar	1/8 oz.
as needed	purple decorating sugar	1/8 oz.

preparation:
1. Mix the dough:
   a. In a very small bowl mix together the yeast, lukewarm water, and sugar. Set aside in a warm place for 5 minutes.
   b. Mix together the egg yolks, milk, granulated sugar, salt, lemon and orange zest, and yeast mixture.
   c. Stir in enough flour to make a soft dough.
   d. Spread the dough out on a heavily floured work surface, smear the butter on it, and use a bench scraper to fold and turn the dough to incorporate the butter and complete flour absorption.
   e. Spray a bowl with pan coating and place the dough in it. Cover with a kitchen towel and set aside in a cool place to rise for about an hour.
2. Make the filling:
   a. Mix together the pecans, 1/2 beaten egg, brown sugar, salt, vanilla, cinnamon, and allspice.
3. Make up the cakes:
   a. Prepare a half-sheet tray with pan liner.
   b. Turn the dough out onto a floured work surface and use the bench scraper to divide it into 4 pieces. Set 3 pieces aside.
   c. On a floured surface, with a floured pin, roll out a piece of dough into a rectangle about 3" × 8."
   d. Place 1/4 of the pecan filling in a line down the center of the dough.
   e. Fold the top edge of the dough over the filling and then roll the dough into a cylinder with the filling in the center. Pinch together the edges of the dough to seal them, then turn the cylinder over so that the seam is on the bottom.
   f. Trim the ends of the dough cylinder so that the filling extends to the cut edges.
   g. Shape the cylinder into a ring, tucking one end inside the other. Pinch the dough together to secure it.
   h. Using the pastry scraper, transfer the dough ring to the lined half-sheet tray.
   i. Repeat with the remaining dough and filling to make a total of 4 individual king's cakes.
   j. Cover the tray with a kitchen towel and set aside in a cool place to rise 1 hour.
4. Preheat an oven to 375°F.
5. Brush the cakes lightly with egg wash.
6. Bake in the center of the oven about 20 minutes, until the crusts are golden and the cakes sound hollow when tapped.
7. Transfer the cakes to a rack and cool to room temperature.
8. Glaze each cake with Royal Icing.
9. Immediately decorate each cake with 9 alternating stripes of gold, green, and purple sugar.

holding: at room temperature on the rack up to 6 hours

DESSERTS

COMPONENT RECIPE
QUEEN'S SAUCE

yield: approx. 2 1/2 c.

production		costing only
2 1/2 c.	Vanilla Custard Sauce	1 recipe
1 Tbsp.	Bourbon whiskey	1/2 fl. oz.
1 Tbsp.	praline liqueur	1/2 fl. oz.

preparation:
1. Mix all ingredients.

holding: refrigerate in a freshly sanitized, covered, nonreactive container up to 5 days

Dough rectangle with filling.

Folding the top edge of the dough over the filling.

Forming a ring.

King's cake on a sheet tray.

RECIPE VARIATION
Large King's Cake with Queen's Sauce
Make up the cake as a single large ring. Present the Queen's Sauce in a sauceboat.

☐ TABLE 6.2 LOUISIANA REGIONAL INGREDIENTS

ITEM	MARKET FORMS	USES	SEASONALITY	OTHER	STORAGE
CORNMEAL, YELLOW AND WHITE	see p. 80				
LONG-GRAIN WHITE RICE	see p. 80				
WILD PECAN RICE OR POPCORN RICE	Related neither to wild rice nor pecans, this fragrant, ivory-grained rice is a hybrid derived from crossing several aromatic rices. Developed by the Conrad Rice Mill, it is sold under their Konriko label in 2-lb. and 10-lb. bags.	Serve as a distinctive side dish. Its nutty flavor may be augmented by tossing with chopped, toasted pecans just before serving. Wild pecan rice usually needs slightly less than a 2:1 ratio of liquid to rice whether cooked by pan-steaming or by the pilaf method.	N/A	Its toasty, nutty aroma is reminiscent of popping corn, hence the alternative name *popcorn rice*.	Store at room temperature; freeze for long-term storage.
HOLLAND RUSKS	Originally part of a sailing ship's food store, these thick, round bread slices were dried to prevent the formation of mold and extend storage. They became known as *Holland rusks* because several Dutch companies specialized in their production.	Holland rusks are the classic base for New Orleans poached-egg dishes and for Chicken Rochambeau.	N/A	Toasted or fried bread croutons are a suitable substitute.	Store tightly sealed at room temperature.
LOUISIANA RED BEANS	Louisiana red beans are smaller, more rounded, and lighter in color than the standard American light red kidney bean. Camellia brand beans are available in 1-lb. and 4-lb. bags.	Used primarily for red beans 'n' rice, Louisiana red beans cook just a little more quickly and require a little less liquid than standard kidney beans.	N/A	Standard light red kidney beans are an adequate substitute.	Store at room temperature.
CANE SYRUP	The premier Louisiana brand Steen's is available in 16-fl.-oz. bottles and 12-fl.-oz. and 25-fl.-oz. cans.	Cane syrup is used as a topping for breakfast foods or as an ingredient in baking.	N/A	This thick, dark syrup is made by extracting the juice from sugarcane, then boiling it down until it thickens.	Store at room temperature.
GROUND, DRIED CHICORY ROOT	Chicory is sold in 1-lb., 5-lb. and 25-lb. bags.	Brewed along with dark-roast coffee, chicory adds a distinctive Creole flavor.		To make Louisiana chicory, the root of a local chicory cultivar is dried and ground to a fine powder.	Store frozen.
CREOLE MUSTARD	The region's most prominent brand, Zatarain's, is sold in jars of many sizes.	A key ingredient in Creole Rèmoulade, Creole mustard is used on sandwiches, and in sauces, dressings, and marinades. It gives Louisiana crab cakes a distinctive flavor.	N/A	Creole mustard is made from crushed brown mustard seeds blended with salt and vinegar. French brands are an adequate substitute.	Store at room temperature.
FILÉ POWDER	Sold in small jars and in bulk by the pound. Strong, pungent aroma indicates freshness.	Stirred into a hot liquid, it imparts a gelatinous texture similar to that of tapioca. However, the filé must be added off the heat at the last minute before serving, and the liquid never allowed to cook any longer.	N/A	Ground from dried sassafras leaves, this aromatic powder has a distinctive taste similar to dried thyme with a hint of eucalyptus. It is also a powerful thickening agent.	Store tightly sealed at room temperature; freeze for prolonged storage.

☐ TABLE 6.2 LOUISIANA REGIONAL INGREDIENTS (continued)

ITEM	MARKET FORMS	USES	SEASONALITY	OTHER	STORAGE
LOUISIANA HOT PEPPER SAUCE	A Louisiana product still made on Avery Island, classic red Tabasco is America's best-known bottled hot sauce. Crystal brand is a regional favorite. Hot pepper sauces are available in bottles ranging from 1/2-fl.-oz. miniatures to gallon jugs.	A bottle of hot pepper sauce is placed on the table in Louisiana homes and restaurants. This tangy, spicy-hot condiment seasons virtually all savory foods.	N/A	Alternative sauces, such as a milder green Tabasco made from jalapeño chiles, are now available.	Store at room temperature.
LOUISIANA SEAFOOD BOIL	La Cherche's and Zatarain's are prominent brands marketed in individual-use net "bouquets garnis" bags or in bulk. Concentrated liquid seafood seasoning, made by steeping the whole spices and herbs in water, is also available in bottles.	Seafood boil is added to poaching and steaming liquids when preparing crabs, shrimp, or crawfish.	N/A	Seafood boil is a mixture of whole black and white peppercorns, coriander and celery seeds, dried red chiles, broken bay leaves, and other herbs and spices.	Store tightly sealed at room temperature.
ANDOUILLE (ahn-DOO-ee)	Andouille is sold fresh by the pound in the region. Vacuum-packed frozen andouille is shipped around the country.	Andouille is simmered into soups, gumbos, and red beans 'n' rice. Grilled and sliced, andouille may be eaten as an hors d'oeuvre or snack accompanied by Creole mustard or coated with a sweet fruit glaze.	N/A	Louisiana andouille is a coarse-ground sausage seasoned with vinegar, black pepper, and cayenne pepper; lightly cured; then smoked.	Store refrigerated or frozen.
CHAURICE (shore-EECE)	See andouille.	Chaurice may be grilled or fried and served in a roll as a sandwich, or simmered with beans or greens.	N/A	A variation of Spanish chorizo, Louisiana chaurice is a highly spiced, red pepper–spiked, garlic–scented fresh pork sausage.	Store refrigerated or frozen.
TASSO (TAH-so)	See andouille.	May be sliced thin and used as a sandwich ingredient or wrapped around hors d'oeuvre items. More commonly used as a stuffing ingredient or as a seasoning meat.	N/A	Heavily cured, cayenne-rubbed slices of pork butt are finished with pecan or hickory smoke.	Store refrigerated; although its texture deteriorates, frozen tasso may be used as a seasoning meat.
'TI SALÉ (tee sah-LAY)	See andouille.	As a seasoning meat, it is usually diced and fried to render the fat and then simmered with greens, green beans, or dried beans.	N/A	Slangy French for "a little bit salted," 'ti salé is a cayenne-spiked version of salt pork.	Store refrigerated or frozen.
ALLIGATOR MEAT	Cleaned, tenderized alligator tail and loin meat is available frozen in 1-lb. packs and 10-lb. cartons.	Alligator meat is grilled, sautéed, and stewed in gumbos. Grilled 'gator on a stick is a popular appetizer or snack.	Available year round.	The meat is very clean and ready to use with no waste. Virtually all alligator is farm raised.	Store frozen until needed; refrigerate after thawing.

(continued)

☐ **TABLE 6.2 LOUISIANA REGIONAL INGREDIENTS**   *(continued)*

ITEM	MARKET FORMS	USES	SEASONALITY	OTHER	STORAGE
CRAWFISH	In Louisiana, fresh live crawfish are sold in 50-lb. burlap bags called *onion sacks.* Frozen whole crawfish are sold in 10-lb. packs. Whole crawfish are graded by count to pound: true select are under 12/lb.; #1 select are 12-15/lb.; select are 15-20/lb. "Field run" means mixed sizes. Frozen tail meat is available in 2-lb. packs.	Live crawfish are boiled or steamed and eaten "in the rough" with melted butter, boiled potatoes, and corn on the cob. Crawfish tail meat is made into ètoufées, Creoles, gumbos, and other classic dishes. It is featured in rice dressings and salads.	Peak season for live crawfish is March through June. Farmed crawfish season runs from Nov. to July; wild crawfish season runs from late Jan. to June, depending on the weather. A few farm producers offer live crawfish out of season.	Crawfish are now raised throughout the United States, in South and Central America, and in Asia; however, Louisiana crawfish are considered the finest. Whole crawfish are graded by count/lb. Most producers of crawfish tail meat offer it with and without the fat. Cooked crawfish fat appears with the meat as pale-pink to coral-colored nuggets clinging to the front ends of the tails. Fat enhances the flavor and richness of étouffées and other simmered dishes.	Keep fresh crawfish moist under refrigeration. Store processed crawfish frozen until needed; refrigerate after thawing.
GULF SHRIMP	Three types of Gulf shrimp are available: white, brown, and pink. *White Gulf shrimp:* Frozen, head-on white shrimp are packed primarily for the Asian-American market and available from Asian purveyors. Yield is about 60 percent; they commonly range in size from 51–60 to 16–20 count. Deheaded IQF white shrimp are available in sizes from 51–60 to U-16 count. *Deheaded, IQF brown shrimp:* Sizes range from 51–60 to U-16 count. Less expensive than white Gulf shrimp. *Pink Gulf shrimp:* Available locally during their brief spring season; they are small, ranging from 50–60 to 41–45 head-on count.	Many uses.	Peak season is spring and summer months. Frozen shrimp are available year round.	Shrimp from the waters off Louisiana and the related Mississippi, Alabama, and Texas Gulf coasts are among the finest in the world.	Refrigerate fresh shrimp 1 or 2 days only. Store frozen until needed; refrigerate after thawing.
GULF BLUE CRABS/CRAB MEAT	Live crabs are sold regionally. Most Louisiana crabs are steamed and picked to produce pasteurized crabmeat sold in 1-lb. containers.	In Louisiana most crabmeat is made into crab cakes or used in stuffings and dips.	In good weather cycles, live Gulf crabs are available throughout the year but are best in summer months.	For general blue crab/crab meat information, see pp. 199, 200, and 231.	Keep live crabs refrigerated and moist. Store crab meat refrigerated. Freezing destroys texture.
GULF OYSTERS	Gulf oysters are sold live by count or shucked in jars and tubs.	Most Louisiana oysters are eaten raw on the half shell or topped and baked. Oysters are also used in gratins, soups, gumbos, and dressings.	Gulf oysters are abundant and available virtually year-round.	For general oyster information, see pp. 200 and 231.	Keep live oysters refrigerated and moist.

☐ TABLE 6.2 LOUISIANA REGIONAL INGREDIENTS (continued)

ITEM	MARKET FORMS	USES	SEASONALITY	OTHER	STORAGE
GULF REDFISH OR RED DRUM	Three to 5-lb. Gulf redfish are sold whole and as fillets.	Today most redfish is blackened. Small, single service–size redfish, called *puppy drums*, are presented whole either grilled or in *courtbouillon*.	In season winter through spring.	Red drum was virtually fished out by the early 1990s and was put on the endangered species list, but it is making a comeback and is once again legal.	Store whole fish refrigerated in ice; keep fillets in ice in a bag or container.
GULF RED SNAPPER	Although they grow up to 25 lb., snappers of the 4- to 6-lb. size are most common. Small 1- to 2-lb. "baby" snappers are sold whole; larger fish are fabricated into fillets.	Snapper fillets are used in many preparations; baby snappers are grilled or stuffed and baked.	Peak season is early summer.	Gulf snappers are prized for their firm texture and good flavor.	See Gulf redfish.
POMPANO	Small, 1- to 2-lb. pompanos are sold whole; larger fish up to 4 lb. are filleted.	This firm, dark, full-flavored fish is teamed with assertive sauces and is a favorite for Asian presentations. Small, milder fillets are baked in parchment for the classic dish Pompano en Papillote.	Peak season is spring and summer.		See Gulf redfish.
MIRLITON	Fresh mirliton is sold in flats of 12 to 18 pieces..	In Louisiana this pear-shaped member of the squash family is most commonly split, hollowed, and stuffed with a spicy, savory dressing. It may also be peeled, sliced, and steamed or stir-fried.	Peak season is late summer through fall.	For general mirliton information, see chayote, p. 356.	Refrigerate, separately wrapped in cellophane or paper towels.
LOUISIANA "YAMS"	Sold fresh in 40-lb. boxes.	Often simply baked and topped with butter, Louisiana "yams" are also boiled and puréed for casseroles or soups and made into French fries.	In peak season spring through fall, Louisiana "yams" are available year round.	Not a true yam, this tuber is basically the same orange sweet potato grown elsewhere in the United States; those grown in Louisiana soil are noted for their sweetness and full flavor.	Store at cool room temperature in darkness.
ARTICHOKES	See p. 596.				
JERUSALEM ARTICHOKES/ SUNCHOKES	See p. 82.				
CREOLE TOMATOES	Picked ripe and fragile, Creole tomatoes are a regional specialty rarely shipped nationwide.	Used in raw and cooked preparations.	Marketed locally June through October.	The locally prized Creole tomato is not a particular cultivar, but rather any small, round tomato grown in Louisiana where the rich, alluvial soil produces a thin-skinned, low-acid, juicy tomato.	Store at cool room temperature; refrigeration destroys flavor and texture.

■ □ ■ chapter seven

The Mexican Border

southern Texas, New Mexico, Arizona, southern Utah, southern Colorado, and Hispanic California

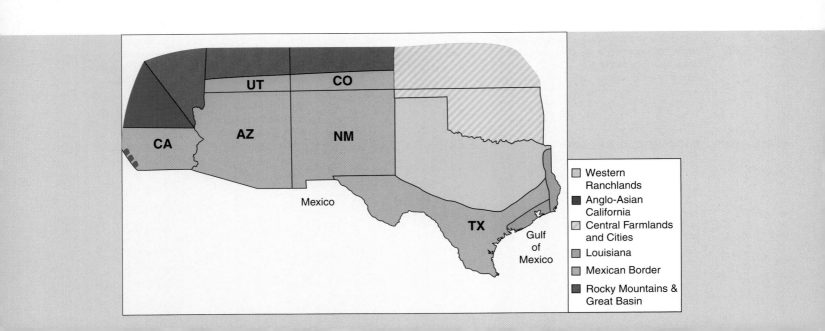

UT   CO

CA   AZ   NM

Mexico

TX   Gulf
of
Mexico

- ☐ Western Ranchlands
- ☐ Anglo-Asian California
- ☐ Central Farmlands and Cities
- ☐ Louisiana
- ☐ Mexican Border
- ☐ Rocky Mountains & Great Basin

THIS CHAPTER EXPLORES an American culinary region with foodways closely connected to Mexico. Within this region you'll discover two distinctive subcuisines as well as a chef-driven modern cuisine and a thriving Native American microcuisine.

In the 1600s, Mexican cooking marched north along with Catholic missionaries settling new land for Spain. Mission cooks adopted the ingredients and cooking techniques of the highly developed Southwestern Native American cultures, blending them with their own colonial Mexican cuisine. In the early 1800s Americans introduced pioneer provisions and beef-based Ranchlands cuisine. The result of this culinary overlay is American Southwestern cuisine, a unique cooking style little known outside the region.

Mexican-American cuisine is exactly what its name implies: a hybrid cooking style based on traditional Mexican cuisine modified with American ingredients and technology. This well-known cuisine is known across the nation and around the globe.

In the late 20th century, restaurant chefs expanded Southwestern cuisine, cooking with Mexican ingredients and world cuisines techniques to create contemporary Mexican Border cuisine. This cutting-edge cooking style is still evolving.

On this book's companion website you'll also discover the Southwestern Native American microcuisine, the most sophisticated and widely practiced of all modern native cooking styles.

AFTER STUDYING THIS CHAPTER YOU SHOULD BE ABLE TO:

- describe the climate and topography of the American Southwest (Factor 1) and explain their impact on the development of American Southwestern cuisine
- discuss Southwestern Native American culture and cuisine (Factor 2)
- discuss the role of the Spanish missions in American Southwestern cuisine (Factor 2 and Factor 3)
- explain traditional alkaline processing of corn as practiced in Mexican (Factor 3) and Southwest Native American (Factor 2) cuisines
- outline the evolution of Mexican-American cuisine and describe its most prominent dishes (Factor 4)
- list and describe the ingredients, cooking methods, and flavor profiles of traditional Southwestern cuisine
- explain the impact of late 20th century economic development on the development of Mexican Border cuisine (Factor 5)
- discuss the Southwestern Native American microcuisine and list its defining dishes
- identify and prepare traditional Southwestern, Mexican-American, Southwestern Native American dishes, and contemporary Mexican Border cuisine dishes

APPETIZERS

Creamy Corn and Green Chile Soup with Flour Tortillas

Nopal Cactus Salad

Guacamole and Chips for Two

Southwest Cheese Chile Relleno with Spiced Tomato Sauce

Texas Gulf Coast Shrimp Cocktail

Green Chile Quesadilla with Fresh Tomato Salsa

Twin Tostadas

California Crab Meat Corn Crêpes in Creamy Tomato Sauce

Border-Style Beef Tamal with Red and Green Salsas

Zuñi Stuffed Squash Blossoms with Roasted Tomato Sauce

ENTRÉES

Southern California Mahimahi Tamal with Jalapeño-Citrus Butter Sauce, Herbed Posole,
and Steamed Chayote

Santa Fe Red Chile Cheese Enchiladas with Olla Beans and Avocado Salad

New Mexico Pork *Chile Verde* with Flour Tortillas and Pepper-Squash Medley

Baja Border Chicken Green Enchiladas with Refried Beans and Desert Salad

Chicken Monterey with Green Chile Potatoes and Black Bean Pico de Gallo

Hopi Blue Corn Smoked Rabbit Stacked Enchilada

Fajitas

Navajo Mutton Stew with Fry Bread and Three Sisters Vegetable Medley

***Chile con Carne* in Tortilla Basket** with Olla Beans and Avocado Pico de Gallo

White Posole with Crisp Vegetable Garnish

DESSERTS

Piñon Pine Nut Torte with Prickly Pear Sauce and Crema

Flan with Cactus Cut-Out Cookie

Sopaipillas with Brown Sugar Apple Compote

WEBSITE EXTRAS

Basic Preparations

Breakfasts   Sandwiches and Tacos   Hors d'Oeuvres   Thanksgiving Menu

■
□ AMERICAN
■ SOUTHWESTERN
CUISINE

We begin our study of the Mexican Border culinary region with the cooking of the American Southwest because it predates the region's other cuisines by several hundred years. In fact, Southwestern cuisine existed well before the settlement of Jamestown, making it the North American continent's first regional cooking style. However, at the time the region belonged to another country. Long before the English landed in Virginia, the Spanish had colonized Mexico and were settling California and the Southwestern high desert. Although America as a nation did not yet exist, American Southwestern cuisine had already been born.

The cuisine of the American Southwest was shaped by its geographical limitations. Much of this area has beautiful, yet challenging topography. Its climate is **arid,** having little rainfall. Much of the American Southwest is an extension of the great Sonoran Desert of northern Mexico, one of the driest places in the world. However, this land was not always dry; in prehistoric times it was covered with water.

The Southwestern High Desert

When the North American continent was still being formed and the Appalachian Mountains were still young, much of the American Southwest was the level floor of a vast ocean. Over millions of years, layers of sediment built up on the seabed in random strata. Compression caused by the weight of water gradually changed these layers into sedimentary rock composed of diverse minerals and in varied colors. Then the same geological forces that had previously built the Appalachians pushed the Rocky Mountains high into the sky. The water receded, and dry land emerged. The former ocean floor was now the surface of a high plateau.

Over millennia, wind and water transformed this plateau, wearing away the softer bedrock and leaving harder rock unscathed. In some areas massive erosion created thousand-foot-high pillars, called *buttes* (Figure 7.1), and larger tablelands, called *mesas*. The wind-blasted sides of these formations are striped in shades of red, brown, tan, ocher, and gold, revealing layers of the ancient seabed. Some of these strata contain fossilized marine plants and animals buried in the sediment millions of years ago. In other places water erosion from melting glaciers carved deep, narrow trenches, called *canyons*, into the bedrock. At the bottom of these ancient water courses, modern streams and rivers flow far below the level of the surrounding land.

Much of the American Southwest is classified as **high desert,** arid land at an elevation of more than 4,000 feet, high enough for frost and occasional snow. The Southwest is dry because of its location within the **rain shadow** of the Sierra Nevada mountain range, which blocks westerly moist air from the Pacific (Figure 7.2, p. 304). In many areas the air is so dry that rainfall often *sublimates*, or changes from liquid form into vapor, before reaching the ground. As a result of the Sierra Nevada rain

FIGURE 7.1

Buttes are striking features of the Southwest's high desert topography.
Nagel Photography/Shutterstock

shadow, annual precipitation in most of the Southwest is less than 13 inches. The region's streams and rivers are full to their banks only in springtime when they rush with mountain snowmelt; most of the year only a trickle of water flows in the center of their dry beds.

Not the entire Southwest is high desert. In southeastern Texas the land flattens out to sea level near the Gulf, where it's typically hot and humid. On the Pacific slope of the Sierra Nevadas and along the coast, southern California has a Mediterranean climate. However, high desert topography and climate primarily shaped the agriculture and, thus, the foodways of the region.

FACTOR 1

The Southwest's arid climate shaped its agriculture and cuisine.

Throughout most of the Southwest, the soil is thin and the vegetation sparse. South of the Rocky Mountains, thin groves of yellow pine crest the tops of low foothills. Piñon pines, scrub oaks, mesquite, and juniper bushes dot the hillsides, and cottonwoods and black walnut trees line canyon bottom riverbanks. Sagebrush and nopal cactus are scattered across the desert floor, and here and there a giant saguaro cactus lifts its fleshy arms into the cloudless blue sky.

Such land is inhospitable to animal life; only the hardiest thrive. Jackrabbits, squirrels, and small, piglike peccaries make their homes on the flatlands and mesas; mule deer range the hillsides and mountain lions prowl the ridge tops. Here you'll also find snakes, armadillos, and lizards. Eagles, owls, hawks, roadrunners, and vultures are among the few birds attracted to the desert topography.

Indigenous foods of the Mexican Border region include seeds (acorns, black walnuts, jojoba, sunflower roots and seeds, pine nuts, and grass seeds), wild fruits (chokecherry, hackberry, manzanita, squawberry, and mesquite beans), and wild vegetables (cattail, cota, dock, dandelion, purslane, lamb's quarter, and tumbleweed). Although they appear forbidding, cactus and cactuslike plants, such as agave, cholla, yucca, barrel cactus, and ocotillo, provide nutrition in many forms. The giant saguaro

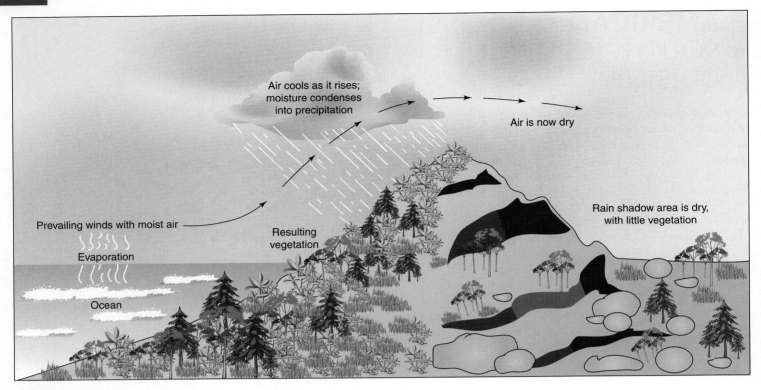

FIGURE 7.2
Rain Shadow

cactus provides fruits, eaten fresh or preserved, and juice drunk fresh or fermented into an alcoholic beverage. Although agriculture was the primary food source for many of the region's Native Americans, these indigenous wild foods added both variety and essential nutrients to the native diet.

Native Americans of the Southwest

The cradle of Southwestern Native American civilization—and the birthplace of Southwestern cuisine—lies just south of the **Four Corners,** the place where the states of New Mexico, Arizona, Colorado, and Utah meet.

Archaeological evidence proves that humans have inhabited the American Southwest for more than 6,000 years. In fact, by the time of European contact in the early 1500s, three widespread and complex civilizations had already flourished and then disappeared (Figure 7.3). Known to the region's natives as the Ancient Ones, these groups left behind numerous dwelling sites, artifacts, and legends passed down through the centuries to the modern Native American cultures that followed them. Some of these civilizations are believed to be the ancestors of modern pueblo tribes (Figure 7.4).

The Pueblo Tribes

In this book Native American groups thought to be the descendants of the ancient Southwest civilizations are known

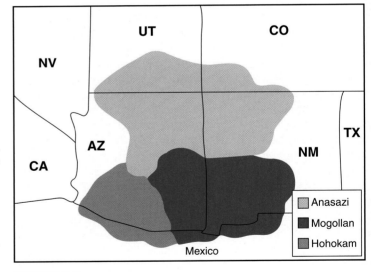

FIGURE 7.3
Ancient Cultures of the Four Corners Area

collectively as the *pueblo tribes*, named for their distinctive architectural style. These tribes lived in **pueblos** (PWEB-lows), or permanent fortified villages on high mesa tops, the rims of canyons, or the desert floor near rivers. A typical pueblo consists of multistory houses constructed of *adobe*, or clay bricks, with timber rafters and roofs of mud-and-brush thatch (Figure 7.5).

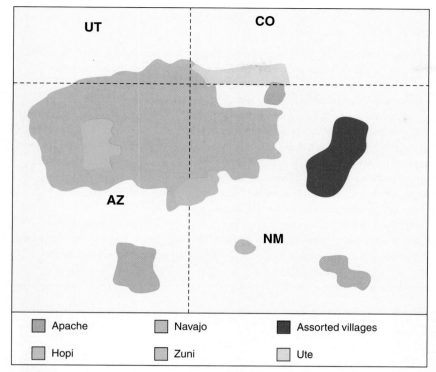

FIGURE 7.4
Native American Settlement in the Southwest

FIGURE 7.5
Ruins of a Southwestern pueblo. Caitlin Mirra/Shutterstock

The Ancient Ones	Their Descendants
The Hohokam	Pimas, Papagosx
The Anasazi	Hopi, Zuni, Pueblo
The Mogollan	no known descendants

ceremonial chamber. During the height of pueblo culture, the surrounding canyon bottoms were highly cultivated land that supplied the inhabitants with most of their food. Both food and water were carried up the sides of the mesa on narrow pathways, and up primitive ladders, to the mesa top.

Although the various pueblo tribes had different languages, religious practices, and social customs, they all had three important things in common: the pueblo style of building permanent villages, similarly designed handicrafts, and the effective methods of desert agriculture that gave rise to their distinctive cuisine.

The Birth of Corn Culture

Knowing about the agriculture and cooking of the pueblo tribes is key to understanding both American Southwestern cuisine and the modern microcuisine of the Southwestern Native American tribes. Moreover, the food culture of these Native American groups is a significant part of the food history of the entire nation because the pueblo tribes were the first Americans to receive and transmit corn culture. From their ancestors, corn cultivation and cooking spread throughout the North American continent and the world.

FACTOR 2
Ancestors of pueblo Native American tribes initiated the spread of corn culture throughout the North American continent.

Food historians believe that the ancestors of American Southwestern pueblo tribes learned desert agriculture, including corn cultivation, from the ancient civilizations of central Mexico. The Aztecs, Mayas, and other ancient people of the area are collectively called **Meso-Americans.**

As early as 3500 B.C.E., Meso-Americans discovered that a particular species of wild grass could be planted, tended, and harvested to create a dependable, sustainable source of food. After many centuries this grass became a cultivated grain plant, called corn or maize. Over centuries, Meso-Americans adapted the corn plant to human needs and preferences by selective breeding.

From its beginning in Central America, the cultivation and cooking of corn gradually moved north, spreading to the ancient Mayas and Aztecs of present-day Mexico and then to the ancient civilizations of the American Southwest. There, knowledge of corn culture was handed down from generation to generation, its cultivation improving over time. In the American Southwest, pueblo tribes learned to grow many cultivars of corn in a variety of colors: white, yellow, red, multicolored, and blue—the latter considered most sacred of all. Both dried corn as a food and corn seed for planting were valuable trade goods. Through precontact Native Americans' expanding system of trade, corn culture gradually spread throughout North America until many Native American tribes had embraced corn as their staff of life.

Early pueblo houses had no doors or windows and were entered from rooftop access holes equipped with pole ladders (Figure 7.6). Unlike most Native American dwellings, pueblo houses were designed with kitchens containing both food preparation and food storage areas. Traditional pueblo houses were arranged around courtyards, each having a central *kiva*, or underground

THE IMPORTANCE OF CORN

Corn, or maize, is the New World's most important contribution to the human diet. Corn is high in carbohydrates; is rich in vitamins A, B, and C; and contains potassium, magnesium, phosphorus, and iron. When corn is subjected to traditional alkaline processing and combined with legumes, the resulting protein rivals that of meat.

Corn kernels are large and durable, valuable qualities in a plant seed. Corn can be planted without plowing, requiring only drilling, or making shallow holes in the ground. It can thrive in mediocre soil, it withstands both cold and heat, and it gives a remarkably high yield per acre: two to even three times that of wheat. Thus, corn provides a lot of nutrition for a relatively small amount of work.

When Europeans discovered this nutritious, easily grown grain during the Age of Exploration, they instantly recognized it as a useful food for both people and animals. Within a hundred years corn culture had traveled around the world. Cornmeal dishes became a staple food for many of Europe's poor and for most sub-Saharan Africans. Cornmeal sustained America's colonists and pioneers and fed the slaves of the Plantation South, Caribbean, and South America. Corn fattens American hogs, producing succulent pork and smoked pork products; fed to feedlot steers, it produces prime beef. Corn is the raw material from which Bourbon and sour mash whiskies are made.

Today the world eats corn in many forms, some of them "hidden." Corn syrup and other corn derivatives are included in thousands of industrially produced foods, a practice that has become the subject of controversy among health and nutrition experts. In addition, corn-based ethanol is fueling farm machinery and automobiles, a use that threatens its availability as a food crop and may have negative environmental consequences.

FIGURE 7.6
Pueblo dwellings were entered from the roof via ladders.
sydcinema/Shutterstock

FIGURE 7.7
Terracing creates supported beds that retain water and prevent erosion. apdesign/Shutterstock

Desert Agriculture and Three Sisters Crops

Unlike most Native American groups, the pueblo tribes didn't engage in seasonal migration but instead remained in permanent villages tending crops year round and practicing routine fertilization. In order to grow crops in the arid high desert, pueblo tribes developed many unique and sophisticated agricultural methods. Of course, the key to desert agriculture is effective use of water.

In the high desert the most readily available water is in streams and rivers. Thus, most pueblo natives farmed narrow canyon bottoms with a central watercourse and ample natural fertilizer deposited during seasonal flooding. Pueblo tribes irrigated this bottomland by digging short ditches diverting water to their fields. More extensive irrigation systems were needed in river flatlands, where surrounding fields stretched for many miles. This challenge didn't daunt the flatland tribes or their ancestors. The ancient Hohokam culture created more than

500 miles of irrigation canals, some of which are still in use near Phoenix, Arizona. Pueblo farmers also used natural subsurface irrigation. They knew how to deep-plant seeds in areas where groundwater rises or snowmelt and rainwater collect. Deep planting is particularly suited to corn cultivation. Specialized techniques, such as terracing (Figure 7.7) and companion planting (Figure 2.4), are hallmarks of Native American desert agriculture. Today these ancient methods are being adopted by modern agriculture.

Because their diet included little meat, Southwest Native Americans relied heavily on the corn-bean protein synergy (p. 35), and thus grew a wide variety of beans. Among the most ancient Southwest bean cultivars are Anasazi beans and tepary beans, today considered heirloom varieties and gaining rapidly in popularity. Over time, pink beans, pinto beans, appaloosa

FACTOR 2
Three Sisters crops formed the foundation of the Southwestern native diet.

FIGURE 7.8

A variety of dried beans are featured in traditional Southwestern cooking.
Elena Elisseeva/Shutterstock

beans, and red beans were added to the Southwestern legume pantry (Figure 7.8).

Squashes additionally complemented bean and corn dishes, adding important vitamins to the traditional diet. Southwestern tribes raised several types of pumpkin and other hard winter squashes.

Precontact Pueblo Cooking

Before the Spanish arrived in the 1500s, pueblo tribes already had developed a cuisine much more sophisticated than that of most other Native American groups. Contact with advanced Meso-American civilizations had resulted in superior technology that the pueblo people applied to cooking as well as other endeavors. Their sophisticated cooking equipment resulted in more highly refined dishes.

Pueblo tribes were master potters, crafting clay vessels of remarkable durability and beauty. Pueblo-made, fire baked clay cooking pots can withstand high, direct heat and thus are useful for many different cooking methods. In addition to preparing long-simmered soups and stews, pueblo cooks could also sear and steam over high heat. Foods cooked in clay acquire subtle, earthy flavors and mineral nutrients from it. Another useful quality of clay is its cooling properties, especially in the desert. Porous clay vessels soaked in water keep their contents cool as the moisture in the clay slowly evaporates.

Pueblo tribes applied advanced technology to grinding as well. Accounts written by Spanish explorers extol the smooth, powdery consistency of cornmeal ground by pueblo women. The typical pueblo kitchen was stocked with a three-part grinding system consisting of rectangular grinding stones graduated coarse, medium, and fine in texture. This technologically superior grinding equipment enabled pueblo cooks to prepare alkaline-treated corn flatbreads, later called **tortillas,** using a different method than Meso-American cooks. The pueblo method of making tortillas is discussed later in this chapter on p. 309.

Because game animals are scarce in the high desert, the settled pueblo tribes could not depend on hunted game as a foundation food in their diet. Pueblo cooks used their limited game meat by preparing bean- and corn-based stews flavored with a small amount of meat, rather than using meat as a main ingredient. The low availability of game meat resulted in little fat for cooking or flavoring foods and, thus, a virtually fat-free diet.

FACTOR 2
Alkaline processing of corn spread north from Mexico to the Southwest Native American tribes.

Foraged foods complemented agricultural products. Cacti were important both as a food and for the life-giving moisture they held. Piñon pine nuts added much-needed fat to the diet. Mesquite beans were boiled into a sauce or jelly or could be dried and ground into a sweet-tasting flour. All of the indigenous wild foods listed on p. 303 were incorporated into pueblo cooking.

An important legacy of the Meso-Americans is the fruit of the **capsicum** plant, the all-important **chile.** Indigenous to Mexico and South America, wild chile plants (Figure 7.9) traveled north at the same time as Meso-American agriculture to become an essential element in the diet of Southwestern Native Americans. Replete with vitamins A and C and a good source of other important vitamins and minerals, chiles provided not only nutrition but also flavor to bland bean and corn dishes. In addition, their antiseptic properties helped minimize spoilage in the foods to which they were added. Pueblo grinding technology made possible a wide range of sophisticated chile-based dishes. Fresh chiles were ground with seeds and desert fruits to make sauces. Dried chiles were ground into powder for use as a seasoning, or softened in water and ground into a paste for use in soups and stews.

A great benefit of the arid high desert climate was the ease with which all manner of foods could be dried. Dried meats, corn, beans, chiles, squashes, fruits, and other vegetables were stored for use in winter and spring or used as trade goods.

Navajos and Apaches

In the late 1400s, shortly before Spanish contact, a linguistically and culturally different group of Native Americans, possibly from Canada, arrived in the American Southwest. This group had not yet achieved agricultural status and lived by hunting and foraging. Those who settled in the mountains eventually became

FIGURE 7.9

The tiny pequín chile is similar to the indigenous wild chiles of the precontact Pueblo diet. Courtesy Hazel L. Toopoleski

ELEMENTS OF PRECONTACT PUEBLO CUISINE

FOUNDATION FOODS

principal starch: dried corn (maize)

principal protein: dried beans

principal produce: squashes, pumpkins, cacti, wild vegetables and fruits

FAVORED SEASONINGS: wild chiles, wild herbs, wild fruits

PRINCIPAL COOKING MEDIUM: water

PRIMARY COOKING METHODS: stone-griddling, poaching, stewing, boiling, grilling

FOOD ATTITUDES: strong food culture, culinary liberals

known as the Apache tribes and those who settled near the desert pueblos became known as the Navajos.

When the Navajos and Apaches encountered the prosperous, settled pueblo tribes, they saw easy plunder. From the time of their arrival through Spanish rule and into American governance, they periodically raided pueblo villages, stealing textiles, pottery, baskets, jewelry, and tools and frequently taking pueblo women and children into slavery.

Eventually both Navajos and Apaches adopted many of the customs, mythologies, and technologies of their pueblo captives. However, neither group chose permanent settlement. Most remained primarily hunter-gatherers, with cooking similar to Plains Native Americans (Chapter 10), until the arrival of the Spanish in the 1500s.

The acquisition of Spanish horses and sheep revolutionized the Navajo way of life. Sheepherding on horseback suited the Navajo sensibility, offering a reliable source of food as well as the freedom and mobility to which they were accustomed (Figure 7.10). Thus, mutton became the primary protein in the Navajo diet, and hunted game became far less essential. Sheep fat enriched corn dough products and was used for frying. Sheepskins were made into coats, and wool dyed in vivid desert colors was used to weave blankets and rugs in distinctive patterns.

When Americans arrived in the 1800s, Navajos embraced pioneer provisions (p. 364), including white flour, sugar, baking soda, refined salt, and pork lard. The availability of white wheat

FIGURE 7.10

Herding sheep on horseback is a Navajo tradition.

Coral Coolahan/Shutterstock

flour eliminated the drudgery of grinding corn. Wheat-flour flatbreads could be griddle-baked over campfires while herding. Navajos preferred the mild flavor of pork lard to the strong taste of mutton fat and used it for frying meats, vegetables, and bread doughs. Foraged foods, particularly wild fruits and herbs, added distinction to Navajo cooking.

In the late 1800s, pressure from the U.S. government forced many Navajos to settle on reservations. Although sheepherding continued, most Navajos eventually settled into permanent villages. Pioneer provisions supplied by the government became the foundation of the Navajo diet.

Unlike the Navajos, the Apache tribes were not attracted to sheepherding. Horses enabled them to hunt wild game more efficiently and made them fearsome raiders. As American settlement in the high desert increased, Apaches largely withdrew into the mountains and plains. Their traditional cooking remains similar to that of the Plains tribes, discussed in Chapter 10.

A Nutritional Time Bomb

Southwestern Native American groups faced varying fates after the arrival of the Spanish and, later, Americans. As in the East, European diseases greatly reduced the native population. In Southern California, Native Americans were effectively assimilated into the prevailing white culture. Texas tribes were pushed northwest into the plains and mountains. However, the tribes of the Four Corners area did not suffer large-scale assimilation or relocation because they lived in an arid, desolate area not highly coveted by white settlers.

Continuing contact with American settlers during the 1800s significantly changed the Southwestern Native American diet. First purchased from settlers, and later doled out by the U.S. government, pioneer provisions entered the traditional Southwestern native diet. At first, these foods enriched the cuisine, making possible flour tortillas, wheat breads, and other baked goods. Salt pork and bacon added protein and flavor. Pork lard made frying a viable cooking method. The combination of white-flour dough and pork lard led to the creation of Native American fried breads that are delicious, but not very healthful. Even less beneficial was American whiskey, which gave rise to rampant alcoholism.

More insidious than alcohol, however, was the long-term result of pioneer provisions entering the Southwestern Native American diet. From the late 1800s through the 1940s, government-sponsored initiatives sought to eradicate native culture, including native cuisine. The resulting lack of cultural self-esteem made traditional, indigenous ingredients less acceptable and mainstream American foods more desirable. Though white flour, sugar, salt, and pork lard merely enriched other Native American cuisines, for Southwestern Native Americans these products created a health crisis. By the end of the 20th century, thousands of Southwest Native Americans, particularly those of pueblo ancestry, faced serious obesity and other diet-related health problems.

<table>
<tr><td>

ELEMENTS OF PRECONTACT NAVAJO AND APACHE CUISINES

FOUNDATION FOODS

    principal starch: dried corn (maize), acquired from others

    principal protein: small and large game

    principal produce: cacti, wild vegetables and fruits

FAVORED SEASONINGS: wild herbs, wild fruits

PRINCIPAL COOKING MEDIUM: water

PRIMARY COOKING METHODS: grilling, sling-bag simmering

FOOD ATTITUDES: minimized food culture, culinary liberals

</td></tr>
</table>

Why were Southwestern Native Americans so profoundly affected by adopting pioneer provisions when other native groups were not? Nutritionists believe that natural selection genetically hard-wired these desert dwellers with the ability to survive on very few calories. Simply eating three meals a day of processed white-flour breads, fried foods, meat dishes, and sweets caused an alarming number of Southwest Native Americans to become morbidly obese. Today obesity-related health problems such as diabetes, heart disease, and arteriosclerosis are rampant in the Southwestern native population, and most Southwest Native Americans are aware of this dietary health risk. Nutritionists are encouraging them to adopt a more traditional diet featuring whole-kernel corn products, a high proportion of fresh vegetables, less meat, and low-fat cooking methods.

Spanish/Mexican Colonial Cuisine

By the mid-1500s, Spanish conquistadores had subjugated the Aztecs and Mayas. Spain's rule over Mexico was firmly established, Spanish settlement was widespread, and intermarriage between Spaniards and native Mexicans had created a signifi-

cant *mestizo*, or mixed heritage, population. A lively colonial cuisine had been established, and the development of traditional Mexican cuisine was well underway. Soon Spanish missionaries, and the Mexicans that accompanied them, were bringing colonial Mexican cuisine north into the American Southwest.

To understand both American Southwestern cuisine and Mexican-American cuisine, you need rudimentary knowledge of Mexican cuisine because both are based on it. Mexican cuisine is a hybrid of precontact Meso-American cuisine and Old World Spanish cuisine. An important difference between Mexican cooking and Native American cooking is the way each cuisine handled traditional alkaline processing of corn, explained in the following box. Perhaps you've already studied the cooking of Mexico in a world cuisines class. If you're unfamiliar with Mexican cuisine, refer to this book's companion website for a brief introduction to it.

Once Mexico's central and southern regions were firmly under control, the Spanish were ready for colonial expansion. Hearing of "cities of gold" 500 miles to the north, in 1540 Francisco Vasquez de Coronado mounted a 2-year expedition to claim these northern lands for Spain, conquer the natives, and bring back their fabled riches. Coronado explored virtually the entire American Southwest, venturing as far north and east as present-day Kansas. Although he discovered prosperous farming pueblos and brought back a few silver-and-turquoise native trinkets, he never found great riches. However, Coronado's reports of endless open land spurred further exploration, resulting in Spanish claim to virtually the entire western third of North America. The area north of the Sonoran desert was named *Nuevo Mexico* (New Mexico). Land north of the Gulf of Mexico became *Tejas* (Texas), bounded on the east by France's Louisiana colony. The West Coast was divided into a southern peninsula called *Baja*

TWO WAYS TO ALKALIZE CORN

As the name implies, traditional alkaline processing of corn requires an alkali. Most Meso-Americans used calcium hydroxide, commonly referred to as *slaked lime* or *cal*, for processing corn. This alkaline substance was derived from a mineral found in volcanic rock, prevalent in parts of Mexico. Today industrially produced calcium hydroxide is used for alkaline processing corn throughout Mexico and the United States. Conversely, most Native Americans used sodium hydroxide, commonly called *lye*, derived from plant ashes. Each of these alkalis gives corn products a different flavor.

Both groups prepared hominy (p. 34) by the same basic method of simmering dried corn kernels in alkalized water. In Spanish, hominy for eating is called **posole** (poh-SO-lay). However, most Meso-American alkaline-processed corn was ground into dough for making bread-like dishes.

Meso-American and modern Mexican-style hominy boiled with calcium hydroxide to make corn dough is called **nixtamal** (NEECE-tah-mal) and the calcium hydroxide alkaline process is called **nixtamalization**. Fresh, moist *nixtamal* is ground into a cohesive dough called **masa** that is formed by patting out or pressing into tortillas or other shapes and then baked or fried. Conversely, Southwestern Native Americans prepared alkalized corn doughs by grinding whole, unprocessed corn kernels into flour, and then mixing the flour with alkalized water.

Today calcium hydroxide and the nixtamalization process are used to make both handmade and industrially produced tortillas throughout Mexico and the American Mexican Border culinary region.

◼️◻️◻️ ELEMENTS OF COLONIAL MEXICAN CUISINE

FOUNDATION FOODS

principal starch: nixtamalized dried corn (maize) tortillas and other corn products

principal proteins: dried beans, pork, cheese

principal produce: squashes, pumpkins, avocados, wild greens

FAVORED SEASONINGS: many kinds of domesticated chiles, cinnamon, cumin, cloves, anise, black pepper, vanilla, oregano, cilantro, epazote

PRINCIPAL COOKING MEDIA: lard, stock

PRIMARY COOKING METHODS: stewing (clay pot), griddle-baking, deep-frying, grilling

FOOD ATTITUDES: strong food culture, culinary liberals

California (lower California) and the remaining coast, called *Alta California* (upper California), stretching indefinitely north. None of these territories had northern boundaries.

The Missions

Although the Spanish government sponsored further exploration, settlement of the Southwest did not begin until Franciscan Catholic missionaries ventured north to convert indigenous people to Christianity. The Franciscan brothers established a system of interrelated missions stretching across New Mexico on the *Camino Real*, or Royal Road. Another chain of missions penetrated California as far north as present-day San Francisco. Yet more missions were established in present-day Arizona and Texas.

The mission system proved to be an economically effective way for Spain to loosely control its vast North American domain.

Each mission was anchored by a simply designed adobe church surrounded by houses and outbuildings built in the pueblo style but with wooden window frames and doors (Figure 7.11). Using a blend of Native American and European agriculture, missionaries established gardens and raised pigs, goats, sheep, and chickens. However, colonial domesticate plant varieties had only limited success in the desert climate. Most of the fruits and vegetables grown on early missions were indigenous.

The missions had both positive and negative impact on Southwestern Native Americans. Along with religion, Spanish missionar-

FIGURE 7.11

Mission architecture blended pueblo construction methods with European details such as wooden doors and windows.

Caitlin Mirra/Shutterstock

ies introduced European education; native children living near missions learned to read and write Spanish. The Navajos profited most, acquiring both sheep and horses lost or stolen from mission lands. However, the Franciscan priests did their best to destroy indigenous Native American religious beliefs and culture, suppressing native languages and customs. Yet many Southwest tribes, although appearing to conform, privately retained their separate cultural identities and passed down their native cultural heritage to their progeny. In this way both indigenous culture and cuisine survived.

Most important to students of cuisine, the missions were the birthplace of American Southwestern cooking. In mission kitchens, indigenous Southwestern pueblo ingredients and cooking methods were blended with colonial Mexican cuisine.

Colonial Southwestern Cuisine

A mission's head cook was typically a Mexican lay brother or a female Mexican housekeeper. Either would likely be of mestizo heritage and would have had some degree of training in both Old World Spanish and colonial Mexican cuisines. Once the mission was established, the cook hired a team of local indigenous people as kitchen workers.

The early missions adopted pueblo-style agriculture and raised Three Sisters crops to feed the brothers and the mission workers. Southwestern native kitchen helpers learned Mexican corn cuisine while using many of their own cooking methods in their work.

Early missions raised both hogs and chickens; when these became plentiful, meat-based stews claimed a place of honor on the mission table. Pork lard made corn dough products tastier, more pliable, and longer keeping. More important, the use of lard as a frying medium transformed the lean corn tortilla into a product that could be fried crisp to make foods such as tostada shells and tortilla chips.

Mission cooks served Mexican bean varieties, such as pinto and pink beans, as well as indigenous anasazi and tepary beans. Slow-simmered in clay pots and flavored with lard or smoked pork products, beans were served as a side dish or as a supper entrée accompanied by corn tortillas. As in Mexican cuisine, mission cooks used leftover beans to make refried beans.

Because shipments of goods from Mexico were infrequent, mission cooks worked with a limited palette of seasonings. Whereas in Mexico a cook could choose from a wide variety of herbs and spices, the mission cook was usually limited to black pepper, cumin, cinnamon, and wild sage.

FACTOR 2   FACTOR 3

Indigenous Southwest Native American cooking blended with hybrid colonial Mexican cooking to create multihybrid Southwestern cuisine.

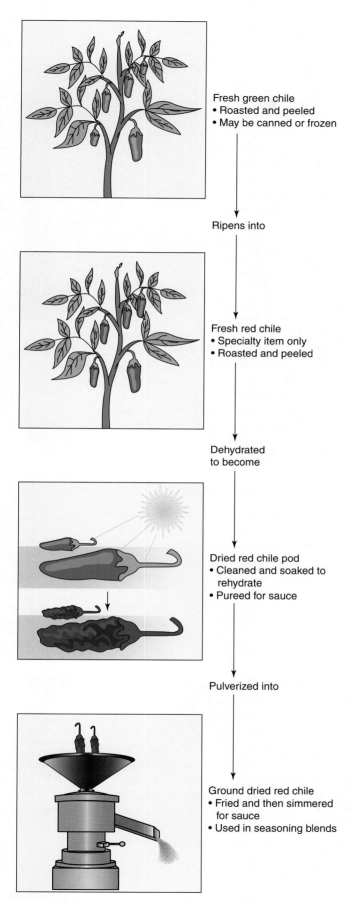

Fresh green chile
• Roasted and peeled
• May be canned or frozen

Ripens into

Fresh red chile
• Specialty item only
• Roasted and peeled

Dehydrated
to become

Dried red chile pod
• Cleaned and soaked to
  rehydrate
• Pureed for sauce

Pulverized into

Ground dried red chile
• Fried and then simmered
  for sauce
• Used in seasoning blends

FIGURE 7.12
Stages of Chile Production

In the desert it was difficult to grow Mexican chile varieties. However, by 1600 New Mexico farmers had developed a type of large, flavorful chile that thrived in the thin soil and dry climate. Today this chile cultivar is known simply as the **long green chile,** grown throughout the American Southwest in different varieties with varying characteristics. The long green variety grown in New Mexico is considered the nation's finest; these are referred to as *New Mexico chiles*. New Mexico long green chiles range in heat from medium to very spicy-hot.

The New Mexico Chile: Green and Red

The New Mexico chile harvest begins in late August and, depending on the weather, can last into October. Growers decide at which stage of ripeness to pick the chiles and then subject them to different processes resulting in various chile products described in this section. Figure 7.12 illustrates the stages of chile production in a graphic organizer.

Like all capsicum fruits, the New Mexico long green chile is green at maturity (Figure 7.13.a) but loses its green color as it ripens. When fully ripe, a New Mexico long green chile is vivid orange-red in color. As a chile ripens, its flavor changes as well, becoming more complex and acquiring a subtle sweetness. Though long green chiles from other areas are typically harvested green, slightly less than half of the New Mexico long green chile crop is harvested at the green stage.

The skin of fresh long green chiles is thick and fibrous, but their flesh is tender. Before they are served or further cooked in other ways, fresh long green chiles are always roasted and their skins removed. In New Mexico during the harvest season, roadside chile markets offer consumers roasting services at no charge (Figure 7.14). Chile-processing plants roast and peel long green chiles before canning or freezing them.

Roasted and peeled fresh long green chile is diced or julienned and used in sandwiches, tacos, burritos, quesadillas, and many other preparations. When ground into a thick purée, it becomes the base of *chile verde* (CHEE-lay VAIR-day), or New Mexico green chile sauce, one of the signature dishes of American Southwestern cuisine. Whole roasted and peeled long green chile pods are stuffed with cheese or a savory meat filling, then

(a) Fresh New Mexico long green chile pods. **Courtesy Biad Chilesh,** biadchili.com

(b) A dried New Mexico chile pod. Steve Snowden/Shutterstock

FIGURE 7.13

FIGURE 7.14

During the late-summer harvest season, produce stands offer complimentary roasting for customers buying long green chiles. Courtesy Harold Zoschke

FIGURE 7.15

In traditional drying, mature red chile pods are braided into ristras and hung in the desert sunshine. Natalia Bratslavsky/Shutterstock

breaded and deep-fried to make New Mexico-style *chiles rellenos* (CHEE-lays ray-YAY-nohs), or stuffed chiles.

In New Mexico, more than half of the long green chile crop is allowed to ripen to bright red maturity. Almost all of these ripe chiles are then dried (Figure 7.13.b). The best quality dried chile is air-dried outdoors spread on racks. However, today much of the crop is mechanically dehydrated in drying sheds. Some of the pods are hand-braided into traditional **ristras** (REE-strahs) today primarily used for decoration (Figure 7.15). A significant portion of the dried chile harvest is pulverized into pure New Mexico chile powder (not to be confused with chili powder, a proprietary spice blend discussed on p. 470).

Whether whole or powdered, dried chile is primarily used to make sauces. The traditional Mexican method of preparing a red chile sauce involves steeping whole cleaned dried chiles in hot water until softened, and then grinding them into a smooth purée. The purée is fried in lard and then simmered with stock. A simplified method uses pure chile powder, flour, and lard to make a spicy roux that is then simmered with stock.

Fresh red chiles are a local delicacy. Used in place of fresh long green chiles, their sweet, bright flavor produces extraordinary dishes. Each season a limited amount of ripe red chile is air-freighted to chile connoisseurs around the country.

Flour Tortillas

In Mexico, Spanish colonists yearned for the yeast-leavened wheat breads and rich pastries of their homeland, and initially they imported expensive European wheat flour to make them.

By the late 1600s, wheat cultivation in north-central Mexico had proven successful, and Mexico and her northern territories had access to domestic wheat. However, yeast bread baking—using temperamental yeasts, requiring time for fermentation, and using oven technology—was too complicated for everyday mission fare. Instead of baking yeast breads, mission cooks made flatbreads by mixing wheat flour, lard, salt, and water to make a gluten-rich dough. Unlike corn masa that is patted out or pressed, wheat-flour dough is rolled and stretched. The resulting large, thin rounds of dough are baked on a griddle in the manner of corn tortillas. Although corn tortillas remained in the cuisine, the flour tortilla eventually became the staple bread of colonial Southwestern cooking (Figure 7.16).

Traditional Southwestern Cuisine

The first 200 years of Spanish settlement in the American Southwest saw limited growth and gradual expansion in Texas and the Californias. On the West Texas plains, longhorn cattle introduced by Coronado in the 1500s multiplied into sizable herds. By the mid-1700s, Spanish and Mexican entrepreneurs had begun cattle ranching in the region. By the 1800s, ranching was the predominant occupation in Texas and in many of California's interior valleys. In ranching areas, beef became a foundation food.

Along the California coast, Spanish missions concentrated on farming, achieving success with subtropical and Mediterranean crops such as avocados, olives, and citrus fruits. In addition to Three Sisters crops, New Mexico concentrated on the cultivation of long green chiles and warm-climate fruits, such as peaches, grapes, and melons.

As the three main population areas of the Southwest evolved and their cultures matured, three distinctive Southwestern cooking styles emerged: New Mexico cuisine, traditional Texas cuisine, and Hispanic California cuisine.

New Mexico Cuisine

Traditional New Mexico cooking reflects the austerity and clarity of the Southwestern desert. For example, New Mexico chile

FIGURE 7.16

Wheat flour tortillas are rolled and stretched into thin discs and then griddle-baked. rj lerich/Shutterstock

FACTOR 3

Wheat, a Spanish colonial domesticate, became an important element of American Southwestern cuisine. Wheat-flour tortillas are a signature starch.

FACTOR 3

Beef became a foundation food in ranching areas.

sauces typically have few ingredients: chile purée or powder, lard for frying the chile, perhaps some onion or a hint of garlic, and a light meat or poultry broth. Seasonings are kept to a minimum so that the flavor of the chile shines through. A few desert-foraged foods, such as nopal cactus paddles, pine nuts, and prickly pear fruits, are used in the modern cuisine.

New Mexico cuisine favors wheat and corn equally. Flour tortillas are preferred for tacos and quesadillas and as a table bread to accompany sauced foods. Corn tortillas are used for enchiladas and tostadas.

Fillings for tacos and enchiladas are typically meat-based, made with pork, beef, or chicken that has been poached or braised and then shredded. Ground meats are rarely used.

Cheese is used sparingly. When cheese tops tacos or fills enchiladas, typically a crumbly fresh-type cheese is used. Mild domestic Cheddars are used for melting.

New Mexico long green and dried red chiles are the principal seasonings of New Mexico cuisine and are the basis of its two primary sauces: chile verde (CHEE-lay VAIR-day), or green chile sauce, and chile rojo (CHEE-lay RO-ho), or red chile sauce. In New Mexico the term chile refers not only to the chile pod, purée, or powder but also to the sauce made from them. Many New Mexico dishes are served with a choice of sauces; when you order them, you'll be asked "red or green?" The undecided typically order "half and half."

After ranching arrived in the Southwest, New Mexico cooks began serving beef dishes. In addition to savory beef stews and fillings, grilled steaks became popular fare. Southwest steaks are typically seasoned with pure New Mexico red chile powder and topped with sautéed fresh long green chile. The taste of mesquite wood smoke is a signature flavor for steaks and other grilled foods.

Traditional New Mexico cooking doesn't boast a large repertoire of desserts and baked goods. The Spanish caramel custard, flan (p. 350), is popular in New Mexico and throughout the Southwest. New Mexico is well known for sopaipillas, fluffy pillows of fried dough similar to New Orleans beignets (p. 261).

Through the 1800s, traditional New Mexico cooking changed very little, a remarkable fact considering the influx of travelers that passed through the area on the Santa Fe Trail and the Spanish Camino Real. The purity of the cuisine reflects the strong food culture and culinary conservatism of traditional New Mexicans. Through the era of the wagon trails, the city of Santa Fe boasted hotels and inns serving both New Mexico and Mexican fare. With the closing of the trail in 1880, the region suffered economic decline and languished for about a hundred years. The American Southwest would not again achieve economic viability until the 1980s. Until then, New Mexico cuisine garnered little attention outside the region.

Texas Cuisine

Unlike the cuisine of New Mexico, Texas cuisine didn't benefit from large, settled Native American communities having advanced food cultures. Most of the tribes associated with Texas history were relative latecomers to the region, pushed westward by population pressure in the East.

The traditional cuisine of Texas began in the 1700s on Spanish ranchos, typically huge operations boasting as many as 40,000 head of longhorns. Spanish ranches were isolated and largely self-sufficient, raising most of the food needed for the owner's family and scores of employees.

With an unlimited supply of cattle in Spanish Texas, the meat of choice was beef. Spanish-born landowners got the pick of the slaughter, enjoying tender cuts such as filet and sirloin typically spit-roasted or grilled over mesquite coals. The juicy, savory meats were accented with piquant salsas made from fresh tomatoes in season and with preserved tomatoes in the winter. Mexican vaqueros, or cowboys (Figure 7.17), made do with the tougher cuts. One of their favorites was the cut we now call skirt steak. Spanish cowboys called this wide, thin band of meat a fajita (fah-HEE-tah), or "little belt," because its shape resembled a cowboy's wide sash. Fajitas are marinated for tenderization, grilled, and sliced thin across the grain to wrap in hot flour tortillas.

Locally grown dried red chiles were a signature seasoning of the early Texas style. Ranch cooks created spicy beef stews called chile con carne (CHEE-lay kon KAR-nay), or chile sauce with meat, using reconstituted puréed dried chile pods. Beans, slow cooked in an earthenware pot, accompanied virtually every meal—but were never included in the chile. In 1894 a Texas café owner named William Gebhardt combined pure Texas red chile powder with other seasonings to create a spice blend for chile con carne. Both the name of the dish and the name of the spice powder were eventually spelled chili. Today much Texas chili is made with chili powder—but still no beans.

Corn dough products were the staff of life in early Texas. However, by the mid-1800s Texas was positioned between two

FIGURE 7.17
Mexican cowboys stop for coffee on the open range.
Herbert C. Lanks/European Tourists Services

FACTOR 4
Americans from the Mid-Atlantic, Plantation South, and Louisiana began settling the new state of Texas.

of the Western Hemisphere's most important wheat-producing regions and, thus, wheat flour became readily available. Flour tortillas became the universal bread product, with corn dough reserved for making tamales and corn tortillas for enchiladas.

Although most Texas cattle were beef breeds, in the late 1800s immigrant German farmers introduced dairy cows and began producing mild, Cheddar-type cheeses. Prized for its melting quality, such cheese was frequently used to make *chile con queso* (CHEE-lay kon KAY-soh), a gratin of broiled cheese and roasted long green chile meant for wrapping in flour tortillas.

In the mid-1800s a complex series of political events led to Texas finally becoming an American territory and then a state. Through the late 1800s an influx of American settlement changed the face of Texas culture and cuisine. American settlers added a strong element of Ranchlands cooking to the prevailing Mexican-based traditional Texas cuisine.

Many of the new Texans hailed from the Plantation South; these settlers applied Southern barbeque and frying techniques to the region's plentiful beef. German immigrants began making beer and sausages and opened food-based businesses such as restaurants and grocery stores.

Today traditional Texas cuisine is frequently confused with Tex-Mex cooking, a late-20th-century, commercialized form of Mexican-American cuisine discussed on p. 317. However, in many parts of the state—particularly on ranches and in rural towns—the traditional cuisine of Texas still thrives.

Hispanic California Cuisine

The State of California is home to two distinctive cuisine styles thriving side by side. Anglo-Asian California cuisine is covered in Chapter 12. Equally prevalent in California is Mexican Border cuisine, both the Southwestern-style cooking of its earliest settlers and the Mexican-American cuisine of today's Mexican immigrants.

Geographically, southern California is part of the American Southwest, although it doesn't share the region's high desert climate. Because it lies west of the Sierra Nevadas and benefits from proximity to the Pacific Ocean, coastal southern California has a Mediterranean climate, with mild, warm winters and hot, sunny summers.

When Spanish missionaries began settling California's coastal plain and interior valleys, they encountered loosely organized Native American groups of primarily hunter-gatherer status. Because the region's abundant wild food resources were available year round, California native groups did not develop agriculture or complex foodways. Lacking the strong cultural identity of the New Mexico natives, California's indigenous groups were easily overcome by Spanish culture and religion. Thus, early California cooking was almost purely Mexican, exhibiting virtually no Native American influence.

California's mild climate and good soil enabled missions to grow a wide variety of produce crops. Citrus fruits thrived; their juice

and zest are important seasonings in Hispanic California cuisine. Avocado trees transplanted from central Mexico grew well in southern California (Figure 7.18). Thus, California cooks were able to prepare *guacamole* (hwa-kah-MOH-lay), a chunky purée of avocado seasoned with onions, cilantro, lime juice, and green chile. The *jalapeño* was the area's primary chile cultivar until around 1900, when the long green chile was introduced to California. Southern California's soil and climate produced the mild-tasting *Anaheim chile*, a long green chile cultivar named after its primary growing location. The Anaheim was the

FIGURE 7.18
Avocados thrived in southern California, making guacamole a popular dish.
AntoinetteW/Shutterstock

first chile to be commercially canned, and today it is also available frozen. Flame-roasted and peeled, this versatile long green chile gives California-Mexican cooking a special flavor.

Unlike the high desert, southern California provided plentiful protein food resources in the form of seafood. The ocean yielded Pacific rockfish, mahimahi, calico bass, yellowtail (Japanese amberjack), various types of tuna, spot prawns, spiny lobster, Pacific littleneck and pismo clams, and rock and Dungeness crabs. Inland streams and lakes contributed crayfish, trout, and perch. Today fish and shellfish remain an important element in Hispanic California cuisine. Fish tacos are a traditional dish that has become popular once again.

When the Spanish began cattle ranching in California's inland valleys, beef became the meat of choice. In addition, California dairies produced rich milk that made superlative cheeses. Today Hispanic California cooking features Monterey Jack cheese (p. 357) in quesadillas, *queso fundido* (a casserole of melted cheese and chiles), or any dish that requires a supple melting cheese is needed.

As you'll learn in Chapter 12, Californians have a reputation for innovation and for starting trends. In matters of cuisine Californians are well known culinary liberals having a strong food culture. Thus, Hispanic California cuisine is a constantly evolving cooking style that readily embraces new ingredients and techniques.

Contemporary Southwestern Cuisine

Although mining and ranching spurred early economic development in the American Southwest, for such a remote and climatically challenging area true economic viability was not possible until the construction of the interstate highway system and the development of affordable air conditioning in the mid-20th century. However, at that time traditional

Southwestern cuisine was largely overshadowed by Mexican-American cuisine. Southwestern cuisine remained a regional secret.

In the 1980s, Southwestern cuisine began drawing public attention when the nation experienced a surge of general interest in the American Southwest. The rediscovery and popularization of the paintings of Georgia O'Keeffe and other Southwest artists led to a nationwide trend for Southwestern home décor and Southwestern crafts and jewelry, as well as for Southwestern cooking. Concurrently, America was beginning its love affair with spicy-hot foods, a romance that hasn't waned. Sales of all types of salsas and hot-spicy condiments skyrocketed. *Chile Pepper* magazine, a publication entirely devoted to spicy-hot foods, was read nationwide. The Southwest became America's locus of hot and spicy cooking, and its formerly little-known cuisine suddenly became all the rage. A new generation of restaurant chefs discovered and popularized traditional American Southwestern cuisine. For a list of noteworthy restaurants, including those featuring New Mexico, Texas, and Hispanic California cuisines, refer to this book's companion website.

By the 1990s many of the chefs responsible for popularizing traditional American Southwestern cuisine became restless with its limitations and began its transformation into a broader, more inclusive cooking style we call contemporary Mexican Border cuisine. In doing so they also drew upon elements of Mexican-American cuisine, discussed in the next section. Figure 7.19 is a graphic organizer illustrating the development of both branches of Mexican Border cuisine.

■ MEXICAN-AMERICAN
□ CUISINE

Although the land north of the Mexican border was initially settled by Spaniards and Mexicans, after it became American property in the mid-1800s the region's Hispanic population percentage declined as Americans from the East Coast and Midwest flooded the region. Some came to try their luck as Texas ranchers, some came to work New Mexico's mines, and others were attracted to California agriculture. The region's Hispanic first settlers called these new arrivals **Anglos,** or "English people," although not all were of English origin. By the late 1800s, second-settler Anglo culture and cuisine dominated America's Mexican Border region.

Americans were not the only ones drawn to the region's vitality. Through the 20th century, nearly a million Mexicans crossed the border in search of economic opportunity. These second-wave immigrants—some documented, others not—joined the region's workforce and contributed to its economic growth. More important to students of cuisine, they created a new, hybrid cooking style: Mexican-American cuisine.

Like other settler groups you've studied, Mexican immigrants yearned for the familiar dishes of their homeland. Like the others, they had no choice but to adapt their cooking to ingredients readily available in their new country. Although Mexico was often only a few miles away, many immigrants found it problematic to recross

FIGURE 7.19
Development of Mexican Border Cuisine

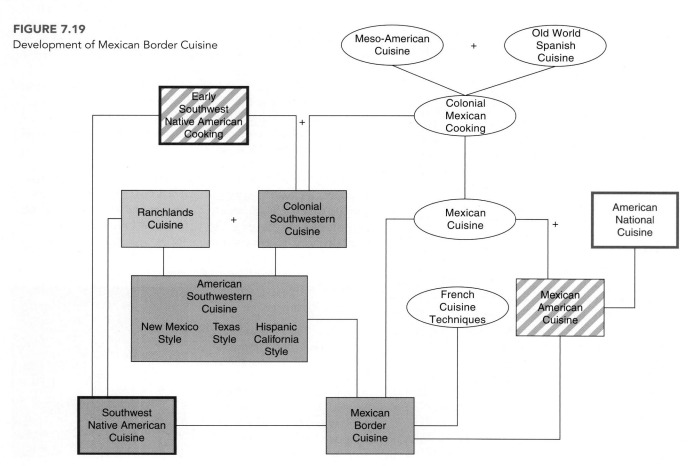

the border for groceries. In addition, many hailed from central and southern Mexico and thus were accustomed to ingredients not available in the north. Shipping food products from Mexico was slow and expensive. Finally, most immigrants were too busy working outside the home to spend time on laborious cooking processes required by traditional Mexican ingredients. These factors led to the development of a simpler cooking style based on few seasonings and inexpensive ingredients.

Mexican-American immigrants frequently followed the same pattern as immigrants from other countries, opening restaurants and food shops catering to fellow displaced Mexicans. Soon Anglos were patronizing these businesses, drawn to the spicy flavors, large portions, and cheap prices. These restaurants were responsible for many aspects of Mexican-American cuisine as we know it today.

Mexican-American Convenience Foods

Both Mexican-American home cooks and owners of Mexican-American restaurants needed inexpensive, laborsaving food products. In response, American industrial food-processing companies began developing convenience foods aimed at the Mexican-American market.

The Tortilla Revolution

Fresh, handmade corn tortillas are the gold standard of Mexican cuisine. Nothing comes close to the flavor, texture, and aroma of a tortilla made from fresh-ground masa and served straight from the griddle. However, few cooks have time to prepare their own masa. In Mexico, consumers can buy fresh-ground masa as well as fresh corn tortillas from artisan shops and small industrial producers. However, masa dough spoils rapidly and corn tortillas stale quickly. Neither product transports well, especially in a hot climate. Nonetheless, early Mexican immigrants wanted fresh corn tortillas—or a way to make their own tortillas quickly and easily.

In 1904 Mexican entrepreneurs invented the first industrial tortilla-making machine. Within a few years Mexican-American companies were selling packaged corn tortillas. The availability of premade tortillas made it faster and easier to prepare tacos, enchiladas, and other popular foods.

In 1909 San Antonio-based Azteca Mills developed a process for dehydrating and pulverizing masa dough. Quaker Oats was the first national food-processing company to recognize the need for a nonperishable nixtamalized corn product for making tortillas and other corn-based foods. They began marketing powdered masa as **masa harina,** literally "corn dough flour." Mixed with cool water, masa harina rehydrates into a dough acceptably similar to fresh masa. With masa harina, early Mexican-American cooks had the option of making their own tortillas from a shelf-stable product. Today masa harina is produced and used in Mexico as well.

In traditional Mexican cuisine, chips made by deep-frying tortilla strips or wedges are used as a crunchy garnish. To please Anglo customers, Mexican-American restaurants began offering crisp fried tortilla chips and salsa as a complimentary appetizer. American snack food companies soon made tortilla chips a national favorite.

Today the many forms of fried corn tortilla are signature ingredients in Mexican-American cuisine. Second in popularity only to tortilla chips, taco shells are a thoroughly American product not used in Mexico. The taco shell evolved from a Mexican dish called the *taco dorado,* meaning "golden or fried taco," a soft corn tortilla that is first filled, then rolled or folded, and finally fried semi-crisp. Producers reasoned that consumers would find a prefried shell easier to work with. Around 1950 the Mexican-American food industry developed a machine that molds corn tortillas into a U shape while frying. The industrial taco shell made possible the Mexican-American crispy taco consisting of shell, filling, garnishes, and a thin, spicy-hot tomato sauce.

Corn tortillas fried flat are topped with spreads and garnishes to become *tostadas.* Today prefried tostada shells are gaining in popularity.

Prefried tortilla chips and shells could be packaged, stored for long periods without refrigeration, and distributed nationwide. They lowered labor costs for Mexican-American restaurants and made Mexican-American cuisine accessible to mainstream Americans looking for a new "fun food."

Entrepreneurs developed machines for producing flour tortillas, as well. In addition to large industrial producers, small stores and restaurants were able to offer fresh, machine-made flour tortillas (Figure 7.20). Specialty sizes were developed to accommodate popular Mexican-American dishes. For example, small flour tortillas are used to accompany fajitas. The Mexican-American adaptation of the northern Mexican burrito led to the creation of 10" and even 12" flour tortillas.

The *burrito* (literally "little donkey") is a flour tortilla wrapped around a hot filling, such as refried beans and/or cooked meats. Mexican-Americans adapted the burrito to include additional fillings such as cheese, rice, salsa, guacamole, and sour cream. Mexican-American restaurants further modified the burrito by offering a "wet" version topped with enchilada sauce and melted cheese, and by deep-frying it to create the *chimichanga.*

Fillings, Salsas, and Seasonings

Industrial food processing also played a role in fillings for crispy tacos. In traditional Mexican and Southwestern cuisines, fillings are made from meats and poultry that are first cooked and then shredded or chopped. This requires time and skilled labor, resources in

FIGURE 7.20

At this Mexican-American restaurant, a flour tortilla machine provides guests with fresh, hot tortillas.

Courtesy BE&SC Manufacturing, 1623 N. San Marcos, San Antonio, TX, 1-800-683-0928, www.flourtortilla .machine.com

short supply for Mexican-American immigrants. Home cooks and restaurant owners looking for a shortcut found it with ground beef. By the 1920s, electric meat grinders were in widespread use, transforming America's overabundance of tough beef cuts into inexpensive ground beef. When Mexican-American restaurateurs began using cooked, seasoned ground beef as a filling for the new prefried taco shells, the Mexican-American crispy taco took its present form. Home cooks began serving these easy-to-prepare tacos as everyday fare. American food producers responded with packaged taco-seasoning mixes that flavored and thickened the ground beef as it cooked.

The canning industry seized the opportunity to market premade, shelf-stable salsas and other sauces. Taco sauce, a smooth, thin, chile-spiked tomato sauce, was among the first products to be bottled. As consumer tastes became more sophisticated, chunky tomato salsas, green chile salsas, and green tomatillo salsas followed. Canned enchilada sauce and canned refried beans became popular convenience foods.

In addition to domestic Cheddars and Monterey Jack, pasteurized process cheeses were adopted into Mexican-American cuisine. When Kraft foods introduced Velveeta processed cheese in 1928, its melting quality made easily curdled *chile con queso* cheese dip much easier to prepare. When Cheez Whiz cheese sauce was introduced in 1953, preparation of melted cheese dishes became foolproof.

Mexican-American Restaurant Fare

Throughout the first half of the 20th century, Mexican-American restaurants and food stands could be found in virtually every border town and city, and by the 1960s they had spread throughout the nation. To keep menu prices low, Mexican-American restaurants offered menus composed almost entirely of corn dishes, such as crispy or soft tacos, enchiladas, and tamales. Today Mexican-American restaurants specialize in the **combination plate,** a menu item featuring the diner's choice of corn-based dishes served on one large platter, and typically including refried beans and Mexican rice.

Nachos, the well-known appetizer, is a Mexican-American restaurant specialty that has become part of America's national cuisine. Although many Mexican-American home cooks likely prepared quick snacks of tortilla chips baked with cheese, this appetizer was popularized in Mexican-American restaurants. Today nachos may be embellished with scores of toppings, such as pickled jalapeños, refried beans, or grilled chicken.

Fajitas, the skirt steak dish developed by Mexican *vaqueros*, was introduced to the American dining public in 1973 at Ninfa's in Houston. Originally made with beef, fajitas so captured the public's imagination that now the term *fajitas* has come to mean a presentation of almost any grilled food served with sautéed onions and peppers, refried beans, salsa, and flour tortillas. Today restaurant menus feature chicken fajitas and even seafood and vegetable fajitas.

Many Mexican-American dishes are ideal fast foods. As early as 1890, Mexican-American "chili queens" sold tacos, enchiladas, and tamales from street carts in San Antonio and other Southwestern cities. Mexican fast food went nationwide in 1962, when Glen Bell, Jr., launched the Taco Bell chain of franchise restaurants that would eventually popularize Mexican-American cuisine throughout the world. Today other fast-food chains offer Mexican-American dishes as well.

TEX-MEX COOKING

Because so many of today's popular Mexican-American dishes were developed in Texas, the catchy term *Tex-Mex* was coined to describe them. Although a discernible Texas style of Mexican-American cuisine exists, in general, *Tex-Mex* is synonymous with *Mexican-American* in referring to food and cooking.

■ CONTEMPORARY MEXICAN BORDER CUISINE

Thus far we've followed the development of American Southwestern cooking from its Meso-American and Native American roots through the colonial Mexican mission era and American pioneer influence and into traditional Southwestern cuisine. We've also learned about the creation of Mexican-American cuisine. Now let's discover how these two cooking styles are evolving and merging in the hands of modern chefs.

In the 1980s the American Southwest underwent a surge of economic growth. The region became a vacation destination, boasting fine hotels, resorts, and health spas. Increased tourism brought a more demanding clientele of restaurant diners and a new generation of Southwestern chefs to cook for them. Sophisticated diners were enchanted by the flavors of spicy chiles

ELEMENTS OF MEXICAN BORDER CUISINE

FOUNDATION FOODS

principal starches: flour tortillas, corn tortillas, and related products

principal proteins: beef, pork, poultry, dried beans, cheese

principal produce: tomatoes, tomatillos, long green chiles, nopal cactus, sweet corn, crisp lettuces, avocados

FAVORED SEASONINGS: dried red chiles, long green chiles, serrano and jalapeño chiles, chipotle chiles, cumin, oregano, sage, juniper

PRINCIPAL COOKING MEDIA: lard, vegetable oil

PRIMARY COOKING METHODS: grilling, griddling, braising, stewing/simmering

FOOD ATTITUDES: strong food culture, culinary liberals

FACTOR 5
Late-20th-century economic development attracted a new generation of chefs responsible for creating contemporary Mexican Border cuisine.

and savory corn dishes elevated by the techniques of modern French cuisine. The new Southwestern chefs were noted for dramatic presentations, stacking food high on the plate like desert rock formations and using sauces to paint plates in subtle desert colors. Many expanded their repertoire to include dishes from the Southwest Native American microcuisine. Centuries-old dishes, such as blue corn dumplings and cactus salads, were refined and updated to suit the tastes of contemporary diners.

When these creative chefs began to chafe under the limitations of the traditional Southwestern ingredients palette, they began adding seasonings adopted from Mexican cuisine. Although the region's signature long green chile remained a foundation ingredient, Mexican poblano, serrano, ancho, and chipotle chiles quickly came into wide use. Mexican cheeses became important ingredients. Chefs began using complex Mexican cooking methods to create sophisticated sauces and corn dishes. They embraced the earthy taste of mesquite smoke and the pure flavors achieved by steaming. Not content to work only with local freshwater fish, chefs added seafood, such as shrimp, crabmeat, scallops, salmon, swordfish, and other ocean fish to their menus. They began using avocados, pineapples, mangoes, and other tropical fruits. French elements such as butter, cream, demi-glace, and wines added rich flavors. A few Mexican-American cuisine elements, such as nachos and pre-fried tortilla shells, were embraced—but in more sophisticated, updated forms. By the late 20th century the contemporary restaurant cooking of the American Southwest was no longer solely Southwestern.

Nor was this type of cooking confined to the Southwest. Like Mexican-American cuisine, this new cooking style soon spread throughout the nation. However, it was not limited to areas of significant Hispanic population. Instead, restaurants offering the new cuisine opened in affluent urban areas and catered to upscale customers looking for the latest trend in restaurant dining.

Having moved so far beyond its Southwestern roots, this new, multihybrid cooking style needs a more accurate name. You may hear it referred to as "New Southwestern," but those who understand cooking know that name is too limited. Because its root cuisines—Mexican and American Southwestern—are found on either side of the border, and because it's new and constantly evolving, we call it *contemporary Mexican Border cuisine*.

Although the 1980s craze for Southwestern art and crafts has waned, the popularity of contemporary Mexican Border cuisine endures. Diners enjoy the cuisine's bold flavors and dramatic presentations. The cuisine is livened by a constant underlying tension among its practitioners: innovative chefs constantly redefine the cuisine, and traditional chefs strive to maintain its desert purity. Today adventurous diners can sample many styles of contemporary Mexican Border cuisine, along the border and around the globe.

For a list of noteworthy contemporary Mexican Border cuisine restaurants, refer to this book's companion website.

■□■ THE SOUTHWESTERN NATIVE AMERICAN MICROCUISINE

Despite attempts at assimilation by Spanish conquerors and American settlers, the culture and cuisine of Southwestern Native Americans endured through the mid-20th century and experienced a renaissance beginning in the 1980s. Unlike other Native American cuisines, which are largely featured only on special occasions, Southwestern Native American cooking is practiced daily in thousands of homes throughout New Mexico, Arizona, southern Colorado, and southern Utah.

Because of its wide range of defining dishes and its status as a living cuisine widely practiced both in private homes and in public venues, Southwestern Native American cooking is considered a modern microcuisine.

Visit this book's companion website at www.pearsonhighered.com/sackett to learn more about the Southwestern Native American microcuisine. Following are two photos relating to that microcuisine.

Piki bread is made by smearing a thin corn batter by hand onto a 700°F baking stone.
Courtesy of Steve Forbis

Beehive-shaped adobe ovens, called *hornos*, are used to bake yeasted wheat breads.
Francesca Yorke/© Dorling Kindersley

☐ TABLE 7.1 MEXICAN BORDER DEFINING DISHES

ITEM NAME	HISTORY	DOMINANT INGREDIENTS AND METHOD	MORE
HOUSE-MADE TORTILLA CHIPS	Called *totopos* (toe-TOE-pohs) in Mexican Spanish, wedges or strips of crisp-fried tortilla are a favorite snack food on both sides of the border. Chips are served with appetizer dips such as salsa, *chile con queso*, and guacamole.	House-made chips are prepared with thin yellow, white, or blue corn tortillas cut, fried, drained well, and tossed with fine salt. Today tortillas and chip wedges are available in additional colors produced by adding food dyes to the masa. Chips fried in oil containing a proportion of lard are especially tasty but have a heavier mouthfeel and are more perishable.	Hot, house-made chips require a fryer dedicated only to chip-making and extra labor to ensure that they are fried virtually to order. The labor involved in handmade chips makes them a higher-cost item, but chips fried to order yield virtually no breakage waste. Using whole tortillas, creative chefs cut interesting shapes for chips intended as a garnish.
FRESH SALSA ALSO CALLED: *SALSA FRESCA* (FRAY-skah)/ OR *SALSA CRUDA* (CROO-dah)	Fresh salsas accompany tacos and other tortilla-based dishes. Contemporary Southwestern chefs also serve fresh salsa as a topping for grilled meats, poultry, and seafood. When salsa ingredients are diced and tossed together, the result is called *pico de gallo* (PEE-ko day GUY-oh), or "rooster's beak," a relishlike topping.	Properly made salsa is pounded in a mortar, resulting in a rough purée in which all of the flavors have melded together. Traditional Mexican Border fresh salsa is based on uncooked ripe tomatoes mashed with serrano or jalapeño chiles, onions, garlic, cilantro, and salt. Green salsa/*salsa verde* (VAIR-day) is based on a mixture of cooked and raw tomatillos with similar seasonings. New Southwestern cuisine also uses other fruits and vegetables, such as yellow tomatoes, zucchini, or even mangoes.	Salsas are quite perishable, losing quality in a few hours. Use only freshly chopped ingredients and prepare only enough salsa for service.
COOKED SALSAS	During the summer and fall harvest seasons, Mexican Border cooks traditionally canned batches of cooked salsa in anticipation of the winter months when fresh tomatoes and tomatillos were not available. By the 1980s, industrial bottled salsa had become America's favorite condiment, surpassing even ketchup in annual sales.	The same ingredients found in fresh salsa are boiled together until thick. Cooked salsas may be prepared in-house or bought ready-made.	Cooked salsa is used in Mexican-American cuisine as a topping for all types of tortilla-based dishes and also as a complimentary appetizer served with tortilla chips at the beginning of the meal.
NACHOS	Nachos officially premiered in 1943 when Ignacio "Nacho" Anaya of the Victory Club, just across the border from Eagle Pass, Texas, prepared them for a group of American service wives.	At its best, nachos is made with fresh tortilla chips arranged in a single layer on an ovenproof plate, topped with shredded Monterey Jack or sharp Cheddar cheese, and broiled or baked until the cheese melts and bubbles. Cooked toppings such as shredded or chopped meats, refried beans, or roasted chiles may be added before baking. Fresh raw toppings such as diced tomatoes, chopped onions, or green chiles are added after baking.	The addition of seafood, although common in many restaurants, is problematic to some who feel that the taste of seafood is not compatible with sharp, tangy cheeses.
GUACAMOLE (hwa-ka-MOLE-ay)	This dish of seasoned, mashed avocadoes dates from pre-Colombian times. The word *guacamole* is derived from the Aztec language Nahuatl.	Chilled, firm-ripe, Western avocados are blended with chopped and mashed white onion, garlic, and fresh serrano chiles. The mixture is seasoned with fresh lime juice, diced ripe tomatoes, chopped cilantro, and salt.	Freshness is key to serving good guacamole, which ideally should be made to order. Some restaurants prepare it tableside.
CHILE CON QUESO (CHEE-lay con KAY-soh)	Literally "chile with cheese," *chile con queso* has many interpretations.	The traditional Mexican-American version of *chile con queso* is a fondue-like dip made from cream or unsweetened condensed milk, cream cheese, and sharp Cheddar cheese with the addition of onion, tomato, and chopped, fresh roasted green chile. Served hot, usually in a chafing dish, this savory dip is served with tortilla chips.	Today a more common curdle-proof version melts pasteurized process cheese or cheese spread with canned diced green chile and chopped tomatoes.

(continued)

☐ **TABLE 7.1 MEXICAN BORDER DEFINING DISHES** *(continued)*

ITEM NAME	HISTORY	DOMINANT INGREDIENTS AND METHOD	MORE
CHILES RELLENOS (CHEE-lays ray-YAY-nos)	Stuffed chiles originated in Mexican cuisine, in which the chile of choice is the poblano. The Southwestern version features fresh New Mexico or Anaheim chiles, commonly used green but extraordinary when they are fresh red-ripe.	Chiles are flame-roasted, peeled, slit open with the stem intact, and seeded, then stuffed with Cheddar or Monterey Jack cheese or other fillings. Once filled, traditional rellenos are dipped into flour, coated with a delicate soufflé batter, and fried golden brown. Southwestern restaurants sometimes use an alternative coating of flour, egg, and cornmeal.	Chiles rellenos are traditionally served in a pool of light, fresh tomato sauce subtly seasoned with bay leaf, cinnamon, and clove. Alternative fillings include *picadillo*, a sweet-and-savory mixture of ground beef, raisins, olives, almonds, and tomatoes.
QUESADILLAS (KAY-sah-DEE-yas)	Original Mexican quesadillas encase a soft melting cheese in a corn masa turnover pan-fried in lard.	Mexican Border cooks make quesadillas by folding shredded Cheddar or Monterey Jack cheese in large, thin flour tortillas. They are then toasted on a griddle or char-grill until the tortilla crisps at the edges and the cheese melts.	Filling enhancements include roasted chiles; cooked, crumbled chorizo sausage; sautéed mushrooms; and squash blossoms. Quesadillas are often accompanied by a fresh salsa designed to complement the filling ingredients. Quesadillas are served as appetizers or snacks. Cut into wedges, they make easy hors d'oeuvres.
TAMALES (TAH-MAH-lays)	One of Mexico's most ancient foods, the tamal is a leaf-wrapped packet of corn masa dough, cooked by steaming. The leaf wrapper encases and flavors the dough; it is not meant to be eaten. Sweet tamales, made with brown sugar and raisins, are a specialty in Mexico and are served for a snack or for supper. Some chefs even make dessert tamales filled with chocolate, dried fruits, or other sweet fillings.	Traditional Mexican Border cooks beat masa with pork lard and poultry stock to make a light, fluffy dough which is then wrapped in dried cornhusks with a savory filling, such as cooked beef or chicken. Tamales are steamed and served hot, sometimes with a complementary salsa.	Tamales are endlessly variable. Banana leaves may replace cornhusks. Fresh corn tamales are a seasonal treat. Contemporary chefs add herbs, chiles, and other seasonings to the dough and use alternative meats, vegetables, or seafood as fillings. Sweetened dessert tamales replace lard with butter and stock with cream, and incorporate fillings such as dried fruits or chocolate.
SIMMERED DRIED BEANS *FRIJOLES DE OLLA*/(free-HOE-lays day OH-yah)	Portable and packed with protein, *frijoles de olla* is a dish of tender beans in their lightly thickened cooking broth. Beans were an important source of nutrition for the early inhabitants of the Mexican Border region—Native American, Spanish, Mexican, and Anglo alike.	Flavored with salt pork, smoked pork bones, or bacon, and then seasoned with onion, garlic, chiles, and herbs, beans are traditionally simmered in an earthenware pot, or *olla* (OH-yah). For vegetarian diners, omit the smoked pork, enrich with oil, and season with a hint of chipotle chile for a smoky flavor. Pinto beans, pink beans, or heirloom beans are traditional. Contemporary chefs may use black beans.	*Frijoles de olla* is usually served as a side dish. When times are lean, a plate of beans topped with cheese, chopped onions, and green chiles makes an economical and nutritious meal accompanied by flour tortillas. Leftover beans may be thinned with stock to make soup.
REFRIED BEANS/ *FRIJOLES REFRITOS* (free-HOE-lays ray-FREE-toes)	"Refrieds" are the Mexican Border's most popular bean dish. The English term *refried* is a misnomer, as they are fried only once.	A heavy sauté pan or brazier is heated, fresh pork lard is melted, and brothy *olla* beans are poured sizzling into the pan. (For vegetarian refrieds, use a flavorful oil.) After the beans are fried and mashed into a purée, they become "refried" beans. Handmade refrieds have a chunky texture with visible bits of bean.	Refried beans are a popular side dish and an essential component of burritos and tostadas.
TOSTADAS (toe-STAH-das)	These snacks became popular when the Spanish introduced fats and frying to Mexico. A simple tostada is a thin corn tortilla fried crisp, spread with refried beans and garnished with assorted toppings—most typically cheese, salsa, and shredded lettuce.	Additional toppings, such as shredded or chopped meat and poultry or seafood, add substance and interest.	Simple tostadas are served as snacks or appetizers. Layered tostadas, stacked high on the plate, are substantial enough to serve as casual entrées and make a dramatic presentation.

☐ **TABLE 7.1 MEXICAN BORDER DEFINING DISHES** *(continued)*

ITEM NAME	HISTORY	DOMINANT INGREDIENTS AND METHOD	MORE
ENCHILADAS (ain-chee-LAH-dahs)	*Enchilada* roughly translates as "enveloped in chile." This dish essentially consists of a corn tortilla covered with a chile-based sauce. Even in the flour-loving Southwest, only corn tortillas are used to make enchiladas. Traditionally accompanied by refried beans and shredded lettuce or cabbage, and garnished with chopped onion and cilantro and crumbled cheese.	Corn tortillas are fried soft in lard or oil, dipped in sauce, rolled or folded with a filling such as crumbled fresh cheese; cooked, shredded beef, pork, or chicken; ground meat picadillo; cooked vegetables; or even seafood, and then baked. *Enchiladas rancheras*: fresh white cheese and tomato sauce with green chiles. *Enchildas rojas*: any filling with New Mexico red chile sauce. *Southwestern enchiladas verdes*: any filling with New Mexico green chile sauce. *Mexican-American enchiladas verdes*: chicken or cheese filling with tomatillo sauce.	In Mexican Border cuisine enchiladas are served as an entrée accompanied by refried beans and shredded lettuce. A single enchilada may be served as an appetizer or side dish.
CACTUS SALAD	Fleshy paddles of the nopal cactus are a desert specialty dating back to pre-Aztec cultures. Cleaned cactus paddles are available and rapidly becoming the industry standard—at a premium price.	With tiny thorns, cactus is literally a pain to prepare; each paddle must be trimmed of all thorns before cooking. Traditionally cut batonnet and steamed or boiled, cactus exudes a sticky substance similar to that produced by okra. Modern chefs often brush the cleaned paddles with oil and char-grill them whole before cutting in order to minimize this substance.	Tossed in a light, slightly sweet, cumin-laced cider vinaigrette with onions, tomatoes, string cheese, and roasted chiles, grilled cactus makes an unusual and delicious salad. Grilled cactus is an unusual side dish.
STUFFED SQUASH BLOSSOMS	Delicate yellow blossoms from summer squash plants are a seasonal delicacy in the Mexican Border region and in Mexico.	Blossoms are filled with a tangy melting cheese and roasted green chiles, deep-fried in a soufflé batter, and served on a pool of light, fresh tomato sauce. Contemporary chefs improvise with other delicate fillings, such as shrimp or crab meat.	A high-cost, high-labor dish, stuffed squash blossoms is an appetizer suitable for a fine-dining restaurant operation.
BURRITOS	*Burrito* means "little donkey," alluding to the plump, cylindrical shape of this popular dish. Originally street food, burritos were eaten on the run like sandwiches.	A large flour tortilla is warmed on a griddle and then rolled around hot refried beans, cheese, salsa, and other fillings. Breakfast burritos include scrambled eggs along with the beans and cheese. "Wet" burritos are napped with a sauce.	Contemporary burritos can be elegant, featuring exotic ingredients such as lobster, cactus paddles, or venison.
CHIMICHANGAS (CHIVICHANGAS)	Reputedly created in the 1950s at the El Charro restaurant in Tucson, Arizona, the original chimichanga was a flour tortilla rolled around a filling of cooked, diced beef, green chiles, and potatoes and then pan-fried.	The modern Mexican-American chimichanga is essentially a deep-fried burrito. It is typically napped with red chile sauce and garnished with sour cream.	Chimichangas must be made to order and served immediately.
SOFT TACOS	In traditional Mexican and Southwestern cuisines, a taco consists of chopped or shredded meat, poultry, seafood, or vegetables folded or rolled into a soft corn or flour tortilla—the Mexican equivalent of a sandwich.	In Southwestern and Mexican-American cuisine, flour tortillas are the most popular choice.	Salsas—either fresh and chunky or thin and fiery—accompany soft tacos. Shredded cheese, shredded lettuce, chopped onion, and sour cream are optional garnishes.
FRIED TACOS AND FLAUTAS (FLOUT-ahs)	Simple fried tacos are made to order from thin corn tortillas and cooked fillings as described earlier.	After folding the tortilla over the filling, the taco is shallow-fried in oil and/or lard until it begins to crisp at the edges yet is still a little soft in the center. Salsas and garnishes are similar to those served with soft tacos.	If the tortilla is rolled into a thin cylinder and fried in the same manner, it becomes a *flauta*. Flautas are traditionally accompanied by fresh tomato salsa and guacamole.

(continued)

☐ TABLE 7.1 MEXICAN BORDER DEFINING DISHES (continued)

ITEM NAME	HISTORY	DOMINANT INGREDIENTS AND METHOD	MORE
CRISPY TACOS/ "HARD" TACOS	Mexican-American crispy tacos or "hard" tacos became popular in the 1950s when industrial food producers developed machines to fry corn tortillas in the now-familiar "U" shape.	Crisp, pre-fried taco shells are filled with cooked, seasoned ground beef or refried beans, then heated in an oven or a microwave. Crispy tacos are topped with shredded cheese, cooked salsa, diced tomatoes, chopped onions, and shredded lettuce.	Sour cream and pickled jalapeños are frequent additions.
FAJITAS (fah-HEE-tahs)	Introduced to American diners in 1973 at Ninfa's in Houston, Texas, these tacos made of char-grilled beef originally appeared on the menu under the Mexican Spanish name *tacos al carbon* (TAH-koes ahl kar-BONE). (See p. 313 for more historical information.)	Skirt steak is tenderized in a spicy, acidic marinade, char-grilled, diagonally sliced thin across the grain, and served sizzling on a hot platter. Accompanied by sautéed peppers and onions, salsa, and shredded lettuce, fajitas are eaten as tacos wrapped in warm flour tortillas.	Named for the cut of beef, fajitas so captured the public's imagination that now the term represents any grilled food so presented. Today restaurant menus feature chicken fajitas and even seafood and vegetable fajitas.
NEW MEXICO *CHILE VERDE* (CHEE-lay VAIR-day)	Sauces and stews flavored with roasted, ground fresh green chile date back to Southwestern civilizations that flourished before Spanish conquest. Before refrigeration, green chile dishes were seasonal to late summer and fall.	Roasted, peeled, seeded New Mexico green chile is puréed or chopped before simmering in a roux-thickened sauce usually based on poultry stock. The ultimate heat of the finished dish depends on the heat of the chile variety used and the amount of chile added.	This distinctive sauce may be simmered with beef, chicken, pork, or game. *Chile verde* also sauces eggs and a variety of tortilla dishes.
NEW MEXICO *CHILE ROJO* (CHEE-lay ROE-hoe)	Southwestern Native Americans air-dried ripe, red chiles and used them throughout the year to make spicy, rustic sauces. Red chile sauces were an important source of vitamins.	The traditional method involves soaking cleaned chile pods in hot water and then grinding them into a purée, which is then fried in pork lard. Flour is stirred into the frying chile to make a roux, and hot stock is added. Some recipes simply add pure New Mexico red chile powder to the roux.	*Chile rojo* sauce is simmered into a spicy stew with beef, goat, lamb, pork, chicken, or game. It frequently sauces enchiladas or egg dishes.
POSOLE (poe-SOH-lay)	These whole, alkaline-treated hominy kernels are simmered in a classic trio of hearty entrée soups based on beef, pork, or poultry.	Posole soups are named after the color of their seasoning ingredients. *Red posole* is flavored with red chile and tomatoes. *Green posole* is flavored with green chile and tomatillos. *White posole* remains natural to be flavored at table with the seasonings of the diner's choice.	Contemporary chefs sometimes serve seasoned, buttered posole as a side dish.
HUEVOS RANCHEROS (WAY-vose rahn-CHAIR-ohs)	A dish of tortillas topped with eggs is the classic Mexican and Mexican Border breakfast dish.	Two thick corn tortillas fried chewy-crisp in pork lard, spread with refried beans, sprinkled with grated sharp Cheddar cheese, topped with two fried eggs, and napped with a green chile-spiked tomato sauce. Hot corn or flour tortillas accompany the dish.	In New Mexico, huevos rancheros is sauced with *chile verde* or *chile rojo*. New Mexicans call huevos rancheros ordered with half red sauce and half green sauce "Christmas style."
SOPAIPILLAS (soap-ah-PEE-yas)	These rectangle-shaped pillows of deep-fried dough were made in Albuquerque as early as the 17th century.	Sopaipilla dough is made from white flour enriched with pork lard or shortening and is leavened with baking powder. The dough is cut into rectangular shapes and deep-fried, emerging from the oil light, puffy, and golden brown.	Sopaipillas drizzled with honey or dusted with confectioner's sugar are a breakfast or afternoon snack. Dressed up with ice creams, fruits, and/or dessert sauces, sopaipillas are a component of contemporary Mexican Border desserts.
FLAN (FLAHN)	Flan is found throughout Latin cuisines and in classic French cuisine is known as *crème renversée au caramel*.	Sweet custard is baked in ramekins lined with caramelized sugar. European versions are made with fresh cream, eggs, sugar, and vanilla. In Mexico and the Mexican Border region recipes often replace perishable cream with condensed milk.	After chilling, the custard is turned out of its mold bottom-up on the plate to showcase the deep-brown caramel, which becomes a sauce.

■ □ ■   # STUDY QUESTIONS

1. Describe the climate and topography of the Mexican Border region. How did these land factors affect the region's cuisine?

2. Name and describe the two main Native American groups that inhabited the Four Corners area at the time of Spanish contact. Discuss their indigenous ingredients and the legacy of their cooking in traditional American Southwestern and contemporary Mexican Border cuisines.

3. Explain why the corn-bean synergy (p. 35) was vitally important to Southwestern Native Americans. Compare their method of alkaline processing corn to that practiced in Mexican cuisine.

4. Explain how the Spanish missions combined colonial Mexican cuisine with Southwestern Native American cuisine. List and describe three hybrid dishes that resulted from this blending of cuisines.

5. Discuss the development and use of the long green chile. Include in your discussion the various forms in which this chile cultivar is available and how you, as a chef, might use them.

6. List and describe the three styles of traditional American Southwestern cooking.

7. Outline the history of Mexican-American cuisine. List and describe the convenience foods that have become its primary ingredients.

8. Describe the Southwestern Native American microcuisine and list three of its defining foods or dishes.

9. Discuss the creation of contemporary Mexican Border cuisine. Include in your discussion the various culinary influences it comprises and explain the economic forces that made it possible.

10. List and describe five defining dishes of the Mexican Border culinary region and identify the subcuisines to which they belong.

11. Using your imagination and the information learned in this chapter, develop a five-course special-occasion menu of traditional American Southwestern cuisine or contemporary Mexican Border cuisine.

Creamy Corn and Green Chile Soup
with Flour Tortillas

yield: 1 (8-fl.-oz.) appetizer serving
(multiply × 4 for classroom turnout; adjust equipment sizes
accordingly)

MASTER RECIPE

production		costing only
1 c.	Creamy Corn and Green Chile Soup	1/4 recipe
2	7" Flour Tortillas or commercial tortillas	1/4 recipe or % of pkg.
1	cocktail napkin or 6" doily	1 each
2 tsp.	minced cilantro	1/40 bunch a.p.
1 Tbsp.	brunoise-cut red bell pepper	1/4 oz. a.p.

service turnout:
1. Stir the Creamy Corn and Green Chile Soup to redistribute its contents, then ladle it into a small saucepan. Heat to just under the boil.
2. Toast the Flour Tortillas on a grill or griddle just until pliant and flecked with brown.
3. Plate the dish:
   a. Pour the soup into a hot 10-oz. soup plate.
   b. Place the plate on a cool 10" plate lined with a cocktail napkin.
   c. Fold the tortillas into quarters and tuck them under the soup plate rim.
   d. Sprinkle the soup with the cilantro and red bell pepper.

COMPONENT RECIPE
CREAMY CORN AND GREEN CHILE SOUP

yield: 1 qt.

production		costing only
3 ears	fresh corn on the cob	3 ears a.p.
3/4 c.	3/8" diced Flame-Roasted Long Green Chiles, preferably New Mexico variety	1/2 recipe
2 Tbsp.	butter	1 oz.
1/2 c.	chopped white onion	2 1/2 oz. a.p.
1 tsp.	minced garlic	1/9 oz. a.p.
2/3 c.	vine-ripe tomato, coarse concassée	10 oz. a.p.
2 1/2 c.	Poultry Stock	1/6 recipe
tt	kosher salt	1/8 oz.
2/3 c.	heavy cream	5 1/3 fl. oz.
tt	sugar, optional**	1/4 oz.

preparation:
1. Prepare the corn:
   a. Husk the corn and remove the silk.
   b. Cut the kernels from the cobs.
   c. Using the back of a knife, scrape the milky liquid from the cobs into a small bowl.
   d. Place about 2/3 of the raw corn kernels and the corn liquid in a blender or food processor and grind to a smooth purée.
2. Cook the soup:
   a. Place the butter, onion, garlic, and chiles in a 4-qt. nonreactive saucepot and sweat them over low heat, stirring occasionally, about 2 minutes, until soft.
   b. Add the tomato and cook until almost dry.*
   c. Add the corn purée, raw corn kernels, Poultry Stock, and a little salt. Simmer 15 minutes, until the corn is tender and the flavors are melded.
   d. Stir in the heavy cream and remove from heat. Correct the salt and add a little sugar if needed.**

holding: open-pan cool and immediately refrigerate in a freshly sanitized, covered container up to 5 days

CHEF'S NOTES:
*Make sure to reduce excess moisture from the tomatoes to minimize their acidity. Acidic broth or prolonged heating may cause the cream to curdle. Slightly curdled soup can be partially corrected with an arrowroot slurry.
**Sugar may be needed to replace sweetness lost in storing and shipping corn. Fresh-picked corn should not need sugar.

Nopal Cactus Salad

yield: 1 (5-oz.) appetizer serving
(multiply × 4 for classroom turnout)

MASTER RECIPE

production		costing only
1/2 c.	batonnet-cut Grilled Cactus	1/6 recipe
2 Tbsp.	slivered red onion	1/2 oz. a.p.
1/4 c.	batonnet-cut vine-ripe tomato	2 oz. a.p.
1/4 c.	thick-julienne Flame-Roasted Long Green Chiles	1/6 recipe
1/4 c.	finely pulled Mexican string cheese	1/2 oz.
1/4 c.	Southwest-Style Vinaigrette	1/4 recipe
2 tsp.	chopped cilantro	1/40 bunch a.p.
2	7" Flour Tortillas or commercial tortillas	1/4 recipe or % of pkg.

service turnout:
1. Toss together all ingredients except the cilantro and Flour Tortillas.
2. Plate the dish:
   a. Mound the salad toward the front of a cool 10" plate.
   b. Sprinkle with cilantro.
   c. Toast the tortillas on a grill or griddle until pliant and flecked with brown.
   d. Fold the tortillas in quarters and overlap them on the back of the plate.

COMPONENT RECIPE
GRILLED CACTUS

yield: 3 c. (about 12 oz.)

production		costing only
6	nopal cactus paddles	1 lb. a.p.
2 Tbsp.	gold-color pure olive oil	1 fl. oz.
tt	kosher salt	1/4 oz.

preparation:
1. Prepare a charcoal grill or gas grill set to medium heat.
2. Clean the cactus:
   a. Using a sharp paring knife, trim and discard a 1/4" rim around edges of each paddle.
   b. Using the tip of the knife, cut out and discard every spine.
   c. Wash the paddles thoroughly and pat dry.
   d. Make sure to discard all of the spiny residue. Thoroughly scrub and rinse the knife, glove, and cutting board.
3. Brush the paddles with oil and grill them on both sides until they turn olive green in color, are charred with a few black flecks, and yield easily when pierced with a knife.
4. Season the cactus paddles with salt and cool them to room temperature on a rack.
5. Fabricate each paddle into the type of knife cut designated in your recipe.

holding: refrigerate in a freshly sanitized, covered container lined with paper towels to absorb moisture, up to 3 days; change the towels daily

Trimming the edges of the paddles.

Cutting out the spines.

COMPONENT RECIPE
SOUTHWEST-STYLE VINAIGRETTE

yield: 1 c.

production		costing only
1/2 tsp.	fresh-toasted, fresh-ground cumin	1/16 oz.
1/4 tsp.	dried oregano, preferably Mexican	1/16 oz.
1/4 tsp.	pure New Mexico red chile powder	1/16 oz.
1 c.	American Cider Vinaigrette	1 recipe

preparation:
1. Whisk the cumin, oregano, and chile powder into the American Cider Vinaigrette.
2. Taste and adjust the seasonings.

holding: in a freshly sanitized squeeze bottle at room temperature up to 1 week; refrigerate up to 1 month; will separate; re-emulsify in a blender or with an immersion blender

---

RECIPE VARIATION
Southwestern String Bean Salad
Replace the cactus with an equal volume of cooked, French-cut string beans.

Guacamole and Chips for Two

yield: 2 (4-oz.) appetizer servings (1 1/2 c.)
(double for classroom turnout)

MASTER RECIPE

production		costing only
5	thin white or yellow corn tortillas, each cut into 6 wedges	% of pkg
as needed	frying compound or oil for deep frying	% used
tt	fine salt	1/16 oz.
1	minced serrano chile	1/4 oz. a.p.
1/3 c.	fine-chopped sweet onion	1 2/3 oz. a.p.
1 tsp.	minced fresh garlic	1/9 oz. a.p.
tt	kosher salt	1/16 oz.
1	cold, firm-ripe Western avocado	1 [24 ct.] avocado
tt	fresh lime juice	1/4 [63 ct.] lime
1/3 c.	3/8"-diced vine-ripe tomato	3 oz. a.p.
1 Tbsp.	chopped cilantro	1/20 bunch a.p.
1	cocktail napkin, optional	1 each
1 leaf	lettuce, preferably red leaf, optional	1/20 head a.p.
1	lime wedge	1/8 [63 ct.] lime

service turnout:

1. Fry the chips:
   a. Using the basket method, deep-fry the tortilla wedges at 400°F until light golden.
   b. Shake off excess oil and transfer to a hotel pan lined with paper towels.
   c. Season with fine salt.
2. Prepare the guacamole:
   a. Place the chile, onion, garlic, and kosher salt into a foodservice-approved plastic *molcajete* (mortar) or small stainless steel bowl.
   b. Using the *mano* (pestle) or a heavy spoon, pound the vegetables until well mashed and the flavors blended.
   c. Cut open the avocado and discard the pit. Cube the avocado flesh and add it to the *molcajete* or bowl along with a little lime juice.
   d. Using a fork, lightly mash the avocado into a very rough, chunky purée.
   e. Mix in the tomato and about 2/3 of the cilantro; add kosher salt and lime juice to taste.
3. Plate the dish:
   a. If serving in the molcajete, wipe its rim clean with a clean, damp towel. Sprinkle with the remaining cilantro and stick three tortilla chips upright out of the back of the guacamole. Place the lime wedge on the rim. Serve the remaining chips in a small basket lined with a cocktail napkin.
      —or—
   b. Place the lettuce leaf slightly front center on a cool 10" plate. Mound the guacamole on the leaf and sprinkle with the remaining cilantro. Place the lime wedge alongside. Mound the chips in an arc across the back of the plate.

RECIPE VARIATIONS

Guacamole Shrimp Cocktail
Line a 12-fl.-oz. martini glass with 1/2 c. chiffonade romaine. Scoop 1/2 recipe guacamole into the glass. Hang 4 cooked and peeled cocktail shrimp and a lime wedge on the rim of the glass. Place the glass on an underliner plate and stick 3 tortilla chip strips upright in it. Serve additional chips in a basket.

Guacamole Green Sauce
Omit the tomatoes and lime juice. Mash the avocado smooth. Mix in 1 c. poached, chilled, puréed tomatillos. Serve as a sauce for tacos, flautas, or grilled chicken or seafood.

Southwest Cheese Chile Relleno
with Spiced Tomato Sauce

yield: 1 (5-oz.) appetizer serving
(multiply × 4 for classroom turnout; adjust equipment sizes accordingly)

MASTER RECIPE

production		costing only
3/4 c.	Fresh Tomato Sauce, Mexican-American variation	about 1/5 recipe
1	egg yolk	1 each or 2/3 oz.
1 Tbsp.	flour	1/3 oz.
tt	fine salt	1/16 oz.
1	egg white	n/c or 1 oz.
1	Southwest Cheese Chile Relleno	1/4 recipe
as needed	flour for dredging	1/2 oz.
as needed	frying compound or oil for frying	% used
1 large sprig	fresh cilantro	1/20 bunch a.p.

service turnout:
1. Heat the Fresh Tomato Sauce in a small sauté pan or in the microwave.
2. Mix the batter:
   a. Use a fork to beat together the egg yolk, 1 Tbsp. flour, and a little salt in a small bowl.
   b. Place the egg white and a little salt in a separate bowl and use a whip to beat it to just under firm peaks.
   c. Use a rubber spatula to fold together the yolk and white.
3. Fry the relleno:
   a. If necessary, remove the basket(s) from the fryer to allow the chile to float freely in the oil.
   b. Dredge the Southwest Cheese Chile Relleno in flour and shake off the excess.
   c. Dip the relleno into the batter, using a spoon to help coat it completely.
   d. Place the relleno into 400°F oil. Fry the relleno until the bottom is golden.
   e. Using two perforated hotel spoons, carefully turn over the relleno. ⚠ Do not puncture the coating. Fry until the new bottom is golden.
   f. Using one of the perforated hotel spoons, lift the relleno out of the oil and drain it briefly on a rack.
   g. Remove the cocktail picks.
4. Plate the dish:
   a. Spoon the sauce onto a hot 10" pasta plate.
   b. Place the relleno diagonally in the center of the plate.
   c. Garnish with the cilantro sprig at 11 o'clock.

COMPONENT RECIPE
SOUTHWEST CHEESE CHILES RELLENOS

yield: 4 (5-oz.) stuffed chiles

production		costing only
4	large, fresh long green chiles, preferably New Mexico variety*	about 12 oz.
5 oz.	grated extra-sharp white Cheddar cheese	5 oz.
as needed	plain cocktail picks	% of pkg. or each

preparation:
1. Prepare the chiles as described in the recipe for Flame-Roasted Long Green Chiles, option b.
2. Stuff the chiles:
   a. Wearing foodservice gloves, divide the cheese into 4 portions and, using the palm of your hand, squeeze and shape each portion into a tight, elongated cone similar to the shape and size of each chile.
   b. Insert a cheese cone into each chile.
   c. Secure each chile shut with one or two cocktail picks. Make sure that the ends of the picks will be visible after the chiles are batter-fried.

holding: refrigerate in a freshly sanitized, covered container, with pan liner between layers, up to 5 days

CHEF'S NOTES:
*Chiles rellenos are best made with fresh chiles. For ease of handling and attractive presentation, choose chiles that are uniform in size, are smooth and convex in shape, and have long stems firmly attached. If frozen roasted chiles must be used, search through the package for chiles that have thick flesh and are intact. If frozen chiles are small, present two per serving. If frozen chiles are not peeled, peel them and make sure no seeds remain inside.

RECIPE VARIATIONS

Picadillo Chiles Rellenos
Omit the cheese. Prepare a thick filling of ground beef and pork simmered with onions, garlic, raisins, slivered almonds, green olives, ground cinnamon, toasted ground cumin, and tomato concassée. Chill the filling and stuff the chiles.

Crumb-Crusted Southwest Chiles Rellenos
Prepare Cheese or Picadillo Chiles Rellenos. As part of preparation, dredge the stuffed chiles in flour, coat them with egg wash, and then roll them in dried bread crumbs to coat completely. Place on a rack set on a sheet tray and refrigerate at least 1 hour before frying.

Corn-Crumb-Crusted Baked Chiles Rellenos
Prepare Cheese or Picadillo Chiles Rellenos. In a food processor, grind broken tortilla chips into fine, even crumbs. As part of preparation, dredge the stuffed chiles in flour, coat them with egg wash, and then roll them in the tortilla chip crumbs to coat completely. Place on a rack set on a sheet tray and refrigerate at least 1 hour. To turn out, place on a sizzle plate, drizzle with melted butter, and bake at 400°F about 8 minutes, until the rellenos are heated through and the crumbs are golden.

Texas Gulf Coast
Shrimp Cocktail

yield: 1 (4-oz.) appetizer serving
(multiply × 4 for classroom turnout)

MASTER RECIPE

production		costing only
1	thin white or yellow tortilla, cut in long, 3/4"-wide strips	% of pkg.
as needed	frying compound or oil for deep-frying	% used
tt	fine salt	1/16 oz.
1/4	cold, firm-ripe Western avocado, 1/2" dice	1/4 [24 ct.] avocado
1 tsp.	fresh lime juice	1/8 [63 ct.] lime
tt	kosher salt	1/16 oz.
1/4 c.	Fresh Tomato Salsa	1/4 recipe
2 Tbsp.	ketchup	1 fl. oz.
(3 oz.)	Creole Poached Gulf Shrimp with Shrimp Glaze, p. 266	1/4 recipe
2 Tbsp.	brunoise-cut jicama	1 oz. a.p.
1 Tbsp.	fine diagonal-sliced scallion	1/16 bunch a.p.
1/2 c.	chiffonade romaine hearts	1/20 head a.p.
1 tsp.	chopped cilantro	1/40 bunch a.p.
1	6" doily or cocktail napkin	1 each
1	(21–25 ct.) shrimp, poached and peeled	3/4 oz. a.p.

service turnout:
1. Fry the tortilla strip garnish:
   a. Using the basket method, deep-fry the tortilla strips at 400°F until light golden.
   b. Shake off excess oil and transfer them to a hotel pan lined with paper towels.
   c. Sprinkle with fine salt.
2. In a small bowl, toss together the avocado, lime juice, and a little kosher salt. Mix in the Fresh Tomato Salsa, ketchup, Creole Poached Gulf Shrimp, 1 tsp. Shrimp Glaze, jicama, and scallion.
3. Plate the dish:
   a. Place the romaine in a 12-oz. martini glass.
   b. Top with the shrimp mixture.
   c. Sprinkle with cilantro.
   d. Place the glass on an 8" plate lined with a 6" doily.
   e. Stick the tortilla strips upright out of the back of the glass.
   f. Prop the poached shrimp against the tortilla strips.

RECIPE VARIATION
Southern California Crab Cocktail
Replace the shrimp with Dungeness crab meat, using 3 oz. per serving.

Green Chile Quesadilla
with Fresh Tomato Salsa

yield: 1 (5-oz.) appetizer serving
(multiply × 4 for classroom turnout; adjust equipment sizes accordingly)

MASTER RECIPE

production		costing only
2	thin 10" Flour Tortillas or commercial tortillas	1/3 recipe or % of pkg.
1/2 c.	extra-sharp white Cheddar cheese	1 1/2 oz.
1/3 c.	julienne Flame-Roasted Long Green Chiles	4 oz. a.p.
1/3 c.	Fresh Tomato Salsa	1/3 recipe
6 sprigs	fresh cilantro	1/8 bunch a.p.

service turnout:

1. Assemble and bake the quesadilla (work quickly so it doesn't burn):
   a. Place one Flour Tortilla on a medium-hot griddle or low-heat gas grill.
   b. Distribute the cheese on the tortilla, leaving a 1/2" rim.
   c. Distribute the chiles on top of the cheese.
   d. Place the remaining tortilla on top and press down with a large metal spatula.
   e. Check the bottom tortilla and, when flecked with brown spots or nicely grill-marked, flip it over.
   f. Press down with the spatula and continue to toast the quesadilla until the new bottom is brown-flecked or grill-marked and the cheese is melted. If using a char-grill, you may rotate the quesadilla 90 degrees to achieve attractive crosshatch grill marks.
2. Transfer the quesadilla to a cutting board and cut it into 8 wedges.
3. Plate the dish:
   a. Arrange the wedges around the edge of the plate well of a warm 12" plate.
   b. Ladle the Fresh Tomato Salsa into a 3-oz. ramekin and place it in the center of the plate.
   c. Arrange the cilantro sprigs around the ramekin.

APPETIZERS

RECIPE VARIATIONS

Border-style quesadillas are subject to endless variation. The only constants are the flour tortillas and the cheese. Some ideas:

Chorizo Quesadillas with Green Salsa
Reduce the chile amount by half and add 2 Tbsp. cooked, crumbled chorizo sausage. Replace the Fresh Tomato Salsa with any of the Green Salsa (p. 331) variations.

Wild Mushroom Quesadillas with Fresh Tomato Salsa
Reduce the chile amount by half and add 1/4 c. very well sautéed, highly seasoned wild mushrooms, sliced if large.

Huitlacoche Quesadillas with Fresh Tomato Salsa
Reduce the chile amount by half and add 1/4 c. very well sautéed, highly seasoned huitlacoche (corn fungus, p. 356).

Squash Blossom Quesadillas with Fresh Tomato Salsa
Reduce the chile amount by half and add 1/4 c. very well sautéed, highly seasoned, prepared squash blossoms (p. 356).

Twin Tostadas

yield: 1 (5-oz.) appetizer or lunch serving
(multiply × 4 for classroom turnout)

MASTER RECIPE

production		costing only
2	4" white Corn Tortillas or commercial tortillas*	1/6 recipe or % of pkg.
3 Tbsp.	pork lard	1 1/2 oz.
1/4 c.	corn oil	2 fl. oz.
1/3 c.	hot, fluid Refried Beans	1/6 recipe
1 Tbsp.	sautéed crumbled Mexican chorizo sausage, drained well	1/2 oz. a.p.
1/4 c.	Green Salsa	1/4 recipe
1/4 c.	Shredded Chicken	1/12 recipe
1/4 c.	Fresh Tomato Salsa	1/4 recipe
2/3 c.	shredded romaine hearts	1/12 head a.p.
2 Tbsp.	crumbled cotija or añejo cheese	1/2 oz.
2 Tbsp.	fine-chopped red onion	3/4 oz. a.p.
2 Tbsp.	Crema, in squeeze bottle	1/8 recipe

service turnout:
1. Pan-fry the Corn Tortillas:
   a. Heat the lard and oil in a 6" sauté pan.
   b. Pan-fry each tortilla on both sides until light brown around the edges and almost crisp.
   c. Blot on paper towels.
2. Plate the dish:
   a. Spread each tortilla with half of the Refried Beans and place them side by side on a warm 10" oval plate.
   b. Sprinkle the left tortilla with the chorizo and spoon the Green Salsa on top.
   c. Sprinkle the right tortilla with the Shredded Chicken and spoon the Fresh Tomato Salsa on top.
   d. Top both tortillas with shredded romaine.
   e. Sprinkle both tortillas with cheese and red onion.
   f. Drizzle both tortillas with Crema.

COMPONENT RECIPE
REFRIED BEANS

yield: 1 pt.

production		costing only	
1/4 c.	pork lard	2 oz.	
2 1/2 c.	Border Beans de Olla	about 1/3 recipe with broth	
as needed	water	n/c	

preparation:
1. Heat a 10" sauté pan, add the lard, and heat it almost to the smoke point.
2. Standing back, and with sleeves down, pour in the beans and immediately begin to stir and mash them with the back of a hotel spoon.
3. As the beans crush and thicken, lower the heat and continue to stir and mash until they become a thick, chunky purée. If necessary, add water to achieve the desired consistency.
4. Taste and correct the seasoning.

holding: open-pan cool and immediately refrigerate in a freshly sanitized, covered container up to 1 week; may be frozen up to 3 months; holds well in a steam table if thinned with boiling water as necessary

---

RECIPE VARIATIONS
Vegetarian Refried Beans
Replace the pork lard with corn oil. Use the Vegetarian version of Border Beans de Olla.
Refried Black Beans
Use the Black Beans version of Border Beans de Olla.

CHEF'S NOTE:
*Standard 5" corn tortillas yield too large a portion. If 4" tortillas are unavailable or not cost effective, simply cut down standard 5" tortillas with scissors.

APPETIZERS

COMPONENT RECIPE
GREEN SALSA

yield: 1 c.

production		costing only
6 oz.	tomatillos	6 oz.
1 Tbsp.	minced serrano chiles	1/4 oz. a.p.
1/4 c.	chopped sweet onion	2 oz. a.p.
1 tsp.	minced fresh garlic	1/8 oz. a.p.
tt	kosher salt	1/16 oz.
1 Tbsp.	chopped cilantro	1/20 bunch a.p.
tt	sugar, optional	1/4 oz.

preparation:
1. Prepare the tomatillo purée:
   a. Remove the paperlike husks from all of the tomatillos and wash them thoroughly.
   b. Poach 4 oz. of the tomatillos in barely simmering water 4 to 8 minutes, until they are soft and olive green in color. ⚠ Do not boil; the tomatillos may disintegrate.
   c. Refresh the tomatillos in ice water and then drain well.
   d. Purée the cooked tomatillos in a blender or food processor.
2. Finish the salsa:
   a. Chop the remaining tomatillos fine.
   b. Place the tomatillos, chiles, onion, garlic, and salt in a *molcajete* (mortar) or small stainless steel bowl. Using the *mano* (pestle) or a heavy spoon, grind the vegetables until they are well mashed and the flavors are blended.
   c. Stir in the tomatillo purée and the cilantro.
   d. Correct the salt and balance the flavor with sugar, if necessary.

holding: refrigerated in a freshly sanitized, covered, nonreactive container up to 3 days

COMPONENT RECIPE
FRESH TOMATO SALSA

yield: approx. 1 c.

production		costing only
1 Tbsp.	seeded, chopped serrano chile	1/4 oz. a.p.
3 Tbsp.	fine-chopped sweet onion	1 oz. a.p.
1 tsp.	minced fresh garlic	1/9 oz. a.p.
tt	kosher salt	1/16 oz.
1 c.	fine-chopped vine-ripe tomato	8 oz. a.p.
1 Tbsp.	chopped cilantro	1/20 bunch a.p.

preparation:
1. Place chiles, onion, garlic, and salt in a foodservice-approved plastic *molcajete* or small stainless steel bowl.
2. Using the *mano* or a spoon, grind the vegetables until they are well mashed and the flavors are blended.
3. Add the tomatoes and grind until blended into a textured, pourable purée.
4. Stir in the cilantro and correct the salt.

holding: refrigerate up to 6 hours

RECIPE VARIATIONS
Tostadas are subject to endless variation; the only constants are the shell, the refried bean layer and the crisp vegetable garnish. A few suggestions:

Lobster, Crab, or Shrimp Tostadas with Guacamole Green Salsa
Top with Refried Beans; cooked lobster, crab, or shrimp; Guacamole Green Salsa (p. 326), shredded lettuce, and Crema. Omit the cheese.

Shredded Pork Tostadas with Roasted Corn and Green Salsa
Top with Refried Beans, Shredded Pork, roasted corn kernels, Green Salsa, shredded lettuce, red onion, crumbled cheese, and Crema.

Tex-Mex Ground Beef Tostadas with Cheddar and Sour Cream
Top with Refried Beans, Tex-Mex Ground Beef Taco Filling, shredded Cheddar, Cooked Tomato Salsa, shredded lettuce, and sour cream.

Southwest Grilled Vegetable Tostadas with Roasted Tomato Salsa
Top with Refried Beans; Monterey Jack cheese; Grilled Cactus (p. 325); marinated grilled eggplant, zucchini, and red bell pepper; Roasted Tomato Sauce; and Crema.

Pico de Gallo
Toss chopped ingredients together rather than grinding into a purée; serve as a relish-like condiment.

Avocado—Tomato Salsa
Toss 1/2 c. small-diced firm-ripe avocado with kosher salt and lime juice and stir into the salsa.

Pineapple Salsa
Substitute chopped fresh pineapple for the tomatoes.

Border-Style Beef Tamal
with Red and Green Salsas

yield: 1 (4-oz.) appetizer serving
(multiply × 4 for classroom turnout)

MASTER RECIPE

production		costing only
1	Beef Tamal	1/4 recipe
1/4 c.	Fresh Tomato Salsa	1/4 recipe
1/4 c.	Green Salsa, p. 331	1/4 recipe
1 sprig	fresh cilantro	1/20 bunch a.p.

service turnout:

1a. Heat the Beef Tamal in a steamer.
—or—
1b. Place the Beef Tamal on a small plate, moisten with a little water, and cover with plastic wrap. Microwave on high power a few seconds only, just until heated through.
2. Open the cornhusk and fold the edges underneath so that the dough filling is cradled in the open husk.
3. Plate the dish:
   a. Place the tamal in the center of a warm 9" plate.
   b. Spoon the Fresh Tomato Salsa diagonally across the tamal.
   c. Spoon the Green Salsa diagonally across the tamal in front of the tomato salsa.
   d. Place the cilantro sprig on the plate at 4 o'clock.

COMPONENT RECIPE
BEEF TAMALES

yield: 6 (3-oz.) tamales (4 appetizer servings plus 2 for practice)

production		costing only
10	large dried cornhusks	2 1/2 oz.
1 c.+	Poultry Stock	1/16 recipe
tt	kosher salt	1/8 oz.
1/2 c.	room-temperature pork lard	4 oz.
2 c.	masa harina	8 oz.
1 c.	Beef Tamal Filling	1 recipe
6	5" lengths kitchen string	% of roll

preparation:

1. Place the cornhusks in a bowl and add boiling water to cover. Weight down with a plate so they are submerged. Soak the husks until pliant, about 20 minutes.
2. Mix the tamal dough:
   a. Bring the Poultry Stock to the simmer, remove it from the heat, and season it with salt. (The stock must be well salted to season the dough.) Cool to lukewarm.
   b. Using the whip attachment of a mixer, beat the lard on high speed 3 minutes, until very light and fluffy.
   c. Reduce the speed to medium and add 1/2 c. masa harina. Return to high speed and beat 20 seconds.
   d. Reduce the speed to medium and add 1/4 c. stock. Return to high speed and beat 20 seconds.
   e. Repeat, using the remaining masa harina and stock, scraping down the sides of the bowl as necessary. The dough should be very light and fluffy, with a loose texture similar to soft cooked oatmeal.
   f. Test the dough by placing 1 tsp. dough on the surface of a small glass of ice-cold water. The dough should float. If it sinks, beat the remaining dough 2 to 4 minutes longer until another spoonful floats.
3. Prepare a steamer:
   a. Start water boiling in the bottom of a stovetop steamer, or prime a commercial pressure steamer.
   b. Line the steamer pan with 2 cornhusks.
4. Assemble the tamales:
   a. Drain and pat dry the remaining cornhusks.
   b. Place a cornhusk opened flat on the work surface with the pointed tip away from you and the straight bottom edge toward you.
   c. Spoon 1/6 of the masa dough in the center of the husk and make an oblong well in the middle of the dough.
   d. Spoon 1/6 of the filling into the well and push up the edges of the dough to encase the filling.
   e. Fold the right side of the husk over the filling and then fold the left side of the husk over it to completely encase the filling.
   f. Fold the squared-off bottom up, and the pointed top down, to make a rectangular packet.
   g. Tie around the middle with string.
   h. Repeat to make 6 tamales.
   i. Prop the tamales upright in the steamer pan and cover them with the remaining cornhusks.
5. Steam the tamales:
   a. If using a stovetop steamer, steam the tamales 40 minutes, checking occasionally to make sure the steamer doesn't run dry. If using a commercial pressure steamer, steam 15 to 20 minutes.
   b. Carefully open the steamer and remove a tamal. Open the tamal and check it for doneness. The tamal should feel firm throughout with no raw dough in the center.
   c. When the tamales are cooked through, remove from the steamer and serve immediately, or cool completely on a rack.
6. Remove the kitchen string from the tamales.
7. Individually wrap each tamal in plastic film.

holding: refrigerate up to 5 days; may be frozen for up to 3 months

COMPONENT RECIPE
BEEF TAMAL FILLING

yield: 1 1/4 c.

production		costing only
1 c.	Shredded Beef	1/3 recipe
1/4 c.	New Mexico Red Chile Sauce, p. 338	1/16 recipe

preparation:

1. Mix the Shredded Beef and New Mexico Red Chile Sauce.

holding: refrigerate in a freshly sanitized, covered container up to 5 days; may be frozen up to 3 months

---

RECIPE VARIATIONS

Navajo Tamales
Replace the beef in the Beef Tamal Filling with shredded cooked shoulder of mutton, lamb, goat, or venison.

Chicken Tamales with Green Salsa
Replace the Beef Tamal Filling with Shredded Chicken in Tomatillo Sauce. Serve each tamal with 1/2 c. Green Salsa only.

Chile Relleno Tamales
Replace the Beef Tamal Filling with 6 (3/4-oz.) thick batons of sharp white cheddar Cheese, each wrapped in a piece of Flame-Roasted New Mexico Long Green Chile. Serve each tamal with 1/2 c. Fresh Tomato Salsa only.

"Blind" Tamales (side dish)
Omit the filling.

Hopi Blue Corn Tamales
Replace the masa harina with blue corn flour mixed to a thick paste with alkalized water. Reduce the amount of Poultry Stock accordingly. Prepare the Beef Tamal Filling with shredded cooked rabbit. Add julienne Grilled Cactus (p. 325) and cooked corn kernels to the filling.

Sweet Dessert Tamales
Replace the lard with butter. Add 1/2 c. brown sugar to the masa harina. Decrease the salt to just a pinch. Replace the Poultry Stock with warm milk. Add 1/2 tsp. cinnamon to the dough. Prepare a sweet filling, such as sautéed apples or poached cherries. Serve with Vanilla Custard Sauce.

Southern California Mahimahi Tamal

with Jalapeño-Citrus Butter Sauce, Herbed Posole, and Steamed Chayote

yield: 1 (7-oz.) entrée serving plus accompaniments
(multiply × 4 for classroom turnout; adjust equipment sizes
accordingly)

MASTER RECIPE

production		costing only
1	Mahimahi Banana Leaf Tamal	1/4 recipe
5	3-oz. Steamed Chayote Wedges	1/4 recipe
tt	kosher salt	1/16 oz.
1 Tbsp.	seeded, minced jalapeño chile	2/3 oz. a.p.
tt	fresh lime juice	1/6 [63 ct.] lime
4 Tbsp.	butter	2 oz.
1 c.	canned Mexican–style posole, hot in steam table	1/8 recipe
1 Tbsp.	chopped fresh mint	1/12 bunch a.p.
1 Tbsp.	chopped cilantro	1/20 bunch a.p.
1	thin slice of small navel orange	1/8 [100 ct.] orange
1	thin slice of small lemon	1/6 [165 ct.] lemon
1	thin slice of small lime	1/6 [63 ct.] lime
1 sprig	fresh mint	1/12 bunch a.p.
1 sprig	fresh cilantro	1/20 bunch a.p.

service turnout:

1. Place the Mahimahi Banana Leaf Tamal on a sizzle pan and bake in a 400°F oven 15 minutes.
2. Heat the Steamed Chayote Wedges with a little water and salt in a covered 8" sauté pan or in a microwave.
3. Finish the tamal and its sauce:
   a. Remove the tamal from the oven. Using scissors, cut an X in the top of the banana leaf wrapper. Open the pointed flaps. Check the doneness and, if necessary, finish the fish in a microwave.
   b. Pour the juices from the mahimahi into an 8" sauté pan by carefully tilting the sizzle pan while holding the tamal in place.
   c. Add the jalapeño and lime juice to the pan and reduce the pan juices to about 1/4 c.
   d. Whisk the butter into the sauce to form an emulsion.
4. Plate the dish:
   a. Place the open tamal on the front of a hot 12" plate and hold warm.
   b. Use a perforated spoon to place the posole on the back left of the plate on top of the banana leaf flap. Sprinkle with the chopped mint and cilantro.
   c. Fan the Chayote Wedges on the back right of the plate on top of the banana leaf flap.
   d. Pour the sauce over the fish and vegetables.
   e. Stack the citrus slices together and cut a slit through them from the center through the edges. Twist the citrus slices into a "butterfly" and place it on top of the fish.
   f. Make a bouquet of the herb sprigs and plant it upright behind the citrus "butterfly."

COMPONENT RECIPE
MAHIMAHI BANANA LEAF TAMALES

yield: 4 (7-oz.) entrée servings

production		costing only
2	dried New Mexico chile pods	1/2 oz.
1/4 c.	chopped white onion	1 1/4 oz. a.p.
1 tsp.	minced garlic	1/9 oz. a.p.
1/2 c.	orange juice	1 [90 ct.] orange
1 Tbsp.	minced orange zest	n/c
tt	kosher salt	1/16 oz.
4	7-oz. mahimahi fillets, pinned and trimmed	2 lb. a.p.
1	large frozen banana leaf, thawed	1/4 pkg.

preparation:
1. Prepare the chile purée:
   a. Using tongs, pass the chiles over a gas flame until they become flexible. ⚠ Do not allow to brown or scorch.
   b. Clean the flexible chiles of stems, seeds, and veins.
   c. Place the chiles in a small, nonreactive bowl and pour boiling water over them. Weight them down with a small plate. Soak for 20 minutes until soft.
   d. Drain the chiles and place them in a blender along with the onion, garlic, orange juice, orange zest, and salt. Grind into a smooth purée.
2. Coat the mahimahi fillets with the purée.
3. Assemble the tamales:
   a. Cut the banana leaf into 4 (approx. 12" × 12") squares.
   b. Wash the banana leaf squares under hot water and pat dry.
   c. Place a banana leaf square on the work surface, shiny side down, and place a coated fish fillet in the center, rounded side down.
   d. Fold the banana leaf around the fish to encase it in a square packet.
   e. Repeat with the remaining ingredients to make a total of 4 banana leaf tamales.

holding: refrigerate in a freshly sanitized, covered container up to 24 hours

COMPONENT RECIPE
STEAMED CHAYOTE WEDGES

yield: approx. 12 oz.

production		costing only
2	chayotes (mirlitons)	2 [24 ct.] a.p. (1 lb.)

preparation:
1. Prepare a stovetop steamer or commercial pressure steamer. Prepare ice water for refreshing.
2. Cut the chayotes in half lengthwise. Place them on the steamer rack, cut side down, and steam about 20 minutes in the stovetop steamer or about 5 minutes in the pressure steamer, until just tender.
3. Refresh the chayotes in ice water and wipe them dry.
4. Remove the pits, pare off the skins, and slice each chayote half into 5 even wedges.

holding: refrigerate in a freshly sanitized, covered, paper towel–lined container up to 3 days; change towels daily

Santa Fe Red Chile Cheese Enchiladas
with Olla Beans and Avocado Salad

yield: 1 (6-oz.) entrée serving plus accompaniments
(multiply × 4 for classroom turnout; adjust equipment sizes
accordingly)

MASTER RECIPE

production		costing only
3	Red Chile Cheese Enchiladas	1/4 recipe
3/4 c.	New Mexico Red Chile Sauce, p. 338, hot in steam table	approx. 1/5 recipe
1	5" thin yellow or white Corn Tortilla or commercial tortilla	1/12 recipe or % of pkg.
as needed	frying compound or corn oil	% used
1/2	cold, firm-ripe Western avocado	1/2 [24 ct.] avocado
1 tsp.	fresh lime juice	1/8 [63 ct.] lime
tt	kosher salt	1/16 oz.
1/4 c.	brunoise-cut jicama	3 oz. a.p.
1/2 c.	3/8"-diced vine-ripe tomato	5 oz. a.p.
2 Tbsp.	fine diagonal-sliced scallion	1/8 bunch a.p.
2 Tbsp.	Southwest-Style Vinaigrette, p. 325	1/8 recipe
3/4 c.	Border Beans de Olla, hot in steam table	1/9 recipe
1 Tbsp.	crumbled *cotija* or *añejo* cheese	1/8 oz.
1 c.	shredded romaine lettuce	1/8 head a.p.
2 Tbsp.	Crema, in squeeze bottle	1/8 recipe
2 Tbsp.	chopped white onion	1 1/4 oz. a.p.
1 Tbsp.	chopped cilantro	1/20 bunch a.p.

service turnout:

1. Place the Red Chile Cheese Enchiladas close together on a sizzle plate and nap the edges with a little New Mexico Red Chile Sauce. Bake in a 400°F oven about 10 minutes.
2. Fry the tortilla basket:
   a. Warm the Corn Tortilla on a griddle or char-grill just until flexible.
   b. Press the tortilla in a potato basket form or between two 5" mesh strainers.
   c. Deep-fry until crisp, then release the tortilla basket upside down on paper towels.
3. Mix the salad:
   a. Cut the avocado into 1/2" dice, place in a small bowl, and season it with lime juice and salt.
   b. Gently toss in the jicama, tomato, scallion, and Southwest-Style Vinaigrette.
4. Plate the dish:
   a. Use a wide spatula to place the enchiladas diagonally on the right side of a warm 12" plate.
   b. Nap the enchiladas with the remaining red chile sauce.
   c. Fill the tortilla basket with the Border Beans de Olla and place the basket on the plate at 10 o'clock. Sprinkle the beans with the cheese.
   d. Place a bed of lettuce to the left of the enchiladas and spoon the avocado salad onto it.
   e. Squeeze a zigzag pattern of Crema across the enchiladas.
   f. Scatter a diagonal stripe of onion and cilantro across the enchiladas.

COMPONENT RECIPE
RED CHILE CHEESE ENCHILADAS

yield: 12 (2-oz.) enchiladas

production		costing only
4 Tbsp.	pork lard	2 oz.
12	5" Corn Tortillas or commercial tortillas	1 recipe
2 c.	crumbled fresco cheese	14 oz.
1 c.	grated extra-sharp white Cheddar cheese	7 oz.
1 c.	hot New Mexico Red Chile Sauce	1/4 recipe

preparation:
1. Heat an 8" sauté pan, heat a little lard, and fry the Corn Tortillas on both sides, one by one, just until softened. ⚠ Do not fry crisp.
2. Mix the cheeses.
3. Assemble the enchiladas:
   a. Dip a fried tortilla into the New Mexico Red Chile Sauce, lightly coating both sides, and place on a plate.
   b. Place 1/12 of the cheese mixture (about 2 Tbsp.) in a horizontal line across the tortilla.
   c. Roll the tortilla into a tight cylinder and place it on a sheet tray covered with pan liner.
   d. Repeat with the remaining ingredients to make a total of 12 enchiladas.
   e. Cover the surface of the enchiladas with plastic film.

holding: refrigerate up to 3 days

COMPONENT RECIPE
NEW MEXICO RED CHILE SAUCE

yield: approx. 1 qt.

production		costing only
4 oz.	dried red New Mexico chile pods	4 oz.
1 c.	chopped white onion	5 oz. a.p.
1 Tbsp.	chopped garlic	1/2 oz. a.p.
1 c.	water	n/c
6 Tbsp.	pure pork lard	3 oz.
2 Tbsp.	flour	2/3 oz.
2 qt.	hot Poultry Stock	1/2 recipe
tt	kosher salt	1/16 oz.
tt	sugar, optional	1/8 oz.

preparation:
1. Prepare the chile purée:
   a. Heat a griddle or dry sauté pan over low heat. Place the chiles on it and press with a spatula to warm them. Turn the chiles and continue pressing just until they are warm and flexible. ⚠ Do not scorch.
   b. While the chiles are still warm, remove the stems, open the pods and remove all seeds and veins.
   c. Place the chiles in a small bowl and pour in boiling water to cover. Weight with a plate to keep them submerged. Soak for about 20 minutes until the chiles are soft.
   d. Drain the chiles and place them in a blender along with the onion and garlic. Blend until smooth.
2. Heat the lard in a heavy, nonreactive 8 qt. saucepan almost to the smoke point. ⚠ Standing back and with sleeves down, add the chile purée. Cook, stirring, about 5 minutes until the purée thickens and becomes fragrant.
3. Stir in the flour and then whisk in the Poultry Stock to make a smooth sauce. Add a little salt.
4. Simmer briskly about 30 minutes until the sauce reaches a light nappé consistency.
5. Correct the salt and add a little sugar if necessary.

holding: open-pan cool and refrigerate in a freshly sanitized, nonreactive, covered container up to 5 days

RECIPE VARIATIONS

Vegetarian Red Chile Cheese Enchiladas
Replace the lard with corn oil. Use the Vegetarian version of New Mexico Red Chile Sauce.

New Mexico Green Chile Cheese Enchiladas
Substitute New Mexico Green Chile Sauce (p. 342) for the Red Chile Sauce.

New Mexico Red Chile Pork or Chicken Enchiladas
Substitute 3 c. Shredded Pork or Shredded Chicken in New Mexico Red Chile Sauce for the cheese. Add 2 Tbsp. crumbled fresco cheese to the garnish for each serving.

Enchiladas Rancheras
Substitute Fresh Tomato Sauce, Ranchera variation for the Red Chile Sauce.

New Mexico Pork
Chile Verde
with Flour Tortillas and Pepper-Squash Medley

yield: 1 (6-oz.) entrée serving plus accompaniments
(multiply × 4 for classroom turnout; adjust equipment sizes accordingly)

MASTER RECIPE

production		costing only
2 c.	Pork *Chile Verde*	1/4 recipe
as needed	water, in squeeze bottle	n/c
2 tsp.	corn oil	1/3 fl. oz.
1/4 c.	1/4"-diced red bell pepper	2 oz. a.p.
3/4 c.	seeded, 1/2"-diced zucchini	4 1/2 oz. a.p.
tt	kosher salt	1/16 oz.
pinch	pure New Mexico chile powder	1/16 oz.
1 Tbsp.	butter	1/2 oz.
2	7" Flour Tortillas or commercial tortillas	1/4 recipe or % of pkg.
1 Tbsp.	chopped cilantro	1/20 bunch a.p.

service turnout:

1. Heat the Pork *Chile Verde* in a covered 10" sauté pan, thinning with water as necessary.
2. Heat a 10" sauté pan, heat the oil, and sauté the red bell pepper and zucchini. Season with salt and chile powder. Remove from the heat and work in the butter to form an emulsion.
3. Plate the dish:
   a. Spoon the *chile verde* into a hot 10" pasta bowl.
   b. Arrange the sautéed vegetables around the edge of the plate well from 4 o'clock to 10 o'clock.
   c. Toast the Flour Tortillas on a char-grill or over an open flame until flexible.
   d. Fold the tortillas into quarters and tuck them, edges upright, into the back of the bowl.
   e. Sprinkle the *chile verde* with cilantro.

COMPONENT RECIPE
PORK *CHILE VERDE*

yield: 1 qt. (approx. 20 oz. cooked pork)

production		costing only
2 lb.	boneless pork shoulder	2 lb.
6 Tbsp.	pork lard	3 oz.
tt	kosher salt	1/8 oz.
1 c.	chopped white onion	5 oz. a.p.
2 tsp.	minced garlic	1/4 oz. a.p.
1/2 tsp.	toasted, ground cumin seeds	1/16 oz.
1/2 tsp.	dried oregano, preferably Mexican	1/16 oz.
3 Tbsp.	flour	1 oz.
1 qt.	hot, strong Poultry Stock	1/4 recipe
2 c.	peeled, 3/4"-diced russet potatoes	12 oz. a.p.
1 1/4 c.	chopped Flame-Roasted Long Green Chiles, New Mexico variety	1 recipe
tt	fresh lemon juice	1/8 [90 ct.] lemon

preparation:

1. Trim the pork of excess fat and silverskin while dividing it into individual muscle bundles. Cut the pork into 1" cubes. Blot dry with paper towels.
2. Heat a 12" sauté pan, heat the lard, and brown the pork cubes. Season with salt and transfer to a heavy, nonreactive saucepan.
3. Add the onion, garlic, cumin, and oregano to the sauté pan. Sauté over low heat until soft.
4. Add the flour to the sauté pan and stir to make a blond roux.
5. Whisk the Poultry Stock into the sauté pan and bring it to the simmer.
6. Pour the sauce over the pork, cover the saucepan, and simmer the pork about 30 minutes, adding a little water if necessary.
7. Add the potatoes and simmer 10 minutes longer.
8. Add the Flame-Roasted Long Green Chiles to the sauce and simmer 15 minutes longer, stirring occasionally, until the flavors blend and the sauce reaches a nappé consistency.
9. Season with lemon juice and correct the salt.

holding: open-pan cool and immediately refrigerate in a freshly sanitized, covered container up to 5 days; loses flavor when frozen

---

RECIPE VARIATION
Chicken *Chile Verde*
Substitute 1 3/4 lb. boneless, skinless chicken thighs for the pork. Reduce the cooking time by 20 minutes.

Chicken Monterey
with Green Chile Potatoes and Black Bean Pico de Gallo

yield: 1 (6-oz.) entrée serving plus accompaniments
(multiply × 4 for classroom turnout; adjust equipment sizes
accordingly)

MASTER RECIPE

production		costing only
2 Tbsp.	corn oil	1 fl. oz.
1 1/2 c.	boiled, peeled, 1/2"-diced new potatoes	8 oz. a.p.
tt	kosher salt	1/16 oz.
1/2 c.	1/4"-diced Roasted, Peeled Long Green Chiles, preferably Anaheim	1/2 recipe
tt	fresh-ground black pepper	1/16 oz.
6 oz.	boneless, skinless chicken breast, trimmed and flattened	6 oz. a.p.
1 Tbsp.	corn oil	1/2 oz.
pinch	chili powder	1/16 oz.
3/4 c.	Pico de Gallo	3/4 recipe
1/4 c.	canned or cooked black beans, drained	2 fl. oz. or a.p.
1	2" × 3" × 1/8" slice Monterey Jack cheese	3/4 oz.
2 pc.	thin-sliced smoked bacon, parcooked	1 oz. a.p.
1/3	cold, firm-ripe Western avocado	1/3 [24 ct.] avocado
tt	fresh lime juice	1/6 [63 ct.] lime
1 sprig	fresh cilantro	1/20 bunch a.p.

service turnout:

1. Fry the potatoes:
   a. Heat an 8" nonstick sauté pan, heat 2 Tbsp. corn oil, and add the potatoes and a little salt. Fry, tossing occasionally, about 6 minutes, until browned.
   b. Toss in the Roasted, Peeled Long Green Chiles, season with pepper, and hold hot.
2. Coat the chicken breast with 1 Tbsp. corn oil, season it with salt and chili powder, and char-grill on both sides just under medium doneness.
3. Mix the Pico de Gallo and black beans.
4. Place the chicken breast on a sizzle pan and top with the cheese. Place the bacon strips alongside. Place the sizzle pan in the top of a 400°F oven to finish cooking, about 2 minutes.
5. Plate the dish:
   a. Mound the potatoes on the back of a hot 12" plate.
   b. Prop the chicken breast against the potatoes and arrange the bacon slices in an X pattern on top of it.
   c. Mound the Pico de Gallo on either side of the chicken.
   d. Peel and pit the avocado, cut it into 3 vertical slices, and season it with lime juice and salt.
   e. Fan the avocado slices across the front of the plate, propped against the chicken.
   f. Stick the cilantro sprig upright just above the avocado slices.

RECIPE VARIATIONS

Pepper Jack Chicken with Green Chile Potatoes and Black Bean Pico de Gallo

Replace the Monterey Jack cheese with pepper jack cheese.

Barbeque Chicken Monterey with Cowboy Beans, Green Chile Potatoes, and Ranch Salad

While grilling, baste the chicken with Kansas City Barbeque Sauce. Replace the black bean Pico de Gallo with Cowboy Beans (p. 493). Omit the avocado and serve a tossed salad with Ranch Dressing (p. 477).

ENTREES

339

Hopi Blue Corn Smoked Rabbit Stacked Enchilada

yield: 1 (10-oz.) entrée serving
(multiply × 4 for classroom turnout; adjust equipment sizes accordingly)

MASTER RECIPE

🕐 Requires minimum 24 hours advance preparation.

🕐 Please read Appendix II, Curing and Smoking.

production		costing only
1/4	Mesquite Smoked Rabbit (3 slices and about 2/3 c. shredded meat)	1/4 recipe
as needed	water	n/c
2 Tbsp.	pork lard	1 oz.
4	4" Blue Corn Tortillas or commercial tortillas*	1/4 recipe
1 c.	New Mexico Green Chile Sauce, p. 342, hot in steam table	1/5 recipe
1/4 c.	cooked, seasoned corn kernels	1/4 ear a.p.
1/4 c.	3/8"-diced Grilled Cactus, p. 325	1/12 recipe
2 Tbsp.	brunoise-cut red bell pepper	1/2 oz. a.p.
1 Tbsp.	toasted green pumpkin seeds	1/4 oz.
1 Tbsp.	chopped cilantro	1/20 bunch a.p.
1/2 c.	New Mexico Red Chile Sauce, p. 338, in squeeze bottle	1/8 recipe
1/2 c.	Crema, in squeeze bottle	1/4 recipe

service turnout:
1. Place the Mesquite Smoked Rabbit (shredded meat and slices) in an 8" sauté pan with a little water. Cover and place over low heat to warm.
2. Assemble the enchilada:
    a. Heat an 8" sauté pan, heat the lard, and fry the Blue Corn Tortillas over medium heat just to soften.
    b. Dip a tortilla in New Mexico Green Chile Sauce and place it on a sizzle plate.
    c. Top with 1/3 of the shredded rabbit.
    d. Repeat twice, using all of the shredded rabbit and ending with a dipped tortilla.
    e. Press the tortilla stack with a wide spatula to firm it, then place the sizzle plate in the oven about 5 minutes, until the enchilada is heated through.
3. Plate the dish:
    a. Transfer the enchilada to the center of a hot 12" plate.
    b. Nap the top with the remaining green chile sauce, allowing the excess to pool in the plate well.
    c. Fan the rabbit slices across the top of the enchilada.
    d. Scatter the corn, cactus, red bell pepper, pumpkin seeds, and cilantro over the top.
    e. Squeeze zigzags of New Mexico Red Chile Sauce and Crema across the enchilada.

*If using commercial tortillas, use scissors to trim to 4" diameter.

ENTREES

COMPONENT RECIPE

MESQUITE SMOKED RABBIT

yield: approx. 3 c. shredded meat and 12 slices loin meat

🕐 Requires 24 hours advance preparation.

production		costing only
1 Tbsp.	kosher salt	1/2 oz.
1 Tbsp.	pure New Mexico chile powder	1/4 oz.
2 tsp.	granulated onion	1/16 oz.
1 tsp.	granulated garlic	1/16 oz.
1/2 tsp.	ground dried sage	1/16 oz.
1/4 tsp.	dried thyme	1/16 oz.
2 tsp.	fresh-ground black pepper	1/8 oz.
1/2 tsp.	toasted, ground cumin seeds	1/16 oz.
1 Tbsp.	sugar	1/2 oz.
1	domestic rabbit	3 lb.
as needed	mesquite wood, chips, or as specified by smoker manufacturer	% of pkg.
1/4 c.	cider vinegar	2 fl. oz.
1/4 c.	fresh lime juice	2 [63 ct.] limes
1 c.	Poultry Stock	1/16 recipe
2 Tbsp.	gold tequila	1 fl. oz.
1 Tbsp.	sugar	1/2 oz.
2 tsp.	kosher salt	1/4 oz.
2 Tbsp.	corn oil	1 fl. oz.

first day preparation:

1. Mix 1 Tbsp. salt and the chile powder, onion, garlic, sage, thyme, pepper, cumin, and sugar to make a dry rub.
2. Fabricate and rub the rabbit:
   a. Remove the rabbit liver and kidneys; reserve the liver for another use and discard the kidneys.
   b. Use a heavy chef's knife to cut through the rabbit's breast-bone and crack the pelvis.
   c. Flatten the forequarter and hind legs to "butterfly" the rabbit.
   d. Coat the rabbit with the spice rub and massage it into the meat.
   e. Place the rabbit in a freshly sanitized, covered, nonreactive container and refrigerate 24 hours.
3. Cover the mesquite chips with cold water and soak until needed.
4. Mix the vinegar, lime juice, Poultry Stock, tequila, sugar, and salt to make a mopping sauce.

second day preparation:

5. Smoke the rabbit:
   a. Place a drip pan on the lower rack of a smoker. Add half of the wood chips and set the smoker to operate at 160°F, or its lowest setting.
   b. When the chips have heated enough to produce strong smoke, brush the rabbit with the oil and place it on the top rack of the smoker. Smoke the rabbit, adding more wet chips as necessary, 15 minutes.
   c. Turn the rabbit over and baste with about 2 fl. oz. of the mopping sauce.
   d. Repeat, basting every 15 minutes, for a total of 1 hour.
   e. Remove the rabbit to a cutting board and cut off the legs. Set the carcass aside to cool.
   f. Return the legs to the smoker and continue to smoke, basting every 15 minutes, 45 minutes longer.
   g. Check the rabbit legs for doneness; if not cooked through, finish, covered, in a low oven.
   h. Cool the rabbit to room temperature. (Reserve the juices in the drip pan.)
6. Fabricate the smoked rabbit meat:
   a. Using a sharp, flexible knife, cut the loin meat from the saddle in two long cylinders. Remove the silverskin from the loin meat and cut the meat into as many slices as possible.
   b. Cut several long, narrow slices of meat from each rabbit leg to make a total of 12 slices (including the slices from the loin).
   c. Remove the forequarter meat and the remaining leg meat from the bones and pull the meat into shreds.
   d. Place all the rabbit meat in a freshly sanitized container and add the flavorful liquids (from both smoked rabbit fabrication and the drip pan) to it.

holding: refrigerate, covered, up to 5 days

COMPONENT RECIPE

NEW MEXICO GREEN CHILE SAUCE

yield: 5 c.

production		costing only
6 Tbsp.	pork lard	3 oz.
1/2 c.	minced white onion	2 1/2 oz. a.p.
1 tsp.	minced garlic	1/8 oz. a.p.
1/4 c.	flour	1 1/2 oz.
1 qt.	hot, strong Poultry Stock	1/4 recipe
1 1/4 c.	minced Flame-Roasted Long Green Chiles, New Mexico variety	1 recipe
tt	kosher salt	1/16 oz.
tt	fresh lemon juice	1/8 [90 ct.] lemon

preparation:

1. Melt the lard in a nonreactive saucepan, add the onion and garlic, and sweat them over low heat until soft.
2. Add the flour to the saucepan and stir to make a blond roux.
3. Whisk the Poultry Stock into the sauté pan and bring it to the simmer. Cook about 15 minutes, stirring occasionally.
4. Add the Flame-Roasted Long Green Chiles and salt to the sauce and simmer 10 minutes longer, stirring occasionally, until the flavors blend and the sauce reaches a nappé consistency.
5. Season with lemon juice and correct the salt.
6. For a smooth consistency, force the sauce and all of its solids through a food mill or coarse-mesh strainer.

holding: open-pan cool and immediately refrigerate in a freshly sanitized, covered container up to 5 days; loses flavor when frozen

---

RECIPE VARIATION

Hopi Blue Corn Stacked Enchiladas with Chicken
Replace the Mesquite Smoked Rabbit with 3 c. Shredded Chicken and 12 slices cooked chicken breast.

Fajitas

yield: 1 (7-oz.) entrée serving plus accompaniments
(multiply × 4 for classroom turnout; adjust equipment sizes
accordingly)

MASTER RECIPE

🕐 Requires 24 hours advance preparation.

production		costing only
7 oz.	Mexican Marinated Skirt Steak	1/4 recipe
2 Tbsp.	corn oil	1 fl. oz.
3 oz.	thick-sliced red onion	3 1/2 oz. a.p.
4 oz.	thick-sliced red bell pepper	4 1/2 oz. a.p.
4 oz.	thick-sliced yellow bell pepper	4 1/2 oz. a.p.
1/2 c.	thick-sliced Flame-Roasted New Mexico or Anaheim Chiles	1/3 recipe
tt	kosher salt	1/8 oz.
tt	pure New Mexico chile powder	1/8 oz.
1/2 c.	Refried Beans, p. 330, hot in steam table	1/4 recipe
2 Tbsp.	grated sharp yellow Cheddar cheese	1/2 oz.
1/2 c.	Fresh Tomato Salsa	1/2 recipe
4	7" Flour Tortillas or commercial tortillas	1/3 recipe or % of pkg.

service turnout:
1. Place a 12" sizzle pan in a 400°F oven to preheat. Have ready the heatproof plastic undertray that fits the sizzle pan, or line a 14" oval platter with a folded linen napkin.
2. Char-grill the Mexican Marinated Skirt Steak to the desired doneness. Hold warm.
3. Heat a 10" sauté pan, heat the oil, and sauté the onion, bell peppers, and Flame-Roasted New Mexico Chiles until crisp-tender. Season with salt and chile powder.
4. Plate the dish:
   a. Remove the sizzle pan from the oven and place it in its tray or on the napkin-lined platter.
   b. Place a bed of sautéed onion and peppers on the sizzle pan, reserving about 1/4 of them for garnish.
   c. Mound the Refried Beans on the back left of the platter and sprinkle with the cheese.
   d. Quickly slice the skirt steak thin across the grain and fan it across the middle of the sizzle pan on top of the onion and peppers.
   e. Spoon the Fresh Tomato Salsa into a 5-oz. ramekin and place it on the back right of the pan.
   f. Mound the remaining onion and peppers behind the meat.
   g. Toast the Flour Tortillas on the grill until flexible and flecked with brown spots. Fold them in half and place them in a basket lined with a linen napkin.

COMPONENT RECIPE
MEXICAN MARINATED SKIRT STEAK

🕐 Requires 24 hours advance preparation.

yield: about 1 3/4 lb.

production		costing only
1/3 c.	fresh lime juice	2 1/2 [63 ct.] limes
2 tsp.	minced lime zest	n/c
2 Tbsp.	minced serrano chile	1 oz. a.p.
1 Tbsp.	honey	1/2 fl. oz.
2 tsp.	toasted, ground cumin seeds	1/8 oz.
1 tsp.	dried oregano, preferably Mexican	1/16 oz.
2 tsp.	kosher salt	1/4 oz.
1/2 c.	corn oil	4 oz.
2 lb.	skirt steak	2 lb.

preparation:
1. Mix all ingredients except the skirt steak in a freshly sanitized, nonreactive container just large enough to hold the meat.
2. Trim the silverskin from the skirt steak and cut it into 4 (7-oz.) pieces.
3. Place the meat in the container and turn the meat to coat well. Refrigerate 24 hours.

holding: after 24 hours, drain the meat to avoid overmarinating; hold refrigerated no more than 4 days total

---

RECIPE VARIATIONS
Chicken Fajitas
Substitute boneless chicken breast for the skirt steak.
Swordfish Fajitas
Substitute a swordfish steak for the skirt steak.

Navajo Mutton Stew
with Fry Bread and Three Sisters Vegetable Medley

yield: 1 (2-c.) entrée serving (about 6 oz. meat) plus accompaniments
(multiply × 4 for classroom turnout; adjust equipment sizes accordingly)

MASTER RECIPE

production		costing only
2 c.	Navajo Mutton Stew	1/4 recipe
1 Tbsp.	corn oil	1/2 fl. oz.
3 oz.	seeded, batonnet-cut yellow squash	3 1/2 oz. a.p.
2 oz.	batonnet-cut red bell pepper	3 oz. a.p.
tt	kosher salt	1/16 oz.
pinch	pure New Mexico chile powder	1/8 oz.
2 oz.	blanched, refreshed green beans, cut into 1" lengths	2 oz. a.p.
1/4 c.	cooked fresh corn kernels	1/4 ear a.p.
as needed	flour	1/4 oz.
3 oz.	Fry Bread Dough	1/6 recipe
as needed	frying compound or oil for deep-frying	% used
1 sprig	fresh mint	1/12 bunch a.p.
1 sprig	fresh sage	1/12 bunch a.p.
1 sprig	fresh thyme	1/20 bunch a.p.

service turnout:

1. Place the Navajo Mutton Stew in a 10" sauté pan, cover, and heat over medium heat, adding a little water if necessary.

2. Cook the vegetable medley:
   a. Heat a 10" sauté pan, heat 1 Tbsp. corn oil, and sauté the squash and red bell pepper for a few seconds. Season with salt and chile powder.
   b. Add the beans, corn, and a little water. Cover and pan-steam for a few seconds longer until the vegetables are hot through.

3. Prepare the fry bread:
   a. Dust a cutting board and rolling pin with flour and roll out the Fry Bread Dough into a thin 6" disc.
   b. Poke a 1/2" hole in the center of the disc.
   c. Lower the fryer basket and float the dough disc on the surface of 375°F oil.
   d. Use a spider or perforated spoon to press the dough under the oil's surface a few times.
   e. Turn over the dough and continue frying, basting with oil, until puffed and golden.
   f. Drain on a rack and then blot on paper towels.

4. Plate the dish:
   a. Spoon the Navajo Mutton Stew into the front of a hot 12" plate.
   b. Mound the vegetable medley on the back left of the plate.
   c. Cut the fry bread into 3 wedges.
   d. Arrange the fry bread wedges, overlapping, on the back right of the plate.
   e. Make a bouquet of the three herb sprigs and stick it upright in the center of the plate.

COMPONENT RECIPE
NAVAJO MUTTON STEW

yield: 2 qt. (approx. 24 oz. cooked meat)

production		costing only
3 1/2 lb.	bone-in shoulder of mutton or lamb	3 1/2 lb.
3 Tbsp.	pork lard	1 1/2 oz.
tt	kosher salt	1/8 oz.
1 c.	chopped white onion	5 oz. a.p.
1 Tbsp.	minced garlic	1/3 oz. a.p.
1 Tbsp.	pure New Mexico chile powder	1/4 oz.
1 qt.	brown lamb stock or Poultry Stock	1/4 recipe
4 Tbsp.	masa harina	1 oz.
1/2 c.	cool water	n/c
2 tsp.	sugar	1/4 oz.
1 1/2 c.	peeled, 3/4"-diced russet potato	9 oz. a.p.
1 Tbsp.	chopped sage	1/16 bunch a.p.
1 Tbsp.	chopped mint	1/12 bunch a.p.
2 tsp.	fresh thyme leaves	1/20 bunch a.p.

preparation:
1. Fabricate the mutton:
   a. Trim off and discard the meat's surface fat.
   b. Remove the meat from the bones and seam out the individual muscle bundles, removing thick silverskin and interior fat.
   c. Cut the meat into 1 1/2" cubes to yield 2 lb. clean meat.
2. Cook the stew:
   a. Heat a 12" sauté pan, heat 1 Tbsp. lard, and brown the mutton cubes. Season with salt during the last few seconds of cooking. If necessary, work in two batches to avoid crowding the pan.
   b. Remove the mutton to a heavy saucepan.
   c. Add the remaining lard to the sauté pan and add the onion. Sauté over medium heat until golden. Add the garlic and chile powder, then sauté a minute longer.
   d. Stir in the hot stock and scrape the pan to deglaze it.
   e. Pour the cooking liquid into the saucepan with the meat and place the pan over high heat. Bring the liquid to a lively simmer.
   f. Place the masa harina in a small bowl and stir in the cool water to make a smooth slurry.
   g. Stir the slurry into the simmering liquid to thicken it.
   h. Season the sauce with a little more salt and add the sugar. Reduce the heat, partially cover the pan, and simmer the stew about 45 minutes (30 minutes for lamb), until the sauce is lightly thickened and the meat is tender.
   i. Add the potatoes and herbs. Simmer 15 minutes longer, until the potatoes are just cooked through.
   j. Taste and correct the seasoning.

holding: open-pan cool and immediately refrigerate in a freshly sanitized, covered container up to 7 days; may be frozen up to 3 months

---

RECIPE VARIATIONS
Navajo Venison Stew
Replace the mutton with 3 lb. bone-in venison shoulder or 1 3/4 lb. boneless venison top round. Sauté 4 oz. bacon lardons until crisp and add the bacon drippings to the stew in step 2c. Garnish the stew with the lardons.

Navajo Stew with Sweet Potatoes
Replace the russet potato with orange-fleshed sweet potatoes.

ENTREES

Chile con Carne
in Tortilla Basket
with Olla Beans and Avocado Pico de Gallo

yield: 1 (1 1/2-c.) entrée serving (approx. 5 oz. meat) plus accompaniments
(multiply × 4 for classroom turnout; adjust equipment sizes accordingly)

MASTER RECIPE

production		costing only
1 1/2 c.	*Chile con Carne*	1/4 recipe
as needed	water, in squeeze bottle	n/c
1	12" Flour Tortilla or commercial tortilla	1/2 recipe
as needed	frying compound or corn oil for frying	% used
1/2	cold, firm-ripe avocado	1/2 [24 ct.] avocado
1 tsp.	fresh lime juice	1/8 [63 ct.] lime
tt	kosher salt	1/16 oz.
1/2 c.	Pico de Gallo	1/2 recipe
2 c.	shredded iceberg lettuce	1/5 head a.p.
2/3 c.	Border Beans de Olla, hot in steam table	1/8 recipe
1 Tbsp.	crumbled *cotija* or *añejo* cheese	1/4 oz.
2 Tbsp.	fine diagonal-sliced scallion	1/8 bunch a.p.

service turnout:

1. Place the *Chile con Carne* in an 8" sauté pan and add a little water. Cover and heat over low heat.
2. Fry the tortilla basket:
   a. Have ready a 16-oz. ladle, a 12" mesh strainer, and a rack set over a half-sheet tray.
   b. Remove the baskets from a deep fryer preheated to 400°F.
   c. Warm the Flour Tortilla on a char-grill or griddle just until pliable.
   d. Place the tortilla in the strainer and press it against the strainer mesh with the ladle. Lower the strainer into the oil and fry the tortilla light golden.
   e. Remove from the oil and release the tortilla upside-down onto the rack.
   f. While the tortilla is still pliable, gently press on its rounded bottom to flatten it slightly, enabling the basket to sit level.
3. Cut the avocado into 1/2" dice and place them in a small bowl. Toss the avocado with the lime juice and salt, and then mix in the Pico de Gallo.
4. Plate the dish:
   a. Mound about 1 1/2 c. shredded lettuce on a cool 12" oval plate and make a well in the center.
   b. Place the tortilla basket in the well and mound the remaining lettuce in it at the 10 o'clock position.
   c. Spoon the *chile con carne* into the front of the tortilla basket.
   d. Ladle the beans into the tortilla basket at the 2 o'clock position and sprinkle them with the cheese.
   e. Spoon the avocado pico de gallo into the tortilla basket on top of the shredded lettuce.
   f. Sprinkle the scallion on the *chile*.

COMPONENT RECIPE

CHILE CON CARNE

yield: 2 qt. (approx. 24 oz. meat)

production		costing only
8	large dried New Mexico chile pods	1 1/2 oz.
as needed	boiling water	n/c
2	white onions, peeled and quartered	10 oz. a.p.
3 large	peeled garlic cloves	1 oz. a.p.
2	small vine-ripe tomatoes	8 oz. a.p.
2 tsp.	cumin seeds	1/8 oz.
1/2 tsp.	anise seeds	1/16 oz.
1"	cinnamon stick, crushed	1/8 oz.
10	black peppercorns	1/4 oz.
2 tsp.	dried oregano, preferably Mexican	1/4 oz.
1/2 tsp.	dried thyme	1/8 oz.
as needed	water	n/c
2 lb.	beef chuck (shoulder)	2 lb. a.p.
6 Tbsp.	pork lard	3 oz.
1 qt.	hot Brown Beef Stock	1/4 recipe
tt	kosher salt	1/8 oz.
tt	sugar	1/4 oz.

preparation:

1. Prepare the chile paste:
   a. Heat a griddle or heavy sauté pan over low heat. Place the chiles on the griddle and press them with a spatula for a second or two. Turn the chiles over and press again for a few seconds just to heat the chiles and make them pliable. ⚠ Do not scorch. Remove the chiles from the griddle and set them aside until cool enough to handle. Leave the griddle on the heat.
   b. Clean the chiles by removing the stems, opening the pods, and removing the seeds and veins.
   c. Place the chiles in a small, nonreactive bowl, pour boiling water over them to cover, and weight them down with a small plate. Soak 20 minutes.
   d. Place the onion quarters, garlic cloves, and whole tomatoes on the hot griddle. Cook them, turning often, until the onion and garlic are lightly charred on the edges and beginning to soften and the tomatoes have brown/black blotches.
   e. Place the cumin, anise, cinnamon, and peppercorns in a small, heavy sauté pan and toast them over low heat, shaking occasionally, until fragrant. Transfer the spices to a mortar or electric spice mill and grind them into a powder.
   f. Drain the chiles and place them in a blender. Remove and discard the tomato cores and add the tomatoes to the blender. Break up the onions and add them to the blender along with the garlic, ground spices, oregano, and thyme. Grind these ingredients into a thick paste, adding just enough water to release the blades.

2. Fabricate the beef:
   a. Trim and discard excess fat and silverskin from the beef while separating it into individual muscles.
   b. Cut the beef into 1/2" dice.

3. Cook the chile:
   a. Heat a 12" sauté pan, heat 2 Tbsp. lard, and brown the beef cubes, if necessary working in two batches to avoid crowding the pan. Remove the beef to a heavy, nonreactive saucepan.
   b. In the same sauté pan, heat the remaining lard. Scrape in the chile paste. ⚠ The chile paste will spatter; keep clear of the pan to avoid burns and staining. Fry the paste, stirring constantly over medium heat, about 5 minutes, until the color darkens slightly and the fat begins to separate out of the paste.
   c. Add the Brown Beef Stock and stir until smooth. Rinse out the blender with a small amount of water and add the resulting liquid to the pan. Bring the sauce to the simmer and season it with salt.
   d. Pour the sauce over the beef in the saucepan. Partially cover the pan and simmer about 1 hour, adding water if the sauce becomes too thick, until the beef is tender and the sauce is a thick nappé consistency.
   e. Season with more salt and a little sugar, if needed.

holding: open-pan cool and immediately refrigerate in a freshly sanitized, nonreactive covered container up to 7 days; may be frozen up to 1 month

---

RECIPE VARIATION

Venison *Chile con Carne*
Substitute any tough cut of venison for the beef. Add a cracked pig's knuckle in step 3c for added richness and body.

Piñon Pine Nut Torte
with Prickly Pear Sauce and Crema

yield: 1 dessert serving
(multiply × 4 for classroom turnout)

MASTER RECIPE

production		costing only
1 slice	Piñon Pine Nut Torte	1/10 recipe
1/3 c.	Prickly Pear Sauce, in squeeze bottle	1/10 recipe
1 Tbsp.	Crema, in squeeze bottle	1/16 recipe
1 Tbsp.	toasted pine nuts	1/4 oz.
1 small sprig	fresh mint	1/12 bunch a.p.

service turnout:
1. Plate the dish:
   a. Place the Piñon Pine Nut Torte slice slightly back of center on a cool 8" plate with the point at 8 o'clock.
   b. Squeeze a pool of Prickly Pear Sauce in front of the Torte.
   c. Squeeze a zigzag pattern of Crema onto the Prickly Pear Sauce.
   d. Draw the tip of a paring knife through the crema to make a hound's-tooth pattern.
   e. Mound the pine nuts against the torte.
   f. Place the mint sprig in the center of the pine nuts.

COMPONENT RECIPE
PIÑON PINE NUT TORTE

yield: 1 (10") cake

production		costing only
as needed	baker's pan coating spray	% of container
2 c.	pine nuts	8 oz.
12	room-temperature egg yolks	12 each or 8 oz.
1 c.	sugar	8 oz.
8	room-temperature egg whites	n/c or 8 oz.
1/4 c.	fine dried bread crumbs	1/2 oz.

preparation:
1. Mise en place:
   a. Preheat an oven to 350°F.
   b. Spray a 10" × 2" round cake pan with pan coating. Place a 10" circle of pan liner in the bottom and spray the liner.
2. Place the pine nuts in a small stainless bowl and, pulsing with an immersion blender, pulverize them into a fine powder. Alternatively, pulse in a food processor. ⚠ Be careful not to grind the nuts into a paste.
3. Mix the batter:
   a. Using the whip attachment of a mixer, beat the egg yolks on high speed until light yellow and fluffy, then beat in the sugar in a thin stream. Continue to beat on high speed 1 minute longer.
   b. In another mixer or by hand, beat the egg whites to just under firm peaks.
   c. Immediately fold 1/4 of the egg whites into the yolk mixture, then begin to fold the yolk mixture back into the whites. As you fold, sprinkle the bread crumbs and pulverized pine nuts over the batter mixture and incorporate them into the batter. Fold only until the batter is homogenous.
4. Scrape the batter into the prepared pan and smooth the top.
5. Bake the torte in the center of the preheated oven about 30 minutes, until golden in color, springy when pressed in the center, and pulling away from the sides of the pan.
6. Cool the pan on a rack in a draft-free area 10 minutes.
7. Turn the cake out of the pan onto the rack and cool to room temperature.

holding: best served the same day; hold wrapped in plastic film at cool room temperature up to 24 hours; may be frozen up to 1 month

COMPONENT RECIPE
PRICKLY PEAR SAUCE

yield: 3 1/2 c.

production		costing only
3 1/3 c.	sweetened prickly pear purée	27 fl. oz.
3 Tbsp.	cornstarch	1/2 oz.
3 Tbsp.	white tequila	1 1/2 fl. oz.

preparation:
1. Place the prickly pear purée in a nonreactive saucepan and bring it to the boil.
2. Place the cornstarch in a small bowl and mix in the tequila to make a thick slurry.
3. Immediately whisk the slurry into the boiling purée. Boil 30 seconds, until the purée thickens into a clear, nappé consistency sauce.
4. Open-pan cool to room temperature and then refrigerate.

holding: refrigerate in a freshly sanitized squeeze bottle up to 5 days

RECIPE VARIATIONS

Pepita Torte with Prickly Pear Sauce
Replace the pine nuts with lightly toasted, ground green pumpkin seeds.

Almond Torte with Raspberry Sauce
Replace the pine nuts with almonds or almond flour, the prickly pear purée with raspberry purée, and the tequila with Chambord liqueur.

Pecan Torte with Persimmon Sauce
Replace the pine nuts with pecans or pecan flour, the prickly pear purée with persimmon purée, and the tequila with Grand Marnier.

Walnut Torte with Apricot Sauce
Replace the pine nuts with walnuts or walnut flour, the prickly pear purée with apricot purée, and the tequila with apricot brandy.

Hazelnut Torte with Cherry Sauce
Replace the pine nuts with hazelnuts or hazelnuts flour, the prickly pear purée with cherry purée, and the tequila with Chambord liqueur.

Flan
with Cactus Cut-Out Cookie

yield: 1 dessert serving
(multiply × 4 for classroom turnout)
🕐 Requires 24 hours advance preparation.

MASTER RECIPE

production		costing only
1	Classic Flan	1/6 recipe
1	Cactus Cut-Out Cookie	1/8 recipe

service turnout:
1. Run a knife around the inside of the Classic Flan ramekin to loosen the flan.
2. Plate the dish:
   a. Place a cool 8" plate on top of the ramekin and flip the vessels upside-down to turn out the flan. Allow all of the caramel sauce to run onto the plate.
   b. Remove any custard scraps that have fallen onto the plate.
   c. Stick the Cactus Cut-Out Cookie upright in the flan.

COMPONENT RECIPE
CLASSIC FLANS

yield: 6 (8-fl.-oz.) flans
🕐 Requires 24 hours advance preparation.

production		costing only
3/4 c.	sugar	6 oz.
1/2 c.	water	n/c
3	eggs	3 each or 6 oz.
4	egg yolks	3 each or 2 2/3 oz.
2/3 c.	sugar	5 oz.
pinch	fine salt	1/16 oz.
1 1/2 c.	half-and-half	12 fl. oz.
1 1/2 c.	heavy cream	12 fl. oz.
1 tsp.	pure vanilla extract	1/6 fl. oz.

preparation:
1. Mise en place:
   a. Preheat an oven to 275°F.
   b. Place 6 (8-fl.-oz.) ramekins in a half-size hotel pan and place the pan near the stove.
   c. Cut out 6 squares of doubled aluminum foil of the correct size to cover the ramekins.
   d. Have ready about 2 qt. very hot water.
2. Line the ramekins with caramel:
   a. Place 3/4 c. sugar and the water in a heavy saucepan and stir until the mixture is homogenous.
   b. Place the pan over medium heat. Cook, watching carefully as the sugar bubbles and begins to caramelize. Do not stir the sugar with any implement. ⚠ Be careful, as the caramel is dangerously hot.
   c. When the sugar syrup caramelizes to a deep, rich brown, quickly pour it into the ramekins, dividing it evenly among them.

3. Mix and pan the custard:
   a. Place the eggs, egg yolks, 2/3 c. sugar, and salt in a bowl and stir to combine well.
   b. Whisk in the half-and-half, cream, and vanilla.
   c. Strain the custard through a fine mesh strainer into a large measuring cup or pitcher.
   d. Pour the custard into the ramekins, dividing it evenly among them.
   e. Cover each ramekin with a double layer of aluminum foil, then fold the edges back up over the top so the foil will not wick water up into the custards.
   f. Pour hot water into the hotel pan to reach 2/3 up the sides of the ramekins.
4. Bake the flans on the center rack of the preheated oven 45 minutes to 1 hour, until the custard is just set.
5. Place the hotel pan on a rack and cool the flans to room temperature.
6. Refrigerate the flans at least 12 hours.

holding: refrigerated up to 3 days

COMPONENT RECIPE
CACTUS CUT-OUT COOKIES

yield: 8 cookies plus dough for practice

production		costing only
as needed	baker's pan coating spray	% of container
as needed	flour	1 oz.
8 oz.	Rolled Cookie Dough	1 recipe
1 Tbsp.	egg wash	1 oz. a.p.
2 Tbsp.	pine nuts	1/2 oz.

preparation:
1. Mise en place:
   a. Preheat an oven to 375°F.
   b. Prepare a half-sheet tray with pan liner. Spray with pan coating.
2. Roll out and make up the cookies:
   a. Lightly flour the work surface and rolling pin.
   b. Roll out the Rolled Cookie Dough 1/8" thick.
   c. Using a cactus-shaped cookie cutter, or cutting freehand with a sharp knife, cut out 8 (3" tall) cactus shapes and place them on the sheet tray.
   d. Brush the cookies with egg wash.
   e. Stick pine nuts into the dough to resemble spines on the cactus.
   f. Refrigerate the cookies at least 15 minutes.
3. Bake the cookies in the center of the preheated oven 8 to 10 minutes, until very light brown around the edges.
4. Cool the pan on a rack 5 minutes.
5. Gently slip the pan liner onto the rack and allow the cookies to cool completely.

holding: in a tightly sealed container at cool room temperature up to 1 week

RECIPE VARIATIONS
Coconut Flan
Replace the half-and-half with unsweetened coconut cream. Omit the vanilla.
Coffee Flan
Replace 4 oz. of the half-and-half with very strong espresso at room temperature.

TABLE 7.2 MEXICAN BORDER REGIONAL INGREDIENTS

ITEM	MARKET FORMS	USES	SEASONALITY	OTHER	STORAGE
FLOUR TORTILLAS	Industrially produced flour tortillas are available in 6" fajita size, 8" soft taco size, 10" burrito size, and 12" wrap size. Pack quantity varies from 10 to 50 count.	Flour tortillas are used as a table bread, as the wrapper for soft tacos, and to make wrap sandwiches. They may be deep-fried in a form to make tortilla baskets for salads and chili.	N/A	Small Hispanic-owned companies typically produce better-quality, fresher flour tortillas.	Store at room temperature or refrigerated. Freeze for long-term storage; thaw completely before using.
CORN TORTILLAS	Industrially produced corn tortillas are available in a thin, yellow corn variety and a thicker, white corn type. Artificially-colored corn tortillas are available in blue and red. Virtually all are 6" in diameter. Package size varies. Pre-cut strips and wedges are also sold.	Thin, yellow corn tortillas are used for frying to make taco shells, toastada shells, and chips. Thicker, white corn tortillas are used for enchiladas and as table tortillas.	N/A	Blue corn tortillas may contain a proportion of blue corn masa and/or may be tinted with food coloring.	Store refrigerated up to 2 weeks. Freeze up to 3 months; thaw before using.
TORTILLA CHIPS	Industrially produced, fried tortilla chip wedges are sold in 10-oz. and 16-oz. consumer packs and in bulk cartons. Most are seasoned with salt; unsalted chips are available. Chip strips and colored chips are available in bulk from some producers.	Tortilla chips are served as a snack food, usually accompanied by salsa or other dips. They may be used as a garnish.	N/A	Breakage is a major factor in the cost of tortilla chips. Factor in breakage percentage when costing dishes containing chips. Thrifty chefs create menu items made with tortilla chip crumbs.	Store tightly sealed at cool room temperature. Check for freshness before using.
TACO SHELLS AND TOSTADA SHELLS	For foodservice, taco and tostada shells are sold in bulk cartons by count or weight. Standard taco shells and extra large shells are available. Tostada shells are 6" in diameter.	Taco shells are used primarily in Mexican-American restaurants to make crispy tacos. Tostada shells are topped with ingredients and garnishes; multiple tostada shells are used to make stacked tostadas.	N/A	Breakage is a major factor in the cost of pre-made shells. Factor in breakage percentage when costing dishes containing them.	Store tightly sealed at cool room temperature. Check for freshness before using.
MASA HARINA (MAH-sah ah-REE-nah)	This dehydrated, powdered form of masa is sold in 5-lb. bags under a variety of brand names, with Maseca the best known.	Masa harina is an alternative to fresh masa dough when making corn tortillas, tamales, and other corn dough products. It is reconstituted with water and sometimes salt.	N/A	Because masa harina contains the oil-rich germ of the corn kernel, it can become rancid. Check for an off-odor similar to that of rancid oil and watch out for insect infestation.	Store at cool room temperature; freeze for long-term storage.
CORNMEAL (SEE P. 80)					
BLUE CORN FLOUR	Powdery, fine-textured blue corn flour is sold by the pound by specialty purveyors in the Southwest.	Blue corn flour is used in conjunction with culinary ash to make blue corn products, such as tortillas, tamales, and piki bread.	N/A	Coarser blue corn meal is not an acceptable substitute.	Store at cool room temperature; freeze for extended storage.
CULINARY ASH	Culinary ash is not currently available from commercial producers.	This calcium-rich ash is used to intensify the color of blue cornmeal and blue corn flour products. It chemically reacts to stabilize the pigments that make corn blue in color. It also adds nutrients to products made from it.	N/A	Burn green juniper or chamisa wood outdoors or in a disposable aluminum tray under a powerful exhaust hood, then sift the ashes to obtain a fine, powdery ash. Alternatively, add 1/8 tsp. pickling lime (calcium hydroxide) to 1 c. blue corn flour.	Store at cool room temperature.

(continued)

☐ TABLE 7.2 MEXICAN BORDER REGIONAL INGREDIENTS *(continued)*

ITEM	MARKET FORMS	USES	SEASONALITY	OTHER	STORAGE
PICKLING LIME (CALCIUM HYDROXIDE)	Pickling lime is powdered calcium hydroxide. It is available by the ounce or pound wherever canning supplies are sold or by mail order.	In the United States pickling lime is used primarily to enhance crisp texture when making pickled vegetables. It is used in the nixtamalization process (see p. 309) for corn. In Southwestern cuisine it is substituted for culinary ash when making blue corn products.	In retail stores stocked during the summer canning season; available by mail order year round.	Incorrect use of pickling lime may pose a health risk; use only as specified in directions from reliable sources.	Store tightly sealed at cool room temperature.
POSOLE (poh-SO-lay)	Posole is hulled corn made by the nixtamalization process (see p. 309). Dried posole is sold by the pound from purveyors of Mexican groceries. Cooked posole is available in 29-oz. and #10 cans. Frozen, semi-cooked posole is sold by the pound.	Posole is traditionally used in soups but may be served as a starch side dish. Sweetened posole is sometimes served as a breakfast cereal with milk.	N/A	Once opened, canned cooked posole spoils quickly. Use within 2 days or freeze.	Store dried and canned posole at room temperature; store frozen posole in the freezer up to 6 months.
CORNHUSKS	Dried cornhusks for culinary use are sold in 8-oz. and 1-lb. packages, or in bulk cartons, from purveyors of Mexican groceries. Fresh cornhusks are obtained from fresh sweet corn.	Cornhusks are used to wrap tamales. Dried cornhusks must be rehydrated in hot water before using.	Dried cornhusks are available year round. Fresh cornhusks are widely available during the summer months.	Because cornhusks vary in size and some may be damaged, soak more than needed. Remove corn silk, insects, and debris. Leftover husks may be re-dried and stored for future use.	Store at room temperature.
DRIED BEANS	Dried beans are widely sold in 1-lb. consumer packs and in 10-lb. boxes. Southwestern heirloom beans are sold by the pound by specialty grocers in the region and may be mail-ordered.	Beans are simmered in soups or served in thick broth as a side dish. The most popular presentation is refried beans.	N/A	Cooking times vary by type of bean and by source. When using a new shipment of dried beans kitchen test a batch to determine length of cooking.	Store at cool room temperature.
DRIED RED NEW MEXICO CHILE PODS	Rarely sold retail outside the region, dried red New Mexico chile pods are available by mail order from specialty purveyors in the Southwest. They are sold by the ounce or pound in medium to extra hot. Decorative dried red chile ristras (see p. 312) are also available.	The pods are cleaned, rehydrated in hot water, and puréed to become the base of Southwestern red chile sauces.	Freshest in fall after the harvest.	Look for pods that are brick red, flexible, and fragrant. Reject lightweight pods that appear translucent as these are old and have lost much of their flavorful flesh. Discard pods that have tiny holes and powdery residue in the container as these are signs of insect infestation.	Store at cool room temperature or frozen for long-term storage, up to 1 year.
NEW MEXICO RED CHILE POWDER	New Mexico red chile powder is available by mail order from specialty purveyors in the Southwest. It is sold by the ounce or pound.	For quick Southwestern sauces, red chile powder is added to a roux and simmered with stock. This brick-red spice is used in rubs, marinades, salad dressings, and may be sprinkled as a garnish.	Freshest in fall after the harvest.	Do not substitute chili powder, as it contains other spices and seasonings as well as red chile.	Store at cool room temperature or frozen for long-term storage, up to 1 year.

☐ TABLE 7.2 MEXICAN BORDER REGIONAL INGREDIENTS (continued)

ITEM	MARKET FORMS	USES	SEASONALITY	OTHER	STORAGE
GREEN CHILE	New Mexico green chile is widely available in the region during harvest season, usually from mid-August through September. There it is purchased fresh and may be roasted to order. During the harvest 20-lb. cartons of fresh New Mexico green chile may be ordered from growers and air-freighted throughout the United States. Frozen New Mexico green chile is available by the pound as roasted whole pods (which must be peeled and seeded) or diced chile. Fresh Anaheim chiles may be found in some supermarkets and from standard produce purveyors. Frozen Anaheim chile is also available. Most canned green chile is the Anaheim variety. Chiles are available in several hotness gradations from medium to extra-hot.	Chopped or puréed green chile flavors, thickens, and colors Southwestern sauces and stews. Diced or sliced chile is used in fillings and as a garnish. Whole roasted and peeled pods are stuffed for chiles rellenos (see p. 327).	Fresh chile is sold only during harvest from mid-August through September. Frozen and canned chile is available year round.	Fresh red-ripe chile is sold fresh and frozen at a higher price. Chile from Hatch, New Mexico, is considered the finest.	Store fresh chile refrigerated up to 2 weeks; roast, peel, and freeze for longer storage. Keep frozen chile in the freezer until needed.
SERRANO CHILES	These small, tapering, dark-green, medium-hot chiles have fewer seeds and more flavor than jalapeños. They are widely available from produce purveyors and in supermarkets where they are sold by the pound.	Frequently used raw, chopped serranos spike salsas and guacamole, and may be used in marinades and dressings. They may be added to cooked sauce recipes for extra heat.	Available year round; most abundant in late summer.	Milder jalapeños may be substituted for serranos, but should be seeded before chopping.	Refrigerate up to 2 weeks.
PICKLED JALAPEÑOS	These spicy pickled chiles are sold in jars of various sizes and in #10 cans in whole pod form or in slices.	Pickled jalapeños are used as a condiment or garnish. Slices are a classic nachos topping.	N/A	Do not substitute picked jalapeños for fresh. Smaller, hotter pickled serranos are available from purveyors of Mexican groceries.	Store at room temperature. After opening, transfer to an unbreakable, nonreactive container and refrigerate up to 6 months.
CHILES CHIPOTLES EN ADOBO	Traditional chiles chipotles en adobo (whole pods in sauce) are sold in 7-oz. cans and larger foodservice cans. A purée form is now available.	The spicy, smoky, tangy taste of chipotles en adobo enhances virtually any savory dish.	N/A	Jalapeño chiles ripen to reddish-brown on the plant and are then dried by smoking to become chiles chipotles. The dried chiles are then hydrated in hot water, drained, and cooked in a red chile tomato sauce flavored with vinegar to make chiles chipotles en adobo.	Store cans at room temperature. After opening, refrigerate in a nonreactive container up to 6 months.
CUMIN SEEDS	For freshness, purchase cumin seeds by the ounce or pound from a spice dealer or South Asian grocery with high turnover.	Toast cumin seeds in a small, dry sauté pan then transfer to a mortar or spice grinder. Grind coarse or fine for use in many Southwestern and Mexican-American dishes.	N/A	Avoid pre-ground cumin as it lacks flavor.	Store seeds at room temperature; freeze for prolonged storage. Use toasted ground cumin within a day or two.

(continued)

☐ **TABLE 7.2 MEXICAN BORDER REGIONAL INGREDIENTS** *(continued)*

ITEM	MARKET FORMS	USES	SEASONALITY	OTHER	STORAGE
DRIED MEXICAN OREGANO	Purchase by the ounce from purveyors of Mexican groceries.	Distinctly different than the standard Italian variety, this type of oregano is a favored seasoning in many Southwestern and Mexican-American dishes.	N/A	Check for freshness: the dried crumbled leaves should be fragrant and dark green.	Store at room temperature; freeze for prolonged storage.
CILANTRO (see-LAHN-tro)	Fresh leaves and stems of the coriander plant are sold in bunches with or without roots.	Chopped raw cilantro is used liberally to flavor salsas, cold sauces, and other Mexican-American and Southwestern dishes. Chopped cilantro and cilantro sprigs are used as garnishes.	Available year round.	Fine-minced cilantro stems have a strong flavor and may be used in cooked sauces or stewed dishes.	Stand bunches upright in a few inches of water and refrigerate. Bunches with roots last longer, up to 1 week.
EPAZOTE (eh-pah-ZOE-tay)	The fresh herb is sold in bunches or by the pound by purveyors of Mexican groceries. Dried epazote is sold by the ounce; check for dark green color and strong fragrance.	Epazote is traditionally used in bean dishes and is believed to counteract their gaseousness.	Available year round in stores.	In certain areas epazote grows wild in vacant lots, along roads, and even in cracks in the sidewalk. It is very easy to grow from seed.	Stand bunches upright in a few inches of water and refrigerate. Bunches with roots last longer, up to 1 week.
JUNIPER	Juniper berries are sold by the ounce by spice dealers. Juniper twigs must be gathered in the wild.	Juniper berries give a high-desert flavor to meat marinades and stews, and are particularly suited to game meats and fowl. Juniper twigs flavor grilled and smoked foods.	N/A	Look for juniper berries that are firm, fragrant, and heavy for their size.	Store juniper berries at room temperature; freeze for long-term storage. Store juniper twigs with cut ends in a few inches of water outdoors in cool weather.
SAGE	Fresh sage is sold in bunches; dried rubbed sage leaves and powdered dried sage are sold by the ounce or pound.	Sage flavors many Southwestern dishes.	Available year round.	Check for dusty-green color and strong fragrance.	Store fresh sage bunches upright in a few inches of water at cool room temperature. Store dried sage at room temperature or freeze for prolonged storage.
PINE NUTS OR PIÑON NUTS (PIN-yun)	These small, oval, ivory-colored nuts are harvested from the cones of certain pine species. They are sold by the pound.	Pine nuts lend a distinctive flavor to baked goods and candies. In Southwestern Native American cooking ground pine nuts are used to thicken savory sauces.	N/A	When purchasing pine nuts check the source. Pine nuts from Asia have been linked to a condition known as *pine mouth*, a lingering metallic taste that is unpleasant but harmless. Some individuals are deathly allergic to pine nuts of any origin; dishes made with pine nuts must be identified on menus.	Due to their high oil content, pine nuts are quite perishable. Store frozen up to 6 months.
GREEN PUMPKIN SEEDS OR *PEPITAS* (pep-EE-tahs)	Hulled raw pumpkin seeds are sold by the pound by purveyors of Mexican groceries.	Lightly toasted green pumpkin seeds are used as a salad garnish. Ground fine, they are used to thicken sauces.	N/A	Do not confuse green pumpkin seeds with the salted, roasted pumpkin seeds used as a snack food.	Store at cool room temperature; freeze for long-term storage.

☐ TABLE 7.2 MEXICAN BORDER REGIONAL INGREDIENTS *(continued)*

ITEM	MARKET FORMS	USES	SEASONALITY	OTHER	STORAGE
TOMATILLOS	This round, pale green fruit has a papery outer husk and sticky surface. Fresh tomatillos are sold by the pound by standard produce dealers and in supermarkets. Choose firm tomatillos with fresh-looking husks. Tomatillos with a yellowish color are riper and, thus, less acidic. Because of their metallic taste and low yield, canned tomatillos are a poor value and are not recommended.	Husked, washed, chopped raw tomatillos are the basis of some salsas. More commonly they are poached and puréed for cooked salsas and sauces.	Available year round.	Although they are sometimes called "Mexican green tomatoes," tomatillos are not a tomato cultivar.	Refrigerate up to 2 weeks; for longer storage husk, wash, poach, and freeze.
NOPAL CACTUS OR *NOPALES* (noh-PAH-lays)	Fresh nopal cactus is sold by produce purveyors in several forms: whole natural paddles, with spines intact; de-thorned paddles; and dethorned dice or batonnet cuts. Canned nopal cactus is not recommended because of metallic taste and poor texture.	Traditionally, dethorned, fabricated nopal cactus is boiled, cooled, fabricated, and served as a salad in a vinaigrette dressing. It may be added to scrambled eggs and layered in casseroles. Modern chefs grill dethorned paddles, slice them, and serve them as a side dish or salad.	Available year round.	Grilling minimizes the viscous substance exuded by cactus paddles.	Refrigerate up to 2 weeks.
PRICKLY PEARS OR CACTUS PEARS	The fresh fruit of the opuntia cactus is small, oval shaped, and has skin ranging from yellow-green to magenta in color; it has numerous thorns that may be partially removed by the packer. Prickly pears are usually sold in flats by count. For consistency and to save labor, many chefs purchase lightly sweetened frozen prickly pear purée in containers of varying sizes.	The deep pink to red pulp is poached in sugar syrup or simmered with sugar and puréed for use in desserts or sweet-savory dishes.	Late summer to fall.	Prickly pear spines can cause skin irritation. To prepare the fruits, wear rubber gloves and scrape them with a sharp knife under running water.	Store fresh fruits refrigerated up to 2 weeks. Keep purée frozen until needed.
AVOCADOS	Fresh avocados from California, Mexico, and South America are preferred for Mexican Border cuisine. Haas and Fuerte are the major cultivars. Avocadoes are sold in flats ranging from 12 to 48 count, with 24 count the most common size. Frozen avocado pulp is available but not recommended.	The most popular avocado dish is guacamole, a dip or sauce of mashed avocadoes. Sliced or diced avocadoes are widely used as a garnish and salad ingredient.	Available year round.	Avocadoes must be carefully managed so they ripen to proper texture. For most uses avocadoes are properly ripe when slightly yielding to the touch. Accelerate ripening by enclosing in a plastic bag with a cut apple.	To hold unripe, store between 40° and 60°F. To ripen, store between 70° and 80°F.

(continued)

☐ TABLE 7.2 MEXICAN BORDER REGIONAL INGREDIENTS (continued)

ITEM	MARKET FORMS	USES	SEASONALITY	OTHER	STORAGE
COOKING PUMPKIN OR *CALABAZA*	Whole fresh cooking pumpkins are available by the pound from purveyors of Latin-American groceries and in supermarkets in areas with Latino populations. Cut and wrapped wedges of pumpkin are sometimes available.	Chunks of pumpkin are simmered in soups and stews. Contemporary chefs feature savory pumpkin purée as a side dish.	Available year round.	Do not substitute decorative jack-o-lantern pumpkins. Acorn, butternut, or other winter squashes are adequate substitutes.	Store whole pumpkins at cool room temperature up to 1 month; check for soft spots or mold. Refrigerate cut pumpkin up to 2 weeks.
SQUASH BLOSSOMS	These delicate vegetable flowers are sold by the piece in farmer's markets and in boxes by specialty purveyors. Male squash blossoms are larger. Female blossoms are smaller and often sold with the immature fruit (usually zucchini) attached.	Squash blossoms may be steamed, chopped, and folded into scrambled eggs. They are layered into casseroles and used as a stuffing for quesadillas. The most popular preparation is batter-fried: Male squash blossoms may be stuffed and fried; female blossoms with fruit are simply fried.	Summer.	Because they are too delicate to wash, squash blossoms must come from a source that does not use chemical pesticides. Inspect carefully for insects.	Refrigerate 1 or 2 days only.
CHAYOTE (cha-YO-tay)	This pale green vegetable is available fresh in flats by count from specialty purveyors. It has many other names, including christophene, cho-cho, choko, mirliton, and vegetable pear.	Chayotes are eaten raw in salads or steamed and served as a cooked vegetable. They are often steamed, halved, hollowed, stuffed, and baked.	Available year round.	All parts of the chayote are edible, including the pit.	Store at cool room temperature or refrigerated up to 2 weeks.
HUITLACOCHE (weet-lah-KO-chay) **OR CORN FUNGUS**	This silver-gray to black fungus that sometimes grows on ears of corn is considered a delicacy in Mexican cuisine. It is available fresh from specialty purveyors and some purveyors of Mexican groceries. It is sometimes sold by farmer's markets in season. Canned and frozen huitlacoche lack texture.	Fresh huitlacoche is a traditional filling for quesadillas and may be used as a garnish. Canned and frozen huitlacoche are suitable for sauces and soups.	Fresh huitlacoche is more widely available in summer.	Huitlacoche is a wild food that occurs spontaneously. It was a high status food for Aztecs and other Meso-Americans.	Refrigerate fresh huitlacoche and use within 1 or 2 days.
PORK LARD	Industrially produced pork lard is sold in 1-lb. blocks or 5-lb. tubs and in 25-lb. metal containers. Artisan lard is sold by the pound.	Pork lard is the traditional fat for frying Mexican-American and Southwestern foods. It is essential for making savory tamal dough.	Industrial pork lard is available year round. Some artisan makers stop producing lard in hot summer months.	A recipe for rendering pork lard appears in this book's companion website.	Industrially produced lard is partially hydrogenated for longer shelf life and may be refrigerated until the manufacturer's expiration date. Artisan lard is best kept frozen and thawed only when needed.
MEXICAN CHORIZO SAUSAGE	This brick-red, heavily-seasoned, fatty sausage is sold by the pound in artificial casing links by purveyors of Mexican groceries.	Crumbled, fried chorizo is used as a topping or seasoning meat.	N/A	Do not substitute the mild, lean Spanish variety of chorizo.	Refrigerate up to 1 month; freeze for long-term storage up to 6 months.

TABLE 7.2 MEXICAN BORDER REGIONAL INGREDIENTS (continued)

ITEM	MARKET FORMS	USES	SEASONALITY	OTHER	STORAGE
MONTEREY JACK CHEESE	This mild-tasting, semi-firm cheese is sold by the pound in vacuum pack or in whole wheels.	Monterey Jack is widely used as a melting cheese in quesadillas, on nachos, and to top casseroles and gratins.	N/A	Most Monterey Jack is factory produced. Artisan cheese makers offer Monterey Jack with superior flavor and mouthfeel. Refrigerate until manufacturer's expiration date. Pepper jack cheese includes roasted, peeled, chopped red and green chile.	Refrigerate until manufacturer's expiration date.
QUESO FRESCO (KAY-soh FRAYS-koh) OR QUESO BLANCO (KAY-soh BLAHN-koh)	This crumbly, fresh white cheese is sold by the pound in vacuum pack or in whole wheels by purveyors of Mexican groceries.	Because queso fresco holds its shape when heated, it is the cheese of choice for making enchiladas. Crumbled queso fresco is used as a topping for tostadas, tacos, refried beans, and other dishes.	N/A	Firm, crumbly domestic farmer cheese may be substituted for queso fresco.	Refrigerate until manufacturer's expiration date.
QUESO COTIJA (KAY-soh koh-TEE-hah)	This aged form of queso fresco is dry and crumbly with a strong flavor and pungent aroma. It is sold by the pound in vacuum pack or in whole wheels by purveyors of Mexican groceries.	Queso Cotija is almost exclusively used as a topping or garnish cheese. It may be added to a queso fresco filling for stronger flavor.	N/A		Refrigerate until manufacturer's expiration date.
MEXICAN STRING CHEESE OR QUESO OAXAQUEÑO (KAY-soh WAH-hah-KANE-yoh)	Braids of this soft, elastic white cheese are sold in 8-oz. vacuum packs by purveyors of Mexican groceries.	Braids unravel into ropes of cheese that pull apart into long, stringy shreds used for garnishing salads or tortillas. This cheese melts into a soft, stringy mass when baked or broiled.	N/A	Eastern European or Middle Eastern string cheese may be substituted, although it may contain spice seeds or other flavorings not traditional in Mexican-American and Southwestern cuisines.	Refrigerate until manufacturer's expiration date.
NATURAL CHEDDAR CHEESE	White or yellow Cheddar cheese is sold by the pound in vacuum pack or in whole wheels. Cheddar is available in mild, sharp, and extra-sharp varieties.	Grated cheddar is used cold as a topping or may be heated to become a melted topping or filling.	N/A	For Mexican-American cooking domestic Cheddar is preferred.	Refrigerate until manufacturer's expiration date.
CREMA (KRAY-mah)	This tangy fermented dairy product is sold in 12 oz. jars and 2 lb. tubs by purveyors of Mexican groceries.	Crema is used as a topping or to enrich sauces.	N/A	Substitute French crème fraîche or commercial sour cream thinned with milk. A recipe for crema appears on this book's companion website.	Refrigerate until manufacturer's expiration date.
MUTTON OR GOAT	Sold boneless or bone-in by the pound from specialty meat dealers, particularly halal butchers.	Tender cuts are marinated and grilled; tough cuts are braised, stewed, or simmered in soups.	N/A	Remove the papery fell, or outer membrane, of the meat before fabricating.	Refrigerate or freeze.
WILD GAME	(See p. 515).		N/A		

■□■ chapter eight

The Appalachian South

western Maryland, West Virginia, parts of southern Ohio, western Virginia, eastern Kentucky, western North Carolina, eastern Tennessee, northwestern South Carolina, northern Georgia, northern Alabama, northeastern Mississippi

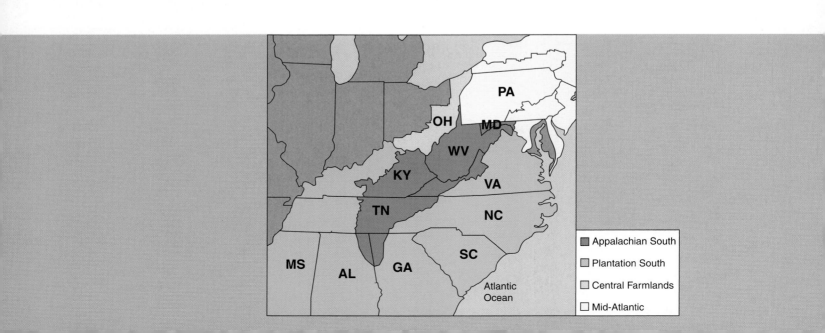

FOR MOST AMERICANS, the word *Appalachia* conjures up visions of remote mountains and secluded valleys, of rustic cabins and moonshiners' stills. Appalachia can be a troubling contradiction, possessing great beauty yet also having a history of poverty and backwardness, violence and suffering. Yet these perceptions are only part of the story. Within this little-known and often misunderstood region exists a thriving folk culture that has produced a distinctive American regional cuisine.

The pioneers who put down roots in the southern Appalachian Mountains were tough, proud, independent people. Seeking to settle after eastern America's prime coastal land already had been claimed, they ventured into the interior mountain ranges to carve farmsteads out of mountain hollows. Later settlers sought work as loggers and miners. For generations mountain isolation preserved their traditional folkways, as well as their cooking.

Despite the wanton destruction of their environment and the encroachments of modern culture, many Appalachian families still preserve the region's traditional customs and cooking. Theirs is a cuisine of both farmland and woodland, a mix of homegrown ingredients, pioneer provisions, and the hunter's and fisherman's catch. Comforting and satisfying, the cooking of the Appalachian South is one of America's best-kept secrets.

AFTER STUDYING THIS CHAPTER YOU SHOULD BE ABLE TO:

- discuss the ways in which the topography and climate of the Appalachian South shaped its culture and cuisine (Factor 1)
- discuss direct and indirect Native American influence on Appalachian South cuisine (Factor 2)
- list the two primary first-settler groups that settled the Appalachian South, and describe their Old-World foodways (Factor 3)
- compare and contrast Plantation South and Appalachian South cuisines
- explain how lack of economic viability influenced the development of Appalachian South cuisine and continues to affect the region today (Factor 5)
- list and describe the important techniques, ingredients, and flavor profiles of Appalachian South cuisine
- prepare authentic Appalachian South dishes

APPETIZERS

Summer Garden Vegetable Soup with Cracklin' Bread

Wilted Salad with Hot Bacon Dressing and Fried Potato Croutons

Buckwheat Rolls with Country Ham, Asparagus, and Herbed Fresh Cheese

Applewood Smoked Trout with Horseradish Cream and Biscuit Crackers

ENTRÉES

Baked Stuffed Trout with Wild Mushroom Cornbread Dressing and Peas 'n' Pearl Onions

Chicken with Brunswick Stew and Corn Pone

'Possum-Style Pork Shoulder with Sweet Potatoes and Creamed Lima Beans

Apple-Maple Pork Sausage with Braised Red Cabbage, Fried Apples, Appalachian Potato Cakes, and Pickled Apple Rings

Kentucky Barbeque Lamb Shank with Creamed Corn, Pole Beans, and Fried Potatoes

Cherokee Venison Stew with Shuck Bread

Maple-Glazed Turkey with Sauerkraut and Hominy

Roast Grouse with Sawmill Gravy, Ramp Home Fries, and Mountain Vegetable Medley

DESSERTS

Apple Stack Cake

Black Walnut Poundcake with Persimmon Sauce

Peach-Filled Half-Moon Fried Pie with Burnt Sugar Ice Cream

WEBSITE EXTRAS

Breakfasts   Sandwiches   Hors d'Oeuvres   Thanksgiving Menu

■ IN SEARCH OF
□ APPALACHIA

What, exactly, is Appalachia? Where is it located and how are its boundaries defined? There are different, and frequently contradictory, answers to these questions. In fact, there's even controversy over how to pronounce the word. South of the Mason-Dixon Line, it's "ap-pel-AT-cha." Northerners usually say "ap-a-LAY-shuh." According to the dictionary, both pronunciations are acceptable. However, historians believe that 16th-century Spanish explorers named the mountains after a northern Florida tribe called the Appalachees, making the Southern pronunciation linguistically correct.

Appalachia is a region shaped—but not solely defined—by the Appalachian Mountains, which stretch from Georgia as far north as Maine. Thus, parts of the Mid-Atlantic and New England are technically Appalachian. However, the Appalachian cultural area, as recognized by the Appalachian Regional Commission, stops short in southern New York. It encompasses a large section of western Pennsylvania as well as eastern Ohio. The ARC demarcation can be considered **geocultural,** as it uses the origin of immigrant groups and their defining cultural characteristics, as well as topography, when defining boundaries.

The Appalachian South culinary region begins at the Mason-Dixon line in western Maryland, where Mid-Atlantic influence is evident. Farther south, the cooking is close cousin to that of the Plantation South, yet different in several fundamental ways: more rustic, much more frugal, and lacking Afro-Caribbean flavors. To see the influence of these two neighboring regions, refer to Figure 8.2.

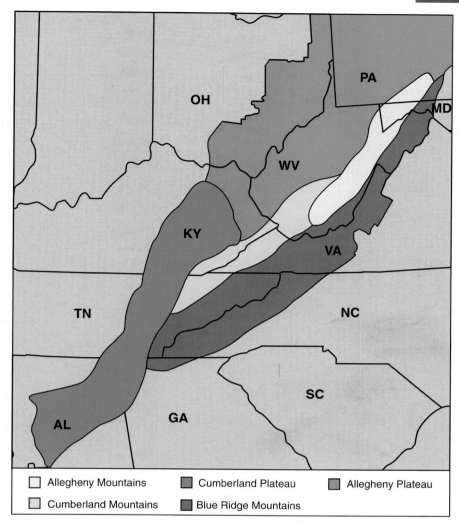

FIGURE 8.1

Mountain Chains of the Southern Appalachians

Legend:
- Allegheny Mountains
- Cumberland Mountains
- Cumberland Plateau
- Blue Ridge Mountains
- Allegheny Plateau

■ TERRAIN SHAPES
□ CUISINE

To begin our exploration of this little-known American regional cuisine, let's take a closer look at the topography and climate of the southern Appalachians and learn how the mountains shaped the cuisine.

Elderly Mountains

The southern Appalachian Mountains are hauntingly beautiful. Unlike the high and rugged Rockies, the Appalachians are old, worn by time into a gentle visage that belies the harsh reality of living in them. Three great mountain chains compose the southern Appalachians: the Alleghenies, the Blue Ridge, and the Cumberlands (Figure 8.1). From western Maryland south to Georgia, the mountains appear as low, parallel ridges stretching to the horizon. Depending on the light, these tree-covered ridges appear blue-green to smoky gray, each separated from the next by a deep, dark valley in between. V-shaped gaps in the ridgelines reveal the paths of rivers, once gateways for pioneers heading west.

Over millions of years, as the Appalachians wore down from wind and water erosion, converging streams formed creeks and rivers coursing swiftly through the steep valleys, carrying soil away. Pockets of fertile soil concentrated only on the floors of river valleys and in **hollows,** small horseshoe-shaped mountainside depressions with streams flowing through them. As erosion did its work on the surface, geologic compression created vast deposits of coal hidden underground in thick strata between layers of shale and sandstone.

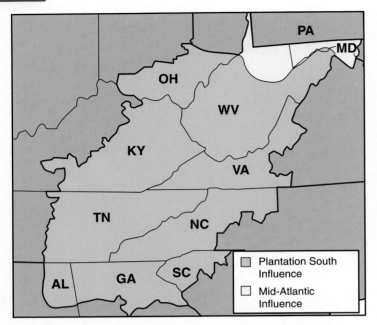

FIGURE 8.2
Mid-Atlantic and Plantation South Influence in Appalachian South Cuisine

Because of the region's steep and rocky terrain, large-scale farming was impossible, and even subsistence farming was problematic. Crops can be grown only in narrow river valleys and on the gentle slopes of cleared hollows. Thus, Appalachian farms are small and often far apart. Rugged terrain between farms and towns made transporting goods to market difficult. Even after railroads connected mountain towns to the outside world, because of lack of tillable acreage most Appalachian farmers barely fed their own families and had little surplus to sell.

Although most Appalachian waterways are too swift and steep for navigation, they were a valuable resource for early settlers. Through the early 20th century Appalachian streams teemed with brook trout and crawfish, and rivers harbored larger trout species, catfish, and turtles. Streams were a source of abundant aquatic greens. Appalachian waterpower turned early millwheels, grinding corn into grits and wheat into flour. Later, the same energy powered sawmills and mining operations.

Like the coastal flatlands and piedmont, before the European incursion the Appalachians were almost totally tree-covered. Unlike other regions that were stripped of trees by the early 1800s, the Appalachians' steep and rocky topography slowed the progress of lumbering to a reasonable rate. Although harvest of the region's timber began as early as the 1700s, regrowth has largely kept pace with harvest. Today hardwood forest covers the region's mountainsides, with walnut, locust, maple, sycamore, oak, poplar, and hickory trees towering in dense profusion. Redbuds, black gums, and dogwoods flourish in the understory. Along the ridgetops, scrub pines and cedars force their roots into the thin, shale-ridden soil. Trees remain an important resource throughout the Appalachians;

FACTOR 1
Erosion removed much of the region's soil, leaving only shallow deposits in lowland areas.

the lumber originally used to build pioneer homesteads is now raw material for paper mills.

Mountain Climate

Mountain topography dictates the region's climate, which is determined as much by altitude as by latitude. In Appalachian Maryland and the Virginias, springtime comes late. Some years snow remains in deep and shady hollows until mid-May. Although short, Appalachian summers are among the world's most pleasant, with warm sunny days, low humidity, and cool nights. Fall arrives quickly, with frost as early as mid-September. Winter can be brutal, with bone-chilling damp punctuated by strong winds whipping down the mountainsides. Frequent storms dump as much as 200 inches of snow in a single year. From the Carolinas southward, the climate is warmer and less extreme. However, the mountains are always cooler and less humid than the eastern or western lowlands.

Appalachian mountainsides and valleys teemed with wildlife through the 1800s. Elk, deer, bears, rabbits, opossums, raccoons, groundhogs, and squirrels were among the plentiful furred game. Wildfowl such as quail, partridge, grouse, wild turkeys, and doves lived in the ground cover. These food resources drew Native Americans of the Southern coastal plains to their mountain hunting grounds.

FACTOR 1
High altitude results in a shorter growing season and cooler weather.

■ NATIVE HUNTING
□ GROUNDS

As you've learned, eastern Native Americans practiced seasonal migration, spending the growing and harvest seasons farming near their lowland villages and moving to higher ground during the hunting seasons. Thus, the Appalachian Mountains were seasonal hunting grounds for numerous tribes, many of which traveled significant distances to reach them. Native Americans from the Mid-Atlantic, the Ohio River Valley, and the Great Lakes region all made semiannual trips into the central Appalachians, and New England coastal tribes moved to the northern Appalachians. In like manner, tribes from the Plantation South and the Chesapeake region, such as the Shawnees, Delawares, and Susquehannocks, ventured west into the southern Appalachians during the hottest weather of the summer and stayed there through the early fall. All tribes regarded the Appalachian Mountains as neutral territory, belonging to none and available to all. Under normal circumstances, tribes that were normally hostile to one another observed a temporary truce while in the mountains.

The Cherokees

Cherokees were the only Native American group to permanently reside in the Appalachians (Figure 8.3). Before the European incursion they lived in more than two hundred well-constructed vil-

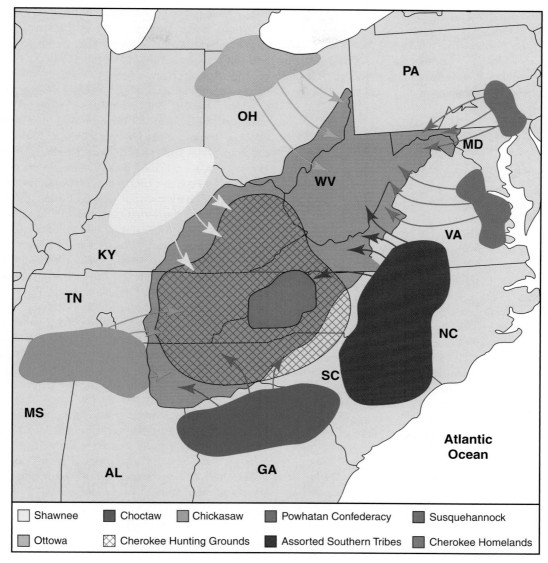

FIGURE 8.3

Map of Cherokee Territory and Native American Seasonal Migration

lages in the far southern Appalachians and their piedmont areas, migrating farther north and to higher altitudes in summer for hunting. Their unique success in Appalachian Mountain living was partly due to the milder climate in the south, but also due to their highly developed farming technology and generally advanced culture. Proximity to the Natchez of northern Louisiana may explain their expertise. In addition, historians believe that the Cherokees' technological advantage is at least partially due to early contact with Spanish explorers in the 1500s.

The Cherokees practiced a balanced blend of farming, hunting, and gathering that resulted in a wide palette of ingredients. In the 1500s, Spanish explorers reported dining on Cherokee shuck breads made of green corn and roasted chestnuts pounded together and steamed in cornhusks. Game-based stews were flavored with mountain herbs and fortified with corn, squash, and beans.

Later, Cherokee cooking was further enriched as British and Rhineland (p. 147) pioneers penetrated the far southern Appalachians. Intermarriage between white settlers and Cherokees was prevalent, and thus their cooking styles mingled. When slaves escaping the Plantation South fled into the mountains, many Cherokee tribes welcomed them, creating an Afro-Cherokee bloodline and introducing Plantation South ingredients and techniques to Cherokee cuisine. This blending of cuisines is evident in modern Appalachian South cuisine that, in its southernmost areas, shows stronger Native American and Plantation South influences.

The U.S. government's forced removal of East Coast Native Americans is one of the great tragedies in

FACTOR 2   FACTOR 4

Native American and African-American influences are important only in the southernmost areas of the region.

American history, and a national disgrace. This policy relocated most of the region's Cherokee population from the far southern Appalachians to present-day Oklahoma in 1838. Although today many residents of the southern Appalachians claim Cherokee blood, after relocation Native American culture and cuisine became virtually extinct in the Appalachians.

■ INTO THE
▢ APPALACHIANS
■

During the initial settlement of America's Plantation South, Chesapeake, and Mid-Atlantic coastal regions, exploration of the inland Appalachians was infrequent. For most early colonists there was no reason to venture into the mountains because there was plenty of better land on the coastal plain and in the piedmont. Early colonists believed the best use for the mountainous interior was as a refuge for displaced natives.

By the mid-1700s, however, a colonial population explosion gave rise to the need for more land. The sons of early colonists had followed the region's rivers inland, establishing farms north and west of the fall line. Eighteenth-century European settlers, primarily from England, also settled the piedmont areas, leaving nothing to the west but an intimidating barrier of mountains.

Lack of flat farmland didn't stop the flow of settlers to the American colonies. However, a vastly different type of person was required to face the Appalachian Mountains.

■ AMERICA'S FIRST
▢ PIONEERS
■

Thus far in our study of America's culinary regions all first-settler groups—those of the Plantation South, New England, the Mid-Atlantic, the Chesapeake, Louisiana, and the Mexican Border region—were colonists who traveled from their home nations to previously unclaimed areas. The Appalachians, however, had been claimed by England as part of her coastal colonies. Moreover, many Appalachian settlers already had been living in the colonies, and thus were migrating from one area of an established state to another. Therefore, the people who settled the Appalachian Mountains in the 1700s were pioneers—America's first pioneers.

In the days before modern transportation, people traveling from one place to settle another had to take along enough food to sustain them until they could grow or raise more. This food is often referred to as *provisions*. In the regions you've previously studied, the travelers discussed were colonists, and

the provisions they carried with them were Old World foods in a form that would keep for long periods without spoiling: grains such as wheat, barley, and buckwheat; cured meats, such as bacon and salt pork; and cured fish such as salt cod. During the settling of the Appalachians, America's most important indigenous foods—cornmeal and dried beans—became fundamental provisions for pioneers. Even Europeans straight off the boat purchased these unfamiliar foods for their journey, mainly because they were cheaper and more readily available than Old World foods. In addition to wheat flour, salt fish, cured meats, pork lard, salt, and coffee, cornmeal and dried beans were carried west with America's pioneers; we call this group of foods **pioneer provisions.**

Two primary pioneer groups began the first great human migration into the American interior: Europeans and colonial Americans. From 1720 until the Revolutionary War, thousands of British settlers landed in Philadelphia en route to the Appalachian Mountains. They were joined by landless workers, many of them freed indentures, from the coastal South and a later wave of settlers from Europe's Rhineland areas. From Philadelphia they headed west along the Great Conestoga Road past Lancaster and then turned southwest on the Great Valley Road through the Shenandoah Valley on the western side of the Blue Ridge Mountains (see Figure 8.4). Other pioneer groups traveled south from Baltimore into Virginia. At Fredericksburg they chose from several wagon roads leading southwest. To reach their chosen tract of land, pioneers left the wagon roads, following the path of rivers and creeks upward into the mountains.

The typical Appalachian pioneer risked his family's life savings to purchase travel needs: a Conestoga wagon, a team of heavy horses or oxen, and pioneer provisions. However, all believed this a risk worth taking. Let's learn who they were and why they became America's first pioneers.

Pioneers from Great Britain

In the early days of Appalachian settlement, most pioneers were of Celtic origin (see the box on p. 365), many of Scottish ancestry. Some arrived in America directly from the mountainous Scottish highlands. To these Scots the Appalachians seemed like home. Many more were **Scots-Irish,** Scottish families that

---

■ ▢
▢ **ELEMENTS OF OLD-WORLD SCOTS
AND SCOTS-IRISH CUISINE**

FOUNDATION FOODS

    principal starches: wheat bread, oatmeal, potatoes

    principal proteins: mutton/lamb, fresh and preserved pork, dairy products

    principal produce: root vegetables, cabbages

FAVORED SEASONINGS: minimal

PRINCIPAL COOKING MEDIA: butter, lard, bacon drippings

PRIMARY COOKING METHODS: boiling, stewing, pan-frying, roasting

FOOD ATTITUDES: minimized food culture, culinary conservatives

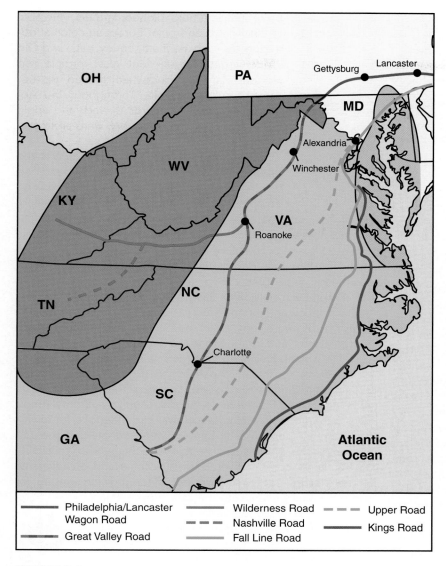

FIGURE 8.4
Eighteenth-Century Wagon Roads Leading to the Appalachians

distilling fine whiskey. They also brought fierce independence and a warlike attitude.

Another group of Celtic-heritage immigrants were drawn to the Appalachians in the early 1800s during the start of the coal-mining industry. To supplement the local workforce, mine owners began recruiting experienced miners from Wales. Sharing many of the same folkways and foodways as earlier settlers, Welsh families fit seamlessly into Appalachian life.

Pioneers from the American Colonies

In the mid-1700s the social order of the American colonies was largely based on land ownership. Even voting rights were tied to the possession of property. Because only first sons inherited land, many descendants of small farmers were landless and therefore poor. Freed indentures had even less chance for success. Particularly in the Plantation South, the lack of towns and cities resulted in limited opportunities for advancement and earnings with which to purchase a farm. Even members of the planter class suffered from landlessness because there was little local land available.

The social inequalities that resulted from landlessness led to growing dissatisfaction among the disenfranchised and created strong motivation to move on. Landless Southerners began looking west to the Appalachians, where unclaimed land lay free for the taking. These pioneers brought cast-iron cooking; smoked pork products; and dishes such as cornbread, greens with seasoning meat, and Southern quick breads to the mountains.

Pioneers from the Rhineland

In the mid-1700s, Protestant Rhineland immigrants arriving in Philadelphia discovered that most of the Pennsylvania Dutch homeland area had been settled. Unlike the separatist groups that preceded them, most of these Rhinelanders sought not religious freedom, but farmland. Finding none in Pennsylvania, they turned to Appalachia. These secular Rhinelanders brought with them their agricultural expertise and the Germanic foodways that would add variety to Appalachian South cuisine. To review the elements of Old-World Rhineland cuisine, refer to this book's companion website.

■□■ APPALACHIAN FARMING

Acquiring a homestead in the Appalachian Mountains was a simple matter. To secure title to a tract of land up to 400 acres, a man needed only make "tomahawk improvements" by chopping his

had been transplanted from Scotland to Irish Ulster by the British Crown in order to wrest Northern Ireland from its indigenous Catholic population. Fleeing political strife and overcrowding in Ulster, they longed for the mountain isolation of their Scottish homeland. Both groups harbored a strong sense of their Celtic heritage and brought with them crafts, music, and storytelling traditions. Along with their folkways they brought Celtic foodways, including a preference for eating oatmeal and potatoes, a love of dairy foods, and the art of

THE CELTS

The term *Celtic* describes the descendants of an ancient European culture today most visibly represented in Ireland, Wales, Scotland, the British county of Cornwall, and the French region of Brittany. Celtic culture is renowned for its music, art, literature, and crafts. Early Celts were known for their skill at hunting and bravery in warfare.

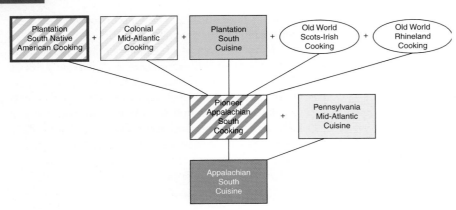

FIGURE 8.5

The Development of Appalachian South Cuisine

FACTOR 2

Three Sisters crops were essential foods for early settlers and remain an important part of the Appalachian Southern diet.

initials into trees at the four corners of his claim, building a cabin, and planting apple trees and a garden (Figure 8.6). An additional thousand acres of adjoining land could be secured later.

Pioneer families built their homesteads in deep hollows near springs or streams. They cleared their first fields using the Native American girdling technique, then planted corn, pumpkins, and beans using swidden agriculture. Hogs, sheep, goats, and chickens transported in the wagon were carefully tended until they had time to breed. Cows that made the long trek tied behind wagons were kept for their dairy products, and the draft animals that pulled the wagons were put to use pulling out tree stumps and hauling stone. Until the first crops came in, Appalachian pioneer families lived solely on hunted and foraged foods and the pioneer provisions brought with them.

After a few years, as they accrued more goods and equipment, and as their large families of children grew old enough to

FIGURE 8.6

A typical Appalachian homestead of the late 1700s. Mark Winfrey
© Shutterstock

be of sufficient help, pioneer farmers were able to clear fields and plant European colonial domesticates such as wheat, barley, oats, and Old World vegetables. In cool West Virginia and western Maryland, buckwheat thrived and became a culinary staple. Throughout the Appalachians, apple orchards thrived, and apple dishes, both sweet and savory, were an important food.

Hunting and trapping brought food to the table, but also yielded furs that could be traded for "necessaries," such as farm tools, cooking equipment, medicine, and cloth. Salt, coffee, wheat flour, and molasses were among the food products considered necessary; other purchased foods were bought rarely and used sparingly. Because a trip to the nearest general store might mean several days' journey over mountainous terrain, it was simply more practical to grow, raise, or process food at home. Appalachian Mountain farms rarely progressed much past self-sufficiency, and thus had few cash crops to purchase luxuries. Many farms were not even borderline successful, making hunted, fished, and foraged foods of vital importance to the diet.

The isolation resulting from mountain settlement suited the worldview of most early Appalachian settlers. Many had left Britain or the Rhineland disgusted with government interference in their lives, and thus were deeply distrustful of authority. Americans left landless by inheritance laws had little love for law or government. Those of Celtic heritage were strongly clan-oriented and suspicious of outsiders. People with this type of sensibility were culinary conservatives both by choice and of necessity. Nonetheless, as a group responsible for growing, raising, or hunting virtually everything they ate, Appalachian Southerners developed a very strong food culture. Once the fundamentals of Appalachian South cuisine were established by the mid-1800s, little change occurred. As yet no second-wave settlers have influenced the cuisine in any meaningful way. Although the poverty and hopelessness generated by industrial exploitation in the early 20th century threatened to diminish the cuisine, the region's foodways have largely prevailed. Today a traditional Appalachian South family meal consists of virtually the same dishes, made the same way, as those on the table a hundred years ago. Let's discover this little-known cuisine.

FACTOR 3

Colonial domesticates such as wheat, barley, oats, buckwheat, apples, chickens, and hogs enhanced the Appalachian diet.

APPALACHIAN SOUTH CUISINE

The cooking of the Appalachian South is characterized by thriftiness and self-reliance and was shaped by deprivation. Unlike those of wealthier culinary regions, Appalachian South cooks worked with a limited palette of ingredients. Mountain farmers had virtually no money, and with few exceptions their families ate only what they could grow, raise, hunt, or forage. In addition to a limited pantry, Appalachian women working farms and raising children often had little time for cooking. The typical Appalachian family had no servants, and there were very few restaurants with professional cooks. This resulted in a cuisine that is straightforward and unfussy but, nonetheless, deeply satisfying.

Limited ingredients meant that Appalachian cooks had to be much more creative in their cooking. Unlike regions with plentiful food resources in which the cuisine is ingredient driven, instead Appalachian South cuisine is technique driven. Using only pioneer provision foods, local indigenous foods, and the hardiest Old World colonial domesticates, Appalachian cooks developed an impressive repertoire of interesting main dishes; unusual desserts; and a wide array of pickles, preserves, and smoked and cured foods.

Before industrialization took its toll, most Appalachian farmers managed to feed their families very well. On a mountain farm, life revolved around food because everyone in the family was constantly preoccupied with foraging it, hunting it, growing it, preserving it, and cooking it. Sitting down to a bountiful table was one of few daily pleasures, and sharing that bounty with neighbors and friends made even a cash-poor person feel rich. During the 1930s, when government-sponsored folklorists recorded the life stories of thousands of Appalachian elders, a common remark was that, as children, "we never knew we were poor."

Appalachian cooks were experts at making a lot out of a little. By using every part of the carcass, Appalachian cooks could make one hog supply enough seasoning meat for hundreds of meals. Most Southern Appalachian dishes have lots of rich gravy or meat-enhanced "pot likker," good for stretching starchy side dishes and feeding many mouths with just a little protein. The synergy of corn and beans made a diet short on meat sufficiently nutritious.

However, in the Southern Appalachians food was far more than just fuel. Sharing food was the ultimate symbol of brotherhood and hospitality. With farms far apart and transportation limited to mere tracks in the woods, travelers relied on the welcome of strangers. Charitable gifts of food to the less fortunate were expected of anyone who could afford them. All of life's milestones, such as christenings, birthdays, weddings, harvests, and funerals, were celebrated with food—the best food the family could offer, and lots of it.

Roots of Appalachian South Cuisine

Like America's other regional cuisines, Appalachian South cooking is a hybrid, in this case a blending of select Plantation South ingredients and techniques with the hunted and foraged foods of the mountains and the foodways of British Isles and Rhineland settlers.

Plantation South Roots

The Appalachian South shares many of the ingredients and defining dishes of the Plantation South, brought to the mountains by Southern pioneers. Cornbread is frequently served as an accom-

paniment indispensable with beans. Cornmeal mush and cornmeal pancakes are served with sorghum syrup (p. 371) or maple syrup. As in the Chesapeake region, steam-processed hominy appears as a side dish. Grits is a relative newcomer to the Appalachian table, becoming popular in the early 20th century. Sweet corn—served on the cob and in fritters, puddings, and casseroles—is a summer treat.

In the Appalachian South a pot of beans is as much a signature dish as in New England. Poverty was the original reason: Legumes are one of the world's most filling and least expensive foods. Today slow-simmered pinto beans flavored with smoked pork neck bones and served with cornbread and buttermilk are considered the ultimate Appalachian comfort food.

FACTOR 2
Native American corn and bean dishes entered Appalachian Southern cuisine through the filter of Plantation South cooking.

Until recently Appalachian people relied on the hog for most of their domesticated meat, and most pork was preserved in some way. Today preserved pork remains a staple of the cuisine. Whole hams are cured and smoked for table meat, and smoked pork hocks and neck bones are used as seasoning meat for soups, vegetables, and beans. Bacon is a favored breakfast food and is used extensively as a seasoning meat. More important, **bacon drippings** (the rendered fat that remains after frying bacon) are the region's preferred frying medium. Almost every Appalachian South cook keeps a crock of bacon drippings near the stove. Fresh pork shoulder, scraps, and fatback are ground, seasoned, and forced into casings to make rope sausage, eaten fresh or hung to dry. To make a traditional preserved food, heavily seasoned cooked sausage patties are packed into sterile crocks and covered with melted lard for long storage in a cool cellar. Fatty side meat, as well as pig's feet, tails, and ears, are pickled in brine. Pure home-rendered lard is stored in tin buckets. Today these traditional Appalachian preserved pork products are purchased from specialty butchers and locally owned supermarkets.

Although they're similar in many ways, Appalachian and Plantation Southern cuisines also differ. One important Plantation food is conspicuously absent: Rice is rarely found on Appalachian menus. Seafood is not part of the cuisine, although freshwater fish are featured. As you've learned, African-American influence, so important in the Plantation South, is far less evident in Appalachian Mountain cooking, and Native American cooking plays a much larger role.

Indigenous Foods

A hidden benefit of poverty and isolation is invention bred by the necessity of using only local ingredients. Although hunted game and foraged fruits and vegetables loomed large in the diet of early Americans of all regions, in the Appalachian South they remain important in the modern cuisine, appearing on traditional families' everyday tables.

Wild Greens

Among the many foraged foods important in modern Appalachian South cuisine is the region's wide variety of wild

Lamb's Quarters Courtesy "Wildman" Steve Brill

Dandelion, shown here with blossom and, thus, overmature for eating. Richard Peterson © Shutterstock

Pokeweed Courtesy of the Bishop Museum

Creasy Greens Courtesy Jill Doughtie

Ramps David Kay © Shutterstock

FIGURE 8.7

greens (Figure 8.7). Before canned and frozen vegetables became widely available, Appalachian families eagerly anticipated the first green vegetables of spring. After a winter diet of salt meat and storage vegetables, fresh greens were a much-needed "tonic," or home remedy, for the digestive system and helped prevent nutrient deficiencies. Long before the earliest garden vegetable was ready to harverd, wild greens began to shoot up from the warming soil in the woods and along streams and creeks. Dock, lamb's quarters, wild mustard, dandelion, branch lettuce, and fiddlehead ferns are among the nutritious greens still gathered in early spring. Various types of watercress, collectively called **creasy greens,** also fill the springtime salad bowl. Two special wild greens are much enjoyed and have become well known as Appalachian specialties. **Poke sallet,** the young shoots of the pokeweed plant, and **ramps,** a particularly odoriferous member of the onion family, are Appalachian specialties.

Wild Fruits and Nuts

Appalachian pioneer families harvested a seasonal progression of wild fruits and nuts. However, despite local beliefs not all were indigenous to the region. As in northern Louisiana, in the far southern Appalachians 18th-century pioneers discovered European fruit trees and berry bushes likely introduced by Spaniards in the 16th century. Called **wildings,** these fruits frequently have an intense flavor not found in cultivated varieties.

Wild or wilding fruits are the basis of many traditional Appalachian desserts. Blackberries, wild blueberries, dewberries, serviceberries, huckleberries, elderberries, wild strawberries, wild cherries, **scuppernong grapes** (an indigenous grape variety), pawpaws, and crabapples are baked into pies and cobblers; boiled into jams, jellies, and preserves; and enjoyed fresh with cream and sugar. The juice of scuppernong grapes and elderberries is

INFAMOUS APPALACHIAN RAMPS

The most infamous of Appalachian wild greens are ramps, known by a variety of nicknames such as *the wild leeks of the mountains* and *Tennessee truffles*. Resembling bulbous scallions with green tops similar to young corn shoots, ramps grow in protected hollows throughout the southern Appalachians from West Virginia to Georgia. Their powerful flavor is likened to a cross between strong onion and pungent garlic. Eaten raw, they are overpowering to most diners; parboiling tames the flavor somewhat. Beloved by many—and despised by equally many—ramps are a seasonal Appalachian delicacy with a significant drawback.

The odor of ramps stays with the human body for an incredibly long time. Ramps on the breath can clear a room. Those who eat copious amounts of ramps perspire ramp odor through their pores. Because of this unfortunate fact, Appalachian husbands commonly prepare to sleep on the couch for a few days after a ramp feast. In the days of one-room schoolhouses, outlander schoolteachers were known to plan weeklong vacations during ramp season.

Social problems notwithstanding, communities throughout the Appalachian South stage ramp feasts and ramp festivals throughout the spring season, and visitors come from around the country to sample this "stinking lily."

FIGURE 8.8
Pawpaws Barnabas Kindersley
© Dorling Kindersley

fermented into sweet wine. Native persimmons are a fall favorite, allowed to ripen on the tree until they are squishy-soft and supremely sweet. Persimmon bread and persimmon puddings are among the dishes made from them. **Pawpaws,** discussed in the box at right and shown in Figure 8.8, are a little-known regional specialty. Black walnuts, discussed on p. 402, are one of the few indigenous tree nuts still featured in modern cuisine.

Unfortunately, today wild fruits and nuts are far less prevalent than in days past. Modern agricultural methods, the indiscriminate use of herbicides, and plant diseases have eradicated many species. But far up in the mountains, in hidden coves and hollows, favorite picking spots still exist.

Wild Game and Fish

Once a necessary element of survival, hunting and eating wild game remains an integral part of life for many Appalachian folks. Today most families have a hunter in the house or know someone who can supply them with their favored game meats. For them, game is not a special-occasion food; although the tenderloin of venison may be reserved for a holiday dinner, ordinary cuts of venison and small game are often the bases of everyday meals. Ground venison is typically mixed with store-bought hamburger to extend it, enrich it, and modify its strong flavor.

Wild game commonly served on Appalachian tables includes venison, bear meat, feral hog, rabbit, squirrel, opossum, raccoon, groundhog, rattlesnake, snapping turtle, wild turkey, pheasant, dove, quail, grouse, partridge, and woodcock. Game may be eaten for breakfast, lunch, or dinner, and is prepared by virtually every cooking method.

For many Appalachian outdoorsmen, fishing is as important as hunting. Although overharvesting and pollution have decimated many local native trout populations, the region's various states have stocking programs that release hatchery-raised rainbow and brown trout into streams and creeks. Indigenous fish also include spots, sunfish, freshwater perch, pike, eel, and mountain catfish. The favored cooking method for these small, freshwater fish is pan-frying in bacon drippings with a cornmeal or cracker crumb crust.

British Foodways

Because most Appalachian South settlers hailed from the British Isles, it's no surprise that British foodways are the primary European influence on Appalachian South cuisine. Refer to the box on p. 39 for elements of Old World English cuisine. However, keep in mind that most Appalachian South settlers were from other parts of the British Isles, and thus their cuisine elements vary slightly from the English norm.

Whereas the preferred meat in lushly pastured England was beef, in the Scottish highlands sheep were more successful. Therefore, in Scotland and Northern Ireland lamb and mutton were the meats of choice. Although other Southerners disdain it, in Scottish-settled parts of the southern Appalachians mutton is frequently served, featured in both Kentucky barbeque and mountain-style Brunswick stew. Because they're easy feeders, hogs were kept on every Appalachian homestead, where the art of smoking was raised to a level rivaling the Plantation South. Though eggs were a breakfast staple and

PAWPAWS

The pawpaw is the largest of America's indigenous tree fruits and the only temperate climate member of the mostly tropical Annonaceae family. Ranging from northern Florida to the Canadian border and from the southern Atlantic coast as far west as Nebraska, the pawpaw is most frequently associated with the Appalachian South, where it is most highly prized. Pawpaws are highly nutritious and a good source of vitamin C.

A favorite food of Native Americans, pawpaws were relished by European settlers as well. Today pawpaws are gaining renewed popularity as regional chefs rediscover them. Kentucky State University leads the nation in research into pawpaw cultivation.

widely used for custards and baking, chicken was considered "company food" and served only on Sundays or for special occasions.

The Celtic Dairy Heritage

In cool Appalachian mountain valleys, dairy products could be made and stored far more easily than in the hot and humid coastal plain. Although the land could not sustain large dairy herds and commercial dairy farming typically was not viable, almost every Appalachian family had at least one milk cow. True to their Celtic heritage, most Appalachian people loved to drink both fresh milk and buttermilk as a beverage. **Clabbered** (lightly fermented) cream and butter were used as table spreads as well as in cooking. Cheese making was a job for the farm wife, who made fresh, cottage-style cheeses as well as pressed, aged cheeses. Traditionally colored with egg yolk (later tinted with powdered annatto coloring tablets), aged homemade cheeses are simply called **yellow cheese.** Yellow cheese is sliced for sandwiches, melted into grits, and used for making macaroni and cheese.

Potatoes

The Appalachian South is the only region below the Mason-Dixon Line where potatoes compete with corn and rice as a staple starch. Especially in West Virginia and western Maryland, home fries rather than grits appear alongside breakfast eggs, and stews are fortified with hefty chunks of potato rather than cornmeal dumplings.

Although potatoes are most closely associated with the Irish, they quickly became the staff of life for the transplanted Scots-Irish in Ulster. By the late 1700s, potatoes also had become a favored food of Germany's working classes. Both immigrant groups brought seed potatoes with them on the wagon trails. Well suited to the climate, potatoes grew easily in the shallow mountain soil without succumbing to rot as they easily did in the humid lowlands. Potatoes kept well throughout the long Appalachian winters stored in root cellars or dug into trenches.

Apples

For the Appalachian pioneer farmer, the most valuable of all European fruits was the apple, often called "the pig of fruits" because its versatility rivaled that of pork. In traditional Appalachian South cooking, fresh apples are used in baked goods, sliced and fried as a side dish, and cooked down into sauces. Apples are pressed into cider and enjoyed as a fresh beverage but are more appreciated when fermented into hard cider or distilled into **applejack,** a potent spirit. A portion of each year's apple cider was soured into cider vinegar, used for salad dressings and for pickling.

For long-term storage, Appalachian apples were traditionally dried. Peeled, cored apples are cut into even rings and spread out between sheets of open-texture muslin cloth on a hot shed roof. When thoroughly dry, they are sewn into muslin bags and hung in the rafters. Dried apples hung over the fireplace hearth acquire a hint of smoky flavor; occasionally families dry some of their apples in the smokehouse or in their chimneys for a more pronounced flavor.

APPLE BUTTER

The art of apple butter making was brought to the mountains by Rhineland Germans but soon was embraced by all. In September and October, when apple season was at its peak, mountain hollows throughout the region were fragrant with wood smoke and the spicy aroma of simmering apples. Neighbors gathered for daylong "apple buttering" parties to share in the laborious peeling, chopping, and stirring involved.

Even today, now that quality commercial and artisan apple butters are produced throughout the Appalachian South, many families still prepare and can their own special home recipes. Appalachian people eat apple butter on hot homemade biscuits, on cornbread, on wheat toast or bread, layered between pancakes, and even on cottage cheese.

As with the hog, every part of the apple was used—and hogs were part of the program. Apple cores and peelings, as well as the pomace, or mash, left over from cider making, were tossed into the hog troughs to help fatten and flavor the pork.

Rhineland Flavors

Settlers from the Rhineland brought Germanic flavors and food preservation techniques to the Appalachians.

Cabbage was foremost among the European vegetables transplanted to the mountains by Rhinelander pioneers; it became the region's staple vegetable and one of few cash crops. Cabbage grows well in cool weather, stores for long periods in the root cellar, and preserves well by several methods. Soon all Appalachian families, regardless of ethnic background, had barrels of German-style sauerkraut fermenting in the cellar. Today both preserved and fresh cabbages are featured on the Appalachian table. Sauerkraut is a cold-weather specialty, and fresh cabbage appears in cool-weather soups and stews and in crisp summer slaws.

Buckwheat also grows well in the cool mountain climate. Rhinelanders brought their love of pancakes to the Appalachian highlands and adapted them to use plentiful locally produced buckwheat flour. Today sourdough buckwheat cakes are a specialty of West Virginia and western Maryland and are perfectly complemented by the excellent local maple syrup.

Homegrown and Homemade

Without doubt the most defining characteristic of Appalachian cooking is the do-it-yourself aspect of the cuisine. *Homegrown, homemade,* and *local* are recurring words in descriptions of Appalachian dishes. Both the Appalachian economy and the Appalachian attitude result in foods made at home or close to it.

The Backyard Garden

Although the Appalachian growing season is short—or perhaps because of that fact—fresh garden vegetables are among the most prized of foods. In Appalachian towns and cities, the backyard

SORGHUM SYRUP

Until the late 1800s, refined cane sugar was expensive and virtually unavailable in the Appalachians. Caribbean molasses was less costly, but heavy to transport into the mountains. Thus, the people of Appalachia initially relied on locally produced honey to sweeten their foods and beverages. However, in the mid-1800s, sweet sorghum, a grasslike food plant native to Africa, was introduced to mountain farms along with the technology for extracting its sap. Boiled like maple sap, sorghum sap reduces into thick, sweet, golden syrup. Before long most Appalachian farms had a sorghum mill, and sorghum syrup became the sweetener of choice. Called *long sweetening* because of its lingering taste in the mouth, sorghum syrup was used in coffee and tea and poured over hot cereals, pancakes, and biscuits. Many traditional Appalachian South desserts and baked goods are flavored with sorghum syrup as well.

garden is the rule rather than the exception. By late May the Appalachian vegetable garden yields a bounty of produce, the harvest beginning with rhubarb, radishes, peas, pearl or knob onions, and young garden greens. Tiny new potatoes are considered a special treat. Asparagus season soon follows, and then the summer vegetables, such as cucumbers, tender squashes, sturdy greens, root vegetables, string beans, shell beans, tomatoes, okra, and sweet corn, take center stage. In the summer months an Appalachian dinner may consist of nothing but vegetables, some made into salads, some breaded and fried, others simmered with a little seasoning meat. Late summer brings sweet potatoes, baked in their skins or stewed with 'possum. Fall brings the cabbage-family vegetables and winter squashes, eaten fresh and preserved for winter cooking.

Foods Preserved at Home

In the Appalachian South, old-time food preservation techniques are part of daily life. More so than in any other American culinary region, in the Appalachian South a typical family is likely to have a smoker on the back porch and a freezer in the basement. A successful hunting trip may result in homemade sausage or jerky, and a hog butchering on a relative's farm yields a home-cured, home-smoked ham. Appalachian women are known for their jams, jellies, and pickles. All summer long families "put up" garden vegetables by both canning and freezing. Although the technique is no longer necessary, traditional Appalachian gardeners often preserve some of their produce by drying it in the traditional manner just for its special taste. Parched corn (p. 35), dried shell beans, dried apples, and **leather britches** (see the box at left and Figure 8.9) are among the region's signature dried foods.

FIGURE 8.9
"Leather Britches" Beans
Courtesy of the Foxfire Museum and Heritage Center, Mountain City, GA, www.foxfire.org

LEATHER BRITCHES

Before the introduction of heatproof glass canning jars in the late 1800s, most garden vegetables were preserved by drying. Appalachian Southerners devised a unique method of drying string beans that is still used in traditional homes today. The fibrous strings of meaty textured, heirloom-variety beans are first carefully removed by hand. Using thick needles and cotton thread, the family sits on the front porch and fashions the beans into long festoons that are hung in the rafters to slowly dry in the cool mountain air. Because of their texture when dry and their resemblance to trousers hanging on a clothesline, these air-dried string beans are called *leather britches*. Long simmered in water with onions and seasoning meat, leather britches cook up tender yet chewy, with a unique texture and savory flavor unlike that of beans cooked fresh.

Spirits Made at Home

A legacy of their Scottish ancestry is Appalachian Southerners' legendary expertise at distilling spirits. Some Appalachian farmers used part of their corn crops to prepare a fermented liquid that was transformed in homemade stills into potent corn whiskey. This strong, clear spirit was called **moonshine** because it was produced in hidden hollows under cover of darkness to avoid the attention of government officials.

Home-Style Desserts

Appalachian South desserts are homey, hearty, and plain. Appalachian bakers take inspiration from neighboring Plantation South and Mid-Atlantic regions, both areas well known for their collective sweet tooth. Southern-style cobblers are everyday desserts, and flaky-crusted fruit pies and rich custard pies are made for special occasions. A fondness for old-fashioned steamed puddings and fruitcakes is a legacy of British cuisine. Preserved fruits are the basis of many Appalachian desserts: dried peaches and dried apples are simmered into thick, sweet fillings, and poundcakes and cookies are laced with raisins and currants. **Fried pies** (p. 400) are pastry turnovers with sweet or savory fillings.

The signature dessert of Appalachian South cuisine is the **stack cake** (p. 396), a tower of thin, dense, poundcake layers filled with fruit purée. Originally served as a wedding cake, today the stack cake is presented with pride at parties, church suppers, and other special events.

■ RAILROADS, INDUSTRY,
□ AND EXPLOITATION
■

In the Appalachian Mountains, tracts of arable land are small and scattered. Into the late 1800s, descendants of the region's early pioneers had fared reasonably well practicing subsistence farming, hunting for food and fur, and logging. By the late 1800s, however, the region's high birthrate resulted in a population too large to be supported by the region's aboveground resources. In isolated Appalachian mountain valleys, there was not enough work, little education, and virtually no way for people to make a living.

The arrival of rail transportation brought industry to the previously inaccessible Appalachians. Finally, the region's millions of acres of hardwood trees could be harvested and shipped to growing urban areas on the East Coast and in the Midwest. Industrialists took advantage of waterpower to run sawmills and paper mills, and large coal mining and natural gas companies moved in. These new industries attracted a small second wave of settlement, largely immigrants from Welsh and English mining towns. Hailing from virtually the same food culture as the region's pioneers, these second settlers reinforced British foodways. Second wave settlers also included immigrants from Southern Italy. As in other regions, Italians opened restaurants, delis, and pizza shops. Although Italian sandwiches, pasta dishes, and pepperoni bread are popular take-out fare, Italian immigrants did not significantly contribute to Appalachian South cuisine.

By the turn of the 20th century the Appalachian Mountains were generating enormous wealth—but that wealth did not stay in the region. Instead, the region was exploited by outsiders doing little to reinvest in its physical or human resources.

Industry brought employment to the Appalachians, but at enormous cost. With few exceptions, the owners of Appalachian mines and mills were wealthy barons of industry who lived elsewhere. Most regarded their employees simply as cheap labor. They built crowded, poorly constructed company towns (Figure 8.10) and required workers to purchase goods from company stores, forcing many into a spiral of debt. Little effort was made to institute safe working standards and benefits were nonexistent. Because of lack of health care and the many dangers facing miners and industrial workers, in the early 1900s the Appalachian Mountain region had one of the lowest life expectancy rates in the developed world.

The fabric of traditional Appalachian life began to unravel with the advent of industry and went into severe decline after 1900, when thousands of Appalachian families began leaving their farms to live in coal towns and mill towns. Living off the farm, many lost the ability to raise and cook the nutritious foods of their heritage. The introduction of industrially processed foods, often the only option available in company stores, further degraded the Appalachian diet.

FIGURE 8.10

Kempton, West Virginia, circa 1920 Courtesy of the Library of Congress, LC-USF33-001364-M4

By the mid-20th century, industry had taken its toll on the ecology of the region. Appalachian rivers ran rusty red or sulfurous yellow with mine runoff. The sharp stench of paper mills hung in the air. Mountaintops were blown apart to yield their minerals; the resulting slag filled valley floors and choked mountain streams. Pollution made once-plentiful fish and game less available as a food source.

Although industrial jobs were essential, many Appalachian South families nonetheless managed to stay on their own land. While men labored in mines and mills, Appalachian women and children worked small, hardscrabble farms to make ends meet. Economic and educational opportunities still were few. But the harshness of Appalachian life honed the tough-spirited independence of these pioneer descendents. Family bonds were tight, people worked together, and families learned to "make do." Although many Appalachian families lived in poverty, those with small farms managed to eat fairly well, relying on traditional pioneer provision foods supplemented with homegrown produce, backyard-raised hogs and chickens, foraged foods, and hunted game. As in the Plantation South after the Civil War, a few dedicated cooks from traditional families managed to keep the cuisine alive.

■ BRINGING THE PAST
□ INTO THE FUTURE
■

In the mid-1900s the rise of labor unions and government antipoverty measures significantly raised the Appalachian standard of living. However, at the same time the promotion of processed foods and convenience ingredients degraded Appalachian cooking as it did other American regional cuisines. Appalachian families needed two incomes to survive, and thus had little time for home cooking. Once again, traditional Appalachian South cuisine was at risk of disappearing.

ELEMENTS OF APPALACHIAN SOUTH CUISINE

FOUNDATION FOODS

principal starches: wheat quick breads, cornbread, potatoes, sourdough buckwheat pancakes

principal proteins: fresh and preserved pork, dried beans, game meats and fowl

principal produce: cabbages, root vegetables, wild greens, wild and wilding fruits, apples

FAVORED SEASONINGS: smoked seasoning meats, black pepper

PRINCIPAL COOKING MEDIA: bacon drippings, lard

PRIMARY COOKING METHODS: pan-frying, stewing/simmering, griddling

FOOD ATTITUDES: strong food culture, culinary conservatives

nation's poorest region. Despite the presence of industry and growing tourism in the region, the Appalachian South has not yet reached Factor 5 economic viability. In response to the bleak economic situation in most of Appalachia, many of the region's young people leave for job opportunities in other parts of the country. The remaining population is graying. American mass culture no longer values old-fashioned, labor-intensive activities such as home food preservation and cooking from scratch. Fast food and convenience foods threaten the region's home cooking. Moreover, Appalachian South cuisine is not widely represented in fine-dining restaurants and remains largely unknown outside the region. For a list of noteworthy Appalachian South restaurants, refer to this book's companion website.

A much-needed period of preservation and revival resulted from the counterculture and back-to-the-land movements of the 1960s and 1970s (pp. 560–561). Young people across the nation recognized Appalachian Southerners to be America's first hippies—they had been living off the land, resisting consumerism, and distrusting government since the 1700s. The popular *Foxfire* book series featured interviews with older Appalachian residents on topics including farming methods, food preservation techniques, and cooking. For a time these books revived interest in, and validated, the Appalachian way of life.

However, interest in Appalachian South culture and cuisine proved short-lived. Today the Appalachian South remains the

Only a few modern chefs and cookbook authors have taken up the cause of preserving and promoting Appalachian South cuisine. Without deeper knowledge and understanding, mainstream Americans are not likely to search it out. Thus, presenting Appalachian South cooking as a restaurant cuisine presents a formidable marketing challenge. However, the cuisine of the Appalachian South deserves to be recognized as a national treasure and preserved for the enjoyment of future generations of Americans.

FACTOR 5
To date, the Appalachian South has not yet fully reached economic viability.

TABLE 8.1 APPALACHIAN SOUTH DEFINING DISHES

ITEM NAME	HISTORY	DOMINANT INGREDIENTS AND METHOD	MORE
WILTED SALADS	Traditional Appalachian households did not have access to vegetable oil for salad dressings. Instead, dressing was made from readily available bacon drippings.	Boiled with cider vinegar, salt, and sugar, the bacon fat forms an emulsion. Cooled slightly, the dressing is poured over sturdy greens, such as escarole, watercress, or dandelions, that wilt from the heat.	Hard-cooked eggs, fried potatoes, or crispy bacon bits serve as garnish, with lots of black pepper for seasoning.
CREAM DRESSING SALADS	A legacy of Irish cuisine, use of cream dressings is the result of plentiful dairy products. Appalachian cream dressings are similar to those made in the British Isles, but apple cider vinegar replaces British malt vinegar.	Vinegar, sugar, salt, mustard, and hard-cooked egg yolks are mashed to a thick purée that is thinned by whisking in light table cream. The dressing may be tossed with delicate greens or used to bind cooked vegetable salads. Boiled dressings are frequently served as an alternative.	In the mid-20th century, commercial cream-type dressings, such as Miracle Whip, replaced homemade cream dressings in some households.
POKE SALLET	*Sallet* is a term for "salad" dating back to Elizabethan England. One of the year's first available fresh foods, poke sallet was a favorite spring meal.	Poke shoots are cleaned, parboiled, then tossed with a hot bacon dressing. Poke sallet is often served with fried potatoes and slow-simmered dried beans.	Parboiled poke is also scrambled with eggs or breaded and fried to serve as a side dish.

(continued)

☐ TABLE 8.1 APPALACHIAN SOUTH DEFINING DISHES *(continued)*

ITEM NAME	HISTORY	DOMINANT INGREDIENTS AND METHOD	MORE
RAMPS	Ramps were a favorite food of Native Americans and were embraced by hardy pioneers. These odorous vegetables are considered a home-style treat not served in polite company.	Ramps are par-boiled, sliced, and then fried with potatoes or scrambled with eggs. They flavor cheese grits and scalloped potatoes. Chopped, cooked ramps are mixed with ground beef to make "rampburgers" or mixed into cornmeal batter to make tasty fritters.	Pickled ramps are a pungent condiment.
"LEATHER BRITCHES" BEANS	Long, broad-podded string beans were strung together with needle and cotton thread and then hung in the sun, attic rafters, or over the wood-stove to dry. Their name comes from their appearance, as they look rather like pants hanging on a clothesline.	The beans are reconstituted by long, slow simmering with a piece of smoked or salted seasoning meat. The tasty "pot likker" is sopped up with cornbread.	Even today, with canned or frozen beans available, traditional Appalachian cooks still put up a few strings of leather britches so that they can enjoy their deeply savory, old-time flavor.
FRIED OR CREAMED POTATOES	Scots-Irish immigrants brought potato culture to the Appalachians during the mid-1700s, and soon it was embraced by all. Today the potato is the staple starch of the Appalachian table.	Home fries are boiled, peeled, sliced potatoes fried in bacon drippings and served for breakfast or supper. The Irish combination of potatoes and dairy remains a mountain favorite, with scalloped potatoes and creamy potato soups the most popular. In spring, tiny new potatoes are steamed in their jackets and glossed with butter or simmered in cream.	The water remaining after soaking peeled potatoes was used as a laundry starch.
SWEET POTATOES	Although not as popular as in the Plantation South, sweet potatoes are an autumn favorite.	Soft-fleshed early sweets are simply baked, pinched open, and served with butter, salt, and pepper. Roasted sweet potatoes with 'possum is a traditional combination. Sweet potatoes are also boiled, mashed, candied, souffléd, and made into pies.	On frosty mornings, many an Appalachian mother put an oven-hot sweet potato in each of her child's pockets as hand warmers, later to be eaten for school lunch.
DUMPLINGS	A good vehicle for "stretching" a dish to feed many mouths, dumplings of all kinds enhance Appalachian soups, stews, vegetables in "pot likker," and desserts.	Made of white flour, cornmeal, or potatoes, dumplings poached in savory or sweet sauces absorb flavor and act as a thickener.	Dessert dumplings may be filled with fruit and baked or dropped into simmering, sweet fruit purée to poach up soft and tinted with the color of the fruit. Clabbered cream (similar to crème fraîche) is a frequent accompaniment.
SAUERKRAUT	Introduced by German settlers, tangy preserved cabbage became a universal mountain favorite.	Prepared as a side dish, sauerkraut may be flavored with apples, caraway, and smoked pork. It is often simmered or baked along with the meat, fowl, or game.	Sauerkraut is an indispensable part of the Appalachian Thanksgiving dinner.
SOUTHERN QUICK BREADS	The same biscuits and corn breads featured in Plantation South cuisine play a vital role in Appalachian cooking.		See pp. 40, 41, and 48.
FRIED APPLES	Blurring the distinction between savory and sweet, pioneers served apples as a side dish as well as for breakfast and dessert.	Firm, tart cooking apples are peeled and cored, cut into thick wedges, and slowly sautéed in bacon drippings or butter. Once the apples soften to tenderness, they are sprinkled with sugar and allowed to caramelize.	The amount of sugar used depends on the tartness of the apples as well as the purpose of the dish; breakfast apples are highly sweetened. Fried apples to accompany pork or game are lightly sweetened and then balanced with salt to make a savory side dish.

☐ **TABLE 8.1 APPALACHIAN SOUTH DEFINING DISHES** *(continued)*

ITEM NAME	HISTORY	DOMINANT INGREDIENTS AND METHOD	MORE
BACKBONE STEW/BACK-BONES AND SAUERKRAUT	The reward for a day of hog butchering, slow-simmered dishes made with fresh pork back-bones were literally "finger-lickin' good," necessitating eating with the hands.	Made from the bones remaining after the loins and tenderloins were re-moved, backbone dishes consist of tasty and tender intercostal meat. Hacked into manageable pieces, they are cooked in a thickened sauce for stew or simmered in the broth of fresh sauerkraut.	Pork spareribs are often added as well.
BRUNSWICK STEW	Brunswick stew was adapted from Native American one-pot meals of small game and vegetables. It's traditionally cooked in large batches for community celebrations and political rallies. "Stew masters," usually men, prepare it outdoors in huge cast-iron cauldrons suspended over wood fires. The taste of the iron and the tang of the wood smoke are essential flavors.	Brunswick stew was originally based on squirrel, with the addition of rabbit and game birds when available. Today chicken is typically substituted for squirrel. Research reveals two major schools of Brunswick stew preparation. Central Appalachian style uses small game meat only, with rabbit a central ingredient. Georgia style adds pork, mutton, or even beef to the mixture. Both contain tomatoes, corn kernels, and shell beans such as limas or butter beans.	Food historians disagree on the origin of the name *Brunswick*. Some believe that the dish was titled in honor of a visiting earl of Brunswick, England. Others assert that it was named in honor of the location where it was first made. Unfortunately, towns named Brunswick are located in Virginia, Georgia, and North Carolina.
KENTUCKY BURGOO	An adaptation of Brunswick stew, burgoo was originally conceived as an attraction to lure crowds to sporting events and political rallies. Burgoo is always served on Kentucky Derby Day.	Similar to a Georgia Brunswick stew, burgoo mixes beef, mutton, and squirrel (or chicken) with tomatoes, corn, and limas. Burgoo also contains carrots, green peppers, and okra. Burgoo can be mild or spicy; its fluid component ranges in consistency from a rich broth to a thick sauce.	Like its predecessor, traditional burgoo depends on outdoor, cast-iron cooking over a wood fire for authentic flavor.
'POSSUM AND SWEET POTATOES	After the first hard frost in early October, opossum comes into season just as the sweet potatoes become fully mature.	A fat possum is skinned, cleaned, par-boiled in several changes of water, and oven-roasted to a sizzling brown. Toward the end of roasting, it is surrounded by sweet potatoes that roast in the pan drippings.	Accompanied by collards and cornbread, this dish is a traditional Appalachian favorite.
WEST VIRGINIA BUCKWHEAT CAKES	This breakfast dish is a specialty of mountainous West Virginia, where cool-climate buckwheat thrives.	A batter of buckwheat flour and water left at room temperature captures ambient yeasts and bacteria and ferments into sourdough. Seasoned with salt and maple syrup, the batter is griddle baked into thin, crisp-edged cakes.	Buckwheat cakes are served with butter, maple syrup, and thick-sliced bacon or country sausage.
HALF-MOON FRIED PIES	Compact and self-contained, these individual pastries were carried in pockets to farm fields or while traveling.	A pastry disc is topped with a cooked fruit filling, and then folded over in a half-moon shape. The pies are shallow-fried in lard and served warm or cool with a dusting of confectioner's sugar.	Fillings include cooked, puréed dried peaches or apples, fruit jams, or apple butter.
APPLE STACK CAKE	According to folk history, apple stack cake was the original Appalachian wedding cake. Each woman attending the wedding was responsible for bringing a layer. The bride's family then filled and assembled the cake.	Dried apples are simmered with sugar, water, and spices until they dissolve into a thick purée. The cooled apple purée fills seven thin white cake layers to make a tall, moist cake. Older versions feature drier, more biscuit-like layers.	Apple stack cake is accompanied by whipped cream or vanilla ice cream.

■ ▢ ■   # STUDY QUESTIONS

1. Define the boundaries of the Appalachian South culinary region. How does the culinary region differ from the Appalachian geocultural region? Explain where this difference becomes evident and why.

2. Explain the lack of direct Native American culinary influence in all but the southernmost parts of the Appalachian South culinary region. Explain why Native American ingredients and techniques are nonetheless foundations of Appalachian South cuisine.

3. List and describe the people of British Isles origin who settled the southern Appalachians. Discuss their food culture. List their colonial domesticates that became key ingredients in Appalachian South cuisine.

4. Describe the people of Rhineland origin who settled the southern Appalachians, list their colonial domesticates, and describe their Germanic cuisine.

5. List six indigenous southern Appalachian foraged foods and describe how they're used in the modern cuisine.

6. Explain why the Appalachian settlers are considered America's first pioneers. List American pioneer provisions and explain why indigenous foods are important among them.

7. Compare and contrast Plantation South cooking and Appalachian South cooking.

8. Explain why, although blessed with bountiful natural resources, the Appalachian South as yet has not fully reached economic viability. How has this affected the cuisine?

9. Discuss the importance of homegrown, home-processed, and homemade foods in Appalachian South cuisine.

10. List and describe six defining dishes of Appalachian South cuisine.

11. Using the information you learned in this chapter and your imagination, plan a four-course special-occasion dinner menu featuring Appalachian South cuisine.

Summer Garden Vegetable Soup
with Cracklin' Bread

yield: 1 (10-fl.-oz.) appetizer serving
(multiply × 4 for classroom turnout; adjust equipment sizes accordingly)

MASTER RECIPE

production		costing only
1 1/4 c.	Summer Garden Vegetable Soup	1/4 recipe
1 Tbsp.	Garden Herb Butter	1/4 recipe
1	6" doily or cocktail napkin	1 each
1 wedge	Cracklin' Bread	1/6 recipe

service turnout:
1. Stir the Summer Garden Vegetable Soup to distribute the vegetables evenly, and then ladle it into a small saucepan. Heat just to boiling.
2. Plate the dish:
   a. Pour the soup into a hot 12-oz. soup cup.
   b. Float the Garden Herb Butter on top.
   c. Place a 6" doily left of center on a cool 10" plate and set the cup on it.
   d. Place the Cracklin' Bread on the plate to the right of the soup cup.

COMPONENT RECIPE
SUMMER GARDEN VEGETABLE SOUP

yield: approx. 5 c.

production		costing only
4 oz.	smoked pork neck bones	4 oz.
1	1" slice beef shin, with bone	8 oz.
2 qt.	water	n/c
1 sprig	fresh thyme	1/20 bunch a.p.
1 sprig	fresh sage	1/20 bunch a.p.
2	ramps or scallions	1/4 bunch a.p.
1/3 c.	3/8"-diced carrot	2 oz. a.p.
1/3 c.	3/8"-diced turnip	2 oz. a.p.
1/2 c.	3/8"-diced white cabbage	1 1/2 oz. a.p.
1/2 c.	3/8"-cut green beans	1 oz. a.p.
1/3 c.	baby lima beans	1 1/2 oz. frozen, 6 oz. in-shell
1/3 c.	corn kernels	1 1/2 oz. frozen, 1/3 ear fresh
1/2 c.	3/8"-cut okra, fresh or frozen	1 1/2 oz. a.p. or 1 3/4 oz.
1/2 c.	peeled and seeded, 3/8"-diced vine-ripe tomatoes	5 oz. a.p.
tt	kosher salt	1/16 oz.

preparation:
1. Place the pork bones, beef shin, and water in a saucepan just large enough to accommodate them. Bring to the simmer and skim. Add the thyme, sage, and ramps and simmer briskly 1 hour.
2. Discard the thyme, sage, and ramps. Remove and cool the pork bones and beef shin.
3. Taste the broth for salt. Add the carrot, turnip, cabbage, green beans, lima beans, okra, tomatoes, and, if needed, a little salt to the broth and simmer about 20 minutes, until the vegetables are soft and the total volume of soup is about 5 cups.
4. Separate the meats from the bones. Pull the meats into small shreds and return the meats to the soup.
5. Correct the seasoning with additional salt if needed.

holding: open-pan cool and immediately refrigerate in a freshly sanitized, covered container up to 5 days

COMPONENT RECIPE
GARDEN HERB BUTTER

yield: 4 Tbsp.

production		costing only
3 Tbsp.	softened butter	1 1/2 oz.
1 Tbsp.	minced flat-leaf parsley	1/40 bunch
1 tsp.	fresh thyme leaves	1/20 bunch
1 tsp.	minced sage leaves	1/20 bunch
1 tsp.	fresh lemon juice	1/16 [90 ct.] lemon
1 tsp.	minced lemon zest	n/c
tt	kosher salt	1/16 oz.
tt	fine-ground white pepper	1/16 oz.

preparation:
1. Mix together all ingredients.
2. Form into 4 discs and refrigerate. (If making a large quantity, form into a 1" diameter log, refrigerate, and slice into discs.)

holding: wrap in plastic film and refrigerate up to 1 week; may be frozen up to 1 month

---

RECIPE VARIATION
Winter Pantry Vegetable Soup
Replace the lima beans with presoaked dried navy beans and the fresh corn with dried sweet corn, such as Cope's brand. Add the dried beans and corn along with the pork bones and beef shin. Replace the fresh herbs in the soup with pinches of dried herbs. Omit the green beans and okra and increase the amount of carrots, turnips, and cabbage accordingly. Replace the fresh tomatoes with canned tomatoes. Omit the Garden Herb Butter.

Wilted Salad
with Hot Bacon Dressing and Fried Potato Croutons

yield: 1 (5-oz.) appetizer serving
(multiply × 4 for classroom turnout)

MASTER RECIPE

production		costing only
2/3 c.	1/2"-diced russet potatoes, soaked in water	4 oz. a.p.
as needed	frying compound or corn oil	% used
tt	fine salt	1/16 oz.
1/2 tsp.	Southern Seasoning for Poultry	1/16 oz.
2 oz.	washed, thoroughly dried escarole	1/4 head or 4 oz. a.p.
1 oz.	washed, thoroughly dried curly endive	1/4 head or 4 oz. a.p.
1 oz.	washed, thoroughly dried dandelion greens	1/6 bunch or 1 1/2 oz. a.p.
1/4 c.+	Hot Bacon Dressing, hot in steam table	1/8+ recipe
tt	fresh-ground black pepper	1/16 oz.
2 slices	red onion, broken into rings	1 oz. a.p.
2 Tbsp.	cooked, crumbled bacon	3/4 oz. a.p.

service turnout:
1. Fry the potatoes:
   a. Drain the potatoes and blot them dry.
   b. Deep-fry the potatoes at 400°F until crisp and golden.
   c. Drain on paper towels.
   d. Toss with salt and Southern Seasoning for Poultry.
2. Dress the salad:
   a. Tear the greens into bite-sized pieces and drop into a bowl.
   b. Stir the Hot Bacon Dressing well, then ladle over the greens just enough dressing to coat them and wilt them slightly. Grind pepper over the top.
   c. Toss the greens gently.
3. Plate the dish:
   a. Mound the greens on a cool 10" plate.
   b. Arrange the onion rings on top.
   c. Scatter the fried potatoes on top.
   d. Drizzle on a little more dressing.
   e. Sprinkle the bacon on top.

COMPONENT RECIPE
HOT BACON DRESSING

yield: 1 pt.

production		costing only
1/2 c.	bacon drippings	n/c
2 Tbsp.	minced yellow onion	1/2 oz. a.p.
1/4 tsp.	celery seeds	1/20 oz.
2 Tbsp.	flour	1/20 oz.
1 c.	hot Poultry Stock	1/16 recipe
±1/2 c.	cider vinegar	±4 fl. oz.
1 Tbsp.	sugar	1/2 oz.
tt	kosher salt	1/16 oz.
as needed	boiling water	n/c

preparation:
1. Heat the bacon drippings in a small saucepan, add the onion and celery seeds, and sauté over medium heat until the onion is soft. Add the flour and make a blond roux.
2. Whisk in the Poultry Stock and vinegar, bring to a brisk simmer, and cook 2 or 3 minutes, stirring, until the dressing thickens to a nappé consistency.
3. Add the sugar and then balance the flavor with salt and vinegar.
4. Thin with water only if necessary.

holding: hold in steam table during service (thin with water as necessary); alternatively, refrigerate in a freshly sanitized, covered non-reactive container up to 5 days; whisk over low heat to rewarm and reemulsify

---

RECIPE VARIATION

Spring Tonic Salad with Hot Bacon Dressing and Hard-Cooked Egg
Replace the escarole and endive with a medley of domestic and foraged spring greens such as tiny mustard leaves; tiny turnip leaves; wild or garden cress; young dandelion; or blanched, refreshed, and drained poke salad. Replace the fried potatoes with sliced hard-cooked eggs.

Buckwheat Rolls
with Country Ham, Asparagus, and Herbed Fresh Cheese

yield: 1 (5-oz.) appetizer serving
(multiply × 4 for classroom turnout; adjust equipment sizes accordingly)

🕐 Requires 3 days advance preparation.

MASTER RECIPE

production		costing only
1 Tbsp.	melted butter	1/2 fl. oz.
2	Buckwheat Pancake Rolls	1/4 recipe
1/2 c.	Cheddar Cheese Sauce, hot in steam table	1/4 recipe
1 Tbsp.	thin-sliced scallion	1/8 bunch a.p.

service turnout:
1. Brush a sizzle plate with a thin coat of butter, place the Buckwheat Pancake Rolls on the sizzle plate, and brush the rolls with the remaining butter.
2. Bake at 400°F about 10 minutes, until heated through.
3. Plate the dish:
   a. Place one roll on a hot 10" plate positioned diagonally from 2 o'clock to 8 o'clock.
   b. Prop the remaining roll on top of the first, positioned on a diagonal from 11 o'clock to 5 o'clock.
   c. Nap the Cheddar Cheese Sauce across the center of the rolls, allowing much of the sauce to pool in the center.
   d. Sprinkle a line of scallion across the sauce.

COMPONENT RECIPE
CHEDDAR CHEESE SAUCE

yield: 2 1/4 c.

production		costing only
1/2 c.	grated sharp yellow Cheddar cheese	1 1/2 oz.
2 c.	hot Basic White Sauce	1 recipe

preparation:
1. Mix the cheese into the Basic White Sauce until melted.

holding: best prepared shortly before service; hold in steam table during service and thin with boiling water as needed (once the cheese has been added, do not heat higher than 180°F)

COMPONENT RECIPE
BUCKWHEAT PANCAKE ROLLS

yield: 8 (2-oz.) rolls

production		costing only
8	Sourdough Buckwheat Cakes	1 recipe
1 c.	Herbed Fresh Cheese	1 recipe
2 oz.	julienne country ham	2 oz.
32	thin asparagus spears, peeled, blanched and refreshed, and blotted dry	12 oz. a.p.

preparation:
1. Place a Sourdough Buckwheat Cake on the work surface, browned side down.
2. Spread with a thin, even layer (2 Tbsp.) of Herbed Fresh Cheese.
3. Sprinkle with 1/4 oz. ham.
4. Place 4 asparagus spears on the cake and roll up tight.
5. Repeat with the remaining ingredients to make 8 Buckwheat Pancake Rolls.

holding: refrigerate on a tray with pan liner, covered with a clean, damp towel and plastic film, up to 2 days

COMPONENT RECIPE
SOURDOUGH BUCKWHEAT CAKES

yield: 8 (4"-diameter) pancakes plus extra for practice

production		costing only
1 tsp.	baking powder	1/16 oz.
1/2 c.	buckwheat flour	2 3/4 oz.
1 tsp.	fine salt	1/6 oz.
1 c.	room-temperature Buckwheat Sourdough Starter	about 1/2 recipe
1 Tbsp.	pure maple syrup	1/2 fl. oz.
1 Tbsp.	melted butter	1/2 fl. oz.
±1 1/4 c.	lukewarm water	n/c
2 Tbsp.	melted clarified butter, in squeeze bottle	1 1/4 oz. a.p.

preparation:
1. Mix the batter:
   a. Mix together the baking powder, buckwheat flour, and salt in a medium bowl.
   b. Stir in the Buckwheat Sourdough Starter, syrup, and melted butter, then stir in enough lukewarm water to achieve a consistency like thick crêpe batter.
   c. Rest the batter at room temperature about 20 minutes.
2. Prepare the pancakes:
   a. Heat a 6" nonstick sauté pan very hot, squeeze in a few drops of clarified butter, and ladle in about 2 fl. oz. batter to make a thin pancake. Bake about 30 seconds, until browned on the bottom.
   b. Flip the pancake and bake the other side about 20 seconds, until cooked through.
   c. Slide the pancake onto a rack to cool.
   d. Repeat with the remaining batter to make a total of 12 pancakes.

holding: stack the pancakes with sheets of parchment or deli paper between them; wrap in plastic film and refrigerate up to 3 days; may be frozen up to 1 month

COMPONENT RECIPE
BUCKWHEAT SOURDOUGH STARTER

yield: approx. 3 c.

🕐 Requires 3 days advance preparation.

production		costing only
1 1/2 tsp.	active dry yeast	1/5 oz.
pinch	sugar	1/16 oz.
as needed	lukewarm water	n/c
1 1/2 c.	buckwheat flour	8 1/2 oz.

first day preparation:
1. In a small ramekin, mix the yeast, sugar, and 1/8 c. lukewarm water. Condition until bubbly.
2. Scrape the yeast mixture into a bowl. Add 1/2 c. lukewarm water. Stir in approximately 1/2 c. buckwheat flour to make a thick batter (sponge). Beat 1 minute. Cover with a kitchen towel and ferment in a warm place 1 hour.
3. Stir 1 c. lukewarm water into the sponge and then whisk in 1/2 c. buckwheat flour to make a thin batter.
4. Cover with loose plastic film and ferment in a warm place for 24 hours.

second day preparation:
5. "Feed" the starter by whisking in 1/4 c. lukewarm water and 1/4 c. buckwheat flour. Replace the loose plastic film and ferment in a warm place for another 24 hours.

third day preparation:
6. Repeat the feeding process and allow to ferment in a warm place for yet another 24 hours. When fermentation is complete, the batter should have a slightly sour aroma and tangy taste.

holding: refrigerate in a freshly sanitized, covered plastic container; once per week, "feed" the starter with 1/8 c. of lukewarm water and 1/8 c. buckwheat flour (the starter is viable as long as it produces CO_2 gas bubbles); bring to warm room temperature before using; reserve at least 1 c. starter for the next batch

APPETIZERS

COMPONENT RECIPE
HERBED FRESH CHEESE

yield: approx. 1 c. (8 to 10 oz.)

production		costing only
1 qt.	whole milk, preferably unpasteurized	1 qt.
1 Tbsp.	fresh lemon juice	1/5 [90 ct.] lemon
1/4 to 1/3 c.	heavy cream	2 to 3 fl. oz.
tt	fine salt	1/16 oz.
2 tsp.	minced flat-leaf parsley	1/40 bunch a.p.
2 tsp.	minced chives	1/20 bunch a.p.
1 tsp.	minced thyme leaves	1/40 bunch a.p.

preparation:
1. Curdle the milk:
   a. In a nonreactive pan, heat the milk to 195°F.
   b. Remove the milk from the heat and stir in the lemon juice. Allow to rest at room temperature until curdled. (Unpasteurized milk should curdle within about 15 minutes; pasteurized milk may take up to 1 hour and may need additional lemon juice if it does not curdle within that time.)
2. Drain the curds:
   a. Line a colander with several layers of cheesecloth, set it in a bowl, and pour in the curds and whey.
   b. Lift up the corners of the cheesecloth to make a bag and tie the bag closed with approximately 12" of kitchen string.
   c. Hang the bag of cheese over a bowl to drain for 1 hour.*
3. Finish the cheese:
   a. Remove the curds from the bag and place in a bowl.
   b. Stir in enough heavy cream to achieve a moist, spreadable texture.
   c. Season with salt.
   d. Mix in the parsley, chives, and thyme.

*The whey may be reserved for use in place of water in bread making.

holding: refrigerate in a freshly sanitized, covered nonreactive container up to 5 days

Applewood Smoked Trout
with Horseradish Cream and Biscuit Crackers

yield: 1 (4-oz.) appetizer serving plus accompaniments (multiply × 4 for classroom turnout)

🕐 Requires 1 day advance preparation.

MASTER RECIPE

production		costing only
1	Boston lettuce leaf	1/12 head
3 Tbsp.	Horseradish Cream	1/5 recipe
1/2	Applewood Smoked Trout	1/4 recipe
3 slices	red apple	1/6 [60 ct.] apple
1 Tbsp.	brunoise-cut red onion	1 oz. a.p.
1 sprig	fresh dill	1/40 bunch
1	lemon wedge	1/8 [90 ct.] lemon
5	Biscuit Crackers	1/4 recipe

service turnout:
1. Plate the dish:
   a. Place the lettuce leaf on a cool 10" plate at 2 o'clock.
   b. Spoon the Horseradish Cream into a dip dish and place it on the base of the leaf near the center of the plate.
   c. Peel the skin off the Applewood Smoked Trout and place it diagonally across the plate, propped against the dip dish, with the pointed tail end to the right.
   d. Fan the apple slices on the trout tail section at 4 o'clock.
   e. Mound the red onion in front of the apple slices.
   f. Arrange the Biscuit Crackers in an overlapping arc behind the dip dish from 12 to 9 o'clock.
   g. Place the lemon wedge between the crackers and the trout.
   h. Stick the dill sprig upright between the dip dish and the trout.

COMPONENT RECIPE
HORSERADISH CREAM

yield: 1 c.

production		costing only
5/8 c.	sour cream	5 fl. oz.
1/4 c.	mayonnaise	2 fl. oz.
±2 Tbsp.	prepared horseradish, drained well	±1 fl. oz.
1 Tbsp.	minced fresh dill	1/20 bunch a.p.
tt	kosher salt	1/16 oz.
tt	sugar	1/16 oz.
tt	fine-ground white pepper	1/16 oz.

preparation:
1. Mix together all ingredients, using more or less horseradish according to its strength. Balance the salt and sugar.

holding: refrigerate in a freshly sanitized, covered container up to 7 days

COMPONENT RECIPE
APPLEWOOD SMOKED TROUT

yield: 2 (9-oz.) trout; 4 (4-oz.) trout fillets

🕐 Requires 2 days advance preparation.

production		costing only
as needed	applewood, form as specified by smoker manufacturer	% of pkg.
as needed	water	n/c
2	10 oz. boneless, head-on whole trout	1 1/2 lb. a.p.
2 1/2 c.	Brine for Curing Trout	1 recipe
as needed	pan coating spray	% of container
1/2 c.	Maple Mop	1 recipe

first day preparation:
1. If necessary, soak the applewood in water to cover for the specified time.
2. Brine the trout:
   a. Remove and discard the heads of the trout.
   b. Open up the trout and place them, skin side down, in a nonreactive container of appropriate size to ensure complete submersion in the Brine for Curing Trout.
   c. Pour the brine over the trout, cover the container, and refrigerate 3 hours only. ⚠ Do not overcure.
   d. If longer holding is necessary, remove the trout from the brine after 3 hours.
3. Remove the trout from the brine and pat them dry. Place the trout on a rack set over a sheet tray, skin side down, and refrigerate, uncovered, 12 hours or overnight.

second day preparation:
4. Prepare the smoker with the wood and set the heat control to 180°F.
5. Spray the smoker rack with pan coating and put it in place.
6. Brush the flesh of the trout with half of the Maple Mop.
7. Place the trout on the smoker rack, flesh side down, and smoke 15 minutes.
8. Carefully turn the trout over, brush with the remaining maple mop, then continue to smoke 10 to 15 minutes longer until the flesh is opaque throughout and the smoke has permeated the flesh.
9. Cool the trout and refrigerate at least 12 hours.

holding: refrigerate in a freshly sanitized, covered, nonreactive container, with pan liner between layers, up to 7 days

CHEF'S NOTE:
Fruitwood is traditional in Appalachian smoking; if applewood is not available, substitute another fruitwood. The more readily available hickory wood is too strong-flavored for use with fish; use only as a last resort and reduce the amount of smoke by venting. Do not use mesquite wood.

RECIPE VARIATION
Applewood Smoked Trout with Toast Points and Honey Mustard Butter
Omit the Horseradish Cream and Biscuit Crackers. Serve with a softened composed butter flavored with Dijon mustard, honey, and salt. Accompany with freshly toasted triangles of American White Bread.

Baked Stuffed Trout

with Wild Mushroom Cornbread Dressing and Peas 'n' Pearl Onions

yield: 1 (10-oz.) entrée serving plus accompaniments (multiply × 4 for classroom turnout; adjust equipment sizes accordingly)

MASTER RECIPE

production		costing only
1	10-oz. boneless, head-on trout	10 oz. a.p.
tt	kosher salt	1/16 oz.
tt	fresh-ground black pepper	1/16 oz.
3/4 c.	Wild Mushroom Cornbread Dressing	1/4 recipe
1 Tbsp.	clarified butter	2/3 oz. a.p.
3/4 c.	shelled fresh peas, blanched and refreshed	3/4 lb. a.p. (in-shell)
2 oz.	peeled pearl onions, poached tender and refreshed	2 oz. a.p.
as needed	water, in squeeze bottle	n/c
6 Tbsp.	butter	3 oz.
2 Tbsp.	fresh lemon juice	3/8 [90 ct.] lemon
1 tsp.	minced lemon zest	n/c
1 Tbsp.	minced flat-leaf parsley	1/40 bunch a.p.

service turnout:
1. Wash the trout under cool running water and pat dry with paper towels.
2. Season the trout inside and out with salt and pepper, then fill its cavity with the Wild Mushroom Cornbread Dressing.
3. Brush a sizzle plate with clarified butter and place the trout on it. Brush the trout with the remaining butter and bake at 400°F about 12 minutes, until the trout is just cooked through and the dressing is hot.
4. In a small, covered sauté pan, heat the peas and onions with a squeeze of water and a pinch of salt. Alternatively, place in a small dish and microwave until hot.
5. Prepare a brown butter pan sauce:
   a. Heat another small sauté pan, add 2 Tbsp. butter, and heat until the milk solids separate out and turn golden brown.
   b. Immediately stop the browning by adding the lemon juice, lemon zest, and a few drops of water.
   c. Work in the remaining butter to form an emulsion.
   d. Season with salt and add the parsley.
6. Plate the dish:
   a. Spoon any loose dressing across the center of a hot 12" oval plate.
   b. Place the trout across the front of the plate, propped against the dressing.
   c. Spoon the peas and onions behind the trout.
   d. Pour the brown butter sauce over the trout and vegetables.

COMPONENT RECIPE

WILD MUSHROOM CORNBREAD DRESSING

yield: 3 c.

production		costing only
2 oz.	assorted wild or woodland mushrooms, such as chanterelles, hen of the woods, black trumpet, or morels	2 oz.
2 Tbsp.	corn oil	1 fl. oz.
tt	kosher salt	1/16 oz.
2 Tbsp.	butter	1 oz.
2 c.	Cornbread Dressing, p. 74	2/3 recipe

preparation:
1. Clean and fabricate the mushrooms:
   a. Pick over the mushrooms for dirt, insects, twigs, and so on.
   b. Wipe the mushrooms clean with a damp paper towel and remove any hard stem ends.
   c. If using morels, slit them open and inspect for insects.
   d. Cut large mushrooms into uniform pieces.
2. Cook the mushrooms:
   a. Heat a sauté pan until very hot, heat the oil, and sear the mushrooms, tossing and adding a little salt, about 1 minute, until just cooked.
   b. Remove from the heat and work in the butter.
   c. Cool to room temperature.
3. Gently mix the mushrooms into the Cornbread Dressing.

holding: open-pan cool and refrigerate in a freshly sanitized, covered container up to 3 days

---

RECIPE VARIATION

Baked Stuffed Trout with Black Walnut–Apple Cornbread Dressing, Cider Cream Sauce, and Brussels Sprouts
Replace the wild mushrooms in the dressing with 1 c. sautéed chopped apples and 1/4 c. toasted black walnut pieces. Replace the peas and pearl onions with boiled and refreshed Brussels sprouts. Replace the brown butter sauce with a cream reduction based on shallots, fish stock, and apple cider.

Chicken with Brunswick Stew

and Corn Pone

yield: 1 (10-oz.) entrée serving plus accompaniment
(multiply × 4 for classroom turnout; adjust equipment sizes
accordingly)

MASTER RECIPE

production		costing only
2 c.	Chicken Brunswick Stew (with 1 chicken leg)	1/4 recipe
1	Corn Pone	1/4 recipe
1 Tbsp.	bacon drippings	n/c
3 oz.	boneless, skinless chicken breast	3 oz.
1 tsp.	Southern Seasoning for Chicken	1/16 oz.
as needed	water, in squeeze bottle	n/c
1 Tbsp.	butter	1/2 oz.
tt	fresh-ground black pepper	1/16 oz.
1 sprig	fresh thyme	1/20 bunch
1 sprig	fresh sage	1/20 bunch
1 sprig	celery leaves	n/c

service turnout:

1. Finish the dish:
   a. Remove the chicken leg from the Chicken Brunswick Stew and place it on a sizzle pan with the Corn Pone. Heat in a 400°F oven about 10 minutes.
   b. Heat a 10" sauté pan and add the bacon drippings.
   c. Sprinkle the Southern Seasoning for Chicken on the chicken breast and sear it on both sides.
   d. Ladle in the Brunswick stew, squeeze in a little water, cover the pan, reduce the heat, and simmer until the stew is hot.
2. Plate the dish:
   a. Remove the chicken breast from the stew to a cutting board.
   b. Work the butter into the stew and season with pepper.
   c. Spoon the stew into a hot 12" pasta plate.
   d. Place the corn pone on a slight angle at the back of the plate at 12 o'clock.
   e. Prop the chicken leg against the pone with the bone end pointing upward.
   f. Slice the chicken breast into diagonal slices and fan them against the front of the leg.
   g. Make a bouquet of the herb sprigs and stick it upright between the chicken leg and the pone.

COMPONENT RECIPE
CHICKEN BRUNSWICK STEW

yield: 2 qt. plus 4 chicken legs

production		costing only
4	6-oz. skinless chicken legs	1 1/2 lb.
1 Tbsp.	Southern Seasoning for Poultry	1/16 recipe
1/4 c.	bacon drippings	n/c
1 qt.	Poultry Stock	1/4 recipe
1 qt.	water	n/c
1/2 c.	3/8"-diced country ham	1 1/2 oz.
1 c.	fine-chopped yellow onion	2 1/2 oz. a.p.
3/4 c.	1/2"-diced carrot	3 oz. a.p.
3/4 c.	peeled, 3/8"-diced celery	2 1/2 oz. a.p.
1/2 c.	canned petite diced tomatoes with juice	4 fl. oz.
2 sprigs	fresh thyme	1/20 bunch
1	bay leaf	1/16 oz.
tt	kosher salt	1/16 oz.
1 drop	liquid smoke	1/40 oz.
2 c.	3/4"-diced russet potatoes	12 oz. a.p.
1 c.	shelled lima beans, fresh or frozen	1 1/4 lb. a.p. or 4 oz.
1 1/4 c.	corn kernels, fresh or frozen	1 large ear a.p. or 4 oz.
1 c.	peeled and seeded, 1/2"-diced vine-ripe tomato	10 oz. a.p.
tt	bottled hot sauce (such as Crystal brand)	1/16 fl. oz.

preparation:
1. Season the chicken legs with Southern Seasoning for Poultry.
2. Heat a sauté pan, heat 2 Tbsp. bacon drippings, and sauté the chicken legs until browned on all sides. Remove the legs to a 4-qt. saucepan.
3. Add some of the Poultry Stock to the sauté pan, deglaze the browned bits, and then pour the deglazings over the chicken legs.
4. Add the remaining stock, water, ham, onion, carrots, celery, canned tomatoes, thyme, bay leaf, some salt, and liquid smoke to the saucepan. ⚠ Add the salt and liquid smoke carefully; do not overseason. Bring the mixture to the simmer and cook, uncovered, about 20 minutes, until the chicken legs are tender, adding water and partially covering the pan if the broth reduces too much.
5. Remove and discard the thyme stems and bay leaf. Remove the chicken legs from the broth, place in a freshly sanitized container, and spoon a small amount of broth on top. Open-pan cool and immediately cover and refrigerate.
6. Add the potatoes, lima beans, and corn to the broth and simmer about 10 minutes, until the potatoes are almost tender.
7. Add the fresh tomatoes and simmer 2 to 3 minutes longer.
8. Crush a few of the potatoes to lightly thicken the broth. Season with bottled hot sauce and correct the salt.

holding: open-pan cool and immediately refrigerate in a freshly sanitized, covered container up to 3 days

RECIPE VARIATIONS
Traditional Brunswick Stew
Replace the chicken and ham with 1 (3-lb.) disjointed wild rabbit, 1 (2-lb.) disjointed pheasant or grouse, and 1 lb. 2"-diced pork shoulder meat. When cooked, remove the meat from the bones, pull it into large shreds, and return it to the stew.

Kentucky Burgoo
Prepare Traditional Brunswick Stew, but with chicken, pork shoulder, and mutton shoulder. Add garlic, diced green bell pepper, and sliced okra along with the other vegetables.

ENTREES

'Possum-Style Pork Shoulder
with Sweet Potatoes and Creamed Lima Beans

yield: 1 (5-oz.) entrée serving plus accompaniments
(multiply × 4 or 6 for classroom turnout; adjust equipment sizes accordingly)

MASTER RECIPE

production		costing only
1 portion	'Possum-Style Pork Shoulder with Sweet Potatoes (meat, sweet potato, and 1/2 c. sauce)	1/6 recipe
as needed	water, in squeeze bottle	n/c
1 c.	Creamed Lima Beans	1/6 recipe
1 bouquet	watercress	1/3 bunch

service turnout:
1. Place the 'Possum-Style Pork Shoulder, sweet potato, sauce, and a little water in a small sauté pan, cover, and cook over low heat about 8 minutes, until heated through.
2. Heat the Creamed Lima Beans in a small, covered saucepan or in the microwave, adding a little water as needed.
3. Uncover the pork and bake it in a 400°F oven 2 to 3 minutes to crisp the crust.
4. Plate the dish:
   a. Mound the pork in the center of a hot 12" plate and pour the sauce around it.
   b. Lean the sweet potato against the back right of the pork.
   c. Spoon the lima beans onto the front right of the plate.
   d. Stick the watercress bouquet upright between the pork and the sweet potato.

COMPONENT RECIPE
'POSSUM-STYLE PORK SHOULDER WITH SWEET POTATOES

yield: approx. 2 lb.

production		costing only
2 Tbsp.	bacon drippings	n/c
1	3 1/2-lb. boneless pork shoulder, trussed	3 1/2 lb.
tt	kosher salt	1/16 oz.
tt	fresh-ground black pepper	1/16 oz.
2	small onions, peeled and quartered	7 oz. a.p.
2 c.	Poultry Stock	1/8 recipe
1/4 c.	cider vinegar	2 fl. oz.
1/2 c.	flour	2 1/2 oz.
as needed	water	n/c
6	5-oz. orange-fleshed sweet potatoes, peeled	2 lb.

preparation:
1. Heat a heavy braising pan of appropriate size to accommodate the pork and sweet potatoes without excess space. Add the bacon drippings and brown the pork shoulder on all sides.
2. Season the pork liberally with salt and pepper, scatter the onions around it, add the Poultry Stock and vinegar, and cover the pan.
3. Braise the pork in a 325°F oven 30 to 40 minutes, until almost tender.
4. Place the flour in a small bowl and whisk in enough water to make a pastelike wash. Season with salt.
5. Remove the pan from the oven and increase the oven temperature to 400°F.
6. Uncover the pan and brush the pork shoulder with the flour wash.
7. Add the potatoes to the pan and turn them to coat each one in the braising liquid.
8. Return the pan to the oven and roast the pork and potatoes, turning the potatoes occasionally, about 20 minutes longer, until the pork is very tender and the sweet potatoes are cooked through. Add additional stock or water as needed to maintain the sauce.
9. If not serving immediately, open-pan cool the pork and sweet potatoes. Portion and pack per the holding instructions that follow.
10. Remove the pork to a cutting board and the sweet potatoes to a freshly sanitized container. Cut the pork into 6 (5-oz.) portions, each including some of the crust. Place the pork servings into the container.
11. Strain the sauce, pressing on the solids.
12. Deglaze the pan with a little water or stock and add the deglazings to the sauce, which should total about 3 c.
13. Season the sauce and correct the flavor with salt and more vinegar if needed.
14. If not serving immediately, chill and defat the sauce. If serving immediately, skim off the excess fat while the sauce is hot.

holding: open-pan cool the pork, potatoes, and sauce; refrigerate in covered, freshly sanitized containers up to 5 days

COMPONENT RECIPE
CREAMED LIMA BEANS

yield: 6 c.

production		costing only
2 Tbsp.	butter	1 oz.
1/2 c.	fine-chopped yellow onion	2 1/2 oz. a.p.
1 c.	water	8 fl. oz.
1 qt.	shelled lima beans, fresh or frozen	4 lb. a.p. or 2 lb.
tt	kosher salt	1/16 oz.
2 c.	Basic White Sauce	1 recipe
tt	fresh-ground white pepper	1/16 oz.

preparation:
1. Place the butter and onion in a heavy saucepan, cover, and sweat over low heat about 1 minute until the onions soften but do not brown.
2. Add the water, lima beans, and a little salt. Stir well, cover the pan, and simmer briskly 6 to 8 minutes, until the limas are tender.
3. Add the Basic White Sauce to the pan, increase the heat, and cook, stirring and scraping with a heatproof rubber spatula, until the sauce reduces just enough to cling to the lima beans.
4. Correct the salt and season with white pepper.

holding: open-pan cool and immediately refrigerate in a covered, freshly sanitized container up to 3 days

Kentucky Barbeque Lamb Shank
with Creamed Corn, Pole Beans, and Fried Potatoes

yield: 1 (8-oz.) bone-in entrée serving plus accompaniments (multiply × 4 for classroom turnout; adjust equipment sizes accordingly)

🕐 Requires 24 hours advance preparation.

MASTER RECIPE

production		costing only
1	Kentucky Barbeque Lamb Shank	1/4 recipe
1/4 c.	Kentucky Barbeque Mopping Sauce	1/20 recipe
as needed	water, in squeeze bottle	n/c
1 small	russet potato, peeled, sliced thin, soaked in water	5 oz. a.p.
2 Tbsp.	corn oil	1 fl. oz.
tt	kosher salt	1/16 oz.
1 c.	Creamed Corn	1/4 recipe
1 c.	Appalachian-Style Pole Beans	1/4 recipe
1 Tbsp.	butter	1/2 oz.
1 Tbsp.	chopped flat-leaf parsley	1/20 bunch a.p.
1 Tbsp.	brunoise-cut red bell pepper	1/2 oz. a.p.

service turnout:

1. Place the Kentucky Barbeque Lamb Shank in a 10" sauté pan, add the Kentucky Barbeque Mopping Sauce and a little water, cover the pan, and heat over medium heat until heated through. ⚠ Do not allow the pan to run dry and scorch. Check and add more water if necessary.
2. Fry the potatoes:
   a. Drain the potato slices and blot them dry.
   b. Heat an 8" nonstick sauté pan, heat the oil, quickly add the potato slices in a concentric circle to cover the bottom of the pan, and season with salt.
   c. Place a lid on the pan, reduce the heat to medium, and cook 3 or 4 minutes, until the bottom is crisp and brown.
   d. Uncover the potatoes and flip over. Sauté uncovered until the new bottom is crisp and brown.
3. Separately heat the Creamed Corn and Appalachian-Style Pole Beans in covered pans or in a microwave oven.
4. Remove the lamb shank to a sizzle pan and brown it in a 400°F oven 1 to 2 minutes.
5. Reduce the lamb's pan juices to a nappé consistency, then work in the butter to create an emulsion.
6. Plate the dish:
   a. Flip the potatoes again so the better side is up, then slide them onto the center of a hot 12" plate.
   b. Place the lamb shank upright on the potatoes and remove the trussing string.
   c. Spoon the corn to the right of the shank and the pole beans to the left.
   d. Nap the lamb shank with the sauce.
   e. Sprinkle the lamb and the corn with the parsley and red bell pepper.

COMPONENT RECIPE
KENTUCKY BARBEQUE LAMB SHANKS

yield: 4 (10-oz.) shanks

🕐 Requires 24 hours advance preparation.

production		costing only
4	16-oz. lamb shanks	4 lb. a.p.
5 Tbsp.	Kentucky Rub	1 recipe
as needed	hickory wood per smoker manufacturer's specifications	% of pkg.
5 c.	Kentucky Barbeque and Mopping Sauce	5/6 recipe

first day preparation:

1. Fabricate and season the shanks:
   a. Using a meat saw, trim the wide ends of the lamb shanks so they'll stand upright at a slight slant. Wipe away any bone chips.
   b. French the shanks by scoring the meat around the bone at the halfway point. Scrape the thin end of the bone clean.
   c. Trim away excess fat from the meat.
   d. Tie the shanks securely with kitchen string.
   e. Coat each shank with Kentucky Rub and massage the rub in well.
   f. Place the shanks in a freshly sanitized, covered container and refrigerate at least 24 hours but not longer than 3 days.
2. Soak the hickory wood in cool water overnight or for at least 4 hours.

second day preparation:

3. Prepare a smoker, covered grill, or improvised stovetop smoking equipment using 1/3 of the hickory wood. Adjust the temperature to approximately 225°F. Have the Kentucky Barbeque and Mopping Sauce warm and at hand.
4. Place the lamb shanks on the rack and baste with a little sauce. Close the chamber and smoke about 3 hours, basting and turning the shanks every 20 minutes, until the shanks are cooked through and very tender. Replenish the hickory wood as necessary. If preparing more than a few hours in advance, reserve a little sauce for holding.

holding: open-pan cool and refrigerate up to 5 days in a freshly sanitized, covered container with a little sauce spooned over the top

COMPONENT RECIPE
CREAMED CORN

yield: 1 qt.

production		costing only
8 ears	fresh sweet corn	8 ears a.p.
4 Tbsp.	butter	2 oz.
1/2 c.	water	n/c
tt	kosher salt	1/16 oz.
1/2 c.	half-and-half	4 fl. oz.
tt	fine-ground white pepper	1/16 oz.

preparation:
1. Fabricate the corn:
   a. Shuck the corn and carefully remove all silk.
   b. Place a cutting board on a sheet tray to catch stray kernels and corn juices.
   c. Using a sharp boning knife, cut the kernels from the cobs.
   d. Using the back of the knife, firmly scrape down each ear to remove every last bit of corn pulp and juices.
   e. Place 1/3 of the corn kernels in a blender and purée.
2. Heat a 10" nonstick sauté pan, melt the butter, and then stir in the corn kernels, corn pulp and juices, and water. Add a little salt and then cook the corn about 15 minutes, stirring and scraping often with a heatproof rubber spatula, until the mixture cooks through and thickens.
3. Add the half-and-half and continue to cook, stirring and scraping, 5 minutes longer, until the mixture thickens enough to stand softly in a spoon.
4. Correct the salt and season with white pepper.

holding: open-pan cool and immediately refrigerate in a freshly sanitized, covered container up to 3 days

COMPONENT RECIPE
APPALACHIAN-STYLE POLE BEANS

yield: 1 qt.

production		costing only
1/2 c.	salt pork, cut into 1/8" × 1/8" × 1/2" lardons	2 oz.
1 1/2 lb.	pole beans or green beans, trimmed, stringed if necessary, cut into 2" lengths	1 1/2 lb. a.p.
2/3 c.	water	n/c
tt	kosher salt	1/16 oz.
tt	fresh-ground black pepper	1/16 oz.

preparation:
1. Place the salt pork in a heavy saucepan, place it over low heat, and fry it gently until the fat renders out and the lardons are brown.
2. Add the beans and water, cover, and simmer briskly, stirring occasionally, 10 to 20 minutes, until the beans are tender.
3. Remove the beans.
4. Bring the cooking liquid to a boil and reduce it to 1/4 c.
5. Return the beans to the saucepan and toss to coat with the cooking liquid.
6. Correct the salt and season with pepper.

holding: open-pan cool and immediately refrigerate in a freshly sanitized, covered container up to 3 days

---

RECIPE VARIATION

Kentucky Barbeque Mutton with "Leather Britches" Beans, Creamed Corn, and Fried Potatoes
Replace the lamb shanks with 4-lb. shoulder of mutton in one piece. Double the amount of rub, sauce, and hickory wood. Increase the cooking time to 6 hours. Chop or pull (shred) to serve. Replace the pole beans with dried "leather britches" beans. Increase the water to 1 qt. and simmer at least 1 hour, until the beans are reconstituted and tender.

ENTREES

Cherokee Venison Stew
with Shuck Bread

yield: 1 (8-oz.) entrée serving plus accompaniments (multiply × 4 for classroom turnout; adjust equipment sizes accordingly)

🕐 Best with 24 hours advance preparation.

MASTER RECIPE

production		costing only
1	Butternut Squash "Calabash"	1/4 recipe
1 Tbsp.	melted butter	1/2 oz.
tt	kosher salt	1/16 oz.
2 1/2 c.	Cherokee Venison Stew (with garnish vegetables)	1/4 recipe
as needed	water, in squeeze bottle	n/c
1	Shuck Bread	1/4 recipe
1 bouquet	watercress	1/4 bunch

service turnout:

1. Place the Butternut Squash "Calabash" on a sizzle plate, brush it with butter, season it with salt, and bake it in a 400°F oven 10 minutes, until browned.
2. Place the Cherokee Venison Stew in a 10" sauté pan and add a little water. Add the garnish vegetables, making sure each portion gets 1/2 c. sunchoke cubes, 3 onions, 5 squash Parisiennes, and 3 chestnuts. Cover the pan and place over medium heat until heated through.
3. Heat the Shuck Bread in a steamer or on medium power in a microwave oven.
4. Plate the dish:
   a. Place the "calabash" on a warm 12" oval plate with the small end at 7 o'clock.
   b. Fill the "calabash" with the stew, making sure that some colorful vegetables are visible on the surface.
   c. Place the watercress on the plate at 3 o'clock. Fold back the husks of the shuck bread and lean it against the cress and the "calabash."

COMPONENT RECIPE
BUTTERNUT SQUASH "CALABASHES"

yield: 4 "calabash" presentation containers and approx. 12 oz. Parisienne squash

production		costing only
2	small (1-lb.) butternut squashes	2 lb.

preparation:

1. Cut each squash in half lengthwise and scrape out the seeds and membranes.
2. Use the large end of a Parisienne scoop to cut out squash Parisiennes. Reserve for use as a garnish vegetable for the stew.
3. Preheat a commercial pressure steamer or set up a stovetop steamer.
4. Place the squash shells on the steamer tray, cut side down, and steam until the flesh is just cooked through, about 3 minutes in a commercial steamer and 10 minutes in a stovetop steamer.
5. Cool the squash shells to room temperature.
6. Scrape out the remaining squash flesh from each shell to create an attractive, even interior surface and a 1/4" wall.

holding: wrap the "calabash" shells in plastic film and refrigerate up to 4 days

COMPONENT RECIPE
CHEROKEE VENISON STEW

yield: approx. 2 1/2 qt.

🕐 Best with 24 hours advance preparation.

production		costing only
2 lb.	boneless venison shoulder or bottom round	2 lb. a.p.
1/2 c.	minced yellow onion	2 1/2 oz. a.p.
2 Tbsp.	minced garlic	1/3 oz. a.p.
2 Tbsp.	chopped sage leaves	1/6 bunch a.p.
1 Tbsp.	thyme leaves	1/10 bunch a.p.
1 Tbsp.	crushed juniper berries	1/10 oz.
1 tsp.	crushed black peppercorns	1/16 oz.
2 tsp.	kosher salt	1/5 oz.
1/4 c.	cider vinegar	2 fl. oz.
1/2 c.	corn oil	4 fl. oz.
2 oz.	rindless salt pork, cut into 1/4" × 1/4" × 3/4" lardons	2 3/4 oz. a.p.
5 Tbsp.	flour	1/2 oz.
2 Tbsp.	corn oil	1 fl. oz.
5 c.	hot Brown Beef Stock	1/3 recipe
1 Tbsp.	tomato paste	1/2 fl. oz.
1 Tbsp.	honey	1/2 fl. oz.
tt	kosher salt	1/16 oz.
10 oz.	peeled, 1"-diced sunchokes	12 oz. a.p.
12	boiling onions, peeled and scored with an X	8 oz. a.p.
20 pc.	butternut squash Parisiennes (from "Calabash" recipe)	n/c
12	chestnuts, roasted, shelled, and peeled	6 oz. a.p.

first day preparation:
1. Trim the venison of excess silverskin and cut into 2" cubes.
2. In a freshly sanitized plastic container just large enough to hold the venison, combine the onion, garlic, sage, thyme, juniper berries, peppercorns, 2 tsp. salt, vinegar, and 1/2 c. oil. Mix in the venison, cover, and marinate, refrigerated, 24 hours or as time allows.

second day preparation:
3. Place the salt pork in a 12" sauté pan and fry it over medium heat until the fat renders out and the lardons are browned. Remove and reserve the lardons.
4. Remove the venison from the marinade, brushing off any clinging herbs and vegetables and returning them to the marinade. Blot the venison dry on paper towels.
5. Increase the heat under the sauté pan and sauté the venison cubes. When browned, remove the venison to a heavy 2 1/2-qt. saucepot.
6. Add the flour to the sauté pan along with enough corn oil to make a thick roux. Cook the roux to light brown. Whisk in the Brown Beef Stock and bring to the simmer.
7. Scrape the sauce into the saucepot with the venison. Add the reserved marinade, lardons, tomato paste, and honey and a little salt. Bring to a bare simmer and cook, uncovered, 45 minutes to 1 1/4 hours, until the venison is tender. Skim any fat that rises to the surface.

8. Prepare the vegetable garnish:
   a. Separately simmer the sunchokes, boiling onions, and squash in salted water until just tender.
   b. Drain but do not refresh. Cool completely.
   c. For à la carte service, portion the vegetables, including the chestnuts, as specified in step 2 of the master recipe.
9. When the venison is tender, evaluate the consistency of the sauce and, if necessary, thin it with stock or water or thicken it by reduction.
10. Taste the sauce and correct the seasoning.

holding: open-pan cool and separately refrigerate the stew and vegetables in freshly sanitized, covered containers

COMPONENT RECIPE
SHUCK BREAD

yield: 4 breads

production		costing only
8	large dried cornhusks	1 oz.
as needed	boiling water	n/c
1 c.	stone-ground white cornmeal	3 3/4 oz.
1 tsp.	kosher salt	1/10 oz.
3/4 c.	boiling water	n/c
1/2 c.	cooked, drained black-eyed peas	1 oz. dried, 3 1/2 oz. canned
1/4 tsp.	baking powder	1/16 oz.
1/4 c.	warm bacon drippings	n/c

preparation:
1. Place the cornhusks in a bowl and pour over them enough boiling water to cover. Weight them down with a plate so that they are submerged. Soak until pliant, about 20 minutes.
2. Prepare the dough:
   a. Place the cornmeal and salt in a small bowl.
   b. Pour 3/4 c. boiling water into the cornmeal, stir well, and allow the mixture to stand about 20 minutes, until the water is absorbed.
   c. Place the black-eyed peas in a food processor and grind to a coarse purée.
   d. Add the baking powder and the cornmeal mixture to the food processor and purée.
   e. With the machine running, pour in the bacon drippings through the feed tube.
   f. Taste and, if necessary, season with salt.
3. Assemble the shuck breads in the same manner as the tamales on p. 332, but without the meat filling.
4. Steam the shuck breads in the same manner as the tamales.
5. Cool the shuck breads and prepare them for service as for the tamales.

holding: refrigerate wrapped in plastic film up to 5 days; may be frozen for up to 1 month, in which case postpone step 5 until the breads are thawed for service

---

RECIPE VARIATIONS

Cherokee Venison Stew with Corn Pone
Replace the Shuck Bread with Corn Pone.

Cherokee Beef Stew with Shuck Bread
Replace the venison with 2 1/4 lb. beef chuck.

ENTRÉES

Maple-Glazed Turkey
with Sauerkraut and Hominy

yield: 1 (7-oz.) entrée serving plus accompaniments (multiply × 4 for classroom turnout; adjust equipment sizes accordingly)

MASTER RECIPE

production		costing only
1 Tbsp.	clarified butter	2/3 oz. a.p.
1	5-oz. Seasoned Turkey Breast Portion	1/4 recipe
1/3 c.	Maple Glaze, hot in steam table	1/4 recipe
as needed	water, in squeeze bottle	n/c
1/2 c.	Pulled Turkey Leg	1/4 recipe
3 pc.	blanched and refreshed baby carrots	2 oz. a.p.
1 1/2 c.	Appalachian-Style Sauerkraut, hot in steam table	1/4 recipe
1 c.	Home-Style Buttered Hominy, hot in steam table	1/4 recipe
1 sprig	flat-leaf parsley	1/40 bunch

service turnout:
1. Cook the Seasoned Turkey Breast Portion:
   a. Heat a small sauté pan, add the clarified butter, and add the turkey breast, skin side down.
   b. Sear the turkey breast until the skin is brown, and then turn it over.
   c. Brush with half of the Maple Glaze and then squeeze a little water into the bottom of the pan.
   d. Finish in a 400°F oven about 8 minutes.
2. Place the Pulled Turkey Leg and the carrots in another small sauté pan, add a little water, cover the pan, and warm over low heat.
3. Plate the dish:
   a. Place a 2 1/2" × 1 1/2" entremet ring back center of a hot 12" plate and pack in the turkey leg. Remove the ring.
   b. Use tongs to place the Appalachian-Style Sauerkraut in the plate well around the pulled turkey, and then spoon in some of the sauerkraut juices.
   c. Pack a 3-fl.-oz. portion scoop with the Home-Style Buttered Hominy and mound it on top of the turkey leg.
   d. Slice the turkey breast across the grain and fan the slices across the front of the plate, propped against the turkey leg. Brush with the remaining maple glaze.
   e. Prop the carrots against the turkey breast slices with the tips at 5 o'clock.
   f. Place the parsley sprig at the top of the carrots.

COMPONENT RECIPE
SEASONED TURKEY BREAST PORTIONS

yield: at least 4 (5-oz.) raw-weight portions

production		costing only
2 tsp.	kosher salt	3/4 oz.
2 tsp.	ground dried sage	1/8 oz.
1 tsp.	dried thyme	1/16 oz.
1 tsp.	fine-ground white pepper	1/16 oz.
1	2 1/2-lb. bone-in raw turkey breast half	2 1/2 lb.

preparation:
1. Mix the salt, sage, thyme, and white pepper.
2. Remove the turkey breast meat from the bones in one piece. Trim away excess fat and skin tags, leaving as much skin attached to the breast meat as possible.
3. Place the turkey breast between two sheets of parchment and pound the thick section gently to flatten the breast into an equal thickness.
4. Weigh the meat and determine how many 5-oz. portions it will yield.
5. Cut the turkey breast into even-sized, blocklike, 5-oz. portions, each with some skin attached. Reserve scraps for another use.
6. Rub each portion with the seasoning mix.

holding: wrap individually in plastic film and refrigerate up to 3 days

COMPONENT RECIPE
MAPLE GLAZE

yield: 1 1/3 c.

production		costing only
3 c.	Poultry Stock	3/16 recipe
1/2 c.	pure maple syrup	4 fl. oz.
1/4 c.	butter	2 oz.

preparation:
1. In a 1 1/2-qt. saucepan, reduce the Poultry Stock to 3/4 c.
2. Add the maple syrup and work in the butter.

holding: refrigerate in a freshly sanitized, covered container up to 5 days

COMPONENT RECIPE
PULLED TURKEY LEG

yield: approx. 1 pt. (approx. 8 oz.)

production		costing only
1	20 oz. turkey leg	20 oz.
1 Tbsp.	Southern Seasoning for Poultry	1/16 recipe
1 Tbsp.	bacon drippings	n/c
1/2 c.	water	n/c
2 Tbsp.	cider vinegar	1 fl. oz.
1 drop	liquid smoke	% of container

preparation:
1. Cut the turkey leg through the joint into a drumstick and thigh. Remove excess skin and fat, but do not remove all of the skin.
2. Rub the turkey pieces with the Southern Seasoning for Poultry.
3. Heat a small sauté pan, heat the bacon drippings, and brown the turkey pieces on all sides. Add the remaining ingredients, cover the pan, and simmer about 15 minutes, until the turkey is cooked but slightly pink at the bone.
4. Uncover the pan and transfer it to a 400°F oven. Bake the turkey about 15 minutes longer, until cooked through. Add a little water if the pan juices reduce too much.
5. Open-pan cool the turkey to room temperature.
6. Remove and discard the turkey skin. Pick the meat from the bones. Pull the meat into medium-size shreds. Discard the bones.
7. Toss the turkey meat with the pan juices.

holding: refrigerate in a freshly sanitized, covered container up to 3 days

ENTREES

COMPONENT RECIPE
APPALACHIAN-STYLE SAUERKRAUT

yield: 5 c.

production		costing only
10 oz.	smoked pork neck bones	10 oz.
3 c.	water	n/c
3 Tbsp.	bacon drippings	n/c
1 1/2 c.	thin-sliced yellow onion	7 oz. a.p.
1 1/2 c.	hard apple cider	12 fl. oz.
6 c.	drained fresh sauerkraut	2 lb. a.p.

preparation:
1. Rinse the pork bones in cold water and place them in a heavy, nonreactive saucepan large enough to hold them and the sauerkraut. Add the water and simmer, covered, 20 minutes.
2. Heat a sauté pan, heat the bacon drippings, and sauté the onion over medium heat about 1 minute until softened and barely beginning to brown.
3. Scrape the onion into the pan with the pork bones and deglaze the sauté pan with some of the cider.
4. Add the sauerkraut to the saucepan along with the deglazings and the remaining cider. Stir to combine, cover the pan, and cook over medium heat about 30 minutes, until the sauerkraut is tender.
5. Remove the pork bones and cool them to room temperature.
6. Increase the heat under the sauerkraut and reduce the cooking liquid, leaving just enough to keep the sauerkraut juicy, but not wet.
7. Pick the meat from the pork bones and mix it into the sauerkraut.

holding: open-pan cool and immediately refrigerate in a freshly sanitized, covered container up to 5 days

COMPONENT RECIPE
HOME-STYLE BUTTERED HOMINY

yield: 1 qt.

production		costing only
1 qt.	canned pearl hominy, such as Manning's brand, with liquid	32 fl. oz.
tt	kosher salt	1/16 oz.
tt	fine-ground white pepper	1/16 oz.
4 Tbsp.	butter	2 oz.

preparation:
1. In a 12" sauté pan, heat the hominy with its liquid.
2. If necessary, reduce the canning liquid so that the hominy is juicy but without excess liquid.
3. Season the hominy with salt and white pepper, and then work in the butter.

holding: hold in a steam table during service, or open-pan cool and immediately refrigerate in a freshly sanitized, covered container up to 3 days

---

RECIPE VARIATION

Maple-Glazed Cornish Hens with Sauerkraut and Hominy
Replace all of the turkey with 4 (14-oz.) Cornish hens. Season, truss, sear, and flash-chill the hens during preparation, and then finish roasting to order.

Roast Grouse

with Sawmill Gravy, Ramp Home Fries, and Mountain Vegetable Medley

yield: 1 (12-oz.) bone-in entrée serving plus accompaniments (multiply × 4 for classroom turnout; adjust equipment sizes accordingly)

MASTER RECIPE

production		costing only
1	Seared Grouse Half	1/4 recipe
1 Tbsp.	clarified butter	2/3 oz. a.p.
2 Tbsp.	bacon drippings	n/c
1 1/2 c.	boiled, peeled, 1/2"-diced waxy potatoes	6 oz. a.p.
1 oz.	1/2" diagonal-cut ramps or large scallions, boiled and refreshed	2 oz. a.p. or 1/2 bunch
tt	kosher salt	1/16 oz.
tt	fresh-ground black pepper	1/16 oz.
1/4 c.	cooked corn kernels, fresh or frozen	1/4 ear or 1 oz.
1/4 c.	cooked baby lima beans, fresh or frozen	1/4 lb. or 1 oz.
1/4 c.	3/8"-diced carrots, blanched and refreshed	1 1/2 oz. a.p.
1/4 c.	3/8" diced zucchini	1 1/4 oz. a.p.
1/4 c.	3/8" lengths green beans, blanched and refreshed	1 oz. a.p.
1/4 c.	water, in squeeze bottle	n/c
1 Tbsp.	butter	1/2 oz.
3/4 c.	Sawmill Gravy, hot in steam table	1/4 recipe

service turnout:

1. Place the Seared Grouse Half on a sizzle plate and brush with clarified butter. Finish roasting in a 400°F oven about 12 minutes.
2. Finish the Ramp Home Fries:
   a. Heat a 10" nonstick sauté pan, heat the bacon drippings, and sauté the potatoes over medium heat, flipping occasionally, about 5 minutes, until well browned.
   b. Add the ramps and toss until heated through.
   c. Season with salt and a generous amount of pepper.
3. Heat the vegetables:
   a. Place the corn, lima beans, carrots, zucchini, green beans, 1/4 c. water, and a little salt in a small sauté pan, cover, and heat over medium heat until hot.
   b. Uncover and reduce away most of the liquid.
   c. Work in the butter to create an emulsion.
4. Plate the dish:
   a. Mound the home fries on the back left of a hot 12" oval plate.
   b. Place the grouse half diagonally on the plate, propped against the home fries. Scrape any pan juices over the top.
   c. Spoon the vegetables onto the right front of the plate.
   d. Nap the grouse with the Sawmill Gravy.

COMPONENT RECIPE

SEARED GROUSE HALVES AND SAWMILL GRAVY

yield: 4 (12-oz.) bone-in entrée portions plus 3 c. gravy

production		costing only
2	2-lb. grouse	4 lb.
tt	kosher salt	1/16 oz.
tt	fine-ground white pepper	1/16 oz.
2 Tbsp.	corn oil	1 fl. oz.
3 Tbsp.	bacon drippings	n/c
1/4 c.	fine-ground white cornmeal	1 oz.
2 c.	hot Poultry Stock, preferably made with game bird carcasses	1/8 recipe
2 c.	half-and-half	16 fl. oz.

preparation:

1. Fabricate and season the grouse:
   a. Remove the backbones of the grouse and split them in half down the breastbone.*
   b. Chop off the drumstick knuckles and the wing tips.*
   c. Remove the thigh bones, rib bones, and any other small bones, leaving only the drumstick bones and breastbones.*
   d. Use foodservice tweezers to pluck out any visible pinfeathers.
   e. Season with salt and white pepper.
2. Heat a 14" sauté pan, heat the oil, and sear the grouse halves, skin side down, about 1 minute, until golden brown. Turn and sear the flesh sides 30 seconds. Remove to a half-sheet tray and immediately refrigerate, uncovered, until cold.
3. Make the gravy:
   a. Add the bacon drippings to the sauté pan. Stir in the cornmeal and cook over low heat about 20 seconds, until light brown, stirring and scraping up the pan glaze.
   b. Add the Poultry Stock, whisking constantly to avoid lumps. Simmer briskly, whisking occasionally, about 5 minutes until reduced by half.
   c. Add the half-and-half and bring to the simmer. Cook about 1 minute, until reduced to a light nappé consistency.
   d. Season with salt and white pepper.

*Reserve the bones and any giblets for stock.

holding: store grouse halves and open-pan-cooled gravy refrigerated separately in freshly sanitized, covered containers up to 3 days

---

RECIPE VARIATION

Roast Pheasant with Sawmill Gravy, Ramp Home Fries, and Mountain Vegetable Medley

Replace the grouse with pheasants.

Apple Stack Cake

yield: 1 dessert serving
(multiply × 4 for classroom turnout)

🕐 Best prepared 24 hours in advance.

MASTER RECIPE

production		costing only
1 slice	Apple Stack Cake	1/10 recipe

service turnout:
1. Place the Apple Stack Cake slice in the center of a cool 10" plate.

COMPONENT RECIPE

APPLE STACK CAKE ASSEMBLY

yield: 10 dessert servings: 1 (9") cake

🕐 Best prepared 24 hours in advance.

production		costing only
1 c.	apple syrup (from Apple Filling recipe)	n/c
2 Tbsp.	applejack	1 fl. oz.
7	Cake Layers for Apple Stack Cake	1 recipe
1	(9") cardboard cake circle	1 each
4 c.	Apple Filling for Apple Stack Cake	1 recipe
1/4 c.	confectioner's sugar	1 oz.

preparation:
1. Moisten the cake layers:
   a. Place the apple syrup in a squeeze bottle and add the applejack.
   b. Place a sheet of pan liner on a work surface. Remove the pan liner circles from the Cake Layers and place them on the pan liner sheet in one layer.
   c. Using a sharp-tined fork or pastry docker, poke holes all over the layers.
   d. Slowly drizzle each layer with a little more than 1 fl. oz. of the applejack syrup, waiting for it to absorb and adding more as needed.
2. Assemble the cake:
   a. Place one cake layer on the cake circle.
   b. Spread with 2/3 c. Apple Filling and top with another cake layer.
   c. Repeat with the remaining cake layers, pressing gently but firmly on each layer to make a solid, cylindrical cake.
3. Wrap the cake in plastic film and allow it to mellow at cool room temperature for at least 2 hours and up to 48 hours.
4. Just before serving, sift confectioner's sugar onto the top surface of the cake.

holding: store under a cake dome at cool room temperature up to 2 days

CAKE LAYERS FOR APPLE STACK CAKE

yield: 7 (9") cake layers

production		costing only
as needed	baker's spray pan coating	% of container
22 oz.	flour	22 oz.
1 tsp.	fine salt	1/16 oz.
1/2 tsp.	ground ginger	1/16 oz.
1/2 tsp.	baking soda	1/16 oz.
2 tsp.	baking powder	1/8 oz.
8 oz.	room-temperature butter	8 oz.
8 oz.	sugar	8 oz.
1 c.	sorghum syrup	8 fl. oz.
3	room-temperature eggs	3 each or 6 oz.
2 tsp.	pure vanilla extract	1/3 fl. oz.
1 c.	buttermilk	8 fl. oz.

preparation:
1. Preheat an oven to 425°F.
2. Prepare the cake pans:
   a. Spray the inside of 7 (9") cake pans* with pan coating.
   b. Press a 9" circle of pan liner into the bottom of each pan.
   c. Spray again.
3. Mix the batter:
   a. Sift together the flour, salt, ginger, baking soda, and baking powder.
   b. Using the paddle attachment of a mixer, cream the butter and sugar on medium speed until light and fluffy.
   c. Beat in the sorghum syrup.
   d. Beat in the eggs, one at a time.
   e. Add the vanilla.
   f. On low speed, alternately pulse in the flour mixture and buttermilk to make a smooth batter. ⚠ Do not overmix.
4. Spread 1/7 of the batter into each pan. Tap each pan on the work surface to force out air pockets.
5. Bake about 10 minutes, or until springy to the touch and very lightly browned.
6. Cool the pans on racks 10 minutes.
7. Remove the layers from the pans and return them to the racks. Cool to room temperature.

*If 7 cake pans are not available bake in batches, holding remaining batter in a cool place. Wash and prepare pans before proceeding.

holding: store each layer individually wrapped in plastic film at cool room temperature 24 hours; may be frozen up to 1 month

APPLE FILLING FOR APPLE STACK CAKE

yield: 4 c. filling plus 1 c. syrup

production		costing only
1 lb.	coarse-chopped dried apples	1 lb.
pinch	fine salt	1/16 oz.
1 c.	brown sugar	5 1/2 oz.
as needed	water	n/c
4 tsp.	ground cinnamon	1/4 oz.
1 tsp.	ground cloves	1/16 oz.
1 tsp.	ground allspice	1/16 oz.
4 Tbsp.	butter	2 oz.

preparation:
1. Cook the apples:
   a. Place the apples in a 4-qt. nonreactive saucepan and add the salt, sugar, and enough water to cover by 1/2".
   b. Bring to the simmer, partially cover, and cook until softened, 15 to 30 minutes depending on the texture of the apples.
   c. Ladle off 1 c. of the resulting apple syrup and reserve it for cake assembly.
2. Purée the apples:
   a. Cool the apples until they can be safely handled.
   b. Purée the apples with an immersion blender. Alternatively, purée them in a food processor and then return them to the pan.
3. Reduce the purée:
   a. Add the cinnamon, cloves, allspice, and butter to the apple purée.
   b. Simmer briskly over medium heat, stirring frequently, until the mixture thickens enough to hold its shape on a spoon.
4. Open-pan cool to room temperature and then refrigerate until cold.

holding: refrigerate in a freshly sanitized, covered container up to 5 days

Black Walnut Poundcake

with Persimmon Sauce

yield: 1 dessert serving
(multiply × 4 for classroom turnout)

MASTER RECIPE

production		costing only
2	1/2" slices Black Walnut Poundcake	1/8 recipe
1/2 c.	Persimmon Sauce	1/4 recipe
1/4 c.	Sweetened Whipped Cream, in a pastry bag fitted with a star tip	1/4 recipe
1 sprig	fresh mint	1/20 bunch a.p.

service turnout:

1. Plate the dessert:
   a. Diagonally overlap the Black Walnut Poundcake slices slightly left of center on a cool 10" plate.
   b. Pool the Persimmon Sauce on the right front of the plate.
   c. Pipe a rosette of Sweetened Whipped Cream at 2 o'clock.
   d. Stick the mint sprig upright between the cake and the rosette.

COMPONENT RECIPE

BLACK WALNUT POUNDCAKE

yield: 1 (4" × 8" loaf)

production		costing only
as needed	baker's pan coating spray	% of container
8 oz.	room-temperature butter	8 oz.
8 oz.	sugar	8 oz.
1 tsp.	pure vanilla extract	1/6 fl. oz.
1 Tbsp.	sour mash whiskey, such as Jack Daniels	1/2 fl. oz.
1/2 tsp.	fine salt	1/16 oz.
4	room-temperature eggs	4 each or 8 oz.
7 1/2 oz.	flour	7 1/2 oz.
1/2 c.	fine-chopped black walnuts	2 oz.

preparation:

1. Preheat an oven to 350°F.
2. Prepare the pan:
   a. Cut a 7" × 15" rectangle of pan liner.
   b. Spray the inside of a 4" × 8" loaf pan with pan coating.
   c. Press the pan liner crosswise into the pan, creasing so the edges hang over the long sides.
   d. Spray the parchment.
3. Mix the batter:
   a. Using the paddle attachment of a mixer, cream the butter, sugar, vanilla, whiskey, and salt on high speed about 3 minutes, until very light and fluffy.
   b. On medium speed, beat in the eggs, one at a time. Continue to beat 2 minutes longer, until the mixture has expanded in volume and is very light.
   c. On low speed, pulse in the flour and the black walnuts. ⚠ Don't overmix.
4. Scrape the batter into the prepared pan. Gently tap the pan on the work surface to force out air pockets.
5. Place in the middle of the oven and bake about 40 minutes, until the cake is lightly browned on top and only a few small, moist crumbs cling to a cake tester.
6. Cool in the pan on a rack 15 minutes.
7. Turn the cake out of the pan onto the rack and cool to room temperature.

holding: wrap in plastic film and store at cool room temperature up to 2 days; freeze up to 1 month

COMPONENT RECIPE

PERSIMMON SAUCE

yield: approx. 2 c.

production		costing only
1/2 c.	sugar	4 oz.
1/2 c.	water	n/c
12	very ripe American persimmons	1 lb.
—or—		
6	very ripe Japanese persimmons	1 lb.
—or—		
1 1/2 c.	canned, sweetened American persimmon pulp	12 fl. oz.
1 Tbsp.	peach schnapps	1/2 fl. oz.
as needed	fresh lemon juice	1/4 [90 ct.] lemon

preparation:
1. Prepare the syrup:
   a. Place the sugar and water in a 1-qt. saucepan.
   b. Bring to the boil and simmer until the sugar is dissolved. Cool.
2. If using fresh persimmons, prepare the purée:
   a. Cut open the persimmons and scoop out the flesh.
   b. Pass the flesh through a food mill to remove seeds. (The persimmons should yield approximately 2 c. purée.)
   c. Taste the purée and evaluate its sweetness.
3. Whisk enough sugar syrup into the persimmon purée to sweeten it and thin it into a sauce having a light nappé consistency. If the canned purée is very sweet, use water in place of some of the syrup.
4. Add the schnapps and adjust the flavor balance with lemon juice.

holding: refrigerate in a freshly sanitized, covered container up to 3 days; freeze up to 1 month

RECIPE VARIATION

Walnut Poundcake with Peach Sauce
Replace the black walnuts with walnuts. Replace the persimmon purée with peach purée.

Peach-Filled Half-Moon Fried Pie
with Burnt Sugar Ice Cream

yield: 1 dessert serving
(multiply × 4 for classroom turnout)

MASTER RECIPE

production		costing only
1	Peach-Filled Half-Moon Fried Pie	1/4 recipe
1	4-oz. scoop Burnt Sugar Ice Cream	1/8 recipe
1 tsp.	confectioner's sugar, in shaker	1/16 oz.
1 sprig	fresh mint	1/20 bunch

service turnout:
1. Place the Peach-Filled Half-Moon Fried Pie on a sizzle plate and heat in a 400°F oven about 5 minutes, until warm.
2. Plate the dessert:
   a. Place the pie toward the front of a cold 10" plate.
   b. Place the scoop of Burnt Sugar Ice Cream behind the pie.
   c. Shake a diagonal stripe of confectioner's sugar across the pie.
   d. Place the mint sprig between the pie and the ice cream.

COMPONENT RECIPE
PEACH-FILLED HALF-MOON FRIED PIES

yield: 4 pies

production		costing only
1 1/4 lb.	American Flaky Pastry Dough, lard reduced by 2 Tbsp.	1 recipe
1 1/3 c.	Dried Peach Filling	1 recipe
1 Tbsp.	egg wash	1/3 egg
2 c.	corn oil	16 fl. oz.*
1/4 c.	pork lard	2 oz.*

preparation:
1. Make up the pies:
   a. Divide the American Flaky Pastry Dough into 4 equal-size discs.
   b. Roll a disc out into an approximately 4" × 5" oval, with the dough slightly less than 1/8" thick.
   c. Place 1/3 c. Dried Peach Filling in the center of the dough.
   d. Brush the edges with a little egg wash and fold into a half-moon shape.
   e. Cut the rounded edge of the dough into an even semicircle.
   f. Crimp the edges with a fork.
   g. Repeat to make a total of 4 pies.
   h. Place the pies on a half-sheet tray with pan liner and refrigerate at least 20 minutes.
2. Fry the pies:
   a. Heat a heavy 10" sauté pan and add the corn oil and lard. Heat to 350°F.
   b. Add two pies to the oil and fry them about 2 minutes on each side, until golden brown.
   c. Drain on a rack and then blot with paper towels.
   d. Fry and drain the remaining two pies.
   e. Cool the pies to room temperature on the rack.

*The oil and lard may be re-used to fry 8 to 10 pies. Calculate cost accordingly.

holding: best served the same day; hold covered with a kitchen towel at room temperature up to 12 hours; may be refrigerated in a sealed container with pan liner between layers up to 2 days

COMPONENT RECIPE
DRIED PEACH FILLING

yield: 1 1/3 c.

production		costing only
12 oz.	chopped dried peaches	12 oz.
as needed	water	n/c
1/4 to 1/2 c.	sugar	2 to 4 oz.
1/2 tsp.	ground cinnamon	1/20 oz.
1/4 tsp.	ground nutmeg	1/20 oz.
1 Tbsp.	butter	1/2 oz.
as needed	fresh lemon juice	1/4 [90 ct.] lemon

preparation:
1. Place the peaches in a small nonreactive saucepan and add enough water just to cover them. Bring the water to the simmer and cook until the peaches are very soft, 15 to 30 minutes depending on their texture.
2. Purée the peaches with an immersion blender. Alternatively, purée in a food processor and return to the pan.
3. Add 1/4 c. sugar and the cinnamon, nutmeg, and butter. Bring to the simmer, taste for sweetness, and add more sugar if necessary (remember that the mixture will concentrate through reduction). Simmer briskly over medium heat, stirring frequently, until the mixture thickens into a purée that will hold its shape on a spoon.
4. Balance the flavor with lemon juice.
5. Open-pan cool to room temperature and then refrigerate until cold.

holding: refrigerate in a freshly sanitized, covered container up to 7 days

COMPONENT RECIPE
BURNT SUGAR ICE CREAM

yield: approx. 1 qt.

production		costing only
1 c.	sugar	8 oz.
1/4 c.	cold water	n/c
1 qt.	Vanilla Ice Cream unfrozen base	1 recipe
pinch	fine salt	1/16 oz.

preparation:
1. Prepare the caramel syrup:
   a. Have ready an ice-water bath and a small pan of simmering water.
   b. Combine the sugar and water in a small, heavy saucepan.
   c. Place the pan over medium heat and allow the sugar to melt. Tilt and swirl the pan to facilitate melting, but do not stir.
   d. Continue cooking the syrup until it caramelizes to a deep, rich brown. ⚠ Do not allow the syrup to burn. Use care, as the syrup is dangerously hot.
   e. Immediately remove the pan from the heat and stop the cooking by placing the pan in the ice-water bath for a few seconds only.
   f. Add a little simmering water to the caramel to loosen its consistency.
   g. Return the pan to the heat and simmer until reduced to a pourable syrup.
   h. Cool to room temperature.
2. Whisk the caramel syrup into the Vanilla Ice Cream base and add the salt.
3. Freeze according to the instructions of the ice cream machine manufacturer.
4. Transfer the ice cream to a freshly sanitized, chilled container and place plastic film directly on the surface. Place the lid on the container.
5. Firm the ice cream in the freezer at least 1 hour.

holding: store frozen up to 2 days

RECIPE VARIATIONS

Apple-Filled Half-Moon Fried Pies with Vanilla Ice Cream
Replace the dried peaches with dried apples and serve with vanilla ice cream.

Blackberry-Filled Half-Moon Fried Pies with Vanilla Ice Cream
Replace the Dried Peach Filling with seedless blackberry preserves and serve with vanilla ice cream.

DESSERTS

INGREDIENTS OF THE APPALACHIAN SOUTH

With a few notable exceptions, the Appalachian South pantry is stocked with the same ingredients as is the pantry of the Plantation South. Products noteworthy for their absence are rice in all its forms, cane syrup, sesame seeds, and smoked turkey seasoning meat. Following is a list of additional Appalachian ingredients.

TABLE 8.2 APPALACHIAN SOUTH REGIONAL INGREDIENTS

ITEM	MARKET FORMS	USES	SEASONALITY	OTHER	STORAGE
RAMPS	Fresh ramps are available in season from specialty purveyors. In the region they may be purchased from local foragers.	Ramps are used as a pungent aromatic vegetable added to potato dishes, egg dishes, and hamburger meat.	Late spring	Ramps should be trimmed, washed, parboiled, and refreshed before using.	Once parboiled, they may be frozen up to 3 months.
APPLE BUTTER	Quality, home-style apple butter is sold in jars of varying sizes by Appalachian artisan producers, many of Amish or Mennonite heritage.	Apple butter is used as a spread for toast and biscuits. It may be used as a filling for apple stack cake. Mountain people enjoy it as a topping for ice cream and cottage cheese.	N/A	Foodservice operations can make apple butter in a steam jacketed kettle.	Refrigerate after opening.
BLACK WALNUTS	Black walnuts are sold by the pound by nut dealers and specialty purveyors. Check for freshness upon arrival. In the region they are sold at farmers' markets.	Black walnuts can replace standard English walnuts in baked goods and candies for a distinctive regional flavor.	Freshest in fall.	Notoriously hard to crack, the shells of black walnuts produce a dark-brown stain that, despite repeated washing, stays on the hands for days.	Store frozen.
BUCKWHEAT FLOUR	For authentic Appalachian taste and texture use buckwheat flour produced in regional roller mills and sold by mail order in 2-lb. packages or in bulk.	Buckwheat flour is primarily used to make pancakes.	Fall	Buckwheat contains gluten-forming proteins and, thus, batters and doughs made from it can rise.	Store frozen.
DRIED FRUIT	Commercial dried fruit is available by the pound in both supermarkets and from nut/candy purveyors. Most has been treated with sulfur dioxide to prevent discoloration. Dried fruits marketed as "natural" must be free from sulfur products.	Elsewhere used primarily as a snack food, dried fruit is featured in Appalachian desserts and savory stuffings.	N/A	Though supermarkets stock snack-sized pieces, wholesalers can supply diced and chopped product that is more economical when making dried fruit purées.	Store tightly sealed at cool room temperature.
FRESH SAUERKRAUT	See p. 184.				
FARM-RAISED GAME	USDA inspected frozen game meats and fowl are sold by the pound or piece by specialty purveyors.	Game is featured in Appalachian appetizers and entrées.	Although now available year round, game is traditionally seasonal to fall and winter.	Farmed game is less flavorful than wild, but more consistent in size, flavor, texture, and availability.	Store frozen until needed. Thaw in the refrigerator.

chapter nine

The Central Farmlands and Cities

extreme northwestern Pennsylvania, Ohio, Michigan, Indiana, Wisconsin, Illinois, Minnesota, Iowa, Missouri, Arkansas, North Dakota, South Dakota, Nebraska, Kansas, Oklahoma, eastern Montana, eastern Wyoming, northeastern Colorado

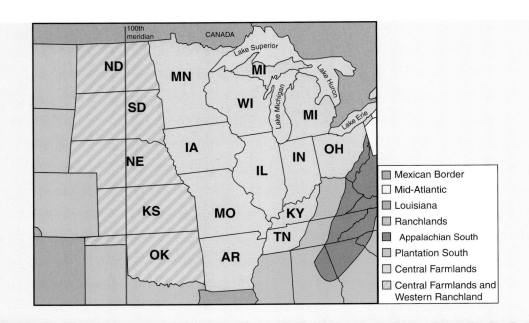

IN THE CENTER OF AMERICA lies a geographical region commonly known as the Midwest. Throughout the 1800s this vast expanse of flat, fertile land attracted generations of American pioneers. Those who settled the eastern half were primarily farmers. Those settling the western plateau became cattle ranchers. Because these two first-settler groups had access to different ingredients and led vastly different lives, their cooking styles were—and are—quite different from each other. Thus, the Midwest is home to two very different cuisine styles.

In the early days of settlement it was easy to divide the Midwest into two separate culinary regions, with farm cuisine in the east and ranch cuisine in the west. However, by the late 1800s technological advances made farming possible on the western plateau, and demand for beef brought ranching farther east. Thus, in parts of the American Midwest farming and farm cuisine exist side by side with ranching and ranch cuisine.

In Chapter 10 you'll learn about Western Ranchlands cuisine. In this chapter we focus on the cooking of Midwestern farmers, a style we call Central Farmlands cuisine. In addition, you'll explore the cooking of major Midwestern cities built to process and pack the region's agricultural products. Finally, on this book's companion website you'll discover the cooking of the Midwest's primary immigrant groups represented by the German-American, Polish-American, and Scandinavian-American microcuisines.

AFTER STUDYING THIS CHAPTER YOU SHOULD BE ABLE TO:

- describe the climate and topography of the Midwest's three subregions (Factor 1) and explain their impact on agriculture and cuisine (Factor 5)
- explain the lack of Native American influence on Farmlands cuisine (Factor 2) and discuss the one Farmlands Native American ingredient featured in the American pantry
- discuss the food culture of the Farmlands region's two main first-settler groups (Factor 3) and the agricultural products that formed the foundation of Farmlands cuisine
- explain the impact of late-19th-century immigration on the cuisine of the Farmlands cities (Factor 4) and discuss the cuisine styles that resulted from it
- list the Farmlands region's primary food products, favored seasonings, and predominant cooking methods
- prepare authentic Farmlands dishes
- discuss the German-American microcuisine (Factor 4) and prepare authentic German-American dishes
- discuss the Scandinavian-American microcuisine (Factor 4) and prepare authentic Scandinavian-American dishes
- discuss the Polish-American microcuisine (Factor 4) and prepare authentic Polish-American dishes

APPETIZERS

Scandinavian Beet Soup with Knäckebrød

Beef Barley Soup with Farmhouse White Bread and Butter

Wisconsin Cheddar Broccoli Rarebit

Gravlax with Dilled Mustard Sauce and Toast Points

Wild Mushroom Ragout in Herbed Tartelette Shell

Triple Onion Potato Pierogies

Red, White, and Maytag Blue Salad with Pickled Beets and Egg

Heartland Relish Tray for Two

ENTRÉES

Ten Thousand Lakes Fish Stew with Root Vegetables and Pike Dumplings

Escalopes of Goose with Dried Cherry Demi-Glace and Ojibwa Goose Ragout in Baby Pumpkin, with Braised Kale and Wild Rice

Deep-Dish Flaky Pastry Chicken Pie

Breaded Pork Chops with Stewed Tomatoes and Baked Macaroni 'n' Cheese

Minnesota Fruit-Stuffed Pork Loin with Jansson's Temptation and Watercress

Grilled Veal Sausages with Hot German Potato Salad and Red Cabbage Slaw

Cincinnati Five-Way Chili with a Frank

Classic Meat Loaf with Mashed Potatoes, Mushroom Gravy, and Heartland Vegetable Medley

All-American Beef Stew

Chicago Steakhouse Sirloin Strip with Cottage Fries and Creamed Spinach

DESSERTS

Lattice-Top Cherry Pie with Buttermilk Ice Cream

Devil's Food Cake with Vanilla Custard Ice Cream

Angel Food Cake with Tipsy Fruit Compote

Carrot Cake with Cream Cheese Frosting

Pineapple Upside-Down Cake

Butterscotch Pudding with Whipped Cream and Wafer Cookie

Wells Kringle with Lingonberry Sauce

Apple Brown Betty with Hard Sauce

WEBSITE EXTRAS

Breakfasts   Sandwiches   Hors d'Oeuvres   Thanksgiving Menu

A FLAT AND FERTILE LAND

More than sixty million years ago, the center of the North American continent was a vast inland sea. However, the lifting effect that occurred when the Appalachian and Rocky Mountains rose eventually drained this sea and blocked the entrance of new waters. The mountains' rise created a wide, level plain extending from the older, lower Appalachians in the east to the lofty Rockies in the west, and bounded on the north by the higher Canadian central plateau.

Because it was once under seawater, this central plain already had been covered with sediment consisting of pulverized minerals and organic matter created by marine plants and animals. After the Appalachians and Rockies rose, additional minerals and organic matter flowed with mountain runoff down the slopes and into the plain. During successive ice ages, glaciers expanded south into the plain and then retreated, scraping up loose rock, soil, and organic matter from northern areas and churning it into a rich, loamy type of soil called *loess* (LOHS). Pushed south by the glaciers and then blown farther south and east by prevailing winds, glacial loess eventually blanketed North America's central plain with nutrient-laden soil. The result is a region blessed with some of the world's best soil that, in some places, is 20 feet deep.

A Network of Lakes and Rivers

As rainwater and glacial melt flowed downhill, it carved out channels in the deep, soft soil. The resulting network of rivers eventually converged along a north-south corridor to form America's preeminent river, the Mississippi, which drains the Midwest into the Gulf of Mexico (Figure 9.1).

FIGURE 9.1
Mississippi River System

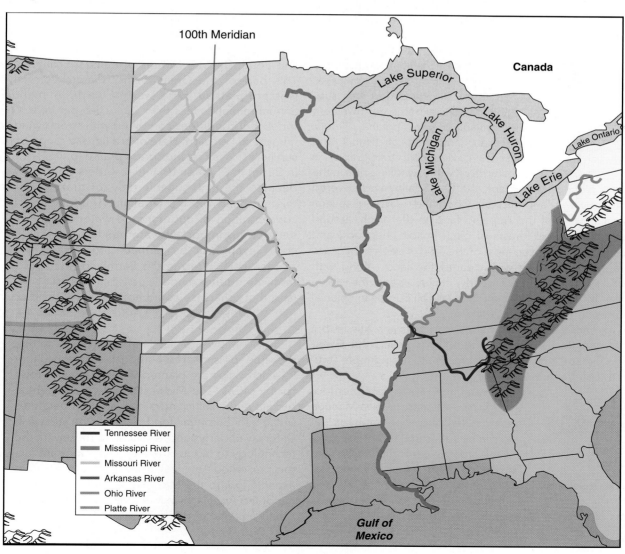

▬▬	Tennessee River
▬▬	Mississippi River
▬▬	Missouri River
▬▬	Arkansas River
▬▬	Ohio River
▬▬	Platte River

West of the central Appalachians, a cluster of five massive glacial gouges filled with water to become the Great Lakes. As a group, these lakes contain one-fifth of the world's fresh surface water. The Great Lakes served as links in the St. Lawrence Seaway water route, enabling explorers to travel from Nova Scotia's Atlantic coast to the Midwest primarily by water (Figure 9.2). In addition, Great Lakes fish were an important source of food.

The Midwest's network of lakes and rivers provided reliable water transportation for pioneers heading west. Once farms and ranches were established, these waterways were key to transporting goods to market in the days before railroads. Human-made canals completed the system. Boats on the Ohio River and Great Lakes carried goods east; the Mississippi brought them south to the Port of New Orleans. Thus, the region's waterways were largely responsible for its early economic viability.

Flatlands, Plains, and Plateau

The Midwest comprises three subregions: the trans-Appalachian flatlands, the central plains, and the western plateau (Figure 9.3). Although all three have relatively flat topography, each has its own unique climate.

FACTOR 1   FACTOR 5
The trans-Appalachian flatlands are ideal for diversified agriculture and dairy production.

The **trans-Appalachian flatlands** are bounded on the south by the Ohio River Valley and in the north by Lakes Erie, Huron, and Superior. This subregion includes extreme northwestern Pennsylvania, Ohio, Indiana, Illinois, Michigan, and half of Illinois and Wisconsin. Here the topography is mostly level, with low rolling hills in the east. Before pioneer settlement, the Ohio Valley was covered with deciduous oak and hickory woodland reaching several hundred miles west of the Appalachians. In the north, around the Great Lakes, stood forests of birch, maple, hemlock, and white pine. Today, however, most of this land is treeless because of generations of farmers who cleared the land. Along with fertile soil, the area's ample yearly rainfall made the trans-Appalachian flatlands hospitable to virtually all European colonial domesticates and ideal for dairy farming.

The immense area of land stretching from the Mississippi corridor to the Rocky Mountain foothills is called the **Great Plains.** The Great Plains is divided by climate, being more temperate in the east and more arid in the west.

FACTOR 1   FACTOR 5
The central plains are ideal for large-scale grain cultivation.

From the Mississippi corridor through the Minnesota-Iowa-Missouri tier of states, the topography is flat and the climate semitemperate. We'll call this area the **central plains,** a vast, largely treeless tract of land extending northward well into Canada and southward into northern Louisiana and Texas. This once was America's **tallgrass prairie,** a land carpeted with waist-high vegetation as far as the eye could see. Tallgrass prairie includes switchgrass, Indian grass, and bluestems, plants that can survive on moderate amounts of rainfall and endure powerful winds and subzero temperatures. Until the arrival of pioneer farmers and their plows, the thick tallgrass roots held the region's loose soil in place. Tallgrass sustained tens of millions of bison, hardy animals that were the primary protein food for the region's Native American population. Manure deposited by bison herds and ash from occasional grassfires fertilized the soil, keeping the land in a delicate environmental balance. As in the trans-Appalachian flatlands, however, the effects of nearly 200 years of farming have greatly changed the face of the land. Today only scattered pockets of tallgrass prairie survive. Instead of grasslands, today the central plains are covered with corn, soybeans, and wheat.

Moving yet farther west, the land slopes gradually upward for hundreds of miles until it meets the foothills of the Rocky Mountains. As altitude increases, annual rainfall decreases because the Rockies cast a massive rain shadow (p. 304). Moisture-laden clouds moving east from the Pacific are blocked by the tall mountains, leaving the land on the inland side dry. The effect of the Rocky Mountain rain shadow becomes apparent as you approach the **100th longitudinal meridian,** a north-south geographical line bisecting North and South Dakota, Nebraska, Kansas, Oklahoma, and Texas. This part of the Great Plains is more correctly called the **western plateau.** Here, west of the 100th meridian, average annual rainfall is less than 20 inches per year. Over the centuries, dry conditions combined with strong winds caused significant soil erosion. Here only a limited range of plant life can survive. This is the *shortgrass prairie* (p. 461), a topic covered in depth in Chapter 10. Initial settlers on the western plateau deemed the land suitable only for grazing. However, under this arid land lies the **Ogallala Aquifer,** the nation's largest concentration of underground water (Figure 9.4). The presence of this important water resource explains why the land could eventually be farmed and, thus, why the western plateau is included in the Farmlands culinary region. Water from the aquifer made it possible to grow certain crops in a land that otherwise could not sustain agriculture. More information about the Ogallala Aquifer can be found on this book's companion website.

The Midwest's flat land with deep, fertile, rock-free soil is ideal for European-style agriculture in which crops are planted in long, straight rows cut by plows. The Midwest's eastern and central sectors enjoy sufficient rainfall and temperatures suitable for European food plants. In the arid west, water lay underground, available to those with the technology to tap it. However, two important factors prevented America's East Coast colonists from expanding into the Midwest: the forbidding barrier of the Appalachian Mountains, and the Native Americans who populated the land (Figure 9.5).

FACTOR 1
Before well-drilling technology, the arid western plateau was suited only for grazing.

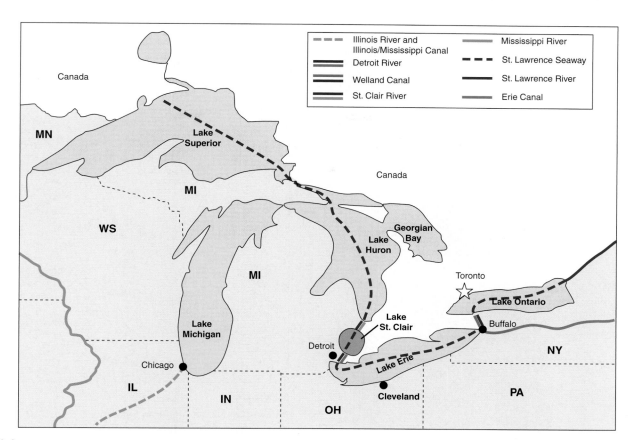

FIGURE 9.2
Great Lakes Waterways

FIGURE 9.3
Midwest Climatic Subregions

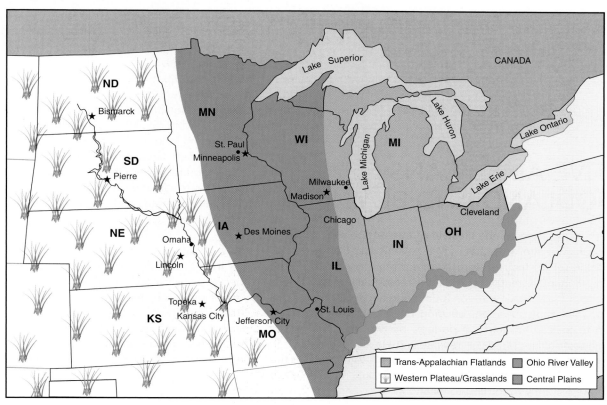

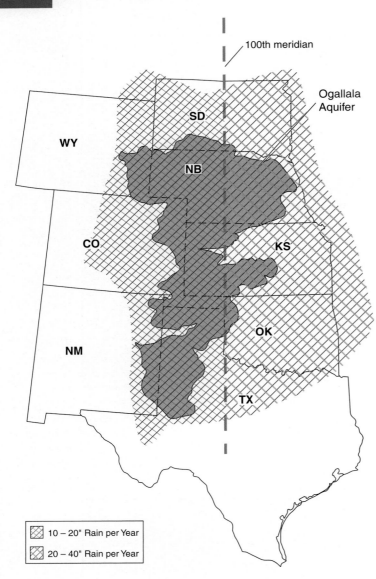

FIGURE 9.4
The Ogallala Aquifer

Legend:
- 10 – 20" Rain per Year
- 20 – 40" Rain per Year

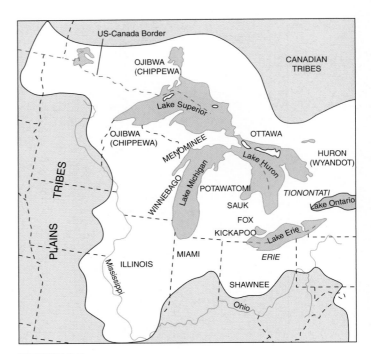

FIGURE 9.5
Midwestern Native American Settlement, circa 1750
(Before Displacement of East Coast Tribes)

◼ NATIVE AMERICANS OF
◻ WOODLAND AND PLAIN
◼

Before the arrival of pioneers, the lifestyle of trans-Appalachian Native Americans was similar to that of Mid-Atlantic and Plantation South natives. Like their eastern counterparts, they maintained semipermanent farming villages on the region's rivers and lakes and practiced seasonal migration for hunting and foraging. All relied on water transportation, building birch bark canoes light enough to be carried across a portage by two men, yet sturdy enough to ride river rapids or traverse large lakes. The region's waterways facilitated an efficient trade system. Although food products were important trade items, individual tribes' foodways differed slightly according to location.

The trans-Appalachian was home to Algonquian language groups such as the Shawnee, Kickapoo, Fox, Sauk, and Miami. These tribes spent the agricultural season in large river valley settlements, some as populous as modern towns. In spring and summer women raised Three Sisters crops while men fished and hunted small game. In fall and winter, settlements broke up into smaller groups and traveled onto the prairie to hunt bison and other large game.

The original Great Lakes tribes, among them Ottawas, Potawatomies, Ojibwas, Chippewas, Winnebagos, and Menominees, were of Algonquian and Siouxan language groups. These northern tribes lived in smaller villages; although they engaged in farming, hunting and gathering were far more important sources of sustenance. Great Lakes tribes traveled north to their winter hunting grounds, where they primarily sought beaver and moose. In their seasonal food cycle, the final event before heading north was the important wild rice harvest.

Wild Rice

Wild rice is the seed of an aquatic grass indigenous to the Great Lakes region. Although called "rice," it is not related to the many rice cultivars native to Asia. The wild rice plant grows in mud beneath shallow lake water. At maturity, stalks of wild rice can reach 6 feet, each stalk topped with a tassel of small seedpods. In late summer, when the seedpods are ripe and swollen, the wild rice is ready for harvest.

FACTOR 2
Wild rice is the primary Native American contribution to Central Farmlands cuisine.

The traditional Native American method of harvesting wild rice involves teams of two or three harvesters riding in a canoe. As the teams glide through thick stands of wild rice, the person in back poles the canoe while those in front bend the stalks over the side of the canoe and beat the tops with wooden flails. About half of the seedpods fall into the bottom of the canoe, and the rest fly into the lake when the stalks are released. This hand-harvesting method ensures reseeding of the lake bed so the crop grows again next season (Figure 9.6).

After harvesting, the seedpods are processed. Returning to the village with laden canoes, harvesters spread the seedpods on mats placed in the sun. Once thoroughly dry, the seedpods are hulled by treading on them or beating them to loosen the outer husk. The seedpods are then winnowed by tossing them in the air on a windy day to blow away the husks, leaving only the long, slender, brown grains. Only after these laborious procedures is the wild rice ready to cook.

The quality of a wild rice crop is judged by both flavor and length of grain; longer grains are considered texturally superior. Most wild rice is boiled in water until the individual grains swell and burst, revealing the gray-beige interior. Unlike most other grains, wild rice may be cooked to different degrees of doneness, ranging from intact and quite chewy to almost completely burst and more tender. Boiled wild rice has a unique nutty-earthy flavor much prized by Great Lakes tribes and by connoisseurs today. Although it is not widely known, wild rice can also be popped in oil in the same manner as popcorn (Figure 9.7).

Wild rice was harvested and processed by only a few Great Lakes tribes, for whom it was a valuable trade good and a staple food. For these tribes, wild rice also had religious significance similar to that of corn. However, all trans-Appalachian and central plains tribes enjoyed wild rice, as did early pioneer settlers. Through the 1800s, pioneer farmers frequently called wild rice "pocket money" because it was a valuable trade commodity.

Through the mid-20th century, wild rice was considered a luxury food because it was rare and, therefore, expensive. By the

FIGURE 9.7

(a) Uncooked wild rice grains, (b) Boiled wild rice, (c) Popped wild rice. Photo by David Haynes

1950s a combination of pollution, uncontrolled flooding, and competing aquatic plants had significantly reduced America's harvest of natural wild rice, making it even more costly. At that time entrepreneur farmers began experimenting with cultivated wild rice, discussed at more length on this book's companion website. Today most commercially available wild rice is cultivated. However, connoisseurs seek out the small amount of traditionally produced Native American harvested wild rice available from tribal stores or online. This high-quality product is both better in flavor and texture and more environmentally sound because of its low carbon footprint and its sustainability. Purchasing Native American–harvested wild rice also contributes much-needed revenue to tribal economies.

Indigenous Fish and Game

Native Americans of the trans-Appalachian flatlands and central plains were expert fishermen. Great Lakes tribes harvested lake fish, such as yellow perch, muskellunge, and walleye, with nets. Large lake fish frequently were cooked by the planking method (p. 608), in which sides of fish are affixed to slabs of wood and placed near a wood fire. This Native American cooking method, prominent in modern Pacific Northwest cooking, is discussed in greater detail in Chapter 13. Central plains natives fished the Mississippi and the region's rivers and smaller lakes for freshwater trout, sunfish, freshwater bass, and crappies as well as freshwater crayfish and mussels. Through the 1800s, the region's freshwater fish were an important protein food for both Native Americans and pioneer farmers.

When the trans-Appalachian flatlands were still wooded, the area abounded with small and large game. Along with deer, bears, and northern moose, grasslands bison were known to enter the woodlands from time to time. The region's Native Americans enjoyed small game fresh, whereas the yield of a communal bison or moose hunt was typically dried or smoked.

FACTOR 1

In the 1800s, freshwater fish were an important protein food.

FIGURE 9.6

The centuries-old Native American method of harvesting wild rice ensures the sustainability of the crop. Courtesy Minnesota Department of Natural Resources

■ EUROPEAN
□ INFLUENCE

European explorers entered the trans-Appalachian region as early as the mid-1600s. The French followed the St. Lawrence Seaway into the northern interior and then paddled the length of the Mississippi. Soon French *voyageurs* (voy-ah-ZHUR), or entrepreneur explorers, roamed the trans-Appalachian woodland in search of furs. Black-robed French friars established Catholic missions that functioned primarily as trading posts. In response, the region's Native Americans turned from hunting for food to hunting for fur. Native-caught pelts were exchanged for trade goods such as metal knives and cooking vessels. Although these items expanded native culinary technology, because of transportation problems European food goods were not prevalent. However, trade for guns and alcoholic beverages set the stage for future difficulties. Early French presence in the Midwest was largely male and trade oriented—and thus not conducive to the development of cuisine. Although the French left behind many place names, they made no significant culinary contribution.

After the French and Indian War, the 1763 Treaty of Paris ceded the trans-Appalachian area to England. Acquisition of new land ordinarily would have sparked colonial expansion even though mountains and armed Native Americans stood in the way. However, Britain would soon have its hands full on another front with the beginning of the Revolutionary War.

■ AMERICA PUSHES
□ WEST

In 1783, citizens of the newly formed United States of America began looking west to the trans-Appalachian flatlands. Determined to make these lands safe for settlement, the young American government sent troops into the Ohio Valley to remove the area's native population. Upon their success, thousands of pioneer families crossed the Appalachians in wagon trains and began to create farms out of wilderness.

America's trans-Appalachian pioneer settlers had little contact with the region's remaining Native Americans and, in any case, would have had little to learn from them. Almost all of the region's indigenous foods, such as corn, beans, squashes, foraged plants, and game animals, had already been in their culinary repertoire for generations. Thus, only indirect Native American influence appears in the region's cooking. Wild rice is virtually the only new Native American food to enter Central Farmlands cuisine.

In the years between the Revolutionary War and the beginning of the 20th century, a flood of humanity poured across the Appalachians. After the trans-Appalachian area became saturated, pioneers began looking farther west to the Mississippi corridor and beyond. The Homestead Act of 1862 turned over vast amounts of public land to private citizens. Pioneers began crossing the Mississippi and settling the central plains. Historians estimate that in the decades following the Homestead Act, the frontier moved west at a rate of 10 to 40 miles per year.

■ MIDWEST
□ AGRICULTURE

Within a hundred years the American Midwest evolved from virtually unexplored wilderness into one of the most productive and profitable agricultural areas in the world. Let's discover how this transformation occurred.

Pioneer Farmers

The Midwest welcomed two distinct groups of first-settler pioneer farmers: Americans from the East Coast and immigrants from Europe.

East Coast Americans

Americans from the East Coast were the first group of pioneers to settle the trans-Appalachian flatlands and central plains. Many were former New England farmers escaping a region where manufacturing now drove the economy and whose farms were too small to be profitable. Others were landless farm laborers and tenant farmers from the Mid-Atlantic. Among the Mid-Atlantic contingent were sons of large Pennsylvania Dutch families unable to find acreage in their traditional homeland areas. Many Amish and Mennonites settled in Indiana, Ohio, Illinois, and Iowa. Following in their wagon tracks were entrepreneurs of all types traveling west to service the new farming communities that sprang up virtually overnight.

Pioneers traveling to the Midwest used the same type of wagon transportation and carried the same provisions as Appalachian pioneers (p. 364). However, in the Midwest, pioneer cuisine was short-lived because Midwestern farms met with quick success, and Farmlands cooks soon abandoned their pioneer provisions. Although Midwestern farms produced thousands of tons of dried corn, by the end of the 19th century virtually all of it was either exported or used to finish cattle (p. 419). Traditional pioneer ingredients such as cornmeal, salt-preserved meats, and molasses rarely appear in modern Farmlands cuisine.

FACTOR 3
Pioneers from the East Coast brought New England and Mid-Atlantic cuisines to the Midwest.

Immigrants from Europe

Early settlers from Europe arrived after 1869 with the completion of the transcontinental railroad. Land-hungry immigrant farmers could literally get off the boat from Europe and board a train bound for the Midwest. Upon arriving at the rail stop nearest their allotted claim, pioneers unloaded their wagons, animals, tools, and personal possessions and set forth across the prairie to reach their homesteads.

German farmers were among the first immigrant pioneers, settling in Missouri, Nebraska, and Iowa. Hardy immigrants from Scandinavian countries gravitated north to establish dairy farms in Minnesota and other Great Lakes states. Scandinavians were also instrumental in lumbering, which eventually provided wood for building structures on the treeless prairie.

Arriving a little later, Eastern Europeans traveled even farther west, among the first farmers to venture across the 100th meridian.

Although the treeless prairie required no clearing, the tough sod required strenuous work with specialized implements in order to break it up for planting European crops. The region's ranchers looked upon these early farmers doing hard manual labor with disdain, derisively calling them "sod busters." Because of the prairie's lack of trees, there was no locally available wood for building barns and houses. In Kansas and Nebraska, Russian Mennonites and Czechs built semisubterranean houses and farm structures out of sod (Figure 9.8). Only later, when cash crops brought in money, could they build houses with lumber transported from the Great Lakes region by rail.

FACTOR 3

Early Eastern European immigrants advanced wheat cultivation in the central plains and on the western plateau.

The impact of pioneer settlement was dramatic. In less than 100 years after the American Revolution, the trans-Appalachian woodlands virtually vanished; almost the entire area became well-tended, profitable farmland. The settlement of the central plains was well underway. By the end of the 19th century, farming extended even farther west, across the 100th meridian into the western plateau. The American Midwest became the world's premier agricultural area.

History played a major role in the relocation of American agriculture to the Midwest. After the Civil War, virtually no export food was produced in the devastated Plantation South. Of the remaining eastern regions, only Pennsylvania could grow large volumes of grain crops. Other states began concentrating on specialty agriculture such as truck farming and dairy farming. America now looked to the Midwest for commodity crops to feed its growing population.

Let's take a brief look at Midwestern agriculture and discover how it differs from the farming practices of other regions.

Early Farming

For farm families throughout the Midwest, life was an unending cycle of work. In the early years, virtually every task was accomplished by physical labor of people or animals. Farmers and their sons worked from before dawn to after dark tending animals, breaking ground for new fields, sowing seeds, fighting weeds, digging wells and irrigation ditches, repairing broken machinery, and constructing fences and farm buildings. In late summer and fall, farm families faced the exhausting, time-sensitive work of harvesting crops. Even young children were expected to put in a full day's work (Figure 9.9).

Women and girls carried water, gathered firewood or dried manure fuel, and kept the house clean and the laundry done without benefit of modern conveniences. However, on a Midwestern farm, a woman's most important activities involved food. While the men typically focused on the cash crop—usually wheat or corn—and the hoofed animals, women were responsible for growing or raising virtually all other food. They tended vegetable gardens and orchards and raised chickens for eggs and meat. Produce harvested in season was preserved for winter by drying, curing, and canning (Figure 9.10). In addition, farm women were expected to cook three large meals per day, often for as many as twenty hungry family members and hired workers.

FIGURE 9.8

On the treeless prairie, pioneer settlers built semi-subterranean sod houses and barns. Courtesy USDA Forest Service

FIGURE 9.9

Women and children remove strings from beans before canning. Courtesy of the Library of Congress, lot 7475, v. 1, no. 0855

FIGURE 9.10
Canning fruits and vegetables was an essential task for farm women. Courtesy of the Library of Congress, LC=H25-2746

Through hard work and skill, early Midwestern farmers produced plenty of food for their families and the surrounding towns, as well as excess food to sell. However, the challenge was getting the food to market. The only available method of transporting goods was via a combination of wagon and water. Early water transportation was based on a north-south axis. To reach the American East Coast, Midwestern products first traveled by wagon to river docks, then by boat down the Mississippi system to the port of New Orleans, and finally by ship around the Florida peninsula and northward along the Atlantic coast. With the completion of the Erie and Ohio Canals by 1831, goods could travel east through the Great Lakes. However, this route was often closed during the winter months, when the lakes and canals were impassable because of ice and storms.

By the end of the Civil War, the Midwest had reached a modest level of economic viability and was poised for greater success. Only two final elements were needed for the Midwest to become an agricultural giant: labor to plant, tend, and harvest even more crops; and an efficient, reliable way to get crops to market. Both elements were put in place by the American Industrial Revolution.

Technology Revolutionizes Farming

In the 1860s, the American Industrial Revolution began introducing technology that created profound changes in American agriculture. One of the most important was mechanization. Think back to the pre–Civil War South, when labor to produce cash crops was provided by tens of thousands of slaves. After the 1860s, on Midwestern farms machinery took the place of slaves. One farm machine—even an early, primitive type—could replace many workers. American inventors mechanized agricultural production

with a variety of new tools and equipment. John Deere mounted a steel blade onto a wrought-iron moldboard, creating a plow that swiftly cut through the heaviest sod (Figure 9.11). Automatic planters and reapers were not far behind. Initially these new farm implements were drawn by horses. Later, steam engines powered farm machinery until the de-

FIGURE 9.11
John Deere's "singing" plow cut through heavy prairie sod. Courtesy of U.S. Department of Agriculture

velopment of the internal combustion engine made possible gasoline-powered tractors and other agricultural equipment. Grain cultivation evolved from hand planting and harvesting to operations fully mechanized from start to finish.

Horticultural technology greatly advanced agriculture, as well. On the western plateau, German and Russian immigrant farmers could grow wheat where others failed because of dry farming technology previously developed on the Eurasian steppes. They introduced drought- and disease-resistant Crimean wheat that became the foundation of American cultivars. New drilling technology enabled wells to reach deep into the Ogallala Aquifer, providing water for animals and crops.

As the tractor gradually replaced horses and mules, demand for hay and oats diminished, and the resulting extra land was used for cash crops. Because farmers had far less manure to nourish the land, industry developed chemical fertilizers. The same companies created pesticides to minimize crop loss and herbicides to control weeds. Rather than producing a variety of grains, vegetables, and food animals, most farmers began to specialize in a single cash crop, a system called **monoculture.** Through science and technology, farming became an industry and Midwestern farms became agribusinesses, enabling American farmers to produce more food far more cheaply than ever before. By 1850 the Midwest was ready to feed the world. The final challenge, then, was getting the food to market.

Started in 1848, the construction of the Galena and Chicago Railroad marked the beginning of a rail network that would open up the Midwest to an unprecedented economic boom (Figure 9.12). Chicago became the hub of the system and the region's largest and most important city. In addition to shortening travel time and lowering transportation costs, rail transport also changed the way grain was handled and sold (Figure 9.13). This substantially lowered the cost of wheat and made corn cheap enough to use as animal food— a crucial development for America's beef industry and for the Ranchlands culinary region, discussed in Chapter 10.

By the early 20th century, grain cultivation had moved to the central plains and western plateau, and trans-Appalachian farmers began specializing in large-scale dairy production. By 1800, Wisconsin had surpassed New York State in cheese production.

FACTOR 5
Agriculture technology combined with rail transport finalized economic viability.

FIGURE 9.12
Midwest Rail Network with Chicago as the Hub

FIGURE 9.13
Railroad container cars revolutionized the way grain was shipped and sold.
Mike Bossman © Shutterstock

Let's take a closer look at the Central Farmlands culinary region's two most important food products.

Midwestern Grain

In the late 1800s the Midwest became America's breadbasket, growing vast amounts of wheat for various uses. Wheat is the raw material from which flour is milled. Different types of flour are used to make breads, baked goods, pasta, and cereals; as a thickener; and in many processed foods. More information on Midwestern wheat cultivation is presented on this book's companion website.

Corn became the second most important grain after wheat. During this time, corn became an important animal feed, a practice discussed in Chapter 10. Plentiful and inexpensive to produce, corn is now used to fatten cattle, hogs, and chickens for the table. In the early 20th century, food scientists developed a process for extracting cooking oil from corn and for producing cornstarch, a valuable culinary thickener with additional industrial uses. In the mid-20th century, the food industry began converting cornstarch into corn syrup, creating a variety of low-cost sweeteners. Today new technology is converting corn into *biofuels*, organically based combustible substances used for both heating and automotive use. Although today few people eat cornmeal dishes on a daily basis, Americans are consuming more corn than ever—but in the form of "hidden" corn found in soft drinks, cereals, breads, snack foods, and almost all processed foods.

In the 20th century, soybeans completed the Midwestern commodity crop trinity. Although soybeans are indigenous to Asia, today the United States leads the world in soybean cultivation. Although one variety of soybeans, known as *edamame*, is enjoyed as a vegetable, very little of the American soybean crop is directly consumed by humans. Most soybeans are processed into soybean oil, used for cooking and as a salad oil. The solid residue that remains after processing is used as a high-protein animal feed. Soy protein is also used in processed foods and meat replacement items and to make soy milk.

Dairy and Cheese

Wisconsin and the surrounding Great Lakes states produce a wide variety of cheeses ranging from fine, handcrafted products made by small artisan dairies to mass-produced process cheese food. Farmlands cheese makers traditionally produce cheeses in the style of established European types. These are referred to as **copycat cheeses,** American-made products bearing the same name as, and having characteristics similar to, European cheeses. Most prominent among copycat cheeses is Cheddar, accounting for more than half of Wisconsin's production. Wisconsin artisan Cheddar is produced by traditional methods and coated in colored wax (see p. 457).

Cheese curds, a fresh form of Cheddar, are unique to the Central Farmlands region. In the cheddaring process, curdled milk is packed into forms, salted, and pressed in a special way. Normally the formed curd is then aged for 6 months to several years to become Cheddar cheese. For cheese curds, the newly pressed, unaged cheese is simply cut into nuggets of approximately an inch in size and sold fresh. Cheese curds may be eaten as is, straight from the bag. Truly fresh cheese curds squeak when you bite into them; however, this sign of freshness disappears after a day or so. In Canada, cheese curds are tossed with French fries and topped with brown gravy to make *poutine* (poo-TEEN). However, the most popular way to serve cheese curds is breaded and fried, a specialty featured at fairs, festivals, and other outdoor events.

Three distinctive, truly American cheeses deserve special notice in any discussion of Farmlands cheese making. Colby, brick, and Maytag blue are described in the table on p. 457. Today the Farmlands region is home to a growing number of artisan cheese makers who create unique products in both the American and European style.

The Downside of Industrial Agriculture

Despite the financial success of industrial agriculture, many of its advances proved less beneficial than originally thought. Chemicals applied to farmland created pollution and decimated wildlife. Pests and weeds became resistant to pesticides and herbicides. By the 1930s extensive plowing for monoculture crops combined with unusual weather conditions produced the **dust bowl,** an

FIGURE 9.14
In the 1930s, poor agricultural practices combined with unusual weather created the dust bowl. Courtesy USDA/NRCS/Natural Resources Conservation Service

ecological disaster in which drought and wind erosion virtually destroyed Midwestern agriculture (Figure 9.14). To learn more about the dust bowl years, refer to this book's companion website.

The lessons of the dust bowl years ushered in a new era of soil conservation. The U.S. Department of Agriculture funded research into improved dry-farming techniques and educational programs for farmers. Agronomists developed "no-till" methods of planting for use in areas subject to wind erosion, and contour plowing techniques were instituted to prevent water erosion. Soil replenishment programs nurtured existing fields, and millions of acres of abandoned fields were returned to grassland.

In addition to ecological damage, by the turn of the 21st century significant social damage also had been done. As farms became larger and more mechanized, the cost of operating them became prohibitively high—in many cases too much for individual farmers to bear. In the late 20th century, corporate-owned agribusiness began crowding out individual operators, many of whom had worked the land for generations. The mid-size, diversified family farm, once the foundation of rural Midwestern society, is now in danger of extinction. You'll learn more about the endangered family farm and measures being taken to save it in the section on America's National Cuisine on this book's companion website.

■ TRADITIONAL
□
■ FARMLANDS CUISINE

The cooking of the Central Farmlands is the model of "American" food. Central Farmlands cuisine was based on the New England and Mid-Atlantic cooking of the region's first settlers,

enhanced with abundant, high-quality ingredients, and solidified by the conservative outlook of its inhabitants. Its development coincided with the birth of America's national cuisine, and therefore its dishes were promoted nationwide.

In Farmlands cuisine, meals focus on protein. Meats and poultry are served in large portions. Starchy side dishes add bulk and substance. In essence, Farmlands cuisine is "meat and potatoes" food, with the emphasis on meat. Fresh-vegetable accompaniments are served in season, with home-canned vegetables traditionally replacing them during the winter. Throughout the 1900s, freshwater fish from the region's rivers and the Great Lakes were important protein foods; however, pollution and overharvesting has made fish less available and, thus, less frequently served in the modern cuisine.

Because Central Farmlands cooking is a cuisine of plenty, sauces and seasonings are minimal. Unlike frugal New Englanders and many impoverished Southern cooks, Central Farmlands cooks had no need to "stretch" the protein food with sauces and gravies, or make highly seasoned foods to liven a diet based on starches. Complex cooking methods are rare because

FACTOR 3 FACTOR 4
Conservative attitudes of both early settlers and later immigrants resulted in simple, ingredient-driven cuisine.

ample, high-quality ingredients stand on their own merit. Presentations are simple and garnishes few. Moreover, the Midwestern mindset resists spending too much time and attention on food.

The simplicity of Farmlands cuisine is primarily a matter of attitude. New Englanders are well known for simple living and frugality, a legacy of their Puritan heritage. Mid-Atlantic culture has roots in Quaker simplicity and Pennsylvania Dutch practicality. Both groups favor hearty, straightforward cooking. Most of the Midwest's second settlers shared this mindset. Hailing from Eastern Europe and Scandinavia, many had suffered deprivation and hardship in their former homelands and valued thrift and plain living. Therefore, a culinarily conservative attitude is pervasive throughout the Central Farmlands culinary region.

Despite a conservative culinary outlook, the Central Farmlands region has developed a strong food culture because of its citizens' close connection to food. Although in the past hundred years the number of Midwesterners directly involved in farming has continued to shrink, virtually everyone native to the region has a parent or grandparent who worked on a farm or in a food-processing factory. A result of the region's strong food culture is the almost universal preference for home-style food. With the exception of the Central Cities' contemporary dining scene, most Midwestern restaurants attempt to emulate home cooking.

Farmlands Favorite Foods

Beef, pork, and chicken are the most frequently served protein foods in Farmlands cuisine. Several Farmlands cities are meat-packing centers that process Ranchlands beef. Although it's shipped from the central cities around the nation and the world, much fine beef remains on Midwest tables. Farmland cooks prepare well-marbled tender cuts as traditional roast beef and broiled or grilled steaks. Tough cuts become pot roast, beef stew, meat loaf, and hamburgers. Pork raised on Midwest farms is roasted, braised, and fabricated into cutlets for pan frying. Locally produced chickens are roasted, sautéed, and simmered into stews.

The most widely available regional fish is **walleye,** a large Great Lakes species with firm, white, mild-tasting flesh. Walleye is typically broiled with butter and seasoned simply with lemon juice and salt. Breaded and fried walleye is also popular. Few other regional freshwater fish are sold commercially. Although today fish and shellfish are frequently served in Midwestern restaurants, little of it is local.

Cheese is an important ingredient in Farmlands cuisine. Regionally produced Cheddar accents starch dishes, such as macaroni and cheese, Welsh rarebit, and potatoes au gratin. Farmlands-style cheese sauce (béchamel-like white sauce with Cheddar) is served on vegetables.

Although accorded side-dish status, vegetables play a large role in Farmlands cuisine. Fresh, homegrown vegetables are the gold standard of Midwestern cooking, with home-canned vegetables considered a close second. Traditional cooks without gardens search out farm markets with just-picked produce and follow the seasons from early spring peas to the pumpkins of fall. By far the region's most popular vegetable is sweet corn. Whole ears are consumed as corn on the cob, or made into simple dishes such as creamed corn and corn fritters. Much of the large Midwestern sweet corn crop is processed into commercially frozen or canned corn kernels. Potatoes are the region's favorite side starch, served boiled, baked, fried, or mashed.

Farmlands cuisine is known for casseroles, composed dishes that can be prepared ahead and easily transported. Bringing a casserole (in Minnesota, called a *hotdish*) is expected when attending parties, potluck dinners, and church functions. Sending a casserole is a duty when friends, neighbors, or relatives fall ill or have a death in the family.

A legacy of the region's German immigrants, breaded and fried foods are popular in both Farmlands and cities. Bread crumbs, cracker crumbs, and slightly sweet cornflake crumbs are used as coatings. Inspired by Wiener schnitzel, Farmlands cooks apply this technique to a variety of foods, including pork cutlets, boneless chicken breasts, freshwater fish fillets, summer squash, and eggplant. Midwestern state fairs are infamous for breaded and fried foods "on a stick"—corn dogs, pork chops, and even candy bars and Twinkies.

Preserved foods were not life-or-death necessities in Farmlands cuisine. Although ham, bacon, and sausages figure in the cuisine, they're typically served as breakfast foods and sandwich fillings rather than as seasoning meats or main-course protein foods. Cured fish was a favored food in areas of Scandinavian settlement. Traditional Farmlands cooks prepare homemade jams, jellies, preserves, pickles, and relishes.

CHARACTERISTICS OF FARMLANDS CUISINE

- abundant, high-quality protein foods
- simple recipes and methods
- culinary conservatism

Farmlands Baking

New England and Mid-Atlantic settlers brought their pie-making skills to the Midwest, and immigrants expanded the region's pie repertoire. Farmlands cuisine abounds in pies both savory and sweet.

Stews made with chicken or beef are baked under flaky pastry crusts to become savory pies, sometimes called pot pies. Ground beef cottage pie is baked with a mashed potato topping. Immigrants introduced smaller, turnover-style meat pies, such as Cornish pasties, Bohemian (Czech) *runzas*, and Russian *pirozhki*. Today miniaturized versions are popular cocktail hors d'oeuvres.

Farmlands bakers make a wide variety of fruit pies ranging from strawberry in the spring to apple and pumpkin in the fall. Certainly the most beloved of all Midwestern fruit pies is cherry, traditionally made with a lattice top for a glimpse of the bright-red filling. The Great Lakes states are America's most important commercial source of sour pie cherries, most of which are sweetened and canned as pie filling.

Farmlands cuisine abounds in layer cakes of many kinds. Once baking powder became widely available in the late 1800s, both home bakers and pastry shops featured towering creations of multiple layers boasting luscious fillings and rich frostings. Many of America's favorites, such as devil's food, pineapple upside-down cake, and carrot cake, are attributed to Midwest bakers.

In the early 1900s commercial bakeries developed the traditional American white bread loaf modeled after the milk-and-butter-enriched, round-topped loaves of the Midwestern farmwife (Figure 9.15). The **Pullman loaf** is bread baked in a lidded pan to ensure a uniform oblong shape to be stacked in the dining galleys of Pullman train cars. The resulting perfectly square slices are preferred for sandwich making.

FIGURE 9.15

Traditional American white bread is enriched with milk, butter, sugar, and sometimes eggs to ensure long keeping. Courtesy Prepared Pantry, www.preparedpantry.com

□ ELEMENTS OF CENTRAL FARMLANDS AND CITIES CUISINE

FOUNDATION FOODS

principal starches: yeasted wheat breads, potatoes

principal proteins: beef, pork, poultry

principal produce: all varieties of European and indigenous vegetables and fruits

FAVORED SEASONINGS: minimal

PRINCIPAL COOKING MEDIA: butter, water, stock

PRIMARY COOKING METHODS: roasting, sautéing, pan-frying, stewing/simmering

FOOD ATTITUDES: strong food culture, culinary conservatives

Eastern European Influence

Among the earliest of second-wave settlers, immigrants from Eastern European nations significantly influenced Farmlands cooking.

Hungarian paprika lends a bold, piquant flavor to *goulash* (GOO-lahsh), a hearty meat stew. In Farmlands cooking, mild paprika is used as a universal garnish, sprinkled on potato salad, deviled eggs, and numerous other savory dishes. The use of sautéed bell peppers, tomato sauces, and smoked sausages reflects Hungarian cuisine. Rich Hungarian desserts, such as seven-layer Dobos torte and fruit strudels, are Midwestern pastry shop favorites.

The lavish use of sour cream is a legacy of many Eastern European cuisines and has become a hallmark of Farmlands cuisine. Hungarian-inspired chicken paprikash and Russian-inspired beef Stroganoff have rich sour cream sauces. Eastern European–style soups—hot and cold, savory and sweet—are often dolloped with sour cream. After American dairies began producing commercial cultured sour cream in the late 1800s, salad dressings made from sour cream became nationally popular and today are a feature of Farmlands cooking. In the 1950s, sour cream–based dips dominated the cocktail hour, and Americans began to top baked potatoes with sour cream and chives.

■ THE CENTRAL
□ CITIES

While pioneer farmers were settling the trans-Appalachian flatlands and central plains, entrepreneurs were building centers of trade where the Midwestern agricultural products could be amassed and sold. During the era of water transport, market towns were located along the region's canals, rivers, and lakeshores, frequently at the confluence of two navigable waterways. As the number of farms increased and more food was produced, towns grew into cities. Cleveland, Toledo, Detroit, Chicago, and Milwaukee grew up along the Great Lakes trade network; Cincinnati, St. Louis, Kansas City, Omaha, and

Minneapolis lined the river routes. When railroads reached the region, America's central cities became hubs in the nation's rail network. Even today, when most meat and dairy travels by truck, the region's central cities still handle the packing, marketing, sale, and distribution of Midwestern food products.

Meat Production and Packing

Until the advent of railroads, meat was delivered to market "on the hoof," or in the form of live animals. In Chapter 10 you'll learn about the era of long cattle drives and the cowboy lifestyle of which they were a part. During the years of the great cattle drives Western beef was tasty, but lean and tough because of weight loss and muscle development during the long trip to slaughter. When railroads reached the western plateau, steers could be loaded into railroad cattle cars and transported to slaughter without the physical effects of making a long journey. Chicago became the destination for millions of beef cattle and, in response, built massive stockyards to receive them and large slaughter/packinghouses where the animals were butchered (Figure 9.16). After fabrication into primal cuts, the meat was packed in cartons and shipped east by rail in boxcars chilled with block ice.

Although with rail transport the steers arrived in good condition, Western beef grazed on the shortgrass prairie were still rather lean for Eastern tastes. After the Civil War, Chicago packers pioneered the practice of finishing beef cattle in stockyards before slaughtering them.

FIGURE 9.16

Chicago's Union Stockyards consolidated the city's meatpacking industry in one area. Courtesy of U.S. Department of Agriculture

CONTROVERSY OVER CATTLE FINISHING

Both health experts and animal rights advocates question the wisdom of the cattle-finishing process. Although it produces a desirable and highly marketable product, it creates both health concerns and ethical problems.

America's recent epidemic of obesity has led nutritionists to champion leaner, grass-fed beef. Moreover, they express concerns about the possible transfer to humans of hormones, antibiotics, and other medications today given to stockyard steers to speed growth and prevent diseases caused by overcrowding.

Animal rights groups protest the inhumane conditions found in stockyards, where hundreds of animals are penned closely together on concrete slabs, often without shade or breeze. They also cite the damage done to the digestive systems of cattle when they are deprived of their natural grass-based diet and instead fed only grain.

The decision whether to serve grain-finished beef must be made by individual chefs and consumers armed with awareness and knowledge of the process.

Finishing is a meat improvement technique involving two related physical processes that occur simultaneously. To finish a steer before slaughter, for several weeks the animal is confined in a space too small for physical exercise and fed a high-fat diet. Lack of physical activity causes the animal to lose muscle tone, making the meat more tender. Combined with lack of exercise, feeding the animal a high-fat diet—typically based on dried corn—results in a buildup of fat both on the exterior and in the interior of the muscles. Veins of interior fat are called **marbling,** a characteristic that makes meat taste rich and succulent. However, finishing is not universally accepted as a good animal husbandry practice. The box on this page outlines the controversy over finishing meat animals.

Finished beef proved so profitable that ranchers were soon raising cattle in great numbers across the western plateau and also in the central plains. Stockyards sprang up in other Midwestern cities, although Chicago remained the primary meat-processing center. The finishing process created increased demand for corn, creating a positive relationship between farmer and rancher.

Until railroads arrived, most of the pork raised in the Central Farmlands region was consumed locally. Hogs were typically raised as a sideline by farmers who fed them table scraps and slaughtered them for family food or for sale to neighbors. Despite a growing market for fresh pork and preserved pork products in the East, the logistics of moving stubborn and easily injured hogs long distances on the hoof simply did not make economic sense.

After the arrival of railroads, hogs could be butchered at local stockyards and the perishable pork shipped quickly to eastern markets. Hog rearing shifted from individual husbandry to large-scale feedlot production. On feedlot farms, hogs are fed heat-sterilized food refuse and finished on corn.

Cincinnati, Ohio, became the nation's first large-scale center for meatpacking, specializing in salt pork and lard and earning the nickname *Porkopolis*. Cincinnati pork producers created the world's first automated production line for meat slaughter and processing. The system was later perfected in the Chicago stockyards.

Although the new system of meat production resulted in cheaper, more readily available protein food for a hungry nation, it would not develop without problems. Through the late 1800s well into the 20th century, issues of sanitation, safety, and ethics plagued the industry. For more information on the Midwestern meatpacking industry, refer to this book's companion website.

Industrial Food Production

America's transition from fresh to processed foods began in 19th-century New England and continued in the Central Farmlands region with the development of a massive agro-industrial food complex. Large canning plants gave Midwestern farmers an unlimited market for fruits and vegetables. A significant proportion of Midwestern grain becomes processed cereals developed by industrial giants such as Kellogg's and Post. James L. Kraft created pasteurized process cheese. Meat processing evolved to include canned products such as soups, stews, and chili. Hormel produced the first canned ham and later created Spam, a canned luncheon loaf that would become popular worldwide. Automation and the perfection of the canning process soon led to the production of a wide variety of canned, bottled, and packaged foods. Today's brand names such as General Mills, Armour, Swift, Pillsbury, Procter & Gamble, Land o' Lakes, Smuckers, and Green Giant were all born in the late 1800s. Job opportunities in food processing drew immigrants to Central Farmlands cities.

City Cuisine

The Central Farmlands cities developed a restaurant cuisine separate—and quite different—from the home cooking of the surrounding farmlands. In the cities, economic development created a business aristocracy that supported expensive restaurants serving the best of the region's food products. However, until the end of the 20th century, Midwestern restaurant food preparation and presentation remained simple and straightforward. Best known among Midwestern restaurant concepts is the steakhouse.

Chicago Steakhouses

America's central cities are noted for restaurants serving fine beef. Chicago pioneered the **steakhouse,** a restaurant concept based on

FIGURE 9.17

One of the Midwest's premier steakhouses, St. Elmo's is an Indianapolis landmark. Courtesy St. Elmo's Steakhouse, Indianapolis, IN

serving prime, house-aged beefsteaks. Famous Midwestern steakhouses include the Chicago Chop House, Morton's of Chicago, and St. Elmo's (see Figure 9.17).

In a classic steakhouse operation, sirloin strip, T-bone, porterhouse, rib, and filet steaks are cooked under an intensely hot broiler and served with no embellishment other than an optional topping of fried onions or sautéed mushrooms. Prime rib is slow roasted and served au jus. Lamb chops, pork chops, and fish steaks are also offered, but usually make up only a small percentage of sales. In the 1970s the introduction of gas-fired grills replaced broiling as the cooking method of choice. In the 1980s wood-fired grills became popular, allowing chefs to subtly flavor steaks and chops by using different woods for fuel.

Unlike Continental and European restaurants where the main entrée includes starch and vegetable accompaniments planned by the chef, the classic steakhouse menu is strictly à la carte, with side dishes listed and priced separately to be chosen by the individual diner. The star of steakhouse side dishes is the potato: traditionally baked, twice-baked, hash browned, cottage-fried, home-fried, au gratin, and mashed. Steakhouse fries, better known as **steak fries,** are thick wedges of skin-on russet potatoes deep-fried crisp. Side vegetables are often sauced, as in asparagus hollandaise or creamed spinach.

In the 1920s steakhouses began offering salads as appetizers in the California style (p. 558). The American **tossed salad,** iceberg lettuce with assorted vegetable garnishes and dressing on the side, is a steakhouse signature dish. *Garbage salad*, an antipasto-like mixture of lettuces, fresh and pickled vegetables, salami, and provolone, is a Chicago favorite despite its unappetizing name. Caesar salad (p. 559) is now a standard offering. In addition to salads, steakhouse appetizers include signature soups and seafood. The most popular seafood appetizer is shrimp cocktail, followed by oysters and clams on the half shell and smoked salmon. Steakhouses feature all-American desserts such as apple pie, chocolate cake, ice cream, and cheesecake.

City Soul Food

During the African-American diaspora following the Civil War, tens of thousands of newly emancipated African-Americans migrated north to find economic opportunity in Midwestern cities. Seeking the shortest route, many gravitated to the cities closest

to them: primarily Cincinnati, St. Louis, and Kansas City. Although farther away, Chicago drew a large African-American population as well.

Along with the blues and jazz music traditions, African-Americans brought Plantation South cooking and soul food to the central cities. However, their cooking style largely remained separate—found in African-American homes and black-owned restaurants but not assimilated into the regional cuisine. Only one Plantation South dish significantly affected Farmlands cuisine: barbeque.

Midwestern Barbeque

Today barbeque is almost as popular in the Midwest as in the South, and distinct regional variations exist there as well. Two central cities compete for barbeque supremacy: Kansas City and St. Louis (Figure 9.18).

Kansas City, Missouri, is a crossroads of barbeque culture. Situated between beef-loving Texas and the pork-loving South, located on the northward path to freedom for African-American slaves, once surrounded by smoke-producing hardwood forests, and in America's largest meat-producing region, Kansas City is world famous for barbeque. Kansas City is eclectic in its choice of meats. In addition to pork ribs, baby back ribs, and pulled pork shoulder, beef ribs and beef brisket are also featured. Split broiler chickens and chicken wings are offered for those who prefer poultry. Tomato-based Kansas City barbeque sauce is sweet, mild, and thick "so it don't fall off the meat." Diners preferring a spicy-hot flavor add bottled hot sauce to taste.

The city of St. Louis developed a different style of barbeque. **St. Louis–cut ribs** (photo on p. 71) are squared off and have the brisket bones removed. Tasty, chewy barbeque brisket bones are

FIGURE 9.18

Kansas City is the self-proclaimed barbeque capital of the world, and Fiorella's Jack Stack Barbecue is consistently ranked as one of the best. Courtesy Jack Stack Barbecue

now marketed as **rib tips,** a popular appetizer. In addition to ribs, St. Louis barbeque features barbeque pork steaks, inch-thick slices cut from the picnic shoulder. "Crispy snoots," barbequed meat and skin from the hog's muzzle, are a regional specialty. Tomato-based St. Louis barbeque sauce is thinner, tangier, and less sweet than Kansas City sauce.

Chicago Deep-Dish Pizza

By the early 20th century, Italian-Americans had opened food shops and restaurants in virtually every Midwestern town and city. Among several Italian-inspired dishes created in Chicago, deep-dish pizza is most famous. Originated in 1943 by a displaced Texan in a tiny bar and grill called Pizzeria Uno, deep-dish pizza gained instant popularity because it was perceived as a good value well suited to the hearty eating habits of Midwesterners. This rich, multilayered concoction is more like a bread-lined casserole than a true Italian pizza, typically containing several types of meat as well as cheese, tomato sauce, and vegetables. The popularity of deep-dish pizza soon caused Pizzeria Uno to expand and, by the 1970s, the restaurant had become a national chain. Today Chicago has more than 2,000 pizzerias, most serving the deep-dish style. Connoisseurs agree that the best Chicago deep-dish is found at Lou Malnati's, a restaurant opened by a former employee of the original Uno.

Cincinnati Chili

Cincinnati is home to America's most imaginative version of chili, created in 1922 by a Macedonian immigrant. Cincinnati chili is made with ground beef flavored with cinnamon, turmeric, cocoa, and black pepper as well as the traditional cumin, oregano, and chili powder. Cincinnati chili can be eaten as is, in a bowl accompanied by oyster crackers, but is usually served over spaghetti. Refer to the table on p. 424 to learn the "ways" of Cincinnati chili.

■ FUTURE CUISINE OF THE
□ CENTRAL FARMLANDS
■ AND CITIES

Just as the family farm is in danger of extinction, so is traditional Farmlands cuisine. As older farmers retire and fewer young people go into farming, large agricultural corporations are buying up Midwestern land at an unprecedented rate. As fewer Midwesterners lead the farming lifestyle, Farmlands cuisine may simply fade into the past. Like the rest of America, many modern Midwestern families have turned to restaurant meals and industrially processed convenience foods. One reason is the decreasing availability of fine raw materials. Without full-flavored, naturally raised meats and garden-fresh vegetables grown by traditional methods, the simple cooking and straightforward presentation so representative of Farmlands cuisine can be bland and unexciting. Because high-quality ingredients are essential for this ingredient-driven cuisine, its future depends on a return to localized food production on the artisan level.

FACTOR 4
Into the 21st century, Latin American and Asian immigrants enrich the cuisine of the Farmlands' central cities.

A number of Midwestern chefs are championing the movement toward local, sustainable agriculture. By purchasing the region's best ingredients and preparing them with simplicity and respect, they best represent the future of Farmlands cuisine. For a list of noteworthy Farmlands cuisine restaurants, refer to this book's companion website.

The outlook in the Farmlands' central cities also reflects change, but in a more positive direction. Continuing immigration has created a lively cuisine scene in many neighborhoods. After the Vietnam War, thousands of Asian immigrants came to the Midwest. Africans and Middle Easterners followed. Farmlands cities soon sprouted neighborhoods of almost entirely homogenous ethnic settlement, often seeing one cultural group survive, flourish, move on to the suburbs, and be replaced by another. Through the end of the 20th century, a steady stream of immigrants, primarily Latin Americans from Mexico and the Spanish-speaking Caribbean, brought their lively foodways.

Chicago stands out among the most vital immigrant cities. Modern Chicago is a city of ethnic neighborhoods, such as the African-American South Side, Scandinavian Andersonville, Indian/Pakistani Devon Avenue, Greek Town on Halstead Street, Little Italy on Taylor, and Little Mexico in formerly Eastern European Pilsen. Dearborn, Michigan, has the nation's second-largest Arab-American population and scores of Middle Eastern restaurants. Minneapolis–St. Paul has welcomed immigrants from around the globe; Minneapolis's "Eat Street" offers a veritable United Nations of ethnic restaurants.

FIGURE 9.19
Development of Central Farmlands and Cities Cuisine

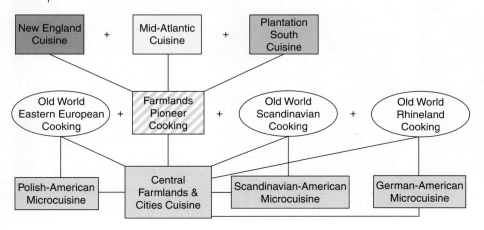

In addition to the wealth of foreign cuisines brought by immigrants, in the future Farmlands cities may also see the development of new American hybrid cuisines. Because many immigrants typically enter foodservice, their culinary influence is sure to affect mainstream cuisine.

■ MICROCUISINES OF THE
□ CENTRAL FARMLANDS
■ AND CITIES

Late 19th-century immigration to the Central Farmlands region resulted in three important American microcuisines: German-American, Scandinavian-American, and Polish-American.

Unlike the early Rhineland immigrants to the east coast who became known as the Pennsylvania Dutch, Germans who arrived in the Midwest after the Civil War had no need for indigenous cornmeal, dried beans, squashes, and foraged foods. Instead they embraced abundant Midwestern meats and dairy products, modifying their Old World foodways to feature the colonial domesticates already prevalent in the region. Thus, the German-American and Pennsylvania Dutch microcuisines have the same Rhineland roots but are distinctly different.

Scandinavians settling the Great Lakes area modified their seafood-based cuisine to suit the region's freshwater fish and shellfish. They produced a variety of dairy products and raised fruits, both vital elements of their microcuisine and important in the regional style, as well. Scandinavians made coffee one of America's most popular beverages and instituted the habit of drinking it all day long.

Polish immigrants concentrated in Midwestern cities, where they developed a thrifty hybrid cooking style based on Old World Polish recipes simplified for quick preparation and made with inexpensive regional ingredients.

Visit this book's companion website at www.pearsonhighered.com/sackett to learn more about the German, Polish, and Scandinavian microcuisines. Following are some photos relating to these microcuisines.

German immigrants excelled at sausage production.
Jo Chambers © Shutterstock

German-American restaurants are primarily located in areas with large German immigrant populations.
Harry B. Lamb © Shutterstock

Polish-Americans prepare pierogies.
Courtesy of Poland Culinary Vacations, Inc., www.polandculinaryvacations.com

Ice fishing is popular among Scandinavian-Americans.
Denis Pepin © Shutterstock

A Door County fish boil.
Courtesy DoorCounty.com/
Door County Visitor Bureau

Hors d'oeuvres presented as part of a Scandinavian smorgasbord.
© Shutterstock

◻ TABLE 9.1 CENTRAL FARMLANDS DEFINING DISHES

ITEM NAME	HISTORY	DOMINANT INGREDIENTS AND METHOD	MORE
RELISH TRAYS	Traditional Farmlands meals did not include appetizers, but tables were often set with "relishes" such as raw vegetables, pickled vegetables, composed salads, or other cold items. Diners nibbled on these offerings while awaiting the arrival of the hot dishes.	Traditional relish trays consist of celery and carrot sticks, scallions, and radishes, sometimes accompanied by a dip and perhaps deviled eggs. In the 1950s canned California olives, both black and green, became popular.	Options may include pickled eggs and beets, plain or seasoned cottage cheese, or a vinegary pepper slaw.
FARMLANDS SOUPS	Based on English, New England, and Mid-Atlantic traditions, the soups of the Central Farmlands region can be called the soups of America. Soups may be served as appetizers to begin a special-occasion meal, but are more often served for lunch with a salad or sandwich. Hearty soups become supper entrées served with bread and butter.	Soups are made in large quantity and slow-simmered over low heat. A steam-jacketed kettle avoids scorching. With choices such as creamy mushroom, chunky vegetable, and hearty beef barley, Farmlands soups are represented by a wide variety of well-known recipes.	Immigrants from Germany and Poland added new recipes to the Farmlands repertoire. Scandinavians introduced semi-sweet fruit soups served hot or chilled.
DEEP-FRIED CHEESE CURDS	Deep-fried cheese curds likely debuted at a Midwestern fair or carnival, venues well known for serving a wide variety of fried foods.	Nuggets of fresh, unaged Wisconsin Cheddar are dipped in a beer batter or coated with bread crumbs. Deep-fried golden, they're served with mustard sauce or ketchup.	This dish is a regional specialty rarely found outside the Midwest.
SAVORY PIES	First- and second-wave settlers of the Central Farmlands region brought along culinary traditions of baking savory ingredients into flaky pastry crusts. Americans of Anglo-Saxon background continued the English practice of sealing a meat or poultry stew under a dome of pastry and baking it golden brown.	Stewed meat or poultry is baked in a casserole sealed with flaky pastry or puff pastry. This type of dish is often called "pot pie," although the term correctly refers to a stew simmered with large, square noodles (see Pennsylvania Dutch Bot Boi on p. 169). Cottage pie (made with ground beef) and shepherd's pie (made with ground lamb) are baked with a mashed potato topping.	Smaller, turnover-style pies include ground-beef-filled Cornish pasties; Bohemian (Czech) *runzas*; and chopped-ham-filled Russian *pirozhki*. These portable snacks were perfect for toting to the fields in pocket or rucksack. Today miniaturized versions of these turnovers are popular cocktail hors d'oeuvres.

(continued)

☐ **TABLE 9.1 CENTRAL FARMLANDS DEFINING DISHES** *(continued)*

ITEM NAME	HISTORY	DOMINANT INGREDIENTS AND METHOD	MORE
HAMBURGER AND SALISBURY STEAK	The "hamburger steak," or ground beef patty, is named after Hamburg, Germany. Originally promoted by German butchers as a low-cost alternative to cutlets, it was sautéed, plated, and napped with gravy. The hamburger became popular as a sandwich after it was served on a bun at the St. Louis Exposition of 1904. Cheese was first added around 1930.	Freshly ground beef is pressed into a patty by hand or with a machine. Fat content up to 20% gives flavor and good mouthfeel. Hamburgers were originally sautéed or pan-seared. Today many prefer a grilled burger.	Today a ground meat patty served in a sauce or gravy is known as Salisbury steak, named after Salisbury, England.
MEAT LOAF	After 1900, electric meat grinders enabled butchers to produce ground meat quickly and at a low cost. By forming ground meat into a loaf shape, thrifty cooks simulated a meat roast for a fraction of the cost. Today the classic meat loaf is a signature dish of American home cooking.	Traditionally made with a mixture of ground beef, pork, and veal, meat loaf is often topped with sliced bacon for richness and savor. Seasoned sparingly with grated onion, herbs, ketchup, and Worcestershire sauce, the loaf's pure meat flavor is evident.	Served hot with gravy and mashed potatoes, or chilled as a sandwich filling, meat loaf ranks high on the list of American comfort foods.
GROUND BEEF 'N' BEAN CHILI	A Mexican dish of diced pork simmered in a puréed red chile sauce, *chile con carne* traveled north into the Spanish-held American Southwest, where the meat of choice was beef. From there it spread into the Anglo Ranchlands, where it was made of fine-diced or hand-chopped beef seasoned with a powdered chile blend and where the *e* became an *i*. The Farmlands region is the scene of its final transformation.	Midwest cooks turned to ground beef, added tomato, and put kidney beans in the dish instead of serving pinto beans on the side.	Farmlands chili is accompanied by saltine crackers and may be topped with grated Cheddar cheese, chopped onions, and sour cream.
CINCINNATI CHILI	Cincinnati chili was created by a restaurateur of Middle Eastern origin.	Subtly flavored with cinnamon, cocoa, and Worcestershire sauce as well as the traditional cumin, oregano, and chili powder, this ground beef chili includes tomatoes but not beans.	Cincinnati chili is traditionally served over spaghetti with various toppings. Variations are called "ways." Skyline Chili, the region's best-known chili restaurant, offers 5 "ways:" (1) plain, or chili bowl; (2) chili spaghetti; (3) 3-Way, chili spaghetti topped with grated Cheddar cheese; (4) 4-Way, chili spaghetti with cheese and kidney beans *or* chopped onions; (5) 5-Way, chili spaghetti with cheese, beans, *and* onions. Oyster crackers are a traditional accompaniment.
CHICAGO DEEP-DISH PIZZA	Created at Chicago's Pizzeria Uno in 1943, deep-dish pizza is like a casserole baked in a crust.	Pizza dough is hand-patted into a deep, round pan and covered with grated mozzarella cheese. Tomato sauce, meat and vegetable toppings, and more cheese are added, then the pizza is baked. Deep-dish pizza is served in the pan and eaten with knife and fork.	The popular "meat lover's" option includes sausage, pepperoni, ham, and ground beef. Vegetarian combinations may include mushrooms, spinach, peppers, onion, and broccoli.
CHEESE SAUCES AND TOPPINGS	Sauces enriched with cheese are a legacy of British cuisine. Welsh rarebit, toasted white bread topped with a beer-based cheese sauce, is also a British heritage dish. "Au gratin" dishes arrived from France with Contenental cuisine (Chapter 16).	White sauce, a simplified béchamel, is flavored and colored with yellow Cheddar. Broccoli and asparagus spears, cauliflower, and Brussels sprouts are often topped with a béchamel-based cheese sauce. Baked potatoes, French fries, and deep-fried potato skins may be topped with Cheddar sauce or melted blue cheese.	The word "rarebit" is a modification of "rabbit." A dish of melted cheese over toast was originally called *Welsh rabbit*, likely because Welsh peasants were forbidden to hunt for meat on the estates of the aristocracy and had to eat cheese, instead.

☐ **TABLE 9.1 CENTRAL FARMLANDS DEFINING DISHES** *(continued)*

ITEM NAME	HISTORY	DOMINANT INGREDIENTS AND METHOD	MORE
MACARONI 'N' CHEESE	Thomas Jefferson served macaroni 'n' cheese in the White House around 1800. Although Italian in origin, it was popular in Victorian Britain and frequently appeared in American cookbooks after the Civil War.	Cooked macaroni 'n' cheese is composed of elbow macaroni tossed in a white sauce flavored with sharp yellow Cheddar cheese.	For baked macaroni 'n' cheese, this basic mixture is bound with beaten egg and baked under a golden bread crumb crust.
STEWS AND BRAISES	Inexpensive tough cuts of meat and older chickens required low, slow, moist cooking that resulted in lots of tasty sauce.	Beef stew is emblematic of Farmlands cooking, combining cubes of beef chuck with sturdy root vegetables—carrots, boiling onions, and potatoes—in a roux-thickened gravy. Farmlands pot roast is a large cut of beef braised in a casserole and then served in thin slices surrounded by vegetables and napped in a light pan sauce.	Tough cuts of pork and lamb, as well as elderly chickens and game birds, are also cooked by stewing and braising. Seasonings are minimal to showcase the flavor of fine ingredients.
DUMPLINGS	Although they rarely needed to "stretch" the meat, Farmlands cooks sometimes added fluffy dumplings to stews and saucy braises.	Wheat dumplings are preferred over the cornmeal variety; often, mashed potato is added to the dumpling dough for flavor.	Sharp cheese and/or fresh herbs add color and savor to dumplings.
BREADED FRIED FOODS	Farmlands cooks learned to make golden, crumb-crusted fried foods from their German neighbors. After the introduction of industrially processed cereals, cornflake crumbs became a favored breading medium, adding deep color and a hint of sweetness.	Foods are seasoned, dredged in flour, dipped in beaten egg, and then coated with crumbs before shallow-frying or deep frying.	At state fairs and carnivals, food vendors married Plantation South cornmeal frying with the Farmlands' favorite frankfurter sausage to produce the corn dog—a cornmeal-coated, deep-fried wiener-on-a-stick. Today breaded, deep-fried foods—especially those on a stick—are a main attraction of Midwestern fairs.
FRUIT PIES	Farmlands bakers continued the tradition of British, New England, and Mid-Atlantic cooks, making a wide variety of fruit pies, from strawberry in the spring to apple and pumpkin in the fall.	Flaky pastry lines a pie pan, which is then filled with sweetened fruit. Raw fruit fillings are tossed with flour or cornstarch and dotted with bits of butter. Cooked fruit fillings are more prevalent in bakeries and restaurants. Fruit pies may be topped with a lid of pastry or a lattice top. German-style streusel toppings are also popular.	As America's only significant commercial source of sour pie cherries, the Great Lakes states naturally feature cherry pie as a signature dish. Lattice-top cherry pies are especially attractive because the bright-red fruit is visible between the woven strips of pastry.
CHEMICALLY LEAVENED CAKES	After baking powder became widely available in the late 1800s, Midwestern bakers began making tall cakes of many layers.	*Carrot Cake:* spiced yellow cake flavored and moistened with grated carrot and iced with cream cheese frosting. *Upside-Down Cake:* yellow cake made in a skillet with fruit in the bottom; before serving the cake is inverted so that the fruit is on top *Angel Food Cake:* a tall, light white cake made from egg whites. *Devil's Food Cake:* chocolate cake originally colored slightly red by a reaction of chemical leavener and today tinted with food coloring; iced with a chocolate fudge frosting.	Midwestern farmwives enter their best layer cakes in baking contests at county and state fairs.
CHERRY CHEESECAKE	Combining two Farmlands specialties, cherry-topped cheesecake became popular in the early 1900s after the introduction of industrially processed cream cheese.	Farmlands cheesecake is lighter and less tangy than the New York variety, and typically has a graham cracker crust. The chilled cheesecake is topped with shiny, cornstarch-thickened cherry pie filling.	Today "no-bake" cheesecakes thickened with gelatin are also popular.

■ ◻ ■   # STUDY QUESTIONS

1. Relate the geological events that created Midwestern topography and the Farmlands region's thick, fertile soil. Discuss how these land characteristics influenced the region's economy and cuisine.

2. Draw a map of the United States, showing the Midwest in its center. Indicate the Farmland region's three subregions. Label the 100th longitudinal meridian on your map. At the bottom of the map, describe the climate and primary agricultural products of each subregion.

3. Discuss the Farmlands region's two first-settler groups. Include in your discussion where they came from, their food cultures and taste preferences, and their culinary outlooks (conservative or liberal).

4. Explain the lack of Native American influence in Farmlands cuisine. Identify the one indigenous Native American food product that has entered American cuisine, and describe its traditional method of harvest.

5. Compare and contrast the agricultural methods of the Plantation South and the Farmlands region. Relate the differences in agricultural practices to differences in culture and cuisine.

6. Explain the relationship between the economies of the Farmlands cities and the Ranchlands region. Explain the two regions' culinary relationship.

7. List the three main characteristics of Farmlands cuisine, and explain their origins.

8. Discuss the effects of the post–Civil War African-American diaspora on the Farmlands central cities. Identify the most popular African-American contribution to Farmlands cuisine, and describe its two distinctive Midwestern styles.

9. Write a brief profile of the German-American microcuisine. Include its foundation protein foods, foundation grains/starch dishes, foundation vegetables, and flavor preferences. Explain why German-American cuisine is not widely popular outside areas of German immigration heritage.

10. Write a brief profile of the Scandinavian-American microcuisine. Include its foundation protein foods, foundation grains/starch dishes, foundation vegetables, and flavor preferences. Identify and describe the distinctive foodservice style brought to the United States by Scandinavian immigrants.

11. Write a brief profile of the Polish-American microcuisine. Include its foundation protein foods, foundation grains/starch dishes, foundation vegetables, and flavor preferences. List three Polish-American dishes that have become part of the American national cuisine.

12. Using your imagination and the information presented in this chapter, develop a five-course special-occasion menu of Central Farmlands and Cities cuisine.

Scandinavian Beet Soup
with Knäckebrød

yield: 1 (10-fl.-oz.) appetizer serving
(multiply × 4 for classroom turnout; adjust equipment sizes accordingly)

MASTER RECIPE

production		costing only
1 1/4 c.	Scandinavian Beet Soup	1/4 recipe
1	6" doily or cocktail napkin	1 each
2 tsp.	minced dill	1/40 bunch a.p.
1	hard-cooked egg slice	1/4 each
1 Tbsp.	sour cream, in pastry bag fitted with a medium star tip	1/2 fl. oz.
1 pc.	Knäckebrød	1/8 recipe
1 Tbsp.	butter, in butter chip or ramekin	1/2 oz.

service turnout:

1. Stir the Scandinavian Beet Soup well to distribute the solids, ladle it into a small saucepan, and heat the soup just to the boil.
2. Plate the dish:
   a. Ladle the soup into a hot 12-oz. soup cup.
   b. Place a 6" doily on a cool 8" plate and place the cup on it.
   c. Sprinkle the soup with dill.
   d. Place the egg slice on the tip of a metal spatula and pipe a rosette of sour cream on it.
   e. Float the egg slice on the surface of the soup.
   f. Serve the Knäckebrød and butter in a napkin-lined basket.

COMPONENT RECIPE
SCANDINAVIAN BEET SOUP

yield: 5 c.

production		costing only
3 Tbsp.	butter	1 1/2 oz.
1 c.	fine-chopped red onion	5 oz. a.p.
1/2 c.	minced carrot	2 oz. a.p.
2 c.	peeled, grated beet	16 oz. a.p.
tt	kosher salt	1/8 oz.
2 or 3	dill stems	n/c
1 qt.	brown poultry or veal stock	1/4 recipe
2 c.	water	n/c
2 c.	fine-shredded Savoy or other cabbage	10 oz. a.p.
tt	cider vinegar	1/2 fl. oz.
tt	sugar	1/8 oz.

preparation:

1. Heat the butter in a nonreactive saucepan. Add the onion, carrot, beet, and a little salt. Sweat the vegetables about 5 minutes, until soft but not brown.
2. Add the dill stems, stock, and water. Simmer uncovered, stirring occasionally, 1 hour, until the vegetables are very tender.
3. Cool slightly.
4. Strain the soup, reserving both solids and liquid. Remove and discard the dill stems.
5. Place the solids in a blender or food processor and purée them, adding some of the liquid as necessary.
6. Return the purée to the pan and whisk in the remaining liquid.
7. Add the cabbage and simmer 30 minutes longer, until the cabbage is tender and the soup is reduced to about 5 c.
8. Season with vinegar and sugar, and adjust the salt to achieve a slightly sweet, tangy flavor.

holding: open-pan cool and immediately refrigerate in a freshly-sanitized, covered, nonreactive container

---

RECIPE VARIATIONS

Chilled Scandinavian Beet Soup with Knäckebrød
Replace the butter with corn oil. Reduce the water by 1 c. Omit the cabbage. Omit step 7. Cool and chill the soup and then readjust the seasoning. Omit the egg slice and instead pipe the sour cream onto a thin slice of cucumber.

Chilled Scandinavian Beet and Crayfish Soup with Knäckebrød
Prepare Chilled Scandinavian Beet Soup, but replace the meat stock with Shellfish Stock. Add 1/2 oz. chopped cooked crayfish tails before garnishing.

Beef Barley Soup
with Farmhouse White Bread and Butter

yield: 1 (10-fl.-oz.) appetizer serving
(multiply × 4 for classroom turnout; adjust equipment sizes accordingly)

MASTER RECIPE

production		costing only
1 1/4 c.	Beef Barley Soup	1/4 recipe
1	6" doily or cocktail napkin	1 each
1 Tbsp.	chopped flat-leaf parsley	1/40 bunch a.p.
1	small Boston lettuce leaf	1/12 head a.p.
1 Tbsp.	salted butter, piped into a rosette and chilled	1/2 oz.
1	3/4"-thick slice American White Bread, cut in half on the diagonal	1/12 recipe

service turnout:
1. Stir the Beef Barley Soup well to distribute the solids. Ladle it into a small saucepan and heat it just to the boil.
2. Plate the dish:
   a. Place a 6" doily on a cool 6" plate.
   b. Ladle the soup into a hot 12-oz. soup cup and place the cup on the plate.
   c. Sprinkle the soup with parsley.
   d. Place the lettuce leaf on the left side of a cool 5" plate and place the butter rosette on it. Overlap the bread slices on the right side of the plate.

COMPONENT RECIPE
BEEF BARLEY SOUP

yield: 5 c.

production		costing only
1	1"-thick slice beef shank, with marrow bone	8 oz. a.p.
as needed	water	n/c
1 qt.	Brown Beef Stock	1/4 recipe
2 c.	water	n/c
1/2 c.	fine-chopped yellow onion	2 1/2 oz. a.p.
1/4 c.	minced carrot	1 oz. a.p.
1/4 c.	peeled, minced celery	1/40 head a.p.
1/4 c.	pearl barley, rinsed and drained	1 3/4 oz.
1 tsp.	tomato paste	1/6 fl. oz.
pinch	dried thyme	1/16 oz.
pinch	dried savory	1/16 oz.
tt	kosher salt	1/8 oz.
1/2 c.	3/8"-diced carrot	2 oz. a.p.
1/2 c.	3/8"-diced turnip	4 oz. a.p.
1/4 c.	peeled, 3/8"-diced celery	1/40 head a.p.

preparation:
1. Trim the beef shank of fat and score the silverskin around its edges.
2. Blanch the beef shank:
   a. Place the shank in a saucepan, add water to cover by 3", and bring just to the boil.
   b. Pour out the water and rinse off the beef shank.
   c. Wipe the pan clean and return the beef shank to it.
3. Add the Brown Beef Stock, 2 c. water, onion, minced carrot and celery, barley, tomato paste, thyme, savory, and a little salt. Simmer, uncovered, stirring occasionally, 40 minutes, until the meat is tender.
4. Add the diced carrot, turnip, and celery and simmer 10 minutes longer, until the vegetables are just tender.
5. Fabricate the beef:
   a. Remove the beef shank from the soup and cool it enough to handle.
   b. Remove the marrow from the bone and chop it fine. Discard the bone.
   c. Trim the gristle from the meat and discard it.
   d. Cut the meat into 3/8" dice.
   e. Return the meat and marrow to the soup.
   f. Taste the soup and correct the seasoning.

holding: open-pan cool and immediately refrigerate in a freshly sanitized, covered container

---

RECIPE VARIATIONS
Vegetable Beef Soup
Omit the barley. Reduce the amount of diced vegetables to 1/4 c. each. Add 1/4 c. each of similar-size mixed cut vegetables, such as green beans, baby lima beans, corn kernels, and potatoes, in step 4.

Beef Noodle Soup
Omit the barley. Separately parboil, refresh, and drain 1/4 oz. fine-cut, dry egg noodles per serving. Add the noodles to the soup when heating for service.

Wisconsin Cheddar Broccoli Rarebit

yield: 1 (5-oz.) appetizer serving
(multiply × 4 for classroom turnout; adjust equipment sizes accordingly)

MASTER RECIPE

production		costing only
2	3"-diameter, 3/8"-thick rounds cut from American White Bread	1/12 recipe
3/4 c. (6 pc.)	small broccoli florets, blanched and refreshed	1/4 bunch or 4 oz. a.p.
1/2 c.	julienne broccoli (fabricated from peeled stems), blanched and refreshed	n/c
tt	kosher salt	1/16 oz.
1/2 c.	lager beer	4 fl. oz.
1 c.	grated sharp yellow Cheddar cheese	4 oz.
1/4 c.	Maquechoux Liaison, p. 280	1/4 recipe
pinch	cayenne pepper	1/16 oz.
pinch	dry mustard	1/16 oz.
1 drop	Worcestershire sauce	1/16 fl. oz.
pinch	fine-ground white pepper	1/16 oz.
1/4 c.	peeled and seeded, brunoise-cut vine-ripe tomato	3 oz. a.p.
1 Tbsp.	fine-sliced chives	1/20 bunch a.p.

service turnout:

1. Toast the American White Bread rounds crisp and hold them warm on a rack.
2. Season the broccoli florets and stems with salt and heat them in a steamer or microwave oven.
3. Prepare the sauce:
   a. Heat the beer in a small, nonreactive saucepan, add the cheese, and whisk over low heat just until the cheese is melted.
   b. Whisk the Maquechoux Liaison into the cheese and cook over low heat, whisking constantly, about 30 seconds, just until the mixture thickens and the yolk loses its raw taste. ⚠ Don't allow the sauce to overheat, or it will curdle.
   c. Season with cayenne, mustard, Worcestershire, white pepper and salt.
4. Plate the dish:
   a. Spoon a dab of the cheese sauce in the center of a hot 10" plate.
   b. Place a toast round in the center, top it with the broccoli stems, and nap them with about 1/3 of the cheese sauce.
   c. Place the second toast round on top and press gently. Nap with half of the remaining cheese sauce.
   d. Arrange the broccoli florets in a compact mound on the top toast round and press gently to firm them.
   e. Drizzle the broccoli florets with the remaining cheese sauce.
   f. Sprinkle a ring of tomato around the plate well.
   g. Sprinkle a ring of chives just outside the tomato ring.

RECIPE VARIATION

Wisconsin Cheddar Woodchuck (Tomato-Bacon Rarebit)
Add 2 Tbsp. canned tomato purée to the cheese sauce in step 3c. Replace the broccoli with 2 thick slices peeled vine-ripe tomato and 4 half-slices cooked bacon. Omit the chives and replace the brunoise-cut tomato with diagonal-sliced scallion.

Gravlax
with Dilled Mustard Sauce and Toast Points

yield: 1 (3-oz.) appetizer serving plus accompaniments (multiply × 4 for classroom turnout)

🕐 Requires 3 days advance preparation.

MASTER RECIPE

production		costing only
3 oz.	Gravlax, sliced to order	1/4 recipe
5	Toast Points	1/4 recipe
1	Boston lettuce leaf	1/20 head a.p.
2 Tbsp.	Dilled Mustard Sauce, in squeeze bottle	1/4 recipe
1	small hollowed lemon crown	1/2 [120 ct.] lemon
1 Tbsp.	drained nonpareil capers	1/2 fl. oz.
2 Tbsp.	brunoise-cut red onion	3/4 oz. a.p.
1 sprig	fresh dill	1/40 bunch a.p.

service turnout:

1. Using a sharp, flexible knife, and cutting on the diagonal, cut 5 thin slices of Gravlax weighing 3 oz. total.
2. Plate the dish:
   a. Overlap the gravlax slices vertically in the center of a cool 10" rectangular plate.
   b. Arrange the Toast Points, overlapping, on the right side of the plate.
   c. Place the lettuce leaf on the left side of the plate.
   d. Squeeze the Dilled Mustard Sauce into the lemon crown and place it slightly right of center on the lettuce leaf.
   e. Mound the capers to the right of the lemon crown.
   f. Mound the red onion to the left of the lemon crown.
   g. Place the dill sprig to the right of the toast points.

COMPONENT RECIPE
GRAVLAX

yield: approx. 12 oz.

🕐 Requires 3 days advance preparation.

production		costing only
18 oz.	skin-on salmon fillet cut from the thick end	18 oz.
1 Tbsp.	fresh lemon juice	3/8 [90 ct.] lemon
1 Tbsp.	aquavit or brandy	1/2 fl. oz.
1/4 c.	kosher salt	2 oz.
1/2 c.	brown sugar	2 3/4 oz.
1 Tbsp.	crushed peppercorns, preferably white	1/4 oz.
1 Tbsp.	crushed coriander seeds	1/4 oz.
1 Tbsp.	minced lemon zest	n/c
2 c.	coarse-chopped fresh dill leaves	3/4 bunch a.p.

first day preparation:
1. Wash and dry the salmon fillet.
2. Using kitchen tweezers or clean needle-nose pliers, remove any pin bones in the salmon flesh.
3. Using a sharp knife, cut shallow slits through the salmon skin in a crosshatch pattern. ⚠ Do not cut into the flesh.
4. Lay out a long piece of plastic wrap on the work surface and place the salmon fillet on it, skin side down.
5. Rub the lemon juice and aquavit into the salmon flesh.
6. Mix together the salt, sugar, peppercorns, coriander seeds, and lemon zest.
7. Rub the seasoning mixture onto the salmon, using less than half on the skin side and more on the flesh side.
8. Coat both sides with dill leaves.
9. Wrap the salmon in the plastic wrap.
10. Place the salmon packet in a half-size hotel pan, skin side up; place another half-size hotel pan on top and weight the top pan with a heavy object.
11. Refrigerate the salmon for 12 hours.

second day preparation:
12. Remove the weight and pan from the salmon and drain off the liquid. Turn the salmon packet over so that the flesh side is up. Return the top pan, replace the weight, and refrigerate 12 hours longer.
13. Repeat, turning the salmon skin side up. Refrigerate 12 hours longer.

third day preparation:
14. Unwrap the salmon and check the cure. The salmon flesh should retain a raw appearance but feel firm throughout.
15. Brush off the curing ingredients and place the gravlax on a rack set over a sheet tray, skin side down.
16. Refrigerate, uncovered, up to 6 hours to air-dry.

holding: wrapped in butcher paper or pan liner and refrigerated up to 5 days longer

COMPONENT RECIPE
DILLED MUSTARD SAUCE

yield: approx. 1/2 c.

production		costing only
3/8 c.	sour cream	3 fl. oz.
2 Tbsp.	mayonnaise	1 fl. oz.
1 Tbsp.	Dijon mustard	1/2 oz.
1 Tbsp.	minced dill	1/40 bunch a.p.
1 tsp.	sugar	1/6 oz.
tt	kosher salt	1/16 oz.
tt	fine-ground white pepper	1/16 oz.

preparation:
1. Mix all ingredients.
2. Refrigerate and allow the flavors to mellow for at least 1/2 hour.
3. Taste and correct the seasoning.

holding: refrigerated in a freshly sanitized, covered container up to 5 days

---

RECIPE VARIATION
Southwestern Gravlax on Corn Cakes with Salsa Sour Cream
Replace the aquavit with tequila, the white pepper with pure New Mexico dried red chile powder, and the dill with cilantro. Replace the Dilled Mustard Sauce with a sauce made by combining equal parts Cooked Tomato Salsa and sour cream. Replace the toast points with Granddaddy's Corn Cakes.

Triple Onion Potato Pierogies

yield: 1 (4-oz.) appetizer serving
(multiply × 4 for classroom turnout; adjust equipment sizes accordingly)

MASTER RECIPE

production		costing only
as needed	water	n/c
3	Potato-Leek Pierogies	1/4 recipe
1/4 c.	Caramelized Onions	1/4 recipe
1 Tbsp.	fresh lemon juice	3/8 [90 ct.] lemon
tt	kosher salt	1/16 oz.
tt	fine-ground white pepper	1/16 oz.
4 Tbsp.	butter	2 oz.
2 Tbsp.	thin diagonal-sliced scallion	1/8 bunch a.p.
1 Tbsp.	brunoise-cut red bell pepper	1/2 oz. a.p.

service turnout:

1. Heat the Potato-Leek Pierogies:
   a. Bring 1" of water to the boil in an 8" sauté pan.
   b. Add the pierogies and simmer about 1 minute, until heated through.
2. Plate the pierogies and make the sauce:
   a. Using tongs, lift each pierogi out of the simmering water, blot it with a clean kitchen towel, and arrange it on a hot 10" plate to make a spoke pattern with all three pierogies. Hold hot.
   b. Pour off all but 1/3 c. water from the pan.
   c. Add the Caramelized Onions, lemon juice, salt, and white pepper.
   d. Bring the mixture to the boil and reduce it until only about 2 Tbsp. liquid remains.
   e. Remove the pan from the heat and work in the butter to create an emulsion.
   f. Correct the seasoning.
   g. Pour the sauce over the pierogies, mounding the onions in the center.
   h. Sprinkle the scallion and red bell pepper around the edge of the plate well.

COMPONENT RECIPE
POTATO-LEEK PIEROGIES

yield: 12 or more (1 1/2-oz.) pierogies

production		costing only
1 Tbsp.	kosher salt	1/2 oz.
as needed	flour	2 oz.
1 lb.	Pierogi Dough	1 recipe
2 c.	Potato-Leek Pierogi Filling	1 recipe
2 Tbsp.	melted butter	1 oz.

preparation:

1. Bring about 1 gal. water to the boil and add the salt.
2. Make up the pierogies:
   a. Flour the work surface and a rolling pin.
   b. Roll out the Pierogi Dough a little thicker than 1/8". (You may wish to divide the dough in half and work in two batches.)
   c. Using a 3 1/2" round cutter, punch out 12 or more rounds. (If necessary, the dough scraps may be rested 15 minutes and then re-rolled.)
   d. To make each pierogi, spoon a heaping tablespoon of Potato-Leek Pierogi Filling in the center of a dough round. Fold the dough into a half-moon shape and crimp the edges shut with the tines of a fork.
   e. Repeat to make at least 12 pierogies. (You may have extra filling and dough with which to make more.)
3. Parboil the pierogies:
   a. Drop the pierogies into the boiling water and cook at a lively boil 4 to 5 minutes, until the pierogies float to the top and the dough is al dente.
   b. Using a perforated lifter, remove the pierogies from the water into a colander.
   c. Rinse the pierogies under lukewarm water, drain, and blot dry on a clean, lint-free towel.
   d. Place the pierogies on a half-sheet tray with pan liner.
   e. Brush both sides of each pierogi with melted butter.
   f. Cool to room temperature.

holding: cover and refrigerate up to 3 days; may be frozen up to 1 month with slight loss of quality

COMPONENT RECIPE
PIEROGI DOUGH

yield: approx. 1 lb.

production		costing only
1 3/4 c.+	flour, plus additional	10 oz.+
1/2 tsp.	fine salt	1/12 oz.
1	room-temperature egg	1 each or 2 oz.
2/3 c.	sour cream	5 1/3 fl. oz.

preparation:
1. Place the flour in a large bowl and mix in the salt.
2. Make a well in the center and crack in the egg.
3. Using a fork, beat the egg to mix it well, then stir in the sour cream.
4. Begin stirring the flour into the egg mixture, a little at a time, to make a medium-soft dough. Add additional flour as necessary.
5. When the dough forms a ball, dust the work surface with flour and knead the dough 2 to 3 minutes, until smooth and slightly elastic.
6. Dust the dough mass with flour, wrap it in plastic film, and rest at room temperature 20 minutes.

holding: at cool room temperature up to 3 hours; if longer holding is necessary, refrigerate; bring to room temperature before using

COMPONENT RECIPE
POTATO-LEEK PIEROGI FILLING

yield: approx. 2 c.

production		costing only
12 oz.	russet potatoes	12 oz. a.p.
2 tsp.	kosher salt	1/3 oz.
as needed	water	n/c
2	large leeks	2/3 bunch or 14 oz.
2 Tbsp.	butter	1 oz.
tt	fine-ground white pepper	1/8 oz.

preparation:
1. Fabricate, cook, and mash the potatoes:
   a. Peel the potatoes, cut them into 1" chunks, and place them in a saucepan with the salt and cold water to cover.
   b. Boil the potatoes just until tender.
   c. Drain the potatoes, transfer them to a bowl, and mash them into a rough purée.
2. Fabricate and cook the leeks:
   a. Cut off and discard the root ends of the leeks.
   b. Cut off the dark green tops, leaving only the white and pale green parts. (The green tops may be saved for stock.)
   c. Cut a lengthwise slit in each leek, open out the layers, and wash under cool running water to remove all traces of soil.
   d. Chop the leeks into approximately 1/4" pieces.
   e. Heat a nonstick sauté pan, heat the butter, and sauté the leeks with a little salt until wilted and light brown at the edges.
   f. Add about 1 c. water, cover the pan, and simmer about 10 minutes, until the leeks are very tender.
   g. Uncover the pan and cook over high heat, stirring, until the excess water reduces away and the leeks begin to sizzle.
3. Mix together the leek and potato.
4. Correct the salt and add the white pepper to make a highly seasoned filling.
5. Cool the filling to room temperature.

holding: refrigerated in a freshly sanitized, covered container up to 5 days

---

RECIPE VARIATIONS

Potato-Cheddar Pierogies with Onion Butter Sauce
For the pierogies, replace the cooked leeks with 1 c. grated extra-sharp white Cheddar cheese. For the sauce, replace the Caramelized Onions with sautéed chopped red onions.

Sauerkraut Pierogies with Onion Butter Sauce
Replace the filling with the following mixture: 1 1/2 c. mashed potatoes; 1/2 c. cooked, drained, chopped sauerkraut; 2 Tbsp. chopped, sautéed onions. For the sauce, replace the Caramelized Onions with sautéed chopped red onions.

Pierogi Medley with Onion Butter Sauce
Serve one Potato-Leek Pierogi, one Potato-Cheddar Pierogi, and one Sauerkraut Pierogi with Onion Butter Sauce.

Golden Fried Pierogies
Omit the butter sauce. Sauté the pierogies in clarified butter until crisp and golden. Garnish with chopped scallion, brunoise-cut red bell pepper, and a dollop of sour cream.

Red, White, and Maytag Blue Salad
with Pickled Beets and Egg

yield: 1 (approx. 5-oz.) appetizer serving
(multiply × 4 for classroom turnout)

🕐 Requires 24 hours advance preparation.

APPETIZERS

MASTER RECIPE

production		costing only
2 oz.	washed and dried red leaf lettuce	1/6 head a.p.
1/3 c.	1/2"-diced White Bread Croutons	1/12 recipe
3 Tbsp.	American Cider Vinaigrette, in squeeze bottle	3/16 recipe
1 slice	sweet onion	1 oz. a.p.
4 wedges	Pickled Beets, drained	1/6 recipe
1	Pickled Egg	1/4 recipe
2 Tbsp.	crumbled Maytag Blue cheese	1/2 oz.
1 Tbsp.	fine-sliced chives	1/20 bunch a.p.

service turnout:
1. Tear the lettuce into bite-sized pieces and place it in a bowl.
2. Toss the lettuce and White Bread Croutons with about 2 Tbsp. American Cider Vinaigrette.
3. Plate the dish:
   a. Mound the lettuce on a cool 10" plate.
   b. Break the onion into rings and arrange the rings on the lettuce.
   c. Arrange the Pickled Beets in a circle on top of the onion.
   d. Cut the Pickled Egg into 4 wedges and arrange the wedges between the beets.
   e. Drizzle the remaining vinaigrette over the top.
   f. Sprinkle the cheese and chives on top.

COMPONENT RECIPE
PICKLED BEETS AND EGGS

yield: 24 beet wedges (approx. 8 oz.) plus 4 eggs

🕐 Requires 24 hours advance preparation.

production		costing only
4	small beets (greens removed)	1 bunch or 12 oz.
tt	kosher salt	1/4 oz.
as needed	water	n/c
4	peeled hard-cooked eggs	4 each
1 1/2 c.	cider vinegar	12 fl. oz.
3/4 c.	brown sugar	3 3/8 oz.
4	peeled, slightly crushed garlic cloves	1 oz. a.p.
1/2 c.	thin-sliced yellow onion	2 1/2 oz. a.p.
1/2 tsp.	coriander seeds	1/16 oz.
1 tsp.	black peppercorns	1/8 oz.
1/2 tsp.	dill seeds	1/16 oz.

preparation:
1. Prepare the beets and eggs:
   a. Trim and peel the beets. Cut each into 6 even wedges.
   b. Place the beets and a little salt in a small saucepan and add water to cover by 1". Simmer 10 to 12 minutes, until the beets are tender.
   c. Using a slotted spoon, lift out the beets and transfer them to a bowl.
2. Prepare the pickling liquid:
   a. Pour out and discard all but 1 c. of the beet liquid.
   b. Add the vinegar, sugar, and a little salt, and bring the liquid to the boil. Cook at a rolling boil 5 minutes.
   c. Remove from the heat and correct the seasoning to achieve a sweet-salty-tart flavor balance.
3. Add the garlic, onion, coriander seeds, black peppercorns, and dill seeds to the bowl with the beets and toss to combine.
4. Pack the beets, eggs, and seasonings into a freshly sanitized, nonreactive container of the correct size to hold them snug. Pour the pickling liquid over the beets and eggs. Make sure the beets and eggs are completely submerged. If necessary, weight them down with a small plate or dish.
5. Cool the beets and eggs to room temperature, cover the container, and refrigerate at least 24 hours.

holding: refrigerated for 1 to 2 days longer (if held too long in the liquid, the egg whites will toughen and the yolks will discolor)

RECIPE VARIATION
Roasted Beet and Blue Cheese Salad with Quail Eggs
Roast and peel the beets rather than boiling them. Omit the pickling liquid ingredients. Marinate the beets in 1/2 c. American Cider Vinaigrette. Replace the pickled eggs with 5 quail eggs per serving, poached to order.

Escalopes of Goose
with Dried Cherry Demi-Glace and
Ojibwa Goose Ragout in Baby Pumpkin,
with Braised Kale and Wild Rice

yield: 1 (8-oz.) entrée serving plus accompaniments
(multiply × 4 for classroom turnout; adjust equipment sizes
accordingly)

MASTER RECIPE

production		costing only
1	Steamed Baby Pumpkin	1/4 recipe
2 tsp.	melted butter	1/3 oz.
tt	kosher salt	1/16 oz.
1/2 c.	Ojibwa Goose Ragout	1/4 recipe
as needed	water	n/c
1 Tbsp.	clarified butter	2/3 oz. a.p.
2 c.	tightly packed chiffonade kale	6 oz. a.p.
1 Tbsp.	clarified butter	2/3 oz. a.p.
3 oz. (4 pc.)	Escalopes of Goose	1/4 recipe
1/2 c.	Demi-Glace	1/8 recipe
1/4 c.	Goose Reduction	1/4 recipe
2 Tbsp.	Reconstituted Cherries	1/4 recipe
3/4 c.	Wild Rice, hot in steam table	1/4 recipe

service turnout:

1. Brush the inside of the Steamed Baby Pumpkin with melted
   butter, season it with salt, place it on a sizzle pan, and bake
   in a 400°F oven about 10 minutes, until heated through.
2. Place the Ojibwa Goose Ragout and a little water in an
   8" sauté pan, cover, and simmer just until heated through.
3. Heat a 10" sauté pan, heat 1 Tbsp. clarified butter, and
   sauté the kale with a little salt until wilted. Add a little water,
   cover the pan, and braise about 3 minutes, until the kale is
   tender and the liquid absorbed.
4. Sear the Escalopes of Goose and finish the sauce:
   a. Heat an 8" sauté pan until very hot, add 1 Tbsp. clari-
      fied butter, and quickly sear the escalopes a few sec-
      onds on each side for a browned exterior but rare
      interior. Hold warm.
   b. Deglaze the pan with the Demi-Glace, Goose Reduc-
      tion, and Reconstituted Cherries to make the sauce.
   c. Season the sauce with salt.
5. Plate the dish:
   a. Mound the Wild Rice on the back of a hot 12" plate.
   b. Mound the kale to the right of the wild rice.
   c. Spoon the goose ragout into the pumpkin and place it
      on top of the wild rice.
   d. Overlap the escalopes on the front of the plate, leaning
      against the rice and pumpkin.
   e. Pour the sauce over the escalopes.

COMPONENT RECIPE

OJIBWA GOOSE RAGOUT, ESCALOPES OF GOOSE, AND GOOSE REDUCTION

yield: 1 qt. ragout, 12 escalopes of goose, 1 c. reduction

production		costing only
1/2	12-lb. domestic goose (from whole carcass split lengthwise down the center)	6 lb.
as needed	pan coating spray or vegetable oil	% of container or 1/4 fl. oz.
as needed	water	n/c
2 Tbsp.	clarified butter	1 1/3 oz. a.p.
4 oz.	button mushrooms (or large ones, quartered)	4 oz.
tt	kosher salt	1/8 oz.
1 tsp.	minced garlic	1/9 oz. a.p.
2 c.	Brown Poultry Stock	1/8 recipe
1 tsp.	balsamic vinegar	1/6 oz.
3/4 c.	Demi-Glace	3/16 recipe
3/4 c.	3/8"-diced sunchokes (Jerusalem artichokes), blanched and refreshed	5 oz. a.p.
1 c.	full-bodied, dry red wine	8 fl. oz.
1 tsp.	minced sage	1/40 bunch a.p.
1 tsp.	minced thyme leaves	1/40 bunch a.p.
tt	fresh-ground black pepper	1/16 oz.

preparation:

1. Preheat an oven to 400°F.
2. Fabricate the goose:
   a. Remove the wing and whole leg from the goose half-carcass.
   b. Cut the wing through the joints into three pieces and remove as much fat and skin as possible. Place the pieces in a 12" sauté pan.
   c. Skin the leg and remove the meat from the bone, trimming off as much fat* as possible. Cut the meat into 3/4" dice. Chop the bone into three pieces and add them to the sauté pan.
   d. Skin the breast and remove the breast meat from the carcass. Separate the tendon from the main muscle and remove the tendon. Defat* the remaining carcass and chop it into several pieces. Add the carcass pieces to the sauté pan.
   e. Cutting on the diagonal, slice the breast meat into 12 flat, even escalopes totaling 12 oz. meat. Cut any remaining breast meat into 3/4" dice and add it to the leg meat.
   f. Spray a sheet of pan liner with pan coating and place the escalopes on one side of it. Fold the paper over the escalopes. Flatten the escalopes by pounding gently with a meat mallet.
   g. Divide the escalopes into 4 (3-oz.) portions, wrap individually, and refrigerate.
3. Place the sauté pan of goose bones in the preheated oven and roast them about 30 minutes, until browned.
4. Prepare the ragout:
   a. Heat a 10" sauté pan, heat half the clarified butter, and sear the mushrooms with a little salt until browned. Remove.
   b. Add the remaining clarified butter and sear the goose meat cubes.
   c. Reduce the heat and add the garlic, Brown Poultry Stock, and vinegar. Simmer uncovered about 15 minutes, until the goose is tender.
   d. Remove the goose meat and reduce the cooking liquid to about 1/2 c.
   e. Add the Demi-Glace, mushrooms, sunchokes, and goose meat. Bring to the simmer.
   f. Correct the salt and vinegar. Season with sage, thyme, and pepper.
5. Prepare the goose reduction:
   a. Remove the sauté pan of roasted bones from the oven and press down on them with a spatula to flatten them.
   b. Add the red wine and enough water to cover the bones.
   c. Place the pan over medium heat. Simmer briskly up to 1 hour, adding water as needed to keep the bones barely covered.
   d. Strain the liquid and discard the bones.
   e. Return the liquid to the pan and reduce over high heat, scraping to release the pan glaze, and reduce to about 1 c. goose reduction.

holding: open-pan cool and immediately refrigerate in a freshly sanitized, covered container up to 5 days

*Goose fat may be rendered in the same manner as pork fat to make an excellent frying medium for potatoes and other foods.

COMPONENT RECIPE
RECONSTITUTED CHERRIES

yield: 1/2 c.

production		costing only
1/3 c.	dried cherries	1 3/4 oz.
1/2 c.	white wine	4 fl. oz.
1/3 c.	ruby Port wine	2 2/3 oz.

preparation:
1. Combine the cherries, white wine, and Port in a small, non-reactive saucepan. Bring to the simmer and reduce to 1/2 c.

holding: open-pan cool and refrigerate in a freshly sanitized, non-reactive container up to 5 days

COMPONENT RECIPE
WILD RICE

yield: approx. 3 c.

production		costing only
1 c.	wild rice	6 oz.
6 c.	water	n/c
tt	kosher salt	1/8 oz.
4 Tbsp.	butter	2 oz.
1/2 c.	peeled, minced celery	1/20 bunch a.p.
3/4 c.	fine-chopped yellow onion	3 3/4 oz. a.p.
1 tsp.	minced lemon zest	n/c
1 c.	Brown Poultry Stock	1/16 recipe
tt	fresh lemon juice	1/6 [90 ct.] lemon

preparation:
1. Rinse the wild rice in several changes of water and drain.
2. In a heavy saucepan, bring 6 c. water to the boil and add some salt. Stir in the rice and simmer briskly, stirring occasionally, about 35 minutes, until the grains have swollen and the ends burst open. Taste to ensure that the rice has cooked al dente.
3. Heat a 10" sauté pan, heat the butter, and add the celery, onion, and a little salt. Sweat over low heat until soft.
4. Drain the wild rice and add it to the sauté pan along with the lemon zest and Brown Poultry Stock. Cook over high heat, scraping and tossing, until the liquid absorbs.
5. Season with lemon juice and correct the salt.

holding: open-pan cool and refrigerate in a freshly sanitized, covered container up to 5 days

---

RECIPE VARIATIONS

Escalopes of Duck with Dried Cherry Demi-Glace and Ojibwa Goose Ragout in Baby Pumpkin, with Braised Kale and Wild Rice
Replace the goose with a 5-lb. Long Island duck.

Ojibwa Escalopes of Duck with Dried Cherry Demi-Glace, Braised Kale, and Wild Rice
Omit the Pumpkin and Goose Ragout. Prepare escalopes of Long Island, Muscovy, or Moulard duck breast, allowing 5 oz. per serving. Increase the sauce ingredients to make 3/4 c. sauce per serving.

Deep-Dish Flaky Pastry Chicken Pie

yield: 1 entrée serving: 6 oz. chicken plus vegetables
(multiply × 4 for classroom turnout; adjust equipment sizes
accordingly)

MASTER RECIPE

production		costing only
2 c.	Chicken Pie Filling	1/4 recipe
as needed	water, in squeeze bottle	n/c
2 tsp.	Egg Wash	1/9 recipe
1	disc prerolled puff pastry sheet, cut to fit a 16-fl.-oz. individual casserole, very cold	1/10 sheet
1	cocktail napkin or 8" doily	1 each
1 bouquet	watercress	1/6 bunch a.p.

service turnout:

1. Place 2 c. Chicken Pie Filling into a 10" sauté pan (make sure ingredients are evenly distributed). Add a little water, cover, and bring just to the boil.
2. Assemble the casserole:
   a. Place a 16-fl.-oz. individual casserole on a half-sheet tray and spoon the hot filling into it.
   b. Wipe the casserole of any drips, brush the inside rim with egg wash, and place the puff pastry disc on top. Press gently so the top of the pastry is level with the rim of the casserole.
   c. Brush the pastry with egg wash.
   d. Using a sharp paring knife, cut 3 slashes into the pastry in a decorative pattern.
3. Place the casserole in a 400°F oven. Bake about 10 minutes, until the pastry is puffed and golden.
4. Plate the dish:
   a. Place the cocktail napkin on a cool 12" plate.
   b. Place the casserole on the plate slightly left of center.
   c. Arrange the watercress bouquet on the right of the casserole.

COMPONENT RECIPE

CHICKEN PIE FILLING

yield: 8 c.

production		costing only
1	3-lb. fryer/broiler chicken	3 lb.
5 c.	Poultry Stock	1/3 recipe
1/2	lemon	1/2 [90 ct.] lemon
2 sprigs	fresh thyme	1/10 bunch a.p.
2 sprigs	flat-leaf parsley	1/10 bunch a.p.
2 sprigs	celery leaves	n/c
2 or 3	leek greens, washed well	n/c
1 Tbsp.	clarified butter	2/3 oz. a.p.
6 oz.	button mushrooms (or large ones, quartered)	6 oz.
tt	kosher salt	1/8 oz.
6 Tbsp.	butter	3 oz.
6 Tbsp.	flour	2 oz.
2 tsp.	minced lemon zest	n/c
pinch	fine-ground white pepper	1/16 oz.
1 c.	1" batonnet-cut carrots, blanched and refreshed	4 oz. a.p.
2/3 c.	peeled, poached pearl onions (or frozen)	1/2 pt. a.p. or 3 oz.
1/2 c.	shelled peas, blanched and refreshed (or frozen)	1/2 lb. a.p. or 2 oz.
2 tsp.	chopped flat-leaf parsley	1/40 bunch a.p.
2 tsp.	chopped tarragon leaves	1/20 bunch a.p.

preparation:

1. Fabricate the raw chicken:
   a. Cut the chicken into 2 bone-in breast halves, 2 legs, 2 wings, and the backbone.
   b. Remove the skin and as much fat as possible from the entire carcass.
   c. Remove any bits of internal organ clinging to the backbone.
   d. Wash all pieces and pat dry.

2. Cook the chicken:
   a. Bring the Poultry Stock to the boil in a saucepan. Add the chicken pieces. Squeeze in the juice from the lemon half and drop it into the pan.
   b. Return the stock to a brisk simmer, skim off the foam, and add the thyme, parsley, celery leaves, and leek greens. Poach the chicken until just cooked through, removing the breast halves at about 12 minutes and the legs at 20 minutes. (Leave the wings and the backbone to simmer until the stock is needed.)
   c. When the chicken is cool enough to handle, remove the meat from the bones and cut it into 1" pieces, trimming and discarding any bits of fat and gristle. Cover and refrigerate.
   d. Return the bones to the pan and continue simmering the stock about 30 minutes longer.

3. Heat a 10" sauté pan, heat the clarified butter, and sauté the mushrooms with a little salt until they are just cooked but not brown. Cool.

4. Make the sauce:
   a. Melt the butter in a large, heavy saucepan. Add the flour and stir over medium heat to make a blond roux.
   b. Strain the stock.
   c. Whisk in the hot stock to make a smooth velouté. Season lightly with salt and simmer briskly about 30 minutes to make about 1 qt. thick sauce.
   d. Add the lemon zest, correct the salt, and season with white pepper.
   e. If not serving immediately, cool the sauce quickly in an ice-water bath, stirring occasionally, to room temperature.

5. Fold the chicken, mushrooms, carrots, onions, peas, parsley, and tarragon into the sauce.

holding: refrigerate in a freshly sanitized, covered container up to 3 days

---

RECIPE VARIATIONS

Deep-Dish Flaky Pastry Turkey Pie
Replace the chicken with 12 oz. turkey breast cut in 1" dice. Adjust the poaching time accordingly.

Deep-Dish Flaky Pastry Pheasant Pie
Replace the chicken with 4 lb. bone-in pheasant. Enrich the sauce with reduced heavy cream to taste.

Breaded Pork Chops
with Stewed Tomatoes and Baked Macaroni 'n' Cheese

yield: 1 (7-oz.) entrée serving plus accompaniments
(multiply × 4 for classroom turnout; adjust equipment sizes accordingly)

MASTER RECIPE

production		costing only
as needed	pan coating spray	% of container
1 c.	Macaroni 'n' Cheese	1/4 recipe
1/2 c.	corn oil	4 fl. oz.
1	Breaded Pork Chop	1/4 recipe
1 1/4 c.	Stewed Tomatoes	1/4 recipe
1 Tbsp.	butter	1/2 oz.
dash	sweet paprika	1/16 oz.
1 large leaf	flat-leaf parsley	1/40 bunch a.p.

service turnout:
1. Bake the Macaroni 'n' Cheese:
   a. Spray a sizzle pan and the inside of a 3" entremet ring with pan coating.
   b. Place the ring on the sizzle pan and pack in the Macaroni 'n' Cheese.
   c. Place on the top rack of a 400°F oven and bake 10 to 12 minutes, until set and golden on top.
2. Cook the Breaded Pork Chop:
   a. Place the oil in an 8" nonstick sauté pan and heat over medium heat to about 350°F.
   b. Pan-fry the chop about 3 minutes on each side, until crisp.
   c. Drain on a rack and hold hot.
3. Heat the Stewed Tomatoes in a covered 8" sauté pan or in a microwave oven. Work in the butter to form an emulsion.
4. Plate the dish:
   a. Using an offset spatula, lift the macaroni in its ring from the sizzle pan onto the back left of a hot 12" plate. Remove the ring, running a knife around the inside if necessary to loosen the macaroni.
   b. Dust the top of the macaroni with paprika.
   c. Prop the pork chop against the macaroni with the bone pointing upward.
   d. Spoon the stewed tomatoes onto the front of the plate.
   e. Stick the parsley leaf upright between the pork chop and the macaroni.

COMPONENT RECIPE
MACARONI 'N' CHEESE

yield: 1 qt.

production		costing only
2 c.	elbow macaroni	5 1/4 oz.
1 gal.	water	n/c
tt	kosher salt	1/8 oz.
2 c.	milk	16 fl. oz.
1/2	bay leaf	1/16 oz.
1 sprig	fresh thyme	1/40 bunch a.p.
1 thick slice	onion	1 oz. a.p.
2 Tbsp.	butter	1 oz.
3 Tbsp.	flour	1 oz.
tt	fine-ground white pepper	1/16 oz.
1/2 tsp.	dry mustard	1/8 oz.
1 c.	grated extra-sharp white Cheddar cheese	4 oz.
as needed	half-and-half	2 fl. oz.

preparation:
1. Cook the macaroni:
   a. Bring the water to a rolling boil and add the salt.
   b. Stir in the macaroni and boil just until it reaches al dente.
   c. Drain the macaroni in a colander and refresh it briefly under cold running water. Shake the colander to further drain the macaroni.
2. Make the sauce:
   a. Combine the milk, bay leaf, thyme, and onion in a nonreactive saucepan and scald it over medium heat until bubbles form around the edge and steam rises.
   b. Remove the pan from the heat and steep 10 minutes.
   c. Combine the butter and flour in a heavy nonreactive saucepan and cook, stirring, to make a white roux. Remove from heat.
   d. Remove the bay leaf, thyme, and onion from the scalded milk.
   e. Whisk the hot milk into the roux and simmer 20 minutes to make a thick béchamel.
   f. Season the béchamel with salt, white pepper, and mustard.
   g. Cool to room temperature.
3. Mix together the macaroni, béchamel, and cheese. Taste and correct the salt. If the mixture seems very thick, stir in a little half-and-half.

holding: refrigerated in a freshly sanitized, covered container up to 5 days

COMPONENT RECIPE
BREADED PORK CHOPS

yield: 4 (7-oz.) chops

production		costing only
4	8-oz. rib pork chops	2 lb.
1 Tbsp.	Southern Seasoning for Pork	1/6 recipe
as needed	flour	1 oz.
6 Tbsp.	Egg Wash	2 recipes
2 c.	cornflake crumbs	9 oz.

preparation:
1. Fabricate and season the chops:
   a. French a chop by scraping away the meat and fat from the upper third of the bone.
   b. Score the rounded edge by cutting through the silverskin.
   c. Rub the meat surfaces of the chop with 1/4 of the Southern Seasoning for Pork.
   d. Repeat, to fabricate and season a total of 4 chops.
2. Bread the chops:
   a. Set up a breading station with pans of flour, Egg Wash, and cornflake crumbs, and a rack set on a half-sheet tray.
   b. Dredge a chop on all surfaces in flour and tap off the excess.
   c. Dip all surfaces of the chop in the egg wash and allow the excess to drip off.
   d. Dredge the chop on all surfaces in the cornflake crumbs, pressing firmly so they adhere.
   e. Place the chop on the rack.
   f. Repeat, breading a total of 4 chops.
   g. Refrigerate the chops, uncovered, at least 30 minutes.

holding: refrigerated on the rack, covered loosely with plastic film, up to 3 days

COMPONENT RECIPE
STEWED TOMATOES

yield: approx. 5 c.

production		costing only
1 1/4 lb.	firm-ripe plum tomatoes or other small tomatoes	1 1/4 lb.
3 Tbsp.	butter	1 1/2 oz.
1/2 c.	peeled, 3/8"-diced celery	1/10 head a.p.
1/2 c.	medium-chopped yellow onion	2 1/2 oz. a.p.
1/4 c.	3/8"-diced green bell pepper	1 1/2 oz. a.p.
1 c.	canned tomato juice	8 fl. oz.
tt	kosher salt	1/8 oz.
tt	sugar	1/2 oz.
tt	fresh-ground black pepper	1/16 oz.

preparation:
1. Fabricate the tomatoes:
   a. Blanch, refresh, peel, and core the tomatoes.
   b. Cut the tomatoes in half lengthwise.
   c. Place a strainer in a bowl and, holding the tomatoes over the strainer, scrape out the seeds and juice. Force the juice through the strainer and discard the seeds.
2. Melt the butter in a heavy nonreactive saucepan. Add the celery, onion, and green bell pepper. Sweat the vegetables over low heat about 3 minutes, until soft.
3. Add the canned tomato juice and the juice from the fresh tomatoes. Bring to the simmer and season lightly with salt and sugar (remember that the sauce will later be reduced and the flavor concentrated).
4. Add the tomato pieces and simmer gently about 5 minutes, until the tomatoes are softened but not falling apart.
5. Using a perforated spoon, lift out the tomatoes and reserve them.
6. Increase the heat and reduce the cooking liquid into a moderately thick sauce.
7. Correct the seasoning with salt and sugar (this dish should be relatively sweet).
8. Return the tomatoes to the sauce.

holding: open-pan cool and refrigerate in a freshly sanitized, covered container up to 5 days

---

RECIPE VARIATIONS

Breaded Pork Medallions with Stewed Tomatoes and Macaroni 'n' Cheese
Replace each pork chop with 3 (1 1/2-oz.) pork medallions cut from the loin.

Midwestern Wiener Schnitzel
Replace the pork chops with 2 (3-oz.) flattened veal cutlets. Replace the cornflake crumbs with fresh bread crumbs. Serve with lemon wedges, Egg Potato Salad (p. 60), and green salad with Sweet Cider Vinaigrette.

Minnesota Fruit-Stuffed Pork Loin

with Jansson's Temptation and Watercress

yield: 1 (7 1/2-oz.) entrée serving plus accompaniments (multiply × 4 for classroom turnout; adjust equipment sizes accordingly)

MASTER RECIPE

production		costing only
5 oz.	Jansson's Temptation	1/4 recipe
as needed	pan coating spray	% of container
3	2 1/2-oz. slices Minnesota Fruit-Stuffed Pork Loin	1/4 recipe
3/4 c	jus (from Pork Loin recipe)	n/c
1 Tbsp.	Butter-Toasted Bread Crumbs	1/32 recipe
1 Tbsp.	butter	1/2 oz.
1 bouquet	watercress	1/3 bunch a.p.

service turnout:

1. Spoon the Jansson's Temptation onto a sizzle pan sprayed with pan coating. Heat in a 400°F oven until hot and beginning to brown.
2. Place the Minnesota Fruit-Stuffed Pork Loin slices in a 10" sauté pan along with the jus. Cover and heat over very low heat.
3. Plate the dish and finish the sauce:
   a. Mound the Jansson's Temptation on the back right of a warm 12" plate. Sprinkle with Butter-Toasted Bread Crumbs.
   b. Overlap the pork loin slices across the front of the plate.
   c. Bring the jus to the boil, remove from the heat, and work in the butter to create an emulsion.
   d. Nap the pork loin slices with the jus.
   e. Arrange the watercress bouquet upright on the back left of the plate.

COMPONENT RECIPE

JANSSON'S (YAHN-senz) TEMPTATION

yield: about 1 1/4 lb.

production		costing only
3 Tbsp.	butter	1 1/2 oz.
1 c.	thin-sliced yellow onion	4 1/2 oz. a.p.
1 lb.	russet potatoes	1 1/4 lb.
2 Tbsp.	chopped anchovy fillets	1/4 oz.
tt	fine-ground white pepper	1/8 oz.
2 c.	half-and-half	16 fl. oz.
as needed	kosher salt	1/16 oz.

preparation:

1. Melt the butter in a 12" nonstick sauté pan and add the onion. Sauté over medium heat about 1 minute until soft but not brown.
2. Fabricate the potatoes:
   a. Peel the potatoes, wash them, and blot them dry.
   b. Cut the potatoes into rough batonnet shapes. As you work, cover the batonnets with a clean, damp towel to prevent browning. Do not soak in water.
3. Add the anchovies, white pepper, and potatoes to the onion and toss to coat the potatoes with the seasonings.
4. Pour in the half-and-half, cover the pan, and simmer briskly about 15 minutes, until the potatoes are just tender and the half-and-half has thickened. During the cooking time, turn over the potatoes with a heatproof rubber spatula once or twice to ensure even cooking.
5. Correct the seasoning, adding salt only if necessary.

holding: open-pan cool and immediately refrigerate in a freshly sanitized, covered container

Scoring the fat in a crosshatch pattern.

The butterflied roast.

The roast formed into a cylinder.

The trussed roast.

COMPONENT RECIPE

MINNESOTA FRUIT-STUFFED PORK LOIN

yield: 12 (2 1/2-oz.) slices

production		costing only
1 c.	red Port wine	8 fl. oz.
1 c.	water	n/c
1/2 c.	3/8"-diced dried apples	2 oz.
1/2 c.	3/8"-diced pitted prunes	3 1/2 oz.
1/2 c.	pitted dried cherries	2 1/2 oz.
1/2 c.	3/8"-diced dried apricots	2 1/2 oz.
1/4 c.	butter	2 oz.
1 c.	fine-chopped yellow onion	5 oz. a.p.
1/2 c.	peeled, fine-chopped celery	1/10 head a.p.
1 1/2 c.	Butter-Toasted Bread Crumbs	3/4 recipe
±1/2 c.	warm Poultry Stock	1/32 recipe
1	egg, beaten	1 each or 2 oz.
tt	kosher salt	1/8 oz.
tt	fresh-ground black pepper	1/8 oz.
2 Tbsp.	chopped flat-leaf parsley	1/10 bunch a.p.
1	2-lb. center-cut boneless pork loin roast	2 lb.
2 c.	apple cider	1 pt.
1 qt.	Poultry Stock	1/4 recipe
1 Tbsp.	fresh lemon juice	1/6 [90 ct.] lemon
1 Tbsp.	minced lemon zest	n/c
1 c.	medium-diced yellow onion	4 oz. a.p.
1/2 c.	medium-diced celery	1/10 head a.p.
1/2 c.	fine-diced carrot	2 oz. a.p.

preparation:

1. Preheat an oven to 450°F.
2. Reconstitute the dried fruits:
   a. Place the Port; water; and dried apples, prunes, cherries, and apricots in a small, nonreactive saucepan and bring to the boil.
   b. Remove from the heat and steep until cool.
   c. Remove the fruits from the liquid, squeezing them dry, and reserving both fruits and liquid.
3. Prepare the stuffing:
   a. In a 10" sauté pan heat the butter and sauté the fine-chopped onion and celery until soft but not brown.
   b. Add the reconstituted fruits to the pan along with the Butter-Toasted Bread Crumbs. Mix well and cool to room temperature.
   c. Stir in half of the egg and just enough of the 1/2 c. Poultry Stock to moisten the crumbs.
   d. Season highly with salt and pepper, and mix in the parsley.
4. Fabricate and stuff the pork roast:
   a. Trim the pork loin's surface fat to an even 3/8" layer.
   b. Using a sharp, flexible knife, score the fat in a 3/8" crosshatch pattern. (Cut through only the fat and silverskin; do not cut into the meat itself.)
   c. Turn the roast over, fat side down, and cut a lengthwise slit halfway through the meat. Butterfly the meat open by cutting parallel to the work surface from the center out to within about 1" of each side.
   d. Brush the interior of the roast with the remaining beaten egg, and season it highly with salt and pepper.
   e. Form a cylinder of fruit stuffing down the center of the roast, pressing firmly so that the stuffing holds its shape.
   f. Bring up the sides of the roast and, using a trussing needle and kitchen string, sew the roast shut into its original cylindrical shape.
   g. Cut two 4" circles of pan liner and press them onto either end of the roast to hold in the filling.
   h. Truss the roast with kitchen string, making sure to truss the ends of the roast to hold the pan liner circles in place.
   i. Season the exterior of the roast with salt and pepper.
5. Prepare the basting liquid:
   a. Combine the cider, 1 qt. Poultry Stock, lemon juice, and lemon zest in a small, nonreactive saucepan.
   b. Add the reserved fruit-steeping liquid.
   c. Bring to the simmer and season with salt (remember that the basting sauce will later be reduced and its flavor concentrated).
6. Roast the pork loin:
   a. Place the diced mirepoix (onion, celery, and carrot) in a roasting pan just large enough to hold the pork.
   b. Place the pork in the pan on the mirepoix vegetables, fat side up, and add 1 c. of the basting sauce.
   c. Place the pan in the oven and roast the pork about 15 minutes, until the top becomes golden brown.
   d. Reduce the heat to 325°F and continue to roast about 40 minutes to an internal temperature of 150°F. Baste occasionally, using half of the remaining basting liquid. ⚠ Be sure to insert the thermometer into the meat and not the filling. Do not allow the roasting pan to become dry.
   e. Remove the roast from the pan and allow it to rest at least 10 minutes for immediate service, or open-pan cool to room temperature.
7. Prepare the jus:
   a. Place a strainer in the pan holding the basting liquid, and scrape the roasting pan juices and mirepoix into it. Press to extract as much liquid as possible, then discard the solids.
   b. Reduce the jus to a light nappé consistency. (You will need 3 c. jus.)
   c. Deglaze the roasting pan with a little water and add to the basting liquid as it reduces.
   d. Taste the jus and correct the seasoning.
8. Cut the roast into 12 (approx. 1/2" thick) slices.
9. If not serving immediately, place the pork slices into a freshly sanitized, covered container with pan liner between layers. Cool the jus and place in a freshly sanitized, covered container.

holding: refrigerate, covered, up to 5 days

RECIPE VARIATIONS

Roast Pork Loin with Fruit Sauce, Jansson's Temptation, and Watercress
Omit the stuffing ingredients and roast the pork loin whole. Add the Port-steeped fruit to the jus in step 7 after straining and before reducing.

Minnesota Fruit-Stuffed Pork Chop with Jansson's Temptation and Watercress
Replace the pork loin with 4 (10-oz.) center-cut rib pork chops. Cut a pocket in each chop, fill with the fruit stuffing, and secure shut. Sear the chops to order in clarified butter, then braise in the basting liquid.

Cincinnati Five-Way Chili

with a Frank

yield: 1 (7-oz.) entrée serving plus accompaniments
(multiply × 4 for classroom turnout; adjust equipment sizes
accordingly)

MASTER RECIPE

production		costing only
1	pork-and-beef natural casing frankfurter	3 oz.
1 tsp.	corn oil	1/6 fl. oz.
1 1/2 c.	Cincinnati Chili	1/4 recipe
as needed	water, in squeeze bottle	n/c
2 c.	cooked, refreshed, drained spaghetti	2 1/2 oz. a.p.
1 c.	water	n/c
tt	kosher salt	1/16 oz.
1 Tbsp.	butter	1/2 oz.
1/2 c.	cooked or canned red kidney beans, hot in steam table	1 oz. dry or 2 oz. canned
1/3 c.	grated sharp yellow Cheddar cheese	1 oz.
1/3 c.	medium-chopped sweet onion	1 1/2 oz. a.p.
1 Tbsp.	chopped flat-leaf parsley	1/40 bunch a.p.

service turnout:

1. Cook the frankfurter:
   a. Score the frankfurter with five shallow slits on one side only (so it curls as it cooks).
   b. Brush the frankfurter with oil and grill over medium heat until it curls and chars slightly.
   c. Hold hot.
2. Heat the Cincinnati Chili with a little water in a covered 10" sauté pan.
3. Heat the spaghetti:
   a. Place the spaghetti in a 10" sauté pan with about 1 c. water and a little salt. Cover and cook over high heat about 3 minutes, until the water boils.
   b. Drain off all but 2 Tbsp. water. Remove from the heat and work in the butter.
   c. Replace the cover and hold hot.
4. Plate the dish:
   a. Mound the spaghetti in a hot 12" pasta plate.
   b. Top with the chili, the beans, and the cheese.
   c. Position the frankfurter, in a U shape, on top of all.
   d. Sprinkle with the onion and parsley.

COMPONENT RECIPE
CINCINNATI CHILI

yield: approx. 6 c.

production		costing only
1 1/2 lb.	ground beef (85 percent lean)	1 1/2 lb.
1/4 c.	bacon drippings or corn oil	2 fl. oz.
1 1/2 c.	fine-chopped yellow onion	7 1/2 oz. a.p.
4 Tbsp.	chili powder	3/4 oz.
1/2 tsp.	cayenne pepper	1/16 oz.
1/2 tsp.	ground turmeric	1/16 oz.
1 tsp.	ground cinnamon	1/8 oz.
1 tsp.	crushed dried oregano	1/16 oz.
1 Tbsp.	minced garlic	1/3 oz. a.p.
3 Tbsp.	flour	1 oz.
2 tsp.	unsweetened cocoa powder	1/16 oz.
2 c.	hot Brown Beef Stock	1/8 recipe
1/2 c.	lager beer	4 fl. oz.
1/2 c.	light tomato purée	4 fl. oz.
1/4 c.	ketchup	2 fl. oz.
dash	Worcestershire sauce	1/4 fl. oz.
tt	kosher salt	1/8 oz.
tt	sugar	1/4 oz.

preparation:
1. Set a colander in a bowl and place it near the stove.
2. Crumble the ground beef into a 12" nonstick sauté pan. Place the pan over medium heat and cook the beef, stirring and breaking up lumps, about 1 minute, until it loses most of its red color and renders out some of its fat content. Do not brown the meat.
3. Transfer the meat to the colander and allow it to drain.
4. Heat a heavy, nonreactive saucepan, add the bacon drippings, and then add the onion. Sauté the onion until it softens and begins to brown.
5. Add the chili powder, cayenne, turmeric, cinnamon, oregano, and garlic to the pan and sauté a few seconds, until fragrant.
6. Stir in the flour and cocoa powder.
7. Whisk in the Brown Beef Stock, followed by the beer, tomato purée, ketchup, Worcestershire sauce, and a little salt. Bring to the boil.
8. Stir in the ground beef and simmer about 10 minutes.
9. Correct the seasoning, adding more salt if needed, and a little sugar if necessary to balance the flavor.

holding: open-pan cool and refrigerate in a freshly sanitized, covered container up to 5 days; may be frozen up to 3 months

---

RECIPE VARIATIONS

Cincinnati Four-Way Chili
Serve the chili over spaghetti with onion or beans and cheese. (Omit the frank.)

Cincinnati Three-Way Chili
Serve the chili over spaghetti with cheese. (Omit the frank.)

Cincinnati Two-Way Chili
Serve the chili over spaghetti. (No frank or toppings.)

Cincinnati Chili Bowl
Serve the chili in a bowl accompanied by oyster crackers.

Classic Meat Loaf

with Mashed Potatoes, Mushroom Gravy, and Heartland Vegetable Medley

yield: 1 (7-oz.) entrée serving plus accompaniments (multiply × 4 for classroom turnout; adjust equipment sizes accordingly)

MASTER RECIPE

production		costing only
2	3/4" slices Classic Meat Loaf	1/4 recipe
2 Tbsp.	Brown Beef Stock, in squeeze bottle	1/128 recipe
1 1/2 oz.	cauliflower florets, blanched and refreshed	1/12 head a.p.
1 1/2 oz.	1" diagonal-cut green beans, blanched and refreshed	2 oz. a.p.
1 1/2 oz.	1" batonnet carrots, blanched and refreshed	2 oz. a.p.
1/4 c.	cooked corn kernels	1/4 ear or 1 1/2 oz.
1/4 c.	water, in squeeze bottle	n/c
tt	kosher salt	1/16 oz.
1 c.	Mushroom Gravy	1/4 recipe
1 1/4 c.	Classic Mashed Potatoes, hot in steam table	1/4 recipe
1 Tbsp.	butter	1/2 oz.
1 sprig	flat-leaf parsley	1/40 bunch a.p.

service turnout:

1. Place the meat loaf slices on a sizzle pan, drizzle with the Brown Beef Stock, cover with foil, and heat in a 400°F oven about 8 minutes, until heated through. Hold hot.
2. Place the cauliflower, green beans, carrots, and corn in a 10" sauté pan with the water and a little salt. Cover the pan and heat over medium heat. Hold hot.
3. Stirring well to distribute the ingredients, ladle the Mushroom Gravy into an 8" sauté pan and heat to just under the boil. Thin with water if necessary.
4. Plate the dish:
   a. Spoon the Classic Mashed Potatoes into a pastry bag fitted with a star tip*. Pipe a tall ring of potatoes onto the back center of a hot 12" plate, leaving a well inside for the gravy.
   b. Drain all but 1 Tbsp. water from the vegetables and work in the butter to create an emulsion.
   c. Mound the vegetables on either side of the potatoes.
   d. Prop one meat loaf slice against the front of the potatoes, then prop the other slice against it.
   e. Spoon the mushroom gravy into the well in the potatoes, allowing some to run down the front of the meat loaf.
   f. Stick the parsley sprig upright between the meat loaf slices and the potatoes.

*If a large plastic star tip is available, the mashed potatoes may be held in the pastry bag in a steam table pan and microwaved hot before each plating.

COMPONENT RECIPE

CLASSIC MEAT LOAF

yield: 1 (4" × 8") loaf, about 1 3/4 lb.

production		costing only
1 1/4 lb.	meat loaf mix (equal parts ground beef, veal, and pork)	1 1/4 lb.
1/2 c.	grated yellow onion	3 oz. a.p.
1	egg, beaten	1 each or 2 oz.
2 tsp.	minced garlic	1/5 oz. a.p.
pinch	dried thyme	1/16 oz.
pinch	dried marjoram	1/16 oz.
pinch	dried savory	1/16 oz.
1/4 tsp.	fresh-ground black pepper	1/16 oz.
1 tsp.	Worcestershire sauce	1/6 fl. oz.
2 Tbsp.	ketchup	1 fl. oz.
1/2 c.	fine, dried bread crumbs	1 3/4 oz.
2 1/2 strips	thin-sliced smoked bacon	1 1/4 oz.

preparation:

1. Preheat an oven to 375°F.
2. Mix together all ingredients except the bacon.
3. Poach a small patty of meat, taste, and correct the seasoning.
4. Cut a piece of pan liner to fit across the bottom and long sides of a 4" × 8" loaf pan.
5. Place the pan on a sheet tray, line the pan, and then pack in the meat mixture. Press to firm the meat, and tap the pan on the work surface to force out any pockets of air.
6. Bard the surface of the meat loaf with the bacon strips.
7. Bake the meat loaf in the center of the oven about 20 minutes.
8. Remove the bacon strips and discard them.
9. Invert the meat loaf onto the sheet tray and remove the pan liner. Return the meat loaf to the oven and bake about 20 minutes longer to an internal temperature of 150°F. (When the meat loaf is done, reserve the pan glaze on the sheet tray for making the gravy.)
10. If serving immediately, allow to rest in a warm place 5 minutes before slicing, or cool to room temperature and then refrigerate until cold.
11. Cut the meat loaf into 8 (3/4") slices.

holding: individually wrap 2 slices of cold meat loaf in plastic film and refrigerate up to 5 days

COMPONENT RECIPE
MUSHROOM GRAVY

yield: 1 qt.

production		costing only
6 Tbsp.	butter	3 oz.
2 c.	chopped mushrooms (clean stems and trimmings may be used)	6 oz. or n/c
tt	kosher salt	1/16 oz.
6 Tbsp.	flour	2 oz.
1 qt.	hot Brown Beef Stock	1/4 recipe
as available	pan glaze from a meat loaf or roast	n/c
as needed	water	n/c
2 Tbsp.	butter	1 oz.
6 oz.	3/8"-sliced small mushrooms	6 oz.

preparation:

1. Place 6 Tbsp. butter in a saucepan, heat the butter to foaming, and add the chopped mushrooms with a little salt. Sauté the mushrooms until they brown.
2. Add the flour and stir to make a brown roux. Remove from heat.
3. Whisk in the Brown Beef Stock. Simmer briskly 30 minutes.
4. Deglaze the meat loaf roasting pan with water and add the deglazings to the gravy.
5. Heat a 10" sauté pan, heat 2 Tbsp. butter, and sauté the sliced mushrooms with a little salt until browned.
6. Strain the sauce, pressing firmly on the chopped mushrooms. Discard the mushrooms.
7. Return the sauce to the pan and correct the consistency, if necessary, by thinning with stock or water or by reducing over high heat to make a moderately thick gravy.
8. Add the sliced mushrooms and correct the salt.

holding: open-pan cool and refrigerate in a freshly sanitized, covered container up to 5 days

RECIPE VARIATIONS

Cottage Pie with Heartland Vegetable Medley
Pack the meat loaf mixture into 4 (16-fl.-oz.) casserole dishes. Cover with foil and bake about 30 minutes to an internal temperature of 150°F. Invert on a rack set over a drip pan to drain and cool. Pipe a decorative swirl of Classic Mashed Potatoes on top of each casserole and brush them with melted butter. Bake to reheat until the meat is hot through and the potatoes are golden. Serve the vegetables on the side. Omit the Mushroom Gravy.

Hot Meat Loaf Sandwich
Overlap the hot meat loaf slices on a slice of American White Bread. Omit the mushrooms from the gravy, and increase the amount per serving to 1 1/2 c. Nap the meat loaf and bread with the gravy. Omit the Classic Mashed Potatoes. Accompany with French fries and the vegetable medley.

Diner-Style Meat Loaf with French Fries
Omit the Mushroom Gravy, Classic Mashed Potatoes, and vegetable medley. Serve with French fries, Homemade Ketchup, and Creamy Cole Slaw.

All-American Beef Stew

yield: 1 entrée serving: 6 oz. beef plus vegetables
(multiply × 4 for classroom turnout; adjust equipment sizes
accordingly)

MASTER RECIPE

production		costing only
2 c. + 5 pc.	Beef Stew Base (sauce plus beef cubes)	1/4 recipe
as needed	water, in squeeze bottle	n/c
4	peeled 1-oz. new potatoes, steamed and cooled	4 oz. a.p.
6	peeled 1 1/4" carrot lengths, blanched and refreshed	3 oz. a.p.
3	peeled boiling onions, poached and cooled	2 oz. a.p.
1/2 tsp.	minced thyme leaves	1/40 bunch a.p.
1 Tbsp.	chopped flat-leaf parsley	1/40 bunch a.p.
1 sprig	flat-leaf parsley	1/40 bunch a.p.
1 sprig	fresh thyme	1/20 bunch a.p.
1 sprig	celery leaves	n/c

service turnout:

1. Place the Beef Stew Base, water, potatoes, carrots, and onions in a 10" sauté pan, cover, and simmer about 5 minutes, until heated through.
2. Mix in the thyme leaves and half of the chopped parsley.
3. Plate the dish:
   a. Spoon the stew into a hot 12" pasta plate, arranging the vegetables in an attractive pattern.
   b. Sprinkle the stew with the remaining chopped parsley.
   c. Make a bouquet of the herb and celery sprigs and stick it upright at 2 o'clock.

COMPONENT RECIPE
BEEF STEW BASE

yield: 2 qt. sauce plus 20 beef cubes (approx. 24 oz.)

production		costing only
2 lb.	trimmed beef chuck, cut into 2 1/2" cubes	2 3/4 lb. a.p.
3 Tbsp.	corn oil	1 1/2 fl. oz.
3 Tbsp.	bacon drippings	n/c
as needed	flour for dredging	2 oz.
tt	kosher salt	1/8 oz.
3/4 c.	fine-chopped yellow onion	4 oz. a.p.
1/3 c.	minced carrot	2 oz. a.p.
1/3 c.	peeled, fine-chopped celery	1/15 head a.p.
6 Tbsp.	flour	2 oz.
2 qt.	hot Brown Beef Stock	1/2 recipe
1 c.	lager beer	8 fl. oz.
1 Tbsp.	minced garlic	1/3 oz. a.p.
1/2 c.	tomato concassée	6 oz. a.p.
2	bay leaves	1/8 oz.
pinch	dried thyme	1/16 oz.

preparation:

1. Pat the beef cubes dry on paper towels.
2. Heat a 14" sauté pan over medium heat, then add the oil and bacon drippings.
3. Dredge the beef cubes in the flour and brown them on all sides. Season with salt and remove the browned beef cubes to a heavy saucepan.
4. Add the mirepoix (onions, carrot, and celery) to the sauté pan and cook over low heat, stirring, about 2 minutes, until softened and lightly browned.
5. Add the flour and stir it into the mirepoix, adding more oil only if necessary to make a thick roux. Cook the roux to light brown.
6. Whisk in the Brown Beef Stock, stirring to avoid lumps. Add the beer, garlic, tomato, bay leaves, and thyme. Bring the sauce to the simmer and season it with salt.
7. Pour the sauce over the beef, place the saucepan over low heat, and bring the sauce to a gentle simmer. Cook about 1 hour, stirring occasionally, until the beef is tender. Add more stock or water if the sauce becomes too thick.
8. When the beef is tender remove the bay leaf and, if necessary, adjust the thickness to a full-bodied nappé consistency. (You may need to thin the sauce with water or stock, or you may need to remove the beef cubes and reduce the sauce by boiling it.)
9. Taste and correct the seasoning.

holding: open-pan cool and refrigerate in a freshly sanitized, covered container up to 5 days; freeze up to 1 month

RECIPE VARIATIONS

Great Plains Bison Stew
Replace the beef with shoulder of bison. Cut 4-oz. slab of bacon into 3/8" dice, sauté almost crisp, and add to the sauce in step 6.

Basque Lamb or Mutton Stew
Replace the beef with lamb or mutton shoulder. Replace the beer with 1/2 c. Reduced Red Wine. Replace the carrots with sautéed button mushrooms. Omit the potatoes and serve over Rice Pilaf flavored with saffron. Garnish with sautéed red, green, and yellow bell pepper strips.

Hungarian-American Goulash
Replace the beef with pork shoulder. Add 1 Tbsp. hot or sweet Hungarian paprika to the roux in step 5. Replace the Brown Beef Stock with Poultry Stock. Add 1"-diced, sautéed red and green bell peppers to the sauce at turnout. Omit the potatoes and serve over Fresh Pasta cut into 1/2" × 1 1/2" noodles.

Lattice-Top Cherry Pie
with Buttermilk Ice Cream

yield: 1 dessert serving
(multiply × 4 for classroom turnout)

MASTER RECIPE

production		costing only
1 slice	Lattice-Top Cherry Pie	1/8 recipe
1	3-oz. scoop Buttermilk Ice Cream	1/10 recipe

service turnout:
1. Place the Lattice-Top Cherry Pie slice slightly left of center on a cool 10" plate.
2. Place the Buttermilk Ice Cream scoop to the right of the pie.

COMPONENT RECIPE
LATTICE-TOP CHERRY PIE

yield: 8 dessert servings: 1 (9") pie

production		costing only
18 oz.	American Flaky Pastry Dough	1 1/2 recipe
as needed	flour for dusting	
1/4 c.	dried bread crumbs	n/c or 3/4 oz.
15 oz.	canned cherry pie filling*	15 oz.
2 oz.	cold butter, 1/4" dice	2 oz.
1 Tbsp.	sugar	1/2 oz.

preparation:
1. Mise en place:
   a. Preheat an oven to 400°F.
   b. Have ready a 9" pie pan, a half-sheet tray with pan liner, and another half sheet of pan liner.
2. Begin making up the pie shell:
   a. Divide and shape the American Flaky Pastry Dough into a 10-oz. disc and an 8-oz. square.
   b. Flour the work surface and a rolling pin. Roll out the dough square a little thicker than 1/8" and place the pastry square on the sheet tray. Cover it with the half sheet of pan liner.
   c. Roll out the dough disc a little thicker than 1/8" and fit the pastry into a 9" pie pan. Trim the edges to an even 1/2" overhang. Place the pan on the sheet tray.
   d. Refrigerate the shell and pastry square 20 minutes.
3. Assemble the pie:
   a. Using a fluted pastry wheel, cut the pastry square into long, 1/2"-wide lattice strips.
   b. Scatter the bread crumbs over the bottom of the pie shell.
   c. Spoon in the cherry pie filling.
   d. Scatter the butter dice on top of the filling.
   e. Very lightly moisten the edge of the pastry shell with water.
   f. Beginning in the center of the pie, arrange the pastry strips on top, weaving them in a lattice pattern.
   g. Roll up the edges of the pie shell pastry dough to enclose the lattice edges and form a rim.
   h. Flute the rim.
   i. Sprinkle the lattice top with 1 Tbsp. sugar.
4. Bake the pie:
   a. Place the pie pan on the lined sheet tray and bake about 30 minutes, until the pastry is golden.
   b. Cool the pie to room temperature on a rack.

holding: at cool room temperature up to 3 hours

*If fresh or frozen red sour cherries are available, proceed as follows:

a. Pit 1 1/2 lb. cherries (omit for frozen cherries).
b. Mix with 2 c. sugar and refrigerate overnight.
c. Place the cherries and their juices into a nonreactive saucepan and boil 5 minutes.
d. Strain the cherries and return the juice to the pan.
e. Bring the juice to the boil and thicken it by whisking in a slurry consisting of approximately 1/4 c. cornstarch and 1/4 c. cold water. Cook until translucent. The juice should thicken to a puddinglike consistency.
f. Cool to room temperature and fold the cherries into the thickened juice.

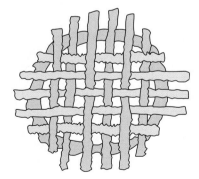

Lattice-top crust.

RECIPE VARIATIONS

Lattice-Top Peach Pie with Buttermilk Ice Cream
Replace the cherry pie filling with 1 lb. IQF sliced peaches, thawed, tossed with 1/2 c. sugar and 1/4 c. flour.

Lattice-Top Blueberry Pie with Buttermilk Ice Cream
Replace the cherry pie filling with 1 lb. blueberries tossed with 2/3 c. sugar and 1/4 c. flour.

Devil's Food Cake
with Vanilla Custard Ice Cream

yield: 1 dessert serving
(multiply × 4 for classroom turnout)

MASTER RECIPE

production		costing only
1 slice	Devil's Food Cake	1/8 recipe
1	3 oz. scoop Vanilla Custard Ice Cream	1/10 recipe

service turnout:
1. Plate the dish:
   a. Place the Devil's Food Cake slice slightly left of center on a cool 8" plate.
   b. Using a #12 portion scoop, form a sphere of Vanilla Custard Ice Cream and place it next to the cake.

COMPONENT RECIPE
DEVIL'S FOOD CAKE ASSEMBLY

yield: 10 dessert servings: 1 (9") layer cake

production		costing only
2	(9") round Devil's Food Cake Layers	1 recipe
4 to 5 c.	Chocolate Fudge Frosting	1 recipe

preparation:
1. Remove the pan liner circles from the Devil's Food Cake Layers. If necessary, trim the cake layer tops flat and brush away any crumbs.
2. Spoon about 1/3 of the Chocolate Fudge Frosting on one of the cake layers and use an offset spatula to smooth it to the edges. ⚠ Work quickly, as the frosting will begin to set up as it cools.
3. Invert the other cake layer on top of the filling and remove the cake board. Press down to firm the layers and flatten the top surface.
4. Use about half of the remaining frosting to coat the sides of the cake, extending the frosting about 3/8" higher than the top layer.
5. Scrape the remaining frosting on top and smooth it even.

holding: at cool room temperature under a cake dome up to 8 hours; refrigerated up to 3 days; to prevent drying, place plastic wrap directly on any cut surface

COMPONENT RECIPE
DEVIL'S FOOD CAKE LAYERS

yield: 2 (9" round) cake layers

production		costing only
as needed	baker's pan coating spray	% of container
2	9" round cake boards	2 each
4 oz.	unsweetened chocolate, chopped	4 oz.
3 oz.	standard cocoa powder	3 oz.
1 c.	boiling water	n/c
4 oz.	all-purpose flour	4 oz.
3 oz.	cake flour	3 oz.
1 tsp.	baking soda	1/6 oz.
1/2 tsp.	fine salt	1/6 oz.
5 oz.	brown sugar	5 oz.
8 oz.	room-temperature unsalted butter	8 oz.
3	room-temperature eggs	3 each or 6 oz.
1 tsp.	pure vanilla extract	1/6 fl. oz.
8 fl. oz.	sour cream	8 fl. oz.

preparation:
1. Mise en place:
   a. Preheat an oven to 350°F.
   b. Cut out 2 (9") circles of pan liner, and have ready 2 (9") round cake boards.
   c. Spray 2 (9") round cake pans with pan coating, place the pan liner circles in the bottoms of the pans, and spray again.
2. Combine the chocolate and cocoa powder in a small bowl, pour the boiling water over them, and stir until smooth. Cool to room temperature.
3. Sift together the flours, baking soda, and salt.
4. Mix the batter:
   a. Using the paddle attachment of a mixer, cream the sugar and butter on medium speed until light and fluffy.
   b. Beat in the eggs one at a time, scraping down the sides after each addition. Add the vanilla.
   c. Reduce the mixer speed to low and add the chocolate mixture.
   d. Pulse in half of the flour mixture, then the sour cream, and then the rest of the flour mixture, mixing only enough to make a smooth batter. ⚠ Do not overmix.
5. Pan the batter:
   a. Divide the batter between the two prepared pans.
   b. Using an offset spatula, smooth the batter surfaces, making the centers a little lower than the edges.
6. Bake the layers about 35 minutes, until the centers test clean with a toothpick.
7. Cool the layers in the pans about 10 minutes.
8. Turn the cakes out of the pans onto the cake boards, and cool to room temperature.

holding: wrapped in plastic film at cool room temperature up to 3 days; freeze up to 1 month

COMPONENT RECIPE
CHOCOLATE FUDGE FROSTING

yield: approx. 5 c.

production		costing only
6 oz.	unsweetened chocolate, chopped	6 oz.
2 oz.	emulsified vegetable shortening	2 oz.
1 1/2 oz.	light corn syrup	1 1/2 oz.
1/2 tsp.	salt	1/8 oz.
4 fl. oz.	water	n/c
2 lb.	sifted confectioner's sugar	2 lb.
1 Tbsp.	pure vanilla extract	1/2 fl. oz.
as needed	simmering water	n/c

preparation:
1. Melt the chocolate in a hot-water bath over low heat, stirring occasionally, until smooth.
2. Combine the shortening, corn syrup, salt, and water in a saucepan and bring to the boil.
3. Place the confectioner's sugar in the bowl of a mixer fitted with the paddle attachment. Turn the mixer on low speed and pour the boiling syrup mixture into the bowl in a thin stream.
4. Increase the speed to medium and beat 1 minute.
5. Reduce the speed to low and stir in the vanilla and chocolate.
6. If necessary, thin with simmering water.

holding: use immediately, before the icing hardens

RECIPE VARIATION

German-American Black Forest Cake
Omit the Chocolate Fudge Frosting and Vanilla Custard Ice Cream. Perforate the cake layers with a docker or a fork, and moisten them with 3 fl. oz. kirsch. Fill the layers with 1 c. Sweetened Whipped Cream and 2 c. cherry pie filling. Frost and decorate with 3 c. Sweetened Whipped Cream. Decorate the top with drained cherries from the cherry pie filling.

Carrot Cake
with Cream Cheese Frosting

yield: 1 dessert serving
(multiply × 4 for classroom turnout)

MASTER RECIPE

production		costing only
1 slice	Carrot Cake	1/10 recipe

service turnout:
1. Place the Carrot Cake slice on a cool 8" plate.

COMPONENT RECIPE
CARROT CAKE ASSEMBLY

yield: 10 dessert servings: 1 (9") cake

production		costing only
1 1/2 c.	walnut pieces	6 oz.
1 qt.	Cream Cheese Frosting	1 recipe
as needed	orange (or red and yellow) icing color	% of container
as needed	green icing color	% of container
2	Carrot Cake Layers	1 recipe

preparation:
1. Mise en place:
   a. Preheat an oven to 400°F.
   b. Place about 1/2 c. Cream Cheese Frosting in a small bowl and mix in enough orange (or red and yellow) food coloring to achieve a bright orange color.
   c. Place about 1/3 c. frosting in another bowl and mix in enough green food coloring to achieve a bright green color.
   d. Transfer the tinted frostings into parchment piping cones or 12" disposable pastry bags with #4 round tube tips.
   e. Have ready a 12" disposable pastry bag or durable bag fitted with a medium star tip.
   f. Spread the walnut pieces on a half-sheet tray and toast them in the oven about 8 minutes, until crisp. Cool, and then chop to a medium consistency.
2. Assemble and frost the cake:
   a. Spoon about 1/4 of the remaining frosting on one of the cake layers and spread it evenly to the edges.
   b. Place the top layer on the bottom layer and remove the cake board. Press to firm the layers and create an even top surface.
   c. Frost the sides of the cake, using another 1/4 of the frosting, and extending a 1/4" rim of frosting above the top surface.
   d. Spoon another 1/4 of the frosting on top of the cake and spread it evenly to the edges.
   e. Smooth the top and sides of the cake to make it a perfect cylinder.

3. Portion and decorate the cake:
   a. Score the top of the cake to mark 10 portions.
   b. Mask the sides of the cake with the chopped walnuts.
   c. Place the remaining 1/4 of the frosting in the star tip pastry bag.
   d. Decorate the cake with a star crown border and star base border.
   e. Decorate each slice with an icing "carrot," as shown in the photo.

holding: refrigerated under a cake dome up to 2 days; after cutting, protect the cut edges of the cake with plastic film

COMPONENT RECIPE
CREAM CHEESE FROSTING

yield: approx. 1 qt.

production		costing only
12 oz.	room-temperature cream cheese	12 oz.
8 oz.	room-temperature unsalted butter	8 oz.
1 Tbsp.	minced lemon zest	1/4 [90 ct.] lemon
1 Tbsp.	pure vanilla extract	1/2 fl. oz.
1 1/2 lb.	confectioner's sugar	1 1/2 lb.
as needed	milk	about 2 fl. oz.

preparation:
1. Using the paddle attachment of a mixer, beat the cream cheese, butter, lemon zest, and vanilla until light and fluffy.
2. Reduce the speed to low and mix in the confectioner's sugar.
3. Increase the speed to medium and beat until well blended.
4. Beat in a little milk as needed to achieve a consistency that will spread and pipe easily.

holding: refrigerated in a freshly sanitized, covered container up to 5 days; freeze up to 3 months; to use, bring to room temperature and beat using a mixer

COMPONENT RECIPE
CARROT CAKE LAYERS

yield: 2 (9" round) cake layers

production		costing only
as needed	baker's pan coating spray	% of container
2	9" round cake boards	2 each
8 oz.	flour	8 oz.
1/2 tsp.	baking powder	1/12 oz.
1 tsp.	ground cinnamon	1/8 oz.
pinch	fine salt	1/16 oz.
2 oz.	room-temperature unsalted butter	2 oz.
1 c.	sugar	8 oz.
2	egg yolks	2 each or 1 1/3 oz.
3 Tbsp.	corn oil	1 1/2 fl. oz.
2 c.	fine-grated peeled carrots	9 oz. a.p.
1/2 c.	fine-chopped walnuts	2 oz.
1/4 c.	currants	1/2 oz.
2	room-temperature egg whites	n/c or 2 oz.

preparation:

1. Mise en place:
   a. Preheat an oven to 375°F.
   b. Cut 2 circles of pan liner to fit the bottoms of 9" cake pans, and have ready 2 (9") round cake boards.
   c. Spray the bottoms and sides of the cake pan with pan coating, press the pan liner circles onto the bottoms of the pans, and spray again.
2. Sift together the flour, baking powder, cinnamon, and salt.
3. Mix the batter:
   a. Using the paddle attachment of a mixer, cream the butter and sugar on medium speed until very light and smooth.
   b. Add the egg yolks, one at a time, beating until fluffy.
   c. Beat in the oil, and then continue to beat 1 minute longer.
   d. Reduce the speed to low and pulse in half of the flour mixture.
   e. Pulse in the carrots, walnuts, and currants.
   f. Pulse in the remaining flour mixture.
   g. In a clean, dry bowl, beat the egg whites just to firm peaks.
   h. Fold about 1/3 of the egg whites into the batter, and then fold the batter into the remaining whites.
4. Pan the batter, dividing it evenly between the two pans and smoothing the tops. Make the centers just a little lower than the edges.
5. Bake about 35 minutes, until a cake tester comes out clean.
6. Cool the layers in the pans on a rack 10 minutes.
7. Turn the layers out onto the cake boards and cool completely.

holding: tightly wrapped in plastic film at cool room temperature up to 24 hours; refrigerate up to 5 days; freeze up to 3 months

---

RECIPE VARIATIONS

Carrot Cupcakes
Bake the batter in muffin tins. Reduce the amount of Cream Cheese Frosting to 1/2 recipe. Omit the walnuts for masking.

Southern-Style Carrot Cake
Substitute pecans for the walnuts. Add 1 oz. Bourbon whiskey to the batter.

Pineapple Upside-Down Cake

yield: 1 dessert serving
(multiply × 4 for classroom turnout)

MASTER RECIPE

production		costing only
1	Pineapple Upside-Down Cake slice	1/8 recipe
1/2	maraschino cherry, blotted dry	1/8 oz.

service turnout:
1. Place the Pineapple Upside-Down Cake slice on a cool 8" plate.
2. Place the cherry in the center of the pineapple ring.

COMPONENT RECIPE

PINEAPPLE UPSIDE-DOWN CAKE

yield: 8 dessert servings: 1 (10") cake

production		costing only
4 oz.	butter	4 oz.
5 oz.	brown sugar	5 oz.
3 Tbsp.	juice from canned pineapple	n/c
8 rings	100–110 ct. canned pineapple rings (slices) in juice	1/12 #10 can
2 c.	canned crushed pineapple, thoroughly drained	1/6 #10 can
10 oz.	flour	10 oz.
2 tsp.	baking powder	1/3 oz.
1/2 tsp.	salt	1/12 oz.
4 oz.	softened butter	4 oz.
8 oz.	sugar	8 oz.
2	egg yolks	2 each or 1 1/3 oz.
2 tsp.	minced lemon zest	1/6 [90 ct.] lemon
1 tsp.	pure vanilla extract	1/6 fl. oz.
4 fl. oz.	milk	4 fl. oz.
2	room-temperature egg whites	n/c or 2 oz.

preparation:
1. Preheat an oven to 375°F.
2. Prepare the topping:
   a. Melt the butter in a 10" cast-iron skillet or heavy 10" cake pan.
   b. Stir in the brown sugar and pineapple juice.
   c. Spread the sugar mixture evenly over the bottom of the pan and remove from the heat.
   d. Arrange the pineapple slices in the bottom of the pan, in a circle, touching the side of the pan.
   e. Pack the crushed pineapple in the middle, between the slices, and inside the rings.
3. Sift together the flour, baking powder, and salt.
4. Mix the batter:
   a. Using the paddle attachment of a mixer, cream the butter and sugar on medium speed until light and fluffy.
   b. Add the egg yolks, zest, and vanilla and beat 1 minute longer.
   c. Reduce the speed to low. Pulse in the flour mixture and milk in 4 alternate additions. (The batter will be quite thick.)
   d. In a clean, dry bowl, beat the egg whites to just under firm peaks.
   e. Fold 1/3 of the egg whites into the batter, then fold the batter into the remaining whites.
5. Spoon the batter into the skillet without disturbing the pineapple. Smooth the top, making the center a little lower than the edges.
6. Bake in the center of the oven 35 to 40 minutes, until a tester comes out clean.
7. Cool on a rack 10 minutes. ⚠ Do not allow the cake to cool completely; if the topping cools and hardens, it may stick to the pan.
8. Run a knife around the edge of the cake to loosen it from the pan. Place a serving tray on top of the skillet or cake pan and invert it. The cake should come out with topping intact.
9. Cool to room temperature.

holding: up to 24 hours at cool room temperature under a plastic dome

If presenting the entire cake, decorate it with 8 well-drained maraschino cherries placed inside the pineapple rings.

Pineapple slices and crushed pineapple in the pan.

RECIPE VARIATIONS

Apple-Cinnamon Upside-Down Cake
Add 1/2 tsp. ground cinnamon to the butter-sugar mixture. Replace the pineapple juice with apple cider. Replace the pineapple with 4 c. peeled, thin-sliced Granny Smith apples arranged overlapping in concentric rings. Omit the maraschino cherry garnish.

Peach Upside-Down Cake
Add 1 tsp. pure vanilla extract to the butter-sugar mixture. Replace the pineapple juice with peach schnapps. Replace the pineapple with 4 c. peeled, thin-sliced firm-ripe peaches arranged overlapping in concentric rings. Omit the maraschino cherry garnish.

Pear Upside-Down Cake
Replace the pineapple juice with ruby Port wine. Replace the pineapple with 4 c. peeled, thin-sliced firm-ripe pears arranged overlapping in concentric rings. Omit the maraschino cherry garnish.

DESSERTS

Wells Kringle
with Lingonberry Sauce

yield: 1 dessert serving
(multiply × 4 for classroom turnout)

MASTER RECIPE

production		costing only
1/2 c.	lingonberry sauce	4 fl. oz.
1	Individual Wells Kringle	1/4 recipe
1 sprig	fresh mint	1/12 bunch a.p.

service turnout:
1. Spoon a dab of lingonberry sauce slightly left of center on a cool 10" plate.
2. Place the Individual Wells Kringle on the sauce.
3. Spoon the remaining sauce on the plate to the right of the kringle.
4. Place the mint sprig on the sauce next to the kringle.

COMPONENT RECIPE
INDIVIDUAL WELLS KRINGLES

yield: 4 (4") pastries

production		costing only
5 oz.	flour	5 oz.
1 oz.	almond flour or fine-ground almonds	1 oz.
2 Tbsp.	granulated sugar	1 oz.
1/4 tsp.	fine salt	1/16 oz.
4 oz.	cold butter, 1/2" dice	4 oz.
as needed	very cold water	n/c
1 c.	water	n/c
1/2 tsp.	fine salt	1/12 oz.
4 oz.	cold butter 1/2" dice	4 oz.
6 oz.	flour	6 oz.
3	eggs	3 each or 6 oz.
1/2 tsp.	almond extract	1/12 fl. oz.
as needed	flour for dusting	1 oz.
1 Tbsp.	very soft butter	1/2 oz.
3 oz.	confectioner's sugar	3 oz.
1/4 tsp.	almond extract	1/16 fl. oz.
1/4 c.	heavy cream	2 fl. oz.
1/2 c.	sliced almonds, toasted and cooled	2 oz.

preparation:
1. Mix the flaky pastry:
   a. On the work surface mix 5 oz. flour with the almond flour, granulated sugar, and 1/4 tsp. salt.
   b. Use a pastry scraper to cut 4 oz. butter into the flour mixture until the butter is the size of small peas.
   c. Scrape the flour mixture into a bowl.
   d. Drizzle in 2 to 4 Tbsp. cold water while mixing the flour with a fork to make a cohesive dough that is moist but not sticky.
   e. Form the dough into a disc, wrap in plastic film, and refrigerate at least 20 minutes.

2. Mise en place:
   a. Preheat an oven to 400°F.
   b. Prepare a half-sheet tray with pan liner.
   c. Cut out a plastic or cardboard oval template 4" long and 2 3/4" wide.
3. Mix the choux paste:
   a. Have ready a mixer fitted with the paddle attachment.
   b. Place 1 c. water, 1/2 tsp. salt, and 4 oz. butter in a heavy saucepan and bring to the boil.
   c. Remove the pan from the heat and immediately dump in 6 oz. flour. Beat vigorously with a wooden spoon until the mixture forms into a smooth mass.
   d. Return the pan to low heat and beat about 1 minute, until the dough dries out slightly and forms a film on the bottom of the pan.
   e. Transfer the dough to the mixer and beat on medium speed about 1 minute longer, until the mixture cools slightly.
   f. Beat in the eggs, one at a time, to make a smooth, shiny dough.
   g. Add 1/2 tsp. almond extract.
   h. Transfer the dough to a heavy pastry bag fitted with a medium star tip.
4. Make up the pastries:
   a. Divide the flaky pastry dough into 4 quarters.
   b. Dust the work surface with flour and roll out each dough quarter a little thicker than 1/8". Using the template, cut out 4 dough ovals.
   c. Place the dough ovals on the sheet tray.
   d. Refrigerate the dough ovals 20 minutes.
   e. Pipe concentric ovals of choux paste onto the pastry ovals.
5. Bake the pastries:
   a. Place the pan on the lowest rack of the oven and bake about 30 minutes, until the flaky pastry bases are crisp and the choux paste tops are puffed and golden.
   b. Turn off the oven, open the oven door, and allow the pastries to dry out until the pan is cool enough to touch.
   c. Transfer the pastries to a rack and cool to room temperature.
6. Make the icing glaze:
   a. In a small bowl mix together the soft butter, confectioner's sugar, and 1/4 tsp. almond extract.
   b. Whisk in enough heavy cream to make a smooth, thick, but pourable icing.
7. Decorate the pastries:
   a. Spoon about 1/4 of the icing glaze on top of each pastry and use a small offset spatula to smooth it over the surface.
   b. Sprinkle each pastry with toasted sliced almonds.

holding: store in one layer in a tightly sealed plastic container at cool room temperature up to 12 hours

Side View

Choux paste

Flaky pastry

Piping choux paste onto the pastry oval.

RECIPE VARIATION
Wells Kringle with Raspberry Sauce
Replace the lingonberry sauce with sweetened raspberry purée.

☐ **TABLE 9.2 CENTRAL FARMLANDS REGIONAL INGREDIENTS**

ITEM	MARKET FORMS	USES	SEASONALITY	OTHER	STORAGE
WHEAT BERRIES	Wheat kernels polished to remove the cellulose hulls are sold in 1-lb. packages and in bulk.	Wheat berries are added to baked goods, salads, casseroles and pilafs to add flavor, a chewy texture, and nutrients.	N/A	Wheat berries require moisture to soften to palatability. To use in baked goods or salads, soak them in water 24 hours, then simmer to the desired texture.	Store at room temperature for a few weeks; freeze for longer keeping.
WILD RICE	Paddy-grown and mechanically harvested wild rice is sold in 1-lb. packages and in bulk. True wild rice is available by mail order from Native American tribes. Wild rice is graded by the length of the grain, with the longest and most intact grains considered finest.	Wild rice is boiled in salted water to the desired texture, then drained and seasoned. Because of its cost, wild rice is often blended with other grains for pilafs and stuffings.	N/A	Preblended wild rice mixtures usually contain inferior-quality wild rice and may be based on parboiled (converted) white rice. It is best to purchase pure wild rice and make your own custom rice blend.	Store at room temperature or freeze for extended storage.
BLACK WALNUTS	See p. 402.				
PERSIMMONS	See p. 83.				
SOUR OR PIE CHERRIES	Fresh sour cherries may be available from specialty produce purveyors in season. Pitting them requires hand labor. Whole, pitted IQF sour cherries are selectively available and may be used in the same manner as fresh cherries.	Sour cherries are sweetened and cooked for preserves or pie fillings.	Summer (fresh).	Industrially produced cherry pie filling may have a low proportion of cherries and a high proportion of thickened sauce.	Refrigerate fresh cherries and use within 1 week. Store frozen cherries in the freezer and thaw only the amount needed.
SUNCHOKES/ JERUSALEM ARTICHOKES	See p. 82.				
HONEY	For foodservice, honey is sold in 5-lb. jugs. Some types are modified with glucose and maintain a clear, pourable texture.	Honey is most often used as a table sweetener, taken in tea, spooned onto cereals, or spread on biscuits or toast. When an assertive honey flavor is desired, choose a darker, more strongly flavored variety such as wildflower or buckwheat honey.	N/A	If honey crystallizes, it can be reliquefied by gently heating the container in a hot water bath. Honey, not even the pasteurized variety, should not be fed to children younger than 1 year. It is a suspected source of infant botulism.	Store tightly sealed at room temperature; because of a naturally occurring antimold enzyme, honey keeps for a very long time.
WALLEYE	Fresh walleye fillets may be available from specialty seafood dealers. The Great Lakes walleye may be available as fresh or frozen fillets.	Walleye fillets are sautéed or broiled and served with lemon and butter. Breaded and pan-fried walleye is accompanied by tartar sauce.	Available year round.	Most Farmlands wild fish species are available only to sport fishermen.	Store fresh walleye fillets in plastic bags on ice in the refrigerator one to two days only. Thaw frozen walleye in the refrigerator and use immediately.

☐ **TABLE 9.2 CENTRAL FARMLANDS REGIONAL INGREDIENTS** *(continued)*

ITEM	MARKET FORMS	USES	SEASONALITY	OTHER	STORAGE
CENTRAL FARMLANDS SAUSAGES	Central Farmlands sausage varieties range from spicy to mild, coarse to smooth, tiny to hefty, and raw to cooked and smoked. Sausage is sold by the pound.	Mild sage-scented link sausages are served as a breakfast meat. Other types are used in sandwiches and featured in casseroles and other composed dishes.	N/A	Polish kielbasa, both fresh and smoked, is popular in the region as are German franks and wursts. The late-20th-century influx of Mexican immigrants brought spicy fresh chorizo to the region.	Store fresh sausage as directed by the producer; freeze sausage as necessary.
FARMLANDS CHEESES	Factory-produced and artisan-made Farmlands cheeses are sold by the pound in vacuum-packed blocks and whole wheels.	Cheese is featured on cheese boards, in sandwiches, in gratinée dishes, and melted into sauces.	N/A	*Wisconsin Cheddar:* mild (clear wax); medium (red wax); extra-sharp (black wax). Midwesterners prefer yellow Cheddar. *Brick Cheese:* a moist, semi-firm cheese with a slightly pungent flavor and strong aroma. *Colby/Colby Longhorn:* mild flavored, deep yellow in color with a crumbly texture. *Maytag Blue:* America's best-known blue cheese derives its rich, tangy flavor from a full 5 months' aging.	Store wrapped tightly in refrigerator. Length of storage depends on type.
CHEESE CURDS	Fresh cheese curds are sold in 1-lb. bags at cheese factories and cheese shops, primarily in Wisconsin.	Cheese curds are eaten as a snack or may be batter fried.	N/A	After 24 hours of refrigeration, fresh cheese curds become rubbery in texture and lose their delicate flavor.	Frozen for shipping, they still have a short shelf life of 1 to 2 weeks.

■□■ chapter ten

The Western and Central Ranchlands

North Dakota, South Dakota, Nebraska, Kansas, Oklahoma, northern and central Texas, Oklahoma, Kansas, eastern Montana, eastern Wyoming, eastern Colorado

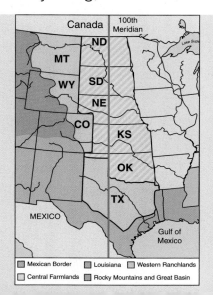

AMERICA'S PIONEER TRAVELERS encountered a changing landscape as their wagons moved west across the Great Plains. Leaving the Mississippi behind, they passed through miles of temperate tallgrass prairie where waist-high grasses undulated in the wind. After the central plains were claimed, later pioneers pushed farther west toward the Rocky Mountains, crossing an imaginary line called the 100th longitudinal meridian into the western plateau. As they progressed westward, the land became drier and the soil layer thinner. Grasses became shorter and less green. There, on land many believed to be useless, the hardiest pioneers became cattle ranchers and sod-busting wheat farmers.

You learned about the culture and cuisine of Midwestern farmers in Chapter 9. This chapter tells the culinary story of the region's ranchers and their hired help, the iconic American cowboy. Their cooking is called Western Ranchlands cuisine, a style that spread to other areas of America as well. Ranchlands cooking is based on pioneer provisions and features beef, an ingredient they possessed in virtually limitless supply. Ranchlands cooking is often done outdoors and uses many Native American cooking methods. Simple, straightforward, and masculine, Ranchlands cooking is favored by many home cooks and is featured in casual restaurants throughout the region. Western-themed restaurants are popular nationwide, offering fine aged beef—and, today, bison—to a public eager for red meat and a taste of America's cowboy heritage.

AFTER STUDYING THIS CHAPTER YOU SHOULD BE ABLE TO:

- describe the climate and topography (Factor 1) of the western plateau and explain how they affected the region's culture and cuisine
- recount the history of the region's Native American groups (Factor 2) and explain how it affected their foodways and the cooking of the region
- recount the development of the Ranchlands cattle industry (Factor 5) and explain how it essentially created Ranchlands cuisine
- discuss the impact of Mexican Border cuisine (Factor 3) on traditional and modern Ranchlands cuisine
- list and describe the ingredients, cooking methods, and flavor profiles of Ranchlands cuisine
- prepare authentic Ranchlands dishes

APPETIZERS

Smoky Beef 'n' Bean Soup with Biscuit-on-a-Stick

Tossed Salad with Buttermilk Ranch Dressing

Chicory Salad with Beef Jerky, Spiced Pecans, and Smoked Tomato Vinaigrette

Texas "Caviar" with Tortilla Chips

Armadillo Egg with Fresh Tomato Salsa

Cannibal Steak

ENTRÉES

Campfire Brook Trout with Corn Relish Tartar Sauce, Annie's Skillet Potatoes, and Grilled Western Vegetables

Ranch House Chicken 'n' Dumplings

Oklahoma Chicken-Fried Steak with Cream Gravy, Mashed Potatoes, and Western-Style Greens

Grilled Filet of Bison with Smoky Steak Sauce, Beer-Batter Onion Rings, Hash Brown Potatoes, and Vegetable Roundup

Smoke-Roasted Prime Rib of Beef with Twice-Baked Potato and Smothered Squash

Barbeque Beef Brisket with Cowboy Beans and Ranch-Style Slaw

Beer-Braised Beef Short Ribs with Chuck Wagon Macaroni and Wilted Spinach

Trail-Drive Chili over Texmati Rice with Cowboy Beans, Longhorn Cheddar, and Sweet Corn Pico de Gallo

DESSERTS

Apple Pandowdy with Honey Sour Cream Sauce

Rum-Raisin Texmati Rice Pudding with Apricot Sauce

S'mores Pie

WEBSITE EXTRAS

Breakfasts   Sandwiches   Hors d'Oeuvres   Thanksgiving Menu

■ THE WESTERN
□ PLATEAU
■

America's western plateau lies between the 100th longitudinal meridian and the Rocky Mountain foothills. This area is classified as a *steppe*, or a high plateau region with a semiarid climate, shallow sedimentary soil, and extreme weather. Such land supports only the hardiest vegetation: tough, low-growing shrubs and a limited variety of grasses.

Shortgrass Prairie

The change in vegetation at the 100th meridian is primarily due to a change in precipitation patterns. Although land east of the meridian normally receives enough rainfall to support temperate grasses and grain cultivation, from the 100th meridian west to the Rockies, average yearly rainfall measures less than 20 inches per year—far too little for most food crops (Figure 10.1). The region's lack of rainfall is largely due to the Rocky Mountain rain shadow (see p. 304). Here the towering Rockies block westerly rain clouds moving inland from the Pacific Ocean. Upon reaching the Rockies, storm clouds typically stall and drop most of their moisture on the mountains' western slopes, leaving the land on the eastern side dry.

In addition to lack of rainfall, the western plateau also suffers from poor soil. Although much of the region's soil is mineral-rich loess, in most places there is very little of it because dry conditions and prevailing weather patterns cause wind erosion. In some areas of the western plateau, soil is quite saline (containing high amounts of mineral salts) and/or highly alkaline. In these areas, called *badlands*, virtually no vegetation grows.

FACTOR 1
Poor soil and lack of water made food crop cultivation problematic.

As a result of these climate and soil conditions, most of the western plateau is covered with a thick carpet of short, sturdy grasses, among them buffalo grass, gamma shortgrass, wheatgrass, and needlegrass. Low shrubs such as sagebrush, tumbleweed, and rabbitbrush are scattered throughout. Because of its vegetation this area is called the **shortgrass prairie.**

In order to survive, shortgrass prairie plants evolved to tolerate very dry conditions. Their roots penetrate deep into the soil in search of water, and their short growth minimizes evaporation. During the winter and in periods of summer drought, prairie shortgrasses go dormant, appearing dry and dead on the surface but clinging to life underground. Thus, during most of the year, the shortgrass prairie is painted in shades of brown, gold, and sage green. In spring it explodes with color when wildflowers such as blazingstar, white prickly poppy, and wild sunflowers bloom.

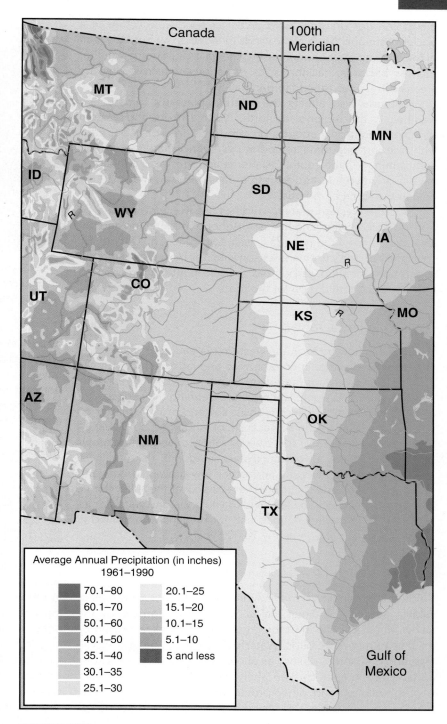

Average Annual Precipitation (in inches) 1961–1990

70.1–80	20.1–25
60.1–70	15.1–20
50.1–60	10.1–15
40.1–50	5.1–10
35.1–40	5 and less
30.1–35	
25.1–30	

FIGURE 10.1

The 100th longitudinal meridian separates the temperate tallgrass prairie to its east from the semiarid shortgrass prairie to its west.

A Climate of Extremes

The Rocky Mountains are also the primary cause of the western plateau's infamous wind and stormy weather. The Rockies block warm Pacific breezes, creating a continental climate lacking moderating ocean effects. In addition, the mountains create a broad corridor drawing frigid arctic air southward, often in a powerful stream. When arctic winds meet warm air from the Gulf of Mexico and the Sonoran desert, the result is extreme weather such as blizzards, hailstorms, or tornadoes—which is why the area is sometimes called "tornado alley."

Latitude also affects the western plateau's climate and weather. In the region's far north, North Dakota and eastern Montana count only about a hundred frost-free days per year, with freezing nighttime temperatures even in late spring and early autumn. In the south, Oklahoma and the Texas panhandle have nearly two hundred frost-free days per year, with extreme heat in the summer months.

On the western plateau wildfires are frequent, caused by both lightning strikes and humans. Although frightening and destructive, these fires provide a valuable function. During the shortgrass prairie's dormant season wildfires burn off the old top vegetation, creating carbonized organic matter that provides much-needed fertilization for the roots.

FIGURE 10.2
An American short-horn bison on the shortgrass prairie.
Doug James/Shutterstock

River Valley Oases

Where rivers flow through the western plateau, their valleys create oases of moisture in an otherwise arid land. Although these riverbeds are nearly empty much of the year, they hold significant moisture beneath the surface. Annual flooding deposits soil and organic matter on valley floors. Because of underground moisture and better soil, a wider variety of vegetation grows there. River courses are lined with oaks, willows, cottonwoods, and other low-growing trees, and mixed tall and short grasses cover the valley floors. Valley habitat provided vital food and water for indigenous animals and for humans who arrived in the region nearly 10,000 years ago.

FACTOR 1
River valleys provided water and fertile soil to support limited animal and human populations.

Prairie Wildlife

Before European arrival in the Americas, a staggering variety of wildlife ranged the Great Plains. The corridor formed by the Rocky Mountains is part of the great north-south flyway used by millions of migratory birds. Waterfowl found refuge in river valleys, and dry-land birds such as pheasants, grouse, and the now-endangered prairie chicken sheltered on the plains. Hawks, eagles, vultures, and other predatory birds cruised the wide prairie sky. Jackrabbits and prairie dogs lived among the shrubs and grasses. Deer, elk, and antelope migrated through the river valleys and traversed the Rocky Mountain foothills. Wolves ranged the grasslands in search of prey.

Although these other animals were important parts of the region's ecosystem, one animal almost totally dominated the shortgrass prairie landscape: the great short-horned **bison,** commonly known as the American buffalo (Figure 10.2). This immense bovine was perfectly suited to the climate and topography of the western plateau. Standing more than 8 feet tall at the crest of its hump, with a huge, powerful head and sharp horns, a healthy adult bison had no reason to fear a wolf pack.

Its thick skin and dense, insulating coat allowed the bison to tolerate prairie blizzards and subzero temperatures. Capable of traveling many miles without water and subsisting even on dry, dormant shortgrasses, bison thrived in the plateau's arid climate. At the time of European contact, nearly sixty million bison roamed the Great Plains. These remarkable animals provided virtually every necessity of life for the region's first human beings and their descendants.

■□■ NATIVE AMERICANS OF THE WESTERN PLATEAU

Anthropologists believe that the first humans in America were Asians who entered the North American continent somewhere in the west, traveling across the Beringan land bridge or sailing across the Pacific in prehistoric times. After the last ice ages, some of these humans arrived in the Great Plains and evolved into various Native American groups (Figure 10.3). Chapter 9 introduced the river valley tribes, semi-settled groups alternating Three Sisters agriculture with hunting and gathering on a seasonal cycle. In this chapter you'll learn about the hunting tribes of the western plateau that strongly influenced Ranchlands cuisine.

Before the arrival of American and European settlers only a few Native Americans actually lived on the western plateau. The Sioux, Crows, Cheyennes, Comanches, Blackfoots, Kiowa-Apaches, and Arapahos ranged the shortgrass prairie full-time, leading a nomadic lifestyle similar to that of their prehistoric ancestors. Except for a few foraged foods and food goods acquired from agricultural river valley tribes, their diet was based almost exclusively on game meat—primarily bison.

Before the arrival of Europeans, Great Plains tribes used prehistoric methods of communal hunting, using only wood and

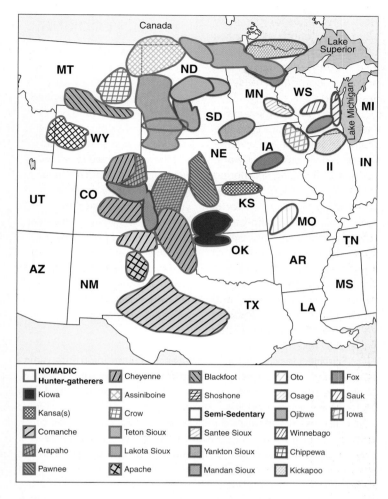

FIGURE 10.3

Great Plains Native American Population, circa 1750

Each harvested bison was used in its entirety. The fat was used for cooking or cosmetics; hides were made into clothing, blankets, tents, and cooking vessels; and bones were fashioned into tools. After a hunt the tribe feasted on fresh meat, especially enjoying the delectable but highly perishable organs. But most of the meat was preserved in order to establish a secure food supply for winter and for use in trade.

Plains Equestrians

Despite the iconic image of the American Indian astride his pinto pony, for most of their history Native Americans had no horses. However, the arrival of horses in the New World drastically changed the lives of Great Plains Native Americans. Although all Native Americans valued horses and acquired them when they could, on the Great Plains many tribes made horses and horse-back transportation the central aspect of their lives. These tribes are classified as **plains equestrians.**

Natives of the western plateau were among the first to acquire horses descended from those lost or abandoned by Spanish explorers in the 1500s. Mobility afforded by horses made hunting far easier and, thus, the food supply more secure. Horses also allowed Native Americans to raid each other's villages and camps, stealing both goods and human chattel.

Throughout the 1600s, the acquisition of horses caused more than a few central plains tribes to abandon the hard work of agriculture and revert to a nomadic hunter-gatherer lifestyle. In the 1700s this trend increased because of the domino effect of population pressure in the east; when displaced East Coast tribes pushed Ohio Valley natives out of their traditional territories, Ohio Valley tribes moved westward, in turn displacing central plains river valley natives. Forced out of their ancestral homelands, many stopped engaging in traditional agriculture. Finally, in the 1800s pioneers began settling the central plains, and the U.S. government sought to remove any remaining settled plains natives from valuable river valley land. By the 19th century most Midwestern Native Americans lived as plains equestrians.

When the Great Plains tribes went mobile, their architecture, crafts, and cooking all changed. The sod-constructed lodge was replaced by the conical, pole-and-hide tepee that could be dismantled, pulled long distances behind a horse, and quickly reassembled. Possessions, including cooking equipment, were minimized and designed for easy transport.

Because they acquired most of their food by hunting, plains equestrians ate a lot of meat. The typical male plains native consumed as much as 10 pounds of meat per day. However, this high meat consumption accompanied a low consumption of carbohydrates—similar to the late-20th-century Atkins diet discussed on this book's companion website. Although today this diet is considered unbalanced, plains equestrian tribes adapted to it and, until their eating habits were forcibly altered by the actions of the U.S. government in the late 1800s, they remained uniformly strong, healthy, and lean.

Although they no longer produced their own agricultural products, plains equestrians had access to a limited amount of

stone tools and traveling on foot. On a large hunt, many bison were killed. Plains hunters used ingenious methods to capture their prey, including pit traps and fencelike snares. The most dramatic method was the *buffalo jump*, in which teams of hunters guided a running herd of bison over a cliff (Figure 10.4). Bison carcasses were butchered on site and the hunt's bounty transported to the village or hunting camp on pole travoises pulled by humans or dogs.

FIGURE 10.4

This sculpture at the Tatanka Museum depicts Native Americans using the buffalo jump hunting method. Courtesy Peggie Detmers Studio.

Photo taken by Mike Wolforth

Three Sisters foods through trade with remaining settled tribes—or by stealing them during raids. Foraging for a limited number of wild foods supplied additional nutrients to a diet largely based on meat.

The equestrian nomadic life resulted in a different, more primitive style of Native American cuisine. To begin our study of Ranchlands cooking, let's examine the Native American cuisine that strongly influenced it.

Plains Equestrian Native American Cuisine

During the golden age of the plains equestrian tribes, roughly between 1750 and 1870, bison was the foundation food for all western plateau tribes. Rather than engaging in large-scale organized hunts, in good weather the typical extended family group sent out small hunting parties every few days, harvesting a single animal for immediate consumption.

For constantly roaming plains natives, cooking technology was simple yet ingenious. On the treeless shortgrass prairie, wood was scarce. Instead of burning firewood, plains equestrians used dried bison dung as fuel for both heat and cooking fires. Grilling was the cooking method of choice for tender cuts. However, applying the moist heat needed to tenderize tough cuts required more ingenuity. Clearly, nomads traveling on horseback couldn't carry around fragile clay pots. Instead, they used sling-bag simmering (p. 33) and paunch cooking, described in the box.

Although plains equestrians had ready access to fresh meat for most of the year, preserved meat products remained important as traveling provisions and for use during bad weather. As winter approached, a significant portion of each harvested animal was preserved by drying (Figure 10.5).

The best-known Native American preserved meat product is **jerky,** thin strips of salted, dried meat. The word *jerky* is derived from the Mexican Spanish word *charqui,* itself derived from a South American native language. In the American West and the Caribbean, *to jerk* means to preserve meat (see Chapter 15).

FIGURE 10.5
Bison meat drying in a Cheyenne camp. Courtesy of The Denver Public Library

As today, strips of dry jerky were often eaten as a snack or traveling food. Plains tribes also made *pemmican* (p. 89), another compact, easy-to-carry food.

Jerky and other dried meat products could be the main ingredient of winter meals. Slowly cooked in water using the sling-bag simmering method, the dried meat reconstituted into a flavorful stew. *Wakapapi,* stone-baked meat pounded with bone marrow, was used as a kind of soup base, reconstituted with boiling water to make a thick hash or to flavor soups and stews. Purchased or foraged vegetable components added flavor and texture.

Foraged foods added much-needed vitamins to the plains equestrians' meat-based diet. Wild fruits, such as sand cherries, chokecherries, serviceberries, currants, buffalo berries, and wild plums, were eaten ripe in season and dried for future use. Dried fruit pulp was reconstituted into soups or sauces and was often combined with meat to make dishes with sweet-savory flavors. Wild vegetables, among them buffalo gourd, a turniplike tuber, a wild variety of onion, and a potato-like tuber, were eaten fresh as well as dried. Spring brought nettles, purslane, lamb's quarter, dock, pigweed, and tumbleweed shoots, all good digestive tonics after a winter of heavy protein foods. Wild mushrooms were gathered in spring and fall. In the southwestern reaches of the plains, where the grasslands verged on desert, plains equestrians harvested various types of edible cacti.

Many plains equestrian Native American cooking and food preservation methods were adopted by the western plateau's rancher first settlers. In many ways their lives were similar: Both groups spent long periods on the move and needed easily transportable foods and cooking implements. Both relied on red meat as the foundation of their diets and used provisions to supplement it. Thus, Native American cooking strongly influenced the cuisine of the Western Ranchlands.

PAUNCH COOKING

An animal's **paunch,** or stomach, can be used as a cooking vessel. In Native American paunch cooking the stomach is emptied and thoroughly cleaned out; filled with cubes of meat, seasonings, and a little water; and then suspended over low embers. Bovine stomach tissue is sturdy enough to contain simmering liquid and thick enough to withstand gentle heat for an extended period. By the time the contents are simmered tender, the paunch becomes brown and crisp on the bottom. The entire package is consumed with much appreciation.

FACTOR 2
Ranchlands cuisine is strongly influenced by the foodways of plains equestrian Native Americans.

■ WESTERN
□
■ RANCHING

In Texas, ranchers of Mexican and Spanish origin had been running longhorn cattle on the southern shortgrass prairie for nearly 200 years. Thus, the true first settlers of the Ranchlands culinary region were Meso-Spanish colonists, whose food-ways are discussed in Chapter 7. Their colonial Meso-Spanish cooking is one of the roots of modern Ranchlands cuisine.

Although the Mexican government had encouraged American settlement in Texas, after it became part of the United States in the mid-1800s greater numbers of Americans began establishing ranches there. To sell their cattle, Texas ranchers drove them primarily to New Orleans and cities in the Plantation South. However, the Civil War seriously disrupted commerce throughout the South and stopped cattle from reaching market. Incurring the loss of many cattle, and with no market for those that remained, many early Texans simply walked away from their ranches. By 1866, large herds of abandoned longhorn cattle roamed the plains, unclaimed and free for the taking.

The U.S. Desert Land Act of 1877 opened land beyond the 100th meridian to free-claim settlement. With no capital other than money to buy lumber, anyone could claim a parcel of land and build a ranch house on it. To establish a herd, the aspiring rancher simply rounded up some cattle and burned his brand in their hides. Enterprising easterners, including newly discharged soldiers and newly freed African-Americans, began migrating west to take advantage of this irresistible opportunity. Soon the western plateau was dotted with cattle ranches from Texas to the Dakotas.

In 1863 the dream of building a railroad connecting America's East Coast with its rapidly developing West Coast became reality when work on the Transcontinental Railroad was begun. Rail transport would become the key factor in establishing economic viability for the Western Ranchlands.

By the 1870s well-established Midwestern farms were producing grain, hogs, and other food products. Railroads had reached Midwestern hub cities, and meatpacking companies were building stockyards and slaughterhouses. Cattle were driven to market by cowboys on horseback over long distances to Midwestern markets in Kansas City and Chicago. This form of cattle transport became known as the *long drive* (Figure 10.6). Long drives followed famous cattle routes such as the Goodnight-Loving Trail, the Chisholm Trail, and the Abilene Trail. At the end of the summer grazing season, these trails were flooded with mile-long drives of cattle numbering in the thousands.

FIGURE 10.6

Cowboys and steers stop for water on a cattle drive.

Courtesy of The Denver Public Library

However, the long drive of cattle on the hoof was an inefficient way to transport meat. Because of the excessive exercise the animals endured during a typical thousand-mile trip, they typically became tough and lost valuable poundage en route. As work on the Transcontinental Railroad progressed, ranchers negotiated the construction of rail spurs leading from the main rail line into the western grasslands. Rail spurs ended in railheads where live cattle were loaded into boxcars and shipped to Midwestern stockyards without facing the rigors of a thousand-mile trail drive. There the range-fed cattle were finished on corn and other grains in stockyard holding pens, acquiring the marbling demanded by Eastern beef consumers. Demand and price soared, causing more Americans to travel west to make their fortunes in cattle.

Only one problem now stood in the way of western ranching: the region's Native American population. The government-forced expulsion of Native American tribes from the central plains in the early 1800s had pushed numerous tribes west of the 100th meridian. With the Rocky Mountains to the west, desert to the southwest, and cold climate to the north, Native American tribal leaders realized there was nowhere left to go. Correctly viewing their situation as a last stand, many tribes turned to violence. As skirmishes between settlers and Native Americans became more and more frequent, the U.S. Army was mobilized to protect the West.

In addition to traditional fighting with firearms, the U.S. government began a systematic program intended to solve the "Indian problem" for good. The primary tactic was to remove the Native American's main food source, the bison, as recounted in the box on p. 466. Without their principal source of food, clothing, and shelter, most of the region's Native Americans were reduced to weakness or starvation. Native American tribes were relocated to confined areas of settlement, called *reservations*. In this way the western plateau was cleared of both Native Americans and bison to make room for ranchers and their cattle.

Ranchers and Cattle Barons

Once the "Indian problem" had been resolved and the Great Plains virtually cleared of bison, word got out that millions could be made in cattle ranching. Before long, a higher class of entrepreneurs began settling the western plateau. Wealthy Easterners, Englishmen, and Europeans claimed huge tracts of Western land and established great ranches. Called **cattle barons,** these landowners lived as aristocrats in rambling ranch houses filled with servants. Mexican-Americans and laid-off Chinese railroad workers cooked, cleaned, and tended vegetable gardens for the ranch houses. Situated on a tract as large as 50,000 acres, a great western ranch functioned as an independent entity, producing much of its own food and equipment. Preserved and processed foods such as wheat flour, coffee, and sugar as well as raw materials for building were shipped in by rail to towns that sprang up at the railheads. Each ranch needed many employees to maintain the ranch buildings and perform skilled crafts such as horse shoeing, saddle making, and woodworking.

THE DESTRUCTION OF THE AMERICAN BISON HERD

Estimates vary as to how many bison populated the Great Plains in the early 1800s; some historians estimate as many as 60 million. Throughout the century, bison were harvested at an unprecedented rate. Increasing numbers of Native Americans living on the plains were responsible for killing millions of bison for food. A period of drought further reduced numbers. During the building of the Transcontinental Railroad, millions more were harvested to feed railroad workers. By 1870 America's bison population had been reduced to about 13 million. However, the real decimation of the herds began in the 1870s when buffalo leather became fashionable. Professional hunters swarmed the Great Plains: Individual hunters killed as many as one hundred bison per day; teams of "hiders" skinned the animals and left the meat to rot in the sun. Passenger trains brought wealthy Easterners to the western plateau for "buffalo hunts" in which bison were shot from the windows of luxury railroad cars purely for sport. Soon the land was littered with bison skeletons that were eventually collected for use in the production of fertilizer (Figure 10.7).

U.S. government officials clearly understood the correlation between the destruction of the bison herd and the removal of Native Americans' primary food source. Encouraged by the government, by 1890 professional and amateur hunters had reduced the bison population to fewer than one thousand.

FIGURE 10.7
After the destruction of the American bison population, their bones were shipped east by rail to be ground into fertilizer. Courtesy Saskatchewan Archives Board, R-B677-2

Small-time ranchers claimed more modest spreads and took out bank loans to build and furnish them. These ranchers scratched out their livings with only their families and a few hired hands to help. Life was dangerous for both ranchers and cowboys; working long hours in the wilderness in the company of large, often intractable animals resulted in many accidents. Disputes over grazing territory sometimes led to violence and even full-scale range wars. If a small rancher had several years of bad luck, he could easily default on his bank loan and face foreclosure. Many were forced to sell out to a local cattle baron and become hired hands on their own former ranches.

Ranching on the western plateau was initially based on the open range concept. Although under the Desert Land Act millions of acres of grasslands were owned by individual ranchers, only areas directly surrounding homesteads were fenced. Even more land belonged to the U.S. government and was available to all.

FACTOR 3
American settlers' pioneer cooking forms the foundation of Ranchlands cuisine.

During the days of the open range, ranchers and cowboys on horseback followed the cattle herds as they progressed on their seasonal migration in search of food. In spring and fall, marketable cattle were rounded up and driven to a railhead to be shipped east. Along the way, cowboys hauled their own provisions, medical supplies, and weapons in a wagon or on packhorses. To feed the crew, each rancher sent along a cook and *chuck wagon*, the precursor of today's lunch truck (pp. 468 and 469). Thus, chuck wagon cooking is a foundation of Western Ranchlands cuisine.

The Cattle Boom Goes Bust

Advances in agricultural technology and the development of drought-resistant wheat eventually made it possible to farm many parts of the western plateau. In the 1890s, "sod-busting" farmers began settling the shortgrass prairie and planting wheat. Clearly, cattle had to be kept out of their wheat fields. The invention of barbed wire made possible cheap, easily constructed fences that ended the era of the open range.

Because ranchers were now bounded by property lines and subject to growing government restrictions, they reluctantly began confining their cattle in fenced pastures and feeding them hay. European cattle breeds were introduced, with Angus and Hereford among the most popular. Ranchers developed new American crossbreeds, blending the European characteristics of tenderness and high meat-to-bone ratio with Longhorn sturdiness. Prime western beef became the protein food of choice for many Americans and was exported to England and Europe. However, the cattle boom was about to go bust.

Concentrated cattle ranching began to destroy the fragile prairie ecosystem. Although the shortgrass prairie could support roaming bands of bison moving cyclically over thousands of miles of territory, it could not sustain concentrated

ELEMENTS OF RANCHLANDS CUISINE

FOUNDATION FOODS

principal starches: wheat breads and quick breads, potatoes

principal proteins: beef, dried beans, bison

principal produce: carrots, cabbage

FAVORED SEASONINGS: sage, thyme, onions, bacon, smoke

PRINCIPAL COOKING MEDIA: bacon drippings, lard

PRIMARY COOKING METHODS: grilling, barbeque, braising, stewing

FOOD ATTITUDES: minimized food culture, culinary conservatives

potatoes and other root vegetables that grew easily and could be stored for long periods of time. Because they weren't widely cultivated, vegetables thus play a lesser role in Ranchlands cuisine.

Cooking technology wasn't a priority on the typical ranch. Ranch house kitchens were adequate for simple cooking, but were not designed for producing elaborate meals or for formal entertaining. Even on the homestead, much cooking was done outdoors. Grilling, stewing, and barbeque are the Ranchlands' most favored cooking methods. Then and now, ranchers prefer simple food, plainly cooked, served in large portions.

populations of cattle confined in fenced ranges. Unusually high rainfall between 1877 and 1886 had given false confidence to both ranchers and farmers. With the return to normal weather, overgrazing led to destruction of prairie habitat, leaving little forage for cattle.

The cattle boom abruptly busted during the winter of 1886–1887, when the coldest weather in recorded history froze cattle in their tracks and blizzards buried them in snowdrifts. Ranchers lost as much as 85 percent of their stock. Most of the grand cattle barons packed up and moved on to other enterprises, leaving only the toughest and most determined ranchers behind.

From start to finish, the great American cattle boom lasted only 20 years. However, ranching and the cowboy lifestyle are the subject of many popular books and films and have become major elements in American popular culture. More important to students of cuisine, ranching created a unique American regional cooking style.

TRADITIONAL RANCHLANDS COOKING

Most of the pioneer ranchers that settled the western plateau in late 1800s were of British Isles origin, typically of English and Scots-Irish heritage. Although some were immigrants direct from Europe, many more were Americans from the East Coast or Midwest. Thus, they were accustomed to cooking with American indigenous foods and colonial domesticates. Their cooking repertoire and taste preferences were primarily derived from Old World British, New England, Mid-Atlantic, Appalachian South, and Central Farmlands cuisines.

In general, early ranchers did not have a strong food culture. Few planted extensive vegetable gardens or established orchards. This was partly due to the poor quality of the region's soil, but even more so to the rancher mindset. To most ranchers, beef cattle were the sole cash crop and therefore demanded all the attention. About the only food crops a typical ranch produced were

Despite the physically and financially daring act of establishing agricultural operations in the arid west, most early ranchers were culinary conservatives. This food attitude prevails today. Although the cuisine has embraced some elements of Mexican-American cooking, for the most part it resists foreign flavors. Instead the cuisine focuses on meat and potatoes, mainly supported by pioneer provisions.

Cooking with Provisions

Wheat flour is the primary starch in Ranchlands cuisine. By the mid-1800s, white wheat flour from newly established Midwest farms was the ranch cook's most important provision, surpassing cornmeal in popularity. For bread making, Ranchlands cooks used natural yeasts and the sourdough method, discussed on p. 469. After the Civil War, fast-acting baking soda was used to leaven biscuits, pancakes, and other quick breads. Ease of preparation made these baked goods even more prevalent than yeast breads.

Salt pork and bacon were shipped to railheads from back east, and later from the Midwest. Bacon remains a favored breakfast meat and is used as a seasoning or topping for many Ranchlands dishes. The region's frying media include both bacon drippings and lard. In the Ranchlands, bacon is an indispensable seasoning meat for beans.

Dried beans were among the ranchers' most important pioneer provisions. Pinto beans were most popular, with navy beans and kidney beans a close second. In the Ranchlands beans may be cooked in the Mexican style with lard, tomatoes, and chiles, or in the New England style with salt pork or bacon, molasses, and mustard. Beans cooked with seasoning meat and served with biscuits or cornbread made a frugal yet nourishing and satisfying meal. Beans are also an indispensable side dish with Ranchlands barbeque (p. 471). Leftovers from a dinner of beans might become bean soup or a layer in a casserole. In winter many ranch cooks prepared large tubs of cooked beans and left them outdoors to freeze; when they needed a quick meal, cooks hacked off chunks of frozen beans with an ax and thawed them on the stove or over a campfire.

FACTOR 3

Ranchlands cooking is based on Anglo-American foodways and pioneer provisions.

FACTOR 3
Pioneer provisions remain important ingredients in Ranchlands cuisine.

In the late 1800s, industrially produced canned goods became widely available. These products supplemented the traditional provisions in the ranch house pantry and broadened the cuisine. Canned fruits were especially welcome, providing sweetness and nutrients in a diet based primarily on red meat and starch.

In most American culinary regions, reliance on pioneer provisions waned as economic viability increased. Not so in the Ranchlands region. Even financially successful ranchers relied on provision foods because of the long distance to the nearest town and frequent isolation due to bad weather. Thus, pioneer provisions remain a cornerstone of traditional Western Ranchlands cuisine.

A Diet Based on Beef

Because beef cattle are the main product of a typical western ranch, it's no surprise that in Ranchlands cuisine the main protein food is beef. Although cattlemen were careful not to overconsume their only cash crop, weak or injured animals frequently ended up on the table. The rancher's family and guests ate the tender cuts, while the hired help made do with the tougher, less valued parts.

Although most ranches had a flock of chickens, they were kept primarily for eggs. Chicken was considered a special-occasion food and served infrequently. In Ranchlands cuisine, beef is often substituted for chicken in favorite dishes, as in chicken-fried steak (p. 486) or beef pot pie. In the early days of cattle ranching, bison and other wild game were abundant and helped vary the Ranchlands diet.

Cooking by Professionals

Ranch life was hard on women. Ranchers' wives were largely isolated from the company of other women, and their husbands were away working on the range for weeks at a time. Many wives, tiring of hard work, boredom, and loneliness, gave up and went back east. Without readily available medical help, many others died in childbirth. Thus the single rancher running his own home was more the rule than the exception.

Unlike other American culinary regions where women traditionally do the cooking, Ranchlands cuisine was primarily developed by men. Most ranch house kitchens were run by a paid employee who was frequently a retired cowboy and almost always a man. Thus, Ranchlands cuisine was developed largely by male professional cooks. The ranch cook, or **coosie** (from the Spanish *cocinero*), was among its highest-paid employees, usually second only to the foreman in salary.

In the early days of ranching, the working conditions of the typical coosie were primitive at best. The job of providing three meals a day, seven days a week, for a bunch of demanding, complaining cowboys was thankless and tiring work. Often exhausted and irritable, ranch cooks got the reputation of being bitter and ornery. However, good food was so important to the successful operation of a ranch that the coosie was indulged in all manner of eccentric, unpleasant, and abusive behavior in exchange for providing the comfort of a well-cooked meal.

Despite having a minimized food culture, ranchers and cowboys nonetheless demanded well-cooked, substantial meals. Ranches that served poor food had a hard time keeping help and, once word got around that their cooking was bad, had a hard time hiring good workers. Celebrations such as holidays and weddings caused the cookhouse to swing into high gear, forcing reluctant cowboys into kitchen duty and frequently involving barbeque (p. 471).

By the late1800s most ranch house kitchens were furnished with a cast-iron woodstove complete with an oven and warming box. In addition, many had a stone fireplace with a rotisserie and cooking hearth. Large ranches maintained separate structures, called *cookhouses*, which contained both a kitchen and a staff dining room. In the hot summer months, much of the cooking was done outdoors in a fire pit near the kitchen. Outdoor cooking remains a hallmark of Ranchlands cuisine.

Chuck Wagon Grub

Because a typical western ranch extends more than 5,000 acres, and big operations are much larger, cowboys spent much time away from the actual ranchstead. Cowboys working alone or in pairs carried their food on horseback, often munching on jerky for a quick protein meal. In the evening they relied on primitive campfire cooking, grilling meat on a greenwood rack, heating cans of beans directly in the coals, and baking biscuit dough by wrapping it around a stick and suspending it over the fire, marshmallow-style. On the range where trees were scarce, cowboys adopted the Native American method of using dried bison dung, known as **buffalo chips,** for fuel.

Cowboys also copied Native American hunting and food preservation practices. When they needed meat, a group of cowboys working the range typically killed a single large animal and butchered it on the spot. A bison, deer, or steer became several days' meals for the crew. Tender cuts and organs were eaten first, simply grilled over coals, and the tough cuts were seasoned highly with salt, wrapped in the animal's hide, and stored for a few days to trigger enzymatic tenderization. When able to camp in one place for a few days' time, they made jerky.

Major trail drives required large parties of men to work far away from the ranch for many months. In the early days, teams of cowboys traveled with just a cook and a provisions wagon; meals were prepared on the ground and cooked over a campfire. In the 1870s, ranchers began refitting surplus Civil War military supply wagons to become mobile kitchens, complete with food storage bins, equipment racks, and fold-down tailgate work counters (Figure 10.8). Known as a **chuck wagon,** this ingenious mobile kitchen was equipped and stocked to serve three meals a day for several months' time as well as to serve as a makeshift barbershop and medical office. Even after the era of long trail drives was over, ranchers used chuck

Native American cooking methods and food preservation techniques were essential elements of cowboy cooking.

FIGURE 10.8
A traditional chuck wagon has storage compartments and a drop-down tailgate that functions as a worktable. Courtesy of the Library of Congress, LC-D4-13756

wagons to accompany their cowboys to and from far-flung grazing lands and distant railheads. By the turn of the 20th century, some chuck wagons even boasted built-in tin woodstoves.

Cowboy Food Slang

The term *chuck wagon* is derived from cowboy slang, a rich vocabulary of humorous terms developed by cowboys for their own amusement. Beef chuck, or shoulder, was considered a lesser cut of beef. By extension cowboys took to calling all cheap, low-grade foodstuffs *chuck* and used the term *chuck wagon* to insult the coosie. Many other cowboy slang terms are food-related. A few of the best known are listed in the box.

Cast-Iron Baking

Cowboys on horseback could carry only lightweight tin pots and pans. However, the chuck wagon made it possible to use heavier cooking equipment. Though tin pots were used to boil water

for coffee and washing up, for most chuck wagon dishes the cooking vessel of choice was the black cast-iron Dutch oven. Although it is well known for slow simmering soups, stews, and beans, the versatile Dutch oven also can be used for rustic baking (Figure 10.9). To make quick breads or simple cakes, the Dutch oven is preheated over the fire, greased, filled with dough or batter, and covered with its heavy lid. The Dutch oven is then nestled into a bed of hot coals and more coals piled onto its lid to ensure even heating. This method results in a moist, tasty product with a crusty, well-browned exterior.

FIGURE 10.9
The cast-iron Dutch oven is a versatile cooking vessel that can be used for outdoor baking as well as for soups and stews. Courtesy Lee Raine, www.cowboyshowcase.com

Sourdough

Before the availability of chemical leaveners in the late 1800s, yeast was the only ingredient capable of transforming wheat-flour dough into a palatable and long-keeping leavened bread. However, at that time commercial bakers' yeast did not exist. To leaven their homemade breads, bakers relied on wild yeasts captured from their surroundings. On farms and in villages, settled bakers could capture free-floating wild yeasts simply by setting out a bowl of flour-and-water batter. Soon this mixture became a bubbly mass called a **starter** because it contained yeast and could be used to start a batch of bread dough. If a piece of yeasted bread dough was reserved from the day's baking and kept under the right conditions, the yeast living within it could be used to start another batch of bread. Because most yeasts are rather fussy about the conditions under which they are stored, bakers needed to be careful with their starters and use them quickly.

However, pioneers traveling through the wilderness in all kinds of weather could not be so careful about the conditions under which their starters were stored. Nor could they bake on a regular schedule. In all starters, ever-present bacteria enter the dough mass along with the wild yeasts. When the bacteria in a particular dough mass become too numerous, the acids they produce create conditions that kill many kinds of yeasts. Luckily, a few types of wild yeast thrive in acidic conditions. This fact makes possible a special type of bread that has become a signature dish of Ranchlands cooking and other cuisines of the American West. Because this unique bread has a tangy, acidic flavor, it's called **sourdough.**

Until the late 1800s, sourdough starter was an essential element of both ranch kitchen and chuck wagon baking. A sour-smelling, bubbly mass of soft dough, the sourdough starter was carefully watched and coddled, kept warm in the winter and cool in the summer, and "fed" with fresh flour and water on a daily basis. On the trail in cold weather, many a ranch cook tucked a

A COWBOY CULINARY LEXICON

bacon	overland trout
beef	slow elk
biscuits	hot rocks, soda sinkers, dough gods
canned goods	airtights
coffee	brown gargle
fancy food	fluff duffs
gravy	Texas butter
onions	skunk eggs
pancakes	splatter dabs, belly pads
pinto beans	whistle berries, Pecos strawberries
waitress	biscuit shooter

HOW YEAST WORKS

Yeast is a living microorganism. When yeast is introduced into a dough made from wheat flour and water, it feeds on the carbohydrates in the flour. As the yeast "eats," it produces carbon dioxide, or CO_2 gas, as a waste product. This gas remains trapped within the dough in the form of tiny bubbles. When the dough is held at an optimal temperature, around 80°F, the yeast produces more and more CO_2 bubbles, causing the dough to expand, or rise. This action is called *fermentation*; when it occurs, the dough becomes light and puffy. When the dough is placed in a hot oven, the CO_2 gas expands rapidly and the dough rises yet again. When the internal temperature of the loaf reaches about 140°F, the oven heat kills the yeast, whose work is done. At about 190°F the crust is golden brown and the interior set. The finished loaf is larger and lighter than the original dough mass, and its interior crumb has an open, airy texture. In this way yeast **leavens,** or lightens, bread.

leather pouch of starter inside his clothing so his body heat would keep the yeast alive and active.

Sourdough starter was used not only for making bread, but also to leaven biscuits and pancakes. As sourdough baking traveled westward with America's pioneers, each region they settled acquired a special group of sourdough products all its own. Although chemical leaveners and commercial yeasts are faster and easier to handle, the tangy taste of sourdough remains an important part of the Ranchlands flavor profile.

The Mexican Connection

On the southern plains, Mexicans and Mexican-Americans frequently took jobs as cowboys on Anglo ranches and often became ranch cooks. To suit their own tastes and lend variety to a limited palette of ingredients, Mexican ranch cooks rubbed meat for the grill with Mexican seasonings and served it with salsa and flour tortillas, fajita style. They added powdered dried red chile to bean dishes and meat stews, resulting in cowboy beans and, eventually, Anglo-style chili.

Chili with an *i*

The correct term for a hot and spicy member of the capsicum family is *chile*, spelled with an *e* as in the Spanish language. The names of Mexican and Mexican Border cuisine dishes based on chiles use this spelling, as in *chile con carne*.

Chili spelled with an *i* is an Anglo dish that originated on Texas ranches when Anglo coosies began imitating the *chile con carne* of their Mexican counterparts. To make the dish quicker and easier to prepare, Anglo cooks replaced rehydrated, puréed dried red chiles with a ground dried spice mixture they called *chili powder*. Chili powder typically contains ground dried red chile, ground cumin, dried oregano, and other seasonings.

Ranchlands chili is a stew made from tough but flavorful cuts of beef simmered in a rich sauce made with beef stock. Authentic Texas chili is made with beef cut into small dice, not with ground beef. It does not contain tomatoes. Flavored with onions, garlic, and chili powder, Texas chili is slow-simmered until the beef is tender and bound with a spicy, deep-red sauce (Figure 10.10).

Chili garnered national attention during the Chicago World's Fair in 1893 when the San Antonio Chilley [sic] Stand introduced the spicy red stew to visitors from all over America. Chili soon underwent many adaptations as the recipe made its way around the country. After the invention of the electric grinding machine around 1900, cooks began using widely available ground beef to make chili. Ranging from bland cafeteria versions to imaginatively prepared, award-winning signature dishes, chili is now an American national dish, affectionately called "a bowl o' red" from Maine to California.

Today many ardent chili lovers join chili cooking clubs such as the Chili Appreciation Society International, which boasts scores of "pods," or chapters, all over the United States and Canada. Local chili-cooking competitions lead to the International Championship Chili Cookoff, held annually in Terlingua, Texas.

Mexican-American Dishes

In the second half of the 20th century, many Mexican-American dishes such as nachos, *chile con queso*, and guacamole entered the Ranchlands repertoire. So where does Mexican Border cooking end and Ranchlands cooking begin? Hard to say—but in general, Ranchlands cooking remains more Anglo-oriented in technique, ingredients, and attitude. Ranchlands cooking is simpler and less labor-intensive than true Mexican Border cuisine. The Ranchlands cook is more likely to reach for a blended chili powder than for the pure ground chile used by a Mexican Border cook. He often uses canned beans or bottled salsa in place of homemade. Like a baked potato topped with sour cream and salsa, Mexican-influenced Ranchlands dishes are based on

FIGURE 10.10

Texas chili is a defining dish of Ranchlands cuisine. Photo by David Haynes.

mainstream American cooking with just a touch of Mexican-American flair.

German Influence

In the late 1800s, northern and central Texas welcomed a substantial number of German immigrants. They enriched Ranchlands cuisine with German-style smoked sausages. Ranchlands cooks readily adopted German coleslaw, both creamy-style and vinegar-based types. Beer is a German specialty much appreciated by thirsty cowboys. Ranch cooks use beer as a cooking medium as well, braising beef in it and frequently adding a splash to chili. Germans adapted Wiener schnitzel (breaded veal cutlets) to Ranchlands beef and created Chicken-Fried Steak (p. 486), today claimed by Oklahoma as a state dish. And it was a German, William Gephardt, who first marketed prepared chili powder; today Gephardt's brand is Texas's best-selling chili powder.

Barbeque Goes West

FACTOR 4
Second-settlers from the Plantation South brought fried foods and barbeque.

After the Civil War, thousands of freed African-Americans headed west and became cowboys. Newly landless white Southerners claimed ranches. The art of Southern barbeque traveled west with both groups.

Although Ranchlands cooks already followed the Native American practice of grilling tender meats outdoors over coals, Southerners applied their moist-heat barbeque techniques to tough cuts of beef and even whole beef carcasses (Figure 10.11). Rubbed with a Western-flavored seasoning mix and periodically doused with a Western-style mop, barbequed beef cooks to steamy, succulent perfection.

For Ranchlands barbeque, the beef cut of choice is brisket, preferably the fattier second-cut section. Briskets are heavily

FIGURE 10.11
At a Texas barbeque, a whole bull is slowly cooked over glowing coals.
Bonnie Walton/Shutterstock

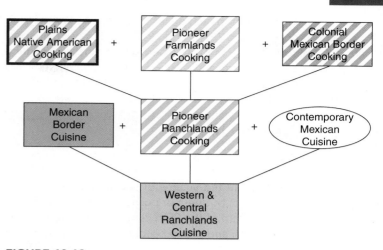

FIGURE 10.12
Development of Western and Central Ranchlands Cuisine

coated with a dry spice rub and cured for several days. A mesquite wood fire is burned down to glowing coals over which low wire racks are positioned. The briskets are placed on the racks and cooked slowly for hours, basted frequently with a sweet-and-tangy mopping sauce, and turned often for even cooking. Sliced thin across the grain and served with the reduced mopping sauce, Ranchlands barbeque is juicy, deeply flavored, and succulent. Ranchlands mopping sauce is sweeter and less acidic than most Southern mops. In the Ranchlands, barbequed beef is served with a thick, slightly sweet, tomato-based barbeque sauce.

Today's Ranchlands barbeque restaurants offer more than just the traditional brisket. Beef ribs, chicken, and smoked sausages make popular barbeque fare. Accompaniments to Ranchlands barbeque include coleslaw, cowboy-style beans, and biscuits. In eastern Texas, Kansas City, and Oklahoma, barbeque joints also offer Plantation South–style pork ribs and pulled pork shoulder, and cornbread and collard greens compete with Ranchlands accompaniments.

■ ALTERNATIVE AND □ SPECIALTY ■ RANCHING

The rise of industrial agriculture in the 20th century greatly affected ranching. Both increased demand for beef and consumer preference for highly marbled beef led to the practice of finishing beef cattle in feedlots. Because confined animal feeding operations, or CAFOs, don't require thousands of acres of rangeland, entrepreneurs began establishing cattle operations in other parts of the country. Ranching expanded eastward into the central plains and Florida, and westward into California's interior valleys.

By the end of the 20th century, highly capitalized corporate megaranches were proving more profitable than small family operations. Fluctuations in beef prices and a decline in American beef consumption in the 1970s and 1980s led many small operators to sell out. Today the top 7 percent of ranches produce 75 percent of industry revenue. However, many family ranches still remain viable, typically because of expansion into innovative specialty products and agritourism.

Alternative Ranching

As early as the 1770s, a few western plateau settlers chose to raise sheep rather than cattle. Despised by cattle ranchers, sheep ranchers became the victims of several range wars and were often forced out of business or pushed west into the Rocky Mountains. After the turn of the 20th century, sheep operations became more common and proved economically viable. By the 1950s Western lamb was sold all over the United States and exported to Europe. However, in the latter part of the 20th century, stiff competition from New Zealand and Australia sheep ranchers slowed European trade.

Beginning in the early 20th century, conservationists in America's western national parks began work to restore the bison population. In the 1970s a few ranchers began crossbreeding cattle and bison. Called *beefalo*, the meat exhibited the worst characteristics of both animals and, thus, was not well received. By the 1990s consumers seeking a leaner, all-natural substitute for beef turned to bison meat. In response, some western ranchers began raising bison for market. Easy keepers on grass alone, bison need not be finished with grain and have a high meat-to-bone ratio. Promoted as a natural, hormone-free product, bison meat has become a popular menu item for steakhouses and Western-themed restaurants.

A few ranchers specialize in ostrich and emu. The meat of these large, exotic birds is marketed as a lean, low-cholesterol red meat alternative. Although it's a strange sight to see cowboys on horseback herding gawky, long-necked birds, production of these dark-meat fowl is on the rise. Some alternative ranches operate as game farms, raising red deer for venison as well as various African and American species of antelope.

■ RANCHLANDS
▫ TOURISM

FACTOR 5
Tourism brings renewed prosperity to the Ranchlands region.

In the second half of the 20th century, America's love affair with the automobile and the Old West led to a new source of income for the Ranchlands. The interstate highway system, low gas prices, and comfortable, air-conditioned cars put a Western vacation within reach for the American middle class. National parks and Native American reservations became tourist attractions, bringing in much-needed revenue.

The most popular Western vacation destination is the **dude ranch**—more politely called a

FIGURE 10.13
Ranchlands tourism is anchored by the dude ranch, where guests participate in ranch activities and enjoy Ranchlands cuisine. Alan Keohane © Dorling Kindersley

guest ranch—a resort where visitors participate in ranch activities such as horseback trail riding and herding cattle. Western-style entertainment, such as square dancing, two-step dancing, country-western music concerts, and rodeo exhibitions, adds to the fun. Dude ranches were the first foodservice operations to popularize Ranchlands cooking, serving casual, hearty dishes in buffet or family-style service. Today many guest ranches have professional chefs and offer lavish meals featuring contemporary Ranchlands cuisine (Figure 10.13).

■ CONTEMPORARY
▫ RANCHLANDS
■ CUISINE

Today ranch culture and ranch-style cuisine is found not only throughout the shortgrass prairie but also in central Florida, the American Southwest, the Rocky Mountains, and California's interior valleys—all of which have a venerable tradition of ranching. Ranch-style barbeque brisket, cowboy beans, steaks, and "ranch" dressing have become part of the national cuisine.

As America's preference turns toward leaner grass-fed meat, independent ranchers are responding with breeds of cattle that pack more flavor with less fat. Bison is growing in popularity as a beef alternative. Selected producers are specializing in animals raised on organic feed and without the use of hormones and antibiotics. As the 21st century unfolds, increasing domestic tourism and the popularization of high-protein diets portend a promising future for ranchers and Ranchlands cuisine. Refer to this book's companion website for a list of noteworthy Western Ranchlands cuisine restaurants.

☐ TABLE 10.1 WESTERN AND CENTRAL RANCHLANDS DEFINING DISHES

ITEM NAME	HISTORY	DOMINANT INGREDIENTS AND METHOD	MORE
BISCUITS	Yeasted sourdough biscuits predate chemically leavened ones. On the trail they were baked in cast-iron Dutch ovens.	Lard or butter is cut into flour mixed with baking soda and salt. The mixture is moistened with buttermilk to make a soft dough. Round biscuits are punched out with a cutter or dropped with a spoon. Campers wrap dough around a stick and bake it over coals like marshmallows.	As a bread accompaniment, biscuits complement soups, stews, or any saucy dish. Topped with red-eye gravy or sausage cream gravy, biscuits are the base of a hearty breakfast entrée. Large biscuits are split and stuffed with ham or other cold cuts to make interesting sandwiches. Miniature stuffed biscuits serve as casual hors d'oeuvres. Biscuit dough may be flavored with cooked sausage, sharp Cheddar cheese, or a variety of fresh herbs.
SOURDOUGH BAKED GOODS	Since the days of the wagon train and the chuck wagon, Ranchlands cooks have been using a leavening starter made from wild yeasts cultivated in a fermented dough base.	See pp. 469–470 for a detailed discussion of sourdough baking and baked goods.	Sourdough breads, biscuits, and pancakes are Ranchlands favorites.
RANCH DRESSING	Many Ranchlands settlers were from the British Isles where salad dressings based on eggs and dairy products are traditional. In the Ranchlands, thick, tangy buttermilk was used.	Thick buttermilk (or a combination of buttermilk and mayonnaise) is flavored with granulated onion and garlic, and a variety of dried herbs. Cider vinegar contributes tart flavor.	Buttermilk salad dressing captured the public's imagination in the 1950s at the Hidden Valley Ranch, a dude ranch with a restaurant and nightclub "hidden" in the hills outside Santa Barbara, California. Served on a steakhouse-style tossed salad (p. 420), ranch dressing was an instant hit.
COWBOY BEANS	Mexican *cocineros* simmered pinto beans with onions, garlic, tomatoes, dried or fresh chile, and sometimes spicy sausage. Anglo coosies cooked white beans with salt pork or bacon, molasses, onions, and sage.	Today both Mexican Border and Anglo ingredients are used in Ranchlands beans. Ketchup or barbeque sauce is sometimes added. A drop of liquid smoke lends a campfire flavor.	With cowboys eager to ingest beer in any guise, the *borracha* or drunken style of adding beer to the beans was another favorite.
BRAISED MACARONI/ GOULASH	On the trail where water was scarce, coosies were unwilling to use and then discard gallons of water to boil pasta. Instead, they used the braising technique borrowed from Mexican *cocineros*.	Dry macaroni is browned in bacon drippings or oil and then cooked with canned tomatoes and all their juices to make a saucy, casserole-like pasta dish. Prepared in this manner, the pasta becomes soft and absorbs much of the sauce. The casserole is usually topped with cheese and gratinéed.	For a one-pot meal, ground beef is browned and then simmered along with the macaroni. For unknown reasons, this dish is sometimes called *goulash*.
DRY-RUBBED, WOOD-FIRE GRILLED STEAKS	When a steer was slaughtered for ranch consumption, the ranch owner reserved the steer's tender cuts for his own use. Sirloin, tenderloin, and rib steaks were favored for grilling.	A thick, well-marbled, dry-aged beefsteak is rubbed with salt and other seasonings. Held refrigerated for a short period, the steak partially cures as the seasonings penetrate it. For true Ranchlands flavor the steak is then grilled over smoky mesquite coals. A typical rub for steak may include salt, granulated onion, granulated garlic, dried herbs, ground black pepper, dried powdered chile, and other ground dry spices.	Traditional accompaniments include cowboy beans, home fries, and coleslaw. Modern diners prefer French fries or baked potatoes and green salad with ranch dressing.
BEEF BARBEQUE	Second-settlers from the Plantation South brought barbeque to the Ranchlands, where the meat of choice was beef. The traditional cut for barbeque is brisket, preferably the fattier second-cut section.	Beef briskets are cured with a mixture of salt, sugar, dry spices, and aromatics. The meat is slow-cooked for hours over glowing coals and basted with a vinegar-based mopping sauce. Mesquite wood provides a distinctive flavor.	Ranchlands barbeque sauce is a thick, tangy-sweet mixture of ketchup, mustard, molasses, beer, garlic, onion, brown sugar or honey, cider vinegar, and bottled hot sauce. Authentic Ranchlands barbeque is always accompanied by cowboy beans, biscuits, and cole slaw. Optional sides include Western-style potato salad, macaroni salad, bean salad, or corn on the cob. Chilled longneck bottles of beer wash it all down.

(continued)

☐ **TABLE 10.1 WESTERN AND CENTRAL RANCHLANDS DEFINING DISHES** *(continued)*

ITEM NAME	HISTORY	DOMINANT INGREDIENTS AND METHOD	MORE
RANCHLANDS CHILI	Texas ranchers adapted Mexican and Southwestern red chile stews, using abundant beef and a pre-blended mixture of dried, ground red chile and other spices.	Diced beef is browned and then simmered in a roux-thickened sauce colored and flavored with prepared chili powder or a house-made proprietary spice blend containing red chile. "Secret" ingredients include chocolate or cocoa, chipotle chiles en adobo (p. 353), liquid smoke, beer, and tequila. Today bison chili is popular, its leanness often counteracted by the addition of pork. True Texas chili contains neither tomatoes nor beans.	Chili toppings include grated Cheddar cheese, chopped onion or scallion, chopped cilantro, chopped green chiles, sour cream, and bottled hot sauces. Starch accompaniments include saltine crackers, flour tortillas, corn tortilla chips, white rice, and cornbread. Pinto beans or black beans may be served on the side.
CHICKEN-FRIED STEAK	The state dish of Oklahoma, chicken-fried steak is a menu favorite throughout the Ranchlands region. This hybrid dish applies a Plantation South breading to Western beef prepared in the same manner as German Wiener schnitzel.	Half-inch slices of beef top round are scored and pounded for tenderness, seasoned with salt and pepper, breaded in a Southern egg-flour-egg coating, and then pan-fried in lard. Chicken-fried steak is always served with mashed potatoes and a black pepper–spiked cream gravy made fron the drippings.	Accompaniments vary. In most of the Ranchlands region, a plate of chicken-fried steak with mashed potatoes and gravy is completed with corn or corn relish and pinto beans. In eastern Oklahoma and the Deep South, the dish includes black-eyed peas, collard greens, and cornbread.
PRAIRIE OYSTERS	During the spring roundup, when new calves are caught, counted, and branded, most of the male calves are gelded, or castrated, to become steers. The resulting calves' testicles are considered a delicacy. Today they are a featured food at several festivals held in the Ranchlands culinary region.	Calf testicles are peeled, sliced, coated in seasoned bread crumbs, and pan-fried. To some, the golden-brown discs resemble fried oysters—hence the name.	Prairie oysters are traditionally eaten unaccompanied or served with tomato ketchup. Today, many chefs serve them with a spicy salsa.
DUTCH OVEN DESSERTS	Trail coosies developed an ingenious method of baking desserts in Dutch ovens buried in and topped with hot coals.	*Fruit Cobblers:* Fresh or reconstituted dried fruit is placed in a Dutch oven with sugar and butter. Dollops of sweetened biscuit dough are placed on top. The dessert is baked in campfire coals with more coals on the lid. *Pudding-in-a-Sack:* A variation on English steamed puddings, a dense, sweet batter studded with nuts and dried fruits and spiked with whiskey is placed in a cotton flour sack and poached in gently simmering water for several hours until it becomes a firm, chewy sphere. The poaching liquid is reduced, sweetened, and thickened to become a sauce.	Although sometimes prepared by ambitious campers, today these desserts are most often made in the oven or on the stove.

■ ◻ ■   # STUDY QUESTIONS

1. Describe the climate and topography of the western plateau. How have these factors affected Ranchlands food products and food culture?

2. Discuss the importance of Native American cooking and food preservation techniques in traditional Ranchlands cuisine. Name two plains equestrian food preparation techniques that became part of Ranchlands cooking.

3. How did Mexican Border cooking become part of Ranchlands cuisine? Compare and contrast Mexican Border cuisine and Ranchlands cuisine.

4. Explain why, in many areas of the Midwest, Ranchlands cooking exists side by side with Farmlands cooking. Compare and contrast Ranchlands cuisine and Farmlands cuisine.

5. Why, until recent times, were preserved products so important to Ranchlands cooking? Name some of these products and explain how they were/are used.

6. Explain why outdoor cooking was an important element in traditional Ranchlands cuisine. Describe some of the equipment and techniques used in Ranchlands outdoor cooking. How has this legacy influenced modern Ranchlands cooking? How has it affected American cooking in general?

7. Discuss sourdough baking. Include in your discussion how wild yeasts leaven bread doughs, and how bacteria create a tangy, sour taste. Explain why the sourdough process was favored by Ranchlands pioneers.

8. Discuss the Ranchlands region's primary food product and explain the processes it undergoes from field to table. List and describe two alternative foods produced in the Ranchlands today.

9. Explain how Plantation South barbeque led to the development of Ranchlands barbeque. Compare and contrast the two.

10. Discuss Ranchlands tourism. How has it affected the culture and cuisine of the ranchlands? Describe the most prevalent type of Ranchlands tourist attraction and the cuisine it offers.

11. Using your imagination and the information in this chapter, plan a four-course special-occasion dinner menu featurig Ranchlands cuisine.

Smoky Beef 'n' Bean Soup
with Biscuit-on-a-Stick

yield: 1 (10-fl.-oz.) appetizer serving
(multiply × 4 for classroom turnout; adjust equipment sizes accordingly)

MASTER RECIPE

production		costing only
1	Biscuit-on-a-Stick	1/6 recipe
1 1/4 c.	Smoky Beef 'n' Bean Soup	1/4 recipe
1	cocktail napkin	1 each
1 Tbsp.	chopped flat-leaf parsley	1/40 bunch a.p.

service turnout:
1. Place the Biscuit-on-a-Stick on a sizzle pan and heat it about 5 minutes in a 400°F oven.
2. Stir the Smoky Beef 'n' Bean Soup well to distribute the solids. Ladle it into a small saucepan and heat it just to the boil.
3. Plate the dish:
   a. Place the cocktail napkin on a cool 10" plate.
   b. Pour the soup into a hot 12-oz. soup cup and place the cup to the left of the plate.
   c. Sprinkle with parsley.
   d. Place the biscuit on the right of the plate.

COMPONENT RECIPE
SMOKY BEEF 'N' BEAN SOUP

yield: 5 c.

production		costing only
1	1" slice beef shank, with marrow bone	8 oz. a.p.
2 Tbsp.	pork lard	1 oz.
3/4 c.	dry pinto beans, quick-soaked or soaked overnight and drained	4 3/4 oz. a.p.
1/4 c.	dried sweet corn, such as Cope's brand	1 oz.
1 qt.	Brown Beef Stock	1/4 recipe
2 c.	water	n/c
5 oz.	3/8"-diced rindless smoked slab bacon	6 oz. a.p.
1/2 c.	fine-chopped yellow onion	2 1/2 oz. a.p.
1/4 c.	peeled, 3/8"-diced celery	1/20 head a.p.
1/2 c.	3/8"-diced carrot	3 oz. a.p.
1/4 c.	seeded, chopped jalapeño chile	2 oz. a.p.
1 c.	coarse-chopped tomato concassée	9 oz. a.p.
1 sprig	fresh thyme	1/20 bunch a.p.
1 sprig	fresh sage	1/12 bunch a.p.
1 drop	liquid smoke	1/16 fl. oz.
tt	kosher salt	1/16 oz.

preparation:
1. Trim the beef shank of all fat and score the silverskin around its edges to prevent curling.
2. Heat a 10" sauté pan, heat 1 Tbsp. lard, and brown the beef shank on both sides.
3. Place the shank, beans, corn, Brown Beef Stock, and water in a 3-qt. saucepan and bring to the simmer.
4. Skim away the foam and simmer, uncovered, 30 to 40 minutes, until the beans are almost tender.
5. In the same 10" sauté pan, heat the remaining lard and sauté the bacon until it is almost crisp and its fat renders out.
6. Add the onion, celery, carrot, and jalapeño and sauté until soft.
7. Add the tomato and cook, stirring, until almost dry.
8. Scrape the bacon and vegetables into the soup. Add the thyme, sage, liquid smoke, and a little salt. Simmer, uncovered, stirring occasionally, 30 minutes longer, until the meat and beans are tender.
9. Remove the beef shank and cool it enough to handle. Discard the herb sprigs.
10. Remove the marrow from the beef bone and chop it fine. Cut the meat into 3/8" dice, discarding the bone and gristle.
11. Return the meat and marrow to the soup.
12. Taste and correct the seasoning.

holding: open-pan cool and immediately refrigerate in a freshly sanitized, covered container

---

RECIPE VARIATION

Vaquero Beef 'n' Bean Soup
Replace the dried corn with 1/2 c. cooked corn kernels added in step 8. Replace the liquid smoke with 1 Tbsp. minced *chiles chipotles en adobo*. Replace the parsley with cilantro. Replace the Biscuit-on-a-Stick with 2 warm Flour Tortillas.

Tossed Salad
with Buttermilk Ranch Dressing

yield: 1 (5-oz.) appetizer serving
(multiply × 4 for classroom turnout)

MASTER RECIPE

production		costing only
1 1/2 oz.	cleaned, thoroughly dry, torn romaine hearts	1/4 head a.p.
2 oz.	cleaned, thoroughly dry, torn iceberg lettuce	1/6 head a.p.
1/4 c.	Buttermilk Ranch Dressing, in squeeze bottle	1/4 recipe
1/4 c.	chiffonade-cut red cabbage	1/2 oz. a.p.
1/8 c.	slivered sweet onion	3/4 oz. a.p.
1/8 c.	thin-sliced radish	1/6 bunch a.p.
1/8 c.	julienne red bell pepper	1 oz. a.p.
1/8 c.	drained, cooked or canned chickpeas	1/2 oz. or 1 fl. oz.
1/8 c.	sliced pitted California black olives	1/2 oz.
1/2 c.	Garlic Croutons	1/4 recipe
1 tsp.	chopped flat-leaf parsley	1/40 bunch a.p.
2 1/2 pc.	cherry tomato halves	1/8 pt. a.p.

service turnout:
1. Toss the romaine and iceberg lettuces with 2/3 of the Buttermilk Ranch Dressing.
2. Plate the dish:
   a. Mound the lettuce in a cool 10" pasta plate or 8" salad bowl.
   b. Top the salad in order with the cabbage, onion, radish, red bell pepper, chickpeas, olives, croutons, parsley, and tomatoes, arranging the cherry tomato halves around the edge of the plate well.
   c. Drizzle the salad with the remaining dressing.

COMPONENT RECIPE
BUTTERMILK RANCH DRESSING

yield: approx. 1 c.

production		costing only
2/3 c.	mayonnaise	5 1/3 fl. oz.
1 tsp.	granulated onion	1/16 oz.
1 tsp.	granulated garlic	1/16 oz.
1/2 tsp.	white pepper	1/16 oz.
1/2 tsp.	dried thyme	1/16 oz.
1/4 tsp.	dried powdered sage	1/16 oz.
2 Tbsp.	cider vinegar	1 fl. oz.
2 tsp.	sugar	1/6 oz.
2 drops	Worcestershire sauce	1/16 fl. oz.
dash	hot pepper sauce	1/16 fl. oz.
2 Tbsp.	minced scallion	1/16 bunch a.p.
1/3 c.	buttermilk	2 1/3 fl. oz.
tt	kosher salt	1/16 oz.

preparation:
1. Whisk together the mayonnaise, onion, garlic, white pepper, thyme, sage, vinegar, sugar, Worcestershire sauce, hot pepper sauce, and scallion.
2. Whisk in the buttermilk.
3. Refrigerate 30 minutes to meld the flavors.
4. Taste and correct the seasonings and flavor balance.

holding: refrigerate in a freshly sanitized, covered container up to 5 days

APPETIZERS

RECIPE VARIATION

Fiesta Salad with Ranch Dressing and Salsa
Shred rather than tear both types of lettuce. Replace the toppings with 1/8 c. each julienne radishes, julienne jicama, cooked corn kernels, chopped red onion, toasted *pepitas* (green pumpkin seeds), and sliced California black olives. Top with a dollop of Cooked Tomato Salsa.

Chicory Salad
with Beef Jerky, Spiced Pecans, and Smoked Tomato Vinaigrette

yield: 1 (5-oz.) appetizer serving
(multiply × 4 for classroom turnout)

🕐 With house-made jerky, requires 3 days advance preparation.

MASTER RECIPE

production		costing only
2 oz.	cleaned, thoroughly dry, torn escarole	1/5 head a.p.
1 1/2 oz.	cleaned, thoroughly dry, torn curly endive	1/5 head a.p.
1/4 c.	Smoked Tomato Vinaigrette, in squeeze bottle	1/4 recipe
2 slices	sweet onion, separated into rings	1 oz. a.p.
1/2 c.	tomato filet, cut in thick julienne	3 oz. a.p.
1/3 c.	loosely packed shredded Beef Jerky or commercially produced jerky	1/5 recipe
5 pc.	Spiced Pecans	<1/4 recipe
1 Tbsp.	fine diagonal-sliced chives	1/20 bunch a.p.

service turnout:
1. Toss the escarole and endive with the Smoked Tomato Vinaigrette.
2. Plate the dish:
   a. Mound the greens in a cool 10" pasta plate.
   b. Top the salad in order with the onion, tomato, jerky, Spiced Pecans, and chives.

COMPONENT RECIPE
SMOKED TOMATO VINAIGRETTE

yield: approx. 1 c.

production		costing only
1 Tbsp.	tomato paste	1/2 fl. oz.
1 Tbsp.	minced shallot	1/4 oz. a.p.
1 tsp.	minced garlic	1/9 oz. a.p.
1 Tbsp.	sugar	1/2 oz.
1/4 c.	cider vinegar	2 fl. oz.
1 to 2 drops	liquid smoke	1/16 fl. oz.
tt	kosher salt	1/16 oz.
2/3 c.	room-temperature corn oil	5 1/3 fl. oz.

preparation:
1. Place all ingredients except the oil in a blender.
2. Blend on high speed and, with the blender running, remove the insert from the blender lid and pour in the oil in a thin stream to create an emulsion.
3. Taste and correct the seasoning to achieve a tart, well-salted, slightly sweet dressing with just a hint of smoke.

holding: refrigerate in a freshly sanitized squeeze bottle at room temperature up to 3 hours; refrigerate up to 1 week; if the dressing separates under refrigeration, reblend

COMPONENT RECIPE
BEEF JERKY

yield: approx. 4 oz.

🕐 Requires 3 days advance preparation.

production		costing only
1/4 c.	Japanese soy sauce	2 fl. oz.
1 tsp.	pure New Mexico red chili powder	1/16 oz.
1 tsp.	fresh-ground black pepper	1/16 oz.
1 tsp.	granulated onion	1/16 oz.
1 tsp.	granulated garlic	1/16 oz.
1/2 tsp.	dried powdered sage	1/16 oz.
8 oz.	thin (3/8") slice of beef top round, trimmed of all fat	9 oz. a.p.

first day preparation:
1. Mix together the soy sauce, chile, pepper, onion, garlic, and sage.
2. Place the meat between two sheets of pan liner and pound it with a meat mallet to 1/4" thickness.
3. Rub the seasonings into the meat.
4. Place the meat in a sealed plastic bag, place it flat in the refrigerator, and marinate at least 12 hours.

second day preparation:
5. Preheat a food dehydrator, smoker (using no wood product), or holding oven to 180°F.
6. Drain the meat and blot it dry.
7. Cut the meat into 3/4" strips.
8. Arrange the meat strips flat, in one layer, on the smoker rack or on a cooling rack placed over a sheet tray.
9. Dry the meat about 24 hours until it has lost approximately half its original weight and is leathery in texture but still flexible.

third day preparation:
10. If using as a salad garnish, pull the jerky apart into short shreds.

holding: store in a tightly sealed container at cool room temperature for about 1 month

COMPONENT RECIPE
SPICED PECANS

yield: approx. 1 1/2 c.

production		costing only
6 Tbsp.	butter	3 oz.
1 tsp.	pure New Mexico red chile powder	1/16 oz.
1 tsp.	fresh-ground black pepper	1/16 oz.
1 tsp.	granulated garlic	1/16 oz.
1 tsp.	granulated onion	1/16 oz.
1 Tbsp.	sugar	1/2 oz.
1 1/2 c.	pecan halves	8 oz.

preparation:
1. Line a half-sheet tray with a sheet of pan liner.
2. Melt together the butter, chile, pepper, garlic, onion, and sugar in a 10" sauté pan.
3. Add the pecans and sauté them over low heat, tossing constantly, about 2 minutes, until the pecans are well coated with seasonings and just beginning to darken.
4. Spread the pecans on the pan liner and cool to room temperature.

holding: store in a tightly sealed container at cool room temperature about 1 month

---

RECIPE VARIATION
Chicory Salad with Grilled Steak, Spiced Pecans, and Smoked Tomato Vinaigrette
Omit the Beef Jerky. Top the salad with 2 to 3 oz. thin-sliced grilled steak of choice. Drizzle the meat with a little extra vinaigrette.

Texas "Caviar"

with Tortilla Chips

yield: 1 (4-oz.) appetizer serving plus accompaniments
(multiply × 4 for classroom turnout)

MASTER RECIPE

production		costing only
2	thin yellow or white corn tortillas, each cut into 8 wedges	% of pkg.
as needed	frying compound or vegetable oil	% used
tt	fine salt	1/16 oz.
1 leaf	green leaf lettuce	1/20 head a.p.
3/4 c.	Texas "Caviar"	1/4 recipe
1 Tbsp.	chopped cilantro	1/20 bunch a.p.
1	lime wedge	1/6 [63 ct.] lime

service turnout:

1. Deep-fry the tortilla chips in a 400°F fryer. Drain on paper towels and sprinkle with salt.
2. Plate the dish:
   a. Place the lettuce leaf on the left front of a cool 10" plate.
   b. Mound the Texas "Caviar" on the leaf.
   c. Sprinkle with the cilantro.
   d. Place the lime wedge next to the "caviar."
   e. Mound the tortilla chips on the back right of the plate.

COMPONENT RECIPE

TEXAS "CAVIAR"

yield: approx. 3 c.

production		costing only
1 Tbsp.	seeded, chopped jalapeño chile	1/2 oz. a.p.
1/4 c.	fine-chopped white onion	1 1/4 oz.
1 tsp.	minced fresh garlic	1/9 oz. a.p.
tt	kosher salt	1/16 oz.
1/2 c.	tomato concassée	6 oz. a.p.
1 1/2 c.	cooked or canned black-eyed peas, drained	3 oz. dry or 12 fl. oz.
2 Tbsp.	gold-color pure olive oil	1 fl. oz.
1/3 c.	1/4"-diced green bell pepper	2 2/3 oz. a.p.
1/3 c.	1/4"-diced pitted California black olives	1 1/4 oz.
1 Tbsp.	chopped cilantro	1/40 bunch a.p.
tt	fresh-ground black pepper	1/16 oz.
tt	fresh lime juice	1/4 [63 ct.] lime

preparation:

1. In a large mortar or small, heavy bowl, mix the jalapeño, onion, and garlic with a little salt.
2. Using the pestle or a heavy spoon, mash the aromatics together into a rough paste.
3. Add the tomato, half of the black-eyed peas, and the oil. Mash to a rough purée.
4. Stir in the remaining black-eyed peas and the green bell pepper, olives, and cilantro.
5. Season with pepper, lime juice, and more salt if needed.

holding: best made the same day; prepare only enough for one service; hold refrigerated in a freshly sanitized, covered container up to 8 hours

---

RECIPE VARIATIONS

Texas "Caviar" Salad in Tortilla Bowl
Omit the tortilla chips. Using a tortilla bowl form or two mesh strainers, deep-fry a 10" flour tortilla to make a tortilla bowl. Place shredded romaine in the bottom of the tortilla bowl and fill with Texas "Caviar."

Corny Texas "Caviar"
Replace half of the black-eyed peas with cooked fresh corn kernels. Garnish with popcorn.

Armadillo Egg
with Fresh Tomato Salsa

yield: 1 (4-oz.) appetizer serving plus accompaniments (multiply × 4 for classroom turnout; adjust equipment sizes accordingly)

MASTER RECIPE

production		costing only
1 tsp.	corn oil	1/6 oz.
1	Armadillo Egg	1/4 recipe
1	small Boston lettuce leaf	1/10 head a.p.
2 fl. oz.	Fresh Tomato Salsa (p. 331)	1/4 recipe

service turnout:
1. Brush a sizzle plate with oil, place the Armadillo Egg on it, and bake in a 400°F oven about 10 minutes, until heated through.
2. Plate the dish:
   a. Place the lettuce leaf on the left side of a cool 10" plate and fill it with Fresh Tomato Salsa.
   b. Cut the Armadillo Egg in half and arrange it on the plate to the right of the salsa.

COMPONENT RECIPE
ARMADILLO EGGS

yield: 4 (4-oz.) "eggs"

production		costing only
4	jalapeño chiles	3 oz. a.p.
1/4 c.	cider vinegar, optional	2 fl. oz.
1 1/4 oz.	Monterey Jack cheese, cut into 4 (1 1/4" × 1/2" × 1/2") rods	1 1/4 oz.
5 oz.	bulk breakfast sausage	5 oz.
1/2 recipe	Buttermilk Biscuit ingredients	1/2 recipe
1/2 tsp.	fine salt	1/12 oz.
1/2 c.	grated sharp Cheddar cheese	2 oz.
as needed	flour	1 oz.
1	egg mixed with 1 Tbsp. water	1 each or 2 oz.
2/3 c.	cornflake crumbs	3 oz.

preparation:
1. Prepare the chiles:
   a. Place a cooling rack over a gas flame, place the jalapeños on the rack over the flame, and char them, turning often.
   b. Immediately wrap the chiles in a piece of aluminum foil and allow them to steam in their own heat about 15 minutes, until cool enough to handle.
   c. Wearing foodservice gloves, remove the stems from the chiles and scrape away the charred skin.
   d. Slit each chile open and use a tomato coring tool or small spoon to scrape out all seeds and white membrane.
   e. If the chiles are too spicy-hot, soak them in cool water mixed with 1/4 c. vinegar 30 minutes to 1 hour, then blot them dry inside and out with paper towels.
   f. Stuff each chile with a piece of Monterey Jack cheese and squeeze it closed.

2. Cook the sausage:
   a. Crumble the sausage into a cold sauté pan and place the pan over low heat.
   b. Cook, stirring to break up the lumps, until the sausage is cooked through and has rendered its fat.
   c. Drain in a strainer, discarding the fat.
3. Prepare the Buttermilk Biscuit dough, adding the salt, sausage, and cheese.
4. Make up the "eggs":
   a. Divide the dough into 4 even-size spheres.
   b. Flour the work surface and your hands.
   c. Flatten the spheres into oval discs.
   d. Encase each chile in a portion of the dough, forming the dough into the shape of an egg.
   e. Dip each "egg" in the egg wash, then roll it firmly in cornflake crumbs.
   f. Place the "eggs" on a rack set over a sheet tray and refrigerate them, uncovered, at least 30 minutes.
5. Preheat an oven to 375°F.
6. Place the tray and rack of "eggs" in the middle of the oven and bake about 25 minutes, until the dough is cooked through.
7. If not serving immediately, cool to room temperature on the rack.

holding: refrigerate in a freshly sanitized, covered container with pan liner between layers up to 3 days

---

RECIPE VARIATIONS
Triple Threat Armadillo Eggs
Replace the Monterey Jack cheese with hot pepper jack. Replace the breakfast sausage with hot Italian sausage.

Deep-Fried Armadillo Eggs
Omit the egg wash and cornflake crumbs. Deep-fry to order at 375°F.

Cannibal Steak

yield: 1 (3-oz.) appetizer serving plus accompaniment
(multiply × 4 for classroom turnout)

MASTER RECIPE

production		costing only
3	3/8" baguette slices	2 oz. a.p.
2 Tbsp.	Texas Butter	1/4 recipe
2 1/2 oz.	thoroughly trimmed filet of beef, very cold	3 oz. a.p.
1 tsp.	Dijon mustard	1/6 fl. oz.
dash	hot pepper sauce (such as Crystal brand)	1/16 oz.
dash	Worcestershire sauce	1/16 oz.
1 tsp.	anchovy paste	1/6 fl. oz.
1 Tbsp.	minced shallot	1/2 oz. a.p.
2 tsp.	minced flat-leaf parsley	1/40 bunch a.p.
2 tsp.	minced chives	1/40 bunch a.p.
2 tsp.	chopped nonpareil capers	1/4 oz.
tt	fresh-ground black pepper	1/16 oz.
2 Tbsp.	extra virgin olive oil	1 fl. oz.
tt	liquid from the caper jar	n/c
tt	kosher salt	1/16 oz.
1 leaf	cleaned and dried leaf lettuce	1/20 head a.p.
3	grape tomatoes	1/8 pint a.p.

service turnout:
1. Prepare the toast:
   a. Spread one side of each baguette slice with Texas Butter.
   b. Place the toasts on a rack and bake in a 400°F oven about 2 minutes, until crisp and golden.
   c. Cool on the rack.
2. Wearing foodservice gloves, prepare the meat:
   a. Using a very sharp knife, fabricate the filet into brunoise cuts, then chop through it a few times.
   b. Transfer the meat to a bowl and add the mustard, hot pepper sauce, Worcestershire sauce, anchovy paste, shallot, parsley, chives, capers, black pepper, oil, caper liquid, and salt. Toss lightly to combine.
   c. Taste and correct the seasoning.
3. Plate the dish:
   a. Place the lettuce leaf on the left front of a cool 10" plate.
   b. Mound the beef on the leaf.
   c. Arrange the toast slices overlapping on the rear of the plate.
   d. Arrange the grape tomatoes on the right of the steak.

COMPONENT RECIPE

TEXAS BUTTER

yield: 1/2 c.

production		costing only
7 Tbsp.	room-temperature butter	3 1/2 oz.
2 tsp.	granulated garlic	1/8 oz.
2 tsp.	granulated onion	1/8 oz.
1 tsp.	pure New Mexico red chili powder	1/16 oz.
1 Tbsp.	minced flat-leaf parsley	1/40 bunch a.p.
2 tsp.	minced lemon zest	n/c
1 tsp.	fresh lemon juice	1/16 [90 ct.] lemon
tt	fine-ground white pepper	1/16 oz.
tt	kosher salt	1/16 oz.

preparation:
1. Mix together all ingredients.

holding: store at room temperature up to 3 hours; refrigerate in a freshly sanitized, covered container up to 1 week; freeze up to 1 month; bring to room temperature before using as a spread

CHEF'S NOTE:
Follow local health department guidelines when serving uncooked meat.

RECIPE VARIATION
Charred Rare Filet Steak, Cannibal Style
Coat the piece of filet with oil and char-grill it rare. Cool it to room temperature, then cut brunoise, but do not chop. Proceed with seasoning and presentation.

APPETIZERS

Campfire Brook Trout

with Corn Relish Tartar Sauce, Annie's Skillet Potatoes, and Grilled Western Vegetables

yield: 1 (12-oz.) entrée serving plus accompaniments (multiply × 4 for classroom turnout; adjust equipment sizes accordingly)

MASTER RECIPE

production		costing only
1 tsp.	corn oil	1/6 fl. oz.
1 wedge	Annie's Skillet Potatoes	1/4 recipe
1/2	egg, beaten	1/2 each or 1 oz.
2 Tbsp.	buttermilk	1 fl. oz.
1	12-oz. boneless head-on brook trout, washed inside and out, blotted dry	12 oz.
tt	fine salt	1/16 oz.
1/4 c.	Campfire Fish Dredge	1/4 recipe
1/4 c.	bacon drippings	n/c
1/4 c.	corn oil	2 fl. oz.
1/2	nopal cactus paddle, thorns removed	2 oz. a.p.
2	3/8"-thick red bell pepper rings	2 oz. a.p.
1	3/8"-thick lengthwise slice zucchini	2 oz. a.p.
2	scallions, root end removed	1/4 bunch a.p.
2 Tbsp.	gold-color pure olive oil	1 fl. oz.
tt	kosher salt	1/16 oz.
1 Tbsp.	cider vinegar	1/2 fl. oz.
1/4 c.	Corn Relish Tartar Sauce	1/4 recipe
1	small red bell pepper cup (see photo)	3 oz. a.p.

service turnout:

1. Brush a sizzle pan with 1 tsp. corn oil, place the Annie's Skillet Potatoes on it, and bake them in a 400°F oven about 8 minutes, until they are heated through and the bacon is recrisped.
2. Fry the trout:
   a. Mix together the egg and buttermilk.
   b. Place a 10" nonstick sauté pan over medium heat.
   c. Season the trout inside and out with fine salt and close it.
   d. Coat both sides of the trout in Campfire Fish Dredge, dip in the egg wash, and coat with the dredge again.
   e. Add the bacon drippings and 1/4 c. corn oil to the pan and heat to about 375°F.
   f. Shake excess dredge off the trout and place it in the pan. Pan-fry about 1 1/2 minutes per side, until crisp and just done through.
   g. Drain the trout on a rack and hold hot.
3. Grill the vegetables:
   a. Toss the cactus, red bell pepper, zucchini, and scallions with the olive oil, kosher salt, and vinegar.
   b. Cook on a hot char-grill, turning occasionally, until marked with grill lines and cooked al dente.
4. Plate the dish:
   a. Place the potato wedge on a hot 12" plate at 12 o'clock, point in the center of the plate.
   b. Place the trout horizontally across the center of the plate, leaning against the potato wedge.
   c. Arrange the grilled vegetables in front of the trout from 1 o'clock to 7 o'clock.
   d. Spoon the Corn Relish Tartar Sauce into the red bell pepper cup and place it at 8 o'clock.

COMPONENT RECIPE
ANNIE'S SKILLET POTATOES

yield: 1 (8") cake

production		costing only
1/4 c.	clarified butter	2 1/4 oz. a.p.
2 pc.	thin-sliced smoked bacon	3/4 oz.
3	peeled russet potatoes	1 1/4 lb. a.p.
tt	kosher salt	1/16 oz.
tt	fine-ground white pepper	1/16 oz.
1/4 c.	julienne green bell pepper	2 oz. a.p.
1/3 c.	slivered yellow onion	2 3/4 oz. a.p.

preparation:
1. Mise en place:
   a. Preheat an oven to 425°F.
   b. Cut out a 6" circle of pan liner and brush one side with a little butter.
   c. Have ready a piece of aluminum foil.
   d. Have ready an 8" nonstick sauté pan with an ovenproof handle.
2. Prepare the bacon garnish:
   a. Cut the bacon slices in half and score the edges to prevent curling.
   b. Cook the bacon in the pan over low heat just until the fat renders out and the bacon is beginning to brown.
   c. Remove from the heat and pour the bacon drippings into the remaining melted butter.
3. Assemble the potato cake:
   a. Arrange the bacon slices in the 8" nonstick pan like the spokes of a wheel.
   b. Slice the potatoes thin and even.
   c. Arrange a layer of potato slices in the bottom of the pan on top of the bacon slices. For this first layer only, arrange the potatoes in attractive overlapping circles.
   d. Sprinkle the potatoes very lightly with salt and white pepper.
   e. Scatter a few pieces of green bell pepper and onion on top.
   f. Sprinkle with a little butter and bacon drippings.
   g. Repeat steps 3c through 3f, layering the remaining ingredients into the pan, and ending with potatoes.
   h. Place the buttered pan liner on the potatoes and press gently to firm.
   i. Cover the pan with a double layer of foil and seal the edges.
4. Bake the potato cake:
   a. Place the pan in the center of the oven and bake about 20 minutes, until a knife pierces the potatoes with a little resistance.
   b. Press gently on the potatoes to firm them, then continue baking 10 minutes longer.
   c. Loosen the foil and pour off any liquid from the pan.
   d. Cool the pan on a rack 5 minutes.
5. Portion the potato cake:
   a. Remove the foil and pan liner, place a plate on top of the sauté pan, and flip it over. Remove the pan.
   b. If preparing ahead, cool to room temperature, then refrigerate uncovered until cold.
   c. Cut the potato cake into 4 even wedges, each having a bacon slice in the center.

holding: refrigerate in a covered container, with pan liner between layers, up to 5 days

COMPONENT RECIPE
CAMPFIRE FISH DREDGE

yield: 1 c.

production		costing only
2/3 c.	corn flour	3 oz.
1/4 c.	stone-ground yellow cornmeal	1 oz.
2 tsp.	granulated onion	1/8 oz.
1 tsp.	fresh-ground black pepper	1/16 oz.
1/2 tsp.	dried thyme	1/16 oz.
1/2 tsp.	dried powdered sage	1/16 oz.
2 tsp.	fine salt	1/3 oz.

preparation:
1. Mix together all ingredients.

holding: store in a tightly sealed container at room temperature up to 3 months; dredge that has been contaminated through use must be held frozen or discarded

COMPONENT RECIPE
CORN RELISH TARTAR SAUCE

yield: 1 1/4 c.

production		costing only
3/4 c.	Corn Relish (or commercial corn relish)	1 recipe or 6 fl. oz.
1/2 c.	mayonnaise	4 fl. oz.

preparation:
1. Drain the liquid from the Corn Relish.
2. Mix the relish with the mayonnaise.

holding: refrigerate in a freshly sanitized, covered container up to 1 week

COMPONENT RECIPE
CORN RELISH

yield: approx. 3/4 c.

production		costing only
3/4 c.	lightly cooked or frozen corn kernels	3/4 ear a.p. or 4 1/2 oz.
1/4 c.	fine-chopped yellow onion	1 3/4 oz. a.p.
1/4 c.	brunoise-cut red bell pepper	1 1/4 oz. a.p.
pinch	celery seeds	1/16 oz.
pinch	yellow mustard seeds	1/16 oz.
pinch	crushed dried red pepper	1/16 oz.
2 Tbsp.	sugar	1 oz.
1/2 c.	cider vinegar	4 fl. oz.
1/4 c.	water	n/c
tt	kosher salt	1/4 oz.

preparation:
1. Place all ingredients in a 1-qt. nonreactive saucepan.
2. Cover and bring to the simmer.
3. Taste and correct the seasoning to achieve a sweet-tart-salty flavor balance.
4. Simmer, uncovered, over low heat about 8 minutes, until the liquid reduces level with the vegetables.
5. Open-pan cool to room temperature.

holding: refrigerate in a freshly sanitized, covered, nonreactive container up to 2 weeks

---

RECIPE VARIATION
Campfire Brook Trout with Corn Relish, Cowboy Beans, and Ranch Slaw
Replace the Annie's Skillet Potatoes and the grilled vegetables with Cowboy Beans (p. 493) and Ranch-Style Slaw (p. 493).

Oklahoma Chicken-Fried Steak

with Cream Gravy, Mashed Potatoes, and Western-Style Greens

yield: 1 (6-oz.) entrée serving plus accompaniments (multiply × 4 for classroom turnout; adjust equipment sizes accordingly)

MASTER RECIPE

production		costing only
1 1/4 c.	Western-Style Greens	1/4 recipe
1/4 c.	corn oil	2 fl. oz.
1/4 c.	pork lard	2 oz.
1/2	egg, beaten	1/2 each or 1 oz.
1 Tbsp.	milk	1/2 fl. oz.
1	6-oz. Frying Steak	1/4 recipe
tt	kosher salt	1/16 oz.
tt	fresh-ground black pepper	1/8 oz.
1/3 c.	Chicken-Fried Steak Dredge	1/4 recipe
2 Tbsp.	flour	1/3 oz.
1/2 c.	strong Poultry Stock, hot in steam table	1/32 recipe
3/4 c.	half-and-half, hot in steam table	6 fl. oz.
1 1/4 c.	Classic Mashed Potatoes, hot in steam table	1/4 recipe
1 Tbsp.	chopped flat-leaf parsley	1/40 bunch a.p.
1 Tbsp.	brunoise-cut red bell pepper	1/2 oz. a.p.

service turnout:

1. Heat the Western-Style Greens in a covered 8" sauté pan or in a microwave oven.
2. Fry the steak:
   a. Place a 10" sauté pan over medium heat, add the oil and lard, and heat to about 350°F.
   b. Mix the egg and milk to make egg wash.
   c. Season the Frying Steak with salt and pepper.
   d. Coat the steak with Chicken-Fried Steak Dredge, dip in egg wash, and coat with the dredge once again.
   e. Shake excess dredge off the steak and place it in the pan. Fry about 2 minutes on each side, until golden brown.
   f. Drain on a rack and hold hot.
3. Make the gravy:
   a. Pour off all but 2 Tbsp. fat from the pan.
   b. Stir in 2 Tbsp. flour and cook, stirring, to make a blond roux.
   c. Whisk in the Poultry Stock and half-and-half, bring to the boil, and reduce to a full-bodied nappé consistency.
   d. Season with salt and a generous amount of pepper.
4. Plate the dish:
   a. Spoon a tall mound of Classic Mashed Potatoes on the back of a hot 12" plate.
   b. Mound the greens on both sides of the potatoes.
   c. Place the steak on the front of the plate, leaning against the potatoes.
   d. Nap the steak with a stripe of gravy, allowing most to pool on the front of the plate.
   e. Sprinkle the steak with the parsley and brunoise-cut red bell pepper.

COMPONENT RECIPE
WESTERN-STYLE GREENS

yield: 5 c.

production		costing only
4 Tbsp.	butter	2 oz.
2 1/2 oz.	3/8"-diced rindless smoked slab bacon	3 oz. a.p.
1 c.	fine-chopped yellow onion	5 oz. a.p.
1/4 c.	seeded, chopped jalapeño chile	2 oz. a.p.
1 Tbsp.	minced garlic	1/3 oz.
10 oz.	destemmed, coarse-chopped collard greens	1 (14-oz.) bunch a.p.
8 oz.	destemmed, coarse-chopped kale	3/4 (14-oz.) bunch a.p.
8 oz.	destemmed, coarse-chopped turnip greens	3/4 (14-oz.) bunch a.p.
as needed	water	n/c
tt	kosher salt	1/16 oz.
tt	cider vinegar	1/16 oz.

preparation:
1. Place the butter in a large, heavy saucepan, add the bacon, and fry gently until the bacon fat is rendered and the bacon is almost crisp.
2. Add the onion and fry over low heat until soft.
3. Add the jalapeño and garlic and fry a few seconds longer.
4. Wash all the greens by submerging them together in cool water, then drain in a colander.
5. Pack the greens into the saucepan, stirring to coat them with the fat and seasonings.
6. Add 1 c. water and a little salt. Cover the pan and cook at a brisk simmer, stirring occasionally and adding water as necessary, about 30 minutes, until the greens are tender.
7. Remove the greens to a container and reduce the pan liquid to 1/2 c.
8. Return the greens to the pan, season them lightly with vinegar, and season them with more salt if needed.

holding: open-pan cool and immediately refrigerate in a freshly sanitized, covered container up to 7 days; freeze up to 3 months

COMPONENT RECIPE
FRYING STEAKS

yield: 4 (6-oz.) steaks

production		costing only
2	14-oz. slices beef top round, 1/2" thick	28 oz. a.p.

preparation:
1. Trim away all fat and connective tissue from the beef.
2. Cut the beef into 4 pieces of equal weight, each about 6 oz.
3. Using a very sharp boning knife, score a very shallow 3/8" crosshatch pattern on both sides of each slice.
4. Place the slices between two sheets of pan liner and, using a meat mallet, gently flatten the steaks on both sides to a thickness of just a little greater than 1/4".

holding: refrigerate in a freshly sanitized, covered container up to 3 days

COMPONENT RECIPE
CHICKEN-FRIED STEAK DREDGE

yield: approx. 1 1/3 c.

production		costing only
1 c.	flour	5 oz.
1/4 c.	Southern Seasoning for Chicken	1/2 recipe
2 tsp.	fresh-ground black pepper	1/8 oz.
1 Tbsp.	dried parsley	1/16 oz.

preparation:
1. Mix together all ingredients.

holding: store at room temperature in a tightly sealed container up to 1 month

---

RECIPE VARIATION

Chicken-Fried Turkey with Cream Gravy, Mashed Potatoes, and Western-Style Greens
Replace the beef with boneless turkey breast. Do not score before flattening.

Grilled Filet of Bison

with Smoky Steak Sauce, Beer-Batter Onion Rings, Hash Brown Potatoes, and Vegetable Roundup

yield: 1 (6-oz.) entrée serving plus accompaniments (multiply × 4 for classroom turnout; adjust equipment sizes accordingly)

MASTER RECIPE

production		costing only
1 1/2 c.	cooked, 3/8"-diced russet potato	9 oz. a.p.
1/4 c.	fine-chopped yellow onion	1 1/4 oz. a.p.
1 Tbsp.	chopped flat-leaf parsley	1/40 bunch a.p.
tt	kosher salt	1/16 oz.
tt	fresh-ground black pepper	1/16 oz.
2 Tbsp.	bacon drippings	n/c
1 Tbsp.	heavy cream, in squeeze bottle	1/2 fl. oz.
1 1/2 c.	Vegetable Roundup	1/4 recipe
1/4 c.	water	n/c
1 Tbsp.	corn oil	1/2 fl. oz.
1	6-oz. trimmed filet of bison	6 oz.
3	1/2"-thick rings of small sweet onion, such as Vidalia*	2 oz. a.p.
1/3 c.	Beer Batter, held in ice-water bath	1/4 recipe
as needed	frying compound or corn oil	% used
tt	fine salt	1/16 oz.
1 Tbsp.	butter	1/2 oz.
1/2 c.	Smoky Steak Sauce, hot in steam table	1/4 recipe
1 sprig	fresh thyme	1/20 bunch a.p.
1 sprig	fresh sage	1/10 bunch a.p.

*For best presentation, choose onion rings of graduated size.

service turnout:

1. Cook the hash browns:
   a. Place a 6" nonstick sauté pan over medium heat.
   b. In a small bowl, toss together the potato, onion, and parsley. Season with kosher salt and pepper.
   c. Add the bacon drippings to the pan and pack in the potato mixture. Drizzle the cream onto the potatoes without letting it run into the pan.
   d. Press a small plate on the surface of the potatoes and cook them over low heat about 5 minutes, until the bottom is browned.
   e. Remove the plate, flip the potatoes over, and cook another 5 minutes, until the new bottom is browned.
   f. Hold hot.
2. Heat the Vegetable Roundup with the water and a little salt in a covered 10" sauté pan or microwave oven.
3. Oil the bison filet and char-grill it to medium-rare or the customer's specified doneness, creating diagonal grill marks on the presentation surface. Season with kosher salt and pepper.
4. Fry the onion rings:
   a. Lower the fryer basket into 400°F oil.
   b. Dip the onion rings in the Beer Batter and then lower them into the oil. Deep-fry about 1 minute, until golden.
   c. Drain on a rack and season with fine salt.
5. Plate the dish:
   a. Slide the hash browns onto the center of a hot 12" plate.
   b. Place the bison filet on top.
   c. Work the butter into the vegetables and spoon them around the hash browns.
   d. Nap the bison with the Smoky Steak Sauce.
   e. Stack the onion rings on top of the bison filet.
   f. Make a bouquet of the herb sprigs and stick it upright out of the onion rings.

COMPONENT RECIPE
VEGETABLE ROUNDUP

yield: 6 c.

production		costing only
3/4 c.	cooked corn kernels, fresh or frozen	1 ear a.p. or 4 1/2 oz.
3/4 c.	shelled, cooked baby lima beans, fresh or frozen	3/4 lb. a.p. or 4 oz.
3/4 c.	1/2" diced, seeded zucchini, blanched and refreshed	4 oz. a.p.
3/4 c.	3/8" lengths green beans, blanched and refreshed	4 oz. a.p.
3/4 c.	3/8" squares red bell pepper, blanched and refreshed	5 oz. a.p.
3/4 c.	3/8" diced, peeled carrots, blanched and refreshed	4 oz. a.p.
3/4 c.	3/8" diced, peeled turnips, blanched and refreshed	4 oz. a.p.
3/4 c.	rinsed and drained cooked or canned pinto beans	1 oz. a.p. dry or 6 fl. oz.

preparation:
1. Mix.

holding: refrigerate in a freshly sanitized, covered container up to 2 days

COMPONENT RECIPE
SMOKY STEAK SAUCE

yield: 1 c.

production		costing only
1 Tbsp.	bacon drippings	n/c
1/4 c	minced yellow onion	1 1/4 oz. a.p.
1 tsp.	minced garlic	1/9 oz. a.p.
1/2 c.	Demi-Glace	1/8 recipe
1 Tbsp.	molasses	1/2 fl. oz.
1 Tbsp.	brown sugar	1/3 oz.
1 Tbsp.	light tomato purée	1/2 fl. oz.
1 tsp.	Dijon mustard	1/6 fl. oz.
2 c.	water	n/c
1 drop	liquid smoke	1/16 oz.
tt	kosher salt	1/16 oz.

preparation:
1. Place the bacon drippings, onion, and garlic in a 2-qt. saucepan and sauté until soft.
2. Add the remaining ingredients and simmer briskly about 15 minutes, until reduced to 1 c.
3. Taste and correct the seasoning to create a tangy, slightly sweet flavor balance.

holding: open-pan cool and refrigerate in a freshly sanitized, covered container up to 5 days

COMPONENT RECIPE
BEER BATTER

yield: 1 1/2 c.

production		costing only
1 c.	flour	5 oz.
2 tsp.	fine salt	1/3 oz.
1 tsp.	baking powder	1/16 oz.
1	egg yolk	1 each or 2/3 oz.
1/2 c.+	flat beer	±4 fl. oz.

preparation:
1. In a small bowl mix together the flour, salt, and baking powder and make a well in the center.
2. Add the egg yolk to the well and begin whisking in the flour and incorporating the beer a little at a time, to make a thick, smooth batter.
3. Cover the bowl and refrigerate at least 1 hour.
4. Correct the batter's consistency, adding more beer if necessary to make a thick yet pourable batter.

holding: prepare 1 hour before service and hold in an ice-water bath; discard after service

---

RECIPE VARIATION
Grilled Filet of Beef with Smoky Steak Sauce, Beer-Batter Onion Rings, Hash Brown Potatoes, and Vegetable Roundup
Replace the bison with beef filet.

Smoke-Roasted Prime Rib of Beef

with Twice-Baked Potato and Smothered Squash

yield: 1 (10-oz.) entrée serving plus accompaniments
(multiply × 4 for classroom turnout; adjust equipment sizes
accordingly)

🕐 Requires 3 days advance preparation.

(review smoking information on this book's companion website)

MASTER RECIPE

production		costing only
1 Tbsp.	melted butter	1/2 oz.
1	Twice-Baked Potato Setup	1/4 recipe
1	10-oz. portion Smoke-Roasted Prime Rib of Beef	1/4 recipe
2 Tbsp.	bacon drippings	n/c
1 c.	seeded, 1/2"-diced zucchini	6 oz. a.p.
1 c.	seeded, 1/2"-diced yellow summer squash	6 oz. a.p.
tt	kosher salt	1/16 oz.
1/4 c.	slivered yellow onion	1 1/4 oz. a.p.
1 c.	fine-chopped tomato concassée	12 oz. a.p.
tt	fresh-ground black pepper	1/16 oz.
pinch	minced fresh thyme leaves	1/40 bunch a.p.
2/3 c.	Braised Garlic Jus	1/4 recipe
1/2 tsp.	arrowroot	1/16 oz.
1 Tbsp.	water	n/c
1 Tbsp.	butter	1/2 oz.
dash	sweet Hungarian paprika	1/16 oz.
1 Tbsp.	fine diagonal-cut chives	1/20 bunch a.p.
2 Tbsp.	sour cream, in a pastry bag fitted with a star tip	1 fl. oz.
1 bundle	chive tips	1/10 bunch a.p.

service turnout:

1. Heat the meat and potato:
   a. Brush two sizzle pans with the melted butter.
   b. Place the Twice-Baked Potato Setup on one sizzle plate and the Smoke-Roasted Prime Rib of Beef on the other.
   c. Heat the potato and prime rib in a 400°F oven until the prime rib reaches medium rare or the customer's specified doneness.
   d. Remove the prime rib and hold warm; continue baking the potato about 15 minutes total, until golden brown.
2. Cook the vegetables:
   a. Heat a 10" sauté pan, heat the bacon drippings very hot and sear the squashes with a little salt, tossing constantly.
   b. Add the onion and toss a few seconds longer.
   c. Add the tomato and cook, tossing often, until the squash is coated in a light tomato sauce.
   d. Correct the salt and add the pepper and thyme.
3. Finish the sauce:
   a. Heat the Braised Garlic Jus in a 6" sauté pan.
   b. Mix the arrowroot and water to make a slurry.
   c. Stir enough arrowroot slurry into the jus to achieve a light nappé consistency.
4. Plate the dish:
   a. Place the potato on the back center of a hot 12" plate with the taller end at 12 o'clock.
   b. Spoon a mound of vegetables on either side of the potato.
   c. Slice the prime rib and fan it across the front of the plate, propped against the potato and vegetables.
   d. Nap the prime rib with the jus.
   e. Dust the potato with paprika, sprinkle it with chives, then pipe a decorative line of sour cream down its length.
   f. Make a bouquet of the chive tips and stick it upright out of the back of the potato.

COMPONENT RECIPE
TWICE-BAKED POTATO SETUPS

yield: 4 side-dish servings

production		costing only
4	8-oz. russet potatoes	2 lb. a.p.
1 Tbsp.	corn oil	1/2 fl. oz.
as needed	kosher salt	1/16 oz.
4 Tbsp.	room-temperature butter	2 oz.
1/2 c.	sour cream	4 fl. oz.
tt	fine-ground white pepper	1/16 oz.
as needed	sweet Hungarian paprika	1/16 oz.

preparation:
1. Mise en place:
   a. Preheat an oven to 450°F.
   b. Place a half-sheet tray lined with aluminum foil on the bottom rack.
2. Bake the potatoes:
   a. Scrub the potatoes under cool running water and blot them dry.
   b. Use the point of a knife to prick several small holes in each.
   c. Rub the potatoes with the oil.
   d. Sprinkle the potatoes with salt.
   e. Place the potatoes directly on the middle rack of the oven. Bake about 35 minutes, until the potatoes are cooked through but not too soft.
   f. Transfer the potatoes to a rack and cool just enough to handle.
3. Prepare the filling while the potatoes are still hot:
   a. Cut off the top of each potato on the diagonal, making one end taller than the other.
   b. Scoop the hot potato flesh from the potato top and bottom shells into a ricer or coarse mesh strainer, leaving each potato shell with about 3/8" of potato flesh. Discard the top skins.
   c. While it is still hot, push the potato flesh through the ricer or strainer.
   d. Immediately whisk in the butter and sour cream, and season with salt and white pepper.
   e. Scoop the warm potato filling into a pastry bag fitted with a large star tip.
   f. Pipe the filling into the potato shells in a decorative pattern.
4. If not using immediately, place the setups in a half-size hotel pan and refrigerate, uncovered, until cold.

holding: cover and refrigerate up to 5 days

RECIPE VARIATION

Roast Prime Rib of Beef with Twice-Baked Potato and Vegetable Roundup

Cut the trimmed raw rib eye into quarters (not slices). Season each with 1 Tbsp. Western Rub for Beef. Do not cure or smoke the meat. For service, pan-sear the exterior of each piece in oil, then finish in a 400°F oven to medium-rare or the customer's specified doneness.

COMPONENT RECIPE
SMOKE-ROASTED PRIME RIB OF BEEF

yield: 4 (7-oz.) servings

🕐 Requires 3 days advance preparation.

production		costing only
1	2 1/4-lb. boneless rib eye beef roast	2 1/4 lb.
9 Tbsp.	Western Rub for Beef	1 recipe
as needed	hickory wood for smoking, prepared according to manufacturer's directions	% of package
3 c.	Western Mopping Sauce	1 recipe

first day preparation:
1. Trim the surface fat of the rib eye into an even 3/8" layer and score the fat in a 1/2" crosshatch.
2. Massage the Western Rub for Beef into the meat, seal it in a heavy plastic bag, and refrigerate 48 hours.

third day preparation:
3. Prepare a smoker with hickory wood and a drip pan, and set the heat to 200°F.
4. Place the rib eye on the rack, baste it with a little Western Mopping Sauce, close the smoker, and smoke the rib eye for about 1 1/2 hours, basting with mopping sauce every 20 minutes and turning the rib eye halfway through the smoking. The rib eye must reach an internal temperature of 125°F.
5. If not serving immediately, transfer the rib eye on its rack to a sheet tray and immediately refrigerate it until cold.
6. Cut the rib eye into even-sized quarters and, if not serving immediately, wrap each in plastic film.

holding: refrigerate up to 5 days

COMPONENT RECIPE
BRAISED GARLIC JUS

yield: 2 c.

production		costing only
1/2 c.	fresh garlic cloves	3 oz. a.p.
2 Tbsp.	butter	1 oz.
tt	kosher salt	1/16 oz.
3 c.	Brown Beef Stock	3/16 recipe

preparation:
1. Remove the root ends of the garlic cloves, smash them lightly, and slip off the skins. If the cloves are large, cut each into 3 lengthwise slices.
2. Heat an 8" sauté pan, heat the butter, and sauté the garlic over low heat about 3 minutes, until golden brown.
3. Add a little salt and the Brown Beef Stock. Cover and simmer gently about 12 minutes, until the garlic is very tender.
4. Press any remaining large pieces of garlic with the back of a spoon to break them up.

holding: open-pan cool and immediately refrigerate in a freshly sanitized, covered container up to 5 days

Barbeque Beef Brisket

with Cowboy Beans and Ranch-Style Slaw

yield: 1 (7-oz.) entrée serving plus accompaniments (multiply × 4 for classroom turnout; adjust equipment sizes accordingly)

🕐 Requires 3 days' advance preparation.

(review barbeque information on this book's companion website)

MASTER RECIPE

production		costing only
1	5" flour tortilla	% of pkg.
as needed	frying compound or corn oil	% used
8 oz.	Barbeque Beef Brisket	1/4 recipe
1/2 c.	Texas Barbeque Sauce	1/4 recipe
1 c.	Cowboy Beans, hot in steam table	1/4 recipe
1 c.	Ranch-Style Slaw	1/4 recipe
2 tsp.	chopped flat-leaf parsley	1/40 bunch a.p.
1 Tbsp.	brunoise-cut red bell pepper	1/2 oz. a.p.

service turnout:

1. Prepare the tortilla cup:
   a. Form the tortilla into a cup shape in a potato nest form or in a small mesh strainer held in place with a ladle.
   b. Deep-fry the tortilla cup at 400°F for a few seconds until light golden.
   c. Unmold and place upside down onto paper towels to drain.
   d. Immediately, while the tortilla is still warm and pliable, press on it with the ladle to flatten the bottom.
2. Place the Barbeque Beef Brisket and Texas Barbeque Sauce in an 8" sauté pan, cover the pan, and heat gently, turning once, until heated through.
3. Plate the dish:
   a. Spoon the Cowboy Beans into the tortilla cup and place the cup on the back left of a warm 12" plate.
   b. Remove the brisket from the sauté pan to a cutting board.
   c. Increase the heat and reduce the barbeque sauce by 1/3.
   d. Slice the brisket thin, across the grain, on the diagonal.
   e. Pile the brisket on the front of the plate and pour the barbeque sauce over the top.
   f. Mound the Ranch-Style Slaw on the back right of the plate and sprinkle it with the parsley and red bell pepper.

COMPONENT RECIPE

BARBEQUE BEEF BRISKET

yield: approx. 1 3/4 lb.

🕐 Requires 3 days' advance preparation.

(review barbeque information on this book's companion website)

production		costing only
1	second-cut beef brisket with a 1/2" layer of surface fat	2 1/2 lb. a.p.
3/4 c.	Texas Rub	1 recipe
as needed	mesquite wood, prepared according to manufacturer's directions	% of pkg.
3 c.	Texas Mop	1 recipe

first day preparation:

1. Cure the brisket:
   a. Trim excessive fat from the top of the brisket, leaving an even layer of fat measuring at least 1/2" thick.
   b. Score the fat in a 1/2" crosshatch pattern.
   c. Massage the Texas Rub into the beef on all sides.
   d. Place the beef into a sealed plastic bag and refrigerate 48 hours.

third day preparation:

2. Prepare the smoker:
   a. Place 1/3 of the hickory wood on the heat source.
   b. Place a drip pan filled with at least 2" of water on the lower rack.
   c. Set the smoker to 190°F.
   d. Close the lid of the smoker and wait until a strong head of smoke develops.
3. Place the brisket on the rack above the drip pan. Close the lid and allow the brisket to smoke 30 minutes.
4. Turn the brisket over and smoke 30 minutes longer. Begin basting at 20-minute intervals with the Texas Mop.
5. After 2 hours, add half of the remaining wood to the heat source and turn the brisket over again. Continue to baste with the mopping sauce at 20-minute intervals.
6. After 2 more hours, add the remaining wood, and turn the brisket over, smoking and basting for a total of 6 hours or until tender.
7. If preparing ahead of time, cool the brisket to room temperature and cut it into 4 quarters.

holding: place in individual plastic bags and refrigerate up to 5 days; hot brisket may be held at 150°F in a warming box up to 4 hours.

COMPONENT RECIPE
COWBOY BEANS

yield: 1 qt.

🕐 Requires 24 hours' advance preparation.

production		costing only
1 1/2 c.	pinto beans, soaked overnight	8 oz. a.p.
16 oz.	water	n/c
1 1/2 oz.	1/4"-diced rindless smoked slab bacon	1 3/4 oz. a.p.
6 fl. oz.	beer	6 fl. oz.
3 Tbsp.	seeded, minced jalapeño chile	1 1/2 oz. a.p.
1 tsp.	toasted, ground cumin	1/16 oz.
1 tsp.	minced garlic	1/6 oz.
1 tsp.	crushed dried Mexican oregano	1/16 oz.
1 tsp.	pure New Mexico red chile powder	1/16 oz.
1 tsp.	dry mustard	1/16 oz.
tt	kosher salt	1/16 oz.

preparation:
1. Drain the beans and rinse well, then drain again.
2. Place the beans in a 2 1/2-qt. saucepot and add the water. Bring to the simmer and skim off the foam.
3. Fry the bacon gently in a small sauté pan until almost crisp.
4. Add the bacon and its rendered drippings to the beans along with the beer, chiles, cumin, garlic, oregano, red chile powder, and mustard. Bring to the simmer and cook, stirring occasionally, 1 hour, until the beans are tender and the sauce lightly thickened.
5. Add salt and simmer 5 minutes longer.

holding: open-pan cool and refrigerate in a freshly sanitized, covered container up to 5 days; freeze up to 3 months

COMPONENT RECIPE
RANCH-STYLE SLAW

yield: 6 c.

production		costing only
1 small head	Savoy or other tender cabbage	1 1/2 lb. a.p.
1 tsp.	kosher salt	1/6 oz.
1/2 c.	fine-julienne red bell pepper	4 oz. a.p.
1/2 c.	fine-julienne yellow bell pepper	4 oz. a.p.
1/2 c.	fine-slivered red onion	2 1/2 oz. a.p.
1 c.	Buttermilk Ranch Dressing, p. 477	1 recipe

preparation:
1. Remove and discard the dark outer leaves of the cabbage.
2. Cut the cabbage in quarters, remove the cores, and slice thin to make very fine shreds.
3. Place the cabbage in a bowl and toss with the salt.
4. Transfer the cabbage into a colander. Select a plate of the correct size to weight down the cabbage. Place the plate on top of the cabbage and place a heavy weight on top of the plate. Allow the cabbage to drain 20 minutes at room temperature.
5. Wearing foodservice gloves, squeeze the excess moisture out of the cabbage.
6. Place the cabbage in a nonreactive bowl and mix it with the bell peppers, onion, and Buttermilk Ranch Dressing.

holding: best served the same day; refrigerate in a freshly sanitized, covered container up to 2 days

---

RECIPE VARIATION

Oven-Barbequed Beef Brisket with Cowboy Beans and Ranch-Style Slaw
Omit the mesquite wood. Reduce the amount of Texas Mop by half. Brown the rubbed brisket in corn oil, then braise it with the mopping sauce in a 325°F oven for about 2 hours until tender. Reduce the braising liquid into a sauce.

Beer-Braised Beef Short Ribs

with Chuck Wagon Macaroni and Wilted Spinach

yield: 1 (12-oz.) bone-in entrée serving plus accompaniments (multiply × 4 for classroom turnout; adjust equipment sizes accordingly)

MASTER RECIPE

production		costing only
1 section	Beer-Braised Beef Short Ribs (with sauce)	1/4 recipe
1/4 c.	water	n/c
1 1/2 c.	Chuck Wagon Macaroni	1/4 recipe
1/4 c.	water	n/c
1 Tbsp.	Dijon mustard	1/2 fl. oz.
1/2 Tbsp.	brown sugar	1/4 oz.
2 Tbsp.	bacon drippings	n/c
1/4 c.	slivered red onion	1 1/4 oz. a.p.
6 oz.	cleaned baby spinach	6 oz.
tt	kosher salt	1/16 oz.
dash	cider vinegar	1/16 fl. oz.
1/4 c.	grated Monterey Jack cheese	1 oz.
2 tsp.	chopped flat-leaf parsley	1/40 bunch a.p.

service turnout:
1. Place the Beer-Braised Short Ribs, their sauce, and 1/4 c. water in a 10" sauté pan, cover, and heat over medium heat until heated through.
2. Place the Chuck Wagon Macaroni in an 8" nonstick sauté pan with 1/4 c. water, cover, and heat over medium heat.
3. Remove the short ribs to a sizzle pan, brush the presentation side with mustard, sprinkle with brown sugar, and glaze briefly under a broiler. Hold hot.
4. Cook the spinach:
   a. Heat a 10" nonstick sauté pan, heat the bacon drippings, and sauté the onion a few seconds.
   b. Toss in the spinach and a little salt and turn constantly until wilted.
   c. Season with a little vinegar and correct the salt.
5. Plate the dish:
   a. Stir the cheese and parsley into the macaroni and immediately mound it on the back right of a hot 12" plate.
   b. Mound the spinach at back left.
   c. Place the short ribs diagonally across the plate, leaning against the macaroni.
   d. Spoon the sauce over the ribs.

COMPONENT RECIPE

BEER-BRAISED BEEF SHORT RIBS

yield: 4 (12-oz.) bone-in entrée servings plus 3 c. sauce

production		costing only
4	12-oz. 2-bone beef short rib sections	3 lb.
2 Tbsp.	corn oil	1 fl. oz.
tt	kosher salt	1/16 oz.
2 c.	slivered yellow onion	10 oz. a.p.
1/4 c.	sliced garlic cloves	1 1/3 oz. a.p.
4 Tbsp.	flour	1 1/4 oz.
2 c.	hot Brown Beef Stock	1/8 recipe
1 1/2 c	dark beer	12 fl. oz.
1 Tbsp.	brown sugar	1/3 oz.
1 Tbsp.	Dijon mustard	1/2 fl. oz.
2 sprigs	fresh sage	1/5 bunch a.p.

preparation:
1. Trim the short ribs of excess fat. Wipe with a paper towel.
2. Heat a 12" sauté pan, heat the oil, and brown the short ribs on both sides. Season with salt and remove.
3. Make the sauce:
   a. Add the onion to the fat remaining in the pan and cook, stirring, over low heat until the onion softens.
   b. Add the garlic and continue to cook until the onion is a rich brown.
   c. Add the flour and stir to make a light brown roux. Remove from heat. (If the ribs are very lean and did not produce enough fat, add bacon drippings or oil.)
   d. Stir in the Brown Beef Stock to make a smooth sauce, then add the remaining ingredients.
   e. Season the sauce with a little salt, return the ribs to the pan, cover partially, and braise over low heat about 40 minutes, until the meat is tender.
4. Remove the ribs from the sauce. Remove and discard the sage.
5. Reduce the braising liquid to 3 c. full-bodied, nappé consistency sauce.
6. Return the ribs to the pan and baste with the sauce.

holding: open-pan cool and immediately refrigerate the ribs and their sauce in a freshly sanitized, covered container up to 5 days

COMPONENT RECIPE
CHUCK WAGON MACARONI

yield: 1 1/2 qt.

production		costing only
2 1/2 oz.	3/8"-diced rindless smoked slab bacon	3 oz. a.p.
2 c.	elbow macaroni	7 oz.
1 Tbsp.	butter	1/2 oz.
1 c.	fine-chopped yellow onion	5 oz. a.p.
2 tsp.	minced garlic	1/6 oz. a.p.
1/4 c.	seeded, minced jalapeño chile	1 1/2 oz. a.p.
1 qt.	canned, peeled tomatoes in light juice, chopped coarse	1 qt.
1 qt.	Poultry Stock	1/4 recipe
tt	kosher salt	1/16 oz.

preparation:
1. Heat a heavy 4-qt. saucepan, add the bacon, and fry over low heat until the bacon is almost crisp and the fat renders out. Remove and reserve the bacon.
2. Add the macaroni to the pan and sauté, stirring constantly, until lightly browned. Remove and reserve the macaroni.
3. Add the butter, onion, garlic, and jalapeño to the pan and cook, stirring, over medium heat until the onion softens.
4. Add the tomatoes, their juice, and the Poultry Stock, and bring to the boil. Season with a little salt.
5. Stir in the macaroni and cook, stirring often, about 20 minutes, until the macaroni is al dente and the tomato juices have thickened into a light sauce. (Add water if the sauce becomes too thick, and scrape the bottom of the pan often to prevent sticking.)
6. Taste and correct the seasoning, then stir in the bacon.

holding: open-pan cool and immediately refrigerate in a freshly sanitized, covered container up to 5 days

ENTREES

RECIPE VARIATIONS

Beer-Braised Beef Short Ribs with Yukon Gold Potatoes and Wilted Spinach
Omit the macaroni. Brown 12 small, peeled Yukon gold potatoes along with the ribs and braise them in the sauce.

"Goulash"
Omit the Short Ribs recipe and spinach. Prepare only the macaroni, adding 1 lb. lean ground beef to the bacon, onion, garlic, and jalapeño and browning it lightly. Add cubed Monterey Jack cheese and chopped parsley just before serving. Accompany with a tossed salad dressed with Sweet Cider Vinaigrette.

Trail-Drive Chili

over Texmati Rice with Cowboy Beans, Longhorn Cheddar, and Sweet Corn Pico de Gallo

yield: 1 (12-fl.-oz.) entrée serving plus accompaniments (Multiply by 4 for classroom turnout; adjust equipment sizes accordingly.)

MASTER RECIPE

production		costing only
1/2	white or yellow corn tortilla, cut into 3 wedges	% of pkg.
as needed	frying compound or oil for frying	% used
tt	fine salt	1/16 oz.
1 1/2 c.	Trail Drive Chili	1/4 recipe
1/4 c.	water	n/c
1 1/2 c.	cooked Texmati Rice, hot in steam table	1/4 recipe
1/2 c.	Cowboy Beans, p. 493	1/8 recipe
1/2 c.	Pico de Gallo	1/2 recipe
1/4 c.	cooked corn kernels, fresh or frozen	1/4 ear a.p. or 1 1/2 oz.
1/4 c.	grated Longhorn cheddar cheese	1 oz.
1/4 c.	chopped red onion	1 1/4 oz. a.p.
1 Tbsp.	chopped cilantro	1/20 bunch a.p.

service turnout:

1. Deep-fry the tortilla wedges in 400°F oil until light golden. Shake off excess oil and transfer to a hotel pan lined with paper towels. Sprinkle with salt.
2. Heat the Trail Drive Chili with the water in a covered 10" sauté pan or in a microwave oven.
3. Plate the dish:
   a. Spoon the Texmati Rice into a hot 12" pasta bowl and make a well in the center.
   b. Spoon the chili into the well.
   c. Create a small depression in the rice at 2 o'clock and spoon the Cowboy Beans into it.
   d. Toss the Pico de Gallo with the corn kernels and mound the mixture on the rice at 3 o'clock.
   e. Sprinkle the chili with the cheese, onion, and cilantro.
   f. Stick the tortilla chips upright into the beans.

COMPONENT RECIPE

TRAIL DRIVE CHILI

yield: approximately 1 1/2 qt.

production		costing only
2 1/4 lb.	beef chuck	2 1/4 lb.
4 Tbsp.	pork lard or bacon drippings	2 oz. or nc
1 1/2 c.	fine-chopped white onion	7 1/2 oz. a.p.
1 Tbsp.	minced garlic	1/3 oz. a.p.
2	seeded, minced jalapeño chiles	1 1/2 oz. a.p.
1 tsp.	toasted, ground cumin	1/16 oz.
1/4 tsp.	ground cinnamon	1/16 oz.
1 tsp.	fresh-ground black pepper	1/16 oz.
2 tsp.	dried oregano	1/16 oz.
1/4 c.	Texas chili powder (such as Gebhardt's brand)	4/5 oz.
3 Tbsp.	flour	1 oz.
2 c.	hot Brown Beef Stock	1/8 recipe
3/4 c.	beer	6 fl. oz.
tt	kosher salt	1/16 oz.
tt	sugar	1/16 oz.

preparation:

1. Trim all fat and thick silverskin from the beef and cut it into 1/2" dice.
2. Heat a 12" sauté pan, heat 2 Tbsp. lard, and brown half of the beef. Remove it to a heavy 6-qt. nonreactive saucepot. Add 1 Tbsp. additional lard, brown the remaining beef, and add it to the pot.
3. Prepare the sauce:
   a. In the same sauté pan, heat the remaining 1 Tbsp. lard and sauté the onion and garlic until light golden.
   b. Add the jalapeños, cumin, cinnamon, pepper, oregano, and chili powder and sauté a few seconds longer, until slightly darkened and very fragrant.
   c. Add the flour and stir to make a blond roux. Remove from heat.
   d. Whisk in the Brown Beef Stock in a thin stream to make a smooth, thick sauce.
   e. Whisk in the beer and bring the sauce to the simmer.
4. Pour the sauce over the beef in the saucepot. Deglaze the sauté pan with a little water and pour the deglazings into the saucepot. Add a little salt.
5. Simmer the chili 1 hour, adding a very small amount of water if the sauce becomes too thick. Stir occasionally, watching carefully to prevent scorching.
6. When the beef is tender, balance the flavor with more salt and a little sugar if needed.

holding: open-pan cool and refrigerate in a freshly sanitized, covered container up to 7 days; may be frozen

RECIPE VARIATIONS

Borracha **Chili**
In step 2, after the beef is browned, return all to the sauté pan and flambé with 2 oz. gold tequila.

Deep-Dark Secret Chili
Add 1 oz. or less, to taste, grated bitter chocolate at the end of step 5.

Venison Chili
Replace the beef with 1 lb. venison shoulder or venison bottom round and 1 lb. ground pork. Stir in the raw ground pork toward the end of step 5.

Apple Pandowdy
with Honey Sour Cream Sauce

yield: 1 dessert serving
(multiply × 4 for classroom turnout)

MASTER RECIPE

production		costing only
1	Apple Pandowdy	1/4 recipe
1	8" doily or cocktail napkin	1 each
3 fl. oz.	Honey Sour Cream Sauce	1/4 recipe
1 bouquet	fresh mint	1/5 bunch a.p.

service turnout:
1. Heat the Apple Pandowdy in a 400°F oven about 8 minutes, until very warm.
2. Plate the dish:
   a. Place an 8" doily on a 10" oval plate and set the Apple Pandowdy on the left side.
   b. Ladle the Honey Sour Cream Sauce into a 4-oz. pitcher and set the pitcher on the right side.
   c. Place the mint bouquet between the pandowdy and the pitcher.

RECIPE VARIATIONS
Apple-Whiskey-Raisin Pandowdy with Honey Sour Cream Sauce
Heat together 1/2 c. black raisins and 1/4 c. Bourbon whiskey. Steep until cool. Mix with the apples.

Pawpaw Pandowdy with Honey Sour Cream Sauce
Replace the apples with pawpaws.

COMPONENT RECIPE
APPLE PANDOWDY

yield: 4 (6") gratins

production		costing only
2 oz.	cold butter, cut into small bits	2 oz.
1/2 c.	brown sugar	2 3/4 oz.
1 tsp.	ground cinnamon	1/16 oz.
1/2 tsp.	ground nutmeg	1/16 oz.
1 Tbsp.	cornstarch	1/2 oz.
1 Tbsp.	flour	1/3 oz.
3	Granny Smith apples, peeled and cored	20 oz. a.p.
1/4 c.	apple cider	2 fl. oz.
1/4 recipe	Buttermilk Biscuit, sweet Shortcake variation, dough only	1/4 recipe
4 Tbsp.	granulated brown sugar	1/4 oz.

preparation:
1. Mise en place:
   a. Preheat an oven to 400°F.
   b. Using about 1 Tbsp. of the butter, heavily butter 4 deep, (6") round gratin dishes.
2. Mix 1/2 c. brown sugar with the cinnamon, nutmeg, cornstarch, and flour in a medium bowl.
3. Cut the apples into 1/2" dice and toss them with the brown sugar mixture. Toss in the cider and the remaining butter, distributing the pieces evenly.
4. Divide the apples among the gratin dishes, packing them in firmly.
5. Crumble the Buttermilk Biscuit dough over the top and press it down gently.
6. Place the gratins on a half-sheet tray with pan liner and bake in the center of the oven about 20 minutes, until the apples are almost tender and the biscuit dough is set but not brown.
7. Remove the gratins from the oven and press on the top of the dough to break it up slightly and push it down into the apples. Sprinkle 1 Tbsp. granulated brown sugar on each gratin and return the tray to the oven.
8. Bake 10 to 15 minutes longer, until the pastry is crisp and golden.

holding: best made fresh for each service; hold at room temperature covered with a kitchen towel up to 6 hours; refrigerate, loosely covered with plastic wrap, up to 24 hours with loss of quality

COMPONENT RECIPE
HONEY SOUR CREAM SAUCE

yield: approx. 1 1/3 c.

production		costing only
2/3 c.	sour cream	5 2/3 fl. oz.
4 Tbsp.	honey	2 fl. oz.
±1/2 c.	half-and-half	±4 fl. oz.

preparation:
1. Whisk together the sour cream and honey, then whisk in enough half-and-half to make a smooth sauce that is thick yet pourable.

holding: refrigerate in a freshly sanitized, covered container up to 3 days

DESSERTS

Rum-Raisin Texmati Rice Pudding

with Apricot Sauce

yield: 1 dessert serving
(multiply × 4 for classroom turnout)

MASTER RECIPE

production		costing only
1	Rum-Raisin Texmati Rice Pudding	1/4 recipe
1/2 c.	Apricot Sauce	1/4 recipe
1/4 c.	Rummed Raisins	1/6 recipe
2 Tbsp.	Sweetened Whipped Cream, in pastry bag with medium star tip	1/8 recipe
1 small sprig	fresh mint	1/20 bunch a.p.

service turnout:

1. Run a thin-bladed knife around the inside of the Rum-Raisin Texmati Rice Pudding ramekin to release it.
2. Plate the dish:
   a. Invert the ramekin in the center of a cool 10" plate and unmold the pudding. Peel off the pan liner circle.
   b. Pour the Apricot Sauce over the pudding, allowing it to run onto the plate.
   c. Scatter the Rummed Raisins around the plate well.
   d. Pipe a rosette of Sweetened Whipped Cream on top of the pudding.
   e. Stick the mint sprig upright out of the rosette.

COMPONENT RECIPE

RUM-RAISIN TEXMATI RICE PUDDING

yield: 4 (10-fl.-oz.) ramekins (5 c. custard)

production		costing only
as needed	butter	1 Tbsp.
1 1/2 c.	cooked Texmati Rice, made with butter and only a pinch of salt, at room temperature	1/3 recipe
1/2 c.	Rummed Raisins	1/3 recipe
1	egg	1 each or 2 oz.
2	egg yolks	2 each or 1 1/3 oz.
3/4 c.	half-and-half	6 fl. oz.
3/4 c.	heavy cream	6 fl. oz.
1/2 tsp.	pure vanilla extract	1/12 fl. oz.

preparation:

1. Mise en place:
   a. Preheat an oven to 325°F.
   b. Cut out 4 pan liner circles of the correct size to fit the bottoms of 4 (10-fl.-oz.) ramekins.
   c. Butter one side of each of the circles.
   d. Cut out 4 foil circles slightly larger than the ramekin tops.
   e. Heavily butter 4 (10-fl.-oz.) ramekins and place the pan liner circles in the bottoms, butter side up.
   f. Place the ramekins in a half-size hotel pan lined with a clean, damp kitchen towel.
2. Mix together the Texmati Rice and the Rummed Raisins. Divide the mixture evenly among the ramekins.
3. Beat together the egg and egg yolks, then stir in the half-and-half, cream, and vanilla.
4. Pour the custard into the ramekins. Seal the tops with foil.
5. Fill the hotel pan with hot tap water 3/4 up the sides of the ramekins.
6. Bake the puddings in the center of the oven 30 to 40 minutes, until the custard is just set.
7. Remove the ramekins to a rack and cool to room temperature.
8. Refrigerate at least 1 hour, until cold.

holding: refrigerate up to 5 days

COMPONENT RECIPE
APRICOT SAUCE

yield: approx. 2 c.

production		costing only
2 c.	apricot preserves	16 fl. oz.
1 c.	water	n/c
1/4 c.	dark rum	2 fl. oz.
tt	fresh lemon juice	1/8 [90 ct.] lemon

preparation:
1. In a 1 1/2-qt. nonreactive saucepan, melt together the apricot preserves and water.
2. Strain the preserves into another pan, pressing firmly on the solids. Discard the solids.
3. Reduce the sauce over medium heat to a light nappé consistency.
4. Cool to room temperature.
5. Stir in the rum and balance the flavor with lemon juice.

holding: refrigerate in a freshly sanitized, covered container up to 2 weeks

COMPONENT RECIPE
RUMMED RAISINS

yield: 1 1/2 c.

production		costing only
1 1/4 c.	black raisins	8 oz.
1/2 c.	dark rum	4 fl. oz.

preparation:
1. Mix the raisins and rum in a 1-qt. saucepan. Place over low heat and heat just to steaming. ⚠ Do not overheat and allow the rum to flame. Keep a lid at hand to extinguish flames if the rum overheats.
2. Remove the pan from the heat and allow the raisins to steep about 30 minutes, until they absorb the rum.

holding: store in a freshly sanitized, covered container at cool room temperature up to 1 week

---

RECIPE VARIATION

Cherry Vanilla Texmati Rice Pudding with Cherry Sauce
Replace the raisins with dried cherries and the rum with kirsch. Increase the vanilla extract to 1 tsp. Replace the apricot preserves with cherry jelly (no need to strain).

S'mores Pie

yield: 1 dessert serving
(multiply × 4 for classroom turnout)

MASTER RECIPE

production		costing only
2 Tbsp.	Chocolate Sauce, in squeeze bottle	1/8 recipe
1 slice	S'Mores Pie	1/8 recipe
1	miniature marshmallow	1/4 oz.
2	1" rounds punched out of a graham cracker	1/4 recipe

service turnout:
1. Plate the dish:
   a. Squeeze a dot of Chocolate Sauce slightly back of center on a cool 8" plate.
   b. Place the S'Mores Pie slice on it with the point facing 8 o'clock.
   c. Place the marshmallow on a sizzle plate and brown it with a foodservice torch. Alternatively, impale the marshmallow with a metal skewer and toast it over a gas grill.
   d. Squeeze a teaspoon of Chocolate Sauce on each of the graham cracker rounds and sandwich the marshmallow between them to make a "mini s'more."
   e. Place the "mini s'more" upright on the topping of the Pie.
   f. Squeeze three Chocolate Sauce dots of graduating size on the plate.

COMPONENT RECIPE

S'MORES PIE ASSEMBLY

yield: 1 (9") pie

production		costing only
3 c.	freshly-made Chocolate Chiffon Filling	1 recipe
1	(9") baked and cooled Graham Cracker Pie Shell	1 recipe
1 1/2 c.	Marshmallow Topping	1 recipe

preparation:
1. Pour the Chocolate Chiffon Filling into the Graham Cracker Pie Shell and smooth it flat.
2. Refrigerate, uncovered, about 30 minutes until set.
3. Place the marshmallow topping in a pastry bag fitted with a large star tip.
4. Pipe stars of marshmallow topping all over the surface of the pie, completely covering the filling.

holding: best served the same day; refrigerate the pie under a cake dome up to 2 days

DESSERTS

COMPONENT RECIPE
CHOCOLATE CHIFFON FILLING

yield: 3 c. filling, for 1 (9") pie

production		costing only
1 Tbsp. + 2 tsp.	powdered gelatin	1/2 oz.
1/4 c.	coffee liqueur	2 fl. oz.
2 oz.	unsweetened chocolate	2 oz.
2 oz.	bittersweet chocolate	2 oz.
2 Tbsp.	brandy	1 fl. oz.
4	egg yolks	4 each or 2 2/3 oz.
1/2 c.	sugar	4 oz.
1/2 c.	boiling water	n/c
1 tsp.	pure vanilla extract	1/6 fl. oz.
4	room-temperature egg whites	n/c or 4 oz.
1/2 c.	sugar	4 oz.

preparation:
1. Mise en place:
   a. Prepare a hot-water bath with barely simmering water and make sure the bowl is clean and dry.
   b. Prepare an ice-water bath.
   c. Have ready an electric mixer fitted with the whip attachment. Make sure the bowl and whip are clean, grease-free, and dry.
   d. Make sure the Graham Cracker Pie Shell is cool and ready at hand.
2. Mix the gelatin with the coffee liqueur and allow it to bloom 10 minutes.
3. If necessary, chop the chocolates into small, even-sized pieces.
4. Melt together the chocolates and brandy over the hot-water bath, stirring constantly with a rubber spatula. Cool to room temperature.
5. Prepare the custard:
   a. Place the egg yolks and 1/2 c. sugar in a large mixing bowl and beat with a whisk until fluffy and light yellow.
   b. Beat in the boiling water.
   c. Place the bowl over the hot-water bath and increase the heat to medium. Whisk the mixture constantly until the yolks thicken enough to form a ribbon.
   d. Whisk in the gelatin and stir until smooth.
   e. Remove from the heat and whisk in the chocolates and vanilla.
6. Beat the egg whites in the mixer to foamy consistency, then beat in the remaining sugar. Continue beating the whites to firm peaks.
7. Place the chocolate custard in the ice-water bath and stir constantly until it thickens enough to form a ribbon.
8. Immediately fold the whites into the chocolate mixture. (If lumps begin to form, whisk gently until they break up.)
9. ⚠ Use immediately to fill a pie shell or for another application. If held, the mixture will stiffen and set.

holding: use immediately

COMPONENT RECIPE
MARSHMALLOW TOPPING

yield: approx. 1 1/2 c.

production		costing only
1 Tbsp.	powdered gelatin	1/4 oz.
1/4 c.	light rum	2 fl. oz.
1/4 c.	boiling water	n/c
2	room-temperature egg whites	2 each or 2 oz.
1/2 c.	sugar	4 oz.
1/2 tsp.	pure vanilla extract	1/12 fl. oz.

preparation:
1. Mix the gelatin and rum and allow to bloom 10 minutes.
2. Stir the boiling water into the gelatin to liquefy it, then cool to room temperature.
3. Mix the topping:
   a. Place the egg whites in a mixer with a grease-free, dry bowl and whip attachment.
   b. Beat the whites to just under soft peaks, then quickly beat in the gelatin, then beat in the sugar in a thin stream.
   c. Beat in the vanilla.
   d. Continue to beat about 3 minutes, until the mixture becomes thick and fluffy.

holding: use as soon as possible

RECIPE VARIATION
Chocolate Chiffon Pie
Replace the Graham Cracker Pie Shell with a blind baked 9" American Flaky Pastry pie shell. Replace the Marshmallow Topping with 2 c. Sweetened Whipped Cream. Replace the mini s'more garnish with chocolate curls.

☐ TABLE 10.2 WESTERN AND CENTRAL RANCHLANDS INGREDIENTS

ITEM	MARKET FORMS	USES	SEASONALITY	OTHER	STORAGE
PINTO BEANS	See p. 352, dried beans.				
CORNMEAL	See p. 80.				
TEXMATI RICE	A proprietary brand of Asian basmati rice grown in Texas, Texmati rice is an upland, long-grain variety that requires less water than traditional paddy rice. It is sold by the pound from specialty purveyors and in supermarkets.	Texmati rice can be used in place of any other long grain rice. When prepared correctly it cooks up fluffy with al dente texture.	N/A	Prepare by washing, soaking 20 minutes in hot water, then cooking in a 1:1 ratio of water.	Store at cool room temperature; freeze for extended storage.
LIQUID SMOKE	This natural seasoning is sold in small consumer bottles and in gallon jugs for foodservice. Some producers offer various flavors, such as hickory, mesquite, pecan, and fruitwoods.	Liquid smoke is added in small quantity to marinades, mopping sauces, barbeque sauces, and to any dish in which a smoky flavor is appropriate.	N/A	During the traditional smoking process moisture-laden smoke vapor condenses, forming smoke infused droplets on the food and other surfaces. In the mid-20th century producers began distilling this liquid and marketing it as a seasoning.	Store at room temperature.
CHILI POWDER	Sold by the ounce or pound, proprietary blends usually contain cumin, black pepper, oregano, and granulated onion and garlic powder as well as unidentified ground dried red chile.	Used primarily to flavor and color chili, chili powder also may be used in rubs and marinades.	N/A	Small companies throughout the American Southwest and especially in Texas offer high-quality blends, with Gephardt's among the most popular.	Dry store 3 to 6 months; freeze for extended storage.
JERKY	Commercial jerky is made from beef, bison, or venison. Seasonings vary. All contain salt in some form; many modern producers use soy sauce. Jerky is sold in strips and shreds.	Jerky strips are typically served as a snack food. Chopped or shredded jerky is used as a salad topping. Jerky shreds may be added to stocks, soups, sauces, and fillings.	N/A	Jerky strips are more costly, as they require special packaging and handling to hold their shape.	Store tightly sealed at cool room temperature.
BREED-SPECIFIC BEEF	Specialty ranches offer premium beef from specific cattle breeds, typically Angus, Charolais, and "heirloom" Longhorn crossbreeds. Specify grass-fed or grain finished as well as type and length of aging.	Serve in high-end operations with customers willing to pay a high price for quality.	N/A	Many types are raised organically and processed at small, local slaughterhouses.	Refrigerate vacuum-sealed cuts up to 3 weeks. Freeze if necessary.
BISON	Fresh and frozen grass-fed bison is available by the pound from specialty purveyors and from a growing number of mainstream meat suppliers. Much is organically raised. Cuts are the same as beef cuts, with the exception of hump meat, a tough cut often marketed for its novelty value.	Offer bison as a beef alternative. Known for leanness, bison is popular with health-conscious customers.	N/A	Cook tender cuts by dry methods to rare or medium-rare doneness; enhance with an oil or butter baste, or accompany with a butter sauce. Braise tough cuts in a rich sauce.	Refrigerate vacuum-sealed cuts up to 3 weeks. Thaw frozen bison slowly in the refrigerator.

☐ **TABLE 10.2 WESTERN AND CENTRAL RANCHLANDS INGREDIENTS** *(continued)*

ITEM	MARKET FORMS	USES	SEASONALITY	OTHER	STORAGE
CHOKECHERRY JELLY AND SYRUP	Made from the prairie chokecherry, jellies and syrups are sold in small consumer jars and bottles. These sweet preserved products are a specialty of Native American reservations, where their preparation has become an important cottage industry.	Used in desserts, on breakfast dishes, and as a sweet glaze, chokecherry products lend an Old West feeling to menus.	N/A		Store at room temperature; refrigerate ofter opening.

■□■ chapter eleven

The Rocky Mountains and Great Basin

Montana, Wyoming, Colorado, Idaho, Utah, Nevada

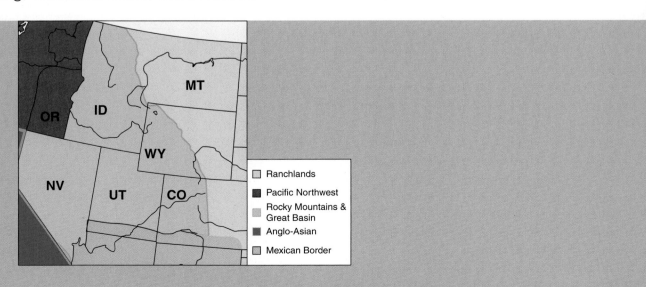

Ranchlands

Pacific Northwest

Rocky Mountains & Great Basin

Anglo-Asian

Mexican Border

DURING PIONEER DAYS the Rocky Mountains were a crossroads of many cultures as people from far-flung places converged on the American West. On the wagon trails pioneer families prepared simple meals using game meat and the most basic pioneer provisions. However, at trading forts and in hub towns and cities, they experienced multiethnic foodways, dining with travelers from around the world. Acquiring liberal culinary outlooks in the Rockies, pioneers went on to shape the adventurous palate of the American West.

Although most of the Rocky Mountain region's early pioneers were merely passing through, one group found their promised land where others saw only wilderness. Mormons escaping religious persecution back east settled the arid Great Basin and, through hard work and perseverance, made the desert bloom. Their cuisine reflects the practicality of their lifestyle.

Today the Rocky Mountains are a playground for Americans who love nature and outdoor sports. In the Great Basin, farming gave way to tourism as entrepreneurs built casino cities and world-class desert resorts. Both areas developed a 20th-century regional cuisine based on pioneer cooking enriched by locally produced ingredients and modern techniques.

AFTER STUDYING THIS CHAPTER YOU SHOULD BE ABLE TO:

- list the ways in which the Rocky Mountain and Great Basin region's climate and topography (Factor 1) affected its culture and cuisine
- explain the indirect effect of Native American cooking (Factor 2) in the Rocky Mountain and Great Basin region
- explain why the Rocky Mountains became a culinary crossroads during the age of the great wagon trails, and how this intermingling of foodways changed the culinary sensibilities of many American pioneers (Factor 3)
- discuss the importance of freshwater fish and wild game in Rocky Mountain and Great Basin cuisine
- describe the impact of tourism (Factor 5) on Rocky Mountain and Great Basin cuisine
- list and describe the ingredients, cooking methods, and flavor profiles of Rocky Mountain and Great Basin cuisine
- prepare authentic Rocky Mountain and Great Basin dishes

APPETIZERS

Pioneer Vegetable Soup with Salt-Rising Bread

Russet Potato Skins with Montana Whitefish Caviar and Dilled Sour Cream

Blue Cheese Potato Chip Mountain for Two

ENTRÉES

Sautéed Rainbow Trout in Pine Nut Butter Sauce with Black Quinoa, French-Cut Green Beans,
and Herb-Grilled Tomato

Poached Montana Whitefish with Crawfish Tails in Buttermilk Velouté with Steamed Mountain Rose Potatoes
and Fresh Peas

Basque Chicken and Sausage in Spicy Tomato Sauce over Pan-Steamed Rice with Three-Pepper Medley

Shepherd's Pie with Pine Nut Romesco Sauce and Julienne Vegetables

Medallions of Venison in Chokecherry Demi-Glace with Garlic Mashed Potatoes, Root Vegetables,
and Wild Mushroom Ragout

DESSERTS

Huckleberry Pie with Whipped Cream

Basque Tostada with Brandied Peach

Sheep's Milk Cheesecake with Chokecherry Sauce

WEBSITE EXTRAS

Breakfasts   Sandwiches   Hors d'Oeuvres   Thanksgiving Menu

THE ROCKY MOUNTAINS

The Rockies are young mountains, formed only around five million years ago. During their birth, geological upheavals beneath western North America shoved masses of rock upward, breaking the earth's crust and thrusting them into the sky. The resulting tectonic shifting formed a network of mountain systems extending from the Arctic Circle in west-central Canada south into Mexico (Figure 11.1). As California-bound pioneers discovered, the Rocky Mountain foothills mark the end of the shortgrass prairie. The mountains beyond extend west for nearly a thousand miles, reaching an elevation of more than 14,000 feet above sea level. Within these vast mountain systems lie countless valleys, some small and narrow and others wide and large.

Mountain Climates and Varied Vegetation

The Rocky Mountains include areas of widely differing altitude, which directly affects climate. Areas of lower altitude are generally warmer, and higher-altitude areas are colder. However, other conditions also affect climate. The Rocky Mountains' roughly north-south orientation exposes their western slopes to warm, moist, Pacific Ocean weather patterns, while the eastern slopes lie within the mountains' rain shadow (p. 304) and thus have a drier, more extreme continental climate. In addition, the Rockies comprise many valleys and basins, often having different microclimates resulting in differences in vegetation.

As the Rockies' foothills rise from the western plateau, prairie shortgrass gives way to mixed evergreen and scrub deciduous forest. Between 8,000 and 9,500 feet, larger trees such as aspens, Douglas firs, and ponderosa, timber, and lodge pole pines thrive in temperatures cool even in high summer. Subalpine snow forest begins at 11,500 feet. Here spruce and fir trees capture moisture primarily from snowfall remaining on the ground as late as July. Above 11,500 feet the climate is alpine (Figure 11.2). Vegetation is low and sparse, including mosses and lichens similar to those of the Arctic tundra. Snow remains year round. On the Rockies' western slopes, climate is similarly dependent on elevation, although warm winds and precipitation from the Pacific create denser vegetation.

At higher altitudes and on steep mountainsides, the soil is quite shallow and rocky. Although the tree-covered mountains produce ample organic material from decomposing leaves, because of the steep terrain much of this soil is carried downhill by erosion and settles into the region's valleys, forming moderately thick deposits of fertile soil. These steep valleys are drained by thousands of small, fast-flowing streams and creeks, none of which are navigable by commercial boat traffic. This rugged, often impenetrable terrain made the Rocky Mountains a barrier to America's westward expansion. Lack of arable soil and difficulty of transportation made the region unsuitable for commercial agriculture and initially

FACTOR 1
Altitude and orientation create varied climates and varied vegetation.

FACTOR 1
The Rocky Mountains' climate and terrain were not considered suitable for farming.

FIGURE 11.1
Mountain Systems of the American West

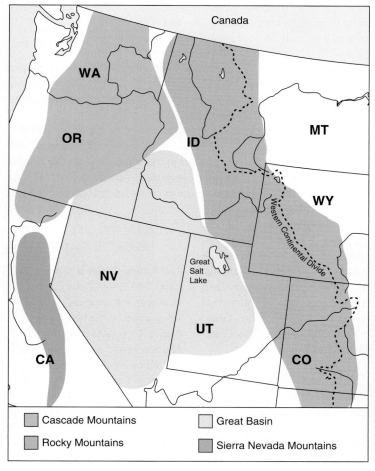

Canada

WA

OR

ID

MT

WY

Western Continental Divide

Great Salt Lake

NV

UT

CA

CO

☐ Cascade Mountains   ☐ Great Basin
☐ Rocky Mountains   ☐ Sierra Nevada Mountains

FIGURE 11.2
At 14,433 feet, Mt. Elbert is the highest peak in the Rocky Mountains.
Paul Cowan/Shutterstock

undesirable for settlement. For most pioneers, the mountains represented nothing more than a final—and formidable—challenge to overcome before reaching the good land that lay beyond. Even today, much of the Rocky Mountain region remains uninhabited.

Mountain Wildlife

The Rocky Mountains are home to many wild animals virtually unknown elsewhere in the United States, including Rocky Mountain elk, mule deer, Rocky Mountain bighorn sheep, mountain goats, mountain lions, and bobcats. Grizzly bears and moose are found in the northern Rockies. Mountains and foothills shelter coyotes, red foxes, wolverines, muskrats, otters, weasels, badgers, snowshoe rabbits, jackrabbits, gophers, minks, marmots, raccoons, martens, and fishers. Although by the 1840s beavers were virtually wiped out by fur hunters, today they have made a vigorous comeback. Lying between the central and Pacific migratory flyways, in season the Rockies host mallard and pintail ducks, Canada geese, and whistling swans. Resident game birds include grouse, quail, partridges, and pheasants. Predatory birds include eagles, ospreys, owls, shrikes, and hawks. Mountain streams harbor brook, cutthroat, brown, and rainbow trout. These food animals were vital to the survival of the region's early pioneers and remain an important part of contemporary Rocky Mountain cuisine.

■ THE GREAT
□ BASIN
■

Geological forces similar to those that formed the Rocky Mountains created the Sierra Nevadas, a chain of mountains running parallel to the Rockies along America's Pacific coast from Mexico's Baja California to north central California. At roughly the same time, volcanic activity created the Cascade system of cone-shaped volcanic mountains located in Washington and Oregon (Chapter 13), Between these mountain ranges is a roughly circular depression called the Great Basin. Not totally flat, the Basin is actually a series of low ridges, roughly oriented southwest to northeast and separated by valleys from fifty to two hundred miles wide. Although the exact boundaries vary according to different map-makers, the Great Basin generally comprises most of Nevada, about half of Utah, and parts of other contiguous states.

The Great Basin is classified as **cold desert,** a dry area with extreme hot and cold temperatures and dry conditions caused by multiple factors. Cold temperatures are partially due to elevation. Although low in comparison to the surrounding mountains, the Great Basin ranges from 4,000 to 12,000 feet above sea level. In addition, mountains block the area from Pacific Ocean warmth and moisture and Canadian precipitation. As a result, most of the Great Basin receives only 10 to 15 inches of precipitation per year. The resulting dry conditions help create temperature extremes: With little cloud cover to hold in warmth or block sun, temperatures can dip to −50°F on winter nights and soar to 125°F on sum-

FIGURE 11.3

The Bonneville Salt Flats are an extreme example of the Great Basin's arid climate and highly mineral soil. mdd © Shutterstock

mer days. These temperature challenges are significant; however, lack of water is the most crucial factor affecting the Great Basin.

Although the Great Basin's annual rainfall is about the same as some shortgrass prairie areas, distribution is different. After a long, dry winter, spring brings sudden, violent rainstorms. Because rainfall typically cannot penetrate the hard, dry soil, virtually all of it flows downhill and collects in low-lying areas, creating seasonal marshes that gradually evaporate away. Evaporation also affects the basin's creeks and rivers, many of which simply peter out into gullies. In many places the resulting concentration of minerals creates highly saline and/or alkaline soil (Figure 11.3).

In such an inhospitable land, only specific types of drought-tolerant vegetation can survive. Sagebrush and saltbrush are among low-growing shrubs found in the basin, along with juniper and piñon pine trees at higher elevations. As in the Great Plains, aspen and cottonwood trees grow in creek beds and river valleys, where they depend on underground water during the dry season. Except during the short spring season when sparse vegetation blooms, the area appears brown and barren. It's little surprise that before irrigation, the Great Basin was called "the Great American Desert."

With little vegetation for food, few creatures could survive in the Great Basin. Jackrabbits, coyotes, and various rodents are among the limited number of animals indigenous to the region.

A NOTE ON THE PALOUSE VALLEY

The Palouse Valley is technically part of the Great Basin. However, the area was frequented by the Nez Perce Native Americans of the Pacific Northwest and was eventually settled by Pacific Northwest pioneers. Because it belongs to the Pacific Northwest both culturally and culinarily, we discuss the Palouse Valley in Chapter 13.

NATIVE AMERICANS OF THE MOUNTAINS AND BASIN

Like the Appalachians, the Rocky Mountains were not permanently settled by Native American tribes but rather were used as hunting grounds in late summer and fall. Shared by the tribes of the western plateau, the Great Basin, and the Pacific Northwest, the Rockies offered foraged foods, game animals, and fur-bearing animals whose pelts were a valuable trading commodity. However, because of harsh winter weather, no tribe permanently settled the Rockies.

Several Native American tribes inhabited the arid, forbidding Great Basin. All were nomadic foragers and hunters of small game. In the eastern basin, the Western Shoshone and Gosiute ranged near the Great Salt Lake, while the Ute and Bannock traveled the Rockies' western foothills. Northern and Southern Paiutes roamed the central basin, while the Washo and Mono traversed the western basin near Lake Tahoe and the foothills of the Sierra Nevada (Figure 11.4).

Great Basin tribes were the most primitive of all Native American groups, living in a virtually prehistoric manner as late as the mid-1800s. The inhospitable desert environment not only made agriculture impossible but also restricted the number and size of animal life that could be supported. Unable to rely on farming or hunting as a primary source of food, the Great Basin tribes were forced into exceptional nutritional diversity, eating a wide range of plant and animal foods including reptiles and insects and devising ingenious methods of getting the most basic shelter and nutrition.

The extreme lack of resources in the Great Basin kept Native American population numbers low and social organization quite loose. For most of the year, Great Basin tribes traveled in small family groups rarely exceeding twenty adults. Following the cyclical rhythms of their environment, tribes moved from place to place according to the availability of food, water, and shelter.

The initial contact between primitive Great Basin tribes and well-provisioned, self-sufficient American pioneers did not result in any meaningful exchange of foodways. To the Mormons and other western pioneers, the Great Basin tribes were virtually beneath notice. Thus, indigenous foods and Native American foodways had no influence on Great Basin cuisine. However, modern cultural anthropologists marvel at the ingenuity and perseverance shown by Great Basin tribes. Flexible and highly adaptable, they were able to live in a brutally hostile environment and coexisted peacefully even in times of great deprivation.

Because no Native American groups settled the Rockies, Native American foodways had no direct impact on Rocky Mountain cuisine. However, the foodways of earlier-encountered Native American groups strongly influenced pioneer cuisines in general, and Rocky Mountain cuisine in particular. Remember that pioneer provisions, such as cornmeal and dried beans, are legacies of East Coast Native American food culture. Game meats eaten fresh and preserved by salting and smoking are likewise Native American derived. Thus, Native American cooking is an indirect but influential element in Rocky Mountain cuisine.

FIGURE 11.4
A Paiute Native American woman uses indigenous seeds and grasses in basket weaving. Courtesy of the Library of Congress, LC-USZ62-104705

PIONEER COOKING

Through the late 1700s and early 1800s, few nonnatives dared broach the formidable barrier of the Rocky Mountains. The region was explored only by a few rugged mountain men in search of furs. However, the 1804 Lewis and Clark expedition captured the nation's imagination with reports of endless open prairie in the Midwest and fertile green valleys along America's Pacific shore. By 1830 wagon trains were moving west, settlement of the American heartland was well on its way, and pioneers were focusing on the land beyond the mountains. In 1848 news of the California gold strike turned the river of migration into a flood. Americans from all over the eastern United States and immigrants from Europe converged on Independence, Missouri, to begin the journey west. Lone miners and merchants set out to make their fortunes. Families staked their life savings to purchase covered wagons, draft animals, and provisions. Once outfitted, travelers obtained a paid guide to lead them across the prairie, over the mountains, and on to their chosen land (Figure 11.5).

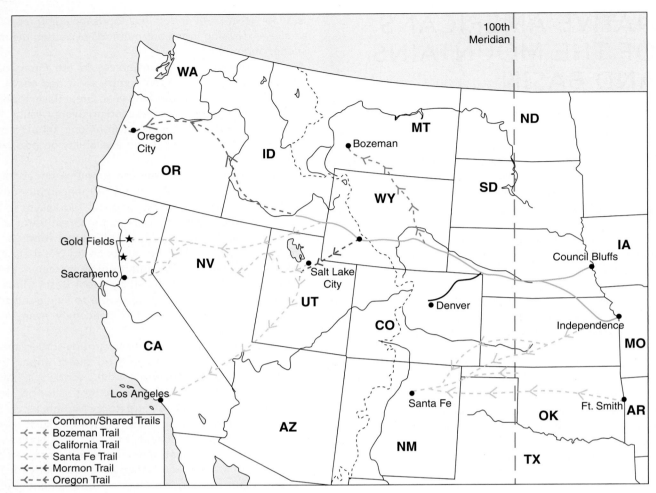

FIGURE 11.5
America's Western Wagon Trails

Many of the pioneers traveling through the Rockies were third- or fourth-generation Americans accustomed to the foodways of their home regions. Except in Appalachia, most Americans ate wild game or foraged foods rarely, if at all. Few American pioneers had experience with foreign cuisines, or even with the cooking of neighboring regions. At the beginning of the journey, most would have been classified as culinary conservatives. However, conditions on the wagon trails were not conducive to maintaining rigid attitudes. Wagon trail pioneers had to be flexible about what they ate; the alternative was to go hungry.

Cooking on the Wagon Trails

Early wagon trail travelers relied on pioneer provisions such as salt pork, cornmeal, wheat flour, and dried beans supplemented with wild game and foraged foods. In fact, on the plains their cooking was virtually identical to early Ranchlands cuisine, but with bison replacing beef. Once they reached the mountains, pioneers ate white-tailed deer, elk, antelope, and wildfowl. Mountain streams yielded a variety of trout. As a people on the move, pioneers were obliged to keep food preparation simple and fast. All cooking was done outdoors, with grilling, griddle-baking, and Dutch oven cooking among the most common methods. Seasonings were minimal, often consisting only of salt and mountain herbs foraged along the way. Pioneer women cooked only in the morning and evening. When the wagon train camped for the night, women prepared a hot meal while the men fished or hunted for game. The men's catch might be supplemented with a pot of beans or boiled hominy. In the morning they cooked a hearty breakfast, such as cornmeal mush or pancakes and fried bacon, and prepared additional foods that could be eaten cold during the day without stopping. As in the Ranchlands region, sourdough bread baking was the norm.

Good Eating at the Forts

In the early years of western migration, the great wagon trails were protected from outlaws and hostile Native Americans by a series of military forts set up by the U.S. government. Before

OYSTERS IN THE ROCKIES

By the mid-1800s, seafood merchants were shipping Atlantic oysters to the Midwest and even as far as the Rockies. Packed in wooden barrels between layers of sawdust and ice, the oysters traveled first by train and then by wagon. At each station stop, fresh ice from underground storage houses was added to the barrels along with cornmeal on which the oysters fed. Arriving fresh, plump, and juicy as far west as Denver and Santa Fe, the oysters fetched top dollar from diners hungry for a taste of the sea.

long the forts expanded, adding trading posts and inns where travelers could take on provisions and enjoy the pleasures of a hot bath, a solid meal, and a soft bed.

As the wagon trails became safer, a more affluent group of travelers began to make their way west. Commercial provisioners traveled the trails to supply them with goods and services. As the years went by, wagon trail supply posts carried a more varied and sophisticated selection of trade goods, including a fancier grade of foodstuffs.

Connecting the East with the civilized Southwest, the Santa Fe Trail was the most cosmopolitan of all the western wagon roads. Along with pioneers headed west, merchants from America's southern seaports, French and French-Canadian traders, and affluent Mexicans of Spanish heritage traveled the Santa Fe Trail. Chiles, pine nuts, chocolate, and Spanish wines moved north and east, while Asian and European trade goods such as Chinese ginger, East Indian spices, Italian olive oils and cheeses, and French wines moved west and south.

Private entrepreneurs began opening wagon trail forts that were more like resort hotels than military outposts. The most famous of all was Bent's Fort, built in 1835 in the Rocky Mountain foothills on the Arkansas River near present-day La Junta, Colorado (Figure 11.6). A large and imposing structure, the adobe fort was a rendezvous point for mountain men, Native Americans, and traders from Mexico and the American East.

At Bent's Fort, as at other wagon trail stopovers, the clash of many cultures and cuisines made for an interesting menu. Charlotte Green, the fort's African-American cook during the 1840s, was equally proficient in making Mexican tortillas, tamales, and refried beans as in baking pumpkin pies and griddlecakes. Native American cooks added indigenous ingredients and cooking methods. Records from the fort indicate that ingredients as diverse as balsam bitters, lemon syrup, capers, and Cantonese preserved ginger could be found in its storehouses.

Although such exotic ingredients were available, local products were the mainstay of the fort's menu. Bison from the prairie was consumed both fresh and dried. All manner of wild game found its way from the mountains into the fort's kitchen, with beaver tail a special favorite. Mountain streams provided trout and crayfish. The fort's farmyard included pigsties and chicken coops, and beef and mutton were readily available from Spanish ranchers and Navajo herders. Neighboring pueblo tribes provided pine nuts, chiles, squash, and even grapes and watermelons in season.

FIGURE 11.6

Bent's Fort was also a trading post, inn, and restaurant. Courtesy of The Colorado Department of Transportation

The era of the western wagon train forts ended with the completion of the Transcontinental Railroad in 1869. Most of the region's forts and trading posts gradually fell out of use, deteriorated, and finally crumbled to the ground. Only a few remain, now historical sites and tourist attractions.

Although it lasted less than forty years, the wagon train era had a profound impact on the American psyche. The image of hardy pioneers enduring numerous hardships to reach the goal of western settlement pervades our national consciousness. West Coast Americans of pioneer heritage typically exhibit independence and rugged individualism. Mingling with people of many races, creeds, and colors on the trails and in early West Coast settlements led to the multicultural society for which the American West is well known. Cultural diversity also led to culinary diversity and the impulse to try new foods. Although most Rocky Mountain pioneers began their journeys as culinary conservatives, many became culinary liberals as a result of their time on the trails and, later, in the teeming boomtowns of the West.

■ EARLY ROCKY ▫ ■ MOUNTAIN COOKING

After the demise of the great western wagon trails and the advent of rail transport, cooking in the mountains became less challenging and more diverse. However, the region remained sparsely settled, populous only in towns and cities that grew up around mines or rail hubs. The Rockies had yet to attract the volume of settlement and a sufficiently homogenous first-settler group necessary to develop a discrete regional cuisine. Nonetheless, there was some good cooking going on. In the late 1800s, much of the region's culinary success was related to the railroad.

Transcontinental Travel and Transport

In 1862 the Pacific Railway Act authorized the building of the first railway linking the American East Coast to the West Coast. The Union Pacific Railroad began building west from Omaha, Nebraska, employing primarily Americans and immigrants from Europe. The Central Pacific Railroad built east from Sacramento, California. Among the Central Pacific's workforce were thousands of Chinese immigrants. Together the two companies laid approximately 2,000 miles of track, much of it over rugged Rocky Mountain terrain. On May 10, 1869, the two tracks were joined with the pounding of the golden spike at Promontory, Utah (Figure 11.7). America was now connected coast to coast by rail.

The construction of the nation's first transcontinental railroad dramatically changed America's patterns of migration. A journey that previously took many dangerous months now could be completed in four days. Tools, farming implements, and personal items no longer lumbered west in wagons; instead, pioneers' possessions traveled with them in boxcars.

Foodstuffs also rode the rails. Train transport brought a wide variety of ingredients to the mountains, making pioneer provisions less important. Spices, seasonings, condiments, and spirits were easily transported. Even fresh foods made the trip packed on ice. The Rocky Mountain cooking that began with rough-and-ready trail food could now be transformed into a unique, multicultural cuisine.

International Dining in Denver

In Chapter 12 you'll learn more about the 1849 California gold rush that opened the floodgates of western migration. A few years later gold was discovered in the hills of Colorado, and a humble mining camp on the banks of Cherry Creek quickly grew into the city of Denver. While the miners prospected the Colorado mountains, Denver prospered from "mining the miners," selling supplies and provisions to the hopeful and providing world-class luxuries to those who had already struck it rich.

By 1860 Denver boasted scores of restaurants, saloons, and gambling houses. Nickel beers and free lunches lured prospectors and railroad workers to spend their newfound money. As prospectors and merchants arrived from the American East Coast and Europe and laid-off Chinese railroad workers settled in, Denver quickly became a city of immigrants. Entrepreneurs opened restaurants featuring ethnic cuisines to feed their countrymen. For example, Maria Anna Capelli's Highland House served pasta dishes and Italian wines to homesick Italians. As in gold rush California, Chinese cooks opened inexpensive restaurants serving a rudimentary version of Cantonese food using local ingredients. Their local version of egg foo yong—peppers, onions, ham, and eggs cooked together in a wok—soon became known as the Denver omelet.

In the late 1800s the Brown Palace Hotel became Denver's most famous landmark (Figure 11.8). Built by Henry C. Brown as a monument to himself, the Brown Palace was constructed from the finest materials, including Colorado red granite and Mexican golden onyx. Its eight-story atrium hosted receptions for European royalty, East Coast millionaires, and the Colorado nouveau riche. The Brown Palace dining room presented lavish banquets and parties, serving the best local beef and game, imported European wines and cheeses, and East Coast fish and shellfish. The Palace's French chefs prepared elegant hors d'oeuvres, sophisticated sauces, and fancy desserts rivaling any in the world.

The discovery of gold in the Rocky Mountains began an economic boom later sustained by other types of mining. Thanks to mining revenues and the railroads, Denver remained a cosmopolitan city despite its remote location.

FIGURE 11.8

Denver's Brown Palace Hotel, circa 1890 Courtesy of The Denver Public Library

FACTOR 5

The discovery of gold brought wealth and sophisticated cuisine to the region.

◼ THE CUISINE OF ◻ ◼ BASQUE IMMIGRANTS

The Rocky Mountains region attracted settlers from Europe as well as from the American East Coast and Midwest. Among them were thousands of **Basques** (BASKS) originally from the Pyrenees

FIGURE 11.7

The completion of the Transcontinental Railroad linked the East Coast with the West and ended the era of the great wagon trails. Courtesy of Library of Congress, LC-USZ62-57524

FIGURE 11.9
Basque sheepherders lived in their wagons, tending sheep for months at a time. Lee O'Dell © Shutterstock

Mountains in southwestern France and northern Spain. Basques are a distinct race of people with a unique language unrelated to any other in the world. Seeking cultural freedom and economic opportunity, they arrived in the Rocky Mountains and Great Basin, some to work in the mines and on the railroads, others to try their luck at sheep ranching (Figure 11.9). Arriving primarily from the late 1800s through the beginning of the 20th century, Basque immigrants became an integral part of the American West, eventually settling in central California as well.

Basque sheepherders were known for remarkably sophisticated outdoor cooking. While watching their flocks, sheepherders had virtually unlimited time to forage and cook. Seasonings and condiments from Spain enlivened their dishes, which were prepared with skill and care. Even finer cuisine was served in boardinghouses and hotels opened by Basque families in the late 1800s. These operations served three meals a day to their residents as well as offering meals to outside guests. In Basque boardinghouses, dinner guests were seated at long, communal tables. Foods were served on platters from which diners helped themselves. Called **boardinghouse service,** this family-style type of dining is still featured today in many of western America's Basque restaurants. Hospitality was equally important in private homes, where setting a fine table was a matter of pride that transcended economic status. The highest compliment a Basque could pay to a meal or dish was to call it "good enough for a sheepherder."

Basque Flavors and Ingredients

As befits a people whose traditional occupation is sheepherding, mutton and lamb are the Basques' foundation proteins, served roasted, stewed, and braised. Until recently lamb was a seasonal treat enjoyed only in springtime, and its consumption is still closely associated with the Easter holiday. Basques roast whole, milk-fed baby lambs in brick ovens, usually surrounded by new potatoes and young carrots, and flavored with mountain herbs. Another seasonal dish, Basque-style Rocky Mountain oysters (lamb testicles) are consumed after the spring castration of young rams. Larger, more mature sheep are often spit-barbequed to serve a crowd.

Garlic plays a major role in Basque cooking. In Basque barbeque, the meat is both basted and served with *ajolio* (ah-OH-lee-oh), a sauce made primarily of pounded garlic and olive oil. Basques share the Spanish love for tomatoes, olive oil, and bell peppers, as well as a preference for drinking wine. A fondness for saffron and other eastern spices is derived from the Moors, people of Arabic origin who conquered Spain around 700 C.E. Condiments such as pickled peppers, olives, pimentos, capers, and sherry wine vinegar add a distinctive Spanish influence. Preserved pork products are important as appetizers and cooking ingredients. Imported Spanish smoked ham as well as *longaniza* and chorizo sausages are favored ingredients. However, American salt pork, bacon, and country-style ham are often substituted when European products are unavailable. Basque cooks soon began making their own domestic pork and lamb sausages in the European style.

Basques adapted many of their traditional seafood recipes to use freshwater fish from local mountain streams. In addition, dried salt cod, or **bacalao** (bah-kah-LAH oh), is a staple of the cuisine. Because it can be stored for long periods of time, bacalao was convenient while traveling or at the sheep camp.

Basque-American cooking relies heavily on legumes. Among those favored by Basque cooks are brown, and green lentils; red, white, kidney, pinto, lima, fava, and cranberry beans; and most important, chickpeas. Teamed with a preserved pork product or lamb sausages, legumes are simmered into soups or served as a side dish.

Basque cuisine relies on starchy side dishes to extend the sauces of its many stews and braised dishes. Basques share the Spanish love of rice, preparing fluffy long-grain pilafs and soft, saucy, risotto-like dishes. Fried potatoes are a staple of Basque home cooking, served as a side dish or as the filling for a Spanish-style tortilla, a flat omelet. Potatoes thicken and extend lamb, chicken, and fish stews. To accompany their meals, Basques prefer a European-style bread with crisp crust and airy interior.

Like Portuguese cooking in New England, the cooking of Basque immigrants did not develop into a Basque-American

---

ELEMENTS OF OLD WORLD BASQUE CUISINE

FOUNDATION FOODS:

principal starches: wheat flour bread, rice, potatoes

principal proteins: mutton/lamb, preserved pork and pork sausages, seafood

principal produce: bell peppers, tomatoes, shell beans, cabbages, greens

FAVORED SEASONINGS: onions, garlic, bay leaf, thyme, marjoram, chiles, seasoning meats

PRINCIPAL COOKING MEDIA: lard, olive oil

PRIMARY COOKING METHODS: grilling, roasting, stewing, braising

FOOD ATTITUDES: strong food culture, culinary liberals

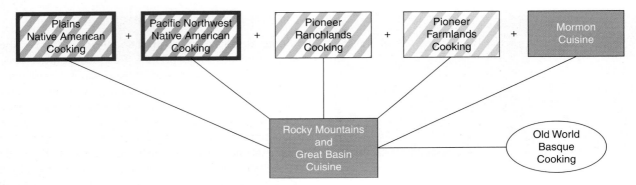

FIGURE 11.10
Development of Rocky Mountains and Great Basin Cuisine

cuisine. Because Basque immigration corresponded with the development of railroads and steamship transport, virtually all the ingredients necessary to produce an authentic version of Basque cuisine were available. Most Basques had the resources to purchase authentic foodstuffs and were not forced to make extensive substitutions. Therefore, Basque cooking in America remained substantially pure, and Basque cuisine did not influence the cooking of the Rocky Mountain and Great Basin culinary region in any meaningful way. However, the existence of Basque cooking in the Rocky Mountains contributed to the liberal culinary sensibility of the American West.

MORMON CUISINE IN THE GREAT BASIN

Among the many East Coast Americans traveling westward in search of land was a Christian religious group known as the **Mormons.** Founded in upstate New York by Joseph Young in 1830, the Mormons soon attracted religious persecution in the East due to their unusual doctrines and practices. Thus, the group relocated successively westward during the 1830s and, led by Joseph Young's son, Brigham Young, eventually traveled to the Great Basin in 1838 (Figure 11.11). There, through relentless work and extreme physical endurance, they literally made the desert bloom through irrigation and good agricultural methods. Much of the modern Great Basin area was settled and farmed by Mormons and their descendants, and today the area is frequently referred to as the Mormon cultural zone.

The cuisine of Great Basin cultural Mormons is based on the inland style of New England cooking practiced in upstate New York blended with Midwestern Farmlands-style dishes and pioneer provisions. Unlike many other Rocky Mountain settlers, Mormon pioneers remained culinary conservatives because of their religious beliefs. Traditional Mormon culture and cuisine are focused on thrift, simplicity, and generosity. Thus, traditional Mormon dishes are plainly seasoned and easy to prepare and serve to large groups. With the exception of Great Lakes fish

FIGURE 11.11
Mormon pioneers crossed the mountains in wagons en route to the Great Basin. Victorian Traditions © Shutterstock

dishes, virtually all of the Farmlands recipes presented in Chapter 9 might be found on a Great Basin Mormon table.

Until Mormon settlers' farms began producing, pioneer foods were their mainstay. When game meats were not available, fried salt pork or bacon was served with thick gravy and cornbread or wheat-flour bread. Slow-simmered dried beans frequently replaced meat. **Salt-rising bread,** a leavened wheat-flour loaf made by a unique natural fermentation process, was baked in cast-iron Dutch ovens. Further information and a recipe for salt-rising bread appear on this book's companion website.

Since the mid-20th century, Mormon cooking has been shaped by the desire for easy, convenient preparations. Casseroles and other potluck-style dishes feature prominently in the cuisine. Among the best known of these are gelatin salads and funeral potatoes, a gratin of diced potatoes enriched with cream cheese, cheddar cheese, and sour cream. Another tradition is the Sunday roast, almost always beef. When Mormon cooks adapted the quick breads of New England to the demands of campfire cooking, the result was Mormon scones, actually a type of fry bread. Because their religion forbids the use of alcohol or caffeine, Mormons serve a variety of homemade beverages, among them lemonade, fruit punches, and Mormon tea, a pioneer brew made from the herb ephedra.

Today the mainstream Mormon religion is known as the Church of Jesus Christ of Latter Day Saints, or LDS. The LDS church has grown far beyond the Great Basin region and has followers around the world. One of the tenets of the LDS religion is the practice of missionary work; thus, young adult Mormons are required to spend time away from home, often across the globe, fulfilling this obligation. Although some Mormon missionaries have returned from their service with a taste for foreign foods, most cultural Mormons retain the foodways of their pioneer forebears and remain culinary conservatives.

FIGURE 11.12

Elk Lake Resort, Montana. Courtesy of Elk Lake Resort, serving delicious Rocky Mountain Cuisine, www.elklakeresortmontana.com

■ TRADITIONAL ROCKY
□
■ MOUNTAIN AND GREAT BASIN CUISINES

FACTOR 5
Tourism drives both the region's economy and cuisine.

Mining, sheep ranching, and upland farming became important sources of income for the inhabitants of the Rocky Mountains and Great Basin. However, today the region's economy is strongly driven by tourism. In the Great Basin state of Nevada, casino gambling generates billions of tourist dollars. In the mountains, breathtaking scenery, rare and abundant wildlife, and the opportunity for outdoor activities create destinations for hikers, rock climbers, skiers, and hunters.

Hunting Lodge Dining

As early as 1900, the mystique of the Rocky Mountain wilderness began drawing wealthy tourists from America's East and West Coasts and from Europe. Once a necessity, in the 20th century hunting and eating wild game had become a luxury. Originally catering to railroad tycoons and mining barons, hunting lodges now offer vacation packages to visitors from all walks of life. At exclusive mountain hunting lodges, amateur hunters spend their days stalking elk, antelope, and deer in the care of a seasoned guide, then feast on sumptuous wild game dinners prepared by a professional chef.

Today's hunting lodge restaurants feature sophisticated menus presented in the European or New American style and offer fine wines to accompany the food. Hunters with the skill and luck necessary to kill a game animal may have their catch fabricated, cooked, and served to them courtesy of the chef. However, because of health restrictions, all others must dine on farm-raised game that has passed USDA inspection.

Casino Dining

In the mid-20th century, legalization of gambling in Las Vegas and Reno, Nevada, transformed these formerly quiet desert towns into bustling tourist centers with elaborate resort hotels. Nevada casinos attracted wealthy high rollers from across the country and around the world for gambling, top-level entertainment, and elaborate, expensive dining.

Today casino tourism in Las Vegas and Reno draws millions of visitors annually to these Great Basin cities. Although the main attraction is gambling, food has become a major part of the experience. Modern casino hotels now offer a multitude of dining options.

On the low end of casino dining is the budget buffet. Subsidized by casino revenues, casino buffet restaurants offer an array of appetizers, main dishes, and desserts arranged in

ROCKY MOUNTAIN FARMED GAME

In the late 20th century a more sophisticated American consumer created growing demand for game meats and fowl. In response, Western ranchers began raising wild game animals in a controlled environment. Game produced in this manner is called **farmed game.** In addition to benefits such as consistency in size, weight, and tenderness, all farmed game is USDA inspected to ensure food safety. Virtually all farmed game is free-range raised in a natural habitat without the use of antibiotics or growth hormones, important qualities for many health-conscious consumers. Although modern game ranches sell primarily to the restaurant industry, Internet mail-order sales of wild game meats is on the rise.

seemingly endless buffet lines. As well as traditional American foods, casino buffets now offer world cuisines dishes as diverse as Japanese sushi, Italian pasta, and Chinese stir-fry. Theme restaurants are a casino specialty. At the high end of the spectrum are flagship restaurants of world-renowned chefs such as Wolfgang Puck, Charlie Palmer, Emeril Lagasse, and the Brennan and Maccioni families.

Despite the large number of fine-dining restaurants in the Great Basin's casino cities, few are dedicated to the area's regional cuisine.

■ MODERN ROCKY
□ MOUNTAIN CUISINE
■

Although its food history dates back to the 1830s, the Rocky Mountain region did not develop a distinctive modern cuisine until the late 20th century. As in the Mexican Border region, the automobile and the interstate highway system did much to increase tourism to the area, primarily by making mountain ski facilities more accessible. As exclusive resort towns grew up around the ski areas, they attracted an affluent and sophisticated clientele ready to support a renaissance of traditional regional cooking. Thus, modern Rocky Mountain cooking is primarily a restaurant cuisine.

In creating modern Rocky Mountain regional cuisine, chefs looked back to pioneer days, often featuring traditional campfire cooking methods such as grilling and smoke roasting. Although no native tribe actually inhabited the region, Rocky Mountain chefs borrow Native American Three Sisters ingredients such as cornmeal-based side dishes, soups made of dried beans, and garnitures of both winter and summer squashes. The region's Mexican heritage is reflected by the use of chiles in sauces, rubs, and marinades. Tortillas and other masa dough products appear frequently.

Modern Rocky Mountain cuisine is intensely ingredient driven. Contemporary Rocky Mountain chefs typically apply European and world cuisines cooking techniques to the region's fine game meats and freshwater fish. Local wild mushrooms, greens, berries, and tree fruits enhance the seasonality of their menus. Rocky Mountain agriculture now produces fine Western lamb, exceptional potatoes, and specialty foods such as black quinoa (p. 536) and farmed caviar.

The future of Rocky Mountain and Great Basin cuisines depends on tourism and ecological sustainability—in many cases, competing interests. Continuing development of high-end ski lodges, hotels, and mountain resort communities brings new restaurants and innovative chefs to the region. However, such development also threatens wilderness areas and the region's scarce farmland that are the source of the region's best ingredients. This new cuisine with old roots will continue to flourish in the hands of chefs and private citizens knowledgeable enough to balance the demands of progress and the requirements of nature.

For a list of noteworthy restaurants serving traditional and contemporary Rocky Mountain and Great Basin cuisines, refer to this book's companion website.

☐ TABLE 11.1 ROCKY MOUNTAINS AND GREAT BASIN DEFINING DISHES

Beginning with the rough-and-ready cooking of explorers and prospectors and blooming only lately into a sophisticated regional cuisine, Rocky Mountain and Great Basin cuisines lack the long list of traditional dishes found in other, more venerable American regions. First cousin to Ranchlands cuisine, the Rocky Mountain style shares many of its defining dishes (listed on pp. 473 and 474). With rare exceptions, the defining dishes of the Rocky Mountain and Great Basin region must be noted as types of dishes rather than specific ones.

ITEM NAME	HISTORY	DOMINANT INGREDIENTS AND METHOD	MORE
LEGUME DISHES	Long-keeping, portable dried beans, peas, and lentils were essential pioneer provisions.	Lentil soups based on lamb broth; white bean soup with ham; split pea soup with bacon. Side-dish beans prepared cowboy style with Mexican seasonings or with salt pork and molasses in the New England manner.	In the mid-20th century, Rockies cooks began serving cool, tangy salads made from cooked beans and crunchy vegetables.
POTATO DISHES	Potatoes are one of the few vegetable crops that thrive in the Rocky Mountains and Great Basin. Idaho is world famous for russet potatoes; in the late 20th century, Colorado farmers began growing many specialty and heirloom potatoes.	Among the dishes made with the Idaho russet are light, fluffy mashed potatoes; twice-baked Potatoes Royale; stuffed baked potatoes; and deep-fried potato skins with assorted toppings. Specialty and heirloom potatoes, particularly tiny fingerlings, are steamed or pan roasted.	
FRESHWATER FISH DISHES	For pioneers, the region's freshwater fish provided a welcome change from game meats. Today streams harbor indigenous and stocked trout including cutthroat, rainbow, and brook trout. In the late 20th century, Lake Superior whitefish were introduced into Montana lakes.	Trout are grilled or pan-fried whole or fabricated into fillets. In a regional variation on the classic trout amandine, almonds are replaced by pine nuts. Lake whitefish fillets are frequently poached.	
WOOD-GRILLED BISON AND VENISON	Contemporary chefs adopted and popularized the pioneer method of grilling over fragrant hardwoods.	Mountain chefs prefer oak to the more common prairie hickory and cottonwood. Alder wood imparts a unique flavor prized by Native Americans.	Juniper berries, laurel, thyme, and mountain sage add a haunting note to a rub or marinade.
ROASTED GAME BIRDS	Wild duck, grouse, guinea fowl, partridge, quail, and dove are among indigenous wildfowl of the Rocky Mountain region.	The same mountain herbs that enhance grilled meats are used to flavor game birds. More strongly flavored birds may be glazed with chokecherry syrup or a wild fruit jam.	
GAME OR BISON STEW	Stews tenderize tough cuts from older game animals and make easy one-pot meals.	Tough cuts of venison, elk, or bison, as well as elderly rabbits and game birds, are slow-simmered with carrots, potatoes, and mountain herbs to make hearty stews.	
ROCKY MOUNTAIN LAMB	Lamb dishes arrived in the region with Basque sheepherders.	Western lamb is known for both flavor and size. Rack of lamb is the cut of choice in high-end restaurants; each large, meaty eight-rib rack serves two diners. Grilled "steaks" cross-cut from lamb leg have become popular in recent years. Tough cuts make succulent stews and braises.	
HUCKLEBERRY PIE	Pioneers found indigenous huckleberries to be a delicious substitute for blueberries.	Tiny, tart berries are heavily sugared, thickened with flour or cornstarch, dotted with butter, and baked in a traditional double crust.	Whipped cream or vanilla ice cream counterpoints the berries' astringent flavor.
DRIED FRUIT COMPOTE	Compotes made of dried fruits were served throughout the winter and early spring, when fresh fruits were not available.	Assorted dried fruits are simmered in water or wine with honey or sugar to make a warm, satisfying dessert. For a more substantial dish, sweet cornmeal or wheat flour dumplings may be poached in the syrup.	Made with less sugar, dried fruit compote is served as a sauce for roasted game meat and fowl.

■ □ ■ **STUDY QUESTIONS**

1. Describe the climate and topography of the Rocky Mountains. Describe the climate and topography of the Great Basin. Why are these two areas grouped together as one culinary region?

2. Why was there no *direct* Native American influence on Rocky Mountain and Great Basin cuisine? Explain how the cuisine was *indirectly* affected by Native American foodways.

3. List the preserved food products that formed the basis of the Rocky Mountain and Great Basin pioneer diet. List the hunted and foraged foods that augmented these products.

4. Compare and contrast wagon train cooking with the chuck wagon cooking of the Ranchlands region. Discuss the forts that sprang up along the trails and explain how they functioned as culinary crossroads.

5. Describe the gold rush cuisine of Denver, Colorado. Explain the origins of its international cooking.

6. Explain why the Rocky Mountain experience helped create the adventurous palate of the American West and resulted in a Western population primarily comprised of culinary liberals.

7. Discuss early Great Basin culture and cuisine. What group comprised the region's primary settlers? Describe their traditional culture and their original foodways. Explain how and why their cuisine evolved as it did.

8. Describe the ways in which tourism affected modern Rocky Mountain and Great Basin cuisine. Describe the foodservice operations of today's Rocky Mountain and Great Basin resorts.

9. Explain why modern Rocky Mountain and Great Basin cuisine is strongly ingredient driven. List the region's most important ingredients.

10. List and describe five types of dishes that define the Rocky Mountain and Great Basin culinary region.

11. Using the information you learned in this chapter and your imagination, plan a four-course special-occasion dinner menu featuring Rocky Mountains and Great Basin cuisine.

Pioneer Vegetable Soup

with Salt-Rising Bread

yield: 1 (10-fl.-oz.) appetizer serving
(multiply × 4 for classroom turnout; adjust equipment sizes accordingly)

MASTER RECIPE

production		costing only
1 1/2 c.	Pioneer Vegetable Soup	1/4 recipe
1	cocktail napkin	1 each
1 Tbsp.	chopped parsley	1/40 bunch a.p.
1 slice	Salt-Rising Bread, cut diagonally in half	1/12 recipe
1 Tbsp.	butter, in a butter chip or small ramekin	1/2 oz.

service turnout:

1. Stir the Pioneer Vegetable Soup thoroughly to distribute the solids, then ladle into a small saucepan and heat just to the boil.
2. Plate the dish:
   a. Ladle the soup into a hot 8" pasta plate.
   b. Line a 9" underliner plate with the cocktail napkin and place the soup on it slightly left of center.
   c. Sprinkle the parsley on top.
   d. Place the Salt-Rising Bread and butter on the right side of the underliner plate.

COMPONENT RECIPE

PIONEER VEGETABLE SOUP

yield: approx. 6 c.

production		costing only
1/2 c.	navy beans, soaked overnight	3 oz.
1 qt.	water	n/c
1 Tbsp.	bacon drippings	n/c
4 oz.	3/8"-diced rindless slab bacon	5 oz. a.p.
1/2 tsp.	dried marjoram	1/16 oz.
1/4 tsp.	dried thyme	1/16 oz.
1	bay leaf	1/16 oz.
1 c.	fine-chopped onion	6 oz. a.p.
1 Tbsp.	minced garlic	1/2 oz. a.p.
6 oz.	fine-shredded cabbage	8 oz. a.p.
1/2 c.	fine-diced carrot	3 oz. a.p.
1/2 c.	fine-diced turnip	3 oz. a.p.
1/2 c.	fine-diced potatoes	2 1/2 oz. a.p.
as needed	water	n/c
tt	kosher salt	1/8 oz.
1 drop	liquid smoke, optional	1/16 oz.

preparation:

1. Drain the beans and place them in a small saucepan with 1 qt. water. Bring to the simmer, skim the foam, and add the bacon drippings. Simmer 30 to 40 minutes, until the beans are almost tender.
2. Place the bacon in a heavy 2 1/2-qt. saucepan and fry it over low heat about 2 minutes, until the fat is rendered out and the bacon dice are browned.
3. Stir the marjoram, thyme, bay leaf, onion, and garlic into the bacon drippings. Cook over low heat about 1 minute until softened.
4. Add the carrot, turnip, potatoes, the beans and their cooking water, and just enough additional water to keep the solids submerged. Simmer about 30 minutes longer, until the beans and vegetables are tender.
5. Remove and discard the bay leaf. Season with salt and liquid smoke, if using.
6. If not serving immediately, open-pan cool to room temperature.

holding: refrigerate in a freshly sanitized, covered container up to 5 days; freeze up to 1 month

---

RECIPE VARIATION

Basque Garbure

Replace the navy beans with shelled fresh cranberry beans or lima beans. Add 1/2 tsp. crushed dried red pepper in step 3. Omit the Salt-Rising Bread. Before serving, fry a 1/2"-thick slice of French bread in bacon drippings and place in the bottom of the bowl. Top it with 1 1/2 oz. grated Manchego cheese, then ladle in the hot soup.

Russet Potato Skins
with Montana Whitefish Caviar and Dilled Sour Cream

yield: 1 (5-oz.) appetizer serving
(multiply × 4 for classroom turnout; adjust equipment sizes accordingly)

MASTER RECIPE

production		costing only
4	Potato Skin Wedges	1/4 recipe
2 Tbsp.	melted butter	1 oz.
tt	kosher salt	1/16 oz.
tt	fresh-ground white pepper	1/16 oz.
4 Tbsp.	Dilled Sour Cream, in a pastry bag fitted with a medium star tip	1/4 recipe
2 Tbsp.	brunoise-cut tomato	1 oz. a.p.
2 Tbsp.	golden Montana whitefish caviar	1 oz.
1	plum tomato crown	1 1/2 oz. a.p.
1 sprig	fresh dill	1/40 bunch a.p.

service turnout:
1. Bake the Potato Skin Wedges:
   a. Bush the wedges inside and out with melted butter, season with salt and white pepper, and place on a sizzle pan.
   b. Bake in a 400°F oven about 8 minutes, until crisped and golden.
   c. Remove and cool slightly.
2. Assemble the wedges:
   a. Pipe a line of Dilled Sour Cream down the length of each wedge.
   b. Mound a dot of brunoise-cut tomato in one tip of each wedge.
   c. Carefully spoon a line of caviar down the length of each wedge.
3. Plate the dish:
   a. Place the tomato crown in the center of a cool 10" plate, season it with salt and white pepper, and pipe a dot of dilled sour cream in the middle.
   b. Arrange the wedges around the tomato crown in a spoke pattern.
   c. Stick the dill sprig upright out of the tomato crown.

COMPONENT RECIPE
POTATO SKIN WEDGES

yield: 16 wedges

production		costing only
4	(5-oz.) blemish-free russet potatoes	1 1/4 lb. a.p.

preparation:
1. Bake the potatoes:
   a. Preheat an oven to 400°F.
   b. Wash the potatoes under cool running water, scrubbing thoroughly with a vegetable brush.
   c. Using a sharp-tined fork, prick several sets of holes in each potato.
   d. Arrange the potatoes on a rack set on a sheet tray, and place them in the oven.
   e. Bake about 30 minutes, until cooked through.
   f. Cool to room temperature.
2. Fabricate the potatoes:
   a. Cut each potato lengthwise into 4 quarters.
   b. Cut away some of the potato flesh to leave a 1/4" shell. (Reserve the cooked potato flesh for another purpose.)

holding: refrigerate in a freshly sanitized, covered container with pan liner between layers up to 4 days

COMPONENT RECIPE
DILLED SOUR CREAM

yield: 1 c.

production		costing only
7 fl. oz.	sour cream	7 fl. oz.
2 Tbsp.	fine-minced fresh dill leaves	1/16 bunch a.p.
tt	kosher salt	1/16 oz.
tt	fine-ground white pepper	1/16 oz.

preparation:
1. Mix the sour cream and dill.
2. Season lightly with salt and white pepper.

holding: refrigerate in a freshly sanitized, covered plastic container up to 4 days

---

RECIPE VARIATION

Basque Potato Skins with Peppers and Bacalao
Replace the Dilled Sour Cream with a purée made of 4 oz. soaked and drained salt cod, 4 oz. cooked potato, and approximately 4 fl. oz. mayonnaise. Replace the caviar with 4 oz. brunoise-cut roasted and peeled red bell peppers tossed with olive oil, garlic, and red wine vinegar. Omit the tomatoes.

APPETIZERS

Blue Cheese Potato Chip Mountain for Two

yield: 2 (5-oz.) appetizer servings
(multiply × 2 for classroom turnout)

🕐 Best prepared 24 hours in advance.

MASTER RECIPE

production		costing only
5 oz.	Potato Slices for Chips, stored in cold water	1/3 recipe
as needed	frying compound or corn oil	% used
tt	fine salt	1/16 oz.
2 oz.	crumbled blue cheese	2 oz.
1/2 c.	medium-diced sweet onion	2 1/2 oz. a.p.
2/3 c.	seeded, medium-diced vine-ripe tomato	7 oz. a.p.
1 Tbsp.	chopped flat-leaf parsley	1/16 bunch a.p.
1 Tbsp.	minced chives	1/16 bunch a.p.
1 tsp.	fresh thyme leaves	1/40 bunch a.p.

service turnout:

1. Fry the potato chips:
   a. Blot the Potato Slices for Chips completely dry in clean, lint-free towels.
   b. Deep-fry at 400°F until golden, then drain on a rack.
   c. Season with salt.
2. Bake the chip "mountain":
   a. On a sizzle pan, construct a conical pile of chips layered with the blue cheese, half of the onion, and half of the tomato. Make the pile as tall as possible.
   b. Place the sizzle pan in a 400°F oven and bake about 6 minutes, just until the cheese is melted.
3. Plate the dish:
   a. Using a wide offset spatula, transfer the chip mountain to a cool 10" plate.
   b. Sprinkle with the herbs and the remaining onion and tomato, allowing some to fall onto the plate well.

COMPONENT RECIPE
POTATO SLICES FOR CHIPS

yield: 4 appetizer servings plus extra for practice

🕐 Best prepared 24 hours in advance.

production		costing only
1 lb.	russet potatoes, preferably aged	1 lb.

preparation:

1. Wash the potatoes, scrubbing well with a vegetable brush. Pat them dry.
2. Using a mandoline or electric slicer, cut round slices of potato of even 1/8" thickness. ⚠ Be sure to use the guard. Discard the ends.
3. Immediately place the potato slices in a freshly sanitized bucket of cold water.
4. Refrigerate at least 2 hours, preferably 24 hours.

holding: refrigerate in the soaking water up to 36 hours, changing the water daily

---

RECIPE VARIATIONS

Bacon and Cheddar Cheese Potato Chip Mountain for Two
Replace the blue cheese with 4 oz. grated sharp yellow Cheddar cheese. Add 4 Tbsp. crumbled cooked bacon in step 2.

Southern Sweet Potato Chip Mountain for Two
Replace the russet potatoes with orange-fleshed sweet potatoes. Replace the blue cheese with 4 oz. grated mild yellow Cheddar cheese. Replace the tomatoes with 3 fl. oz. tomato-based barbeque sauce of choice.

Sautéed Rainbow Trout in Pine Nut Butter Sauce

with Black Quinoa, French-Cut Green Beans, and Herb-Roasted Tomato

yield: 1 (10-oz. bone-in) entrée serving plus accompaniments (multiply × 4 for classroom turnout; adjust equipment sizes accordingly)

MASTER RECIPE

production		costing only
1	plum tomato crown	3 oz. a.p.
1 Tbsp.	Mountain Herb Butter	1/4 recipe
1	10-oz. boneless, head-on rainbow trout	10 oz. a.p.
few drops	fresh lemon juice	1/8 [90 ct.] lemon
tt	kosher salt	1/16 oz.
tt	fresh-ground black pepper	1/16 oz.
1 tsp.	chopped fresh sage	1/40 bunch a.p.
1 tsp.	fresh thyme leaves	1/40 bunch a.p.
as needed	flour	1/4 oz.
2 Tbsp.	clarified butter	1 1/3 oz. a.p.
1 1/2 c.	Black Quinoa	1/4 recipe
4 oz.	blanched and refreshed green beans, French cut	5 oz. a.p.
1 tsp.	clarified butter	1/5 oz. a.p.
2 Tbsp.	pine nuts	1/2 oz.
1 Tbsp.	minced shallot	1/2 oz. a.p.
1/4 c.	Fish Stock	1/64 recipe
2 Tbsp.	fresh lemon juice	3/8 [90 ct.] lemon
6 Tbsp.	cold butter	3 oz.
tt	fine-ground white pepper	1/16 oz.
1 sprig	flat-leaf parsley	1/20 bunch a.p.
1 sprig	fresh sage	1/10 bunch a.p.
1 sprig	fresh thyme	1/16 bunch a.p.

service turnout:

1. Bake the tomato:
   a. Top the tomato crown with the Mountain Herb Butter and place it on a sizzle pan.
   b. Bake the tomato crown in a 400°F oven about 5 minutes.
2. Sauté the trout:
   a. Place a 10" sauté pan over medium heat.
   b. Season the inside of the fish with a few drops lemon juice, salt, pepper, sage, and thyme, and then fold it closed.
   c. Dredge the fish in the flour and shake off the excess.
   d. Place the clarified butter in the pan, add the fish, and sauté about 1 minute on each side, until the skin is crisp and brown.
   e. Remove the fish to the sizzle pan with the tomato and finish in the oven about 5 minutes, until the fish is lightly cooked through. Reserve the sauté pan for step 5.
3. If necessary, heat the Black Quinoa in a microwave oven or steamer.
4. Heat the green beans in a microwave oven or steamer, or with a little water over high heat in a covered sauté pan.
5. Prepare the sauce:
   a. Wipe out the fish pan, add 1 tsp. clarified butter, and sauté the pine nuts over medium heat until golden.
   b. Add the shallot, Fish Stock, and 2 Tbsp. lemon juice to the pan and reduce by half.
   c. Work in the cold butter to form an emulsion.
6. Plate the dish:
   a. Spoon a mound of quinoa onto the back left of a hot 12" oval plate.
   b. Mound the green beans on the back right of the plate.
   c. Place the trout horizontally across the plate, propped against the quinoa, with its head to the left.
   d. Place the tomato crown on the left front of the plate next to the trout's throat cavity.
   e. Nap the trout and green beans with the pine nut butter sauce.
   f. Make a bouquet of the herb sprigs and stick it upright next to the tomato, covering the trout's cavity.

ENTREES

COMPONENT RECIPE
MOUNTAIN HERB BUTTER

yield: 4 Tbsp.

production		costing only
2 tsp.	minced chives	1/16 bunch a.p.
1 tsp.	minced thyme leaves	1/20 bunch a.p.
1 tsp.	minced sage	1/20 bunch a.p.
3 Tbsp.	room-temperature butter	1 1/2 oz.
tt	kosher salt	1/16 oz.
tt	fine-ground white pepper	1/16 oz.

preparation:
1. Mix together all ingredients.
2. Taste and correct the seasoning.

holding: refrigerate in a freshly sanitized, covered container up to 5 days; freeze up to 1 month

COMPONENT RECIPE
BLACK QUINOA

yield: 6 c.

production		costing only
1 1/4 c.	black quinoa	3 1/4 oz.
1 Tbsp.	butter	1/2 oz.
2 Tbsp.	minced shallot	1 oz. a.p.
1 3/4 c.	water	n/c
tt	kosher salt	1/4 oz.

preparation:
1. Preheat an oven to 400°F.
2. Rinse the quinoa:
   a. Place the quinoa in a large, fine-mesh strainer set across the top of a deep bowl or saucepan.
   b. Place the quinoa under a gentle stream of cold water and rinse it, allowing the water to overflow without washing away the grains, about 5 minutes.
   c. Drain and shake off any excess water.
3. Cook the quinoa:
   a. Heat the butter in a 1 1/2-qt. saucepan with a heatproof handle. Add the shallot and sauté until soft.
   b. Add the water and season it with salt.
   c. Bring the water just to the boil, stir in the quinoa, and cover the pot.
   d. Adjust the heat to medium and simmer briskly about 15 minutes, until the liquid absorbs.
   e. Transfer the saucepan to the oven and bake about 10 minutes, until the quinoa is al dente in texture and the germ sprout has separated slightly from the kernel, appearing as a C shape curled around the kernel's center.

holding: open-pan cool and refrigerate in a freshly sanitized, covered container up to 3 days

RECIPE VARIATION
Replace the black quinoa with white quinoa cooked to the producer's specifications.

Poached Montana Whitefish

with Crawfish Tails in Buttermilk Velouté with Steamed Mountain Rose Potatoes and Fresh Peas

yield: 1 (7-oz.) entrée serving plus accompaniments
(multiply × 4 for classroom turnout; adjust equipment sizes accordingly)

MASTER RECIPE

production		costing only
1	5-oz. Montana whitefish fillet, skinned, pinned, and trimmed	6 oz. a.p.
1	cooked whole crawfish for garnish	approx. 1 oz.
as needed	Court Bouillon, simmering in a small braising pan or deep sauté pan	% of recipe
1 1/4 c.	fresh peas	1 1/4 lb. a.p.
1/2 c.	water	n/c
1 Tbsp.	butter	1/2 oz.
tt	kosher salt	1/16 oz.
3 to 5 pc.	Mountain Rose or other red-fleshed potatoes, steamed	4 oz.
1 c.	Buttermilk Velouté for Fish	1/4 recipe
2 oz.	cooked crawfish tails	2 oz. a.p.
1 tsp.	minced tarragon leaves	1/40 bunch a.p.
1 sprig	fresh tarragon	1/12 bunch a.p.

service turnout:

1. Submerge the whitefish and whole crawfish in the simmering Court Bouillon. Poach 6 to 8 minutes, until the fish is just done.
2. Cook the peas:
   a. Place the peas in an 8" sauté pan with the water, butter, and salt. Cover the pan and simmer briskly until the peas are just tender.
   b. Uncover and reduce the cooking liquid to a glaze.
3. Heat the potatoes in a microwave oven or steamer. Season them with salt.
4. Finish the sauce:
   a. Ladle the Buttermilk Velouté for Fish into an 8" sauté pan and add the crawfish tails.
   b. Heat the velouté, adding a little water if necessary to achieve a nappé consistency.
5. Plate the dish:
   a. Place the potatoes on the back center of a hot 12" plate.
   b. Blot the fish dry and prop it against the potatoes on the front of the plate.
   c. Mix the tarragon leaves into the peas and spoon them on both sides of the potatoes.
   d. Nap the velouté over the potatoes and fish, arranging the crawfish tails on top of the fish.
   e. Stick the tarragon sprig upright between the fish and potatoes, slightly to the right.
   f. Place the whole crawfish on the edge of the fish near the sprig.

COMPONENT RECIPE
BUTTERMILK VELOUTÉ FOR FISH

yield: 1 qt.

production		costing only
6 Tbsp.	butter	3 oz.
2 Tbsp.	minced shallot	1 oz. a.p.
4 Tbsp.	flour	2/3 oz.
5 c.	hot Fish Stock	5/16 recipe
tt	kosher salt	1/16 oz.
1 c.	buttermilk	8 fl. oz.
tt	fine-ground white pepper	1/16 oz.

preparation:
1. Melt the butter in a heavy 2 1/2-qt. saucepan.
2. Add the shallot and sauté until soft.
3. Add the flour and make a blond roux. Remove from heat.
4. Whisk in the Fish Stock to achieve a smooth consistency.
5. Season lightly with salt and simmer briskly about 30 minutes to result in about 3 c. thick sauce.
6. Thin the sauce to a nappé consistency with the buttermilk and return to the simmer.
7. Season with salt and white pepper.

holding: open-pan cool and immediately refrigerate in a freshly sanitized, covered container up to 4 days; upon reheating, strain to remove lumps and then thin the consistency as necessary

---

RECIPE VARIATIONS

Poached Steelhead Trout with Crawfish Tails in Buttermilk Velouté with Steamed Mountain Rose Potatoes and Fresh Peas
Replace the Montana whitefish fillet with steelhead trout fillet.

Poached Montana Whitefish with Whitefish Caviar in Dilled Butter Sauce with Steamed New Potatoes and Fresh Peas
Omit the crawfish. Replace the Mountain Rose potatoes with small Red Bliss potatoes. Replace the Buttermilk Velouté for Fish with a lemon butter sauce flavored with minced dill. Replace the tarragon sprig with a dill sprig. Just before serving, spoon 1 oz. Montana whitefish caviar over the fish.

Basque Chicken and Sausage in Spicy Tomato Sauce

over Pan-Steamed Rice
with Three-Pepper Medley

yield: 1 (10-oz. bone-in) entrée serving plus accompaniments
(multiply × 4 for classroom turnout; adjust equipment sizes
accordingly)

MASTER RECIPE

production		costing only
1 serving	Basque Chicken and Sausage, plus sauce	1/4 recipe
as needed	water, in squeeze bottle	n/c
1 Tbsp.	olive oil	1/2 fl. oz.
2 oz.	1/4"-sliced red bell pepper	3 oz. a.p.
2 oz.	1/4"-sliced green bell pepper	3 oz. a.p.
2 oz.	1/4"-sliced yellow bell pepper	3 oz. a.p.
tt	kosher salt	1/16 oz.
1 1/2 c.	Pan-Steamed Rice, hot in steam table	1/4 recipe
1 Tbsp.	butter	1/2 oz.
1 Tbsp.	chopped flat-leaf parsley	1/40 bunch a.p.

service turnout:

1. Finish the dish:
   a. Place the Basque Chicken and Sausage with its sauce in a 10" sauté pan, cover, and heat, adding a little water if necessary.
   b. Heat a 10" sauté pan, heat the oil, and sauté the bell peppers until crisp-tender. Season with salt.
2. Plate the dish:
   a. Mound a bed of Pan-Steamed Rice slightly left center of a hot 12" plate and make a well in the center.
   b. Mound the bell pepper medley in the back of the well.
   c. Place the chicken leg in the well, presentation side up, with the knuckle end upright at 2 o'clock or 10 o'clock.
   d. Fan the sausage slices in front of the chicken leg.
   e. Work the butter into the sauce and pour it over the chicken.
   f. Sprinkle the chicken with chopped parsley.

COMPONENT RECIPE

BASQUE CHICKEN AND SAUSAGE

yield: 4 (8-oz.) bone-in chicken legs plus 12 (1/2-oz.) sausage slices

production		costing only
4	10-oz. chicken legs	2 1/2 lb.
tt	kosher salt	1/16 oz.
tt	fresh-ground black pepper	1/16 oz.
1/2 tsp.	dried thyme	1/16 oz.
1/2 tsp.	dried oregano	1/16 oz.
10 oz.	Spanish *longaniza* or *chorizo** sausage, in one piece	10 oz.
2 Tbsp.	light olive oil	1 fl. oz.
1 1/4 c.	fine-chopped yellow onion	6 oz. a.p.
1/4 c.	fine-diced green bell pepper	2 oz. a.p.
2 Tbsp.	chopped long green Italian chile	1/2 oz. a.p.
1 Tbsp.	minced garlic	1/3 oz. a.p.
3 Tbsp.	flour	1 oz.
2 tsp.	Spanish paprika	1/8 oz.
1/2 c.	red wine	4 fl. oz.
1 qt.	vine-ripe tomato concassée	2 1/2 lb. a.p.
3 c.	Poultry Stock	3/16 recipe
1/2 tsp.	crumbled saffron threads	0.01 oz. or 0.35 g

preparation:

1. Fabricate the chicken:
   a. Use a meat cleaver or the heel of a heavy chef's knife to chop off the knuckle of each chicken leg. Make a clean cut and remove any bone fragments.
   b. Skin the chicken legs and remove any excess fat.
   c. Season the chicken with salt, pepper, thyme, and oregano.
2. Heat a 12" sauté pan over medium heat, heat the oil, and brown the sausage on all sides. Remove.
3. Add the chicken legs and brown them on both sides. Remove.
4. Make the sauce:
   a. Add the onion, green bell pepper, and chile to the fat in the pan. Sauté about 1 minute, until soft.
   b. Stir in the garlic, flour, and paprika and cook to a blond roux.
   c. Add the wine and tomato, stir well, and cook about 2 minutes, until the tomato is almost dry.
   d. Add the Poultry Stock, saffron, and a little salt. Bring to the simmer.
5. Add the chicken to the pan, cover, and braise about 10 minutes.
6. Slice the sausage on the diagonal into 12 pieces.
7. Turn the chicken legs over and add the sausage slices to the pan. Cover and simmer about 5 minutes longer, until the chicken is just done.
8. If necessary, adjust the sauce to a nappé consistency: Thin it with water or stock, or remove the chicken and sausage and reduce it.
9. Correct the salt.
10. If preparing ahead of time, portion as follows: 1 chicken leg, 3 sausage slices, and 1 c. sauce per serving.

holding: open-pan cool and store the chicken and sausage refrigerated in the sauce in a freshly sanitized, covered container up to 5 days

*Do not use Mexican chorizo sausage. If necessary, substitute Portuguese linguiça or mild Italian sausage.

RECIPE VARIATION

Basque-Style Lamb in Spicy Tomato Sauce over Pan-Steamed Rice with Three-Pepper Medley

Replace the chicken with 2 lb. lamb shoulder, trimmed and cut into 1 1/2" cubes. Omit the sausage. Increase the cooking time to about 40 minutes.

Shepherd's Pie
with Pine Nut Romesco Sauce and Julienne Vegetables

yield: 1 (8-oz.) entrée serving plus accompaniments (multiply × 4 for classroom turnout; adjust equipment sizes accordingly)

MASTER RECIPE

production		costing only
1 Tbsp.	melted butter	1/2 oz.
1	Shepherd's Pie	1/4 recipe
tt	Spanish paprika	1/16 oz.
1 Tbsp.	gold-color pure olive oil	1/2 fl. oz.
1 oz.	fine julienne carrot	1 1/4 oz. a.p.
1 oz.	julienne red bell pepper	1 1/2 oz. a.p.
1 oz.	slivered sweet onion	1 1/2 oz. a.p.
1 oz.	seeded, julienne zucchini	2 oz. a.p.
1 oz.	seeded, julienne yellow summer squash	2 oz. a.p.
1 oz.	julienne blanched and refreshed green beans	1 1/4 oz. a.p.
tt	kosher salt	1/16 oz.
tt	fresh lemon juice	1/6 [90 ct.] lemon
1/4 c.	water, in squeeze bottle	n/c
2 Tbsp.	butter	1 oz.
1/2 c.	Pine Nut Romesco Sauce, in squeeze bottle	1/4 recipe
1 sprig	fresh thyme	1/16 bunch a.p.
1 sprig	fresh sage	1/16 bunch a.p.
1 sprig	flat-leaf parsley	1/20 bunch a.p.

service turnout:

1. Finish the Shepherd's Pie:
   a. Brush the center of a sizzle pan with a little melted butter and place the pie on it.
   b. Brush the mashed potato topping with the remaining butter.
   c. Dust the topping with paprika.
   d. Place the sizzle pan in the top of a 400°F oven and bake about 8 minutes, until the pie is heated through and its topping is golden brown.
2. Sauté the vegetables:
   a. Heat a 10" sauté pan, heat the oil, and add the julienne vegetables in the order listed.
   b. Sauté, tossing constantly, a few seconds only until the vegetables are crisp-tender in texture and heated through.
   c. Season the vegetables with salt and lemon juice.
   d. Add a squeeze of water, remove from the heat, and work in the butter to form an emulsion. Hold warm.
3. Plate the dish:
   a. Place the shepherd's pie in the center of a hot 12" plate.
   b. Run a thin-bladed knife around the inside of the entremet ring to loosen it, then lift off the ring.
   c. Arrange the julienne vegetables in the plate well around the pie.
   d. Squeeze Pine Nut Romesco Sauce around the edge of the plate well.
   e. Form a bouquet with the herb sprigs and stick it upright out of the back right of the pie's topping.

ENTREES

528

COMPONENT RECIPE

SHEPHERD'S PIES

yield: 4 (8-oz.) pies

production		costing only
2 oz.	fresh wild-type mushrooms of choice, cleaned	2 oz.
1 Tbsp.	gold-color pure olive oil	1/2 fl. oz.
1 Tbsp.	butter	1/2 oz.
tt	kosher salt	1/16 oz.
tt	fresh lemon juice	1/8 [90 ct.] lemon
1 lb.	ground lamb (85% lean)	1 lb.
1/2 c.	minced yellow onion	2 1/2 oz. a.p.
1 tsp.	minced garlic	1/9 oz. a.p.
1/2 c.	fresh bread crumbs	2 oz. a.p.
2 tsp.	minced flat-leaf parsley	1/16 bunch a.p.
1 tsp.	minced fresh sage	1/16 bunch a.p.
1 tsp.	minced fresh thyme leaves	1/16 bunch a.p.
2 tsp.	tomato paste	1/3 fl. oz.
dash	Worcestershire sauce	1/3 fl. oz.
tt	fresh-ground black pepper	1/16 oz.
2	eggs, beaten	2 each or 4 fl. oz.
3 c.	room-temperature Classic Mashed Potatoes (reduce the amount of half-and-half by about 3 fl. oz.)	1/2 recipe

preparation:

1. Mise en place:
   a. Preheat an oven to 375°F.
   b. Place pan liner on a half-sheet tray and place 4 (2 1/2" diameter × 2" tall) entremet rings on it, spaced well apart.
   c. Cut out 4 (2 1/2") circles of pan liner and 4 (4") circles of foil.
   d. Fill a small sauté pan with water and maintain it at a simmer.
2. Prepare the lamb forcemeat:
   a. Chop the mushrooms fine.
   b. Heat an 8" sauté pan, heat the oil and butter, and sauté the mushrooms over high heat until almost dry. Season with salt and lemon juice. Cool to room temperature.
   c. Mix together the lamb, cooled mushrooms, onion, garlic, bread crumbs, parsley, sage, thyme, tomato paste, Worcestershire sauce, salt, and pepper. Mix in half of the eggs.
   d. Slap the meat against the sides of the bowl several times to compact it and remove air pockets.
   e. Poach a patty of forcemeat in the simmering water and taste for seasoning.
   f. If necessary, correct the seasoning and repeat step 2d.
3. Assemble the pies:
   a. Pack the lamb mixture into the rings, mounding the tops slightly.
   b. Place a pan liner circle on top of each ring.
   c. Cover each ring with a foil circle and fold the circles down around the sides of the rings.
4. Bake the pies in the center of the oven about 30 minutes, to an internal temperature of 145°F.
5. Cool the pies:
   a. Place the sheet tray of pies on a cooling rack.
   b. Place another sheet tray on top, and then weight the tray with heavy objects.
   c. Cool about 1 hour to room temperature.
6. Add the topping:
   a. Unwrap the pies.
   b. Run a flexible knife between the meat and the entremet rings and wipe the edges.
   c. Brush the tops with the remaining beaten eggs.
   d. Scoop the Classic Mashed Potatoes into a pastry bag fitted with a large star tip.
   e. Pipe 1/2 c. potatoes onto each pie in a star pattern, covering the entire top surface of each pie.
   f. Place the tray of pies in the refrigerator and chill about 30 minutes, until the potatoes are set.

holding: wrap in a loose covering of plastic film and refrigerate up to 4 days

COMPONENT RECIPE
PINE NUT ROMESCO SAUCE

yield: 2 c.

production		costing only
1	red bell pepper	7 oz. a.p.
1	serrano or jalapeño chile	1/4 oz. a.p.
4 Tbsp.	gold-color pure olive oil	2 fl. oz.
1/2 c.	pine nuts	3/4 oz.
3 cloves	peeled, gently crushed garlic	1 oz. a.p.
1/4 c.	fresh bread crumbs	2 oz. a.p.
1 c.	vine-ripe tomato concassée	12 oz.
4 Tbsp.	extra virgin olive oil	2 fl. oz.
tt	kosher salt	1/16 oz.
tt	fresh-ground black pepper	1/16 oz.
tt	red wine vinegar	1/4 oz.

preparation:
1. Roast the red bell pepper and chile directly over the flame of a gas range or gas grill. Immediately wrap in aluminum foil and allow the pepper and chile to steam in their own heat until cool.
2. Brown the solid ingredients:
   a. In an 8" sauté pan, warm the pure olive oil over low heat and add the pine nuts. Cook, stirring, about 2 minutes, until the pine nuts become golden brown. Use a perforated spoon to remove the pine nuts to a blender.
   b. Add the garlic to the pan and cook about 3 minutes, occasionally pressing on the cloves to flatten them, until golden on both sides. Use the perforated spoon to remove the garlic to the blender.
   c. Add the bread crumbs and cook, tossing, until golden. Scrape the bread and any remaining oil into the blender.
3. Scrape the blackened skin from the pepper and chile. (Do not wash.) Remove the seeds and veins, then chop the pepper and chile coarse. Add to the blender.
4. Add the tomato to the blender.
5. Blend the mixture to a coarse purée.
6. Remove the plug from the blender lid and, on high speed, add the extra virgin olive oil through the feed tube.
7. Season the purée with salt, pepper, and vinegar.

holding: refrigerate in a freshly sanitized squeeze bottle or covered container up to 3 days

---

RECIPE VARIATIONS

Cottage Pie with Brown Gravy and Heartland Vegetable Medley
Replace the ground lamb with ground beef. Replace the olive oil with corn oil or butter. Omit the mushrooms from the forcemeat. Replace the tomato paste with 1 Tbsp. ketchup. Omit the julienne vegetables and Pine Nut Romesco Sauce. Accompany each serving with 3/4 c. brown gravy and 1 c. mixed vegetables, including corn kernels, baby lima beans, cut green beans, diced carrot, and diced turnip or rutabaga.

Cajun Cottage Pie with Spicy Tomato Sauce
Prepare Cottage Pie, but additionally season the forcemeat with cayenne pepper, white pepper, and bottled hot sauce. Serve with julienne vegetables as in Shepherd's Pie and accompany with 3/4 c. fresh tomato sauce seasoned with brown sugar and cayenne pepper.

ENTREES

Medallions of Venison in Chokecherry Demi-Glace

with Garlic Mashed Potatoes, Root Vegetables, and Wild Mushroom Ragout

yield: 1 (6-oz.) entrée serving plus accompaniments
(multiply × 4 for classroom turnout; adjust equipment sizes accordingly)

MASTER RECIPE

production		costing only
as needed	pan coating spray	% of container
1 c.	Garlic Mashed Potatoes	1/5 recipe
1	Mushroom Cup	1/4 recipe
3 Tbsp.	clarified butter, in squeeze bottle	2 oz. a.p.
tt	kosher salt	1/16 oz.
1 1/2 oz.	Parisienne carrot, blanched and refreshed	4 oz. a.p.
1 1/2 oz.	Parisienne rutabaga, blanched and refreshed	5 oz. a.p.
1 oz.	peeled pearl onions, blanched and refreshed	1 1/2 oz. a.p.
1 to 2 oz.	assorted fresh wild-type mushrooms, cleaned and trimmed to even sizes	1 to 2 oz. a.p.
1 Tbsp.	minced shallot	1/4 oz. a.p.
1 tsp.	minced garlic	1/9 oz. a.p.
1 Tbsp.	red Port wine	1/2 fl. oz.
tt	fresh lemon juice	1/8 [90 ct.] lemon
2 Tbsp.	Demi-Glace	1/32 recipe
1/4 c.	heavy cream	2 fl. oz.
pinch	minced fresh thyme leaves	1/20 bunch a.p.
4	1 1/2-oz. farm-raised venison loin or rib medallions	6 oz. a.p.
1 Tbsp.	minced shallot	1/2 oz. a.p.
3 Tbsp.	white wine	1 1/2 fl. oz.
3/4 c.	Demi-Glace	3/4 recipe
3 Tbsp.	chokecherry syrup	1 1/2 fl. oz.
tt	fine-ground white pepper	1/16 oz.
1 sprig	fresh thyme	1/20 bunch a.p.
1 sprig	fresh sage	1/10 bunch a.p.
1 sprig	flat-leaf parsley	1/20 bunch a.p.

service turnout:

1. Finish the accompaniments:
   a. Spray a sizzle pan and the inside of a (2 1/2" diameter × 2" tall) entremet ring with pan coating.
   b. Place the entremet ring on the sizzle pan and pack it full of Garlic Mashed Potatoes.
   c. Drizzle the Mushroom Cup inside and out with a little of the clarified butter, season it with salt, and place it on the sizzle pan, hollow side up.
   d. Bake the potatoes and the mushroom cup in a 400°F oven about 10 minutes, until heated through.
   e. Heat the carrot, rutabaga, and pearl onions in a steamer or microwave oven.
2. Prepare the Wild Mushroom Ragout:
   a. Heat an 8" sauté pan, heat 1 Tbsp. clarified butter, and sear the mushrooms with a pinch of salt until they wilt slightly.
   b. Add 1 Tbsp. shallot and the garlic, Port, lemon juice, 2 Tbsp. Demi-Glace, cream, and thyme.
   c. Reduce to the sauce to a nappé consistency.
3. Prepare the venison and its sauce:
   a. Heat an 8" sauté pan until very hot, add 1 Tbsp. clarified butter, and sear the venison medallions until rare. Remove and hold warm.
   b. Add 1 Tbsp. shallot and the white wine, 3/4 c. demi-glace, and chokecherry syrup to the pan, bring to the simmer, and season with salt and white pepper.
4. Plate the dish:
   a. Using an offset spatula, lift the mashed potato ring off the sizzle pan and place it on the back center of a hot 12" plate.
   b. Run a paring knife around the inside of the entremet ring and remove it.
   c. Pour any juices accumulated in the mushroom cup into the venison sauce, then place the cup on top of the mashed potatoes.
   d. Fill the cup with mushroom ragout.
   e. Fan the venison medallions across the front center of the plate, propped against the mashed potatoes. Scrape any accumulated venison juices into the venison sauce.
   f. Arrange the carrot, rutabaga, and onions around the plate well.
   g. If necessary, adjust the consistency of the sauce with water or by reduction, and then nap the venison with the sauce.
   h. Make a bouquet of the herb sprigs and stick the bouquet upright out of the back of the mashed potatoes.

COMPONENT RECIPE
MUSHROOM CUPS

yield: 4 cups

production		costing only
4	large (3 1/2"-diameter) white mushrooms	1/2 lb. a.p.
2 Tbsp.	clarified butter	1 1/4 oz. a.p.
tt	kosher salt	1/16 oz.

preparation:
1. Remove the stems from the mushrooms and reserve for another use.
2. Wipe the mushrooms clean with a damp paper towel.
3. Heat an 8" sauté pan until very hot, heat the clarified butter, and quickly sear the bottoms of the mushrooms until golden brown.
4. Immediately transfer the mushrooms to a sheet tray or sizzle plate, hollow side down, and refrigerate until cold.

holding: refrigerate in a freshly sanitized, covered container with pan liner between layers up to 3 days

---

RECIPE VARIATION

Pan-Seared Bear Chop in Cranberry Demi-Glace with Garlic Mashed Potatoes, Root Vegetables, and Wild Mushroom Ragout
Replace the venison with an 8-oz. rib chop of bear. Replace the *
chokecherry syrup with cranberry juice concentrate.

Huckleberry Pie
with Whipped Cream

yield: 1 dessert serving
(multiply × 4 for classroom turnout)

MASTER RECIPE

production		costing only
1 slice	Huckleberry Pie	1/8 recipe
1/4 c.	Sweetened Whipped Cream, in a pastry bag fitted with a star tip	1/8 recipe
1 sprig	fresh mint	1/12 bunch a.p.

service turnout:
1. Plate the dish:
   a. Place the Huckleberry Pie slice on the left center of a cool 10" plate.
   b. Pipe a rosette of Sweetened Whipped Cream to the right of the pie.
   c. Stick the mint sprig upright between the whipped cream and the pie.

COMPONENT RECIPE
HUCKLEBERRY PIE

yield: 1 (9") pie

production		costing only
as needed	flour	1 oz.
18 oz.	American Flaky Pastry, divided into a 10-oz. disc and an 8-oz. disc, refrigerated at least 20 minutes	1 1/2 recipe
1 c.	sugar	8 oz.
1 tsp.	ground cinnamon	1/8 oz.
3 Tbsp.	cornstarch	1 oz.
3 Tbsp.	flour	1 oz.
5 c.	fresh or frozen huckleberries	2 1/2 pt. or 1 lb.
1/2 c.	unseasoned dried bread crumbs	1 oz.
4 Tbsp.	cold butter, 1/4" dice	2 oz.
1 Tbsp.	sugar	1/2 oz.

preparation:
1. Make up the pie shell and lid:
   a. Flour the work surface and a rolling pin.
   b. Roll out the larger American Flaky Pastry disc into a circle a little thicker than 1/8", and fit it into a 9" × 1 1/2" pie pan.
   c. Trim the dough edges to an even 3/4" overhang.
   d. Roll out the smaller disc into a 9 1/2" circle a little thicker than 1/8".
   e. Place the dough circle and pie shell on a sheet tray and refrigerate at least 20 minutes.
2. Preheat an oven to 400°F.
3. Prepare the filling:
   a. In a large bowl, mix together 1 c. sugar with the cinnamon, cornstarch, and 3 Tbsp. flour.
   b. Toss the huckleberries with the sugar mixture.
4. Assemble the pie:
   a. Scatter the bread crumbs into the bottom of the pie shell.
   b. Add the huckleberries and press gently to pack them in.
   c. Distribute the diced butter evenly on top of the huckleberry filling.
   d. Brush the edge of the pastry shell very lightly with water.
   e. Fit the dough circle on top and trim it even with the edge of the bottom shell.
   f. Turn under the edges of the pie shell dough to create a roll of dough resting on the lip of the pan. Flute decoratively.
   g. Cut six vents in the top of the crust in a spoke pattern.
   h. Sprinkle the top of the pie with 1 Tbsp. sugar.
5. Place the pie on a half-sheet tray with pan liner and bake 30 to 40 minutes, until the fruit is cooked and the pastry is golden brown.
6. Cool to room temperature on a rack.

holding: best served the same day; hold at room temperature covered with a kitchen towel up to 6 hours

---

RECIPE VARIATION
Blueberry Pie with Whipped Cream
Replace the huckleberries with wild or domestic blueberries.

Basque Tostada
with Brandied Peach Half

yield: 1 dessert serving
(multiply × 4 for classroom turnout; adjust equipment sizes accordingly)

🕐 Accompaniment requires 24 hours advance preparation.

MASTER RECIPE

production		costing only
5 Tbsp.	clarified butter	3 oz. a.p.
1	Basque Tostada	1/4 recipe
1 tsp.	Cinnamon Sugar	1/6 recipe
2 Tbsp.	Sweetened Whipped Cream, in a pastry bag fitted with a small star tip	1/16 recipe
1	Brandied Peach Half	1/4 recipe
1 sprig	fresh mint	1/12 bunch a.p.

service turnout:

1. Fry the Basque Tostada:
   a. Heat an 8" nonstick sauté pan over medium heat, then heat the clarified butter.
   b. Use a wide, flexible spatula to place the tostada in the pan. Reduce the heat and fry it about 1 minute, until the crumbs are deep golden brown.
   c. Turn the tostada over and continue to fry about 1 minute more, until the new bottom side is deep golden brown.
2. Plate the dish:
   a. Lift the tostada out of the pan onto the left center of a room-temperature 10" plate.
   b. Sprinkle with Cinnamon Sugar.
   c. Pipe a rosette of Sweetened Whipped Cream next to the tostada.
   d. Prop the Brandied Peach Half against the whipped cream.
   e. Stick the mint sprig upright behind the peach.

COMPONENT RECIPE
BASQUE TOSTADAS

yield: 4 dessert servings plus scraps

🕐 Requires 4 to 5 hours advance preparation.

production		costing only
as needed	pan coating spray	% of container
2 c.	half-and-half	16 fl. oz.
1/2 c.	sugar	4 oz.
3	egg yolks	3 each or 2 oz.
1/4 c.	sugar	2 oz.
1/4 c.	half-and-half	2 fl. oz.
1/3 c.	clarified butter	3 1/4 oz. a.p.
1/3 c.	flour	1 3/4 oz.
pinch	fine salt	1/16 oz.
2 tsp.	pure vanilla extract	1/3 fl. oz.
1/4 c.	flour	1 1/3 oz.
1	egg, beaten	1 each or 2 oz.
1 1/2 c.	fine fresh bread crumbs	5 oz. a.p.

preparation:
1. Mise en place:
   a. Cut out 2 (9") circles of pan liner.
   b. Place one circle in a 9" cake pan.
   c. Spray the cake pan with pan coating.
   d. Spray one side of the remaining pan liner circle with pan coating.
   e. Prepare an ice bain-marie placed near the stove.
2. Cook the custard:
   a. Combine 2 c. half-and-half and 1/2 c. sugar in a 1-qt. saucepan. Heat gently, stirring occasionally, until the half-and-half is hot and the sugar is dissolved.
   b. In a 6 qt. heavy-duty stainless bowl, whisk together the egg yolks and 1/4 c. sugar until very light and fluffy. Whisk in 1/4 c. half-and-half.
   c. Combine 1/3 c. clarified butter and 1/3 c. flour in a 1 1/2-qt. saucepan. Cook, stirring constantly, about 1 minute to make a white roux.
   d. Whisk the hot half-and-half mixture into the roux, add a pinch of salt, and then stir over medium heat about 5 minutes to make a thick cream sauce.
   e. Whisk the hot cream sauce into the egg yolk mixture.
   f. Place the bowl directly over low heat and whisk constantly about 3 minutes, until the mixture thickens even more and the raw egg yolk taste is gone.
   g. Move the bowl to the ice bain-marie, add the vanilla, and continue to whisk until the custard is cool and very thick.
3. Form the custard:
   a. Scrape the custard into the lined cake pan.
   b. Use a small offset spatula to smooth it into the pan.
   c. Tap the pan on the work surface to force out any air pockets.
   d. Place the remaining pan liner circle on top of the custard, coating side down.
   e. Refrigerate the custard at least 2 hours until set.

4. Fabricate the tostadas:
   a. Run a flexible knife around the edge of the custard to loosen it.
   b. Turn the custard out of its pan onto a work surface.
   c. Peel off the top layer of pan liner.
   d. Trim the custard disk into a square, and then cut this large square into 4 even-size smaller squares. Be careful not to cut the pan liner underneath.
5. Bread the tostadas:
   a. Lift a custard square off the paper liner, dredge it in flour, dip it in beaten egg, and then coat it thoroughly with bread crumbs.
   b. Place on a cooling rack set over a sheet tray.
   c. Repeat with the remaining squares, making a total of 4 tostadas. (You may bread the scraps and use them to practice frying.)
   d. Refrigerate, uncovered, at least 1 hour.

holding: refrigerate on the rack covered by a dish towel in a dedicated dessert refrigerator up to 48 hours

COMPONENT RECIPE
BRANDIED PEACH HALVES

yield: 4 peach halves

🕐 Requires 24 hours advance preparation.

production		costing only
2	small, slightly underripe freestone peaches	8 oz. a.p.
1 c.	sugar	8 oz.
3"	cinnamon stick	1/8 oz.
2	cloves	1/16 oz.
1 c.	water	n/c
4 Tbsp.	brandy	2 fl. oz.
tt	fresh lemon juice	1/4 [90 ct.] lemon

preparation:
1. Fabricate the peaches:
   a. Blanch the peaches in boiling water 15 to 20 seconds and check one to ascertain that the skin has loosened.
   b. When the skin slips off easily, immediately refresh the peaches in ice water.
   c. Remove the peach skins.
   d. Cut each peach into 2 even halves.
   e. Remove and discard the pits.
2. Poach the peaches:
   a. Place the sugar, cinnamon stick, cloves, and water in a 3/4-qt. nonreactive saucepan and bring to the boil.
   b. Add the peaches and simmer about 5 minutes, until the peaches are just tender when tested with a sharp knife.
   c. Transfer the peaches and syrup to a freshly sanitized container just large enough to hold them completely submerged.
   d. Cool to room temperature.
   e. Mix in the brandy and balance the flavor with lemon juice.
3. Cover and refrigerate the peaches at least 24 hours.

holding: refrigerate up to 2 weeks

☐ TABLE 11.2 ROCKY MOUNTAINS AND GREAT BASIN REGIONAL INGREDIENTS

Settlers of the Rocky Mountain and Great Basin region shared many of the experiences of Western ranchers; they employed many of the same techniques and ingredients, and their cuisines are closely related. In addition to the ingredients listed in Table 11.2, please review Ingredients of the Western and Central Ranchlands, p. 502.

ITEM	MARKET FORMS	USES	SEASONALITY	OTHER	STORAGE
SOURDOUGH STARTER	Refer to the companion website for more information.				
BLACK QUINOA (KEEN-wah)	Colorado black quinoa, a true American product, is sold by the pound at a regional markets and by mail order. White Mountain Farm is the primary Colorado producer.	Rinse thoroughly and cook in 2 parts salted water to 1 part black quinoa. Serve hot as a unique starchy side dish or use as a bed for stews and other saucy dishes. To make an unusual composed salad, toss cooled quinoa with crisp vegetables and vinaigrette dressing.	N/A	If black quinoa is unavailable, substitute white quinoa from South America. Use slightly less water.	Store at cool room temperature; freeze for extended storage.
IDAHO RUSSET POTATOES	Purchase Idaho russets from produce purveyors in 40-lb. cartons. Aged Idaho russets must be special-ordered.	Russet potatoes are best for dry method potato dishes. For superior baked potatoes and French fries, specify aged potatoes. Russets also make light, fluffy mashed potatoes.	Available year round.	For whole presentation, an 8 oz. potato yields a proper portion. Larger potatoes are useful for dishes in which they will be peeled and cut, as they require less labor.	Store uncut potatoes in a dark, cool area; do not refrigerate.
SPECIALTY POTATOES	Colorado's San Luis Valley produces colored, fingerling, and heirloom potatoes marketed nationwide. Purchase by the pound from specialty purveyors.	Serve specialty potatoes as a starchy side dish or use in potato salads. Many types may be served skin-on.	Available year round. Stock may run low in late spring and summer.	Types include: red bliss, Yukon gold, French fingerling, purple Peruvian, rose Finn, Mountain rose, ozette.	Store uncut potatoes in a dark, cool area; do not refrigerate.
PINE NUTS	See p. 354.				
WILD FRUIT SYRUPS, JAMS, AND JELLIES	These specialty products are available in small retail jars or bottles. Mail order from Internet sources. Supply and quality vary.	Jams and jellies are used as table spreads or for topping desserts and pancakes. Savory uses include glazing meats and adding to sauces.	N/A	Types include chokecherry syrup, buffaloberry jam, and huckleberry products.	Store unopened products in a cool, dark place; refrigerate after opening.
MONTANA WHITEFISH	Fresh and frozen whitefish fillets are available by the pound from selected Montana producers.	Prepare as any lean, white fish fillets.	Available year round.	Regional chefs often garnish whitefish fillets with golden whitefish caviar.	
GOLDEN WHITEFISH CAVIAR	Golden whitefish caviar is widely available from seafood purveyors as well as through mail-order sources. Packs include 1-oz., 4-oz., and 14-oz. jars.	Serve on toast rounds with lemon wedges as a featured appetizer. Use as a garnish for both hot and cold foods.	Available year round.	Wasabi flavored golden caviar is now available.	Store refrigerated until producer's expiration date. After opening use within two days.

☐ **TABLE 11.2 ROCKY MOUNTAINS AND GREAT BASIN REGIONAL INGREDIENTS** *(continued)*

ITEM	MARKET FORMS	USES	SEASONALITY	OTHER	STORAGE
FARM-RAISED RAINBOW TROUT	Frozen trout is usually sold boneless, both head-on and pan-ready, in 10- to 12-oz. sizes. Golden trout, a recently developed hybrid, has shiny golden skin and pale ivory flesh.	Sauté or pan-fry. May be stuffed and baked.	Available year round.		Store frozen until needed. Frozen trout thaw quickly.
COLORADO LAMB	Colorado lamb is widely available from meat purveyors. Popular restaurant cuts include "frenched" racks, rib and loin chops, leg steaks, and lamb shanks.	Tender cuts are typically roasted or grilled. Lamb shanks are braised.	Available year round; supply and price are best in spring and summer.	Colorado lambs are larger than Eastern lambs, giving them a high meat-to-bone ratio; their racks have particularly large eyes, yielding as much as 12 oz. clean meat per rack.	Refrigerate vacuum-packed cuts up to 1 month.
ROCKY MOUNTAIN OYSTERS OR LAMB FRIES	Skinned, trimmed, and frozen lamb testicles are sold by the pound by specialty meat purveyors.	The most popular preparation is breaded and deep-fried, accompanied by ketchup or hot sauce. Sautéed Rocky Mountain oysters are served in a cream sauce or demi-glace sauce.	Traditionally served in the spring, the frozen product is available year round.		Store frozen until needed. After thawing, use within 1 or 2 days.

■ □ ■ chapter twelve

Anglo-Asian California

the non-Hispanic cuisine of California

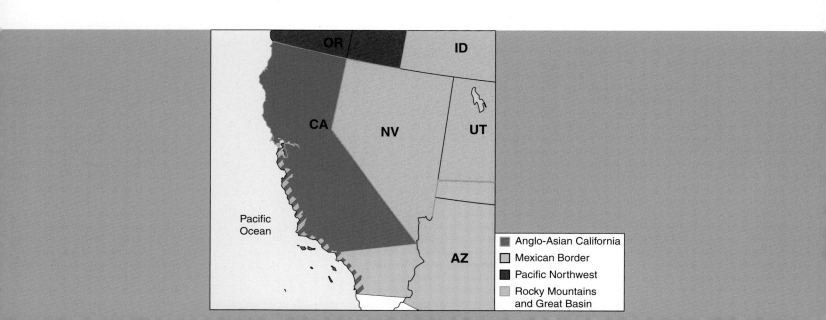

- Anglo-Asian California
- Mexican Border
- Pacific Northwest
- Rocky Mountains and Great Basin

CALIFORNIA CAPTURES AMERICA'S imagination as "The Golden State"—promised land for early pioneers, home to film stars and sun seekers, and domain of dot-com billionaires. Today California not only nourishes dreams but also feeds the nation, yielding a bounty of fine food products that drive its regional cuisine and sustain the rest of the country, enabling Americans to enjoy fresh produce all year long.

Living with the threat of earthquakes, wildfires, and mudslides, Californians are accustomed to flirting with disaster. Their risk-taking mentality also extends to food: California cooks are leaders in culinary innovation, creating new products, developing new ideas, and starting trends.

Today California is home to two major cooking styles. Mexican Border cuisine, explored in Chapter 7, is the legacy of California's Spanish first settlers and was refined by Mexican immigrants. However, California's international group of second settlers developed a separate cuisine. Americans from the East were called *Anglos*, meaning "English." These settlers brought New England, Mid-Atlantic, and Farmlands cuisines. Asian immigrants added new ingredients and a light, fresh touch. In recognition of this culinary blend, we coin the term "Anglo-Asian" to designate the non-Hispanic cuisine of California.

AFTER STUDYING THIS CHAPTER YOU SHOULD BE ABLE TO:

- describe the topography and climate of California (Factor 1) and explain how they affected the region's food production and cuisine
- explain why the contributions of California's first-settler group (Factor 3) rightfully belong to another American culinary region
- discuss the region's international second-settler group (Factor 4), identify the two main food cultures it comprises, and describe the culinary contributions of each
- list the major event that initiated the region's initial economic viability (Factor 5) and describe subsequent events that added to it
- describe traditional California cuisine and list its most important defining dishes
- describe contemporary California cuisine and list its primary elements
- discuss the history of Chinese-American cuisine and list its most important defining dishes
- identify and work with a variety of California ingredients and seasonings
- prepare authentic Anglo-Asian California cuisine dishes and Chinese-American dishes

APPETIZERS

Gilroy Garlic Soup with Sun-Dried Tomato–Black Olive Focaccia

Chilled Avocado Soup with Tobiko Caviar and Poppy Seed Lavash

Salad of Organic Baby Greens with Almond-Crusted Goat Cheese and Napa Valley Verjus Vinaigrette

Salad of Shaved Artichokes, Mushrooms, and Dry Jack Cheese with First-Press Olive Oil–Meyer Lemon Dressing

Classic Cobb Salad

Southeast Asian Spring Rolls with Sweet 'n' Hot Dipping Sauce

Wild Mushroom Risotto with Tricolor Tomato *Sugo Crudo*

Designer Pizzetta with Shredded Duck, Confit Tomatoes, and Mascarpone Cheese

Shrimp-Stuffed Artichoke with Creamy Red Bell Pepper Sauce

California Roll Sushi with Wasabi-Soy Dip

Dungeness Crab Louis in Avocado Half

Safe Caesar Salad

ENTRÉES

San Francisco Cioppino with North Beach Escarole Salad and Sourdough Roll

Tea-Smoked Ahi Tuna with Wasabi Mashed Potatoes and Braised Baby Bok Choy

Toor Dal Tofu Bundles in Red Curry Broth with Brown Rice and Steamed California Vegetables

Crisp-Fried Whole Petrale Sole for Two in Sweet 'n' Sour Sauce with Stir-Fry Chinese Vegetables and Pan-Steamed Rice

Chicken Chop Suey in Crispy Noodle Nest

Pan-Seared Breast of Petaluma Duck in Zinfandel Demi-Glace with Sautéed Flame Grapes, Roasted Garlic Flan, and Wilted Baby Spinach

Escalopes of Sonoma Lamb in Blush Wine–Rhubarb Cream Reduction with Rhubarb Compote, Potato "Risotto," and Four-Pea Medley

DESSERTS

Meyer Lemon Ice Cream with Pistachio Lace Cookie

Santa Rosa Plum Galette with Almond Custard Sauce

Blood Orange Tart with Marmalade Glaze and Dark Chocolate Drizzle

Green Tea Ice Cream with Fortune Cookie

Bittersweet Chocolate Mousse with Chocolate-Covered Strawberry

WEBSITE EXTRAS

Breakfasts   Sandwiches   Hors d'Oeuvres   Thanksgiving Menu

A SLICE OF THE PACIFIC RIM

Hundreds of millions of years ago, the geological activity that formed the earth's landmasses created the Pacific Ocean by sinking its giant basin and raising a circular border of land around it. This land border, comprising the west coasts of North and South America and the east coasts of Australia and Asia, is called the **Pacific Rim** (Figure 12.1).

The structure of Pacific Rim landmasses and the Pacific Ocean floor is seismically unstable. In many areas volcanoes remain active on land and underwater. In other places huge underground slabs of the earth's crust, called *tectonic plates*, occasionally shift, causing earthquakes. Pacific Rim landmasses

are also subject to localized activity such as erosion and the resulting redeposition of soil. All of these geological forces contributed to California's topography (Figure 12.2).

California accounts for more than 800 miles of the Pacific Rim. Its southern and central coastlines comprise both sand and pebble beaches; the northern coast becomes rocky in places. The state's coastal plain forms a narrow strip backed by two major mountain chains. California's Coastal Range stretches more than 450 miles from Santa Barbara in the south to the Klamath Mountains in the north. Running roughly parallel to it, the taller and wider Sierra Nevada mountain chain runs almost 300 miles from slightly north of Bakersfield in the south to just beyond Lake Tahoe in the north. Between these two major ranges lies the Central Valley, actually a series of long, narrow valleys separated by low ridges.

FIGURE 12.1

The Pacific Rim.

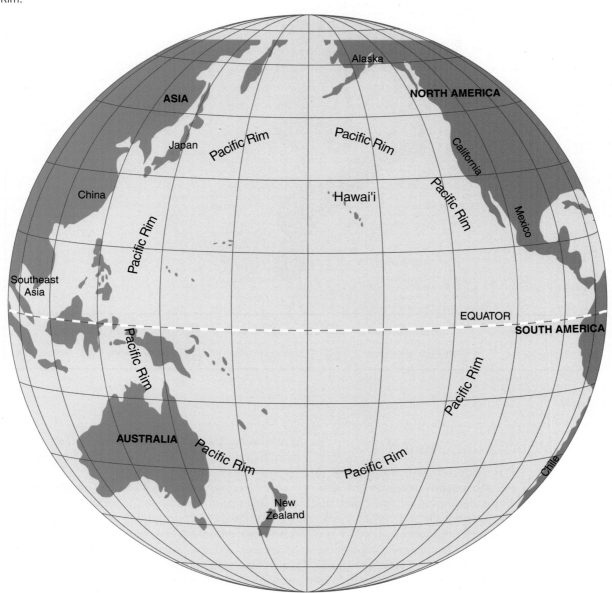

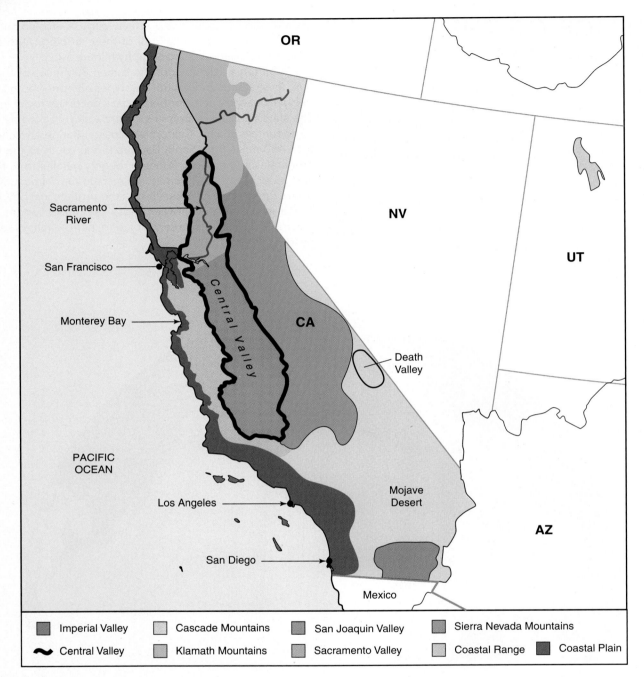

FIGURE 12.2
California Topography.

Wealth and Danger in the Ground

The wealth in California's soil and subsoil layers was integral to the state's early settlement and subsequent development. California's gold deposits and other underground minerals were the primary attraction for the region's historically and culinarily influential second-settler group. In addition, the topsoil of central and Northern California contains a wide variety of essential plant nutrient minerals. With the region's mild climate, modern irrigation technology, and rich soil, California would become an agricultural powerhouse. California's minerals spurred an unprecedented human migration to the region and played an enormous role in its history, culture, and food culture.

In addition to mineral wealth, geological movement has been an important factor in California's history and culture. California's Pacific Rim instability is manifested primarily in the form of earthquakes. The region is intercrossed by many *faults*, or seams in the earth's substrata that have been the sites of many modern seismic events (Figure 12.3). The region regularly experiences minor earthquakes and has suffered

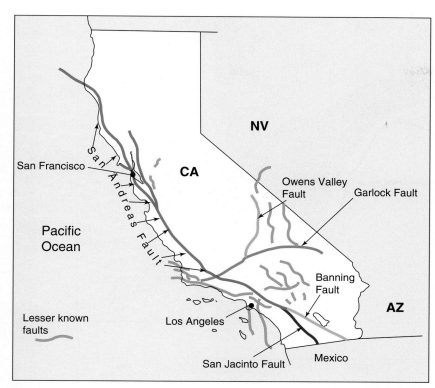

FIGURE 12.3
Locations of Seismic Activity in California.

several major ones, including the 1906 quake that caused the great San Francisco fire and the 1999 quake that did significant damage to the city's infrastructure.

Moreover, earthquakes such as these are not the worst that could happen. Part of the California mindset is the underlying knowledge that, sooner or later, there's going to be "a really big one." California life is underscored by the possibility that one day, much of California could split off the mainland and disappear into the Pacific Ocean.

Climatic Diversity

California has not one climate, but many. At 42 degrees N, the northernmost reaches of California are roughly on the same line as New York City, whereas at 32 degrees N, the Southern California town of Calexico shares the latitude of northern Florida. However, topographical factors are even more influential than latitude.

Based on altitude alone, California's combination of sea level coastal plain, foothills, elevated interior valleys, and mountaintops would be enough to give California wide-ranging temperatures. For example, at nearly 14,500 feet, the peak of Mt. Whitney in the Sierra Nevada is snow-covered year round. Completely land-locked and lying 282 feet below sea level, Death Valley's record high temperature is a scorching 134°F. However, in California temperatures are determined by more than even latitude and altitude combined. Because of its unique geographical position, Califor-

nia can be divided into four distinct climate areas and several microclimate areas, all of which directly affect agriculture and cuisine.

The Central and Northern Coasts

The climate of California's central and northern coasts is the result of Pacific water and air currents. The *California current* is a band of surface water 20 to 50 miles wide that forms along the Gulf of Alaska and flows south along the coast. The *jet stream*, or global air current, that affects California primarily flows west to east but can be deflected by seasonal atmospheric pressure patterns. From late spring though fall, strong northwesterly winds and the force of the California current push warmer surface waters south. The removal of surface water creates *upwelling*, the rising up of very cold waters that lie just above the ocean floor. Upwelling along the northern and central California coast is some of the most dramatic in the world, causing surface water temperatures to drop as much as 10°F. Upwelling water brings with it a rich variety of marine organisms that provide food for fish and shellfish. It also affects the air temperature along the coast; ocean breezes passing over cold surface water cool down significantly and lower the temperature of the land. As breezes pass over the cool water, they pick up moisture and hold it in the form of clouds until the hot midday sun evaporates it away. Because of these climatic phenomena, the central and Northern California coasts enjoy cool summers with foggy mornings and brilliantly sunny afternoons.

In winter, weather conditions reduce the amount of upwelling, and ocean water along California's coast remains relatively warm. As the jet stream moves air across the warm water, the air warms up, attracting moisture as it moves east. When the moisture-laden air eventually moves over land, it cools down and can no longer hold as much moisture. The result is precipitation ranging from dense fog to driving rain, in some areas up to 160 inches per year. However, winter along the California coast is rarely cold. The proximity of the warm Pacific Ocean typically keeps temperatures above 60°F, and frost is rare.

These warm, wet winters and cool summers are similar to those found in Italy and the south of France. Thus, California's central and northern coasts are said to have a **Mediterranean climate,** which makes the region ideal for cultivating many European food plants, and in particular for growing wine grapes (Figure 12.4).

California's Mountains

The climate of California's mountains ranges from temperate in the foothills to alpine on the mountaintops. Like the larger Rocky Mountains, the California Coastal Range stops rain clouds from

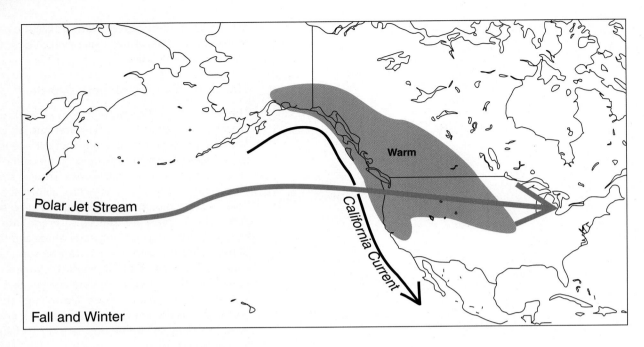

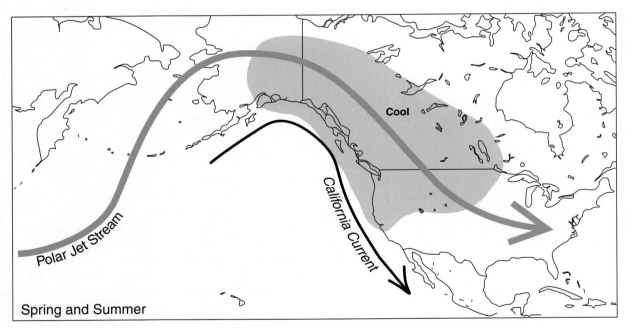

FIGURE 12.4
Air and Ocean Currents Creating California's Mediterranean Climate.

moving inland, creating a significant rain shadow (p. 304). Thus, western mountain slopes enjoy average annual rainfall of about 50 inches, whereas the eastern slopes are much drier. Initially settled by miners, today California's mountains are primarily used for recreation and are famous for ski resorts.

The Central Valley

Blocked from ocean winds and precipitation by the Coastal Range, California's Central Valley experiences hotter and drier weather than the coast. Lacking the moderating effects of Pacific up-

welling, the Central Valley has average summer high temperatures from 80°F to 90°F, with occasional winter lows in the 30s. Much of the Central Valley receives only 10 to 15 inches of rainfall per year and is technically considered high desert. This lack of moisture precluded much of the valley from agricultural use until the development of efficient irrigation systems in the early 20th century.

Southern California

The Southern California coast stretches from Santa Barbara south through Los Angeles and San Diego to the Mexican bor-

FACTOR 1
California's Central Valley has a high desert climate in which agriculture is possible only with irrigation.

FACTOR 1
Southern California's coast and foothills enjoy a subtropical climate suited to citrus and other hot-weather crops.

FACTOR 1
Southern California's Imperial Valley has a desert climate that, with irrigation, accommodates a variety of food crops.

der. Enjoying a subtropical climate, the Southern California coast is hot in summer and warm in winter, with nearly constant sunshine. This is postcard California, where palm trees and citrus groves flourish. With irrigation Southern California grows heat-tolerant fruits and vegetables year-round.

Although the climate is nearly perfect, the Southern California coastal plain and foothills frequently experience weather-related disasters. In fall and early spring, climatic conditions create powerful Santa Ana winds originating in the Great Basin and Mojave Deserts and streaming west through mountain passes. Blowing hot and dry, these winds fuel the region's frequent wildfires. From November to April, heavy rains result in flash floods that race down canyons. Moisture saturates the area's porous, unstable hills and cliffs, causing massive mudslides. Nonetheless, Southern Californians continue to build multimillion-dollar homes in the path of these dangers.

Southern California's interior includes the Mojave Desert and the northern reaches of the Sonoran Desert. Here the climate is extreme; daytime temperatures may reach 130°F, and at night the thermometer plunges below freezing. The less extreme Imperial Valley, once desert, is now a thriving agricultural area because of irrigation.

■□■ CALIFORNIA'S NATIVE AMERICANS: THE MISSING MULTITUDE

Few Americans realize that California once had more Native Americans, and a larger number of Native American tribes, than any other state. It's estimated that, before European contact, California was home to more than 300,000 indigenous people belonging to seven different language groups with as many as 120 dialects and grouped into as many as five hundred tribes (Figure 12.5).

By the mid-1700s, just before Spanish penetration into southern and central California, Native American groups lived along the California coast, in the foothills of the coastal mountain ranges, and in the interior valleys. Because of the region's mild climate and abundant resources, most of them had no need to practice agriculture, instead living by hunting and gathering—and there was plenty of food to go around.

Central and Southern California coastal tribes primarily lived on fish and shellfish as well as sea mammals and the eggs of waterfowl. Interior tribes harvested game and fished inland lakes and streams. Wild food plants grew throughout the year.

The foundation starch for central and Southern California tribes was the acorn, which they processed by an ingenious method: After grinding the meat of the acorn, natives leached out the nuts' bitter tannins by repeatedly pouring water through the acorn meal. Once processed, the product was dried for storage. Nutritious acorn meal was mixed with water and simmered into gruel, or moistened to make dough cakes baked on hot stones.

The foodways of Northern California coastal tribes were virtually identical to those of Pacific Northwest Native Americans, discussed at length in Chapter 13.

Most central and Southern California tribes lived in small, loosely organized groups and usually stayed within their own territories. The same ample resources that made farming unnecessary also created little need for intertribal politics or warfare. The resulting peaceful, isolated existence and loosely organized social structure made them extremely vulnerable.

Well-provisioned Spanish and American settlers had no reason to observe or adopt the foodways of California Native Americans. For them, the region's indigenous people initially were valuable only as laborers and later were considered nuisances to be removed. Within one hundred years of the first Spanish settlement, virtually no organized Native American tribes remained. Thus, virtually none of California's Native American foodways influenced the region's pioneer, traditional, or modern cuisines.

The destruction of California's Native American societies happened so quickly and so thoroughly that the history, culture, and even the names of these tribes are virtually unknown to mainstream Americans. Not until the 1960s, after a group of California Native American college students occupied Alcatraz Island in protest of U.S. government policies, did California's Native Americans begin to organize and activate for their rights.

■□■ SPANISH AND MEXICAN CALIFORNIA

In Chapter 7 you learned about the Spanish missions as a foundation of Mexican Border cuisine. The missions were also a foundation of California's Anglo-Asian cuisine, but indirectly through agriculture.

In 1769, the Franciscan friar **Junipero Serra** (hoo-nee-PAY-roh SAY-rah) set forth from Mexico to establish the first in a string of twenty-one missions that would reach from San Diego to Sonoma, just north of San Francisco. As in the Southwest, the official purpose of the Spanish missions in California was to civilize the region's native population, converting them to Christianity and teaching them basic agriculture. The missions were to operate for 10 years and then relinquish their agriculturally developed lands to the original Native American inhabitants. However, the southern and central California coastal plain proved to be far more valuable farmland than the arid Southwest.

FIGURE 12.5

California's Precontact Native American Tribes. John D. Berry

FACTOR 3

Spanish missionaries established food crop agriculture in coastal areas and cattle ranching in the interior valleys.

Soon California was producing an abundance of food crops, including citrus fruits introduced from Spain's tropical territories. The Spanish planted the region's first vineyards; Junipero Serra is frequently called "the father of the California wine industry." In addition to Spanish introduction of European colonial domesticates, the Mexican brothers who accompanied them introduced corn, beans, squash, and chiles. Spanish missionaries and the Spanish and Mexican ranchers who followed them raised beef cattle in the region's interior valleys, beginning the tradition of California ranching.

Thus, California's Spanish first settlers left two important legacies: the California style of Mexican Border cuisine, and the establishment of agriculture that is the foundation of California's Anglo-Asian cuisine.

Rather than giving productive mission lands back to the natives, the Franciscans retained them and virtually enslaved coastal tribes to work them. Within a few years, thousands of Native Americans died from European diseases, overwork, and malnutrition. In 1823 the Republic of Mexico replaced Spain in governing the missions, and the next year it declared California's Native Americans to be Mexican citizens. However, in practice little changed. The government began granting coastal mission lands and interior tracts to Mexican colonists. Although food crops could not be grown in the dry interior valleys, cattle ranching proved successful there. The introduction of cattle and other European livestock drove out most of the region's indigenous animals and virtually destroyed the oak groves that had provided local Native Americans' foundation starch. By 1836 more than 100,000 California Native Americans—one-third of the precontact population—had perished.

■ AMERICAN
□ CALIFORNIA

Until 1840, most Americans had never even heard of California. However, by the middle of the 19th century the nation was experiencing a groundswell of expansionist sentiment. According to the doctrine of Manifest Destiny, the United States had the right to ownership of the North American continent "from sea to shining sea." Expansionism, combined with other political factors, culminated in war with Mexico and, in 1848, the United States acquired California along with Utah, Nevada, and most of Arizona and New Mexico. The balance of Arizona and New Mexico were added by the Gadsden Purchase in 1854.

Normally America's acquisition of California would have resulted in slow and steady pioneer settlement. However, on January 24, 1848, a foreman working at John Sutter's sawmill in the mountains east of San Francisco reached into the American River and picked up a small, shiny flake of gold.

■ PIONEER COOKING
□ OF THE GOLD RUSH

FACTOR 4
The gold rush attracted second settlers from around the world, giving rise to California's multicultural society.

Within weeks of the gold discovery, central California was inundated by prospectors in search of their fortunes (Figure 12.6). Although gold rush miners were called "49ers," by the end of 1848 more than 6,000 prospectors had already arrived, mainly from the Pacific Northwest, Hawai'i, Mexico, Chile, and Peru. The faraway Easterners got there in 1849; those who could afford to book passage on steamships arrived by sea, while the less fortunate made the 2,000-mile journey overland in wagons.

By 1850 more than 100,000 immigrants had arrived in California from all over the globe. Indeed, the gold rush attracted America's most heterogeneous, or varied, settler group. In the gold fields, Americans from the East Coast and Midwest rubbed shoulders with people from South America, Europe, and Asia, marking the birth of California's multicultural society.

As thousands of would-be prospectors arrived, entrepreneurs saw the opportunity to make a profit on them. San Francisco was the port of entry for those arriving by sea. Formerly a sleepy fishing village, the town quickly grew into a city, its population exploding from six hundred to more than 25,000 in one year.

At the site of the most recent gold strikes, settlements called *boomtowns* grew up virtually overnight. Often little more than tent encampments, gold rush mining towns offered supplies and provisions for those setting out to search for gold as well as restaurants, bars, and brothels for those with gold to spend (Figure 12.7). When local gold fields played out and were abandoned, many of these towns disappeared just as quickly. However, a number survived and grew, among them Sacramento and Stockton.

Mining Camp Cooking

Prospectors camping in the mountains near the gold deposits subsisted primarily on pioneer provisions. They packed bacon and pork lard, dried beans, cornmeal, wheat flour, coffee beans, and sugar on their mules along with picks and shovels needed for mining. At first prospectors could add to these meager provisions by shooting wild game. Bear meat was especially popular for its abundance and flavor. However, wild game soon virtually disappeared. With the foothills full of noisy mining operations, animals that escaped hunters' guns soon fled to the mountains.

FIGURE 12.6
In early Gold Rush days, the precious metal was so abundant that it could be collected in streams simply by panning. P44-3-015 Alaska State Library, Skinner Foundation Photograph Collection

By the height of gold fever, demand for provisions exceeded supply. Thus, what little food was available sold for outrageously high prices. Moreover, few prospectors were willing to spend time on food preparation, so their grub was extremely basic. Many subsisted almost entirely on beans and sourdough biscuits.

When they finally accumulated a little gold, prospectors made their way to the nearest boomtown for rest and recreation. At hastily built hotels they could take a bath and enjoy a hot meal, often the first good food they'd had in months. Miners treated themselves to thick, juicy steaks; fried potatoes; and pies made from fresh or preserved fruits, the meal typically washed down with beer or whiskey. Virtually all of the food served in boomtown

FIGURE 12.7
In California's mining boomtowns, restaurants frequently operated in hastily erected tents. Courtesy Denver Public Library

restaurants was transported from San Francisco, first by steamboat and then by pack mule, making food costs very high. Restaurant owners added a hefty markup as well; when an ounce of gold was worth $5, a full-course dinner could top $10. Drinks were equally expensive. According to local lore, the first Martini cocktail was served to a prospector in the boomtown of Martinez, California, in exchange for a bag of gold nuggets.

In gold rush boomtowns, getting a job as a cook often required no qualifications other than willingness to do the work. Moreover, both cooks and customers were of widely disparate national origins. Many had experienced diverse foodways and strange dishes along the wagon trails en route to California. Because of scarce ingredients and the clash of many food cultures, boomtown cooking became known for unusual combinations. Restaurant cooks frequently created new dishes by throwing together whatever ingredients were on hand. Cooks from foreign countries modified traditional dishes of their home cuisines using available foods. No matter the outcome, their hungry customers were happy to eat the results. Thus, early Californians were culinary liberals willing to try new foods and unusual combinations. Many of traditional California cuisine's best-known dishes had their beginnings in gold rush boomtowns. Arguably the most famous dish of the gold rush era is Hangtown fry, an unlikely mixture of eggs, bacon, and oysters.

Gold Rush San Francisco

San Francisco was perfectly situated as the center of gold rush commerce. Located on the shore of San Francisco Bay, the city has one of the world's deepest and best-protected natural harbors. Then navigable, the Sacramento River connected the bay with interior valleys where gold was being mined. In San Francisco, goods were offloaded from oceangoing vessels onto river steamships and transported inland. Lumber, tools, clothing, and food provisions arrived from the American East Coast and also from as far away as Europe and Hawai'i.

In addition to acting as a transportation hub, San Francisco became a hospitality center with scores of hotels, bars, restaurants, gambling houses, and brothels. In the early days many of these businesses were housed in hastily built wooden shacks

HANGTOWN FRY

During the gold rush, the California town of Placerville was called Hangtown to discourage criminal activity. One day a miner who had finally struck it rich after months of hard work and bad food walked into the El Dorado hotel and asked for the most expensive dish the restaurant could produce.

The three most costly foods in the kitchen were bacon (in scarce supply), oysters (shipped all the way from Portland, Oregon), and eggs (so breakable that almost none survived transport). The cook combined all three delicacies in a hot skillet and named the resulting dish Hangtown Fry.

or canvas tents. Crates and barrels of trade goods were stacked in the open street for want of storage. Construction materials were everywhere as entrepreneurs scrambled to build.

With immigrants pouring in from all over the globe, gold rush San Francisco became one of the world's most racially and ethnically diverse cities. Italians, French Canadians, Hawai'ians, Mexicans, Latin Americans, and Chinese were among the city's diverse immigrant groups. Chinese immigrants virtually flooded the region, at one point amounting to nearly one-fourth of miners working claims. When the U.S. government began imposing heavy fees and taxes on non-American prospectors, most Chinese returned to San Francisco and founded one of the nation's largest Chinatown neighborhoods. Both Chinese and Italian immigrants opened restaurants, initiating the city's longstanding tradition of Chinese-American and Italian-American cooking. Many Italians became fishermen, operating the fleets sailing out of docks that would become Fisherman's Wharf. Settling in nearby North Beach, Italian-Americans opened restaurants, grocery stores, pastry shops, and bakeries. Using the venerable techniques of Old World European bread baking and catering to the region's pioneer taste for sourdough baked goods, Italians were instrumental in developing one of San Francisco's signature foods: sourdough bread.

San Francisco Sourdough Bread

Gold rush prospectors maintained the pioneer tradition of using sourdough starters both en route to the gold fields and while working their claims. In fact, so prevalent was sourdough baking that the prospectors themselves were often called "sourdoughs."

A sourdough starter is created when free-floating ambient yeasts and bacteria land on a mass of wheat-flour dough. The flavor of products made from any starter is a result of the types of yeast and bacteria that drift into it. The characteristic taste of San Francisco sourdough bread results from the special combination of yeasts and bacteria present in the atmosphere of San Francisco during the gold rush years. Those yeasts and bacteria were captured and preserved by San Francisco's Italian and French bakers. Long after other regions largely abandoned this traditional baking method, San Francisco bakeries retained and perfected it. Today the flavor of sourdough bread is an indispensable part of San Francisco cuisine (Figure 12.8). For

FIGURE 12.8
San Francisco sourdough breads.
Noam Armonn/Shutterstock

more information on San Francisco sourdough bread, its artisan producers, and how to reproduce it in your kitchen, refer to this book's companion website.

◼ SAN FRANCISCO
◻
◼ CUISINE

Within 25 years of the region's first gold strike, San Francisco had become a world-class city, boasting hotels and restaurants rivaling those of New York City and London. The extension of the Transcontinental Railroad through to nearby Oakland made overland travel from the East Coast and Midwest to San Francisco fast and affordable. At the same time, increased Pacific Ocean trade opened Asian markets. In addition, the city imported European goods and culture, welcoming not only actors and musicians, but also chefs. Thus, San Francisco's cooking developed as quickly as its commerce and arts scene.

San Francisco's Continental Cuisine

FACTOR 5
Gold rush commerce made San Francisco a wealthy city with expensive restaurants and world-class food.

In 1875 William Ralston set out to build the largest and most luxurious hotel in the world. San Francisco's Palace Hotel was eight stories tall, boasted 755 rooms, and was furnished with the most modern conveniences of the day, including hydraulic elevators. French chefs staffed the kitchens, applying classic cuisine techniques to local food products to create a California version of Continental cuisine. European servers staffed the dining rooms, where sumptuous meals were served at extravagant prices. European royalty as well as American presidents and business tycoons frequented the hotel for its fine food and gracious service. Damaged in the 1906 earthquake and fire, the Palace reopened after an extensive renovation in which its former carriage entrance was sealed under a soaring glass dome to become the Garden Court restaurant.

GREEN GODDESS

A San Francisco signature dish, Dungeness crab salad is frequently enhanced with Green Goddess dressing. Created by Palace Hotel chef Philip Roemer in 1915, this mayonnaise-based salad dressing is tinted an appealing pale green color by a mixture of minced fresh herbs. The dressing was named in honor of a popular stage play titled *The Green Goddess*.

The newly constructed Fairmont Hotel withstood the earthquake but succumbed to the resulting fire. Rebuilt within a year, it soon rivaled the Palace for excellent cuisine (Figure 12.9).

San Francisco's cuisine developed along with the region's agriculture and fishing industry. San Francisco was particularly noted for French cuisine; among the best-loved early French restaurants was La Poule d'Or (la pool DOOR), affectionately known as "the Poodle Dog."

FIGURE 12.9
San Francisco's Fairmont Hotel was world famous for the comfort and style of its accommodations and for the excellence of its cuisine.
Courtesy of the Library of Congress

Hotels continued to offer fine food enhanced by luxurious ambience. The Sir Francis Drake Hotel on Union Square became famous for its innovative restaurants such as the Starlight Roof, where patrons dined and danced in an open-air rooftop garden, and the Middle Eastern–décor Persian Room nightclub. In addition to the grand temples of cuisine, small, independent restaurants served simple fare made exceptional with the region's fine local seafood, meats, and produce.

Good Eating in Ethnic Enclaves

Although known for top-level cuisine in its expensive hotels and restaurants, San Francisco is also a city of neighborhoods, many

RIVAL GRILLS

San Francisco's first restaurant, the Tadich Grill, began as a coffee shop in 1849 but after the 1906 earthquake was rebuilt as a full-service restaurant (Figure 12.10). Today the Tadich retains its early 20th-century décor, with pressed tin ceilings and curtained booths equipped with buzzers to summon waiters. Specializing in seafood, the Tadich became famous for serving local specialties such as sand dabs, petrale sole, spot prawns, abalone, and Dungeness crab. Today most of the Tadich's menu items are still prepared simply, using time-honored methods such as broiling and "grilling" (actually pan-searing).

Sam's Grill and Seafood Restaurant is the Tadich's only rival, offering virtually the same menu in a similar vintage San Francisco atmosphere. Beginning as an oyster saloon in 1867, Sam's is known for its open kitchen and brusque but efficient service. Sam's is well known as a meeting place for politicians and businessmen who hammer out secret deals in enclosed, private booths.

FIGURE 12.10
San Francisco's first restaurant, the Tadich Grill, still serves fine seafood to locals and tourists alike. Courtesy the Tadich Grill, San Francisco, California

CIOPPINO

San Francisco's most famous seafood dish is cioppino (chip-EE-noh), an Italian-style seafood stew. Although the name *cioppino* is well known, popular culture and food historians disagree about its origin.

Legend says the name comes from the fishing community's tradition of communal cooking. After docking with their catch, the fleet typically elected one of the fishermen to prepare dinner. The chosen cook then walked up and down the wharf carrying a basket, calling out "Chip in! Chip in!" asking the other fishermen to donate part of their catch to the meal. From a variable collection of seafood—such as shrimp, mussels, clams, Dungeness crab, squid, snapper, sole, or halibut—the chosen cook made a savory stew accented with Italian ingredients such as tomatoes, onions, peppers, garlic, basil, oregano, and olive oil.

Although the "chip in" story is both plausible and colorful, early records attribute the dish to Giuseppe Buzzaro, a Genoan sailor who created a version of *ciupin* (choo-PEEN), a traditional Ligurian fisherman's stew, with local ingredients.

FACTOR 4

San Francisco's diverse immigrant population gave rise to several ethnic neighborhoods with lively restaurant scenes and good home cooking.

with unique food cultures developed by the immigrant groups that settled in them.

Fisherman's Wharf and North Beach

On the city's north shore, Fisherman's Wharf (Figure 12.11) was once the lively hub of the region's fishing industry. At the wharf San Franciscans of all social backgrounds mingled with commercial fishermen, eager to sample the fresh local seafood at raw bars and rustic restaurants crowding the docks. Looming overhead, the giant Ghirardelli chocolate factory processed cacao beans from South America into chocolate bars and cocoa powder. In the late 1960s Fisherman's Wharf and Ghirardelli Square were developed into a tourist attraction housing trendy shops, amuse-

ments, and scores of restaurants varying from Mexican to sushi. However, the area is still home base to a small working fishing fleet. Today the discriminating diner can enjoy a fine seafood meal or a "walk-away crab salad" from an open-air seafood stand.

Just south of Fisherman's Wharf is San Francisco's North Beach neighborhood. North Beach rivals Manhattan's Little Italy for the number and quality of its Italian markets, cafés, and restaurants. Here San Francisco's first Italian restaurant, Fior d'Italia (fee-ohr deh-TAHL-ee-ah), opened in 1886. Today in North Beach you'll find authentic Italian regional cuisine as well as Italian-American cuisine prepared San Francisco style.

The Mission District

One of California's original Spanish missions, the Mission Dolores anchors the San Francisco neighborhood that bears its name. The Mission District is the city's original Mexican enclave and is best known for its many restaurants and taquerias serving California-style Mexican-American cuisine. Today the Mission District is home to immigrants from virtually every Latin American country and offers an array of restaurants and food stalls with Colombian and Dominican, as well as authentic regional Mexican cuisines.

Chinatown

San Francisco has America's oldest and one of its liveliest Chinatowns (Figure 12.12). Shortly after the first Chinese immigrants arrived in San Francisco in 1848, Chinese settlement began to grow up around Portsmouth Plaza. Stretching along Grant and Stockton Streets, today San Francisco's Chinatown encompasses a twenty-four-block area and is the world's largest Chinese enclave outside Asia. Along with New York's Chinatown, San Francisco's Chinatown is recognized as the birthplace of Chinese-American cuisine, discussed in depth on this book's companion website. In the late 20th century, the neighborhood

FIGURE 12.11
San Francisco's Fisherman's Wharf. Chee-Onn Leong / Shutterstock

FIGURE 12.12
San Francisco Chinatown market c. 1887. © Huntington Library / SuperStock

became a magnet for immigrants from many other Asian countries; today it boasts restaurants and markets offering the food of virtually every Asian nation.

■ CALIFORNIA
□ AGRICULTURE
■

By the late 1800s, advancements in American agricultural science and technology were making large-scale farming profitable. In California, dry farming techniques transformed former Central Valley cattle ranches into wheat farms producing half a million bushels per year. New farm machinery developed in California made such productivity possible. The Stockton gang plow, pulled by a team of eight mules, could turn nearly a hundred acres of soil per day. In 1886 the nation's first steam-powered tractor was put to use in the San Joaquin Valley. A Stockton engineer developed the first tractor powered by an internal combustion engine.

Despite technical innovation, in California large-scale diversified food crop agriculture could not succeed without one essential element: water. Most of California's interior land received far too little rainfall to sustain food production other than wheat and cattle. However, technology initially developed for mining would help transform California into one of the world's most productive food-producing regions.

Watering the West

By the height of the gold rush, easily obtained surface gold was depleted. Instead of panning for gold in streams or chipping away at exposed veins along hillsides, prospectors had to dig into the substrata and separate mineral ore from sand and gravel. Using a sys-

THE CALIFORNIA WATER CONTROVERSY

The benefits of irrigation in California's interior valleys had an ecological cost. Watering the state's farmland and the nearby towns and cities diverts billions of gallons of water from natural habitats. For example, Tulare Lake, once western America's largest body of fresh water and an important regional fishery, was completely drained by the early 20th century. Damming in Northern California and the Pacific Northwest has caused serious population decline in salmon and other food fish.

In the 21st century, environmentalists have persuaded the U.S. government to allot more water for natural habitats. However, these efforts are being countered by California farmers who have turned to the courts to secure their rights to water.

tem called hydraulic mining, prospectors diverted stream water through downhill sluices to literally wash away hillsides. The ecological impact of hydraulic mining, namely clogged waterways and chemical pollution, proved devastating.

When hydraulic mining was finally banned in 1884, the remaining hydraulic infrastructure was used for irrigation. Even with only primitive pumps and hand-dug channels, California's valleys bloomed. Soon deep wells tapped underground aquifers, and advanced pumping systems carried water to fields on the valley floors. The most ambitious project irrigated California's southeastern desert by harnessing the Colorado River with the Hoover Dam, creating the Coachella and Imperial Valley farmlands.

FACTOR 5
Gold rush technology was used for early irrigation systems, initiating massive irrigation projects that made California's dry interior valleys bloom.

Water made it possible for California farmers to grow virtually any type of fruit or vegetable. In addition, the mild climate allowed two full growing seasons, one for hot-weather crops and another for cool-weather crops. Figure 12.13 illustrates areas of crop specialization. Fast rail transportation enabled California-grown fruits and vegetables to be packed on ice—later in refrigerated rail cars—and shipped to the Midwest and East Coast.

California Citrus

Citrus trees have been cultivated along the Southern California coast since the 1700s, when they were introduced by Spanish missionaries. However, on the coast lack of acreage deterred large-scale citrus production. Although year-round temperatures were suitable, citrus trees could not successfully be grown in the interior valleys without irrigation. Moreover, before rail transportation, the cost of shipping citrus fruits to the East Coast by sea made them prohibitively expensive. Citrus would not become commercially viable until irrigation systems were developed and railroads reached the West Coast.

In the late 1800s, technology provided water and transportation, and the California citrus industry was born. The introduction of a winter-ripening orange variety meant that California oranges could be marketed year-round. The taste of sweet and

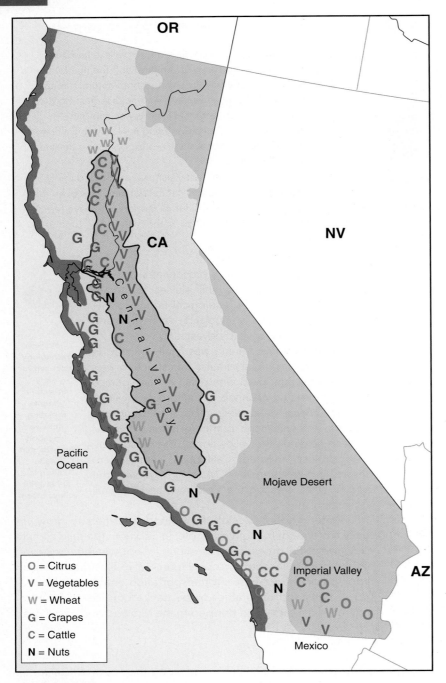

FIGURE 12.13

California Agricultural Areas

Legend:
- O = Citrus
- V = Vegetables
- W = Wheat
- G = Grapes
- C = Cattle
- N = Nuts

FIGURE 12.14

California horticulturalist Luther Burbank. Courtesy of the Library of Congress, LC-USZ62-55143

etable varieties that could withstand the rigors of long-distance shipping to eastern markets. Horticulturalists began experimenting with specialized food plant cultivars sturdy enough to arrive on the East Coast in good shape. Their work would soon transform the eating habits of the nation.

Horticulturalist **Luther Burbank** developed many of California's most important modern fruit, vegetable, and flower cultivars (Figure 12.14). Born in Massachusetts, Burbank moved to California in 1875 and settled in Santa Rosa. There he developed experimental gardens and greenhouses in which he developed more than eight hundred new plant varieties.

Burbank's fundamental goal was to improve food plants in order to better feed the world. One of his most important projects was the Burbank potato, developed in response to potato blight that had devastated Ireland in the 1840s. The Burbank is the precursor to the modern Idaho russet. Other Burbank vegetable cultivars include improved strains of tomato, sweet corn, squash, and asparagus. Among the fruit cultivars he created are several breeds of apples, hundreds of plums, ten different berries, and the freestone peach.

tangy, vitamin-rich California oranges during the long eastern winters made them an instant hit, and citrus production soared. Lemon groves soon followed; although standard lemons make up the bulk of the crop, today juicy and distinctively perfumed Meyer lemons are gaining in popularity.

Horticultural Advances

With irrigation California's farmers could grow fruits and vegetables throughout the year. However, they needed fruit and veg-

California Agro-Industry

Through horticultural and technological advances in the 20th century, California became the nation's leading producer of vegetables and fruits. By the late 20th century California also became the nation's leading dairy-producing state. With its grain crops and cattle ranching, California is an agricultural powerhouse providing Americans with virtually every type of food grown in the United States.

The development of large-scale commercial agriculture in California was paralleled by the rise of industrial food produc-

ICEBERG LETTUCE

Traditional lettuce varieties are highly temperature sensitive, growing only in cool weather but easily destroyed by frost. Because of their delicate cell structure, once picked they wilt easily and spoil quickly. Thus, until the late 1800s lettuce was grown locally and available only in the spring and early fall.

In 1894 the W. Atlee Burpee Company developed a sturdy lettuce that could be packed in ice and shipped cross-country by rail. The new lettuce was called *iceberg*, a name suggestive of its solid texture and ability to withstand cold temperatures. Grown in California and shipped nationwide, iceberg lettuce revolutionized American dining. For the first time ordinary Americans could enjoy salads in the depths of winter and during the hottest summers.

Although it has little flavor, iceberg lettuce is valued for its crunchy texture and durability. Restaurateurs soon discovered that iceberg lettuce salads could be fabricated and plated far in advance. Leaves of iceberg were added to sandwiches to provide textural interest and as an inexpensive filler. When cooks realized that the new lettuce was sturdy enough to be cut on an electric meat slicer, shredded iceberg became a popular sandwich garnish. Most important for foodservice operations, heads of iceberg could be refrigerated for weeks with little loss of quality.

From the beginning of the 20th century through the 1960s, virtually all of America's commercially grown lettuce was of the iceberg variety. Not until the American food revolution of the 1970s would other salad greens challenge iceberg's position as America's favorite lettuce.

FIGURE 12.15

In 1975, labor leader César Chávez organized a 1,000-mile march for awareness of migrant workers' rights. Getty Images, Inc.

However, the development of California's produce industry would ultimately have negative results as well. Produce bred for its appearance and keeping quality does not have the flavor or mouthfeel of traditional varieties. Using petroleum-based transportation to ship food thousands of miles severely impacts the nation's level of carbon emissions. The development of California's specialized food plant cultivars contributed to America's monoculture agricultural system, discussed in Chapter 17. Finally, California's large-scale agriculture involves serious social questions about the employment of migrant workers (Figure 12.15). California restaurateurs and food writers were among the first to promote awareness of today's food policy issues.

Specialty Produce

Although California produces a percentage of virtually every crop grown in America, several items are considered California specialties.

Salad Greens

Through the 1960s, California's lettuce crop was dominated by iceberg lettuce. However, in the early 1970s the emergence of contemporary California cuisine (p. 563) and the American food revolution changed the nation's eating habits. New lettuce cultivars, innovative packaging, better refrigeration, and faster transport made it possible to offer a wider variety of salad greens to a newly appreciative public. The initial variety to challenge iceberg's hold on the market was romaine lettuce. The public's acceptance of romaine led to increased production of Boston, Bibb, and looseleaf lettuces as well as pigment-enhanced lettuces such as red leaf. These varieties are more tender, flavorful, and nutritious than iceberg.

Prompted by contemporary California cuisine restaurants, small growers began offering nonlettuce salad greens such as arugula, radicchio, frisée, mâche, and Asian greens as well as edible flowers. These began appearing in proprietary greens mixtures, the best known of which is called *spring mix*. In the 1980s

---

tion. Although in the early 20th century much of the region's fruit and vegetable harvest was shipped to Midwest and East Coast markets, soon much more was processed in canning plants near the growing fields. Later, technological advances created the frozen food industry and made available a fresher-tasting, less-processed product. The resulting year-round availability of nutrient-rich produce profoundly improved the winter diets of all but the poorest Americans.

MIGRANT WORKERS

Central and Southern California produce growers look to Mexico for field workers. Migrant agricultural workers are employed primarily to pick crops, typically following a region's harvest cycle by moving from one area to another as crops ripen. Accurate information about migrant workers is difficult to obtain, as more than half of them are undocumented, entering or remaining in the United States illegally. However, most work at or below minimum wage, live in substandard conditions, and suffer medical problems that are the direct result of field work. Although illegal immigration has become the subject of political controversy, Americans must recognize that without migrant agricultural workers, much of the food we eat would never reach market.

the availability of prewashed, prefabricated greens made salads virtually effortless to prepare. By the turn of the 21st century, supermarkets were devoting more space to packaged salad mixes than to traditional fresh greens. In the 1990s, **hydroponics,** a production method in which greens are grown in water enhanced with dissolved nutrients, made possible **living greens,** lettuces sold with intact roots packaged in water. Sprouts and **microgreens,** a food plant's first two true leaves, added more choices for both chefs and home cooks.

California Avocados

Although native to Mexico, today 95 percent of the world's avocados are grown in California—and Californians are the world's greatest consumers of them. The California avocado industry began in the late 1800s when several Mexican avocado cultivars were introduced to Southern California. When one cultivar survived the great freeze of 1913, it became known as the *Fuerte* (FWAYR-tay), meaning "strong" in Spanish. Later, horticulturalists developed the Hass avocado, a cultivar that produces year-round.

Avocados are an important element in California's Mexican Border cuisine, discussed in Chapter 7. In addition to guacamole, avocados are used for salads and as sandwich ingredients. Anglo-Asian chefs are even more inventive with avocados, using them for foods such as sushi, sauces, and even ice cream.

Artichokes

California supplies the nation with virtually all of its artichokes. Although the Spanish planted artichokes during the mission period, this formidable-looking vegetable did not catch on with Anglo settlers. At the beginning of the 20th century, Italian immigrants reintroduced artichoke plants around Half Moon Bay. Today the town of Castroville is the center of California's artichoke production.

Asparagus

California's many microclimates make it possible for produce farmers to harvest asparagus during two separate, extended seasons. Although this perennial plant sends up its edible shoots for only 60 to 90 days in the springtime, variations in the California climate create sprouting conditions from January through May. Another, smaller crop is artificially induced to shoot in September and October. California asparagus accounts for 70 percent of the nation's crop.

Olives and Olive Oil

During the Spanish colonial period, olive trees were planted around the missions. Although the moist coastal climate was not the best for olive cultivation, the hardy trees survived and produced enough oil for the mission kitchens and for sacramental use. In the 1860s cuttings from these original mission trees were propagated and planted in the San Joaquin and northern Sacramento Valleys, where they received irrigation from abandoned mining channels. There the trees flourished and produced sizable harvests. This abundant olive harvest would be used in different ways by two separate groups of Californians.

Italian-Americans grew olive trees to make olive oil. By 1885 California was producing olive oils of excellent quality, most of which were enjoyed locally by Italian-American cooks and chefs. California olive oil production continued through World War II. However, when European trade resumed after the war, low-cost Italian and Spanish olive oils flooded the market and the California olive oil industry virtually disappeared. Today renewed interest in California artisan olive oils is prompting more producers to enter the market. California olive oils are noteworthy for their high quality and distinctive taste. However, California still accounts for only 1 percent of the world's production.

In addition to making olive oil, Italian immigrants cured California-grown olives for table use. Following the styles of their home regions, they prepared pungent, salty, slightly bitter olives in both black and green varieties. However, these products proved too exotic for mainstream consumers. In response, American olive growers perfected methods for leaching out virtually all of the olives' natural bitterness to create a milder-flavored olive. Called "California ripe black olives," this product was canned and marketed nationwide. Before long producers also developed a mild-flavored green California olive packed in a tangy brine. After the development of mechanical olive pitters, pitted California black and green olives became a popular snack and condiment. Stuffed with bright red pimiento, the green variety became a standard American garnish.

An aggressive marketing campaign brought California olives into national prominence as a "gourmet" food that virtually everyone could afford. Soon green olives were an indispensable ingredient in Martinis, black olives appeared in every relish tray, and deviled eggs looked naked without pimiento-stuffed olive halves as their garnish.

Today California has more than 36,000 acres of olive trees. Ninety percent of the crop is processed into ripe black olives. With America's renewed interest in regional and artisan products, California producers may begin producing European-style olives for a more sophisticated market.

Grapes for Wine and Table

Home to one of the world's most respected wine industries, California produces more wine grapes than table grapes. From Santa Barbara in the south through the Central Coast region and north through Napa, Sonoma, and into Mendocino counties, California produces almost three million tons of wine grapes annually. Although hundreds of grape varietals are grown in California, the "big four" types are Chardonnay, Sauvignon Blanc, Pinot Noir, and Cabernet Sauvignon; from these grapes California vintners make some of the world's finest wines. The history of California winemaking is discussed on pp. 556 and 557.

In addition to wine grapes, California is responsible for more than 90 percent of U.S. table grape production. California grapes are also made into raisins, both black and white.

Meat and Dairy

California ranching began with the Spanish missions and continued with Anglo settlement of the interior valleys. Even before irrigation, the region provided adequate grazing for hardy beef cattle. Today California produces free-range and feedlot cattle. California is also known for lamb production. This market is dominated by smaller specialty producers using an integrated approach to farming, selling both meat and wool. Milk-fed spring lamb is one of California's premier products. Poultry and eggs are also important. Sonoma County—particularly the area surrounding Petaluma—is known for poultry production, with many operators now specializing in free-range birds.

Dairy production grew steadily throughout the 20th century, and in 1993 California became the nation's leading dairy-producing state. Many of California's milk producers operate large confined animal feeding operations, or CAFOs. Although much of the state's output is sold as fresh milk, a significant portion is used to make cheese.

The California cheese industry traces its beginnings back to the Spanish missions. The Franciscan brothers brought dairy cattle from Mexico and preserved their milk by making simple fresh cheeses. California's commercial cheese industry began just south of San Francisco in the late 1850s, when a woman entrepreneur rounded up locally ranging feral cows and used their milk to produce a cheddar-type cheese. Through most of the 19th century, simple fresh and firm-ripened cheeses were made by individual farmers, many on the Point Reyes Peninsula north of San Francisco.

California's best-known cheese is *Monterey Jack*, a firm cow's-milk variety appreciated for its mild, mellow flavor and its superior melting quality. Though often enjoyed as a table cheese, Monterey Jack is also used extensively in cooking and is an indispensable ingredient in California-Mexican cuisine. *Dry jack*, an aged version of Monterey Jack cheese, was created by accident when a San Francisco wholesaler was overstocked with young Monterey Jack cheese and, in order to preserve it, salted the wheels and allowed them to age in a cellar. In the mid-20th century, industrial dairies began mass-producing cheeses in the style of Monterey Jack. These commercial jack cheeses bear little resemblance to traditional, artisan-made Monterey Jack available in fine cheese shops or directly from producers. *Pepper jack* is a commercial variety flavored with green and red chiles.

Another California cheese creation was first developed in the 1920s, allegedly by a Greek immigrant trying to duplicate feta. However, the result was quite different. The process was adopted by an Italian-American dairyman who called the cheese *Teleme* (TELL-ah-may). Teleme begins as a semisoft fresh cheese and may be purchased in fresh form. However, to make traditional Teleme the cheese is then dusted with rice flour and allowed to ripen under controlled conditions. As it ripens, the cheese becomes more flavorful and softens to a runny interior consistency. To distinguish cheese produced in this manner, the product is called *rice flour Teleme*, today marketed by a descendant of the originator as *Franklin's Teleme*.

Although California dairy production continued to grow, the region saw little innovation in cheese making until the 1970s, when Sonoma native Laura Chenel began raising a herd of dairy goats in order to attempt making her own cheese. After studying cheese-making techniques in France, she began producing America's first recognized brand of *chèvre*, or goat cheese.

Today California's artisan cheeses include widely disparate styles such as Humboldt Fog, a firm cheese sporting a distinctive horizontal line of ash; Point Reyes Blue, a traditional blue-veined cheese; and Cowgirl Creamery Red Hawk, a strong-flavored, highly aromatic washed rind cheese.

■□■ CALIFORNIA SEAFOOD

California's 800 miles of coastline give the region's fishermen ample opportunity to harvest Pacific fish and shellfish. Beginning with fishing fleets sailing out of San Francisco harbor during gold rush days, California's fishing industry has sustained the region's economy and provided food for the entire nation.

The Monterey Peninsula became the center of Northern California's fishing industry in the 1850s. Immigrants dominated California's fisheries, settling in enclaves along the coast and specializing in a particular type of seafood. The town of Monterey became a supplier of seafood to the world in the early 1900s (Figure 12.16).

To exploit the region's abundant sardines, both Anglo and Japanese-American entrepreneurs built canning factories along Monterey's wharf on a street called Cannery Row. For almost three decades, Cannery Row was a state-of-the-art food processing plant, sending its products all over the world. However, as early as the late 1930s, the sardine industry began feeling the effects of overfishing; the annual catch fell from 75,000 tons in 1937 to only 17 tons in 1958. Cannery Row fell into disuse and was later rehabilitated as a shopping mall and tourist attraction. Today sardine fishing in California is strictly controlled and the species is rebounding to abundance.

California's modern fishing industry specializes in halibut, Pacific mackerel, salmon, and swordfish. Between 1906 and

FIGURE 12.16

An early 20th-century sardine processing plant in Monterey Bay, California. Courtesy of the National Archives

1980, tuna canning was an important California industry; however, major companies have moved operations elsewhere. Today California's tuna catch is sold fresh for both the local and international market. In addition to these nationally distributed fish, lesser-known but equally delicious species are caught and sold for local use. Rex sole, sand dabs, Pacific rockfish, sablefish, black cod, shark, and bonito are featured on California menus.

The cool waters off California's central and northern coasts are prime habitat for a variety of crustaceans and mollusks. Many of the oyster species discussed in Chapter 13 are also caught and farmed in California waters. By far the best-known California shellfish is the Dungeness crab (Figure 12.17). Although fished from central California to the Gulf of Alaska, Dungeness crabs are most closely associated with San Francisco, where they are featured on restaurant menus and in "walk-away" cocktails on Fisherman's Wharf. Large and exceptionally meaty, Dungeness crab is served hot with butter and lemon, or cold with mayonnaise. California waters produce scores of shrimp varieties, ranging from large prawns to tiny bay shrimp. Spot prawns are a specialty, as is California spiny lobster.

Abalone (AB-ah-lone-ee) is a large mollusk primarily harvested for the tasty meat of its muscular "foot," the part of its body that propels it forward. In addition to its use for food, the abalone's iridescent, multihued inner shell material, called *mother-of-pearl*, is used in decorative arts. During the early days of California fishing, abalone were incredibly abundant and unpopular with Anglo diners; Japanese and Chinese fishermen specialized in catching abalone and processed it by drying or canning for shipment to Asian consumers. In the 1960s, California's abalone population declined because of habitat issues and overfishing as Anglos finally discovered the delectable flavor of fresh abalone steaks. Today commercial harvesting of wild abalone is banned in California waters. However, demand from American and Asian markets prompted California entrepreneurs to pioneer abalone aquaculture. California abalone is now raised in on-shore facilities, where the valuable mollusks are reared to market size in 3 to 4 years.

■ CALIFORNIA
□
■ WINES

California is considered the premier wine region of the United States. The region's wine making tradition began with the Spanish missions that produced altar wine from the Mission grape, now used as a table fruit.

California's modern wine industry began with Sonoma's Buena Vista Winery, founded in the late 1840s by a Hungarian winemaker and still in operation today. Italian-American immigrants established vineyards as well (Figure 12.18); the noted Gallo family built what would eventually become the largest wine-making company in the world. California wine making grew slowly through the 19th century and into the early 20th century when phylloxera, a root parasite, began infesting the vines. Then Prohibition shut down the industry until its repeal in 1933. Post-Prohibition recovery was slow because makers of

FIGURE 12.18
Bottling wine in California, 1920. Robert Zerkowitz W.I. Archives

FIGURE 12.17
Dungeness crab is a renowned regional specialty.

fine wines were no longer in business. Most wines produced in California between repeal and the late 1960s were mass-produced generic types sold in gallon jugs. However, the American food revolution provided the impetus for a California wine revolution. Beginning in the 1970s, winemakers from European countries as well as self-taught American winemakers established vineyards and wineries dedicated to producing high-quality wines.

In central and Northern California, cool coastal breezes, foggy nights, and hot, sunny days make the interior valleys ideal for wine making. The region's topography creates individual microclimates that give wines special characteristics. California's most important viticulture areas are Napa, Sonoma, Carneros, and Monterey Counties, the Central Coast, the Central Valley, and Santa Barbara County. Today California wines garner awards in world-class wine competitions and are in demand worldwide.

> ## ELEMENTS OF GUANGZHOU CHINESE CUISINE
>
> **FOUNDATION FOODS**
>
> principal starch: steamed long-grain white rice
>
> principal proteins: pork, seafood, soy products
>
> principal produce: a wide variety of Asian and some European vegetables
>
> **FAVORED SEASONINGS:** fresh ginger, garlic, scallions, soy sauce
>
> **PRINCIPAL COOKING MEDIUM:** vegetable oil
>
> **PRIMARY COOKING METHODS:** stir-frying, steaming, stewing
>
> **FOOD ATTITUDES:** strong food culture, culinary liberals

■ TRADITIONAL
□ CALIFORNIA CUISINE

FACTOR 5
Widespread economic viability arrived around the turn of the 20th century, giving rise to traditional California cuisine.

The seeds of traditional California cuisine were planted as early as pioneer gold rush days. Most of California's Anglo second settlers came from culinarily conservative regions, but most were adventurous individuals willing to break free of conventions and take considerable risks. For them, eating new foods came easily. When confronted with new foods and unusual cooking methods, California's Anglos were ready to take a chance.

Pioneer cooking typically transitions into a region's traditional cuisine when most of its citizens achieve economic viability. In California this occurred around the 1880s and continued through the 1920s. During these four decades, many of California's signature dishes and cooking styles were developed. California foodservice enjoyed an additional burst of creativity in the late 1940s after World War II.

Though it's based on Anglo pioneer cooking, traditional California cuisine is strongly influenced by the cuisines of its non-Anglo second settlers. Among the first new foods introduced to California were dishes and ingredients from Asia. These continue to enrich and expand the cuisine today.

Asian Influence

Chinese immigrants initially arrived in California to become prospectors or railroad workers. When both types of employment declined, many went into foodservice. Some opened Chinese restaurants and eventually developed the Chinese-American microcuisine discussed on this book's companion website. Many more obtained jobs as restaurant workers or domestic cooks in Anglo businesses and homes. Though few employees in Anglo kitchens were permitted to prepare Chinese food on a regular basis, their cooking techniques and taste preferences profoundly influenced California's developing traditional cuisine.

At the turn of the 20th century, California's better restaurants and homes were preparing local food products in the Continental cuisine style. Asian cooks working under European-trained chefs gradually lightened and freshened the prevailing cuisine, shortening the cooking times of vegetables and giving sauces a thinner consistency. Early 20th-century visitors to California reported eating lightly cooked foods and an abundance of fresh vegetables—dining habits that would not be adopted by the rest of the nation until the 1970s.

Japanese immigrants added their influence to mainstream cuisine in the fishing industry and agriculture. Japanese fishermen supplied much of the region's specialty seafood, creating a regional taste for unusual items such as squid, mussels, and abalone. California's Japanese truck farmers were instrumental in developing the California produce industry, applying their horticultural knowledge and hard work to California's rich soil (Figure 12.19). At first Japanese farmers concentrated on growing European and American fruit and vegetable cultivars for Anglo customers. In response to the region's increasing Chinese and Japanese population, they imported seeds and began growing Asian produce. Soon Anglo customers were buying snow peas, bok choy, and other specialty items that changed the way mainstream Californians cooked and ate.

California-Style Sushi

By the mid-1960s, Japanese restaurants had become popular with non-Japanese customers in New York City and throughout Hawai'i. However, it was in California that the greatest number of mainstream Americans discovered sushi—the Japanese dish of vinegared rice usually garnished with raw fish—and made it their own (Figure 12.20). Japanese-American chefs working in California restaurants modified time-honored sushi methods and combinations to create new, Americanized versions of sushi.

Several factors contributed to the development of California's Anglo-Asian sushi repertoire. In California, Japanese sushi chefs were introduced to a whole new palette of ingredients, such as avocados, Dungeness crab, mayonnaise, and cream cheese. Such items were included in new, nontraditional preparations. For their Anglo clientele, Japanese chefs began featuring sushi creations made with vegetables and cooked seafood. (Although Californians were by nature more adventurous than other Americans, many were still squeamish

---

□ ELEMENTS OF JAPANESE CUISINE

FOUNDATION FOODS

principal starch: steamed short-grain white rice

principal proteins: seafood, soy products

principal produce: a wide variety of Asian and some European vegetables

FAVORED SEASONINGS: fresh ginger, scallions, soy sauce, sesame oil

PRINCIPAL COOKING MEDIA: dashi stock, water

PRIMARY COOKING METHODS: steaming, poaching, boiling

FOOD ATTITUDES: strong food culture, culinary conservatives

FIGURE 12.19

A Japanese-American truck farmer tends seedlings started under protective coverings. Courtesy of the Library of Congress, LC-USF34-016175-C

FIGURE 12.20

Californians were among the first Americans to discover the pleasures of dining at a sushi bar. bikeriderlondon / Shutterstock

about eating raw fish.) The best-known sushi item of this type is the *California roll*, originally filled with cooked Dungeness crab meat and avocado. By the 1970s many Californians had become vegetarians, and sushi chefs responded with vegetarian and vegan options.

Pan-Asian Ingredients

Throughout the 20th century, a steady progression of Asian immigrants settled in California. People from Korea, Vietnam, Thailand, Indonesia, the Pacific Islands, and many other Asian nations all added their ingredients to the mainstream mix. Today seasonings such as soy sauce, fish sauce, miso, and curry paste are accepted items in the Anglo-Asian California pantry. In addition to their use in traditional Asian dishes, these ingredients frequently enhance non-Asian preparations, such as sauces and marinades. Californians also enjoy a wide variety of rice types, including jasmine and basmati. Asian noodles, both wheat and rice, are an everyday staple.

Salad Eaters

Long before other Americans, Californians made salads an important part of their diets. In doing so, they changed the prevailing American perception of the salad and its place in the meal.

Until Californians revolutionized it, the American salad was a seasonal dish primarily served in spring when lettuce was in season. Country people ate salads of leafy greens as a spring tonic, typically served along with the main dish. Upper-class diners followed the European custom of eating salads after the main course. Salads were dressed with a simple vinaigrette or a dairy-based boiled dressing. However, at the beginning of the 20th century, Californians began changing the way a salad was served, and by the 1920s they had drastically altered the composition of the salad itself.

In the cooler climates of Europe and the American East Coast, a cup of hot soup constituted the traditional first course of a formal meal. Warm-weather Californians began serving salads at the beginning of the meal, instead of soup. Soon salad became the standard opening to American meals, both in homes and in restaurants.

CAESAR SALAD

During Prohibition, Southern Californians frequently crossed the border into Tijuana, Mexico, where they could drink alcohol legally. Among the border-hopping Americans were Hollywood movie stars, directors, and film executives who frequented an Italian restaurant owned by Cesar Cardini. On the busy Fourth of July weekend in 1924, Cardini was running low on appetizers and decided to offer a special salad made with ingredients on hand. He combined crisp leaves of locally grown romaine hearts with a dressing made of lemon juice, Parmesan cheese, Worcestershire sauce, garlic, olive oil, and a soft-cooked egg, and instructed guests to eat the romaine leaves with their fingers. Cesar's salad became the rage among Hollywood society and was copied in virtually every California restaurant. Created in Mexico for a California clientele by an Italian immigrant, today Caesar salad is an American national cuisine signature dish known worldwide.

Not content with serving only leafy greens, Californians began embellishing salads with other raw and cooked vegetables, such as carrot slices, bell pepper strips, radish slices, rings of raw onion, sliced beets, tomato wedges, cauliflower and broccoli florets, and even bean sprouts. This type of green salad, topped with a variety of colorful vegetables, became known as a **tossed salad.**

In addition to the European-style vinaigrette, Californians began serving rich, thick salad dressings based on mayonnaise and sour cream. Among the earliest of this dressing type were Green Goddess and ranch, soon to be commercially bottled and sold nationwide. Russian dressing, Thousand Island dressing, and blue cheese dressing became popular options, as well.

To accommodate varying customer preferences, restaurants began serving salad dressings on the side rather than mixing salads in the kitchen. Dressings were presented on the table in a dressing caddy. Because each diner was expected to dress and mix his or her salad at the table, salads were served in bowls rather than on plates.

Californians loved their salads enough to make them a meal. Originally considered acceptable only for ladies' luncheons, entrée salads soon became standard menu items ordered by men as well as women. To satisfy as a main dish, an **entrée salad** typically includes one or more protein items, such as cheese and cold cooked meat or poultry, as well as greens and vegetables. Though such dishes have been known since the Middle Ages, Californians popularized entrée salads in America and expanded them to include salads topped with warm grilled meats, poultry, and seafood.

Fruit First

In their quest for cool and refreshing starters, Californians began serving fresh fruit as an appetizer. At the time considered unusual and exotic, grapefruit halves were served as a first course, sometimes sprinkled with sugar, broiled, and topped with a maraschino cherry. Avocado halves were sugared or drizzled with vinaigrette dressing. Diced or sliced California fruits were combined to make appetizer fruit salads, called **fruit cocktail** when served in martini glasses. The California custom of serving fruit-based first courses entered America's national cuisine, and was practiced well into the 1960s. Today a vestige of this practice can be seen in composed-salad appetizers containing a fruit element.

Grilled Foods

By the middle of the 20th century, California promoters were touting the region's healthful outdoor lifestyle. Cooking outdoors was part of the California mystique, and grilling was perceived as a healthful, low-fat cooking method. The wood-fired or charcoal grill became the premier backyard cooking implement, considered a status symbol in suburban communities across America.

The popularity of grilled foods quickly influenced restaurant cooking as well. In the 1960s, restaurant equipment manufacturers began marketing gas-fired grills that soon became an indispensable part of the hot line. In steakhouses, grilling replaced broiling.

California restaurant chefs began grilling seafood as well as meats and poultry. Firm fish such as tuna and swordfish were marinated and grilled. Large shrimp and cubes of fish were threaded onto skewers and grilled to make seafood kabobs. Grilled vegetables were offered to vegetarian diners and became a popular side dish.

Burgers, Car Culture, and the Drive-In

California rivals New England as America's sandwich capital, and many consider it the birthplace of fast food. In California the ultimate fast-food sandwich is the hamburger.

Although the hamburger was invented back east, the history of hamburgers in California dates to the late 19th century, when burger-loving Anglos moving to California from New England and the Midwest brought their favorite sandwich along with them. In California's growing towns and cities, hamburgers were popular fare in lunchrooms, family restaurants, and snack bars. Most food historians credit California as the birthplace of the cheese hamburger, or cheeseburger.

The birth of the fast-food hamburger occurred in the 1920s when, for the first time, middle-class Americans could afford to buy automobiles. In response, Los Angeles and other Southern California cities were planned for driving rather than walking, designed with broad boulevards and low, widely spaced buildings. By this time the pace of life was picking up, and everyone was in a hurry. The region was ripe for a new dining concept: the drive-in restaurant (Figure 12.21).

The original 1920s drive-in restaurant was a small building surrounded by parking spaces. Patrons drove in, parked, and were served in their cars. Teenage servers, sometimes on roller skates, took orders and brought food to the cars on specially constructed trays that could be suspended from the driver's-side window. Hamburgers, hot dogs, and French fries were the standard bill of fare.

FIGURE 12.21

At a Stewart's Root Beer drive-in restaurant, Southern Californians enjoy a quick meal without leaving the comfort of their cars. Jerry Waters

FIGURE 12.22

The Brown Derby restaurant is an example of mimetic architecture, popularized in California to attract the attention of people driving by in cars. © Bettmann/CORBIS

In 1948 the California chain In-N-Out Burger opened the nation's first drive-through window featuring two-way speakers. Although drive-ins remained popular through the 1950s, by the 1960s fast-food restaurants with drive-through windows had largely replaced them. By the mid-1970s only a few drive-ins remained.

Dining in Glamorous Hollywood

The city of Los Angeles began as the Mission of San Gabriel, established by Junipero Serra as part of the California mission chain. Originally settled by Spanish farmers, the mission area was irrigated with water from the Los Angeles River and soon became productive farmland. A farming community grew up around the mission, by 1850 becoming a city.

Los Angeles could well have remained an agricultural center practicing basic Farmlands-style cuisine if not for one important development: the film industry. Through the 19th century, most of America's films were made on the East Coast. However, by the early 20th century Southern California's mild climate and varied topography began attracting movie directors eager to film year-round. A Los Angeles suburb named Hollywood became the center of American filmmaking, and soon the world's most glamorous movie stars called Los Angeles home.

Movie stars and Hollywood producers loved the high life and for publicity purposes needed to be seen about town. In response, foodservice entrepreneurs opened expensive, exclusive restaurants. Newspaper gossip columnists ran almost daily reports of stars dining at swanky eateries such as Romanoff's, run by a pseudo Russian prince, and the elegant Perino's. Many of these restaurants were known more for their ambience and clientele than for their food. However, some offered truly fine cooking and were instrumental in developing traditional California cuisine.

Opened in 1921, the Coconut Grove Lounge became Hollywood's most glamorous restaurant. Decorated with artificial palm trees and stuffed monkeys from a movie set, the Coconut Grove became *the* meeting place for stars and film industry power brokers and even hosted Academy Award presentations. Although the Coconut Grove hired a French chef and served pri-

marily Continental cuisine, the restaurant made a point of serving local California products such as avocados, figs, citrus fruits, sand dabs, and abalone.

The Brown Derby restaurants became another Hollywood institution. Following an architecture fad that began in California, the front section of the original restaurant was constructed in the shape of a derby hat (Figure 12.22). The Brown Derby is remembered as the birthplace of the Cobb salad (p. 572).

Despite its upscale atmosphere and star-powered clientele, Chasen's restaurant was best known for its chili. Fans of Chasen's chili included President Richard Nixon and actress Elizabeth Taylor, who ordered the chili sent to Rome during the filming of the movie *Cleopatra*.

■ THE BIRTH OF MODERN
□ ANGLO-ASIAN
■ CALIFORNIA CUISINE

In most of America's other regional cuisines, the transition from traditional cooking to a modern cuisine happened slowly through the efforts of many unknown cooks. However, the emergence of California's contemporary cuisine can be traced to a single decade, and is largely attributed to one extraordinary chef.

Counterculture Ideas

The 1960s ushered in a period of radical change in which young Americans initiated a cultural and political movement unlike any other. Opposition to the Vietnam War sparked general resistance to authority and rejection of the repressive social mores of

THE TIKI BAR

Hawai'i's annexation to the United States in the late 1800s led to a growing fascination with all things Polynesian. In the 1920s and 1930s, Hollywood movies gave American audiences their first glimpse of South Pacific island ambience in the form of grass-thatched huts, potted palms, flickering torches, and fantastically carved Polynesian statues called *tikis* (TEE-kees). The stage was set for a visionary entrepreneur to open a Polynesian-themed restaurant (Figure 12.23).

Don the Beachcomber's opened in 1933 as America's first tiki bar. The bar's restaurant featured exotic rum-based cocktails, some served in hollowed pineapples. The food menu offered basic Chinese-American food and Polynesian-inspired specialty dishes. Presentation was foremost at this fantasy restaurant, where the most popular appetizer was the pupu platter (Chapter 14), a sampler of Chinese-American and Polynesian-inspired hors d'oeuvres presented with a miniature hibachi grill. In the 1930s as today, American diners loved to toast these skewered appetizers over flames. In 1936 "Trader Vic" Bergeron converted his Oakland saloon into a tropical tiki-themed restaurant. Trader Vic's served Polynesian and Asian dishes modified to suit the American palate, arguably the nation's first Asian fusion food.

FIGURE 12.23

Tiki restaurants served America's first Asian fusion food. Courtesy Original Tiki Bar, Ft. Pierce, Florida

the 1950s. Although young people have always rebelled against the older generation, for the first time in history they rebelled publicly and in an organized manner. Moreover, they were able to attract the media coverage necessary to spread their message to the nation and eventually to the world. In doing so, they created a social movement called the **counterculture.**

Historians cite San Francisco's Haight-Ashbury district as the birthplace of America's 1960s counterculture and its values regarding food. In addition to rejecting traditional prohibitions about sex and drugs, counterculture values also included the rejection of the American agricultural-industrial-energy complex that had become the nation's primary source of food. In the eyes of the counterculture, large agribusinesses and food-processing companies were harming the ecology, mistreating animals, and ruining the health of the American public by promoting highly refined and processed foods. These ideas led to the popularity of natural foods and gave rise to the back-to-the-earth movement, in which thousands of urban and suburban young people moved to rural areas and tried their hand at organic subsistence farming in an attempt to become self-sufficient. Back-to-earthers baked their own bread from hand-milled flour, grew and canned their own vegetables, and made their own yogurt and cheese.

The counterculture also promoted the vegetarian lifestyle. Some young people became vegetarians because of the negative ecological impact of raising animals for meat. Others embraced vegetarianism along with Eastern religions, primarily Hinduism and Buddhism. In San Francisco, hundreds of innovative vegetarian restaurants opened, often staffed by amateur cooks and operated on communal or cooperative principles (Figure 12.25).

FIGURE 12.24

Development of Anglo-Asian California Cuisine

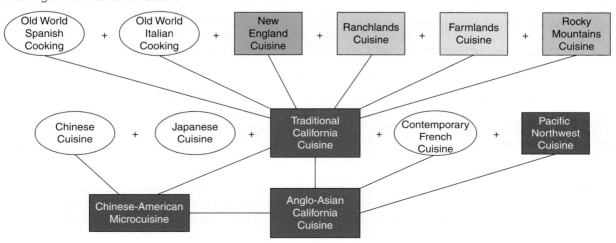

FIGURE 12.25

San Francisco's Greens was the nation's first critically acclaimed vegetarian restaurant. Courtesy Paul Berg, Sebastopol, California

Most important, counterculture thinking led a new generation of cooks and chefs to question authority and challenge traditional ideas about cooking. No longer willing to slavishly follow recipes, they struck out on their own to create new combinations and apply unconventional techniques. Many were influenced by the discovery of world cuisines.

World Cuisines Influences

Although traditional California cooking had been shaped by the cuisines of its Meso-Spanish pioneers and Asian immigrants, the 1960s opened California's cooking to an entire world of ingredients and techniques. Servicemen returning from the Vietnam War brought back a taste for Southeast Asian cooking. Immigrants from Vietnam, Thailand, and Indonesia opened restaurants and grocery stores throughout the region. Interest in Eastern religions created growing appreciation of India's cuisines. Mediterranean Rim cuisines were a perfect match for California's fine wines and food products. All of these influences were absorbed into California's emerging contemporary cuisine.

Alice Waters and Chez Panisse

The culinary philosophies of the early contemporary California cuisine chefs were formed by counterculture ideals and enriched by knowledge of world cuisines. The best known of these chefs is **Alice Waters**, considered the founder of contemporary California cuisine.

After graduating from the University of California at Berkeley and traveling and studying food in France, Alice Waters returned to the Bay area and in 1971 opened a restaurant called Chez Panisse (shay pah-NEECE). The ideals and philosophies behind Chez Panisse were extraordinary for its time. Initially the most daring thing Waters did was to open with a table d'hôte menu that changed each day and that was based on local, seasonal food products. The rationale behind the table d'hôte

menu was twofold. A single set menu allows a restaurant to purchase only what is needed for the day, eliminating waste and making it possible to choose foods at the peak of freshness and quality. It also allows the chef to compose a meal in the same way a musician composes a symphony, leading the diner from the opening appetizer to the final dessert in a logical progression of courses that lead to discovery and delight.

Alice Waters's most radical and enduring principle was to use only meats, poultry, fish, and produce that were fresh, seasonal, local, and ethically raised or caught. Although this policy does not seem so unusual today, you must remember that by the 1960s, most American restaurants were using frozen foods and commercially grown produce shipped from hundreds of miles away. Alice Waters's culinary philosophy was formed by her experiences in France, where restaurants used local, seasonal produce and traditionally raised meats. To find similar food products for Chez Panisse, she began searching for the region's most flavorful fruits and vegetables—and found them on small farms where food was grown using organic practices. With her help, farmers and ranchers purchased land or otherwise expanded their farming operations. With her encouragement and support, they began experimenting with traditional and heirloom plant cultivars and producing naturally raised food animals. Over the decades, Chez Panisse helped develop a network of farmers and ranchers dedicated to natural, ethical practices and sustainable agriculture that produces a steady supply of pure, fresh, local foods for Chez Panisse and other fine restaurants in the area.

Though the cuisine of Chez Panisse was originally French and remains European in inspiration, today at Chez Panisse and its affiliate restaurants the cuisine has evolved to embrace the best of traditional and modern American cooking as well. This mixture of European sensibilities and American products, leavened with the influence of Asian flavors and techniques, is representative of contemporary California cuisine.

Alice Waters's legacy is a new generation of California chefs and restaurants. Many talented chefs who staffed the stoves at Chez Panisse went on to open their own restaurants and break new culinary ground. Among the most respected of Chez Panisse alumni are chefs Paul Bertolli, Jeremiah Tower, Deborah Madison, Mark Miller, and Joyce Goldstein. Alice Waters's philosophy of shared knowledge, respect

TABLE D'HÔTE

Table d'hôte (tah-blah DOTE) translates as "table of the host." Guests are offered one set menu, typically of several courses, with no choices.

THE CHEZ PANISSE FOUNDATION

The Chez Panisse Foundation, a nonprofit organization headed by Alice Waters, promotes gastronomy and good nutrition through education for children, including the concept of the schoolyard garden (Figure 12.26). By teaching healthful eating habits and respect for food, the foundation works to combat childhood obesity and related diseases. In addition, the foundation supports family farms and sustainable agriculture.

FIGURE 12.26
Alice Waters (left) helps children make the connection between farm and table in the Edible Schoolyard. Courtesy Hannah Johnson

for food producers, and seasonal cooking has laid the foundation for one of America's most vital regional cuisines. From this beginning in the 1970s emerged a new style of cooking perfectly suited to California's Mediterranean climate, diverse population, and adventurous spirit.

Celebrity Chef Wolfgang Puck

By the late 1970s, contemporary California cuisine had spread from its birthplace in the Bay Area throughout the region. Contemporary restaurants in Southern California were preparing innovative California dishes, many incorporating Mexican Border cuisine influences as well as Asian and Mediterranean ideas. In Los Angeles, a young chef named Wolfgang Puck opened Ma Maison, where he applied new techniques and ingredients to classic foods such as pasta and pizza, calling them **designer dishes.** He mingled freely with Ma Maison's star-studded clientele and, through a campaign of press releases, television interviews, and magazine articles, soon became known worldwide. Promoting himself as much as his food, Puck became the na-

CULINARY EDUCATION IN CALIFORNIA

As the birthplace of the American food revolution, California is home to some of the nation's most respected culinary schools. San Francisco's California Culinary Academy opened in 1977 and soon developed into a degree-granting institution with programs in culinary and pastry arts. Founded in 1995, the Culinary Institute of America at Greystone is a campus of the CIA in Hyde Park, New York. Initially the world's only center dedicated exclusively to continuing education for foodservice professionals, Greystone now offers undergraduate degree programs as well. CIA Greystone is located in the Napa Valley in the former home of the Christian Brothers Winery. The University of California at Davis offers the nation's most comprehensive education for aspiring winemakers with its Viticulture and Enology Program.

tion's first **celebrity chef.** In doing so, he almost single-handedly changed America's perception of foodservice workers and inspired another generation of young Americans to become chefs.

Three Pillars of Contemporary California Cuisine

Three pillars made possible—and continue to support—contemporary California cuisine: superior regional ingredients; adventurous, affluent diners; and innovative cooks and chefs.

Superior Regional Ingredients

California's specialty foods are the foundation of the region's contemporary cuisine. The best California restaurants and discerning home cooks work exclusively with the region's naturally raised meats and poultry, specialty vegetables, and heirloom fruits, all raised locally and served in season. Thus, contemporary California cuisine is highly ingredient driven.

Adventurous, Affluent Diners

Most Californians are culinary liberals. From gold rush pioneers to the computer innovators of the dot-com era, most people who migrate to California are adventurers. The very act of living in California—where "the big one" could happen at any time—is a form of risk taking. Add to this adventurous mindset the eclectic mix of cultures and cuisines brought on by successive waves of immigration and it's easy to see why Californians are eager to try new foods and experiment with new dishes.

California's economic viability arrived early in the region's history and rarely wanes. No matter how the nation's economy stands, California always has a large population of affluent citizens ready to spend money on fine ingredients for home cooking and able to dine out often and well. California restaurants typically thrive in good times and survive economic downturns unscathed. Thus, the best professional cooking continues to develop, and chefs continue to create.

Innovative Cooks and Chefs

The men and women now standing at California's stoves continue the region's tradition of breaking tradition. New techniques, new ingredients, and new flavor combinations are constantly evolving in contemporary California cuisine. Moreover, California chefs frequently initiate trends that sweep the entire nation.

FACTOR 5
California's ongoing economic viability ensures continuing development of fine cuisine.

■ CONTEMPORARY ANGLO-ASIAN CALIFORNIA CUISINE TODAY

Like its traditional forbear, contemporary California cuisine continues to emphasize lightness. On the West Coast, both the climate and the public's heightened body awareness demand that food be less filling, more lightly cooked, and lower in fat. Thus, meats, poultry, and especially seafood are cooked to a lesser degree of doneness than in other regional styles. Cooked vegetables are left on the crisper side of tender, which works only because California's locally grown vegetables are fresh and not overmature. Raw foods are an important element of the cuisine: crudités, sushi, and meat carpaccios and tartares. This lighter cooking style has affected higher-level restaurant cooking in almost every region.

The art of cooking meats, fish, poultry, and breads with aromatic hardwoods was first popularized in restaurant cooking by California chefs (Figure 12.27). Alice Waters and Wolfgang Puck were leaders in featuring wood-fired grills as well as wood ovens for roasting meats and baking pizzas. Now wood grilling is featured even in America's national chain restaurants.

Borrowing from Mediterranean cuisines, California chefs began replacing butter with olive oil in cooking. In the 1980s they began the custom—unknown in European restaurants—of offering a dish of olive oil at table as an accompaniment to bread. The oil served may be a pure, first-press variety from California or Italy; sometimes it is flavored with herbs, vinegars, or condiments.

Following the lead of nouvelle cuisine chefs and using one of the favored new tools of the health food movement, California chefs make smooth, vividly colored vegetable and herb essences with juice extractors. Today, immersion blenders are used to create silky sauces, and pressure canisters create frothy foams or spumes. Imaginatively conceived vinaigrettes made from specialty oils and vinegars are used not only on salads but also to dress grilled fish, meats, and poultry as well as hot vegetables.

California cuisine desserts are also light. Perfectly ripe, raw fresh fruit often stars on platters, in tarts, and as toppings and garnishes. Fruit-based ice creams and sorbets are among the most popular dessert items. Fruit sauces typically replace heavy buttercream icings. Contemporary desserts are often individual units rather than slices from a larger, prepared unit.

FIGURE 12.27
California chefs popularized the technique of wood-fired grilling in restaurant cooking. Denis Tabler / Shutterstock

Always innovators, California cooks and chefs borrow freely from around the Pacific Rim and across Asia. The result of this culinary exchange is dishes that are neither Asian nor American, but an amalgam of both; today these dishes are described as **fusion cuisine**. Among the first chefs to practice Asian-American fusion were Hidemasa Yamamoto at La Petite Chay Brasserie and Richard Krause and Wolfgang Puck at Chinois on Main, both in Los Angeles. Latin fusion is a natural result of California's Mexican Border culinary heritage. Both Mexican chiles and boldly seasoned salsas have been embraced by California cuisine chefs.

More than any other region, in California chefs cook with wine in mind. The region's world-class wines are considered both as an accompaniment to the food and as an ingredient in cooking. Some of the best cooking in California is done in the kitchens of the wineries themselves, where buyers and wine journalists are treated to dishes created to showcase the fine wines produced on the estates. California's best-known wine-producing area, north of San Francisco, boasts some of the region's finest restaurants, such as John Ash & Company in Santa Rosa, Terra in St. Helena, and the French Laundry in Yountville.

■ THE FUTURE OF
□
■ CALIFORNIA CUISINE

Today California chefs lead the nation in creating cutting-edge dishes with fine, fresh ingredients available virtually year-round. Many are also committed to practicing good food ethics, increasing their customers' awareness about the healthfulness and sustainability of modern food production. As California welcomes more immigrants from around the world, new foodways are sure to enter the cuisine. These elements, combined with the adventurous nature of California cooks and diners, suggest that California cuisine will continue its tradition of innovation.

Although the signature ingredients and methods of contemporary California cuisine are well represented in the region's home cooking, this ever-changing cooking style remains primarily a restaurant phenomenon. For a list of noteworthy contemporary Anglo-Asian California cuisine restaurants, refer to this book's companion website.

■ THE CHINESE-
□
■ AMERICAN
MICROCUISINE

In the mid-1800s thousands of Chinese men, primarily from southern Guangdong province, immigrated to California to search for gold or to work on the Transcontinental Railroad. When the work was done many remained in the United States, eventually sending for their wives and children. Many opened rudimentary restaurants, blending Chinese cooking techniques with American food products and a few imported seasonings.

From this beginning Chinese-American cuisine was born. Originally a restaurant cuisine, in the 1970s Chinese-American cooking—and the stir-fry technique in particular—were embraced by mainstream home cooks. Today Chinese-American cuisine is evolving under the influence of continued Asian immigration and the adoption of new ingredients.

Visit this book's companion website at www.pearsonhighered .com/sackett to learn more about the Chinese-American microcuisine. Following are some photos relating to that microcuisine.

An early Chinese restaurant. © Photo Collection Alexander Alland, Sr./CORBIS

Chinese restaurant owners recognized that their preferred customer base consisted of a non-Chinese clientele. Three Lions/Getty Images

☐ TABLE 12.1 ANGLO-ASIAN CALIFORNIA DEFINING DISHES

ITEM NAME	HISTORY	DOMINANT INGREDIENTS AND METHOD	MORE
CHILLED AVOCADO SOUP	In the late 1930s, the American public embraced the newly available Waring blender primarily for beverages. California cooks also used blenders to prepare cold soups, among them a smooth purée of avocados and cream.	Ripe avocados are puréed with chilled, defatted chicken stock and heavy cream, then seasoned with lemon juice. The soup is traditionally served in an ice-lined bowl.	Garnishes include red or orange tobiko caviar; minced herbs; or a dollop of salsa.
GARLIC SOUP	Soups flavored and thickened with garlic are popular throughout the Mediterranean Rim and are a legacy of Spanish, Italian, and French immigrants.	Mild young garlic cloves are braised in olive oil and chicken stock, then puréed into a light-textured soup thickened with an egg yolk–lemon juice liaison. Some versions are enriched with heavy cream.	The soup is often finished with a cheese-topped crouton or a poached egg.
CRAB LOUIS	Attributed to San Francisco's Solari's restaurant around the turn of the 20th century, Crab Louis was later featured as a signature dish at the Palace Hotel.	This famous California salad teams Dungeness crab meat with romaine lettuce, hard-cooked egg, and tomatoes in a mayonnaise-based dressing spiked with bottled chili sauce.	Modern versions often include avocado.

(continued)

☐ TABLE 12.1 ANGLO-ASIAN CALIFORNIA DEFINING DISHES   *(continued)*

ITEM NAME	HISTORY	DOMINANT INGREDIENTS AND METHOD	MORE
COBB SALAD	The Cobb salad was invented at Los Angeles's Brown Derby restaurant in 1937, when hungry manager Bob Cobb was searching through the restaurant's refrigerators for a quick lunch. When the salad eventually appeared on the menu, it became an instant hit.	The classic presentation tops a volcano-shaped mound of iceberg lettuce and watercress with vertical stripes of diced chicken, tomatoes, avocados, crumbled bacon, blue cheese, and chopped hard-cooked egg.	A vegetarian version replaces the chicken with fried diced tofu and and uses soy "bacon" bits.
GREEN GODDESS DRESSING	Invented in the 1920s by a chef at San Francisco's Palace Hotel, this pale green salad dressing was named after a play called *The Green Goddess* starring actor George Arliss, who was staying at the hotel.	Mayonnaise is blended with minced anchovies, chives, parsley, scallions, tarragon, and vinegar.	Green Goddess became the dressing of choice on a wedge of crisp iceberg lettuce. Now that iceberg has fallen out of favor, Green Goddess dresses romaine or other sturdy greens. At the Palace it enhances Dungeness crab salad. It is also used as a dip for artichokes and as a topping for poached or broiled fish.
CAESAR SALAD	America's most popular salad, this classic was created in 1924 in Tijuana, Mexico, by an Italian chef named Cesar Cardini for a Hollywood clientele. Caesar salad was popularized in Europe by American Wallis Simpson, who would later marry Prince Edward VIII of Wales.	Traditionally prepared tableside, the dish begins with a dressing based on a lightly coddled egg whisked with lemon juice, olive oil, garlic, Parmesan cheese, and Worcestershire sauce or anchovies. Whole leaves of romaine heart are coated with the dressing and garnished with croutons and shaved Parmesan.	The original version of the dressing did not contain anchovies; contemporary recipes usually include them. Cesar intended the salad to be eaten with the fingers in a manner that had become fashionable in California with asparagus and artichokes.
SALAD TOPPED WITH BAKED GOAT CHEESE	Introduced by Alice Waters at Chez Panisse, this dish became an icon of the new California cuisine of the 1970s.	A round or wedge of California chèvre is dipped in egg wash and coated with fresh bread crumbs, then baked until the crumbs are golden and the cheese warmed. The baked cheese tops young greens tossed with a light vinaigrette dressing.	Variations include other cheeses, such as blue or Brie, and alternative coatings, such as tortilla chip crumbs or chopped nuts.
"DESIGNER" PIZZA/ PIZZETTA	Wolfgang Puck popularized the small appetizer pizza (pizzetta) at Spago in Los Angeles in the 1980s. Adding unusual toppings made them "designer" pizzas.	Thin discs of yeast dough are topped with various ingredients and hearth-baked in a wood-fired oven. Toppings include: ■ sun-dried tomato, mozzarella, and frizzled prosciutto ■ smoked salmon, mascarpone, and caviar ■ roasted peppers, Asiago, and black olives ■ spinach, goat cheese, and confit tomato	Sourdough crust is a popular option.
"DESIGNER" PASTA	Wolfgang Puck also started the trend of teaming pasta with ingredients formerly thought by Americans to be exotic and unusual. One of Puck's most famous pasta dishes is angel hair pasta with smoked salmon, crème fraîche, and golden caviar.	Freed from tomato sauce, California pasta may be tossed with fresh artichoke hearts, smoked fish, olive pesto, broccoli rabe, smoked duck, or caviar, and may be dressed with nut oils, vegetable coulis or essences, fruit vinegars, or stock-based sauces.	California chefs returned pasta to its Italian roots by offering it as an appetizer as well as an entrée.

■ TABLE 12.1 ANGLO-ASIAN CALIFORNIA DEFINING DISHES   *(continued)*

ITEM NAME	HISTORY	DOMINANT INGREDIENTS AND METHOD	MORE
CALIFORNIA ROLL SUSHI	In the 1970s Japanese restaurant chefs in Los Angeles developed this sushi roll to showcase local ingredients as well as to provide a non–raw fish option for Anglo diners. Eventually the roll was made "inside-out" to hide the nori seaweed.	Cool vinegared rice is spread on a sheet of nori seaweed, which is then turned over, rolled with a filling of cucumber, crabmeat, and avocado, and finally cut into cylindrical slices. The budget version uses "crab stick," or imitation crab. The exterior of the roll may be garnished with toasted sesame seeds or tobiko caviar.	California roll sushi is accompanied by soy sauce, wasabi (p. 710) paste, and sweet pickled ginger (p. 709). Some chefs replace the Japanese soy sauce with tamari (p. 594).
ROASTED GARLIC	In the late 1970s, California chefs stunned their customers by serving whole, golden-brown heads of roasted garlic. Presented as an amusée or appetizer, the garlic's soft, mild-flavored pulp was meant to be squeezed out and spread on crusty bread.	Whole heads of garlic are roasted in olive oil with salt and a dash of lemon juice.	Chefs went on to use roasted garlic pulp as a thickener in sauces, as an ingredient in composed dishes, and as the base for flans and soufflés.
GARLIC MASHED POTATOES	Although flavoring mashed potatoes with garlic was known as early as colonial times, in the 1980s California chefs "pushed the envelope" by increasing the amount of garlic.	Whole cloves of fresh garlic are boiled along with russet potatoes, which are then riced or mashed with butter and cream into a thick, fluffy purée. The garlic:potato ratio may be as high as 1:4.	For a Mediterranean flavor, butter and cream may be replaced with a fruity California olive oil.
GARLIC SCAPES/ GARLIC SHOOTS	These curly green shoots of the hard-neck garlic plant were introduced by Asian cooks and are a favorite in Korean cuisine. Garlic scapes have a mellow garlic flavor and a satisfying meaty texture.	The tough ends of garlic scapes are snapped off in the same manner as done with asparagus spears. The scapes are cut into 2" lengths and stir-fried with fresh ginger and a touch of soy sauce.	Alternatively, they are boiled tender, refreshed, and used in Western dishes such as pastas and risottos. They may be tossed with lemon and butter and served as an unusual side dish.
WHOLE ARTICHOKES	Before 1900, few Americans outside California had seen an artichoke. In the early 20th century upper-class homes and high-end restaurants offered whole boiled artichokes served hot with Hollandaise sauce or cool with a dressing or dip. People who would never have been caught eating with their fingers in public had fun plucking off the leaves and dipping them into the sauce.	First, the pointed top third of the artichoke is removed. The spiny leaf tips are trimmed with scissors, and the choke is scooped out. The whole artichokes are boiled in acidulated water to prevent darkening.	In the 1970s, chefs grilled quartered, parboiled artichokes, basting them with garlic-scented olive oil.
GRILLED VEGETABLES	In the 1970s California chefs expanded the possibilities of grilling, first experimenting with marinated vegetables.	Tender-textured vegetables such as zucchini, red and yellow bell peppers, eggplant, onions, and mushrooms are marinated in seasoned olive oil and carefully grilled over wood coals or charcoal.	California chefs were the first to grill asparagus. Thick spears are peeled, dipped in water, and then char-grilled over moderate heat. Basting with water and olive oil creates steam to soften the fibers and lubrication to prevent sticking.
STIR-FRY DISHES	In 1962 Grace Zia Chu published *The Pleasures of Chinese Cooking*, a seminal volume that brought the stir-fry technique to the mainstream American public. California cooks embraced stir-frying, applying it to virtually every local product. By the mid-1970s most California kitchens included a wok.	Meat, poultry, seafood, or a soy product plus a selection of tender-textured vegetables are cut into bite-sized pieces and cooked by tossing them over high heat in a small amount of oil. Traditional seasonings include ginger, garlic, scallions, and soy sauce or tamari (p. 594). Most stir-fries are finished with a light pan sauce based on poultry stock and thickened with a cornstarch slurry.	Stir-fry dishes are served over pan-steamed white or brown rice.
HANGTOWN FRY	This classic dish is the result of a Gold Rush prospector's request for a Hangtown restaurant's most expensive dish. (See p. 548)	Diced bacon is fried until the fat renders out, usually with some chopped onions. Shucked oysters and beaten eggs are added to the pan. The mixture may be scrambled or cooked into a cakelike frittata.	Hangtown fry is served with buttered sourdough biscuits.

(continued)

☐ **TABLE 12.1 ANGLO-ASIAN CALIFORNIA DEFINING DISHES** *(continued)*

ITEM NAME	HISTORY	DOMINANT INGREDIENTS AND METHOD	MORE
JOE'S SPECIAL	Created at Original Joe's restaurant in San Francisco's Marina District, this dish has many variations.	Sautéed mushrooms, spinach, and ground beef are scrambled with eggs and enriched with Romano cheese.	This brunch or supper dish is served with crusty sourdough bread.
CIOPPINO (chip-PEE-noh)	According to legend, this seafood soup/stew was created by the fishermen at San Francisco's Fisherman's Wharf. (See p. 550)	Fish and shellfish are simmered in broth with tomatoes, peppers, onions, garlic, olive oil, wine, and Italian herbs such as basil and oregano. Seafood choices include halibut, swordfish, Pacific rockfish, in-shell Dungeness crab, clams, mussels, calamari, spot prawns, and sea scallops.	The classic accompaniments to cioppino are hot sourdough bread and a green salad vinaigrette.
SAUTÉED ABALONE	Historically prized by Asian diners, abalone was discovered by Anglo Californians in the early 20th century. Demand led to overfishing, a ban on commerical harvest, and aquaculture production.	Thin "steaks" of abalone are pounded for tenderization, working from the center to the outer edge. They are then dredged in flour, sautéed, and served in a light lemon butter sauce.	Because of its scarcity and high cost, abalone is today often served in smaller portions as an appetizer.
"GRILLED" PAN FISH	In classic San Francisco seafood houses, such as Sam's Grill and the Tadich Grill, the term *grill* as applied to fish actually means to pan-fry in butter.	Whole, head-and-tail-on sand dabs (p. 599) and small rex sole are dredged in flour, seasoned with salt, and sautéed in clarified butter.	To showcase their rich, full flavor, the fish are served with nothing more than lemon wedges.
WOOD-GRILLED AND WOOD-ROASTED MEATS	In the 1980s California chefs pioneered the use of hand-crafted, built-in wood ovens used for grilling and roasting the best local meats.	Bathed in marinades based on California wines and olive oils, or lightly cured with a spiced or herbed rub, beef, lamb, pork, and poultry acquire the flavor and aroma of selected hardwoods.	Fuel choices include fruitwoods, alder, and mesquite.
MEYER LEMON DESSERTS	Desserts made from fragrant Meyer lemons (p. 598) were popularized at Alice Waters's restaurant, Chez Panisse, in the 1970s.	Replace standard lemons with Meyer lemons to make signature California desserts. Both juice and zest are used in ice creams, sorbets, pies, tarts, cakes, and other pastry products.	Formerly a backyard fruit, by the 1980s demand led to commercial production.
FRUIT AND FRUIT SORBET MEDLEYS	In the 1980s Californians embraced spa cuisine, in which sliced fresh fruit and fruit-based sorbets replaced high-calorie desserts. The development of small, efficient ice cream batch freezers enabled restaurants to produce sorbets in-house.	To make fruit sorbet, fresh fruit pulp or fruit purée is mixed with sugar syrup and churn-frozen. Attractively fabricated fruit and scoops of sorbet are presented on chilled plates.	Plates may be garnished with mint sprigs and accented with a tuile cookie.
DESSERT PIZZAS/ GALETTES	California's fascination with "designer" pizza led to experimentation with sweet doughs and sweet toppings.	Based on yeasted doughs enriched with butter, sugar, and eggs, dessert pizzas are topped with California fruits and often sweetened mascarpone cheese.	Dessert pizzas may be topped with a scoop of house-made ice cream.

■ □ ■   STUDY QUESTIONS

1. How does California's topography affect its climate? Describe the weather patterns and the ocean current that contribute to California's climate and weather. List and describe California's four climate areas.

2. Discuss the postcontact history of California's Native Americans and explain why they had no impact on Anglo-Asian cuisine.

3. Describe California's first settlers and explain why their foodways rightfully belong to another American culinary region.

4. Discuss the California gold rush and describe gold rush cuisine.

5. Explain the importance of irrigation to California's agricultural centers and cities.

6. List and describe five of California's most important produce crops; list and describe three California artisan food products; list and describe three important California fish and/or shellfish.

7. Describe the impact of Asian influence on traditional and contemporary California cuisine and list three dishes that exhibit it.

8. Trace the evolution of salads in California's culinary history. How did Californians change American attitudes regarding salads? How did developments in horticulture and transportation change America's eating patterns in regard to salads?

9. Describe the 1960s counterculture movement and explain how it affected America's ideas about food, food production, and health.

10. Discuss the birth of contemporary California cuisine. Who was its founder? Who was the nation's first celebrity chef? Discuss the ideas and philosophies behind contemporary California cuisine and list its three pillars.

11. List and describe three defining dishes of traditional California cuisine; list and describe three defining dishes of contemporary California cuisine.

12. Discuss the history and philosophy of Chinese-American cuisine; list and describe three dishes unique to it.

13. Using the information you learned in this chapter and your imagination, plan a four-course special-occasion dinner menu featuring traditional or contemporary Anglo-Asian California cuisine.

Chilled Avocado Soup
with Tobiko Caviar and Poppy Seed Lavash

yield: 1 (10-fl.-oz.) appetizer serving
(multiply × 4 for classroom turnout)

MASTER RECIPE

production		costing only
as needed	crushed ice	n/c
1 1/4 c.	Chilled Avocado Soup	1/4 recipe
1 tsp.	minced chives	1/40 bunch a.p.
2 tsp.	red tobiko caviar	1/4 oz.
2 pc.	Poppy Seed Lavash	approx. 1/5 recipe
5	chive stalks	1/10 bunch a.p.

service turnout:
1. Plate the dish:
   a. Partially fill a 16-fl.-oz. soup bowl with crushed ice and press a 12-fl.-oz. soup cup into the ice.
   b. Ladle the Chilled Avocado Soup into the cup and place the entire assembly on the left side of an appropriate underliner plate.
   c. Sprinkle the soup's surface with minced chives and float the caviar in the center.
   d. Arrange the Poppy Seed Lavash pieces on the right side of the plate and garnish with the chive stalks.

COMPONENT RECIPE
CHILLED AVOCADO SOUP

yield: 5 c.

production		costing only
2	firm-ripe California avocados, cold	2 [24 ct.] avocados
2 Tbsp.	minced shallot	1 oz. a.p.
2 Tbsp.	fresh lemon juice	3/8 [90 ct.] lemon
1 Tbsp.	minced lemon zest	n/c
tt	fine-ground salt	1/16 oz.
3 c.	cold, defatted Poultry Stock	3/16 recipe
1/2 c.	cold crème fraîche	4 fl. oz.
tt	fresh-ground white pepper	1/40 oz.

preparation:
1. Peel and pit the avocados, cut into large dice, and place in a blender with the shallot, lemon juice, lemon zest, and a little salt.
2. Purée these ingredients, adding the Poultry Stock through the feed tube to achieve a smooth consistency.
3. Add the crème fraîche and pulse to blend. If necessary, adjust the thickness with more stock to thin the soup to a spoonable consistency.
4. Correct the flavor balance with salt and/or lemon juice and season with white pepper.
5. Immediately transfer the soup to a freshly sanitized, covered plastic container and refrigerate it.

holding: prepare just enough for service; hold refrigerated in an ice bain-marie for maximum coldness; discard leftovers

---

RECIPE VARIATIONS

Chilled Avocado Soup with Dungeness Crab and Rosemary Flatbread
Replace the black sesame seeds in the Poppy Seed Lavash with 2 Tbsp. chopped fresh rosemary leaves. Omit the chives and caviar. Top each serving with 1 oz. shredded Dungeness crab meat, 1 Tbsp. brunoise-cut red bell pepper, and 1 tsp. chopped flat-leaf parsley.

New Mexico Chilled Avocado Soup
Replace the lemon juice and zest in the soup with lime juice and zest. Omit the chives and caviar. Top each serving with 2 Tbsp. Fresh Tomato Salsa. Replace the Poppy Seed Lavash with fresh-fried corn tortilla chips (p. 331).

Salad of Organic Baby Greens

with Almond-Crusted Goat Cheese and Napa Valley Verjus Vinaigrette

yield: 1 (4-oz.) appetizer serving
(multiply × 4 for classroom turnout)

MASTER RECIPE

production		costing only
1 Tbsp.	melted butter	1/2 oz.
1	Almond-Crusted Goat Cheese Disc	1/4 recipe
2 oz.	mixed organic baby greens, such as mâche, mizuna, baby bok choy, arugula, lolla rossa, frisée, treviso, or radicchio	2 oz.
1/4 c.	Napa Valley Verjus Vinaigrette	1/4 recipe
2	organic nasturtium or pansy blossoms	1/4 oz. a.p.
5 to 6	chervil leaves	1/20 bunch a.p.

service turnout:

1. Brush a sizzle plate with a little butter, place the Almond-Crusted Goat Cheese Disc on top, and brush it with the remaining butter.
2. Bake the cheese disc in a 400°F oven about 5 minutes, until the almond crust is golden brown and the cheese is heated through.
3. Toss the greens with enough of the Napa Valley Verjus Vinaigrette to coat them lightly.
4. Plate the dish:
   a. Mound the greens on a cool 10" plate.
   b. Place the cheese disc in the center of the greens.
   c. Pull the petals from the flowers and scatter them on the salad.
   d. Pull the chervil leaves into bits and scatter them on the salad.
   e. Drizzle any remaining dressing over the top.

RECIPE VARIATION

Salad of Organic Baby Greens with Walnut-Crusted Monterey Jack Cheese and Walnut-Verjus Vinaigrette
Replace the almonds with walnuts. Replace the goat cheese with 1 oz. triangles of artisan Monterey Jack cheese. Replace half the olive oil with walnut oil.

COMPONENT RECIPE
ALMOND-CRUSTED GOAT CHEESE DISCS

yield: 4 (1-oz.) pc.

production		costing only
4 oz.	goat cheese, 1 1/2" diameter log	4 oz.
as needed	flour	1 oz.
1	egg, beaten with 1 Tbsp. water	1 each or 2 oz.
1 c.	crushed sliced almonds	2 1/2 oz.

preparation:

1. Cut out 4 (approx. 5" square) pieces of pan liner.
2. Using a sharp, thin-bladed knife heated with a torch or over a gas flame, cut the log of cheese into 4 (1-oz.) discs.
3. Press each disc with a wide spatula to flatten it slightly.
4. Dredge each disc in flour, coat with egg wash, and roll in almonds to coat evenly and completely. Place each disc on a piece of pan liner when coated.
5. Refrigerate the discs, uncovered, 1 hour.

holding: refrigerate in one layer in a covered container up to 3 days

COMPONENT RECIPE
NAPA VALLEY VERJUS VINAIGRETTE

yield: 1 c.

production		costing only
2 Tbsp.	minced shallot	1 oz. a.p.
1	hard-cooked egg yolk	1 each
1 Tbsp.	Dijon mustard	1/2 fl. oz.
1/3 c.	California white or red verjus	2 2/3 fl. oz.
tt	kosher salt	1/40 oz.
tt	fine-ground white pepper	1/40 oz.
1/2 c.	gold-color pure olive oil	4 fl. oz.

preparation:

1. Place all ingredients except the oil in a blender.
2. Purée, adding the oil in a thin stream through the top opening to create an emulsion.
3. Taste and adjust the flavor balance.
4. Transfer to a freshly sanitized squeeze bottle.

holding: store at room temperature up to 3 hours; refrigerate up to 5 days; bring to room temperature before using; if dressing separates, repurée in a blender

Classic Cobb Salad

yield: 1 (8-oz.) luncheon or appetizer serving
(multiply × 4 for classroom turnout)

MASTER RECIPE

production		costing only
1 c.	shredded iceberg lettuce	1/8 head a.p.
2 c.	shredded romaine lettuce	1/3 head a.p.
1 c.	stemmed and torn watercress	1/3 bunch a.p.
1/4 c.	Basic Vinaigrette Dressing, in squeeze bottle	1/4 recipe
1	cocktail napkin	1 each
1/4	firm-ripe California avocado	1/4 [24 ct.] avocado
1/8	lemon	1/8 [90 ct.] lemon
tt	kosher salt	1/40 oz.
1/4 c.	3/8"-diced vine-ripe tomato	2 1/2 oz. a.p.
1/3 c.	3/8"-diced cold poached chicken breast	3 oz. a.p.
1/4 c.	crumbled blue cheese	1/2 oz.
1/4 c.	fine diagonal-sliced scallion	1/6 bunch a.p.
1/3 c.	crumbled crisp-cooked bacon	3/4 oz.
1/3 c.	chopped hard-cooked egg	1/2 each
1	colossal California black olive with pit	1/2 oz.

service turnout:

1. Combine the lettuces and watercress in a bowl and toss with just enough Basic Vinaigrette Dressing to moisten.
2. Pour the remaining vinaigrette into a 2-oz. pitcher or cruet and place it on a small plate lined with a cocktail napkin.
3. If beginning with a whole avocado, cut a 1/4 wedge out of it, peel the wedge, and cut it into 3/8" dice. Squeeze lemon juice over it and season it with salt. (If not using the remaining avocado, squeeze lemon juice on the flesh, wrap it in plastic film, and refrigerate it.)
4. Plate the dish:
   a. Mound the greens in the center of a cool 12" plate in a conical shape.
   b. Arrange 7 vertical stripes of garnish ingredients on the greens (in order: tomato, chicken, blue cheese, scallion, bacon, egg, and avocado).
   c. Place the olive on the top.

RECIPE VARIATION

Vegetarian Cobb Salad
Replace the chicken with diced, deep-fried tofu or Chinese marinated pressed tofu. Replace the bacon with soy bacon bits.

Southeast Asian Spring Rolls
with Sweet 'n' Hot Dipping Sauce

yield: 1 (4-oz.) appetizer serving
(multiply × 4 for classroom turnout; adjust equipment sizes accordingly)

MASTER RECIPE

production		costing only
1 c.	peanut oil	8 fl. oz. (may be reused)
3	Southeast Asian Spring Rolls	1/5 recipe
3	small Boston lettuce leaves, cleaned and dried	1/8 head a.p.
1/2 c.	Carrot-Daikon Tangle	1/4 recipe
1 Tbsp.	fine diagonal-sliced scallion	1/16 bunch a.p.
1 tsp.	black sesame seeds	1/8 oz.
1/4 c.	Sweet 'n' Hot Dipping Sauce, in squeeze bottle with large tip opening	1/4 recipe

service turnout:
1. Fry the Southeast Asian Spring Rolls:
   a. Heat the oil to about 325°F in an 8" sauté pan.
   b. Shallow-fry the spring rolls about 90 seconds on each side until golden and cooked through.
   c. Drain on a rack and blot with paper towels.
2. Plate the dish:
   a. Fan the lettuce leaves across the back left of the plate.
   b. Mound the Carrot-Daikon Tangle at 2 o'clock and sprinkle with the scallion and sesame seeds.
   c. Shake up the Sweet 'n' Hot Dipping Sauce and squeeze it into a 1 1/2-oz. dip dish. Place the dish on the front of the plate.
   d. Place a spring roll in each lettuce leaf.

APPETIZERS

COMPONENT RECIPE
SOUTHEAST ASIAN SPRING ROLLS

yield: 15 rolls (12 for presentation and 3 for practice)

production		costing only
1/2 oz.	bean thread (cellophane) noodles	1/2 oz.
as needed	boiling water	n/c
2 c.	water	n/c
2 Tbsp.	sugar	1 oz.
1/2 lb.	unpeeled raw white shrimp, any size	1/2 lb.
6 oz.	ground pork	6 oz.
2 tsp.	minced lemongrass (core only), frozen or fresh	1/4 oz. or 1 stalk a.p.
2 tsp.	minced garlic	1/3 oz. a.p.
1 Tbsp.	minced shallot	1/2 oz. a.p.
1 Tbsp.	chopped cilantro	1/40 bunch a.p.
2 tsp.	fresh-ground black pepper	1/4 oz.
1 Tbsp.	sugar	1/2 oz.
2 Tbsp.	Thai or Vietnamese fish sauce	1 fl. oz.
tt	kosher salt	1/10 oz.
15	5" rice paper rounds	3/4 pkg.

preparation:

1. Rehydrate the rice noodles:
   a. Place the noodles in a very small bowl and pour boiling water over them to cover.
   b. Soak the noodles 2 to 3 minutes, until pliable.
   c. Drain in a strainer and rinse under cold water. Shake to remove as much water as possible.
   d. Chop the noodles into rough 1" lengths.

2. Prepare sweetened water for brushing the rice papers:
   a. Combine 2 c. water and 2 Tbsp. sugar in a small saucepan and bring to the boil.
   b. Cool to room temperature.
3. Peel and devein the shrimp. Chop into rough 1/4" dice.
4. To make the filling, combine the shrimp, pork, noodles, lemongrass, garlic, shallot, cilantro, pepper, 1 Tbsp. sugar, fish sauce, and salt in a bowl. Wearing a foodservice glove, mix these ingredients together and knead like bread to firm and compact the mixture.
5. Check the filling's seasoning by poaching a tiny ball of it in simmering water. Taste and adjust the seasoning if necessary.
6. Make up the spring rolls:
   a. Prepare a half-sheet tray with pan liner. Have ready a clean, damp kitchen towel and a pastry brush. Sanitize the work surface.
   b. Place 3 rice papers on the work surface.
   c. Brush the rice papers with sweetened water, then turn them over and brush again.
   d. Wait for the papers to soften, brushing with more water if necessary.
   e. Place about 2 Tbsp. filling in a horizontal row across the bottom of each paper.
   f. Fold the bottom edge of each paper over the filling, fold in the sides of the paper, and roll up the spring roll.
   g. Place the spring rolls on the lined sheet tray and cover with the damp towel. Don't allow the rolls to touch each other.
   h. Repeat to make at least 15 spring rolls.

holding: wrap the tray in plastic film and refrigerate up to 2 days

Place filling in a horizontal row across the bottom of the paper.

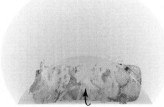

Fold the bottom edge of the paper over the filling.

Fold in the sides of the paper and then roll up the spring roll.

COMPONENT RECIPE
CARROT-DAIKON TANGLE

yield: about 2 c.

production		costing only
1 large	carrot, peeled and trimmed	6 oz. a.p.
4" section	daikon, peeled	about 5 oz. a.p.

preparation:
1. Using the finest julienne blade of a mandoline (preferably Asian-style), shred the vegetables into long, extremely fine filaments.
2. Mix together the carrot and daikon shreds.
3. Soak the shreds in ice water at least 30 minutes.

holding: refrigerate in ice water up to 24 hours

COMPONENT RECIPE
SWEET 'N' HOT DIPPING SAUCE

yield: 1 c.

production		costing only
3 Tbsp	sugar	1 1/2 oz.
3 Tbsp.	water	n/c
3 Tbsp	white rice wine vinegar	1 1/2 fl. oz.
1 Tbsp.	crushed dried red pepper	1/10 oz.
2 tsp.	minced fresh garlic	1/4 oz. a.p.
1 Tbsp.	minced scallion	1/16 bunch a.p.
1 Tbsp.	ketchup	1/2 fl. oz.
1/4 c.	Thai or Vietnamese fish sauce	2 fl. oz.

preparation:
1. Combine the sugar, water, vinegar, and dried red pepper in a small nonreactive saucepan. Heat just to the boil and then cool to room temperature.
2. Stir in the remaining ingredients.
3. Taste and correct the seasoning to achieve a sweet-tart-salty flavor balance.
4. For service, transfer to a freshly sanitized squeeze bottle with a large tip opening.

holding: refrigerate in a freshly sanitized, covered squeeze bottle or nonreactive container up to 1 week

APPETIZERS

RECIPE VARIATION

Southeast Asian Summer Rolls with Sweet 'n' Hot Dipping Sauce
Omit all filling ingredients and frying oil. Do not fry the spring rolls. Instead, fill each moistened wrapper with 1 Tbsp. rehydrated bean thread noodles; 1 Tbsp. poached, peeled, sliced shrimp; 1 Tbsp. julienne Chinese roast pork; a mint leaf and a coriander leaf; a few scallion shreds; and 1 tsp. chopped roasted peanuts. Tie each roll with a 4" length of blanched and refreshed scallion green.

Designer Pizzetta
with Shredded Duck, Confit Tomatoes, and Mascarpone Cheese

yield: 1 (7-oz.) appetizer serving
(multiply × 4 for classroom turnout)

MASTER RECIPE

production		costing only
as needed	cornmeal	1/8 oz.
as needed	flour	1/4 oz.
6 oz.	Pizza Dough	1/4 recipe
1/2 c.	Shredded Duck	1/4 recipe
1/4 c.	mascarpone cheese	2 oz.
1/4 c.	grated Parmigiano-Reggiano cheese	1 oz. a.p.
large pinch	chopped rosemary leaves	1/40 bunch a.p.
3 pc.	Confit Tomatoes, with pan juices	1/4 recipe

service turnout:
1. Mise en place:
   a. Preheat a pizza oven to 500°F, or place a baking stone* in a convection oven and preheat it to 500°F.
   b. Sanitize the work surface and have ready a bench scraper and rolling pin.
   c. Have all ingredients ready at hand.
2. Make up the pizzetta:
   a. Sprinkle the center of a baker's peel* with cornmeal and dust the work surface with flour.
   b. Use a bench scraper to cut the Pizza Dough into 4 equal portions. (If making up only 1 pizzetta, cover the remaining dough and refrigerate it.)
   c. On the floured work surface round the dough and then roll/stretch the dough into a thin, even 10" disc. Place the dough on the baker's peel. Throughout the remaining makeup steps, make sure the dough disc slides freely on the peel.
   d. Scatter most of the Shredded Duck on the dough and press to help it adhere.
   e. Spread mascarpone on the dough in an even layer extending to 1/2" from the edge.
   f. Sprinkle with Parmigiano-Reggiano, rosemary, and the remaining duck.
   g. Arrange the Confit Tomatoes on the dough, and then drizzle their juices over the top.
3. Slide the pizzetta from the peel onto the floor of the pizza oven, or onto the baking stone. Bake 6 to 8 minutes, until the crust is crisp.
4. Plate the dish:
   a. Use the peel to remove the pizzetta from the oven and transfer it to a hot 12" plate.
   b. Provide a steak knife.

*If a baking stone and/or baker's peel are unavailable, you may improvise with inverted half-sheet trays.

COMPONENT RECIPE
SHREDDED DUCK

yield: about 2 c. (5 to 6 oz.)

production		costing only
1/2 c.	California Pinot Noir (or other red wine)	4 fl. oz.
2	5-oz. Petaluma duck legs, or other variety	10 oz.
1 Tbsp.	gold-color pure olive oil	1/2 oz.
tt	kosher salt	1/4 oz.
1 c.	Brown Stock	1/16 recipe
1 sprig	fresh sage	1/10 bunch a.p.
1	bay leaf	1/12 oz.

preparation:
1. Place the Pinot Noir in a small, nonreactive sauté pan and reduce by half over low heat.
2. Skin the duck legs and remove all visible fat.
3. Cook the duck:
   a. Heat a sauté pan just large enough to accommodate the duck legs. Add the oil and sear the duck legs on both sides.
   b. Season the duck with salt. Add the Brown Stock, reduced wine, sage, and bay leaf. Cover and simmer about 30 minutes, until the duck is very tender.
   c. Open-pan cool the duck in its cooking liquid.
4. Finish the duck:
   a. Remove and discard the sage sprig and bay leaf from the cooking liquid, then remove and reserve the duck. Reduce the liquid to a glaze over moderate heat.
   b. Remove the duck meat from the bones and discard the bones.
   c. Pull the duck meat into shreds.
   d. Mix the glaze into the shredded duck.
   e. Taste and, if necessary, season with additional salt.

holding: refrigerate in a freshly sanitized, covered container up to 5 days

COMPONENT RECIPE
CONFIT TOMATOES

yield: 12 pc. (approx. 10 oz.)

production		costing only
3	firm, medium-size vine-ripe tomatoes	1 lb.
as needed	kosher salt	1/2 oz.
2 tsp.	Four-Spice Mix	1/10 recipe
1 c.	extra virgin olive oil	8 fl. oz.

preparation:
1. Fabricate and drain the tomatoes:
   a. Blanch the tomatoes in boiling water for a few seconds only to loosen the skins, then refresh in ice water.
   b. Core and peel the tomatoes.
   c. Cut each tomato into 4 thick, even slices.
   d. Line a half-sheet tray with a triple layer of paper towels. Place the tomato slices on the towels and salt them generously.
   e. Turn over the tomatoes and salt the new top surfaces.
   f. Place a triple layer of paper towels on the tomatoes' surface and place another sheet tray on top. Weight with a 2- to 3-lb. object to press the tomatoes and force out excess liquid.
   g. Allow to stand at room temperature about 30 minutes.
2. Preheat an oven to 275°F.
3. Finish seasoning the tomatoes:
   a. Uncover the tomatoes and remove the top layer of towels. Season with half of the Four-Spice Mix.
   b. Flip over the tomatoes, remove the towels, and season with the remaining spice mix.
   c. Drizzle the tomatoes with the oil.
4. Bake the tomatoes:
   a. Place the tray in the oven and bake 30 minutes to 1 hour, until the tomatoes soften and release their juices.
   b. Increase the oven temperature to 450°F and bake off the liquid. Watch carefully and, after 5 to 15 minutes, remove the tray from the oven when the tomatoes begin to sizzle.
5. Cool to room temperature.

holding: refrigerate in a freshly sanitized, nonreactive container up to 1 week

---

RECIPE VARIATIONS

Designer Pizzetta is subject to endless variation; here are some California classics:

- pesto, fresh mozzarella, and sliced fresh tomatoes (peeled, salted, pressed)
- Monterey Jack, chorizo, and Fresh Tomato Salsa (p. 331)
- marinara sauce, braised broccoli rabe, and Asiago cheese
- smoked salmon, cream cheese, and caviar (added after baking)
- grilled red onions, blue cheese, and walnuts
- cooked chopped spinach, goat cheese, and roasted red bell peppers
- lamb sausage, feta cheese, and sliced fresh tomatoes (peeled, salted, pressed)

California Roll Sushi
with Wasabi-Soy Dip

yield: 1 (4-oz.) appetizer serving
(multiply × 4 for classroom turnout)

APPETIZERS

MASTER RECIPE

production		costing only
1/2	Inside-Out California Roll	1/4 recipe
2	Scallion Brushes (p. 276)	1/4 recipe
1/4 oz.	pink pickled ginger	1/4 oz.
1 Tbsp.	Wasabi-Soy Dip, in squeeze bottle	1/4 recipe
1 tsp.	black sesame seeds	1/8 oz.

service turnout:

1. Cut the Inside-Out California Roll:
   a. Dip the blade of a sharp, flexible knife in cold water and, if necessary, cut a full, plastic-wrapped California roll in half. Return one half to its container and return it to the refrigerator. Wipe the knife clean.
   b. Unwrap the remaining half California roll. Cut the half California roll into three even-size pieces, wiping the knife and dipping it in water after each cut.
2. Plate the dish:
   a. Place one Scallion Brush in the front right corner of a 10" rectangular plate and the other brush on the left side of the plate.
   b. Arrange the California roll pieces on the plate slightly right of center.
   c. Arrange the pickled ginger slices on the work surface overlapping in a row, and then roll them into a loose roll. Open out one side of the roll to make a "rose," and place it on the back left corner of the plate.
   d. Squeeze the Wasabi-Soy Dip into a 1/2-oz. dip dish and place it on the plate to the left of the California roll pieces.
   e. Sprinkle the plate with black sesame seeds.

COMPONENT RECIPE

INSIDE-OUT CALIFORNIA ROLLS

yield: 2 (8-oz.) rolls

production		costing only
1/4	cold, firm-ripe California avocado	1/4 [24 ct.] avocado
tt	fresh lemon juice	1/8 [90 ct.] lemon
tt	kosher salt	1/20 oz.
2 sheets	best-quality sushi nori	1/5 pkg.
1 1/2 c.	fresh-made Sushi Rice, room temperature	1/3 recipe
2 Tbsp.	orange tobiko caviar	1/2 oz.
1 Tbsp.	black sesame seeds	2/3 oz.
2 oz.	shredded Dungeness crab meat (or other crab meat)	2 oz.
1 Tbsp.	mayonnaise, in squeeze bottle	1/2 fl. oz.
tt	shichimi togarishi seasoning	1/8 oz.
1 1/2 oz.	peeled seeded cucumber, 3/8" × 3/8" × 4" batonnets	4 oz. a.p.

preparation:

1. Peel the avocado and slice it into slender strips. Coat the slices with lemon juice and season with salt.
2. Assemble an inside-out California roll:
   a. Cover a sushi mat with a piece of plastic film. Place a sheet of nori on it horizontally.
   b. Dip your fingers in cool water, pick up half of the Sushi Rice, and press the rice onto the surface of the nori in a thin, even layer, leaving a 3/4" exposed edge at the back. Extend the rice fully into the corners and to the front and side edges (see photo on p. 678).
   c. Sprinkle half of the tobiko and half of the black sesame seeds, evenly distributed, on the rice.
   d. Press a sheet of plastic film on the surface of the rice and then turn the rice-covered nori sheet over, upside-down, on the mat. Remove the plastic film, exposing the nori sheet.
   e. Arrange half of the crab meat across the nori in a horizontal line about 2 1/2" from the nearest edge. (The photo on p. 678 illustrates this technique but with the rice, rather than the nori, on top).
   f. Squeeze half of the mayonnaise on the crab meat and sprinkle with shichimi seasoning.
   g. Arrange half of the avocado slices on the crab meat and press to help them adhere.
   h. Arrange half of the cucumber batonnets on the avocado and press to help them adhere.
   i. Using the mat to get started, and holding the filling in place with your fingertips, begin rolling up the sushi roll as you peel back the plastic film. (The photos on p. 678 illustrate this technique but with the rice, rather than the nori, on top).
   j. When almost rolled, moisten the back edge very lightly with water and then finish rolling.
   k. Wrap the plastic film up around the California roll, and then wrap the roll in the bamboo mat. Squeeze gently along its length to firm the roll.
   l. Unroll the mat and tip the California roll onto the work surface.
3. Repeat, using the remaining ingredients and making another roll in the same manner.

holding: prepare just before service, making only the amount needed for the service; refrigerate up to 6 hours only

Note: Japanese sushi is traditionally made to order because sushi rice hardens under refrigeration. However, in non-Japanese California restaurants it is frequently prepared ahead of time.

COMPONENT RECIPE

WASABI-SOY DIP

yield: approx. 4 Tbsp.

production		costing only
2 tsp.	wasabi powder	1/8 oz.
4 Tbsp.	Japanese soy sauce	2 fl. oz.

preparation:

1. Mix the wasabi paste with the soy sauce.
2. Let stand at room temperature, stirring occasionally, at least 30 minutes.
3. For service, place in a freshly sanitized squeeze bottle.

holding: at cool room temperature up to 3 hours; refrigerated up to 1 week

---

RECIPE VARIATIONS

Philadelphia Roll Sushi with Ponzu Sauce
Replace the crab meat with julienne smoked salmon. Replace the cucumber with red onion slivers. Replace the avocado with cream cheese. Omit the mayonnaise. When making the dipping sauce, replace the wasabi with 1 Tbsp. fresh lime juice and the juice of 1/4 oz. fresh ginger squeezed through a garlic press. Hydrate 1/2 tsp. wasabi powder with a few drops of water and add to the plate.

Dungeness Crab Louis in Avocado Half

yield: 1 (8-oz.) luncheon or appetizer serving
(multiply × 4 for classroom turnout)

MASTER RECIPE

production		costing only
3/4 c.	shredded Dungeness crab meat (or other)	8 oz. crab claw clusters or 3 oz. crab meat
1/2 c.	Louis Dressing, in squeeze bottle	1/4 recipe
3 leaves	romaine lettuce	1/6 head a.p.
1 c.	shredded romaine lettuce hearts	1/6 head a.p.
1/2	cold firm-ripe California avocado	1/2 [24 ct.] avocado
1 Tbsp.	fresh lemon juice	1/6 [90 ct.] lemon
tt	kosher salt	1/40 oz.
2 oz.	San Francisco Sourdough baguette, cut in 3/8" slices and toasted	1/12 recipe
1	hard-cooked egg, peeled and halved	1 each
3	grape tomatoes	1/12 pt.
3	canned California black olives	1/2 oz.
2 tsp.	chopped flat-leaf parsley	1/40 bunch a.p.

service turnout:

1. Toss the crab meat with half of the Louis Dressing.
2. Plate the dish:
   a. Line a cool 10" plate with the romaine leaves.
   b. Mound the shredded romaine hearts slightly left of center on the plate.
   c. If beginning with a whole avocado, quickly cut it in half lengthwise and remove the pit. Peel the avocado half, coat its surfaces with lemon juice, and season it with salt. (If not using the other avocado half immediately, leave the pit in it, coat it with lemon juice, wrap it in plastic film, and refrigerate.)
   d. Fill the avocado half with the crab meat and press it into the shredded lettuce with the pointed end toward 11 o'clock.
   e. Drizzle the remaining dressing over the crab meat and the shredded lettuce.
   f. Fan the toasted San Francisco Sourdough slices behind the avocado at 1 o'clock.
   g. Arrange the egg halves, tomatoes, and olives around the avocado.
   h. Sprinkle a diagonal line of parsley across the crab meat.

COMPONENT RECIPE
LOUIS DRESSING

yield: 2 c.

production		costing only
1/4 c.	fine-chopped scallion	1/4 bunch a.p.
1/4 c.	fine-diced green bell pepper	1 1/2 oz. a.p.
2 Tbsp.	bottled chili sauce	1 fl. oz.
dash	Worcestershire sauce	1/8 fl. oz.
1 Tbsp.	fresh lemon juice	1/6 [90 ct.] lemon
1 Tbsp.	minced lemon zest	n/c
1 c.	mayonnaise	8 fl. oz.
1/3 c.	heavy cream	2 2/3 fl. oz.
tt	kosher salt	1/40 oz.
tt	fine-ground white pepper	1/40 oz.

preparation:

1. Mix together all ingredients and allow to stand at room temperature about 15 minutes, until the flavors meld.
2. Taste and balance the seasonings.
3. Transfer to a freshly sanitized squeeze bottle with a large opening.

holding: refrigerate up to 5 days

RECIPE VARIATION

Crab Louis–Stuffed Artichoke

Omit the lettuce, avocado, lemon, egg, tomatoes, olives, and toast. Stuff the dressed crab meat into the hollow of a cleaned, boiled, refreshed, and drained artichoke. Present the remaining sauce in a dip dish. Garnish with brunoise-cut red bell pepper and chopped flat-leaf parsley.

San Francisco Cioppino

with North Beach Escarole Salad and Sourdough Roll

yield: 1 (9-oz.) entrée serving plus accompaniments
(multiply × 4 for classroom turnout; adjust equipment sizes accordingly)

MASTER RECIPE

production		costing only
2 c.	Cioppino Base	1/4 recipe
1	Dungeness crab cluster, cracked	4 oz.
3	Pacific littleneck clams, scrubbed	3 each
1	1-oz. cube trimmed Pacific swordfish steak	1 1/2 oz. a.p.
1	1-oz. strip Pacific rockfish fillet, skin on, pinned	1 oz.
2 to 4	Pacific spot prawns or other shrimp, peeled	2 oz. a.p.
3	Pacific mussels, scrubbed	1 oz.
1/2 oz.	cleaned calamari tubes, cut in 3/8" rings	1/2 oz.
2 Tbsp.	chopped hard-cooked egg	1/2 each or 1 oz.
3 Tbsp.	North Beach Italian Dressing, in squeeze bottle	1/4 recipe
2 oz.	escarole, trimmed, washed and dried	1/6 head a.p.
1 Tbsp.	brunoise-cut red bell pepper	1/4 oz. a.p.
1	San Francisco Sourdough Roll	1/8 recipe
1 Tbsp.	chopped flat-leaf parsley	1/40 bunch a.p.

service turnout:

1. Finish the cioppino:
   a. Place the Cioppino Base and crab cluster in a covered 10" sauté pan and bring to the boil.
   b. Add the clams, swordfish, rockfish, prawns, and mussels, cover, and simmer 3 minutes.
   c. Stir in the calamari and remove from heat.
2. Dress and plate the salad:
   a. Place the egg in a large work bowl and mash it.
   b. Thoroughly shake the dressing bottle and squeeze the North Beach Italian Dressing into the work bowl.
   c. Tear the escarole into bite-size pieces and drop it into the work bowl.
   d. Toss the escarole with the dressing.
   e. Mound the salad on the left side of a cool 8" plate.
   f. Sprinkle the salad with the brunoise red bell pepper.
   g. Place the San Francisco Sourdough Roll on the right side of the plate.
3. Plate the cioppino:
   a. Use tongs and a perforated spoon to mound the seafood into a hot 12" pasta plate.
   b. Ladle the broth over the top.
   c. Sprinkle with parsley.
   d. Provide a soup spoon, seafood fork, seafood cracker, and finger bowl or wet wipe.

COMPONENT RECIPE

CIOPPINO BASE

yield: 2 qt.

production		costing only
1/2 c.	gold-color pure olive oil	4 fl. oz.
1 c.	medium-chopped yellow onion	5 oz. a.p.
3/4 c.	trimmed, medium-chopped fennel bulb	3 oz. a.p.
1/2 c.	fine-chopped green bell pepper	4 oz. a.p.
1/2 c.	peeled, fine-chopped celery	1/10 head a.p.
1/4 c.	peeled, fine-chopped carrot	2 oz. a.p.
2 Tbsp.	minced garlic	1/2 oz. a.p.
2 tsp.	crushed dried red pepper	1/16 oz.
1 tsp.	dried oregano	1/16 oz.
pinch	dried thyme	1/16 oz.
1 sprig	fresh rosemary	1/10 bunch a.p.
2	bay leaves	1/30 oz.
1/2 c.	California Zinfandel (or other red wine)	4 fl. oz.
3 c.	petite canned diced tomatoes in juice	24 fl. oz.
tt	kosher salt	1/4 oz.
6 c.	Fish Stock or Shellfish Stock	3/8 recipe
2 Tbsp.	chopped flat-leaf parsley	1/20 bunch a.p.

preparation:

1. Combine the oil, onion, fennel, green bell pepper, celery, and carrot in a large, nonreactive saucepan. Sauté over low heat about 5 minutes, until the vegetables are soft and light golden in color.
2. Add the garlic, dried red pepper, oregano, and thyme. Sauté 1 minute longer.
3. Add the rosemary, bay leaves, and wine. Cook until almost dry. ⚠ Watch carefully; do not allow to scorch.
4. Add the tomatoes and a little salt, increase the heat, and cook until almost dry.
5. Add the Fish Stock, bring to the simmer, and cook about 35 minutes, until the flavors are melded and the mixture is reduced to about 2 qt. of light, brothlike sauce.
6. Add the parsley and correct the salt, keeping in mind that seafood of varying salinity will be cooked in the sauce base.

holding: open-pan cool and immediately refrigerate in a freshly sanitized, covered, nonreactive container up to 4 days

Tea-Smoked Ahi Tuna

with Wasabi Mashed Potatoes and Braised Baby Bok Choy

yield: 1 (6-oz.) entrée serving plus accompaniments
(multiply × 4 for classroom turnout; adjust equipment sizes
accordingly*)

MASTER RECIPE

production		costing only
as needed	pan coating spray	% of container
1/4 c.	raw basmati rice	1/4 oz.
2 Tbsp.	Chinese black tea leaves	1/4 oz.
1	Tea-Marinated Tuna Steak	1/4 recipe
4 or 6	baby bok choy, trimmed, washed, thoroughly drained	3 oz. a.p.
1/2 c.	water	n/c
1/2 c.	Chinese Vegetable Glaze	1/4 recipe
1 1/4 c.	Wasabi Mashed Potatoes, hot in steam table	1/4 recipe
1/3 c.	Teriyaki Sauce, p. 691, hot in steam table	1/6 recipe
1/2 c.	Pickled Vegetable Shreds	1/4 recipe

service turnout:

1. Mise en place:
   a. Line the inside of a 12" wok with a double layer of heavy-duty aluminum foil.
   b. Combine the raw rice and tea leaves in the bottom of the wok.
   c. Spray a 10" round cake cooling rack with pan coating and fit it into the wok.
   d. Cover the wok with a tight-fitting lid and place it on a turned-off stove burner. Make sure the ventilation system is activated.
   e. Have ready a 10" sauté pan with a tight-fitting lid.

2. Smoke-roast the Tea-Marinated Tuna Steak:
   a. Turn the burner under the wok to high heat and allow the rice-tea mixture to heat and build smoke under the lid for 5 minutes.
   b. Quickly lift the wok lid, place the tuna on the rack inside the wok, and immediately replace the cover. Reduce the heat to medium and smoke-roast the tuna 2 1/2 to 3 minutes to a rare doneness.

3. Cook the baby bok choy:
   a. Place the baby bok choy and water in the sauté pan, cover with the lid, and pan-steam it on high heat about 3 minutes, until crisp-tender. Uncover the pan.
   b. Stir the Chinese Vegetable Glaze to redistribute the ingredients, then ladle 1/2 c. glaze into the pan. Stir and toss the bok choy until it is coated with the glaze.

4. Plate the dish:
   a. Place a 2 1/2" entremet ring slightly back of center on a hot 12" plate. Pack it with the Wasabi Mashed Potatoes, then remove the ring.
   b. Place the tuna steak on top of the mashed potatoes and nap it with Teriyaki Sauce.
   c. Arrange the bok choy on either side of the mashed potatoes.
   d. Mound the Pickled Vegetable Shreds on top of the tuna.

*Two tuna steaks can be smoke-roasted in the designated setup; to prepare all 4 tuna steaks, increase the wok size to 14" and the rack to 12"; double the raw rice and tea amounts.

COMPONENT RECIPE
TEA-MARINATED TUNA STEAKS

yield: 4 (6-oz.) tuna steaks

production		costing only
2 Tbsp.	Chinese black tea leaves	1/4 oz.
3/4 c.	boiling water	n/c
1/4 c.	chopped fresh ginger	1 1/2 oz. a.p.
1 Tbsp.	chopped garlic	1/3 oz. a.p.
1/2 c.	chopped scallion	1/4 bunch a.p.
1/2 c.	Chinese rice wine or dry sherry	4 fl. oz.
1/4 c.	peanut oil	2 fl. oz.
1/4 c.	Chinese soy sauce	2 fl. oz.
2 drops	Chinese sesame oil	1/16 fl. oz.
4	6-oz. ahi tuna steaks, at least 1" thick	1 1/2 lb. a.p.

preparation:
1. Prepare the marinade:
   a. Place the tea leaves in a small, nonreactive bowl. Pour the boiling water over them and allow them to steep 30 minutes, until cool.
   b. Place the ginger, garlic, scallion, wine, peanut oil, soy sauce, and sesame oil in a blender and grind to a paste.
   c. Strain the liquid tea into the blender and purée the mixture.
2. Place the tuna steaks in a freshly sanitized container just large enough to hold them in one layer. Pour in the marinade and turn the steaks to coat them.
3. Cover and refrigerate 1 hour.
4. Turn over the tuna steaks, re-cover, and marinate 1 hour longer.

holding: after 2 hours, drain the tuna steaks of marinade; refrigerate up to 2 days

COMPONENT RECIPE
CHINESE VEGETABLE GLAZE

yield: approx. 2 c.

production		costing only
3 Tbsp.	cornstarch	2/3 oz.
1 1/3 c.	water	n/c
1/4 c.	minced fresh ginger	1 oz. a.p.
1 Tbsp.	minced garlic	1/2 oz. a.p.
3 Tbsp.	Chinese soy sauce	1 1/2 fl. oz.
1/4 c.	Chinese oyster sauce	2 fl. oz.
1 Tbsp.	sugar	1/2 oz.

preparation:
1. Place the cornstarch in a small bowl and whisk in the water.
2. Mix in the remaining ingredients.

holding: prepare just enough for service; hold at cool room temperature up to 3 hours; stir frequently

COMPONENT RECIPE
WASABI MASHED POTATOES

yield: approx. 5 c.

production		costing only
1 Tbsp.	wasabi powder	1/4 oz.
1/3 c. or more	boiling water	n/c
5 c.	Classic Mashed Potatoes, firm variation	1 recipe
1/2 c.	commercial mayonnaise	4 fl. oz.

preparation:
1. Place the wasabi powder in a small bowl and stir in enough boiling water to make a pourable paste.
2. If necessary, heat the Classic Mashed Potatoes.
3. Stir together the wasabi paste and mayonnaise, then stir this mixture into the potatoes.
4. Taste and correct the seasoning.

holding: during service, hold in a steam table or hot bain-marie; for longer holding, open-pan cool and immediately refrigerate in a freshly sanitized, covered container up to 3 days

COMPONENT RECIPE
PICKLED VEGETABLE SHREDS

yield: 2 c.

production		costing only
2	peeled, trimmed carrots	7 oz. a.p.
1	large red bell pepper	6 oz. a.p.
4	scallions, trimmed	1/2 bunch a.p.
1/2 c.	Japanese pink pickled ginger, with pickling liquid	4 fl. oz.
tt	white rice wine vinegar	1/2 fl. oz.
tt	kosher salt	1/8 oz.

preparation:
1. Fabricate the vegetables:
   a. Using the finest julienne blade of a mandoline (preferably Asian-style), cut the carrots into fine julienne about 3" in length.
   b. Core the red bell pepper, cut it into sections along its contours, and remove all white membrane. Using a swivel peeler, peel away the skin. Cut the pepper flesh into fine julienne about 3" in length.
   c. Cut the scallions into 3" lengths, then cut the lengths into fine julienne.
   d. Drain the pickled ginger, reserving the liquid. Cut into fine julienne.
2. Place the pickling liquid in a bowl and toss in the julienne vegetables and ginger. Cover and refrigerate 1 hour, mixing occasionally.
3. Taste and balance the seasoning with vinegar and salt.

holding: refrigerate in a freshly sanitized, covered, nonreactive container up to 12 hours

---

RECIPE VARIATION
Tea-Smoked Ahi Tuna with Pickled Vegetable Shreds (appetizer)
Smoke-roast 4 (3-oz.) Tea-Marinated Tuna Steaks, cool, and chill. Present each serving sliced, with 1/2 c. Pickled Vegetable Shreds, 5 or 6 rice crackers, and 3 Tbsp. mayonnaise flavored with cayenne, sugar, light soy sauce, and shichimi togarishi seasoning.

Toor Dal Tofu Bundles in Red Curry Broth

with Brown Rice and Steamed California Vegetables

yield: 1 (5 oz.) entrée serving plus accompaniments
(multiply × 4 for classroom turnout; adjust equipment sizes
accordingly)

MASTER RECIPE

production		costing only
3 Tbsp.	unsweetened coconut cream or thick coconut milk	1 1/2 fl. oz.
2 tsp.	Thai red curry paste	1/3 fl. oz.
1 c.	Vegetable Broth, Asian variation	1/4 recipe
tt	kosher salt	1/16 oz.
tt	brown sugar	1/8 oz.
3	Toor Dal Tofu Bundles	1/4 recipe
as needed	frying compound or peanut oil	% used
5 oz.	fresh vegetables, such as cauliflower, carrots, asparagus, snap peas, haricots verts, etc., fabricated to cook evenly together	6 oz. a.p.
1 1/2 c.	Pan-Steamed Brown Rice, hot in steamtable	1/4 recipe
1 Tbsp.	cornstarch mixed with 2 Tbsp. water	1/4 oz. a.p.
2	cilantro sprigs	1/10 bunch

service turnout:

1. Prepare the sauce:
   a. Heat the coconut cream in an 8" sauté pan, add the curry paste and fry, stirring, a few seconds until fragrant.
   b. Stir in the Vegetable Broth and bring to the simmer.
   c. Season with salt.
2. Deep-fry the Tofu Bundles:
   a. Blot the tofu bundles dry and lower them into the oil of a fryer set at 400°F. Fry about 40 seconds until golden.
   b. Drain on paper towels and remove the picks.
3. Add the tofu bundles to the simmering curry broth, cover, and cook at a simmer for about 3 minutes.
4. Steam the vegetables in a range-top steamer for about 2 minutes or in a pressure steamer about 30 seconds until just al dente.
5. Finish and plate the dish:
   a. Place a 3 1/2" × 2" entremet ring in the center of a hot 12" pasta plate, pack the Pan-Steamed Brown Rice into the ring, and lift the ring.
   b. Arrange the vegetables around the rice.
   c. Arrange the tofu bundles on top of the rice.
   d. Bring the curry broth to the boil. Stir the cornstarch and water to mix it thoroughly, then stir it into the broth, adding just enough to thicken it to thinner than nappé consistency.
   e. Spoon the broth over the tofu bundles and allow it to flow into the plate well.
   f. Pull the cilantro into leaflets and scatter them over the dish.

COMPONENT RECIPE

TOOR DAL TOFU BUNDLES

yield: 12 (1 1/2 oz.) pieces

production		costing only
1 c.	toor dal (non-oily type yellow split legume)	6 oz.
1 tsp.	turmeric	1/8 oz.
pinch	cayenne powder	1/16 oz.
tt	kosher salt	1/8 oz.
1/2 c.	bulgar wheat	3 oz.
3/4 c.	boiling water	n/c
12	6" × 6" squares dried tofu sheets (bean curd skins)	3/4 pkg.
as needed	boiling water	n/c
1/2 c.	peanut oil	4 fl. oz.
1 tsp.	black mustard seeds	1/8 oz.
2 tsp.	crushed coriander seeds	1/4 oz.
2 tsp.	crushed black peppercorns	1/4 oz.
2 Tbsp.	chiffonade fresh curry leaves	1/10 pkg.
1 1/4 c.	fine-chopped yellow onions	6 oz.
1/3 c.	minced ginger, peeled	1 1/2 oz.
1	firm tofu square (bean curd), 1/4" dice	about 4 oz.
+/− 1/4 c.	gram flour (besan, chick pea flour)	+/−1/2 oz.

preparation:

1. Precook the toor dal:
   a. Pick over the toor dal for stones or foreign matter.
   b. Place the dal in a small saucepan and rinse well. Drain, cover with water by 1 inch, and bring to the boil. Reduce the heat to medium, skim off the foam, and add the turmeric and cayenne.
   c. Simmer 20 to 30 minutes until the dal is tender and the cooking liquid reduced to almost dry. Add water only if necessary to keep the dal moist until cooked through.
   d. Season with salt.
2. Place the bulgar wheat in a small bowl, mix with a little salt, and add the boiling water. Stir until combined. Cool to room temperature. The grains should absorb all the liquid and become tender.
3. Place the tofu sheets in a large bowl and cover with boiling water. Soak about 15 minutes until softened. Drain, rinse under cool water, and drain again.

4. Finish the toor dal filling:
   a. Heat the oil in an 8" sauté pan, add the mustard seeds and swirl over low heat until the seeds turn gray and just begin to pop. ⚠ Do not allow the seeds to turn black.
   b. Quickly add the coriander seeds, black peppercorns, and curry leaves, swirl them in the pan, then add the onions, ginger, and a pinch of salt.
   c. Cook, stirring, over medium heat until the onions turn golden brown.
   d. Add the diced tofu and continue to cook about 1 minute longer until the flavors meld.
   e. Pour the hot spice/tofu mixture into the dal, stir, then stir in the bulgar wheat. Correct the salt and cool to room temperature.
   f. Sift some gram flour over the mixture and mix it in. Continue sifting and mixing until the mixture binds enough to hold a soft shape.
   g. Refrigerate 1 hour.
5. Assemble the tofu bundles:
   a. Wearing foodservice gloves, divide the toor dal filling into 12 equal portions and gently squeeze each portion into a cylinder about 2 1/2" long.
   b. Spread a tofu sheet out on a clean, lint-free kitchen towel and blot the surface dry.
   c. Place a cylinder of toor dal filling onto the sheet and roll it up into a bundle, tucking in the ends. Secure with a wooden pick.
   d. Repeat to make 12 bundles.

holding: refrigerated in a covered plastic container with pan liner between layers up to 3 days

---

RECIPE VARIATIONS

Toor Dal Cabbage Bundles in Red Curry Broth with Brown Rice and Steamed California Vegetables
Replace the dried tofu sheets with cabbage leaves prepared as on p. 825. Do not deep-fry; instead, sauté the cabbage bundles in peanut oil before adding to the curry sauce.

Chicken Chop Suey
in Crispy Noodle Nest

yield: 1 (8-oz.) entrée serving plus accompaniments
(for classroom turnout, separately stir-fry 2 double batches)

MASTER RECIPE

production		costing only
3 Tbsp.	peanut oil, in squeeze bottle	1 1/2 fl. oz.
1 1/2 oz.	large, firm mushrooms, sliced 1/4" thick	1 1/2 oz.
tt	kosher salt	1/8 oz.
1 oz.	peeled carrot, sliced 1/8" thick on the diagonal, blanched and refreshed	2 oz. a.p.
1 oz.	peeled celery, sliced 1/8" thick on the diagonal	1/10 head a.p.
1/2 oz.	peeled sweet onion, cut into 3/4" squares	1 oz. a.p.
1/2 oz.	peeled fresh water chestnuts, sliced 3/8" thick (or jicama fabricated in 3/4" paysanne cuts)	1 oz. a.p.
4 oz.	Chinese Marinated Chicken Breast	1/4 recipe
1/4 c.	Asian Aromatics Mix	1/4 recipe
1 c.	Stir-Fry Sauce	1/4 recipe
1/4 c.	Cornstarch Slurry	1/4 recipe
1 oz.	mung bean sprouts, green seed casings removed	1 oz.
1 c.	Jasmine Rice, hot in steam table	1/5 recipe
1	Crispy Noodle Nest	1/4 recipe
1 Tbsp.	fine diagonal-sliced scallion	1/10 bunch a.p.

service turnout:

1. Mise en place:
   a. Have all ingredients at the stove. Put a small spoon in the Cornstarch Slurry container.
   b. Place a sizzle plate or pie pan at the stove.
2. Stir-fry the dish:
   a. Heat a 14" wok over high heat, squeeze in about 1 Tbsp. peanut oil, and add the mushrooms with a little salt. Stir and toss, cooking the mushrooms about 15 seconds, until lightly browned at the edges. Remove to the sizzle pan.
   b. Heat 1 Tbsp. additional oil and add the carrot, celery, onion, and water chestnuts. Stir and toss, cooking about 20 seconds. Remove to the sizzle pan.
   c. Heat the remaining 1 Tbsp. oil and add the Chinese Marinated Chicken Breast. Stir and toss about 10 seconds, then add the Asian Aromatics Mix. Continue stir-frying about 10 seconds longer until the chicken is firm.
   d. Return the stir-fried vegetables to the wok along with the Stir-Fry Sauce. Bring to the boil.
   e. Stir the Cornstarch Slurry to recombine it. Push aside the solids in the wok and then stir in just enough slurry to thicken the sauce to a full-bodied nappé consistency as it returns to the boil.
   f. Fold in the bean sprouts and remove from heat.
3. Plate the dish:
   a. Spoon the Jasmine Rice onto a hot 12" plate and make a well in the center.
   b. Place the Crispy Noodle Nest in the well.
   c. Spoon the chop suey and sauce into the Noodle Nest.
   d. Sprinkle with scallion.

COMPONENT RECIPE
CHINESE MARINATED CHICKEN BREAST

yield: 1 lb.

production		costing only
1/4 c.	cornstarch	1 1/4 oz.
1/2 c.	Chinese rice wine or dry sherry	4 fl. oz.
1 tsp.	kosher salt	1/3 oz.
1 lb.	skinless, well-trimmed boneless chicken breast	1 lb.

preparation:
1. Mix together the cornstarch, wine, and salt.
2. Cut the chicken breast across the grain into 3/8"-thick slices.
3. Add the chicken to the cornstarch mixture and toss well to combine.
4. Refrigerate at least 30 minutes.

holding: refrigerate in a freshly sanitized, covered container up to 3 days

COMPONENT RECIPE
STIR-FRY SAUCE

yield: 1 qt.

production		costing only
1 qt.	Poultry Stock	1/4 recipe
2 Tbsp.	sugar	1 oz.
2 tsp.	salt	1/3 oz.
1/4 c.	Chinese soy sauce	2 fl. oz.

preparation:
1. Bring the Poultry Stock to the simmer.
2. Add the sugar and salt and stir until dissolved.
3. Add the soy sauce.

holding: may be held in a steam table during service; top off with water to counter evaporation; open-pan cool and refrigerate in a freshly sanitized, covered container up to 5 days

COMPONENT RECIPE
ASIAN AROMATICS MIX

yield: about 1 c.

production		costing only
1/3 c.	peeled, minced ginger	2 oz. a.p.
1/2 c.	fine-chopped scallion	1/2 bunch a.p.
2 Tbsp.	minced fresh garlic	2/3 oz.

preparation:
1. Mix together the ginger, scallion, and garlic.

holding: refrigerate in a freshly sanitized, covered container up to 12 hours

---

RECIPE VARIATION

Sub Gum Chop Suey in Crispy Noodle Nest
For each serving, use 1 oz. sliced chicken breast, 1 oz. sliced pork loin, 1 oz. sliced beef flank or top round, and 1 oz. peeled, deveined shrimp. Separately prepare each ingredient in the same marinade as the chicken.

Pan-Seared Breast of Petaluma Duck in Zinfandel Demi-Glace

with Sautéed Flame Grapes, Roasted Garlic Flan, and Wilted Baby Spinach

yield: 1 (6-oz.) entrée serving plus accompaniments (multiply × 4 for classroom turnout; adjust equipment sizes accordingly)

MASTER RECIPE

production		costing only
1	Roasted Garlic Flan	1/4 recipe
1 Tbsp.	corn oil, in squeeze bottle	1/2 fl. oz.
1	6-oz. boneless duck breast, skin scored in 1/8" crosshatch, trimmed (see p. 442)	6 oz.
tt	kosher salt	1/16 oz.
tt	fresh-ground black pepper	1/16 oz.
1	3/8"-thick slice baguette, cut on a sharp diagonal to make an elongated oval	3/4 oz.
2 Tbsp.	butter	1 oz.
3 to 5	flame grapes	1 oz. a.p.
3 oz.	cleaned baby spinach	3 oz.
1 Tbsp.	minced shallot	1/2 oz. a.p.
1/4 c.	Reduced Red Wine, made with Zinfandel	1/4 recipe
2/3 c.	Demi-Glace, hot in steam table	1/6 recipe
1 tsp.	fresh thyme leaves	1/40 bunch a.p.
as needed	water, in squeeze bottle	n/c
1 Tbsp.	butter	1/2 oz.
1 sprig	fresh thyme	1/20 bunch a.p.

service turnout:

1. Place the Roasted Garlic Flan on a sizzle plate and heat it in a 400°F oven about 5 minutes.
2. Pan-sear the duck breast:
   a. Heat an 8" sauté pan until very hot, add the oil, then add the duck breast, skin side down. Sear about 1 minute, until the skin is golden brown and much of the fat has rendered out.
   b. Pour off the fat, turn over the duck breast, and season with salt and pepper. Sear about 30 seconds longer.
   c. Use the touch test to judge the doneness and, if necessary, place the pan with the duck breast in the oven to finish cooking to a rare doneness. Hold warm.
3. Toast the baguette slice on the grill and hold warm.
4. Cook the remaining accompaniments:
   a. Heat a 10" sauté pan, heat the butter, and sauté the grapes, rolling and turning them, just until hot.
   b. Push the grapes aside and add the spinach to the empty side of the pan. Turn it with tongs just until wilted and season it with salt. Hold warm.
5. Finish and plate the dish:
   a. Remove the flan from the oven. Take off the foil cap and remove the pan liner. Run a paring knife around the edge to loosen it from the ramekin. Unmold the flan onto a hot 12" plate at 2 o'clock and peel off the pan liner from the top.
   b. Mound the spinach on the plate at 11 and 3 o'clock.
   c. Place the toasted baguette slice in the center of the plate.
   d. Slice the duck breast thin on a sharp diagonal and fan it across the toast slice.
   e. Add the shallot, Reduced Red Wine, Demi-Glace, and thyme leaves to the duck pan. Bring this sauce to the simmer and correct the seasoning. Thin with water if necessary, and then stir in the butter to create an emulsion.
   f. Add the grapes to the sauce.
   g. Nap the duck with the sauce and allow the grapes to fall into the front of the plate well.
   h. Stick the thyme sprig upright in front of the flan.

ROASTED GARLIC FLANS

yield: 4 (5-fl.-oz.) flans

production		costing only
2 tsp.	butter	1/3 oz.
1	egg	1 each or 2 oz.
2	egg yolks	2 each or 1 1/3 oz.
1/2 c.	room-temperature Roasted Garlic pulp, mashed smooth	1/2 recipe
2 tsp.	minced lemon zest	1/4 [90 ct.] lemon
1 1/2 c.	half-and-half	12 fl. oz.
tt	fine-ground salt	1/16 oz.
tt	fine-ground white pepper	1/16 oz.

preparation:

1. Preheat an oven to 325°F.
2. Prepare the ramekins:
   a. Heavily coat the inside of 4 (5-fl.-oz.) ramekins with butter.
   b. Cut out 4 circles of pan liner that exactly fit the bottoms of the ramekins.
   c. Press these circles into the ramekins and turn the circles over.
   d. Place the ramekins in a half-size hotel pan.
   e. Cut out 4 more pan liner circles that exactly fit the tops of the ramekins.
   f. Cut out 4 squares of aluminum foil just a little bigger than the tops of the ramekins.
   g. Have ready about a quart of simmering water.
3. Prepare the custard:
   a. Beat together the egg and egg yolks.
   b. Stir in the Roasted Garlic pulp, lemon zest, and half-and-half.
   c. Season with salt and white pepper.
4. Pan the custard:
   a. Ladle the custard into the ramekins.
   b. Place the remaining pan liner circles on the surface of the custard, butter side down.
   c. Place the aluminum foil squares on top, turn up the edges, and seal tight onto the rim of the ramekins.
   d. Pour enough simmering water into the hotel pan to reach 3/4 of the way up the sides of the ramekins. ⚠ Make sure the aluminum foil caps don't extend into the water.
5. Place the pan in the center of the oven and bake about 40 minutes, until the custard is just set.
6. Remove the pan from the oven. Wait at least 15 minutes before unmolding. If not using immediately, place the pan on a rack and cool to room temperature.

holding: refrigerate, intact, up to 5 days

RECIPE VARIATION

Pan-Seared Breast of Petaluma Duck in Red Wine Roasted Garlic Demi-Glace with Sautéed Flame Grapes, Mashed Potatoes, and Wilted Baby Spinach

Replace the Roasted Garlic Flan with 1 1/4 c. Classic Mashed Potatoes. Stir 2 Tbsp. Roasted Garlic pulp into the Demi-Glace.

Santa Rosa Plum Galette
with Almond Custard Sauce

yield: 1 dessert serving
(multiply × 4 for classroom turnout)

MASTER RECIPE

production		costing only
1/2 c.	Vanilla Custard Sauce, made without vanilla and subtly flavored with almond extract, in squeeze bottle	1/4 recipe
1 slice	Santa Rosa Plum Galette	1/8 recipe
1 sprig	fresh mint	1/12 bunch a.p.

service turnout:
1. Plate the dish:
   a. Squeeze a dot of Almond Custard Sauce slightly back of center on a cool 8" plate.
   b. Place the Santa Rosa Plum Galette slice back center on the plate.
   c. Squeeze a pool of custard sauce to the right and in front of the galette.
   d. Place the mint sprig to the right of the galette near the crust.

COMPONENT RECIPE
SANTA ROSA PLUM GALETTE

yield: 1 (10") galette

production		costing only
1 tsp.	active dry yeast	1/9 oz.
pinch	sugar	1/10 oz.
1/4 c.	water, 105°F	n/c
1	egg	1 each or 2 oz.
1 tsp.	water	n/c
5 oz.	flour	5 oz.
pinch	fine salt	1/10 oz.
2 oz.	sugar	2 oz.
1/4 c.	sour cream	2 fl. oz.
2 oz.	room-temperature unsalted butter	2 oz.
as needed	additional flour	1 to 2 oz.
1/2 c.	dry vanilla cake crumbs or cookie crumbs	1/2 oz. or n/c
1 c.	sliced almonds	5 oz.
5	firm-ripe Santa Rosa plums	1 1/4 lb.
1/4 to 1/2 c.	sugar	2 to 4 oz.
3 Tbsp.	cold butter, cut in 3/8" dice	1 1/2 oz.

preparation:
1. Activate the yeast:
   a. Place the yeast and a pinch of sugar in a small bowl or ramekin. Add the 105°F water and stir until smooth.
   b. Set aside in a warm place 10 minutes, after which time it should bubble.
2. Mix the dough:
   a. In a small bowl beat the egg until well mixed. Pour half of the egg into another small bowl and mix in 1 tsp. water to make egg wash. Refrigerate the egg wash.
   b. Combine 5 oz. flour, the salt, and 2 oz. sugar in a medium bowl. Make a well in the center.
   c. Place the beaten half egg, the sour cream, and the yeast mixture in the well and begin stirring in the flour, drawing it in from the edges.
   d. When the mixture forms a shaggy mass, stir in the butter to make a soft, slightly sticky dough. Add additional flour if needed. For a tender product, work the dough as little as possible.
3. Place the dough in a bowl, cover loosely with plastic wrap, and allow to ferment 40 minutes at cool room temperature.
4. Place a baking stone or inverted half-sheet tray on the bottom rack of an oven and preheat it to 375°F. Prepare a half-sheet tray with pan liner.
5. Combine the crumbs and almonds, crushing them together with your fingers.
6. Wash, halve, and pit the plums, then cut them into 3/8" wedges.
7. Assemble the galette:
   a. On a floured work surface, pat out the dough into an even 11" circle.
   b. Gently transfer the dough to the lined sheet tray.
   c. Sprinkle the crumb-almond mixture on the dough in an even layer.
   d. Arrange the plum slices on the dough in concentric circles, overlapping the slices and leaving a 1/2" rim. Press to firm the fruit into the dough.
   e. Sprinkle the plums with sugar, the amount depending on the sweetness of the fruit.
   f. Evenly distribute the butter cubes on the fruit.
   g. Brush the galette's rim with the egg wash and sprinkle it with sugar.
8. Bake the galette:
   a. Place the sheet tray on the middle rack of the oven and bake the galette about 20 minutes, until the crust is set.
   b. Remove the sheet tray from the oven and place it on a rack.
   c. Increase the oven temperature to 500°F.
   d. After 10 minutes, lift the galette onto a baker's peel or the back of a sheet tray and slide it onto the baking stone. Bake 10 to 15 minutes longer, until the fruit is soft and the bottom is crisp.
   e. Remove the galette from the oven and cool to room temperature on the rack.

holding: prepare the same day as service; hold at room temperature, covered with a kitchen towel, up to 6 hours

---

RECIPE VARIATIONS
Amaretto Plum Galette with Vanilla Custard Sauce
Replace the crumbs and almonds with 2 c. crushed amaretti cookies. Replace the almond extract in the custard sauce with pure vanilla extract.

Italian Plum Galette with Vanilla Custard Sauce
Omit the almonds and increase the crumbs to 1 c. Replace the Santa Rosa Plums with small Italian prune plums, halved and pitted. Mix 1/2 tsp. ground cinnamon with the sugar topping.

DESSERTS

Blood Orange Tart
with Marmalade Glaze and Dark Chocolate Drizzle

yield: 1 dessert serving
(multiply × 4 for classroom turnout)

MASTER RECIPE

production		costing only
1/4 c.	Chocolate Sauce, in squeeze bottle	1/4 recipe
1 slice	Blood Orange Tart with Marmalade Glaze	1/8 recipe

service turnout:
1. Plate the dish:
   a. Squeeze a drop of Chocolate Sauce on the center of a cool 8" plate.
   b. Place the Blood Orange Tart wedge in the center of the plate.
   c. Drizzle parallel lines of Chocolate Sauce over the tart and the plate well.

COMPONENT RECIPE
BLOOD ORANGE TART WITH MARMALADE GLAZE

yield: 1 (10") tart

production		costing only
12 oz.	Sweet Dough, chilled at least 20 minutes	1 recipe
as needed	flour	1 oz.
5	large blood oranges	20 oz.
2 tsp.	granular gelatin	1/4 oz.
3 Tbsp.	Grand Marnier or other orange liqueur	1 1/2 fl. oz.
3 c.	hot freshly made Pastry Cream	1 recipe
1 c.	orange marmalade	8 fl. oz.
2 Tbsp.	Grand Marnier or other orange liqueur	1 fl. oz.
as needed	water	n/c
1	10" round cake board	1 each

preparation:
1. Make up the tart shell:
   a. Roll out the Sweet Dough on a floured work surface and fit it into a 10" round fluted tart pan. Place the tart shell on a half-sheet tray.
   b. Refrigerate the raw shell at least 20 minutes.
   c. Preheat an oven to 400°F.
2. Using a zester or swivel peeler, remove the zest of half of a blood orange. Mince the zest very fine.
3. Fabricate the oranges:
   a. Place a cutting board in a sheet tray in order to retain the oranges' juice.
   b. Using a sharp, flexible boning knife, cut the tops and bottoms off the oranges, then pare off both the peel and its underlying membrane, leaving only the flesh of the oranges.
   c. Cut the oranges horizontally into 1/4" slices, removing all seeds.
   d. Refrigerate until needed.

4. Blind-bake the tart shell:
   a. Cut out a 12" circle of pan liner and press it into the tart shell.
   b. Fill the shell with baking weights or dried beans and place in the center of the oven. Bake about 12 minutes, until the dough is set. Remove the weights and liner and continue to bake 5 to 8 minutes more, until the pastry is light golden.
   c. Cool to room temperature on a rack.
5. Finish the filling:
   a. Combine the gelatin and 3 Tbsp. Grand Marnier in a small stainless bowl and allow to bloom about 5 minutes.
   b. Place the bowl over a small pan of hot water and melt the gelatin.
   c. As indicated in the Pastry Cream recipe, prepare an ice-water bath.
   d. Stir the bloomed gelatin, orange zest, and juices from the blood oranges into the hot Pastry Cream.
   e. Chill the Pastry Cream in the ice-water bath, stirring often.
6. Prepare the glaze:
   a. Combine the marmalade and 2 Tbsp. Grand Marnier in a small nonreactive saucepan and melt the mixture over low heat.
   b. Stir in enough water to achieve a pourable consistency. Hold warm.
7. Assemble the tart:
   a. Using a pastry brush, paint a dot of glaze on the cake board.
   b. Carefully remove the tart shell from its pan and place it on the cake board.
   c. Paint the bottom and sides of the shell with about 1/3 of the marmalade glaze, distributing the solids evenly.
   d. Refrigerate the shell and keep the glaze warm.
   e. Spread the chilled orange pastry cream into the cooled tart shell.
   f. Arrange the orange slices in concentric circles on the surface of the tart.
   g. Blot the surface of the orange topping with a paper towel, then paint it with the remaining glaze, distributing the solids evenly.
   h. Use a knife to score the top of the crust edge, indicating cut lines for 8 servings.
   i. Refrigerate at least 30 minutes.

holding: refrigerate under a plastic cake dome up to 12 hours

---

RECIPE VARIATION
Orange Tart with Marmalade Glaze and Dark Chocolate Drizzle
Replace the blood oranges with navel oranges.

Green Tea Ice Cream
with Fortune Cookie

yield: 1 dessert serving
(multiply × 4 for classroom turnout)

🕐 Best prepared 24 hours in advance.

MASTER RECIPE

production		costing only
1	6-fl.-oz. scoop Green Tea Ice Cream	1/5 recipe
1	Fortune Cookie	1/8 recipe

service turnout:
1. Plate the dish:
   a. Scoop the Green Tea Ice Cream into a cold 8-fl.-oz. bowl.
   b. Place the bowl on the left side of a rectangular or oval underliner plate.
   c. Place the Fortune Cookie on the right side of the plate.

COMPONENT RECIPE
GREEN TEA ICE CREAM

yield: approx. 1 qt.

🕐 Best prepared 24 hours in advance.

production		costing only
1 recipe	ingredients for Philadelphia-Style Ice Cream	1 recipe
1 Tbsp.	Japanese green tea powder	1/3 oz.

preparation:
1. Prepare the ice cream base, whisking in the green tea powder while the ice cream base is still hot.
2. Cool the ice cream base and refrigerate it overnight, if possible.
3. Freeze according to the ice cream machine's instructions.
4. Pack into a chilled container. Cover the ice cream's surface with plastic film and then put on the container lid.
5. Harden in a freezer at least 1 hour.

holding: freeze up to 3 days

COMPONENT RECIPE
FORTUNE COOKIES

yield: approx. 10 cookies

production		costing only
1 c.	flour	5 oz.
1/2 tsp.	fine salt	1/6 oz.
2 Tbsp.	cornstarch	2/3 oz.
1/2 c.	sugar	4 oz.
4	room-temperature egg whites	4 each or 4 oz.
7 Tbsp.	peanut oil	3 1/2 fl. oz.
1 Tbsp.	pure vanilla extract	1/2 fl. oz.
±3 Tbsp.	water	n/c

preparation:

1. Mise en place (set up as close to the oven as possible):
   a. Cut out 8 (3/8" × 2") slips of paper and write fortunes on them.
   b. Preheat an oven to 325°F.
   c. Have ready a plastic 3 1/2" round tuile stencil; alternatively, fabricate a stencil from a piece of flexible plastic such as a plastic box lid or plastic coffee can lid.
   d. Place a silicone mat on a sheet tray.
   e. Have ready an oven mitt, a 1/2-fl.-oz. scoop or a tablespoon, two metal offset spatulas, and foodservice gloves.
   f. Have ready an ungreased standard muffin pan with 4-fl.-oz. cups.
2. Mix the batter:
   a. Sift the flour, salt, cornstarch, and sugar into a bowl.
   b. Beat the egg whites just to soft peaks.
   c. Whisk the peanut oil and the vanilla into the flour mixture, then whisk in just enough water to make a spreadable batter.
   d. Fold in the beaten egg whites.

3. Preferably working with a partner, spread, bake, and form the cookies. Ideally have one person do steps a. through d. and the other person do steps e. through h.
   a. Place the stencil on the silicone pad, drop about 1 Tbsp. batter into the stencil opening, and use an offset spatula to spread the batter to the stencil opening's edge. Lift off the stencil.
   b. Immediately place the tray in the oven. Bake about 5 minutes, until light golden around the edges.
   c. Immediately remove the tray from the oven. From this point on you must work very quickly as the cookie will begin to harden.
   d. Release the cookie disc from the silicone pad with a clean offset spatula and flip it over.
   e. Wearing foodservice gloves, place a fortune across the center of the cookie disc with one end placed to extend out of the cookie after it's folded.
   f. Fold the cookie into a semicircle without creasing the fold.
   g. Grasping the two pointed ends with thumbs and forefingers, bring the pointed ends together to form the cookie's characteristic shape.
   h. Place the folded cookie in a muffin cup to hold its shape while it cools.
   i. Repeat with the remaining batter, making at least eight cookies. (If you're working with a partner, or if you've become proficient at forming the cookies, you can spread and bake two at a time.)

holding: store in a tightly sealed container at cool room temperature and low humidity up to 1 week

Place the stencil on the silicone pad and drop about 1 Tbsp. batter into the stencil opening.

Using an offset spatula, spread the batter to the stencil opening's edge.

Release the cookie disc from the silicone pad with a clean offset spatula and flip it over.

Place a fortune across the center of the cookie disc with one end placed to extend out of the cookie after it's folded. Fold the cookie into a semicircle without creasing the fold.

Grasping the two pointed ends with thumbs and forefingers, bring the pointed ends together to form the cookie's characteristic shape.

RECIPE VARIATION

Ginger Crème Brûlée with Fortune Cookie
Replace the Green Tea Ice Cream with a Crème Brûlée (p. 837) modified by steeping the cream with 1 c. grated fresh ginger and then straining it.

☐ **TABLE 12.2 ANGLO-ASIAN CALIFORNIA REGIONAL INGREDIENTS**

The majority of Asian ingredients used in this chapter are listed and defined in Chapter 14, pp. 671–673. For information on Asian ingredients not listed in the following table, please refer to those pages.

ITEM	MARKET FORMS	USES	SEASONALITY	OTHER	STORAGE
CALIFORNIA RICE	More than 90 percent of California-grown rice is the medium-grain variety favored by Asian diners. Specialty rices include domestic basmati-type, domestic Arborio-type, Japanese short-grain-types, black and red Japonica. Most are available in unpolished, brown form, as well.	Steamed, unseasoned white rice is the foundation of many Asian dishes, including stir-fries. Basmati is appropriate for Asian curries, pilafs, and biriyanis. Arborio rice is used for risottos and rice puddings. Specialty rices make interesting side dishes. Substitute brown rice for white to please health-conscious customers.	N/A	Be sure to use the correct liquid ratio and cooking method for the chosen type of rice.	Store at cool room temperature; freeze for extended storage.
BULGUR WHEAT	In processing this popular Middle Eastern staple, wheat berries (p. 456) are steamed, dried, and then crushed. Available by the pound in coarse, medium, and fine textures.	This highly nutritious starch is used as a side dish and can be added to stuffings and other composed dishes.	N/A	Fully cooked as purchased, it needs only be reconstituted in water before using.	Store at cool room temperature; freeze for extended storage.
THAI/ VIETNAMESE RICE WRAPPERS	These paper-thin, round, translucent discs are made from a batter of rice flour and water. Rice wrappers are available in consumer packs as round discs of varying size and in triangular form.	Rice wrappers are used to make uncooked summer rolls filled with cool cooked pork or shrimp and fresh vegetables. They are also the wrapper for crisp-fried Thai and Vietnamese spring rolls filled with ground pork and vegetables.	N/A	Brittle when dry, rice wrappers are moistened by brushing with water in order to soften them for filling and rolling.	Store tightly sealed at room temperature.
SOUTH ASIAN DALS	Various South Asian legumes, called *dals*, became popular in California during the 1960s health food movement. Types include toor dal, split moong dal, channa dal, and whole urad dal. All are available in bulk by the pound and in consumer packs from Indian/Pakistani markets.	Simmer with water to make soups and side dishes. Dal is traditionally finished by "tempering" with spices and aromatics cooked in ghee, or clarified butter.	N/A	Served with rice, breads, or other grain-based dishes, dals add valuable protein to vegetarian diets.	Store at cool room temperature.
TOFU (BEAN CURD)	This staple of Asian and American vegetarian diets is processed from soybeans. Varieties include: soft Japanese-style; firm Chinese style; seasoned, pressed tofu; deep-fried aburage.	Add to soups, stews, and stir-fries for textural interest and added nutrients. An important source of protein in vegetarian diets.	N/A	Soybeans are boiled in water, mashed, and strained to produce a milky liquid. It is then coagulated into a soft curd-like mass that is very high in protein. The curd is then drained and pressed.	Refrigerate soft and firm tofu submerged in cold water in a sealed container. Store up to 1 week with water changed daily.
TAMARI	Introduced to California in the 1960s, this type of fermented soy sauce is brewed from whole soybeans, sea salt, water, and koji, a type of yeast. Unlike standard soy sauce, true tamari is wheat-free.	Use in place of soy sauce in dips, dressings, marinades, and stir-fry dishes.	N/A	Tamari has a more assertive flavor than regular soy sauce. It is a favorite in California health food cooking. Check the label to make sure what is sold as "tamari" is the genuine article.	Store at cool room temperature.

☐ **TABLE 12.2 ANGLO-ASIAN CALIFORNIA REGIONAL INGREDIENTS** *(continued)*

ITEM	MARKET FORMS	USES	SEASONALITY	OTHER	STORAGE
CHINESE MUSTARD	A particularly pungent variety of ground yellow mustard seed is sold by the ounce or pound in Asian markets.	Prepared Chinese mustard is used as a dip for spring rolls and other fried foods. It enhances dressings and marinades.	N/A	For table use, the mustard powder is prepared by mixing with water into a thick paste.	Store mustard powder tightly sealed at cool room temperature. Refrigerate prepared mustard up to 1 month, after which it begins to lose pungency.
BLACK MUSTARD SEEDS	Black mustard seeds are sold by the ounce or pound by Indian/Pakistani markets. Yellow mustard seeds may be substituted.	The whole mustard seeds flavor South Asian-inspired dishes and are traditional in the "tempering" for dals.	N/A	To release their flavor, the seeds must be fried in oil or ghee (clarified butter) until they turn gray and make a "popping" sound. If the seeds are allowed to burn they acquire a very bitter, unpleasant flavor.	Store tightly sealed at cool room temperature.
POWDERED JAPANESE GREEN TEA	Powdered Japanese green tea is sold in small consumer packs in Asian markets.	Traditionally used to make tea for Japanese tea ceremonies, this tea is not brewed, but rather is reconstituted by whisking boiling water into it. California chefs use it to make green tea-flavored broths, sauces, and desserts.	N/A	Powdered green tea is made by steaming fresh green tea leaves, drying them, and crushing them into a fine powder.	Store tightly sealed at cool room temperature.
THAI CURRY PASTES	These aromatic seasoning pastes are made by grinding red or green chiles, lemongrass, galangal, garlic, shallots, and spices. Varieties include red, green, yellow, and Masaman. Curry pastes are available in 4-oz. cans, 14-oz. containers, and larger foodservice tubs.	Begin Thai-inspired dishes by frying curry paste in oil or thick, oily coconut milk, then fry the protein item in the curry-flavored oil.	N/A	Fried curry paste can be added to dressings, sauces, and marinades to add fragrance and heat.	Refrigerate after opening or freeze for extended storage.
CURRY LEAF	Fronds of curry leaf are sold fresh in Indian markets. The olive-green, oval leaves have a warm, mysterious flavor much prized in South Indian cooking.	Use whole to impart a mild flavor to sauces in the same manner as bay leaves. May be chopped or julienned and added to a dish for a stronger flavor. Add to the "tempering" for dal.	N/A	Despite the name, curry leaf is not a component of curry powder.	Store frozen.
SUN-DRIED TOMATOES	Originally a product of Italy, sun-dried tomatoes are now produced in California. The dry product is sold by the ounce or pound in a variety of fabrications, including halves, dice, and powder. Reconstituted sun-dried tomatoes packed in olive oil are sold in consumer-size jars and in 1-liter foodservice packs.	Reconstituted in boiling water, then drained and enriched with oil, sun-dried tomatoes lend their concentrated flavor to salads, cold sauces, egg dishes, pastas, breads, and pizzas.	N/A	Plum tomatoes are halved, lightly salted, and set out in the sun under protective netting and allowed to dehydrate. Oven-dried tomatoes are less expensive but inferior in flavor and texture.	Store tightly sealed at cool room temperature; freeze for extended storage.

(continued)

☐ **TABLE 12.2 ANGLO-ASIAN CALIFORNIA REGIONAL INGREDIENTS** *(continued)*

ITEM	MARKET FORMS	USES	SEASONALITY	OTHER	STORAGE
CALIFORNIA OLIVES	California black ripe olives are sold in cans ranging from 13-oz. to #10. They are available with pits and pitted, in sizes ranging from colossal to small, and in fabrications including sliced, chopped, and wedged. California green ripe olives are available with pits and pitted in small consumer jars on a limited basis.	Because of their mild flavor, California black olives are used primarily as a garnish. Mellow green ripe olives are enjoyed as a table olive.	N/A	In the 1940s California olives became an indispensable part of the American relish tray.	Store cans and jars at cool room temperature; once opened, refrigerate in a sanitized nonreactive container.
CALIFORNIA OLIVE OIL	California olive oil is made by small, artisan producers, many of whom grow their own olives. Grades include pure (a blend of refined and virgin oils), virgin (extracted at low temperature by physical means), and extra-virgin (the highest grade of virgin, with less than 1 percent oleic acidity). California oils are sold in small, consumer bottles but may be purchased in bulk by special arrangement with the producer.	Pure olive oil is used for sautéing and pan frying. Virgin and extra-virgin oils are used in salad dressings and other cold preparations. Californians enjoy fine olive oil as a dip for bread.	N/A	Olive oil may be flavored by steeping herbs, aromatics, or spices in it.	Refrigerate extra virgin and virgin olive oils; bring to room temperature before using.
VERJUS (vair-ZHOO)	*Verjus* means "green juice," or the juice of unripe grapes. California red and white verjus is sold in 750-mL bottles.	Less acidic than vinegar, verjus is a wine-friendly alternative to wine vinegar in salad dressings and pan sauces.	N/A	Wine grapes are picked at midsummer, when their skin color has just begun to develop. The grapes are crushed and the fresh, nonalcoholic juice is filtered and bottled.	Use verjus within a year of bottling; refrigerate after opening.
SAN FRANCISCO SOURDOUGH STARTER	A culture containing the yeast strain *saccharomyces exiguus* and the bacteria *Lactobacillus San Franciscoensis* is available in a powdered medium from several California-based companies.	Refer to this book's companion website for information and recipes using sourdough starter.	N/A		Store frozen.
SPECIALTY GREENS	European varieties include mâche (lamb's lettuce or corn salad), arugula (rocket), cresses, frisée, lolla rossa, radicchio, and treviso. Asian types include minimizuna, choy sum, and mini-mustard greens. *Mesclun* (MESS-klun) is the French name for mixed specialty greens, also called *spring mix*.	Use in salads and sandwiches, and as a fresh, raw garnish for a variety of dishes.	N/A		Refrigerate in the original packaging a few days only. Pick over and discard wilted specimens.

☐ TABLE 12.2 ANGLO-ASIAN CALIFORNIA REGIONAL INGREDIENTS (continued)

ITEM	MARKET FORMS	USES	SEASONALITY	OTHER	STORAGE
SPROUTS AND MICROGREENS	Sprouts are the first growth that emerges from a plant seed. Micro-greens are the first two true leaves of a food plant. Cleaned, ready-to-use sprouts and micro-greens are sold in clamshells and flats from specialty purveyors or shipped directly from the producer.	Use in salads and sandwiches or as a fresh, raw garnish.	Available year round.	Sprout types include: bean, radish, corn, alfalfa, sunflower, wheat, broccoli, and lentil. Microgreen types include: amaranth, arugula, basil, cilantro, dandelion, celery, lemon basil, Thai basil, nasturtium leaves, opal basil, purslane, sage, shiso, hungiku, sorrel, kohlrabi, purple cabbage, and lemon balm.	Refrigerate in the orig-inal packaging a few days only. Pick over and discard wilted specimens.
EDIBLE FLOWERS	Edible flowers are pur-chased by the piece or by the ounce from a de-pendable culinary source, preferably certified organic.	Whole edible flowers are used as a garnish. The petals of some edible flowers have a distinctive taste that en-hances the flavor of salads or other dishes.	Least expensive and most widely available in sum-mer; available from greenhouse and hy-droponic sources year round.	Popular flowers include angelica, anise hyssop, bee balm, calendula, car-nation, cornflower, hibis-cus, jasmine, lavender, nasturtium, pansy, and rose geranium. The flow-ers of standard culinary herbs may be used as well: borage, burnet, chamomile, chives, lemon verbena, and thyme.	Refrigerate in the orig-inal packaging a few days only. Pick over and discard wilted specimens.
CALIFORNIA AVOCADOS	California avocados are packed in 12 1/2-lb. flats typically in counts rang-ing from 12 to 36 and in 25-lb., two-layer lugs in counts typically ranging from 24 to 60. Purchase slightly underripe.	Avocados are used in salads and sandwiches, for soups, dips, and sauces, and even in desserts. Size is important in preparations when half an av-ocado is served stuffed or fanned and when guacamole is prepared to order.	In season spring to fall; off-season substitute chilean or Mexican avocados.	Avocados are ready to eat when they yield to gentle pressure at the stem end. To avoid bruising, they must be handled gently.	To slow ripening, hold at cool room tempera-ture, ideally between 55° and 60°F. To has-ten ripening, store around 80°F. Avoid refrigerating.
ARTICHOKES	Most of the California crop consists of "globe"-type cultivars: Green Globe, Desert Globe, and Big Heart. Artichokes are packed in 25-lb. boxes and are sized by count, ranging from 18 to 60 per box. Canned and frozen hearts and bot-toms are available in vari-ous packs. Fresh, fabricated, and par-cooked hearts and bot-toms are vacuum sealed and sold refrigerated. These products have a flavor and texture similar to that of freshly pre-pared artichokes.	Jumbo artichokes are used for steaming and stuffing as lunch entrées; medium and small artichokes are used for appetizers and side dishes. Baby artichokes that grow on the plant as side shoots are tender and have no fuzzy choke; they may be trimmed, boiled or steamed, and served whole.	March through May, and October.	Because of the labor re-quired to prepare fresh ar-tichokes, few restaurant operations are willing to offer them.	Refrigerate fresh arti-chokes 1 week; use before the edges of the leaves begin to darken.

(continued)

☐ **TABLE 12.2 ANGLO-ASIAN CALIFORNIA REGIONAL INGREDIENTS** (*continued*)

ITEM	MARKET FORMS	USES	SEASONALITY	OTHER	STORAGE
ASPARAGUS	Asparagus packs vary; size is graded by count per pound. *Jumbo:* 7–9 per pound *Large:* 9–10 per pound *Medium:* 10–12 per pound *Small:* 12–16 per pound *Pencil/grass:* 16–28 per pound.	Jumbo asparagus can be featured as an appetizer served hot with Hollandaise or cold with a thick vinaigrette dressing. Serve asparagus as a side dish, or toss cut asparagus into pastas, risottos, and salads.	January to May; September to October.	Jumbo and standard asparagus spears should be peeled for tenderness and even cooking.	Refrigerate several days. For longer storage cut 1/2" off the butt ends and stand the spears in a container in 1" water. Cover the tips with a damp towel.
ALMONDS	Whole roasted almonds are sold skin-on or blanched, sized by count per ounce ranging from 18 to 40. Almonds are also available split, sliced (skin-on or blanched), slivered, diced in several sizes, ground, and powdered (almond flour).	Whole almonds are used for eating and as garnishes. Slivered and sliced almonds top salads and are used as a garnish. Diced and ground almonds are used in baking and as a coating.	N/A		Store at cool room temperature; freeze for prolonged storage.
BLOOD ORANGES	The California blood orange crop is predominantly of the Moro cultivar. Blood oranges are smaller than standard oranges, at about 100 count to a 40-lb. carton.	Use in desserts, salads, as an accent to savory dishes, and in any preparation that showcases the fruit's scarlet flesh.	December through March.	Frozen blood orange juice is available from specialty purveyors.	Refrigerate up to 1 month.
MEYER LEMONS	These delicate lemons are sold in 18-lb. cartons and smaller consumer packs.	California Meyer lemons lend an aromatic sweetness to desserts, sauces, marinades, and salad dressings.	November to May.	This specialty lemon has a thin skin, lots of juice, and a sweet, low-acid flavor.	Refrigerate up to 1 month.
CALIFORNIA FIGS	California produces two main fig varieties: the blue-black Mission and the golden Calimyrna. Fresh figs are sold in flats of 12 1-pt. containers. Dried figs are sold in cello packs of varying sizes and in bulk by the pound.	Serve fresh figs as a table fruit or team with smoked meats, such as prosciutto, for a sweet-savory appetizer.	Fresh figs, late June to August; dried figs are classified as *new crop* from November to January.	Old-crop figs may develop white sugar crystallization on their skins; this does not impair quality and may be wiped away with a damp cloth.	Refrigerate fresh figs in their original container. Store dried figs tightly sealed at cool room temperature.
CALIFORNIA DATES	This sweet dried fruit product is available in a variety of forms, including whole pitted and unpitted, dehydrated pieces, diced dates, extruded date pieces, macerated, date paste, and syrup.	Dates add sweetness and rich mouthfeel to baked goods and may be used to enhance savory preparations such as sauces and stuffings.	Available year round.		Refrigerate after opening.

☐ TABLE 12.2 ANGLO-ASIAN CALIFORNIA REGIONAL INGREDIENTS (continued)

ITEM	MARKET FORMS	USES	SEASONALITY	OTHER	STORAGE
MONTEREY JACK	Factory-produced Monterrey jack is widely available in vacuum packs in block form and grated. Pepper jack is flavored with red and green chiles. Artisan Monterey jack is available from specialty purveyors and direct from producers.	Factory jack is widely used as a cooking cheese; it melts easily on nachos, in grilled sandwiches and quesadillas, and on gratins. Artisan jack is served as a table cheese.	N/A	Dry jack is aged Monterey jack that is hard enough for grating and shaving; its strong, complex flavor makes it a good replacement for Parmigiano-Reggiano.	Refrigerate.
CALIFORNIA CHÈVRE	California is known for its artisan-produced goat cheeses. Purchase from cheese dealers or direct from the producer.	Serve as a table cheese or use in cooking. Toss with pasta, use in hot and cold sandwiches, or layer into composed dishes. Crumble onto salads or roll in a crunchy coating and bake as a salad topping.	N/A	Noteworthy producers include: Laura Chenel's Chèvre; Cypress Grove (Humboldt Fog); Point Reyes Farmstead Cheese Company; North Valley Farms Chèvre.	Refrigerate.
PACIFIC SAND DABS	These tiny flatfish typically dress out under 8 oz. They are rarely sold outside the region.	Sand dabs are sautéed or pan-fried whole and served with butter and lemon. Two to three fish make up an entrée portion.	Available year round; avoid females harvested in the summer spawning season.		Refrigerate on ice in a self-draining container.
TOBIKO (FLYING FISH CAVIAR)	The tiny, crunchy roe of flying fish is processed with food dyes, most commonly to a bright orange or red color. Tobiko is also flavored with wasabi (p. 710) and tinted green. One type is flavored and colored black with squid ink. Tobiko is sold in jars of varying sizes. Asian dealers offer the best prices.	Because of its bright color, tobiko is a popular garnish. It is used in many sushi items.	N/A	Lesser-quality capelin roe is sometimes substituted.	Refrigerate or freeze for prolonged storage.
DUNGENESS CRAB	See p. 645.				
SPOT PRAWNS	See p. 645.				
ABALONE	Commercially sold California abalone is farm-raised, with red abalone the primary product. Most are harvested when they are 3" to 4" long and weigh in at 4 to 5 per lb. Abalone is available in two forms: live in the shell and frozen meat.	For raw presentation, the fresh meat is sliced very thin and served very cold. For cooking, it is physically tenderized by pounding lightly with a mallet, beginning in the center and moving outward to the edge. Pretenderized steaks are available. Sauté in butter and season with lemon.	Available year round.	Due to its expense, abalone is often served in small portions as an appetizer.	Live abalone are very perishable; store on ice and use the same day they are received.

■■□■ chapter thirteen

The Pacific Northwest

Washington State, Oregon, Alaska

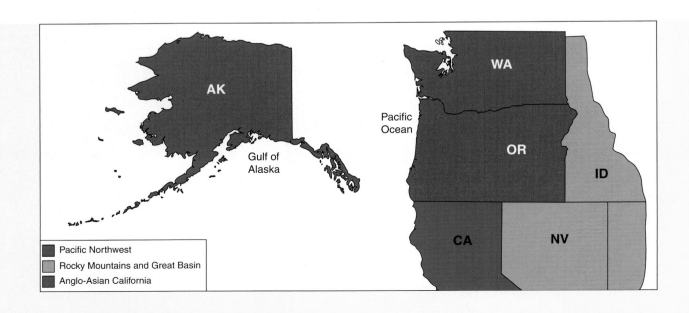

BY THE MID-1800s America stretched from sea to sea, and the Pacific Northwest had become a desirable destination for settlers, primarily fishermen and farmers. A wealth of indigenous food resources and significant Native American food roots influenced an early cooking style primarily based on New England and Midwestern cuisines.

In 1867 America's purchase of Alaska added a massive new tract of land even farther to the north and west. Here, limited food resources led to a rough-and-ready, pioneer cooking style that can be described as varied or even fragmented. However, the Pacific's bounty of seafood brought economic prosperity and culinarily linked Alaska to the lower Northwest.

Despite its fine food resources, the Pacific Northwest was among the last parts of the country to develop a distinctive cuisine. Only in the past three decades have the region's chefs—inspired by fine local wines, microbrew beers, superb seafood, quality meats, and a diverse array of local fruits and vegetables—developed a definitive Pacific Northwest cuisine. In this chapter you'll discover this new, ingredient-driven cuisine style that honors its Native American heritage while incorporating world cuisines techniques.

AFTER STUDYING THIS CHAPTER YOU SHOULD BE ABLE TO:

- describe the lower Pacific Northwest's two distinctive geographical areas (Factor 1) and explain why the two are grouped together as a unified culinary region
- discuss the unique nature of Pacific Northwest Native American food culture and describe its impact on the region's modern cuisine (Factor 2)
- list the region's first settlers and describe their homeland cuisines (Factor 3)
- explain the importance of both commercial fishing and aquaculture (Factor 5) to the Pacific Northwest's economy and cuisine
- list the region's second-settler immigrant groups (Factor 4) and discuss their influence on both traditional Pacific Northwest cooking and modern Pacific Northwest cuisine
- discuss Alaska's food culture and cuisine
- list and describe the ingredients, cooking methods, and flavor profiles of Pacific Northwest cuisine
- prepare authentic Pacific Northwest dishes

APPETIZERS

Creamy Cauliflower Soup with Cracked Hazelnuts and Cougar Gold Cheddar Wafers

Palouse Valley Brown Lentil Soup with Wheatberry Biscuit

Salad of Watercress, Pears, Rogue River Blue Cheese, and Walnuts in Walnut Vinaigrette

Pink Singing Scallops with Pinot Noir Beurre Rouge and Wilted Baby Spinach

Chilled Raw Olympia Oysters with Merlot Mignonette, Grilled "Pemmican" Venison Sausages, and Walla Walla Onion Salad

Warm Spring Salad of Asparagus, Morels, Fingerling Potatoes, and Seared Rare Duck Breast

ENTRÉES

Gitksan Planked Salmon with Berry Barbeque Sauce, Roasted Fennel–Yukon Gold Potato Purée, and Northwest Vegetable Medley

Steelhead Trout and Pacific Littlenecks in Gewürztraminer Saffron Cream with Apple-Rice Pilaf and Braised Brussels Sprouts

Smoke-Roasted Duck Leg in Cider Sauce with Pumpkin Gnocchi and Arugula

Roast Rack of Northwestern Lamb with Pinot Noir Demi-Glace, Porcini Bread Pudding, and Baked Walla Walla Onion Filled with Carrot Purée

Pan-Seared Elk Steak in Chanterelle Cream with Barley–Wheat Berry Pilaf, Braised Kale, and Salmonberry Compote

DESSERTS

Poached Pear on Frangipane Cake with Almond Crunch Filling and Pinot Noir Syrup

Chocolate Cream Cheese Hazelnut Tart

Seattle Coffeehouse Pot de Crème with Chocolate-Dipped Biscotto

WEBSITE EXTRAS

Breakfasts   Sandwiches   Hors d'Oeuvres   Thanksgiving Menu

A LAND OF CONTRASTS

The land of the lower Pacific Northwest culinary region comprises two distinctly different geographical areas: a moist, temperate coastal plain and a semiarid interior plateau. Few other culinary regions include land of such dramatic contrast; you may wonder why they're grouped together as one region. The answer is that this particular culinary region is defined more by cultural criteria than geographical ones—an explanation you'll understand more fully as you read on. First, though, let's look at the land of the Pacific Northwest and the forces that shaped it.

The Pacific Northwest culinary region is bounded on the west by the Pacific Ocean, beginning at the region's southernmost point on the Oregon-California border and stretching hundreds of miles north along the Oregon and Washington State shores. Separated from the lower part of the region by Canada, the northern section of America's Pacific Northwest coast resumes along the Alaska panhandle, reaches west along the Aleutian Island chain, and then proceeds north to the Arctic Circle. The Pacific Ocean effectively defines the region, contributing its name as well as its climate, primary protein foods, and initial settlement gateway.

The region's inland areas extend east. The lower Pacific Northwest includes the Cascade Mountains and a wide interior plateau that meets the Rockies. Alaska spreads inland across a subarctic wilderness where it joins British Columbia and the Canadian Yukon.

Varied Topography

The topography of the Pacific Northwest region was shaped by the same geological events that formed California, described in Chapter 12. Its position on the Pacific Rim gives the lower Pacific Northwest a climate similar to California's northern and central coasts.

The Cascade Mountains cut through Oregon and Washington in ridges running parallel to the coast, bisecting the lower Pacific Northwest region into coastal plain and interior plateau. The Cascades and the Alaskan Olympic and Cascade extensions were formed by volcanic activity and tectonic thrusting. Dotted throughout these mountain chains are distinctive, cone-shaped volcanoes, some of which—like Washington's Mt. St. Helens—are still active (Figure 13.1).

The region's interior was shaped by volcanic activity and sedimentary action. Prehistoric volcanic eruptions created massive basalt lava flows that solidified in low-lying areas and later were covered by wind-borne loess soil, creating fertile valleys. However, during successive ice ages, glaciers advanced over the region; in the warm cycles between ice ages, they receded. A cataclysmic flood resulting from the breakup of a glacial lake dam scoured parts of inland Washington State bare, leaving stark lunar landscapes called *scablands*. However, most of the interior remained covered with enough soil to support grasslands.

Paleontologists believe that during the last ice age, the Pacific receded and the Beringan land bridge between Alaska and eastern Russia appeared. Thus, many suggest that the Pacific Northwest was the entry point for the first human beings of the Americas. When the last ice age ended, melting ice caused the ocean to rise and the Beringan land bridge disappeared. North America and Asia took on their modern outlines, with Alaska and eastern Russia separated by the Bering Strait.

Today the Pacific Northwest is laced with clear, fast-flowing rivers (Figure 13.2). The wide and powerful Columbia River rises in Canada and flows south to become the region's most important waterway. Turning sharply west, it forms part of the Washington-Oregon border as it crosses the Cascade Range through the dramatic Columbia River Gorge and empties into the Pacific. Its tributaries, the Snake, Salmon, and Willamette Rivers, are also vital waterways. Throughout the region's history its rivers were essential for food and transportation.

FACTOR 1
The Pacific Northwest's rivers provided both food and transportation.

FIGURE 13.1
Lower Pacific Northwest Topography

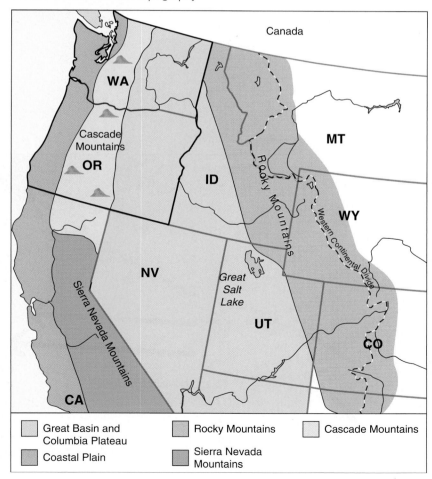

Great Basin and Columbia Plateau	Rocky Mountains	Cascade Mountains
Coastal Plain	Sierra Nevada Mountains	

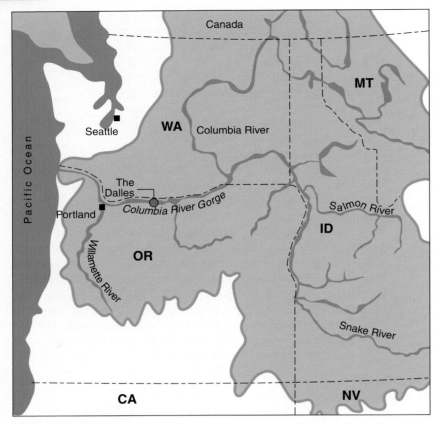

FIGURE 13.2
Pacific Northwest Rivers and Watershed Area

Climatic Diversity

Because of the region's varied topography and its position on the Pacific Rim, the Pacific Northwest has several distinctive climates.

Temperate Rain Forest on the Coast

The coastal plain of Oregon and Washington has one of the world's most unusual microclimates. As along the central and Northern California coast, ocean water upwelling (p. 543) causes cool summers, and the modifying effects of the ocean and jet stream result in warm winters. The Pacific Northwest is strongly influenced by the **Japan Current,** a warm flow of water originating in the Philippine Sea and swirling clockwise along the northern Pacific Ocean (Figure 13.3). These combined phenomena override latitude: at 47 degrees N, Seattle's latitude is the same as that of northern Maine; however, Seattle's climate is remarkably similar to that of coastal North Carolina at 35 degrees N. Even as far north as the Alaska panhandle, the effects of Pacific wind and water produce unusual warming.

In addition to warmth, the Pacific also contributes moisture. Especially in winter, when westerly airflow meets the tall Cascade range, the mountains effectively block it, stalling rain clouds that then drop moisture on the western slopes and coastal plain. Although rarely cooler than 40°F, coastal Pacific Northwest winters are gray and foggy, with almost constant rain.

FIGURE 13.3
Ocean Currents Affecting the Pacific Northwest

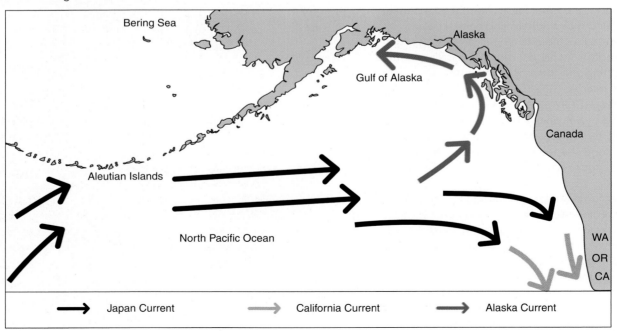

FIGURE 13.4
Giant redwoods thrive in the temperate rain forests of coastal Oregon and Washington. Sahani Photography/Shutterstock

FACTOR 1
Plant life thrives in the warm, moist coastal climate.

Because of this combination of warmth and moisture, in certain coastal areas of the lower Pacific Northwest plant life thrives, and evergreen trees such as Douglas fir, western hemlock, pine, spruce, and red cedar trees grow to massive size. These areas are classified as temperate rain forest. Old-growth forests undisturbed by logging may contain trees over 450 years old with trunks up to 100 feet in circumference (Figure 13.4).

These tall trees with straight trunks were a valuable lumber resource for the region's Native Americans and first settlers alike. Rapid, virtually year-round plant growth caused by the warm, moist climate proved conducive to both foraging and farming.

PANHANDLE

A **panhandle** is an elongated section of land belonging to a particular geopolitical state that extends into the territory of one or more other states.

Alaska's Panhandle

Although much farther north than the Oregon and Washington coasts, Alaska's southern panhandle similarly benefits from the warming effects of the Pacific Ocean. The area's high latitude is responsible for extended daylight during the summer months; during the June solstice Anchorage enjoys 20 hours of sunlight per day. However, this comes with the drawback of fewer than 8 hours of daylight in winter and a growing season of fewer than 100 days.

Alpine Climate in the Mountains

The western slopes of the Cascade mountain range are temperate and experience moderate rainfall; the eastern slopes are warmer and drier. As you ascend past the foothills and into higher elevations the climate turns alpine (p. 507), with snow remaining on the highest peaks year round.

Semiarid Grasslands on the Interior Plateau

East of the Cascade range, the climate and terrain are strikingly different from those of the coast. The Cascades' eastern slopes are temperate piedmont (p. 27) that descends to high plateau originally covered with shortgrass prairie (p. 461). The northern part of this plateau extends through Canada and into Alaska. In eastern Washington State and Idaho, the plateau forms a unique area called the Palouse Valley, an area of dune-shaped hills of fine-grained loess soil that holds moisture more efficiently than the surrounding land. The southernmost part of the plateau, in eastern Oregon, is technically part of the Great Basin and thus quite arid.

Lying in the Cascades' rain shadow (p. 303), the interior plateau receives little Pacific rainfall. Here the prevailing winds are from the north; high pressure over Canada frequently pulls Arctic winds south, lowering temperatures. Like the shortgrass prairie of the Ranchlands region, this area originally supported massive bison herds and later was used for grazing. Only after drought-tolerant wheat cultivars were developed in the mid-1800s did this land become valuable for agriculture.

Tundra in the Alaskan North

In Alaska's far northern interior, the terrain is described as **tundra.** This treeless, flat or rolling land is composed of black, silt/clay earth spread in a thin layer over *permafrost*, subsoil that remains frozen year-round. Both cold and dry, tundra supports only low-growing shrubs, scrub grasses, and various mosses and lichens. Deep snow covers the ground throughout northern Alaska's 6-month winter. Mid-December brings 20 hours of darkness per day. Blizzards are frequent.

■ PACIFIC NORTHWEST
■ NATIVE AMERICANS

Most anthropologists agree that many of the humans who became America's indigenous peoples crossed the Beringan passage in the far northwestern reaches of the Pacific Northwest. However, an important consideration in our study of this culinary region is whether some of these first Americans remained in the Pacific Northwest. If so, the Pacific Northwest tribes represent the oldest of all Native American cultures. However, an alternative theory, based on comparisons of culture and artifacts, suggests that the region's natives arrived from coastal northern Asia much later, riding the Japan Current in boats.

No matter their origin, Native American tribes of the lower Pacific Northwest and Alaska panhandle are divided into two basic groups: coastal tribes and tribes of the interior plateau. Differences in climate and topography led to different lifestyles for these two groups. Nonetheless, because of trade and cultural contact, they share many foodways. Central and northern Alaska is home to a third Native American group with its own, totally different culture and cooking style. Figure 13.5 shows Native American territories in the Pacific Northwest.

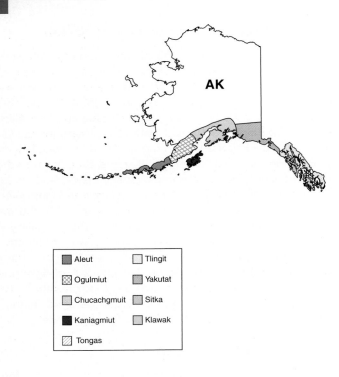

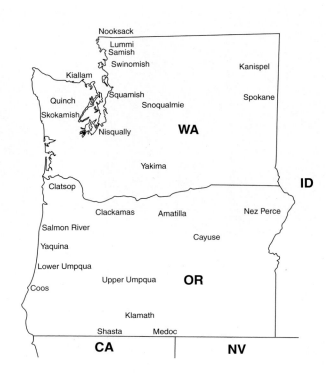

FIGURE 13.5
Pacific Northwest Native American Tribes

Tribes of the Lower Pacific Northwest

Because of the wealth of natural resources in the lower Pacific Northwest, before European contact neither coastal Native Americans nor tribes of the interior plateau practiced agriculture. Although early explorers report a few tribes growing tobacco for recreational, ceremonial, and trade use, none raised Three Sisters food crops. There simply was no need to do so.

Coast and plateau provided different, but equally abundant wild foods that were easy to harvest and preserve. Therefore, foraging was an important activity for native women. Coastal tribes had the advantage of warm weather almost year-round, minimizing the need for food preservation.

Both coastal and plateau tribes relied on aquatic animals for protein. The region's long coastline yielded halibut, cod, clams, mussels, crabs, oysters, and sea urchins as well as seals, sea lions, and whales. Rivers provided both freshwater and anadromous fish, such as sturgeon, herring, smelts, eulachon, trout, and the all-important salmon. Both groups used ingenious methods of fishing, described shortly.

All Pacific Northwest tribes were expert boaters and boat builders. Coastal tribes constructed elaborately carved wooden longboats; plateau tribes fabricated canoes of wood and hides. In their excellent watercraft the Native Americans of the region traveled the inland waterways and the seacoast for fishing and trade.

Unique among Native American groups, and an important unifying factor among lower Pacific Northwest tribes, was their highly developed trading system. The two groups constantly traded raw materials, handicrafts, and food products with each other and with Plains natives farther east. When European explorers began venturing into the region by land and sea, coastal tribes welcomed them as new customers and as a source of unusual trade goods.

The close cultural, commercial, and culinary relationship between Pacific Northwest coastal and plateau Native American tribes marks the beginning of the two areas' shared history. Later, after European settlement, coast and plateau continued this shared culture despite geographical differences. That's why, although geographically similar to the shortgrass prairie of the Ranchlands and Farmlands regions, the northwest interior plateau is considered part of the Pacific Northwest culinary region.

Now that you understand the customs and characteristics shared by the lower Pacific Northwest Native American groups, let's look at the two groups individually.

Coastal Tribes

In anthropology, conventional wisdom holds that agriculturalist groups are more highly civilized than hunter-gatherers. Although in most cases this is true, Native American tribes of the coastal Pacific Northwest defy convention. Indeed, the coastal Pacific Northwest tribes' highly organized trade-based culture is unique among preagricultural societies.

Coastal tribes include the Makah, Klallam, Chinooks, and Tillamooks of Oregon and Washington, and the Tlingits of the Alaska panhandle. Although they belong to various language groups and vary in some aspects of culture, in general these tribes shared a common lifestyle based on the natural world

FIGURE 13.6

Totem poles represent clan lineage and history. Steve Rosset/Shutterstock

around them and its abundant resources. Among the most important were trees that provided ample lumber for building structures and boats.

Coastal tribes lived in permanent villages along navigable waterways, where they erected elaborately decorated communal longhouses situated in precise rows. Wood, particularly soft, easy-to-work cedar, was the preferred craft material for tools, furniture, storage chests, and even woven bark clothing. Families carved elaborate totem poles representing their clan lineage and history (Figure 13.6).

Because of mild weather, the region's seasonal cycle of wild fruit, such as salmonberries, cloudberries, and chokecherries, is long and varied. Wild vegetables, such as mushrooms, onions, hemlock-parsley root, sunflower roots, and bitterroot, were found in natural clearings. Most important among foraged vegetables was *camas*, the root of a wild lily described on p. 609. Wildlife included bear, elk, deer, squirrel, rabbits, and beaver, providing both fur and food. Situated along the route of the western flyway, the region welcomed the biannual arrival of migratory waterfowl.

Spring and summer brought the annual migration of anadromous fish leaving the Pacific Ocean to swim upstream to their spawning grounds. At the time of European contact, these fish swarmed in such abundance that coastal natives could catch and preserve their annual supply of fish—and plenty more for trade—in a matter of weeks. Moreover, gentle weather meant that fishing and foraging could be practiced virtually year-round.

Living in such an abundant land, coastal tribes did not need to spend most of their time obtaining food. Instead, they constructed a highly developed culture based on a strict class hierarchy, commerce, and the acquisition and conspicuous consumption of material goods. The most potent symbol of coastal Pacific Northwest tribes' wealth was the **potlatch,** a ceremonial feast primarily given to solidify the power of a clan and glorify its leader.

Interior Plateau Tribes

The Pacific Northwest's interior plateau was home to the Wenatchi, Columbia, Spokane, Walla Walla, Klamath, Cayuse, Coeur d'Alene, Flathead, and Nez Perce tribes. Living on the semiarid plateau, these groups found obtaining food more challenging. Therefore, they spent more time fishing, hunting, and foraging and less time engaged in crafts and tribal politics.

Like many other Native American groups you've studied, plateau tribes were seminomadic. In winter and early spring they lived in riverfront villages. The region's annual spring fish run provided salmon, their all-important foundation food, which was preserved by salting and smoking. Trout, sturgeon, eel, and whitefish were caught and preserved as well. Once the spring fishing season was over, they ranged the plateau in search of game and foraged plants. Hunters bagged deer, elk, antelope, and small game that were eaten fresh and preserved by traditional methods. Some tribes, such as the Nez Perce and the Flathead, traveled as far east as the bison hunting grounds of the Plains tribes.

Although plateau tribes harvested a more limited range of food products, through trade they acquired foods and other products from the coastal tribes and even some European trade goods brought by Pacific-sailing ships. Each year's most important event was the Dalles rendezvous, a trade fair on the Columbia River where coastal and inland Native Americans mingled.

Native American Legacy Foods

Many indigenous foods enjoyed by Pacific Northwest natives remain in the region's modern cuisine. In addition, one type of wild food not yet adopted by mainstream Americans has the potential for discovery. Let's take a closer look at these foods and how Pacific Northwest natives prepared them.

Sacred Salmon

For both coastal and plateau Native Americans, fish was the primary foundation food, and salmon the most prized of all fish. In fact, to the region's Native Americans, the salmon was and still is considered sacred. According to traditional Pacific Northwest

---

THE TRADITIONAL POTLATCH

For a coastal Pacific Northwest Native American clan, hosting a potlatch was similar in planning, expense, and stress to a modern formal wedding—only lasting many days longer. Virtually all of the clan's resources were used to produce this weeklong event, to which all members of one or more rival clans were invited. Religious and cultural ceremonies, singing and dancing, sports, and exhibitions of physical endurance were held between each day's lavish feasts. The best of the clan's fresh and preserved foods were served in copious portions far exceeding the amounts needed to feed the assembled crowd. Each day culminated in a show of extravagant gift giving, wherein the host clan presented every guest with presents appropriate to his or her rank.

Today Native Americans of the coastal Pacific Northwest have renewed and refined the custom of potlatch and use the event to reflect their traditional values of hospitality and generosity as well as to highlight their distinctive regional Native American culture and cuisine.

FIGURE 13.7

Native Americans of the Yakima tribe harvest salmon at Celilo Falls on the Columbia River. *Courtesy of the Library of Congress, LC-USF346-070154-D*

Native American religious beliefs, salmon are a race of immortal men who turned themselves into fish in order to feed humans. If each harvested salmon is properly thanked and honored, when its bones are thrown back into the water they will miraculously regenerate into another fish. Formal tribal ceremonies are held each spring when the first fish is taken, and throughout the season each fisherman performs a private ceremony whenever he harvests a fish.

Like the shad discussed in Chapter 4, salmon are an anadromous species. After living most of their lives in salt water, they return to their original freshwater spawning grounds in early spring, heading upriver, swimming hard against rushing waters created by spring rains and melting snow. With flesh firm from vigorous exercise and bodies fat from feeding on ocean plankton, wild salmon caught during the springtime run are a true delicacy. Coastal and plateau tribes were experts at harvesting salmon (Figure 13.7). During the annual run upstream, native fishermen penned salmon in wooden traps and then caught them with spears or nets.

Pacific Northwest Native Americans often cooked salmon by planking, today a signature cooking style of the region.

PLANKING

Planking is a cooking method that uses a plank, or board, fabricated from fragrant wood that imparts a special flavor when heated. In the Pacific Northwest the typical choice of wood is alder or cedar. The planks and thin strips of leather are soaked overnight in cool water so they don't burn. Before planking, Pacific Northwest native cooks seasoned salmon sides with sea salt, wild herbs, and juniper berries. When the cooking fire burns down to hot embers, the seasoned salmon sides are lashed to the planks with leather and the planks are staked upright near the fire. Planking involves two successive cooking methods. The salmon initially steams as the moisture in the plank heats up and turns to vapor. When the moisture is gone, the salmon then smoke-roasts, basted with its own fat.

Although most of a salmon's edible portion comprises the sides, to Pacific Northwest natives the most prized part of the salmon is found in the salmon's head. **Salmon cheeks** are tender round nuggets of flesh found just behind the gills. Salmon cheeks were sautéed in fish oil or bear fat. Today salmon cheeks are a local specialty rarely found outside the region.

In spring and early summer, Pacific Northwest natives preserved hundreds of pounds of salmon for later use and for trade. Women specialized in preserving the fish using methods ingeniously adapted to their environment.

FIGURE 13.8

A Pacific Northwest Native American dries salmon over a smoky fire. *University of Washington Libraries, Special Collections*

On the dry and generally sunny interior plateau, fish could be air-dried or open-air smoke-dried, as in Figure 13.8, year round. However, on the coast early spring weather is too cloudy and misty for successful open-air preservation. To compensate for spring weather conditions, coastal Pacific Northwest tribes developed a special drying method called **hot smoking.** Salmon and other fish are first cured with salt and other seasonings. A low fire of cedar or alder wood is built inside a specially designed smoking hut and the fish hung inside. The antibacterial properties of salt and smoke combined with gentle heat from low embers made it possible to preserve fish when sun drying was not possible. Before refrigeration the fish was smoked until thoroughly dry; today fish is smoked for less time and then refrigerated. In its modern form, hot-smoked salmon is a signature dish of the Pacific Northwest culinary region.

By the height of salmon season, even the coastal Pacific Northwest is clear and sunny enough for traditional drying. Heavily salted sides of salmon were spread on drying racks. When fully dehydrated, the sides were at least 50 percent lighter and as flat and hard as boards. Dried salmon sides were tied up in bundles for long-term storage, or trade and transport. When needed, the salmon was simply soaked in water to rehydrate it, after which it was ready for eating or further cooking.

SALMON GOES TO HAWAI'I

Portability and ease of preparation made Pacific Northwest dried salmon the ultimate convenience food of its era—a fact not lost on European sea captains. Shortly after the first European ship landed on the Pacific Northwest coast, Native American–produced dried salmon was being shipped to Hawai'i. There it became the main ingredient in lomi-lomi salmon, a signature dish of traditional Hawai'ian cuisine. A recipe for Lomi-Lomi Salmon appears on p. 680.

In addition to drying and smoking, salmon and other fish were processed for oil. Dark, fatty fish flesh was simmered in water to render out the oil. Then the water was boiled away, leaving only pure fish oil behind. Fish oil was the region's primary cooking fat and was used as a sauce or dressing in the same way we use olive oil today.

Wild Berries

The Pacific Northwest has more indigenous berries and vine fruits than any other American culinary region. Among these are salmonberries, various trailing blackberries, thimbleberries, huckleberries, salal berries, elderberries, beach strawberries, wild currants, and wild grapes. All were enjoyed by Pacific Northwest Native Americans, who ate them fresh in season and preserved them in various ways. Berries were sun-dried and eaten like raisins, or simmered into savory stews. They were also pounded into pastes with fish oil and used as a condiment.

Today foraged Pacific Northwest wild fruits demand high prices in farmer's markets and are used in fine restaurants to make sweet-savory sauces, ice creams, pies, and other desserts.

Wild Roots

Nonagricultural Pacific Northwest tribes relied on indigenous plants for the starch component of their diets. As did many other Native Americans, Pacific Northwest tribes processed flour from acorns. However, wild roots were the foundation starch of the region's native diet. Of the many wild roots prepared by native cooks, two were most favored: camas root and bitterroot. Both grow prolifically throughout the interior plateau.

Camas is a member of the lily family that produces a tasty, starchy root bulb (Figure 13.9). In spring the plant stem shoots up from the bulb and eventually forms a beautiful pale-blue flower. However, camas bulbs should be harvested in the early spring before the plants begin to bloom. Native foragers dug camas bulbs out of the ground, wiped them clean of soil, and then transported them to storage bins or pits. Like most root vegetables, under correct conditions camas can be stored for long periods.

Freshly dug camas can be eaten raw, in which state its taste and texture resemble those of jicama or mild turnips. However, native cooks usually roast the bulbs in the embers of a fire or steam them in fire pits lined with stones and wet leaves. Once cooked, camas bulbs can be eaten in the same manner as baked sweet potatoes and have a similar taste and texture. For even longer keeping, native cooks compress the cooked flesh into cakes and dry them in the sun. Dehydrated camas cakes, called *pasheco* (pah-SHEH-ko), can be eaten dry as a snack food or can be reconstituted by simmering in soups or stews.

Bitterroot, a plant similar to camas, also grows prolifically throughout the interior plateau and across Montana, where it has been adopted as the state flower. Bitterroot's delicate pink blossoms alert native foragers to massive beds where the roots are easily dug. The name *bitterroot* refers to the root's bitter flavor and indigestibility when eaten raw. However, when cooked in the same manner as camas, the root of bitterroot acquires a neutral flavor and pleasant mealy texture like that of a russet potato. Bitterroot is typically peeled and boiled, then mashed and formed into cakes. The cakes may be enhanced with fish and berries, or with wild herbs and bison or venison fat. The most important qualities of bitterroot are its portability and high nutrient value; as little as 1 ounce of the cooked product provided a traveling Native American enough nourishment for a meal.

Neither camas root nor bitterroot has been embraced by modern Pacific Northwest cooks. Today these root foods are primarily prepared by the region's Native American population for special events and ceremonial use. However, a hungry world in need of easily grown, sustainable food crops may soon discover these highly nutritious plant foods.

Native American Influence on Modern Northwest Cuisine

Early explorers such as Lewis and Clark were impressed by the indigenous food products of the Pacific Northwest as well as by the skill and imagination of the region's native cooks. The region's culinarily adventurous first settlers adopted many native foodways and prepared many native dishes—at first out of necessity but later out of preference.

FACTOR 2

Native American foods and cooking methods are an important element in modern Pacific Northwest cuisine.

Today Native American influence in modern Pacific Northwest cuisine is still strong. For example, planked salmon and hot-smoked salmon continue to be regional specialties. Following the Native American custom of mixing meat and berries, modern Pacific Northwest chefs often flavor savory dishes with the region's abundant wild and cultivated fruits. Wood-fire grilling and smoke roasting have become popular cooking techniques, and the traditional fragrance of cedar and alderwood still flavors many modern dishes.

Subarctic Native Americans and the Inuit

In addition to the Native American tribes discussed earlier, a number of native groups inhabit northern Alaska and the Aleutian Islands. Best known among them are the Inuit (IN-oo-it), a group that inhabits a vast area rimming the northern coast of Alaska and stretching across the Canadian Arctic. The Inuit acquired the name *Eskimo*, meaning "eaters of raw meat" in Algonquian,

FIGURE 13.9

Camas leaf, flowers, stalk, and roots.

Marilyn Angel, Wynn/Nativestock.com

ELEMENTS OF PACIFIC NORTHWEST NATIVE AMERICAN CUISINE

FOUNDATION FOODS

principal starches: camas, bitterroot

principal proteins: fresh and preserved fish (especially salmon)

principal produce: wild fruits (especially berries), wild greens, wild mushrooms

FAVORED SEASONINGS: sea salt, fish oil, wild berries

PRINCIPAL COOKING MEDIA: water, fish oil

PRIMARY COOKING METHODS: planking, grilling, hot-smoking, stewing

FOOD ATTITUDES: strong food culture, culinary liberals

THE INUIT: LAST OF THE FIRST

Anthropologists believe the Inuit were among the last Asians to enter the Americas, arriving sometime after the submerging of the Beringan land bridge, about 15,000 BC, by floating across the Bering Straits in canoes or on ice floes. Living proof of the Asian-American connection, a small group of Inuit remain on the extreme tip of eastern Siberia.

because lack of fuel on the tundra often made it impossible for them to cook. Because of its negative connotation, this term is no longer used.

The Inuit and other subarctic Native American tribes exist in a tundra climate barren of vegetable foods for as long as 10 months per year. Traditionally nomadic hunters, before European intervention interior tribes lived by following herds of wild ruminants, carrying their possessions on toboggans pulled by dogs. Thus, they subsisted on a largely protein diet of caribou, elk, and moose meat. Coastal groups harvested seals, whales, walruses, and a variety of fish (Figure 13.10). Many of these foods were eaten raw.

Living in a frigid climate and often traveling hundreds of miles on foot, Alaska's far northern native people expended

enormous amounts of energy simply to survive. Fat provided the calories necessary to do so. *Muktuk*, or **blubber,** is the fat of certain marine animals. Rich in nutrients and heart-healthy fatty acids, blubber was a staple food for far northern natives. The eulachon (YOO-lah-chon) fish provided a different type of fat. During the seasonal eulachon run, thousands were harvested, fermented, and then boiled down to release the oil, called *hooligan oil* by English-speaking settlers. For the Inuit and subarctic tribes, hooligan oil was the primary cooking fat and was used as a dip to enrich both cooked and raw fish.

Beginning in the late 1800s, the American and Canadian governments initiated programs to settle northern natives. In doing so, they changed the traditional far northern diet to include pioneer provisions and, later, canned foods. However, some groups have retained at least a vestige of traditional cooking. Their special foods are still prepared in their own communities and are showcased at ceremonial events. However, Inuit and far north cuisine has had virtually no impact on traditional or modern Pacific Northwest cuisine.

FIGURE 13.10

An Inuit family butchers a whale. University of Washington Libraries, Special Collections

■ EUROPEAN AND AMERICAN SETTLEMENT

The Pacific Northwest was colonized by a European nation and later settled by American pioneers. The first Europeans arrived on the coast by ship, whereas most Americans entered the interior traveling overland by wagon.

English Traders and Russian Farmers

British explorer Sir Francis Drake sailed the Oregon coast in 1579, and by 1600 both British and Spanish sailing ships were cruising the Pacific Ocean in search of new resources to exploit. By the 1700s New England merchant clippers were sailing the coast as well. For Europeans, the Pacific Northwest's most important resource was lumber, particularly trees with tall, straight trunks that could be fashioned into ship's masts and building beams. However, furs and preserved fish purchased from the region's Native Americans also became valuable trade goods.

At the same time, Europeans were also exploring the South Pacific islands and, venturing north, arrived in Hawai'i. You'll learn about the European discovery of Hawai'i in Chapter 14. The economic fortunes of the Pacific Northwest and Hawai'i became intertwined because of the forces of wind and water, as so frequently happened during the Age of Exploration. After rounding Cape Horn and entering the Pacific Ocean, a navigator's natural instinct was to sail directly north, hugging the coast of South America. When ships attempted to do so, they found themselves battling a strong south-flowing current. But if they headed west into the open Pacific, both the ocean current and the prevailing winds pushed them northwest, toward Hawai'i. From there they could sail across the placid central ocean and reach the Pacific Northwest. Thus emerged a new, Pacific Ocean triangle of trade (Figure 13.11). European and American ships brought manufactured goods, spirits, spices, and other European preserved foods into the Pacific. They bought Hawai'ian lumber, tropical fruits, and, later, beef. They sold previously acquired Pacific Northwest dried fish to Hawai'ians. Hawai'ian beef, pineapples, and other food ingredients were transported to the Pacific Northwest. Finally, ships laden with lumber, furs, and preserved food products sailed down the North and South American coasts, rounded the cape, and returned to their American or European home ports. The Pacific triangle of trade introduced dried salmon into Hawai'ian cuisine and enabled Hawai'ian food products to feed the growing population of the Pacific Northwest.

The region's Native Americans benefited from European and American contact by receiving trade goods such as metal tools and weapons. Through the 1700s they didn't experience displacement because neither the Europeans nor the Americans chose to settle the region. Nonetheless, as in other parts of the Americas, contact brought European diseases, particularly smallpox, against which Native Americans had no immunity. In the 1770s a massive epidemic swept the Pacific Northwest, killing approximately 30 percent of the region's indigenous population. Later epidemics, including measles and influenza, brought the population to an all-time low by 1900.

The first settlers of the Pacific Northwest culinary region came from a country much closer to it: Russia. Although most Americans think of Russia as a European nation, at the time the Russian Empire stretched across Asia to include Russian Siberia, whose eastern tip is only 59 miles from Alaska. In the mid-1700s Russian hunters began sailing into Alaskan waters in search of fashionable seal and otter furs. At first they set up semipermanent camps, slowly expanding throughout the Aleutian Islands and into the Alaska panhandle. Russian sealers had a devastating effect on Alaska's ecology and indigenous population. Relentless hunting drastically reduced the region's seal and sea otter populations. Enslaving many Native Alaskans to work at hunting and skinning seals, Russian sealers introduced foreign

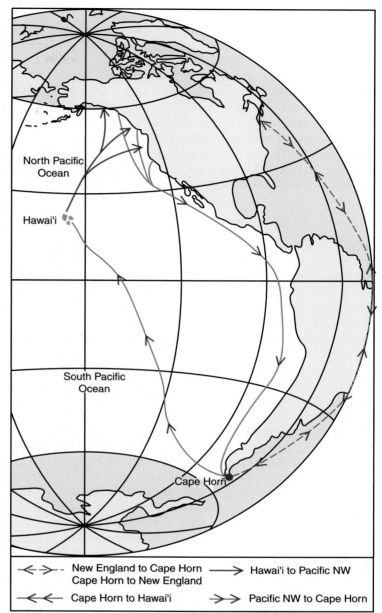

FIGURE 13.11
Pacific Triangle of Trade

diseases that, along with brutal treatment, decimated the Aleuts and severely impacted many panhandle tribes.

As fur became more profitable, the expanding number of hunters needed a more accessible source of provisions. In the 1800s the Russian government began settling farming families along the Pacific Northwest coast, eventually penetrating as far south as northern California. With colonists to occupy and defend the land, Russia claimed the far northern Pacific Northwest as its "American Empire."

The Russian presence in North America made America's leaders more than a little nervous. Russia's claim additionally stood in the way of Manifest Destiny, the prevailing national ideal of an America stretching from sea to sea. In 1867 President

Andrew Johnson's secretary of state, William Seward, concluded a deal with Russia that effectively removed its claim to the region. In what became known as "Seward's Folly," the United States purchased Alaska for the price of $7 million, a cost amounting to fewer than 2 cents per acre.

Although the Alaska Purchase effectively halted Russian immigration to the Pacific Northwest, many Russian settler families remained in the region. The cooking of Russian fur hunters had been primitive at best, but settler families contributed a legacy of frontier-style Russian cuisine that primarily impacted Alaskan cooking. Therefore, we'll discuss Russian-inspired dishes in the section on traditional Alaska cuisine on pp. 617 and 618.

American Pioneers

As you've learned, the Lewis and Clark expedition of 1804 began the era of America's trans-Appalachian westward expansion. Their reporting on the lower Pacific Northwest—the grasslands of the interior plateau and the lush, fertile coast—awakened the American public to the region's agricultural potential. In 1843 the opening of the Oregon Trail launched the migration of hundreds of thousands of settlers to the Pacific Northwest (Figure 13.12).

Most early pioneers settled in Oregon's Willamette Valley, an area of superb farmland. Having struggled with farming the played-out soils of New England or the arid western plains, the new settlers considered Oregon an agricultural paradise. Virtually every crop proved successful. In addition to European grains and vegetable crops, orchards of apples, pears, and other tree fruits grew quickly and soon produced superior fruit. Dairy cattle thrived. Moreover, settlement was for the most part peaceful as local Native American tribes generally accepted the newcomers without resistance. So hospitable was the Willamette Valley that most of Oregon's early population settled within it; even today, two-thirds of the state's population is centered there.

Along the Oregon Trail, Pacific Northwest settlers suffered hardships similar to those of other regions' pioneers. On the move, they made do with pioneer provisions, foraged foods, and game meats. However, once settled in the Pacific Northwest, farmers produced a bounty of fine ingredients. Additionally, the Pacific Northwest reached economic viability early in its history. Therefore, the region had no prolonged period of pioneer cooking.

FIGURE 13.12
Oregon-bound pioneers are depicted on a mural. Alami

■ TRADITIONAL
□ COOKING IN THE
■ PACIFIC NORTHWEST

Within one or two generations after settlement, the lower Pacific Northwest was producing superb seafood and agricultural products. However, the elements needed to spark a new and distinctive regional cuisine were not yet in place. The region's American settlers and the immigrants who followed largely retained their original cuisine styles, using locally produced ingredients that were very similar to the foods of home.

First Settler Foods

Most first settlers in the Pacific Northwest culinary region hailed from two geographically different, but culinarily similar, parts of America: New England and the Midwest.

FACTOR 3
Settlers from New England and the Midwest retained their cooking styles using indigenous ingredients.

New Englanders found the northern Pacific coast and its indigenous foods comfortably familiar. Their cooking adapted seamlessly to the region's climate conditions and indigenous ingredients. Indeed, much traditional Pacific Northwest cooking has a distinctly New England flavor. Dried salmon is prepared in virtually the same manner as New England salt cod. New England–style chowders are delicious when prepared with Pacific clams or salmon and enriched with cream from local dairy herds. The combination of smoked pork and seafood, as in New England clam chowder, is a popular flavor profile. When New Englanders tired of seafood, abundant game meats provided variety. The region's wild and cultivated berries become New England–style cobblers and crisps. Both fruit and seafood are baked into pies.

Midwestern settlers drew on their own cooking heritage, creating Pacific Northwest versions of Farmlands and Ranchlands cuisines. Farmlands-style biscuits and pancakes, as well as sourdough breads, are part of traditional Pacific Northwestern cooking. On the eastern plateau, cattle ranching provided beef, prepared in Farmlands-style roasts and stews as well as grilled in the Ranchlands manner.

The mixture of food cultures encountered on the wagon trails and in the forts gave rise to the liberal palate of the American West. Although most New Englanders and Midwesterners are culinary conservatives, by the time these groups arrived in northern California and the Pacific Northwest, they had become culinary liberals more than happy to try the indigenous foods of their new home.

Technology played a major role in Pacific Northwest farming and led to the region's early economic viability. The development of drought-resistant strains of wheat, mechanization of farm machinery, and construction of dams on the region's rivers enabled the interior plateau to support grain crops. As industrial canning became more efficient and rail transportation less expensive, fruits and vegetables from the Pacific Northwest could be shipped to eastern tables.

FACTOR 5
Economic
viability
arrived quickly
in the Pacific
Northwest,
spurred by a
combination
of agriculture,
logging,
fishing, and
prospecting.

By the late 1800s, railroads reached north from San Francisco, connecting it with Oregon's coast and its agricultural interior. Now the region's established settlers had a ready market for both lumber and food products. Soon millions of pounds of Pacific Northwest salmon were being canned in the region's processing plants. Fish parts unsuitable for canning became local delicacies.

A legacy of the region's Native Americans, salmon cheeks are a Pacific Northwest specialty. These tender disks are frequently wrapped in bacon, skewered, and grilled over a wood fire. Alternatively, they're pan-seared in bacon drippings. **Salmon bellies,** the fatty flesh found near the ventral fins, are first cured in salt brine and then fried as a breakfast or supper dish accompanied by boiled potatoes.

Another food with native origins, hot-smoked or **kippered** salmon is a renowned Pacific Northwest product. In this method, the fish is lightly cured with a salt-spice-sugar rub or brine and then smoked between 165 and 185°F. The kippering method produces a lightly smoked flavor and a somewhat flaky, "cooked" texture.

Immigrants' Influence

When word of the Pacific Northwest's seemingly limitless opportunities reached the East Coast, thousands of immigrants headed for the region, ready and willing to work. Many went into food-related occupations.

Italians from the south of Italy and Italian-Americans from the East Coast had perhaps the most profound influence on the region's ingredients. Arriving in significant numbers after the completion of the railroads in the late 1800s, many Italians went into business as truck farmers and produce purveyors. In addition to growing and selling the standard American produce of the era, they also introduced Italian vegetables and fruits—such as broccoli, broccoli rabe, zucchini, various types of bell peppers, table grapes, and Italian prune plums—that were considered quite exotic at the time. Discovering the mild, moist climate of the Oregon and Washington coasts, they began growing Mediterranean food plants such as artichokes, cardoons, figs, and dates. As culinary liberals, mainstream Pacific Northwesterners were willing to add these new vegetables and fruits to their repertoire. Italians were also among the nation's first successful commercial growers of vinifera wine grapes and helped found the Pacific Northwest wine industry.

Although these Italians brought many new produce items to the region, their cuisine style did not significantly affect the seasonings or techniques of traditional Pacific Northwest cooking.

Thousands of Chinese men immigrated to America's West Coast to work on the Transcontinental Railroad. When it was completed, many started businesses and prospered, eventually bringing their wives and families to America. In the Pacific Northwest, as in California, many opened

FACTOR 4
Italian
immigrants
brought
Mediterranean
vegetables
and founded
the region's
wine industry.

FIGURE 13.13
Pacific Northwest oyster beds. Courtesy Taylor Shellfish Farms

restaurants and helped develop the Chinese-American microcuisine you studied on this book's companion website.

Japanese immigrants were among the earliest developers of Pacific Northwest aquaculture. Using the region's bays and inlets as protected areas in which to construct cultivation beds, they introduced both Pacific and Kumamoto oysters as well as Japanese littleneck clams (Figure 13.13).

Asian immigrants were among the first to plant truck gardens and fruit orchards in the region's coastal valleys. Many were experts at plant propagation and were instrumental in developing new varieties of vegetable and fruit cultivars suited to the region. Most of these immigrant horticulturalists remained unknown. However, in 1875 an Oregon grower named a superior new cherry cultivar after the Chinese worker who developed it. Today the Pacific Northwest Bing cherry is prized worldwide.

Asian immigrants became a significant force in the region's commercial and domestic foodservice industry. Upon the completion of the railroads, many Chinese laborers became domestic servants. Those with talent for cooking soon headed the kitchens of large farms, boardinghouses, and estates of wealthy merchants. Many more entered commercial foodservice, working in the kitchens of hotels, saloons, and non-Asian restaurants.

As the region's level of wealth and sophistication rose, so did the level of the region's cooking. Many Chinese cooks became skilled chefs, proficient in preparing both American and European dishes. As in California, Asian cooking methods and taste preferences lightened and improved Pacific Northwest cooking. Similarly, Japanese chefs introduced Pacific Northwest diners to the concept of eating raw seafood.

Northern Gold Creates European-Style Opulence

The discovery of gold in Alaska in 1872 caused an unprecedented boom for the entire Pacific Northwest. Miners from the San Francisco gold fields

FACTOR 4
Asian cooking
methods and
taste
preferences
lightened and
improved
Pacific
Northwest
cooking.

headed to Alaska in droves and were soon joined by hopeful prospectors from around the world. These new Alaskans depended almost entirely on foods and equipment produced in the lower Pacific Northwest.

Alaska miners who struck it rich returned south for rest and recreation and to spend their newfound fortunes. Soon Portland and Seattle became cities of wealth and sophistication. Along with the influx of money from the gold rush came East Coast and European entrepreneurs, many of whom were world travelers with refined tastes. In hotels and restaurants built to accommodate them, and later in their own homes, these newcomers raised standards of Pacific Northwest cooking to a new level.

Ships from the Pacific and railcars from the East Coast brought the world's delicacies to the doors of hotels and restaurants. Restaurant and hotel proprietors recruited chefs from Boston, New York City, Philadelphia, and Baltimore as well as from Europe, luring them with high salaries and unheard-of benefits. European-trained chefs, many from France and Switzerland, prepared classic French dishes with the region's fine ingredients. At the request of their patrons, they also turned their skills to producing extraordinary versions of English and American dishes as well. Thus, Pacific Northwest restaurants featured European dishes such as salmis of duck and oyster vol-au-vent as well as American classics such as terrapin stew and clam chowder.

Food Production Anchors an Emerging Cuisine

Although the Pacific Northwest's refined restaurant cuisine and fine home cooking required imported seasonings brought by rail or sea, its main ingredients were local. Yaquina Bay oysters, Columbia River salmon, plateau-raised beef and lamb, and Willamette Valley vegetables and fruits were among the raw materials that made fine meals. However, virtually all of the dishes served in the region's restaurants and homes belonged to the national or regional cuisine of another place. Despite having a few noteworthy local food specialties, the Pacific Northwest lacked a repertoire of unique defining dishes. Nor had a distinctive Pacific Northwest style yet developed. Through the mid-20th century and into the early 1980s, traditional Pacific Northwest cooking must be considered a work in progress, having not yet evolved into a fully mature cuisine. During this time entrepreneur farmers, foragers, fishermen, and merchants continued developing the region's first-rate food resources.

The Nation's Fruit Basket

Commercial fruit growing became a major business in the Pacific Northwest in the 1880s, when railroads connected the region to the rest of the country. In the early 20th century, irrigation in the Yakima Valley opened up thousands of acres to new orchards (Figure 13.14). Today, more than half of the fresh apples consumed in the United States are produced in Washington State.

In addition to apples and pears, the region boasts a variety of sweet cherries, among them the Oregon Bing cherry and Washington's golden Rainier cherry. In the United States fruit market, Washington ranks first in production of apples, cherries, and pears. Oregon ranks second in pears and cherries.

Nuts are also an important crop in the Pacific Northwest, with Oregon hazelnuts among the most valuable. Traditional berry cultivars are supplemented with local specialty items such as cloudberries, salmonberries, marionberries, and lingonberries introduced from Scandinavia.

FIGURE 13.14

Irrigation made the Yakima Valley bloom with fruit orchards.

@erics/Shutterstock

Wild Mushrooms

In the late 1980s, mushroom foraging became a commercial enterprise in the Pacific Northwest. Still a cottage industry, mushrooming is a seasonal occupation that provides much-needed extra income in the region's rural areas. Throughout the spring, summer, and fall mushroom seasons, foragers go out in search of wild mushrooms, most often on federally owned land. The U.S. Forest Service monitors foraging activity, conducting research on the impact of commercial mushrooming on the lands it protects. Most of the mushroom harvest is purchased by large produce companies that set up seasonal buying stations in rural towns (Figure 13.15). The most commonly found mushrooms are boletes, morels, chanterelles, and the American matsutake. Fresh Pacific Northwest mushrooms are air-freighted to urban specialty markets across the country and throughout the world.

FIGURE 13.15

Produce companies set up mushroom-buying stations where foragers can sell their day's harvest.

Todd Bigelow/Aurora Photos, Inc.

Regional Cheeses

As befits a region perfectly suited to dairy production, the Pacific Northwest boasted fine local cheeses as early as the mid-1800s. At that time, Dutch farmers who settled Oregon's Tillamook County began producing European-style cheeses as well as a high-quality English-style Cheddar that still bears the Tillamook name. The Tillamook County Creamery Association was founded as a cooperative in 1909 and continues producing fine cheeses famous across the country.

Washington State University's Creamery has been famous for dairy products since its founding. In the 1940s, food scientists at WSU perfected the technology for sealing cheeses in metal cans. The most popular of these cheeses is a pale yellow sharp Cheddar known as Cougar Gold, named in honor of the school mascot and the cheese's creator, Dr. N. S. Golding.

The Rogue Creamery specializes in blue-veined cheeses. Its Rogue River Blue was awarded the title "World's Best Blue" at the 2003 World Cheese Awards in London.

Palouse Valley Crops

The combination of dry-land farming techniques and mechanized agricultural equipment made the Palouse Valley into one of the nation's most productive sources of commodities crops (Figure 13.16). Today the Palouse is a leader in the production of potatoes, barley, hops, and legumes such as lentils and dried beans.

FIGURE 13.16
Pacific Northwest Agricultural Areas

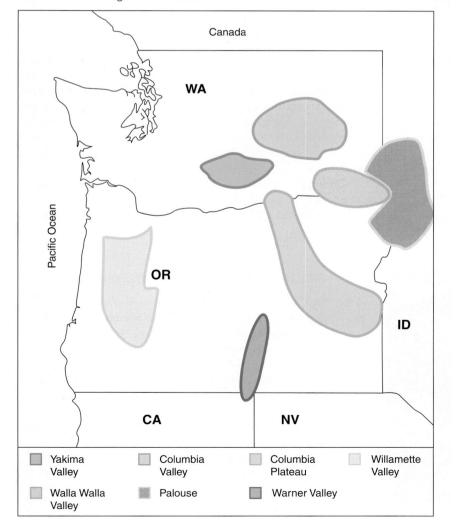

Fishing and Aquaculture

The Pacific Northwest coast provides habitat for more than 80 species of crab, including Dungeness, king, snow, tanner, and rock crab. The region boasts more than 160 varieties of clams, including razor, butter, pink necks, Pacific littlenecks, and various cockles. **Pink singing scallops** is a marketing name for small Pacific Northwest scallops harvested by divers and sold in the shell. Both the adductor muscle and coral are eaten.

Among the region's primary food fish are steelhead trout, rock cod, Pacific rockfish, canary rockfish, halibut, and several varieties of char and sturgeon. However, in the lower Pacific Northwest and Alaska, salmon are the most highly prized fish. The four major varieties of salmon caught in the wild are Chinook, silver, sockeye, and chum.

Through the mid-1900s, most of the Pacific Northwest salmon catch was processed in canning facilities. Through the end of the century, sales of fresh and frozen salmon became equally important. However, the Pacific Northwest's river fisheries went into severe decline as a result of water loss to agriculture and pollution from a growing population. Scarcity of salmon combined with growing national and international demand drove prices sky-high. By the 1960s most of the region's catch was being shipped out of the area, and it became difficult to find local salmon in restaurants. In response, aquaculture became one of the region's biggest businesses.

In the Pacific Northwest, aquaculture includes raising Atlantic mussels, Atlantic and Asian oysters, and various clams. Aquaculture of geoduck (p. 644) and abalone (p. 599) is a growing business as well. However, most Pacific Northwest aquaculture involves raising Atlantic salmon in Pacific waters. In fact, farmed Atlantic salmon from Pacific waters makes up most fresh salmon found in America's restaurants and supermarkets.

Various methods and equipment are used by the aquaculture industry, some of which are safe and environmentally friendly and others that are not. Most methods of shellfish aquaculture are considered acceptable. However, in the Pacific Northwest, certain types of salmon farming have raised concerns and led to a ban on salmon aquaculture in Alaska. Refer to this book's companion website for more information on salmon aquaculture.

Seattle's Pike Place Market

One of the best places to experience the bounty of Pacific Northwest foods is at Seattle's Pike Place Market. This public food market was founded in 1907 to provide a venue where consumers could buy produce and meats directly from the region's farmers, many of Japanese origin. Shortly thereafter the Pike Place Fish Market was added and, by 1917, the market had grown into a complex of stores, wholesale halls, restaurants, crafts workshops, and

PIKE PLACE FLYING FISH

The Pike Place Fish Market is a tourist attraction in its own right. In addition to gazing at an astounding variety of sparkling-fresh Pacific seafood, visitors flock to see the market's famous "flying fish." The practice began with harried fishmongers rushing to fill their orders by tossing 20-pound salmon across the market aisles to each other. Today vendors throw fish to amuse visitors and maintain a venerable Pike Place tradition.

even a dance hall. The market reached its peak of activity in 1926, housing more than 600 farmers as well as numerous other food producers, and welcoming as many as 50,000 shoppers on a weekend day.

However, the market fell on hard times beginning with World War II and the internment of the region's Japanese immigrants, to which the market lost more than half of its truck farmers. The 1950s saw the American public abandon city public markets in general as many fled to the suburbs and embraced supermarket shopping. By 1963 the market was largely empty, derelict, and scheduled for demolition. However, a group of Seattle citizens, recognizing the market's value as a civic institution and historic site, formed a nonprofit preservation group that brought the market back to life.

Today the sprawling Pike Place Market covers nine acres of prime Seattle real estate (Figure 13.17). Within this assembly of market halls crowned with the iconic Pike Place sign and clock, several hundred merchants and food purveyors sell local produce, most of which is picked the same day it is sold. Several fine butchers provide cut-to-order meats, and grocers offer spices, seasonings, condiments, and cooking equipment. For the hungry shopper, scores of restaurants complete the scene.

FIGURE 13.17
Seafood dealers at Seattle's Pike Place Market. Paul Costinsky/Shutterstock

■ MODERN PACIFIC □ NORTHWEST CUISINE ■

Many chefs and food historians believe the birth of Pacific Northwest regional cuisine occurred in the 1980s as a result of the region's burgeoning wine industry. Therefore, we'll begin our section on the region's modern cuisine with Pacific Northwest wines and wine making.

Pacific Northwest Wine Making

In the late 1960s, Northern California once again began growing high-quality vinifera wine grapes and making world-class wines. In the 1970s, growers began looking north to Oregon and Washington State, where the mild climate and volcanic soil were suitable for Chardonnay and Pinot Noir, the classic grape varietals of France's Burgundy region.

At the same time, the American food revolution that began in California was expanding north as well. As the San Francisco dining market became saturated and rents went sky-high, Portland and Seattle began attracting entrepreneur chefs eager to open fine dining restaurants.

Chef-Driven Cuisine

Each of the American regional cuisines you've studied thus far is rooted in a fully-developed traditional cuisine created primarily by home cooks and later refined by restaurant chefs. However, most food authorities agree that Pacific Northwest regional cuisine began in restaurant kitchens. Having no long and continuous regional culinary tradition to draw on, Pacific Northwest chefs initially focused on local ingredients to forge their region's new cuisine.

During the middle of the 20th century, the Pacific Northwest underwent the same culinary homogenization as the rest of the nation. In most of the region's restaurants, local foods had

MICROBREWERIES AND BREW PUBS

In the 1970s, Pacific Northwest entrepreneurs began opening small, independent beer companies. Called **microbreweries,** they specialize in making small batches of specialty "craft-brewed" beers using traditional methods and, often, regionally grown ingredients. Today the Pacific Northwest is home to more than a hundred microbreweries, and Portland, Oregon, is recognized as the microbrewery capital of America.

In an effort to showcase their beers and bring in extra revenue, many Pacific Northwest microbreweries opened brew pubs. A **brew pub** is a casual restaurant located on the premises of a microbrewery serving its specialty beers fresh on draft. Brew pubs offer dishes designed to be paired with beer.

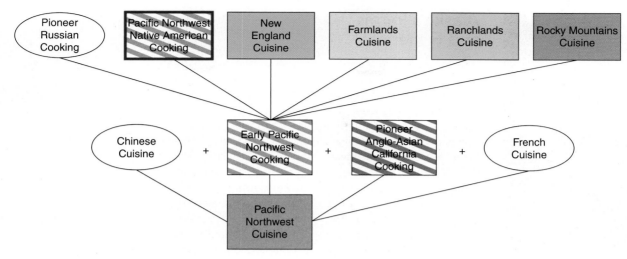

FIGURE 13.18
Development of Pacific Northwest Cuisine

been replaced with mass-market industrial foods, including frozen seafood from faraway sources. Chef Charles Ramseyer of Ray's Boathouse in Seattle is credited with reintroducing Olympia oysters, pink singing scallops, Alaska spot prawns, and Copper River salmon to restaurant menus. One of his most revolutionary ideas was obtaining a wholesale fish buyer's license, enabling his restaurant to buy directly from the boats and thus to serve the freshest available seafood at the most reasonable prices. Soon diners were asking for local seafood, and supply returned to meet the demand.

Pacific Northwest chefs then began sourcing regionally raised lamb and beef. Foraged wild mushrooms became a signature ingredient of the region. The region's bounty of fresh fruits and vegetables returned to restaurant tables, this time prepared in unusual new ways.

Fortunately, Pacific Northwest diners are an adventurous group eager to try new foods and dishes. Moreover, the region's restaurant chefs are of diverse backgrounds, using world cuisines techniques as well as classic cooking methods. All of these chefs bring a unique sensibility to their personal interpretations of Pacific Northwest cuisine. For example, Chef Cory Schreiber, formerly of Wildwood in Portland, Oregon, smoke-roasts meat and fish in an authentic North Indian tandoor oven. Many others use Pacific Rim techniques and ingredients from Japan, China, and Southeast Asia.

Pacific Northwest chefs pay homage to the region's culinary roots by using Native American ingredients and cooking methods. Planking is more popular than ever: Local salmon is treated to innovative seasoning rubs or marinades and then smoke-roasted with the flavor of alder or cedar. Chefs strive to achieve wild flavors in their dishes, using foraged mushrooms, herbs, and indigenous vegetables. Berries and other fruits are used in savory dishes as well as desserts.

Although Native American and world cuisines techniques are part of modern Pacific Northwest cuisine, at heart the style is

BIRTHPLACE OF AMERICA'S COFFEE CRAZE

In the 1980s, Pacific Northwesterners became discerning coffee drinkers demanding authentic espressos, cappuccinos, and café lattes. Entrepreneurs responded by opening hundreds of neighborhood cafés, many of which roast their own coffee beans and create their own signature blends. Most prominent among Seattle's coffee businesses is Starbucks, now an international company with outlets around the world.

based on ingredients. Pacific Northwest chefs were among the nation's first to credit producers on their menus, naming dishes after the farm, town, county, or body of water where the main ingredient was sourced.

Refer to this book's companion website for a listing of noteworthy Pacific Northwest regional cuisine restaurants.

ALASKAN COOKING

The gold rush that initially lured thousands of prospectors to Alaska was short-lived. However, after the gold mines played out, other minerals continued to attract the mining industry. In the 1960s the discovery of oil—and the development of technology for delivering it—created an unprecedented economic boom. The Alaska oil pipeline, constructed between 1975 and 1977, brought a new influx of settlers to the region. Drawn by high wages and the challenge of America's last wilderness, these latest Alaska pioneers brought with them a sense of adventure that extended to food and cooking and created the beginnings of a modern Alaskan cooking style.

Alaska's Farms and Fisheries

By the mid-20th century, developments in horticulture enabled at least some Alaskans to enjoy local produce. With cold-tolerant fruit and vegetable cultivars bred to mature in fewer than 100 days, Alaska's river valleys and coastal plains became viable for truck farming. In fact, the combination of 20-hours-per-day sunlight and fertile volcanic soil sometimes produces vegetables of extraordinary size; the Alaska State Fair regularly exhibits record-setting vegetables such as a 100-pound cabbage or a pumpkin bigger than a wheelbarrow (Figure 13.19).

FIGURE 13.19

Alaska's fertile soil and long hours of summer daylight frequently result in giant vegetables.
ARENA Creative/Shutterstock

Improvements in boat-building and food-processing technology created a thriving Alaskan fishing industry. Advancements making fishing boats safer and more dependable allowed fishermen to travel far out into the Gulf of Alaska in search of fish and shellfish. Alaskan halibut is considered one of the continent's finest food fish. Abundant Alaskan pollack is used to make frozen breaded fish sticks and is a component of **surimi,** an industrially processed imitation crab product. Using onboard processing plants and freezers, fishermen harvest and preserve Alaskan king crab and snow crab, once local specialties unknown outside the region. However, Alaskan crab fishing is the nation's most dangerous occupation. Each year hundreds of crab fishermen are injured or killed.

Traditional Alaskan Cooking

As late as the 1960s, Alaskan food was truly pioneer food. Outside the cities, Alaskans relied as much on pioneer provisions and preserved products as did wagon train travelers of a hundred years before. Dried, smoked, and brined meats; dried beans; dried corn products; crackers and biscuits; flour; sugar; and coffee were essential supplies. In addition, mid-20th-century Alaskans subsisted on many canned products, including vegetables, fruits, milk products, meats, seafood, and prepared items. To protect their food supply from hungry bears, wolves, and other wild animals, the typical Alaskan settler built a *cache* (KASH), or elevated storage shed, raised high on posts (Figure 13.20).

Alaska's Native Americans contributed numerous methods of preparing fish and wild game to traditional Alaskan cooking. In addition to planking, they taught early settlers to cure, smoke, dry, freeze, and even ferment these foods both for preservation and for flavor. Halibut "popcorn," chewy morsels of salted and dried fish, remains a popular snack. The practice of combining indigenous berries with meats and other savory foods is a native foodway that remains in many forms. Cloudberries, salmonberries, huckleberries, nagoonberries, and low-bush blueberries and cranberries are popular not only in desserts and breakfast dishes but also in savory stuffings, sauces, and glazes for roasted meats, game, poultry, and planked fish. At festivals and traditional outdoor events, one can sample *agutuk*, or Eskimo ice cream, a fluffy mixture of game fat, seal oil, crushed berries, and sugar whipped with snow.

FIGURE 13.20

The *cache*, or elevated storage shed, protects food supplies from wild animals. LC-USZ62-107327, Library of Congress

Early Russian settlers left a lasting impression on Alaska's cuisine with their love of sturdy, cool-weather vegetables such as cabbage, potatoes, carrots, and especially rutabagas. *Borscht*, the hearty soup based on cabbage and beets, is a regional favorite made in many different ways. *Golubtsy*, or Russian stuffed cabbage, is enjoyed by many Alaskans no matter their heritage. Virtually every Alaskan cook has a recipe for *peroche* (pe-ROACH), the classic Russian pastry turnovers that can be filled with ground meat, mushrooms, cabbage, or fish. Russian sweet pastries include *kulich* (koo-LEECH), tall cylinders of briochelike cake studded with dried fruits that are served with *pashka*, a spread of fresh cheese mixed with confectioner's sugar and vanilla. And many Alaskans enjoy Russian tea, a strong infusion of black tea leaves served in tiny glasses with a dollop of berry jelly and an optional shot of vodka.

Settlers from Sweden, Norway, and Finland added their foodways to the local cuisine. Sweet-and-tangy pickled herring served with beets or cucumbers is an Alaskan favorite. *Sillsalat* blends salt herring with beets, potatoes, apples, dill pickles, and hard-cooked eggs in a sour cream dressing. Salted salmon bellies are simmered in a rich cream sauce with egg and dill, then served with boiled potatoes. Fish pudding (basically a large molded fish mousseline) and *fiskesuppe* (a creamy fish soup with fish dumplings) are Scandinavian-inspired dishes that have become part of the Alaska repertoire.

As late as the 1960s, wild game was the only fresh meat available in rural Alaska. Today the taste for game remains, although other types of meat are now readily available. Among the game meats and fowl enjoyed by Alaskans are deer, elk, caribou, reindeer, moose, bear, beaver, muskrat, squirrel, hare, lynx, mountain goat, Dall sheep, scores of goose and duck species, ptarmigan, and grouse, as well as seal, walrus, and whale.

The discovery of oil in Alaska, and the subsequent construction of the Alaska oil pipeline in the 1970s, brought a new influx of settlers to the region along with millions of dollars and new technology. Even Alaskans living in remote areas gained access to fresh foods shipped by air, and Alaska's cities acquired supermarkets and restaurants.

☐ TABLE 13.1 PACIFIC NORTHWEST DEFINING DISHES

ITEM NAME	HISTORY	DOMINANT INGREDIENTS AND METHOD	MORE
TILLAMOOK CHEDDAR SOUP WITH ALE	This smooth, rich soup was popularized in the region's brew pubs.	A velouté soup based on poultry stock and fresh microbrew ale is enriched with artisanal Tillamook Cheddar cheese.	The soup may be garnished with minced fresh herbs, crumbled bacon, or croutons.
PACIFIC NORTHWEST SEAFOOD CHOWDER	Transplanted New Englanders prepared chowders similar to those of home but using local seafood.	These cream-based soups include potatoes and a preserved pork product. They feature razor or Pacific littleneck clams, scallops, local fish, or Dungeness crab.	Pacific Northwest chowder is accompanied by crackers or sourdough bread.
OYSTER PAN ROAST	An East Coast legacy, this dish was popular in Northwest gold rush–era hotels.	Oyster liquor is simmered with a base of sweated onion and celery, enriched with cream, and seasoned with Worcestershire sauce and bottled chili sauce. Shucked oysters are poached in the sauce and then served over toast points.	Oyster pan roast is frequently prepared at the table in a chafing dish.
OYSTERS ON THE HALF SHELL	The region's indigenous Olympia oysters were prized by Native Americans and settlers alike.	Freshly shucked oysters traditionally are served with a wedge of lemon.	Modern chefs create signature toppings, or pair chilled raw oysters with hot grilled sausages as in Bordeaux.
CHILLED CRACKED DUNGENESS CRAB	This delectable crab is named for the coastal town of Dungeness, Washington, itself named after England's Dungeness headland by explorer George Vancouver.	Freshly steamed whole Dungeness crabs are cooled and cleaned, and their legs are cracked for easy eating. A sauce is prepared by mixing the crab's tomalley with mayonnaise and bottled hot sauce.	The crab is accompanied by a vinaigrette salad and crisp sourdough bread.
HOT-SMOKED (KIPPERED) SALMON	Made by the traditional Pacific Northwest Native American method of smoking, this salmon has a pale pink color and a cooked texture.	Hot-smoked salmon is served at cool room temperature with crackers or toast points; it is often accompanied by lemon wedges and capers or served with a mayonnaise-based sauce.	Hot-smoked salmon may be flaked and mixed with cream cheese to make a tasty spread.
SALTED SALMON BELLIES IN EGG SAUCE	This regional dish makes use of trimmings from the production of salted or smoked salmon sides.	Fatty sections of the ventral portion of the salmon are cured in a light brine, then poached in a court bouillon. The fish is served in a light velouté with lemon, dill, and chopped hard-cooked egg.	This dish is served over toast points or with boiled potatoes.
PLANKED SALMON	This regional signature dish is a Native American legacy. See p. 608 for more information.	A salmon side or fillet is seasoned, placed on a presoaked alder or cedar plank, and roasted in a wood-fired oven or a closed charcoal grill.	The traditional presentation includes a border of potato purée piped around the fish near the end of the roasting time. Vegetable accompaniments are placed within the potato border just before serving and the plank is presented on an underliner tray.
STEAMED KING CRAB LEGS/SNOW CRAB LEGS	This delicacy was enjoyed only in Alaska until the development of frozen food technology.	The large and meaty legs of the king crab are steamed and served with lemon and melted butter.	Today frozen king crab and snow crab legs are available throughout the nation. Locals agree that nothing compares to the flavor and texture of fresh Alaska crab enjoyed right off the boat.
HALIBUT CADDY GANTY	Named for the female owner of Alaska's Pelican Cold Storage Company, who is said to have invented the recipe. This simple dish has been an Alaska favorite for nearly 50 years.	Halibut fillets are marinated in white wine, dredged in bread crumbs, and baked under a topping of mayonnaise, sour cream, minced onion, and paprika.	

(continued)

☐ **TABLE 13.1 PACIFIC NORTHWEST DEFINING DISHES** (*continued*)

ITEM NAME	HISTORY	DOMINANT INGREDIENTS AND METHOD	MORE
FIDDLEHEADS AND MORELS	These two foraged foods of the region's woodlands come into season at the same time.	These seasonal specialties are combined in dishes such as pastry-encased appetizer ragouts, pastas, salads, and side dishes.	The combination has become a seasonal signature found on spring menus in virtually all of the region's fine-dining restaurants.
LEAFY SALADS COMBINING FRUIT, NUTS, AND/OR ARTISANAL CHEESES	Modern Pacific Northwest chefs have created various salads featuring fruit combined with nuts and local cheeses.	Examples include young spinach combined with Braeburn apples, walnuts, and Tillamook Cheddar; watercress teamed with ripe Comice pears, hazelnuts, and Rogue River Blue.	
WILD MUSHROOM BREAD PUDDING	This unique side dish began appearing on Pacific Northwest menus in the early 1990s and has become a regional signature dish.	Highly seasoned, sautéed wild mushrooms are layered with slices of firm bread in a savory custard and baked until set.	Modern chefs use rounds or diamonds of the bread pudding as a base to add height to meat, game, or poultry presentations.
LEGUME DISHES	Northwest chefs showcase the Palouse Valley's various legumes in dishes both traditional and modern.	In classic soups and innovative salads and side dishes, lentils and beans are an important element in the cuisine.	
BAKED STUFFED WALLA WALLA ONIONS	Stuffed onions traditionally accompany roasted meats and fowl.	Local chefs hollow the onions and fill them with a variety of stuffings, such as Italian bread crumb and sausage mixtures and Creole-inspired rice dressings.	The high sugar content of the onions caramelizes to a deep, rich sweetness that perfectly offsets a savory stuffing.
BERRY SAUCES FOR SAVORY DISHES	Modern chefs are inspired by the Native American custom of seasoning meats, fowl, and fish with indigenous berries.	Wild duck is served in a huckleberry demi-glace; wood-roasted salmon is accompanied by a cloudberry compote; grilled venison is teamed with a salal berry game essence.	Berries find their way into salad dressings both sweet and tart. Berry barbeque sauce enhances grilled meat, poultry, and even fish.
HUCKLEBERRY PIE	Settlers from America's East Coast brought the legacy of English pie-making to the Pacific Northwest.	Small, deep-blue Northwest huckleberries are baked in a double crust of traditional American pastry dough with butter, sugar, and a thickener of flour and/or cornstarch.	Aficionados ignore the many tiny seeds.
FRUIT AND NUT DESSERTS	The region that produces more than half of America's fresh table fruit and a significant portion of America's domestic nuts features these products in its signature desserts.	Fruits and nuts are showcased in tarts, tortes, mousses, soufflés, and frozen desserts.	

■□■ STUDY QUESTIONS

1. Contrast the climate and topography of the coastal Pacific Northwest with those of the region's interior plateau. Describe the agricultural products of each area.

2. Describe the food culture and cooking of lower Pacific Northwest Native American tribes. Explain why these groups are exceptions to the rule regarding agriculture and cultural advancement. Discuss Native American ingredients and cooking techniques that have influenced modern Pacific Northwest cuisine.

3. Describe the colonist first-settler group that arrived in Alaska by boat and eventually penetrated into the coastal lower Pacific Northwest. Briefly describe their cuisine and its influence on Alaskan cooking.

4. Describe the pioneer first-settler group that arrived in the lower Pacific Northwest via the overland wagon trails. Where did they come from? How did their food attitudes change? Describe their cooking styles.

5. List and describe the second-wave immigrant groups of the Pacific Northwest. How did they influence traditional Pacific Northwest cooking?

6. Discuss Pacific Northwest seafood as a regional industry and as signature items of the region's modern cuisine. Include in your discussion the history of various preserved seafood products as well as modern aquaculture.

7. Separately list the Pacific Northwest's most important agricultural and foraged food products. Explain how these ingredients became the inspiration for modern Pacific Northwest cuisine.

8. List the three types of beverages for which the Pacific Northwest is famous, and explain their impact on Pacific Northwest cuisine.

9. Recount the history of Alaskan cooking and explain its diversity.

10. Discuss modern Pacific Northwest cuisine as prepared in restaurants. Explain why, in this particular regional cuisine, flavor combinations and cooking methods are more important than defining dishes.

11. Using the information you learned in this chapter and your imagination, plan a four-course special-occasion dinner menu featuring Pacific Northwest cuisine.

Creamy Cauliflower Soup
with Cracked Hazelnuts and Cougar Gold Cheddar Wafers

yield: 1 (10-fl.-oz.) appetizer serving
(multiply × 4 for classroom turnout; adjust equipment sizes accordingly)

MASTER RECIPE

production		costing only
1 1/4 c.	Creamy Cauliflower Soup	1/4 recipe
1 Tbsp.	toasted, crushed hazelnuts	1/8 oz.
1 tsp.	minced chives	1/40 bunch a.p.
1	6" doily or cocktail napkin	1 each
3	Cougar Gold Cheddar Wafers	1/8 recipe

service turnout:
1. Stir the cold Creamy Cauliflower Soup to redistribute the solids, then ladle it into a small saucepan. Heat the soup to just under the boil.
2. Plate the dish:
   a. Ladle the soup into a hot 12-fl.-oz. soup cup.
   b. Garnish with the hazelnuts and chives.
   c. Place the cup slightly left of center on an 8" plate lined with a 6" doily.
   d. Arrange the wafers on the plate to the right of the cup.

COMPONENT RECIPE
CREAMY CAULIFLOWER SOUP

yield: 5 c.

production		costing only
2 Tbsp.	butter	1 oz.
1 c.	fine-chopped yellow onion	5 oz. a.p.
3 c.	coarse-chopped cauliflower florets and stems	3/8 [12 ct.] head
1/2 c.	peeled, 1/2"-diced russet potato	3 oz. a.p.
tt	kosher salt	1/16 oz.
1 qt.	Poultry Stock	1/4 recipe
pinch	ground mace	1/16 oz.
1	fresh sage sprig	1/10 bunch a.p.
2/3 c.	tiny cauliflower florets	1/8 [12 ct.] head
1/2 c.	heavy cream	4 fl. oz.
tt	fine-ground white pepper	1/16 oz.

preparation:
1. Heat the butter in a heavy 4-qt. saucepan, add the onion, and cook over low heat until the onion softens.
2. Add the chopped cauliflower, potato, and salt. Stir well to coat the vegetables with the butter, then cover the pan and sweat them over low heat, stirring often, about 3 minutes.
3. Add the stock, mace, and sage sprig. Bring to the simmer and cook at a brisk simmer, partially covered, about 20 minutes, until the vegetables are very soft.
4. Remove the sage sprig and purée the soup with an immersion blender or in a food processor. If using a processor, return the soup to the pan. If necessary, adjust the soup to a nappé consistency, adding water or stock to thin it, or reducing to thicken it.
5. Add the tiny cauliflower florets and the cream, then return to the simmer for 1 minute only.
6. Season with white pepper and correct the salt.

holding: open-pan cool and immediately refrigerate in a freshly sanitized, covered container up to 5 days

---

RECIPE VARIATION
Creamy Broccoli Soup with Cracked Hazelnuts and Cougar Gold Cheddar Wafers
Replace the 3 c. cauliflower florets with peeled, diced broccoli stems. Omit the mace and sage. Replace the tiny cauliflower florets with tiny broccoli florets.

Palouse Valley Brown Lentil Soup
with Wheatberry Biscuit

yield: 1 (10-fl.-oz.) appetizer
(multiply × 4 for classroom turn-out; adjust equipment sizes accordingly)

MASTER RECIPE

production		costing only
1 1/4 c.	Palouse Valley Brown Lentil Soup	1/4 recipe
1	6" doily or cocktail napkin	a.p.
1 Tbsp.	chopped flat-leaf parsley	1/40 bunch a.p.
1	Wheatberry Biscuit	1/8 recipe

service turnout:
1. Stir the soup to distribute the solids. Ladle into a small saucepan and heat just to the boil.
2. Plate the dish:
   a. Place the doily on a cool 8" plate.
   b. Ladle the soup into a hot 12-fl. oz. soup cup and place on the left side of the plate.
   c. Sprinkle with parsley.
   d. Place the Biscuit to the right of the soup.

COMPONENT RECIPE
PALOUSE VALLEY BROWN LENTIL SOUP

yield: 5 c.

production		costing only
2 Tbsp.	corn oil	1 fl. oz.
1 lb.	lamb bones and fat-free lamb trimmings	1 lb. a.p. or n/c
1 qt.	Brown Beef Stock	1/4 recipe
2 c.	water	n/c
1	thyme sprig	1/20 bunch a.p.
1	sage sprig	1/10 bunch a.p.
2	bay leaves	1/8 oz.
2 Tbsp.	butter	1 oz.
1/2 c.	chopped yellow onion	2 1/2 oz. a.p.
1/2 c.	washed, drained, brown lentils	3 oz.
1/4 c.	peeled, 3/8"-diced celery	1/20 bunch a.p.
1/2 c.	peeled, 3/8"-diced russet potato	3 oz. a.p.
1/2 c.	peeled, seeded, 3/8"-diced tomato	5 oz. a.p.
tt	kosher salt	1/8 oz.
tt	fresh lemon juice	1/6 (90 ct.) lemon

preparation:
1. Prepare lamb stock:
   a. Using a heavy cleaver, chop the bones into 2" pieces. Wash to remove any bone chips and blot dry.
   b. Heat a 12" sauté pan, heat the oil, and brown the lamb bones and trimmings.
   c. Transfer the bones and trimmings to a 4 qt. saucepan and add the Brown Beef Stock.
   d. Deglaze the sauté pan with 2 c. water and add to the saucepan. Bring to the simmer, skim, and add the thyme, sage, and bay leaves. Simmer for 20 minutes.
2. Finish the soup:
   a. Heat a 2 1/2 qt. saucepan, add the butter and onion, and cook, stirring, over medium heat until the onion browns.
   b. Strain the lamb stock into the pan with the onions. Add the lentils and celery, cover, and simmer gently for 30 minutes until the lentils are tender.
   c. Add the potato, tomato, and a little salt. Simmer 5 minutes longer until the potatoes are tender.
   d. Season with salt and balance the flavor with lemon juice.

holding: open-pan cool and immediately refrigerate in a covered, freshly-sanitized, nonreactive container

---

RECIPE VARIATION
Basque Red Bean Soup with Garlic Crouton
Replace the lentils with 2/3 c. red beans or red kidney beans soaked and partially cooked in water; omit the potatoes; add 1 c. diced Spanish chorizo sausage along with the beans; reduce 1/2 c. red wine to 1/4 c. and add along with the tomatoes; omit the biscuit; serve in a 10" pasta bowl ladled over a baguette slice fried in garlic-scented olive oil.

Salad of Watercress, Pears, Rogue River Blue Cheese, and Walnuts in Walnut Vinaigrette

yield: 1 (5-oz.) appetizer serving
(multiply × 4 for classroom turnout)

APPETIZERS

MASTER RECIPE

production		costing only
1 bunch	watercress	1 bunch a.p.
1 oz.	slivered Walla Walla onion (or other sweet onion)	1 1/4 oz. a.p.
1/4 c.	Walnut Vinaigrette, in squeeze bottle	1/4 recipe
3 oz.	Riesling Poached Pear Slices	1/4 recipe
3/4 oz.	crumbled Rogue River blue cheese	3/4 oz.
2 Tbsp.	coarse-chopped toasted walnuts	1/4 oz.

service turnout:
1. Dress the watercress:
   a. Remove and discard the large watercress stems.
   b. Gently tear the watercress into bite-size pieces and place in a work bowl along with the onion.
   c. Squeeze 2/3 of the Walnut Vinaigrette over the watercress and toss to coat it evenly.
2. Plate the dish:
   a. Mound the watercress in the center of a cool 10" plate.
   b. Arrange the Riesling Poached Pear Slices in a spoke pattern over the watercress.
   c. Drizzle the remaining dressing over the pears.
   d. Scatter the cheese and walnuts over the top.

COMPONENT RECIPE
WALNUT VINAIGRETTE

yield: 1 c.

production		costing only
1 Tbsp.	minced shallot	1/2 oz. a.p.
1 Tbsp.	Dijon mustard	1/2 fl. oz.
1/4 c.	Champagne vinegar	2 fl. oz.
tt	kosher salt	1/16 oz.
tt	sugar	1/16 oz.
3/4 c.	room-temperature walnut oil	6 fl. oz.

preparation:
1. Whisk together the shallot, mustard, vinegar, salt, and sugar.
2. Whisk the oil into the vinegar mixture in a thin stream to form an emulsion.
3. Correct the balance of salt and sugar.

holding: at cool room temperature in a freshly sanitized squeeze bottle up to 3 hours; refrigerate for longer storage; bring to room temperature and reemulsify before using

COMPONENT RECIPE
RIESLING POACHED PEAR SLICES

yield: approx. 12 oz.

production		costing only
2 1/2 c.	Washington or Oregon Riesling	20 oz.
1/4 c.	sugar	1 1/4 oz.
4	small, firm, slightly underripe pears	18 oz.
as needed	water	n/c

preparation:
1. Make the wine poaching syrup:
   a. Combine the wine and sugar in a 1 1/2-qt. nonreactive saucepan, place it over low heat, and stir until the sugar dissolves.
   b. Cool to room temperature.
2. Peel the pears, quarter and core them, and cut them into lengthwise slices about 3/8" thick. As you work, drop the pear slices into the wine syrup, adding water to keep them barely submerged.
3. Return the pan to the heat and poach the pears at a gentle simmer until tender. Depending on the type and ripeness of the pears, this may take 5 to 20 minutes.
4. Cool the pears in the syrup to room temperature.
5. Transfer the pears and syrup to a small, nonreactive container of the correct size to keep the pears submerged.

holding: refrigerate covered up to 3 days

RECIPE VARIATION
Salad of Watercress, Plums, Goat Cheese, and Hazelnuts in Hazelnut Vinaigrette
Replace the poached pear slices with sliced raw, ripe plums; replace the blue cheese with goat cheese; replace the walnuts with hazelnuts; replace the walnut oil with hazelnut oil; and serve the tossed greens topped with an attractive arrangement of the garnishes.

Pink Singing Scallops

with Pinot Noir Beurre Rouge and Wilted Baby Spinach

yield: 1 (4-oz.) appetizer serving
(multiply × 4 for classroom turnout; adjust equipment sizes accordingly)

MASTER RECIPE

production		costing only
2 tsp.	clarified butter, in squeeze bottle	1/2 oz. a.p.
3 oz.	cleaned baby spinach	3 oz.
1 tsp.	minced fresh garlic	1/9 oz. a.p.
tt	kosher salt	1/16 oz.
1/3 c.	Washington or Oregon Pinot Noir	2 2/3 fl. oz.
1/2 c.	juice pressed from Red Flame grapes	3 oz. grapes
1 Tbsp.	minced shallot	1/2 oz. a.p.
3 oz. (8 pc.)	live pink singing scallops in the shell, scrubbed	3 oz.
tt	fine-ground white pepper	1/16 oz.
1/4 c.	butter	2 oz.
1/2 oz. (3 pc.)	Red Flame grapes, quartered	1/2 oz.
2 sprigs	fresh chervil, leaves only	1/20 bunch a.p.

service turnout:

1. Finish and plate the dish:
   a. Heat a 10" sauté pan until very hot, add the clarified butter, then add the spinach. Turn the spinach constantly with tongs, and add the garlic and a pinch of salt when the spinach is just wilted.
   b. Transfer the spinach to a warm 10" soup plate and push it outward toward the plate rim, making a well in the center.
   c. Place the wine, grape juice, shallot, and scallops in the pan, cover, and steam the scallops over high heat a few seconds, until they open.
   d. Arrange the scallops in the center of the plate.
   e. Reduce the pan juices to about 3 Tbsp., season with salt and white pepper, and work in the butter to form an emulsion.
   f. Pour the sauce over the scallops and return the sauté pan to high heat.
   g. Sear the grape quarters for 1 or 2 seconds and scatter them over the scallops.
   h. Pull the chervil leaves apart and scatter the pieces over the scallops.

RECIPE VARIATION

Bay Scallops with Pinot Noir Beurre Rouge and Wilted Baby Spinach
Replace the singing scallops with 2 to 3 oz. dry-pack bay scallops. Sauté and plate the scallops, then prepare the beurre rouge sauce in the sauté pan.

Chilled Raw Olympia Oysters

with Merlot Mignonette, Grilled "Pemmican" Venison Sausages, and Walla Walla Onion Salad

yield: 1 (5-oz.) appetizer serving
(multiply × 4 for classroom turnout)

🕐 Best prepared 24 hours in advance.

MASTER RECIPE

production		costing only
3 links	"Pemmican" Venison Sausage	1/4 recipe
1 tsp.	corn oil	1/6 fl. oz.
1	romaine lettuce leaf	1/10 head a.p.
2 Tbsp.	Merlot Mignonette	1/4 recipe
1/2 c.	shredded romaine lettuce	1/20 head a.p.
5	live Olympia oysters, scrubbed well	5 each
1/2 c.	Walla Walla Onion Salad	1/4 recipe
3	toasted baguette slices	1/12 baguette, approx. 1 oz.

service turnout:

1. Brush the "Pemmican" Venison Sausage links with corn oil and grill them over medium heat, turning once, about 5 minutes, until cooked through and lightly browned.
2. Plate the dish:
   a. Line a cool 10" plate with the lettuce leaf.
   b. Stir the Merlot Mignonette to redistribute the solids, then ladle it into a dip dish or small ramekin. Place the dish on the plate at 9 o'clock.
   c. Mound the shredded lettuce slightly front center of the plate.
   d. Quickly open the oysters,* retaining as much oyster liquor as possible, and arrange them across the front of the plate.
   e. Mound the Walla Walla Onion Salad on the plate at 1 o'clock.
   f. Fan the baguette toasts from 10 to 12 o'clock.
   g. Arrange the sausages in the center of the plate, leaning against the toasts.

*If you are new to opening oysters or are preparing this dish in large volume, you may open the oysters ahead of time and hold them refrigerated for 1 to 2 hours.

COMPONENT RECIPE
"PEMMICAN" VENISON SAUSAGES

yield: 1 lb.; 12 (1 1/3-oz.) links

🕐 Best prepared 24 hours in advance.

production		costing only
12 oz.	well-trimmed venison leg or shoulder	1 lb. a.p.
4 oz.	unsalted pork fatback without rind	5 oz. a.p.
1/4 oz.	dried cherries	1/4 oz.
1/2 c.	Washington or Oregon Merlot	4 fl. oz.
1 Tbsp.	minced shallot	1/2 oz. a.p.
1 tsp.	minced garlic	1/9 oz. a.p.
1 Tbsp.	minced parsley	1/40 bunch a.p.
1/2 tsp.	minced thyme leaves	1/40 bunch a.p.
tt	kosher salt	1/8 oz.
1 tsp.	fresh-ground black pepper	1/8 oz.
36"	lamb casings, soaked in cold water	a.p.

preparation:
1. Cut the venison and fatback into 1" dice and place in the freezer for a few minutes only.
2. Place the parts of a meat grinder and a small mixer bowl and paddle attachment in the freezer.
3. Prepare the cherries:
   a. Place the cherries and wine in a small saucepan and simmer over low heat about 5 minutes, until the cherries are softened and the wine reduced by half.
   b. Cool to room temperature.
   c. Remove the cherries from the wine and reserve both.
   d. Fabricate the cherries into rough brunoise cuts and return them to the wine.
4. Prepare the forcemeat:
   a. Separately grind the venison and fatback using the coarse die of the grinder.
   b. Grind the coarse-ground fatback again, this time using the fine die of the grinder.
   c. Combine the venison, fatback, shallot, garlic, parsley, thyme, cherries and liquid, salt, and pepper in the chilled mixer bowl and beat with the paddle attachment until well combined and cohesive.
5. Poach a tiny ball of the sausage, cool, and taste. If necessary, correct the seasoning.
6. Encase the sausage:
   a. Drain the casings and rinse them.
   b. Thread the casings onto the horn of a sausage stuffer and force the sausage into the casing. Don't pack the casing too tightly.
   c. Divide the sausage into 12 links and tie off the lengths with kitchen string.
   d. Prick each link with a sterilized pin in 6 to 8 places.
   e. Rub the links with a light coating of salt.
   f. If time allows, hang the sausages or place them on a rack over a drip pan in the refrigerator up to 24 hours.

holding: after 24 hours, store in a freshly sanitized, covered container or plastic bag up to 3 days longer; freeze up to 1 month

COMPONENT RECIPE
MERLOT MIGNONETTE

yield: 1/2 c.

production		costing only
3/4 c.	Washington or Oregon Merlot	6 fl. oz.
1 tsp.	kosher salt	1/8 oz.
3 Tbsp.	minced shallot	1 1/2 oz. a.p.
2 tsp.	cracked black pepper	1/4 oz.

preparation:
1. Place the wine in a small, nonreactive sauté pan and, over very low heat, reduce slowly by almost half, scraping the sides of the pan with a heatproof rubber spatula.
2. Add the salt and cool to room temperature.
3. Mix in the shallot and pepper.

holding: at cool room temperature in a freshly sanitized, covered, nonreactive container up to 5 days

COMPONENT RECIPE
WALLA WALLA ONION SALAD

yield: 2 c.

production		costing only
10 oz.	slivered Walla Walla onion (or other sweet onion)	12 oz. a.p.
3/4 oz.	very fine julienne carrot	1 oz. a.p.
2 Tbsp.	fresh lemon juice	3/8 [90 ct.] lemon
tt	kosher salt	1/16 oz.
2 Tbsp.	gold-color pure olive oil	1 fl. oz.
2 tsp.	chopped tarragon leaves	1/16 bunch a.p.
dash	sweet Hungarian paprika	1/16 oz.

preparation:
1. Mix the onion and carrot with the lemon juice and season highly with salt. Refrigerate 1 hour.
2. Drain the liquid from the onion and toss with the oil, tarragon, and paprika.

holding: prepare just enough for service; hold refrigerated up to 5 hours

---

RECIPE VARIATION

Wood-Roasted Olympia Oysters with Merlot Beurre Rouge and Crispy Bacon
Place a small handful of presoaked fruitwood chips on the hot coals of a charcoal or gas grill and allow smoke to build. Place 6 live Olympia oysters on a grill rack over the wood chips and cover them with a metal dome. Roast about 5 minutes, until the oysters open. Remove the top shells, plate, and nap with a beurre rouge sauce (p. 623) made with Washington or Oregon Merlot. Top with crisp crumbled bacon and pulled chervil.

Gitksan Planked Salmon

with Berry Barbeque Sauce, Roasted Fennel–Yukon Gold Potato Purée, and Northwest Vegetable Medley

yield: 1 (6-oz.) entrée serving plus accompaniments (multiply × 4 for classroom turnout; adjust equipment sizes accordingly)

MASTER RECIPE

production		costing only
2 sprigs	fresh thyme	1/10 bunch a.p.
1 sprig	fresh rosemary	1/10 bunch a.p.
1	individual-size cedar or alder plank, soaked in water overnight	a.p.
6 oz.	salmon fillet, skinned and pinned	7 oz. a.p.
1 Tbsp.	corn oil	1/2 fl. oz.
tt	kosher salt	1/16 oz.
tt	fine-ground white pepper	1/16 oz.
1/4 c.	Gitksan Baste	1/4 recipe
1 Tbsp.	corn oil	1/2 fl. oz.
1/4 c.	fresh wild mushrooms, wiped clean	3/4 oz. a.p.
1/2 c.	trimmed baby pattypan squash, blanched and refreshed	1 3/4 oz. a.p.
1/2 c.	peeled, 1" diagonal-cut, thick asparagus, blanched and refreshed	2 oz. a.p.
1/2 c.	peeled baby carrots, halved lengthwise, blanched and refreshed	3 oz. a.p.
1/2 c.	trimmed young green beans, blanched and refreshed	2 oz. a.p.
as needed	water	n/c
1 1/2 c.	Roasted Fennel–Yukon Gold Potato Purée, hot in steam table	1/4 recipe
2 Tbsp.	butter	1 oz.
1/2 c.	Berry Barbeque Sauce, hot in steam table	1/4 recipe

service turnout:

1. Roast the salmon:
   a. Arrange the thyme and rosemary sprigs slightly left of center on the cedar plank and place the salmon on top of them, shiny side down.
   b. Brush the salmon with 1 Tbsp. oil, season it with salt and white pepper, and moisten it with half of the Gitksan Baste.
   c. Place the plank on the top rack of a 450°F oven and roast about 8 minutes.
   d. Check the salmon's doneness and brush with the remaining baste. The salmon is done when heated through but still slightly translucent in the center.
2. Finish the vegetables:
   a. Heat a 10" sauté pan, heat 1 Tbsp. oil until very hot, and sear the mushrooms with a little salt for a few seconds until slightly darkened and fragrant.
   b. Add the squash, asparagus, carrots, and green beans with a little salt and a little water. Cover the pan and steam until heated through.
3. Plate the dish:
   a. Place the cedar plank on a 14" oval presentation platter lined with a folded linen napkin.
   b. Scoop the hot Roasted Fennel–Yukon Gold Potato Purée into a pastry bag fitted with a large star tip and pipe a decorative border around the edge of the plank.
   c. Work the butter into the vegetables and spoon them onto the plank inside the potato purée border.
   d. Ladle the Berry Barbeque Sauce into a hot ramekin and place it on the platter behind the plank.

ENTREES

COMPONENT RECIPE
GITSKAN BASTE

yield: approx. 1 c.

production		costing only
1/4 c.	cider vinegar	2 fl. oz.
2 Tbsp.	ketchup	1 fl. oz.
1 Tbsp.	sugar	1/8 oz.
2 tsp.	kosher salt	1/6 oz.
1 c.	water	n/c
2 drops	liquid smoke	1/16 fl. oz.

preparation:
1. Bring all ingredients to the boil in an 8" sauté pan while stirring to help dissolve the solids.
2. Cool to room temperature.

holding: refrigerated in a freshly sanitized, covered container up to 2 weeks

COMPONENT RECIPE
ROASTED FENNEL–YUKON GOLD POTATO PURÉE

yield: 6 c.

production		costing only
14 oz.	young fennel bulb, including tops	14 oz. a.p.
as needed	water	n/c
1/4 c.	gold-color pure olive oil	2 fl. oz.
2 Tbsp.	fresh lemon juice	3/8 [90 ct.] lemon
tt	kosher salt	1/8 oz.
1 lb.	Yukon gold potatoes	1 lb. a.p.
3 Tbsp.	room-temperature butter	1 1/2 oz.
1/2 c.	hot half-and-half	4 fl. oz.
tt	fine-ground white pepper	1/16 oz.

preparation:
1. Preheat an oven to 425°F.
2. Roast and purée the fennel:
   a. Remove the stalks from the fennel and reserve for another use.
   b. Quarter the bulb and remove the core.
   c. Place the fennel in a quarter-size hotel pan, cut side up, with 1/4" water in the bottom of the pan. Drizzle the fennel with oil and lemon juice, season it with salt, and cover the pan with foil.
   d. Roast the fennel about 40 minutes, until very tender, adding a little more water if necessary to prevent scorching.
   e. Cool slightly.
   f. Purée the fennel and its pan juices in a food processor.
3. Boil and purée the potatoes:
   a. Peel the potatoes and cut them into even-size chunks.
   b. Boil the potatoes in salted water until just tender.
   c. Drain the potatoes, and then immediately press them through a ricer or coarse-mesh strainer.
   d. Beat in the butter and half-and-half, but don't overmix.
4. Combine the fennel purée and the potato purée into a smooth mixture, but don't overmix. When hot, the mixture should be soft and smooth enough to pipe from a pastry bag yet firm enough to hold a shape.
5. Correct the salt and season with white pepper.

holding: open-pan cool and immediately refrigerate in a freshly sanitized, covered container up to 5 days

COMPONENT RECIPE
BERRY BARBEQUE SAUCE

yield: 2 c.

production		costing only
2 Tbsp.	bacon drippings or corn oil	n/c or 1 fl. oz.
1/4 c.	minced shallot	2 oz. a.p.
2 tsp.	minced garlic	1/6 oz. a.p.
1 tsp.	crushed dried red pepper	1/8 oz.
1 c.	unsweetened raspberry purée	8 fl. oz.
1/2 c.	Washington or Oregon Pinot Noir	4 fl. oz.
1/2 c.	Fish Stock	1/32 recipe
1/2 c.	Poultry Stock	1/32 recipe
2 Tbsp.	Dijon mustard	1 fl. oz.
tt	kosher salt	1/16 oz.
tt	brown sugar	1/4 oz.

preparation:
1. Melt the bacon drippings in a small, nonreactive saucepan, add the shallot, and sweat over low heat about 1 minute, until softened.
2. Add the garlic and dried red pepper, sauté a few seconds more, then add the remaining ingredients.
3. Simmer over low heat about 15 minutes.
4. If necessary, increase the heat and reduce, stirring constantly, to a full-bodied nappé consistency.
5. Correct the seasoning to achieve a balanced sweet-salty-tart flavor.

holding: open-pan cool and immediately refrigerate in a freshly sanitized, covered, nonreactive container up to 1 week

---

RECIPE VARIATION

Grilled Salmon Steak with Berry Barbeque Sauce, Roasted Fennel–Yukon Gold Potato Purée, and Northwest Vegetable Medley
Replace the salmon fillet with a salmon steak. Omit the cedar plank. Add a little minced thyme and rosemary to the Gitskan Baste. Mound the potato purée on the plate along with the salmon, vegetables, and sauce.

Steelhead Trout and Pacific Littlenecks in Gewürztraminer Saffron Cream

with Apple-Rice Pilaf and Braised Brussels Sprouts

yield: 1 (7-oz.) entrée serving plus accompaniments (multiply × 4 for classroom turnout; adjust equipment sizes accordingly)

MASTER RECIPE

production		costing only
2 Tbsp.	clarified butter	1 1/3 oz. a.p.
5 oz.	steelhead trout fillet, skinned and pinned	6 oz. a.p.
tt	kosher salt	1/16 oz.
1/2 c.	Washington or Oregon Gewürztraminer	4 fl. oz.
1/2 c.	Fish Stock or clam juice	1/32 recipe or 4 fl. oz.
8	Pacific littleneck clams, scrubbed and purged*	8 each
1 Tbsp.	butter	1/2 oz.
1/4 c.	julienne leeks	1/20 bunch a.p.
pinch	saffron threads	0.25 g**
3/4 c.	heavy cream	6 fl. oz.
tt	fine-ground white pepper	1/16 oz.
1 1/2 c.	Apple-Rice Pilaf	1/4 recipe
6 to 8 pc.	Braised Brussels Sprouts	1/4 recipe
1/4	firm, red-skinned apple	1 1/4 oz. a.p.

service turnout:

1. Sear the trout:
   a. Heat an 8" sauté pan, heat the clarified butter, and sear the trout about 2 minutes per side, until rare.
   b. Season with salt.
   c. Remove to a sizzle pan and hold hot.

*To purge the clams, place them in a bowl under a light stream of cold water; allow the water to run over the rim of the bowl, flushing the clams of grit, about 5 minutes.

**Saffron is often sold by the gram. If purchased in ounce units, multiply the ounce cost × 0.009.

2. Steam the clams:
   a. Pour out any fat left in the pan. Add the wine, fish stock, and clams, cover, and pan-steam over high heat for less than a minute, just until the clams open.
   b. Use a slotted spoon to lift the clams out to the sizzle pan.
   c. Reserve the juices in the pan.
3. Prepare the sauce:
   a. Heat another 8" sauté pan, heat the butter, and sauté the leeks a few seconds.
   b. Pour the pan juices from the clams through a fine strainer into the pan with the leeks.
   c. Add the saffron, bring to the boil, and reduce to 1/4 c.
   d. Add the cream and reduce the sauce to a light nappé consistency.
   e. Pour any accumulated juices from the clam and trout pan into the sauce and again correct the consistency.
   f. Season with white pepper and salt, if needed.
4. Heat the Apple-Rice Pilaf and the Braised Brussels Sprouts in a microwave or individual covered sauté pans.
5. Plate the dish:
   a. Place a 3 1/2" entremet ring on the back center of a hot 12" pasta plate. Pack in the pilaf and remove the ring.
   b. Prop the trout fillet against the pilaf.
   c. Arrange the Brussels sprouts on either side of the pilaf.
   d. Arrange the clams in front of the trout.
   e. Nap the trout and clams with the sauce.
   f. Quickly cut the apple into fine julienne and mound it on top of the pilaf.

COMPONENT RECIPE
APPLE-RICE PILAF

yield: 6 c.

production		costing only
3 Tbsp.	butter	1 1/2 oz.
12 oz.	tart cooking apples	12 oz. a.p.
1 Tbsp.	lemon juice	1/6 [90 ct.] lemon
3 Tbsp.	butter	1 1/2 oz.
1/2 c.	fine-chopped yellow onion	2 1/2 oz. a.p.
1 3/4 c.	long-grain white rice	10 1/2 oz.
2 1/4 c.	water	n/c
tt	kosher salt	1/8 oz.
2 tsp.	chopped fresh sage	1/20 bunch a.p.

preparation:
1. Preheat an oven to 400°F.
2. Prepare the apples:
   a. Melt 3 Tbsp. butter in a 10" nonreactive sauté pan.
   b. Quickly peel and core the apples and cut them into 3/8" dice, adding them to the sauté pan and sprinkling with lemon juice as you work.
   c. Cover the pan and sweat the apples over low heat about 1 minute, until they soften and produce a little liquid.
   d. Uncover the pan, increase the heat, and sauté the apples about 1 minute longer, until light golden.
3. Cook the rice:
   a. Melt 3 Tbsp. butter in a heavy, ovenproof 1 1/2-qt. saucepan with a tight-fitting lid.
   b. Add the onion and sauté over medium heat until softened.
   c. Add the rice and sauté it until the grains are opaque and well coated with butter.
   d. Add the water and salt, cover the pot, bring to the boil, and then reduce the heat. Simmer about 15 minutes, until the liquid is absorbed.
   e. Fold the apples and sage into the rice, smooth the surface, and re-cover the pan.
   f. Bake about 10 minutes.
4. If not using it immediately, turn the rice out to a half hotel pan, spread it into an even layer, cover it with a damp towel, and cool to room temperature.

holding: refrigerated in a freshly sanitized, covered container up to 3 days

COMPONENT RECIPE
BRAISED BRUSSELS SPROUTS

yield: 24 to 32 pc.

production		costing only
2 pt.	Brussels sprouts	2 pt.
1/4 c.	butter	2 oz.
1/4 c.	minced shallot	2 oz. a.p.
tt	kosher salt	1/8 oz.
2 c.	sweet apple cider	16 fl. oz.
tt	fresh-ground black pepper	1/16 oz.

preparation:
1. Trim the base of each sprout and cut an X in it.
2. Cook the sprouts in lots of rapidly boiling water until just tender, then refresh in ice water. Drain the sprouts and gently squeeze each one to remove residual water.
3. Finish the sprouts:
   a. Heat the butter in a 10" sauté pan and allow it to become golden brown. Add the sprouts and shallot and cook over low heat, swirling the pan, until the sprouts are well coated with butter.
   b. Season with salt and add the cider. Cook at a brisk simmer until the cider reduces to a glaze and the sprouts are fully tender.
   c. Season with pepper.

holding: open-pan cool and refrigerate in a freshly sanitized, covered container up to 5 days

---

RECIPE VARIATION

Spot Prawns and Pacific Littlenecks in Gewürztraminer Cream (appetizer)
Omit the trout and accompaniments. Sauté 2 oz. peeled Pacific spot prawns in butter. Steam the clams and make the sauce, adding the prawns before plating.

Smoke-Roasted Duck Leg in Cider Sauce
with Pumpkin Gnocchi and Arugula

yield: 1 (7-oz.) entrée serving plus accompaniments (multiply × 4 for classroom turnout; adjust equipment sizes accordingly)

🕐 Best prepared 24 hours in advance.

MASTER RECIPE

production		costing only
1	Smoke-Roasted Duck Leg	1/4 recipe
1 Tbsp.	clarified butter	2/3 oz. a.p.
4 oz.	Pumpkin Gnocchi	1/6 recipe
as needed	kosher salt	1/16 oz.
3 Tbsp.	softened butter	1 1/2 oz.
1/4 c.	grated Parmigiano-Reggiano cheese	3/4 oz. a.p.
tt	fresh-ground black pepper	1/16 oz.
1 tsp.	minced flat-leaf parsley	1/40 bunch a.p.
3/4 c.	Cider Pan Reduction	1/4 recipe
2 tsp.	arrowroot dissolved in 1 Tbsp. water	1/16 oz.
2 Tbsp.	butter	1 oz.
2 1/2 oz.	cleaned and stemmed arugula	3 oz. a.p.

service turnout:
1. Place the Smoke-Roasted Duck Leg on a sizzle plate, brush it with clarified butter, and heat it in a 400°F oven about 8 minutes, until crisped and heated through.
2. Cook the Pumpkin Gnocchi:
   a. Drop the gnocchi into at least 3 qt. salted boiling water and cook, stirring occasionally, about 6 minutes, until floating and done through.
   b. Remove the gnocchi with a spider or slotted spoon, drain a few seconds, then place in a warm stainless steel bowl.
   c. Toss the gnocchi with the softened butter, cheese, pepper, parsley, and salt as needed.
   d. Hold hot.
3. Finish the sauce:
   a. Bring the Cider Pan Reduction to the boil in a small sauté pan and thicken it to a light nappé consistency by whisking in the arrowroot slurry.
   b. Work in the remaining butter to form an emulsion.
   c. Hold warm.
4. Plate the dish:
   a. Mound the arugula on the back center of a hot 12" plate.
   b. Prop the duck leg against the arugula with the bone end upright.
   c. Spoon the gnocchi in two mounds on either side of the arugula.
   d. Pool the sauce in the front of the plate well.

COMPONENT RECIPE
SMOKE-ROASTED DUCK LEGS

yield: 4 (7-oz.) duck legs

🕐 Best prepared 24 hours in advance.

production		costing only
4	10-oz. duck legs	2 1/2 lb. a.p.
1/2 c.	fine-chopped yellow onion	5 oz. a.p.
1 Tbsp.	minced garlic	1/3 oz. a.p.
2 sprigs	fresh thyme	1/10 bunch a.p.
1 sprig	fresh sage	1/10 bunch a.p.
2 Tbsp.	kosher salt	1 oz.
2 tsp.	cracked black pepper	1/8 oz.
12 fl. oz.	hard apple cider	12 fl. oz.
as needed	fruitwood, form specified by manufacturer, soaked in water overnight	% of package
1 c.	apple cider	8 fl. oz.

first day preparation:
1. Fabricate the duck legs:
   a. Chop off the knuckles* of the duck legs, leaving a clean break with no fragments.
   b. Bone out the thighs* of the duck legs, separating the joint between the thigh and drumstick, and leaving the drumstick bone intact.
   c. Trim off excess fat from the duck legs and make several small, parallel slashes in the skin of each leg.
2. Marinate the duck legs:
   a. In a freshly sanitized, nonreactive container just large enough to hold the duck legs snug, crush together the onion, garlic, thyme, sage, salt, and pepper. Stir in the cider and allow the salt to dissolve.
   b. Add the duck legs and turn them to coat well.
   c. Cover and refrigerate overnight.

second day preparation:
3. Smoke the duck legs:
   a. Prepare a smoker set to 180°F, using the soaked fruitwood per the manufacturer's specifications.
   b. Drain the duck legs and pat dry. Discard the marinade.
   c. Place the duck legs in the smoker, skin side down, and smoke them 20 minutes, basting once with 1/3 of the apple cider.
   d. Turn the legs over, baste with another 1/3 of the cider, and continue smoking 20 minutes longer.
   e. Baste again with the rest of the cider and smoke another 10 to 15 minutes, until the legs reach an internal temperature of 145°F.
   f. Immediately remove the duck legs from the smoker, place them on a rack set over a half-sheet tray, and refrigerate them, uncovered, until cold.

*Knuckles and thigh bones may be reserved for stock.

holding: refrigerated in a freshly sanitized, covered container or in plastic bags up to 1 week

COMPONENT RECIPE
PUMPKIN GNOCCHI

yield: approx. 1 1/2 lb.

production		costing only
12 oz.	peeled, 1"-diced Yukon gold potatoes	14 oz. a.p.
tt	kosher salt	1/4 oz.
4 oz.	canned, unsweetened pumpkin purée	4 oz.
±1 c.	flour	±5 oz.

preparation:
1. Preheat an oven to 400°F.
2. Prepare the potatoes:
   a. Boil the potatoes in generously salted water until just tender.
   b. Drain the potatoes and spread them on a sheet tray.
   c. Place the tray in the oven about 5 minutes, until the potatoes are dry but not browned.
   d. Force the potatoes through a ricer, or push them through a coarse mesh strainer, into a large bowl.
3. Mix the gnocchi while the ingredients are still warm:
   a. Bring a small pan of water to the boil.
   b. Place the flour in a sifter or strainer.
   c. Use a fork to gently mix the pumpkin purée into the riced potatoes.
   d. As you mix, sift in enough flour to bind the mixture.
   e. Taste for salt and add more if needed.
   f. On a floured work surface, knead the mixture a few strokes to achieve a soft, supple dough.
   g. Test the consistency of the dough by boiling a small ball of it 5 minutes until it floats. The dough should hold its shape. If the dough is too slack, add more flour to it.
4. Fabricate the gnocchi:
   a. Form the dough into a ropelike shape about 5/8" thick.
   b. Cut the dough rope into 3/4" lengths.
   c. Working over a half-sheet tray covered with a kitchen towel, and holding a dinner fork in one hand, press a dough length against the tines with your index finger, then use your thumb to roll it against the fork tines and off the fork tip to make a gnoccho that is deeply indented on one side and ridged on the other side.
   d. Repeat with the remaining dough.
   e. Spread the gnocchi in one layer and cover with another kitchen towel. Refrigerate until needed.

holding: refrigerate on the sheet tray (on and under towels), loosely wrapped with plastic wrap up to 3 days; freeze up to 1 month

COMPONENT RECIPE
CIDER PAN REDUCTION

yield: 3 c.

production		costing only
2 Tbsp.	minced shallot	1 oz. a.p.
12 fl. oz.	hard apple cider	12 fl. oz.
1 c.	apple cider	8 fl. oz.
1 qt.	Poultry Stock	1/4 recipe
tt	kosher salt	1/16 oz.
tt	fine-ground white pepper	1/16 oz.

preparation:
1. Place the shallot, hard cider, apple cider, Poultry Stock, and a little salt in a sauté pan and reduce over high heat to a light nappé consistency, about 3 c. in volume.
2. Season with additional salt and white pepper.

holding: open-pan cool and refrigerate in a freshly sanitized, covered container up to 5 days

---

RECIPE VARIATION

Roast Duck Leg in Cider Sauce with Pumpkin Gnocchi and Wilted Arugula
Omit the marinade. Brown the duck leg in corn oil, season it with salt and pepper, and then roast it, basting occasionally with apple cider.

Roast Rack of Northwestern Lamb

with Pinot Noir Demi-Glace, Porcini Bread Pudding, and Baked Walla Walla Onion Filled with Carrot Purée

yield: 1 (9-oz. bone-in) entrée serving plus accompaniments (multiply × 4 for classroom turnout; adjust equipment sizes accordingly)

MASTER RECIPE

production		costing only
1 Tbsp.	corn oil	1/2 fl. oz.
1/2	8-rib rack of lamb, frenched	9 oz. prefabricated or a.p.
tt	kosher salt	1/16 oz.
tt	fresh-ground black pepper	1/16 oz.
2 Tbsp.	melted butter	1 oz.
1	Porcini Bread Pudding Disk	1/4 recipe
1	Walla Walla Onion Cup	1/4 recipe
2/3 c.	Pinot Noir Demi-Glace	1/4 recipe
3/4 c.	Carrot Purée, hot in steam table	1/4 recipe
1/2 bunch	watercress	1/2 bunch a.p.
1 Tbsp.	butter	1/2 oz.

service turnout:
1. Roast the lamb rack and accompaniments:
   a. Heat an 8" sauté pan, heat the oil until very hot, and sear the lamb rack on all sides. Season it with salt and pepper.
   b. Brush a sizzle pan with some of the melted butter and transfer the lamb rack to it, along with the Porcini Bread Pudding Disk and the Walla Walla Onion Cup. Brush the bread pudding and onion cup with the remaining melted butter.
   c. Finish the lamb rack, bread pudding, and onion cup in a 400°F oven 5 to 8 minutes, to the desired doneness.
   d. Ladle the Pinot Noir Demi-Glace into the lamb sauté pan and place it over low heat.
   e. If necessary, remove the lamb rack and continue baking the bread pudding and onion cup until lightly browned.
2. Plate the dish:
   a. Cut the lamb rack into 4 chops of even thickness. Scrape any juices that accumulate around the lamb into the pan with the demi-glace.
   b. Place the bread pudding on the back center of a warm 12" plate.
   c. Scoop the Carrot Purée into a pastry bag fitted with a large star tip and pipe it into the onion cup.
   d. Place the onion cup on top of the bread pudding.
   e. Divide the watercress into 2 bouquets and arrange them on either side of the bread pudding.
   f. Arrange the chops, bones upright and interlocking, on the front of the plate, leaning against the bread pudding.
   g. Whisk the butter into the demi-glace and spoon it into the plate well.

COMPONENT RECIPE
CARROT PURÉE

yield: 3 c.

production		costing only
15 oz.	peeled, trimmed, thick-sliced carrots	1 lb. a.p.
tt	kosher salt	1/8 oz.
3 Tbsp.	softened butter	1 1/2 oz.
1/3 c.	heavy cream	2 2/3 oz.
tt	fine-ground white pepper	1/16 oz.

preparation:
1. Boil the carrots in heavily salted water about 10 minutes, until very tender. Drain.
2. While still hot, purée the carrots in a food processor or with an immersion blender until smooth.
3. If necessary, run the carrot purée through a food mill or medium-mesh strainer.
4. Return the carrots to their cooking pan and stir over low heat to thicken them, if necessary.
5. Stir in the butter and cream to achieve a purée thick enough to hold a shape.
6. Correct the salt and season with white pepper.

holding: open-pan cool and immediately refrigerate in a freshly sanitized, covered plastic container up to 5 days

COMPONENT RECIPE
PINOT NOIR DEMI-GLACE

yield: 2 2/3 c.

production		costing only
1 1/2 c.	Washington or Oregon Pinot Noir	12 fl. oz.
2 c.	Demi-Glace	1/2 recipe
tt	kosher salt	1/8 oz.

preparation:
1. Place the wine in a small, nonreactive sauté pan and cook at a bare simmer over very low heat until reduced by almost half.
2. Add the wine reduction to the Demi-Glace and season with salt.

holding: open-pan cool and immediately refrigerate in a freshly sanitized, covered, nonreactive container up to 5 days

COMPONENT RECIPE
PORCINI BREAD PUDDING DISKS

yield: 4 (3 1/2") disks plus scraps

production		costing only
2 tsp.	softened butter	1/3 oz.
1/4 oz.	dried porcini mushrooms	1/4 oz.
1/2 c.	hot Poultry Stock	1/32 recipe
8 oz.	firm, day-old French or Italian bread	8 oz.
2 Tbsp.	clarified butter	1 1/3 oz. a.p.
6 oz.	stemmed, cleaned, fresh porcini mushrooms, 1/2" dice	7 oz. a.p.
tt	kosher salt	1/16 oz.
1 Tbsp.	Port wine	1/2 fl. oz.
2 tsp.	fresh lemon juice	1/8 [90 ct.] lemon
2	eggs	2 each or 4 fl. oz.
2 c.	half-and-half	16 fl. oz.
1 Tbsp.	minced lemon zest	n/c
2 tsp.	chopped sage leaves	1/16 bunch a.p.

preparation:
1. Mise en place:
   a. Preheat an oven to 350°F.
   b. Thoroughly butter the bottom and sides of a 9" × 2 1/2" round cake pan and place the pan in a half-size hotel pan.
2. Prepare the dried mushrooms:
   a. Place the dried mushrooms in a ramekin and cover them with the Poultry Stock. Allow them to steep for about 15 minutes, until rehydrated.
   b. Remove the mushrooms from the stock, rinse them, and chop them fine.
   c. Strain the stock through a coffee filter or fine-mesh strainer and reserve.
3. Prepare the bread cubes:
   a. Without removing the crust, cut the bread into 1/2" dice.
   b. Spread the diced bread on a half-sheet tray and toast in the oven about 5 minutes. Cool.
4. Precook the fresh mushrooms:
   a. Heat a 10" sauté pan until very hot, heat the clarified butter, and sauté the fresh mushrooms with a little salt until browned. No liquid should remain in the pan.
   b. Add the reconstituted dried mushrooms and continue to cook until the mushrooms are sizzling.
   c. Remove from the heat, add the Port and lemon juice, and correct the salt.
   d. Cool to room temperature.
5. Mix the custard:
   a. Beat together the eggs, half-and-half, mushroom-flavored stock, lemon zest, sage, and salt.
   b. Mix in the bread cubes and refrigerate about 20 minutes, stirring occasionally.
   c. Toss in the mushroom mixture.
6. Bake the bread pudding:
   a. Pour the bread-custard mixture into the prepared cake pan and smooth the top.
   b. Fill the hotel pan with hot water halfway up the side of the cake pan and place it in the center of the oven.
   c. Bake about 40 minutes, until the custard is set.
   d. Remove the cake pan from the hotel pan and cool to room temperature.
   e. Refrigerate the bread pudding uncovered about 2 hours, until completely cold and firm.
7. Fabricate the cylinders:
   a. Using a 3 1/2" round cutter, punch out 4 cylinders of bread pudding.
   b. If not using immediately, wrap each cylinder in plastic film.

holding: refrigerate up to 5 days

COMPONENT RECIPE
WALLA WALLA ONION CUPS

yield: 4 cups

production		costing only
4	(5-oz.) Walla Walla or other sweet onions	1 1/4 lb. a.p.

preparation:
1. Fabricate the onions:
   a. Cut the top third off each onion.
   b. Peel each onion and trim away just enough of the root end so that it rests flat on the work surface.
   c. Using a Parisienne scoop, hollow out the center of each onion, leaving a 3/8" shell.*
2. Steam the onions until just tender. Cool.

*Reserve the onion flesh for another use.

holding: refrigerate in one layer in a freshly sanitized, covered container up to 5 days

---

RECIPE VARIATION

Char-Grilled Northwestern Lamb Chops with Pinot Noir Demi-Glace, Porcini Mushrooms, Roasted Potatoes, and Carrot Purée
Replace the lamb rack with 2 char-grilled (4 oz.) loin chops. Replace the bread pudding with roasted potatoes. Sauté fresh porcini mushroom caps with diced Walla Walla onions and add to the plate.

Poached Pear on Frangipane Cake
with Almond Crunch Filling and Pinot Noir Syrup

yield: 1 dessert serving
(multiply × 4 for classroom turnout)

🕐 Requires 24 hours advance preparation.

MASTER RECIPE

production		costing only
1	Frangipane Cake Disk	1/4 to 1/6 recipe
1	Pinot Noir Poached Pear	1/4 recipe
1/3 c.	Almond Crunch Filling, in a pastry bag fitted with a large round tip	1/4 recipe
2/3 c.	Pinot Noir Syrup, in squeeze bottle	1/4 recipe
1 sprig	fresh mint	1/12 bunch

service turnout:

1. Plate the dish:
   a. Place the Frangipane Cake Disk on a cool 10" plate. Drain the Pinot Noir Poached Pear and place it firmly upright on top of the cake.
   b. Pipe the Almond Crunch Filling into the center hollow of the pear.
   c. Squeeze the Pinot Noir Syrup around the cake.
   d. Stick the mint sprig out of the top of the pear.

COMPONENT RECIPE
FRANGIPANE CAKE DISKS

yield: 4 to 6 (3") rounds

production		costing only
as needed	baker's pan coating spray, optional	% of container
1 oz.	flour	1 oz.
1/4 tsp.	baking powder	1/16 oz.
pinch	salt	1/16 oz.
3 oz.	almond flour (fine-ground almonds)	3 oz.
3 oz.	softened butter	3 oz.
1/2 c.	sugar	4 oz.
6 oz.	room-temperature almond paste	6 oz.
3	egg yolks	3 each or 2 fl. oz.
1 Tbsp.	dark rum	1/2 oz.
3	room-temperature egg whites	n/c or 3 fl. oz.
1/4 c.	apricot preserves, melted	2 fl. oz.
2 oz.	toasted, sliced almonds, crushed	2 oz.

preparation:

1. Mise en place:
   a. Preheat an oven to 300°F.
   b. Place a 3" cylinder silicone baking form on a sheet tray.
      —or—
      Spray a 9" × 2 1/2" round cake pan with pan coating. Press in a 9" pan liner circle, then spray again.
2. Mix the batter:
   a. Combine the flour, baking powder, salt, and almond flour.
   b. Using the paddle attachment of a mixer, cream the butter and sugar until very light and fluffy. Add the almond paste a little at a time, creaming until smooth. Add the egg yolks one at a time, and then add the rum.
   c. In a clean, dry mixer or bowl, beat the egg whites to firm peaks.
   d. Fold 1/4 of the egg whites into the creamed mixture, then fold the creamed mixture back into the whites, sprinkling on the flour-almond mixture as you fold.
3. Scrape the batter into 6 of the silicone cylinder forms or the prepared cake pan and smooth the surface(s).
4. Immediately place the tray or pan in the center of the oven. Bake the cylinder pan about 20 minutes or the cake pan about 35 minutes, until firm and light golden.
5. Cool the cake(s) in the form or pan set on a rack for 15 minutes, then turn the cake(s) out to the rack. Cool to room temperature.
6. Fabricate the cake rounds:
   a. If the cake was baked in a 9" round pan, use a 3" round cutter to punch out 4 disks of cake. (Reserve the scraps for another use.)
   b. Brush the edges of the cake disks with the melted preserves.
   c. Roll the coated edges in the toasted almonds.
   d. Place the cake rounds on squares of pan liner.

holding: in a tightly sealed container at cool room temperature up to 2 days

PINOT NOIR POACHED PEARS
AND PINOT NOIR SYRUP

yield: 4 pears and 3 c. syrup

🕐 Requires 24 hours advance preparation.

production		costing only
2 1/2 c.	Washington or Oregon Pinot Noir	20 oz.
±2 oz.	sugar	±2 oz.
2"	vanilla bean, slit open	1/3 bean
4	5-oz. firm, slightly underripe pears	1 1/4 lb. a.p.
as needed	water	n/c
1 oz.	cornstarch dissolved in 1/4 c. water	1 oz.

first day preparation:
1. Place the wine, sugar, and vanilla bean in a 1 1/2-qt. nonreactive saucepan and place the pan over low heat. Stir until the sugar dissolves, and then remove from the heat.
2. Fabricate the pears:
   a. Peel each pear and, using an apple corer, cut down through the top of the pear to remove the stem and core, leaving a cylinder of space in the middle. Immediately drop the pear into the wine syrup.
   b. Repeat with the 3 remaining pears.
   c. When all pears are done, add enough water to the pan to just cover the pears.
   d. Place a small plate or nonreactive object on top of the pears to weight them.
3. Return the pears to the heat and poach them at a gentle simmer about 30 minutes, until the pears are very tender.
4. Remove the pears to a freshly sanitized, nonreactive container just large enough to hold them snugly upright.
5. Cool the syrup to room temperature and pour it over the pears along with the vanilla bean. Cover the container, and refrigerate the pears overnight.

second day preparation:
6. Pour the syrup off the pears into a nonreactive saucepan, removing and discarding the vanilla bean. Bring the syrup to the boil and reduce it to about 3 c.
7. Stir the cornstarch mixture together and whisk just enough of it into the boiling syrup to thicken it to a light nappé consistency.
8. Remove the syrup from the heat and cool it to room temperature.
9. Pour the syrup into a freshly sanitized squeeze bottle.

holding: refrigerate pears and sauce separately, up to 4 days

ALMOND CRUNCH FILLING

yield: 1 c.

production		costing only
1/2 c.	sliced almonds	1 1/4 oz.
4 oz.	sugar	4 oz.
1/4 c.	water	n/c
1/2 c.	Vanilla Pastry Cream	1/5 recipe
—or—		
1/2 c.	Sweetened Whipped Cream	1/4 recipe

preparation:
1. Spread the almonds close together in a thin layer on a silicone pad placed on a sheet tray.
2. Prepare the caramel:
   a. Place the sugar in a small sauté pan and stir in the water.
   b. Cook the syrup over high heat, without stirring, about 2 minutes until it forms large bubbles.
   c. Continue to cook, swirling occasionally, about a minute longer until the sugar caramelizes to a rich brown color.
3. Immediately pour the caramel over the almonds. ⚠ Be careful, as caramel is dangerously hot. Cool the almond praline to room temperature.
4. Chop the almond praline into coarse crumbs.
5. Fold the praline crumbs into the Vanilla Pastry Cream or Sweetened Whipped Cream.

holding: refrigerate in a freshly sanitized, covered plastic container up to 4 days

---

RECIPE VARIATION
Raspberry Frangipane Cakes
Omit the Poached Pears. Split the cake rounds and fill with the Almond Crunch Filling. Pipe a rosette of Sweetened Whipped Cream on top of each cake disk and top with fresh raspberries. Squeeze sweetened raspberry purée onto the plates.

Chocolate Cream Cheese Hazelnut Tart

yield: 1 dessert serving
(multiply × 4 for classroom turnout)

MASTER RECIPE

production		costing only
2 tsp.	warm Brown Butter, in squeeze bottle	1/8 recipe
2 Tbsp.	fine-chopped toasted hazelnuts	1/4 oz.
2 Tbsp.	Chocolate Sauce, in squeeze bottle	1/8 recipe
1 slice	Chocolate Cream Cheese Hazelnut Tart	1/8 recipe

service turnout:
1. Plate the dish:
   a. Shake the Brown Butter squeeze bottle to redistribute the solids, then squeeze a circle of brown butter around the edge of the plate well of a cool 10" plate.
   b. Sprinkle half of the hazelnuts on the brown butter to make a neat border.
   c. Squeeze a dot of Chocolate Sauce in the center of the plate.
   d. Place the Chocolate Cream Cheese Hazelnut Tart slice in the center of the plate on the chocolate sauce.
   e. Sprinkle the remaining hazelnuts on the rim of the tart slice.
   f. Squeeze a zigzag pattern of chocolate sauce across the tart slice.

COMPONENT RECIPE
BROWN BUTTER

yield: 4 Tbsp.

production		costing only
4 Tbsp.	butter	2 oz.

preparation:
1. Prepare an ice-water bath of the correct size to accommodate an 8" sauté pan.
2. Brown the butter:
   a. Place the butter in an 8" sauté pan and melt it over low heat.
   b. Cook the butter, swirling constantly, until the milk solids turn a rich, deep brown.
   c. Immediately cool the pan in the ice-water bath to stop the browning.
   d. Pour the butter while still liquid into a freshly sanitized squeeze bottle, scraping in all the browned solids.

holding: at cool room temperature up to 3 hours; refrigerate up to 2 weeks; bring to room temperature before using

COMPONENT RECIPE
CHOCOLATE CREAM CHEESE HAZELNUT TART ASSEMBLY

yield: 1 (10") tart

production		costing only
2 c.	whole blanched (skinless) hazelnuts	6 1/2 oz.
1	Cocoa Sweet Dough Pastry Shell	1 recipe
6 oz.	bittersweet chocolate, chopped into 3/8" chunks	6 oz.
2 c.	Hazelnut Cream Cheese Filling	1 recipe

preparation:
1. Preheat an oven to 400°F.
2. Place the hazelnuts on a half-sheet tray and toast them in the oven about 8 minutes, until light golden. Cool.
3. Reduce the oven temperature to 300°F.
4. Scatter the hazelnuts and chocolate into the Cocoa Sweet Dough Pastry Shell and pour the Hazelnut Cream Cheese Filling evenly over the top.
5. Bake in the center of the oven about 40 minutes, until the filling is lightly set and the chocolate chunks melted.
6. Cool on a rack to room temperature and then refrigerate, uncovered, until cold.

holding: best served the same day; hold refrigerated under a plastic dome up to 2 days

COMPONENT RECIPE
COCOA SWEET DOUGH PASTRY SHELL

yield: 1 (10") tart shell

production		costing only
6 1/2 oz.	flour	6 1/2 oz.
2 1/2 oz.	confectioner's sugar	2 1/2 oz.
3/4 oz.	cocoa powder	3/4 oz.
1/4 tsp.	salt	1/16 oz.
4 oz.	room-temperature butter	4 oz.
2 oz.	granulated sugar	2 oz.
1 Tbsp.	chocolate liqueur	1/2 fl. oz.
±2 Tbsp.	ice water	n/c
as needed	cocoa powder	1 oz.

preparation:
1. Mix the dough:
   a. Sift together the flour, confectioner's sugar, 3/4 oz. cocoa powder, and salt. Repeat two to three times until the color of the mixture is a homogenous brown.
   b. Using the paddle attachment of a mixer, cream the butter and granulated sugar on medium speed until combined.
   c. Add the flour-cocoa mixture and pulse to combine.
   d. Add the liqueur and a little water and pulse to achieve a smooth dough.
2. Form the dough into a disk, wrap it in plastic film, and refrigerate 30 minutes.
3. Make up the tart shell:
   a. Dust the work surface and rolling pin with cocoa powder.
   b. Roll out the dough and fit it into a 10" removable-bottom fluted tart pan, preferably nonstick.
   c. Refrigerate 30 minutes.
4. Bake the shell:
   a. Preheat an oven to 375°F.
   b. Line the tart shell with pan liner and fill it with baking weights.
   c. Bake 15 to 20 minutes, until lightly set.
   d. Remove from the oven, then remove the baking weights and pan liner.
   e. Cool at least 15 minutes.

holding: at cool room temperature loosely wrapped in plastic film up to 2 days

COMPONENT RECIPE
HAZELNUT CREAM CHEESE FILLING

yield: approx. 2 c.

production		costing only
6 oz.	room-temperature cream cheese	6 oz.
2 oz.	sugar	2 oz.
1	beaten egg	1 each or 2 oz.
1 Tbsp.	Frangelico liqueur	1/2 fl. oz.
1/4 tsp.	salt	1/16 oz.

preparation:
1. Using the paddle attachment of a mixer, beat the cream cheese and sugar on medium speed until smooth.
2. Stir in the remaining ingredients on low speed.

holding: refrigerate in a freshly sanitized, covered container up to 24 hours

Seattle Coffeehouse Pot de Crème

with Chocolate-Dipped Biscotto

yield: 1 dessert serving
(multiply × 4 for classroom turnout)

MASTER RECIPE

production		costing only
2 Tbsp.	Sweetened Whipped Cream, in pastry bag with a star tip	1/8 recipe
1	Coffee Pot de Crème	1/4 recipe
dash	cocoa, in a shaker or small sifter	1/16 oz.
1	coffee bean	1/16 recipe
1	cocktail napkin	1 each
1	Chocolate-Dipped Biscotto or purchased biscotto	1/12 recipe or a.p.

service turnout:
1. Plate the dish:
   a. Pipe a rosette of whipped cream on the surface of the Coffee Pot de Crème.
   b. Dust the top lightly with cocoa and place the coffee bean in the center.
   c. Place the cocktail napkin on a saucer and put the Pot de Crème cup on top.
   d. Place the Chocolate-Dipped Biscotto on the right side of the saucer.

COMPONENT RECIPE

COFFEE POTS DE CRÈME

yield: 4 dessert servings.

production		costing only
1 1/2 c.	heavy cream	12 fl. oz.
1/4 c.	espresso beans, crushed	1/4 oz.
3	egg yolks	3 each or 2 fl. oz.
1/2 c.	sugar	4 oz.
pinch	fine salt	1/16 oz.
1/4 c.	brewed espresso coffee, room temperature	2 fl. oz.
1/2 tsp.	pure vanilla extract	1/12 fl. oz.

preparation:
1. Mise en place:
   a. Preheat an oven to 275°F.
   b. Place 4 (8-fl. oz.) coffee cups into a half-size hotel pan.
   c. Cut out 4 (4"-diameter) circles of aluminum foil.
   d. Have ready about a quart of boiling water.
2. Combine the cream and crushed espresso beans in a small saucepan, bring to the simmer, and remove from heat. Steep for 20 minutes and then pass through a fine-mesh strainer. Discard the espresso beans.
3. Whip together the yolks, sugar, and salt until light yellow and fluffy. Stir in the espresso-flavored cream, brewed espresso coffee, and vanilla.
4. Pan and bake the custard:
   a. Divide the custard among the coffee cups.
   b. Cover each cup with foil, folding up the foil to prevent it touching the water bath.
   c. Pour boiling water into the pan reaching 2/3 up the sides of the cups.
   d. Place the pan in the oven and bake 30 to 40 minutes until the custard is almost set, yet slightly wobbly in the center.
   e. Gently remove the pan from the oven and cool on a rack for 1 hour.
5. Remove the foil and clean the cup rims and exterior with a damp towel. Cover each cup with plastic wrap. Refrigerate at least 2 hours until cold.

holding: refrigerate up to 4 days

RECIPE VARIATION

Classic Pots de Crème
Omit the espresso beans. Increase the amount of heavy cream by 1 fl. oz. Replace the brewed espresso coffee and vanilla with 1 fl. oz. Grand Marnier. Top each chilled custard with a candied violet petal and serve with a tuile cookie.

Chocolate Pots de Crème
Omit the espresso beans and brewed espresso coffee. Add 4 oz. melted bittersweet chocolate in step 3. Top each chilled custard with a rosette of whipped cream and chocolate curls.

☐ TABLE 13.2 PACIFIC NORTHWEST REGIONAL INGREDIENTS

ITEM	MARKET FORMS	USES	SEASONALITY	OTHER	STORAGE
WHEAT BERRIES	See p. 456.				
LENTILS	The Palouse Valley produces standard brown lentils; small, greenish Pardina lentils; and quick-cooking Red Chief lentils, all sold by the pound and in 20- or 25-bulk bags.	Lentils are used primarily in soups. They may be cooked in limited liquid and served as a side dish.	Available year round. Late fall and winter new-crop lentils cook much more quickly than storage lentils.	Lentils benefit from a small amount of fat added to the liquid. Salt lentils at the end of cooking to ensure tenderness.	Store at room temperature or freeze for prolonged storage.
FIDDLEHEADS	See p. 89.				
WALLA WALLA ONIONS	These sweet onions are sold by the pound or in 35- to 40-lb. cartons.	Use raw in salads and sandwiches. To caramelize, cook slowly in butter or olive oil.	Mid-June through early September.	This onion variety was brought from Corsica to the Walla Walla Valley in the beginning of the 20th century.	These high-moisture onions are more perishable than other types. Store in a cool, dark, well-ventilated area a few weeks only.
WILD MUSHROOMS	True wild mushrooms are available by the pound from specialty purveyors. Many foragers also produce dried mushrooms. Types include boletes, chanterelles, matsutake, lobster, oyster, hen-of-the-woods, and morels.	Rare and expensive wild mushrooms are showcased in toppings and sauces for meats, poultry, and game. They flavor pastas and risottos. Sautéed wild mushrooms may be served on toast points or in a pastry case for a lavish appetizer.	Spring to fall; consult your dealer for availability of each type.	Buy wild mushrooms from a reputable source and cook them fully before serving.	Purchase fresh wild mushrooms in small amounts only as needed. Store refrigerated in the container in which they were packed a few days only.
OREGON TRUFFLES	Oregon produces two varieties of white truffles: *Tuber oregonense* and *Tuber gibbosum*. The Oregon black truffle is *Leucangium carthusianum*. Both types can be mail-ordered from foragers that advertise on the Internet. Ripe truffles "give" slightly when squeezed and have a pronounced aroma.	Truffles are shaved over buttered pasta, risotto, and mashed potatoes. Chopped truffles flavor sauces and enhance soft scrambled eggs. Truffles infuse their flavor into oils and essences.	Black truffles: November; white truffles: May through June.	Use truffles raw; add to hot preparations at the last minute before serving.	Store refrigerated, buried in Arborio rice, several days to two weeks depending on ripeness. (Use the resulting flavored rice for risottos.)
APPLES	Hundreds of apple varieties are grown in the region. Purchase fresh apples by the pound or in 40-lb. cartons. Dried apples are available in many fabrication types, including rings and pieces. Individually quick frozen apple slices are also available.	Apples are used raw as a salad ingredient, garnish, and snack. Cooking varieties are used for applesauce, fried apple dishes, and in desserts and baked goods.	August through November.	Washington is the source of more than half the fresh apples consumed in the United States.	Refrigerate.
PEARS	Pears grown in the Pacific Northwest include Bartlett, Anjou, Bosc, and Comice. Purchase by the pound or in 40-lb. cartons.	Ripe raw pears are used in salads and as a snack food. Depending on the sweetness of the cooking liquid, poached pears are used as a dessert item or a sweet-savory addition to salads or main dishes.	August through November.	Choose pears with a pronounced aroma.	Pears are picked firm and will sweeten, soften, and mellow if stored at room temperature. Once pears reach your preferred texture, refrigerate them.

(continued)

☐ **TABLE 13.2 PACIFIC NORTHWEST REGIONAL INGREDIENTS** *(continued)*

ITEM	MARKET FORMS	USES	SEASONALITY	OTHER	STORAGE
SWEET CHERRIES	Bing cherries are large, with deep-red skin and flesh. Rainier cherries (also known as Queen Anne) are golden yellow blushed with pale red, and smaller. Other varieties include Chelan, Tieton, Lapin, and Sweetheart. Purchase by the pound or in 15-lb. and 20-lb. boxes. Look for firm, taut-skinned cherries. Dark color indicates sweetness.	Fresh sweet cherries are primarily eaten as a snack food. Pitted whole or sliced raw cherries may be added to fruit salads and savory salads. They top or fill desserts.	June through August.	Some of each year's crop is canned.	Refrigerate.
OTHER STONE FRUITS	Products include fresh plums, peaches, nectarines, and apricots. Look for new varieties and specialty items, such as white-fleshed and donut peaches and Italian prune plums.	Use perfect ripe fruit raw. Blanch and refresh to remove skins, then fabricate and add to fruit salads and savory salads or as a garnish. Use in dessert work as a topping or filling, or purée for sauce. Firm specimens may be poached in light syrup.	June through August, depending on type.	Pacific Northwest chefs feature sweet fruits in savory preparations.	Refrigerate.
CULTIVATED BERRIES	Cranberries, blueberries, strawberries, blackberries, and raspberries are sold in various packs. Crossbred specialty cultivars include loganberries, boysenberries, and marionberries. Jams and preserves are available in jars of many sizes.	Top tarts, pies, and other desserts with fresh raw berries. Use in fruit salads and toss into savory salads. Use berry purées in sweet and savory sauces. Garnish with fresh berries.	Summer.	Lingonberries were introduced to the Pacific Northwest by Scandinavian settlers. Most are processed into jam and preserves. A limited amount of fresh lingonberries is sold in the fall, from mid-October to mid-November.	Buy in small amounts and refrigerate; wash and blot dry just before using.
FORAGED WILD BERRIES	Indigenous berries include Western huckleberries, salal berries, cloudberries, nagoon berries, and salmon berries. Purchase by special order from foragers.	Use in the same manner as cultivated berries.	Summer.	Wild berries are delicate, highly perishable, and expensive.	Buy in small amounts and refrigerate 1 or 2 days only; wash and blot dry just before using.
HAZELNUTS	Shelled hazelnuts are available whole (blanched or skin-on) in various sizes; in pieces; or ground into a product called *hazelnut flour*.	Use hazelnuts in baked goods and desserts. Savory applications include use as a coating, breading, or topping.	Available year round.	Until 1986, hazelnuts were alternatively called *filberts*.	Store at cool room temperature; refrigerate or freeze for extended storage.
ARTISAN CHEESES	Cougar Gold (p. 615); Tillamook Cheddar (mild yellow, medium yellow, vintage extra-sharp white, and smoked); Rogue River Blue (soft-ripening, soaked in pear brandy and wrapped in grape leaves).	Serve as table cheese or use in cooking in dishes showcasing their unique flavor and texture.	Most cheeses are available year round; some are seasonally available.	Many other artisan cheeses are currently developing.	Purchase ripe and refrigerate a few days only.

☐ TABLE 13.2 PACIFIC NORTHWEST REGIONAL INGREDIENTS (continued)

ITEM	MARKET FORMS	USES	SEASONALITY	OTHER	STORAGE
WILD PACIFIC SALMON	King (Chinook) salmon is available in large sides with pale color and coarse flesh. Sockeye salmon is sold in smaller, 3-lb. to 5-lb. sides with fine-grained, bright red flesh. Coho salmon is similar to sockeye with a more robust flavor. Keta and pink salmon are rarely available outside the region. Wild salmon is sold fresh and frozen.	Poach, pan-sear, or grill fillets or sides. Full-flavored wild salmon stands up to robust sauces. Whole poached salmon may be served chilled for buffets.	Spring and summer.	Copper River sockeye is one of the region's most prized fish.	Store refrigerated on ice in a self-draining container 1 to 2 days only. Thaw frozen salmon overnight in the refrigerator and use immediately.
FARM-RAISED ATLANTIC SALMON	Atlantic salmon is aquaculture-raised along the Pacific Northwest coast. Sides consistently weighing 4 lb. to 5 lb. are widely available fresh and frozen.	Use in the same manner as wild salmon.	Available year round.	Farm-raised salmon may contain artificial coloring and may be subjected to antibiotics and growth hormones. Check your source for production practices and compliance with environmental regulations.	Store refrigerated on ice in a self-draining container 1 to 2 days only. Thaw frozen salmon overnight in the refrigerator and use immediately.
PACIFIC HOT-SMOKED SALMON	Small artisan producers market hot-smoked salmon vacuum sealed in 3-oz. consumer packs and 3-lb. to 4-lb. whole sides. Many producers offer specialty cures, such as black pepper, honey, or herbs.	Serve at cool room temperature as an appetizer with lemon wedges and crackers or toast points. Alternatively, accompany with classic mayonnaise-based sauces or create modern sauces using wild fruits.	Available year round.	For information on hot-smoking see (p. 608).	Refrigerate unopened, up to 6 months; after opening, use within one week.
PACIFIC STEELHEAD TROUT	Three- to 4-lb. steelhead sides have bright red to pale pink flesh. Most commercially sold steelhead is farm raised.	Use in the same manner as salmon.	Available year round.	Farmed steelhead trout raise the same concerns as farm-raised salmon.	Store refrigerated on ice in a self-draining container 1 to 2 days only. Thaw frozen steelhead overnight in the refrigerator and use immediately.
ALASKA HALIBUT	Mild, white-fleshed halibut is cut into thick fillets. The tail sections of smaller fish are cut crosswise into elongated steaks. A high percentage of the catch is frozen.	Sauté, pan-sear, bake, or broil fillets. Steaks are typically grilled. Halibut's mild flavor and fine texture suggest simple lemon butter sauce or light cream sauces.	Fresh halibut is available mid-spring into November. Frozen halibut is sold year round.	Halibut cheeks are an Alaskan delicacy.	Store refrigerated on ice in a self-draining container 1 to 2 days only. Thaw frozen halibut overnight in the refrigerator and use immediately.
PETRALE SOLE	This popular flatfish is most commonly sold as fresh or frozen fillets. It is occasionally sold in whole, headed and gutted form.	Sauté or broil with butter and lemon.	Limited year-round availability.		Store refrigerated on ice in a self-draining container 1 to 2 days only. Thaw frozen petrale sole overnight in the refrigerator and use immediately.
OTHER PACIFIC WHITEFISH	Types include: Pacific cod; ling cod; Pacific rockfish or snapper (canary, vermillion, and yelloweye); Pacific white sturgeon (Columbia River sturgeon).	Prepare by any method.	Seasons vary.	Pacific sturgeon roe is processed as caviar.	Store refrigerated on ice in a self-draining container 1 to 2 days only. Thaw frozen fish overnight in the refrigerator and use immediately.

(continued)

☐ **TABLE 13.2 PACIFIC NORTHWEST REGIONAL INGREDIENTS** *(continued)*

ITEM	MARKET FORMS	USES	SEASONALITY	OTHER	STORAGE
PACIFIC RAZOR CLAMS	These large, elongated soft-shell clams are sold live to foodservice operations by the "bushel" carton. For additional clam information see pp. 97 and 144.	Razor clams are scalded and shucked; the tender body meat is butterflied and the tough "digger" neck is skinned, butterflied, and pounded for tenderization. The meat is then sautéed, steamed, or stir-fried.	Controlled digging throughout the year, depending on environmental conditions.		Refrigerate in the carton covered by layers of damp newspaper. Pick through daily and discard dead specimens. Refrigerate up to 1 week depending on freshness when purchased.
GEODUCK (GOO-ee-duck or GO-ee-duck)	This large soft-shell clam is harvested primarily for its thick, meaty neck that can reach 12" long and 3 1/2" in diameter. Weighing 1 1/2 lb. to 4 lb., geoducks are sold live and fresh, cleaned. Obtain from specialty seafood dealers, especially those supplying Japanese restaurants.	The neck is scalded and peeled, butterflied, scraped clean, and then sliced thin. It is typically served raw as sashimi. Alternatively it may be stir-fried or lightly sautéed.	Farmed geoduck is available year round.	Due to high demand from Asian markets, geoduck is now widely farmed around Puget Sound.	Refrigerate live geoduck in the carton covered by layers of damp newspaper. Pick through daily and discard dead specimens. Refrigerate up to 1 week depending on freshness when purchased.
PACIFIC HARD-SHELL CLAMS	Types include Pacific littlenecks and Manila clams. Wild-caught clams must be 1 1/2" in diameter; farmed clams may be smaller. Clams are sold live in "bushel" cartons or 50-count net bags.	Pacific hardshell clams may be served raw on the half shell with lemon, or steamed and servd hot with melted butter and lemon. Clams may be steamed in a tomato-based broth and/or teamed with sausage. Manila clams are usually steamed.	Available year round.		Refrigerate in the carton covered by layers of damp newspaper. Pick through daily and discard dead specimens. Refrigerate up to 1 week depending on freshness when purchased.
PACIFIC OYSTERS	Small, crisp, briny Olympias are the region's only indigenous oysters. Aquaculture types include Kumamotos and European flats (called belons), Purchase live oysters in "bushel" cartons. For additional oyster information see pp. 194 and 225.	Serve raw on the half shell with lemon, or in cooked preparations.	Farmed oysters are available year round. All oysters are best in cold months.	Pacific Northwest oysters are often named after the location where they are grown.	Refrigerate in the carton covered by layers of damp newspaper. Pick though daily and discard dead specimens. Refrigerate up to 1 week depending on freshness when purchased.
PINK SINGING SCALLOPS	These small, live scallops have shells ranging from 2" to 4" in diameter. They are sold by the pound in cartons or net bags. For additional scallop information see pp. 97 and 145.	Steam lightly and serve with their broth. In addition to the sweet and tender adductor muscle, the pale pink roe is also eaten.	The season begins in summer; fall harvested scallops are considered superior.	Serve these costly scallops as an appetizer.	Refrigerate in the carton covered by layers of damp newspaper. Pick through daily and discard dead specimens. Refrigerate a few days only.
ALASKA WEATHERVANE SCALLOPS	These large sea scallops are dredged offshore from Cape Spencer to Yakutat. Shucked, cleaned, and frozen on the boats, they are available in U-10, 10-20, and 20–30 sizes in 5-lb. boxes.	Broil or pan-sear. Accompany with a light sauce.	Available year round.	With accompaniment and garnish, one large, U-10 scallop makes an adequate appetizer portion.	Thaw overnight in the refrigerator in a self-draining container. Once thawed use within 24 hours.

☐ TABLE 13.2 PACIFIC NORTHWEST REGIONAL INGREDIENTS (continued)

ITEM	MARKET FORMS	USES	SEASONALITY	OTHER	STORAGE
FARMED MUSSELS	Indigenous blue mussels and Mediterranean mussels are sold in 2-lb. net bags or perforated plastic sleeves. For additional mussel information see pp. 98 and 144.	Steam mussels in white wine or a tomato-based broth with varying seasonings. Very fresh mussels may be served raw on the half shell with lemon wedges or mignonette sauce.	Available year round.	Penn Cove Shellfish of Washington's Whidbey Island was the nation's first producer of farm-raised mussels. Both indigenous Pacific blue mussels and Mediterranean mussels are farmed in the Pacific Northwest; Penn Cove mussels are considered the region's finest.	Refrigerate in the carton covered by layers of damp newspaper. Pick through daily and discard dead specimens. Refrigerate a few days only.
DUNGENESS CRAB	In the region, 2-lb. to 4-lb. live Dungeness crabs are sold by the pound. Steamed and picked crabmeat is sold in 1-lb. tubs. Frozen steamed crab clusters are also available. For general crab information, see pp. 193, 194, and 225.	Steam and serve hot with lemon wedges and melted butter or chill and serve with a mayonnaise-based sauce.	Fresh crabs are in season from November to June, with most of the catch in by the end of December. Frozen clusters are available year round.		Refrigerate live crabs in the carton covered by layers of damp newspaper. Pick through daily and discard dead specimens. Refrigerate a few days only. Refrigerate crabmeat containers on ice up to three days. Thaw frozen clusters overnight and use immediately.
ALASKA KING CRAB AND SNOW CRAB	Alaska king crab is sold fresh only in Alaska. Elsewhere the meaty legs are steamed, flash frozen, and sold by the pound. Frozen snow crab clusters comprise legs and backfin sections. Look for vividly colored shells and packages with minimal interior frost.	Steam just until hot through; serve with lemon wedges and melted butter.	Frozen crab legs and clusters are available year round.		Thaw overnight in the refrigerator and use immediately. With adjusted cooking time the product may be steamed directly out of the freezer.
SHRIMP AND SPOT PRAWNS	Of several varieties of shrimp harvested in the Pacific Northwest, spot prawns are the largest. In the region they are sold fresh, head-on as well as headed. Smaller shrimp are typically headed and individually quick frozen in 2-lb. packs or frozen in 5-lb packs. Shrimp are sized by count per pound (see p. 298).	Steam, boil, broil, or grill in shell. Shelled shrimp may be poached, sautéed, or coated and deep-fried.	Fresh spot prawns are harvested in spring and summer.	Petersburg, Alaska, is the shrimping capital of the region.	Store frozen; thaw as needed in a colander placed in a sink under cool running water.
PACIFIC NORTHWEST FARMED GAME	In addition to farmed game listed in Chapter 11 on p. 515, Alaska yields caribou and reindeer.	Various preparations.	Available year round.	Moose meat is popular with Alaskan home cooks but is unavailable commercially.	Store frozen; thaw overnight in the refrigerator.

■ ■ □ ■ chapter fourteen

Hawai'i

the islands of Hawai'i, Maui, O'ahu, Lanai, Kaua'i, Moloka'i, Ni'ihau, and Kaho'olawe

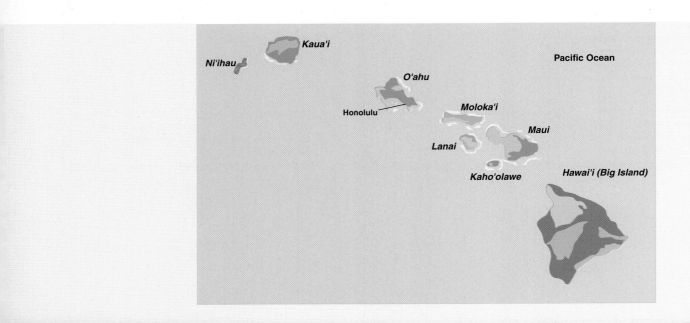

THE HAWAI'IAN ISLANDS are located in the center of the Pacific Ocean, 2,000 miles from mainland United States. This distance can be measured not only in miles, but also in geography and culture. Hawai'i's topography and climate are profoundly different from those of any other American culinary region. Hawai'i's population is unlike that of mainland America as well: far more ethnically diverse and having a more multicultural worldview. As a result, Hawai'i's cooking is vastly different from that of any other American regional cuisine.

The first Hawai'ians, Polynesian colonists, developed a cooking style based on Pacific seafood, a few domesticated food animals, and a few Asian plant cultivars. For nearly 1,500 years their cuisine evolved in isolation. Then, within a span of only 120 years, seven major settler groups burst on the scene. Most had strong food cultures, and all brought new ingredients and cooking techniques.

As a result Hawai'i developed three dynamic cooking styles. Traditional Hawai'ian cuisine blends the ingredients and techniques of precontact First Hawai'ians with the foodways of late-18th-century American and European settlers. Local food is a multicultural mixture of traditional Hawai'ian, Japanese, Chinese, Portuguese, Korean, and Filipino cooking combined with exuberance and a no-rules attitude. Still evolving, Hawai'i regional cuisine was created in the late 20th century by professional chefs.

AFTER STUDYING THIS CHAPTER YOU SHOULD BE ABLE TO:

- describe the location, topography, and climates of the Hawai'ian Islands (Factor 1) and explain their impact on the region's agriculture and cuisine (Factor 5)
- list the domesticated food plants and animals brought by Hawai'i's first-settler group (Factor 3) and discuss this group's food culture
- discuss the development of traditional Hawai'ian cuisine (Factor 3 and Factor 4), and describe its defining dishes
- trace the evolution of local food (Factor 3, Factor 4, and Factor 5), list its contributing food cultures, and describe its defining dishes
- explain the creation of Hawai'i regional cuisine and list its primary characteristics and elements (Factors 1, 3, 4, and 5)
- prepare traditional Hawai'ian cuisine dishes, local food dishes, and Hawai'i regional cuisine dishes.

APPETIZERS

Big Island Lemongrass Seafood Soup with Lotus Root Chips

Ahi Nori Tempura Roll with Shoyu Butter Sauce and Radish Sprouts

Squid Lu'au in Crunchy Lumpia Shell

***Lomi Lomi* Salmon Salad**

Ahi *Poke* with Shrimp Chips

Pau Hana *Pupu* Platter for Two: Rumaki, Shrimp on Sugarcane, Korean Mandoo Dumplings, Chinese Barbeque Baby Back Ribs, *Poke*-Stuffed Mini-Skins, Edamame, and Shichimi Wings

ENTRÉES

Macadamia-Crusted Mahimahi with *Liliko'i* Sauce, Garlic *"Poi,"* and Steamed Baby Bok Choy

Seared Rare Ahi Tuna with Teriyaki Sauce, Pacific Vegetable Medley, and Bento Rice Balls

Yellowtail Snapper Laulau with Coconut Sweet Potatoes and Stir-Fry Vegetable Shreds

Chicken Hekka with Jasmine Rice

Chicken Adobo with Vegetable Pancit

Shoyu-Braised and Grilled Duck with Macadamia-Pineapple Pilaf and Black Goma Asparagus

Kalua Pork Baked in Banana Leaf with Island Fried Rice and Stir-Fry Cabbage

Chinese-Style Tomato Beef with Sticky Rice

DESSERTS

Banana Spring Rolls with Rum Sauce and Grilled Pineapple

Kona Coffee Choco-Mac Tart with Macadamia Brittle

Waikiki Sunset Guava Cake with *Liliko'i* Purée

Fire and Ice *Haupia* Custard with Pineapple Compote

WEBSITE EXTRAS

Breakfasts   Plate Lunches   Pupu   Thanksgiving Menu

A UNIQUE AND ISOLATED LAND

The Hawai'ian Islands form the top point of the giant Polynesian Triangle, a geographic area encompassing a large segment of the Pacific Ocean (Figure 14.1). The triangle is completed by Rapa Nui (Easter Island) in its southeastern corner and New Zealand in its southwestern corner. Samoa, Tahiti, Tonga, the Marquesas, and a thousand other islands lie within the triangle. Together these islands constitute a geographic region called Polynesia.

Within the Polynesian Triangle, landmasses are grouped in clusters of small islands with miles of ocean between groups. Although its total landmass is small, the area encompassed by the Polynesian Triangle is huge, equaling more than one-fifth of the earth's surface.

FACTOR 1

Hawai'i's isolation profoundly affected its history and foodways.

Like many other Polynesian island groups, the Hawai'ian Islands form an *archipelago*, a chain or elongated cluster of islands. The Hawai'ian archipelago consists of 132 islands stretching 1,500 miles southeast to northwest and extending across the Tropic of Cancer. However, the eight main islands of Hawai'i lie just within the tropical zone, at latitude similar to that of Cuba. Situated roughly in the middle of the Pacific Ocean, far from other island groups or the Pacific Rim mainlands, the Hawai'ian Island group is one of the most isolated places in the world.

FIGURE 14.1

The Polynesian Triangle

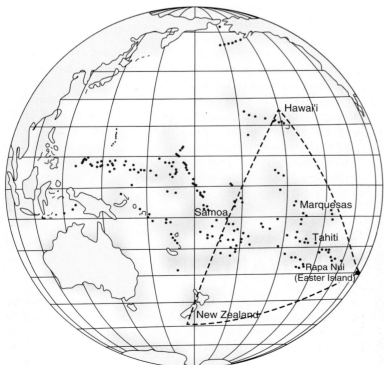

FIGURE 14.2

Blue water, beautiful beaches, tall mountains, and near-perfect weather make Hawai'i a virtual paradise. James M. House/Shutterstock

The Hawai'ian Islands were formed by volcanic magma eruptions arising from the bottom of the ocean, occurrences that are extremely rare. Although most volcanic activity happens at the edges of two overlapping tectonic plates, Hawai'i's magma escaped from the center of a tectonic plate at a place called the *Hawai'ian hot spot*. The archipelago's older islands—those formed from earlier eruptions—are located at the northwestern end of the chain; the newer islands are located in the southeast, where volcanic activity is still ongoing. The size of volcanic islands is determined by the amount of magma that escapes from the earth, often over a succession of eruptions. Hawai'i's eight main islands vary widely in size. The chain's largest island, called Hawai'i, measures about 4,000 square miles; the smallest of the main islands, Kaho'olawe, is only 44 square miles. To avoid confusion between the island of Hawai'i and Hawai'i the state or island group, the island of Hawai'i is often called **the Big Island.**

The Hawai'ian Islands are known for varied topography, fertile soil, and nearly perfect weather. This combination of land factors made life easy for the region's first settlers, and today it attracts tourists hoping for the vacation of a lifetime. Hawai'i, like other Polynesian islands, has often been described as paradise (Figure 14.2).

The mineral composition of Hawai'i's soil is derived from volcanic rock slowly broken down by the action of wind, rain, and geological activity. The region's lush vegetation grew up from seeds and spores that arrived on the newly formed islands carried by wind, borne by ocean currents, and deposited by the droppings of birds. Botanists refer to this type of plant transfer as "the three Ws": wind, waves, and wings. As the plants grew, died, and

FACTOR 1
Hawai'i's fertile volcanic soil enables plants to thrive.

FACTOR 1
Hawai'i comprises several climate zones, accommodating many food plant species.

decayed, Hawai'i's soil became rich with organic material. Over centuries the islands were visited by millions of birds, whose droppings further enriched the soil. The combination of volcanic minerals and organic matter resulted in exceptionally fertile soil.

Because the Hawai'ian Islands are actually the tops of volcanoes they are steeply mountainous, some reaching altitudes of nearly 14,000 feet above sea level. You've learned that climate grows cooler as altitude rises. Thus, mountainous Hawai'i has not one climate but many.

You've also learned that proximity to water has a moderating effect on climate. Although at sea level, and within the hot tropical zone, Hawai'i's beaches and coastal lowlands are subject to ocean breezes and ambient cooling from ocean currents from the temperate southern Pacific. Thus, coastal Hawai'i enjoys a year-round average temperature of 75°F that rarely fluctuates. Tropical vegetation—such as palm trees and wild orchids—thrives, but people are cool and comfortable. This is postcard Hawai'i, the one with which most Americans are familiar.

However, Hawai'i offers two other primary climate zones and a variety of microclimates. As you travel inland and upland the weather becomes more temperate, similar to that of New England but with far milder weather in winter. Here European food crop cultivars flourish. Climbing yet higher into Hawai'i's mountains, it's not uncommon to see snow; in Mauna Kea on the Big Island, skiing is a popular winter sport. Indeed, some of Hawai'i's mountains are snow-capped year-round, having alpine climates at their summits (Figure 14.3).

Hawai'i's annual rainfall and, thus, its vegetation differ according to location. In Hawai'i the prevailing weather brings wind and lots of moisture from the east. The eastern, windward sides of the Hawai'ian Islands receive an average 475 inches of

FIGURE 14.3
Hawai'i's climatic diversity includes alpine regions; some peaks have snow year-round. George Burba/Shutterstock

rain per year. In the coastal lowlands, this moisture combined with fertile soil and warm temperatures results in dense tropical rain forest. Higher up, it causes temperate-climate grasses, shrubs, and trees to thrive. Asian and pan-American plant species originally transferred by the three Ws in many cases found Hawai'i more hospitable than the lands from which they came. Over time, these transferred species evolved into new cultivars that, at the time of European contact, were unique to Hawai'i. However, except for a few marginally nutritious fern species, none produced food capable of sustaining human life.

On the western sides of the islands, vegetation is vastly different. Hawai'i's tall mountains create a dramatic rain shadow (p. 304) that stops moist easterly winds and the rain clouds they transport. Areas of the leeward, western sides sometimes receive as little as 6 inches annual rainfall and, before irrigation, were virtual deserts. Thus, throughout Hawai'i's history the allocation of water rights has always been a vital issue.

Although the Hawai'ian Islands boasted fertile soil, lush vegetation, and one of the world's most perfect climates, they remained virtually empty of land-based life for most of their history. Until the arrival of Polynesian first settlers the islands' only animal life consisted of migratory sea birds and the fish, shellfish, and reptiles living in the surrounding waters.

The absence of mammals, including humans, can be attributed to the Hawai'ian Islands' complete isolation in the center of a vast ocean. These volcanic islands emerged far from older landmasses where animal life was previously established. After the islands formed, the only way for animals to reach them was by air or water. Flying birds and swimming sea creatures could do so; land animals—including early humans—could not. Hawai'i had no human inhabitants until the Polynesians because, without open-ocean sailing technology, humans simply couldn't get there.

FACTOR 1
The windward eastern sides of the Hawai'ian islands have ample rainfall whereas the leeward western sides have arid climates.

FACTOR 1
Isolated presettlement Hawai'i had no mammals.

PRONOUNCING HAWAI'IAN WORDS

By remembering a few simple rules, you can easily pronounce any Hawai'ian word. For this reason, pronunciations are not given for this chapter's individual Hawai'ian terms. Please refer to this book's companion website for an easy-to-follow Hawai'ian language pronunciation guide.

■ FIRST
□
■ HAWAI'IANS

Hawai'i is unique among American culinary regions in that it has no indigenous people. An indigenous population consists of the descendants of humans who arrived in a particular place in prehistoric times. These humans filtered gradually into their respective regions over thousands of years, adapting to the local climate and topography and learning to harvest, cook, and eat the local plants and animals. In many places they domesticated both animals and plants, thus developing the region's indigenous agriculture. This was not the case in Hawai'i. Although the first Europeans to visit the Hawai'ian Islands found an established and highly developed cultural group living there, this group was not indigenous. The first people to inhabit the Hawai'ian Islands arrived suddenly, late in human history, in a carefully planned, state-sponsored expedition. Thus, Hawai'i's first residents were colonists.

Let's find out who these colonists were, where they came from, and what motivated them to undertake their extraordinary journey to the Hawai'ian Islands.

Early Polynesians

The first people to arrive in the Hawai'ian Islands were Polynesians from islands in the southern part of the Polynesian Triangle. These people are considered indigenous to Polynesia because their prehistoric ancestors migrated over millenia to southern Polynesia from Asia (Figure 14.4).

As their migration progressed, the prehistoric humans who eventually became native Polynesians acquired agricultural knowledge. By the time they began inter-island migration, they had begun to domesticate wild food plants in their new environment. However, the terrain of South Pacific islands is quite different from that of mainland Asia. Most South Pacific islands are volcanic in origin, with fertile but thin and easily depleted topsoil and a narrow band of coastal lowland encircling steep interior highlands. Adapting to island topography, early Polynesians developed agricultural techniques such as terracing (p. 654) and companion planting (p. 30).

During their migration from Asia, these prehistoric humans also domesticated three food animals: pigs, dogs, and an early form of chicken. Additionally, the Pacific Ocean provided a limitless supply of protein food, including fish, shellfish, and marine mammals. However, agriculture based on limited animal husbandry typically results in lack of fertilizer and, thus, soil depletion—a situation that would eventually lead to the colonization of the Hawai'ian Islands.

The South Pacific island climate is similar to that of Hawai'i. Subtropical at sea level, the climate becomes more temperate as one ascends through the foothills into the mountains. On the windward sides, rainfall is ample. As in Hawai'i, these varied climates and abundant natural resources made acquiring food relatively easy.

However, because of restricted physical space and easily depleted soil, South Pacific islands could sustain only small human populations. Although they lived under favorable conditions, as their numbers grew Polynesians found it necessary to move some of their population to other islands. When an island got too crowded, by common consent an adventurous group simply took to their canoes and moved. Such migrations became the subject of stories and songs, passed down in the oral history of various

FIGURE 14.4
Prehistoric Migration Routes

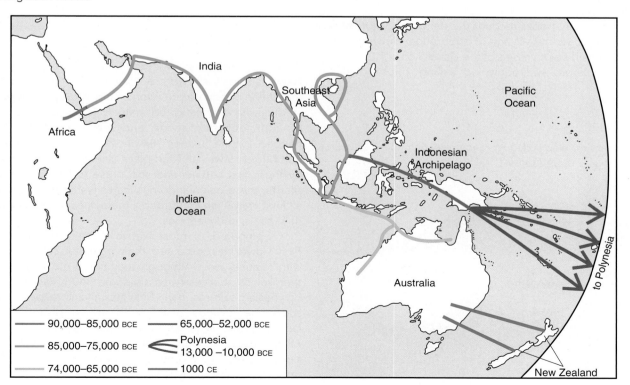

Polynesian cultures. Anthropologists partially base their assumptions about Polynesian settlement on these migration legends.

South Pacific islanders traveled the open ocean in 40-foot dugout canoes fitted with outriggers or lashed together in pairs for stability (Figure 14.5). These canoes were propelled both by oars and by sails woven from plant fibers. Some of the canoes carried only passengers. Others were loaded with provisions and possessions, including live animals and plant seedlings. In good weather these canoe fleets could remain in open water for months.

Polynesian colonists often moved to known islands. During the day they navigated by the position of the sun and by the feel of currents, waves, and winds. At night they practiced celestial navigation, using familiar stars to guide them. Just as often the voyagers set forth with no known destination, simply trusting their fates to their gods. New islands were discovered, explored, and evaluated for suitability. Protected harbors, good soil, and ample building materials were among the qualities needed for successful colonization. However, the primary requirement was life-sustaining fresh water.

The Voyage to Hawai'i

Sometime in the first millennium, possibly as early as 300 to 400 C.E., a group of South Pacific natives embarked on one of the most extraordinary of all human migrations (Figure 14.6). Anthropologists believe they departed from the island group now known as the Marquesas and headed north. At first the stars were familiar, but after they crossed the equator into the Northern Hemisphere, the constellations were new and, therefore, meaningless. In unknown territory they crossed thousands of miles of open ocean, encountering no islands. Finally, led by currents, wave systems, and the flight patterns of birds, they discovered the islands today called Hawai'i.

Western history books recount the dangers and privations faced by Columbus on his voyage of exploration. However, compared to the small, open vessels of the Hawai'i colonists, Columbus's fleet of large, well-equipped sailing ships could be considered safe and comfortable. Even modern sailors with advanced navigational instruments might think twice before making this remarkable 2,000-mile journey.

According to First Hawai'ian oral history, some of these first settlers went back to the Marquesas and then returned, bringing more colonist families and additional seeds, plants, and breeding animals to ensure the success of the colony. However, many anthropologists believe Hawai'i experienced a second wave of settlement by Tahitian colonists around the year 1000. These more aggressive and culturally advanced settlers likely established the islands' hereditary chieftainships and became the Hawai'ian nobility.

No matter which historical version you support, there's no doubt that Polynesians were Hawai'i's first settlers. For nearly 1,500 years the Polynesian-based culture of Hawai'i existed without outside influence. Eventually all of the archipelago's eight main islands were populated. Hawai'ians developed a rich culture with a complex class structure that included hereditary chieftainships and the establishment of a ruling class based on genealogy. Europeans making first contact in the 1770s believed these people were indigenous. However, we now know that's not the case. Because they were actually first settlers, and not indigenous natives, we call these people and their descendants First Hawai'ians.

FIRST HAWAI'IANS AS NATIVE AMERICANS

When Hawai'i became America's 50th state in 1959, its citizens of First Hawai'ian heritage were recognized as a separate and independent cultural group and welcomed into the nation's Native American community. Although not technically an indigenous people, First Hawai'ians are now frequently referred to as Native Hawai'ians.

First Hawai'ian Agriculture

Lack of indigenous wild foods was not a problem for First Hawai'ians, as they had prepared well for their journey and had more than adequate provisions. They brought breeding pairs to start raising domesticated animals for meat. In addition they brought rootstock, seeds, and seedlings of the food plants needed for life in their new home. Ethnobotanists identify a number of Hawai'ian food plant cultivars brought to the islands by these first settlers and still in use today. Designated **canoe plants,** these colonial domesticates were the source of virtually all First Hawai'ian plant foods, medicines, fibers, building materials, tools, and weapons.

Compared to most Native Americans, the First Hawai'ians sustained their complex culture with relative ease. Although they could not feed themselves effortlessly, as did some South Pacific Polynesian cultures, early First Hawai'ians reaped substantial rewards for a limited amount of agricultural work. With an average temperature of 75°F, rich soil, and ample rainfall on the windward sides of the islands, growing enough food for the population was rarely a problem. Although First

FIGURE 14.5
Early Polynesians traveled in dugout canoes with outriggers. Courtesy of the Library of Congress, LC-USZ62-105953

FACTOR 1
Polynesian canoe plants thrived in Hawai'i's rich soil and varied climates.

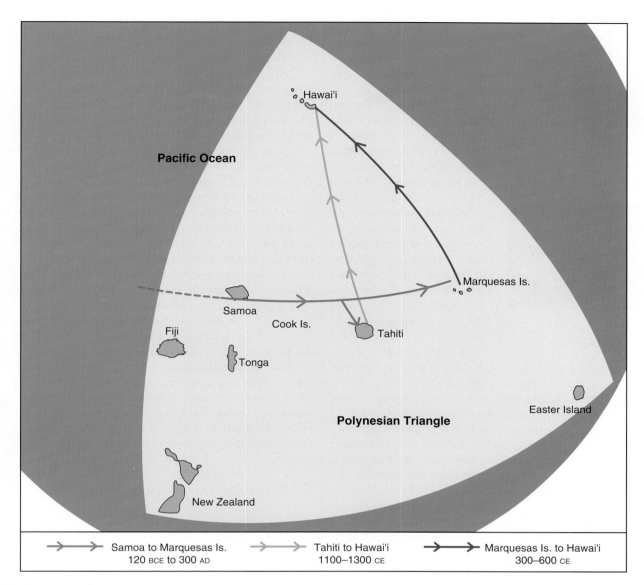

FIGURE 14.6
Polynesian Migration to Hawai'i

PRIMARY HAWAI'IAN CANOE PLANTS

English	Hawai'ian
Taro root and taro leaves	Kalo and lu'au
Breadfruit	'Ulu
True yams	Uhi
Hawai'ian arrowroot	Pia
Turmeric	'Olena
Hawai'ian ginger	'Awapuhi 'ai
Candlenut (kemiri nut)	Kukui
Ti (TEE)	Ki
Banana	Mai'a
Coconut	Niu
Mountain apples	'Ohi'a
Sugarcane	Ko

Hawai'ian oral history mentions drought and corresponding famine, these occurrences were infrequent. Considering the abundance of local seafood and the skill of First Hawai'ian fishermen, it seems unlikely that the population suffered from lack of sustenance. The occasional reference to certain roots and leaves as "famine foods" implies that the "famine" consisted more of a lack of preferred foodstuffs than actual starvation.

Because the islands offered a variety of climates ranging from rain forest to alpine, First Hawai'ians could choose a temperature zone for their crops simply by ascending the mountainsides. On the windward sides of the islands there was plenty of rainfall, and virtually every acre of soil was fertile. In addition, clearing agricultural fields was relatively easy as Hawai'i didn't harbor massive hardwood forests like those covering many of our mainland culinary regions. Some of the agricultural methods

FIGURE 14.7
Taro root. Digitaldepth/Shutterstock

FIGURE 14.8
Taro leaf. limpid/Shutterstock

used by First Hawai'ians were unique to the Hawai'ian climate and to the canoe plants that were their sole food crop cultivars.

The most important food crop for First Hawai'-ians was **taro,** a plant that produces a starchy root veg-etable as well as edible leaves (Figures 14.7 and 14.8). In other parts of the world, indigenous wetland taro grows naturally in marshes and along stream-beds. However, growing cultivated taro in Hawai'i required the construction of pond-fields that First Hawai'ians called *lo'i.* To construct a *lo'i,* farmers dug out a sunken soil plot rimmed by embankments of stone and earth and planted taro seedlings in it. Using an ingenious companion system, farmers then planted bananas, ti, and sugarcane around the edges of the *lo'i* so that the roots of the companion plants strengthened the embankments and their stalks and leaves acted as windbreaks. Once the embankments were planted, farmers diverted stream water into the *lo'i* and stocked it with freshwater fish that quickly grew and multiplied. Counting the taro itself, the bananas and other crops growing in the embankments, and the fish living in the water, a single acre of *lo'i* could produce 3 to 5 tons of food per year (Figure 14.9).

Because much of Hawai'i's temperate climate land is steeply sloping, First Hawai'ians constructed terraced agricultural plots.

Both standard agricultural plots and *lo'i* were terraced, ascending the hillsides in neat rows (Figure 14.10).

As their population grew, First Hawai'ians realized the need to grow crops on the drier, leeward sides of the islands. Hawai'ian chiefs organized mandatory communal work parties, first to build crop terraces and then to construct sophisticated irrigation systems leading to them. A typical system consisted of stone channels and wooden sluices made from hollowed tree trunks, diverting water from springs and streams often several miles away. Although these irrigation systems were successful, they were eventually replaced as Hawai'ians developed dryland taro cultivars needing less water than the original types.

First Hawai'ians raised taro and other canoe plants using a complex system of communal agriculture driven by a complicated social hierarchy. The Hawai'ian hereditary nobility, a group of chieftains and their immediate families, owned much of the land. Commoners also owned land and farmed it in extended family groups. In addition, commoners were required to work the nobles' land a specific number of days each year as a form of tribute.

Food animals were considered outside the communal system; each family raised pigs, chickens, and dogs for its own consumption. However, farmers were expected to give food animals in tribute to the nobility. For example, a chief had the right to requisition a pig or a dozen chickens for his own use or for a communal feast. Because of their relative scarcity, domestic food animals were typically reserved for special-occasion meals. For precontact First Hawai'ians, the everyday protein food was seafood.

First Hawai'ian Fishing

Early European explorers recorded more than two hundred ocean fish species in Hawai'ian waters. First Hawai'ians were superb fishermen, ranging

FACTOR 1
More than two hundred species of fish became the foundation protein of First Hawai'ian cuisine.

FIGURE 14.9
Food crops companion planted in the *lo'i* system. Keoke Stender, www.Marinelifephotography.com

FIGURE 14.10
Terraced agricultural fields. Steve Heap/Shutterstock

TRADITIONAL HAWAI'IAN FISH CATEGORIES

Tuna

To First Hawai'ians the tuna is the most revered of all fish, honored as a separate category (Figure 14.11). These large, oily-fleshed fish have firm and meaty flesh ranging from grayish pink to bright coral to deep maroon in color. Tuna is grilled, roasted, and enjoyed raw in traditional Hawai'ian preparations as well as in Japanese sashimi and sushi. Among the most prized tunas are the yellowfin and bigeye (*ahi*), the albacore (*tombo*), and the skipjack (*aku*).

Billfish

First Hawai'ians recognized billfish, a sword-nosed species, as a separate category. These large, scary-looking fish are ferocious fighters today highly prized as sport fish. Although in the Western world these fish are usually served cooked—most often grilled or broiled—in Hawai'i and Japan they are also served raw. In modern Hawai'ian usage some of these fish have Japanese names: the shortbill spearfish (*hebi*), the Pacific blue marlin (*kajiki*), and the broadbill swordfish (*shutome*) (Figure 14.12). The striped marlin retains its Hawai'ian-language name, *a'u*.

Bottom Fish

Bottom fish dwell along the ocean floor, often in very deep water. Most prized is the Pacific pink or crimson snapper (*opakapaka*), a large snapper variety often cooked whole for special occasion (Figure 14.13). The smaller pink or ruby snapper, *onaga* in Japanese, is a smaller fish with a delicate flesh; another snapper family member, the jobfish (*uku*) is rich and fatty. Pacific grouper (*hapu'upu'u*) is sometimes called Pacific sea bass.

Open-Ocean Fish

The open-ocean fish category includes some of the Pacific's most beloved species. In the West the best-known fish of the open-ocean category is now universally labeled by its Hawai'ian name, *mahimahi*. Formerly known as dolphin fish and in Latin American countries called *dorado*, the mahimahi has firm, mild-tasting white flesh. Pomfret, *monchong* in Cantonese, is a favorite of Hawai'i's Chinese community. Its light-pink, oily flesh has a rich, distinctive flavor, and its firm texture stands up to wok braising and grilling. The moonfish (*opah*) is beautifully colorful and considered good luck by Hawai'ian fishermen. Like fowl, moonfish have flesh of different color and texture depending on the location of the particular muscle group within the body. The wahoo, a type of mackerel, is another Hawai'ian favorite (Figure 14.14). Its Hawai'ian name, *ono*, is also the Hawai'ian word for "delicious."

FIGURE 14.11
Tuna on sale at Honolulu Fish Market. Keoke Stender, www.Marinelifephotography.com

FIGURE 14.12
Broadbill swordfish.
tonobalaguerf/Shutterstock

FIGURE 14.13
Pacific pink snapper. Keoke Stender, www.Marinelifephotography.com

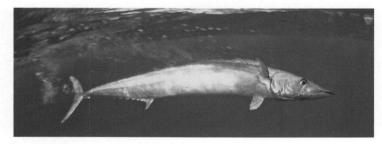

FIGURE 14.14
Wahoo, or *ono*. Keoke Stender, www.Marinelifephotography.com

FIGURE 14.15
Hawai'ian *Opihi.* Keoke Stender,
www.Marinelifephotography.com

far out into the open ocean to catch them. Their unique classification system divided ocean fish into four categories.

Although Hawai'i's waters abound with fish, only a few varieties of shellfish are indigenous to the islands. Kona crab, spiny and slipper lobster, and shrimp are commercially harvested. Limpets, or *opihi*, are an indigenous mollusk (Figure 14.15). This delicacy is eaten raw, steamed, or sautéed. Octopus, or *tako*, is an important part of the traditional Hawai'ian diet, served grilled, steamed, or simmered into soups and stews. Confusingly, in Hawai'i English speakers refer to octopus as squid. Sea urchin is known both by its Japanese name, *uni*, and its Hawai'ian name, *wana*.

Hawai'i's natural mountain pools are home to unique varieties of freshwater crustaceans. Small black shrimp are harvested by amateur shrimpers who catch them for family dining or sell them to fine restaurants. Crayfish grow in natural pools as well as in *lo'i*.

Seaweed

An important food for early Hawai'ians and later immigrant groups, today only a few types of seaweed remain in the modern cuisine, and only one is commercially available. *Ogo*,

FIGURE 14.16
Ogo seaweed. Keoke Stender,
www.Marinelifephotography.com

now farm-raised in the islands, is found in virtually every Hawai'ian food store (Figure 14.16). Appearing as a tangle of stringy reddish filaments, *ogo* has a mildly briny flavor and a crunchy texture. Primarily used in salads and pokes (pp. 666, 671, and 682), *ogo* is also pickled or made into candy. Today imported Japanese seaweeds are an important cuisine element, as well.

HAWAI'IAN ALAEA SALT

First Hawai'ians obtained salt from seawater. Sometimes they found salt in tidal pools that had dried up naturally. They also constructed shallow lagoons and allowed the water to evaporate. In some places the evaporating seawater mixed with red volcanic clay, contributing a variety of minerals, a mild but distinctive flavor, and a salmon-color tint to the salt. This unique product is called **alaea salt.**

■ THE CUISINE OF THE
□
■ FIRST HAWAI'IANS

The food culture of precontact First Hawai'ians was markedly different from that of any Native American group. Like many Native American cultures, First Hawai'ians had clearly defined gender roles. In other words, men and women were responsible for different tasks. Hawai'ian women tended the animals, cultivated and harvested the crops, and cared for the children. Because there were no indigenous food plants, gathering wild foods was not a seasonal occupation as it was for Native American women. Like Native American men, Hawai'ian men were hunters who caught the fish and shellfish that supplied their families with protein. However, unlike Native American men, Hawai'ian men also did virtually all the cooking. Women took over culinary duties only after European planters arrived and Hawai'ian men were hired to work on sugar and pineapple plantations.

The diet of precontact First Hawai'ians was strongly influenced by *kapus*. A **kapu** is a taboo or restriction. Some *kapus* were traditional and permanent, invoked in the early days of Hawai'ian culture by chieftains and priests and then handed down through the generations. Other *kapus* were temporary, instituted for a specific reason or on a whim by current leaders. Many *kapus* involved food. For example, certain fishing areas were permanently *kapu* to commoners. Seafood harvested from those areas could be eaten only by the nobility. A temporary *kapu* might be placed on a particular fish if its numbers appeared to be dwindling. One important traditional *kapu* involved dining. Men and women were not permitted to eat together; the sexes were segregated into separate dining structures with the men eating first, and the women and young children eating later.

First Hawai'ians had clearly defined dining practices. Diners knelt or sat cross-legged around dining mats placed on the ground outdoors or on the dirt floor of an extended family dining hut. Foods were served in large bowls, on wooden trays, or in large gourd calabashes. Sections of banana leaf served as plates. Most foods were eaten with the hands. Soups and other liquid foods were eaten from coconut shells or wooden bowls with spoons fashioned out of gourds. Although today people of First Hawai'ian descent dine in the modern American fashion, for special occasions such as *lu'aus* (p. 658) or religious observations traditional precontact dining customs are still followed.

FACTOR 3
First Hawai'ians developed a complex and varied cuisine with a limited ingredients palette.

Despite *kapus* and a limited ingredients palette, First Hawai'ians were exceptionally creative cooks. First Hawai'ian cuisine involved several unique cooking methods and techniques, many of which are still popular today.

Pit Roasting in the Imu

Along with conventional fire cooking methods such as grilling and spit roasting, First Hawai'ians commonly practiced pit roasting in an underground oven called an **imu.** Hawai'ian pit roasting is virtually identical to Native American pit roasting, such as the early New England clambake described on p. 91.

In compliance with a traditional *kapu*, foods for men and women were cooked in separate *imus* (Figure 14.17). The size of these circular roasting pits varied according to the number of people to be fed; a typical extended family *imu* might be 6 feet across and 3 feet deep. *Imus* for a large, communal feast might be three or four times larger and a few feet deeper.

Several hours before cooking, men built a wood fire in the pit and allowed it to burn down to coals. Stones were placed in the coals, where they became extremely hot. Some of these stones also might be used to fill the cavity of a whole pig, fish, or chicken, or they could be dropped into a wooden vessel to boil water. The cooks arranged a thick layer of banana or ti leaves on the coals, placed the seasoned food on top, added more leaves, and then covered the pit with sand or soil. The size of the fire and the cooking time depended on the size and quantity of the foods to be cooked. After the appropriate amount of time, the cooks removed the sand and opened up the leaves to reveal the moist, tender food within.

Roots and Tubers

Roots and tubers were the foundation starches of the First Hawai'ian diet, prepared boiled, steamed, or pit-baked. Serving as a bland base for other, more highly seasoned foods, they were eaten in remarkable quantity. A full-grown Hawai'ian man commonly ate 10 pounds of roots and tubers per day, choosing among taro, sweet potatoes, yams, and breadfruit. After European contact, white potatoes became popular as well. Although

---

ELEMENTS OF FIRST HAWAI'IAN CUISINE

FOUNDATION FOODS

principal starches: taro, true yam, sweet potatoes

principal proteins: seafood, pork

principal produce: tropical fruits, taro leaves, seaweeds

FAVORED SEASONINGS: sea salt, ginger, turmeric, kukui nut, sugarcane

PRINCIPAL COOKING MEDIA: water, coconut water, coconut milk

PRIMARY COOKING METHODS: grilling, spit roasting, boiling, poaching, pit roasting

FOOD ATTITUDES: strong food culture, culinary liberals (after contact)

---

these starchy vegetables could be baked or steamed and eaten without further preparation, they were most commonly transformed into *poi*, the Hawai'ian staff of life. Although technically *poi* can be made from any starchy root or tuber, in modern usage **poi** is cooked, pounded taro root.

Poi is infamous among traditional Hawai'ian foods, a dish about which people have strong opinions. To modern Hawai'ians that grew up eating it, *poi* is the ultimate comfort food. To most non-Hawai'ians—whose first experience with *poi* is typically at a commercially prepared *lu'au* feast—the bowlful of sticky, gray starch seems the least appealing food on the buffet and is usually avoided.

The color of a particular batch or brand of *poi* depends on the variety of taro used. Like the flesh of taro, *poi* may be white, beige, ivory, tan, gray, yellow, purplish, or reddish in color. Commercially prepared *poi* is typically beige or gray. To prepare *poi* from scratch, peeled taro is boiled until soft, pounded into a paste in a wooden mortar, and then mixed with water (Figure 14.18). At

FIGURE 14.18

To make *poi*, the boiled, peeled roots are pounded in a large wooden mortar. LC-USZ62-24005, Courtesy of Library of Congress

FIGURE 14.17

Reenactment of First Hawai'ian *imu* cooking. Photo by Alissa Everett, courtesy of Kona Village

HOW MANY FINGERS?

Poi may be served thick, or it may be thinned out with water according to preference. The thickness of a particular batch of *poi* is described by the number of fingers used to eat it. "One-finger *poi*" is very thick, "two-finger *poi*" has the consistency of a vegetable purée, and "three-finger *poi*" is quite runny.

this stage the product is called fresh *poi*, and to keep it fresh it is immediately refrigerated or frozen. However, true *poi* lovers prefer fermented *poi*. To prepare the fermented variety, the mashed taro is allowed to stand at warm temperatures for one to several days in order for bacterial action to occur. The flavor of fermented *poi* ranges from mildly tangy to quite sour and pungent.

Today most Hawai'i residents purchase commercially prepared *poi*. Each brand has its supporters. Most commercial *poi* is sold fresh and is fermented to taste by the consumer.

Like the staple starches of many traditional cuisines, *poi* may be used in both savory and sweet applications. Hawai'ians eat *poi* for breakfast sweetened with sugar or cane syrup. Most often, however, *poi* serves as a starchy base or side dish for savory foods.

Preserved Foods

Living in a tropical paradise with a year-round growing season and consistently available seafood, First Hawai'ians did not need to preserve foods to sustain them through winter as many Native Americans did. Nonetheless, Hawai'ians often needed light, compact provisions that could be packed into canoes and taken on ocean journeys. For this reason they developed a number of dried food products. Many of these foods were enjoyed by non-traveling Hawai'ians as well, who ate them out of preference rather than necessity.

First Hawai'ians cured fish and meats with sea salt and set them out on racks to dry. Fruits and vegetables were sliced and sun dried as well. However, the special properties of many canoe plants gave rise to preservation methods unique to Hawai'ian cuisine. Ripe raw breadfruit was mashed with coconut cream, wrapped in ti leaves, and then pit-baked at low temperature to make rich, oily cakes. In another preservation method, breadfruit was cooked, peeled, seeded, mashed, flattened into sheets, sun dried, and then finally rolled into cylinders like fruit leather. Firm cakes of dried fermented *poi* were packed in baskets to be carried on voyages. Although many of these traditional dried foods are no longer prepared, many types of preserved fish and meats remain staples of the modern cuisine.

Fresh Fish Dishes

First Hawai'ians enjoyed the region's abundant fish in cooked and raw preparations. Whole small fish were scaled, gutted, and scored to absorb seasonings. Larger fish were cut into steaks or fillets. Once fabricated, fish were seasoned with sea salt and enhanced with canoe plant seasonings, including turmeric, Hawai'ian ginger, coconut, and sugar. Fish was grilled over wood fire embers, simmered in water with canoe plant vegetables to make soups and stews, or wrapped in fragrant leaves and pit-steamed.

Certain types of fish were preferred raw. Fillets were diced or sliced thin; mixed with alaea salt, kukui nuts, and chopped seaweed; and eaten cold. First Hawai'ian methods for preparing raw fish remained an important part of all Hawai'i cuisines and today are represented by various forms of *poke*.

The *Lu'au*

Hawai'i's chieftains and kings traditionally celebrated momentous occasions such as weddings, leadership successions, and war victories by hosting a large communal feast today called a **lu'au.** Families also hosted smaller *lu'aus* for their own, private celebrations. (The term *lu'au* describing a dinner is derived from the term *lu'au*, or taro leaf, because this leaf is frequently used in *imu* cooking.)

The *lu'au* is a tradition that has remained a vital part of Hawai'ian food culture and, indeed, is known worldwide. Today the two events most commonly celebrated with a full-blown family *lu'au* are marriages and the first birthday of a child. Contemporary family *lu'aus* are often catered affairs, prepared and served by professionals. *Lu'aus* are also hosted by churches and other community organizations as celebrations and fund-raisers. Hotels stage elaborate *lu'aus* for tourist guests.

Most *lu'au* cooking is done in the traditional *imu*, or fire pit. The centerpiece of both the precontact and modern *lu'au* is kalua pig, a whole piglet or young hog rubbed with seasonings and pit-baked in the *imu*. Precontact Hawai'ian cooks seasoned the meat only with sea salt, but today's cooks also add ginger, soy sauce, and a variety of other flavorings. Other *lu'au* dishes baked in the *imu* might include a dish of pork belly and salt fish wrapped in ti leaves called *laulau*, fresh fish wrapped in ti leaves, whole crabs, and vegetables such as sweet potatoes, breadfruit, and bananas.

Poi is the essential starchy side dish that always accompanies *lu'au* food. Other separately prepared dishes not cooked in the *imu* may include *lomi lomi* (p. 680) or shredded salt fish tossed with ginger and tomatoes; *opihi 'a me limu*, or raw limpets with seaweed; and *poke* (p. 682), or diced, seasoned raw fish. Individual portions of various seasonings, such as candlenut relish, red alaea sea salt, shredded dried fish or meat, and chopped fresh chiles, are part of each place setting. Liquid foods are served in individual, hand-carved wooden bowls, gourds, or coconut shells. Desserts, such as coconut custard and baked bananas, are set out along with the savory dishes. When the *imu* is first uncovered, smaller foods from the top layer are placed on the table steaming hot for all to sample. Then, as the climax of the meal, the roasted pig is paraded around the tables on a special wooden tray constructed like a litter and carried on the shoulders of two men.

FACTOR 3

First Hawai'ian foods and cooking techniques are important elements of Hawai'i's modern cuisines.

A Lasting Food Legacy

The highly developed cuisine of the First Hawai'ians is a lasting legacy that influences contemporary cooking today. Just as the Pilgrims' Thanksgiving feast is recreated yearly throughout the nation, the First Hawai'ians' *lu'au* is a food celebration staged many times throughout the year in Hawai'i's homes and restaurants. First Hawai'ian foods such as *poi* and kalua pig are regularly served, and their cooking methods have stood the test of time. In addition, many canoe plants remain staple foods or favored seasonings.

Although subsequent settlers would modify and enhance many First Hawai'ian dishes, First Hawai'ian cooking remains the foundation of Hawai'i's three modern cuisines.

■□■ EUROPEANS AND AMERICANS IN HAWAI'I

Although some historians believe the islands had been visited by Portuguese sailors some time earlier in the decade, the first recorded landing of a European ship was in 1778 with the arrival of Captain James Cook. Ignoring the islands' long-established names, Cook called the Hawai'ian archipelago "the Sandwich Islands" in honor of an English earl.

Because of his appearance and advanced technology, First Hawai'ians believed Cook to be a god and received him with reverence and hospitality. Unfortunately, Cook and his men were insensitive to local customs and beliefs. They violated numerous *kapus*, took advantage of the open sexuality of the Hawai'ian culture, and engaged in unfair trade dealings. When they departed, they left behind a resentful population and a host of European diseases. Like Native Americans, First Hawai'ians had no immunity to these diseases, and many perished.

Cook and his crew returned to the Hawai'ian Islands for two more visits. Before long other European ships began to call on a regular basis. Caucasian visitors from Europe and later, from America, were called **haoles** (today pronounced HOWL-ee), meaning "outsiders." Although *haoles* brought diseases and cultural disruption, First Hawai'ians tolerated them because of the trade goods they brought. In addition to manufactured goods, tools, and weapons, Europeans introduced a variety of new foods. After centuries of cooking with the same palette of ingredients, First Hawai'ians now had access to preserved products from around the globe and became enthusiastic culinary liberals, adopting virtually every new food they encountered.

At least in part because of the exciting new foods they offered, European visitors and settlers were soon accepted and even welcomed by ordinary Hawai'ians. However, the nobility rightly feared that the more technologically advanced newcomers might depose them and seize control. In response, the noble families of the main islands united under a single king, Kamehameha I, in 1795 (Figure 14.19).

Thus began the Hawai'ian monarchy that initiated the hereditary succession of Kamehameha I through V. Although the Hawai'ian kings ruled the islands in name, the nobility had no choice but to cooperate with the increasing number of Europeans settling the islands. Many European and American men married high-ranking Hawai'ian women and in doing so acquired prime agricultural lands and fishing grounds. Although the intent of unification was to protect the islands from European colonization, by the 1870s Hawai'i's kings were mere figureheads. Hawai'i's last monarch was Queen Liliuokalani, a proud yet tragic figure who was forced to surrender her kingdom to the United States in 1893 (Figure 14.20).

By 1800, many Europeans and Americans were arriving in the Hawai'ian Islands, establishing businesses and intermarrying with the local population. In addition to changing the economy and social structure of Hawai'i, these *haole* second-wave settlers would also have a profound influence on the cooking of the First Hawai'ians. They added new ingredients and introduced new foodways that combined with First Hawai'ian food culture to create traditional Hawai'ian cuisine.

Traders, Planters, and Ranchers

Despite the fact that Hawai'i was discovered by the British and settled by quite a few British citizens, New England Yankees made the most lasting impact on Hawai'i's early history. Swift Yankee clippers making the

FIGURE 14.19

Statue of King Kamehameha I.
Chee-Onn Leong/Shutterstock

FIGURE 14.20

Queen Liliuokalani. Courtesy of the Library of Congress, LC-USZ62-59774

FACTOR 4
American and British second settlers expanded First Hawai'ian cuisine.

FACTOR 5
Cash crops sugarcane and pineapples brought wealth to Hawai'i's early planters.

long voyage around the Cape of Good Hope on their way to China invariably stopped in Hawai'i to take on provisions and to give their sailors shore leave. Later, as the whaling industry boomed, New England whalers joined the merchant ships plying the Pacific and Arctic Oceans. Even ships bound for the Pacific Northwest found it easier to ride the prevailing winds and currents to Hawai'i before turning northeast to their destination. Many Americans traveled to Hawai'i with the goal of opening stores and chandlers' shops servicing the sailing ships. Others opened taverns, inns, and brothels to accommodate the sailors.

Hawai'i's immense agricultural potential attracted entrepreneurs eager to establish plantations growing sugarcane and, later, pineapples. Needing labor, plantations gave rise to subsequent immigration that would transform Hawai'i into a multicultural region with an interesting and complex cuisine.

Although most American Yankees in Hawai'i had a purely financial agenda, some had a spiritual one. Christian missionaries from New England arrived in Hawai'i intent on instilling Puritan morals into the First Hawai'ian population. These Americans sought to eradicate Hawai'ian culture and cuisine but met with little success.

In keeping with their Puritan heritage, these New England missionaries were culinary conservatives. They introduced American dishes such as corned beef and cabbage, boiled ham, and fish chowder and insisted on eating these heavy foods even in the hottest weather. However, Hawai'i's island climate and the population's easy attitude soon softened their austere sensibilities. Missionary wives intent on producing traditional New England meals began adapting many of their recipes to use Hawai'ian ingredients.

HAWAI'IAN PINEAPPLE

Although pineapples were introduced to Hawai'i in the 1790s, successful commercial cultivation didn't begin until nearly one hundred years later, when reliable steamship transportation made long-distance shipping of fresh fruits viable. When a devastating freeze in 1894–1895 ruined the Florida pineapple crop, America looked to Hawai'i for pineapple production. James D. Dole planted his first pineapples on Oahu in 1901 and soon after founded the Hawaiian Pineapple Company. In 1903, Dole began canning pineapple and shipping it worldwide. By 1922, when Dole purchased the island of Lanai and established vast plantations, pineapple was the most important crop in Hawai'i, far outstripping sugarcane (Figure 14.21). Dole was eventually bought out by a company called Castle & Cooke, which still owns much of Lanai. Pineapple remained one of the state's most important industries until the mid-1940s.

FIGURE 14.21
By 1922 pineapple was Hawai'i's most important crop.
Keysurfing/ Shutterstock

Secular Americans and Europeans were far more influential on Hawai'ian cuisine. Many of the *haole* merchants and planters were both socially and culinarily liberal. They frequently married women of the Hawai'ian nobility and were accepted into the Hawai'ian social hierarchy, forming a unique societal niche somewhere between royals and commoners. Their descendants became known as **kama'ainas,** literally "children of the land." These long-established families became the moving force in the social and economic life of 19th- and early-20th-century Hawai'i. While promoting modernization, they were staunch supporters of First Hawai'ian culture and cuisine. In their kitchens American and European foods, as well as imports from around the globe, entered the pantry of First Hawai'ian cuisine.

Anglo-American Preserved Foods

Despite the fact that First Hawai'ians were already expert at preserving their own foodstuffs—or possibly because of it—the introduction of even more preserved foods was greeted with enthusiasm. Although Hawai'i abounded with indigenous seafood, salt cod from New England and salted and smoked salmon from the Pacific Northwest became immensely popular. Hawai'ians coined a new term for these imported fish: *kamano* literally means "fish from elsewhere," but now refers solely to salmon. Corned beef, salt pork, and bacon became everyday foods for First Hawai'ians. At first these products were shipped in from the American mainland but later were produced on the islands for domestic use and trade.

Preserved foods remained popular throughout Hawai'i's history. By the end of the 19th century, the growing New England food industry was producing canned meats and found Hawai'i a ready customer. By the mid-1930s industrial food plants offered a full array of canned meats, with Hormel's Spam foremost among them. Hawai'i residents are notoriously fond of Spam, consuming more of it than any other Americans. At the turn of the 21st century, Hawai'i residents annually devoured 6 cans of Spam per person.

The Cooked Breakfast

Both the British and the Americans taught Hawai'ians to love hearty breakfasts based on eggs, preserved meats, and wheat-bread toast. To distinguish this type of morning fare from the European Continental breakfast of coffee and bread and from the typical Polynesian breakfast of fresh fruit, Hawai'i residents refer to the Anglo-American meal as a **cooked breakfast.** Later, Asians replaced toasted bread with steamed rice.

Beef and the Hawai'ian Cowboy

In the 1800s, British Captain George Vancouver introduced European livestock to Hawai'i. Having first seen the islands as a member of Cook's crew, when he was granted command of his own fleet he returned to Hawai'i bringing horses, goats, sheep, geese, and, most important, cattle. He persuaded First Hawai'ian chiefs to declare a 10-year *kapu* on slaughtering the animals in order to allow them time to multiply.

These cattle eventually became so numerous that Mexican vaqueros were recruited to come to Hawai'i and teach First Hawai'ians how to manage them. Mexican cowboys were initially called *Españoles*, or Spanish, because of the language they spoke. In the Hawai'ian language the term became **paniolo.** Later many Americans became *paniolos*, first working as paid help and eventually founding ranches of their own. One such cattle entrepreneur was John Palmer Parker, a New Englander who arrived in Hawai'i in the early 1800s. Although he started out as a lowly *paniolo*, he married into the Hawai'ian nobility and established the Parker Ranch, today one of the largest cattle operations in the United States. When most mainland Americans think about Hawai'i, cattle ranching seldom comes to mind. However, the Hawai'ian *paniolo* predates the American cowboy by almost 50 years (Figure 14.22). By the late 19th century, Hawai'i was known for raising fine beef. Before refrigeration, Hawai'ian beef was typically salt cured and packed for use on sailing vessels. During the California gold rush it was easier and cheaper for San Francisco purveyors to import Hawai'ian beef than to transport Midwestern beef over the Rockies. Later, Hawai'ian beef was shipped to Japan and Korea. Through the mid-20th century Hawai'i was one of the world's largest exporters of beef.

FACTOR 5
Hawai'ian beef, raised for export, created wealth for ranchers.

Although *haole* ranchers, planters, and merchants frequently enjoyed roast beef and grilled steaks, beef was not widely popular with First Hawai'ians and subsequent Asian immigrants. Thus, beef never became a major ingredient in traditional

FIGURE 14.22
Hawai'ian *paniolos* round up cattle in the surf. Courtesy Bishop Museum

Hawai'ian cuisine. Instead, it helped finance the comfortable and elegant *kama'aina* lifestyle.

■ TRADITIONAL HAWAI'IAN CUISINE

The transformation of First Hawai'ian cooking into traditional Hawai'ian cuisine is attributed to the *kama'ainas*. In *kama'aina* homes, British and American ingredients such as salted and smoked fish, pumpkins, and melons entered the First Hawai'ian pantry along with pineapples, mangoes, passion fruits, citrus, and other tropical fruits. *Kama'ainas* used a wide variety of Asian spices, such as black pepper, cinnamon, and coriander, as well as chiles from the Americas. Soy sauce became a favored seasoning. They also imported fresh and cured salmon from the Pacific Northwest.

Kama'ainas typically added new ingredients to traditional First Hawai'ian dishes. For example, meats and fish to be roasted in the *imu* were enhanced with spices, aromatics, and soy sauce. Tropical fruits from other lands were eaten for dessert and used to season savory foods. New World chiles were blended with canoe plant kukui nuts and indigenous red Hawai'ian alaea salt to make *'inamona*, a savory relish. Diced raw fish benefited from the addition of citrus juice, scallions, and minced fresh chiles. Salt-cured salmon from the Pacific Northwest was shredded and mixed with Hawai'ian, Western and, later, Asian ingredients to make **lomi lomi** salmon, a dish named for the technique used to shred it.

Wealthy *kama'aina* families typically alternated between traditional Hawai'ian cuisine and American or European cooking, sometimes mixing the two in one meal. In the late 1800s, Hawai'i's upper classes entertained guests at elegant **poi suppers,** formal meals of traditional Hawai'ian cuisine fare presented on both European china and silver and heirloom traditional Hawai'ian serving pieces.

Although culinary liberals at the outset, at a crucial point near the end of the 19th century *kama'ainas* became more culinarily conservative. In a largely unconscious attempt to preserve their unique heritage, they gradually stopped adding new ingredients and cooking methods to their cuisine. Because of them, traditional Hawai'ian cuisine was not significantly affected by the rapid succession of five additional second-settler groups that would quickly change Hawai'i's popular cooking into an almost unrecognizable fusion cuisine. Thus, traditional Hawai'ian cuisine remains frozen in time, basically First Hawai'ian cooking enriched with a selected group of ingredients derived from other places.

Today one primarily encounters traditional Hawai'ian cuisine at *lu'aus* and ceremonial banquets. Although some traditional Hawai'ian cuisine dishes, such as *poi* and *laulaus*, remain everyday Hawai'i fare, in its pure form traditional Hawai'ian cuisine appears primarily on special occasions.

ELEMENTS OF PORTUGUESE CUISINE

FOUNDATION FOODS

principal starches: wheat bread, potatoes, long-grain rice

principal proteins: seafood, pork and pork sausages, poultry, cheese, legumes

principal produce: kale, cabbages, tomatoes, bell peppers

FAVORED SEASONINGS: garlic, onions, parsley, saffron, black pepper, piri-piri chiles, wine, vinegar

PRINCIPAL COOKING MEDIA: olive oil, pork lard, stock

PRIMARY COOKING METHODS: grilling, sautéing, deep-frying, braising, stewing

FOOD ATTITUDES: strong food culture, culinary conservatives

HAWAI'I'S IMMIGRANT CUISINES

Now that we've traced the evolution of First Hawai'ian cooking into traditional Hawai'ian cuisine, let's look at the five immigrant food cultures whose ingredients and techniques transformed Hawai'i's everyday cooking.

The Portuguese

FACTOR 4
Portuguese settlers expanded Hawai'i's repertoire with European dishes.

During the century of exploration that opened up the Pacific, Portuguese navigators were known as the world's boldest and farthest-ranging seafarers. By the late 1600s, Portuguese navigators were capable of reaching the Pacific from both sides of the globe. Thus, they probably reached the Hawai'ian Islands before Cook. However, they were far more interested in trade than in settlement. The first recorded Portuguese arrival in Hawai'i coincides with that of other early European traders. However, this first group did little to influence Hawai'i's cuisine.

A second, much more culinarily influential group of Portuguese arrived in Hawai'i around 1880. These were true settlers, in Hawai'i with the intention of staying. This group brought the cuisine of the Iberian Peninsula to the Hawai'ian Islands. Largely because of the strong Portuguese food culture and the availability of ingredients shipped from Portugal, their cuisine did not change significantly. As in New England, in Hawai'i Portuguese cuisine remains almost identical to the mother cuisine, undergoing little or no modification.

Portuguese sausages—particularly linguiça—have become widely popular. They are often the meat component of cooked breakfasts, they become sausage sandwiches, and are used in soups and stews. Hearty Portuguese bean soup is a favorite in Hawai'i's hill towns and is served throughout the islands whenever the weather turns cool. Before refrigeration, Portuguese cooks simmered meat in an acidic sauce to preserve it from spoiling. In Hawai'i this method is represented by *carne vinha d'alhos* (CAR-nay VEEN-ah DOESH), literally "meat in wine and garlic." As in New England, Portuguese immigrants introduced salt cod, potatoes, kale, and sweet pastries. *Malasadas* (mah-la-SAH-dahs), traditional Portuguese Shrove Tuesday doughnuts, are an everyday treat in Hawai'i.

The Chinese

By 1850, the need for labor on Hawai'i's expanding sugar and pineapple plantations had outgrown the First Hawai'ian population. At the same time war, drought, and famine in southern China created population pressure strong enough to force hundreds of thousands of Cantonese men to emigrate in search of work. Beginning with a boatload of Chinese contract workers recruited in 1852, a virtual tidal wave of Chinese laborers poured into the islands until Hawai'i became an American possession in 1898.

As on the American mainland, most Chinese immigrants to Hawai'i were men intent on earning their fortunes and then returning home to China. Although some did just that, many others remained after their contracts were fulfilled.

Like mainland Chinese immigrants, most Chinese immigrants to Hawai'i were working-class male laborers with no special training in Chinese cooking. However, from watching Chinese women cook they had a basic understanding of the stir-fry technique and were familiar with common Chinese seasonings such as soy sauce, oyster sauce, scallions, garlic, and ginger. Unlike mainland Chinese immigrants who suffered from a shortage of available women, Chinese men staying on in Hawai'i typically married First Hawai'ian women. By teaching their wives Chinese cooking methods and importing Chinese ingredients, these men initiated a unique fusion of Polynesian and Asian cuisines. The extremely strong Chinese food culture had a dramatic impact on culinarily liberal Hawai'ian cooks, who readily adopted Chinese ingredients and techniques (p. 557). In turn, culinarily liberal Chinese men were happy to incorporate First Hawai'ian foods into their diets. This blending of Chinese and First Hawai'ian cooking marked the beginning of a new, widely popular, uniquely Hawai'ian cooking style that, as yet, had no name.

Chinese foodways were almost instantly adopted throughout the Hawai'ian Islands. The change was dramatic. When Chinese spun-steel woks arrived in the islands, stir-fry became one of Hawai'i's most important cooking techniques. Rice quickly became Hawai'i's foundation starch, supplanting *poi* and other starchy roots within a single generation. Noodles, made from both wheat and rice, became everyday foods. Tofu (bean curd) found its way into soups, stews, and salads. Dim sum (Chinese dumplings and other snacks) was sold in shops and restaurants and by street vendors. Specialty restaurants introduced Chinese barbeque, displaying mahogany-colored roast ducks, red-tinted pork strips, and glistening sparerib racks in their windows. Chinese soy sauce became a ubiquitous seasoning for Hawai'i's foods, flavoring pit-roasted meats, shaken onto seaweed salads, and placed on tables as a condiment. Although canoe plant Hawai'ian ginger was already a preferred seasoning, Chinese ginger root soon supplanted the locally grown variety. The Chinese combination of ginger, garlic, and scallions flavored traditional Hawai'ian foods.

Culinary blending went both ways. Soon traditional Chinese dishes acquired a decidedly Hawai'ian flavor. For example: Chinese cooks added pineapple chunks to stir-fries and fried rice; and mixed pineapple juice into glazes and marinades, creating new versions of sweet-and-sour dishes. Local seafood was subjected to Chinese cooking techniques, seasonings, and sauces.

Because their ingredients, seasonings, and cooking methods were highly complementary, the fusion of Chinese cuisine and traditional Hawai'ian cuisine was successful. However, a separate and distinct Chinese-Hawai'ian microcuisine would not have time to develop because the next wave of Asian immigrants had already arrived, adding new and different elements to Hawai'i's emerging popular cuisine.

The Japanese

In 1868, Japanese contract workers began arriving in Hawai'i to staff the islands' sugar plantations. Many were skilled farmers, and virtually all had valuable skills and a strong work ethic. Within eight years more than 30,000 Japanese were living in Hawai'i, and by 1924 Hawai'i's ethnic Japanese numbered more than 200,000. About half of Hawai'i's Japanese contract workers remained in the islands, and many brought over Japanese wives.

Most of these Japanese women had been trained by their mothers in Japanese home cooking. Moreover, Japan has a strong food culture. Until quite recently the Japanese were culinary conservatives, preferring their own cuisine above all others. These factors helped Japanese cooking in Hawai'i remain relatively pure. Thus, only a few Japanese dishes evolved into Japanese-Hawai'ian hybrid creations. However, many elements of Japanese cuisine quickly entered Hawai'i's cooking (p. 558).

Already accustomed to eating raw seafood, Hawai'i residents were more than ready to accept sashimi and raw forms of sushi. Similarly, Hawai'i residents accustomed to eating local seaweeds embraced the Japanese seaweeds *hijiki* (hee-jee-kee) and *nori* (noh-ree) with gusto. Tofu, or bean curd—already popularized by the Chinese—became even more popular with the introduction of many Japanese variations such as fried tofu *aburage* (ah-boo-rah-gee) and dried *koridofu* (koh-ree-doh-foo). Fermented soy products, such as *miso* (mee-soh) and *natto* (nah-toe), became Hawai'i staples, as did *edamame* (a-dah-mah-may), or green soybeans. The Japanese stock *dashi* (dah-shee), made by steeping dried seaweed and dried fish flakes in hot water, flavors many Hawai'i soups and stir-fries. Japanese soy sauce, which tastes slightly different from the Chinese product, became Hawai'i's dominant seasoning, to the extent that the Japanese word *shoyu* (sho-yoo) became the Hawai'i term for it.

Among the most important Japanese contributions to Hawai'i's popular cuisine are the introduction of Asian vegetables and the practice of cooking them to a crisp-tender texture. Today Japanese-American truck farmers grow a wide variety of both Asian and European vegetables in Hawai'i. Fresh vegetables such as snow peas, bok choy, and Chinese broccoli typically accompany Hawai'i cuisine main dishes.

As Hawai'ians began assimilating Chinese and Japanese cooking into their foodways, the lines of distinction between the two cuisines began to blur. An example is hekka (p. 694), a Hawai'i created dish that can be called a cross between a stir-fry and sukiyaki. In this preparation, Chinese-style stir-fried meats and vegetables are simmered in a Japanese soy and *dashi* base, bean thread noodles are added, and then the dish is served over rice.

The Koreans

Relative latecomers to Hawai'i, Korean immigrant workers brought their distinctive cooking style to the Hawai'ian Islands in the early 20th century. Korean cooking can be described as a blend of northern Chinese and Japanese cuisines. Korean food culture is strong, and most Koreans are culinary conservatives.

■□ ELEMENTS OF KOREAN CUISINE

FOUNDATION FOODS

principal starch: medium-grain white rice

principal proteins: beef, seafood, soy products

principal produce: cabbages, spinach, turnips

FAVORED SEASONINGS: garlic, ginger, scallions, dried chiles, sesame seeds, sesame oil

PRINCIPAL COOKING MEDIA: soy oil, water

PRIMARY COOKING METHODS: stir-frying, grilling, boiling, poaching

FOOD ATTITUDES: strong food culture, culinary conservatives

Korean immigrants were delighted to discover that Hawai'i ranching provided ample beef, considered a luxury food in Korea. In Hawai'i the most popular style of Korean restaurant cooking is **Korean barbeque.** In this cooking method, which is not true barbeque, thin-sliced beef, or *bul kogi* (bull KOH-kee), and sliced strips of beef short ribs, or *kalbi* (KAHL-bee), are flavored with a soy-based marinade, grilled, and then served with a spicy sesame-soy dip. Korean pickles, especially spicy cabbage kim chee, have become a Hawai'i staple found in every supermarket and often accompany plate lunches (p. 667).

The Filipinos

Filipino immigrants began arriving in Hawai'i around the turn of the 20th century, when the United States annexed the Philippines after the Spanish-American War. Although small in number, Filipino immigrants made a significant mark on Hawai'i's popular cuisine. Blending Spanish, Polynesian, and Southeast Asian foodways, Filipino cooking is a hybrid cuisine known for surprising combinations. Although they have a strong food culture, Filipinos are culinary liberals.

Filipino dishes exhibit the wide range of ingredients and cooking methods implicit in a triple-hybrid cuisine. *Pancit* (pahn-SEET) is an Asian-inspired dish of fried noodles flavored with Spanish chorizo sausage and Polynesian coconut milk. Both chicken and pork are prepared *en adobo* (ehn ah-DOH-boh), simmered in coconut milk with vinegar, black pepper, and bay leaf, after which the sauce is reduced to an almost dry texture with a highly concentrated flavor.

FACTOR 4
Filipino cuisine combines Spanish and Polynesian foodways, reinforcing Hawai'i's Polynesian cuisine roots.

Paella-like Filipino rice dishes mix pork, chicken, and seafood. *Lechon* (lay-CHONE), or Spanish-seasoned suckling pig, is stuffed and spit-roasted. Fish is preserved *en escabeche* (ehn es-kah-BAY-chay), or pickled in a vinaigrette. Filipinos prepare stews and soups that blend Polynesian and European ingredients, such as *pochero* (po-CHAIR-oh), a meat stew that includes bananas, chickpeas, potatoes, and papayas. Filipino cooks use Southeast Asian–style condiments such as a fermented fish paste called *bagoong* (bah-GOONG) and a clear fish sauce called *patis* (pah-TEECE). Spanish-style baked and fried pastries are served as afternoon snacks, and hot chocolate is a favored beverage.

For the most part local ingredients did not significantly alter Filipino cooking in the Hawai'ian Islands. Most Hawai'i Filipinos have eclectic dining habits, enjoying both Hawai'i's popular cuisine and their own traditional fare. Filipino restaurants and food trucks are favorite dining spots throughout the islands.

■□ WORLD WAR II ■ AND POSTWAR DEVELOPMENT

In 1898 Hawai'i was officially annexed to the United States, largely because of its strategic position in the center of the Pacific. Just after 1900 the U.S. military began building a naval base at Pearl Bay, later to be called Pearl Harbor. Before and during World War II, the Hawai'ian Islands welcomed hundreds of thousands of U.S. military personnel and civilian workers. Along with them arrived the popular American national cuisine foods of the day: hamburgers, French fries, and milk shakes; spaghetti with

■□ ELEMENTS OF FILIPINO CUISINE

FOUNDATION FOODS

principal starches: medium-grain rice, wheat noodles, wheat bread

principal proteins: pork, seafood

principal produce: cabbages, tropical tubers, tropical fruits

FAVORED SEASONINGS: bay leaf, black pepper, chiles, fish sauce, coconut

PRINCIPAL COOKING MEDIA: olive oil, lard, soy oil

PRIMARY COOKING METHODS: stir-frying, grilling, stewing

FOOD ATTITUDES: strong food culture, culinary liberals

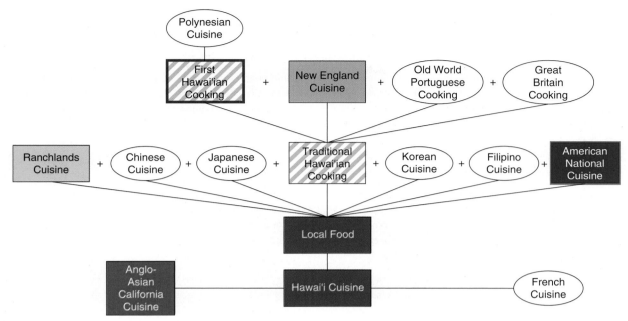

FIGURE 14.23
Development of Local Food and Hawai'i Cuisine.

meat sauce; macaroni salad and potato salad side dishes; and ketchup and brown gravy used as universal sauces.

After the war, faster planes and inexpensive airfare made Hawai'i a popular tourist destination. However, visitors to Hawai'i were coming for sand and sunshine, not for the food. In Hawai'i's newly built resort hotels, American chefs offered the same Continental cuisine served in Manhattan, Los Angeles, and Miami Beach. But in isolated Hawai'i this food was typically made from canned and frozen vegetables and an array of industrially produced convenience foods. A formula hotel *lu'au* was the only regional food the typical visitor experienced.

The stagnation of Hawai'i's cuisine development was at least partially due to the prevailing allocation of agricultural land. In the mid-1900s most was dedicated to large-scale export agriculture, with little thought given to the domestic market. Progress was also dampened by the postwar decline in cooking affecting the rest of the nation. Although local fish, pork, beef, and other protein foods were available and tropical fruit abounded, other types of fresh food had to be imported via air freight, making it prohibitively expensive. Like many Americans of the period, most middle-class Hawai'i residents ate vegetables out of cans—if at all. Because meat, poultry, and fish were plentiful, everyday Hawai'i meals consisted of large protein portions teamed with an even larger amount of starch side dishes.

Despite the lack of fresh produce, throughout the 20th century most of the food made in Hawai'i's private homes and small family restaurants was tasty and boldly seasoned. Hawai'i's multicultural population and freewheeling food attitudes sometimes led to weird culinary combinations, such as spaghetti with a side of kim chee or teriyaki beef served with macaroni salad.

As the 20th century wore on, Hawai'i's mixed-up, polyethnic popular cooking gradually coalesced into a definitive cuisine. Because this cooking style was unknown outside the region, and unrecognized within, no one even bothered to give it a name.

◼ LOCAL
◻ FOOD
◼

The American food revolution reached Hawai'i a little later than the mainland. By the late 1970s, growing awareness of cuisine and increased regional pride resulted in general recognition of Hawai'i's popular cooking as a true cuisine. Nonetheless, there was both confusion and indecision about what to call it. The term *Hawai'ian cuisine* correctly refers to First Hawai'ian and *kama'aina* cooking. This new, spontaneous style was far more complex and inclusive. Like modern Hawai'i itself, this new cooking style reflected a liberal outlook and didn't take itself too seriously. It wasn't prepared in high-end restaurants or tourist hotels but in private homes and small food-service operations where only locals ate. Although no one knows who first coined the term, by the 1980s Hawai'i's popular cuisine was called **local food.**

Local food is constantly changing and follows no rules. However, local food can be defined by a number of characteristics: colliding cuisines, a "no rules" attitude, the use of preserved foods, rice as the principal starch, and a preference for fish.

FACTOR 4
Local food is the product of Hawai'i's many waves of immigration.

CHARACTERISTICS OF LOCAL FOOD

Colliding Cuisines

In Hawai'i seven major food cultures came together in a little more than a hundred years. As a result, Hawai'i's cooking is more than a melting pot—it could be described as a whirling blender. Culinary assimilation occurred so quickly that by the middle of the 20th century, many Hawai'i residents were unaware of the ethnic origins of many of their favorite dishes. Just as people of different ethnic origins met, married, and had children who considered themselves "local," so did recipes traded across the back fence adapt and change according to the ingredients available and the taste of the cook, becoming part of the local food repertoire.

No Rules

Local food has absolutely no rules. When preparing local food, Hawai'i residents have no problem mixing foods of vastly different ethnic origins. Hawai'I residents flavor Japanese teriyaki sauce with pineapple juice, and roll American smoked salmon or canned tuna into *norimaki* sushi. Why not garnish a Portuguese sausage sandwich with Korean kim chee? Or serve an American hamburger over Japanese rice with brown gravy and Thai Sriracha sauce? The philosophy is simple: if it tastes good, do it.

Preserved Foods

A legacy of the islands' history as provisioning port of call, Hawai'i residents use a wide array of foods preserved by canning, drying, and curing. These foods may be Western or Asian in origin.

Ham, bacon, sausages, dried beef, and corned beef are used in soups and stews and are often eaten as main-dish foods. Canned meats such as Spam and Vienna sausages are defining ingredients. New England pilot crackers soaked in sweetened condensed milk—yet another preserved food—are a favorite snack. Softened in custard and topped with sugar, baked pilot crackers become a tasty dessert pudding.

Hawai'i residents of Asian origin introduced an entire array of preserved foods, such as canned bamboo shoots and water chestnuts, pickled vegetables, and dried mushrooms and seaweed. Although many of these foods are now grown on the islands and, thus, are available fresh at reasonable prices, preserved varieties have become part of the local food tradition and their use endures.

Rice as the Principal Starch

Hawai'i residents eat more rice than any other Americans, eclipsing even Louisianans and Lowcountry Southerners in their fondness for the grain. Rice is the foundation of virtually every local food meal, including breakfast. Rice noodles (called "long rice") and rice flour dishes are popular as well.

Hawai'i residents prefer a medium-grain white rice that cooks up firm-grained yet sticky enough to cling together. The most popular brand is Calrose, grown in California from Japanese seed stock. Local food rice is cooked in the Asian manner by washing it thoroughly before cooking and then pan-steaming it in water with no salt or fat. Virtually all Hawai'i kitchens, both domestic and commercial, are equipped with automatic rice cookers.

A Preference for Fish

Hawai'i residents eat more than twice as much fish as mainland Americans; many eat at least one fish meal per day. Grilling, pan-frying, and sautéing are typical methods of cooking fish. Instead of purchasing expensive tuna, snapper, and billfish, many Hawai'i residents prefer local reef fish for everyday meals. Today much of Hawai'i's fish and seafood is imported, including aquacultured salmon from the Pacific Northwest and shrimp from Asia and South America.

Although Hawai'i residents had been enjoying diced, seasoned raw fish since the islands' earliest habitation, in the 1970s fish prepared in this manner became known as **poke**, meaning "cut into small pieces." Served as an appetizer or snack, *poke* appears in many variations throughout the islands. Home cooks prepare family recipes; restaurants create signature variations. Seafood shops may offer more than 20 varieties of *poke* to suit every taste. Today *poke* may be made from both raw and cooked seafood. Fried *poke*, in which the diced fish is formed into a patty and sautéed, serves as a transition dish for diners unsure about trying raw seafood.

Japanese sushi and sashimi have become Hawai'i staples. Many of these preparations are purely Japanese, whereas others have been modified with Hawai'ian ingredients. For example, Spam *musubi* is a rectangle of sushi rice topped with Spam and garnished with *nori* seaweed (Figure 14.24).

FIGURE 14.24
Spam *musubi*. Courtesy of David Haynes

FIGURE 14.25

This typical Hawai'i plate lunch includes two scoops of rice, teriyaki chicken, kim chee, and macaroni salad. Courtesy of David Haynes

The Plate Lunch

Because five of Hawai'i's seven food cultures are not bread-based, many Hawai'i residents prefer to eat a hot lunch served on a plate rather than grab a sandwich. Catering to the lunchtime crowds at Hawai'i's plantations and food-processing plants, entrepreneurs began outfitting panel trucks with woks, rice cookers, charcoal grills, and other equipment needed to make the most popular local food dishes. These vendors created the Hawai'i **plate lunch,** comprising a local food main course, steamed white rice, and one or more side dishes—all served on a disposable plate (Figure 14.25).

In any plate lunch, rice is the primary starch, a given element ordered by the number of portion scoops desired. The two-scoop lunch is standard; a three-scoop portion is available for the really hungry. Most plate lunches feature a single main dish, but some come with more than one protein item. The ethnicity of plate lunch main dishes varies according to cook and clientele, with Chinese-style stir-fries, Korean barbeque, Japanese-inspired "teri" dishes (discussed shortly), American fried fish or spaghetti and meat sauce, Filipino adobos, and hybrid dishes such as shoyu chicken and hekka (p. 694) among the favorites. In addition to rice and a main dish, a plate lunch always includes mayonnaise-based macaroni salad or potato salad. Many operations offer brown gravy as an optional topping. Some plate lunches are garnished with a Japanese salad or Korean kim chee.

Hawai'ian Barbeque

Although *imu*-baked foods constitute the true barbeque of Hawai'i, in the local food cuisine style "barbeque" means food grilled over coals. Two of local food's contributing food cultures have long traditions of such cooking, and their most popular grilled foods have become part of the local food repertoire.

Teri is local slang for **teriyaki,** a Japanese cooking method in which food is both marinated and basted with a mixture of soy sauce, rice wine, and sugar. Main ingredients for teri include fish, shrimp, beef, chicken, or even tofu (bean curd). Food for teri may be fabricated into thin slices or cubes and threaded onto bamboo skewers, cut into hefty steaks, or even ground and formed into patties. Hawai'i local food teri is quite different than Japanese teriyaki: it's sweeter, more highly seasoned, and finished with a thick, glazy sauce. Teri is an important element in both plate lunches and *saimin* (p. 668).

A later addition to the local food repertoire, Korean barbeque has become widely popular. The char-grilled meat is served with rice and kim chee.

Pupu

The Hawai'ian word *pupu* means "small round object." When European settlers introduced the custom of serving hors d'oeuvres—in particular, canapés—at cocktail parties, Hawai'ians used the word *pupu* to describe the little round finger foods. By extension the term **pupu** now refers to all finger foods, no matter the shape.

By the 1950s, all of Hawai'i's cultural groups had embraced the idea of enjoying hors d'oeuvres after work, before dinner, and at parties. Each contributing cuisine had its own finger foods: Portuguese sausages, Chinese dim sum, Japanese sushi and rumaki (p. 684), Korean mandoo dumplings (p. 686), and Filipino lumpia spring rolls are just a few examples of foods that became Hawai'i's *pupu.*

In the early 20th century, California restaurant entrepreneurs adopted the Hawai'ian term *pupu* to describe an appetizer sampler presented with a tabletop hibachi grill. Many of Hawai'i's restaurants followed this trend, and today the *pupu* platter has become part of Hawai'i's restaurant repertoire. Today, Hawai'i residents continue to enjoy a variety of *pupu* from local and world cuisines.

LOCAL TALK

In addition to uniting seven disparate food cultures, Hawai'i's multiple waves of immigration also brought together seven languages, creating a virtual Tower of Babel where residents frequently struggled to understand one another. Although today virtually all Hawai'i residents speak standard English, nonetheless everyday conversation is peppered with "local talk," fragments of pidgin dialect that combines Hawai'ian words and language structure, English slang, and a smattering of Japanese and Chinese terms. Here are some food-related local talk terms:

broke da mout': great food

bussum out: share your food

da kine: literally "the kind"; when referring to food, typically means "good" or "appropriate"

grind: to eat

grinds: food

ono-licious: doubly delicious

ono-ono-licious: extremely delicious

pau hana: literally "done work"; describes after-work happy hour drinks and snacks

pupu: literally "shell," or by extension "small round thing"; refers to hors d'oeuvres or appetizers

---

Snack Foods

Hawai'i residents love to eat on the go, frequently patronizing outdoor food stands, food trucks, food courts, and convenience stores. Today these operations serve much the same fast food found in other American culinary regions; however, most also offer a variety of special snacks unique to Hawai'i.

■□ HAWAI'I REGIONAL
■ CUISINE

By the 1960s, high labor costs and a changing world economy spelled the end of Hawai'i's sugar and pineapple industries. Large-scale growers had gradually shifted production to Asia, South America, and the Caribbean to benefit from inexpensive labor. In response, Hawai'i's economy turned from agriculture to tourism.

Technological advances after World War II had already made fast, low-cost air travel widely available. During the Korean and Vietnam Wars, many Americans were stationed in or passed through the Hawai'ian Islands, and they brought home glowing reports of Hawai'i's pristine beaches and balmy weather. The combination of cheap airfares and a booming economy made Hawai'i an attainable vacation destination for the American middle classes. In the 1970s international hotel and resort chains opened world-class properties catering to a flood of new tourists.

Although the weather and accommodations were spectacular, the cuisine offered to Hawai'i's tourists was not. Hawai'i residents continued to develop and enjoy local food, but the average tourist was not adventurous enough to seek it out. For the most part, hotel restaurants were still serving up "Continental from a can," with a commercialized *lu'au* featured on weekends.

Finally, in the late 1980s Hawai'i's restaurant cuisine began to change for the better. With the departure of sugarcane and pineapple, thousands of acres of prime farmland lay vacant and ready for other crops. By this time tourists had become more sophisticated in their food preferences and were demanding a more exciting dining experience. Hotels began recruiting innovative chefs to enliven their restaurant menus, and both local and imported talent responded to the challenge. In addition, chef-entrepreneurs began opening freestanding restaurants. These chefs supported the islands' new generation of farmers, featuring locally grown produce and locally raised meats on their menus. To these Hawai'i-raised products they added ingredients, seasonings, and techniques sourced from around the globe. Many researched First Hawai'ian cooking and traditional Hawai'ian cuisine dishes, reviving old recipes and cooking methods. These developments set the stage for the birth of a new cuisine.

FACTOR 5
In the late 20th century, tourism created renewed interest in fine cuisine.

HAWAI'I'S SNACKS

Saimin

This noodle soup is Hawai'i's premier comfort food. Chinese wheat-flour noodles are simmered in poultry broth or *dashi* stock, then topped with Chinese roast pork, Japanese fish cake, teri, or Spam. *Saimin* is garnished with bean sprouts, scallions, and fresh herbs, such as cilantro or Thai basil.

Musubi

Similar to sushi, Japanese-style compressed rice cakes are topped with savory items such as katsu pork or chicken, cooked shrimp, or teriyaki-grilled Spam, and then wrapped with nori seaweed.

Manapua

Cantonese-style steamed yeast buns filled with Chinese roast pork are served warm or at room temperature.

Mochi

Sweet cakes of rice-flour dough filled with sweetened red bean paste or fruit pastes are steamed and served at room temperature.

Crack Seed

Preserved fruits and candied seeds have flavors ranging from spicy-sweet to salty-sour.

Shave Ice

Specially fabricated shaved ice is topped with a variety of fruit-flavored syrups and served in a paper cone.

FIGURE 14.26
Chef Sam Choy and Chef Roy Yamaguchi. Courtesy Sam Choy and Roy Yamaguchi

In 1992 a group of Hawai'i resident chefs banded together to define and promote Hawai'i's new style of cooking. Sam Choy, Roger Dikon, Amy Ferguson Ota, Mark Ellman, Beverly Gannon, Jean-Marie Josselin, George Mavrothalassitis, Peter Merriman, Philippe Padovani, Gary Strehl, Alan Wong, and Roy Yamaguchi were the founding twelve chefs of Hawai'i regional cuisine, a fresh and lively cooking style intended to reflect the true spirit of the islands (Figure 14.26).

Because this cuisine style has existed for little more than 20 years, it's too early to identify a list of defining dishes. However, certain characteristics are recognized as markers of Hawai'i regional cuisine: strong First Hawai'ian roots, the use of locally raised ingredients, pan-Asian flavors and techniques, and Euro-American techniques and presentations.

For a list of noteworthy Hawai'i regional cuisine restaurants, go to this book's companion website.

MACADAMIA NUTS

Macadamia trees are native to Australia, but appreciation of macadamia nuts as a food did not occur until the trees were introduced to Hawai'i in the late 1800s. Although these tasty nuts were embraced as a local delicacy, macadamias were not commercially cultivated until the 1920s. Today Hawai'i is one of the world's largest producers of macadamia nuts. Most expensive of all premium nuts, macadamias are prized for their crisp, somewhat waxy texture and rich, buttery flavor. Because they're similar in texture, macadamia nuts are often substituted for kukui nuts in traditional Hawai'ian cuisine.

THE FUTURE OF HAWAI'I'S CUISINES

In a region whose main industry is tourism, the economic recession that began in 2008 hit hard. During this period, vacation travel to Hawai'i, never inexpensive, became beyond the reach of many middle-class tourists. The resulting job losses meant less local business as well. As a result, revenues plunged in Hawai'i's hotels and restaurants. Without a broad and sophisticated customer base, Hawai'i regional cuisine chefs will find it difficult to further the development of their nascent cuisine. For high-end restaurants serving Hawai'i regional cuisine, the future depends on restored economic prosperity.

More important to the evolution of Hawai'i regional cuisine and local food is the renewed use of Hawai'i's agricultural lands. Hawai'i still has thousands of acres of dormant farmland that could support specialty crops. Unfortunately, water allocation remains a point of contention; increased residential development threatens the water supply to traditional agricultural lands. To attain economic success, Hawai'i's specialty farmers traditionally needed to export their products as well as sell them domestically. This remains a problem because of high transportation costs. In addition, the USDA requires pest quarantine procedures before accepting Hawai'i produce into the U.S. mainland, adding to production costs. Instead of focusing on the export market, today's growers hope to increase local demand for fine food products, a goal that can be achieved only by raising the standard of Hawai'i's popular cooking.

Hawai'i's entrepreneur farmers are experimenting with new products. Hawai'i's sloping mountainsides are proving ideal for dairy goats, and Hawai'i goat cheese is an upcoming product. Locally raised lamb, chickens, and ducks are becoming available. Herbs, in particular lavender, have both culinary and cosmetic uses. In addition to pineapples, Hawai'i is now an important producer of a variety of tropical fruits, including mangosteens, jackfruits, papayas, rambutans, lychees, longans, and star fruits. The availability of fine, locally grown food products is sure to enhance both Hawai'i regional cuisine and local food.

Another factor in Hawai'i's evolving cuisine is ongoing immigration. As new cultural groups arrive in the islands, Hawai'i's liberal culinary outlook makes it likely that their unique foodways will be embraced and assimilated.

Finally, growing cultural pride and awareness among residents of both *kama'aina* and First Hawai'ian ancestry may lead to a renaissance of traditional Hawai'ian cuisine. Accomplished chefs and home cooks alike may rise to the challenge of bringing this venerable cooking style out of the museum and into the mainstream of fine dining.

CHARACTERISTICS OF HAWAI'I REGIONAL CUISINE

Strong First Hawai'ian Roots

First Hawai'ian foodways play an important role in Hawai'i regional cuisine. Literally returning to their roots, Hawai'i regional cuisine chefs feature tropical tubers in many dishes. Taro root is boiled and lightly mashed to make an updated—and more widely palatable—version of *poi*, often formed into cakes and pan-fried. Raw taro root is thin-sliced or julienned and then deep-fried to make taro chips or taro baskets to hold stir-fried seafood or salads. Breadfruit, sweet potatoes, and true yams are used in similar ways. Leafy vegetables are used in traditional and new ways. Cooked taro leaves are used in salads, as a side vegetable, and as an edible food wrapper. Ti leaves also wrap foods for steaming or pit roasting. Coconut milk appears in savory sauces and desserts. Similarly, bananas and plantains have sweet and savory applications. Many Hawai'i regional cuisine savory dishes have a hint of sweetness from sugar or sugarcane juice. Kukui nuts are a frequent garnish.

Locally Raised Ingredients

As in other modern American regional cuisines, Hawai'i regional cuisine is strongly ingredient driven and features locally raised products whenever possible. Hawai'i has become known for specialty agriculture (Figure 14.27), particularly Maui sweet onions, Asian herbs and microgreens, purple-fleshed Okinawa sweet potatoes, watercress, radicchio, and a variety of berries.

Hawai'i's aquaculture took off in the 1990s. In addition to the islands' traditional fishery, Hawai'i's chefs now have access to aquaculture products such as Kauai shrimp and Kona cold lobster. The Tamashiro Fish Market stands out among many sources for fine seafood, supplying chefs and home cooks alike.

Coffee grown on the island of Kona is known worldwide for its robust flavor. Today Kona coffee production is in the hands of about six hundred small, independent farms, and Kona coffee is rare and expensive. Used not only as a beverage, Kona coffee is also an ingredient in world-class desserts.

Hawai'ian chocolate is among the newest of local products. Unlike shade-grown cacao, in Hawai'i cacao trees are grown in full sunlight and are extremely prolific producers. Although the beans are harvested and aged in Hawai'i, most are shipped to California for processing into the final premium chocolate product. However, several producers process Hawai'i-grown chocolate preferred by Hawai'i regional cuisine chefs to make imaginative desserts and confections.

FIGURE 14.27
Hawai'i produces herbs for culinary and cosmetic use. Shen Armstrong/ Shutterstock

Pan-Asian Flavors and Techniques

Hawai'i regional cuisine chefs use ingredients and techniques from all over Asia. Although the cuisine's primary flavors are derived from Chinese and Japanese immigrant ingredients, Hawai'i's new chefs borrow freely from Thai, Malaysian, Indonesian, and Indian pantries, adding fire and spice to their dishes. Hawai'i's chefs often add unusual twists to traditional Asian dishes—for example, stacking squares of sushi rice with cooked seafood or filling spring rolls with sweet dessert fillings. Macadamia nuts are featured in savory dishes, such as macadamia-crusted fish, and in sweet desserts. Tropical fruits such as lychees, mangoes, papayas, kiwifruit, and passion fruit grace Hawai'i's dessert menus.

In Hawai'i regional cuisine, stir-frying is a prominent technique for composed dishes and is the most important cooking method for vegetables. A quick tumble in searing-hot oil leaves Asian and European vegetables crisp-tender and vividly colored. Steaming is also favored for vegetables and is a perfect method to showcase fresh local seafood.

Euro-American Techniques and Presentations

Most Hawai'i regional cuisine chefs are classically trained, having mastered French and American cuisines before choosing to specialize. Thus, French sauces and French cooking and baking techniques are a vital part of the cuisine. The saucier's arts are an important element: demi-glace and raw butter emulsion sauces add richness and depth to Hawai'i regional cuisine dishes. Strong American influence makes grilling and smoke roasting among the most popular cooking methods. Grilled meats, fish, and vegetables figure prominently on restaurant menus.

Hawai'i regional cuisine is always presented with flair. Artistic plate arrangements combine striking juxtapositions of color and texture and use architectural layering of food elements. Brilliantly colored tropical fruits and edible flowers add visual interest, and black seaweeds and black sesame seeds add dramatic contrast. Banana leaves and ti leaves are used as plate liners, creating interesting presentations.

☐ TABLE 14.1 HAWAI'I CUISINES DEFINING DISHES

ITEM NAME	HISTORY	DOMINANT INGREDIENTS AND METHOD	MORE
INAMONA (ee-nah-MOH-nah)	*Inamona* is served as a table seasoning to be added to traditional Hawai'ian foods at the discretion of the diner.	Kukui nuts, red alaea salt, and fresh red chiles are pounded to a coarse paste in a mortar.	
LIMU (LEE-moo)	*Limu* is a generic term for edible seaweed. Hawai'i's many varieties of edible seaweed were a source of valuable nutrients for precontact First Hawai'ians.	Seaweed is served raw or lightly cooked and chilled as a relish or side dish salad. Modern *limu* salads are usually tossed with a citrus dressing.	*Limu* may be embellished with other raw or cooked vegetables.
LOMI LOMI FISH (loh-mee LOH-mee)	By the late 1700s European and American merchant ships were transporting salt-cured salmon from the Pacific Northwest to Hawai'i, where it became a favored food.	Salt-cured fish, usually salmon, is pulled into shreds and tossed with citrus juice, ginger, scallions, tomatoes, and chipped or shaved ice. Served as an appetizer, *lomi lomi* is often bedded on salad greens or seaweed salad.	The Hawai'ian term *lomi lomi* means "to massage," referring to the action of pulling the fish into shreds.
POKE (POH-kay or POH-kee)	Although seasoned raw fish dates back to precontact First Hawai'ian cooking, the local food dish *poke* emerged around 1970.	Raw fish is cut into small dice or thin slices and seasoned with soy sauce and chopped seaweed. Additional seasonings include ginger, citrus juice, and *inamona*.	To make fried poke, the seasoned, diced fish is formed into patties, breaded, and pan-fried golden outside, raw or very rare inside.
OPIHI (oh-PEE-hee)	*Opihi* are Hawai'ian limpets, univalves similar to abalone but much smaller. They are a traditional First Hawai'ian food.	Loosen the meat from the shell with a spoon and serve raw with lemon wedges. Raw *opihi* meat may be diced and used in *poke*. Alternatively, *opihi* may be cooked in their shells on a charcoal grill and served with lemon and melted butter.	Because *opihi* cling tenaciously to surf-pounded rocks, collecting them can be a dangerous activity.
LU'AU (LOO-ahw)	*Lu'au*, meaning "taro leaves," is the name of the taro leaf vegetable and, confusingly, also the name of the traditional Hawai'ian feast.	To make the dish *lu'au*, taro leaves are parboiled, chopped, and simmered in coconut milk.	Fish or shellfish may be poached in the sauce to transform this side dish into an entrée.
POI (POY)	The Hawai'ian staff of life, *poi* is technically a thick paste made from any tropical tuber. Today *poi* is made with taro root.	Taro root is peeled, boiled soft, and pounded in a mortar. The paste is blended with water and allowed to steep, drawing off any bitter flavor. The water is strained off and the *poi* is served immediately or refrigerated. For fermented *poi*, the paste is allowed to age at a warm temperature one to several days, depending on the degree of acidity desired.	"One-finger" *poi* is thick; "two-finger" *poi* is medium consistency; and "three-finger" *poi* is thin.
SWEET POTATOES	Sweet potatoes are a First Hawai'ian canoe plant.	Steamed, oven-baked, or pit-baked, sweet potatoes in their jackets are a Hawai'i staple and are commonly served as a side starch.	
KALUA PIG (kah-LOO-ah)	The centerpiece of the *lu'au*, or traditional Hawai'ian feast, the kalua pig may range from a 25-lb. suckling piglet to a 100-lb. hog big enough to feed a large crowd.	The pig is cleaned and seasoned with salt, ginger, and other optional aromatics and spices, its cavity is filled with blazing hot stones, and the entire carcass is lowered into an *imu*, or fire pit, lined with hot stones, leaves, and seaweed. Covered with more leaves and seaweed, the pig slowly roasts in the smoky steam.	

(continued)

◻ **TABLE 14.1 HAWAI'I CUISINES DEFINING DISHES** *(continued)*

ITEM NAME	HISTORY	DOMINANT INGREDIENTS AND METHOD	MORE
HAUPIA (ha-OO-pee-ah)	First Hawai'ians combined three canoe plant foods (coconut, sugarcane, and Hawai'ian arrowroot) to make this pudding.	Coconut milk is sweetened with cane sugar and cooked into a firm pudding. Traditionally thickened with *pia*, or Hawai'ian "arrowroot," today *haupia* is usually thickened with cornstarch. Cut into squares and served cold on a ti leaf, *haupia* is a favored dessert at *lu'aus*. Contemporary chefs often enrich the custard mix with cream.	The firm custard squares may be breaded and fried golden to make a hot dessert.
PUPU (POO-poo)	Meaning "shell," or by extension "small round thing," the Hawai'ian word *pupu* has come to mean "finger food" or "appetizer." The Hawai'ian name and concept of *pupu* were hijacked by 1950s American-Polynesian restaurants such as Trader Vic's (p. 561).	In Hawai'i, *pupu* covers a broad category of finger foods and light dishes. Raw fish dishes, such as *poke*, sushi, and sashimi, are favored *pupu*. A restaurant *pupu* platter consists of a number of Hawai'ian-style and Asian finger foods rewarmed at the table over a miniature hibachi grill.	Popular hibachi *pupu* include Asian dumplings, rumaki, Chinese barbeque spareribs, and fried wontons.
HAWAI'I'S SUSHI	In addition to serving classic Japanese sushi items, Hawai'i's sushi chefs have developed purely Hawai'i sushi creations.	*Cone Sushi:* sushi rice and assorted seasonings are wrapped in a cone of fried *aburage*, a spongy tofu sheet that crisps and puffs when it contacts hot oil. *Canned Tuna Maki:* this lunch truck special features canned tuna fish, dried shrimp flakes, pickled daikon radish, and sushi rice in a nori-wrapped roll. *Spam Musubi:* sushi rice is topped with a slice of teriyaki broiled Spam and a nori seaweed sash.	
PORTUGUESE BEAN SOUP	This hearty soup is a legacy of late 19th-century Portuguese settlers.	Red, pinto, or navy beans are simmered in a stock made from smoked ham hocks or pork neck bones. Onions, carrots, celery, turnips, and other aromatic vegetables are added along with tomatoes, potatoes, and Portuguese chauriço sausage.	
STIR-FRY	Featured in Chinese, Japanese, and Korean cuisines, this fast, high-heat cooking method inspired a number of local food dishes and has become a generic term for dishes cooked in a wok.	Uniformly fabricated vegetables are quickly cooked by tossing in hot vegetable oil in a wok, then removed. Similarly fabricated meat, poultry, or seafood is then tossed in the hot oil along with aromatics such as garlic, ginger, and scallions. The vegetables and meat are then finished in a pan sauce made from stock and Asian seasonings and thickened with a cornstarch slurry.	Hawai'i's stir-fries are usually served over rice rather than separately from the rice, as is done in Asia.
TERIYAKI DISHES	Local food cooks adapted Japanese teriyaki to suit Hawai'i residents' taste preferences.	Meat, fish, or poultry is grilled with a sweet glaze of soy sauce, sugar, and mirin rice wine. In Hawai'i teriyaki is often heavily glazed and served with an additional, separate teriyaki sauce.	"Teri" is popular lunch truck fare.

☐ TABLE 14.1 HAWAI'I CUISINES DEFINING DISHES (continued)

ITEM NAME	HISTORY	DOMINANT INGREDIENTS AND METHOD	MORE
KOREAN BARBEQUE	In response to cold Korean winters, a small charcoal grill, or *hibachi*, was brought to the table both for warmth and to cook food.	The most popular meat choices, thin-sliced beef rib steak (*bul kogi*) or beef short ribs (*kalbi*), are soy-marinated and charred on the grill along with mushrooms and onions. The meat is served with steamed rice, various dipping sauces, and lettuce leaves to wrap it. Accompaniments include a selection of vegetable salads and kim chee, a spicy pickled cabbage.	Diners grill meat to their preferred doneness.
ADOBO DISHES	Portuguese and Spanish settlers learned that meats cooked in spicy, acidic sauces kept longer in hot climates. Filipino cooks added coconut milk.	Pork or chicken is simmered in vinegar and coconut milk with garlic, bay leaf, and black pepper until the meat is very tender and the sauce is reduced almost to a glaze.	Adobo is served with rice.
THE PLATE LUNCH	In the early 20th century, entrepreneurs catered to field workers and canning factory workers by providing hot lunches cooked on site in mobile kitchens set up in carts and, later, in trucks. Served on paper plates, their fare became known as a "plate lunch."	A Hawai'i plate lunch always includes "two scoops and a salad," meaning two rounded foodservice scoops of steamed white rice and a scoop of mayonnaise-bound macaroni or potato salad. The choice of main dish is as diverse as Hawai'i's cultural melting pot; options include shoyu chicken; teriyaki beef; Korean kalbi and kim chee; a chicken, beef, or pork stir-fry; or adobo pork.	
THE COOKED BREAKFAST	British settlers introduced the custom of eating a substantial hot breakfast. Various immigrant groups modified the British breakfast to suit their own tastes.	Steamed or fried rice is topped with fried eggs and accompanied with ham, bacon, Spam, or Portuguese sausage. Fresh fruit is a favored garnish.	Served throughout the day, a *loco moco* features steamed rice, a fried hamburger patty, and a fried egg covered in a thick brown gravy.
RAW SEAFOOD DISHES	Hawai'i cuisine continues the Polynesian custom of serving fresh seafood raw, adding the Japanese sashimi tradition and the European discovery of raw seafood in tartares and carpaccios.	With dishes such as aquacultured oysters on the half shell, sliced raw snapper tossed with seaweed, and a seared-on-the-outside/raw-on-the-inside tuna steak, Hawai'i regional cuisine encompasses the entire East-West spectrum of raw seafood preparations.	Hawai'i's chefs embellish local food *poke* and Japanese sashimi with tropical flavors and New World spices.
COCONUT DISHES	Coconut was one of the most important First Hawai'ian canoe plants.	Coconut milk and cream are the base of savory and sweet sauces, as well as adding a subtle flavor to soups of all kinds. Grated coconut meat is used as a filling and a coating. Coconut water is a poaching medium and flavors rice. Coconut custards and confections are popular.	Coconut-flavored soups and appetizers may be served in coconut shells.
TROPICAL FRUITS	European explorers introduced fruit cultivars from other tropical areas.	Used in both sweet and savory dishes, indigenous and imported tropical fruits play a starring role in the new Hawai'i cuisine. Pineapples, passion fruit, guavas, bananas, mangoes, papayas, mountain apples, kiwifruit, atemoyas, lychees, rambutans, and jackfruits are among the fruits used in both sweet and savory dishes.	

■ □ ■ STUDY QUESTIONS

1. Draw a map of the Pacific Rim, showing the west coasts of North and South America and the east coasts of Australia and Asia. Include the Polynesian Triangle, labeling the Hawai'ian Islands placed in their proper position.

2. Describe the topography of the Hawai'ian Islands and explain how the islands' topography creates several different climate zones.

3. Explain why the Hawai'i culinary region has no indigenous people and recount the story of Hawai'i's settlement by Polynesian colonists.

4. Discuss the cooking of the First Hawai'ians, including ways in which they prepared canoe plant foods and used special cooking methods.

5. Name the societal group that resulted from early British/American settlers' contact with First Hawai'ian nobility and describe the traditional Hawai'ian cuisine they developed. Include in your discussion at least five traditional Hawai'ian dishes.

6. Discuss Hawai'i's agriculture "then and now." Include Hawai'i's traditional cash crops and modern specialty agricultural products.

7. List in order the five successive ethnic groups that arrived in Hawai'i after British/American first contact. List the elements of each group's cuisine and explain the impact of each group's foodways on Hawai'i's popular cuisine.

8. Describe local food. How did this cuisine develop? When was it first recognized? Include in your description at least five local food dishes.

9. Discuss the birth of Hawai'i regional cuisine and describe its characteristics.

10. Develop a dinner menu for a Hawai'i regional cuisine restaurant comprising five appetizers, six entrées, and four desserts.

Big Island Lemongrass Seafood Soup
with Lotus Root Chips

yield: 1 (10-fl.-oz.) appetizer serving
(multiply × 4 for classroom turnout; adjust equipment sizes accordingly)

MASTER RECIPE

production		costing only
1 Tbsp.	peanut oil	1/2 fl. oz.
3	Manila or other small clams, cleaned and soaked	3 each
1 Tbsp.	minced ginger	1/4 oz. a.p.
3	(36–40 ct.) white shrimp, peeled, deveined, and halved lengthwise	1 1/4 oz. a.p.
1 1/4 oz.	bay scallops	1 1/4 oz. a.p.
1 1/4 c.	Lemongrass Seafood Broth	1/4 recipe
1/2 oz.	fresh or reconstituted* thin rice noodles, cut in 2" lengths	1/4 oz. a.p.
1/2 oz.	snow peas, strings removed, julienne	1/2 oz. a.p.
1/4 oz.	fresh enoki mushrooms, ends trimmed	1/3 oz. a.p.
tt	fresh lime juice	1/6 [63 ct.] lime
tt	kosher salt	1/16 oz.
1	cocktail napkin	1 each
1 Tbsp.	very thin diagonal-sliced scallion	1/16 bunch a.p.
1 sprig	fresh cilantro, leaves pulled apart into bits	1/20 bunch a.p.
1 tsp.	peeled, fine-julienne red bell pepper	1/4 oz. a.p.
3 to 5	Lotus Root Chips	1/8 recipe

service turnout:

1. Finish the soup:
   a. Heat a 10" sauté pan, add the oil, and then add the clams, ginger, shrimp, and scallops in that order. Sauté a few seconds, tossing to coat the seafood with oil and seasonings.
   b. Add the Lemongrass Seafood Broth and rice noodles. Bring to the boil, check to make sure the clams have opened, and then add the snow peas and mushrooms.
   c. Correct the seasoning, adding lime juice and salt only if needed.
2. Plate the dish:
   a. Use tongs to place the noodles and seafood in a hot 12-oz. soup cup.
   b. Pour in the broth.
   c. Place a cocktail napkin on the left side of a cool 9" oval plate and place the soup cup on it.
   d. Sprinkle the soup with scallion, cilantro, and red bell pepper.
   e. Arrange the Lotus Root Chips on the plate to the right of the soup cup.

*To reconstitute dried rice noodles, place them in a bowl and pour boiling water over them. Soak as little as 1 minute, or longer if necessary, until the noodles soften to al dente. Drain and rinse with cool water, then drain again.

COMPONENT RECIPE
LEMONGRASS SEAFOOD BROTH

yield: 5 c.

production		costing only
1/2 oz. or	frozen chopped or fresh	1/2 oz. or 5 oz.
6 stalks	lemongrass	
2 Tbsp.	peanut oil	1 fl. oz.
1/2 oz.	minced ginger	1/3 oz. a.p.
tt	chopped fresh Asian red chile*	1/4 oz. a.p.
1/2 tsp.	black peppercorns	1/16 oz.
2 c.	Shellfish Stock	1/8 recipe
2 c.	Poultry Stock	1/8 recipe
1 Tbsp.	instant *dashi* granules	1/4 oz.
2 c.	water	n/c
6	fresh or frozen Kaffir lime leaves**	1/4 oz.
tt	sugar	1/2 oz.
tt	kosher salt, optional	1/8 oz.

preparation:
1. If necessary, fabricate the lemongrass:
   a. Trim off the root ends and about 3" of the tips of the fresh lemongrass stalks.
   b. Peel off the coarse outer layers until you reach the core, a pliable central stalk that can be easily pierced with a fingernail.
   c. Smash the lemongrass cores with the flat of a knife, and chop them coarse.
2. Prepare the broth:
   a. Heat a nonreactive saucepan, heat the oil, and add the ginger, chile, and peppercorns. Sauté a few seconds only.
   b. Add the Shellfish Stock, Poultry Stock, *dashi*, water, lime leaves, and lemongrass. Bring to the boil, reduce the heat, and simmer briskly 10 minutes, until the flavors are melded.
   c. Strain the broth, pressing on the solids before discarding them.
   d. Taste the broth, and balance the flavor with sugar and more salt (only if needed).

holding: open-pan cool and refrigerate in a freshly sanitized, non-reactive covered container up to 5 days

*If you are unsure of the chiles' hotness, add a little at a time; this soup should be spicy-hot, but not so hot as to be inedible.

**If Kaffir lime leaves are unavailable, substitute 3 Tbsp. minced lime zest.

COMPONENT RECIPE
LOTUS ROOT CHIPS

yield: approx. 36 chips

production		costing only
12 oz.	lotus root	12 oz. a.p.
as needed	frying compound or peanut oil	% used
tt	fine salt	1/16 oz.

preparation:
1. Fabricate the lotus root:
   a. Have ready a bowl of ice water.
   b. Peel the lotus root and trim the ends. Using an electric slicer, mandoline, or sharp knife, cut the lotus root into even 1/8" slices.
   c. Immediately place the slices in the ice water and soak at least 1 hour.
2. Mise en place:
   a. Preheat a fryer or heat frying oil in a large pan on the stove to 400°F.
   b. Have ready a hotel pan lined with paper towels.
3. Fry the lotus root slices:
   a. Blot the lotus root slices completely dry on a clean towel.
   b. Deep-fry the slices, a few at a time, until light golden.
   c. Drain them on the paper towels.
   d. Season with salt while still hot.

holding: store at cool room temperature and low humidity in a tightly sealed plastic container up to 1 week

---

RECIPE VARIATION

Hot and Fragrant Coconut Chicken Soup with Lotus Root Chips
Replace the Shellfish Stock in the Lemongrass Broth with 1 c. additional Poultry Stock and 1 c. unsweetened coconut milk. Replace the clams, shrimp, and scallops with 2 oz. skinned and trimmed boneless chicken breast cut into 3/8" slices.

Ahi Nori Tempura Roll
with Shoyu Butter Sauce and Radish Sprouts

yield: 1 (4-oz.) appetizer serving
(multiply × 4 for classroom turnout; adjust equipment sizes accordingly)

MASTER RECIPE

production		costing only
1 Tbsp.	minced shallot	1/4 oz. a.p.
1 tsp.	minced garlic	1/9 oz. a.p.
1 Tbsp.	minced fresh ginger	1/4 oz. a.p.
2 Tbsp.	mirin	1 fl. oz.
1 Tbsp.	liquid from pickled ginger	n/c
1 Tbsp.	Japanese soy sauce	1/2 fl. oz.
1 Tbsp.	fresh lime juice	1/6 [63 ct.] lime
1 tsp.	minced lime zest	n/c
1/2 c.	Fish Stock	1/32 recipe
1	Ahi Norimaki Sushi Roll	1/4 recipe
as needed	cornstarch	1/2 oz.
1/2 c.	Tempura Batter	1/4 recipe
as needed	frying compound or peanut oil	% used
3 Tbsp.	butter	1 1/2 oz.
1 Tbsp.	thin-sliced pink pickled ginger, well drained	1/2 fl. oz.
1/2 oz.	radish sprouts	1/2 oz.
1 tsp.	Wasabi Sauce, in a small squeeze bottle	1/9 recipe

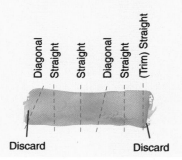

Diagonal | Straight | Straight | Diagonal | Straight | (Trim) Straight

Discard   Discard

service turnout:

1. Start the shoyu butter sauce by preparing the reduction:
   a. Place the shallot, garlic, ginger, mirin, pickled ginger liquid, soy sauce, lime juice, lime zest, and Fish Stock in an 8" sauté pan. Over high heat, reduce by half.
2. Fry the Ahi Norimaki Sushi Roll:
   a. Have ready a draining rack set over a drip pan.
   b. Dredge the sushi roll in cornstarch and tap off the excess.
   c. Coat the sushi roll in the Tempura Batter.
   d. Deep-fry the sushi roll in 400°F oil about 20 seconds, until golden.
   e. Drain on the rack.
3. Cut the Tempura Sushi Roll as illustrated in the figure at left.
   a. Cutting on the diagonal, trim off one end of the roll and discard it.
   b. Make a straight cut, then a diagonal cut, then two more straight cuts and a final diagonal cut to yield 5 pieces: 2 standard cylinders and 3 cylinders with slanting tops. Discard the other end of the roll.
4. Plate the dish:
   a. Work the butter into the shoyu reduction to create an emulsion, then pour the resulting butter sauce onto a warm 9" square plate.
   b. Place the 2 standard sushi roll cylinders on the left side of the plate at 8 o'clock and 10 o'clock. Stack one of the slanted sushi roll cylinders on top of the 10 o'clock cylinder, and then arrange the remaining slanted cylinders next to the stack, in a row.
   c. Quickly arrange the pickled ginger slices on the work surface in an overlapping row and roll them up into a loose cylinder. Fan the tops to create a rose. Place the ginger rose on the plate, front center, against the sushi roll cylinders.
   d. Make a bouquet of the radish sprouts and stick it upright in the center of the sushi roll cylinders.
   e. Squeeze a dot of Wasabi Sauce onto the shoyu sauce at 4 o'clock.

COMPONENT RECIPE

AHI NORIMAKI SUSHI ROLL

yield: 4 (4-oz.) rolls

production		costing only
4 oz.	sashimi-grade ahi tuna	4 oz.
4 sheets	sushi nori	1/3 package
3 c.	Sushi Rice	1 recipe
1 Tbsp.	Wasabi Paste	1/4 recipe
2 Tbsp.	fine diagonal-sliced scallion greens	1/8 bunch a.p.

preparation:

1. Cut the tuna slab on the diagonal into 12 (2 1/2" × 3/8" × 3/8") pieces.
2. Pass the nori sheets over a gas flame to crisp them. ⚠ Do not pass the sheets too close to the flame or they will shrivel and scorch.
3. Wearing food service gloves, assemble the sushi rolls:
   a. Cover a bamboo sushi mat with a piece of foodservice film wrap.
   b. Place one of the nori sheets horizontally on the sushi mat, shiny side down.
   c. Dampen your gloved fingers with water and place about 3/4 c. Sushi Rice on the nori sheet. Spread the rice into an even 3/8" layer, covering the bottom two thirds of the nori out to the edges, but leaving 1" of the far edge exposed.
   d. Arrange three pieces of tuna horizontally across the middle of the rice. Spread with a very small amount of Wasabi Paste, and then sprinkle the tuna with 1/4 of the scallions.
   e. Very lightly moisten the exposed edge of nori with water and then, using the mat as an aid, immediately roll up the nori sheet so that the bottom edge of the rice meets the top edge of the rice, and the moist nori edge seals to the outside of the roll.
   f. Squeeze gently to firm the sushi roll, and then unroll the mat.
   g. Wrap the roll in the plastic film.
   h. Repeat with the remaining ingredients to make 4 sushi rolls.

holding: best refrigerated only a few hours; if necessary, refrigerate up to 24 hours

Spread the rice on the nori.

Place the tuna, wasabi, and scallion in a horizontal row.

Using the mat as an aid, begin rolling.

As you roll, peel back the sushi mat and plastic film.

To firm the roll, wrap it in the sushi mat and squeeze with gentle, even pressure.

The completed sushi roll.

COMPONENT RECIPE
SUSHI RICE

yield: approx. 3 c.

production		costing only
1 c.	Japanese-style short-grain sushi rice	7 oz.
1 3/4 c.	water	n/c
1	2" × 2" square kombu, rinsed of excess salt	1/4 oz.
2 tsp.	kosher salt	1/3 oz.
1 Tbsp.	sugar	1/2 oz.
3 Tbsp.	Japanese rice wine vinegar	1 1/2 fl. oz.
1/4 c.	water	n/c

preparation:
1. Preheat an oven to 350°F.
2. Place the rice in a heavy 1 1/2-qt. saucepan, place the saucepan under cool running water, and wash the rice, swishing the water around with your hand until it changes from milky white to clear. Drain the rice by pouring off the water.
3. Add 1 3/4 c. cold water and the kombu to the pot of rice. Cover the pan, bring the water to the boil, and then reduce the heat to a simmer. After 8 minutes, check the water level; when the water is absorbed, transfer the covered pan to the oven and bake for 10 minutes.
4. Prepare the seasoning liquid:
   a. Place the salt, sugar, vinegar, and 1/4 c. water in a 6" sauté pan.
   b. Cover the pan and place over low heat. Simmer just until the salt and sugar dissolve.
   c. Uncover and cool to room temperature.
5. Season and cool the sushi rice:
   a. Remove the rice from the oven and, using a rubber spatula, turn the rice out into a half-size hotel pan.
   b. Using two rubber spatulas, lift and toss the rice in order to air-cool it, reducing its temperature from hot to warm.
   c. Remove and discard the kombu.
   d. Then, while tossing the rice as before, have a helper sprinkle in the seasoning liquid. The rice should be tender, sticky, and moist, but not wet or mushy.
   e. Cover the rice with a clean, damp towel and hold it at room temperature until needed.

holding: at cool room temperature up to 3 hours

COMPONENT RECIPE
WASABI PASTE AND WASABI SAUCE

yield: approx. 1 Tbsp. paste and 3 Tbsp. sauce

production		costing only
1 Tbsp. + 1 tsp.	wasabi powder	1/3 oz.
approx. 3 Tbsp.	water	n/c

preparation:
1. Place the wasabi powder in a small bowl and mix in just enough water to make a thick paste.
2. Rest at room temperature for at least 1/2 hour.
3. Spoon about 1 Tbsp. wasabi paste into a ramekin or small bowl and reserve.
4. To make the wasabi sauce, adjust the thickness of the remaining wasabi paste by stirring in a little more water to achieve a consistency that will flow from a small squeeze bottle with pressure yet hold its shape on a plate.

holding: at cool room temperature up to 1 week

COMPONENT RECIPE
TEMPURA BATTER

yield: approx. 3 c.

production		costing only
1 c.	flour	5 oz.
1 1/4 c.	cornstarch	6 oz.
1 Tbsp.	baking powder	1/3 oz.
2 tsp.	fine salt	1/3 oz.
1	egg white, beaten to a froth	1 each or 1 oz.
approx. 3/4 c.	ice-cold water	n/c

preparation:
1. Sift the flour, cornstarch, baking powder, and salt into a bowl just large enough to accommodate the finished batter.
2. Make a well in the center of the dry ingredients, then add the egg white and a little water. Whisk the wet and dry ingredients together, drawing in the sides of the well and adding additional water as needed, to make a smooth mixture with the consistency of pancake batter.
3. Place the bowl of batter in an ice bain-marie.

holding: prepare just before service; hold in the ice bain-marie up to 5 hours

---

RECIPE VARIATION
Ahi Norimaki Sushi
Prepare the Ahi Norimaki Sushi Rolls to order and, using a very sharp, wet knife, cut each roll into 8 even cylinders. Stack the cylinders on a plate and serve with pickled ginger, Wasabi Paste, and Japanese soy sauce.

Lomi Lomi Salmon Salad

yield: 1 (2 1/2-oz.) salmon appetizer serving plus accompaniments (multiply × 4 for classroom turnout)

🕐 Requires 48 hours advance preparation.

MASTER RECIPE

production		costing only
2 1/2 oz.	Hawai'ian Salted Salmon	1/4 recipe
1/3 c.	*Lomi Lomi* Dressing, in squeeze bottle	1/4 recipe
3	shiso (perilla) leaves*	3 each
3/4 c.	Japanese seaweed salad** or Hawai'ian *ogo* seaweed salad	2 oz.
1/2 oz.	hulled and tailed mung bean sprouts	3/4 oz. a.p.
3	grape tomatoes	1/12 pint
1 tsp.	fine diagonal-sliced scallions	1/16 bunch a.p.
3	white cocktail napkins or paper towels	3 each
1 c.	crushed ice	n/c

service turnout:

1. Prepare the *Lomi Lomi* Salad:
   a. Tear the Hawai'ian Salted Salmon into shreds and place it in a small bowl.
   b. Mix in the *Lomi Lomi* Dressing.
2. Plate the dish:
   a. Arrange the shiso leaves on a cold 10" plate with the tips at 12, 4, and 8 o'clock.
   b. Place the seaweed salad in the center of the plate.
   c. Mound the salmon salad on the seaweed salad.
   d. Surround the salads with the bean sprouts.
   e. Arrange the grape tomatoes between the shiso leaves.
   f. Place a dot of scallion on top of the salmon salad.
   g. Arrange the cocktail napkins in the center of a cold 12" plate and place the crushed ice on top of them.
   h. Press the salmon plate onto the crushed ice so that it rests stable on the underplate.

*If shiso leaves are unavailable, substitute large, perfect spinach leaves.

**Japanese seaweed salad can be purchased from seafood purveyors. If unavailable, substitute a salad made from julienne cucumber and Ginger-Soy Dipping Sauce (p. 749).

APPETIZERS

COMPONENT RECIPE
HAWAI'IAN SALTED SALMON

yield: approx. 10 oz.

🕐 Requires 48 hours advance preparation.

production		costing only
14 oz.	center-cut skin-on salmon fillet	14 oz.
1 Tbsp.	fresh lime juice	1/6 [63 ct.] lime
1 Tbsp.	vodka	1/2 oz.
1/3 c.	Hawai'ian red alaea salt or other coarse natural salt	3 oz.
1/2 c.	palm sugar or brown sugar	3 oz.
1/4 c.	minced ginger	1 1/2 oz. a.p.
1 Tbsp.	minced lime zest	n/c

first day preparation:
1. Fabricate the salmon:
   a. Remove the salmon skin.
   b. Use foodservice tweezers or clean needle-nose pliers to remove any pin bones.
   c. Wash the salmon fillet and pat it dry with paper towels.
2. Prepare the cure:
   a. Mix the lime juice and vodka.
   b. In a mortar, pound together the salt, sugar, ginger, and lime zest.
3. Apply the cure:
   a. Place a large sheet of foodservice film wrap on the work surface and place the salmon fillet on it.
   b. Rub the lime-vodka mixture onto both sides of the salmon.
   c. Coat both sides of the salmon with the salt mixture and press firmly to help it adhere.
   d. Wrap the salmon tightly in the film wrap, and then place the wrapped salmon in a heavy plastic bag.
   e. Place the salmon in a half-size hotel pan, place another half-size hotel pan on top, and weight the top pan with a heavy object.
   f. Refrigerate 12 hours.
4. Turn the salmon over, place the pan and weight back on top, and refrigerate 12 hours longer.

second day preparation:
5. Early in the day, check the cure:
   a. Unwrap the salmon and look at it. The salmon will have shrunk and lost moisture. Its flesh should still be translucent, but the texture should be almost as firm as smoked salmon.
   b. Cut a slit into the thickest part of the fillet. If the flesh in the center looks different than the flesh near the surface, the cure is not complete.
   c. If additional curing is necessary, rewrap, turn and reweight the salmon and refrigerate up to 12 hours longer.
6. Check the cure as in steps 5a. and 5b. When the cure is complete, wash the salmon under cool running water and pat it dry.
7. If serving within a day or two, you may cut the salmon into 4 (2 1/2-oz.) portions.
8. Wrap in butcher paper or parchment.

holding: refrigerate up to 1 week

COMPONENT RECIPE
LOMI LOMI DRESSING

yield: 1 1/3 c.

production		costing only
2 oz.	peeled fresh ginger	2 1/4 oz. a.p.
1/4 c.	minced scallion, white part only	1/4 bunch a.p.
1 Tbsp.	Japanese white miso	3/4 oz.
1 Tbsp.	Dijon mustard	1/2 fl. oz.
1/3 c.	Japanese sweetened white vinegar	2 2/3 fl. oz.
1 tsp.	fine-ground white pepper	1/8 oz.
2/3 c.	peanut oil	5 1/3 fl. oz.
as needed	fine salt, optional	1/16 oz.
as needed	sugar, optional	1/16 oz.
as needed	white wine vinegar or cider vinegar, optional	1/2 oz.

preparation:
1. Juice the ginger in a juice extractor or by squeezing ginger cubes in a garlic press.
2. Place the ginger juice, scallion, miso, mustard, vinegar, and white pepper in a blender.
3. Blend on high speed and, while blending, add the oil through the lid opening in a thin stream to create an emulsion.
4. Taste and correct the seasoning with salt and sugar as needed, or with more white wine vinegar if necessary.

holding: best prepared the same day; refrigerate in a freshly sanitized squeeze bottle up to 3 days

---

RECIPE VARIATION
Hawai'ian Sashimi Salad
Replace the *Lomi Lomi* Salmon with a mixture of diced raw sashimi-grade tuna and yellowtail snapper.

Ahi Poke
with Shrimp Chips

yield: 1 (3-oz.) appetizer serving plus accompaniments
(multiply × 4 for classroom turnout)

MASTER RECIPE

production		costing only
3 oz.	sashimi-grade ahi or other fresh tuna	3 oz.
1 Tbsp.	fresh lime juice	1/6 [63 ct.] lime
tt	crushed red alaea salt or other natural salt	1/8 oz.
2 Tbsp.	cleaned, chopped *ogo* seaweed*	1/2 oz.
1 Tbsp.	chopped scallion	1/16 bunch a.p.
dash	Japanese soy sauce	1/4 oz.
1 drop	Asian roasted sesame oil	1/16 fl. oz.
tt	fine-ground white pepper	1/16 oz.
1 c.	chiffonade romaine lettuce hearts	1 1/2 oz.
2 tsp.	chopped kukui nuts or macadamia nuts	1/4 oz.
5	Fried Shrimp Chips	1/4 recipe

service turnout:
1. Prepare the *poke*:
   a. Cut the tuna into 1/4" dice.
   b. Mix in the lime juice, salt, seaweed, scallion, soy sauce, sesame oil, and white pepper.
   c. Taste and correct the seasoning.
2. Plate the dish:
   a. Arrange a bed of romaine hearts in the center of a cool 10" plate.
   b. Mound the *poke* on the romaine and sprinkle it with the nuts.
   c. Arrange the Fried Shrimp Chips around the *poke*.

*If Hawai'ian *ogo* seaweed is not available, substitute reconstituted Japanese dried *hijiki* seaweed.

COMPONENT RECIPE
FRIED SHRIMP CHIPS

yield: 20 chips

production		costing only
as needed	frying compound or oil for deep-frying	% used
20	natural (uncolored) small Thai or Indonesian shrimp chips	1/2 oz.

preparation:
1. Mise en place:
   a. Preheat a fryer or pan of frying oil to 400°F.
   b. Have ready a hotel pan lined with paper towels and a "spider" or perforated lifter.
2. Fry the shrimp chips:
   a. Drop a shrimp chip into the hot oil and use the spider to hold the chip under the oil until it expands into a cup shape. ⚠ Do not allow the chip to brown.
   b. Immediately remove the chip to the paper towels and drain it, upside down.
   c. Repeat with the remaining shrimp chips to make a total of 20 fried chips.

holding: at cool room temperature and low humidity in a tightly sealed container up to 3 days

Pau Hana *Pupu* Platter for Two

Rumaki, Shrimp on Sugarcane, Korean Mandoo Dumplings, Chinese Barbeque Baby Back Ribs, *Poke*-Stuffed Mini-Skins, Edamame, and Shichimi Wings

yield: 2 appetizer servings
(multiply × 4 for classroom turnout; adjust equipment sizes accordingly)

MASTER RECIPE

production		costing only
4 pc.	Chinese Marinated Chicken Wings	1/8 recipe
1/2	egg white, beaten to a froth	1/2 each or 1/2 oz.
1/4 c.	*Shichimi* Coating	1/4 recipe
4 pc.	Rumaki	1/4 recipe
2 pc.	Chinese Barbeque Baby Back Ribs	1/6 recipe
4 pc.	Mini-Skin Shells	1/4 recipe
2 pc.	Shrimp on Sugarcane	1/8 recipe
1 Tbsp.	peanut oil	1/2 fl. oz.
4 pc.	Korean Mandoo	1/8 recipe
1	10" × 10" square banana leaf	1/12 pkg.
as needed	liquid fuel, such as Sterno	% used
2 Tbsp.	Mandoo Dip	1/6 recipe
8 pc.	*Furikake* Edamame	1/8 recipe
3/4 oz.	Ahi *Poke*, p. 682, made with brunoise-cut tuna	1/4 recipe
1 Tbsp.	Thai sweet chile sauce, in squeeze bottle	1/2 fl. oz.
2	scallion "brushes," p. 276	1/3 bunch a.p.

service turnout:

1. Deep-fry the Chinese Marinated Chicken Wings:
   a. Remove the wings from their marinade and blot them dry.
   b. Coat the wings with egg white and dredge them heavily in Shichimi Coating.
   c. Deep-fry the wings at 375°F about 3 minutes, until golden and almost cooked through.
   d. Place the wings on a large sizzle plate.
2. Place the Rumaki and Chinese Barbeque Baby Back Ribs on the same sizzle plate as the wings. Place the sizzle plate in a 400°F oven and bake about 8 minutes.

3. Cook the remaining deep-fried foods:
   a. Drop the Mini-Skin Shells and the Shrimp on Sugarcane into the fryer.
   b. After about 30 seconds, remove the shells, place them on the sizzle plate hollow side down, and return it to the oven.
   c. Continue frying the shrimp about 3 minutes longer, until done through and golden.
   d. Add the shrimp to the sizzle pan in the oven.
4. Pan-fry the Korean Mandoo:
   a. Heat a 6" nonstick sauté pan over medium heat, heat 1 Tbsp. oil, and add the mandoo.
   b. Cover the pan and fry over low heat about 30 seconds, until browned on the bottoms.
   c. Turn over the mandoo and fry uncovered until browned on the new bottoms.
   d. Slide the mandoo out onto paper towels and blot the tops.
5. Arrange the *pupu* platter:
   a. Place the banana leaf square on a 12" platter.
   b. Fill a *pupu* hibachi with liquid fuel, place it back center on the platter, and light the fuel.
   c. Arrange the ribs to the left of the hibachi and the shrimp to the right.
   d. Prop the wings upright against the hibachi.
   e. Spoon the Mandoo Dip into a 1-oz. dip dish and place it in front of the wings.
   f. Arrange the *Furikake* Edamame upright behind the dip dish.
   g. Arrange 2 rumaki on each side of the dip dish.
   h. Fan the mandoo across the front of the platter, propped against the dip dish.
   i. Fill the shells with Ahi *Poke*. Place 2 filled shells on each side of the Mandoo.
   j. Drizzle the shrimp with Thai sweet chile sauce.
   k. Stick the scallion brushes upright between the wings and the hibachi.

COMPONENT RECIPE
CHINESE MARINATED CHICKEN WINGS

yield: 16 pc.

production		costing only
8	(10–12 ct.) chicken wings	12 oz.
1/4 c.	Chinese light soy sauce	2 fl. oz.
1/4 c.	Chinese rice wine	2 fl. oz.
2 Tbsp.	minced ginger	2/3 oz. a.p.
2 Tbsp.	minced scallion	1/8 bunch a.p.
1 Tbsp.	sugar	1/2 oz.
2 drops	Chinese roasted sesame oil	1/8 fl. oz.

preparation:
1. Fabricate the chicken wings:
   a. Cut off the wing tips and reserve for stock.
   b. Separate the wings into flats and drumettes by cutting through the center joint.
   c. Remove any pinfeathers and cut away excess skin.
2. Mix together the remaining ingredients to make the marinade.
3. Mix the wings with the marinade.
4. Refrigerate for at least 2 hours.

holding: refrigerate in a nonreactive container up to 12 hours; drain off the marinade and continue holding up to 3 days

COMPONENT RECIPE
SHICHIMI COATING

yield: approx. 1 c.

production		costing only
1 c.	cornstarch	4 1/2 oz.
4 Tbsp.	Japanese *shichimi togarashi* seasoning	1 oz.
1 Tbsp.	fine salt	1/2 oz.

preparation:
1. Mix together all ingredients well.

holding: tightly sealed in a covered container up to 1 week; shake or stir well before using

COMPONENT RECIPE
RUMAKI

yield: 16 pc.

production		costing only
1/4 c.	Chinese soy sauce	2 fl. oz.
1/4 c.	Chinese rice wine	2 fl. oz.
1 tsp.	sugar	1/6 oz.
2 Tbsp.	minced ginger	2/3 oz.
1	garlic clove	1/4 oz. a.p.
16	chicken liver lobes, trimmed well	10 oz. a.p.
8	thin slices bacon, halved widthwise	4 oz. a.p.
8	canned or peeled fresh water chestnuts, halved	2 1/2 oz. a.p. or % of can
16	wooden cocktail picks	% of pkg.

preparation:
1. Marinate the livers:
   a. Combine the soy sauce, rice wine, and sugar in a small, nonreactive container.
   b. Using a garlic press, press the ginger juice and garlic into the soy mixture. Discard the pulp.
   c. Blot the chicken livers on paper towels, then add them to the soy marinade. Cover and refrigerate for 1 hour.
2. Parcook the bacon:
   a. Lay out the bacon slices in a 10" nonstick pan and place over low heat.
   b. Cook very gently for about 1 minute, just until the bacon strips shrink slightly and render out some fat.
   c. Remove to paper towels and cool.
3. Assemble the rumaki:
   a. Drain the livers of marinade and pat dry with paper towels.
   b. Use a paring knife to make a small slit in each liver, and insert a piece of water chestnut into the slit.
   c. Wrap each liver in a bacon slice and secure with a cocktail pick.

holding: refrigerate in a freshly sanitized, covered container up to 2 days

COMPONENT RECIPE

CHINESE BARBEQUE BABY BACK RIBS

yield: approx. 2 lb. bone-in cooked ribs

production		costing only
1/4 c.	Chinese light soy sauce	2 fl. oz.
1/4 c.	Chinese rice wine	2 fl. oz.
1/4 c.	minced ginger	1 1/3 oz. a.p.
1/4 c.	minced scallion	1/4 bunch a.p.
2 Tbsp.	ketchup	1 fl. oz.
1/4 c.	honey	2 fl. oz.
1/4 c.	hoisin sauce	2 fl. oz.
2 Tbsp.	Chinese brown bean paste	1 fl. oz.
1/2 tsp.	Chinese five-spice powder	1/8 oz.
2 drops	Asian roasted sesame oil	1/16 fl. oz.
1 rack	pork baby back ribs	2 1/4 lb.
1/4 c.	honey	2 fl. oz.
1/3 c.	water	n/c

preparation:
1. To make the marinade, mix together the soy sauce, rice wine, ginger, scallion, ketchup, 1/4 c. honey, hoisin sauce, bean paste, five-spice powder, and oil.
2. Marinate the ribs:
   a. Cut the rib rack in half and place in a half-size hotel pan.
   b. Add the marinade and turn the ribs to coat them thoroughly.
   c. Cover the pan and marinate the ribs at cool room temperature for 2 hours, turning often. Alternatively, refrigerate in the marinade overnight, turning occasionally if possible.
3. To make the glaze, combine the remaining 1/4 c. honey and 1/3 c. water in a saucepan. Bring to the boil and cool.
4. Roast the ribs:
   a. Remove all but the top and bottom racks of a convection oven.
   b. Place 1" of water in a hotel pan and place it on the bottom rack.
   c. Preheat the oven to 400°F.
   d. Drain the marinade from the ribs.
   e. Using meat hooks or sanitized large paper clips, hang the ribs from the top rack with the drip pan positioned underneath. Roast the ribs for 10 minutes.
   f. Reduce the temperature to 325°F and continue roasting for about 20 minutes longer, until the ribs reach medium doneness.
   g. Brush the ribs on both sides with the honey glaze.
   h. Raise the temperature to 400°F and continue roasting for 5 to 10 minutes longer, until the glaze is set and beginning to brown.
5. Remove the ribs from the oven. (If not serving immediately, cool to room temperature.)
6. Cut the rack halves into individual ribs.

holding: refrigerate in a freshly sanitized, covered container up to 5 days

COMPONENT RECIPE

MINI-SKIN SHELLS

yield: 16 pc.

production		costing only
8	1 1/4"-diameter Red Bliss or other new potatoes	8 oz.

preparation:
1. Prepare a stovetop steamer or pressure steamer.
2. Scrub the potatoes and cut them in half widthwise.
3. Steam the potatoes until just tender (time will vary according to the type of steamer used).
4. Cool to room temperature.
5. Shave off just enough of the bottom of each potato half so that it will sit solidly on a flat surface.
6. Using a Parisienne scoop, hollow out each potato to create a 1/4"-thick shell. (Reserve the potato flesh for another use.)

holding: refrigerate in a freshly sanitized, covered container with pan liner between layers

COMPONENT RECIPE
SHRIMP ON SUGARCANE

yield: 8 pc.

production		costing only
3 oz.	pure unsalted pork fat, cold	3 oz.
12 oz.	shelled, deveined white shrimp, any size	14 oz. a.p.
2	egg whites, beaten to a froth	2 each or 2 oz.
2 Tbsp.	minced ginger	1 oz. a.p.
1/4 c.	minced scallion	1/4 bunch a.p.
2 tsp.	sugar	1/3 oz.
2 tsp.	kosher salt	1/3 oz.
tt	fine-ground white pepper	1/16 oz.
1 Tbsp.	Chinese rice wine	1/2 fl. oz.
1 Tbsp.	Thai or Vietnamese fish sauce	1/2 fl. oz.
1 Tbsp.	cornstarch	1/4 oz.
1	5" length fresh sugarcane	10 oz.
—or—		
as needed	canned or vacuum-packed sugarcane	% of pkg

preparation:
1. Mix the shrimp paste:
   a. Cut the pork fat into fine dice, then chop it until minced fine. Place the minced fat in a bowl set in an ice-water bath.
   b. Chop the shrimp fine and add it to the bowl in the ice-water bath.
   c. Wearing a foodservice glove, mix the ginger, scallion, sugar, salt, white pepper, rice wine, and fish sauce into the fat/shrimp mixture.
   d. Sift the cornstarch over the fat/shrimp mixture and continue mixing.
2. Test the shrimp paste:
   a. Form a small sample patty of shrimp paste.
   b. Poach the sample in simmering water for about 1 minute.
   c. Taste and correct the seasoning.
3. Compact the shrimp paste:
   a. Steadying the bowl in one hand, pick up the shrimp paste in the other and throw it firmly back into the bowl. Continue slapping the mixture into the bowl (like a ball into a baseball glove) four or five times more to firm and compact the mixture.
4. Fabricate the sugarcane:
   a. If using fresh cane, use a paring knife to peel it.
   b. Using a sharp, heavy chef's knife, split the sugarcane into 8 slender skewerlike lengths.
5. Assemble the pieces:
   a. Divide the shrimp paste into 8 even portions.
   b. Wet your hand and form a portion of shrimp paste around the middle of a cane length to make a 4" sausage-shape with 1/2" cane extending on each side.
   c. Place the finished item in a half-size hotel pan with pan liner.
   d. Repeat with the remaining shrimp paste to make 8 pieces.

holding: cover and refrigerate up to 3 days

COMPONENT RECIPE
KOREAN MANDOO

yield: 16 pc.

production		costing only
1/4 lb.	ground pork shoulder	1/4 lb.
1/4 lb.	ground beef chuck	1/4 lb.
1/4 c.	minced Asian or domestic cabbage	1 oz. a.p.
1 Tbsp.	minced scallion	1/16 bunch a.p.
2 tsp.	minced garlic	1/6 oz. a.p.
1 Tbsp.	Japanese soy sauce	1/2 fl. oz.
1 tsp.	sugar	1/6 oz.
tt	fresh-ground black pepper	1/16 oz.
tt	kosher salt	1/16 oz.
1 drop	sesame oil	1/32 fl. oz.
16 or more	gyoza skins	1/3 pkg.

preparation:
1. Mix the filling:
   a. Combine the pork, beef, cabbage, scallion, garlic, soy sauce, sugar, pepper, salt, and oil.
   b. Knead the mixture for a few seconds and slap it into the bowl a few times to compact it, as in step 3a of Shrimp on Sugarcane.
   c. Test and correct the filling as in step 2 of Shrimp on Sugarcane.
2. Prepare a half-sheet tray lined with a clean, damp, lint-free kitchen towel.
3. Assemble the mandoo:
   a. Moisten the edge of a gyoza skin halfway around.
   b. Place a tablespoon of filling in the center of the gyoza skin, fold it over into a half moon shape, and press the edges shut.
   c. Place the mandoo on one side of the sheet tray and fold over the towel to cover it.
   d. Repeat, making at least 16 mandoo.

holding: refrigerate between towels on a sheet tray up to 4 hours; refrigerate the tray wrapped in plastic film up to 2 days; freeze up to 1 month; bring to refrigerated temperature before cooking

COMPONENT RECIPE
MANDOO DIP

yield: 3/4 c.

production		costing only
1 Tbsp.	white sesame seeds	1/8 oz.
1 tsp.	crushed dried red pepper	1/16 oz.
1 Tbsp.	peanut oil	1/2 fl. oz.
1 Tbsp.	minced ginger	1/3 oz. a.p.
1 Tbsp.	minced scallion	1/16 bunch a.p.
1 Tbsp.	minced fresh garlic	3/8 oz. a.p.
1 Tbsp.	sugar	1/2 oz.
4 Tbsp.	Japanese soy sauce	2 fl. oz.
4 Tbsp.	Japanese rice wine vinegar	2 fl. oz.

preparation:
1. Toast the sesame seeds in a dry 6" sauté pan, shaking constantly for about 20 seconds, until lightly browned. Transfer to a small mortar or spice grinder and pulverize them.
2. Wipe out the 6" sauté pan and place the dried red pepper and oil in it. Warm the oil over low heat until the pepper sizzles and darkens slightly. ⚠ Do not scorch.
3. Immediately remove the pan from the heat and stir the ginger and scallion into the hot pepper oil.
4. Add the garlic, sugar, soy sauce, vinegar, and crushed sesame seeds to the ginger-scallion oil and mix well.
5. Taste and correct the flavor balance.

holding: at cool room temperature in a freshly sanitized, covered container up to 5 hours; refrigerate up to 3 days

COMPONENT RECIPE
FURIKAKE EDAMAME

yield: 12 oz.

production		costing only
2 Tbsp.	peanut oil	1 fl. oz.
12 oz.	frozen edamame pods, thawed	12 oz.
tt	Hawai'ian red alaea salt, crushed	1/8 oz.
3 Tbsp.	Japanese *furikake* seasoning	1/2 oz.

preparation:
1. Heat a 14" wok or sauté pan over medium heat, heat the oil, and then stir-fry the edamame until they are heated through and evenly coated with oil.
2. Remove the edamame from the heat source and toss with alaea salt and *furikake* seasoning.
3. Cool to room temperature.

holding: prepare just before service; hold at cool room temperature up to 4 hours

---

RECIPE VARIATIONS

Any of this recipe's component dishes may be served as a stand-alone *pupu;* **increase the recipe yield accordingly.**

Macadamia-Crusted Mahimahi

with *Liliko'i* Sauce, Garlic *"Poi,"* and Steamed Baby Bok Choy

yield: 1 (7-oz.) entrée serving plus accompaniments (multiply × 4 for classroom turnout; adjust equipment sizes accordingly)

MASTER RECIPE

production		costing only
as needed	pan coating spray	% of container
1	Mac-Panko-Crusted Mahimahi Fillet	1/4 recipe
1 c.	Garlic *"Poi"*	1/4 recipe
1 1/4 c.	cleaned leeks, white and pale green parts, julienne	1/3 bunch a.p.
1/4 c.	fine-julienne young ginger	1 1/4 oz. a.p.
tt	fine salt	1/16 oz.
2 Tbsp.	fine-julienne lime zest	n/c
2 tsp.	fresh lime juice	1/6 [63 ct.] lime
4	1-oz. heads intact baby bok choy, rinsed and soaked to remove sand	4 oz.
2 Tbsp.	minced shallot	1/8 bunch a.p.
3 Tbsp.	frozen sweetened passion fruit purée	1 1/2 fl. oz.
3/4 c.	Fish Stock	1/20 recipe
5 Tbsp.	butter	2 1/2 oz.
tt	fine-ground white pepper	1/16 oz.
1	purple edible flower	1 each

service turnout:

1. Bake the fish:
   a. Spray a sizzle pan with pan coating, place the Mac-Panko-Crusted Mahimahi Fillet on it, and place in the top of a 400°F oven.
   b. Bake for 10 to 12 minutes, until the topping is deep golden and the fish is almost cooked through.
2. Finish the vegetable sides:
   a. Heat the Garlic *"Poi"* in a microwave or on the stovetop in a covered 8" nonstick sauté pan.
   b. Scatter the leeks and ginger into the basket of a fryer set to 400°F and deep-fry for about 10 seconds, until lightly browned at the edges. Dump the contents of the basket into a bowl and toss with the fine salt, lime zest, and lime juice.
   c. Steam the bok choy in a stovetop steamer or pressure steamer until crisp-tender (time varies according to the type of steamer used).
3. Start the sauce:
   a. Place the shallot, passion fruit purée, and Fish Stock in an 8" sauté pan and reduce by two thirds.
4. Plate the dish:
   a. Mound the *"poi"* on the back of a hot 12" plate.
   b. Mound the leek-ginger mixture on top of the *"poi."*
   c. Blot the bok choy dry with a clean, lint-free kitchen towel and arrange 2 heads on either side of the plate.
   d. Place the fillet on the front of the plate, propped against the *"poi."*
   e. Work the butter into the sauce reduction to create an emulsion, season it with white pepper, and correct the salt. Spoon the sauce onto the front of the plate.
   f. Place the edible flower on the fillet.

MAC-PANKO-CRUSTED MAHIMAHI FILLETS

yield: 4 (7-oz.) entrée servings

production		costing only
4	7-oz. skinless mahimahi fillets, pinned and trimmed	2 lb. a.p.
tt	kosher salt	1/16 oz.
1 tsp.	ground turmeric	1/8 oz.
4	1/4"-thick slices ginger	1 1/3 oz. a.p.
2 Tbsp.	fresh lime juice	1/2 [63 ct.] lime
1 1/2 c.	medium-chopped salted macadamia nuts	8 oz.
2/3 c.	panko bread crumbs	2 oz.
6 Tbsp.	softened butter	3 oz.
1/4 c.	chopped fresh cilantro	1/10 bunch a.p.

preparation:
1. Season the fish:
   a. Rub the surfaces of each fish fillet with an equal portion of salt and turmeric.
   b. Using a garlic press, squeeze an equal amount of ginger juice onto each fillet.
   c. Squeeze the lime juice onto the fillets.
   d. Rub the seasonings into the fish.
2. To make the topping, mix together the nuts, bread crumbs, butter, and cilantro.
3. Top the fish:
   a. Place the fillets on a half-sheet tray with pan liner, shiny side down.
   b. Divide the nut topping into 4 portions.
   c. Press a portion of nut topping neatly on the top of each fillet.
   d. Refrigerate uncovered for about 1 hour, until the topping is chilled and set.

holding: refrigerate, covered with a clean, dry kitchen towel, up to 24 hours

GARLIC "POI"

yield: 4 c.

production		costing only
1 1/2 lb.	taro root	1 1/2 lb.
1/2 c.	peeled fresh garlic cloves, halved if large	2 oz. a.p.
3	1/4"-thick slices ginger	1 oz. a.p.
tt	kosher salt	1/8 oz.
1/4 c.	softened butter	2 oz.
1/2 c.	hot half-and-half	4 fl. oz.
tt	fine-ground white pepper	1/8 oz.

preparation:
1. Fabricate the taro:
   a. Have ready a bowl of cold water.
   b. Wash the taro under cold running water and use a vegetable brush to scrub it thoroughly.
   c. Peel the taro, dropping each peeled root into cold water as you work.
   d. Cut each taro root into thirds or quarters, depending on size, to make even-size pieces. Return the pieces to the water as you work.
2. Cook the taro:
   a. Drain the taro and place it in a saucepan with the garlic and ginger and enough water to just cover. Salt the water heavily.
   b. Bring the water to the boil and cook for about 10 minutes until the taro and garlic are soft.
3. Mash the taro:
   a. Drain off all but about 1/2 c. of the cooking water and pick out the ginger pieces.
   b. Run the taro through a ricer, or force it through a coarse strainer, into a large bowl.
   c. Whip in the butter and half-and-half.
   d. Taste, correct the salt, and season with white pepper.

holding: prepare just before service and hold in a 180°F steam table up to 5 hours; leftover "poi" can be made into patties for frying

---

RECIPE VARIATION

Peanut-Crusted Mahimahi with Sticky Rice, Thai Red Curry Sauce, and Baby Bok Choy

Replace the macadamia nuts with salted peanuts. Replace the "poi" with Sticky Rice. Replace the passion fruit sauce with Coconut Red Curry Sauce. Replace the edible flower garnish with peeled, brunoise-cut red bell pepper and fine diagonal-sliced scallions.

Seared Rare Ahi Tuna

with Teriyaki Sauce, Pacific Vegetable Medley, and Bento Rice Balls

yield: 1 (6-oz.) entrée serving plus accompaniments (multiply × 4 for classroom turnout; adjust equipment sizes accordingly)

MASTER RECIPE

production		costing only
2 Tbsp.	peanut oil	1 fl. oz.
6 oz.	2" × 2" × 3" block sashimi-quality ahi tuna	6 oz.
tt	kosher salt	1/4 oz.
tt	fresh-ground black pepper	1/16 oz.
4	Bento Rice Balls	1/4 recipe
1 Tbsp.	Japanese *shichimi togarashi* seasoning	1/4 oz.
2 Tbsp.	peanut oil	1 fl. oz.
2 oz.	snow peas, strings removed, trimmed	2 oz.
1/2 c.	peeled, sliced fresh water chestnuts*, held in water	3 oz. a.p.
2 Tbsp.	minced ginger	2/3 oz. a.p.
3 oz.	batonnet-cut kabocha or other winter squash, boiled and refreshed	5 oz. a.p.
1/2 c.	chopped, cleaned *ogo* seaweed**	1 1/2 oz.
2 Tbsp.	Japanese soy sauce	1 fl. oz.
3/4 c.	Teriyaki Sauce	1/4 recipe
2 Tbsp.	butter	1 oz.
1 tsp.	black sesame seeds	1/8 oz.

service turnout:

1. Cook the tuna:
   a. Heat a 6" sauté pan until very hot, add 2 Tbsp. oil, and sear the block of tuna on all six sides, turning to a new side as soon as one side is browned, so the tuna remains very rare inside.
   b. Season with salt and pepper and hold warm.

2. Roll the Bento Rice Balls in the shichimi, place them on a plate, and heat them gently in a microwave until warm.
3. Stir-fry the vegetable medley:
   a. Heat a 14" wok or 12" sauté pan until very hot and add 2 Tbsp. oil.
   b. Add the snow peas and water chestnuts and stir-fry them with a little salt for about 30 seconds, until just crisp-tender.
   c. Add the ginger and squash and stir-fry for 30 seconds longer.
   d. Toss in the seaweed and drizzle in the soy sauce.
   e. Remove from the heat and hold warm.
4. Finish the sauce:
   a. Heat the Teriyaki Sauce in an 8" sauté pan just until hot. ⚠ Do not allow prolonged boiling or the sauce will thin out.
   b. Work in the butter to create an emulsion.
   c. Hold warm.
5. Plate the dish:
   a. Stack the bento balls in a pyramid shape on the back left of a hot 10" rectangular plate.
   b. Mound the vegetable medley on the back right of the plate.
   c. Spoon the teriyaki butter sauce onto the plate.
   d. Slice the tuna into thick slabs.
   e. Lean the end slab of tuna against the bento balls and fan the remaining slabs on the front of the plate.
   f. Sprinkle the vegetable medley with black sesame seeds.

*If fresh water chestnuts are not available, substitute batonnet-cut jicama.

**If Hawai'ian *ogo* seaweed is not available, substitute reconstituted dried Japanese *tosaka* or *hijiki* seaweed.

COMPONENT RECIPE
BENTO RICE BALLS

yield: 16 (1-oz., 1 1/4") balls

production		costing only
3 c.	warm Sushi Rice (p. 679)	1 recipe
1/4 c.	brunoise-cut Japanese pickled daikon	2 oz.
2 Tbsp.	chopped Japanese pickled umiboshi	1/3 oz.
1/4 c.	chopped scallion	1/8 bunch a.p.

preparation:
1. Mix together all ingredients.
2. Dampen a clean, lint-free kitchen towel and place it on a half-sheet tray.
3. Wet your hands and form the rice into 16 (1-oz.) spheres. As you work, place each finished sphere on one side of the tray and fold the towel over the top.

holding: refrigerate on the tray, covered with the towel and wrapped in plastic film, up to 24 hours

COMPONENT RECIPE
TERIYAKI SAUCE

yield: 3 c.

production		costing only
2 c.	water	n/c
1 Tbsp.	instant *dashi* granules	1/4 oz.
1 c.	Japanese soy sauce	8 fl. oz.
1/4 c.	mirin	2 fl. oz.
1/3 c.	grated palm sugar or brown sugar	1 3/4 oz.
2 Tbsp.	minced ginger	2/3 oz. a.p.
1/3 c.	water	n/c
2 Tbsp.	cornstarch	1/2 oz.

preparation:
1. Combine the water and *dashi* in a small saucepan and bring to the boil.
2. Add the soy sauce, mirin, sugar, and ginger to the dashi. Simmer for 15 minutes.
3. Mix the water into the cornstarch to make a thick slurry.
4. Bring the sauce to the boil, stir the slurry, and then whisk in just enough slurry to thicken the sauce to a nappé consistency.
5. Taste and correct the flavor balance.

holding: open-pan cool and refrigerate in a freshly sanitized, covered container up to 5 days; reheat very gently, and do not boil; sauce may need to be strained to remove lumps

---

RECIPE VARIATION

Seared Rare Duck Breast with Teriyaki Sauce, Pacific Vegetable Medley, and Bento Rice Balls
Replace the ahi tuna with a 7-oz. boneless duck breast, skin scored in a 1/8" crosshatch pattern. Replace the *dashi* granules and water with Poultry Stock.

Yellowtail Snapper Laulau

with Coconut Sweet Potatoes and Stir-Fry Vegetable Shreds

yield: 1 (7-oz.) entrée serving plus accompaniments
(multiply × 4 for classroom turnout and adjust equipment sizes
accordingly)

MASTER RECIPE

production		costing only
2 Tbsp.	peanut oil, in squeeze bottle	1 fl. oz.
1 Tbsp.	peeled, minced fresh ginger	1/3 oz. a.p.
1/4 c.	julienne peeled broccoli stems	2 oz. a.p.
1/4 c.	julienne red bell pepper	2 oz. a.p.
1/4 c.	fine julienne carrot	2 oz. a.p.
1/4 c.	julienne stringed snow peas	2 oz. a.p.
1/4 c.	julienne cooked or canned bamboo shoots	2 oz. a.p.
1/8 c.	reconstituted shredded dried black fungus	1/16 oz. a.p.
2 Tbsp.	water, in squeeze bottle	n/c
1 Tbsp.	Chinese soy sauce, in squeeze bottle	1/2 fl. oz.
1 tsp.	sugar	1/6 oz.
2 Tbsp.	toasted shredded, sweetened coconut	1/8 oz.
1/4 c.	Fish Stock	1/64 recipe
4 Tbsp.	Laulau Butter	1/8 recipe
1 Tbsp.	chopped cilantro	1/40 bunch a.p.
1	Yellowtail Snapper Laulau	1/4 recipe
1 1/2 c.	Coconut Sweet Potatoes	1/4 recipe

service turnout:

1. Mise-en-place:
   a. Place all ingredients except the Coconut Sweet Potatoes and the Yellowtail Snapper LauLau on a half-sheet tray at the stove. (In a culinary class, you may combine the julienne vegetables and shredded fungus.)
   b. Have ready a 14" wok or 12" sauté pan, a hotel spoon, sanitized kitchen scissors, and tongs.
   c. Preheat a pressure steamer or stove-top steamer.
2. Place the film-wrapped laulau on a sizzle plate and steam for about 4 minutes in the pressure steamer or 8 minutes in the stove-top steamer.
3. Reheat the sweet potatoes in a covered 8" nonstick pan or in a microwave oven.
4. Stir-fry the julienne vegetables:
   a. Heat the wok, heat the oil, and add the ginger and julienne vegetables. Stir-fry by tossing with the hotel spoon about 10 seconds.
   b. Squeeze in the water, stir-fry about 15 seconds longer, then season with soy sauce and sugar. Hold hot.
5. Wearing foodservice gloves, finish and plate the dish:
   a. Mound the sweet potatoes on the back of a hot 12" plate and sprinkle them with toasted coconut.
   b. Unwrap the laulau over the sizzle pan to catch its juices. Prop the laulau against the sweet potatoes with the leafy point upward. Using scissors, cut open and remove the string. Fold back the ti leaves. Cut open and fold back the taro leaves to expose the snapper. (At this point, you may remove your gloves.)
   c. Use tongs to arrange the stir-fry vegetables on either side of the laulau.
   d. Add the Fish Stock and laulau juices to the wok, bring to the boil and, if necessary, reduce to 1/4 c. Remove from heat, and work in the Laulau Butter to create an emulsion.
   e. Spoon the sauce over the fish.
   f. Sprinkle the fish with the cilantro.

COMPONENT RECIPE
LAULAU BUTTER

yield: 1 c.

production		costing only
1/4 c.	minced scallions	1/4 bunch a.p.
1/4 c.	minced, peeled fresh ginger	1 1/3 oz. a.p.
tt	minced, seeded fresh Asian chile, preferably red	1/8 oz. a.p.
1 Tbsp.	minced or grated lime zest	1/4 [90 ct.] lime
3/4 c.	room-temperature butter	6 oz.
2 Tbsp.	fresh lime juice	n/c
tt	alaea salt or kosher salt	1/8 oz.
tt	fine-ground white pepper	1/16 oz.

preparation:
1. Place the scallion, ginger, chile, and lime zest in a mortar or small bowl. Using the pestle or the back of a spoon, mash these ingredients into a pulp.
2. Mix in the butter, then season the mixture with the lime juice, a generous amount of salt, and pepper.

holding: refrigerate in a sanitized, covered plastic container up to 5 days; may be frozen up to 1 month; bring to room temperature before using

COMPONENT RECIPE
YELLOWTAIL SNAPPER LAULAUS

yield: 4 (7 oz.) entrée servings

production		costing only
8	fresh organic or dried ti* leaves	4 oz. fresh, 2 oz. dried
12	pre-cooked, frozen luau (taro) leaves, thawed	% of package
	—or—	
8	large Swiss chard leaves	2/3 bunch
4	strips thick-sliced smoked bacon	3 oz.
1 1/2 lb.	yellowtail snapper fillet	1/12 lb.
1/2 c.	Laulau Butter	1/2 recipe

preparation:
1. Blanch fresh ti leaves in lots of rapidly boiling water for 3 to 4 seconds then immediately refresh, drain, and blot dry. (If using dried ti leaves, drop in boiling water, remove from heat, and soak about 1/2 hour until pliable.)
2. If using Swiss chard, remove the stems (reserve for another use) and cut away the thick center vein. Blanch for 1 second, immediately refresh, drain, and press dry between clean kitchen towels.

*Note: *If ti leaves are unavailable, use banana leaves cut into 2" × 12" rectangles.

3. Cut each bacon strip into 5 pieces. Fry in a sauté pan or bake on a half-sheet tray until almost crisp. Drain and cool to room temperature.
4. Cut the yellowtail snapper into 16 squares of equal size and thickness. (If necessary, fold over thinner portions of the fillet.)
5. Cut 4 (6") lengths of kitchen string.
6. Assemble the laulaus:
   a. Place 1 ti leaf on a sanitized work surface, shiny-side-down. Place another ti leaf perpendicular across the first, also shiny-side-down, to make a + pattern.
   b. Arrange 1/4 of the luau (taro) leaves in an overlapping sheet in the center of the ti leaf +.
   c. Place a piece of bacon in the center of the leaves, top it with a snapper square, and spread the snapper with about 1 1/2 tsp. of Laulau Butter.
   d. Repeat, stacking more bacon, snapper, and butter, and using a total of 4 snapper squares and 5 bacon pieces (ending with a bacon piece on top). Press gently to firm the stack.
   e. Fold the luau (taro) leaves up over the stack to make an elongated bundle, then fold the ti leaves up over the bundle. Use a length of kitchen string to tie the leaves at the top of the bundle.
   f. Repeat with the remaining ingredients to make a total of 4 laulaus.
   g. Individually wrap each laulau in plastic film.

holding: refrigerate up to 2 days

COMPONENT RECIPE
COCONUT SWEET POTATOES

yield: 6 c.

production		costing only
4	1/2"-diced, peeled, orange-fleshed sweet potatoes	1 1/2 lb.
6	1/4" slices fresh ginger	2 oz.
1 c.	canned, unsweetened coconut milk	8 fl. oz.
3 c.	water	n/c
to taste	kosher salt	1/8 oz.

preparation:
1. Place the potatoes and ginger in a 10" nonstick sauté pan, add the coconut milk, water, and a generous amount of salt. Cover the pan and simmer about 8 minutes until the potatoes are al dente.
2. Uncover and cook, tossing, until the liquid almost absorbs/evaporates.
3. Correct the salt.
4. Remove and discard the ginger.

holding: open-pan cool and immediately refrigerate in a freshly sanitized, covered container up to 5 days

---

RECIPE VARIATION

Grilled Whole Baby Snapper with Laulau Butter, Coconut Sweet Potatoes, and Stir-Fry Vegetable Shreds
Substitute a whole, head-on, 16 oz. cleaned baby snapper for the laulau; season it with lime juice, salt, turmeric, and ginger; brush with peanut oil and char-grill; top with softened laulau butter or nap with a laulau butter sauce.

Chicken Hekka

with Jasmine Rice

yield: 1 (10-oz.) entrée serving
(to multiply × 4 for classroom turnout, separately prepare
2 double recipes in a 14" or 16" wok)

MASTER RECIPE

production		costing only
4 Tbsp.	peanut oil, in squeeze bottle	2 fl. oz.
6	Flavored *Aburage* Triangles	1/4 recipe
1/2 c.	thick-julienne bamboo shoots (canned or peeled and cooked fresh)	2 oz. or 4 oz. a.p.
1/2 c.	julienne carrot	3 oz. a.p.
1/2 c.	thick-julienne red bell pepper	4 oz. a.p.
1/3 c.	peeled, thick-julienne celery	1/15 head a.p.
1/4 c.	1 1/2" scallion lengths, halved	1/8 bunch a.p.
1/2 c.	thick slivers sweet onion	3 oz. a.p.
1/2 c.	cleaned, medium-sliced fresh shiitake mushrooms	1 oz. a.p.
tt	kosher salt	1/16 oz.
2 Tbsp.	minced ginger	2/3 oz. a.p.
2 tsp.	minced fresh garlic	1/4 oz. a.p.
4 oz.	Hawai'ian Marinated Chicken	1/4 recipe
1/2 c.	reconstituted bean thread (cellophane) noodles*	1/2 oz. a.p.
1 c.	Hekka Sauce	1/4 recipe
1 1/2 c.	Jasmine Rice, hot in steam table	1/4 recipe
1/4 bunch	watercress, large stems removed, 2" lengths	1/4 bunch a.p.
1 tsp.	lightly toasted white sesame seeds	1/16 oz.

service turnout:

1. Mise en place:
   a. Have ready at the stove a wok, a hotel spoon, a small side plate, and a large sizzle plate.
   b. Assemble the Flavored *Aburage* Triangles, bamboo shoots, carrot, red bell pepper, celery, scallion, onion, mushrooms, ginger, garlic, Hawai'ian Marinated Chicken, and noodles on a half-sheet tray near the stove.
   c. Place the container of Hekka Sauce and an 8-oz. ladle near the stove.
   d. Have the service plate and garnishes ready.

2. Cook the stir-fry:
   a. Heat a wok, heat 2 Tbsp. oil, and then add the *aburage* triangles. Press the triangles into the oil with the back of the hotel spoon, then flip and toss them so that they lightly brown on both sides. Remove them to the side plate.
   b. Heat 1 Tbsp. more oil and stir-fry the bamboo shoots, carrot, red bell pepper, celery, scallion, onion, and mushrooms with a little salt for about 30 seconds. Remove to the sizzle plate.
   c. Heat the remaining 1 Tbsp. oil and add the ginger, garlic, and chicken. Stir-fry for about 30 seconds, until lightly browned.
   d. Ladle in the hekka sauce, then add the noodles and stir-fried vegetables. Bring to the boil, tossing constantly, until the sauce thickens/reduces.

3. Plate the dish:
   a. Spoon a bed of Jasmine Rice into a hot 12" pasta bowl and make a well in the center.
   b. Fold the *aburage* triangles and watercress into the stir-fry and immediately spoon it into the well in the rice.
   c. Sprinkle with the sesame seeds.

*To reconstitute dried rice noodles or cellophane noodles, break them into desired lengths, place in a bowl, and pour boiling water over them. Soak for 1 minute, or longer as necessary, until the noodles soften to al dente. Drain and rinse.

ENTREES

COMPONENT RECIPE
FLAVORED *ABURAGE* TRIANGLES

yield: 24 triangles

production		costing only
3 oz. (6 pc.)	1/2-oz. (4" × 4") *aburage* sheets	3 oz.
as needed	boiling water	n/c
1 c.	water	n/c
1 Tbsp.	instant *dashi* granules	1/4 oz.
3 Tbsp.	Japanese soy sauce	1 1/2 fl. oz.
1 Tbsp.	sugar	1/2 oz.

preparation:
1. Fabricate and reconstitute the *aburage*:
   a. Cut each *aburage* square diagonally into 4 triangles.
   b. Place the *aburage* in a stainless steel bowl just large enough to hold them snug.
   c. Pour boiling water over them and weight them with a plate or other small foodservice object. Soak for 5 minutes.
   d. Drain the *aburage* and squeeze them dry.
2. Flavor the *aburage*:
   a. Combine the water, *dashi*, soy sauce, and sugar in a very small saucepan. Bring to the simmer and add the *aburage*.
   b. Cover and simmer, occasionally turning over the *aburage*, for about 15 minutes, until almost all the liquid is absorbed.
   c. Cool to room temperature.
   d. Drain the *aburage* and press out excess liquid.

holding: refrigerate in a freshly sanitized, covered container up to 1 week

COMPONENT RECIPE
HAWAI'IAN MARINATED CHICKEN

yield: 1 lb.

production		costing only
1 lb.	boneless, skinless chicken thighs, very well trimmed	1 1/4 lb. a.p.
1 Tbsp.	cornstarch	1/4 oz.
1/4 c.	Japanese soy sauce	2 fl. oz.
1/4 c.	mirin	2 fl. oz.
tt	fresh-ground black pepper	1/16 oz.
pinch	cayenne pepper	1/16 oz.

preparation:
1. Cut the chicken thighs with the grain into 1 1/2" × 3/8" × 3/8" batonnets and place them in a bowl.
2. Sprinkle the cornstarch over the chicken and toss to coat the chicken evenly.
3. Add the remaining ingredients and toss.

holding: place in a freshly sanitized, covered container and refrigerate in the marinade up to 12 hours; after 12 hours, drain off the marinade and refrigerate up to 2 days longer

COMPONENT RECIPE
HEKKA SAUCE

yield: 1 qt.

production		costing only
1 c.	sake	8 fl. oz.
1 c.	Japanese soy sauce	8 fl. oz.
1 c.	pineapple juice	8 fl. oz.
1 c.	Poultry Stock	1/16 recipe
tt	kosher salt	1/8 oz.

preparation:
1. Mix all ingredients together.

holding: refrigerate in a freshly sanitized, covered container up to 1 week

---

RECIPE VARIATIONS
Hekka may be made with pork, firm fish such as tuna or swordfish, or shrimp. The vegetables may be varied as desired. If *aburage* is not available, omit it or replace it with Chinese seasoned pressed tofu or any firm tofu (omit the soaking and seasoning component recipe).

Chicken Adobo
with Vegetable Pancit

yield: 1 (12-oz.) bone-in entrée serving plus accompaniments (multiply × 4 for classroom turnout; adjust equipment sizes accordingly)

🕐 Requires 24 hours advance preparation.

MASTER RECIPE

production		costing only
1 Tbsp.	Annatto Oil	1/4 recipe
1 portion	Adobo-Marinated Hen	1/4 recipe
2 c.	coconut water	16 fl. oz.
—or—		
1/2 c.	coconut milk mixed with 1 1/2 c. water	4 fl. oz.
1 Tbsp.	red wine vinegar	1/2 fl. oz.
tt	kosher salt	1/8 oz.
2 Tbsp.	peanut oil	1 fl. oz.
1 Tbsp.	minced ginger	1/3 oz. a.p.
2 tsp.	minced fresh garlic	1/4 oz. a.p.
1/2 c.	julienne green beans	2 oz. a.p.
1/2 c.	fine-julienne carrot	2 oz. a.p.
1/2 c.	peeled, julienne celery	1/12 head a.p.
1/2 c.	fine-shredded napa cabbage	1/30 head a.p.
1/4 c.	julienne Braised Chinese Black Mushrooms	1/4 recipe
1 c.	Poultry Stock	1/16 recipe
2 Tbsp.	Philippine, Thai, or Vietnamese fish sauce	1 fl. oz.
1 Tbsp.	grated palm sugar or brown sugar	1/3 oz.
5 oz.	boiled and refreshed Chinese wheat flour noodles	3 oz. a.p.
tt	fresh lime juice	1/4 [63 ct.] lime
5	vine-ripe tomato wedges	2 1/2 oz. a.p.
1/4 c.	julienne scallion	1/4 bunch a.p.
1/8 c.	julienne red bell pepper	2 oz. a.p.
2 Tbsp.	fresh cilantro, pulled into bits	1/20 bunch a.p.

service turnout:

1. Braise the Adobo-Marinated Hen quarters:
   a. Heat an 8" nonstick sauté pan, heat the Annatto Oil, and add the hen pieces, skin side down. Fry over high heat for about 1 minute, until well browned.
   b. Add the coconut water, vinegar, and salt. Cover the pan and simmer briskly for about 2 minutes.
   c. Turn the hen pieces skin side up, cover the pan, and simmer for about 5 minutes longer.
   d. Uncover the pan and turn the hen pieces skin side down. Increase the heat and boil until the liquid reduces away. ⚠ Watch carefully to avoid scorching.
   e. When the liquid evaporates, the hen pieces will begin to fry. Cook, shaking the pan, allowing the skin to brown and crisp. ⚠ Watch carefully to avoid scorching.
2. Stir-fry the noodles:
   a. Heat a 14" wok or sauté pan until very hot, heat the peanut oil, then add the ginger, garlic, green beans, carrot, celery, cabbage, and Braised Chinese Black Mushrooms. Stir-fry for about 30 seconds.
   b. Add the Poultry Stock, fish sauce, sugar, and noodles.
   c. Continue to stir-fry for 1 to 2 minutes more, until the stock is absorbed and reduced to a light glaze.
   d. Add the lime juice, then taste and correct the seasoning, adding more fish sauce or sugar as needed.
3. Plate the dish:
   a. Mound the noodles in the center of a hot 12" plate.
   b. Place the hen pieces on top.
   c. Arrange the tomato wedges around the noodles.
   d. Top the hen pieces with a mound of julienne scallion and red bell pepper.
   e. Scatter the cilantro on top.

COMPONENT RECIPE
ADOBO-MARINATED HEN

yield: 4 (12-oz.) bone-in entrée servings

🕐 Requires 24 hours advance preparation.

production		costing only
8	peeled, crushed garlic cloves	2 1/2 oz. a.p.
1 c.	white wine	8 fl. oz.
1/2 c.	red wine vinegar	4 fl. oz.
1 Tbsp.	kosher salt	1/2 oz.
1 Tbsp.	cracked black pepper	1/4 oz.
1/4 tsp.	powdered bay leaf	1/16 oz.
2	24-oz. Cornish game hens	3 lb. a.p.

first day preparation:
1. Prepare the marinade:
   a. Combine the garlic, wine, vinegar, salt, pepper, and bay leaf in a large bowl.
2. Fabricate each hen into quarters:
   a. Use a heavy boning knife to cut down both sides of the backbone and pelvis, cutting through the hip joints. Remove the back section and reserve it for stock.
   b. Open the hen flat and cut through the breastbone to make 2 halves.
   c. Cut each half into a breast/wing quarter and a leg/thigh quarter.
   d. Repeat with the remaining hen.
   e. Rinse the hen quarters under cool water and blot dry with paper towels.
3. Marinate the hens:
   a. Place the hen quarters in the bowl with the marinade and turn them to thoroughly coat with the marinade.
   b. Pack the hen quarters and any remaining marinade in a freshly sanitized, nonreactive container just large enough to hold them.
   c. Cover and refrigerate for 24 hours.

second day preparation:
4. Portion the hens:
   a. Remove the hen pieces from the marinade and divide them into 4 portions consisting of 1 breast/wing quarter and 1 leg quarter.
   b. Individually wrap each portion in a plastic bag.

holding: refrigerate up to 2 days longer

COMPONENT RECIPE
BRAISED CHINESE BLACK MUSHROOMS

yield: approx. 3 oz.; 6 to 8 whole mushrooms or 1/2 c. julienne mushrooms

production		costing only
1 oz.	Chinese dried black mushrooms	1 oz.
1 c.	boiling water	n/c
1 Tbsp.	rendered chicken fat or peanut oil	n/c or 1/2 fl. oz.
1/4 c.	Chinese rice wine	2 fl. oz.
2 Tbsp.	Chinese light soy sauce	1 fl. oz.
2 tsp.	sugar	1/3 oz.
1/2 c.	strained mushroom soaking liquid	n/c
1 drop	Chinese dark sesame oil	1/32 fl. oz.

preparation:
1. Reconstitute the mushrooms:
   a. Place the mushrooms in a small stainless steel bowl or large ramekin.
   b. Pour the boiling water over the mushrooms and weight them down with a plate or other small foodservice item.
   c. Soak for 30 minutes or until the mushrooms are soft.
   d. Remove the mushrooms from the soaking liquid and rinse them under cool water.
   e. Pass the mushroom liquid through a very fine strainer or coffee filter and reserve it.
   f. Remove the tough mushroom stems. (Discard them, or reserve for making Asian stock.)
2. Braise the mushrooms:
   a. Heat an 8" sauté pan, heat the fat, and stir-fry the mushrooms for about 10 seconds, until they shrink slightly and are well coated with fat.
   b. Add the wine, soy sauce, sugar, mushroom liquid, and sesame oil.
   c. Simmer briskly, stirring occasionally, about 1 minute until the liquid absorbs/reduces to a glaze on the mushrooms. ⚠ Watch carefully to avoid scorching.
   d. Cool to room temperature.

holding: refrigerate in a freshly sanitized, covered container up to 1 week

---

RECIPE VARIATIONS

Filipino Vegetable Pancit with Adobo-Grilled Chicken Breast
Replace the Cornish Hens with 4 (4-oz.) boneless, skin-on chicken breast halves. Reduce the marinade ingredients by half. Marinate the chicken refrigerated for 2 hours. Char-grill the chicken breast, slice on the diagonal, and serve atop the vegetable noodles.

Filipino Seafood-Vegetable Pancit
Replace the Cornish hens with 2 oz. peeled small shrimp, 2 oz. sliced swordfish, and 2 oz. thin-sliced calamari tubes. Reduce the coconut water to 1/2 c. and the vinegar to a few drops. Braise the seafood for a few seconds only.

Kalua Pork Baked in Banana Leaf
with Island Fried Rice and Stir-Fry Cabbage

yield: 1 (8-oz.) bone-in entrée serving plus accompaniments (multiply × 4 for classroom turnout; adjust equipment sizes accordingly)

🕐 Requires 24 hours advance preparation.

MASTER RECIPE

production		costing only
1	Kalua Pork Packet	1/4 recipe
1 Tbsp.	peanut oil	1/2 fl. oz.
2 Tbsp.	fine-julienne young ginger	1 1/2 oz. a.p.
1/2 c.	julienne carrot	2 oz. a.p.
1/2 c.	slivered yellow onion	2 1/2 oz. a.p.
3 c.	shredded napa cabbage	6 oz. a.p.
tt	kosher salt	1/16 oz.
1/4 c.	water	n/c
tt	sugar	1/16 oz.
1 1/4 c.	Island Fried Rice, hot in steam table	1/4 recipe
1/4 c.	Pork Jus (from Kalua Pork Packets recipe), hot in steam table	1/4 recipe
2 Tbsp.	thin diagonal-sliced scallion	1/8 bunch a.p.

service turnout:
1. Heat the Kalua Pork Packet in a stovetop steamer for about 12 minutes or in a pressure steamer for 5 to 8 minutes.
2. Stir-fry the cabbage:
   a. Heat a 14" wok or 12" sauté pan, heat the oil, add the ginger, and then quickly add the carrot, onion, and cabbage.
   b. Stir-fry with a little salt for about 1 minute until just crisp-tender.
   c. Add the water and sugar and continue to stir-fry about 40 seconds until the water absorbs/evaporates.
   d. Taste and correct the salt.
3. Plate the dish:
   a. Place the pork packet on the left side of a hot 12" square plate. Using scissors, cut an X in the top of the packet and open up the banana leaf flaps.
   b. Use an 8-oz. portion scoop to place the Island Fried Rice on the back right of the plate.
   c. Mound the cabbage on the right front of the plate.
   d. Ladle the Pork Jus onto the pork.
   e. Sprinkle the scallion onto the pork.

COMPONENT RECIPE
KALUA MARINATED PORK

yield: 2 lb.

🕐 Requires 24 hours advance preparation.

production		costing only
1/4 c.	chopped ginger	1 1/4 oz. a.p.
2 Tbsp.	chopped garlic	2/3 oz. a.p.
1/4 c.	chopped scallion	1/4 bunch a.p.
1 tsp.	ground turmeric	1/8 oz.
1/4 c.	Japanese soy sauce	2 fl. oz.
2 Tbsp.	fresh lime juice	1/2 [63 ct.] lime
2 Tbsp.	peanut oil	1 fl. oz.
2 tsp.	kosher salt	1/3 oz.
1 Tbsp.	cracked black pepper	1/4 oz.
3 drops	liquid smoke	1/16 fl. oz.
1 c.	pineapple juice	8 fl. oz.
2 lb.	country-style pork ribs, in 1 piece	2 lb.

preparation:
1. Prepare the marinade:
   a. Combine the ginger, garlic, scallion, turmeric, soy sauce, lime juice, oil, salt, pepper, and liquid smoke in a blender and blend smooth.
   b. While blending, add the pineapple juice through the feed tube.
2. Fabricate and marinate the ribs:
   a. Trim excess fat from the ribs.
   b. Cut the ribs into 4 (8-oz.) portions.
   c. Place the ribs in a bowl and pour the marinade over them, scraping in all the solids. Mix well.
   d. Pack the ribs and marinade into a freshly sanitized, non-reactive container just large enough to hold them snug.
   e. Cover and refrigerate for at least 24 hours.

holding: refrigerate in the marinade up to 3 days

RECIPE VARIATION
Kalua Chicken with Island Fried Rice and Stir-Fry Cabbage
Replace the pork ribs with 8 (4-oz.) skinless bone-in chicken thighs. Decrease the steaming time by half.

ENTREES

COMPONENT RECIPE

KALUA PORK PACKETS AND PORK JUS

yield: 4 (8-oz.) bone-in entrée servings

production		costing only
8	15" lengths banana leaf	1/2 pkg.
3	8-oz. orange-fleshed sweet potatoes	1 1/2 lb. a.p.
tt	Hawai'ian red alaea salt or other coarse natural salt	1/8 oz.
4 portions	Kalua Marinated Pork	1 recipe

preparation:

1. Mise en place:
   a. Soak the banana leaves in hot water for about 30 minutes, until pliable.
   b. Prepare a two-tier stovetop steamer or pressure steamer fitted with a drippings pan on the first tier.
2. Fabricate and season the sweet potatoes:
   a. Peel the sweet potatoes and cut them lengthwise into quarters to yield 12 pieces.
   b. Rinse the sweet potatoes under cool water and, while they are still damp, sprinkle them liberally with salt.
3. Assemble the pork packets:
   a. Drain the banana leaves and blot them dry.
   b. Place a banana leaf section horizontally on the work surface, shiny side down.
   c. Lay another leaf section perpendicular across it.
   d. Place a portion of Kalua Marinated Pork, fatty side down, in the center of the leaves. Arrange three sweet potato quarters around it.
   e. Fold the left side of the horizontal banana leaf over the food, and then the right. Fold the far end of the vertical banana leaf over the food, then the near end. Turn the packet upside down. When finished, you should have a square packet with the ends of the leaves underneath and a smooth, seamless top.
   f. Repeat with the remaining ingredients to make a total of four packets.
4. Steam the pork packets in the top tier of the stovetop steamer for 1 1/2 hours (replenish the water as needed) or in the pressure steamer for 20 to 30 minutes.

5. Prepare the jus (pan juices):
   a. If serving immediately, transfer the liquid in the drippings pan to an ice-water bath. Skim the fat from the top and reserve the jus.
   b. If not serving immediately, open-pan cool the pork packets and drippings to room temperature and then refrigerate until cold.
   c. Remove the fat from the drippings and reserve the jus.

holding: refrigerate the pork packets in a freshly sanitized, covered container, or in individual plastic bags, up to 5 days; refrigerate the jus in a freshly sanitized, covered container up to 5 days

COMPONENT RECIPE

ISLAND FRIED RICE

yield: 5 c.

production		costing only
4 c.	cold, cooked Jasmine Rice	2/3 recipe
1	egg, beaten	1 each or 2 oz.
2 Tbsp.	Japanese soy sauce	1 fl. oz.
4 Tbsp.	bacon drippings	n/c
2 Tbsp.	peanut oil	1 fl. oz.
2 Tbsp.	minced ginger	1 oz. a.p.
1 Tbsp.	minced garlic	1/3 oz. a.p.
1/3 c.	3/8"-diced red bell peppers	3 oz. a.p.
1/3 c.	3/8"-diced green bell peppers	3 oz. a.p.
1/3 c.	3/8"-diced smoked ham	2 oz. a.p.
tt	kosher salt	1/16 oz.
1/2 c.	3/8"-diced fresh pineapple	1/12 [10 ct.] pineapple
1/3 c.	thin diagonal-sliced scallion	1/6 bunch a.p.

preparation:

1. Mix together the Jasmine Rice, egg, and soy sauce. Rest at room temperature for 15 minutes, and then mix again.
2. Heat a 14" wok or 12" nonstick sauté pan, heat the bacon drippings and oil, and then add the ginger, garlic, bell peppers, and ham. Stir-fry for a few seconds, then add the rice. Stir-fry constantly for about 1 minute, until the rice is hot and the egg coats each rice grain.
3. Taste and correct the seasoning with salt, if needed.
4. Remove the wok from the heat and toss in the pineapple and scallion.

holding: open-pan cool and immediately refrigerate in a freshly sanitized, covered container up to 3 days

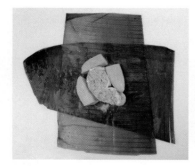

Place a portion of pork and three pieces of sweet potato on the leaves.

Begin wrapping the packet by folding the left side of the horizontal banana leaf over the food.

Turn upside down, making a square packet with a smooth top.

Chinese-Style Tomato Beef
with Sticky Rice

yield: 1 (10-oz.) entrée serving
(to multiply × 4 for classroom turnout, separately prepare
2 double recipes in a 14" or 16" wok)

MASTER RECIPE

production		costing only
3 Tbsp.	peanut oil, in squeeze bottle	1 1/2 fl. oz.
3 oz.	1/4"-thick slices green bell pepper	4 oz. a.p.
3 oz.	1/4"-thick slices yellow bell pepper	4 oz. a.p.
2 oz.	1/4"-thick slices sweet onion	2 1/2 oz. a.p.
2 Tbsp.	minced ginger	1 oz. a.p.
1 Tbsp.	minced garlic	1/3 oz. a.p.
4 oz.	Chinese Marinated Beef	1/4 recipe
2	vine-ripe plum tomatoes, each cut into 6 wedges	6 oz. a.p.
1 c.	Chinese Stir-Fry Sauce for Beef	1/4 recipe
2 Tbsp.	cornstarch dissolved in 1/4 c. water to make a slurry	1/2 oz.
2 drops	Chinese sesame oil	1/16 fl. oz.
tt	kosher salt	1/16 oz.
tt	fresh-ground black pepper	1/8 oz.
2 Tbsp.	thin diagonal-sliced scallion	1/8 bunch a.p.
2 Tbsp.	fresh cilantro, pulled into bits	1/20 bunch a.p.
1 1/2 c.	Sticky Rice, hot in steam table	1/4 recipe
as needed	hot water, in pan or steam table	n/c

service turnout:

1. Mise en place:
   a. Have ready at the stove a wok, a hotel spoon, a small spoon, a sizzle plate, an 8 fl. oz. ladle, the serving plate, an 8 fl. oz. portion scoop, and a pan or steam table pot of hot water.
   b. Assemble the oil, bell peppers, onion, ginger, garlic, Chinese Marinated Beef, tomatoes, cornstarch slurry, sesame oil, salt, pepper, Chinese Stir-Fry Sauce for Beef, scallions, and cilantro on a half-sheet tray near the stove.

2. Cook the stir-fry:
   a. Heat a 14" wok or sauté pan, heat 1 Tbsp. oil, and use the hotel spoon to stir-fry the peppers and onion with a little salt for about 20 seconds, until their color deepens and they are coated with oil. Remove to the sizzle plate.
   b. Add the remaining oil and the ginger and garlic, then immediately add the beef. Stir-fry for about 10 seconds.
   c. Quickly add the tomatoes and stir-fry for a few seconds longer.
   d. Stir the sauce to recombine it, and then ladle it into the wok.
   e. When the sauce boils, stir the slurry with the small spoon to recombine it, then push aside the solids in the wok and stir just enough slurry into the boiling sauce to thicken it.
   f. Immediately remove the wok from the heat, add the pepper and sesame oil, and toss to distribute the seasonings.

3. Plate the dish:
   a. Dip the portion scoop in the hot water, shake off excess water, and take up a heaping scoop of Sticky Rice. Place the rice in the back center of a hot 12" pasta plate.
   b. Spoon the beef stir-fry into the plate.
   c. Sprinkle with the scallion and cilantro.

COMPONENT RECIPE
CHINESE MARINATED BEEF

yield: 1 lb.

production		costing only
1 1/4 lb.	beef flank steak	1 1/4 lb.
1 Tbsp.	cornstarch	1/4 oz.
1/4 c.	Chinese soy sauce	2 fl. oz.
1/4 c.	Chinese rice wine or dry sherry	2 fl. oz.

preparation:
1. Fabricate the beef:
   a. Trim all fat and silverskin from the beef flank steak.
   b. Cut the beef flank steak in half lengthwise to make 2 long strips.
   c. Use a sharp, flexible knife to cut each strip across the grain on a sharp diagonal to make wide, 1/8"-thick slices.
2. Marinate the beef:
   a. Place the cornstarch in a small, freshly sanitized container just large enough to hold the beef slices.
   b. Stir in the soy sauce and wine.
   c. Mix the beef slices into the marinade, cover the container, and refrigerate for at least 1 hour.

holding: refrigerate up to 24 hours

COMPONENT RECIPE
CHINESE STIR-FRY SAUCE FOR BEEF

yield: 1 qt.

production		costing only
3 c.	Poultry Stock	3/16 recipe
1/2 c.	Chinese oyster sauce	4 fl. oz.
1/4 c.	Chinese rice wine or dry sherry	2 fl. oz.
1/4 c.	Chinese soy sauce	2 fl. oz.
2 Tbsp.	sugar	1 oz.

preparation:
1. Mix together all ingredients in a freshly sanitized, nonreactive container.

holding: cover and refrigerate up to 1 week

RECIPE VARIATION
Tomato Chicken
Replace the beef flank steak with trimmed, boneless chicken breast.

Banana Spring Rolls
with Rum Sauce and Grilled Pineapple

yield: 1 dessert serving
(multiply × 4 for classroom turnout; adjust equipment sizes accordingly)

MASTER RECIPE

production		costing only
1 wedge	cored baby golden pineapple (with crown)	1/6 pineapple a.p.
1 Tbsp.	melted butter	1/2 oz.
1 Tbsp.	brown sugar	1/3 oz.
2	Banana Spring Rolls	1/4 recipe
as needed	frying compound or peanut oil	% used
2/3 c.	Rum Sauce	1/4 recipe
2 Tbsp.	toasted unsalted macadamia nut pieces	1/4 oz.

service turnout:
1. Grill the pineapple:
   a. Brush the flesh of the pineapple wedge with half of the melted butter and grill it, flesh side down, until marked.
   b. Place the pineapple wedge on a sizzle pan, flesh side up; brush with the remaining butter, sprinkle with the sugar, and bake in a 400°F oven until the sugar melts.
2. Refry the Banana Spring Rolls in 400°F oil for about 15 seconds to recrisp them. Drain in the fryer basket or on a rack.
3. Plate the dish:
   a. Ladle the Rum Sauce onto a cool 8" plate.
   b. Place 1 spring roll horizontally on the plate, and then prop the other spring roll vertically across it.
   c. Prop the pineapple wedge upright against the intersection of the spring rolls, flesh side facing left.
   d. Sprinkle the plate with the macadamia nuts.

COMPONENT RECIPE
BANANA SPRING ROLLS

yield: 8 spring rolls

production		costing only
as needed	frying compound or peanut oil	% used
1/3 c.	brown sugar	1 3/4 oz.
1/3 c.	light rum	2 2/3 fl. oz.
pinch	kosher salt	1/16 oz.
3	large, ripe bananas	1 lb. a.p.
1 Tbsp.	fresh lemon juice	1/6 [90 ct.] lemon
2 Tbsp.	banana liqueur	1 fl. oz.
8	Chinese spring roll wrappers	3/4 pkg. or a.p.
1 Tbsp.	beaten egg mixed with 1 Tbsp. water	1/4 each or 1/2 oz.

preparation:
1. Mise en place:
   a. Preheat a fryer to 400°F, or fill a heavy saucepan with oil and heat to 400°F.
   b. Have ready a rack set over a sheet tray.
2. Prepare the filling:
   a. Combine the sugar, rum, and salt in a small sauté pan, and stir over low heat until the sugar melts.
   b. Scrape the sugar mixture into a large bowl and cool to room temperature.
   c. Peel the bananas and add them to the bowl along with the lemon juice and banana liqueur.
   d. Use a potato masher or immersion blender to mash the bananas into a coarse purée.
3. Assemble the spring rolls:
   a. Place a spring roll wrapper on the work surface with one corner directly in front of you.
   b. Spoon 1/8 of the banana mixture in a horizontal line just forward of the wrapper's center.
   c. Bring the wrapper corner up over the banana mixture and then roll up the spring roll, tucking in the sides. Seal it by brushing the far corner with egg wash.
   d. Repeat with the remaining ingredients to make 8 spring rolls.
4. Immediately deep-fry the spring rolls until the shells are light golden. Drain on the rack.
5. If not using immediately, cool the spring rolls to room temperature and refrigerate them.

holding: refrigerate on the rack, covered with a clean, lint-free kitchen towel, up to 24 hours

DESSERTS

COMPONENT RECIPE
RUM SAUCE

yield: 2 1/2 c.

production		costing only
4	egg yolks	4 each or 2 2/3 oz.
2/3 c.	brown sugar	3 2/3 oz.
1/2 tsp.	kosher salt	1/6 oz.
1 c.	heavy cream	8 fl. oz.
3 Tbsp.	butter, cut into bits	1 1/2 oz.
2 Tbsp.	fresh lemon juice	3/8 [90 ct.] lemon
1/4 c.	dark rum	2 fl. oz.

preparation:
1. Mise en place:
   a. Prepare a simmering hot-water bath of the correct size to accommodate a 3-qt. stainless steel bowl.
   b. Prepare an ice-water bath that will accommodate the same bowl.
2. In a 3-qt. stainless steel bowl, whisk together the egg yolks, sugar, and salt, and then whisk in the cream.
3. Place the bowl in the hot-water bath and whisk the yolk mixture constantly over simmering water for about 8 minutes, until the sauce thickens and the mixture reaches 180°F.
4. Whisk in the butter and lemon juice.
5. Transfer the bowl from the hot-water bath to the ice-water bath and cool it, whisking occasionally, to room temperature.
6. Whisk in the rum, and then continue chilling until cold.

holding: refrigerate in a freshly sanitized, covered, nonreactive container up to 3 days

RECIPE VARIATION

Banana Spring Rolls with Chocolate Sauce and Macadamia Nut Ice Cream
Replace the Rum Sauce with Vanilla Custard Sauce flavored while hot with melted bittersweet chocolate. Replace the grilled pineapple with a 4-fl.-oz. scoop Vanilla Ice Cream made with 4 oz. toasted, chopped, salted macadamia nuts.

Kona Coffee Choco-Mac Tart

with Macadamia Brittle

yield: 1 dessert serving
(multiply × 4 for classroom turnout)

MASTER RECIPE

production		costing only
1 slice	Kona Coffee Choco-Mac Tart	1/10 recipe
1 Tbsp.	miniature chocolate curls or chocolate shavings	1/4 oz.
1 wedge	Macadamia Brittle	1/8 recipe

service turnout:
1. Plate the dish:
   a. Place the slice of Kona Coffee Choco-Mac Tart in the center of a cool 10" plate.
   b. Garnish the rim of the tart slice with chocolate curls.
   c. Stick the wedge of Macadamia Brittle upright in the top of the tart.

COMPONENT RECIPE
KONA COFFEE CHOCO-MAC TART

yield: 1 (10") tart

production		costing only
1/4 c.	very strong, freshly-brewed Kona coffee, room temperature	2 fl. oz.
2 tsp.	unflavored granular gelatin	1/3 oz.
3 c.	Pastry Cream, fresh-made and still warm	1 recipe
1	Macadamia Frangipane Sweet Dough Shell	1 recipe
4 oz.	bittersweet chocolate, preferably Hawai'ian, chopped if necessary	4 oz.
1 c.	coarse-chopped unsalted macadamia nuts	4 oz.
1 1/2 c.	Sweetened Whipped Cream	3/4 recipe

preparation:
1. Mix the coffee and gelatin in a small bowl. Bloom the gelatin for 5 minutes, and then place the bowl in a saucepan of hot water until the gelatin dissolves.
2. Spoon 1 c. of the Pastry Cream into another bowl and reserve it in a warm place.
3. Whisk the coffee-gelatin mixture into the remaining Pastry Cream.
4. Spoon a dab of the coffee pastry cream in the center of a 10" round cake board. Remove the Macadamia Frangipane Sweet Dough Shell from the tart pan and place it on the cake board.
5. Spread the coffee pastry cream into the shell and freeze it until just set. Do not freeze for longer than 30 minutes.
6. Place the chocolate in a clean, dry bowl and place it over a pan of barely simmering water. Melt the chocolate, stirring frequently with a rubber spatula.
7. Whisk the chocolate and macadamia nuts into the reserved pastry cream.
8. Spread the chocolate–macadamia nut pastry cream onto the coffee filling already in the shell and refrigerate for about 20 minutes, until set.
9. Spread the Sweetened Whipped Cream onto the tart in a smooth, even layer and refrigerate for at least 30 minutes.

holding: refrigerate under a cake dome up to 2 days

COMPONENT RECIPE
MACADAMIA FRANGIPANE SWEET DOUGH SHELL

yield: 1 (10") tart shell

production		costing only
12 oz.	Sweet Dough, chilled for 30 minutes	1 recipe
1 1/2 c.	Macadamia Frangipane	1 recipe

preparation:
1. Mise en place:
   a. Preheat an oven to 400°F.
   b. Have ready a 12"-diameter circle of pan liner and dried beans or other pie weights.
2. Roll out the Sweet Dough and fit it into a 10" removable-bottom fluted tart pan placed on a half-sheet tray.
3. Refrigerate the shell, uncovered, for 20 minutes.
4. Fit the pan liner circle into the shell and fill it with the pie weights.
5. Bake the shell for 15 minutes. (Prepare the Macadamia Frangipane now.)
6. Remove the pie weights and pan liner, and reduce the oven temperature to 350°F.
7. Smooth in the frangipane.
8. Return the shell to the oven and bake for 20 minutes longer, until the frangipane is set and the crust golden.
9. Remove the tart pan to a rack and cool to room temperature.

COMPONENT RECIPE
MACADAMIA FRANGIPANE

yield: approx. 1 1/2 c.

production		costing only
2 oz.	butter	2 oz.
1/2 c.	chopped unsalted macadamia nuts	2 oz.
1/4 c.	flour	1 1/2 oz.
pinch	fine salt	1/16 oz.
1/2 c.	confectioner's sugar	2 1/2 oz.
2	room-temperature egg whites	2 each or 2 oz.

preparation:
1. Prepare brown butter:
   a. Prepare a shallow ice-water bath of the correct size to accommodate an 8" sauté pan.
   b. Melt the butter in an 8" sauté pan.
   c. Continue heating, swirling the pan and watching carefully, until the butter becomes a rich brown color.
   d. Immediately stop the browning by placing the sauté pan in the ice-water bath.
   e. Remove the pan from the ice-water bath and hold the brown butter at warm room temperature. Do not allow it to congeal.
2. Combine the nuts, flour, salt, and confectioner's sugar in a blender or small food processor. Pulse to a coarse powder.
3. In a clean, dry bowl, beat the egg whites to very soft peaks.
4. Immediately fold in the nut mixture, and then fold in the brown butter.

holding: use immediately

COMPONENT RECIPE
MACADAMIA BRITTLE

yield: 10 triangles plus scraps

production		costing only
1 c.	coarse-chopped salted macadamia nuts	4 oz.
1 1/2 c.	sugar	12 oz.
as needed	water	n/c

preparation:
1. Place a silicone pad on a sheet tray and arrange the nuts in the center in a thin, even layer.
2. Prepare the caramel:
   a. Place the sugar in a heavy saucepan and stir in just enough water to moisten it.
   b. Place the saucepan over low heat. Allow the sugar to melt undisturbed, shaking the pan only if necessary for the sugar to melt evenly.
   c. Raise the heat and bring the sugar syrup to the boil. Cook at a full boil until the sugar caramelizes to light brown. ⚠ Watch the sugar syrup constantly and handle carefully.
3. Immediately pour the caramel over the nuts in a thin, even layer.
4. Put on foodservice gloves and, as soon as you can handle the hot caramel, gently stretch it into a thin sheet of macadamia brittle.
5. Allow the brittle to cool and harden.
6. Break the brittle into at least 10 elongated triangles about 1" wide and 2" long.

holding: store at cool room temperature and low humidity in a tightly sealed container up to 2 weeks

---

RECIPE VARIATION
Chocolate–Coffee–Macadamia Nut Pie
Replace the Macadamia Frangipane Sweet Dough Shell with a fully baked 9" American Pastry Dough pie shell. Whisk the bloomed gelatin, melted chocolate, and nuts into 3 c. pastry cream, and then smooth this filling into the pie shell. Pipe rosettes of whipped cream onto each serving. Omit the Macadamia Brittle.

Fire and Ice
Haupia Custard
with Pineapple Compote

yield: 1 dessert serving
(multiply × 4 for classroom turnout; adjust equipment sizes accordingly)

MASTER RECIPE

production		costing only
3 Tbsp.	clarified butter	1 3/4 oz. a.p.
2 Tbsp.	peanut oil	1 fl. oz.
1	Coconut-Breaded *Haupia* Square	1/4 recipe
1	*Haupia* Custard Square, very cold	1/9 recipe
3/4 c.	Pineapple Compote	1/4 recipe

service turnout:
1. Fry the Coconut-Breaded *Haupia* Square*:
   a. Combine the butter and oil in a 6" nonstick sauté pan and heat over medium heat.
   b. Add the Coconut-Breaded *Haupia* Square, reduce the heat, and pan-fry for about 1 minute on each side until golden brown.
   c. Blot on a paper towel.
2. Plate the dish:
   a. Place the hot, fried *haupia* square on the left side of a cool 10" plate (preferably black), with points at 12, 3, 6, and 9 o'clock.
   b. Place the cold *Haupia* Custard Square upside down on the right side of the plate oriented in the same manner as the fried *haupia* square. Peel off the pan liner.
   c. Use a perforated spoon to mound the Pineapple Compote in the center.
   d. Spoon some of the compote syrup onto the plate, evenly distributing the chiffonade lime zest in it.

*Before turnout time, practice frying the extra Coconut-Breaded *Haupia* Square to master heat adjustment and timing.

COMPONENT RECIPE
COCONUT-BREADED *HAUPIA* SQUARES

yield: 4 squares plus 1 for practice

production		costing only
1 1/2 c.	sweetened shredded coconut	2 oz.
1 1/2 c.	coarse-ground fresh bread crumbs	6 to 8 oz. a.p.
5	*Haupia* Custard Squares	5/9 recipe
as needed	cornstarch	1/2 oz.
1	egg, beaten with 1 Tbsp. water	1 each or 2 fl. oz.

preparation:
1. Mix the coconut and bread crumbs in a shallow bowl.
2. Peel the pan liner off of each *Haupia* Custard Square, dredge it in cornstarch, coat with egg wash, and then coat with the coconut-crumb mixture. Press firmly to ensure that the coating adheres.
3. As you work, place the breaded custard squares on a rack set over a sheet tray.
4. Refrigerate the breaded custard squares at least 30 minutes so that the coating adheres.

holding: refrigerate on the rack, covered with a clean, dry kitchen towel, up to 2 days

COMPONENT RECIPE

HAUPIA CUSTARD SQUARES

yield: 9 (2 3/4" × 2 3/4" × 3/4") squares

production		costing only
as needed	pan coating spray	% of container
1 c.	sugar	8 oz.
6 Tbsp.	cornstarch	1 1/2 oz.
pinch	fine salt	1/16 oz.
27 fl. oz.	canned unsweetened coconut milk	2 (13.5-fl.-oz.) cans
1 c.	half-and-half	8 fl. oz.

preparation:
1. Mise en place:
   a. Cut a sheet of pan liner into 2 (9" × 11") rectangles that fit into the bottom of a half-size hotel pan.
   b. Place one of the rectangles in a half-size hotel pan and reserve the other one.
   c. Spray the pan liner and the sides of the pan with pan coating.
   d. Prepare an ice-water bath in a deep full-size hotel pan.
   e. Have ready an oven mitt and a clean, sanitized ruler.
2. Prepare the custard:
   a. Combine the sugar, cornstarch, and salt in a large, heavy, stainless steel bowl.
   b. In a thin stream, whisk in the coconut milk and half-and-half.
   c. Wearing an oven mitt, place the bowl over low heat and whisk constantly, rotating the bowl, for 8 minutes until the mixture thickens. Increase the heat to medium and whisk until the mixture comes to the boil. ⚠ Watch carefully to avoid scorching and to avoid catching the oven mitt on fire.
   d. Immediately pour the custard into the prepared hotel pan and place the pan level in the ice-water bath. Cool to room temperature.
   e. Refrigerate the custard for about 2 hours, until completely cold and firm.
3. Fabricate the custard squares:
   a. Run a flexible rubber spatula between the custard and the sides of the hotel pan to loosen it.
   b. Place the reserved pan liner rectangle on the surface of the custard.
   c. Place a clean cutting board on top of the hotel pan, and then flip over the pan and board. Remove the pan and peel off the pan liner.
   d. Trim off the edges of the custard to create a rectangle with square, rather than rounded, corners. Use the ruler to assist in cutting the custard and its pan liner into 9 (2 3/4" × 2 3/4") squares. Reserve the scraps for practice breading and frying.

holding: refrigerate in one layer in a covered container up to 4 days

COMPONENT RECIPE

PINEAPPLE COMPOTE

yield: 3 c.

production		costing only
1/2	ripe, fragrant pineapple	1/2 [8 ct.] pineapple
2 stalks	lemongrass	a.p.
—or—		
1 Tbsp.	frozen chopped lemongrass	1/4 oz.
6	1/4"-thick slices ginger	1 oz. a.p.
1/2 c.	sugar	4 oz.
as needed	water	n/c
1/4 c.	chiffonade lime zest	1 [63 ct.] lime
tt	fresh lime juice	n/c

preparation:
1. Fabricate the pineapple:
   a. Place a cutting board inside a sheet tray to catch the pineapple's juice.
   b. Cut off and discard the pineapple crown and base.
   c. Pare away the pineapple skin.
   d. Use the tip of a swivel peeler to dig out the eyes.
   e. Cut the pineapple flesh off the core and discard the core.
   f. Cut the pineapple flesh into 1/4" dice.
   g. Place the pineapple juice in a liquid measuring cup and reserve it.
2. Prepare the pineapple syrup:
   a. If necessary, cut off the root ends of the lemongrass stalks and peel away the fibrous outer layers to expose the tender cores. Cut into 1" lengths. Use a meat mallet to crush the lemongrass cores and ginger slices.
   b. Place the sugar in a small, nonreactive saucepan.
   c. Add enough water to the pineapple juice to equal 1 c.
   d. Stir the pineapple water into the sugar and add the lemongrass and ginger. Bring to the boil, cover the pan, and remove from the heat. Steep for 30 minutes.
   e. Pick out and discard (or strain out) the ginger slices and lemongrass stalks. Cool the syrup to room temperature.
3. Finish the compote:
   a. Mix the diced pineapple with the sugar syrup and add the lime zest.
   b. Taste and balance the flavor with lime juice.
   c. Refrigerate for at least 30 minutes.

holding: refrigerate in a freshly sanitized, covered container up to 24 hours

---

RECIPE VARIATIONS

Lu'au-Style Haupia
Omit the dredging and frying ingredients. Serve chilled *Haupia* Custard Squares on ti leaves sprinkled with toasted sweetened coconut and accompanied with a lime wedge.

Haupia Coconut-Custard Coupe
Reduce the cornstarch in the *Haupia* Custard Squares to 4 Tbsp. Portion the warm custard into martini glasses or wineglasses and chill until softly set. Top with Pineapple Compote.

☐ TABLE 14.2 HAWAI'I REGIONAL INGREDIENTS

The pantry of Hawai'i is the pantry of the entire Pacific Rim and, indeed, much of the world. Contemporary Hawai'i chefs and cooks not only use Hawai'ian and Polynesian seafood and agricultural products, but also borrow freely from the huge list of Chinese, Korean, Japanese, Filipino, and Southeast Asian ingredients. Western foods from Portugal, Spain, and the Americas also play an important role in Hawai'i's cooking.

ITEM	MARKET FORMS	USES	SEASONALITY	OTHER	STORAGE
MEDIUM-GRAIN WHITE RICE	Medium-grain white rice is sold by the pound in 20-lb. and 25-lb. bags. The California-produced Calrose variety is Hawai'i's most popular rice. Kokuho rose is preferred for sushi and musubi.	Hawai'i cooks pan-steam medium-grain rice in the Asian manner. The rice is washed, boiled in limited water, and then allowed to steam in its own heat or in a low oven until fluffy but slightly sticky. Pan-steamed rice accompanies virtually every local food entrée.	N/A	To make fried rice, cold, cooked medium-grain rice is coated with raw egg and then stir-fried with Asian seasonings and various ingredients often including bacon, ham, or Spam.	Store at cool room temperature.
JASMINE RICE	As above. Brands vary in mouthfeel and aroma.	After washing, the rice is soaked in hot water for 20 minutes, then drained and cooked in 1:1 ratio water.	N/A		Store at cool room temperature.
STICKY RICE/ GLUTINOUS RICE	As above; 5-lb. bags are also available.	The rice is washed, soaked in water overnight, and then steamed.	N/A		Store at cool room temperature.
RICE NOODLES	Rice noodles are made by extruding a rice flour–water dough through a die. Dried forms range from fine vermicelli to flat 1/8"-wide noodles sold in 12-oz. and 1-lb. bundles. Fresh rice noodles are sold by the pound as flat 1/8"-wide noodles and thick, 1/2" wide chow fun noodles.	Dried rice noodles are reconstituted by steeping in boiling water for a minute or so, then drained and rinsed. Rice noodles are used in soups and salads, and may be stir-fried.	N/A	Dried rice noodles, when deep-fried in oil, puff up and become crisp. They are used as a garnish or as a "nest" for saucy stir-fry dishes.	Store dried rice noodles at room temperature. Refrigerate fresh noodles or freeze for prolonged storage.
OKINAWAN PURPLE SWEET POTATOES	Grown on Molokai, these Asian imports have a deep purple flesh and almost sugary-sweet taste. They are available by the pound from specialty purveyors or mail-ordered on the Internet.	Baked, steamed, fried, or mashed, their unusual color lends interest to plate presentations.	September to October		Store in a cool, dark, well-ventilated place up to 2 weeks.
BEAN THREAD NOODLES/ CELLOPHANE NOODLES	These fine-textured dried noodles are made from a mung bean starch paste extruded through a die. They are sold in bundles of varying sizes.	When reconstituted in boiling water, they become soft, slippery, and translucent, adding interesting texture to soups, salads, and stir-fry dishes.	N/A		Store at room temperature.
FRESH CHINESE WHEAT-FLOUR NOODLES	These soft, spaghetti-like, ivory-colored noodles are made from white wheat flour and water. They are sold in 1-lb. consumer packs and 10-lb. bags.	These noodles are boiled al dente, refreshed, and drained, then stir-fried with Asian seasonings and various ingredients. Alternatively, they are pan-fried crisp and topped with a saucy stir-fry.	N/A	Fresh Chinese wheat flour noodles may be substituted for Filipino *pancit* noodles.	Refrigerate 1 week; freeze up to 3 months.

☐ TABLE 14.2 HAWAI'I REGIONAL INGREDIENTS *(continued)*

ITEM	MARKET FORMS	USES	SEASONALITY	OTHER	STORAGE
CHINESE SPRING ROLL WRAPPERS/ FILIPINO LUMPIA WRAPPERS	Very thin, almost translucent squares or rounds of wheat-flour dough are used to wrap a variety of fillings before deep-frying. They are sold frozen in packages of 10 to 20 wrappers.	Spring roll skins must be thoroughly defrosted before using and, once the package is opened, kept tightly sealed or under a damp towel to prevent drying. The 7" × 7" squares may be used whole to make large spring rolls or cut in quarters to make miniature spring rolls.	N/A	Do not substitute the thicker, pastalike Chinese egg roll wrappers.	Store frozen. Thaw overnight in the refrigerator before using.
JAPANESE GYOZA WRAPPERS/ CHINESE DUMPLING WRAPPERS	Thin, 3" round discs of wheat-flour dough are sold frozen in packages of 40 to 50. Gyoza wrappers are typically thinner, whereas dumpling wrappers are thicker.	These wrappers are used to make a variety of Japanese, Korean, and Chinese dumplings, which are steamed, boiled, or pan-braised.	N/A	Wonton wrappers are square rather than round.	Store frozen. Thaw overnight in the refrigerator before using.
SHRIMP CHIPS/*KRUPUK* (kroo-POOK)	Processed from ground, dried shrimp and rice flour, shrimp chips are sold in small boxes of both Indonesian and Thai manufacture. They are offered in small and large sizes. A multi-colored variety is also available.	The small, translucent dried disks are briefly deep-fried, which causes them to puff up into large, opaque chips with a texture reminiscent of Styrofoam.	N/A	Fried shrimp chips are best served immediately but may be stored in a tightly sealed container at room temperature for up to 1 week.	Store tightly sealed at room temperature.
JAPANESE PANKO BREAD CRUMBS	These very light, flaky bread crumbs are sold in 1-lb. packages and in bulk.	Panko is used as a coating for fried foods.	N/A	If unavailable, substitute coarse-textured dried white bread crumbs or cracker crumbs.	Store at room temperature.
SOY SAUCES	For everyday use, most Hawai'i cooks prefer Japanese-style soy sauce; Kikkoman is the most widely used brand. Soy sauce is sold in various size bottles and in gallon jugs for foodservice. Flavored soy sauces and low-sodium soy sauce are also available.	Soy sauce flavors sauces, salad dressings, and marinades. In many homes and restaurants it is used as a table sauce.	N/A	Soy sauce is made by soaking and steaming soybeans, adding water and a yeast culture, fermenting, and then straining. The soy sauce is then aged for several months up to 2 years.	Store at room temperature.
FISH SAUCE	Hawai'i cooks use Vietnamese *nuoc mam* (nook MAHM), Thai *nam pla* (nahm PLAH), and Filipino *patis* (pah-TEECE) fish sauces interchangeably. It is sold in 25-oz. bottles and 2-liter jugs for foodservice.	Pungent, salty uncooked fish sauce flavors salad dressings, dipping sauces, and marinades. Its flavor mellows when used in hot dishes such as stir-frys and stews.	N/A	This translucent, amber liquid is produced by fermenting salted fish in brine. The liquid is strained off the fish and bottled.	Store at room temperature.
OYSTER SAUCE	This dark brown, viscous, salty-sweet condiment is sold in 18-oz. bottles and gallon jugs for foodservice.	Oyster sauce is used to flavor meat, poultry, and vegetable dishes and is rarely used with seafood.	N/A	Oyster sauce is made by simmering oyster extracts, water, salt, and caramel coloring. It is thickened with cornstarch.	Store unopened bottles at room temperature. Refrigerate after opening.

(continued)

☐ TABLE 14.2 HAWAI'I REGIONAL INGREDIENTS (continued)

ITEM	MARKET FORMS	USES	SEASONALITY	OTHER	STORAGE
JAPANESE RICE WINE VINEGAR	Japanese rice wine vinegar is sold in various size bottles and in gallon jugs for foodservice. Marukkan is a popular brand distributed worldwide.	This light, slightly sweet vinegar is used to flavor sushi rice and in salad dressings and marinades.	N/A	Once a by-product of rice wine production, today rice vinegar is made from rice soaked in water and then fermented.	Store at room temperature.
MIRIN (meer-in)	This clear, slightly sweet cooking wine is sold in bottles of various sizes.	Mirin is used in sauces, dressings, marinades, and glazes.	N/A	Not technically wine, this slightly alcoholic liquid is made from fermented glutinous rice and Japanese distilled grain alcohol.	Store at room temperature.
SAKE (sah-kay)	Sake is available in 750-ml and 1.5-L bottles in stores that sell alcoholic beverages.	Used in sauces, marinades, and stir-fry dishes, sake is normally heated until the alcohol evaporates out, leaving behind a mellow, slightly sweet flavor.	N/A	Sake is brewed from fermented rice in a manner similar to beer. If unavailable, substitute dry vermouth.	Store unopened bottles at room temparature. Refrigerate after opening.
CHINESE RICE WINE	Chinese rice wine flavored with salt is sold in Asian grocery stores in 750-ml bottles. The Shaoxing (shao-ZHING) variety is most commonly available.	Chinese rice wine is used primarily in marinades for foods to be stir-fried. Its mild acidity helps tenderize protein foods and its mellow flavor enhances the flavor of the sauce.	N/A	Chinese rice wine is made in much the same way as sake, but it has a different flavor. If unavailable, substitute dry sherry.	Store unopened bottles at room temperature. Refrigerate after opening.
JAPANESE PICKLED GINGER	Pickled ginger is sold in jars and plastic tubs of various sizes.	Pickled ginger is the traditional accompaniment to sushi and sashimi. Hawai'i cooks use it in salads and as a garnish. The pickling juice flavors sauces and salad dressings.	N/A	Tender young ginger is sliced very thin and immersed in a pickling liquid containing salt, sugar, rice vinegar, and pink food coloring.	Store unopened containers at room temperature. Refrigerate after opening.
ASIAN SESAME OIL	Because it is used sparingly as a seasoning, Asian sesame oil is normally sold in small 5-fl.-oz. bottles.	Use for seasoning foods rather than as a cooking medium. Its rich, nutty flavor can be overpowering if used in excess.	N/A	This dark, aromatic oil is extracted from roasted sesame seeds. Do not confuse it with flavorless sesame oil used for cooking.	Store at room temperature. Refrigerate for prolonged storage.
BROWN BEAN PASTE	Brown bean paste is packed in cans and jars of various sizes. Flavor and texture vary by producer.	This thick seasoning paste is used as an aromatic in stir-frying. It may be included in sauces and marinades. Its pungent, salty flavor mellows when fried in oil.	N/A	Brown bean paste is made from crushed, fermented soybeans, wheat flour, salt, and sugar.	If purchased in a can, transfer to a sanitized plastic container after opening and refrigerate.
HOISIN SAUCE	This thick, smooth, dark brown, highly aromatic Chinese condiment is sold in jars and cans of varying size. Flavor and consistency vary per producer; brands produced in Asia are superior.	Hoisin is used as a table sauce for Peking duck, mooshu pork, and Asian appetizers. When sizzled in the oil of a stir-fry, hoisin sauce lends a deep color and sweet, slightly smoky flavor to the dish. It adds color and flavor to marinades and glazes.	N/A	Hoisin sauce is made from puréed brown bean paste with garlic, red chile, and Chinese five-spice powder.	If purchased in a can, transfer to a sanitized plastic container after opening and refrigerate.

☐ TABLE 14.2 HAWAI'I REGIONAL INGREDIENTS (continued)

ITEM	MARKET FORMS	USES	SEASONALITY	OTHER	STORAGE
MISO (mee-soh)	Red miso is robust in flavor and quite salty; white miso is sweeter and has a more refined flavor. Miso is sold in containers of varying sizes.	Best known as a Japanese soup ingredient, miso is also used in salad dressings, coatings, and marinades. Salty and pungent, it can be used to cure meats or poultry.	N/A	A lightly fermented paste made from soybeans and grains.	Refrigerate up to 1 month. Avoid contamination by using a freshly-sanitized utensil to remove from the container.
STAR ANISE	Star anise is a whole spice available by the ounce or pound from Asian markets and spice purveyors.	Star anise is used whole to lend soups, stews, and sauces an aromatic licorice-like flavor. For foodservice, remove pods before serving.	N/A	Pods of Asian anise have a symmetrical, five-pointed star shape.	Store at room temperature or freeze for prolonged storage.
CHINESE FIVE-SPICE POWDER	This blend of ground star anise, fennel, cinnamon, cloves, and Sichuan peppercorns is sold by the ounce or pound in Asian markets or by spice purveyors.	Five-spice powder flavors marinades and glazes and is used in sauces for slow-simmered pork, beef, or duck dishes. Use sparingly.	N/A		Store frozen to retain flavor and aroma.
TURMERIC	This golden colored, pungent spice is usally sold by the ounce or pound in powdered form. For best price and freshness purchase from a South Asian market.	Turmeric adds a warm, slightly bitter flavor and a deep yellow color to sauces, batters, and coatings.	N/A	Rhizomes of the turmeric plant are boiled, dried, and then ground into a fine yellow-orange powder.	Store tightly sealed at room temperature or freeze for prolonged storage.
WASABI (wah-sah-bee)	The most economical option, pale green, dried wasabi powder is sold in 1-oz. cans or in bulk in Japanese markets. Prepared wasabi is available in small tubes and tubs of varying sizes. Frozen wasabi root is available from specialty purveyors.	This pungent green horseradish is served as a head-clearing accent to sushi and sashimi. It adds kick to sauces, marinades, and salad dressings. Mix wasabi powder with water and wait 15 to 20 minutes for the flavor to develop.	N/A	Wasabi may be prepared stand-up thick or of a thinner, saucelike consistency.	Store dried wasabi powder at room temperature. Refrigerate prepared wasabi up to 1 week.
ANNATTO	See p. 782.				
HAWAI'IAN SALTS	Alaea (ah-la-A-ah) sea salt is colored salmon-red with nutrient-rich clay. Black lava salt contains natural volcanic charcoal. Purchase coarse- or fine-grind salts by the pound from specialty purveyors or on the Internet.	Use as a finishing salt to lend a crunchy texture and unusual color to any savory food.	N/A		Store tightly sealed at room temperature.
OGO (OH-go) SEAWEED	Rarely marketed outside Hawai'i, ogo may be ordered by the pound from specialty purveyors.	The thin, hairlike, brown seaweed is eaten raw or lightly blanched in salads and to accompany raw or cooked fish. When deep-fried, ogo transforms into a crispy tangle with a dramatic appearance.	N/A	An indigenous Hawai'ian food, ogo grows wild along the shorelines and is also aquacultured.	Refrigerate loosely covered up to 1 week.

(continued)

☐ **TABLE 14.2 HAWAI'I REGIONAL INGREDIENTS** *(continued)*

ITEM	MARKET FORMS	USES	SEASONALITY	OTHER	STORAGE
NORI	Thin, crisp, pressed and roasted seaweed ranges in color from black to deep olive green. Nori for sushi comes in packets of 10 to 12 (7 1/2" × 8 1/2") sheets.	Nori is primarily used to wrap sushi rolls. Crumbled nori is sprinkled over rice or in soups. Nori can be used as a wrapping for foods such as fish, chicken, or vegetables. Cut with scissors into chiffonade, it makes a dramatic garnish.	N/A	For most applications, nori is crisped by passing the sheet over a gas flame just until the color darkens slightly.	Packages of nori contain a small packet of desiccant, which should be resealed in the package after opening to keep the nori crisp during room temperature storage.
INSTANT DASHI	These tiny beige granules are sold by the pound in Japanese and Korean markets.	Mix with boiling water to make dashi, the primary soup stock and cooking liquid in Japanese and Korean cuisines.	N/A	This convenience product has largely taken the place of stock made traditionally from kombu seaweed and katsuobushi flaked dried fish.	Store tightly sealed at cool room temperature.
JAPANESE SEASONINGS	*Furikake* (foo-ree-kah-kee) is a blend of dried crushed seaweed, fried fish flakes, sesame seeds, and salt. *Shichimi Togarashi* (shee-chee-mee toe-gah-rah-shee) includes ground red chile, ground Sichuan pepper, dried ground citrus peel, poppy seeds, sesame seeds, rapeseeds, and mustard seeds. Both are sold in small metal tins in Japanese markets.	Japanese seasonings are used as a topping for plain steamed rice, and make a tasty garnish for steamed vegetables and salads. They are added to batters and coatings.	N/A		Store tightly sealed at room temperature.
BLACK SESAME SEEDS	Black sesame seeds are sold by the pound by spice dealers and in Asian markets.	Asian black sesame seeds are primarily used as a garnish.	N/A	Their black color adds a note of drama to many presentations.	Store at room temperature or freeze for extended storage.
JAPANESE PICKLES	Most popular are bright-yellow disks of savory pickled daikon radish and small, pink, puckery-sour umeboshi plums. Japanese pickles are sold in a variety of packs and market forms in Japanese and Korean grocery stores and online.	Served with steamed rice, pickles are a traditional part of the Japanese breakfast. Hawai'i chefs use them as a flavoring ingredient and garnish.	N/A		Refrigerate; once opened, use within 2 weeks.
CHINESE/ JAPANESE DRIED BLACK MUSHROOMS	Dried mushrooms are sold by the ounce or pound in Asian markets.	Reconstitute by steeping in boiled water, then wash and remove stems. Use whole caps or large pieces in stir-fry dishes and stews. Chopped, diced, or julienne mushrooms are used in fillings and composed dishes. Strained soaking liquid is used in sauces and soups. Stems flavor stock.	N/A	Look for firm, whole mushrooms with a minimum of powdery residue and broken bits in the package.	Store tightly sealed at room temperature.

☐ TABLE 14.2 HAWAI'I REGIONAL INGREDIENTS *(continued)*

ITEM	MARKET FORMS	USES	SEASONALITY	OTHER	STORAGE
SHREDDED DRIED BLACK FUNGUS	Large, thin, black tree ear and wood ear fungus are fabricated into fine julienne and dried. This product is sold by the ounce or pound in Asian markets.	Reconstituted in boiled water, they add a crunchy texture and striking black color to stir-fry dishes, fillings, and composed dishes.	N/A	If preshredded fungus isn't available, reconstitute whole black fungus, trim away any hard nodules, and cut into chiffonade.	Store tightly sealed at room temperature.
FRESH ASIAN MUSHROOMS	Delicate, white enoki daki (eh-noh-kee dah-kee) mushrooms have thin, elongated stems, tiny button-shaped heads, and a subtle flavor. Fresh shiitake mushrooms are dark brown with a full flavor and meaty texture. Sold by the pound or in 10-lb. cartons, Asian mushrooms are widely available from produce dealers and in supermarkets.	Enokis are used raw in salads; or, as a dramatic garnish, they add texture and visual appeal. Shiitakes are sautéed or stir-fried.	N/A	Enokis have tough, fibrous ends and shiitakes have tough stems. These must be trimmed and can be used for stock.	Refrigerate up to 1 week.
ABURAGE (ah-boo-rah-gay)	These thin sheets of golden deep-fried tofu are sold by the pound in the refrigerated case of Japanese markets.	In Hawai'i cuisine, *aburage* is used as a wrapper for cone sushi. Cut into decorative shapes, it is added to soups and stir-fries.	N/A		Refrigerate sealed packages up to 1 month; resealed packages up to 1 week longer.
MACADAMIA NUTS	Macadamia nuts are sold roasted and unroasted; salted and unsalted. Shelled market forms include whole nuts graded by size; pieces; and chopped. Sold by the pound, Macadamias are quite expensive. Nut dealers usually offer freshness and best price.	Whole, jumbo nuts are reserved for snacking and chocolate dipping. Pieces and chopped nuts are used in baking. Chopped Macadamia nuts are used as a coating for pan-fried fish fillets and meat or poultry cutlets.	N/A	Macadamias are used as a substitute for kukui nuts in traditional Hawai'ian cuisine.	Store frozen.
COCONUTS AND COCONUT PRODUCTS	See p. 780.				
TARO ROOT	See p. 779.				
POI	Commercially made frozen *poi* is sold by the pound in plastic tubs and vacuum-packaging. Flavor and color vary according to the producer. Hawai'i producers offer specialty *pois* in yellow, beige, and brick red.	*Poi* is thawed, heated, and served as a savory side dish or with milk and sugar as a breakfast dish. To make fermented *poi*, the thawed product is allowed to stand at a warm room temperature until the desired level of acidity is reached.	N/A		Store frozen until needed, then thaw in the refrigerator. Once opened, cover the surface of refrigerated poi with a thin film of water to prevent drying.

(continued)

☐ **TABLE 14.2 HAWAI'I REGIONAL INGREDIENTS** *(continued)*

ITEM	MARKET FORMS	USES	SEASONALITY	OTHER	STORAGE
PINEAPPLES	Fresh pineapples are sold by count per 40-lb. carton: 10, 12, 16, and 18 are most common sizes. Baby golden pineapples weigh 10- to 14-oz.	Modern Hawai'i chefs use pineapple in salads, salsas, sauces, and desserts. Dishes and beverages are sometimes served in a pineapple shell.	Available year round with peak season in April and May.	Although pineapples don't actually ripen after harvest, a few days at room temperature usually makes a hard pineapple with little aroma become more mellow and juicy. Beads of sugar at the cut end are a sign of sweetness.	Store refrigerated.
OTHER TROPICAL FRUITS	See p. 781.				
BANANA LEAVES	Outside the tropics, banana leaves are sold frozen, folded into plastic packages, in Asian and Latin American markets. A typical pack usually contains two large, long leaves.	Banana leaves are used as a food wrapper that holds in steam and lends a distinctive aroma. They also are used as a decorative plate liner.	N/A	To make the leaves more pliable, soak in hot water for 15 to 30 minutes.	Store frozen; after thawing, refrigerate up to 1 week.
TI LEAVES (tee)	Ti leaves are sold frozen in 1-lb. packages in larger Asian markets. Dried ti leaves are sold in bundles of varying size.	Ti leaves are used as a food wrapper, and are the leaf of choice for Hawai'ian *laulau*.	N/A	Dried ti leaves are reconstituted by soaking in water.	Keep frozen; once thawed, refrigerate up to 1 week. Store dried ti leaves at room temperature.
KAFFIR LIME LEAVES	The shiny, deep-green, oval leaves of the Kaffir lime tree are available both fresh and frozen in Asian markets.	Used whole then removed like bay leaves, or chopped or chiffonaded and added to a dish, they impart a brilliant citrus note to soups, sauces, and marinades.	N/A	If unavailable, substitute lime zest.	Refrigerate or freeze for extended storage.
SHISO (shee-soh) LEAVES/ PERILLA (per-EE-yah) LEAVES	Deep-green, corrugated, heart-shaped shiso leaves are sold fresh in bundles in larger Asian markets.	Shiso leaves are used as a flavorful and edible food wrapper, often encasing fish that is to be baked or steamed. Chiffonade leaves are an attractive garnish that lends a minty, gingerlike flavor.	Available year round.		Refrigerate in a perforated plastic bag for about 5 days.
LEMONGRASS	Slender stalks of a tropical grass, fresh lemongrass is widely available in Asian markets and supermarkets. Frozen peeled and chopped lemongrass is sold in 1-lb. containers in Asian markets.	Minced lemongrass flavors stir-fry dishes and Southeast Asian curries. Crushed whole stalks are simmered in stocks and soups.	N/A		Trim root ends of lemongrass stalks and stand in an inch of water. Refrigerate or keep in a cool place. Keep frozen chopped lemongrass in the freezer; chip out as needed.
FRESH CHILES	Modern Hawai'i cooks use virtually all of the world's chile cultivars, including Thai bird chiles, Chinese long reds, and Mexican serranos and jalapeños.	Chiles may enliven virtually any savory dish.	N/A	Chiles introduced to Hawai'i in the 18th and 19th centuries became naturalized and produced a hybrid cultivar called the Hawai'ian chile.	Refrigerate chiles in a paper bag in the refrigerator.

☐ TABLE 14.2 HAWAI'I REGIONAL INGREDIENTS (continued)

ITEM	MARKET FORMS	USES	SEASONALITY	OTHER	STORAGE
LOTUS ROOT	Fresh lotus root is sold by the pound in Asian markets.	Peeled lotus root slices are blanched and refreshed, then served cool in salads or as a garnish. Sautéed or stir-fried, lotus root adds crunch and visual interest. Sliced very thin and deep-fried, it becomes beautiful, lacy chips.	N/A	This tuber grows floating in ponds in jointed sections. Its buoyancy is caused by air pockets that, when it is sliced into rounds, give the slices a decorative, lacy appearance.	Store refrigerated up to 2 weeks. Store peeled and sliced lotus root in water to prevent browning. Store up to 1 week, changing the water daily.
WATER CHESTNUTS	Freshwater chestnuts are sold by the pound in larger Asian markets. Canned water chestnuts are widely available in small consumer cans and in #10 cans for foodservice.	The sweet flavor and crisp texture of fresh water chestnuts makes them desirable in stir-fry dishes and salads despite their high cost and high labor required to prepare them. Less flavorful canned water chestnuts add texture only. They are acceptable in fillings and mixed with other vegetables.	Availability depends on weather conditions in Florida and Southern California where most are grown. If freshwater chestnuts are unavailable, substitute jicama.	Producers often leave a coating of mud on the water chestnuts to help prevent mold. After washing, the skin must be carefully pared away and the white flesh immediately submerged in cool water to prevent enzymatic browning. Edible portion yield may be as low as 50 percent. Rinse canned water chestnuts well to help remove the canning liquid's metallic taste.	Do not wash fresh, intact water chestnuts before storing. Store in paper bags or between layers of dry newspaper in the refrigerator up to 2 weeks. Inspect frequently for mold and soft spots, discarding damaged specimens. After paring away the skin, store cleaned water chestnuts submerged in cold water for 2 to 3 days.
BAMBOO SHOOTS	Peeled, par-boiled fresh bamboo shoots are sold by the pound in larger Asian markets, usually displayed in 5-gallon tubs submerged in water. Canned bamboo shoots are widely available in shredded (julienne), sliced, and whole tips fabrication forms and in cans of many sizes, including foodservice #10.	Fresh bamboo shoots are featured in stir-fry dishes. Canned bamboo shoots may be substituted.	Available year round.	Rinse canned bamboo shoots well to help remove the canning liquid's metallic taste.	Refrigerate fresh prepared and opened canned bamboo shoots submerged in water up to 1 week.
EDAMAME (eh-dah-mah-may)/ GREEN SOYBEANS	Most edamame are sold frozen in 12-oz. or 1-lb. packs as whole pods and shelled beans. Sold primarily in Asian markets, they are now carried by larger supermarkets and health food stores. Fresh edamame are sometimes available at farmer's markets.	Whole pod edamame are steamed to reheat them, tossed with alaea (p. 711) salt or other coarse salt, and served as a snack or appetizer. Diners nibble the tasty, tender beans out of the pods. Shelled edamame are tossed into salads, stir-fry dishes, soups, and vegetable medleys.	Frozen edamame are available year round. Fresh may be available in mid- to late summer.		Keep frozen until needed. Refrigerate fresh edamame up to 1 week.
SPROUTS AND MICROGREENS	See p. 596.				
KABOCHA SQUASH	Kabochas are sold by the pound in Asian markets and many larger supermarkets. Some purveyors offer slices or chunks as well as whole squash. Substitute calabaza (p. 780).	Steam and serve as a side vegetable or add to stir-fries. Purée for soup.	Fall to early winter.	This Japanese winter squash has a deep-green to black, finely striated skin and a flattened globe shape. Its flesh is bright orange and has a fine texture and sweet flavor.	Store at cool room temperature. Inspect frequently for soft spots and, if evident, refrigerate or use quickly.

(continued)

◻ **TABLE 14.2 HAWAI'I REGIONAL INGREDIENTS** *(continued)*

ITEM	MARKET FORMS	USES	SEASONALITY	OTHER	STORAGE
MAUI ONIONS	Maui onions are sold primarily in the region. They may be purchased from specialty produce dealers and ordered on the Internet in 5-lb. and 40-lb. cartons.	These sweet onions are primarily used raw in salads and sandwiches. They may be caramelized to make onion confit.	Available year round.	Maui onions are large and round, with a pale yellow skin and very mild, juicy, white flesh. Substitute other sweet onion varieties.	Store in a cool, dark, well-ventilated area.
TARO LEAVES/ *LU'AU* (LOO-awh)	Fresh taro leaves are sold by the pound by specialty produce dealers. Frozen taro leaves are sold in 1-lb. packs.	Taro leaves are parboiled and refreshed, then chopped and used in sauces or fillings. Blanched leaves may be used whole as an edible food wrapping.	Available year round.	Taro leaves must be thoroughly cooked before eating in order to break down needlelike calcium oxalate crystals that can irritate the gastric system. If unavailable, substitute spinach.	Refrigerate fresh leaves a few days only. For prolonged storage, blanch, refresh, drain, and freeze.
SUGARCANE	Lengths of fresh sugarcane are sold by the pound in Asian, Latin American, and Caribbean markets. Thai producers offer 7" to 8" lengths of split processed sugarcane packed in 48-oz. cans. Frozen split lengths are sold in vacuum packs of varying sizes.	Used as semi-edible skewers for grilling kabobs, the sweet flavor of sugarcane lingers in the taste of the food.	Available year round.	Use a small hacksaw with a cleaned and sanitized blade to saw fresh sugarcane into skewer-size lengths.	Refrigerate or freeze.
FROZEN TROPICAL FRUIT PULP AND PURÉES	Natural, unsweetened or lightly sweetened tropical fruit pulp and purées are widely available in containers of varying sizes.	Tropical fruit pulp and purées are used in dessert work and in savory sauces and salad dressings.	Available year round.	Using frozen pulp rather than fresh fruit saves labor and ensures a consistent product.	Keep frozen until needed. Thaw overnight in the refrigerator or microwave on low power.
HAWAI'IAN CHOCOLATE	Hawai'i grown chocolate is primarily sold as eating chocolate in the form of chocolate bars and molded shapes. Slabs and pistoles of dark baking chocolate are available, but costly. Purchase by the pound directly from the producer.	Showcase Hawai'ian chocolate in specialty desserts.	N/A		Store tightly sealed at cool room temperature with low humidity.
HAWAI'IAN TUNA	Hawai'i's waters yield several varieties of tuna, including skipjack, yellowfin, bigeye, and albacore. Tuna fillet and steak is sold fresh by the pound in the region. Yellowfin and bigeye are called *ahi* tuna. The best and freshest tuna is referred to as "sashimi quality." Frozen tuna steaks are vacuum sealed and sold in 20-lb. boxes.	Serve sashimi-quality tuna raw in sushi, sashimi, or *poke.* Tuna steaks are grilled or broiled.	Available year round.	Except in tuna-producing regions, tuna with bright-red flesh has probably been treated with carbon monoxide gas, a practice deemed "generally regarded as safe" by the US Department of Agriculture.	Refrigerate wrapped fresh tuna bedded in ice in a self-draining container 1 or 2 days only. Thaw frozen tuna in the refrigerator overnight.

☐ TABLE 14.2 HAWAI'I REGIONAL INGREDIENTS (continued)

ITEM	MARKET FORMS	USES	SEASONALITY	OTHER	STORAGE
MAHIMAHI	Mahimahi is available fresh and frozen in various fabrications.	Prepare by virtually any cooking method.	Available year round.		Refrigerate wrapped fresh mahimahi bedded in ice in a self-draining container 1 or 2 days only. Thaw frozen mahimahi in the refrigerator overnight.
HAWAI'IAN PINK SNAPPER/ *OPAKAPAKA* AND PACIFIC RED SNAPPER/ *ONAGA*	These small fish are typically sold whole in the region. Larger specimens may be filleted. They may be available on the mainland from specialty fish dealers.	Use for whole presentation. Grill, broil, bake, pan-fry, or deep-fry. Prepare fillets by any cooking method.	Limited availability.		Refrigerate gutted and gilled whole fish bedded in ice in a self-draining container 1 or 2 days only.
WAHOO/*ONO*	Elongated fillets are sold by the pound in the region and may be available on the mainland from specialty fish dealers.	Prepare by any cooking method.	Limited availability.	Of the mackerel family, wahoo has light flesh and is rich tasting but not oily.	Refrigerate wrapped fresh fillets bedded in ice in a self-draining container 1 or 2 days only.
BROADBILL SWORDFISH/ *SHUTOME* (shoo-toe-may) OR *MEKAJIKI* (meh-kah-jee-kee)	Fresh and frozen steaks are available from specialty purveyors.	Grill or broil.	January to May.		Refrigerate wrapped fresh steaks bedded in ice in a self-draining container 1 or 2 days only. Thaw frozen steaks in the refrigerator overnight.
HAWAI'I AQUACULTURE SHELLFISH	Coldwater lobster, mussels, and abalone are aquaculture raised for comsumption within the region.	Hawai'i shellfish is prepared by various cooking methods.	Aavailale year round.		Refrigerate a few days only. Store in original container.
LIMPETS/*OPIHI*	Fresh, live Hawai'ian opihi are primarily collected by amateur harvesters for personal use. Limpets imported from Ireland to Hawai'i are sold to organizers of commercial *lu'aus*.	Shuck and serve raw with lemon. Dice or slice shucked raw opihi and toss with seasonings for poke. Alternatively, tenderize by pounding and sauté or stir-fry.	Limited availability.		Refrigerate live opihi in the refrigerator between layers of damp newspaper.

chapter fifteen

South Florida and Puerto Rico

Florida's coastal rim and southern interior and the islands of Puerto Rico

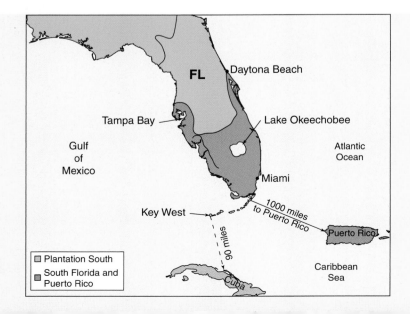

SOUTH FLORIDA IS THE TIP of a great peninsula jutting out like a giant fishing pier into the intersection of three waters: the Atlantic Ocean, the Caribbean Sea, and the Gulf of Mexico. Thus, fishing and maritime trade shaped the region's history and food culture.

Extending nearly into the tropics, South Florida experiences brutally hot summer weather and frequent hurricanes. Nonetheless, the region's warm winters, clear water, and sandy beaches make it a magnet for vacationers and retirees. South Florida's climate is ideal for subtropical and off-season produce: the region's citrus groves and truck farms bring the taste of summer to northern regions frozen in winter's grip.

South Florida's population is multicultural, a fact reflected in its cuisine. In South Florida you'll find dishes as plain and homey as a Cracker fish fry and cutting-edge trendy as a South Beach seviche. Superb seafood, fine local produce, and seasonings from around the globe give South Florida chefs a wealth of ingredients. Add the lively Latin flavors of the Cuban-American microcuisine and the allure of South Florida regional cuisine becomes clear.

Located at the intersection of gulf and ocean trade routes, Puerto Rico was, indeed, a rich port during its colonial era. Here Old World Spanish cuisine combined with Caribbean native foodways and spicy African seasonings to create a distinctive new cuisine. Today Puerto Rican cooking is found throughout the nation, but it remains at its best on the island where it began.

AFTER STUDYING THIS CHAPTER YOU SHOULD BE ABLE TO:

- describe the topography and climate of South Florida (Factor 1) and explain why they hindered the region's early growth and development
- explain why South Florida's Native American groups had little impact on the region's modern cuisine (Factor 2)
- identify the two first-settler groups that began the development of traditional South Florida cuisine (Factor 3) and describe their cooking techniques and ingredients
- explain how engineering and technology transformed the topography of South Florida (Factor 1) into viable farmland and beachfront capable of sustaining a tourism economy (Factor 5)
- discuss the birth and evolution of new South Florida cuisine (Factor 5)
- describe Cuban cuisine and trace the development of Cuban-American cuisine (Factors 4 and 5)
- describe Puerto Rican cuisine and trace its development (Factors 1, 2, 3, and 4)
- identify and work with a variety of South Florida and Caribbean ingredients and seasonings
- prepare authentic South Florida, Cuban-American, and Puerto Rican dishes

APPETIZERS

Caribbean Conch Chowder with Yuca Roll

Ybor City Black Bean Soup with Cuban Bread

Coconut Shrimp with Spicy Ginger-Soy Dipping Sauce and Shredded Salad

South Beach Conch Fritters with Spicy Mango Dip

Key West Conch Seviche

Stone Crab Claws with Miami Beach Mustard Sauce, Fresh Hearts of Palm Salad, and Tropical Chips

Black Bean–Stuffed Plantain Cakes with San Juan Salsa

Ruby Red Grapefruit Salad with Hearts of Palm, Avocado, Moro Crab, and Key West Shrimp

Everglades Frog Legs al Mojo Criollo

ENTRÉES

Panéed Grouper with Mango Aïoli and Tropical Seashell Salad

Yellowtail Snapper with Tricolor Peppers in Coconut Curry with Sticky Rice and Chinese Broccoli

Malanga-Mango-Crusted Red Snapper with Fresh Mango Salsa, Black Beans, and Sautéed Chayote

Cuban Crab-Stuffed Lobster Tails with Florida Watercress and Black-Eyed Pea Bollitos

Grilled Mahimahi with Pineapple-Avocado Salsa and Boniato Fries

Pompano en Escabeche with Ñame Cake

Jamaican-American Jerk Chicken with Rice 'n' Peas, Fried Plantains, and Tropical Slaw

Ropa Vieja with Yellow Rice, Black Beans, Green Papaya Salad, and Tostones

Double-Pork Calle Ocho with Orange Mojo, Yuca, and Okra in Sofrito Tomato Sauce

DESSERTS

Key Lime Pie with Whipped Cream and Candied Lime Zest

Tres Leches Cake with Mandarin Oranges

Coconut Cream Pie with Mango Sauce and Star Fruit

Tropical Fruit Palette with Guava Sorbet in Coconut Tuile

WEBSITE EXTRAS

Breakfasts   Sandwiches   Hors d'Oeuvres   Thanksgiving Menu

◼ A BALMY
▢ PENINSULA

Throughout prehistory the area that is now Florida underwent many changes. During successive ice ages, massive amounts of ocean water were bound up in glaciers, and ocean levels dropped. In warmer periods, glaciers melted and ocean water rose, submerging Florida and other low-lying areas. When Florida was covered with water, the land developed layers of sandy marine sediment that eventually formed soft, porous limestone bedrock. When glaciers melted, runoff from the Appalachian Mountains deposited additional layers of soil. The successive covering and uncovering of Florida's landmass with ocean water, combined with erosion and decomposition of its loosely compacted bedrock, created many unusual topographical features such as caves and sinkholes, disappearing streams, and underground springs.

Florida's topography began acquiring its final form around 20,000 years ago. During the last ice age, ocean water levels were low and the southeastern corner of the United States was a broad cape extending into the ocean. An elongated central plateau roughly bisected this cape, primarily running northwest to southeast, where it changed direction to rim the cape's southwestern shoreline (Figure 15.1).

FIGURE 15.1

Florida Landmass During the Last Ice Age

During this last ice age, temperatures were cooler than today, and the climate much drier. The Florida cape was savannah, semiarid land covered with shrubs and tallgrass. Large, cool-climate creatures, such as woolly mammoths, mastodons, and bison, inhabited the land along with small mammals, reptiles, and birds. At this time the region's first humans arrived.

Global warming at the end of the last ice age caused the earth's glaciers to recede and millions of tons of ice to melt. Rising ocean waters partially submerged the Florida cape, shrinking it by more than half. Florida became an elongated peninsula rimmed with low beaches and wetlands, with slightly higher ground in the center. The peninsula's southern tip comprised coastal lowlands, today a unique ecological area known as the Everglades. The former cape's southwestern rim became islands, now known as the Florida Keys. The remnants of the Florida cape became a wide, underwater continental shelf surrounding the Florida peninsula, providing habitat for a wide variety of marine animals.

As the climate warmed and the waters rose, rising temperatures changed Florida's vegetation and wildlife. As the climate became warmer and wetter, the central savannah became subtropical pine barren and the coastal rim acquired tropical vegetation such as palms and mangroves. Cool-weather animals gradually disappeared, and subtropical species took their place.

FACTOR 1
South Florida is surrounded by ocean water on three sides and contains one of the world's largest freshwater lakes.

A Tropical Climate

Although South Florida is not technically in the tropics, it has a tropical climate. In addition to low latitude, the modifying effects of Florida's three surrounding bodies of water create year-round warmth. Like many tropical areas, South Florida has a definitive wet-dry seasonal rainfall pattern.

Florida summers are hot and rainy. During the summer, South Florida experiences excessive heat, typically 90°F to 100°F, with 90 to 100 percent humidity. From June through September it rains almost every afternoon. Thunderstorms and tornadoes are frequent. From August through November, tropical storms and hurricanes often pass across the peninsula.

In winter the South Florida climate is balmy, with daytime temperatures often in the 70°F to 80°F range with lower humidity. Rainfall is moderate. Winter evenings occasionally are chilly but rarely drop below 50 °F; frost is rare. This pleasant winter weather was the driving force behind South Florida's first substantial development and is today the reason for the region's continuing popularity as a vacation and retirement area.

FACTOR 1
Although South Florida lies just north of the tropics, its climate is tropical.

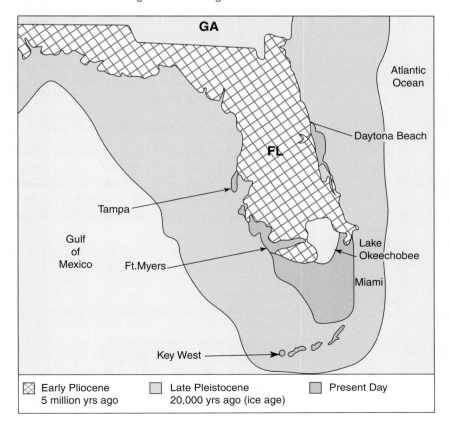

Early Pliocene
5 million yrs ago

Late Pleistocene
20,000 yrs ago (ice age)

Present Day

Varied Topography

South Florida has three distinctive types of topography depending on location (Figure 15.2).

The Coastal Rim

FACTOR 1
Florida's coastal rim provided dry land for fishing villages and, later, beaches for tourism.

Most of Florida's southern coastal rim is protected by long, narrow barrier islands. The outer length of these islands, facing open ocean or gulf, typically consists of white sand beaches backed by dunes (Figure 15.3). The inner length is separated from the mainland by a bay or inlet. On most of Florida's larger barrier islands, the central strip of higher ground has been developed into a resort community. On these islands you'll see tall, graceful sabal palmetto trees as well as other palm species introduced to the area from other tropical areas. Tropical fruit trees, such as mango and citrus, abound. The back bays created by Florida's barrier islands connect to form an inland waterway used by pleasure boaters and commercial fishermen. South Florida's coastal rim is also punctuated by a number of larger bays that form excellent natural harbors.

The Interior Plateau

Moving inland from the coast you'll discover a different Florida: the interior plateau. The middle of the peninsula is a low, elongated tableland with a highest elevation of only about 350 feet

FIGURE 15.3
South Florida's beaches are the foundation of the region's tourism industry. S. Borisov/Shutterstock

above sea level. Here undeveloped ground is covered with low-growing grasses, spiky saw palmetto, and scrub pines. The shallow, sandy soil supports limited agriculture, primarily cattle ranching and citrus. Irrigation is provided by the Floridan and Biscayne aquifers.

Florida's interior is dotted with lakes, of which the most prominent is Lake Okeechobee. This massive body of water has an area of more than seven hundred square miles but in most places is

FACTOR 1
South Florida's low inland plateau supports only specialized agriculture.

no more than 9 feet deep. South of Okeechobee, former wetlands are now drained and used for various forms of agriculture, primarily truck farming, sugar cane, and citrus groves.

The Everglades and the Homestead Area

Much of Florida's southern tip is a vast wetland called the Everglades. Near the center of the peninsula's tip, low-lying land is blanketed with sawgrass—the remnants of the river of grass. Shallow waterways called *sloughs* wind through the grassland, channeling

THE RIVER OF GRASS

Before 20th-century land reclamation projects, in the rainy season Lake Okeechobee discharged its excess water to the southwest in a shallow, slow-moving sheet of water more than 60 miles wide. Much of the low land over which the Okeechobee's water flowed was covered with sawgrass. Because the water was shallow and the vegetation tall, South Florida's early settlers called the area "the river of grass," an apt description. A remnant of this topography is shown in Figure 15.4.

FIGURE 15.2
Florida Topography

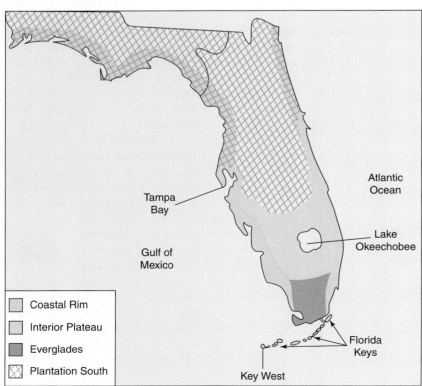

- Coastal Rim
- Interior Plateau
- Everglades
- Plantation South

Tampa Bay
Gulf of Mexico
Atlantic Ocean
Lake Okeechobee
Florida Keys
Key West

FIGURE 15.4
Remnants of the "river of grass" still exist in the Florida Everglades.
FloridaStock/Shutterstock

FACTOR 1
The Everglades is a unique and complex natural wetland.

fresh water out to sea. The peninsula's far southwestern rim is broken by murky brown peat marsh and dense swamps covered with cypress and mangrove trees.

In the mid-20th century, the "river of grass" area and nearly half of the Everglades were drained and reclaimed for agricultural and urban development. Today what remains is protected by a network of national and state parks and nature preserves. The Everglades is valued as one of America's most important natural areas, providing habitat for marine life, amphibians, mammals, and waterfowl.

Just south of Miami, Florida's Atlantic coastal ridge widens to form a low plateau known as the Homestead area. With the exception of the coast and barrier islands, before land reclamation the Homestead area was the only ground firm enough to support extensive South Florida settlement. The Homestead area is now considered the gateway to the Everglades, from which nature tourists embark on wetlands boat tours.

Unusual Wildlife

South Florida is home to some of America's most unusual wildlife. In the central plateau one finds typical Southern woodland mammals such as small deer, jackrabbits, muskrats, skunks, moles, wood rats, and other rodents. In addition, this area has feral hogs, bears, coyotes and the occasional panther. Armadillos are frequently sighted—unfortunately, more often as roadkill than alive. Because Florida is the terminus of the eastern flyway, in winter months the area abounds with wild geese, wild ducks, herons, and other migratory fowl. A multitude of songbirds and other small birds live in or migrate to Florida, along with various birds of prey. Tropical South Florida also has exotic birds such as flamingoes, roseate spoonbills, great blue herons, pelicans, and egrets.

Because of Florida's heat and humidity, reptiles and insects abound. Alligators, crocodiles, freshwater and sea turtles,

caimans, lizards, toads, and frogs thrive in the swamplands, along with snakes such as cottonmouths, rattlesnakes, and black and king snakes. Florida is infamous for insects, ranging from large spiders and scorpions to mosquitoes, tiny gnats, and even tinier "no-see-ums" that plague both man and beast.

Fish and shellfish abound in Florida's coastal waters. Florida saltwater species include redfish, red snapper, grouper, mullet, pompano, snook, shrimp, Moro crab, blue crab, langouste, and Gulf oysters. Manatees, a type of marine mammal once harvested extensively for food, have diminished in population and today are a protected species. Catfish, sunfish, and bass live in freshwater streams, lakes, and wetlands.

FACTOR 1
South Florida's marine life is the region's primary source of food animals.

■ SOUTH FLORIDA
□ NATIVE AMERICANS

Many anthropologists believe that South Florida was the last area of North America to be settled by humans. A longstanding theory holds that prehistoric Native Americans entered the Florida cape during the last ice age, likely following the migration of large game animals southeast from the Great Plains. However, the indigenous presence of Caribbean food plants and the practice of Caribbean cooking methods among original South Florida natives have led others to hypothesize additional human arrival by boat from South America, via the Caribbean.

Foodways of the Four Original Tribes

Four major tribes inhabited South Florida at the time of European contact: the Calousa (ka-LOOSE-ah), the Tekesta (teh-KESS-tah), the Jeaga (hay-AH-gah), and the Ais (AH-eece). These tribes were seminomadic hunter-gatherers that had established territories but seasonally migrated throughout the region following the wet-dry weather cycle (Figure 15.5).

South Florida natives remained hunter-gatherers largely because Florida's tropical climate made farming unnecessary. Florida natives had no need to stockpile grain foods for sustenance through a harsh winter. The region's consistently warm weather ensured that indigenous wild food plants were always available and that fishing and hunting could go on virtually year round.

Food historians estimate that at the time of European contact, more than 80 percent of the South Florida Native American diet was composed of aquatic animals. Native men were expert at fishing by netting and hook-and-line methods. Frogs and other reptiles were harvested by "gigging" or spearing with a sharp stick. Docile, slow-moving manatees were a favored prey, offering both meat and fat.

Both the wetlands and the interior plateau provided hunting grounds. Deer, bear, and boar were trapped and then

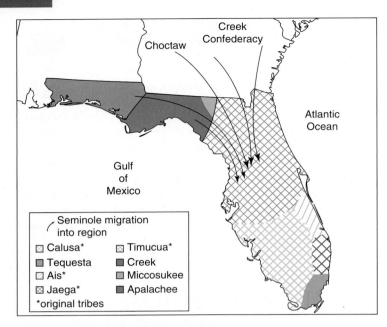

FIGURE 15.5
South Florida Native American Settlement

FACTOR 2
Hearts of palm is the region's only native plant food remaining in the modern cuisine.

speared, frequently using communal hunting methods. Small mammals and wildfowl were trapped or netted. Although alligators were dangerous to catch, their tasty tail meat was a favorite food.

South Florida Native American women occupied themselves with gathering foods such as indigenous berries, sea grapes, amaranth, prickly pear, and pokeweed. One Native American foraged food remains a signature ingredient of modern South Florida cuisine: **Hearts of palm,** or **palm hearts,** is the tender core of the sabal palm tree trunk. Preparation of palm hearts is discussed on p. 733.

Sweet potatoes, the second important foundation of Florida native cuisine, provided Florida natives' primary dietary starch. In addition, hickory nuts, acorns, cattails, and sabal palmetto seeds were ground into coarse flour and made into gruels or cakes. By far the most unusual starch food of South Florida was a flour made from the roots of the arrowroot plant (various members of the *Zamia* botanical family) today known by their Seminole name, **coontie** (Figure 15.6).

During the early days of Florida settlement, coontie flour was produced and eaten only by Native Americans (Figure 15.7). However, when their provisions ran short, American settlers purchased coontie

FIGURE 15.6
Florida's Indigenous Coontie Plant.
Courtesy of Paul Verlander/Landscape Architect

from local natives. Eventually settlers learned to prepare coontie flour and constructed several factories for its production. Coontie flour was commercially produced in Florida from 1845 until 1925, during which time the region's vast stands of indigenous coontie plants were virtually destroyed. Today coontie is no longer used as a food, but several varieties have become popular ornamental plants.

The Birth of Barbeque

As seminomadic hunter-gatherers, South Florida natives could not rely on heavy, breakable pottery vessels for simmering foods. Nor did the soil provide ample clay for making earthenware. Although soups and porridgelike foods were simmered in sling bags, precontact South Florida natives primarily used direct flame grilling for smaller cuts of meat and fish. Larger, tougher cuts and whole animals were cooked with a combination of ember heat and steam, a method likely learned from Native Caribbeans. When studying the Plantation South, you learned about the modern form of this ancient cooking method: barbeque. Now let's learn more about its origins.

To cook larger animals, or several smaller animals at one time, South Florida and Caribbean natives developed and refined the art of **spit barbeque** (Figure 10.11, p. 471). Game animals were gutted, cleaned, seasoned, and then "spitted" by inserting a green wood pole from the tail end through the body cavity and out through the mouth. The animal's

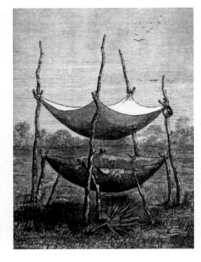

FIGURE 15.7
Seminoles used a tiered cloth strainer to prepare coontie flour.
Courtesy Florida State Archives

FACTOR 2
South Florida and Caribbean native barbeque inspired America's most distinctive cooking method.

PREPARING COONTIE FLOUR

The starchy powder called coontie flour was prepared by drying the plants' roots and then pounding them into fragments. The pounded coontie root was then soaked in several changes of water, during which time poisonous toxins leached out. As the coontie soaked, its starch content separated out and sank to the bottom of the soaking vessel, traditionally a sling made of coarsely woven cloth that allowed the water to slowly drain through it. After the water drained off, the resulting starchy paste was allowed to ferment for a few days and was then dried into a powder resembling white wheat flour. Coontie flour was moistened with water and baked into flatbreads, simmered into a gruel, or used as a nutritious thickener for soups and stews.

legs and head were tightly bound to the pole with wet leather thongs. The carcass was then suspended over a large mound of glowing coals and rotated to ensure slow, even cooking. Liquid seasoning mixtures (later called *mopping sauces* or *mops*) were basted onto the meat for flavor and to create tenderizing steam. Sweet potatoes and, later, plantains were roasted in the coals as accompaniments.

European explorers observed and recorded this interesting local cooking method, and eventually settlers adopted it. The French, reporting that the spit was inserted "from the *barbe* (beard) to the *queue* (tail)," gave us the English word *barbeque*. In Spanish, the term is *barbacoa* (*barba* = beard, *coda* = tail).

For **pit barbeque,** South Florida natives built a wood fire in a shallow hole, then lashed greenwood branches into a gridlike frame that was suspended over the glowing embers. Small game animals or fish were rubbed with seasonings, placed on the frame, and then cooked in the smoky heat and steam resulting from frequent basting (Figure 15.8).

Foodways of the Seminoles

The Native Americans today most frequently associated with Florida, the Seminoles, are relative newcomers to the region. In the 1700s, population pressure in the American South pushed many Native Americans out of the Carolinas and Georgia. A number of native tribes, including Muskogees, Hitchitis, Oconees, and scattered members of the Creek Confederacy, moved into northern Florida and banded together for mutual protection. Over time, escaped African-American slaves joined them, and intermarriage was common. This group became know as the Seminoles, from the Creek/Spanish term *semino-le*, meaning "wild man" or "runaway."

Initially the Seminoles settled in large villages, built permanent houses in the pioneer style, and engaged in Three Sisters farming. In addition to their own diet based on corn, beans, squash, and venison, this native group had adopted European bacon, lard, white flour, sugar, and whiskey. In Florida they added indigenous foods, such as sweet potatoes, coontie flour, palm hearts, alligator, and manatee, to their cuisine. Fish became their most important protein food. The best-known Seminole dish represents a blend of two native food cultures. *Sofkee* is a nourishing gruel made by simmering cracked corn with water and then thickening it with coontie flour. By the mid-1800s, bananas and plantains, tropical domesticates introduced to the Caribbean by Europeans, had entered Seminole cuisine.

In 1830 the Indian Removal Act initiated systematic persecution of Native Americans. The U.S. government wanted the agriculturally promising northern Florida plateau cleared of Seminole villages, and these previously settled tribes were forced to scatter. Some were relocated to the Oklahoma Indian Territories. Others fled south. Constantly on the move to avoid American soldiers, small groups of Seminoles dispersed into the Everglades (Figure 15.9). There they lived in light, open-air shelters, called *chickies*, built of cypress poles and palm thatch. In the humid, marshy Everglades, Seminoles had little success with farming and reverted to a largely hunter-gatherer existence.

Today South Florida's only federally recognized Native American tribes are the Seminoles and the Miccosukee tribe, another late-arriving group originally part of the Creek Nation.

A Limited Legacy

European contact proved disastrous for Florida's original four tribes. Loosely organized and lacking technology, they were decimated by the invading Spanish, slavers, and European diseases. The few survivors fled north and joined other tribes escaping colonial expansion in the Plantation South. By the late 1700s Florida's original four tribes had virtually ceased to exist. Today only a handful of people claiming Tekesta blood remain in South Florida.

FIGURE 15.9

Seminoles traversed South Florida's waterways in dugout canoes.

Ralph Munroe Collection, Historical Museum of Southern Florida

FIGURE 15.8

South Florida natives cooked fish and game over smoky wood fires, the inspiration for Southern barbeque. LC-USZ62-53339. Courtesy of the Library of Congress

With the exception of barbeque and palm hearts, little remains of Florida's Native American cooking. Three reasons account for the lack of Native American influence in the region's modern cuisine:

- As seminomadic hunter-gatherers, Florida's indigenous people did not develop a strong food culture.
- Because they arrived late in the nation's history, Florida's first permanent settlers had little need for indigenous foods, and thus culinary blending of indigenous and first-settler foods did not readily occur.
- By the time of permanent settlement in South Florida, European contact and U.S. government policies had largely removed the region's Native American groups.

■ EUROPEAN
□ EXPLORATION
■ AND SETTLEMENT

Although American schoolchildren are taught that Florida was discovered by Ponce de Leon in search of the fabled "fountain of youth," records indicate that, upon landing in the spring of 1513, he was met with hostile natives who spoke a few words of Spanish. Most likely they had already encountered European slavers, which would certainly account for the hostility.

De Leon claimed the area for Spain and named it *la Florida*—perhaps because of the tropical vegetation in bloom, or in honor of *Pascula Florida*, the Spanish term for the upcoming Easter holiday. De Leon's party did not remain in Florida for long. However, in 1521 he returned and attempted to found a colony in the Tampa Bay area. Arriving with two hundred settlers, he again faced warlike natives, fought back, and this time was mortally wounded. The expedition returned to Cuba, where de Leon died.

Successful Spanish settlement finally occurred in northern Florida, on the gulf in Pensacola, in 1559. Not long after, the French built Fort Caroline at present-day Jacksonville on the Atlantic side. The Spanish responded with another settlement just to the south: St. Augustine, the oldest continuously inhabited European-established city in the United States (Figure 15.10). Nonetheless, Spanish cultural and culinary influence remained slight. Interested more in the strategic value of holding land than in farming, the Spanish did not settle in numbers great enough to establish a cuisine.

Soon Great Britain joined the contest and established a few settlements in Florida. Although three European powers were struggling for control, settlement of Florida was sparse and occurred largely in the north, where the land was better suited to traditional agriculture. Because its early economy, culture, and cuisine were based on the plantation system, northern Florida is identified as part of the Plantation South.

In South Florida, the only truly fertile soil was under water in "the river of grass" for more than half the year. Land along the coastal rim had shallow, sandy soil that could not support

FIGURE 15.10

St. Augustine's colonial-era buildings. Courtesy of the Library of Congress, LC-B811-3546 [P&P] LOT 4164-B

European food crops. Moreover, the hot, humid climate, ravenous insects, dangerous alligators, poisonous snakes, and tropical diseases made the area less than desirable for settlers. Thus, early Florida settlements were established more for their strategic value than for their economic worth. With the exception of Key West, South Florida remained a virtual wilderness until the late 1800s.

Keys Culture and Cuisine

While the rest of South Florida was still virtually uninhabited, a small group of early entrepreneurs was building a thriving economy in the Florida Keys. The Keys are a chain of islands stretching from the peninsula's southern tip westward across the Straits of Florida, the Atlantic seafarer's gateway to the Gulf of Mexico.

During colonial times Florida's Keys were populated primarily by creole settlers from the British Bahamas and other Caribbean islands. After the Revolutionary War, they were joined by exiled New Englanders sympathetic to the British Crown. Keys settlers were called **Conchs** (KONKS) after the shellfish that were an important part of their diet. Conchs were Florida's true first settlers, establishing the region's first economy and its first regional cooking style.

The Keys economy was based on the islands' prime location at the intersection of maritime trade routes. Atlantic ships bound for New Orleans had to pass through the Keys in order to enter the Gulf of Mexico. Ships bound north from Havana, Cuba, to the American East Coast had to pass along the entire chain of Keys. Conchs made good money from these sailing ships by

FACTOR 3
British-influenced Bahamians and American settlers from New England developed the Conch cuisine style in the Florida Keys.

selling them provisions, making repairs, and offering entertainment to sailors on shore leave.

Around the Keys, treacherous shoals and violent weather caused frequent shipwrecks. Many Keys settlers made their livings as ship-wreckers, salvaging the cargo of sunken or run-aground ships and reselling it to other merchants. Some of these wreckers created increased opportunity by extinguishing lighthouse fires or planting false channel markers. The Keys were also a haven for pirates who intercepted ships and demanded money or goods as payment for safe passage.

Known for sheltering pirates and wreckers, and replete with rowdy taverns and brothels, the Florida Keys had a shady reputation that lasted well into the 20th century. Nonetheless, the resulting economic vitality made Key West Florida's largest city, a distinction that it retained until the 1880s.

The inhabitants of Florida's Keys were a tough and independent group whose primary focus was making money from the sea. Because grains, vegetable crops, and livestock did poorly in the hot weather and shallow soil, few Keys residents bothered with farming. The typical Keys diet consisted primarily of seafood, and especially of conch.

FIGURE 15.11
Conch is a univalve shellfish with tough but tasty flesh.

Conch Cookery

Once abundant in the waters around the Florida Keys, **conch** is a univalve shellfish with sweet but tough flesh (Figure 15.11). After the conch is extracted from its shell, the primary challenge is to tenderize it. This can be done physically, by chopping or pounding, or by lengthy moist cooking. Conch's mild flavor lends itself to many seasonings and accompaniments. New Englanders homesick for creamy New England clam chowder created Key West conch chowder, substituting minced conch for clams and coconut milk for cow's milk. Keys cooks of African heritage mixed chopped conch into cornmeal batter to make conch fritters. Caribbean cooks with East Indian foodways simmered it in spicy curry sauces. Chopped or diced conch can be further tenderized with an acidic marinade, as in seviche (p. 753).

Key Limes

Unlike the more common Persian lime today best known in North America, the **Key lime** is small and seeded, with a complex flavor and floral aroma (Figure 15.12). It originated in Southeast Asia, traveled to the Mediterranean region with Arab traders, and was introduced to the Caribbean by the Spanish. Limes were an important cash crop because of de-

mand by sailing ships that rationed lime juice to sailors to prevent scurvy.

Key limes were grown commercially on the Keys and in South Florida until a hurricane wiped out citrus groves in 1926. After the loss of virtually all domestic Key lime groves, the recovering citrus industry turned to the larger, easier-to-grow Persian hybrid. Although American demand for Key lime juice is rising, commercial production of Key limes in the United States remains limited; most Key lime products originate in South America. Many South Florida residents have Key lime trees in their backyards, and often homegrown Key limes can be purchased locally during the citrus season from late fall through spring.

FIGURE 15.12
Key Lime on the Branch
Masonjar/Shutterstock

Key lime juice is the feature ingredient in Key lime pie, one of the defining dishes of traditional South Florida cuisine. It's also the main ingredient in the Key West sauce/marinade called **old sour,** a blend of Key lime juice, salt, and hot chiles. An authentic Cuban mojito cocktail depends on real Key lime juice as well as fresh sugarcane juice.

■ AMERICAN
□ SETTLEMENT

When Spain ceded Florida to Great Britain in the 1760s, Americans were encouraged to settle the area, largely to prevent further incursion by Spanish or French settlers. After the Revolutionary War, American Southerners began looking to Florida in search of land. By that time much of Florida's fertile panhandle and most of its northern interior were already under cultivation as plantations. However, the peninsula's central plateau remained largely vacant. Although its soil was too sandy and shallow for most agricultural crops, the grassy flatlands north of Okeechobee appeared suitable for cattle. Through the early 1800s, a small but influential number of Southerners settled the South Florida interior to become the region's first ranchers.

Florida Crackers

Many of Florida's early cattle ranchers were members of the Plantation South's working class, typically descendants of white indentured servants (Figure 15.13). Others arrived from the far-southern Appalachians. Most were Protestants of English or Scots-Irish ancestry. As a group, these settlers became known as **Crackers.**

FIGURE 15.13
Cracker cowboy on the shore of Lake Okeechobee.
Florida State Archives

(Refer to this book's companion website for an explanation of the origin of this name.) Thus, Crackers are the second of South Florida's two first-settler groups.

Cracker cattlemen built pioneer-style houses with simple kitchens and few comforts. Their cattle were hardy and small, typically weighing less than 600 pounds. As in the early American West, Florida cattlemen ran their stock on the rugged, unclaimed interior lands without fences. Florida cowboys typically drove their cattle from place to place using long bullwhips, snapping and cracking the whips to startle the cattle into moving forward.

Cracker Cooking

When they arrived in the region, South Florida's cattle ranchers brought with them the same pioneer provisions that became foundation foods in other regions. Salt pork, bacon, and lard supplemented beef as protein foods. Because Mid-Atlantic and Midwestern flour were expensive, cornmeal breads and porridges were their primary starch foods.

Cracker cooking blends the foodways of working-class Plantation Southerners, Appalachian Southerners, and Florida Native Americans with tropical ingredients introduced by the Spanish. In tough times Cracker pioneers used coontie flour to make biscuits. Crackers called hearts of palm **swamp cabbage** and prepared it in much the same way as true cabbage. Crackers learned to enjoy frog legs, alligator tail, and local fish and shellfish, often frying these foods Plantation South–style in cornmeal breading. Bananas, coconuts, avocados, and Key limes enlivened their cuisine.

To escape the intense heat, Crackers became masters of outdoor cooking, developing their own distinctive style of barbeque using traditional pork cuts. The tough but tasty meat of small Florida cattle was marinated in Key lime juice and grilled. Sweet potatoes or cornmeal dishes accompanied both meats and seafood.

FACTOR 3
American first settlers from the Plantation and Appalachian South developed Cracker cuisine.

Florida Citrus

Settlers arriving in central Florida in the mid-1700s found wild citrus trees that had naturalized from early Spanish plantings. Recognizing that citrus would thrive in Florida's soil and climate, a few Americans planted experimental orange groves that proved them right. Between the Revolutionary and Civil Wars, small farmers near Tampa and along the St. Johns River began cultivating oranges for the commercial market. Just after the Civil War, Florida's annual citrus production totaled one million boxes. Oranges, lemons, limes, and newcomer grapefruits were sent by steamship along the East Coast and up the Mississippi into the Midwest, providing much needed fresh flavor and nutrients to winter diets.

Florida citrus production suffered a severe setback with the Great Freeze of 1894–1895, when many central Florida groves were destroyed. However, by this time engineers were developing new methods of drainage and controlled irrigation in the "river of grass" area. As newly viable farmland was created from formerly seasonal wetlands, determined Florida citrus growers moved their operations south of Okeechobee, where there is less chance of frost.

ADAMS RANCH AND THE BRAFORD BREED

In 1937, while the United States was in the depths of the Great Depression, Judge Alto Adams bought a large tract of land west of Ft. Pierce and founded the Adams Ranch, where he began one of Florida's first modern large-scale beef production operations. This risky venture ultimately proved successful, aided by an innovative breeding program developed by his son, Alto "Bud" Adams, Jr.

The subtropical climate of Florida's interior plateau had made cattle ranching problematic because modern beef cattle breeds were not well suited to it. Tropical cattle breeds proved too lean for American tastes and too small to yield the poundage needed for commercial success. By crossbreeding American Hereford bulls and South Asian Brahma cows, Adams created the Braford breed of cattle, and the modern Florida beef industry was born. Today Florida ranks 10th in the nation's beef production.

■□■ CUBANS IN FLORIDA

FACTOR 4
Early immigrants from Cuba begin developing the Cuban-American microcuisine.

Cuba is a near neighbor to South Florida, only 90 miles away. Between 1868 and 1878, thousands of Cubans fled civil uprisings in their country and migrated north to the Keys and the Florida mainland. At the time tobacco was an important crop in Cuba, and cigar making one of the island's primary industries. Many exiled Cubans founded cigar factories in Florida; in fact, by the turn of the 20th century, the city of Tampa was producing more cigars than all of Cuba (Figure 15.14).

Along with cigar-making expertise, Cubans brought their own lively and complex food culture to South Florida. Cuban cuisine is a hybrid cooking style based on Spanish cooking, Caribbean ingredients, and African flavor preferences. Cuban cooking acquired another layer of complexity when transplanted to South Florida. The resulting Cuban-American cuisine is discussed on this book's companion website.

■□■ THE DEVELOPMENT OF MODERN SOUTH FLORIDA

Nearly 400 years after Florida's discovery by the Spanish in the early 1500s, much of South Florida remained empty. However, by 1880 new engineering technology was making it possible to drain swampland and pump water for irrigation. These advances, combined with newly developed chemical fertilizers and the region's subtropical climate, had the potential to turn the South Florida wilderness into viable farmland with a year-round growing season. Only one obstacle remained: fast, cheap, reliable transportation.

Railroads Span the Peninsula

South Florida needed a rail system to ship its seafood, citrus, and cattle to a hungry nation and to bring winter-weary northerners south to its sunny beaches. As in other regions you've studied, railroads were the key to Florida's economic viability. A few visionary entrepreneurs invested the capital necessary to link South Florida to the rest of the nation. The results were dramatic. Shortly after Henry Plant's Southern Florida Railroad reached Tampa in the 1880s, the formerly small town grew to a city of more than 2,300 citizens. Two years after Pete Demens built a railroad to St. Petersburg, the village became a major seafood center, processing more than three million pounds of mackerel and snapper each year.

FACTOR 5
Railroads transported Florida produce to the north and brought northern vacationers to Florida's beaches.

Although these railroad magnates spurred commerce, Henry Flagler was the first true promoter of South Florida as a vacation destination. After visiting the Homestead area in 1878, he realized that the region's warm climate and sandy beaches held enormous potential for tourism. The growing economy resulting from the American Industrial Revolution was creating a large middle class with discretionary income that could be spent on vacations. Wealthy Americans were eager for a tropical resort in which to spend the entire winter season. In response, Flagler purchased land and built a network of railroads, by 1894 reaching the coastal town of Palm Beach. There he built his own personal mansion and two grand hotels, the Royal Poinciana and the Breakers. When vacationers to these and other resort hotels experienced the tropical good life, previously worthless land along South Florida's coastal rim became immensely valuable.

Flagler's railroad reached the Biscayne Bay area, the southernmost habitable point on Florida's Atlantic coastal rim, in 1896. Flagler built the Royal Palm Hotel at a spot where a wide, slow-moving river, called the *Mayami*, met the bay at a village called Fort Dallas (Figures 15.15 and 15.16). He began a series of land improvements that forever changed the face of South Florida. Channel dredging; construction of public schools, libraries, and churches; and the introduction of public utilities triggered the fastest economic growth America had ever experienced. In 1896 the town of Miami was incorporated with 344 registered voters; by 1925 the city of Miami counted more than 100,000 residents. Flagler's relentless promotion of South Florida in general and Miami in particular led to an unprecedented land boom. Thousands of entrepreneurs and speculators moved to South Florida in hopes of making a killing in real estate. Demand for building lots soared, and local businesses thrived. Soon, however, the narrow coastal rim was overwhelmed with construction, and real estate agents simply ran out of land to sell.

FIGURE 15.14
Cuban immigrants opened cigar factories in the Tampa area. Courtesy of the Library of Congress, LC-DIG-nclc-04520

FIGURE 15.15

The Miami shoreline, seen here in 1904. Courtesy of the Library of Congress LC-USZ62-91934

FIGURE 15.16

Henry Flagler built the Royal Palm Hotel, Miami's first luxury resort, at the location shown in Figure 15.15. Courtesy of the Library of Congress LC-USZ62-98736

Changing the Face of South Florida

Before the development of Miami and the surrounding Dade County area, the Everglades wetlands came within 3 miles of Biscayne Bay. However, demand for land spurred drastic action among landowners and real estate developers. In the Miami suburbs, engineers began dredging channels and building drainage canals to create more building lots. More farmland was needed to feed South Florida's growing population. To the south of Lake Okeechobee, extensive dredging drained the "river of grass" to create land for citrus groves, pineapple fields, and commercial truck farming plots. The area's wealth of mineral and organic deposits made the newly emerged land immensely fertile. Moving a few latitudinal degrees south protected citrus trees from frost, and the rich soil reclaimed from seasonal flooding enabled crops to flourish. With Florida's warm climate and ample rainfall, many Mediterranean fruits and vegetables and temperate-climate food plants could be grown virtually year-round. Just south of Okeechobee, near Belle Glade, cane fields

were planted and the Florida sugar industry was born. Pineapples were introduced from the Caribbean, and until the 1930s Florida supplied the nation.

Lake Okeechobee, once used only by sportsmen and Native Americans, became the focus of commercial fishing. From both the lake and Florida's coastal waters, thousands of tons of seafood per year were shipped north by rail to East Coast cities.

By the early 1920s, South Florida was able to feed its own population and ship food to the rest of the nation—but at an enormous environmental cost. Uncontrolled harvesting of natural resources and unregulated dredging were the harbinger of an ecological disaster soon to come.

FACTOR 1

Draining the "river of grass" created millions of acres of farmland used for citrus, pineapples, sugarcane, and truck farming.

Carl Fisher Builds a Beach

In 1928 Carl Fisher, a wealthy midwestern automobile tycoon, came to Florida for a winter vacation and was struck by a vision that would drastically change the face of the South Florida coastline. The new resort town of Miami had enormous potential for tourism but was becoming crowded. Moreover, it was separated from the Atlantic Ocean by Biscayne Bay, a shallow, semi-saline estuary bracketed by stands of mangrove trees. A series of swampy, buggy, partially-formed barrier islands stretched across the mouth of the bay. Although the bay was a magnificent example of subtropical marine habitat and an important buffer protecting the mainland from open-ocean wind and waves, it was not conducive to pleasure boating and sunbathing.

Fisher envisioned the bay as a broad lagoon deep enough to accommodate large passenger vessels, with sparkling white beaches lined with hotels and vacation homes stretching across its mouth. To make his dream reality, he persuaded his wealthy friends to finance an incredible venture: the creation of a human-made barrier island across the mouth of Biscayne Bay. Before long massive dredges were digging up the bay bottom and depositing the sandy fill in a long line across the ocean-front, and Miami Beach was born (Figure 15.17).

This strip of land along South Florida's Atlantic coast became the winter home of America's millionaires. No longer a shallow estuary, Biscayne Bay was now a deep lagoon with an even deeper channel, perfect for yachting. Deprived of their breeding grounds, mosquitoes and sand flies diminished in number. Ele-

FIGURE 15.17

Massive dredges dug out a channel in Biscayne Bay and built Miami Beach, an artificial barrier island.

Historical Museum of South Florida

gant mansions and luxurious hotels soon filled the island. On the heels of the millionaires came Hollywood stars, underworld bigwigs, and the upwardly mobile professional class. During Prohibition, Miami largely turned a blind eye to illegal drinking and gambling. Called Fisher's Billion-Dollar Sandbar, Miami Beach became a playground for the rich and famous.

However, the region's newfound prosperity did little to stimulate its cuisine. Though the great resort hotels of Miami and Miami Beach housed elegant restaurants, they largely ignored South Florida's local food products. Nor did their chefs strive to create a distinctive local cuisine. Rather, they served the same standard Continental cuisine fare (p. 791) popularized by high-end New York City restaurants in the late 19th and early 20th centuries.

Continental cuisine was not the only transplant from New York City to Miami. In the 1920s tens of thousands of older New Yorkers retired to South Florida, among them many people of Eastern European Jewish origin. With them came demand for traditional Jewish-American cooking and delicatessen foods. In response, entrepreneurs opened kosher and kosher-style restaurants, Jewish delis, and bagel bakeries. Today the Miami area boasts some of the nation's best Ashkenazi Jewish food.

South Florida's frenzy of development stopped after the stock market crash of 1929. During the Great Depression, however, Miami remained a bustling tourist attraction even as the land boom went bust. From the late 1920s into the 1940s, the slower but still steady construction of homes, businesses, and hotels sustained Miami's economy. The southern end of Miami Beach, called South Beach, became the locus of a distinctive architectural style called Art Deco (Figure 15.18).

FIGURE 15.18
Miami's South Beach Area. FloridaStock/Shutterstock

Ups and Downs in the 20th Century

In the 20th century, South Florida's coastal cities and resort towns rode a roller coaster of fashion. Through the Great Depression, while other vacation spots languished, Miami and Miami Beach remained popular. However, after World War II, Miami's novelty began to wear off. Although the major hotels and resorts retained their loyal, if aging, followers, the new generation of celebrities and jet-setters were going elsewhere. South Florida's top restaurants continued to serve a tired version of Continental cuisine.

ART DECO

Art Deco is a design style created in Weimar Europe that became wildly popular throughout the western world in the 1920s and 1930s. Combining elements of ancient Greek, Egyptian, and Mayan decorative motifs with Cubist and Machine Age sensibilities, this design style refers not only to architecture but also to fine arts, home furnishings, and plate presentations. Art Deco is characterized by pastel colors and streamlined, rectilinear forms.

Although Florida's food culture remained stagnant, its population continued to rise. During World War II and the Cold War, South Florida welcomed thousands of armed services personnel as home to several important military bases. In the 1950s, the process of making frozen concentrated orange juice was perfected, and the Florida citrus industry exploded into a multimillion-dollar agribusiness needing thousands of workers. The introduction of inexpensive window air-conditioning units made year-round Florida residence more attractive, and America's middle-class and working-class families began migrating south. However, the resulting influx of working-class people from all around the country did little to generate a distinctive regional cuisine. Most Floridians were firmly moored in the 1950s culinary doldrums.

Nonetheless, a few dedicated home cooks and independent restaurants preserved many elements of Florida's pioneer Cracker cuisine and blended them with nontraditional ingredients such as newly available tropical fruits and Latin ingredients. In doing so, they created a little-known but interesting and delicious cooking style we'll call traditional South Florida cuisine.

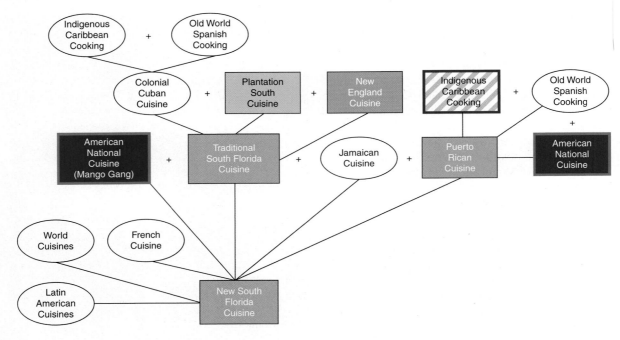

FIGURE 15.19
Development of South Florida Cuisine

■ TRADITIONAL SOUTH
□ FLORIDA CUISINE
■

Few records documenting traditional South Florida cooking exist today. On ranches, in fishing villages, and in the servant-run kitchens of beachfront homes, its recipes and techniques were for the most part passed on orally, from friend to friend and from one generation to another.

The foundation of traditional South Florida cuisine is a basic, working-class version of Plantation South cooking. First brought to the region by Cracker cooks, the preference for this style was compounded by African-Americans who migrated to South Florida to work as house servants and professional cooks.

Cornmeal and smoked pork products are frequent ingredients in many traditional South Florida dishes, biscuits and other Southern quick breads grace many South Florida tables, and Southern-style desserts are enjoyed throughout the state. How-

---

STONE CRAB CLAWS

An enterprising restaurateur introduced Florida residents and visitors to what is now the region's most famous seafood. Until the 1920s, the Moro crab was primarily enjoyed by Caribbean islanders and Hispanic Floridians and largely disdained by mainstream consumers. Joe Weiss, proprietor of a Miami Beach seafood restaurant, got interested in these crabs when a marine biologist suggested they might be good to eat. Joe learned that old-timers sometimes called them "stone" crabs because the shells of the claws were so hard that in order to release the meat, they had to be bashed with heavy stones. Joe began serving steamed and chilled crab claws with a signature mustard-mayonnaise dipping sauce. Under the market name **stone crab claws,** the newly popular seafood became a signature dish not only of Joe's restaurant but also of traditional South Florida cuisine (Figure 15.20). Today Joe's Stone Crab and other Florida restaurants serve thousands of pounds of stone crab claws during their winter season.

FIGURE 15.20
Stone Crab Claws, a South Florida Specialty. rjlerich/Shutterstock

ever, South Florida cooks used local seafood, game, and produce to make their own unique dishes. Conch harvested from coastal waters is made into cornmeal-based conch fritters, typically served with a Southern-style bottled hot sauce. Ocean fish, freshwater fish, alligator tail, and frog legs are breaded in cornmeal and pan-fried, preferably in a combination of oil and bacon drippings or lard. Grouper cheeks fried in this manner are a regional specialty. Alligator tail is also smothered in gravy or fabricated into kabobs for grilling. Tropical fruits replace apples and peaches in pies, cobblers, and cake fillings.

Traditional South Florida cooks look to the Caribbean for ingredients as well. Black beans, bell peppers, spicy tomato sauces, and cooking with sherry are Cuban influences. Bahamians added hot chiles and their love of coconut and bananas in both sweet and savory dishes. Moro crab, often disdained by Anglo newcomers, is enjoyed by islanders and traditional Floridians alike, who not only eat the creatures' large claws but also pick out the meat for salads and hot dishes.

Florida's tropical fruits and vegetables, considered rare and exotic outside the region, are an important part of traditional South Florida cuisine. The Florida avocado, known as the "alligator pear" because of its bumpy green skin, is a popular salad ingredient, served sliced or halved for stuffing. Grapefruits claim a peculiar place in traditional Floridian menus; through the 1960s halved grapefruits were frequently baked with a brown sugar topping and served as an appetizer. Today grapefruit segments are featured in salads and salsas as well as eaten for breakfast. Chayotes (mirlitons) (p. 356) are boiled, sliced, and served au gratin or may be stuffed and baked to become an appetizer or side dish. South Florida's best-known vegetable is hearts of palm, or swamp cabbage.

Traditional South Florida cuisine is not widely represented by high-end restaurants or in current cookbooks. Mostly it's a cuisine of the home cook and the small, local eatery that emulates home cooking. For a list of noteworthy traditional South Florida cuisine restaurants, refer to this book's companion website.

SWAMP CABBAGE BECOMES HEARTS OF PALM

Literally the "heart," or central core, of a young sabal palmetto tree, the vegetable known to Crackers as swamp cabbage is a pale ivory, cylindrical vegetable with a subtle flavor similar to that of artichokes. To harvest a single 16-inch palm heart, an entire tree must be cut down, its trunk peeled open to reveal the edible core (Figure 15.21). The core is then boiled in salted water until tender. The resulting vegetable can be served hot, dressed with butter and lemon juice. Alternatively, it can be breaded and fried. However, the most popular way to present palm hearts is chilled and served as a salad with vinaigrette dressing.

Once considered poor people's food, swamp cabbage of necessity entered the mainstream Florida diet during the Great Depression. After the Depression, chefs and diners were beginning to look for new and unusual food products. Before long, low-class swamp cabbage was discovered by gourmet food producers and became high-class hearts of palm. Sliced palm hearts in vinaigrette dressing was dubbed "Millionaire's Salad" because palm heart had suddenly become an expensive and sought-after product. Entrepreneurs began harvesting, processing, and canning palm hearts and marketing them worldwide.

For a few campers and Cracker farmers to harvest and enjoy swamp cabbage posed no great threat to South Florida's ecosystem. However, by 1940 demand for palm hearts threatened the sabal palmetto's very existence. Marjorie Kinnan Rawlings understood the ecological implications of the palm heart industry early on, mentioning her misgivings in her 1942 cookbook. The State of Florida agreed and eventually passed legislation limiting the harvest of wild sabal palmettos. Today most commercially available wild palm heart comes from South America in canned and vacuum-packed fresh forms. Palm heart is now also harvested from plantation-raised peach palms, a palm variety that produces multiple stalks and thus does not require killing the entire tree to harvest hearts.

FIGURE 15.21
Hearts of palm is the tender core of the sabal palmetto tree. Florida State Archives

■ JAMAICAN-AMERICAN
□ COOKING

Because of its proximity to the islands, in the early 20th century South Florida welcomed a large number of Caribbean immigrants. Thoughout the region, immigrants from Jamaica worked in mainstream foodservice and opened restaurants, grocery stores, and food trucks selling homestyle Jamaican cuisine. In South Florida as in many urban areas throughout the nation, a number of Jamaican dishes have become restaurant favorites. Curry goat or curry chicken served with rice 'n' peas (p. 768), oxtail stew with butter beans, and meat-filled pastry turnovers called *patties* are among the most popular.

Jerk

One Jamaican dish has captured the imagination of the American public more than any other. **Jerk** is the Jamaican version of barbeque in which chicken or pork is coated with a spicy seasoning paste and allowed to cure overnight or up to several days. Jerk seasoning paste is made by individual cooks or is available as commercially produced proprietary blends with varying ingredients. However, all include onion, garlic, Scotch bonnet chile, and Jamaican pimento (allspice). In Jamaica, jerk barbequeing over coals produced by burning the wood of pimento (allspice) trees is preferred because the smoke imparts a special, spicy flavor. As in Plantation South barbeque, while the meat cooks it is basted with a thin, spicy, acidic mopping sauce to create tenderizing steam.

In Jamaica, jerk foods are prepared oudoors and sold in rustic huts, usually with no accompaniment other than a slice of coco bread, a soft, wheat flour bun or loaf made with a small amount of coconut milk. In South Florida and other parts of the United States, Jamaican-American jerk is accompanied by rice 'n' peas, fried plantains, and spicy cooked cabbage or cabbage slaw. Most Jamaican-American cooks offer a spicy, tangy jerk table sauce. A recipe for Jamaican-American jerk appears on p. 768.

■ NEW SOUTH FLORIDA
□ CUISINE

Although South Florida's coastal resorts continued to draw wealthy winter residents and affluent vacationers, from the mid-1960s through the 1970s South Florida was simply not "the place to be" for the cultural or culinary elite. The once-spectacular Art Deco hotels clustered at the southern end of Miami Beach had fallen on hard times. Many were for sale. The time was ripe for shrewd developers to buy at a bargain price—and so began the South Beach real estate renaissance.

By the 1980s Miami's South Beach neighborhood had been totally revitalized. South Beach's Art Deco hotels boasted spec-

FIGURE 15.22

Miami's South Beach, a hotspot for nightlife and new South Florida cuisine. David Davis/Shutterstock

tacularly restored interiors with luxurious amenities. The hotels' new owners added high-end restaurants and hired world-class chefs. Independent restaurants followed suit, and soon Miami's South Beach became not only the chic new spot to party, but also the hottest dining scene around (Figure 15.22). South Florida's contemporary chefs began to blaze a new culinary trail and develop a distinctive regional cuisine.

The Mango Gang

The pioneers of the new South Florida style of restaurant cooking were a group of young, innovative chefs who called themselves the **Mango Gang:** Norman Van Aken (Figure 15.23), Allen Susser, Mark Militello, and Doug Rodriguez. Blending Caribbean, Hispanic, and Asian cuisine elements with traditional South Florida ingredients and techniques, the Mango Gang began creating a light, bold, and colorful South Florida cooking style.

Inspired by the American food renaissance and the movement toward using local ingredients started by Alice Waters (p. 562) in California, the newly arrived South Florida chefs discovered local ingredients previously ignored by Florida restaurant chefs. Soon they were showcasing locally caught seafood, such as grouper and pompano. Local citrus, in particular Key limes, became the preferred acidic ingre-

FIGURE 15.23

Mango Gang Chef Norman Van Aken. s70/ZUMA Press/Newscom

dient in salad dressings and marinades. The chefs engaged the region's truck farmers, previously growing exclusively for the northern trade market, to grow specialty produce for local restaurant use. Finally, they looked to the nearby Caribbean islands—considering them local as well—and added tropical fruits and vegetables to their palette of ingredients.

Ingredients were not the only Caribbean element in this new South Florida cooking style. Cooking methods and flavor preferences of the various islands also entered the cuisine. Because they'd been colonized by different European nations and influenced by various immigrant groups, Caribbean islands embrace a wide range of cooking techniques and seasonings. South Florida chefs borrowed freely from French-based Guadeloupe and Martinique cuisines, East Indian–influenced Jamaican and Trinidadian cuisines, and Spanish-based Puerto Rican and Cuban cuisines. Doug Rodriguez focused on refining and updating the cuisines of South America and the Spanish Caribbean, creating Nuevo Latino cuisine. By the late 1980s, the cooking of many South Florida restaurants was so strongly influenced by the Caribbean that food writers began using the term **Floribbean cuisine** (condensing *Flori*da and *Cari*bbean into one word) to describe it. However, this term is too narrow to accurately describe the new South Florida style.

New South Florida chefs were not content with only Caribbean influences. Classically trained in European cuisines; well versed in regional American cooking; and familiar with Asian, African, and Pan-Hispanic foods, the Mango Gang applied the best of all world cuisines to their menus. Food historians believe Chef Norman Van Aken was the first to apply the term **fusion cuisine** to this global style of cooking. Later, Van Aken adopted the term *New World cuisine* when referring to his menus. No matter the source of culinary inspiration, the new regional cuisine born in the 1980s in South Beach and other South Florida beach towns—and that continues to develop today—is unique to the region. We'll call it new South Florida cuisine.

For a list of noteworthy new South Florida cuisine restaurants, refer to this book's companion website.

Characteristics of New South Florida Cuisine

Less than 30 years old, new South Florida cuisine is still too young to have achieved a large repertoire of defining dishes. As practiced today, this cooking style is still evolving. However, signature techniques, brilliant flavor combinations, and a unique sensibility are part of its current definition. New South Florida cooking typically exhibits the following characteristics.

Bold Flavors and Sharp Contrasts

Strong seasonings are a hallmark of the cuisine. Curry pastes or powders, adobos (p. 741), sofrito, rubs, and marinades add bold flavor to meats, seafood, and poultry. Intensely flavored Key lime and sour (Seville) orange juice are used in sauces and dressings. Ingredients are juxtaposed to create sharp contrasts. Sweet tropical fruits are livened with tart citrus flavors; salty soy sauce or fish sauce accents sweet coconut; hot chiles spike bland tubers.

Light Textures and Consistencies

New South Florida chefs avoid rich sauces and animal-based cooking fats. The cuisine downplays red meats, cheeses, and cream in favor of seafood, vegetables, and fruits. Peanut oil and canola oil are favored frying media. Raw vegetable salads and fruit- or vegetable-based salsas are frequent accompaniments. Fruits, both tropical and temperate, are the foundation of the dessert menu, which typically features many frozen items such as sorbets and ices.

Tropical Tubers

The cuisine showcases a wide array of tropical tubers, often substituting them for potatoes in classic preparations. Ñame/true yam, cassava/yuca, yautía/malanga, boniato/batata, and taro (some shown in Figure 15.24) are among the many tubers used. Shredded and fried into cakes, sliced and prepared au gratin, or boiled and mashed for purées and croquettes, these tubers contribute unique flavors and textures as well as an aura of the exotic.

"Crusted" Foods

To achieve a crunchy coating and an intriguing flavor, new South Florida cuisine chefs use unusual ingredients as breadings. Fish fillets or poultry breasts are coated with chopped or ground nuts,

FIGURE 15.24
Clockwise from left: yautía/malanga; yellow yam; red malanga; cassava/yuca; taro; boniato (center). David Haynes

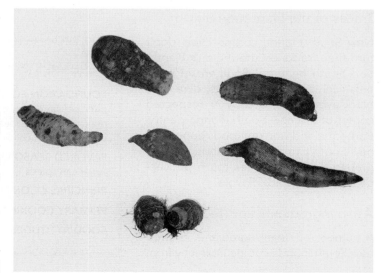

such as peanuts, pecans, macadamias, and pistachios, and baked or pan-fried. Alternatively, fish fillets are wrapped with sliced tropical tubers and fried golden brown. Shrimp are coated with shredded coconut. The term *crusted* is often used to describe these preparations.

Tropical Fruit Sauces and Salsas

New South Florida menus feature a large number of cool, often uncooked sauces made from tropical fruits. Often enhanced with hot chiles, fresh herbs, and citrus juice and zest, this type of sauce is used to enhance seafood, poultry, pork, and various appetizers. Fruit sauces and salsas are welcome when paired with fried foods. Whether presented as smooth purées or chunky, Mexican-style salsas, tropical fruit sauces are light, fresh, and colorful.

Salads as Starters, Sides, and Garnishes

Like California chefs, new South Florida cuisine chefs use leafy salads, crisp-blanched vegetable salads, and fruit salads as both appetizers and accents to hot main dishes. Locally grown leafy greens such as frisée, lolo rosso, and watercress, as well as sprouts and microgreens, are featured.

Coconut Milk in Place of Dairy

Following the time-honored tropical tradition, new South Florida cuisine chefs often substitute coconut milk or coconut cream for dairy milk or cream. Coconut adds tropical flavor and subtle sweetness.

Strong Caribbean Influence

The primary culinary influence in new South Florida cuisine is the cooking of the Caribbean Islands. Caribbean cooking is irresistible to diners who love bold flavors and a broad palette of ingredients. Some chefs lean more strongly toward the Hispanic island cuisines; others favor the flavors and techniques of the French or Anglo-Indian islands.

Traces of the Plantation South

New South Florida cuisine chefs don't turn their backs on the region's Plantation South heritage. Southern ingredients such as cornmeal, grits, okra, and black-eyed peas occupy a respected corner of the new South Florida pantry. Barbeque and smoked foods appear on new South Florida menus, though often prepared with a lighter touch and accented with tropical flavors.

Asian Ingredients and Techniques

A number of Asian ingredients entered new South Florida cuisine indirectly from the Caribbean, the legacy of Asian workers brought to the islands. However, new South Florida cuisine chefs borrow freely from both East Asian and South Asian pantries, using ingredients such as Chinese oyster sauce, Thai curry paste, Vietnamese fish sauce, Japanese seaweeds, and Indian spices. Asian techniques such as stir-frying and steaming have become standard cooking methods. The Japanese preference for raw seafood has made sashimi-style and tartare-style presentations popular.

Art Deco Influence in Plate Presentation

The Mango Gang, and the many South Florida chefs who followed them, responded to their environment by adapting Art Deco South Beach architecture and interior design into their presentation styles. They were among the first to abandon the classic round white plate in favor of unusual serviceware, typically in the Art Deco style. Presenting food on plates of various pastel colors or dramatic black, and in geometric or freeform shapes, was revolutionary at the time. The shapes, colors, and placement of South Florida food also followed the Art Deco model. South Florida chefs featured pastel-color sauces painted on the plate in curving or linear designs and were among the first to present food in tall, stacked assemblages.

■ THE FUTURE OF SOUTH FLORIDA'S CUISINES

Today's South Florida cuisine chefs are developing new dishes and perfecting South Florida signature creations. Agricultural entrepreneurs are branching out into specialty crops, such as microgreens and heirloom tomatoes. Continuing immigration brings new culinary influences and an expanded foodservice workforce. Here, in the birthplace of fusion cuisine, chefs continue combining local seafood and produce with world cuisines ingredients, using classic techniques for a sophisticated clientele.

ELEMENTS OF SOUTH FLORIDA CUISINES

FOUNDATION FOODS:
principal starches: rice, tropical tubers
principal proteins: seafood, pork
principal produce: virtually all vegetables, tropical fruits

FAVORED SEASONINGS: citrus, coconut, chiles, annatto, soy sauce, South Asian and Latin American spices

PRINCIPAL COOKING MEDIA: olive oil, stock, coconut milk

PRIMARY COOKING METHODS: sautéing, pan-frying, steaming, grilling, barbeque

FOOD ATTITUDES: developing food culture, culinary liberals

■ THE CUBAN-AMERICAN
□ MICROCUISINE
■

Throughout South Florida's history, Cuban influence has played a major role in both culture and cuisine. Today Cuban-inspired cooking flourishes in two major enclaves: Tampa's Ybor City (Figure 15.25) and Miami's Little Havana (Figure 15.26) neighborhoods. Itself a hybrid cuisine, the lively cooking of Cuba was enhanced with American cooking technology and fine local ingredients to become Cuban-American cuisine. To discover the roots and evolution of this dynamic American microcuisine, go to www.pearsonhighered .com/sackett.

FIGURE 15.25
Tampa's Ybor City, circa 1890. Florida State Archives

FIGURE 15.26
Miami's Little Havana. Samuel Acosta/Shutterstock

□ TABLE 15.1 SOUTH FLORIDA DEFINING DISHES

ITEM NAME	HISTORY	DOMINANT INGREDIENTS AND METHOD	MORE
CONCH (KONK) SALAD	Conch salad is a form of seviche, a dish in which seafood is "cooked" or denatured by marination in citrus juice. Food historians believe this technique traveled from South Pacific islands to South America, where it was discovered by Spanish explorers. The Spanish introduced it to the Caribbean, where it was used extensively on Bahamian conch. Bahamian immigrants brought conch salad to the Florida Keys.	Fine-diced conch meat is marinated in citrus juice, then tossed in an olive oil dressing with bell peppers, scallions, and tomatoes. New South Florida cuisine chefs sometimes feature dressings based on coconut milk or tropical fruit purées.	Conch salad may be served on a bed of greens, in avocado halves, or in martini glasses to make conch cocktail.
CONCH (KONK) CHOWDER	Tory immigrants who fled New England after the American Revolution and settled in the Florida Keys made chowder by substituting local conch for clams, coconut milk for cow's milk, and tropical tubers for potatoes.	Chopped conch and diced tropical tubers are simmered in coconut milk flavored with salt pork or bacon. Tomatoes and spicy Scotch bonnet chiles may be added.	Similar soups are found throughout the Caribbean, particularly in the Bahamas.

(continued)

☐ **TABLE 15.1 SOUTH FLORIDA DEFINING DISHES** (continued)

ITEM NAME	HISTORY	DOMINANT INGREDIENTS AND METHOD	MORE
CONCH (KONK) FRITTERS	African-American cooks added chopped conch and spicy seasonings to Plantation South hushpuppies.	Chopped conch, onions, bell peppers, and Caribbean seasonings are mixed into a cornmeal batter. Deep-fried golden, the fritters are served as a snack or appetizer accompanied by Caribbean-style bottled hot sauce.	New South Florida chefs accompany conch fritters with spicy mayonnaise-based dips or savory salsas made from tropical fruits.
STONE CRAB CLAWS WITH MUSTARD SAUCE	This signature South Florida seafood was popularized by Joe's Stone Crab restaurant in Miami. (See p. 732)	Steamed, chilled, and cracked Moro crab claws are teamed with a tangy mustard-mayonnaise dip.	
HEARTS OF PALM SALAD	The tender hearts of several palm species are a traditional forage food throughout the tropics. In South Florida they were a subsistence food of poor Cracker settlers and widely eaten during the Great Depression. Hearts of palm became a luxury salad ingredient in the 1940s.	Boiled and refreshed palm hearts are sliced and tossed in a classic vinaigrette dressing. Garnishes include shredded lettuce, tomato wedges, and black olives.	New South Florida chefs often team hearts of palm with cool poached seafood and Caribbean-style dressings.
AVOCADO SALAD	Although avocado trees were introduced by early Spanish explorers, commercial cultivation began around 1900. In the 1920s salads made with "alligator pears" were served as appetizers.	Sliced Florida avocados are served on a bed of lettuce dressed with a classic vinaigrette.	Avocado halves are often filled with seafood salad.
TROPICAL FRUIT SALSAS	New South Florida cuisine's Latin-influenced chefs adapted Mexican-style salsas by replacing tomatoes with ripe tropical fruits. These salsas are served with chips as an appetizer or used as a topping for broiled, grilled, and fried foods.	Onion, chiles, and diced tropical fruit are mashed into a rough purée and then seasoned with citrus juice and zest, cilantro, and other seasonings. Fruits include mango, papaya, pineapple, passion fruit, guava, and others.	Fresh tropical fruit salsas are highly perishable. Prepare just enough for the service and discard leftovers.
COCONUT SHRIMP	This appetizer became wildly popular restaurant fare in the late 1980s.	Large, peeled, tail-on shrimp are breaded with sweetened, shredded coconut and then deep-fried. Dipping sauces include a sweet, marmalade-based mixture, Thai sweet chile sauce, and a tangy soy-and-vinegar blend.	Non-sweet dipping sauces provide better flavor balance.
SEAFOOD-STUFFED CHAYOTE (cha-YOH-tay)	This Meso-American food plant was introduced by the Spanish and, by South Florida settlement in the mid-1800s, had naturalized in many areas.	Chayotes are halved, steamed, and hollowed. The pale green flesh is chopped and mixed with diced seafood, Caribbean seasonings and bread crumbs, then stuffed back into the shell. The baked chayotes are served hot as a main dish or appetizer.	Stuffed chayote may be accompanied by a cream sauce or fresh tomato sauce.
FROG LEGS	South Florida's wetlands produce an abundance of frogs. Early settlers used this resource as a subsistance food. Today frog legs remain a signature regional dish.	Breaded and deep-fried frog legs are served with lemon wedges and tartar sauce. Sautéed frog legs are bathed in a garlicky lemon butter sauce and garnished with chopped parsley.	Fried frog legs are a popular appetizer.

☐ TABLE 15.1 SOUTH FLORIDA DEFINING DISHES *(continued)*

ITEM NAME	HISTORY	DOMINANT INGREDIENTS AND METHOD	MORE
'GATOR STEAK AND 'GATOR KEBABS	A favorite food of South Florida Native Americans, alligator tail meat was eaten by settlers then abandoned until a revival in the 1980s.	Sliced tail meat "steaks" or skewered cubes are marinated and then grilled. Styles include a simple lemon-and-butter baste, Jamaican jerk, Louisiana blackened, and Asian soy-and-ginger.	
"CRUSTED" FISH	Popularized by the Mango Gang (p. 734) in the late 1980s, fish fillets coated in a crispy crust became a signature dish of New South Florida cuisine.	Seasoned fish fillets are dipped in egg wash and then coated with a starchy substance that becomes crisp when cooked. Coatings include: chopped nuts, especially Macadamias; shredded coconut; and tropical tubers.	Crusted fish is often topped with a tropical salsa.
JERK CHICKEN OR PORK	The term *jerk*, as in *jerky*, is derived from the Spanish word *charqui*, meaning "cured." Although precontact Caribbean natives practiced this cooking method, modern-day jerk was created in the 18th century by the Maroons, escaped slaves hiding in Jamaica's mountainous interior.	Meat or chicken is marinated in a spice paste made from ground onion, garlic, Jamaican allspice, Scotch bonnet chiles, soy sauce, and other spices and seasonings. The meat is barbequed "low and slow" with an acidic mopping sauce.	Jamaican-American jerk is usually served with a savory-sweet, tamarind-based table sauce.
KEY LIME PIE	Key Westers from New England adapted custard pie recipes to use the juice of abundant Key limes. In the late 1800s, the availability of canned condensed milk made this pie even more popular. Graham cracker crusts appeared in the early 1900s.	To make the custard, Key lime juice is mixed with sugar, egg yolks, and condensed milk. The acidic lime juice "cooks" and thickens the mixture by coagulating proteins; no need to apply heat. The pie is topped with whipped cream or browned meringue.	Use pasteurized egg yolks to comply with modern food safety regulations.
TROPICAL CREAM PIES	In the early 1900s, meringue-topped cream pies became fashionable. Newly-available Florida tropical fruits made them modern and exotic.	For banana cream pie, vanilla custard is flavored with banana extract and layered with sliced ripe bananas. For Coconut Cream Pie, grated fresh coconut and coconut milk are added to the custard. Lemon Meringue pie is filled w/ tangy lemon curd.	Crumb crusts or traditional flaky pastry crusts may be used.

■ PUERTO RICAN CUISINE

The islands of Puerto Rico form the southern end of the Greater Antilles archipelago (Figure 15.27). These islands are the last vestige of the ancient North American continental shelf and, thus, comprise mainly low plateau land over limestone bedrock. Hills and a few low mountains dot the main island's interior. Puerto Rico's climate is tropical, with year-round average daytime temperatures in the 80s and cooler weather in the interior.

Puerto Rico was a Spanish colony until it became part of the United States in 1898 under the Treaty of Paris. Although it was never an autonomous nation, Puerto Rico's cooking exhibits all the characteristics of a national cuisine. Therefore, in this text we treat Puerto Rican cooking as a unique and separate microcuisine. Because of its close proximity to South Florida, and its cuisine's similarities to the cooking of South Florida, we've chosen to discuss it with the South

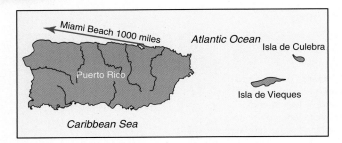

FIGURE 15.27
Puerto Rico

Florida culinary region rather than list it as a separate region in its own right.

Although many Puerto Ricans now live in other parts of the United States, they typically have access to all ingredients necessary to produce a true form of Puerto Rican cooking. Thus, a Puerto Rican-American microcuisine has not developed.

Roots of Puerto Rican Cuisine

Four cultures combined to create traditional Puerto Rican cuisine.

Indigenous Taíno Foodways

At the time of Spanish contact the island of Puerto Rico was occupied by groups of Taíno natives with foodways similar to those of Cuba's Taíno people. Unlike in Cuba, however, indigenous foods became an important element in Puerto Rican cuisine.

As in Cuba, Puerto Rico's Spanish conquerors established plantations and attempted to enslave the indigenous population to work them. Similarly, overwork and European diseases greatly reduced the Taíno population; injury to indigenous culture was compounded by violent retribution after slave revolts and a high rate of suicide among the slaves. As in Cuba and other Caribbean colonies, thousands of Africans were forcibly imported into Puerto Rico to replace indigenous workers. However, in Puerto Rico significant indigenous culture and cuisine was preserved, largely through the intermarriage of Taíno survivors with Africans.

Today much of Puerto Rico's population claims native ancestry. For reasons not completely understood, indigenous ingredients and native foodways were accepted in Puerto Rico far more extensively than in Cuba.

FACTOR 2
Indigenous ingredients and native foodways are an important part of Puerto Rican cuisine.

Because of the preservation of native foodways, many indigenous foods remain in use today. Yuca and yautía are indigenous starchy foundation foods that remain staples of Puerto Rican cuisine, appearing on family tables daily. Three Sisters corn, beans, and squash were additional agricultural products. Although corn was not an important foundation food, beans and squash (especially the Caribbean pumpkin, called *calabaza* [kah-lah-BAH-zah]) have become vital staples in modern Puerto Rican cuisine.

Modern Puerto Rican cooking features many indigenous seasonings, including **annatto** (p. 783), Mexican oregano, several chile varieties, and **culantro** (koo-LAWN-troh), also called **recao** (reh-KAOW), an elongated, saw-toothed herb with a flavor similar to cilantro (Figure 15.28).

Indigenous tropical fruits, such as guavas, guanabanas, and soursops, are featured in modern Puerto Rican cooking.

FIGURE 15.28
Culantro, also known as recao.
Jose Puras/Caribbean Seeds,
www.caribbeanseeds.com

The Spanish: Colonial Domesticates and Tropical Imports

Spanish settlers brought the same foundation foods to Puerto Rico as to Cuba. If necessary, refer to the companion website to refresh your memory of these important colonial domesticates. In Puerto Rican cuisine, Spanish-introduced rice rivals tropical tubers as a foundation starch. However, wheat bread was not an important starch food and was not commonly available until the 20th century.

Puerto Rico was the first landing point for Atlantic sailing ships heading into the Caribbean Sea bound for Central America, and the last port of call for ships leaving the entire Antillean chain. As such, Puerto Rico became a crossroads of trade goods, cultures, and foodways from all over the globe. In addition to foods from Spain, imports from other tropical areas, including breadfruit, bananas and plantains, mangoes, citrus fruits, and sugarcane, enriched the cuisine. The Spanish brought sugar and dairy products, and began a tradition of dessert making that endures in the form of sweet custards. Even foods from Asia, such as soy sauce and ginger, found their way into Puerto Rican kitchens.

FACTOR 3
In Puerto Rican cuisine, Spanish cooking is equal in influence to native and African foodways.

African Influence

The importation of West African slaves brought okra, cornmeal, sesame seeds, true yams, and Guinea hen to Puerto Rico. However, by far the most important African import was pigeon peas, known as **gandules** (gan-DOO-lays). Pigeon peas are cooked with rice and seasoning meat to become *arroz con gandules*, a substantial side dish or, in lean times, a nourishing main course.

As in other parts of America, Africans brought their love of fried foods and expertise at frying. Today many of Puerto Rico's favorite foods—including plantains and pork rinds—are deep-fried.

FACTOR 4
African influence is an important element in Puerto Rican cuisine.

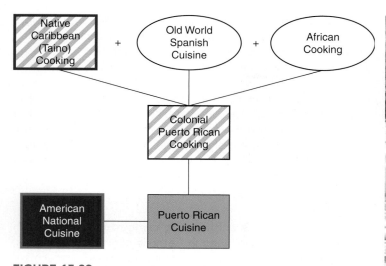

FIGURE 15.29

The Development of Puerto Rican Cuisine

FIGURE 15.30

This mobile vendor specializes in home-style Puerto Rican fare. Courtesy of The Smoke Ring, www.TheSmokeRing.com

FACTOR 5
As part of the United States, Puerto Rico experienced increased economic prosperity and acquired new ingredients.

American Influence

When Puerto Rico became a U.S. territory in the late 1800s, American food products flooded the island. American bacon replaced expensive Spanish ham as the favored seasoning meat. Canned meats, particularly Vienna sausages and corned beef, became staple foods. By the middle of the 20th century Manhattan-based Goya Foods recognized the Puerto Rican market by producing the cuisine's most important seasonings as convenience products. Eventually, American-processed corn oil generally replaced lard as a frying medium. American cooking technology made food preparation faster and easier, and enabled entrepreneurs to open restaurants and food trucks (Figure 15.30).

Characteristics of Puerto Rican Cuisine

Although Cuban and Puerto Rican cuisines evolved from a similar beginning, their significant differences are the result of attitude. In comparison to Cuba, Puerto Rico's population was far more liberal, both socially and culinarily. Unlike Cuba, where the races and classes remained largely segregated, by the mid-1700s Puerto Rico had a strongly established creole culture in the modern sense of the term; most Puerto Ricans were of mixed Spanish, African, and native Caribbean heritage. Puerto Ricans' food preferences were equally liberal. Thus, traditional Puerto Rican cooking is truly a *cocina criolla*, a mixed heritage creole cuisine.

Puerto Rico's creole cooking tradition resulted in a number of characteristic ingredients and cooking methods.

Seasoning Blends

Puerto Rican cooking is noted for its use of premade seasoning blends, both dry and moist. Traditionally these are made in-house and stored for quick use whenever the cook needs them.

Formulas for these seasoning mixtures vary from household to household and are retained as treasured family secrets. Vendors in Puerto Rican food markets sell their own versions of these seasoning blends. Industrial food companies also offer seasoning mixes. The following are Puerto Rican cuisine's most important seasoning blends:

Adobo (ah-DOH-boh) is a dry blend of granulated onion, granulated garlic, ground black pepper, dried Latin American oregano, salt, and sometimes ground cumin. Adobo is rubbed onto meats, poultry, and fish before grilling or frying. It can be included in batters and breadings.

Mojo criollo (mo-ho kree-OH-low) is a marinade based on sour orange juice with onion, garlic, and olive oil.

Sofrito (soh-FREE-toh) in Puerto Rican cuisine contains onions, garlic, green peppers, celery, and tomatoes cooked in olive oil with the addition of culantro/recao and the cook's choice of hot chiles. For many dishes chopped ham, bacon, or salt pork is added. Sofrito is often called the mirepoix of Puerto Rico and is the aromatic base for hundreds of Puerto Rican dishes.

Recaito (reh-KAI-toh) is a rough purée of onions, garlic, green peppers, and culantro/recao. It can be used as a seasoning paste on fish or chicken or added to simmered dishes and casseroles. It enhances the flavor of dried-bean dishes, and its chlorophyll content is said to counteract the digestive problems associated with eating beans.

Patties, Tamales, and Meat Pies

Because Puerto Rican cuisine is based on poor people's cooking, it abounds with recipes that "make something out of nothing," using mashed starches, doughs, and batters to stretch a little bit of flavorful protein food. Refer to p. 743, where Puerto Rican *mofongo*, *pasteles*, *tostones*, and other snack foods are listed and described.

Rice Dishes

Of Arab origin, braised rice dishes came to Puerto Rico with the Spanish and were perfected in African hands. In addition to the signature dish, *arroz con gandules* (p. 743), Puerto Rico also features its own version of the Spanish classic *arroz con pollo*, or rice with chicken. The Puerto Rican version is spicier and richer than its Cuban counterpart. Rice is also simmered in soups to thicken them and make them more substantial. *Asopao* (ah-soh-POW), a broth seasoned with sofrito and thickened with rice, can be made with seafood or chicken.

Soups and Stews

In Puerto Rico the distinction between a soup and a stew can be quite subjective, depending on the ratio of liquid to solids as well as place within the meal. Some of Puerto Rico's most famous stews have African names: *gandinga* (gahn-DING-gah) is a stew of chopped liver, heart, and kidney; *mondongo* (mon-DON-goh) is based on beef tripe flavored with ham, tomatoes, peppers, pumpkin, taro, and chickpeas.

Seafood

Surrounded by both Atlantic and Caribbean waters, Puerto Rico boasts a wide variety of seafood. Fresh fish is served simply grilled and accompanied by one of the island's seasoning sauces. Alternatively, fish is breaded and fried. Shrimp, crab, and spiny lobster are favored, but expensive, seafoods. Octopus salad is a seasonal treat.

Meat Dishes

Pork is the favored meat in Puerto Rican cuisine. For open-air celebrations, Puerto Ricans to this day maintain the Taíno custom of spit barbeque. A whole young pig is marinated in a wet adobo based on sour orange juice and then spitted and slowly revolved over glowing coals while basted with annatto oil. Plantains are roasted in the coals as an accompaniment, and the meat is seasoned at the table with *aji-li-mojili* sauce.

Puerto Rican beef is typically flavorful but tough. Therefore it's usually cooked by a method that tenderizes, such as braising or poaching, followed by shredding. One such dish is *ropa vieja* (ROE-pah vee-YAY-hah), literally "old clothes." The name refers to the similarity in appearance of shredded, cooked beef to tattered rags. Virtually every Latin cuisine has a version of this classic dish. The Puerto Rican variation is served in two courses: The broth from simmering the beef is served as a first-course soup, often fortified with corn, potatoes, squash, and pasta; the shredded meat is then simmered in a tomato sauce and served as a second course with rice or tropical tubers.

Desserts

The tradition of fine Spanish baking came to Puerto Rico with early colonists and continued in Catholic convents. Tarts, pies, cakes, and custards were modified to include island produce, resulting in new creations such as guava cake, pineapple flan, and mango pie. Scores of coconut desserts were developed, among them coconut rice, coconut candy, and coconut cake. As in other tropical areas, the introduction of canned condensed sweetened milk expanded the dessert repertoire.

Puerto Rican Cooking on the Mainland

Around the middle of the 20th century, Puerto Ricans began immigrating to South Florida, New York City, and other large cities throughout the United States. Many found jobs in the hospitality industry, often working in fine restaurants. Gradually their unique blend of Caribbean and Latin foodways is permeating the cooking styles of many kitchens and capturing the imaginations of mainstream chefs. Puerto Rican cooking also has strongly influenced contemporary Nuevo Latino cuisine. As their cuisine blends with that of their host regions, Puerto Ricans living on the mainland may well create a new, hybrid Puerto Rican–American microcuisine, and more mainstream Americans will surely discover the pleasures of Puerto Rican cooking.

☐ TABLE 15.2 PUERTO RICO DEFINING DISHES

ITEM NAME	HISTORY	DOMINANT INGREDIENTS AND METHOD	MORE
AJI-LI-MOJILI (AH-hee-lee-moh-HEE-lee)	*Aji* is a Native Caribbean word for chile. *Mojo* refers to a magic spell or method. So, the name of this signature Puerto Rican table sauce may refer to the cook's artistry in combining chiles with other ingredients.	This thin sauce combines pulverized garlic, black peppercorns, Scotch bonnet, cachucha, or bird chiles, vinegar, lime juice, salt, and olive oil. It is drizzled on mofongo (p. 743) and boiled tropical tubers, and served with roasted and barbequed meats.	
MOJITO ISLEÑO (moh-HEE-toh ee-SLAYN-yoh)	Literally, "small method of the island," this 20th century dipping sauce is similar to a Mexican cooked tomato sauce.	Onions, garlic, capers, green bell peppers, Scotch bonnet or bird chiles, cooked or canned tomatoes, and olive oil are mixed and served cool as a dip or topping.	*Mojito Isleño* is used as a topping for fried, broiled, or grilled fish and has become popular as a dip for fritters.

☐ TABLE 15.2 PUERTO RICO DEFINING DISHES (continued)

ITEM NAME	HISTORY	DOMINANT INGREDIENTS AND METHOD	MORE
PASTELILLOS (pah-stel-EE-yoce)	Pastry turnovers are a legacy of Spanish settlers.	Discs of wheat flour pastry dough are folded over a filling to form a turnover, which may be pan-fried or baked. Fillings include cheese and cooked, seasoned ground meat.	
TOSTONES (toh-STOH-nays)	This Puerto Rican signature dish makes use of an African-inspired double-frying technique.	Yellow-ripe plantain is sliced thick, pan-fried soft on low heat, and cooled. The slices are then flattened into thin discs and soaked in salted water. Before serving they are blotted dry and pan-fried in hot oil until crisp and golden.	Tostones are often served with *mojo criollo* sauce. *Tostones rellenos* are topped with marinated shrimp or *picadillo* and served as hors d'oeuvres.
FRITTERS	Puerto Rican cuisine's many spicy, savory, deep-fried morsels are a blend of African frying technique and indigenous foods.	*Alcapurrias* (ahl-kah-poo-REE-yahs) wrap a dough of mashed plantain and tropical tuber around a filling of pork picadillo (below). *Arañitas* (ah-rahn-YEE-tahs) are made from shredded plantain. *Bacalaitos* (bah-kah-lah-EE-tohs) combine shredded salt cod with a wheat flour or cornmeal batter. Other fritters are made from corn, pumpkin, or eggplant.	Fritters are sometimes served with *mojito isleño* (p. 742).
MOFONGO	A Puerto Rican signature dish, this blend of fried, mashed plantain and pork cracklings is a direct descendant of West African *fufu*, a dish of mashed tubers.	Green plantains are fried soft and then mashed into a thick paste with olive oil, garlic, poultry or meat stock, and seasonings. Crisp pork cracklings or bacon bits are added before serving. It is accompanied by *aji-li-mojilli* (p. 742).	*Mofongo relleno* is stuffed with shredded meat or poultry, picadillo (below), vegetables, or seafood.
PASTELES (bah-STAY-lays)	Puerto Rican *pasteles* are very similar to the banana leaf tamales of southern Mexico.	Yautía and plantain are grated fine and mixed with seasonings to make a thick, pasty dough which is spread on a square of banana leaf. A meat or poultry filling is added, then the leaf is wrapped around the filling to make a bundle that is cooked in boiling water.	*Pasteles* are a traditional Puerto Rican Christmas dish.
ARROZ CON GANDULES (ah-roz kon gahn-DOO-lays)	This signature dish is Puerto Rican comfort food.	Sofrito (p. 741) is cooked in olive oil with diced ham and capers or green olives. Rice is sautéed in the sofrito, then broth and green pigeon peas are added and the rice braised in a covered pot.	*Arroz con Gandules* is served as a thrifty main course or a festive side dish.
ARROZ CON POLLO (ah-ROZ kon PO-yoh)/ ASOPAO (ah-soh-POW)	Spanish dishes of poultry baked in braised rice exhibit Moorish (Arabic) influence.	Rice is braised with sofrito (p. 741) and broth along with adobo (p. 741) marinated chicken. Garnishes include green peas, capers, green olives, pimentos, and diced ham.	*Asopao* is made with more broth (like a soupy risotto) and fewer garnishes.
PICADILLO (pick-ah-DEE-yoh)	This dish is prepared in virtually every Spanish-influenced cuisine, with scores of variations. The original dish is made with cooked, shredded meat. In the mid-20th century ground meat *picadillo* became more popular.	Ground beef or pork is cooked with sofrito (p. 741), tomatoes, green olives, capers, and sometimes raisins.	For shredded meat picadillo, poach or braise the meat, cool, pull with the grain into short lengths and then cook with seasonings.

(continued)

☐ TABLE 15.2 PUERTO RICO DEFINING DISHES (continued)

ITEM NAME	HISTORY	DOMINANT INGREDIENTS AND METHOD	MORE
ROPA VIEJA (roh-pah vee-YAY-hah)	*Ropa Vieja* translates as "old clothes," a reference to its shredded appearance. The Puerto Rican version of this pan-Latin dish is less sweet and more highly spiced than the Cuban dish.	Flank steak is simmered in water or stock with aromatic vegetables, then pulled into fine shreds. The shredded meat is then simmered in a thick tomato sauce flavored with annatto (p. 783), bell peppers, and onions. Depending on the cook's preference, the dish is accented with capers or olives and currants or raisins.	
GANDINGA	In Puerto Rican Spanish, *gandinga* means hog's innards: specifically the liver, kidneys, and heart.	Chopped, boiled *gandinga* is simmered with ham, salt pork, sofrito, and potatoes. The stew is seasoned with vinegar and garnished with stuffed green olives and capers.	
LECHÓN (lay-CHONE)	The term *lechón* is derived from the Spanish word *leche*, meaning "milk," referring to the milk-fed piglet preferred for spit roasting. Puerto Ricans continue the Native Caribbean custom described by the Spanish as *barbacoa*.	A piglet or young hog is seasoned with adobo (p. 741) and spit roasted over hardwood coals. The meat is served with *aji-li-mojilli* (p. 742).	*Lechón* is the centerpiece of special occasion meals for large groups.
TRES LECHES CAKE	*Tres leches* translates as "three milks." This pan-Latin dessert was popularized in the early 1900s by producers of canned milk.	White or yellow cake made by the creaming method is cooled, replaced in its pan, docked with a fork, and soaked with a mixture of sweetened condensed milk, evaporated milk, and heavy cream. Frosting options include meringue-type boiled icing and sweetened whipped cream.	Some Puerto Rican bakers substitute coconut milk for the evaporated milk.

■□■ STUDY QUESTIONS

1. Draw a map of South Florida, showing the location of the region's three distinctive topography areas. Indicate on the map the main economic activities of each topographical area.

2. Discuss South Florida's Native American culinary heritage. Include in your discussion three reasons why Native American cooking had little impact on the region's modern cuisine.

3. Describe Florida Keys culture and cuisine. Include in your description the history of the area and name three dishes typical of its traditional cooking style.

4. Discuss Cracker culture and cuisine. Include in your discussion the main economic activity of Cracker people. Explain the origins of their cooking style and list and describe three Cracker dishes.

5. Explain how technology changed the landscape and economy of South Florida, beginning with developments in the late 1800s and continuing through the 20th century. Include both tourism and agriculture in your explanation.

6. Describe traditional South Florida cuisine and list the neighboring regional and national cuisines that contributed to its development. Name its two most distinctive food products.

7. Outline the birth and development of new South Florida cuisine, including its most prominent chefs. List at least six of its characteristic elements.

8. Discuss the Cuban-American microcuisine. Include in your discussion its history, development, and at least six of its defining dishes.

9. Discuss Puerto Rican cuisine. Include in your discussion its history, development, and at least six of its defining dishes.

10. Using your imagination, and the information you learned in this chapter, create a new South Florida cuisine menu consisting of four appetizers, six entrées, and four desserts.

Caribbean Conch Chowder

with Yuca Roll

yield: 1 (10-fl.-oz.) appetizer serving
(multiply × 4 for classroom turnout; adjust equipment sizes
accordingly)

MASTER RECIPE

production		costing only
1 1/4 c.	Caribbean Conch Chowder	1/4 recipe
2 tsp.	chopped parsley	1/40 bunch a.p.
pinch	chiffonade lime zest	1/8 [63 ct.] lime
1	6" doily or cocktail napkin	1 each
1	Yuca Roll	1/8 recipe

service turnout:
1. Stir the chilled Caribbean Conch Chowder well to distribute the solids and then ladle it into a small saucepan. Heat the soup just to the boil.
2. Plate the dish:
   a. Ladle the soup into a hot 12-fl. oz. soup cup.
   b. Sprinkle the parsley on the soup's surface and then scatter the lime zest on top.
   c. Place a 6" doily on an 8" underliner plate and place the soup cup slightly left of center.
   d. Place the Yuca Roll on the underliner plate to the right of the soup cup.

COMPONENT RECIPE

CARIBBEAN CONCH CHOWDER

yield: 5 c.

production		costing only
2 Tbsp.	gold-color pure olive oil	1 fl. oz.
1 oz.	1/4"-diced rindless smoked bacon	1 1/4 oz. a.p.
2/3 c.	fine-chopped yellow onion	3 1/2 oz. a.p.
1/4 c.	minced carrot	1 1/2 oz. a.p.
1/4 c.	peeled, fine-chopped celery	1/20 head a.p.
1/4 c.	fine-chopped green bell pepper	2 oz. a.p.
8 oz.	cleaned conch meat, ground coarse or chopped fine	8 oz.
2 tsp.	minced garlic	1/8 oz. a.p.
1 2/3 c.	unsweetened canned coconut milk	1 (13.5-fl.-oz.) can
2 1/2 c.	Fish Stock or bottled clam juice	1/6 recipe or 20 fl. oz.
1 sprig	fresh thyme	1/20 bunch a.p.
1	bay leaf	1/16 oz.
1/2 tsp.	seeded, minced Scotch bonnet chile	1/4 oz. a.p.
tt	kosher salt	1/16 oz.
2/3 c.	vine-ripe tomato concassée	8 oz. a.p.
2/3 c.	peeled, 3/8"-diced ñame or yuca	4 oz. a.p.

preparation:
1. Place the oil in a heavy saucepan over medium heat. Add the bacon and fry it until it renders its fat and browns slightly.
2. Add the onion, carrot, celery, and green bell pepper. Sauté over low heat until soft.
3. Add the conch, garlic, coconut milk, Fish Stock, thyme, bay leaf, chile, and a little salt. Bring to a very gentle simmer, cover partially, and simmer for 35 minutes, until the conch is tender and the flavors are melded. Stir occasionally.
4. Add the tomatoes and ñame. Simmer for 15 minutes longer.
5. Remove the bay leaf, taste, and correct the seasonings.

holding: open-pan cool and immediately refrigerate in a freshly sanitized, covered, nonreactive container up to 5 days

---

RECIPE VARIATIONS

Caribbean Shrimp Chowder
Use Shellfish Stock to make the chowder. Omit the conch. Add 1/2 oz. peeled, diced raw shrimp to the soup cup in step 2a of the master recipe.

Old Key West Conch Chowder
Replace 1/2 c. of the stock with canned evaporated milk.

Ybor City Black Bean Soup
with Cuban Bread

yield: 1 (8-fl.-oz.) appetizer serving
(multiply × 4 for classroom turnout; adjust equipment sizes accordingly)

🕐 Best prepared in advance.

APPETIZERS

MASTER RECIPE

production		costing only
1 c.	hot Ybor City Black Bean Soup, in steam table*	1/4 recipe
2 tsp.	brunoise-cut red bell pepper	1/4 oz. a.p.
1 Tbsp.	fine diagonal-sliced scallion	1/16 bunch a.p.
1 Tbsp.	sour cream, in a pastry bag fitted with a star tip	1/2 fl. oz.
1	cocktail napkin or 6" doily	1 each
2 slices	Cuban Bread	1/8 recipe
1 Tbsp.	fino sherry, in a small cruet	1/2 fl. oz.

service turnout:
1. Plate the dish:
   a. Ladle the soup into a hot 10-fl.-oz. soup cup.
   b. Scatter the red bell pepper and scallion on top.
   c. Pipe a rosette of sour cream onto the surface of the soup.
   d. Place the cocktail napkin on an 8" underliner plate and place the soup cup on top.
   e. Serve the Cuban Bread in a cloth-lined basket.
   f. Offer sherry for the customer to stir into the soup.

*When holding in a steam table for prolonged periods, thin with boiling water as necessary.

COMPONENT RECIPE
YBOR CITY BLACK BEAN SOUP

yield: approx. 1 qt.

🕐 Best prepared in advance.

production		costing only
1 c.	black turtle beans	6 oz.
7 oz.	smoked pork neck bones	7 oz.
6 c.+	water	n/c
2	cloves	1/16 oz.
2 oz.	wedge peeled yellow onion	2 1/4 oz. a.p.
2	bay leaves	1/8 oz.
2 sprigs	flat-leaf parsley	1/20 bunch a.p.
6 Tbsp.	gold-color pure olive oil	3 fl. oz.
1 tsp.	fresh-toasted, ground cumin seeds	1/16 oz.
2 tsp.	dried oregano	1/16 oz.
1/2 tsp.	dried thyme	1/16 oz.
3/4 c.	fine-chopped yellow onion	5 oz. a.p.
1/2 c.	fine-chopped green bell pepper	4 oz. a.p.
1/2 c.	fine-chopped red bell pepper	4 oz. .a.p.
1 Tbsp.	minced garlic	1/3 oz. a.p.
1/2 c.	vine-ripe tomato concassée	5 oz. a.p.
tt	kosher salt	1/16 oz.

preparation:

1a. Pick over the beans and remove any foreign matter. Place the beans in a 3-qt. nonreactive saucepan, add a sufficient amount of water to cover them to twice their depth, and soak overnight.

—or—

1b. Alternatively, bring the beans in the water to the boil, remove from the heat, and quick-soak for 1 hour.

2. Drain and rinse the beans, then return them to the pan. Add 6 c. water and the neck bones. Bring to the simmer and skim the foam.

3. Stick the cloves into the onion wedge and tie it in a single-layer cheesecloth sachet along with the bay leaves and parsley sprigs. Cut off any excess cheesecloth and add the sachet to the beans. Simmer for 20 minutes.

4. Heat a 10" sauté pan and add 4 Tbsp. of the oil. Add the cumin, oregano, and thyme; swirl the pan for a few seconds until the seasonings become fragrant; and then add the chopped onion, half of the green bell pepper, half of the red bell pepper, and the garlic. Cook, stirring, over low heat for a few minutes, until the vegetables begin to soften.

5. Scrape the vegetables and oil into the beans. Simmer for 30 to 40 minutes longer, until the beans are very tender and the broth has thickened to a light nappé consistency. Stir occasionally and add water if the soup becomes too thick.

6. Remove and cool the neck bones. Pick off and reserve their meat. Remove and discard the sachet.

7. Use an immersion blender or wooden spoon to mash some of the beans and thicken the broth. ⚠ Do not purée.

8. Heat the remaining 2 Tbsp. oil in a small sauté pan, then add the tomatoes and remaining bell peppers. Cook, stirring, until the tomatoes are almost dry. Scrape the vegetables and oil into the soup, taste, and season with salt.

9. Simmer the soup for 10 minutes longer, adding water if it becomes too thick.

10. Correct the seasoning, adding more salt if necessary.

holding: open-pan cool and immediately refrigerate in a freshly sanitized, covered container up to 5 days; freeze up to 3 months

---

RECIPE VARIATIONS

Coral Gables Black Bean Soup with Orange
Omit the oil, tomatoes, and bell peppers in step 8. Instead, add 1/2 c. orange juice and 1 Tbsp. minced orange zest. Purée the soup, then thin it to a light nappé consistency with Poultry Stock. Omit the brunoise-cut red bell pepper from the garnish. Instead, sprinkle with minced cilantro and chiffonade orange zest.

Cuban Black Beans (side dish)
Prepare the soup through step 6 only, using about 4 1/2 c. water.

Coconut Shrimp

with Spicy Ginger-Soy Dipping Sauce and Shredded Salad

yield: 1 (4-oz.) appetizer serving plus accompaniment
(multiply × 4 for classroom turnout)

MASTER RECIPE

production		costing only
as needed	frying compound or peanut oil	% used
3	Coconut Breaded Shrimp	1/4 recipe
1/8 c.	very fine-julienne carrot	1/4 oz. a.p.
1/4 c.	fine-julienne green papaya flesh or chiffonade Napa cabbage	1/16 [12 ct.] a.p. or 2 oz. a.p.
1/2 c.	seeded and tailed mung bean sprouts	1 oz. a.p.
1 tsp.	peanut oil, in squeeze bottle	1/6 fl oz.
1 tsp.	liquid from Japanese pickled ginger, in squeeze bottle	n/c
1 tsp.	Japanese soy sauce, in squeeze bottle	1/6 fl. oz.
1 pc.	banana leaf, cut into an 8 1/2" triangle	1/20 pkg.
1/2	lime, hollowed out to form a cup	1/2 [63 ct.] lime
2 Tbsp.	Ginger-Soy Dipping Sauce	1/4 recipe
pinch	minced cilantro	1/40 bunch a.p.
pinch	black sesame seeds	1/16 oz.

service turnout:
1. Deep-fry the Coconut Breaded Shrimp in 375°F oil for about 90 seconds. Drain on a rack and then blot on paper towels.
2. Toss together the carrot, papaya, and bean sprouts. Drizzle with peanut oil, pickled ginger liquid, and soy sauce. Toss to dress the vegetables evenly.
3. Plate the dish:
   a. Place the banana leaf triangle on a cool 10" plate with the points at 12, 4, and 8 o'clock.
   b. Mound the salad on the back of the plate.
   c. Place the lime cup slightly right of center on the plate and fill it with Ginger-Soy Dipping Sauce.
   d. Arrange the shrimp to the left of the lime cup.
   e. Sprinkle cilantro and black sesame seeds on the salad.

COMPONENT RECIPE

COCONUT BREADED SHRIMP

yield: 12 (1 1/3-oz.) pc.

production		costing only
12	(16–20 ct.) white shrimp	11 oz. a.p.
1 1/2 c.	sweetened shredded coconut	3 oz.
1/2 c.	flour	2 1/2 oz.
1 tsp.	fine salt	1/6 oz.
1/2 tsp.	cayenne pepper	1/16 oz.
2	egg whites	2 each or 2 oz.

preparation:
1. Fabricate the shrimp:
   a. Peel the shrimp, leaving the tail segments intact as for shrimp cocktail.
   b. Butterfly the shrimp by slitting partway through the curved backs and flattening them.
   c. Remove any visible veins.
2. Prepare the coating:
   a. Chop the coconut to shorten the length of the shreds so they'll properly adhere to the shrimp.
   b. Mix together the flour, salt, and cayenne.
   c. Beat the egg whites to foam.
3. Coat the shrimp, leaving the tails uncoated:
   a. Lightly dip each shrimp in the seasoned flour, dip it in the egg whites, and then roll it firmly in the coconut.
   b. Tap off any excess coconut and then place the shrimp on a half-sheet tray with pan liner.
   c. Repeat with the remaining shrimp.
   d. Refrigerate the shrimp, uncovered, for at least 1 hour.

holding: refrigerate in a covered container with pan liner between layers up to 2 days

COMPONENT RECIPE
GINGER-SOY DIPPING SAUCE

yield: approx. 1/2 c.

production		costing only
1	lime	1 [63 ct.] lime
2 Tbsp.	peeled fresh ginger	1/2 oz. a.p.
1	peeled fresh garlic clove	1/6 oz. a.p.
2 Tbsp.	minced scallion	1/6 bunch a.p.
1 tsp.	seeded, minced Scotch bonnet or habanero chile	1/8 oz. a.p.
1 tsp.	sugar	1/6 oz.
1/2 c.	Japanese soy sauce	4 fl. oz.

preparation:
1. Cut off the ends of the lime and pare away the green zest and white pith. Cut the flesh out of the membrane and place it in a mortar or small bowl. Remove any seeds.
2. Use a garlic press to extract the juice from the ginger, and add the ginger juice to the mortar.
3. Press the garlic into the mortar and then add the scallion, chile, and sugar. Crush the ingredients in the mortar into a rough paste.
4. Stir in the soy sauce and allow the flavors to meld at room temperature for about 15 minutes.
5. Taste and, if necessary, correct the flavor balance.

holding: refrigerated in a freshly sanitized, covered, nonreactive container up to 7 days

---

RECIPE VARIATION
Coconut Shrimp with Spicy Mango Dip
Replace the sweetened shredded coconut with unsweetened desiccated coconut. Replace the Ginger-Soy Dipping Sauce with Spicy Mango Dip (p. 751).

South Beach Conch Fritters
with Spicy Mango Dip

yield: 1 (5-oz.) appetizer serving
(multiply × 4 for classroom turnout)

MASTER RECIPE

production		costing only
as needed	frying compound or peanut oil	% used
5 fl. oz.	Conch Fritter Batter	1/4 recipe
2	cocktail napkins	2 each
3 Tbsp.	Spicy Mango Dip	1/4 recipe
1 bouquet	cilantro	1/10 bunch a.p.

service turnout:
1. Fry the fritters:
   a. Lower the fryer basket into 350°F oil.
   b. Using a #30 (1-fl.-oz.) portion scoop, gently drop 5 fritters into the oil.
   c. Deep-fry for about 2 minutes, turning occasionally, until golden brown and cooked through.
   d. Raise the basket and drain the fritters.
2. Plate the dish:
   a. Arrange the cocktail napkins on a warm 10" oval plate.
   b. Place the Spicy Mango Dip in a small dip dish and place the dish on the left side of the plate.
   c. Arrange the fritters on the right side of the plate.
   d. Arrange the cilantro bouquet between the dip dish and the fritters.

COMPONENT RECIPE
CONCH FRITTER BATTER

yield: 20 fl. oz.

production		costing only
1 Tbsp.	corn oil	1/2 fl. oz.
1/4 c.	fine-diced red bell pepper	2 oz. a.p.
1/4 c.	fine-diced green bell pepper	2 oz. a.p.
tt	kosher salt	1/16 oz.
1/4 c.	chopped scallion	1/8 bunch a.p.
1/2 tsp.	minced fresh thyme leaves	1/40 bunch a.p.
1/2 c.	yellow cornmeal	1 3/4 oz.
1/2 c.	flour	2 1/2 oz.
1/2 tsp.	fine salt	1/6 oz.
1/2 tsp.	seafood seasoning, such as Old Bay	1/16 oz.
1/4 tsp.	baking powder	1/16 oz.
2 tsp.	sugar	1/3 oz.
1/2	egg, beaten	1 oz.
1/4 c.	unsweetened canned coconut milk	2 fl. oz.
as needed	water	n/c
6 oz.	cleaned conch, ground coarse or chopped fine	6 oz.

preparation:
1. Heat a small sauté pan, heat the oil, and sauté the bell pepper with a pinch of salt until crisp-tender. Cool to room temperature, then add the scallion and thyme.
2. Mix the cornmeal, flour, salt, seafood seasoning, baking powder, and sugar in a bowl. Make a well in the center.
3. Combine the egg and coconut milk.
4. Pour the egg mixture into the cornmeal mixture and stir, adding water only if necessary, to make a thick batter. Mix in the conch and pepper mixture.
5. Refrigerate the batter for at least 15 minutes.

holding: refrigerate in a freshly sanitized, covered container up to 12 hours

COMPONENT RECIPE

SPICY MANGO DIP

yield: 3/4 c.

production		costing only
5 fl. oz.	frozen mango purée, thawed	5 fl. oz.
—or—		
1	ripe mango, peeled, pitted, and puréed	1 [12 ct.] mango
2 Tbsp.	minced scallion	1/6 bunch a.p.
1 tsp.	seeded, minced Scotch bonnet or habanero chile	1/8 oz. a.p.
tt	kosher salt	1/16 oz.
as needed	water	n/c
tt	sugar	1/16 oz.
tt	fresh lemon juice	1/6 [90 ct.] lemon

preparation:

1. Combine the mango purée, scallion, chile, and a little salt.
2. Stir in enough water to achieve a consistency slightly thicker than nappé.
3. Let stand for at least 15 minutes to allow the flavors to meld.
4. Taste and correct the flavor balance. (If the mango is very tart, add sugar and then balance with salt; if the mango is sweet, add lemon juice and then balance with salt.)

holding: refrigerated in a freshly sanitized, covered, nonreactive container up to 12 hours; if not to be used same day, freeze immediately and hold frozen up to 1 month

---

RECIPE VARIATION

South Beach Shrimp Fritters
Replace the conch with coarse-chopped raw shrimp.

Key West Conch Seviche

yield: 1 (4-oz.) appetizer serving plus garnishes
(multiply × 4 for classroom turnout)

MASTER RECIPE

production		costing only
1	Fried Plantain Strip	1/8 recipe
3/4 c.	Conch Seviche	1/4 recipe
3 Tbsp.	extra-virgin olive oil	1 1/2 fl. oz.
1/4 c.	3/8"-diced firm-ripe avocado	1/5 [40 ct.] avocado
1/4 c.	3/8"-diced fresh pineapple	1/16 [12 ct.] pineapple a.p.
1 Tbsp.	fine diagonal-sliced scallion	1/16 bunch a.p.
1 Tbsp.	brunoise-cut red bell pepper	1/2 oz. a.p.
tt	seeded, minced Scotch bonnet or habanero chile	1/8 oz.
tt	kosher salt	1/16 oz.
as needed	fresh lime juice, in a saucer	1/8 [63 ct.] lime
as needed	Red Chile Salt, in a saucer	1/8 recipe
1/2 oz.	spring mix salad greens, preferably with frisée	1/2 oz.
1	lime wedge	1/6 [63 ct.] lime
1	cocktail napkin	1 each

service turnout:

1. Place the Fried Plantain Strip on a sizzle plate and crisp it in a 400°F oven for about 3 minutes.
2. Toss together the Conch Seviche with the oil, avocado, pineapple, scallion, red bell pepper, and chile. Season with salt.
3. Plate the dish:
   a. Dip the rim of a 14-fl. oz. margarita glass in lime juice, then in the Red Chile Salt.
   b. Fill the bottom of the glass with spring mix.
   c. Hold the plantain strip upright in the margarita glass while spooning in the seviche mixture, resulting in the plantain strip standing upright toward the back of the glass.
   d. Slit the lime wedge and hang it on the rim of the glass near the plantain strip.
   e. Place the cocktail napkin on an 8" plate and place the margarita glass on it.

COMPONENT RECIPE

FRIED PLANTAIN STRIPS

yield: approx. 8 pc.

production		costing only
as needed	peanut oil	% used
1	firm green plantain	6 oz.
as needed	Red Chile Salt	1/8 recipe

preparation:

1. Pour the oil into a 10" sauté pan to a depth of 1/2" and heat it to approximately 400°F. Line a sheet tray with paper towels.
2. Peel the plantain. Using a mandoline or electric slicing machine, cut it lengthwise into very thin, even slices about 1/16" thick. (One plantain should yield at least 4 perfect, full-sized slices plus others for practice.)
3. Fry the plantain slices, one or two at a time, holding them flat with two perforated spoons as they fry.
4. Drain the fried plantain strips on paper towels.
5. While still hot, sprinkle both sides with Red Chile salt.

holding: store in a tightly sealed, paper towel–lined container at cool room temperature up to 3 days

COMPONENT RECIPE
CONCH SEVICHE

yield: approx. 3 c.

production		costing only
12 oz.	3/8" diced cleaned conch	12 oz.
1 c.	Key lime juice	8 fl. oz.
1 Tbsp.	minced fresh garlic	1/3 oz. a.p.
1/4 c.	minced white onion	1 1/4 oz. a.p.
1 Tbsp.	minced lime zest	1/2 [63 ct.] lime
1/2 tsp.	kosher salt	1/12 oz.
1 Tbsp.	sugar	1/2 oz.

preparation:
1. Mix together all ingredients and place in a freshly sanitized, nonreactive container just large enough to hold the mixture.
2. Cover and marinate in the refrigerator for 3 hours.
3. Drain the mixture, squeezing to remove all liquid.

holding: refrigerate covered up to 3 days

COMPONENT RECIPE
RED CHILE SALT

yield: 4 Tbsp.

production		costing only
3 Tbsp.	fine salt	1 1/2 oz.
1 Tbsp.	pure ancho or New Mexico red chile powder	1/2 oz.

preparation:
1. Mix.

holding: store in a tightly sealed container at cool room temperature up to 3 months

---

RECIPE VARIATIONS

Key West Scallop Seviche
Replace the conch with trimmed, sliced sea scallops. Reduce the marination time to 45 minutes. Hold 24 hours only.

Key West Spanish Mackerel Seviche
Replace the conch with skinned, trimmed, sliced or cubed Spanish mackerel fillet. Reduce the marination time to 1 hour. Hold 24 hours only.

Caribbean Seviche
Prepare Conch Seviche, or either of the preceding variations, but replace the olive oil with thick unsweetened canned coconut milk or unsweetened frozen coconut cream.

Ruby Red Grapefruit Salad

with Hearts of Palm, Avocado, Moro Crab, and Key West Shrimp

yield: 1 (5-oz.) appetizer serving
(multiply × 4 for classroom turnout)

MASTER RECIPE

production		costing only
1/4	cold firm-ripe Florida avocado	1/4 [8 ct.] avocado
—or—		
1/2	cold firm-ripe western avocado	1/2 [24 ct.] avocado
as needed	fresh lime juice	1/6 [63 ct.] lime
1/2	ruby red grapefruit	1/2 [18 ct.] grapefruit
1/2 c.	Ruby Red Marinated Hearts of Palm	1/4 recipe
1 1/2 oz.	Moro or other crab meat, picked over for shell fragments	1 1/2 oz.
5 pc.	(51–60 ct.) white shrimp, poached, peeled, and deveined	1 1/2 oz. a.p.
1/4 c.	Ruby Red Vinaigrette for Seafood, in squeeze bottle	1/6 recipe
1 Tbsp.	brunoise-cut red onion	1/4 oz. a.p.
1 tsp.	minced ruby red grapefruit zest	n/c
2 tsp.	minced flat-leaf parsley	1/20 bunch a.p.

service turnout:

1. Fabricate the avocado:
   a. Peel the avocado and remove the pit.
   b. Slice the avocado into 5 thin wedges.
   c. If not using the entire avocado, coat the cut surface with lime juice, wrap in plastic film, and refrigerate.
2. Fabricate the grapefruit:
   a. Trim the ends of the grapefruit and pare away the rind (both the yellow zest and all of the white pith).
   b. Remove 5 perfect grapefruit sections from the membrane.
   c. If not using the entire grapefruit, wrap in plastic film and refrigerate.
3. Plate the dish:
   a. Arrange the avocado slices and grapefruit sections in an alternating spoke pattern on a cool 10" plate, leaving a 2" space in the center.
   b. Mound the Ruby Red Marinated Hearts of Palm in the center of the plate.
   c. Mound the crab meat on top of the palm hearts.
   d. Arrange a circle of shrimp on top of the crab meat.
   e. Spoon the Ruby Red Vinaigrette for Seafood over all of the salad ingredients.
   f. Scatter the red onion and grapefruit zest over the avocado and grapefruit sections.
   g. Place a dot of parsley in the center of the shrimp.

COMPONENT RECIPE
RUBY RED MARINATED HEARTS OF PALM

yield: 2 c.

production		costing only
12 oz.	cleaned and boiled fresh hearts of palm	12 oz.
—or—		
12 oz.	drained bottled or canned palm hearts	12 oz.
1/2 c.	Ruby Red Vinaigrette for Seafood	1/3 recipe

preparation:
1. Fabricate the palm hearts:
   a. Rinse the palm hearts and blot them dry.
   b. Cut the palm hearts into 1/4" rounds.
2. Mix the palm hearts with the Ruby Red Vinaigrette for Seafood.
3. Refrigerate for at least 30 minutes.

holding: refrigerate in a freshly sanitized, covered, nonreactive container up to 3 days

COMPONENT RECIPE
RUBY RED VINAIGRETTE FOR SEAFOOD

yield: 1 1/2 c.

production		costing only
1 c.	Shellfish Stock	1/16 recipe
2 Tbsp.	minced shallot	1 oz. a.p.
1 Tbsp.	minced ruby red grapefruit zest	n/c
1 Tbsp.	sugar	1/2 oz.
2/3 c.	ruby red grapefruit juice	1 [18 ct.] grapefruit
tt	kosher salt	1/16 oz.
1/2 c.	canola oil	4 fl. oz.

preparation:
1. Prepare the shellfish glaze:
   a. In a small sauté pan over low heat, reduce the Shellfish Stock to 1/4 c., scraping the sides often with a heatproof rubber scraper. ⚠ Do not scorch!
   b. Cool to room temperature.
2. Make the dressing:
   a. Scrape the shellfish glaze into a mixing bowl and add the shallot, grapefruit zest, sugar, grapefruit juice, and a little salt.
   b. Whisk in the oil in a thin stream to create an emulsion.
   c. Taste and correct the flavor balance, adding salt if needed.
   d. For service turnout, pour into a freshly sanitized squeeze bottle.

holding: refrigerate in a freshly sanitized, covered container up to 5 days; bring to room temperature for use. Dressing may separate; to reemulsify, purée in a blender.

RECIPE VARIATIONS
Ruby Red Grapefruit Salad with Hearts of Palm and Avocado
Increase the amount of avocado, grapefruit, and Ruby Red Marinated Hearts of Palm by 25 percent. Replace the reduced Shellfish Stock in the Ruby Red Vinaigrette recipe with reduced Poultry Stock or, for a vegetarian salad, with 2 tsp. Dijon mustard.

Everglades Frog Legs al Mojo Criollo

yield: 1 (5-oz.) appetizer serving
(multiply × 4 for classroom turnout; adjust equipment sizes accordingly)

MASTER RECIPE

production		costing only
as needed	peanut oil	5 fl. oz.
		(may be reused once)
2	(6 ct.) frog leg pairs	5 oz. a.p.
1 tsp.	Sazon-Style Seasoning	1/12 recipe
1 Tbsp.	egg, beaten with 1 Tbsp.	1/2 each or
	water	1 oz. a.p.
as needed	flour	1 oz.
3	cherry tomatoes	1/8 pt. a.p.
1/4 c.	Mojo Criollo	1/4 recipe
1 Tbsp.	butter	1/2 oz.
3 sprigs	flat-leaf parsley	1/20 bunch a.p.

service turnout:

1. Fry the frog legs and cherry tomatoes:
   a. Heat a 10" sauté pan, add 1/2" oil, and heat the oil to about 375°F.
   b. Sprinkle the frog legs with Sazon-Style Seasoning, dip in egg wash, and then dredge in flour.
   c. Pan-fry the frog legs on both sides until crisp and golden.
   d. Drain briefly on paper towels.
   e. Immerse the cherry tomatoes in the hot oil for 1 or 2 seconds, just until shiny and blistered but not soft or collapsed. Drain on the towels.
2. Spoon the Mojo Criollo into an 8" sauté pan and heat to just under the boil. Remove from the heat and stir in the butter to create an emulsion.
3. Plate the dish:
   a. Pour the sauce into the well of a warm 10" plate.
   b. Place the frog legs, with tops overlapping, in the center of the plate.
   c. Arrange the cherry tomatoes in a triangle pattern at the top of the plate.
   d. Place a parsley sprig on either side of the tomatoes, and then stick the third sprig upright in the center.

COMPONENT RECIPE
SAZON-STYLE SEASONING

yield: 4 Tbsp.

production		costing only
1 Tbsp.	granulated garlic	1/4 oz.
1 Tbsp.	granulated onion	1/4 oz.
2 tsp.	toasted, ground cumin seeds	1/8 oz.
1 tsp.	toasted, ground coriander seeds	1/16 oz.
1 tsp.	fine-ground white pepper	1/16 oz.
1 tsp.	powdered annatto (or ground annatto seeds)	1/8 oz.
1 tsp.	fine salt	1/6 oz.

preparation:
1. Mix together all ingredients.

holding: store in a tightly sealed container at cool room temperature up to 3 months

COMPONENT RECIPE
MOJO CRIOLLO

yield: 1 c.

production		costing only
10	Key limes	5 oz.
—or—		
3	standard limes	3 [63 ct.] limes
2 Tbsp.	minced fresh garlic	2/3 oz. a.p.
2 Tbsp.	minced scallion	1/8 bunch a.p.
1 Tbsp.	minced lime zest	n/c
1 Tbsp.	chopped flat-leaf parsley	1/40 bunch a.p.
1 Tbsp.	minced culantro or cilantro	1/10 bunch a.p.
1 tsp.	fresh-ground black pepper	1/8 oz.
2 tsp.	seeded, minced Scotch bonnet or habanero chile	1/4 oz. a.p.
1 Tbsp.+	sugar	1/2 oz.+
tt	kosher salt	1/16 oz.
4 Tbsp.	gold-color pure olive oil	2 fl. oz.

preparation:
1. Prepare the lime pulp:
   a. Cut off the ends of the limes and pare away the rind (green zest and white pith).
   b. Cut the flesh out of the membranes and place it in a mortar or small bowl.
   c. Remove any seeds.
2. Place all of the ingredients except the oil into the mortar or small bowl with the lime pulp. Using the pestle or the back of a spoon, crush the ingredients to a rough purée.
3. Whisk the oil into the lime purée.
4. Taste and balance the flavors. This sauce should be very tart and spicy, as it will be diluted with butter before serving.

holding: refrigerate in a freshly sanitized, covered, nonreactive container up to 24 hours

---

RECIPE VARIATIONS

Alligator Fingers al Mojo Criollo
Replace the frog legs with 3 (1 1/2-oz.) strips trimmed alligator tail steak.

Catfish Fingers al Mojo Criollo
Replace the frog legs with 3 (1 1/2-oz.) strips trimmed catfish fillet.

Panéed Grouper
with Mango Aïoli
and Tropical Seashell Salad

yield: 1 (6-oz.) entrée serving plus accompaniments (multiply × 4 for classroom turnout; adjust oil amount and equipment sizes accordingly)

MASTER RECIPE

production		costing only
as needed	peanut oil	4 fl. oz. (may be reused once)
1	6 oz. grouper fillet, skinned, pinned, and halved lengthwise along the center line	7 oz. a.p.
tt	kosher salt	1/16 oz.
as needed	flour	1 oz.
1 Tbsp.	egg, beaten with 1 Tbsp. water	1/4 each or 1/2 oz.
1/4 c.	Corn Flour Breading for Seafood, p. 60 (replace Chesapeake seasoning with Sazon-Style Seasoning (p. 756)	1/4 recipe
1 bouquet	watercress	1/4 bunch a.p.
1 1/2 c.	Tropical Seashell Salad	1/4 recipe
1/4 c.	Mango Aïoli	1/4 recipe
2 tsp.	chopped flat-leaf parsley	1/40 bunch a.p.
1 tsp.	chopped fresh mint	1/40 bunch a.p.

service turnout:
1. Pan-fry the grouper:
   a. Heat an 8" sauté pan, pour in oil to a depth of 1/2", and heat it to about 350°F.
   b. Season the grouper with salt, dredge in the flour, dip in the egg wash, and roll in the Corn Flour Breading for Seafood, pressing firmly so it adheres well.
   c. Pan-fry the grouper for about 2 minutes on each side until crisp, golden, and cooked through.
   d. Blot the grouper on a paper towel.
2. Plate the dish:
   a. Arrange the watercress bouquet on the back of a warm 12" plate with the leaves near the rim and the stems in the center.
   b. Mound the Tropical Seashell Salad on the back center of the plate covering the watercress stems.
   c. Place the grouper pieces on the front of the plate propped against the salad in an X pattern.
   d. Squeeze a ribbon of Mango Aïoli across the grouper, allowing it to pool in the plate well.
   e. Sprinkle the salad with the parsley and mint.

COMPONENT RECIPE
TROPICAL SEASHELL SALAD

yield: 6 c.

production		costing only
9 oz.	small seashell pasta, preferably Italian-made	9 oz.
1 Tbsp.	kosher salt	1/2 oz.
1 c.	Coconut-Lime Vinaigrette	1 recipe
7 oz.	sugar snap peas, stringed, blanched crisp-tender and refreshed, cut in 1/2" diagonals	7 oz.
1/2 c.	1/4" diagonal-cut scallion	1/4 bunch a.p.
1/2 c.	julienne bamboo shoots (boiled fresh or canned)	2 oz.
1/2 c.	julienne red bell pepper	4 oz. a.p.
1 c.	3/8"-diced fresh pineapple	1/5 [12 ct.] pineapple
1 Tbsp.	chopped mint	1/12 bunch a.p.
tt	fine-ground white pepper	1/16 oz.
tt	kosher salt	1/16 oz.
tt	fresh lime juice	1/4 [63 ct.] lime

preparation:
1. Cook and season the pasta:
   a. Boil the pasta in at least 3 qt. rapidly boiling, heavily salted water to al dente.
   b. Drain in a colander and shake dry.
   c. Place the pasta in a bowl and toss in half of the Coconut-Lime Vinaigrette.
   d. Cool to room temperature, tossing occasionally.
2. Assemble the salad:
   a. Toss the peas, scallion, bamboo shoots, red bell pepper, pineapple, and mint into the salad.
   b. Add enough of the remaining vinaigrette to coat the salad ingredients thoroughly.
   c. Season with white pepper.
   d. Taste and balance the seasonings, adding salt and lime juice if needed.

holding: refrigerate in a freshly sanitized, covered container up to 12 hours

COMPONENT RECIPE
COCONUT-LIME VINAIGRETTE

yield: 1 c.

production		costing only
2 to 3	limes	3 [63 ct.] limes
1/4 c.	frozen coconut cream, thawed	1 1/2 oz. a.p.
1 tsp.	minced fresh garlic	1/9 oz. a.p.
1 Tbsp.	minced shallot	1/2 oz. a.p.
1 Tbsp.	minced lime zest	n/c
1 tsp.	seeded, minced Scotch bonnet or habanero chile	1/8 oz. a.p.
tt	kosher salt	1/16 oz.

preparation:
1. Prepare lime pulp:
   a. Cut off the ends of the limes, and pare away the green zest and white pith.
   b. Cut the flesh out of the membranes and remove any seeds.
   c. Place the pulp in a blender.
2. Add the remaining ingredients to the blender and purée to make a thick, emulsified dressing.
3. Taste and balance the flavors, adding more salt or lime juice if needed.

holding: refrigerate in a freshly sanitized, covered, nonreactive container up to 5 days. (The dressing will separate; to reemulsify, bring to room temperature and purée in a blender.)

COMPONENT RECIPE
MANGO AÏOLI

yield: 1 c.

production		costing only
1/2 c.	frozen mango purée, thawed	4 fl. oz.
—or—		
1/2	ripe mango, peeled, pitted, and puréed	1/2 [12 ct.] mango
3/4 c.	mayonnaise	6 fl. oz.
1 Tbsp.	minced fresh garlic	1/3 oz. a.p.
tt	kosher salt	1/16 oz.
tt	fresh lime juice	1/4 [63 ct.] lime

preparation:
1. Place the mango purée in an 8" sauté pan and reduce over high heat, stirring and scraping constantly with a heatproof rubber spatula, to a thick paste. Cool to room temperature.
2. Combine the cooled mango reduction with the mayonnaise and garlic. Season with salt and lime juice.
3. Refrigerate for at least 30 minutes.
4. Taste and balance the flavors.
5. For service, place in a freshly sanitized squeeze bottle.

holding: refrigerate up to 12 hours (if held for much longer, the garlic flavor becomes too strong and the mixture may separate)

RECIPE VARIATIONS

Panéed Grouper Cheeks with Mango Aïoli and Tropical Seashell Salad
Replace the grouper fillet with grouper cheeks.

Paneéd Alligator with Mango Aïoli and Tropical Seashell Salad
Replace the grouper with trimmed alligator tail steak.

Tropical Seashell Salad with Shrimp (lunch entrée or appetizer)
Prepare Tropical Seashell Salad, adding 2 Tbsp. Shellfish Glace to the Coconut-Lime Vinaigrette. Serve on a bed of watercress. Top each serving with 4 oz. poached, peeled 21–25 ct. white shrimp tossed with additional vinaigrette.

Malanga-Mango-Crusted Red Snapper

with Fresh Mango Salsa, Black Beans, and Sautéed Chayote

yield: 1 (7-oz.) entrée serving plus accompaniments (multiply × 4 for classroom turnout; adjust oil amount and equipment sizes accordingly)

MASTER RECIPE

production		costing only
as needed	peanut oil	5 fl. oz. (may be reused once)
1	Malanga-Mango-Crusted Snapper Fillet	1/4 recipe
3 oz.	chayote, peeled, sliced, blanched and refreshed	4 oz. a.p.
as needed	water	n/c
tt	fresh lemon juice	1/6 [90 ct.] lemon
tt	kosher salt	1/16 oz.
tt	fine-ground white pepper	1/16 oz.
1 Tbsp.	butter	1/2 oz.
1/2 c.	Cuban Black Beans, side-dish variation, p. 747, hot in steam table	1/8 recipe
1/2 c.	Fresh Mango Salsa	1/4 recipe
1 bouquet	cilantro	1/8 bunch a.p.

service turnout:

1. Fry the Malanga-Mango-Crusted Snapper Fillet:
   a. Heat an 8" sauté pan, pour in peanut oil to a depth of 1/2", and heat the peanut oil to about 350°F.
   b. Pan-fry the fillet, malanga side down, for about 3 minutes, until the crust is crisp and golden.
   c. Raise the heat, turn the fillet over, and fry for about 1 minute longer.
   d. Remove the fillet to a sizzle pan and place it in a 375°F oven for 5 minutes longer.
2. Finish the chayote:
   a. Place the chayote slices and a little water in an 8" sauté pan, cover, and pan-steam until hot.
   b. Pour off excess water and season with lemon juice, salt, and white pepper.
   c. Add the butter and toss the chayote to coat it in a light emulsified sauce.
3. Plate the dish:
   a. Spoon the Cuban Black Beans onto the back of a warm 12" plate.
   b. Fan the chayote slices on the right side of the plate from 2 to 5 o'clock.
   c. Place the snapper fillet on the plate, diagonally from 2 to 8 o'clock.
   d. Spoon the Fresh Mango Salsa on the plate to the right of the snapper.
   e. Stick the cilantro bouquet upright between the snapper and the beans at 10 o'clock.

COMPONENT RECIPE
MANGO-MALANGA-CRUSTED SNAPPER FILLETS

yield: 4 (7-oz.) servings

production		costing only
3 c.	peeled and grated malanga, prepared at the last minute before proceeding	1 lb. a.p.
1/2 c.	grated yellow onion	2 1/2 oz. a.p.
1	egg, beaten	1 each or 2 oz.
1/2 c.	flour	2 1/2 oz.
tt	kosher salt	1/8 oz.
4	6-oz. skinned and pinned red snapper fillets	28 oz. a.p.
1/2 c.	Trinidadian or Indian preserved sweet mango chutney, such as Major Grey's	4 fl. oz.

preparation:
1. Prepare the malanga crust:
   a. Grasp the grated malanga in your hands and squeeze to remove as much liquid as possible. Place the drained malanga in a bowl.
   b. Mix the onion, egg, and flour into the malanga and season highly with salt.
2. Apply the crust to the snapper fillets:
   a. Lay a snapper fillet on the work surface, shiny/skin side down.
   b. Spread the top of the fillet with 1/4 of the chutney.
   c. Firmly press 1/4 of the malanga mixture on top of the fillet, sculpting it so the edges of the crust are even with the edges of the fish.
   d. Place the crusted fillet on a sheet tray with pan liner.
   e. Repeat with the remaining ingredients to make 4 crusted fillets.
   f. Refrigerate the crusted fillets, uncovered, for at least 1 hour.

holding: refrigerate in one layer in a tightly covered plastic container 1 day only

COMPONENT RECIPE
FRESH MANGO SALSA

yield: 2 c.

production		costing only
1	firm-ripe mango	1 [12 ct.] mango
1/3 c.	fine-chopped sweet onion	2 oz. a.p.
2 Tbsp.	fine-chopped fresh ginger	1/2 oz. a.p.
1 tsp.	minced fresh garlic	1/9 oz. a.p.
1 tsp.	seeded, minced Scotch bonnet chile	1/8 oz. a.p.
tt	kosher salt	1/16 oz.
1 Tbsp.	chopped cilantro	1/40 bunch a.p.

preparation:
1. Fabricate the mango:
   a. Pare the skin from the mango and remove the flesh from the pit.
   b. Cut the mango flesh into 1/4" dice.
2. Place the onion, ginger, garlic, chile, and salt in a mortar or small bowl.
3. Use the pestle or the back of a spoon to crush the vegetables and release their juices.
4. Add 2/3 of the diced mango to the mortar and crush it into a rough purée.
5. Stir in the remaining diced mango and the cilantro.
6. Taste and correct the seasoning.

holding: refrigerate in a freshly sanitized, covered container up to 12 hours

Cuban Crab-Stuffed Lobster Tails

with Florida Watercress and Black-Eyed Pea Bollitos

yield: 1 (7-oz.) entrée serving plus accompaniments (multiply × 4 for classroom turnout; adjust equipment sizes accordingly)

🕐 Side dish requires 48 hours advance preparation.

MASTER RECIPE

preparation		costing only
2	Crab-Stuffed Lobster Tails	1/4 recipe
1 Tbsp.	melted butter	1/2 oz.
3 fl. oz.	Black-Eyed Pea Bollito Batter	1/4 recipe
as needed	frying compound or peanut oil	% used
3/4 c.	Sofrito Tomato Sauce	1/4 recipe
1 Tbsp.	butter	1/2 oz.
1 bouquet	watercress	1/4 bunch a.p.

service turnout:
1. Bake the Crab-Stuffed Lobster Tails:
   a. Place the lobster tails on a sizzle pan, brush them with butter, and place them in a 400°F oven.
   b. Bake for about 15 minutes, until the lobster meat is just cooked and the stuffing is golden.
2. Fry the bollitos:
   a. Lower the fryer basket into a deep fryer set to 375°F.
   b. Using a #40 (3/4-fl. oz.) portion scoop, portion 4 bollitos into the oil. Deep-fry for about 1 1/2 minutes, until deep golden and cooked through.
   c. Lift the basket and drain.
3. Finish the sauce:
   a. Heat the Sofrito Tomato Sauce in an 8" sauté pan.
   b. Remove from the heat and stir in the butter to create an emulsion.
4. Plate the dish:
   a. Spoon the tomato sauce into the well of a hot 12" plate.
   b. Place the lobster tails side-by-side on the plate at an angle from 11 to 5 o'clock, with tails at 11 o'clock.
   c. Mound the bollitos at the back left.
   d. Arrange the watercress bouquet behind the lobster tails.

COMPONENT RECIPE

CRAB-STUFFED LOBSTER TAILS

yield: 4 (7-oz.) entrée servings; slipper tails also yield 8 (3 1/2-oz.) appetizer servings

production		costing only
8	2-oz. slipper lobster tails	1 lb.
—or—		
4	5-oz. warm-water lobster (langouste) tails	20 oz.
4 Tbsp.	melted butter	2 oz.
tt	kosher salt	1/16 oz.
2 c.	Cuban Crab Stuffing	1 recipe

preparation:
1. Using heavy scissors, cut open the top shell of each lobster tail lengthwise.
2. Use a sharp knife to cut a slit in the tail meat, cutting down to the belly shell.
3. Pull the tails open to make a pouch for the Cuban Crab Stuffing.
4. Brush the exposed tail meat with butter and season it with salt.
5. Divide the stuffing into 8 portions for slipper tails or 4 portions for larger tails.
6. Stuff each tail, pressing gently so the stuffing adheres.

holding: refrigerate, in one layer, in a freshly sanitized, covered container up to 24 hours

COMPONENT RECIPE
CUBAN CRAB STUFFING

yield: approx. 2 c. (12 oz.)

production		costing only
2 Tbsp.	butter	1 oz.
1 c.	fresh bread crumbs	3 oz. a.p.
1 Tbsp.	butter	1/2 oz.
1/3 c.	fine-chopped yellow onion	2 oz. a.p.
1/8 c.	fine-chopped green bell pepper	1 1/2 oz. a.p.
1 tsp.	minced garlic	1/12 oz. a.p.
1/2 c.	heavy cream	4 fl. oz.
1/2 c.	crab meat, picked over for shell fragments	3 oz.
2 tsp.	nonpariel capers	1/3 oz.
1 Tbsp.	chopped pitted Spanish green olives	1/2 oz.
2 tsp.	minced flat-leaf parsley	1/40 bunch a.p.
tt	fresh-ground black pepper	1/16 oz.

preparation:
1. Melt 2 Tbsp. butter in a 10" sauté pan and, over low heat, sauté the bread crumbs until light golden. Remove.
2. Heat the remaining 1 Tbsp. butter; add the onion, green bell pepper, and garlic, and sauté over medium heat until soft.
3. Add the cream, increase the heat, and reduce by half.
4. Cool to room temperature.
5. Combine the bread crumbs, the cream mixture, and the remaining ingredients.
6. Taste and correct the seasoning.

holding: refrigerate in a freshly sanitized, covered container up to 2 days

COMPONENT RECIPE
BLACK-EYED PEA BOLLITO BATTER

yield: approx. 12 fl. oz. (enough dough for about 16 small bollitos)

🕐 Requires 3 days advance preparation.

production		costing only
1 c.	dried black-eyed peas	5 1/2 oz.
as needed	water	n/c
2 tsp.	minced garlic	1/12 oz. a.p.
1 Tbsp.	minced flat-leaf parsley	1/40 bunch a.p.
1 Tbsp.	minced scallion	1/12 bunch a.p.
1 tsp.	toasted, ground cumin seeds	1/16 oz.
1 tsp.	bottled hot pepper sauce, such as Tabasco brand	1/6 oz.
1/4 tsp.	baking soda	1/16 oz.
tt	kosher salt	1/8 oz.

first day preparation:
1. Pick over the peas and remove any foreign matter.
2. Rinse the peas, place them in a bowl, and then cover them with water to twice their depth. Soak for 48 hours.

second day preparation:
3. Skin the black-eyed peas:
   a. Drain the peas in a colander and reserve the bowl.
   b. Take up a small handful of peas and rub them briskly between the palms of your hands. Most of the peas' thick skins will slip off. Return the rubbed peas to the bowl and repeat, until all the peas have been rubbed and skinned.
   c. Place the bowl under a gentle stream of water. The skins will float to the top and wash out of the bowl.
4. Place the drained peas in a blender and grind them into a coarse purée, adding a little water only if necessary to loosen the blades. Remove the top of the blender and run on high speed for 3 minutes to aerate the pea purée batter.
5. Transfer the batter to a nonreactive container, cover loosely with plastic film, and set the container in a warm place. Allow to ferment for 24 hours. When sufficiently fermented, the batter will appear thick and bubbly and will have a slightly sour aroma.

third day preparation:
6. Stir the remaining ingredients into the batter and season it highly with salt.

holding: refrigerate in a freshly sanitized, covered, nonreactive container up to 24 hours

COMPONENT RECIPE
SOFRITO TOMATO SAUCE

yield: 3 c.

production		costing only
1/2 c.	Cuban Sofrito	1/2 recipe
3 c.	vine-ripe tomato concassée	2 1/4 lb. a.p.
as needed	water, optional	n/c
tt	kosher salt	1/16 oz.

preparation:
1. Heat the Cuban Sofrito in a 10" sauté pan until it begins to fry.
2. Add the concassée and a little water if the tomatoes are dry. Stir to blend.
3. Cover the pan and simmer briskly until the tomatoes have softened.
4. Remove the lid, increase the heat, and reduce the sauce to a light nappé consistency.
5. Taste and correct the seasoning, adding salt if needed.

holding: refrigerate in a freshly sanitized, covered, nonreactive container up to 5 days

COMPONENT RECIPE
CUBAN SOFRITO

yield: 1 c.

production		costing only
1/4 c.	gold-color pure olive oil	2 fl. oz.
1 Tbsp.	annatto seeds	1/6 oz.
1/2 tsp.	dried oregano	1/16 oz.
1 small	bay leaf	1/16 oz.
1/2 c.	minced yellow onion	2 1/2 oz. a.p.
1/3 c.	minced carrot	3/4 oz. a.p.
1/3 c.	minced green bell pepper	3 oz. a.p.
1/3 c.	peeled, minced celery	1/15 bunch a.p.
1 Tbsp.	minced garlic	1/3 oz. a.p.
2 Tbsp.	dry sherry	1 fl. oz.
1 c.	vine-ripe tomato concassée	3/4 lb. a.p.
tt	kosher salt	1/8 oz.
1 Tbsp.	chopped flat-leaf parsley	1/40 bunch a.p.

preparation:
1. Prepare annatto oil:
   a. Combine the oil and annatto seeds in a small sauté pan. Place over very low heat for 5 minutes.
   b. Set a strainer over a small bowl and pour in the flavored oil.
   c. Discard the annatto seeds and return the oil to the pan.
2. Add the oregano and bay leaf to the annatto oil and cook over low heat for a few seconds.
3. Add the onion, carrot, green bell pepper, celery, and garlic. Cook over low heat, stirring occasionally, for about 5 minutes, until the vegetables are soft but not brown.
4. Add the sherry, tomatoes, and a little salt. Cook over medium heat, stirring occasionally, until the tomatoes are dry and the oil begins separating out at the edges of the mixture.
5. Stir in the parsley and correct the salt.

holding: open-pan cool and refrigerate in a freshly sanitized, covered, nonreactive container up to 7 days; freeze up to 1 month

---

SOFRITO VARIATIONS

Puerto Rican Sofrito
Omit the sherry, carrot, and parsley. In step 2 add 1/2 tsp. toasted, ground cumin seeds. In step 3 add 1 Tbsp. minced, seeded fresh green chiles. In step 5 add 1 Tbsp. chopped culantro or cilantro.

Sofrito for Beans
To Cuban Sofrito or Puerto Rican Sofrito, add 1 1/2 oz. minced smoked ham or lean bacon in step 3.

MASTER RECIPE VARIATIONS

Cuban Crab-Stuffed Shrimp with Florida Watercress and Black-Eyed Pea Bollitos
Replace the lobster tail with 4 large (U-16) shrimp per portion. Shell the shrimp, leaving the tail section on. Slit the undersides of the shrimp, remove the veins, brush the interior with egg wash, and press a heaping tablespoon of stuffing into each. Reduce the baking time to 10 minutes.

Black-Eyed Pea Bollitos with Sofrito Tomato Sauce (appetizer)
Serve 3 bollitos on a pool of sauce with a parsley sprig garnish.

Grilled Mahimahi

with Pineapple-Avocado Salsa and Boniato Fries

yield: 1 (7 oz.) entrée serving plus accompaniments (multiply × 4 for classroom turnout; adjust equipment sizes accordingly)

MASTER RECIPE

production		costing only
1	(7 oz.) skinned and pinned mahimahi fillet	7 oz.
2 Tbsp.	Mojo Criollo, p. 757	1/8 recipe
5 oz.	preblanched boniato fries (prepared in the manner of Boardwalk French Fries)	10 oz. a.p.
1 tsp.	Sazon-Style Seasoning, p. 756	1/12 recipe
1/8	firm-ripe Florida avocado, cold	1/8 [8 ct.] avocado
	—or—	
1/4	firm-ripe western avocado, cold	1/4 [24 ct.] avocado
3/4 c.	Pineapple Salsa Base	1/4 recipe
1	banana leaf, cut into a 8"× 4"× 4" triangle	1/40 pkg.
1 Tbsp.	chopped cilantro	1/40 bunch a.p.
1 Tbsp.	brunoise-cut red bell pepper	1/2 oz. a.p.

service turnout:
1. Grill the fish:
   a. Coat the mahimahi with the Mojo Criollo and place it diagonally, presentation-side-down, on a hot char-grill.
   b. In about 1 minute, once marks have set, rotate the mahimahi to the other diagonal and grill 1 minute longer.
   c. Turn the mahimahi and finish grilling medium-rare, about 2 minutes longer.
   d. Remove to a sizzle plate and hold hot.
2. Deep-fry the boniato fries in 400°F oil until golden. Drain thoroughly, turn out to a hotel pan lined with paper towels, and sprinkle with Sazon-Style Seasoning.
3. Cut the avocado into 3/8" dice and mix into the Pineapple Salsa Base.
4. Plate the dish:
   a. Place the banana leaf triangle on a warm 12" plate.
   b. Mound the boniato fries on the back of the plate.
   c. Prop the mahimahi against the fries.
   d. Spoon the salsa over the mahimahi, allowing it to fall into the front of the plate well.
   e. Sprinkle the mahimahi with the cilantro and red bell pepper.

COMPONENT RECIPE
PINEAPPLE SALSA BASE

yield: 3 c.

production		costing only
1 Tbsp.	minced, seeded Scotch Bonnet chile	1/2 oz. a.p.
1/2 c.	fine-chopped sweet onion	2 1/2 oz. a.p.
1 tsp.	minced fresh garlic	1/4 oz. a.p.
to taste	kosher salt	1/8 oz.
2 c.	chopped ripe pineapple	1/3 [8 ct.] pineapple
1/4 c.	brunoise-cut red bell pepper	2 oz. a.p.
1 c.	3/8"-diced ripe pineapple	1/6 [8 ct.] pineapple
1 Tbsp.	chopped cilantro	1/40 bunch a.p.

preparation:
1. Place the chile, onion, garlic, and salt in a mortar or small, heavy bowl. Using the mortar or the back of a spoon, crush the vegetables until the flavors blend.
2. Add the chopped pineapple and grind until the mixture blends into a textured, pourable purée.
3. Stir in the red bell pepper, diced pineapple, and cilantro.
4. Correct the salt.

holding: refrigerate in a freshly sanitized, covered, nonreactive container up to 6 hours

---

RECIPE VARIATIONS

Grilled Chicken with Pineapple-Avocado Salsa and Boniato Fries
Replace the mahimahi with skinless, boneless chicken breast.

Grilled Shrimp and Seashell Salad in Pineapple Boat
Omit the boniato fries; replace the mahimahi with peeled, tailed, butterflied 21–25 ct. shrimp; for each serving, toss 1 1/4 c. cool, cooked seashell pasta in the Mojo Criollo, then add the grilled shrimp, diced avocado, and pineapple salsa; serve in a pineapple "boat" made by hollowing out a small pineapple half.

Pompano en Escabeche
with Ñame Cake

yield: 1 (7-oz.) entrée serving plus accompaniments
(multiply × 4 for classroom turnout; adjust equipment sizes
accordingly)

MASTER RECIPE

production		costing only
1	Ñame Cake	1/4 recipe
1 Tbsp.	gold-color pure olive oil	1/2 fl. oz.
1 1/2 oz.	large-julienne red bell pepper	2 oz. a.p.
1 1/2 oz.	large-julienne green bell pepper	2 oz. a.p.
1 1/2 oz.	large-julienne yellow bell pepper	2 oz. a.p.
1 1/2 oz.	large slivers sweet onion	1 3/4 oz. a.p.
tt	kosher salt	1/16 oz.
2 Tbsp.	gold-color pure olive oil	1 fl. oz.
7 oz.	pompano fillet, skinned and pinned	8 oz. a.p.
1 tsp.	Sazon-Style Seasoning, p. 756	1/12 recipe
as needed	flour	1 oz.
1 Tbsp.	minced fresh garlic	1/3 oz. a.p.
1/2 tsp.	toasted, ground cumin seeds	1/16 oz.
1 Tbsp.	flour	1/3 oz.
1/2 tsp.	dried oregano	1/16 oz.
4 Tbsp.	fino sherry	2 fl. oz.
4 Tbsp.	sherry wine vinegar	2 fl. oz.
2 tsp.	sugar	1/6 oz.
1 c.	Fish Stock	1/16 recipe
1 c.	Poultry Stock	1/16 recipe
tt	kosher salt	1/16 oz.
1 Tbsp.	butter	1/2 oz.
2 tsp.	minced fresh oregano leaves	1/40 bunch a.p.
1 bouquet	flat-leaf parsley	1/20 bunch a.p.

service turnout:
1. Place the Ñame Cake on a sizzle pan and heat in a 400°F oven until crisp.
2. Sauté the vegetables:
   a. Heat a 10" sauté pan, heat 1 Tbsp. oil, and sauté the bell peppers until crisp-tender.
   b. Add the onion and sauté for a few seconds more.
   c. Season with salt and place on a sizzle plate.
3. Sauté the pompano:
   a. Heat the same sauté pan and add 2 Tbsp. oil.
   b. Season the pompano with Sazon-Style Seasoning, dredge in flour, and sauté for about 1 minute on both sides.
   c. Place the pompano on the sizzle pan with the pepper mixture and place the pan in a low oven.
4. Prepare the escabeche:
   a. Add the garlic and cumin to the oil in the sauté pan and sizzle for a few seconds without browning.
   b. Stir in 1 Tbsp. flour, then add the sherry, vinegar, sugar, stocks, and a little salt.
   c. Bring to the boil and reduce by half, stirring often, until the sauce reduces to a light nappé consistency.
   d. Remove from the heat, taste, and add salt as needed.
5. Finish and plate the dish:
   a. Cut the Ñame Cake into 3 wedges and fan them across the back of a hot 12" pasta plate.
   b. Place the pompano diagonally across the front of the plate, leaning against the tips of the cake wedges.
   c. Scatter the pepper strips on the pompano and pour the accumulated juices from the sizzle pan into the escabeche.
   d. Heat the escabeche to just under the boil and stir in the butter to create an emulsion.
   e. Add the oregano to the escabeche sauce and pour the sauce over the pompano.
   f. Stick the parsley bouquet upright behind the pompano.

COMPONENT RECIPE
ÑAME CAKES

yield: 4 (3-oz.) cakes

production		costing only
1 1/4 lb.	ñame	1 1/4 lb.
6 Tbsp.	peanut oil	3 fl. oz.
6 Tbsp.	clarified butter, melted	3 oz.
tt	kosher salt	1/16 oz.

preparation:
1. Fabricate the ñame:
   a. Peel the ñame, wash it, and cut it in quarters lengthwise.
   b. Using a mandoline or electric slicing machine, slice the ñame into 1/16" wedge-shaped slices.
   c. Place the slices on a half-sheet tray and cover them with a clean, damp towel.
2. Prepare the ñame cakes:
   a. Combine the oil and butter in a squeeze bottle.
   b. Heat an 8" nonstick sauté pan, add a little of the oil-butter mixture, and arrange a layer of ñame slices in the bottom of the pan in concentric circles with the points in the center.
   c. Season this first layer with a little salt.
   d. Add additional layers of slices in random arrangement, seasoning each layer with a little salt, to make a 3/4"-thick cake.
   e. Cover the pan and cook over low heat for about 3 minutes, until the bottom is golden and the ñame is cooked through.
   f. Remove the lid and press down with an offset spatula to compact the layers.
   g. Increase the heat and squeeze a little more of the oil-butter mixture down the sides of the pan.
   h. Flip the ñame cake and cook over medium heat for about 2 more minutes, until the new bottom is golden brown.
   i. Remove to a rack and cool completely.
   j. Repeat with the remaining ingredients to make 4 ñame cakes.

holding: refrigerate in a covered plastic container with pan liner between layers up to 4 days

---

RECIPE VARIATIONS

Any full-flavored, dark-fleshed fish, such as Spanish mackerel, king mackerel, or small bluefish, may be substituted for the pompano. Other tubers, such as boniato, yuca, malanga, or sweet potatoes may be substituted for the ñame.

Pompano en Escabeche Salad (appetizer or lunch entrée)

Omit the Ñame Cake. Reduce the ingredients by half for an appetizer or by 1/3 for a lunch entrée. When making the escabeche sauce, increase the vinegar to taste and replace the butter with extra-virgin olive oil. Prepare in advance and cool the fish in the sauce. Present the fish and vegetables on a bed of shredded romaine lettuce napped with the cool sauce. Garnish with sliced hard-cooked eggs and green olives.

Jamaican-American Jerk Chicken

with Rice 'n' Peas, Fried Plantains, and Tropical Slaw

yield: 1 (12-oz.) bone-in entrée serving plus accompaniments (multiply × 4 for classroom turnout; adjust equipment sizes accordingly)

🕐 Requires 24 hours advance preparation.

MASTER RECIPE

production		costing only
1	Jerk-Marinated Half Hen	1/4 recipe
1 tsp.	corn oil	1/6 fl. oz.
1/4 c.	Jerk Table Sauce, hot in steam table	1/4 recipe
1/4 c.	corn oil	2 fl. oz.
1 Tbsp.	butter	1/2 oz.
3 pc.	1" thick diagonal slices black-ripe plantain	1/3 each or 4 oz. a.p.
tt	kosher salt	1/16 oz.
1	6" × 10" piece banana leaf	1/20 pkg.
1 1/2 c.	Rice 'n' Peas, hot in steam table	1/4 recipe
1 1/2 c.	Tropical Slaw	1/4 recipe
1 sprig	fresh thyme	1/20 bunch a.p.
1 Tbsp.	brunoise-cut red bell pepper	1/2 oz. a.p.
1 Tbsp.	thin diagonal-sliced scallion	1/16 bunch a.p.
1	cocktail napkin	1 each

service turnout:
1. Cook the Jerk-Marinated Half Hen:
   a. Brush the Jerk-Marinated Half Hen with 1 tsp. oil and place it on a moderately hot gas grill, skin side down.
   b. Grill for about 2 minutes, until the skin browns and acquires grill marks.
   c. Turn the hen, brush with a little Jerk Table Sauce, and grill for 1 minute longer.
   d. Transfer the hen half to a sizzle plate and finish in a 425°F oven for about 12 minutes, until cooked through.
2. Fry the plantains:
   a. Place a 6" sauté pan over low heat, add 1/4 c. oil and the butter, and add the plantain pieces.
   b. Fry the plantains until golden on both sides, about 5 minutes total.
   c. Drain on paper towels, season with salt, and hold warm.
3. Plate the dish:
   a. Place the banana leaf on a hot 12" oval plate.
   b. Spoon the Rice 'n' Peas onto the back left of the plate.
   c. Place the hen half on the front of the plate propped against the rice.
   d. Mound the Tropical Slaw on the back right.
   e. Fan the fried plantains slightly upright between the rice and the slaw.
   f. Sprinkle the hen half with the red bell pepper and scallion.
   g. Serve the remaining sauce in a 2-fl. oz. pitcher or ramekin set on a small underplate lined with a cocktail napkin.

COMPONENT RECIPE

JERK-MARINATED HALF HENS

yield: 4 (12-oz.) bone-in servings

🕐 Requires 24 hours advance preparation.

production		costing only
2	(2-lb.) Cornish hens	4 lb.
3/4 c.	Jerk Paste	3/4 recipe

preparation:
1. Fabricate the hens:
   a. Remove the backbones and pelvic sections and reserve for stock.
   b. Split the hens in half through the breastbone.
   c. Chop off the drumstick knuckles and the wing tips and reserve for stock.
2. Jerk-marinate the hens:
   a. Coat all surfaces of each hen half with 3 Tbsp. Jerk Paste.
   b. Place each hen half in a plastic bag and refrigerate for at least 24 hours.

holding: refrigerate up to 4 days (the longer the chickens jerk-marinate, the stronger and spicier their final flavor will be)

COMPONENT RECIPE

JERK PASTE

yield: 1 c.

production		costing only
1 Tbsp.	whole allspice (Jamaican pimento)	1/4 oz.
1/6	whole nutmeg	1/16 oz.
6	cloves	1/8 oz.
1/2"	cinnamon stick, crushed	1/8 oz.
2 tsp.	black peppercorns	1/8 oz.
3	seeded, chopped Scotch bonnet or habanero chiles	1/3 oz. a.p.
1/3 c.	minced yellow onion	2 oz. a.p.
3 Tbsp.	minced scallion	1/5 bunch a.p.
2 tsp.	minced garlic	1/4 oz. a.p.
2 Tbsp.	peeled, minced fresh ginger	1/2 oz. a.p.
2 tsp.	fresh thyme leaves	1/40 bunch a.p.
2 tsp.	sugar	1/3 oz.
2 tsp.	kosher salt	1/3 oz.
1/4 c.	soy sauce	2 fl. oz.
1/4 c.	corn oil	2 fl. oz.

preparation:
1. In a small mortar or in an electric spice mill, pulverize the allspice, nutmeg, cloves, cinnamon stick, and peppercorns into a coarse powder.
2. Place all of the ingredients except the oil in a blender and grind to a rough paste.
3. With the blender operating, add the oil in a thin stream through the top opening.

holding: refrigerate in a freshly sanitized, covered, nonreactive container up to 1 month; freeze up to 3 months

ENTREES

COMPONENT RECIPE
JERK TABLE SAUCE

yield: 1 c.

production		costing only
3 oz.	very ripe banana	1/4 banana, 1/6 lb. a.p.
1/4 c.	frozen mango purée, thawed	2 fl. oz.
—or—		
1/3 c.	chopped fresh ripe mango	1/6 [12 ct.] mango
1 c.	Poultry Stock	1/16 recipe
1/4 c.	Jerk Paste	1/4 recipe
1 Tbsp.	tamarind concentrate	1/2 fl. oz.
1/4 c.	ketchup	2 fl. oz.
1 c.	water	n/c
tt	kosher salt	1/4 oz.
tt	brown sugar	1/8 oz.

preparation:
1. Grind the banana and mango in a blender. Add the Poultry Stock and purée.
2. Place the fruit-stock mixture in a small, nonreactive saucepan. Whisk in the Jerk Paste, tamarind, ketchup, and water. Bring to the simmer and cook, stirring occasionally, for about 5 minutes, until the flavors are blended and the sauce reduces to a light nappé consistency.
3. Season with salt and sugar to make a balanced, sweet-spicy-tart sauce.

holding: open-pan cool and immediately refrigerate in a freshly sanitized, covered, nonreactive container up to 5 days

COMPONENT RECIPE
RICE 'N' PEAS

yield: 1 1/2 qt.

production		costing only
2 Tbsp.	corn oil	1 fl. oz.
1/2 c.	chopped yellow onion	3 oz. a.p.
1 tsp.	minced garlic	1/9 oz. a.p.
1 1/2 c.	long-grain rice	10 1/2 oz. a.p.
1/2 c.	unsweetened canned coconut milk	4 fl. oz.
1 1/2 c.	water	n/c
1/2 c.	cooked, drained red kidney beans	1 1/2 oz. raw a.p. or 4 fl. oz. canned
tt	kosher salt	1/4 oz.
3	whole allspice (Jamaican pimento)	1/16 oz.
1 sprig	fresh thyme	1/20 bunch a.p.

preparation:
1. Preheat an oven to 350°F.
2. Heat the oil in a heavy, ovenproof, 1 3/4-qt. saucepan with a tight-fitting lid. Add the onion and garlic and sauté until soft.
3. Add the rice and sauté, stirring constantly for about 30 seconds, until the rice grains are opaque and well coated with oil.
4. Add the remaining ingredients, cover tightly, and bring just to the boil.
5. Stir once, reduce the heat as low as possible, and simmer, covered, for about 12 minutes, until the liquid is absorbed.
6. Transfer the saucepan to the oven and bake for 10 minutes.

holding: transfer the rice to a half-size hotel pan and open-pan cool; refrigerate in a freshly sanitized, covered container up to 5 days; freeze up to 3 months

COMPONENT RECIPE

TROPICAL SLAW

yield: 1 qt.

production		costing only
8 oz.	shredded Savoy or other tender white cabbage	10 oz. a.p.
1 tsp.	kosher salt	1/6 oz.
1/2 c.	mayonnaise	4 fl. oz.
1/4 tsp.	granulated onion	1/16 oz.
1/4 tsp.	granulated garlic	1/16 oz.
1/2 tsp.	fresh-ground black pepper	1/8 oz.
1/4 tsp.	ground allspice	1/16 oz.
1/4 tsp.	cayenne pepper	1/16 oz.
1/4 c.	julienne red bell pepper	2 oz. a.p.
1/4 c.	julienne yellow bell pepper	2 oz. a.p.
1/4 c.	shredded scallion	1/4 bunch a.p.
1/2 c.	chopped fresh pineapple	1/10 [12 ct.] pineapple
tt	kosher salt	1/16 oz.

preparation:
1. Drain the cabbage:
   a. Place the cabbage in a bowl and toss with 1 tsp. salt.
   b. Transfer the cabbage to a colander. Select a plate of the correct size to fit into the colander, place it on the cabbage, and place a heavy object on it to weight down the cabbage.
   c. Allow the cabbage to macerate and drain for 20 minutes at room temperature.
2. Mix the mayonnaise with the onion, garlic, black pepper, allspice, and cayenne to make the dressing.
3. Squeeze the cabbage dry and place it in a bowl.
4. Mix the dressing, bell peppers, scallion, and pineapple into the cabbage.
5. Taste and correct the salt.

holding: best served the same day; may be refrigerated in a freshly sanitized, covered container up to 2 days

Ropa Vieja
with Yellow Rice, Black Beans, Green Papaya Salad, and Tostones

yield: 1 (6-oz.) entrée serving plus accompaniments
(multiply × 4 for classroom turnout; adjust equipment sizes
accordingly)

🕐 Best prepared 24 hours in advance.

MASTER RECIPE

production		costing only
1 1/2 c.	Ropa Vieja	1/4 recipe
as needed	water	n/c
as needed	frying compound or peanut oil	% used
2 pc.	Tostones, stored in soaking liquid	1/4 recipe
tt	fine salt	1/16 oz.
1 1/2 c.	Yellow Rice, hot in steam table	1/4 recipe
1 c.	Green Papaya Salad	1/4 recipe
1/2 c.	Cuban Black Beans, side-dish variation, p. 747	1/8 recipe

service turnout:
1. Heat the Ropa Vieja in a small, covered sauté pan, adding a little water if necessary.
2. Fry the Tostones:
   a. Remove the tostones from the soaking liquid and blot them dry.
   b. Lower the tostones into a fryer preheated to 400°F and fry for about 1 minute, until crisp and golden brown.
   c. Drain on paper towels and season with salt.
3. Plate the dish:
   a. Place a 2" ball of aluminum foil into the tip of a 12-fl.-oz. funnel. Pack the Yellow Rice very firmly into the funnel.
   b. Invert the funnel of rice on the back center of a hot 12" plate, remove the funnel, and then remove the foil ball to make a "volcano" of rice with a hollow "crater" in the top.
   c. Spoon the Ropa Vieja around the front of the Rice.
   d. Arrange the Green Papaya Salad around the back of the Rice.
   e. Carefully ladle the Cuban Black Beans into the "crater."
   f. Stick the 2 tostones upright into the rice at 10 o'clock.

COMPONENT RECIPE

ROPA VIEJA

yield: 6 c. (approx. 24 oz.)

production		costing only
1	2-lb. flank steak	2 lb. a.p.
1 qt.	Brown Beef Stock	1/4 recipe
1 qt.	boiling water	n/c
2	cloves	1/16 oz.
3 oz.	yellow onion wedge	3 oz. a.p.
3 oz.	1/2"-sliced carrot	3 oz.
3	garlic cloves, peeled and crushed	1/2 oz. a.p.
2	bay leaves	1/16 oz.
4 sprigs	flat-leaf parsley	1/16 bunch
tt	kosher salt	1/4 oz.
2 Tbsp.	pork lard	1 oz.
2 Tbsp.	gold-color pure olive oil	1 fl. oz.
2 tsp.	annatto seeds	1/8 oz.
3 c.	slivered yellow onion	1 lb. a.p.
1 c.	thin-sliced green bell pepper	8 oz. a.p.
1 Tbsp.	minced garlic	1/3 oz. a.p.
1 tsp.	dried oregano	1/16 oz.
1/2 tsp.	dried thyme	1/16 oz.
1 tsp.	toasted, ground cumin seeds	1/8 oz.
1 tsp.	fresh-ground black pepper	1/8 oz.
3 c.	ripe plum tomato concassée	2 lb. a.p.
2 Tbsp.	currants or coarse-chopped raisins	1/2 oz.
tt	kosher salt	1/16 oz.
1 Tbsp.	nonpariel capers	1/2 fl. oz.
2 Tbsp.	chopped flat-leaf parsley	1/20 bunch a.p.

preparation:

1. Fabricate the flank steak:
   a. Trim away excess silverskin from the flank steak.
   b. Cut the flank steak in half lengthwise, then cut each piece widthwise to make 4 pieces of the correct size to fit into a 10" sauté pan in one layer.
2. Cook the flank steak:
   a. Bring the Brown Beef Stock to the simmer in a 10" sauté pan.
   b. Have ready about 1 qt. boiling water.
   c. Add the flank steak pieces to the stock and add water as needed to cover the meat.
   d. Bring the liquid back to the simmer and skim off any scum that rises to the top.
   e. Stick the cloves into the onion wedge and add it to the pan along with the carrot, crushed garlic, bay leaves, parsley sprigs, and a little salt.
   f. Partially cover the pan and simmer the flank steak at a bare simmer for 1 hour, until the meat is tender, adding boiling water as necessary to keep the meat covered.
   g. Cool the meat in its cooking liquid. (If time allows, refrigerate it in its liquid overnight.)
3. Prepare the sauce:
   a. Combine the lard, oil, and annatto seeds in a 12" sauté pan and place over low heat for 1 minute. Remove from the heat and steep the seeds in the hot fat for 10 minutes.
   b. Pour the lard-oil mixture through a sieve into a small bowl. Discard the annatto seeds and return the lard-oil mixture to the sauté pan.
   c. Place the lard-oil mixture over medium heat and sauté the slivered onion and green bell pepper until soft.
   d. Add the garlic, oregano, thyme, cumin, and pepper and sauté for 1 minute longer.
   e. Add the tomatoes, currants, and a little salt. Cook, stirring occasionally, 2 to 3 minutes, until well reduced and almost dry.
   f. Remove the flank steak from its cooking liquid and reserve it. Discard the vegetables and seasonings.
   g. Add the cooking liquid to the tomato mixture, stir to combine, and place the sauté pan over medium heat. Reduce the resulting sauce, stirring often, to a light nappé consistency.
   h. Taste and correct the seasoning, adding more salt if needed.
4. Finish the dish:
   a. Pull the flank steak into long shreds.
   b. Chop the shreds into approximately 1" lengths.
   c. Add the shredded flank steak to the sauce and simmer gently for 5 minutes.
   d. If not serving immediately, cool the sauced meat to room temperature.
   e. Stir the capers and parsley into the sauced meat.

holding: refrigerate in a freshly sanitized, covered, nonreactive container up to 5 days; freeze up to 1 month

COMPONENT RECIPE
TOSTONES

yield: 8 pc.

production		costing only
1	large green plantain	10 oz. a.p.
1 Tbsp.	kosher salt	1/2 oz.
1 qt.	water	n/c
3	garlic cloves, peeled and crushed	1/2 oz. a.p.
as needed	corn oil	8 fl. oz. (may be reused)

preparation:
1. Fabricate the plantain:
   a. Cut the ends off the plantain.
   b. Cut a lengthwise slit through the plantain skin without cutting the flesh.
   c. Run your thumbs into the slit to pull the skin open and off. Discard the skin.
   d. Cut the plantain on the diagonal into 8 (3/4") pieces.
2. Dissolve the salt in the water, then add the garlic and plantain pieces to the water. Soak for 15 minutes.
3. Fry the plantain pieces:
   a. Remove the plantain pieces from the garlic water and blot them dry. Reserve the water.
   b. In a sauté pan just large enough to hold all the plantain pieces without crowding, heat 1" oil to about 325°F.
   c. Add the plantain pieces and fry them, turning occasionally, for about 8 minutes, until light golden and tender when pierced with a knife.
   d. Drain on paper towels and cool to room temperature.
4. Fabricate the tostones:
   a. Place the plantain pieces on one side of a sheet of pan liner and fold the other side over them.
   b. Using the flat surface of a meat mallet, gently flatten each plantain piece into a 1/4"-thick disk.
   c. Place the tostones in a freshly sanitized container just large enough to accommodate them, and pour in enough garlic water to submerge them. Cover the container and refrigerate until needed.

holding: refrigerate up to 3 days

COMPONENT RECIPE
YELLOW RICE

yield: 6 c.

production		costing only
2 Tbsp.	corn oil	1 fl. oz.
2 tsp.	annatto seeds	1/8 oz.
1/2 c.	fine-chopped yellow onion	2 1/2 oz.
2 c.	long-grain white rice	14 oz.
3 c.	water	n/c
tt	kosher salt	1/4 oz.

preparation:
1. Preheat an oven to 350°F.
2. Place the oil and annatto seeds in a heavy, ovenproof 2-qt. saucepan with a tight-fitting lid. Place over very low heat for 1 minute, then remove from the heat and steep for 10 minutes.
3. Pour the oil mixture through a strainer into a small bowl. Discard the annatto seeds and scrape the oil back into the saucepan.
4. Add the onion to the saucepan and sauté it over medium heat about 30 seconds until soft.
5. Add the rice and sauté it about 30 seconds until the grains are well coated with oil and turning opaque.
6. Add the water and enough salt to make the cooking liquid slightly saltier than you would season soup. Cover the pot and bring to the boil.
7. Uncover the saucepan and stir the rice, then re-cover the pot, reduce the heat to the simmer, and cook, undisturbed, for 10 minutes.
8. Quickly peek under the lid; the liquid should be absorbed.
9. Place the rice in the oven and bake for 12 minutes.
10. If not serving immediately, transfer the rice to a freshly sanitized hotel pan; cover with a clean, damp kitchen towel; and cool to room temperature.

holding: refrigerate covered up to 5 days; freeze up to 1 month

COMPONENT RECIPE

GREEN PAPAYA SALAD

yield: 1 qt.

production		costing only
1 Tbsp.	minced shallot	1/2 oz. a.p.
2 tsp.	minced garlic	1/4 oz. a.p.
2 tsp.	sugar	1/3 oz.
tt	kosher salt	1/8 oz.
tt	fresh-ground black pepper	1/16 oz.
3 Tbsp.	sherry wine vinegar	1 1/2 fl. oz.
1/2 c.	gold-color pure olive oil	4 fl. oz.
3 c.	julienne green papaya* flesh	1 (14-oz.) papaya
1/2 c.	peeled, julienne red bell pepper	4 oz. a.p.
1/2 c.	slivered sweet onion	2 1/2 oz. a.p.

preparation:
1. Combine the shallot, garlic, sugar, salt, black pepper, and vinegar in a bowl.
2. Whisk in the oil in a thin stream to create an emulsion.
3. Taste and correct the flavor balance.
4. Toss the papaya, red bell pepper, and onion with the dressing.
5. Refrigerate for 1 hour.

holding: refrigerate in a freshly sanitized, covered, nonreactive container up to 24 hours

*If green papaya is unavailable, replace it with shredded Savoy or other mild cabbage.

RECIPE VARIATION

Picadillo with Yellow Rice, Black Beans, Green Papaya Salad, and Tostones
Replace the flank steak with 1 1/2 lb. lean ground beef browned in 1 Tbsp. pork lard. Omit steps 1 and 2 in the Ropa Vieja component recipe, also omitting the ingredients used in step 2. In step 3, use only 2 c. stock and no water to make the sauce. Stir the browned ground beef into the finished, thickened sauce.

Key Lime Pie
with Whipped Cream and Candied Lime Zest

yield: 1 dessert serving
(multiply × 4 for classroom turnout)

MASTER RECIPE

production		costing only
1/4 c.	Sweetened Whipped Cream, in a pastry bag fitted with a star tip	1/10 recipe
1 slice	Key Lime Pie	1/8 recipe
1 Tbsp.	Candied Lime Zest	1/8 recipe

service turnout:
1. Plate the dish:
   a. Pipe a small dot of Sweetened Whipped Cream in the center of a cool 8" plate to hold the Key Lime Pie slice in place.
   b. Place the pie slice on top of the whipped cream.
   c. Pipe a rosette of whipped cream on top of the pie.
   d. Scatter Candied Lime Zest on the rosette.

COMPONENT RECIPE
KEY LIME PIE

production		costing only
1 1/2 tsp.	granulated gelatin	1/8 oz.
1/4 c.	dark rum	2 fl. oz.
2 oz.	pasteurized* egg yolks	2 oz.
3/4 c.	Key lime juice	6 fl. oz.
14 fl. oz.	sweetened condensed milk	14 fl. oz.
1 Tbsp.	minced lime zest	1/2 [63 ct.] lime
pinch	fine salt	1/16 oz.
1 Tbsp.	boiling water	n/c
1	fully baked 9" Graham Cracker Pie Crust	1 recipe

preparation:
1. In a small bowl, mix together the gelatin and the rum. Allow the gelatin to bloom for about 10 minutes.
2. Place the egg yolks in a bowl and whip until light yellow and fluffy.
3. Stir the lime juice, condensed milk, lime zest, and salt into the yolks to make the custard.
4. Stir the boiling water into the gelatin to dissolve it.
5. Stir the gelatin into the custard.
6. Pour the custard into the Graham Cracker Pie Crust.
7. Refrigerate, uncovered, for about 3 hours, until the custard is completely set.

holding: refrigerated under a pie dome up to 2 days

*Traditional Key lime pie custard is partially thickened by the action of the lime juice coagulating the proteins in the condensed milk and the egg yolks. Because the custard is not heated, pasteurized egg yolks are required to meet with food safety guidelines. If pasteurized egg yolks are not available, use standard egg yolks and whisk the custard in a double boiler to 180°F.

COMPONENT RECIPE
CANDIED LIME ZEST

yield: approx. 8 Tbsp.

production		costing only
4	limes	4 [63 ct.] limes
1/4 c.	water	n/c
1/2 c.	sugar	4 oz.
2 Tbsp.	sugar	1 oz.

preparation:
1. Fabricate the lime zest:
   a. Wash and dry the limes.
   b. Use a zester or swivel peeler to remove all the zest (dark green outer skin) from the limes. The limes may be reserved for juice for another recipe.
   c. If a swivel peeler was used, cut the zest into very fine julienne.
2. Blanch the zest:
   a. Place the julienne zest in a strainer and lower it into boiling water for 1 minute.
   b. Remove the strainer from the water, shake dry the zest, and drain on paper towels.
3. Candy the zest:
   a. Combine 1/4 c. water and 1/2 c. of the sugar in a very small saucepan. Bring to a boil.
   b. Add the zest and continue boiling, swirling the pan occasionally, until the liquid evaporates and the lime zest is glazed in sugar syrup. ⚠ Watch carefully and do not allow the sugar to caramelize.
   c. Transfer the zest to a silicone pad or a piece of pan liner and use two forks to separate the julienne zest strands.
   d. Sprinkle with the remaining 2 Tbsp. sugar while still warm.
   e. Cool completely.

holding: store at cool room temperature and low humidity in a tightly sealed container up to 1 week

---

RECIPE VARIATION

Key Lime Pie with Meringue Topping
Finish the pie with baked meringue topping as in Coconut Cream Pie, but omit the coconut garnish. Omit the Sweetened Whipped Cream and Candied Lime Zest.

Tres Leches Cake
with Mandarin Oranges

yield: 1 dessert serving
(multiply × 4 for classroom turnout)

MASTER RECIPE

production		costing only
1 slice	Tres Leches Cake	1/12 recipe
1/2 c.	drained canned mandarin oranges	4 fl. oz.
1	mint sprig	1/10 bunch a.p.

service turnout:
1. Place the Tres Leches Cake slice slightly left of center on a cool 8" plate.
2. Mound the oranges to the right of the cake.
3. Place the mint sprig between the cake and the oranges.

COMPONENT RECIPE
TRES LECHES CAKE

yield: 12 dessert servings: 1 (10") cake

production		costing only
2	Tres Leches Cake Layer Halves	1 recipe
2	10" round cardboard cake boards	2 each
1 c.	guava jelly	8 fl. oz.
3 c.	Boiled Icing	3/4 recipe

preparation:
1. Turn out one of the Tres Leches Cake Layer Halves onto one of the cake boards, place another cake board on top, and flip the layer over. Remove the top cake board so that the layer sits on a cake board cut side up.
2. Spread the guava jelly onto the cake layer.
3. Turn out the remaining cake layer half onto the jelly-topped bottom layer, and press gently to firm the two layers together.
4. Frost the cake with Boiled Icing.

holding: refrigerate under a cake dome up to 2 days

COMPONENT RECIPE

TRES LECHES CAKE LAYER HALVES

yield: 2 (10") cake layer halves

production		costing only
as needed	baker's pan coating spray	% of can
11 oz.	flour	11 oz.
1/4 tsp.	fine salt	1/8 oz.
1 Tbsp.	baking powder	1/3 oz.
3	egg yolks	3 each or 2 oz.
1 lb.	sugar	1 lb.
2 tsp.	pure vanilla extract	1/3 oz.
1 c.	milk	8 fl. oz.
3	egg whites	n/c or 3 oz.
pinch	fine salt	1/16 oz.
6 3/4 fl. oz.	unsweetened canned coconut milk	1/2 (13 1/2-fl.-oz.) can
7 fl. oz.	sweetened condensed milk	1/2 (14-fl.-oz.) can
3/4 c.	half-and-half	6 fl. oz.
2 Tbsp.	dark rum	1 fl. oz.
1 tsp.	pure vanilla extract	1/6 fl. oz.

preparation:
1. Mise en place:
   a. Preheat an oven to 350°F.
   b. Spray the inside of a 10" × 3" round cake pan with pan coating, press a circle of pan liner into the bottom, and then spray again.
2. Sift together the flour, fine salt, and baking powder.
3. Mix the batter:
   a. Using the paddle attachment of a mixer, beat the egg yolks on high speed until light yellow and fluffy.
   b. Beat in the sugar in a thin stream.
   c. Add 2 tsp. vanilla.
   d. Reduce the mixer speed to low. Stir in 1/3 of the flour mixture, then stir in half of the milk.
   e. Scrape down the sides of the bowl, then stir in another 1/3 of the flour, the remaining milk, and finally the remaining flour, scraping down after each addition.
4. Lighten the batter with egg whites:
   a. Place the egg whites and the pinch of salt in a clean, dry mixer bowl or standard bowl. With the whip attachment, or by hand with a whip, beat the whites to firm (not stiff) peaks.
   b. Fold 1/4 of the whites into the batter, then fold the batter into the whites.
5. Pan the batter:
   a. Pour the batter into the prepared cake pan.
   b. Smooth the surface.
6. Bake the cake layer in the center of the oven for about 50 minutes, until the cake is set and a tester comes out clean.
7. Cool the cake layer:
   a. Place the cake pan on a rack and cool for 10 minutes.
   b. Turn out the cake layer onto the rack and cool to lukewarm.
8. Soak the cake layer halves:
   a. Combine the coconut milk, condensed milk, half-and-half, rum, and 1 tsp. vanilla. Pour into large squeeze bottles.
   b. Using a serrated knife, split the cake layer in half.
   c. Fit each cake layer half into a 10" cake pan with the cut side up.
   d. Using a skewer, poke holes all through the cake layers.
   e. Slowly drizzle half of the milk mixture over the cake layer halves so that it absorbs evenly. Rest at room temperature for 20 minutes.
   f. Drizzle the remaining milk mixture onto the cake layer halves.
   g. Cover the layer halves with plastic film and refrigerate for at least 3 hours.

holding: refrigerate up to 24 hours

RECIPE VARIATION
Mario's Tres Leches Cake with Lime Marmalade
Replace the guava jelly with lime marmalade.

Tropical Fruit Palette
with Guava Sorbet in Coconut Tuile

yield: 1 dessert serving
(multiply × 4 for classroom turnout)

MASTER RECIPE

production		costing only
1/2	ripe mango	1/2 [12 ct.] mango
tt	fresh lime juice	1/4 [63 ct.] lime
1/4	ripe papaya	3 1/2 oz. a.p.
1/4	small, ripe pineapple (top and base removed, peeled, eyes removed)	1/4 [16 ct.] pineapple
1/4	large yellow star fruit	1 1/2 oz. a.p.
1	Coconut Tuile Cup	1/4 recipe
1	4-fl. oz. scoop Pink Guava Sorbet	1/4 recipe

service turnout:
1. Fabricate the mango:*
   a. Slice the mango in half lengthwise, cutting around and discarding the pit.
   b. Cut a 1/2" crosshatch pattern in the mango flesh, slicing down to the skin.
   c. Turn the mango half inside-out to pop out a pattern of squares.
   d. Sprinkle with lime juice.
2. Fabricate the papaya:*
   a. Cut the papaya quarter into 3 long wedges.
   b. Use a swivel peeler to remove the skin.
   c. Scoop out the seeds and membrane, reserving a few seeds for garnish.
   d. Sprinkle with lime juice.
3. Fabricate the pineapple:*
   a. Remove the core from the pineapple quarter you are using.
   b. Cut the pineapple quarter into 5 wedges.
4. Cut 3 slices of star fruit.*
5. Plate the dish:
   a. Place the Coconut Tuile Cup on the back of a cool 12" plate.
   b. Place the mango half lengthwise in front of the tuile cup.
   c. Arrange the papaya slices on the right side of the plate, tips propped against the mango half.
   d. Fan the pineapple wedges on the left side of the plate, propped against the mango half.
   e. Place a scoop of Pink Guava Sorbet in the tuile cup.
   f. Fan the star fruit slices in the tuile cup behind the sorbet scoop.

*For classroom kitchen turnout you may prefabricate fruit for all 4 servings. Cover and refrigerate.

COMPONENT RECIPE
COCONUT TUILE CUPS

yield: 4 tuile cups plus extra batter for practice

production		costing only
2 oz.	room-temperature butter	2 oz.
1 1/2 oz.	confectioner's sugar	1 1/2 oz.
2 oz.	cake flour	2 oz.
2/3 oz.	sweetened flaked coconut, minced	2/3 oz.
1	egg white, beaten to foam	1 each or 1 oz.

preparation:
1. Mise en place:
   a. Preheat an oven to 375°F.
   b. Place a silicone mat on a sheet tray.
   c. Have ready 4 (8-fl.-oz.) ramekins or an 8-fl.-oz. muffin pan.
2. Mix the batter:
   a. Using the paddle attachment of a mixer, cream the butter and sugar until light and fluffy.
   b. Reduce the speed to low and stir in the flour, coconut, and egg white.
3. Pan, bake, and shape the tuile cups:
   a. Using a #40 (3/4-oz.) portion scoop, place 2 portions of batter well apart on the silicone mat.
   b. Use a small offset spatula to spread the batter into 8" disks.
   c. Bake in the center of the oven for about 5 minutes, until lightly browned on the edges. ⚠ Watch carefully and do not allow to burn.
   d. Run the spatula under one of the disks and flip it over.
   e. Immediately press the disk into the ramekin or muffin pan cup, pleating the edges and firming the bottom to shape the tuile into a flat-bottomed container.
   f. Quickly repeat with the remaining tuile disk. (If it has hardened, return the tray to the oven for a few seconds to soften it.)
   g. Cool the silicone mat and tray to room temperature.
   h. Repeat with the remaining batter to make 4 perfect tuile cups.

holding: store at cool room temperature and low humidity in a tightly sealed container up to 3 days

COMPONENT RECIPE
PINK GUAVA SORBET

yield: approx. 1 qt.

production		costing only
1 c.	orange juice	8 fl. oz.
1/4 c.	water	n/c
1/2 c.	sugar	4 oz.
2 c.	frozen sweetened pink guava purée, thawed	16 fl. oz.
tt	fresh lime juice	1/4 [63 ct.] lime

preparation:
1. Combine the orange juice, water, and sugar in a small, nonreactive saucepan. Bring to the boil, reduce the heat, and simmer for 5 minutes.
2. Cool the orange syrup to room temperature.
3. Stir in the guava purée.
4. Taste and balance the flavor with lime juice, if needed.
5. Place the sorbet base in an ice cream machine and freeze according to the manufacturer's instructions.
6. Place a freshly sanitized 1-qt. container and lid in the freezer.
7. Pack the finished sorbet in the container, cover the surface with plastic film, and close the lid.
8. Freeze for 1 hour to harden.

holding: best served the same day; freeze up to 2 days

☐ **TABLE 15.3 SOUTH FLORIDA AND PUERTO RICO REGIONAL INGREDIENTS**

ITEM	MARKET FORMS	USES	SEASONALITY	OTHER	STORAGE
TROPICAL TUBERS (SEE P. 735 FOR PHOTO OF SELECTED TYPES.)	Tropical tubers are sold in 40- and 45-lb. cartons or burlap sacks, and loose by the pound. Sources include purveyors of Caribbean and Asian produce. Specialty produce dealers typically charge higher prices. Tubers are selectively available in supermarkets with Caribbean clientele.	Most tubers are peeled, diced, and boiled or steamed. They may be eaten as-is or topped with butter or a mojo-style sauce. After preliminary boiling they may be mashed and formed into patties or spheres and fried, stuffed or un-stuffed. Alternatively, tubers are peeled and grated or sliced before pan-frying.	Available year round.	*Boniato* (bone-ee-AH-toe): also batata, batata dulce, camote, Caribbean sweet potato (*Ipomoea batatas*). *Malanga** (mah-LAHN-gah): also yautía (*Xanthosoma sagittaefolium*). *Yuca* (YOO-kah): also cassava, manioc (*Manihot esculenta*). *Ñame* (NYA-may): also African yam, true yam (*Dioscorea alata*). *Taro** (TAH-row): also colocasia (*Colocasia escuelenta*). *Do not serve raw.	Store at cool room temperature in a dark, well-ventilated area for several weeks. Inspect frequently for mold and soft spots; cut these away and use promptly or discard blemished specimens. After peeling immediately submerge in cool water to prevent enzymatic color change, and refrigerate.
PLANTAINS (plan-TAINS or PLAN-tans); ALSO *Plátano* (PLAH-tahn-oh)	Plantains are sold in 40- and 45-lb. cartons by purveyors of Caribbean and Asian produce. When ordering, specify desired degree of ripeness: green or yellow (dealers rarely hold plantains to the black stage). Plantains are widely available by the pound in supermarkets.	Potato-like green plantains are sliced thin and deep-fried for chips, boiled to make a starchy side dish, or simmered in stews. Yellow plantains, with a slightly sweet taste, are usually deep-fried, often smashed and double-fried for tostones. Soft, black plantains are pan-fried, deep-fried, or baked and served salted as a side dish or sugared as a breakfast dish or dessert.	Available year round.	To ripen plantains quickly, place in a single layer on a sheet tray with several cut apples; enclose in a black plastic bag and store at 80°F. Check daily.	Store at cool temperatures (40°F to 50°F) to retard ripening; warm temperatures hasten ripening. Avoid refrigerating to prevent discoloration.
FLORIDA (WEST INDIAN) AVOCADOS	Florida avocodoes are marketed in single-layer, 13-lb. flats; 2-layer, 27-lb. lugs; 35-lb. cartons; and 10-lb. natural packs. Single-layer pack sizes range from 6 to 24 count.	Florida avocados are used primarily in salads and sandwiches, where their lean mouthfeel can be enhanced with a rich dressing.	July through April	Florida avocadoes have a lower fat content and higher sugar content than western avocadoes, giving them a lean, sometimes watery, mouthfeel.	Store at cool temperatures (40°F to 50°F) to retard ripening; warm temperatures hasten ripening. Avoid refrigerating to prevent discoloration. Quick-ripen as for plantains.
FRESH CARIBBEAN CHILES	Fresh chiles are packed in 10-lb. flats but are usually sold by the pound. Most varieties are widely available; lesser-known varieties are sold by purveyors of Caribbean produce.	Fresh Caribbean chiles are used in virtually any savory dish.	Available year round.	*Scotch bonnet chile:* this small, hot, lantern-shaped chile ranges in ripeness from green through yellow, orange, and red. Red color indicates heightened sweetness. *Habanero chiles:* are similar to Scotch bonnets in size, color, and heat, but are slightly smoother and more elongated. *Bird chiles:* this name is used for a variety of small, hot, tapering chiles ranging from green to red. *Banana chile:* a medium-size, elongated, pale yellow, mild chile. *Cubanelle chile:* similar to the banana chile but milder; primarily used for pickling.	Refrigerate in mesh bags or paper bags. Inspect frequently and discard decaying specimens. For extended storage, freeze whole chiles; chop and use while frozen.

☐ **TABLE 15.3 SOUTH FLORIDA AND PUERTO RICO REGIONAL INGREDIENTS** *(continued)*

ITEM	MARKET FORMS	USES	SEASONALITY	OTHER	STORAGE
CALABAZA (kah-la-BAH-za)/ **WEST INDIAN PUMPKIN**	These large pumpkins are sold by the pound by purveyors of Caribbean and Latin American produce. Supermarkets and grocery stores with Caribbean or Latino clientele may offer vacuum-packed slices.	Calabaza is used in soups and stews, as a side vegetable, and as a dessert ingredient. Its bright color adds interest to plate presentations.	Available year round.	Do not substitute decorative jack-o-lantern pumpkin. Winter squash, such as butternut and acorn, is an acceptable substitute.	Store whole *calabaza* in a cool, dark place with good ventilation. Inspect frequently for mold or soft spots. Once cut, wrap in plastic film and refrigerate.
CHAYOTE (cha-YO-tay); **ALSO MIRLITON, CHOKO, CHRISTOPHINE**	Chayotes are sold in 10- and 15-lb. flats by specialty dealers and purveyors of Asian, Caribbean, and Latin American produce. Counts vary, with fruits ranging from 10 oz. to 1 lb. Chayote is available by the piece in larger supermarkets.	Chayote is peeled, sliced, blanched, refreshed, and used cool for salads, or reheated as a side vegetable. Halved, steamed, stuffed, and baked chayote is served as an appetizer or luncheon entrée.	Available year round.	Some individuals experience a contact dermatitis when handling raw, peeled chayotes. To prevent this from occurring, wear foodservice gloves.	Refrigerate up to 2 weeks.
HEARTS OF PALM	Fresh palm hearts from Central and South America are available by the pound in vacuum packaging through specialty purveyors, and may be mail-ordered. Processed palm hearts are widely available sliced in 14-oz. cans and as lengths in tall 28-oz. cans.	Small, young, and tender fresh palm hearts may be served raw in salads. Larger fresh palm hearts are boiled or steamed. They may be refreshed and used in a cold preparation, or served hot as a side dish with butter and lemon or with a mojo-type sauce. Canned palm hearts are ready to eat.	Available year round.	Palm tips, slender palm hearts surrounded by tender, unfurled leaves, are sold fresh with limited availability.	Refrigerate fresh hearts of palm and use within 1 week. Store canned palm hearts at cool room temperature.
COCONUTS	Ripe or mature fresh coconuts are sold in 50-lb. burlap bags in 24 and 30 count, or by the piece. Husk coconuts have the rough, hairy exterior; smooth, "bald" coconuts have had the husk removed. Green coconuts are sold by the piece by purveyors of Caribbean produce.	Ripe fresh coconuts are used primarily for their meat, although the water may be collected and used for cooking or beverages. Availability of frozen coconut meat and milk has resulted in reduced use of fresh coconuts. Green coconuts are sawed open and the sweet water served as a beverage. The jelly-like flesh is eaten with a spoon.	October to December	Ripe coconuts may be sawed in half and used as a rustic cup or bowl for island-style presentations.	Refrigerate up to 1 month; inspect the eyes for signs of mold.
PROCESSED COCONUT PRODUCTS	These convenience products save the high labor cost of opening and cleaning fresh coconuts. Purchase from purveyors of Caribbean and Asian groceries.	Coconut has multiple uses in New South Florida and Puerto Rican cuisines.	N/A	*Sweetened, shredded coconut* is a semi-moist product fabricated in long and short (macaroon) shreds. *Dessicated (dried) coconut* consists of short chips or shreds with no sugar added. *Canned unsweetened coconut milk* is sold in 13.5-oz. cans; do not confuse with sweetened coconut milk for beverage use. *Frozen coconut cream* and *frozen shredded coconut* are sold in vacuum packs of varying sizes.	Store canned products at cool room temperature and refrigerate after opening. Freeze dried coconut for prolonged storage. Keep frozen products in the freezer.

(continued)

☐ **TABLE 15.3 SOUTH FLORIDA AND PUERTO RICO REGIONAL INGREDIENTS** *(continued)*

ITEM	MARKET FORMS	USES	SEASONALITY	OTHER	STORAGE
STANDARD CITRUS FRUITS	Fresh citrus fruits are sold in 40-lb. cartons sized by count. Fresh, not-from-concentrate juice is sold in half-gallon cartons. Frozen, concentrated juice and pulp are sold in containers and tubs. Lightly sugared, frozen grated lemon, lime, and orange zest is available.	Citrus flesh, juice, concentrate, and zest are all important ingredients used in savory and sweet dishes.	Late winter is peak Florida citrus season; however, most types are now available year round from other areas.	Navel and juice oranges, blood oranges, lemons, limes, tangerines, clementines, tangelos, grapefruits, pommelos, Ugli fruit, and kumquats are a few of the market-standard items available.	Refrigerate up to 1 month.
KEY LIMES/ KEY LIME JUICE	Fresh Key limes are sold in 1-lb. mesh bags or loose in 10-lb. boxes. Frozen, not-from-concentrate Key lime juice is sold in quart containers. Processed Key lime juice made from concentrate is sold in 12-oz. bottles.	The juice of Key limes is widey used in table sauces, condiments, salad dressings, marinades, and desserts. It is essential in Key lime pie filling. Wedges of Key lime accent fried foods.	Fresh Key limes are in season June through August.	Ripe Key limes have a yellowish rind; however, most commercially sold Key limes are picked green. Key lime juice is also yellowish in color; Key lime pies with bright-green fillings have been tinted with food coloring.	Refrigerate Key limes up to 1 month. Store processed Key lime juice at cool room temperature up to 1 year; refrigerate or freeze after opening. Keep frozen juice in the freezer until needed; thaw overnight in the refrigerator.
SOUR (SEVILLE) ORANGES/ SOUR ORANGE JUICE	Fresh sour oranges are available in season in 40-lb. cartons from specialty produce purveyors or direct from growers. Processed sour orange juice is sold in 12-oz. and 24-oz. bottles.	Sour orange juice is used in Caribbean marinades and salad dressings. Sour oranges are essential for making authentic orange marmalade.	Winter.		Refrigerate fresh sour oranges up to 1 month. Mark clearly to avoid confusing with sweet table oranges. Store bottled juice at cool room temperature; refrigerate or freeze after opening.
TROPICAL FRUITS AND FROZEN FRUIT PURÉES	A wide variety of indigenous and introduced tropical fruits are featured in New South Florida and Puerto Rican cuisines. Purchase locally in the region or from specialty produce dealers in various pack sizes. Frozen purées are sold in containers and tubs of varying sizes. They require minimal labor and often are of better quality than shipped produce.	Serve fresh tropical fruits in salads and platters, and use as attractive garnishes. Purées are used in dressings, marinades, desserts, and sweet and savory sauces.	Seasons vary; frozen purées are available year round.	*Atemoya* (ah-tay-MOH-ya) has white flesh, custardlike texture, and a sweet, floral flavor. *Cherimoya* (chair-uh-MOY-ah) flesh is custardlike, with a vanilla scent. *Feijoa* (fay-YOH-ah) flesh is slightly granular with an exotic aroma and tart, pineapple-like flavor. *Star fruit or carambola* are sweet and crisp, with distinctive ridges that yield star-shaped slices when cut crosswise. *Sapotes* of several varieties have different characteristics. *Guavas* are sweet and floral; because they have many seeds, they are used in puréed form or in pastes and jellies. *Guanábana* (wan-AH-ban-ah) is primarily used for juice popular in Puerto Rico. *Passion fruit* has sweet flesh and many seeds. *Pineapple* (see p. 714). *Papayas* range from small to huge, with a sultry, musky aroma and sweet flavor. Papaya seeds are edible and may be used as a garnish. *Mangos* have sweet, aromatic flesh perfectly accented with Key lime juice. *Finger bananas* are small and very sweet.	Refrigerate ripe fresh fruit (except bananas). Keep frozen purées in the freezer until needed. Thaw overnight in the refrigerator.

☐ **TABLE 15.3 SOUTH FLORIDA AND PUERTO RICO REGIONAL INGREDIENTS** *(continued)*

ITEM	MARKET FORMS	USES	SEASONALITY	OTHER	STORAGE
BANANA LEAVES	See p. 714.				
TAMARIND CONCEN-TRATE	A processed conven-ience ingredient, smooth, concentrated tamarind paste is sold in jars of varying size. Purchase in South Asian markets.	Add small amounts to sauces, marinades, and chutneys.	N/A	Tamarind is a sour, brown paste de-rived from the beanlike pod of a tropical evergreen tree.	Refrigerate indefinitely.
ANNATTO SEEDS	Small, brick-red an-natto seeds are sold by the ounce or pound by spice dealers or pur-veyors of Latin Ameri-can groceries.	Steep the seeds in hot vegetable oil or lard, and then strain to make a colored, flavored fry-ing medium. Grind the seeds and mix with spices and seasonings to make a spice paste.	N/A	Annatto is widely used in industrial food processing to simulate the yel-low color of butter and egg yolk. It is also used to color cheese.	Store tightly sealed at cool room tempera-ture or freeze for pro-longed storage.
WHOLE ALLSPICE/ JAMAICAN PIMENTO	Purchase whole all-spice berries by the ounce or pound from a spice dealer with a rapid turnover.	Add crushed or ground allspice to spice rubs, stews, and rice dishes.	N/A		Store at cool room temperature; freeze for prolonged storage.
THAI RED CURRY PASTE	See p. 595.				
PICKAPEPPA SAUCE	Pickapeppa is sold in 5-oz. bottles and 1-gal. foodservice jugs.	Pickapeppa sauce is used on sandwiches, as a sauce ingredient, and in marinades. It tops cream cheese canapés and baked or fried plantains.	N/A	This famous Jamaican condiment is made from tomatoes, onions, sugar, vinegar, mangoes, tamarind, and Caribbean spices.	Store at cool room temperature. After opening, refrigerate for prolonged storage.
BLACK TURTLE BEANS/ *FRIJOLES NEGROS* (free-HOH-lays NAY-gross)	Dried black beans are sold in 1-lb. packages and 10-lb. boxes.	Black beans are a signa-ture ingredient in Cuban and Cuban-American cuisines. They are used to make soups, side dishes, and Nuevo Latino salads. Black beans are cooked with rice to make *moros y cristianos*.	N/A	For best texture soak in cool water overnight before cooking.	Store at cool room temperature.
RED KIDNEY BEANS/ JAMAICAN "PEAS"	Dark or light red kid-ney beans are sold in 1-lb. packages and 10-lb. boxes.	Red kidney beans are essential in Jamaican-American rice 'n' peas (p. 769).	N/A	Red kidney beans may be soaked overnight or quick-soaked before cooking.	Store at cool room temperature.
BLACK-EYED PEAS/ FRIJOLES CARITAS (free-HOE-lays kar-EE-tahs)	See p. 82.				

(continued)

☐ **TABLE 15.3 SOUTH FLORIDA AND PUERTO RICO REGIONAL INGREDIENTS** *(continued)*

ITEM	MARKET FORMS	USES	SEASONALITY	OTHER	STORAGE
GANDULES (gahn-DOO-lays)/ PIGEON PEAS; ALSO GUNGO PEAS, GOONGO PEAS	Dried *gandules* are available in 1-lb. packages and in 10-lb. boxes from purveyors of Puerto Rican groceries. Cooked, processed *gandules* are sold in 15-oz. cans widely available in supermarkets. Frozen, lightly processed *gandules* are sold in 14-oz. vacuum packs.	*Gandules* are cooked with rice to make Puerto Rican *arroz con gandules* (p. 743).	N/A		Store dried and canned *gandules* at cool room temperature. Keep frozen *gandules* in the freezer until needed.
CONCH (KONK)	Frozen, cleaned conch is available in 5-lb. block packages and IQF in 2-lb. bags. Purchase from a vendor with a high turnover to ensure quality.	Conch is widely used in soups, salads, seviche, fritters, and stuffings.	N/A	Conch meat must be tenderized physically by pounding or chopping, chemically with an acidic marinade, or through long, slow cooking.	Store frozen; thaw overnight in the refrigerator.
SPINY/ROCK LOBSTER; ALSO *LANGOUSTE* (lahn-GOOST)	Warm-water spiny lobsters caught fresh for the table typically weigh 2 to 5 pounds. Most spiny lobster is processed for frozen shell-on tails in 5-, 6-, 8-, and 10-oz. portion sizes. Slipper lobster tails average 3 ounces. Most are packed in 10-lb. boxes.	In the region, fresh spiny lobsters are steamed and presented whole with butter and lemon, or split and grilled with a mojo-style baste. Spiny lobster tails are grilled or baked, often with a stuffing to enlarge portion size.	Available year round.	Spiny lobsters have very hard shells and no edible claws. Only the tail meat is used.	Store live lobsters in a saltwater tank. To refrigerate, layer in seaweed or damp newspaper 1 or 2 days only. Keep frozen lobster tails in the freezer until needed; thaw overnight in the refrigerator.
STONE CRAB CLAWS	Stone crab claws are sold steamed and chilled, or frozen after steamimg. They are sold by the pound graded by size: *jumbo:* 2 to 3 per pound; *large:* 4 to 5 per pound; *medium:* 7 to 8 per pound.	Carefully crack the shells and serve chilled with a tangy mustard-mayonnaise dip.	October to March	Because of Florida state regulations, stone crabs are a sustainable resource as only one claw is harvested from each crab. Crabs are thrown back into the water, where they regenerate a new claw within about a year.	Refrigerate steamed, chilled claws in plastic bags bedded in ice in a self-draining container 1 or 2 days only. Keep frozen claws in the freezer until needed; thaw overnight in the refrigerator.
FLORIDA GROUPER	Florida grouper is sold fresh by the pound as sides or skinless fillets. Grouper cheeks are a regional specialty.	Firm, mild-tasting, pale-pink grouper fillets may be cooked by virtually any method. The traditional preparation of broiled grouper with lemon and butter showcases its fine flavor.	Seasons vary by fishery.		Refrigerate fresh grouper fillets and cheeks in plastic bags bedded in ice in a self-draining container up to 2 days.
POMPANO	See p. 299.				

▢ TABLE 15.3 SOUTH FLORIDA AND PUERTO RICO REGIONAL INGREDIENTS *(continued)*

ITEM	MARKET FORMS	USES	SEASONALITY	OTHER	STORAGE
FLORIDA GULF MULLET	Mullet is sold by the pound as sides and skin-on fillets.	Mullet's firm, dark flesh lends itself to grilling and broiling. Its full flavor stands up to mojo-type marinades, spicy sauces, and tropical fruit salsas.	Season varies by fishery.	Smoked mullet is an in-house-produced specialty often sold in seafood shops.	Refrigerate fresh mullet fillets in plastic bags bedded in ice in a self-draining container up to 2 days.
FROG LEGS	Fresh frog legs may be available in the region (or in the Plantation South or Ozarks) on a limited basis. Frog legs are graded by size: *jumbo:* 2 to 4 per pound; *large:* 4 to 6 per pound; *medium:* 6 to 8 per pound.	Sauté or coat with breading and pan-fry.	Summer. Frozen frog legs are available year round.	Today most commercially sold frog legs are frozen products imported from Asia.	Refrigerate fresh frog legs in plastic bags bedded in ice in a self-draining container up to 2 days. Thaw frozen frog legs overnight in the refrigerator.
ALLIGATOR TAIL	See p. 297.				

■□■ chapter sixteen

New York City

Manhattan, Brooklyn, Queens, the Bronx, Staten Island

WE END OUR TOUR of America's culinary regions in New York City, considered by many to be the dining capital of the world and home to a global food culture. Shortly after its founding in the early 1600s, the city was already home to scores of ethnic groups speaking 18 different languages; the colony's leader, Peter Stuyvesant, complained that it was "too diverse to govern." Diversity increased during the colonial period and into nationhood, and then exploded during immigration waves starting in the late 1800s and ongoing today, making New York City a glorious cornucopia of cuisines.

New York City is designated as a separate culinary region because, unlike other large American cities, it doesn't reflect the culture or cuisine of its surrounding countryside. Nor is its cuisine founded on home cooking. New York City's best cooking is public—originating in taverns, developed by street vendors and in delicatessens, cooked up in corner cafés and lunch counters, and refined in some of the world's most renowned restaurants. For this reason our discussion of New York City cuisine focuses primarily on the city's foodservice operations and the dishes for which they've become famous.

Two distinctive American microcuisines, Italian-American cooking and Jewish-American cooking, were born in New York City, and there they remain in purest form. To learn about Italian-American and Jewish-American food culture and cooking, go to this book's companion website.

AFTER STUDYING THIS CHAPTER YOU SHOULD BE ABLE TO:

- describe the topography and location of New York City (Factor 1) and explain their effect on the city's physical development, economy, and cuisine
- explain why New York City's original Native American population (Factor 2) and first settlers (Factor 3) had virtually no influence on its cuisine
- discuss the effects of instant and ongoing economic viability (Factor 5) on New York City culture and cuisine
- describe the impact of immigrant foodways on New York City cuisine (Factor 4)
- discuss the conditions that initiated and perpetuated the region's street food, takeout, and restaurant dining traditions
- recount the development of the New York City restaurant scene from the late 1800s to the present
- discuss the Italian-American microcuisine and list its defining dishes
- discuss the Jewish-American microcuisine and list its defining dishes
- prepare selected New York City restaurant dishes and dishes of the Italian-American and Jewish-American microcuisines

APPETIZERS

Manhattan Clam Chowder with Oyster Crackers

Vichyssoise with Onion Twists

Tall Seafood Salad with Avocado and Tobiko

Twenty-First-Century Waldorf Salad

Clams Casino

Potato Latke with Smoked Salmon and Caviar

Tartare of Salmon and Striped Bass with Anchovy Croutons

Ida's Chopped Liver with Bagel Crisps

Pasta Primavera

ENTRÉES

Striped Bass in Potato Crust with Red Wine Sauce, Lentil Ragout, and Leeks

Grilled Swordfish with Preserved Lemon–Black Olive Butter Sauce,
Israeli Couscous, Confit Tomatoes, and Broccolini

Stuffed Savoy Cabbage in Sweet 'n' Sour Sauce with Kasha Varnishkes

Sautéed Sweetbreads in Lemon-Caper Black Butter with Parsley Potatoes,
Glazed Baby Carrots, and Asparagus

Grilled Rare Squab with Green Peppercorn Demi-Glace, Haricots Verts,
and Rutabaga-Mascarpone Purée

Tandoori Lamb Chops with Basmati Pulao, Greens Purée, and Braised Cauliflower

Spaghetti 'n' Meatballs with Braised Broccoli Rabe

Seared Calf's Liver with Balsamic Onion Marmalade, Delmonico Potatoes,
and Wilted Baby Spinach

Veal Parmesan with Fresh Tomato Sauce, Potato Gnocchi, and Vegetable "Spaghetti"

DESSERTS

Crème Brûlée

New York Cheesecake with Strawberries and Strawberry Sauce

Mascarpone Cannolo with Zabaglione Sauce

Park Avenue Fruit Tartelette in Caramel Cage

Frozen Soufflé Grand Marnier with Chocolate-Dipped Burnt-Orange Biscotto

Brooklyn Blackout Cake with Chocolate Whipped Cream

■ ISLANDS
□ OF ROCK

Geologists believe that the earth once consisted of one giant landmass surrounded by ocean. Hundreds of millions of years ago, a cataclysmic seismic event caused it to break apart and its pieces drift away from one another, creating the world's continents as we know them today. At some point during this massive rift, the area now called New York City split from the North American mainland, becoming a cluster of nearby islands. This group of islands, and part of the mainland just north of them, eventually became New York City. The city is divided into five boroughs: Manhattan and Staten Island are discrete islands; Brooklyn and Queens comprise the southern end of Long Island; and the Bronx is part of the New York State mainland.

Manhattan and the Bronx are separated from the New Jersey mainland by the Hudson River. One of the Mid-Atlantic's three pre-eminent waterways, the Hudson rises in upstate New York and flows south to meet the Upper New York Bay and eventually flow into the Atlantic Ocean at the Narrows between Staten Island and Brooklyn. The lower Hudson forms a deep canyon flanked by the New Jersey Palisades, a line of rocky cliffs on the west. Manhattan is separated from the Bronx by the East River, and the Bronx is separated from Queens by Long Island Sound.

The land under much of New York City is primarily bedrock, composed of durable gneiss, granite, and marble. This foundation was key to Manhattan's physical development. Confined by surrounding boundaries of water, Manhattan Island became overcrowded within a hundred years of its founding. And yet, more and more people desired to live and work there. The problem was solved by 20th-century technology: Instead of expanding outward, Manhattan built upward. The heart of New York City eventually rose into the clouds as architects and engineers constructed towering buildings called skyscrapers (Figure 16.1). However, these iconic symbols of New York City could not have been built, nor could Manhattan sustain its dense population, without the island's bedrock foundation.

During successive ice ages the New York City area was scraped bare by advancing glaciers. Between the ice ages, melting glaciers redeposited soil primarily on Long Island and Staten Island, and created the region's broad underwater coastal shelf. Runoff from melting ice deepened the Hudson River channel. After the last ice age, ocean levels once again rose and the land took on its present contours, leaving New York City surrounded by water. As you'll soon learn, the area's topography—islands of solid bedrock surrounded by navigable rivers, bays, inlets, and narrows—determined its destiny (Figure 16.2).

New York City shares the temperate climate of the Mid-Atlantic culinary region to its west. However, its proximity to the Atlantic Ocean lends a moderating effect, resulting in slightly warmer winters and cooling summer breezes when the wind is off the water. The region's firm, dry terrain proved beneficial to the health of local Native Americans and early settlers, minimizing insect pests and diseases carried by them. However, early in the region's history, climate ceased to be a major factor in its economic or culinary development.

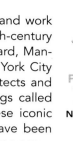

FACTOR 1
The islands comprising New York City have solid bedrock foundations, enabling the construction of skyscrapers and making possible the city's dense population.

FIGURE 16.1

Manhattan's skyscrapers are built on a foundation of solid bedrock. Songquan Deng/Shutterstock

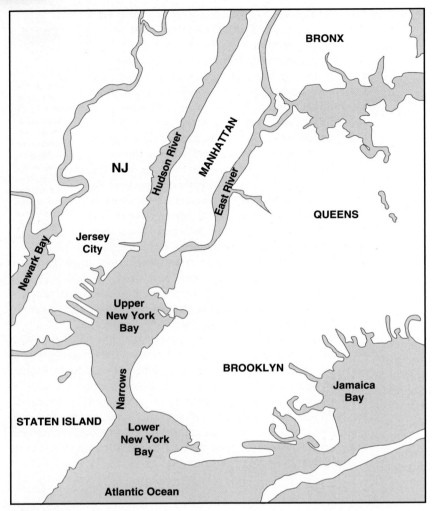

FIGURE 16.2
New York City Boroughs and Waterways

FACTOR 1
New York's island topography surrounded by deep waterways makes it one of the world's best natural harbors.

Upper New York Bay and then sailed north on the river that bears his name.

Hudson immediately recognized the value of the waterways he had just explored and their surrounding land. The New York City area comprised a natural harbor complex that could not have been better planned by a civil engineer. The city's islands are surrounded by channels far deeper than the draft of colonial-era sailing vessels and, indeed, of ample depth for today's giant ships. Protected by arms of land, inner New York Harbor is accessible only through the Narrows. Jamaica Bay is sheltered by a barrier island. At the time the Hudson River was navigable 190 miles inland, the gateway to an interior plateau blessed with seemingly endless natural resources. The region's climate was mild and healthful. The Dutch quickly initiated settlement by purchasing land from local Native Americans rather than attempting to take it by force.

Allegedly the Dutch purchased Manhattan Island for the equivalent of $24. No matter how accurate the legend may be, it's an important clue to understanding the New York City worldview. From the beginning, commerce was New York City's lifeblood and making money its primary preoccupation. Although the Lenapes had no concept of land ownership, they were eager to acquire material goods and thus willing to trade land for decorative objects, metal implements, and firearms. One after another, parcels of land within the boundaries of present-day New York City were sold to the Dutch, who called their settlement New Amsterdam. Later, after the English finally won control of the area in 1674, such transactions continued and, by the late 1600s, Native American presence was negligible. Lower Manhattan quickly built up into a bustling city of shops, warehouses, ship's chandlers, taverns, and townhouses built close together because of limited space. As development increased, the city expanded ever northward, and eventually the outer boroughs were settled.

Although it was founded and governed by the Dutch, New Amsterdam was not a homogenously Dutch city. Nor did the Dutch, known for minimizing food culture, spend significant time or effort on re-creating the foods of their homeland. Interested primarily in founding an international trading port, the Dutch immediately welcomed entrepreneur settlers from all over Europe and around the globe. Thus, New York City has been a cultural and culinary melting pot from its founding.

Indigenous foods and Native American cooking methods were of little interest to New York City settlers. Although local fish and wild game were served in homes and taverns, few

■ NATIVE AMERICANS
□
■ AND COLONISTS

The area that is now New York City was originally Lenape territory. Historians speculate that at the time of European contact, as many as 30,000 Native Americans of the Lenape tribal group lived around the mouth of the Hudson. However, their Native American foodways had literally no impact on the development of New York City cuisine. But the financial transaction that began the transfer of New York City from Native American control into the hands of European first settlers is significant as a portent of the city's overarching preoccupation with trade.

New York Bay was initially explored in 1524 by Giovanni da Verrazzano, an Italian navigator in the service of France. Subsequently, the entire Mid-Atlantic region was unaccountably ignored by European powers until the early 1600s, when Henry Hudson, exploring for the Dutch East India Company, entered

citizens sought out Three Sisters foods. Ships arriving regularly in New York Harbor brought virtually any preserved foodstuff European settlers might want. A few farmers grew Old World colonial domesticates on small farms that were continually pushed outward by the city's rapid expansion.

Initially the Dutch weren't interested in agriculture. Farmers were mandated only to feed the growing city, not to export crops. When New Amsterdam became English New York, policies remained largely the same. By 1700 agriculture had moved to the outer boroughs and then to Long Island, with more room and more suitable soil. Through the early 1800s Long Island supplied most of New York City's meat and produce. Wheat and other grains arrived by boat from central New York State and, after the construction of the Erie Canal, from the Midwest. Thus, by the mid-1800s, the only food produced in New York City was seafood caught in the surrounding waters.

Colonial Cooking

New Amsterdam housewives typically prepared simple, European-style peasant and middle-class foods, each drawing from her own culinary tradition and often borrowing ideas and ingredients from her neighbors. However, home cooking was not the only option. Public dining houses were important fixtures of daily life in New Amsterdam and, later, in New York City. In these early establishments cooking was rarely the main feature. Proprietors made most of their money through sales of alcohol and lodging. As in all colonial dining establishments, New Amsterdam taverns and inns had no menus. Food was served on a *table d'hôte* basis, with only one set meal available. The day's sole offering might be a casserole of salt beef, cabbage, and potatoes baked in the embers; a seafood chowder simmered in a cast-iron cauldron; or a joint of fresh mutton roasted on the spit.

After the English took over, dining options expanded, at least for the affluent. Better establishments, such as Fraunce's Tavern (Figure 16.3) and the Tontine Coffee House, served fresh meats, fowl, game, and seafood dishes, often in private dining rooms. However, recipes remained simple and offerings limited. Through the American Revolution and into the early 1800s, few New Yorkers were interested in fine cuisine.

FIGURE 16.3

Fraunce's Tavern was a center of cultural and political life in early New York City. Courtesy of the Library of Congress – PGA, Society of Iconophiles of New York, Fraunces' Tavern

DELMONICO'S SETS THE STANDARD

By the 1830s, increased commerce resulting from the newly built Erie Canal and advances in ocean transport was producing significant wealth for New York City. European travel had broadened the palates of newly rich merchants and manufacturers. Wealthy New Yorkers were finally ready for the experience of fine dining and willing to pay for it.

New York's tradition as a great restaurant city began with immigrant entrepreneurs. In 1827 Swiss-born brothers Giovanni and Pietro Delmonico opened a European-style café and pastry shop in lower Manhattan. In 1830 it expanded into a formal, full-service restaurant with a French chef. Modeled after the new style of dining establishments opening in France, Delmonico's was among the first American restaurants to feature a **bill of fare,** or à la carte menu, offering a variety of individually priced dishes rather than a set *table d'hôte* menu. Delmonico's imported the best European ingredients and combined them with fine local food products. The restaurant's European chefs initially prepared classic French dishes but eventually began modifying them to suit American ingredients and tastes. Thus, Delmonico's was the birthplace of Continental cuisine.

As New York City expanded, so did the Delmonicos—opening additional locations and offering more elaborate food and more luxurious surroundings in each (Figure 16.4). In the late 1860s Delmonico's began encouraging women to patronize the restaurant without male escorts. Until then, women dining out alone or with other women were considered of questionable reputation. However, all it took to change this deeply ingrained social taboo was the Delmonico seal of approval. Their "women's dining room" was an instant success. By 1870 the Delmonico family was operating four Manhattan locations, and the Delmonico name was known across America to represent the ultimate in luxury dining. Many signature dishes of the American national cuisine repertoire were developed by

FACTOR 5
Always a lucrative trading port, New York City generated increased wealth after the completion of the Erie Canal connected it with the Midwest.

FACTOR 4
New York City's prominence as a restaurant city began when Swiss-born immigrants opened America's first French restaurant and eventually created Continental cuisine.

CONTINENTAL CUISINE

Continental cuisine is a restaurant-driven, hybrid cooking style based on the cuisines of France and other nations of the European continent, though modified to include American ingredients and to accommodate American taste preferences. Refer to this book's companion website for more information on the evolution of Continental cuisine.

FIGURE 16.4
Delmonico's Restaurant, Circa 1900. Superstock Royalty Free

Delmonico chefs and/or bear the Delmonico name: Delmonico steak, Delmonico Potatoes (p. 808, 833), Eggs Benedict, Baked Alaska, and Lobster Newburg are all Delmonico creations.

■ NEW YORK
□ RESTAURANTS
■ OF THE GILDED AGE

The end of the Civil War and the beginning of the American Industrial Revolution ushered in a period of unprecedented economic development. As America's center of commerce, New York City prospered as never before. New Yorkers had money to spend and, finally, the desire to spend it on luxury dining. Inspired by the success of the Delmonico restaurants, entrepreneurs began opening fine restaurants of equal opulence.

The First French Invasion

FACTOR 4
French chefs modified their cooking style to please American customers, popularizing Continental cuisine.

Following the Delmonico's model, New York City restaurateurs hired chefs from France and began serving French cuisine. However, American patrons typically preferred heartier fare in larger portions. Gradually many of New York City's French restaurants adopted the hybrid cooking style developed by Delmonico's and later called Continental cuisine.

Many of the city's luxury hotels opened high-end restaurants. The Metropolitan, the Astor, and the Waldorf Astoria were best known for fine dining. The Waldorf Astoria's maitre d'hotel Oscar Tschirky became world-famous as "Oscar of the Waldorf," creating and/or popularizing many Continental cuisine signature dishes. Waldorf salad (p. 807) and veal Oscar are known Tschirky creations. However, his claim to Eggs Benedict and Thousand Island dressing are disputed. Nonetheless, these dishes were popularized by the Waldorf under Oscar's reign.

Lobster Palaces

By the 1870s, America's East Coast lobster population had been severely overfished, making lobster an expensive delicacy. Largely because lobsters were now rare and costly, a new type of New York restaurant began specializing in them. These large and opulently decorated restaurants, called *lobster palaces*, offered 5-pound lobsters and other expensive seafood items. Rector's was a favorite dining spot of Diamond Jim Brady, a financier known for his gargantuan appetite. Churchill's was even larger and more extravagant than Rector's. By the beginning of the 20th century, scores of imitators were carrying on the lobster palace tradition.

New York Steakhouses

Although affluent New Yorkers were frequent patrons of the city's French and Continental restaurants, as "red-blooded Americans" most were equally fond of a perfectly cooked steak. By the early 1880s rail transport was bringing grain-finished Western beef from Chicago packinghouses to the East Coast, and New York City was one of its largest consumers. The New York steakhouse became a world-renowned institution, rivaling the Chicago steakhouses discussed in Chapter 9.

The most venerable of New York's famous temples to beef is the Old Homestead, founded in 1868 and still operating in the lower Manhattan meatpacking district. Brooklyn's Peter Luger, an American steakhouse with German beer-hall décor, opened in 1887 and is still serving (Figure 16.5). The Palm offers American-style steaks with Italian-American appetizers, sides, and veal dishes. New York's traditional Jewish-style kosher steakhouses are discussed on this book's companion website. The 1960s and 1970s brought a new generation of New York steakhouses, such as Spark's and Smith & Wollensky.

New York Seafood Houses

In its early days, New York City ate seafood caught directly off its shores. Oysters, clams, mussels, lobsters, and scallops filled the bays and coastal shelf. Fish were plentiful in both salt water and in the region's rivers. City-based fishing fleets cruised out into the Atlantic, bringing back seafood to New York's wharves. However, as population increased, demand became so great that additional seafood was shipped in from the Chesapeake Bay, Cape Cod, and Maine.

FIGURE 16.5
Peter Luger steakhouse is a Brooklyn landmark. Courtesy Bob Shepherd

FIGURE 16.6

The Grand Central Oyster Bar, in Manhattan's Grand Central Terminal, serves seafood from all over the world. Courtesy Heidi Hart, Fox Run Farm, Wrightsville, PA

New York City's first seafood houses were oyster bars where rich and poor stood at counters eating raw oysters on the half shell. The Fulton Fish Market, formerly on the water in lower Manhattan, was home to no-frills, sawdust-on-the-floor restaurants serving seafood just off the boat. The historic market was demolished in 2005 and its fish dealers relocated to Hunt's Point in the Bronx. Lundy's, on Sheepshead Bay in Brooklyn, served fine seafood to generations of New Yorkers. The restaurant was famous for its massive shore dinner that included seafood cocktail, steamer clams, lobster, and broiled chicken served with vegetable side dishes and hot biscuits, and then followed by dessert. Although no longer run by the Lundy family, the restaurant is still in operation.

The Grand Central Oyster Bar is the crown jewel of traditional New York seafood restaurants (Figure 16.6). When the Grand Central Railway Terminal was built in 1913, the designers included a traditional oyster bar in the station's cavernous basement. There, under beautiful vaulted and tiled ceilings, travelers and businessmen dined on fresh oysters and other East Coast seafood. However, during the 1960s passenger rail transportation declined; the Oyster Bar grew shabby and neglected and finally closed in 1972. Fortunately, only two years later the Oyster Bar was given a new lease on life by Jerome Brody of Restaurant Associates (p. 798), who restored it to its former glory with a menu featuring seafood from around the world.

New Restaurants for a New Century

The 20th century ushered in a new era for New York City's restaurant industry. Cuisine and culture were merging as never before. Customers dining in expensive restaurants now expected more than just fine food. High-end New York restaurants began offering live music, including classical ensembles and big-band orchestras. Artists were commissioned to decorate restaurants with murals and sculptures.

While the upper classes dined in Gilded Age luxury, a new customer base was emerging. Salespeople and office workers from the growing middle class needed fast lunches. Women entering the workforce were unwilling to come home and cook dinner in a tiny apartment kitchen. Middle-class workers created a strong demand for quick, affordable meals served in respectable surroundings. New York City's foodservice entrepreneurs responded with new kinds of restaurants.

Restaurants for the Common People

Through the 1800s diners looking for inexpensive meals had been limited to taverns, which served food and alcohol to a largely male clientele and were typically dark, smoky, and focused more on beverages than on food. Respectable women with male escorts were served only in the taverns' private dining rooms, where ordering and eating a meal could take hours. In the early 1900s New York entrepreneurs developed a different option.

The urban **lunchroom** was designed to attract office workers and shoppers as regular customers. Lunchrooms featured low-cost sandwiches, soups, salads, desserts, and nonalcoholic beverages served quickly and efficiently in a clean, brightly lit environment. Child's Lunchrooms had spotless white tile interiors and featured pancakes prepared before the public's eyes in the restaurants' front windows. Schrafft's was designed expressly to serve ladies and was one of the first foodservice operations to have women managers. Chock Full o' Nuts featured its proprietary blend of coffee along with breakfast pastries and sandwiches.

Citizens of the new century were obsessed with technology and efficiency. The **Automat** was a restaurant concept that used technology to make service more efficient. Dishes of food were displayed behind coin-operated windows. Customers simply inserted a nickel into the slot, opened the window, and helped themselves. Behind-the-scenes workers refilled the windows as quickly as they emptied. Although founded in Philadelphia, Horn & Hardart's Automats became a fixture of the New York cityscape (Figure 16.7).

FIGURE 16.7

At a Horn & Hardart's Automat, customers purchased prepared dishes of food through coin-operated windows. Courtesy of The New York Public Library

FACTOR 5
During the Great Depression, New York City's fine dining restaurants struggled, but budget restaurants flourished.

Compounding the damage done by Prohibition, the 1929 stock market crash nearly finished New York City's luxury restaurants. Many of their wealthiest patrons lost everything and could no longer afford expensive restaurant meals. Some, like the legendary 21 Club, weathered the Depression by becoming a speakeasy. For more information on Prohibition-era speakeasies and how they emerged as nightclubs after repeal, refer to this book's companion website.

Although the stock market crash and the Great Depression hurt high-end restaurants, these economic challenges actually increased the scope and number of budget foodservice operations. The 1930s became a golden age for New York City street vendors, lunch counters, cafeterias, and inexpensive ethnic restaurants. During the Depression, thousands of out-of-work New Yorkers tried to make money by selling cheap food items on the streets. Tiny "mom-and-pop" restaurants served inexpensive, home-style meals. The city's growing immigrant population offered many New Yorkers their first taste of unfamiliar foreign cuisines.

■ IMMIGRANTS FILL
□
■ THE MELTING POT

The New York City culinary melting pot that began in multicultural New Amsterdam virtually bubbled over in the late 1800s. Entering through Ellis Island, hundreds of thousands of immigrants arrived in New York City hoping for a better life. Although many continued inland to other culinary regions, many others stayed in New York City. They were willing to live in crowded, unsanitary conditions; had the stamina to work up to 18 hours a day for meager pay; and were tough enough to overcome bigotry, injustice, and exclusion in order to survive and prosper.

Immigrants tend to stick together, living in clearly defined enclaves. Thus, New York became a city of neighborhoods often identified by the dominant ethnic group living in each. New York's ethnic neighborhoods eventually became known to outsiders for the exotic and affordable food and drink available in them.

The Irish: Politics and Pubs

The Irish were New York City's first major wave of immigration. Fleeing the Irish potato famine, they topped immigration lists from 1840 to 1852, during which time more than one and a half million entered the country. Such a huge cultural group profoundly affected the city and the nation. Irish-Americans became a powerful political force, eventually entering law enforcement, the judiciary, and politics. Drawing on the Celtic tradition of brewing and distilling, the Irish also became influential in the beverage industry as saloonkeepers and producers of beer and whiskey. By

the late 1800s, it seemed there was an Irish pub on nearly every New York City street corner.

However, Irish-Americans were never known for cuisine. The Irish who came to America in the mid-1800s were the product of more than a hundred years of British agricultural exploitation and a failed monoculture system (p. 414). Thus, they had no food culture from which to draw. In America even the poorest Irish immigrant could afford enough food to eat, but few had the skill or will to create innovative dishes. To the Irish, accustomed to a diet of potatoes and buttermilk, the addition of roasted or boiled meat made the meal a feast. Only one Irish-American hybrid dish comes readily to mind: corned beef and cabbage, an immigrant version of the Irish dish traditionally made with Irish bacon.

The Germans:
Hofbraus and *Rathskellers*

Between 1853 and the outbreak of the Civil War in 1861, Germans topped the immigration rolls. However, many Germans entering through Ellis Island were rural families who moved on into the interior hoping to acquire farms. Germans who remained in New York City initially clustered in a downtown area that became known as *Kleinedeutschland*, or Little Germany. In its heyday Little Germany was home to 800,000 German-American residents; however, by the Civil War many had moved to Yorkville on the Upper West Side. Today that community has also dispersed, leaving no real German-American enclave in New York City.

FACTOR 4
German-Americans introduced the *biergarten* restaurant concept and popularized Germanic cuisine.

German-American *rathskellers*, *hofbraus*, and *biergartens* (Figure 16.8) were an important part of the New York restaurant scene until Prohibition. In these establishments New Yorkers of all ethnic backgrounds enjoyed traditional German and German-American cuisine, described in Chapter 9. There New Yorkers

FIGURE 16.8
Biergarten Zumschneider, in the East Village. Courtesy of www.richardgreene.com

acquired a taste for German-style wines and beers that never waned. Janssen's and the German-American Rathskeller were two of New York's best-known German-American restaurants; however, the most famous and long-lived was Lüchows restaurant and nightclub. Celebrities from around the world made Lüchows a must-visit nightspot. In addition to live entertainment, the Lüchow family was well known for offering a true gustatory experience, hosting weeklong promotional events such as a Venison Festival, Goose Feast, Bock Beer Festival, and May Wine Festival.

The decline and eventual demise of most New York German-American restaurants began with the widespread anti-German sentiment sweeping the country at the beginning of World War I. Prohibition, World War II, and health consciousness combined as final blows. Of the many great New York City German-American restaurants, Lüchows was the only one to survive and thrive, finally closing in 1982. However, the recent popularity of microbreweries has stirred renewed interest in the *biergarten* restaurant concept.

The Italians: Produce and Pasta

Between 1876 and 1924, nearly five million Italians immigrated to America. Most were from the impoverished and drought-ridden southern regions of Campania, Calabria, Puglia, Abruzzi, Basilicata, and Sicily. Although many were farmers from rural villages, by the turn of the 20th century most of America's farmland already had been claimed. Moreover, most Italian immigrants were so poor that they could not afford to travel beyond New York City. Most remained in the city and took menial, physically difficult jobs, often in construction and public works. After 1900 many Italian-American women and children worked in garment manufacturing sweatshops or did piecework sewing in their tiny tenement apartments. Many Italian-American immigrants became hucksters, peddling fruits and vegetables out of pushcarts.

Early Italian settlement centered around Five Points, an infamous slum. By the beginning of the 20th century, Italian-American commerce centered on a downtown neighborhood that became known as Little Italy (Figure 16.9). There, homesick immigrants purchased the pastas, preserved meats, olive oils, and pungent cheeses of home.

Of all second-settler immigrant groups, Italian-Americans had by far the greatest impact on American cooking. Many of their dishes have been so thoroughly incorporated into the American national cuisine that it's difficult to remember they were once foreign foods. The Italian-American microcuisine is discussed on this book's companion website.

FACTOR 4
Italian-Americans had the strongest impact on American cooking of any immigrant group.

The Jews: Bagels and Deli

Jewish settlers arrived in New Amsterdam in 1654, making them the city's earliest immigrant group. Mostly of Spanish and Portuguese descent, they became culturally and politically influential. However, they did little to influence the city's cooking. Not only were their numbers too small, but their cuisine was too eclectic. Often having lived in several different countries before

FIGURE 16.9
Little Italy street scene, circa 1900. Courtesy of the Library of Congress, LC-D4-12683

landing in America, many had adopted a variety of foodways from their host countries. Thus, they didn't project a strong and unified food culture.

The second wave of Jewish immigration began in the early 1800s, comprising mainly German Jews discouraged by growing restrictions being placed on them by the German government. Many more fled revolution in 1848. These were largely merchants and professionals with good educations. Their foodways combined classic German cuisine with kosher law. However, most German Jews aspired to assimilation, wishing to become thoroughly "American." Thus, most eventually gave up the practice of keeping kosher and adopted mainstream American cooking.

FACTOR 4
Eastern European Jews adapted kosher recipes to American ingredients.

The third wave of Jewish immigrants had a real impact on the eating habits of New York City and other urban areas. In the 1880s Eastern European Jews began emigrating to escape pogroms, or systematic, government-sponsored persecutions. Between 1880 and 1924 two million Eastern European Jews entered the United States, most of them semieducated shopkeepers or artisans. Eastern European Jews spoke Yiddish, an expressive language combining colloquial Low German with Hebrew words and featuring uniquely Jewish idioms. Most were highly observant Orthodox Jews who resisted assimilation and clustered together in tightly knit neighborhoods, particularly in Manhattan's Lower East Side and later in Brooklyn's Williamsburg and Borough Park sections.

In addition to founding synagogues, schools, and Yiddish-language newspapers, they also opened food businesses such as kosher slaughterhouses and smokehouses, dairy stores, bakeries, and Jewish delicatessens. Eventually they developed the Jewish-American microcuisine, discussed on this book's companion website.

The Chinese and Other Asians

In 1850 the seaport area of lower Manhattan supported a tiny enclave of about 150 Chinese, mostly former sailors. The completion of the Transcontinental Railroad in 1869 swelled their number as newly unemployed workers headed east on the railroad they had constructed.

In New York City, Chinese men found it difficult to obtain work because of prejudice that outweighed discrimination against other, more-familiar-looking European immigrants. The only industry willing to accept Chinese laborers was commercial laundering, a new business so dirty and physically demanding that few were willing to work in it. In 1882 the U.S. government passed the Chinese Exclusion Act denying Chinese immigrants the right to citizenship and virtually halting Chinese immigration. Even wives and families of established Chinese immigrants were forbidden to enter the country. This edict created a virtual bachelor society of Chinese-American men in New York City.

Nonetheless, a Chinese-operated commercial center, or Chinatown, grew up around lower Manhattan's Mott and Canal Streets (Figure 16.10). The area soon became known outside the Chinese community as an exotic place to be explored by the adventurous. There, as in California, Chinese entrepreneurs opened restaurants serving a simple form of Cantonese food using American ingredients and modified to suit American tastes. The resulting Chinese-American microcuisine is discussed on the website.

When the Exclusion Act was finally lifted in 1943, the low immigration quota set by a still wary U.S. government resulted in slow growth for New York's Chinatown. The neighborhood gradually became residential as well as commercial, with newly arrived families filling the apartments above the street-level stores and restaurants. Manhattan's Chinatown population exploded when quotas were raised in 1968, and the neighborhood expanded to its current boundaries.

FIGURE 16.10
Manhattan's Chinatown, circa 1900. Courtesy of the Library of Congress, LC-D4-13646

The arrival of immigrants from all over China spelled the end of Chinese-American restaurants in Manhattan's Chinatown. Virtually all were replaced by authentic regional cuisine restaurants primarily catering to Chinese diners, but tolerating non-Chinese New Yorkers ready to try duck's feet, tree ear fungus, and other unusual ingredients.

Other Asians, Other Enclaves

In the 1970s the end of the Vietnam War brought thousands of Southeast Asians to New York. Chinatown quickly pushed past its official boundaries, swallowing up much of Little Italy and infiltrating the Lower East Side. Asian enclaves sprang up in other boroughs, particularly in Queens (p. 803). Today New Yorkers can sample the foods of Vietnam Thailand, Burma, Malaysia, Indonesia, and other Southeast Asian countries as well as regional Chinese cuisines from Sichuan, Hunan, Fukien, Guangdong, and Beijing and the cuisines of China's ethnic minorities such as the Hmong and Mongolians.

FACTOR 4
Asians from a variety of nations opened New York City restaurants featuring the authentic cuisines of their homelands.

African-Americans: The Arts and Soul Food

During the colonial period, New York City was home to a significant number of African-American slaves, most employed in construction and crafts and as house servants. By 1746, 21 percent of New York City's population was African-American, and half of its households owned a slave. However, lack of agriculture made large-scale slavery unnecessary, so through the early 1800s the city's black population didn't grow significantly. The State of New York finally abolished slavery in 1827.

After abolition, many of New York's African-Americans sought to acquire education and careers. Before the Civil War, New York City's African-American population ranged from educated professionals to working-class laborers. The African-American professional class built homes in Harlem, where they established a genteel community of doctors, lawyers, and educators as well as artists, musicians, and writers. Many middle-class African-Americans entered foodservice, working in restaurants and hotels and as domestic cooks; in this capacity they profoundly enriched the city's already complex cuisine.

FACTOR 4
After the Civil War, many African-Americans from the South migrated to New York City, introducing a cooking style that would become known as soul food.

After Emancipation, New York's African-American population swelled as tens of thousands migrated north. Many settled in Harlem, opening food stores and restaurants for their fellow displaced Southerners (Figure 16.11). By the 1920s, adventurous whites began visiting Harlem, drawn at first to the neighborhood's jazz clubs and quickly discovering the food scene as well. By the 1960s, when the term *soul food* was coined, Harlem was well known for top-level soul food restaurants such as Sylvia's, Copeland's, and Charles's Southern Kitchen.

FIGURE 16.11

Harlem, street scene circa 1900.
Courtesy of the Library of Congress,
LC-DIG-fsa-8a29959

FACTOR 4
Greek immigrants opened mainstream sandwich shops and diners.

The Greeks: Coffee Shops and Diners

Between 1890 and 1924, approximately 450,000 Greeks arrived in America, with 70,000 more arriving before World War II. Although authentic Greek cuisine is well represented in New York City and other urban areas, Greek immigration most profoundly impacted mainstream foodservice. Through the 20th century, Greek immigrants opened luncheonettes, sandwich shops, and diners serving American national cuisine food at reasonable prices. By the late 1960s, Greek-owned coffee shops were so prevalent that the blue-and-white Hellenic-design cardboard coffee cup was a New York City icon, and the television show *Saturday Night Live* launched a series of skits based on a grouchy Greek restaurateur.

Beyond cheeseburgers and chips, Greek-operated sandwich shops also feature souvlaki, or skewered grilled meat, and gyro (YEE-row), a mixture of ground lamb and beef compressed into a cylinder and roasted on a vertical spit. Both meats typically are wrapped in yeasted flatbread with lettuce, tomatoes, onions, and a garlicky yogurt sauce. By the late 1960s, most East Coast diners were owned and operated by Greek-Americans. Today Greek salads, souvlaki, gyros, hummus, and stuffed grape leaves have entered the American national cuisine repertoire.

FIGURE 16.12

The 1939 World's Fair placed the world's cuisines on New York City's doorstep. Courtesy of The New York City Library

■□■ WORLD CUISINES AT THE WORLD'S FAIR

The 1939 World's Fair, held in New York City's Flushing Meadow, was a seminal event in the history of American dining (Figure 16.12). Although the fair was conceived to showcase the wonders of modern technology, for many visitors it became a gigantic food festival. Twenty nations presented restaurants offering their most representative dishes, literally placing the best of world cuisines on New York City's doorstep. The fair's ethnic restaurants made the strongest impact on middle-class New Yorkers living nearby. Many made repeated visits solely for the purpose of dining out. The World's Fair experience opened a new world of eating to a dining public that previously considered spaghetti an exotic foreign food. At the fair they sampled dishes as diverse as Brazilian *feijoada*, Cuban *arroz con pollo*, and Russian *blinis*—all within the limits of their home city.

The World's Fair experience, combined with foreign travel during and after World War II, gave mainstream New Yorkers a taste for ethnic foods that grew stronger throughout the 20th century. The resulting proliferation of ethnic restaurants and food shops made New York City truly the food capital of the world.

■□■ THE SECOND FRENCH INVASION

Although New York City first experienced French cooking in the 1830s, a hundred years later what passed for French food in most American restaurants was a tired, outdated version of Continental cuisine. For the 1939 World's Fair, the French government assembled a syndicate of restaurateurs and charged them with reproducing a contemporary French restaurant in Flushing Meadow. Called *Le Restaurant du Pavillon de France*, or the French Pavilion, this restaurant introduced New Yorkers to authentic French haute cuisine. In doing so, it launched the second French invasion of New York City.

FACTOR 4
The 1939 World's Fair brought a second wave of French chefs to New York City.

When the World's Fair closed at the end of 1940, many of the French Pavilion's staff elected to stay. Manager Henri Soulé (ahn-REE soo-LAY) opened a restaurant in midtown Manhattan named Le Pavillon (luh pah-vee-OHN) in honor of the restaurant that had brought him to America. For many years Le Pavillon was considered the finest French restaurant in New York—and by extension, in America. Henri Soulé was known as a perfectionist who could be extremely tough on staff and purveyors. But his dedication and attention to detail made the restaurant stand out among its peers. The combination of exquisite food, exemplary service, and Soulé's imperious yet gracious presence in the front of the house made Le Pavillon *the* place to go in New York.

Le Pavillon was a training ground for many of New York City's finest chefs and spawned several other top-level French restaurants. After moving Le Pavillon to a new location, Soulé opened yet another restaurant, La Côte Basque (lah coat BASK), at the original site. After leaving the French Pavilion to enlist in the U.S. Army, chef Pierre Franey (pee-YAIR frah-NAY) returned to New York City as Le Pavillon's executive chef. Franey became world-famous as a chef and food writer, penning the *New York Times*'s popular "60-Minute Gourmet" column for twenty years and teaming with Craig Claiborne to author several cookbooks. Le Pavillon alumnus Fred Decré (duh-KRAY) opened La Caravelle (lah kar-ah-VELL), the favorite restaurant of Jacqueline Onassis. Yet another Le Pavillon chef, Ferdinand Metz, became president of the Culinary Institute of America.

The legacy of Le Pavillon and classical French cuisine lived on in a French restaurant called Lutèce (loo-TESS). In 1961, with consultation from James Beard, Lutèce proprietor André Surmain (ahn-DRAY soor-MAN) hired a young Alsatian chef named André Soltner (ahn-DRAY solt-NAY) and instructed him to prepare regional French food made with seasonal ingredients. Soltner's Alsatian onion tart became one of the restaurant's signature dishes, and the young chef eventually became the restaurant's owner. Lutèce remained New York's most popular and highly respected French restaurant well into the 1990s, finally closing its doors in 2004.

■□■ THE FOUR SEASONS

The late 1950s ushered in some of the most radical social change the nation had ever experienced. Artists and intellectuals led an avant-garde movement that embraced the modern. The post–World War II economic boom was in full swing, and New York City underwent a building frenzy. When European architect Ludwig Mies Van der Rohe was commissioned to design the Seagram Building on Park Avenue, he did so in the stark, elegant International Style for which he was world famous. The owners determined that a building of such architectural significance should house a restaurant of equal stature. Rather than leasing out the restaurant space to a single entrepreneur, Seagram brought in Restaurant Associates, one of the nation's earliest and most important foodservice consulting firms.

JAMES BEARD

Although a native Oregonian, James Beard (Figure 16.13) became a New Yorker at an early age. As a cooking teacher and food writer Beard tirelessly defended and promoted American regional cooking and has been called the Dean of American Cuisine. After his death in 1985, Mr. Beard's Greenwich Village townhouse became headquarters of the James Beard Foundation, a nonprofit organization dedicated to America's culinary heritage and diversity. The foundation awards numerous culinary scholarships and grants. Its many events enable America's best chefs and winemakers to showcase their talents in New York City.

The concept developed by Restaurant Associates was as elegant and modern as the building. Called The Four Seasons, the restaurant featured a menu that changed four times a year to reflect the seasons, and used primarily fresh food products from American sources (Figure 16.14). Although today most fine dining restaurants change their menus seasonally and many use in-season ingredients, at the time this was a revolutionary idea. In the late 1950s most restaurant menus were written at opening and revamped rarely, if ever. Most used the same canned or frozen foods throughout the year. Few featured local specialty items. For New York City, a top-level restaurant serving primarily American dishes, listed on the menu in English, was also a radical idea. Until The Four Seasons, fine food meant French food. Nonetheless, Restaurant Associates selected two European chefs, Executive Chef Albert Stockli (ahl-BARE SHTOCK-lee) and Pastry Chef Albert Kumin (ahl-BARE KOO-man), to lead the kitchens. Although Americans James Beard and Mimi Sheraton were called in as consultants, the United States had not yet produced chefs of the required caliber.

FIGURE 16.13

James Beard Photo by Dan Wynn, © Elizabeth Wynn and Courtesy of the James Beard Foundation

FIGURE 16.14

One of The Four Seasons' two main dining rooms, the pool room is decorated for spring. Courtesy The Four Seasons Restaurant

Despite the fact that The Four Seasons cuisine was based on French techniques and sensibilities, many of the dishes Stockli and Kumin created were thoroughly American in concept. Indeed, a 1959 *Holiday* magazine article dubbed The Four Seasons cooking "The New American Cuisine," the first print citation recognizing this nascent culinary movement.

Although The Four Seasons won critical acclaim and quickly became a New York City institution, it didn't prove financially successful. Beloved by Manhattan's elite, The Four Seasons intimidated many diners, in particular the out-of-town visitors so important to the success of high-end New York City restaurants. As its novelty faded and New York City's upper classes moved on to newer restaurants, revenues declined. However, in 1973 the restaurant was purchased by the team of Tom Margittai (MAR-jet-tie) and Paul Kovi (KOH-vee), who brought in Chef Seppi Renggli (SEP-pee REN-glee) to head the kitchen. This dynamic team breathed new life into The Four Seasons, and continued its tradition of excellence until 1995, when new ownership guided the restaurant into the 21st century.

The importance of The Four Seasons in the evolution of American fine dining can't be overemphasized. Spectacular, audacious, and ahead of its time, The Four Seasons gave birth to modern American cuisine.

■ NOUVELLE CUISINE:
□ THE THIRD FRENCH
■ INVASION

In the late 1970s first New York and then the nation were overtaken by yet another invasion of French cuisine. This time it wasn't French *chefs* taking over New York City's restaurant scene—instead, it was a revolutionary new culinary philosophy called *nouvelle cuisine*. This important culinary movement is discussed in Chapter 17, presented on this book's companion website.

In New York City's restaurants, young American chefs immediately fell under nouvelle cuisine's spell. New Yorkers found early nouvelle cuisine restaurants, such as Le Plaisir (luh play-ZEE), Dodin-Bouffant (doh-dan-boo-FAHN), and Leslie Revsin's Restaurant Leslie, shockingly different from any restaurant they had previously experienced. Yet many nouvelle cuisine ideas and practices soon infiltrated virtually every upscale restaurant in New York. Meats, seafood, and vegetables were cooked more lightly; sauces were thinner; portions were smaller; and food was presented on plates rather than on platters. The nouvelle cuisine movement gave American chefs permission to innovate. Finally—and most important for America's restaurants—it urged a return to regional cooking.

■ AMERICAN COOKING
□ IN NEW YORK CITY

In the late 1970s, New York City chefs and restaurateurs initiated the rediscovery of American regional cooking. Validated by The Four Seasons, blessed by nouvelle cuisine, and promoted by young chefs in search of their roots, the revitalization of American regional cuisines emerged as the nation's most important culinary movement of the late 20th century.

Although traditional regional cuisines are based on home cooking, they were saved by professionals. By 1980, convenience foods and restaurant meals were popular and fewer people were spending time in the kitchen. Cooking as a hobby was declining. Aware that America's regional cuisines were in danger of being lost, chefs and food writers took up the cause of preserving them. Restaurant chefs sought to reproduce the authentic flavors, textures, and food pairings of traditional regional cuisines interpreted as contemporary dishes with modern presentations. Some chefs specialized in a particular region; others opened restaurants showcasing a broad spectrum of American regional cuisines. Many of the best were located in New York City.

In the mid-1970s, America was consumed with preparations for its bicentennial celebration. At the same time unprecedented prosperity had led to a building boom. In 1971 the World Trade Center in lower Manhattan was finished and awaiting foodservice operations equal in stature to the tallest building in the world. Joe Baum and Michael Whiteman headed the firm chosen to tackle the daunting task. In addition to feeding more than 50,000 people a day in multiple venues, they were charged with creating a penthouse restaurant featuring American regional cuisine. With the help of menu consultants James Beard and Barbara Kafka, the restaurant opened in time for the 1976 bicentennial. Windows on the World (Figure 16.15) featured a contemporary American menu based on fresh ingredients from domestic sources. In addition, the concept included two ancillary operations: Cellar in the Sky, dedicated to wine-food pairing; and the Hors d'Oeuverie, featuring a grazing menu. For eighteen years Windows on the World remained a standard-bearer of American regional cuisine.

FIGURE 16.15
Windows on the World occupied a spectacular space on the 106th floor of the North Tower of the World Trade Center. NY Daily News via Getty Images

Windows on the World closed briefly during a 1993 bombing incident, after which it reopened with an international menu. When the World Trade Center was destroyed by terrorists on September 11, 2001, seventy-nine Windows on the World employees perished.

The next champion of American regional cuisines was Culinary Institute of America graduate Larry Forgione, executive chef of Brooklyn's River Café in the late 1970s. Forgione wasn't satisfied with the quality of commercially raised meats and produce and disliked using imported ingredients. Determined to find American sources, he began a search for farm-raised products and seasonal specialties in order to build a menu based on domestic foods. In 1980 he persuaded an upstate New York farmer to produce naturally raised chickens for him and is credited with coining the term *free range*. Forgione was also the first chef to list the provenance of ingredients on the menu, citing not only where the food item came from but also the name of the producer. In 1983 Forgione opened his own restaurant, An American Place, on Manhattan's Upper East Side. Representative of his style are dishes such as cedar-planked salmon with soft corn pudding; and bison carpaccio. After several moves, An American Place is now located in St. Louis, Missouri.

Gotham Bar and Grill is a Greenwich Village landmark (Figure 16.16). Since 1985, when Chef Alfred Portale took over the kitchen, Gotham has been turning out new American cuisine dishes prepared with the freshest and best ingredients. Portale revolutionized modern plate presentation by creating vertical plate arrangements in an architectural style. However, in Portale's kitchen presentation never takes precedence over flavor. A chef with deep understanding of culinary history and tradition, Portale creates combinations that surprise but never confound. Portale's menu changes frequently and features seasonal ingredients. For more than 25 years, Gotham has been praised for excellent ser-

vice and remarkable consistency, making it one of America's finest restaurants.

In 1985 Danny Meyer opened the Union Square Café, an American cuisine restaurant with a strong focus on hospitality (Figure 16.17). The welcoming atmosphere and consistently excellent food are responsible for Union Square Café's record-setting status as the New York City Zagat Survey's number one restaurant for seven consecutive years. In 1994 Meyer expanded his operations to include the Gramercy Tavern, also serving seasonal American fare and, in 2003, an American regional barbeque restaurant called Blue Smoke. Meyer is a strong supporter of New York City's Greenmarkets (p. 801). His progressive employment policies are a model for the industry, providing his staff with a beneficial working environment and ample opportunities for advancement.

In addition to the restaurants profiled here, Jonathan Waxman's Jams, Ann Rosenzweig's Arcadia, and Karen Hubert Allison's Hubert's were instrumental in defining new American cuisine. The 1980s craze for Southwestern art and décor initiated a number of Southwestern cuisine restaurants, among them Arizona 206 and Bobby Flay's Mesa Grill. The decade also brought an influx of Cajun restaurants inspired by Paul Prudhomme.

FIGURE 16.16
Gotham Bar and Grill
Courtesy Bob Shepherd

FIGURE 16.17
Union Square Café Courtesy Union Square Café, New York, NY

NEW YORK CITY FOOD MARKETS

Although New York City residents are better known for eating out and ordering in, dedicated home cooks compensate for small kitchens and busy lives with an incredible selection of ingredients available virtually on their doorsteps. Nearly every block includes a grocery/convenience store offering fresh produce, high-quality cheeses, and respectable wines as well as prepared foods. Small by suburban standards, New York City supermarkets pack a wide array of food products into a limited amount of space.

New York City's love affair with ethnic foods means that New Yorkers have access to ingredients from around the globe. Some ethnic food shops are tiny and obscure; others cover full city blocks. Some cater to only one nationality; others are truly international in scope.

A few New York City food markets can truly be called emporiums, noteworthy for their large inventory of goods. These stand out above other stores for quality, variety, and excellent service. Foremost among them was Balducci's, a Greenwich Village institution that, sadly, closed its doors in 2003 after nearly a hundred years in business. Today Zabar's and Dean & Deluca, profiled below, serve food-loving New Yorkers.

In 1976 the Council on the Environment of New York City opened its first open-air farmer's market in Union Square and changed the way hundreds of thousands of New Yorkers bought their food. New York's officially sponsored venues are called Greenmarkets. The twofold Greenmarket mission is to promote local agriculture and enable city residents to purchase fresh local foods directly from producers. Today New York City has 24 farmer's market locations, with Union Square Greenmarket the largest (Figure 16.19). At Greenmarkets shoppers experience truly seasonal produce, as only fruits and vegetables grown within 100 miles of the city are permitted. In addition, grower-

vendors offer meats and poultry, honey, baked goods, and crafts. Local fishermen display regional seafood. More than 100 restaurants buy produce from New York City Greenmarkets, passing on freshness and value to their customers.

FIGURE 16.18

Zabar's is one of New York City's premier specialty food stores.
Courtesy Heidi Hart, Fox Run Farm, Wrightsville, PA

FIGURE 16.19

Union Square Greenmarket. Courtesy Heidi Hart, Fox Run Farm, Wrightsville, PA

NEW YORK CITY'S FAMOUS FOOD EMPORIUMS

Zabar's is an Upper West Side institution known for smoked fish, fine cheeses, prepared foods, an international selection of groceries, and upscale cookware (Figure 16.18). Founded in 1934 as a Jewish "appetizing", this family-owned business is the food store of choice when neighborhood residents need a ready-to-eat meal or ingredients for a dinner party. On Sunday mornings Zabar's is packed with New Yorkers buying bagels and nova, fresh-squeezed orange juice, and the *New York Times*.

Dean & Deluca brought specialty foods to Soho, a former warehouse district turned residential neighborhood, in 1977. In addition to its diverse selection of food products, Dean & Deluca is known for professional-quality cookware and private-label ingredients marketed in distinctive industrial-style packaging.

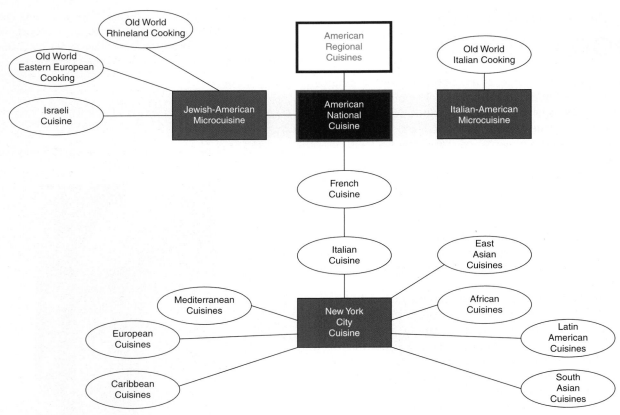

FIGURE 16.20
The Development of New York City Cuisine

FIGURE 16.21
New York City's ethnic enclaves.

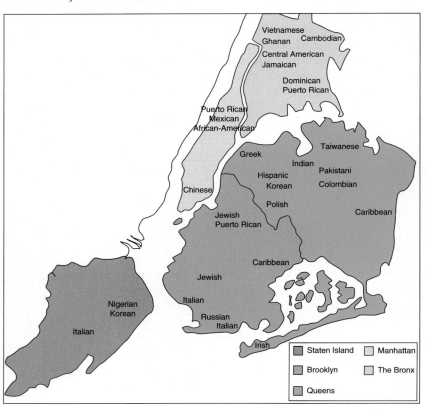

LATE-20th-CENTURY IMMIGRANTS

FACTOR 4
Today immigrants from around the globe ensure a lively food scene in New York City's outer boroughs.

Because of changes in American immigration policy in 1964 and the aftermath of the Vietnam War, a new wave of immigration reached America's shores, increasing exponentially after the elimination of discriminatory quotas in 1976. Many of these late-20th-century immigrants entered the country through New York City, and many stayed there (Figure 16.21). The 2000 census counted nearly three million foreign-born New Yorkers, and the 2010 census is sure to add even more.

Southeast Asians flocked to the city after the Vietnam War and as a result of political unrest in other nations. In addition to Vietnamese, significant numbers of Thai, Indonesian, Malaysian, Burmese, and Cambodian nationals settled in

New York City, many entering foodservice in both ethnic and mainstream restaurants. Restaurants serving Southeast Asian cuisine greatly expanded mainstream New Yorkers' dining choices with dishes such as *pho* soup, *pad Thai* noodles, skewered meat satay, fish and banana heart soup, and green papaya salad.

In the Queens neighborhood of Elmhurst, nearly every shop sign sports Asian-language characters. In addition to corner groceries selling Asian foods, several of the neighborhood's urban strip malls include large supermarkets complete with full-service butcher counters, fish tanks, and produce departments. Shoppers buy blue-footed chickens from China, durians from Indonesia, and pickled baby eels from Korea. Cooks choose from more than 20 kinds of rice and a hundred varieties of noodles. Cookware and tableware fill entire aisles. Take-out counters offer a pan-Asian selection of prepared foods (Figure 16.23). The neighborhood's restaurants are equally pan-Asian in scope, ranging from tiny Vietnamese *pho* joints to large family-style eateries. Elmhurst is the site of the original Penang, a Malaysian restaurant that sprouted a dynasty of hip copies in Manhattan and other East Coast cities.

Flushing, Queens, has excellent Asian food shopping and a lively street scene (Figure 16.22). Flushing's food stores are of similar size and scope to those in Elmhurst. There, vendors offer street food such as fried noodles, steamed dumplings, and tapioca-laced bubble tea. Among a pan-Asian array of restaurants, those serving Thai and Vietnamese food stand out for excellence.

Among the many Asians immigrating to New York City, Koreans profoundly affected the city's foodways by purchasing and operating corner groceries. Today the Korean salad bar includes fruit and vegetable salads as well as an international selection of hot and cold prepared foods priced by the pound. Many Korean restaurants feature Korean barbeque (p. 664).

Immigrants from India and Pakistan arrived in the 1980s, many working in health care, computer technology, and other

FIGURE 16.23

Asian-style roast ducks are a favorite take-home meal. Courtesy Heidi Hart, Fox Run Farm, Wrightsville, PA

science-related pursuits. Pakistani and North Indian Punjabi-style restaurants serve rich, aromatic meat-based dishes, including lamb korma and basmati rice biriyani. South Indian restaurants feature vegetarian fare such as dosai, rice-and-lentil pancakes served with souplike vegetable sambaar and coconut chutney. Jackson Heights, Queens, is the center of New York City's Indian and Pakistani food culture (Figure 16.24). On a typical Saturday afternoon the streets swarm with sari-clad shoppers, Bollywood music blares from loudspeakers, and the aroma of sizzling spices fills the air. Neighborhood businesses include several large supermarkets dedicated entirely to Indo-Pak ingredients. Outdoor

FIGURE 16.22

An open-air Asian vegetable stand in Queens. Courtesy Bob Shepherd

FIGURE 16.24

Jackson Heights shops sell a variety of spices used in Indian and Pakistani cuisines. © Richard Levine / Alamy

displays overflow with Indian produce. Several shops sell **halal** meats: lamb, mutton, or goat slaughtered according to Islamic dietary law. Among the most popular restaurants are halal kabob houses serving Pakistani-style meats grilled on skewers. South Indian vegetarian restaurants serve the observant Hindu population. Tiny storefronts offer Indian sweets and snacks, and Indian buffet restaurants cater to price-conscious families.

Among the new wave's first Latin American immigrants were people from Colombia and the Dominican Republic, bringing sancocho soup, cheese-filled arepa breads, and meat-filled empanada turnovers (Figure 16.25). Today Dominicans are New York City's largest immigrant group, settled primarily in Washington Heights. Puerto Ricans are a major influence in New York City; their food culture and cuisine are discussed in Chapter 15. The late 1980s and 1990s saw a huge influx of Mexicans, many arriving from California. Thus, Mexican and Mexican-American restaurants proliferate. Today Latin American immigrants dominate foodservice in New York City. In addition to working in restaurants featuring their own cuisines, many have risen through the ranks to positions of importance in New York's American, European, and Asian cuisine restaurants.

Numerous immigrants from Jamaica, Trinidad, and Haiti reside in New York City, many in the Bronx. These West Indians have opened grocery stores and small restaurants featuring home cooking. The Jamaican patty, a flaky pastry turnover filled with beef, chicken, or cabbage, is now a New York City street food, often available in corner groceries and pizzerias. Jamaican jerk food (p. 734) is popular take-out fare. Because they speak the language and understand the cuisine, Haitians are frequently on the staffs of the city's French restaurants.

When the Soviet Union relaxed its emigration restrictions in 1971, tens of thousands of Russian immigrants arrived in New York City. Today Brooklyn's Brighton Beach is known as Little Odessa. A ten-block stretch of Coney Island Avenue houses

scores of Russian-owned businesses. Food stores predominate; the largest is M & I International Foods, where diners enjoy smoked salmon, potato pancakes, cucumber salad, and meat-filled *pirozhki* pastry turnovers at bargain prices. Brighton Beach restaurants include huge nightclubs serving Soviet-era Russian food and small cafés serving authentic Uzbek and Georgian cuisine. Russians also patronize Turkish restaurants serving lamacun (Turkish pizzas) and Turkish kabobs.

New York City's late-20th-century immigrants did not create hybrid, ethnic-American cuisines. Nor are 21st-century immigrants likely to do so. In a city where ingredients and cooking equipment from around the world are available virtually next door, today's immigrants have no need to improvise. Instead, home cooks and ethnic restaurants will continue preparing authentic versions of their home cuisines. However, the presence of world cuisines restaurants and food stores in New York City—and throughout the nation—has inspired a new generation of American chefs to expand their repertoires and think about cooking in different ways.

■ NEW YORK
□ HAUTE ETHNIC

Most immigrant cuisines are first represented by casual, inexpensive restaurants opened by nonprofessionals serving simple food to their countrymen. However, as immigrant populations grow and prosper, eventually entrepreneurs with sufficient knowledge, talent, and financial capital launch upscale restaurants serving the finest dishes of their nations' cuisines in comfortable and evocative settings. Food writers call these venues **haute ethnic** (OAT ethnic). New York City leads the nation in haute ethnic restaurants.

Opened in 1966, T. T. Wang's Shun Lee Dynasty featured an elegant interior tastefully decorated with antique Chinese artifacts, flawless service, and an authentic regional Chinese menu (Figure 16.26). Shun Lee was the first Asian restaurant to be awarded a four-star rating by the *New York Times*—an accomplishment that would not be duplicated until the mid-1990s.

The late 1980s through the 1990s was the golden age of New York City haute ethnic. Upscale Indian cuisine was represented by Akbar, Darbar, Dawat, and the glamorous Nirvana, located

FIGURE 16.25
Bodegas offer home-style foods to go as well as Latin American groceries.

FIGURE 16.26
Shun Lee Dynasty was the first of New York's haute ethnic restaurants. Courtesy Heidi Hart, Fox Run Farm, Wrightsville, PA

in a penthouse overlooking Central Park. Rosa Mexicano and Zarela introduced regional Mexican cuisine. David K's rivaled Shun Lee for luxury regional Chinese.

By the end of the 20th century, the food in New York's finest ethnic restaurants had reached a level of sophistication often unknown in the country of their cuisine's origin. American chefs immersed themselves in ethnic cuisines, reproducing dishes from both peasant and royal court recipes. Chefs from other nations created new dishes in their own tradition. The result was a new kind of ethnic restaurant serving one chef's personal interpretation of a foreign cuisine. The first of this type was Vong, a French-Thai fantasy opened by Jean-Georges Vongerichten (zhan-zhorj von-geh-REESH-ten). Japanese Kaiseki cuisine was reinterpreted by Nobuyuki Matsuhisa at his namesake Nobu. Indian cuisine was liberated from classic constraints by Floyd Cardoz at Tabla.

THE NEW YORK CITY MELTING POT IN THE 21st CENTURY

Despite the Wall Street crisis and recession of 2008, New York City continues to thrive as America's capital of cuisine. Along with food fads and temporary trends, the city initiates and supports important culinary movements that eventually resonate throughout the nation.

In 2005 a group of 35 former staff members of Windows on the World opened Colors, the nation's first totally employee-owned restaurant. Hailing from 20 foreign nations, these survivors created a restaurant concept that is the essence of the New York experience. Colors offers a menu of small dishes inspired by world cuisines but made with at least 50 percent locally sourced ingredients. These innovative new entrepreneurs typify the ideals of both the American dream and the New York City melting pot.

THE ITALIAN-AMERICAN AND JEWISH-AMERICAN MICROCUISINES

Of the many immigrants arriving in New York City in the late 1800s, two groups made an indelible mark on the city's culinary landscape.

Escaping a harsh economic situation in the south of Italy, Italian immigrants established an ethnic enclave in lower Manhattan where they created one of America's most popular hybrid cuisines.

At roughly the same time, Eastern European Jews fleeing religious and cultural persecution settled in another part of lower Manhattan. Observing complex dietary restrictions in their new homeland, Jewish-Americans created a hybrid home-cooking style, and opened appetizing stores and delis. These culinary developments became the Jewish-American microcuisine.

Visit this book's companion website at www.pearsonhighered.com/sackett to learn more about the Italian-American and Jewish-American microcuisines. Following are some photos relating to these two microcuisines.

An Italian-American enjoys clams on the half shell purchased from a street vendor's cart, circa 1900. Courtesy of the Library of Congress, LC-D4-13642

Italian-American grocery, circa 1900. Courtesy of the Library of Congress

A Lombardi's pizza emerges from their coal-fired hearth oven.
Courtesy Bob Shepherd

A Jewish family celebrates the Passover seder. Noam Armonn/Shutterstock

An Italian-American bread bakery. Courtesy of the Library of Congress

Falafel. Demark/Shutterstock

Carnegie Deli. Angus Oborn/Rough Guides Dorling Kindersley

◻ **TABLE 16.1 NEW YORK CITY DEFINING DISHES**

The New York City melting pot has a virtually limitless number of ethnic dishes, many of which have become fixtures of the city's cuisine—far too many to be listed. As a city that traditionally embraces and then abandons new food trends, at any given time New York may have had a particular set of defining dishes that lasted for a few years and then vanished. The following table lists the most enduring dishes associated with New York City. Dishes that are part of Continental cuisine are noted with an asterisk (*).

ITEM NAME	HISTORY	DOMINANT INGREDIENTS AND METHOD	MORE
MANHATTAN CLAM CHOWDER	Perhaps because of Italian-American influence, the Manhattan version of this classic American soup replaces New England's cream with tomatoes.	Chopped clams and clam liquor are simmered with bacon, onions, potatoes, thyme, and tomato concassée.	Italian-American cooks may include green bell peppers, oregano, or marjoram.
VICHYSSOISE*	A chilled version of the classic French *potage Parmentièr*, this soup was popularized by Chef Louis Diat (loo-EE dee-AH) at the Ritz-Carlton Hotel.	Leeks, potatoes, and chicken stock are simmered together, puréed smooth with heavy cream, chilled, and garnished with snipped chives.	Vichyssoise is often presented on ice in a shrimp cocktail chiller.
CLAMS CASINO	Chef Julius Keller's claim to creating this famous dish at the Narragansett Pier Casino in 1917 has been disputed. Similar recipes exist in print as early as the 1880s.	Cherrystone or topneck clams on the half shell are topped with a composed butter prepared with shallot or scallion, red and green bell pepper, garlic, and lemon, then topped with a piece of bacon. Baking on a bed of rock salt prevents tipping and maintains temperature.	Although seafood with smoked pork is a New England flavor combination, the inclusion of bell peppers and garlic in the modern version of clams casino—and its popularity in Little Italy restaurants—make it a New York City dish.
WALDORF SALAD*	This salad was created by *maître d'hôtel* Oscar Tschirky (TCHEER-kee) at the Waldorf Hotel in the late 1800s.	Diced raw apples, celery, and walnuts are bound with mayonnaise and served on a bed of greens.	Oscar's original salad did not include walnuts.
ICEBERG WEDGE WITH THOUSAND ISLAND DRESSING	Thousand Island dressing was popularized by Oscar Tschirky at the Waldorf Hotel. When iceberg lettuce became available in the early 20th century (p. 553), this salad became standard New York steakhouse fare. It lost favor during the 1970s and then saw a brief resurgence in the 1990s when nostalgia-themed Continental restaurants came into vogue.	Thousand Island dressing combines mayonnaise with bottled chili sauce, minced pimento-stuffed olives, green bell peppers, scallions, hard-cooked eggs, and parsley.	
SHRIMP COCKTAIL	In the early 20th century popular alcoholic mixed drinks, called cocktails, were served in tall stemmed glasses. During Prohibition, restaurants stocked with useless cocktail glasses began serving chilled seafood in them, and called the resulting dish a "cocktail."	Shredded lettuce and cocktail sauce (p. 206) are placed in the cocktail glass and steamed, chilled, peeled, tail-on shrimp are hung from the rim. Large shrimp are preferred. Saltines or oyster crackers are the traditional accompaniment.	By the 1950s manufacturers of restaurant serviceware were producing shrimp cocktail chillers, presentation vessels consisting of a bottom cup for crushed ice and a top cup for sauce and seafood.
CARPACCIO	Although this dish was invented at Harry's Bar in Venice, Italy, in 1950, it became standard New York City restaurant fare in the 1980s.	Thin-sliced filet of beef is dressed with a light mayonnaise sauce flavored with mustard, shallot, and anchovy paste. Accents include shaved Parmesan cheese, capers, and brunoise-cut onions.	Nouvelle cuisine chefs replaced the beef with bright-red raw tuna.
STEAK TARTARE	This classic dish first appeared on French menus around 1900, but it became widely fashionable after World War II. In the 1980s, lean and carbohydrate-free steak tartare became a staple of the businessman's "power lunch."	Chilled raw filet is hand-chopped and mixed with Dijon mustard, shallots, nonpareil capers, parsley, Worcestershire sauce, bottled hot sauce, sea salt, freshly ground pepper, raw egg yolk, and first-press olive oil.	As an appetizer, steak tartare is served with toast points; as a luncheon entrée, it's accompanied by vinaigrette salad and French fries.

(continued)

☐ TABLE 16.1 NEW YORK CITY DEFINING DISHES (continued)

ITEM NAME	HISTORY	DOMINANT INGREDIENTS AND METHOD	MORE
TUNA TARTARE	In the 1980s, nouvelle cuisine chefs reconstructed steak tartare by substituting raw tuna for beef.	Sashimi-grade, brunoise-cut tuna is mixed with the same seasonings as steak tartare (p. 807).	Tuna tartare is served as an appetizer, often presented in a cocktail glass.
PASTA PRIMAVERA	This much imitated and variously interpreted dish was created in the mid-1970s by Sirio Maccioni (SEE-ree-oh mach-kee-OH-nee), owner of Le Cirque (luh SEERK), a prominent New York City French restaurant.	Recipes vary, but the original, as it was served at the restaurant, is composed of fresh fettuccine tossed in a Parmesan cream reduction with chanterelles, asparagus tips, fresh peas, broccoli florets, and zucchini with diced tomato and basil.	Why a dish literally named after springtime should include summer vegetables and herbs is a question that remains unanswered.
LOBSTER NEWBERG*	This Delmonico's creation was originally named after patron Ben Wenberg, who purportedly taught Chef Charles Ranhofer to prepare it, using then-exotic cayenne pepper; when Wenberg had a falling out with Charles Delmonico, the owner simply changed the name to "Newberg."	Steamed, shelled lobster meat is sautéed in butter and then sauced with a Madeira cream reduction enriched with egg yolk and butter and seasoned with a dash of cayenne.	The dish is often served over toast points or in a *vol-au-vent* pastry shell.
CHICKEN DIVAN*	This elaborate preparation was the signature dish of New York City's Divan (duh-VAN) Parisienne restaurant in the 1950s.	Blanched broccoli florets and poached, sliced chicken are layered in a gratin, then topped with a sauce composed of béchamel and hollandaise mousseline folded together. The dish is then sprinkled with Parmesan cheese and glazed under a broiler.	Modern versions replace the compound sauce with a simple chicken velouté and may include Cheddar cheese and slivered almonds.
STEAK DIANE*	Steak Diane emerged on New York City restaurant menus during the 1950s when tableside preparation of flambée dishes was fashionable. The Colony, the Sherry-Netherland Hotel, and the Drake Hotel all claim to have created the dish.	A thin beef filet or sirloin steak is pan-seared, flambéed with cognac, and then sauced in demi-glace seasoned with shallots and Worcestershire sauce. The sauce is finished with butter, minced parsley, and chives.	Alternative recipes include sherry and Dijon mustard.
STEAK WITH GREEN PEPPERCORN SAUCE	Green peppercorns preserved in vinegar or brine became a popular seasoning in New York City restaurants after they were introduced by nouvelle cuisine chefs in the 1970s.	After a beef filet or sirloin strip steak is pan-seared, the pan is deglazed with white wine and a pan sauce built with shallot, demi-glace, and crushed green peppercorns.	Some versions are finished with crème fraîche or heavy cream.
CORNED BEEF AND CABBAGE	19th century Irish immigrants nostalgic for the traditional dish *bacon and cabbage* were unable to buy Irish-style boiling bacon, a ham-like product. They substituted American corned beef, creating a new, hybrid dish.	Salt-cured beef brisket is poached in water with onions, parsley, peppercorns, and bay leaves. New potatoes and cabbage wedges are added near the end of cooking.	A carrot may be added to the broth for sweetness, but is never served because its orange color reminds Irish Catholics of Protestant Orangemen.
DELMONICO POTATOES*	This rich, creamy preparation is one of Delmonico's earliest dishes, dating to the 1830s.	Russet potatoes are par-boiled; julienned; simmered in cream seasoned with nutmeg, white pepper, and Parmesan cheese; and then gratinéed.	
NEW YORK CHEESECAKE	Cream cheese was first produced in New York in the 1870s. The term "New York" correctly applies to cheesecakes made exclusively with cream cheese, as opposed to the ricotta cheesecakes made by Italian-Americans.	Classic New York cheesecake is baked in a springform pan lined with a sweetened pastry crust. Junior's of Brooklyn introduced the innovation of baking the cheese custard on a spongecake base.	Crumb-crust cheesecakes are made in New York as well but are not considered classic New York fare—nor are flavored or topped cheesecakes.

☐ **TABLE 16.1 NEW YORK CITY DEFINING DISHES** *(continued)*

ITEM NAME	HISTORY	DOMINANT INGREDIENTS AND METHOD	MORE
CRÈME BRÛLÉE	Although similar caramel-glazed custards appear in British and Spanish cuisines, crème brûlée became associated with New York City when Chef Alain Sailhac (ah-LAH sigh-YAH) introduced the dish at Le Cirque in the late 1970s.	Rich vanilla custard is baked in a wide shallow dish and then chilled. The surface is coated with sugar and caramelized under a salamander or with a torch. After a second refrigeration, the caramel crust becomes brittle and crunchy.	Crème brûlée custard is sometimes flavored with mango, passion fruit, ginger, or lemongrass.
BLACKOUT CAKE	This beloved dessert was created by Brooklyn's famous Ebinger's Bakery.	Chocolate cake layers are filled and frosted with a pudding-like chocolate icing. After frosting, the entire cake is masked with chocolate cake crumbs.	

■ □ ■   STUDY QUESTIONS

1. Explain why and how the topography and location of New York City determined its economic and culinary development. Include agriculture, architecture, fishing, commerce, and immigration in your explanation.

2. Discuss the impact of Native American and first-settler foodways on the cuisine of New York City.

3. Discuss New York City's first "French invasion," listing several ways in which it influenced New York City restaurants and American national cuisine.

4. Discuss the impact of the Great Depression on New York City's restaurant scene. Include all types of foodservice operations in your discussion.

5. List three of New York City's most culinarily important immigrant groups and describe their contributions to the city's cooking and dining. (Exclude the Italian-American and Jewish-American microcuisines, on which you will be queried later.)

6. Discuss the impact of the 1939 World's Fair on New York City's restaurant scene.

7. Explain in detail New York City's role in the rediscovery and revitalization of American regional cuisines.

8. Recount the story of late-19th-century Italian-American immigration. Include in your discussion the evolution of Italian-American cuisine.

9. List and describe three defining dishes of the Italian-American microcuisine.

10. Recount the story of late-19th-century Jewish-American immigration. Explain kosher law and describe how its observance affected Jewish-Americans.

11. List and describe three defining dishes of the Jewish-American microcuisine.

12. Using the information in this chapter and your knowledge and imagination, develop a twelve-item New York City cuisine restaurant menu.

Manhattan Clam Chowder
with Oyster Crackers

yield: 1 (10-fl.-oz.) appetizer serving
(multiply × 4 for classroom turnout; adjust equipment sizes accordingly)

MASTER RECIPE

production		costing only
1 1/4 c.	Manhattan Clam Chowder	1/4 recipe
1 tsp.	chopped flat-leaf parsley	1/40 bunch a.p.
1	6" doily or cocktail napkin	1 each
3	Oyster Crackers	1/8 recipe

service turnout:
1. Stir the cold Manhattan Clam Chowder to evenly distribute the solids, and then ladle it into small saucepan. Heat just to the boil.
2. Plate the dish:
   a. Ladle the soup into a hot 12-oz. soup cup.
   b. Sprinkle the parsley on top.
   c. Place the cup on the left side of an 8" plate lined with a 6" doily.
   d. Arrange the Oyster Crackers on the right side of the plate.

RECIPE VARIATION
Quick Manhattan Clam Chowder
Replace the live clams with 10 fl. oz. canned chopped clams in juice. Omit step 1. Reduce the amount of white wine to 2 fl. oz. and add it in step 4.

COMPONENT RECIPE
MANHATTAN CLAM CHOWDER

yield: 5 c.

production		costing only
12	live chowder clams or large cherrystone clams	12 each or 1 doz.
1/2 c.	white wine	4 fl. oz.
±2 c.	bottled clam juice or Fish Stock	±16 fl. oz. or 1/8 recipe
3 oz.	fine-diced rindless smoked slab bacon	3 1/2 oz. a.p.
2 Tbsp.	butter	1 oz.
pinch	crushed dried red pepper	1/16 oz.
1/2 c.	medium-chopped yellow onion	2 1/2 oz. a.p.
1/2 c.	peeled, medium-chopped celery	1/10 head a.p.
1/4 c.	medium-chopped green bell pepper	2 oz. a.p.
1 tsp.	minced garlic	1/9 oz. a.p.
1 c.	canned diced tomatoes in juice	8 fl. oz.
4 oz.	peeled, 3/8"-diced russet potatoes	4 1/2 oz. a.p.
pinch	dried thyme	1/16 oz.
tt	kosher salt, optional	1/16 oz.

preparation:
1. Prepare the clams:
   a. Scrub the clams under cool running water.
   b. Place the clams in a nonreactive saucepan along with the wine. Cover and steam over high heat for about 3 minutes, until the clams have just opened.
   c. Remove the clams to a sheet tray and cool enough to handle.
   d. Strain the clam cooking liquid through damp cheesecloth. Pour it into a measuring cup and add enough clam juice to equal 3 1/2 c.
   e. Remove the clams from their shells and rinse them under cool running water to remove any grit. Blot dry.
   f. Chop the clams coarse and reserve all juices.
2. Combine the bacon and butter in a saucepan and fry over low heat until the bacon fat is rendered and the bacon almost crisp.
3. Add the dried red pepper, onion, celery, green bell pepper, and garlic. Sauté over medium heat until soft but not browned.
4. Add the tomatoes, potatoes, thyme, chopped clams and their juices, and clam juice.
5. Simmer uncovered, stirring occasionally, for about 15 minutes, until the clams and potatoes are tender and the flavors melded.
6. To create a slightly thicker broth, crush some of the potatoes and stir until they dissolve.
7. Taste and season with salt only if needed.

holding: open-pan cool and immediately refrigerate in a freshly sanitized, covered, nonreactive container up to 3 days

Tall Seafood Salad
with Avocado and Tobiko

yield: 1 (5-oz.) appetizer serving
(multiply × 4 for classroom turnout)

MASTER RECIPE

production		costing only
2 1/2 oz.	Poached Seafood for Salad	1/4 recipe
1/2	steamed, chilled, shelled 3/4-lb. lobster, claw meat intact, tail and arm meat diced	6 oz. a.p.
1 tsp.	minced flat-leaf parsley	1/40 bunch a.p.
1 Tbsp.	chiffonade fresh basil	1/40 bunch a.p.
2 Tbsp.	Red and Yellow Bell Pepper Curls, drained, blotted dry	1/8 recipe
1/4 c.	Lemon Vinaigrette, in squeeze bottle	1/4 recipe
1 oz.	baby lettuce mix, cleaned and dried	1 oz.
3	small romaine lettuce heart leaves, whole	1/2 oz.
1/2	cold firm-ripe western avocado	1/2 [40 ct.] avocado
1 tsp.	fresh lemon juice	1/16 [90 ct.] lemon
tt	medium-grind sea salt or kosher salt	1/16 oz.
2 tsp.	orange tobiko caviar	1/4 oz.

service turnout:

1. Place the Poached Seafood for Salad, diced lobster meat, parsley, basil, and about 2/3 of the Red and Yellow Bell Pepper Curls in a bowl and squeeze about half of the Lemon Vinaigrette over the top. Toss gently to combine.

2. Place the lettuce mix and whole romaine leaves in a separate bowl, squeeze about 1 Tbsp. lemon vinaigrette over the top, and toss with a rolling motion to coat lightly.

3. Moisten the lobster claw with the remaining Lemon Vinaigrette.

4. Peel the avocado half and cut it lengthwise into thin slices, placing them in an overlapping line on a piece of parchment as you work. Squeeze the lemon juice over the top and season with salt.

5. Wearing foodservice gloves, plate the dish:

   a. Mound the dressed seafood (except the claw) in the center of a cool 10" plate and form it into a tightly compacted cone. Holding the cone together with one hand, use your index finger to create a hollow center.

   b. Pick up the avocado-topped parchment sheet with your left hand, transfer the avocado slices to your right hand without disturbing their linear arrangement, and peel off the parchment. (Left-handers may do the opposite if it feels more comfortable.)

   c. Pick up the lobster claw with your left (or right) hand, then simultaneously apply the avocado slices and lobster claw to the sides of the seafood cone, wrapping them around the cone tightly and tucking in the ends. Squeeze the ingredients together gently but firmly to create a stable construction.

   d. Make a bouquet of the lettuce leaves and plant it firmly in the cone to make an upright plume.

   e. Place a mound of tobiko on the back side of the tip of a small, flexible offset spatula. Pull back the tip and then release it to fling the tobiko against the avocado slices and onto the plate.

   f. Scatter the remaining bell pepper curls around the plate well.

COMPONENT RECIPE
POACHED SEAFOOD FOR SALAD

yield: approx. 10 oz.

production		costing only
6 oz.	(20–30 ct.) dry-pack sea scallops	6 oz.
6 oz.	baby calamari, tubes only	6 oz.
1/2 c.	white wine	4 fl. oz.
1 c.	water	n/c
1	bay leaf	1/16 oz.
6	black peppercorns	1/16 oz.
1	thin slice yellow onion	1/4 oz. a.p.
tt	kosher salt	1/16 oz.

preparation:
1. Fabricate the seafood:
   a. Remove the tough adductor muscle from the scallops and cut them across the grain into 3/16" slices.
   b. Cut off and discard about 1/4" of the calamari tubes' pointed tips. Rinse the calamari tubes under cool running water inside and out, removing any entrails. Cut into 3/16" slices.
2. Prepare the poaching liquid: Combine the wine, water, bay leaf, peppercorns, onion, and salt in a small, nonreactive saucepan and bring to the simmer.
3. Prepare an ice bath of the correct size to accommodate the poaching saucepan.
4. Stir the scallops and calamari into the simmering poaching liquid, cover the pan, and cook for 20 seconds.
5. Uncover the pan and place it in the ice bath to quickly bring the seafood and poaching liquid to room temperature.
6. Remove the seafood from the saucepan and place it in a freshly sanitized container.
7. Remove and discard the bay leaf, peppercorns, and onion. Bring the poaching liquid to the boil. As it reduces, add to it any liquid that accumulates around the cooled seafood. Reduce to about 1/4 c. seafood glaze, and then cool to room temperature.
8. Mix the seafood glaze with the seafood.

holding: cover and refrigerate up to 2 days

COMPONENT RECIPE
RED AND YELLOW BELL PEPPER CURLS

yield: approx. 1/2 c.

production		costing only
4 oz.	cleaned red bell pepper	4 1/2 oz. a.p.
4 oz.	cleaned yellow bell pepper	4 1/2 oz. a.p.

preparation:
1. Place the peppers skin side down and pressed flat on the work surface. Cutting horizontally, shave off any high spots of flesh to leave each pepper section evenly thick throughout.
2. Cut the peppers into very fine, even julienne.
3. Soak the julienne peppers in ice water for about 1 hour, until they curl.

holding: prepare just enough for service (bell pepper curls become waterlogged after 5 or 6 hours, losing shape and flavor)

COMPONENT RECIPE
LEMON VINAIGRETTE

yield: 1 c.

production		costing only
1 Tbsp.	minced shallot	1/2 oz. a.p.
1 Tbsp.	Dijon mustard	1/2 fl. oz.
1 tsp.	sugar	1/6 oz.
2 tsp.	minced lemon zest	n/c
3 Tbsp.	fresh lemon juice	5/8 [90 ct.] lemon
tt	kosher salt	1/16 oz.
1/2 c.	gold-color pure olive oil	4 fl. oz.
as needed	additional lemon juice, optional	1/2 [90 ct.] lemon

preparation:
1. Place the shallot, mustard, sugar, lemon zest, 3 Tbsp. lemon juice, and salt in a small bowl or blender.
2. Whisk in the oil, or add it through the top opening while the blender is operating, to create an emulsified dressing.
3. Correct the acid-oil balance and correct the salt.

holding: at cool room temperature in a freshly sanitized squeeze bottle up to 3 hours; refrigerate up to 5 days; bring to room temperature and reblend before using

Hold the seafood salad cone together with one hand and use your index finger to create a hollow center.

Transfer the avocado slices to your right hand without disturbing their linear arrangement.

Simultaneously apply the avocado slices and lobster claw to the sides of the seafood cone.

Fling the tobiko against the avocado slices and onto the plate.

Clams Casino

yield: 1 (6-clam) appetizer serving
(multiply × 4 for classroom turnout)

MASTER RECIPE

production		costing only
1 1/2 c.	rock salt	12 oz.
6 pc.	Casino Stuffed Clams	1/4 recipe
1	lemon crown	1/2 [120 ct.] lemon
1	curly parsley sprig	1/20 bunch a.p.

service turnout:
1. Spread the rock salt on a 10" round sizzle pan or heatproof presentation platter. Gently press the Casino Stuffed Clams into the salt, leaving a 2" space in the center.
2. Place the platter in a 400°F oven and bake for 5 to 8 minutes, until the clams are heated through and the topping is bubbling.
3. Present the dish:
   a. Place the sizzle pan in its heatproof undertray, or place the presentation platter on a 12" plate lined with a folded linen napkin.
   b. Place the lemon crown in the center and top the crown with the parsley sprig.

COMPONENT RECIPE
CASINO BUTTER

yield: 12 oz.

production		costing only
2 oz.	medium-chopped red bell pepper	2 1/2 oz. a.p.
2 oz.	medium-chopped green bell pepper	2 1/2 oz. a.p.
1 tsp.	minced garlic	1/9 oz. a.p.
1 Tbsp.	minced shallot	2 oz. a.p.
1 Tbsp.	minced parsley	1/20 bunch a.p.
2 tsp.	minced lemon zest	n/c
2 tsp.	fresh lemon juice	1/8 [90 ct.] lemon
tt	fine-ground white pepper	1/16 oz.
dash	bottled hot sauce, such as Tabasco	1/16 fl. oz.
7 oz.	room-temperature butter	7 oz.

preparation:
1. Mix together all ingredients.

holding: refrigerate in a freshly sanitized, covered plastic container up to 2 days

COMPONENT RECIPE
CASINO STUFFED CLAMS

yield: 24 clams

production		costing only
24	live topneck clams	24
4	thin slices smoked bacon	2 oz.
12 oz.	room-temperature Casino Butter	1 recipe
1 1/2 c.	toasted fresh bread crumbs	3 3/4 oz.

preparation:
1. Scrub and soak the clams:
   a. Rinse the clams under cool running water and scrub them with a foodservice brush.
   b. Soak the clams in a bowl of cold water for 30 minutes to 1 hour.
2. Prepare the bacon:
   a. Score the edges of the bacon slices with shallow cuts to prevent curling.
   b. Place the bacon slices flat in a sauté pan and cook over low heat, turning once, about 3 minutes, until the bacon has rendered some fat and is about half cooked.
   c. Remove the bacon to a cutting board and cut each bacon slice into 6 pieces, yielding 24 pieces.
3. Open and fabricate the clams:
   a. Place a fine-mesh strainer over a bowl and place it on one side of a cutting board placed inside a sheet tray to catch juices.
   b. Using a clam knife and a cut-resistant glove or heavy towel to protect your hand, open the clams over the bowl and strainer to catch the juices. Discard the top shells. Reserve the clam juice for another purpose.
   c. Remove each clam from its bottom shell, cut the clam meat in quarters, and replace it in the shell.
4. Stuff the clams:
   a. Top each clam with 1 Tbsp. Casino Butter.
   b. Top each clam with 1 Tbsp. bread crumbs.
   c. Place a piece of bacon on each clam.

holding: prepare only enough for the day's service; refrigerate in one layer on a sheet tray, loosely covered with plastic film, up to 12 hours

---

RECIPE VARIATION
Clams Oreganata
Reduce the amount of butter in the Casino Butter recipe to 4 oz. Omit the bell peppers and parsley and instead add 1 Tbsp. chopped fresh oregano. Omit the bacon. Drizzle each stuffed clam with 1 tsp. extra virgin olive oil before baking.

Potato Latke
with Smoked Salmon and Caviar

yield: 1 (5-oz.) appetizer serving
(multiply × 4 for classroom turnout; adjust equipment sizes accordingly)

MASTER RECIPE

production		costing only
as needed	corn oil for pan-frying	about 4 fl. oz. (may be reused)
1	Potato Latke	1/4 recipe
1 oz.	thin-sliced smoked salmon, preferably nova	1 oz.
2 Tbsp.	crème fraîche, in a pastry bag fitted with a large star tip	1 fl. oz.
1/2 oz.	American golden whitefish caviar	1/2 oz.
1/4 oz.	black sturgeon caviar	1/4 oz.
1 Tbsp.	minced chives	1/20 bunch a.p.

service turnout:
1. Fry the Potato Latke:
   a. Place a small sauté pan over medium heat and add about 1/2" oil. When the oil is moderately hot, add the latke and fry it for about 10 seconds on each side, until it is golden and heated through.
   b. Blot the latke with paper towels.
   c. Cut the latke into 3 even-size wedges.
2. Plate the dish:
   a. Arrange the latke wedges on a cool 10" plate with the rounded edges at 2, 6, and 10 o'clock, leaving a 2" space in the center of the plate.
   b. Lay out the salmon slices on the work surface in an overlapping line, and then roll them up into a loose cylinder. Pull the edges of the salmon down and outward to make a "rose."
   c. Place the salmon "rose" in the center of the plate.
   d. Pipe a hollow rosette of crème fraîche at the tip of each latke wedge.
   e. Mound a spoonful of golden caviar in each rosette, and then top the golden caviar with a dot of black caviar.
   f. Scatter the chives on the latke wedges.

APPETIZERS

COMPONENT RECIPE
POTATO LATKES

yield: 4 (7") latkes

production		costing only
1 lb.	russet potatoes	1 lb.
4 oz.	peeled yellow onion, in one piece	4 1/2 oz. a.p.
2/3	egg, beaten	2/3 each or 1 1/3 oz.
±1/4 c.	flour	±1 1/3 oz.
1/2 tsp.	baking powder	1/16 oz.
about 1 tsp.	fine salt	1/6 oz.
as needed	corn oil	about 12 fl. oz. (may be reused)

preparation:
1. Prepare the latke batter:
   a. Peel the potatoes, dropping them into a bowl of cold water as you work.
   b. Blot each potato dry and immediately grate it, using the large holes of a box grater or food processor disc.
   c. Pick the grated potatoes up in two hands and, holding them over a bowl, squeeze out as much liquid as possible.
   d. Place the potatoes in a dry bowl and grate the onion over the top. Mix.
   e. Mix in enough egg so that the potato shreds are lightly coated.
   f. Sift together the flour, baking powder, and salt, and then sift the mixture over the potatoes. Mix well. (If the mixture seems too loose, sift in more flour.)
2. Immediately parfry the latkes:
   a. Prepare a rack set over a half-sheet tray.
   b. Heat a 14" sauté pan and add the oil to a level of about 1/2". Heat the oil to 375°F.
   c. Divide the latke batter into 4 portions. Spoon each portion into the oil. Flatten and shape each portion to make an even, round cake.
   d. Fry for about 45 seconds on each side, until light golden and just cooked through.
   e. Drain on the rack and cool to room temperature.

holding: refrigerate in a covered container, with pan liner under and between layers, up to 5 days

---

RECIPE VARIATIONS

Ida's Potato Latkes with Sour Cream and Scallions
Serve 3 (3" round) latkes with 1/3 c. sour cream and 1/4 c. chopped scallions.

German Potato Latkes with Sour Cream and Applesauce
Serve 3 (3" round) latkes with 1/3 c. sour cream and 2/3 c. warm applesauce.

Tartare of Salmon and Striped Bass

with Anchovy Croutons

yield: 1 (4-oz.) appetizer serving plus accompaniments
(multiply × 4 for classroom turnout)

MASTER RECIPE

production		costing only
1 tsp.	minced lemon zest	n/c
2 tsp.	fresh lemon juice	1/8 [90 ct.] lemon
1 tsp.	Dijon mustard	1/6 fl. oz.
1 Tbsp.	minced shallot	1/2 oz. a.p.
2 tsp.	nonpareil capers	1/3 oz.
3 Tbsp.	dark green, unfiltered extra virgin olive oil	1 1/2 fl. oz.
2 oz.	very cold wild salmon fillet, skinned, pinned, and thoroughly trimmed	3 oz. a.p.
2 oz.	very cold wild striped bass fillet, skinned, pinned, and thoroughly trimmed	3 oz. a.p.
tt	medium-grind sea salt or kosher salt	1/16 oz.
tt	fresh-ground black pepper	1/16 oz.
1 tsp.	minced chervil or parsley	1/40 bunch a.p.
5	3/16" diagonal slices French baguette	1/12 loaf
2 Tbsp.	Anchovy Butter	1/4 recipe
1/2 oz.	mild-flavored microgreens or cleaned baby greens	1/2 oz.
1	cocktail napkin	1 each

service turnout:

1. Prepare the tartare:
   a. Place a small bowl in an ice bath and add the lemon zest, lemon juice, mustard, shallot, capers, and oil. Mix well.
   b. Using a very sharp knife, fabricate the fish into 1/4" dice and place it in the bowl.
   c. Toss the fish with the dressing and season it with salt, pepper, and chervil.
2. Prepare the Anchovy Croutons:
   a. Spread the baguette slices with the Anchovy Butter, place on a sizzle pan, and bake in a 400°F oven for about 3 minutes, until crisp.
3. Plate the dish:
   a. Place the microgreens on a chilled 5" scallop shell presentation plate, or other plate, and push them toward the edges to make a well in the center.
   b. Mound the tartare in the center of the plate.
   c. Place the presentation plate toward the front of a 10" underplate lined with a cocktail napkin.
   d. Fan the anchovy croutons across the back of the underplate.

COMPONENT RECIPE

ANCHOVY BUTTER

yield: 1/2 c.

production		costing only
1 Tbsp.	minced shallot	1/4 oz. a.p.
2 tsp.	minced garlic	2/9 oz. a.p.
2 Tbsp.	drained, minced, oil-packed anchovies	1/3 oz.
1/2 c.	white wine	4 fl. oz.
6 Tbsp.	room-temperature butter	3 oz.
1 Tbsp.	minced chervil or parsley	1/12 bunch a.p. or 1/20 bunch a.p.
2 tsp.	minced lemon zest	n/c
tt	fresh lemon juice	1/6 [90 ct.] lemon
tt	fine-ground white pepper	1/16 oz.

preparation:
1. Place the shallot, garlic, anchovies, and wine in a small sauté pan and reduce over medium heat, stirring constantly with a heatproof rubber spatula, until almost dry. Cool to room temperature.
2. Mix in the butter and the remaining seasonings.

holding: at cool room temperature no more than 3 hours during service; refrigerate in a freshly sanitized, covered container up to 5 days; freeze up to 1 month

---

RECIPE VARIATION
Tuna Tartare with Anchovy Croutons
Replace the salmon and striped bass with 4 oz. perfectly trimmed sashimi-grade tuna.

Ida's Chopped Liver
with Bagel Crisps

yield: 1 (3-oz.) appetizer serving
(multiply × 4 for classroom turnout)

MASTER RECIPE

production		costing only
3 oz.	Ida's Chopped Liver	1/4 recipe
1/2	hard-cooked egg yolk	1/2 each
1/4 c.	brunoise-cut red onion	1 1/4 oz. a.p.
1 tsp.	minced flat-leaf parsley	1/40 bunch a.p.
5	Bagel Crisps	1/5 recipe
1	small radish, cleaned, with leaves	1/10 bunch a.p.

service turnout:
1. Plate the dish:
   a. Place a 2 1/2" entremet ring toward the front of a cool 10" plate and pack the Ida's Chopped Liver into it.
   b. Lift the ring, leaving a cylinder of chopped liver on the plate.
   c. Use a small spoon to press the egg yolk through a small, fine-mesh strainer onto the top of the liver cylinder.
   d. Sprinkle a border of red onion around and against the base of the liver.
   e. Place a dot of parsley in the center of the liver's egg topping.
   f. Plant the Bagel Crisps upright into the liver cylinder fanned from 12 o'clock to 2 o'clock.
   g. Place the radish on the left side of the plate with the tip pointing to 6 o'clock.

APPETIZERS

COMPONENT RECIPE
IDA'S CHOPPED LIVER

yield: approx. 12 oz.

production		costing only
1 lb.	chicken livers, preferably kosher	1 lb.
1 Tbsp.	corn oil	1/2 fl. oz.
tt	kosher salt	1/16 oz.
1 Tbsp.	Schmaltz	1/16 recipe
1 1/2 c.	fine-chopped yellow onion	7 1/2 oz. a.p.
2	hard-cooked eggs, peeled	2 each
1/2 c.	fine-chopped raw sweet onion	2 1/2 oz.
2 Tbsp.	Schmaltz, melted and cooled	1/8 recipe
tt	fresh-ground black pepper	1/16 oz.

preparation:
1. Trim the livers, separating the lobes and removing all fat and membrane. Blot the livers completely dry on paper towels.
2. Heat a 12" nonstick pan until very hot, add the oil, and sear the livers for about 20 seconds on each side, until medium rare. Season with a little salt and immediately transfer to a half-sheet tray. Cool to room temperature.
3. Add 1 Tbsp. Schmaltz to the pan, add the yellow onion and a little salt, and cook over medium heat, stirring with a heat-proof rubber scraper, about 3 minutes, until the onion is golden brown. Cool to room temperature.
4. Separate the egg whites and egg yolks. Chop the whites fine and reserve the yolks.
5. Chop the livers into a rough paste.
6. Scrape the livers and their juices into a mixing bowl and add the caramelized onion, raw onion, and chopped egg whites. Using a fork to lightly mix the ingredients together, drizzle in the remaining chicken fat, and then crumble in the egg yolks. Season with pepper and more salt if needed.
7. Refrigerate for at least 1 hour before serving.

holding: best served the same day; hold refrigerated in a freshly sanitized, covered container up to 2 days

---

RECIPE VARIATION
Passover Chopped Liver with Matzohs
Replace the Bagel Crisps with matzohs.

Pasta Primavera

yield: 1 (5-oz.) appetizer serving
(multiply × 4 for classroom turnout; adjust equipment sizes accordingly)

MASTER RECIPE

production		costing only
tt	kosher salt	1/16 oz.
1 Tbsp.	gold-color pure olive oil	1/2 fl. oz.
1 Tbsp.	butter	1/2 oz.
1/2 oz.	fresh chanterelles or other fresh woodland mushrooms, cleaned, sliced if necessary	1/2 oz.
1 tsp.	minced garlic	1/9 oz. a.p.
2 tsp.	minced shallot	3/4 oz. a.p.
2/3 c.	heavy cream	5 1/4 fl. oz.
2 1/2 oz.	fresh fettuccine	2 1/2 oz.
1/4 c.	young peas, shelled, blanched and refreshed	4 oz. a.p.
1 oz.	asparagus tips and peeled stems, cut 1", blanched and refreshed	1 1/4 oz. a.p.
1 oz.	haricots verts or green beans, trimmed, blanched and refreshed, cut in 1" lengths	1 oz. a.p.
1 tsp.	minced lemon zest	1/8 [90 ct.] lemon
1/3 c.	grated Parmigiano-Reggiano cheese	1 1/3 oz. a.p.
tt	fine-ground white pepper	1/16 oz.
1 Tbsp.	minced flat-leaf parsley	1/40 bunch a.p.
2 tsp.	toasted pine nuts	1/16 oz.

service turnout:

1. Have ready a pasta cooker or 6-qt. saucepot filled with salted water at a rolling boil.
2. Heat a 10" sauté pan, heat the oil, add the butter, and sear the mushrooms with a little salt until well browned. Remove and hold warm.
3. Add the garlic, shallot, and cream to the pan and bring to the simmer. Hold warm.
4. Drop the fettuccine into the boiling water, stir once, and cook at a rapid boil for about 30 seconds, or until just al dente.
5. Using a perforated lifter and tongs, remove the fettuccine from the cooking water and place it directly into the heavy cream sauté pan, along with the cooking water clinging to it.
6. Place the sauté pan over high heat. Add the peas, asparagus, haricots verts, and lemon zest, and then toss to mix and reheat.
7. When the sauce thickens enough to barely cling to the pasta, remove the pan from heat and toss in the cheese. Drizzle in boiling pasta water if necessary to maintain a light consistency.
8. Season with salt and white pepper.
9. Plate the dish:
   a. Use tongs to place the pasta in a hot 10" pasta plate.
   b. Arrange some of the vegetables attractively on top.
   c. Use a rubber spatula to scrape every bit of sauce over the top.
   d. Sprinkle with parsley and pine nuts.

RECIPE VARIATIONS

Pasta *al Estate* (ahl eh-STAH-tay)
Replace the peas and asparagus with cooked corn kernels and baby lima beans; add 1/3 c. peeled, seeded, large julienne-cut tomato flesh in step 2; replace the parsley with chiffonade fresh basil.

Pasta *al Autunno* (ahl ah-TUHN-oh)
Replace the chanterelles with porcinis; replace the peas, haricots verts, and asparagus with cooked julienne winter squash, julienne roasted red bell pepper, and spinach leaves; replace the parsley with chiffonade fresh sage.

Striped Bass
in Potato Crust
with Red Wine Sauce, Lentil Ragout, and Leeks

yield: 1 (7-oz.) entrée serving plus accompaniments (multiply × 4 for classroom turnout; adjust equipment sizes accordingly)

MASTER RECIPE

production		costing only
1/4 c.	clarified butter	2 1/4 oz. a.p.
1	Potato-Crusted Bass Fillet	1/4 recipe
2 pc.	Braised Leeks	1/4 recipe
7 pc.	Parisienne carrots, blanched tender and refreshed	6 oz. a.p.
1 c.	Ragout of Green Lentils	1/4 recipe
as needed	water, in squeeze bottle	n/c
1/2 c.	Red Wine Demi-Glace for Fish, hot in steam table	1/4 recipe
1 Tbsp.	butter	1/2 oz.

service turnout:
1. Finish the fish:
   a. Heat an 8" nonstick pan, heat the clarified butter until hot, and add the Potato-Crusted Bass Fillet. Sauté on medium heat for about 45 seconds, until the potatoes are browned on the bottom.
   b. Turn the fillet and sauté for about 30 seconds longer.
   c. Add the Braised Leeks and carrots to the sauté pan along with the fillet and place the sauté pan in a 400°F oven for about 5 minutes, until the fish is just cooked through.
2. Place the Ragout of Green Lentils and a little water in a small sauté pan over low heat, cover, and simmer just to reheat.
3. Plate the dish:
   a. Place the leeks in the center of a hot 12" plate, arranged parallel to each other and spaced about 2" apart, oriented from 10 o'clock to 4 o'clock.
   b. Spoon the lentil ragout in the center of the plate, between and flowing over the leeks.
   c. Place the bass fillet on top of the leeks and lentils, oriented from 2 o'clock to 8 o'clock.
   d. Dip up 1/2 c. Red Wine Demi-Glace for Fish in a large ladle, pick up the butter with tongs, and stir the butter into the demi-glace. (If turning out multiple servings, simply work the butter into the sauce.) Ladle the sauce around the fillet.
   e. Arrange the carrots around the fillet.

COMPONENT RECIPE
POTATO-CRUSTED BASS FILLETS

yield: 4 (7-oz.) entrée servings

production		costing only
4	6-oz. striped bass fillets, skinned, pinned, and trimmed	1 3/4 lb. a.p.
tt	kosher salt	1/8 oz.
tt	fine-ground white pepper	1/16 oz.
2	large, elongated 10-oz. russet potatoes	20 oz.
1/4 c.	clarified butter	2 1/4 oz. a.p.

preparation:
1. Season the bass fillets with salt and white pepper. If necessary, fold the thinner tail and belly flap areas under (shiny side in) to create a rectangular shape. The fillets should measure about 3 1/2" × 4 1/2". If larger, adjust the size of the potato wrap in step 3b.
2. Fabricate the potatoes:
   a. Set up a mandoline over a clean, dry kitchen towel. Adjust the blade to cut very thin slices. ⚠ Be sure to use the guard.
   b. Peel and rinse the potatoes and immediately blot them dry.
   c. Immediately use the mandoline to cut very thin, lengthwise slices.
   d. Wrap the potato slices in the towel and immediately proceed to wrapping the fillets.
3. Wrap the bass fillets:
   a. Place a sheet of plastic film on the work surface.
   b. Place about 1/4 of the large potato slices on the plastic film, overlapping slightly, to make a rectangle about 4" × 8".
   c. Place a bass fillet in the center of the potato rectangle, shiny side up, and wrap it in the potatoes.
   d. Fold the plastic film around the packet and press gently to help the potatoes adhere to the fish.
   e. Repeat with the remaining ingredients to yield a total of 4 wrapped bass fillets.
   f. Refrigerate for 30 minutes only, then proceed to step 4.
4. Parcook the potato-crusted bass fillets:
   a. Heat a 12" nonstick sauté pan, add the clarified butter, and heat the butter until it is moderately hot.
   b. Add the wrapped bass fillets, best side down, and fry over medium heat for about 1 minute, until the potatoes have softened but the fish is still raw.
   c. Turn the fillets and cook for about 1 minute more.
   d. Transfer the fillets to a sheet tray with pan liner and refrigerate them, uncovered, for 30 minutes.

holding: refrigerate individually wrapped in plastic film up to 12 hours

COMPONENT RECIPE
BRAISED LEEKS

yield: 8 pc.

production		costing only
8	leeks	2 bunches
2 Tbsp.	clarified butter	1 1/8 oz. a.p.
2 c.	Poultry Stock	1/8 recipe
tt	kosher salt	1/16 oz.
pinch	sugar	1/8 oz.

preparation:
1. Fabricate the leeks:
   a. Remove the green ends of the leeks (reserve for stock).
   b. Cut off the roots, leaving just enough of the ends to hold the leeks together.
   c. Cut a lengthwise slit halfway into each leek extending from 1/2" from the root to the green end.
   d. Wash the leeks under cool, running water, opening the slit to remove as much grit as possible.
   e. Stand the leeks upright in a tall plastic container, root end up, and cover them completely with cool water. Soak the leeks, shaking them up and down a few times, for about 1 hour to remove any remaining grit.
   f. Drain the leeks and squeeze them dry.
   g. Tie each leek with kitchen string top and bottom to retain its shape.
2. Braise the leeks:
   a. Heat a 10" sauté pan, heat the butter, and sauté the leeks over medium heat about 30 seconds, turning often, until they begin to brown slightly.
   b. Add the Poultry Stock, salt, and sugar. Cover the pan and simmer for about 8 minutes.
   c. Turn over the leeks and continue simmering for about 8 minutes longer, or until very tender.
   d. Remove the leeks to a sheet tray and cool to room temperature.
   e. Remove the strings.
3. Pour any juices accumulated around the leeks into the saucepan and reduce the braising liquid to a glaze.
4. Place the leeks in a freshly sanitized plastic container and cover with the glaze.

holding: cover and refrigerate up to 5 days

COMPONENT RECIPE
RAGOUT OF GREEN LENTILS

yield: approx. 1 qt.

production		costing only
2 c.	green lentils (French, Le Puy)	13 oz.
2 Tbsp.	gold-color pure olive oil	1 fl. oz.
1 Tbsp.	butter	1/2 oz.
1 c.	fine-chopped yellow onion	5 oz. a.p.
2 tsp.	minced garlic	2/9 oz. a.p.
1/2 c.	peeled, fine-chopped celery	1/10 head a.p.
2 c.	Poultry Stock	1/8 recipe
1	fresh thyme sprig	1/20 bunch a.p.
1	fresh sage sprig	1/10 bunch a.p.
as needed	water	n/c
1 c.	3/8"-diced carrots	3 oz. a.p.
tt	kosher salt	1/8 oz.
tt	fresh-ground black pepper	1/16 oz.
tt	fresh lemon juice	1/4 [90 ct.] lemon

preparation:
1. Parcook the lentils:
   a. Place the lentils in a heavy saucepan, cover with water, and bring to the simmer.
   b. Drain the lentils in a strainer, rinse them, and return them to the pan.
   c. Cover with water again and simmer for 10 minutes.
   d. Drain the lentils in a strainer, rinse, and hold. Wipe out the saucepan.
2. Cook the lentils:
   a. Place the oil and butter in the saucepan along with the onion, garlic, and celery. Cover and sweat, stirring once, for about 3 minutes, until the vegetables begin to soften.
   b. Add the lentils, Poultry Stock, thyme, sage, and enough water to cover the lentils by 1/2". Simmer for about 10 minutes.
   c. Add the carrots and continue simmering for about 10 minutes longer, until the lentils are almost tender and the cooking liquid is reduced to a light sauce. (Cooking times vary depending on the type and age of the lentils. If necessary, cook longer and add water if the lentils become too dry.)
   d. Remove the herb sprigs and season with salt, pepper, and lemon juice.

holding: open-pan cool and immediately refrigerate in a freshly sanitized, covered container up to 5 days

COMPONENT RECIPE
RED WINE DEMI-GLACE FOR FISH

yield: 2 c.

production		costing only
3/4 c.	fruity red wine, such as Pinot Noir	6 fl. oz.
1 1/2 c.	Demi-Glace	3/8 recipe
1 c.	Fish Stock	1/16 recipe
1 tsp.	minced lemon zest	n/c
tt	kosher salt	1/16 oz.
tt	fine-ground white pepper	1/16 oz.

preparation:
1. In a small, nonreactive saucepan reduce the wine over very low heat to 1/4 c.
2. Place the Demi-Glace and Fish Stock in a small saucepan and reduce over medium heat to 1 3/4 c. full-bodied sauce.
3. Add the reduced wine and lemon zest.
4. Season with salt and white pepper.

holding: open-pan cool and immediately refrigerate in a covered, freshly sanitized container up to 5 days

---

RECIPE VARIATION

Striped Bass in Potato Crust with Roasted Tomato Sauce, Corn Timbale, and Haricots Verts
Replace the Red Wine Demi-Glace for Fish with Roasted Tomato Sauce. Omit the leeks and lentil ragout. Complete the plate with a Dried Corn Pudding (p. 171) and cooked haricots verts.

Stuffed Savoy Cabbage in Sweet 'n' Sour Sauce

with Kasha Varnishkes

yield: 1 (6-oz.) entrée serving plus accompaniment (multiply × 4 for classroom turnout; adjust equipment sizes accordingly)

MASTER RECIPE

production		costing only
2	3-oz. Stuffed Savoy Cabbage Rolls plus sauce	1/4 recipe
as needed	water	n/c
1/2 c.	water	n/c
2 1/2 oz.	al dente-boiled and cooled bow-tie pasta	1 1/4 oz. a.p.
tt	kosher salt	1/16 oz.
1 c.	Cooked Whole-Grain Kasha	1/4 recipe
1/4 c.	coarse-chopped Caramelized Onions	1/4 recipe
tt	fresh lemon juice	1/8 [90 ct.] lemon
tt	fresh-ground black pepper	1/16 oz.
1	fresh dill sprig	1/20 bunch a.p.

service turnout:

1. Place the Stuffed Savoy Cabbage Rolls and sauce in a small sauté pan along with a little water. Cover and heat over low heat for about 8 minutes, until heated through.
2. Finish the kasha varnishkes:
   a. Place 1/2 c. water in a 12" sauté pan with a pinch of salt. Bring to the boil and add the pasta. Cook, stirring, a few seconds until the pasta is hot.
   b. Add the Cooked Whole-Grain Kasha and Caramelized Onions, stir to separate the kasha grains, and then cover the pan.
   c. Reduce the heat and simmer until the kasha is heated through.
   d. Season with lemon juice and pepper, and correct the salt.
3. Plate the dish:
   a. Spoon a bed of kasha varnishkes onto a hot 12" plate.
   b. Place one cabbage roll horizontally on the left center of the plate atop the kasha varnishkes. Prop the second cabbage roll on the first from 12 o'clock to 7 o'clock.
   c. Spoon the sauce over the top of the cabbage rolls.
   d. Arrange the dill sprig upright between the cabbage rolls.

COMPONENT RECIPE
STUFFED SAVOY CABBAGE ROLLS

yield: 8 (3-oz.) rolls

production		costing only
8	large Savoy cabbage leaves	6 oz. a.p.
2 oz.	Savoy cabbage	2 oz. a.p.
12 oz.	ground beef chuck (80% lean)	12 oz.
1/2 c.	grated yellow onion	3 oz. a.p.
2 tsp.	minced garlic	2/9 oz. a.p.
1 c.	room-temperature cooked long-grain rice	2 oz. a.p.
1/2 c.	matzoh meal or cracker crumbs	1 1/4 oz.
tt	fresh-ground black pepper	1/16 oz.
1 Tbsp.	minced dill	1/40 bunch a.p.
1 Tbsp.	minced flat-leaf parsley	1/40 bunch a.p.
1	egg, beaten	1 each or 2 oz.
tt	kosher salt	1/8 oz.
7 c.	Tomato Sauce for Stuffed Cabbage	1 recipe

preparation:
1. Prepare the cabbage leaf wrappers and cabbage for the filling:
   a. Bring at least 5 qt. water to a rolling boil and prepare a large bowl of ice water for refreshing.
   b. Blanch the cabbage leaves for 1 to 2 minutes until pliable, and then refresh in the ice water until cold. Shake dry and blot on clean kitchen towels.
   c. Boil the additional cabbage tender and refresh until cold. Squeeze dry and chop fine. You should have about 2/3 c. chopped cabbage.
   d. Place each cabbage leaf on the work surface, rounded side up. Shave off and discard the raised, rounded part of its large central vein so the leaf is an even thickness and pliable throughout.
2. Prepare the filling:
   a. Combine the chopped cabbage, ground chuck, onion, garlic, rice, matzoh meal, pepper, dill, parsley, and egg in a large bowl. Mix thoroughly and season with salt.
   b. Poach a small nugget of filling in the cabbage cooking water, taste for seasoning, and make any necessary corrections.
3. Preheat an oven to 350°F.
4. Fabricate the cabbage rolls:
   a. Divide the filling into 8 portions.
   b. Place a cabbage leaf on the work surface, rounded side down, and spoon a portion of filling horizontally across the narrow stem end.
   c. Fold the stem end of the leaf up over the filling, and then fold in only the left side of the leaf.
   d. Roll up the leaf to enclose the filling, leaving loose cabbage ends on the right.
   e. Use your index finger to push the right-side cabbage leaf into the center of the cylinder to secure it shut.
   f. Place the cabbage roll in a half-size hotel pan.
   g. Repeat with the remaining ingredients, making a total of 8 rolls.
5. Cook the cabbage rolls:
   a. Bring the Tomato Sauce for Stuffed Cabbage to the boil and pour it over the cabbage rolls.
   b. Cover the half-size hotel pan with a piece of pan liner and then its lid (or a sheet of aluminum foil).
   c. Bake for about 15 minutes.
   d. Uncover the pan and turn over the cabbage rolls.
   e. Re-cover the pan and bake for about 15 minutes longer, until the cabbage is tender and the filling is just cooked through.
6. Finish the sauce:
   a. Holding the cabbage rolls in the baking pan with a large spatula, pour the sauce out of the pan and into a large sauté pan. Reduce it to nappé consistency, adding any juices that emerge from the cabbage rolls as they cool.
   b. Balance the salt and sugar to achieve a tangy, slightly sweet flavor.
   c. Pour the finished sauce back over the cabbage rolls.

holding: open-pan cool, cover, and immediately refrigerate up to 5 days

COMPONENT RECIPE
TOMATO SAUCE FOR STUFFED CABBAGE

yield: approx. 7 c.

production		costing only
2 Tbsp.	Schmaltz or corn oil	1/8 recipe or 1 fl. oz.
1 c.	minced yellow onion	5 oz. a.p.
2 tsp.	minced garlic	2/9 oz. a.p.
1/4 tsp.	ground ginger	1/16 oz.
2 Tbsp.	flour	1/3 oz.
3 c.	hot Brown Beef Stock	1/5 recipe
2 c.	canned tomato purée	16 fl. oz.
2 c.	water	n/c
tt	kosher salt	1/8 oz.
2 Tbsp.	brown sugar	3/4 oz.

preparation:
1. Heat a deep 12" sauté pan, add the Schmaltz, and heat until it melts.
2. Add the onion, garlic, and ginger. Sauté over medium heat until softened and beginning to brown.
3. Add the flour and cook, stirring, for 30 seconds to make a blond roux, then whisk in the hot Brown Beef Stock. Bring to the simmer.
4. Whisk in the tomato purée and water, return to the simmer, and then season with salt and sugar.
5. Cover and simmer for 15 to 20 minutes, until the flavors meld and the sauce reduces to a light nappé consistency.

holding: if not using immediately, open-pan cool and refrigerate in a freshly sanitized, nonreactive container up to 5 days

COMPONENT RECIPE
COOKED WHOLE-GRAIN KASHA

yield: approx. 1 qt.

production		costing only
1 1/3 c.	whole-grain kasha	11 oz.
2 Tbsp.	Schmaltz or butter	1 oz.
1/4 c.	minced yellow onion	1 1/4 oz. a.p.
2 1/2 c.	hot Poultry Stock	1/6 recipe
tt	kosher salt	1/16 oz.

preparation:

1. Preheat an oven to 400°F.
2. Place the kasha in a 10" sauté pan over low heat. Toast the kasha, stirring often, about 5 minutes until the grains darken slightly and become fragrant. Do not allow the grains to scorch.
3. Place a heavy 1 1/2 qt. saucepan over low heat, add the Schmaltz, and heat it until it melts. Add the onions, sauté them about 20 seconds until softened, add the toasted kasha, and stir to coat the grains with fat.
4. Add the Poultry Stock and salt, cover the pan, and simmer over low heat about 15 minutes until the liquid is absorbed.
5. Transfer the pan to the oven and bake for 10 minutes.
6. Turn the kasha out into a freshly-sanitized half-size hotel pan and fluff it with a fork. Cover the kasha with a clean, damp towel. If using within a few minutes, cover the pan with a lid or a sheet of aluminum foil and hold warm.

holding: if not using immediately, open-pan cool and refrigerate up to 5 days

Shave off and discard the raised, rounded part of the vein.

Spoon the filling across the stem end of the cabbage leaf.

Fold the stem end up over the filling, then fold in the left side of the leaf

Roll up the leaf to enclose the filling, leaving loose cabbage ends on the right.

Push the right-side cabbage leaf into the center of the cylinder to secure it shut.

RECIPE VARIATION

Golabki (Polish-American Stuffed Cabbage)

In the Tomato Sauce for Stuffed Cabbage recipe, replace the Schmaltz with butter and omit the ginger and brown sugar. In the Stuffed Savoy Cabbage Rolls recipe, replace the ground beef chuck with ground beef/pork/veal mix, replace the matzoh meal with dried bread crumbs, replace the dill with 1/4 tsp. dried thyme, and optionally add 1/2 c. sautéed chopped wild mushrooms. Replace the garnish dill with parsley. Omit the kasha varnishkes and serve with boiled or mashed potatoes.

Grilled Rare Squab
with Green Peppercorn Demi-Glace, Haricots Verts, and Rutabaga-Mascarpone Purée

yield: 1 (10-oz. semiboneless) entrée serving plus accompaniments (multiply × 4 for classroom turnout; adjust equipment sizes accordingly)

🕐 Best prepared 24 hours in advance.

MASTER RECIPE

production		costing only
1	Herb-Marinated Semiboneless Squab	1/4 recipe
1 c. as needed	Rutabaga-Mascarpone Purée water	1/4 recipe
3 oz.	trimmed, blanched, and refreshed haricots verts	3 1/4 oz. a.p.
1/2 c.	Port Wine Demi-Glace, p. 178	1/4 recipe
1 Tbsp.	green peppercorns in vinegar, lightly crushed	1/2 oz.
1 Tbsp.	butter	1/2 oz.
1/3 c.	Frizzled Shallots	1/4 recipe

service turnout:

1. Grill the Herb-Marinated Semiboneless Squab:
   a. Place the squab on a hot char-grill, skin-side-down, and cook for 45 seconds to create grill marks.
   b. Rotate 90 degrees and grill for 45 seconds longer.
   c. Turn the squab over and grill for 1 minute longer. The squab should be very rare.
   d. Transfer to an 8" sauté pan and hold hot (but not in an oven).
2. Heat the Rutabaga-Mascarpone Purée in an 8" covered sauté pan, adding a little water if necessary.
3. Heat the haricots verts in a microwave oven or steamer.
4. Finish the squab in a 400°F oven for a few minutes only.
   ⚠ Do not allow to cook beyond a rare doneness.*
5. Finish and plate the dish:
   a. Using a 4-fl.-oz. quenelle scoop or two large tablespoons dipped in boiling water, scoop up and form the rutabaga purée into a quenelle shape and place it on a hot 12" plate at 2 o'clock. Scoop another quenelle and place it at 3 o'clock.
   b. Quickly arrange the haricots verts in a fan pattern across the front of the plate with the tips against the edge of the plate well.
   c. Prop the squab against the rutabaga purée with the wing end covering the back of the haricots verts fan.
   d. Ladle the Port Wine Demi-Glace into the squab sauté pan with the cooking juices and heat it over high heat. Add the green peppercorns, work in the butter, and correct the seasoning. Nap over the squab and into the plate well.
   e. Mound the Frizzled Shallots on the squab's drumstick knuckles.

*Commercially available squabs are slaughtered under sanitary conditions and, if properly handled by the foodservice operation, are safe to consume rare. Squab cooked past medium-rare doneness becomes tough and dry and acquires a flavor similar to overcooked liver.

COMPONENT RECIPE
HERB-MARINATED SEMIBONELESS SQUABS

🕐 Best prepared 24 hours in advance.

yield: 4 (10-oz.) squabs

production		costing only
4	(12-oz.) squabs	3 lb. a.p.
2 Tbsp.	fresh thyme leaves	1/10 bunch a.p.
2 Tbsp.	chopped fresh sage leaves	1/6 bunch a.p.
1 Tbsp.	chopped fresh rosemary leaves	1/20 bunch a.p.
2 Tbsp.	minced garlic	2/3 oz. a.p.
tt	kosher salt	1/4 oz.
tt	fresh-ground black pepper	1/8 oz.
1 Tbsp.	minced lemon zest	n/c
1/2 c.	red Port wine	4 fl. oz.
1/2 c.	gold-color pure olive oil	4 fl. oz.

preparation:
1. Fabricate the squabs:
   a. If necessary, remove the necks, heads, and feet from the squabs. Wash and reserve.
   b. Using the tip of a sharp boning knife, cut out the backbones of the squabs. ⚠ If the squabs are intact and not gutted, be careful not to pierce or crush any of the entrails. Reserve the backbones, cleaning them and rinsing off any blood.
   c. Remove and discard any entrails, reserving the livers for another use.
   d. Crack the breastbones and press the squabs flat.
   e. Remove and reserve the rib bones and any other small, sharp bones, rinsing off any blood.
   f. Rinse the squabs under cool running water and blot dry on several changes of paper towels.
   g. Tuck the wing tips under the wings.
   h. Cut a small slit on either side of the tail and tuck the drumstick knuckles through the slits to secure the legs together.
2. Prepare the marinade:
   a. Crush the thyme, sage, and rosemary between your fingers and place them in a freshly sanitized nonreactive container just large enough to hold the squabs.
   b. Mix in the remaining ingredients.
3. Marinate the squabs:
   a. Place the squabs in the container and turn them to coat well with the marinade.
   b. Cover and refrigerate for 24 hours.

holding: refrigerate up to 3 days total

RECIPE VARIATION
Grilled Rare Duck Breast with Green Peppercorn Demi-Glace, Haricots Verts, and Rutabaga-Mascarpone Purée
Replace each squab with a 6-oz. Muscovy duck breast, skin scored in a tight 1/8" crosshatch pattern.

COMPONENT RECIPE
RUTABAGA-MASCARPONE PURÉE

yield: 1 qt.

production		costing only
12 oz.	peeled, medium-diced rutabaga	1 lb. a.p.
tt	kosher salt	1/2 oz.
as needed	water	n/c
5 oz.	peeled, medium-diced russet potato	6 oz. a.p.
1/2 c.	hot Poultry Stock	1/32 recipe
3/4 c.	mascarpone cheese	4 1/2 oz.
tt	fine-ground white pepper	1/16 oz.

preparation:
1. Boil the rutabaga in heavily salted water to cover for 5 minutes.
2. Add the potato and continue to boil until both vegetables are tender.
3. Drain the vegetables and purée with an immersion blender or force through a food mill into a heavy saucepan.
4. Stir in the Poultry Stock.
5. Return to the heat and simmer briskly, stirring constantly with a heatproof rubber spatula, about 2 minutes until the purée thickens enough to hold a shape.
6. Fold in the mascarpone, season with white pepper, and correct the salt.

holding: open-pan cool and immediately refrigerate in a freshly sanitized, covered plastic container up to 3 days

COMPONENT RECIPE
FRIZZLED SHALLOTS

yield: approx. 2 c.

production		costing only
as needed	frying compound or corn oil	% used
12 oz.	large shallots	12 oz.
tt	fine salt	1/8 oz.

preparation:
1. Preheat a commercial fryer or large saucepan filled with corn oil for deep-frying to 375°F. Line a half-size hotel pan with paper towels.
2. Fabricate the shallots:
   a. Peel the shallots, removing the root ends.
   b. Slice the shallots thin and even.
   c. Separate the slices into rings.
3. Deep-fry the shallots:
   a. Place the shallots in the fryer basket or a strainer, lower them into the hot oil, and fry about 30 seconds until the edges brown and they begin to crisp.
   b. Remove from the oil, shake off any excess oil, and drain the shallots on paper towels.
   c. Toss with salt while still warm.

holding: at cool room temperature in a tightly sealed container lined with paper towels up to 5 days

Tandoori Lamb Chops

with Basmati Pulao, Greens Purée, and Braised Cauliflower

yield: 1 (10-oz. bone-in) entrée serving plus accompaniments (multiply × 4 for classroom turnout; adjust equipment sizes accordingly)

🕐 Best prepared 24 hours in advance.

MASTER RECIPE

production		costing only
2	Tandoori-Marinated Double Lamb Chops	1/4 recipe
3 Tbsp.	clarified butter, in squeeze bottle	1 3/4 oz. a.p.
1/4 c.	slivered yellow onion	1 1/4 oz. a.p.
1 Tbsp.	fine-slivered fresh garlic	1/3 oz. a.p.
2 tsp.	Garam Masala	1/8 recipe
1 c.	Greens Purée	1/4 recipe
2 oz.	North Indian Braised Cauliflower	1/6 recipe
1 1/2 c.	Basmati Pulao, hot in steam table	1/4 recipe
2/3 c.	Fennel-Yogurt Tomato Sauce, hot in steam table	1/4 recipe
1/2	roasted plain papad	1/24 package
1 bouquet	fresh cilantro	1/20 bunch a.p.

service turnout:

1. Grill the Tandoori-Marinated Double Lamb Chops:
   a. Coat the chops on both sides with about 1 Tbsp. of the clarified butter and place on a hot char-grill for about 30 seconds.
   b. Rotate 90 degrees and grill for about 30 seconds longer to mark in a crosshatch pattern.
   c. Turn the chops and grill, rotating after 30 seconds, for a total of 1 minute.
   d. Remove to a sizzle plate and finish to rare to medium rare in a 400°F oven.
   e. Hold warm.

2. Finish the Greens Purée:
   a. Place 2 Tbsp. of the clarified butter and the onion and garlic in a small sauté pan and fry over medium heat about 1 minute, until the onion and garlic are browned.
   b. Add the Garam Masala, swirl the pan, and immediately add the Greens Purée. Using a heatproof rubber spatula, fold the purée into the spiced butter.
   c. Cover the pan, reduce the heat to low, and cook about 1 minute, just until hot.

3. Heat the North Indian Braised Cauliflower in a microwave oven or small covered sauté pan.

4. Plate the dish:
   a. Mound the Basmati Pulao slightly behind the center of a hot 12" plate.
   b. Prop the lamb chops upright, bones interlocking, toward the front of the pulao.
   c. Using a 4-fl.-oz. quenelle scoop or 2 large serving spoons, form the greens purée into 2 quenelles and place them on the plate at 4 o'clock and 8 o'clock.
   d. Spoon the Fennel-Yogurt Tomato Sauce in the plate well between the greens quenelles.
   e. Mound the cauliflower in front of the chops.
   f. Plant the Roasted Papad in the pulao behind the chops.
   g. Arrange the cilantro bouquet on the chops between the bones.

*To roast a papad, use tongs to hold it over the stove burner grid over a low flame for about 20 seconds until it expands and turns lighter in color. Turn it, and roast it a few seconds longer until it is crisp and evenly colored but not scorched. Alternatively, roast several papads at one time under a broiler set to low heat, turning once.

COMPONENT RECIPE
TANDOORI-MARINATED DOUBLE LAMB CHOPS

yield: 8 double chops

production		costing only
1 tsp.	saffron threads	0.02 oz. or 0.7 g
1/4 c.	boiling water	n/c
1/2 c.	chopped yellow onion	2 1/2 oz. a.p.
1/4 c.	chopped ginger	1 1/4 oz. a.p.
1 tsp.	chopped garlic	1/9 oz. a.p.
2 Tbsp.	Garam Masala	1/3 recipe
1 tsp.	cayenne pepper	1/12 oz.
tt	kosher salt	1/8 oz.
1 c.	whole-milk yogurt	8 fl. oz.
2 Tbsp.	fresh lemon juice	3/8 [90 ct.] lemon
2	1-lb. frenched racks of lamb	2 lb.

preparation:
1. Prepare the tandoori marinade:
   a. Place the saffron in a ramekin or small bowl and pour the boiling water over it. Steep for 10 minutes.
   b. Place the onion, ginger, garlic, Garam Masala, cayenne, salt, yogurt, and lemon juice in a blender. Add the saffron water. Purée into a smooth paste.
2. Fabricate and marinate the lamb:
   a. Cut each lamb rack into 4 (4-oz.) double chops to make a total of 8 chops.
   b. Place the chops in a freshly sanitized, nonreactive container just large enough to hold them snug.
   c. Pour the tandoori marinade over the chops, scraping out every last drop from the blender.
   d. Turn the chops to coat thoroughly, then cover and refrigerate for 24 hours.
3. Scrape the marinade off the chops before grilling.

holding: after 24 hours, scrape the marinade off the chops; continue to hold refrigerated up to 2 days longer

COMPONENT RECIPE
GARAM MASALA

yield: 6 Tbsp.

production		costing only
2 Tbsp.	green cardamom pods	1/8 oz.
2 Tbsp.	coriander seeds	1/8 oz.
2 Tbsp.	cumin seeds	1/4 oz.
1 tsp.	fennel seeds	1/10 oz.
1 tsp.	cloves	1/16 oz.
1/2	3" cinnamon stick, crushed	1/8 oz.
1 tsp.	black peppercorns	1/16 oz.

preparation:
1. Open the cardamom pods and extract the seeds. Discard the pods.
2. Place the coriander seeds in a small, dry sauté pan over medium heat. Toast the coriander seeds, shaking and swirling the pan, about 30 seconds, until fragrant and slightly darkened.
3. Transfer the coriander seeds to a small mortar or electric spice mill.
4. Repeat with the cumin seeds, then with the fennel seeds.
5. Place the cloves and crushed cinnamon stick in the sauté pan and toast over low heat, tossing occasionally, about 20 seconds, until the cloves begin to turn gray. Add the peppercorns and cardamom seeds and toast them, shaking the pan, for a few seconds longer. Transfer to the mortar or mill.
6. Grind the spices to a powder.

holding: at cool room temperature in a tightly sealed container up to 2 weeks

GREENS PURÉE

yield: 1 qt.

production		costing only
1 1/4 lb.	fresh mustard greens or 12 oz. frozen mustard greens, thawed and squeezed dry	1 1/4 lb. or 12 oz.
as needed	water	n/c
2 tsp.	ground turmeric	1/8 oz.
1 tsp.	cayenne pepper	1/12 oz.
tt	kosher salt	1/8 oz.

preparation:
1. If using fresh greens, clean and fabricate them:
   a. Remove the stems and large veins from the greens.
   b. Wash the greens by submerging them in cool water and agitating up and down. Remove the greens from the water, drain them, and wash out the sink. Repeat until the water shows no trace of grit.
   c. Chop the greens: The finer they're cut, the faster they'll cook.
2. Cook the greens:
   a. Place the greens in a nonreactive saucepan and pack them down.
   b. Add water just to cover and stir in the remaining ingredients.
   c. Cover the pan and bring to the boil.
   d. Stir to distribute the wilted greens and then cook uncovered at a lively simmer, stirring occasionally, for 10 to 20 minutes, until the greens are very tender and the liquid reduced.
3. Purée the greens using an immersion blender or in a food processor.
4. If necessary, return the purée to the saucepan and reduce, stirring with a heatproof rubber spatula to avoid scorching, from 1 to 3 minutes, until thick enough to hold a shape.
5. Taste and correct the salt.

holding: open-pan cool and immediately refrigerate in a freshly sanitized, covered, nonreactive container up to 5 days; freeze up to 1 month

NORTH INDIAN BRAISED CAULIFLOWER

yield: approx. 12 oz.

production		costing only
1	small head cauliflower	1 [12 ct.] a.p.
1/4 c.	corn oil	2 fl. oz.
2 tsp.	black mustard seeds	1/4 oz.
2 tsp.	toasted, ground coriander seeds*	1/16 oz.
2 tsp.	toasted, ground cumin seeds*	1/8 oz.
2 tsp.	ground turmeric	1/8 oz.
2/3 c.	fine-chopped yellow onion	4 oz. a.p.
1/4 c.	minced ginger	1 1/4 oz. a.p.
1 tsp.	minced garlic	1/9 oz. a.p.
1 Tbsp.	seeded, minced Italian green or serrano chile	1/2 oz. a.p.
1/2 c.	water	n/c
tt	kosher salt	1/8 oz.
1 Tbsp.	fresh lemon juice	3/16 [90 ct.] lemon
2 Tbsp.	butter	1 oz.

preparation:
1. Remove the leaves and core from the cauliflower. Separate it into florets.
2. Heat a 14" wok or 12" sauté pan over medium heat, then add the oil and mustard seeds. Over low heat, swirl the pan about 20 seconds, until the seeds sizzle, turn gray, and begin to pop. ⚠ Do not allow the seeds to blacken.
3. Immediately add the coriander, cumin, turmeric, onion, ginger, garlic, and chile. Stir-fry for 1 to 2 seconds.
4. Immediately add the cauliflower. Stir-fry to coat the florets with the spices and aromatics, season with salt, add the water, and cover the pan.
5. Cook, uncovering and stirring occasionally, for about 6 minutes, until the cauliflower is tender and the liquid almost absorbed/evaporated. ⚠ Watch for scorching; add a little more water if the pan gets completely dry. The cauliflower florets should be tender yet remain intact.
6. Season the cauliflower with lemon juice, correct the salt, remove from heat, and work in the butter.

holding: transfer to a half-sheet tray and open-pan cool; immediately refrigerate in a freshly sanitized, covered container

*The method for toasting and grinding spices appears in the Garam Masala component recipe on p. 829.

COMPONENT RECIPE
BASMATI PULAO

yield: 1 1/2 qt.

production		costing only
2 c.	basmati rice	12 oz.
as needed	hot water	n/c
1/3 c.	butter	2 2/3 oz.
1/2 c.	unsalted cashew nut pieces	3 oz.
1 c.	fine-chopped yellow onion	5 oz. a.p.
4	cloves*	1/16 oz.
1	2" cinnamon stick, broken in half*	1/8 oz.
6	cardamom pods*	1/16 oz.
1	bay leaf*	1/16 oz.
1/2 c.	3/8"-diced carrots	2 oz. a.p.
1/2 c.	fresh raw or frozen peas	8 oz. or 2 1/2 oz.
1/2 c.	3/8"-diced red bell pepper	4 oz. a.p.
2 c.	Poultry Stock	1/8 recipe
tt	kosher salt	1/8 oz.
1 tsp.	crushed saffron threads	0.02 oz. or 0.7 g a.p.

preparation:
1. Wash and soak the rice:
   a. Place the rice in a deep bowl and place the bowl under a gentle stream of warm water. Rinse, stirring gently with your hand, for about 2 minutes, until the water runs clear.
   b. Drain the rice and cover it by 1" with hot tap water. Soak for 20 minutes.
2. Preheat an oven to 400°F.
3. Cook the rice:
   a. Melt the butter in a heavy 3-qt. saucepan with a heat-proof handle and tight-fitting lid.
   b. Fry the cashews for a few seconds, until golden, then lift out with a perforated spoon and reserve.
   c. Add the onion, cloves, cinnamon, cardamom, and bay leaf to the pan and sauté for about 1 minute, until the onion is soft.
   d. Drain the rice and add it to the pan. Stir the rice to coat each grain with the butter, and then cook, stirring, for about 1 minute more, until the grains turn opaque.
   e. Add the carrots, peas, red bell pepper, and Poultry Stock. Bring to the boil, season with salt, and add the saffron. Stir well, cover the pan, and reduce the heat to low.
   f. Simmer for about 10 minutes, until the water is absorbed.
   g. Place the pan in the oven and bake for about 10 minutes.
   h. Immediately turn out the rice into a half-size hotel pan and fluff with a fork, removing the cloves, cinnamon, cardamom, and bay leaf. Stir in the cashews.
   i. Cover with a clean, damp kitchen towel and a lid. (If not using immediately, omit the lid and cool to room temperature.)

holding: immediately place in a freshly sanitized container, cover, and refrigerate up to 5 days

*For restaurant service you may wish to contain the spices in a cheesecloth sachet and add them in step 3e. Remove before serving.

COMPONENT RECIPE
FENNEL-YOGURT TOMATO SAUCE

yield: 2 2/3 c.

production		costing only
1 Tbsp.	butter	1/2 oz.
2 tsp.	toasted, ground fennel seeds*	1/4 oz.
1/3 c.	minced yellow onion	1 2/3 oz. a.p.
1/4 c.	minced ginger	1 1/3 oz. a.p.
1/2 tsp.	minced garlic	1/18 oz. a.p.
3 c.	vine-ripe tomato coulis	2 lb. a.p.
tt	kosher salt	1/8 oz.
as needed	water	n/c
1/2 c.	whole-milk yogurt	4 fl. oz.

preparation:
1. Heat a 10" sauté pan and add the butter and ground fennel. Stir over medium heat for a few seconds, until the fennel becomes fragrant.
2. Add the onion and ginger and sauté about 30 seconds, until softened, but not brown.
3. Add the garlic, tomato coulis, and a little salt. Stir until well blended.
4. Cover the pan and cook over high heat for about 3 minutes.
5. Uncover the pan and reduce the sauce over high heat, stirring, until it reduces almost dry.
6. Stir in the yogurt and correct the salt.

holding: open-pan cool and refrigerate in a freshly sanitized container up to 3 days

*The method for toasting and grinding spices appears in the Garam Masala component recipe on p. 829.

RECIPE VARIATION

Tandoori Quail with Basmati Pulao, Greens Purée, and Braised Cauliflower
Replace the lamb chops with 2 semiboneless, trussed, 3 1/2-oz. quail per serving. Roast in a 400°F oven for 12 minutes.

Seared Calf's Liver

with Balsamic Onion Marmalade,
Delmonico Potatoes, and
Wilted Baby Spinach

yield: 1 (6-oz.) entrée serving plus accompaniments
(multiply × 4 for classroom turnout; adjust equipment sizes
accordingly)

MASTER RECIPE

production		costing only
1	Delmonico Potato Round	1/4 recipe
2/3 c.	Balsamic Onion Marmalade	1/4 recipe
2 Tbsp.	corn oil	1 fl. oz.
1	6-oz. 3/4"-thick slice natural calf's liver, peeled and trimmed	7 oz. a.p.
tt	kosher salt	1/16 oz.
tt	fresh-ground black pepper	1/16 oz.
1 Tbsp.	minced shallot	1/2 oz. a.p.
2 Tbsp.	Reduced Red Wine	1/4 recipe
1/2 c.	Demi-Glace	4 fl. oz.
as needed	water	
2 Tbsp.	butter	1 oz.
1 tsp.	fresh thyme leaves	1/40 bunch a.p.
1 Tbsp.	gold-color pure olive oil	1/2 fl. oz.
1	peeled and crushed garlic clove	1/9 oz. a.p.
8 oz.	baby spinach	8 oz.
1 Tbsp.	peeled, brunoise-cut red bell pepper	1/2 oz. a.p.

service turnout:

1. Place the Delmonico Potato Round on a sizzle pan and bake in the top of a 400°F oven for about 10 minutes, until heated through and golden on top.
2. Warm the Balsamic Onion Marmalade in a microwave oven or small covered sauté pan.
3. Sear the liver:
   a. Heat an 8" sauté pan until very hot.
   b. Add the oil, quickly blot the liver dry, and sear for about 30 seconds on each side to achieve a dark brown exterior and rare interior.
   c. Season with salt and pepper, transfer to a sizzle pan, and hold warm.
4. Finish the sauce:
   a. Add the shallot, Reduced Red Wine, Demi-Glace, and a little water to the liver pan and stir to lift the deglazings.
   b. Reduce the sauce to a light nappé consistency, work in the butter, and add the thyme. Season with salt. Hold warm.
5. Wilt the spinach:
   a. Heat a 10" nonstick pan, add the oil and garlic, and sizzle the garlic for a few seconds.
   b. Remove and discard the garlic and add the spinach. Toss and turn with tongs for a few seconds only until barely wilted, then season with salt.
6. Plate the dish:
   a. Using an offset spatula, lift the Delmonico round off the sizzle plate, place it on the back center of a hot 12" plate, and remove the ring. (You may need to run a paring knife around the edges.)
   b. Place a mound of spinach on either side of the plate.
   c. Prop the liver on an angle against the Delmonico round. Pour any juices accumulated around the liver into the demi-glace.
   d. Spoon the demi-glace over the liver.
   e. Mound the marmalade on the right side of the liver.
   f. Scatter the brunoise red bell pepper over the liver.

COMPONENT RECIPE
DELMONICO POTATO ROUNDS

yield: 4 (2 1/2") rounds

production		costing only
1 lb.	russet potatoes	1 lb.
tt	kosher salt	1/8 oz.
2 c.	half-and-half	16 fl. oz.
1/2 c.	heavy cream	4 fl. oz.
tt	fine-ground white pepper	1/16 oz.
as needed	pan coating spray	% of container
1/2	egg, beaten	1/2 each or 1 oz.
1/2 c.	grated Gruyère cheese	1 1/2 oz. a.p.
1/4 c.	grated Parmigiano-Reggiano cheese	1 oz. a.p.
1/2 c.	fresh bread crumbs	3 oz. bread a.p.
1 Tbsp.	melted butter	1/2 oz.
dash	Hungarian sweet paprika	1/16 oz.

preparation:
1. Peel the potatoes and cut them lengthwise into quarters.
2. Place in a saucepan and add water just to cover. Season liberally with salt and simmer for about 5 minutes, until a sharp knife pierces them with some resistance.
3. Pour off the cooking water, rinse the potatoes briefly with cold water, and blot them dry.
4. Using a mandoline with the julienne blade, cut the potatoes into shreds.
5. Place the potatoes into a 10" nonstick sauté pan, add the half-and-half and cream, and season with white pepper and a little salt. Cook, stirring and scraping with a heatproof rubber spatula, for 3 to 5 minutes, until the sauce is very thick and the potato shreds cling together. Cool to room temperature.
6. Coat a parchment-lined sheet tray and the inside of 4 (1 3/4" × 2 1/2") entremet rings with pan coating.
7. Stir the egg and cheeses into the potatoes.
8. Place the entremet rings on the sheet tray and pack the potatoes into them, pressing to firm and compact the potatoes.
9. Mix the bread crumbs with the melted butter and press them on top of the potatoes.
10. Sprinkle the tops with paprika.

holding: cover with plastic film and refrigerate up to 2 days

COMPONENT RECIPE
BALSAMIC ONION MARMALADE

yield: 2 2/3 c.

production		costing only
2 Tbsp.	gold-color pure olive oil	1 fl. oz.
2 Tbsp.	clarified butter	1 1/4 oz. a.p.
1 lb.	yellow onions, halved and sliced 3/8"	1 lb. 2 oz. a.p.
1 lb.	red onions, halved and sliced 3/8"	1 lb. 2 oz. a.p.
tt	kosher salt	1/4 oz.
2 Tbsp.	sugar	1 oz.
tt	balsamic vinegar	±1 fl. oz.

preparation:
1. Heat the oil and butter in a 12" nonstick sauté pan. Add the onions and a little salt and cook, stirring, for about 1 minute over medium heat.
2. Cover the pan and cook over low heat, stirring occasionally, for about 5 minutes, until the onions are wilted.
3. Uncover the pan, add the sugar, and continue to cook, stirring often, about 3 minutes longer until the onions caramelize to a rich, golden brown. ⚠ Watch carefully as the browning progresses to avoid scorching.
4. Season with salt and balance the flavor with balsamic vinegar, adding enough to make a sweet and tangy condiment.

holding: open-pan cool and immediately refrigerate in a freshly sanitized, covered, nonreactive container up to 1 week

---

RECIPE VARIATION

Seared Foie Gras with Balsamic Onion Marmalade on Straw Potato Cake (appetizer)
Replace the calf's liver with a thick 2-oz. medallion of raw foie gras. Reduce the cooking time to about 15 seconds per side. Omit the accompaniments and instead place the foie gras on a thin, 2 1/2"-diameter Potato Latke (p. 815). Reduce the sauce amounts by half and drizzle it around the foie gras. Reduce the amount of marmalade to 2 Tbsp. and mound it alongside the foie gras. Garnish with microgreens or a sprig of watercress.

Veal Parmesan
with Fresh Tomato Sauce, Potato Gnocchi, and Vegetable "Spaghetti"

yield: 1 (6-oz.) entrée serving plus accompaniments (multiply × 4 for classroom turnout; adjust equipment sizes accordingly)

MASTER RECIPE

production		costing only
1/4 c.	gold-color pure olive oil	2 fl. oz.
2 Tbsp.	clarified butter	1 1/4 oz. a.p.
2	3-oz. Parmesan-Breaded Veal Cutlets	1/4 recipe
4 oz.	Potato Gnocchi	1/4 recipe
as needed	water	n/c
tt	kosher salt	1/16 oz.
2 Tbsp.	gold-color pure olive oil	1 fl. oz.
1	peeled, smashed garlic clove	1/9 oz. a.p.
5 oz.	Vegetable "Spaghetti"	1/4 recipe
2	thin, large 3/4-oz. slices fresh mozzarella	1 1/2 oz.
1 Tbsp.	butter	1/2 oz.
3 Tbsp.	grated Parmigiano-Reggiano cheese	3/4 oz.
1 c.	Fresh Tomato Sauce	1/4 recipe
2 Tbsp.	chiffonade fresh basil leaves	1/20 bunch a.p.

service turnout:

1. Pan-fry the Veal Cutlets:
   a. Heat a 10" sauté pan, add 1/4 c. oil and the clarified butter, and heat to about 375°F.
   b. Add the Parmesan-Breaded Veal Cutlets and pan-fry for about 1 minute, until the bottoms are rich golden brown.
   c. Turn over the cutlets and fry for 1 minute more, until the new bottoms are browned.
   d. Transfer the cutlets to a sizzle pan and hold warm.
2. Place the Potato Gnocchi and a little water in an 8" nonstick sauté pan, season with salt, cover, and heat over low heat.
3. Heat a 10" sauté pan until very hot, add 2 Tbsp. oil and the garlic, then toss in the Vegetable "Spaghetti" and a pinch of salt. Toss, searing over high heat, for about 30 seconds, until wilted but still crisp-tender.
4. Finish and plate the dish:
   a. Place the mozzarella slices on the veal cutlets and heat in a 400°F oven for less than a minute, until the cheese melts.
   b. Work the butter into the gnocchi, toss in the cheese, and immediately mound the gnocchi on the back left of a hot 12" plate.
   c. Mound the "spaghetti" to the right of the gnocchi, removing the garlic clove.
   d. Ladle the Fresh Tomato Sauce into the vegetable pan and heat it.
   e. Prop the veal cutlets overlapping against the "spaghetti" and gnocchi.
   f. Spoon the tomato sauce in a diagonal line across the cutlets and gnocchi from 10 o'clock to 4 o'clock.
   g. Sprinkle the chiffonade basil on top.

COMPONENT RECIPE
PARMESAN-BREADED VEAL CUTLETS

yield: 8 (3-oz.) pc.

production		costing only
2 lb.	top round of veal, preferably a single muscle*	2 lb.
2 c.	fresh bread crumbs from firm, crustless bread	8 oz. bread a.p.
1 c.	grated Parmigiano-Reggiano cheese	4 oz. a.p.
2	eggs, beaten with 2 Tbsp. water	2 each or 4 oz.
1/2 c.	flour	2 1/2 oz.
tt	kosher salt	1/16 oz.
tt	fine-ground white pepper	1/16 oz.

preparation:
1. Fabricate the veal cutlets:
   a. If necessary, trim and discard all of the veal's surface fat.
   b. If necessary, seam out the meat, dividing it into large muscles.
   c. Trim and discard all silverskin and other connective tissue, leaving only clean meat.
   d. For each muscle, determine the direction of the grain. (Seek instructor advice, if necessary.)
   e. Cut each muscle across the grain into large 3-oz. slices of even 1/4" thickness. If necessary, cut on the bias to yield larger pieces. You should have at least 8 (3-oz.) cutlets.
   f. Place a pan liner sheet on the work surface, fold it in half lengthwise, and open it. Arrange the cutlets in a row on the lower half of the sheet and fold the top down over them.
   g. Using the flat surface of a meat mallet, gently flatten the cutlets to an even 3/16" thickness.
2. Bread the cutlets:
   a. Mix together the bread crumbs and cheese in a shallow quarter-size hotel pan or other small vessel.
   b. Place the egg wash and the flour in separate, similar pans and line them up: flour, egg wash, bread crumbs.
   c. Have ready a rack set over a half-sheet tray.
   d. Season both sides of each cutlet with salt and white pepper, dip both sides in flour, dip both sides in egg wash, and then coat both sides with bread crumbs, pressing firmly so the crumbs adhere. Place the breaded cutlets on the rack.
   e. Refrigerate the breaded cutlets uncovered for at least 1 hour to set the coating.

holding: loosely covered with plastic film up to 2 days

*Depending on the trim and muscle configuration of the meat, 2 lb. may yield more than 24 oz. cutlets.

COMPONENT RECIPE
POTATO GNOCCHI

yield: approx. 1 lb.

production		costing only
13 oz.	peeled and quartered russet potatoes	1 lb. a.p.
tt	kosher salt	
1	egg, beaten	1 each or 2 oz.
±3/4 c.	flour	±4 oz.
1 Tbsp.	room-temperature butter	1 oz.

preparation:
1. Cook the potatoes:
   a. Prepare a commercial pressure steamer or stovetop steamer.
   b. Place the potatoes on the steamer tray and steam them until fork-tender (about 5 minutes in a commercial steamer, or as long as 15 minutes in a stovetop steamer).
   c. Force the hot potatoes through a ricer or coarse-mesh strainer into a warm bowl.
2. Mix the dough:
   a. Using a fork, toss a little salt into the potatoes and then lightly work in the egg.
   b. Sift flour over the potatoes and toss with the fork, adding only enough flour to form a cohesive dough.
   c. Turn out the dough onto a floured work surface and lightly knead it a few strokes. The dough should be moist but not sticky.
3. Bring a large pot of salted water to the boil.
4. Fabricate the gnocchi:
   a. Divide the dough in half and, using the palms of your floured hands in a back-and-forth motion, roll each dough half into a long rope about 3/4" in diameter.
   b. Cut each dough rope into 1" sections.
   c. To form a gnocco:
      (1) Hold a fork in your left hand (left-handers do the opposite) over a half-sheet tray lined with a clean, dry kitchen towel.
      (2) Place a dough section on the tines of the fork near the handle and press down on it with your index finger to imprint the bottom of the gnocco with a grooved pattern and create a depression in the top.
      (3) Lift your index finger off the gnocco and, almost simultaneously, use your thumb to roll the gnocco forward off the fork tines onto the tray. If done correctly, you have created a ridged, shell-shaped pasta morsel.
      (4) Repeat with the remaining dough sections.
5. Boil the gnocchi:
   a. Lift the gnocchi up with the towel and drop them into the boiling water.
   b. Reduce the temperature to maintain a brisk simmer, stir, and simmer for about 3 minutes, until the gnocchi float to the surface.
   c. Place the butter in a warm half-size hotel pan.
   d. Using a spider or perforated lifter, lift the gnocchi from the water, shake to drain, and then place them in the hotel pan.
   e. Toss to coat the gnocchi with the butter as they cool.

holding: loosely covered with plastic film at cool room temperature up to 2 hours; refrigerate up to 2 days

COMPONENT RECIPE
VEGETABLE "SPAGHETTI"

yield: approx. 20 oz.

production		costing only
12 oz.	small, slender zucchini with few seeds*	12 oz.
12 oz.	small, slender straight-neck yellow squash with few seeds*	12 oz.
4 oz.	large carrot	4 oz.
8 oz.	large red bell pepper	8 oz.
8 oz.	large yellow bell pepper	8 oz.

preparation:
1. Set up a mandoline to cut 1/8" julienne. ⚠ Be sure to use the guard.
2. Trim and discard the ends of the zucchini and yellow squash. Run the squashes through the mandoline lengthwise to make long, spaghetti-like strands. If necessary, discard the seedy central cores.
3. Reset the mandoline to make 1/16" slices. (If using an Asian mandoline with a 1/16" julienne option, use it instead.)
4. Peel the carrot and trim the ends. Run the carrot through the mandoline lengthwise to make very thin slices. Stack the slices and cut them with a chef's knife to make long, spaghetti-like strands.
5. Core the bell peppers and cut them into sections along the contours. Remove all seeds and veins. Cut lengthwise into long, very slender julienne.
6. Toss the vegetables together.

holding: in a freshly sanitized, covered container, with several layers of paper towels underneath, up to 2 days

*If mature squash with many large seeds must be used, double the amount purchased and use only the flesh, discarding the seedy middle sections.

ENTREES

RECIPE VARIATIONS

Pork Parmesan with Fresh Tomato Sauce, Potato Gnocchi, and Vegetable "Spaghetti"
Replace the veal with boneless pork loin.

Eggplant Parmesan with Fresh Tomato Sauce, Potato Gnocchi, and Vegetable "Spaghetti"
Replace the veal with 1 1/2 lb. very fresh, small eggplants. Peel and slice, but do not flatten. (Hold no longer than 12 hours.)

Crème Brûlée

yield: 1 dessert serving
(multiply × 4 for classroom turnout)

MASTER RECIPE

production		costing only
1	Crème Brûlée	1/4 recipe
1	6" doily	1 each
1	edible flower, optional	1 each

service turnout:
1. Plate the dish:
   a. Place the Crème Brûlée on a doily-lined 8" plate.
   b. Place the flower, if using, on the plate alongside the crème brûlée.

COMPONENT RECIPE
CRÈMES BRÛLÉE

yield: 4 (6-oz.) dessert servings

production		costing only
1 1/2 c.	heavy cream	12 fl. oz.
5	egg yolks	5 each or 3 1/3 oz.
3 1/2 oz.	sugar	3 1/2 oz.
pinch	fine salt	1/16 oz.
4 oz.	sugar	4 oz.

preparation:
1. Mise en place:
   a. Preheat an oven to 300°F.
   b. Choose a hotel pan with a flat, unwarped bottom. Line it with a clean, wet kitchen towel.
   c. Place 4 (8-oz.) shallow crème brûlée dishes into the pan.
   d. Have ready boiling water and a sheet of foil large enough to cover the hotel pan.
2. Mix the custard:
   a. Bring the cream to the simmer in a small saucepan.
   b. Whisk together the yolks, 3 1/2 oz. sugar, and salt, and then whisk the hot cream into the yolks in a thin stream.
3. Bake the crèmes brûlée:
   a. Pour the custard into the crème brûlée dishes.
   b. Pull out the center rack of the oven, place the hotel pan on it, and very carefully pour the boiling water around the dishes to a level of about 1/4".
   c. Place the foil over the pan and secure it on top.
   d. Gently push the rack back into the oven and close the door.
   e. Bake the crèmes brûlée for about 30 minutes, and then begin to check the set at 10-minute intervals. When the custard is almost set but still a little wobbly in the center, remove the foil, turn off the oven, and leave the door open until the pan is cool enough to handle.
   f. Transfer the pan to a refrigerator and chill, uncovered, for about 1 hour until cold.
4. Glaze the crèmes brûlée:
   a. Place the custards on a half-sheet tray lined with foil.
   b. Sprinkle about 2 Tbsp. sugar on the surface of a custard in an even layer.
   c. Using a foodservice torch, caramelize the sugar to a rich, golden brown.
   d. Repeat with the remaining Brûlées.
   e. Refrigerate, uncovered, for at least 1 hour until the caramel hardens.

holding: refrigerate, covered loosely with plastic film, up to 4 hours; hold unglazed custards up to 3 days.

RECIPE VARIATIONS

Ginger Crème Brûlée
Steep the heated cream with 2 Tbsp. peeled fresh ginger and 1 Tbsp. crystallized ginger, both chopped fine. Strain and proceed with the recipe.

Orange Crème Brûlée
Steep the heated cream with the zest of 1 orange, pared off in a strip for 1 hour then remove.. Replace 2 Tbsp. of the cream with Grand Marnier or other orange liqueur.

Mascarpone Cannolo
with Zabaglione Sauce

yield: 1 dessert serving
(multiply × 4 for classroom turnout; adjust equipment sizes accordingly

MASTER RECIPE

production		costing only
1 oz.	pasteurized egg yolk	1 oz.
2 Tbsp.	confectioner's sugar	1/2 oz.
few drops	fresh lemon juice	1/8 [90 ct.] lemon
6 Tbsp.	Italian Marsala wine	3 fl. oz.
1	Mascarpone Cannolo	1/5 to 1/8 recipe
1	orange "butterfly"	1/6 [100 ct.] orange
1	fresh mint sprig	1/12 bunch a.p.

service turnout:

1. Have ready a hot-water bath on the hot line or on a butane burner at the dessert station.
2. Prepare the zabaglione:
   a. Combine the egg yolk and sugar in a small stainless steel bowl and whip vigorously until fluffy.
   b. Add the lemon juice and wine and whip to blend.
   c. Place the bowl over the simmering hot-water bath and whisk for about 1 minute, until the custard thickens into a fluffy sauce and no raw yolk taste remains.
3. Plate the dish:
   a. Pour the sauce into the center of a cool 10" plate.
   b. Place the Mascarpone Cannolo on the plate slightly left of center, oriented from 1 o'clock to 7 o'clock.
   c. Twist the orange "butterfly" and arrange it against the right side of the cannolo.
   d. Stick the mint sprig out of the center of the "butterfly."

COMPONENT RECIPE
MASCARPONE CANNOLI

yield: 5 to 8 cannoli, depending on size of shells

production		costing only
5 to 8	Cannoli Shells	1 recipe
1 qt.	Mascarpone Cannoli Filling, in a pastry bag fitted with a large star tip	1 recipe
1/4 to 1/2 c.	chopped, peeled pistachios	3/4 oz. to 1 1/2 oz.
1 to 2 Tbsp.	confectioner's sugar, in shaker or small, fine-mesh strainer	1/4 oz. to 1/2 oz.

preparation:

1. Fill the shells:
   a. Insert the pastry bag halfway into a Cannolo Shell and squeeze, filling half of the shell with Mascarpone Cannoli Filling and ending with a rosette swirl at the end.
   b. Turn the shell around and repeat to completely fill the shell.
   c. Place the filled cannolo on a half-sheet tray.
   d. Repeat, using all shells and filling.
2. Decorate the cannoli:
   a. Dip the two ends of each cannolo in pistachio nuts.
   b. Dust each cannolo with sugar.

holding: cover loosely with plastic film and refrigerate up to 12 hours

COMPONENT RECIPE
MASCARPONE CANNOLI FILLING

yield: approx. 1 qt.

production		costing only
1 1/2 lb.	mascarpone cheese*	1 1/2 lb.
±1/2 c.	confectioners' sugar	±2 1/2 oz.
1 tsp.	pure vanilla extract	1/6 fl. oz.
2 Tbsp.	orange liqueur	1 fl. oz.
2 Tbsp.	minced citron or candied orange peel	1/4 oz.

preparation:
1. Place the mascarpone in a mixing bowl and whisk in sugar to taste.
2. Stir in the remaining ingredients.

*If the mascarpone's consistency is too thin to hold a shape, whip in 2 to 3 tsp. granular gelatin warmed in the orange liqueur and 2 Tbsp. water. Refrigerate until set.

holding: refrigerate in a freshly sanitized, covered container up to 3 days

COMPONENT RECIPE
CANNOLI SHELLS

yield: 5 to 8 shells, depending on size of tubes

production		costing only
1 c.	flour	5 1/2 oz.
1 Tbsp.	melted, cooled butter	1/2 oz.
pinch	fine salt	1/16 oz.
1 Tbsp.	sugar	1/2 oz.
1	egg yolk	2/3 oz.
1 Tbsp.	red wine	1/2 oz.
as needed	cold water	n/c
as needed	flour	1 oz.
1 Tbsp.	egg, beaten with 2 tsp. water	1/2 each or 1/2 oz.
as needed	frying compound or corn oil	% used

preparation:
1. Mix the dough:
   a. Combine 1 c. flour with the butter, salt, and sugar in a small bowl and mix with a fork.
   b. Stir in the egg yolk, wine, and water to make a medium-firm dough.
   c. Dust the work surface with flour and knead the dough for 1 to 2 minutes, until smooth.
   d. Dust the dough with flour, wrap in plastic film, and rest at room temperature for at least 30 minutes.
2. Make up the shells:
   a. Using a pasta machine or rolling pin, roll the dough slightly thinner than a 1/8" thickness.
   b. Using a fluted pastry wheel, cut the dough into 4" squares.
   c. Wrap each square diagonally around a cannoli tube, sealing the dough cylinder shut with a dab of egg wash.
   d. Place on a sheet tray and refrigerate for 30 minutes.
3. Preheat a fryer or heavy saucepan of oil to 375°F and lower the baskets. Prepare a rack set over a half-sheet tray.
4. Fry the cannoli shells:
   a. As a test batch, carefully lower one of the shells (on the tube) into the hot oil. Deep-fry for about 1 minute, until the shell is golden brown. Gently lift out of the oil and drain on the rack.
   b. Repeat, frying two or more shells at a time until all are fried.
   c. When the shells reach room temperature, remove the tubes.

holding: in a tightly sealed container, with pan liner between layers, at cool room temperature and low humidity, up to 5 days

---

RECIPE VARIATION
Chocolate Chip Cannolo with Mocha Custard Sauce
In the filling, omit the orange liqueur and orange peel. Add 1/2 c. mini chocolate chips to the filling. Replace the pistachio nuts with mini chocolate chips. Replace the zabaglione sauce with Vanilla Custard Sauce flavored with melted bittersweet chocolate and instant espresso.

Frozen Soufflé Grand Marnier
with Chocolate-Dipped Burnt-Orange Biscotto

yield: 1 dessert serving
(multiply × 4 for classroom turnout)

MASTER RECIPE

production		costing only
1	Frozen Soufflé Grand Marnier	1/4 recipe
1 tsp.	cocoa powder, in shaker or small fine-mesh strainer	1/16 oz.
1	8" doily	1 each
1	Chocolate-Dipped Burnt-Orange Biscotto	1/12 recipe
1 Tbsp.	Candied Orange Zest	1/12 recipe

service turnout:
1. Plate the dish:
   a. Dust the top of the Frozen Soufflé Grand Marnier with cocoa powder.
   b. Remove the acetate strip.
   c. Place an 8" doily on the right side of a cool 12" plate.
   d. Place the soufflé on the left side of the plate and set the Chocolate-Dipped Burnt-Orange Biscotto next to it on the right.
   e. Mound the Candied Orange Zest on top of the soufflé.

COMPONENT RECIPE
FROZEN SOUFFLÉ GRAND MARNIER

yield: 4 (10-fl.-oz.) soufflés

production		costing only
1/2 c.	orange juice	4 fl. oz.
1 Tbsp.	granular gelatin	1/5 oz.
3	eggs	3 each or 6 oz.
2 1/2 oz.	sugar	2 1/2 oz.
1 Tbsp.	minced orange zest	n/c
pinch	fine salt	1/16 oz.
2 Tbsp.	Grand Marnier	1 fl. oz.
10 fl. oz.	very cold heavy cream	10 fl. oz.

preparation:
1. Mise en place:
   a. Place 4 (8-fl.-oz.) ramekins on a half-sheet tray.
   b. Cut 4 acetate strips of the correct width to extend 1" higher than the rim of the ramekins, and of the correct length to line the inside of the ramekins. (Alternatively, use folded strips of aluminum foil.)
   c. Line the inside of the ramekins with the acetate strips or foil.
   d. Prepare a hot-water bath of the correct size to accommodate a large mixing bowl.
   e. Set up a mixer fitted with the whip attachment.
   f. If available, place another mixer bowl and whip attachment in the refrigerator. Alternatively, place a large mixing bowl and whip in the refrigerator.
2. In a small sauté pan, reduce the orange juice by half, cool slightly, add the gelatin, and stir to dissolve. Hold warm.
3. Combine the eggs, sugar, orange zest, and salt in a large stainless steel bowl and whip until light and fluffy. Place the bowl over the simmering water bath and whip until the eggs reach 140°F.
4. Immediately scrape the egg mixture into the mixer bowl. Beat on high speed for about 1 minute, until the eggs stand in soft peaks.
5. Beat in the orange juice–gelatin mixture and the Grand Marnier.
6. In the chilled bowl, whip the cream to soft peaks.
7. Fold the whipped cream into the custard.
8. Immediately pour the mixture into the prepared ramekins. Gently tap the ramekins on the work surface to settle the mixture and level the tops.
9. Freeze for at least 4 hours.

holding: cover each ramekin with plastic wrap and freeze up to 3 days

COMPONENT RECIPE
CHOCOLATE-DIPPED BURNT-ORANGE BISCOTTI

yield: 12 to 15 cookies

production		costing only
as needed	baker's pan coating spray	% of container
1/2 c.	Caramelized Orange Zest	2/3 recipe
5 1/2 oz.	flour	5 1/2 oz.
3/4 tsp.	baking powder	1/8 oz.
pinch	fine salt	1/16 oz.
2 oz.	room-temperature butter	2 oz.
3 oz.	sugar	3 oz.
1	egg	1 each or 2 oz.
1/4 c.	minced orange zest	1/2 [100 ct.] orange
1 Tbsp.	orange liqueur	1/2 fl. oz.
3 oz.	bittersweet chocolate, chopped	3 oz.

preparation:
1. Mise en place:
   a. Preheat an oven to 350°F.
   b. Prepare a half-sheet tray with pan liner lightly sprayed with pan coating.
   c. Set up a mixer fitted with the paddle attachment.
   d. Prepare a hot-water bath of the correct size to accommodate a small, shallow stainless steel bowl.
2. Chop the Caramelized Orange Zest fine.
3. Mix the dough:
   a. Sift together the flour, baking powder, and salt.
   b. Combine the butter and sugar in the mixer bowl and cream them on medium speed until light and fluffy.
   c. Mix in the egg, minced orange zest, and chopped caramelized orange zest.
   d. Reduce the speed to low and pulse in the flour mixture and orange liqueur.
4. Form and bake the cookie slab:
   a. Place the dough on the lined sheet tray and form it into a rectangle about 4" × 8" and 3/4" thick.
   b. Bake in the center of the oven for 25 to 30 minutes, until set and light golden.
   c. Reduce the oven temperature to 300°F.
   d. Transfer the sheet tray to a rack and cool the cookie rectangle enough to handle it.
5. Cut and dry the biscotti:
   a. Use two spatulas to transfer the cookie rectangle to a cutting board.
   b. Using a serrated knife, cut it on the bias about 3/8" thick to make 12 perfect biscotti and a few scraps.
   c. Place the biscotti upright on the half-sheet tray and return to the oven for 10 to 15 minutes, until the cookies are dry and crisp.
   d. Cool the biscotti on a rack to room temperature.
6. Glaze the biscotti:
   a. Put the chocolate in the shallow bowl and place the bowl over the hot-water bath. Melt the chocolate, stirring with a rubber spatula, until smooth.
   b. Dip the curved edge of each biscotto in the chocolate and set it upright on the sheet tray until the chocolate hardens.

holding: at cool room temperature and low humidity in a tightly sealed container up to 1 week

COMPONENT RECIPE
CANDIED ORANGE ZEST
AND CARAMELIZED ORANGE ZEST

yield: approx. 1/4 c. candied orange zest and 1/2 c. caramelized orange zest

production		costing only
4	large oranges	4 [100 ct.] oranges
1/2 c.	water	n/c
1/2 c.	sugar	4 oz.

preparation:
1. Use a zesting tool to remove the zest of the oranges in long juliennes.
2. Combine the water and sugar in a small saucepan and heat until the sugar melts. Add the orange zest and simmer for about 30 minutes, until the syrup concentrates and thickens. Do not stir.
3. Using two forks, remove about 1/3 of the zest to a silicone pad (or a sheet of pan liner lightly coated with pan coating spray). Separate the zest into individual strands.
4. Continue cooking the remaining zest, watching carefully, until the sugar syrup caramelizes to a medium brown color. ⚠ Do not stir the syrup, and do not allow the caramel to burn.
5. Use the forks to remove the caramelized zest to the silicone pad (or pan liner) and separate the strands.

holding: in a tightly sealed container, at cool room temperature and low humidity, up to 1 week

---

RECIPE VARIATIONS
Frozen Cappuccino Soufflé with Chocolate-Dipped Hazelnut Biscotto
Omit all orange products from all recipes. Add 1 Tbsp. instant espresso to the soufflé custard. Dust the tops of the soufflés with a little cinnamon in addition to the cocoa powder. Add 2 oz. cracked blanched hazelnuts and 1/2 tsp. pure vanilla extract to the biscotti dough.

Frozen Chocolate Soufflé with Almond Biscotto
Omit all orange products from all recipes. Add 2 oz. melted, cooled bittersweet chocolate to the soufflé custard. Add 2 oz. cracked whole blanched almonds and 1/4 tsp. almond extract to the biscotti dough.

Brooklyn Blackout Cake
with Chocolate Whipped Cream

yield: 1 dessert serving
(multiply × 4 for classroom turnout)

MASTER RECIPE

production		costing only
1 slice	Brooklyn Blackout Cake	1/10 recipe
1/4 c.	Chocolate Whipped Cream, in a pastry bag fitted with a large star tip	1/4 recipe

service turnout:
1. Plate the dish:
   a. Place the Brooklyn Blackout Cake slice slightly left of center on a cool 8" plate.
   b. Pipe a rosette of Chocolate Whipped Cream next to the cake.

COMPONENT RECIPE
BLACKOUT CAKE ASSEMBLY

yield: 10 dessert servings: 1 (8") cake

production		costing only
4	Blackout Cake Layers	1 recipe
2 c.	Blackout Filling	1 recipe
1	(8") round cardboard cake board	1 each
3 c.	Blackout Frosting	1 recipe

preparation:
1. Line a half-sheet tray with ungreased pan liner. Choose the least attractive Blackout Cake Layer and crumble it onto the tray. Try to achieve light, separate, even-sized crumbs.
2. Assemble the cake:
   a. Place a dab of Blackout Filling on the cake board and place a cake layer on it. If available, place it on a decorator's turntable.
   b. Place half of the filling on the cake layer and spread it almost to the edges.
   c. Press another cake layer on top.
   d. Place the remaining filling on the cake layer and spread it almost to the edges.
   e. Press the final cake layer on top.
3. Coat the sides and top of the cake with Blackout Frosting.
4. Mask the sides and top of the cake with cake crumbs.

holding: refrigerate under a cake dome up to 5 days

COMPONENT RECIPE
BLACKOUT CAKE LAYERS

yield: 4 (8") cake layers

production		costing only
as needed	baker's pan coating spray	% of container
2 1/2 oz.	unsweetened chocolate, chopped	2 1/2 oz.
3/4 c.	half-and-half	6 fl. oz.
1/2 c.	Dutch-process cocoa powder	1 1/3 oz.
2 Tbsp.	boiling water	n/c
11 oz.	flour	11 oz.
1 tsp.	baking soda	1/8 oz.
1 tsp.	baking powder	1/8 oz.
1/2 tsp.	fine salt	1/6 oz.
8 oz.	room-temperature butter	8 oz.
16 oz.	sugar	16 oz.
4	egg yolks	4 each or 2 2/3 oz.
2 tsp.	pure vanilla extract	1/3 fl. oz.
4	room-temperature egg whites	n/c or 4 oz.

preparation:
1. Mise en place:
   a. Preheat an oven to 375°F.
   b. Spray 4 (8" × 2") round cake pans with pan coating, press 4 (8") circles of pan liner into the bottoms, and spray again. Place the pans on a sheet tray.
   c. Set up a mixer with the paddle attachment.
   d. If available, obtain another mixer bowl and the whip attachment. (Alternatively, use a bowl and whip.)
2. Place the chocolate and half-and-half in a small saucepan and melt together over low heat, stirring often with a heatproof rubber spatula. Cool to room temperature.
3. Place the cocoa powder in a very small bowl and stir in the boiling water to dissolve it. Scrape the cocoa mixture into the chocolate mixture and stir to blend.
4. Sift together the flour, baking soda, baking powder, and salt.
5. Mix the batter:
   a. Place the butter and sugar in the mixer and cream them on medium speed until light and fluffy.
   b. Beat in the egg yolks and vanilla.
   c. On low speed, pulse in half of the flour mixture, then the chocolate mixture, then the remaining flour mixture to make a smooth batter. Do not overmix.
   d. Whip the egg whites to just under firm peak.
   e. Immediately fold the egg whites into the batter.
6. Pan the batter:
   a. Divide the batter evenly among the 4 pans.
   b. Use a small offset spatula to push the edges of the batter a little way up the sides to help the layers bake flat.
7. Bake the layers in the center of the oven for 20 to 30 minutes until a tester comes out with large, moist crumbs clinging to it, but not with wet batter.
8. Cool the layers for 15 minutes in the pans on racks, then turn out onto the racks and cool to room temperature.

holding: tightly wrapped in plastic film at cool room temperature up to 24 hours; freeze up to 1 month

DESSERTS

COMPONENT RECIPE
BLACKOUT FILLING

yield: approx. 2 c.

production		costing only
3 1/2 oz.	butter	3 1/2 oz.
3 oz.	semisweet chocolate, chopped	3 oz.
1 1/2 oz.	unsweetened chocolate, chopped	1 1/2 oz.
3	eggs	3 each or 6 oz.
3 1/2 oz.	sugar	3 1/2 oz.
pinch	salt	1/16 oz.
3 fl. oz.	chocolate liqueur	3 fl. oz.

preparation:
1. Prepare a hot-water bath and an ice-water bath, both large enough to accommodate a small mixing bowl.
2. Place the butter and chocolates in a small, heavy saucepan and melt together over low heat, stirring with a heatproof rubber spatula until smooth. Remove from the heat.
3. Combine the eggs, sugar, salt, and chocolate liqueur in a small mixing bowl.
4. Place the bowl over the briskly simmering hot-water bath and whisk constantly until the mixture thickens and reaches 180°F.
5. Whisk in the chocolate mixture.
6. Place the bowl in the ice-water bath and cool, whisking constantly, until the filling thickens. Change to a rubber scraper and stir, scraping down the sides of the bowl to prevent the filling from congealing on them.
7. When the filling reaches a thick, puddinglike consistency, remove from the ice-water bath and cover with plastic film.
8. Refrigerate until needed.

holding: up to 3 hours at cool room temperature; if refrigerated the filling will harden and may need to be worked over hot water, then recooled in an ice-water bath

COMPONENT RECIPE
BLACKOUT FROSTING

yield: approx. 3 c.

production		costing only
12 oz.	semisweet chocolate, chopped	12 oz.
1/4 c.	chocolate liqueur	2 fl. oz.
1 Tbsp.	light corn syrup	1/2 fl. oz.
12 oz.	room-temperature unsalted butter	12 oz.
2 tsp.	pure vanilla extract	1/3 fl. oz.

preparation:
1. Prepare a hot-water bath and an ice-water bath, both large enough to accommodate a medium stainless steel bowl.
2. Combine the chopped chocolate and chocolate liqueur in a medium stainless steel bowl placed over the simmering water bath and melt them together, stirring and scraping with a rubber spatula just until smooth.
3. Remove from the heat and cool to room temperature, stirring occasionally.
4. Whisk in the corn syrup, butter, and vanilla.
5. Place the bowl in the ice-water bath and whisk until the frosting thickens. Change to a rubber scraper to keep the frosting from congealing on the sides of the bowl.
6. When the frosting acquires a thick, fudgelike consistency, remove from the ice-water bath and cover loosely with plastic film.
7. Hold at room temperature until needed.

holding: up to 3 hours at cool room temperature; if refrigerated the frosting will harden and may need to be worked over hot water, then recooled in an ice-water bath

---

RECIPE VARIATION
Brooklyn Blackout Cake with Vanilla Ice Cream
Omit the Chocolate Whipped Cream. Serve with a 3-fl.-oz. scoop of Vanilla Custard Ice Cream or Philadelphia-Style Ice Cream.

▢ TABLE 16.2 NEW YORK CITY REGIONAL INGREDIENTS

New York City's pantry includes virtually all of the world's foods. In this section we provide information only for specialty items used in recipes from this chapter and the New York City section on the companion website.

ITEM	MARKET FORMS	USES	SEASONALITY	OTHER	STORAGE
ISRAELI COUSCOUS/ *PTITIM* ([p]tee-TEEM)	These pearl-size, lightly toasted pasta spheres are sold in 1-lb. boxes and in bulk.	Israeli couscous is cooked in a general ratio of 1 1/2 parts liquid to 1 part couscous. It can be boiled in water or cooked by the pilaf method in stock. Hot Israeli couscous is served as a side dish or bed for saucy dishes. It may be cooled and prepared as a salad with crisp vegetables and a variety of dressings. In Israel it is served as a breakfast cereal with milk and sugar.	N/A		Store at cool room temperature.
BASMATI RICE	See p. 594.				
WHOLE-GRAIN KASHA	Small, brown, pyramid-shaped grains of buckwheat are sold by the pound in health food stores.	Whole-grain kasha is cooked in a ratio of 2 parts liquid to 1 part kasha. It may be simmered in water or cooked in stock by the pilaf method. Typically served hot as a starch side dish, it may be cooled, dressed with vinaigrette, and tossed with crisp vegetables to make an unusual salad.	N/A		Store at cool room temperature; freeze for prolonged storage.
MATZOH MEAL	Matzoh is a crackerlike unleavened bread eaten by observant Jews at Passover. Matzoh meal is ground matzoh sold in boxes of various sizes in supermarkets with a Jewish clientle. It can be prepared in-house by grinding matzohs in a food processor.	Matzoh meal is used like cracker crumbs as a coating or binding ingredient.	N/A		Store tightly sealed at cool room temperature.
PAPADS/ POPPADUMS	These round, thin wafers made from lentil dough are available plain or seasoned with black pepper, cumin, or other spices. Standard papads are approximately 7" in diameter and are packed in units of 10 to 24 pieces. Smaller "cocktail" papads are also available. Purchase from Indian/ Pakistani grocers.	Deep-fry papads in 400°F oil until they expand, lighten in color, and become crisp. Alternatively, toast over a gas flame or under a broiler (see p. 828). Serve as a snack or use as a garnish.	N/A		Cooked papads—store at room temperature in tightly sealed containers up to 24 hours. Dried papads—store tightly sealed in a cool place for an indefinite length of time.

☐ TABLE 16.2 NEW YORK CITY REGIONAL INGREDIENTS (continued)

ITEM	MARKET FORMS	USES	SEASONALITY	OTHER	STORAGE
GREEN PEPPERCORNS	Green peppercorns are the immature berries of *Piper nigrum*, the vine that produces familiar black peppercorns. Fresh green peppercorns are packed in brine, a process that best retains their pure flavor. Green peppercorns preserved in vinegar keep longer but have a sharp, acidic flavor. Both are sold in jars and cans of various sizes from 3.5 ounces to 15-ounce foodservice cans. Dehydrated green peppercorns have a slightly different flavor. They are sold in bags by the ounce. Purchase all types from spice dealers or specialty grocers, or mail order on the Internet.	Rinse and drain brined and vinegared peppercorns before using. Crush or chop and add to sauces or dressings. Before using dehydrated green peppercorns, soak them in hot water until soft. Crushed or ground dried green peppercorns are sometimes used in rubs and coatings.	N/A		Store at cool room temperature. Refrigerate soft green peppercorns in liquid after opening or hydrating.
LE PUY GREEN LENTILS	These dark green lentils are imported from France and sold in 500 g boxes by specialty purveyors.	Because they retain their firm, meaty texture after proper cooking, green lentils are typically served as a side dish or dressed with vinaigrette to make salads. To mute their strong flavor, they are usually blanched and drained before final cooking.	N/A		Store at cool room temperature.
SPECIALTY SALAD GREENS	See p. 596.				
BROCCOLI RABE	A favorite vegetable of Italian-American cooks, broccoli rabe is widely available from produce dealers and in supermarkets. A typical bunch weighs 1 lb. or slightly more.	Its deep, slightly bitter taste is enhanced by braising with olive oil, garlic, and lemon. Broccoli rabe is served as a side dish complementing Italian sausage, liver dishes, pork dishes, and foods in rich tomato sauces. Chopped, braised broccoli rabe is a favored pizza topping.	Available year round; best in cool months.	For extended refrigerator storage, cut off 1/2" of the stem ends and stand bunches in water. Cover heads with a damp towel. Change water and towels daily.	Refrigerate.
BROCCOLINI	This modern hybrid vegetable is a cross between standard broccoli and a type of Chinese brassica. It is sold by the bunch or pound in supermarkets and from specialty produce purveyors.	Blanch or steam and refresh before using as a side dish or salad ingredient.	Available year round.	Store in the same manner as broccoli rabe, above.	Refrigerate.

(continued)

☐ **TABLE 16.2 NEW YORK CITY REGIONAL INGREDIENTS** *(continued)*

ITEM	MARKET FORMS	USES	SEASONALITY	OTHER	STORAGE
SAVOY CABBAGE	Distinguish Savoy from other round green cabbages by its prominently veined leaves. This mild, tender cabbage is sold by the pound in supermarkets and from specialty produce purveyors.	Use Savoy cabbage raw in cole slaw or braise and serve as a side dish. Its large, tender leaves are excellent for stuffing.	Available year round; best in cool months.		Refrigerate.
TOBIKO	See p. 599.				
CRÈME FRAÎCHE	This thick, rich, fermented dairy product is sold in small consumer packs of varying size in upscale supermarkets and in bulk tubs for foodservice.	Use as a topping or to enrich sauces; will not curdle when boiled.	N/A	Produce in-house using powdered commercial culture available on the Internet.	Refrigerate until manufacturer's expiration date.
PARMIGIANO-REGGIANO CHEESE	This top-quality grana cheese made in the Emilio-Reggiano region of northern Italy is widely available from cheese dealers and specialty food purveyors. It is sold by the pound in vacuum-pack chunks and as whole, half, or quarter wheels.	Serve as a table cheese or grate for use on pastas, gratins, and pizzas.	Available year round.		Refrigerate small pieces wrapped in plastic film. For prolonged storage of wheel sections, wrap in clean, damp linen tablecloths and hold at 55°F.
PECORINO ROMANO CHEESE	This sharp, salty grana cheese from central Italy is made from sheep's milk. Domestic Romano cheese is usually made from cow's milk. Both are widely available by the pound in vacuum-pack chunks and as whole, half, or quarter wheels.	Use in pasta dishes, gratins, and on pizza whenever a strong flavor is desired.	Available year round.		Store as above.
FRESH MOZZARELLA CHEESE	In the United States, soft fresh mozzarella is prepared from cow's milk. For foodservice it is sold immersed in water in 5-lb. tubs. Fabrication includes 12-oz. spheres or braids, 8-oz. spheres, 3-oz. flat ovals, 1/2-oz. bocconcini, and tiny pearlini. Italian buffalo mozzarella is also available.	Use cool mozzarella in salads, sandwiches, and antipasti. For use as a melting cheese, add mozzarella to pizzas, panini, gratins, and on cutlets at the last moment and heat only until melted.	Available year round.		Refrigerate in a closed container submerged in water. Change water frequently. Avoid contamination by using only sanitized spoons or tongs to remove cheese.

TABLE 16.2 NEW YORK CITY REGIONAL INGREDIENTS (continued)

ITEM	MARKET FORMS	USES	SEASONALITY	OTHER	STORAGE
MASCARPONE CHEESE	A specialty of the Lombardy region of Italy, mascarpone is a fresh cow's-milk cheese similar in texture to ricotta but with a higher fat content, up to 75 percent. For foodservice, domestic mascarpone is sold in 5-lb. tubs.	Use in the same manner as ricotta, for pasta fillings and to enrich purées. Use in baking for cheesecakes and cannoli filling.	Available year round.		Refrigerate for a few days only. Use a sanitized spoon to avoid contamination.
SCHMALTZ	Schmaltz is rendered poultry fat, usually from chickens but also from ducks, turkeys, or geese. Schmaltz is available frozen from kosher poultry processors in 8-oz. consumer packs. Small quantities may be obtained by removing solidified fat from chilled poultry stock. A recipe for schmaltz is presented on this book's companion website.	Schmaltz is used in kosher cooking to replace butter in non-dairy meals. It is an excellent frying medium for tasty sautéed potatoes. Schmaltz is the key ingredient that gives chopped liver a rich mouthfeel.	N/A		Refrigerate up to 2 weeks or freeze for extended storage.
KOSHER POULTRY	Kosher poultry includes chickens, turkeys, and ducks that have been slaughtered and processed according to the laws of kashrut. It is widely available fresh and frozen in whole bird form as well as standard poultry fabrications.	Use in place of standard poultry in any preparation. Due to the koshering process the flesh may retain some salt, so season carefully.	N/A		Refrigerate up to 1 week or freeze.
SQUAB	Squab is domestic pigeon raised for food. Whole, 14- to 19-oz. squabs are sold frozen by the pound by specialty meat dealers and in Asian markets. Standard fabrications include whole, headless and gutted squabs with bones intact; and whole semi-boneless squabs. Asian markets typically stock "Buddhist-style" birds with head and feet on; and "Confucius-exemption" birds intact with heads, feet, and all entrails.	The dark, rich flesh of squab is best enhanced by grilling, broiling, or roasting rare. Because squab is not raised by the battery method and is individually slaughtered, it is safe to serve at 125°F. Squab cooked beyond an internal temperature of 130°F develops an unpleasant "livery" flavor.	Available year round.		Store frozen until needed. Thaw overnight in the refrigerator.

(continued)

☐ **TABLE 16.2 NEW YORK CITY REGIONAL INGREDIENTS** *(continued)*

ITEM	MARKET FORMS	USES	SEASONALITY	OTHER	STORAGE
VEAL SWEETBREADS	"Sweetbreads" is the accepted culinary name for calf thymus gland. Fresh sweetbreads may be special-ordered by the pound from meat dealers; frozen are more widely available. Each veal sweetbread has two sections: the preferred rounded *noix* section and the elongated *gorge* section.	Before cooking, sweetbreads must be carefully trimmed of membrane and soaked in cool water or milk to remove impurities. Sweetbreads are classicly poached, weighted, and peeled before final cooking. Sautéing and pan-frying produce a crisp exterior that contrasts with the soft interior.	Frozen sweetbreads are available year round. Fresh sweetbreads are more abundant in late spring and early summer when more calves are slaughtered.		Fresh sweetbreads are highly perishable: wrap in plastic bags and refrigerate in ice in a self-draining container up to 2 days. Keep frozen sweetbreads in the freezer until needed; thaw under cool running water and use within a day or two.
CALF'S LIVER	The best calf's liver is pale rose-brown to beige in color with a firm texture and fresh aroma. Purchase fresh, whole, 2 1/2- to 3-lb. livers from a reputable meat purveyor. Trim waste may exceed 30 percent. Freezing compromises texture.	Peel and trim the entire liver before cutting into slices or escalopes. Fine liver should be pan-seared or grilled to a medium rare or medium doneness. The rich taste and mouthfeel of liver is complememted by sauces or accompaniments containing citrus juice, vinegar, tomatoes, or other acidic ingredients.	Available year round. Fresh calf's liver is more abundant in late spring and early summer when more calves are slaughtered.		Extremely perishable, calf's liver should be bought the day it is to be served and refrigerated at all times. Do not freeze.
HARICOTS VERTS	Haricots verts are a small, slender French green bean cultivar. Purchase fresh haricots verts in 5-lb. boxes from specialty produce dealers.	For elegance and added value, replace green beans with haricots verts as a side dish and in salads. Trim only the woody stem end; remove the tip only if wilted or wiry. Blanch and refresh before using.	Available year round.		Refrigerate in the orginal box a few days only.

glossary

100th longitudinal meridian   a north-south geographical line bisecting North and South Dakota, Nebraska, Kansas, Oklahoma, and Texas that demarcates the transition between the tallgrass prairie in the east and the shortgrass prairie in the west

Acadian diaspora   migration of Acadians after expulsion from Canada for refusing to swear loyalty to the British government

adobo   a dry blend of granulated onion, granulated garlic, ground black pepper, dried Latin American oregano, salt, and sometimes ground cumin

African-American diaspora   post–Civil War and emancipation migration of former slaves to the Northeast and Midwest

agriculture   the practice of growing plants and raising animals, primarily for food

alaea (ah-lah-A-ah) salt   a Hawai'ian specialty salt produced by evaporating seawater containing red volcanic clay that contributes minerals, a mild but distinctive flavor, and a salmon-color tint

Alice Waters   a California chef who opened a restaurant called Chez Panisse with a daily-changing set menu based on local, seasonal food products; she is considered the founder of contemporary California cuisine

alluvial soil   soil created by river deposits

altitude   land elevation expressed as the number of feet (meters) above sea level

Anglo   Spanish-language word for "English"; in the American Southwest, term used by Spanish and Mexican first settlers when referring to any non-Spanish-speaking person

annatto   yellow dye-producing seeds of a South American plant; flavors and colors Caribbean and Latin American dishes; used in cheesemaking and industrial food production

appetizing store   a market selling Jewish cuisine pareve foods, especially smoked fish and its accompaniments; also known as an *appy*

applejack   a spirit distilled from hard apple cider

appy   *see* appetizing store

apron   the undershell or belly shell of a crab

arid   receiving little rainfall

Art Deco   a design style that combines elements of ancient Greek, Egyptian, and Mayan decorative motifs with Cubist and Machine Age sensibilities; represented in Miami Beach architecture and new South Florida cuisine plate presentation

Ashkenazi cooking   the food of Eastern European Jews, who are called *Ashkenazim*

automat   a restaurant concept developed in the early 20th century that used technology to make service more efficient. Dishes of food were displayed behind coin-operated windows. The customer inserted a coin into the slot, opened the window, and helped himself

bacalao **(bah-kah-LAHoh)**   dried salt cod

bacon drippings   the rendered fat that remains after frying bacon

Basques (BASKS)   originally from the Pyrenees Mountains in southwestern France and northern Spain, Basques are a distinct cultural group with a unique language and cuisine

bayou (BUY-you)   a slow-moving, meandering waterway that empties into a large body of tidal water

beignet **(bain-YAY)**   a French doughnut

Beringan land bridge   a strip of dry land joining Asia and Alaska that emerged during past Ice Ages and then disappeared with the melting of the icecaps

berries   crab roe, or eggs

Big Island,   The term for the island of Hawai'i; used by Hawai'i residents to distinguish the island from the state of Hawai'i

bill of fare   the American 19th-century term for an *á la carte* menu offering a variety of individually priced dishes

bison   the American buffalo, an immense bovine

bitterroot   a plant that grows prolifically throughout the interior northwestern plateau and across Montana; its root was a Native American food

blubber   the fat of certain marine mammals

blue corn   a blue-colored field corn variety sacred in Hopi culture

boardinghouse service   family-style dining: customers seated at long tables help themselves from platters

Boston scrod   a marketing term for small, young cod prized for its fine-grained texture and mild flavor

boucherie **(boo-share-EE)**   a hog processing party, in which home-raised hogs are butchered, fabricated, and then preserved

brewis (BREWS)   a dish made with ship's biscuits or sea biscuits broken up and simmered in broth with meat, poultry, or fish

brew-pub   a casual restaurant located on the premises of a microbrewery; serves its specialty beers fresh on draft

brine   a solution of salt and water used for curing meats

buffalo chips   dried bison manure burned as fuel

Burbank, Luther   famous horticulturalist credited with developing many of California's modern fruit, vegetable, and flower cultivars

buster   *see* peeler

café au lait **(kah-fay-oh-LAY)**   strong, chicory-flavored coffee with hot milk

Cajun   a person of Acadian ancestry born in Louisiana

calamari   Italian term for squid

camas   a plant of the lily family that produces a tasty, starchy root bulb eaten by Pacific Northwest Native Americans

Canadian bacon   cured and smoked pork loin

canoe plants   food plants brought to Hawai'i by Polynesians migrating to the islands in boats

capsaicin   the naturally occurring chemical compound responsible for the "hot" sensation experienced when eating chiles

capsicum   the genus of plants that produces bell peppers and chiles

Carolina Gold   a prized type of long-grain rice produced in the Carolina Lowcountry before the Civil War and once again available in limited quantity

cattle barons   wealthy Easterners, Englishmen, and Europeans who claimed huge tracts of Western land and established great cattle ranches

celebrity chef   a chef who uses marketing and public relations to achieve national or worldwide recognition; typically publishes cookbooks and appears on television and the Internet; Wolfgang Puck became the first celebrity chef in the 1980s.

central plains flat, treeless, semitemperate land of the Mississippi River corridor and the Dakota-Nebraska-Kansas tier of states

charcuterie (shar-koo-tair-EE) the preparation of preserved pork products; also refers to the products themelves

cheese curds newly pressed, unaged Cheddar cheese cut into 1-inch nuggets and sold fresh

Chesapeake seasoning a bold-flavored mixture of ground spices and granulated aromatics best known by the proprietary name Old Bay; seasons many Chesapeake Bay dishes and seafood dishes throughout the nation

chile a fruit of the capsicum plant with a high capsaicin level, making it spicy-hot

chowder an American soup that always includes potatoes and a preserved pork product; the English term is derived from the French word *chaudière*, or "cast-iron cauldron"; clam chowder is the best known variety

chuckwagon a horse-drawn mobile kitchen developed by ranchers who refitted surplus Civil War military supply wagons

clabber thick, tangy fermented cream

clambake a meal consisting of soft-shell or hard-shell clams, lobsters, fish, and corn on the cob steamed in a pit lined with hot rocks and layers of seaweed

clam shack a seaside, open-air stand typically offering a limited menu consisting of clams on the half-shell, steamers, fried clams, and broth-based clam chowder

climate the average weather patterns of a particular area measured over a period of years

coastal plain a flat band of land bordering an ocean

coddies *see* codfish cakes

codfish cakes poached salt cod fillet pulled into shreds, mixed with mashed potatoes, formed into patties, and fried; affectionately called *coddies*

cold desert a dry area that has extreme temperatures, both hot and cold

colonial cuisine the hybrid cooking style resulting when the Old World cuisine of a colonist group is blended with the cuisine of the indigenous group

colonial dish food made with a mixture of indigenous foods and colonial domesticates; may utilize a combination of indigenous and European cooking technology

colonial domesticates food plants and animals that are brought from another place by settlers and established in the new land soon after settlement

colonists people who are sponsored by a sovereign nation to travel to a new, unclaimed land and create permanent settlements under the control of that nation

combination plate in Mexican-American cuisine, a menu item featuring the diner's choice of two or more corn dish items served together on one large platter, typically including refried beans and Mexican rice

common crackers dry, very crunchy, thick, round crackers modeled after, but not as hard as, traditional ship's biscuits

companion plants food plants that grow well when planted together, such as corn, beans, and squash

conch (KONK) (1) a univalve shellfish with sweet-tasting but very tough flesh; (2) also a nickname for Creoles originally from the British Bahamas and other Caribbean islands who settled Key West

Continental cuisine a restaurant-driven, hybrid cooking style based on the cuisines of France and other nations of the European continent, but modified to include American ingredients and to accommodate American taste preferences

convenience food a food product whose cooking preparation, some or all, is done by an industrial food processor

cooked breakfast term used by Hawai'i residents to refer to the standard Anglo-American breakfast meal of eggs, a preserved pork product, and toast

coontie (KOON-tee) flour made from the roots of the arrowroot plant (various members of the *Zamia* botanical family) formerly used by South Florida Native Americans and settlers to make porridge and to replace wheat flour

coosie the ranchhouse or cattle drive cook (from the Spanish *cocinero*)

cooter a freshwater turtle

copycat cheeses American-made products bearing the same name as, and having characteristics similar to, European cheeses

corn-bean synergy the nutritional benefit resulting from eating alkaline-processed corn dishes in conjunction with dried bean dishes; consuming the two together creates a protein source nearly as valuable as that found in animal proteins

corned beef beef brisket cured in brine

counterculture 1960s and early 1970s cultural and political movement that questioned all forms of authority, rejected the military-agricultural-industrial complex, and protested the Vietnam War; influential in the development of the American food revolution and Nouvelle Cuisine

courtbouillon **(Louisiana French: KOO-boo-yon)** (1) classic French cuisine poaching liquid consisting of white wine, water, mirepoix, and bouquet garni; (2) thick, spicy Louisiana sauce made with fish stock, tomatoes, and brown roux; (3) a Louisiana seafood dish featuring this sauce

cover crops plants grown to semimaturity and then tilled back into the soil to increase plant nutrients; a practice of sustainable agriculture

crab pound enclosed floats where "peeler" or "buster" hard-shell crabs are kept until they molt, becoming soft-shell crabs

crackers Florida settlers, primarily of the Plantation South's working class and southern Appalachian farmers of English or Scots-Irish ancestry

cracklings the solid component that remains after lard is rendered out of pork fat; fried crisp, they enhance the flavor and texture of baked goods and are used as a salad garnish

creasy greens various types of wild watercress

Creole in the modern usage, a person of mixed European-African race born in Louisiana, the Caribbean, or Latin America

crop rotation planting a different crop in a particular field each season to balance plant nutrient use

Cubano **(koo-BAN-oh)** *see* Cuban sandwich

Cuban sandwich a South Florida pressed sandwich: roast pork, ham, Swiss cheese, mustard, pickles, and sometimes salami on Cuban bread toasted between two hot metal plates; also called a *Cubano*

cuisine skilled, thoughtful, refined cooking belonging to a particular style

culantro an elongated, sawtoothed herb whose flavor is similar to cilantro

culinary ash an alkaline substance derived from burning indigenous local woody plants that is traditionally used by Native Americans for alkaline-processing corn

culinary conservative   a person who regards new foods and new culinary ideas with suspicion and who is unwilling to experiment with new foods

culinary liberal   a person willing to try a wide variety of foods and to adopt new foods and culinary ideas

culinary region   an area defined by geography that has uniform topography, climate, soil, and proximity to other regions, as well as a homogenous or uniform food culture

cyclical land use   a farming practice in which fields are cultivated until the soil is depleted, then abandoned while the soil regenerates, and then placed under cultivation once again

Deep South   the Plantation South region's southernmost tier of states: Georgia, northern Florida, Alabama, and Mississippi; Louisiana is sometimes included

defining dishes   recipes that unmistakably represent a particular region

DelMarVa Peninsula   teardrop-shaped expanse of land located between the Chesapeake Bay and the Atlantic Ocean; so named because parts of it are claimed by the states of Delaware, Maryland, and Virginia

delta   a triangular expanse of land created by sediment deposited at the mouth of a river where it empties into a larger body of water, such as a bay or a gulf

designer dish   a dish created by an innovative chef who applies new techniques and ingredients to classic foods such as pasta and pizza

diner   a casual restaurant offering American national cuisine dishes, including breakfast foods, served quickly at moderate prices during extended hours; originally recycled railroad dining cars; sometimes new construction designed to resemble a dining car

dressing   the Cajun term for stuffing; frequently prepared in a casserole and served as a side dish

drowned river   an estuary having a deep central channel that formerly, during the ice ages, was a river bed; when polar ice caps melted and ocean water levels rose, the river "drowned," or was covered with water

dude ranch   a guest ranch: a resort where visitors drawn to Western-style entertainment participate in ranch activities such as horseback trail riding and cattle herding, and enjoy Ranchlands cuisine

dust bowl   1930s ecological disaster resulting from extensive plowing for monoculture crops combined with unusually dry weather conditions; wind erosion blew away much of the fertile topsoil, virtually destroying Midwestern agriculture

Eastern Shore   the western half of the DelMarVa Peninsula that borders the Chesapeake Bay

economic viability   the point at which a region has fully utilized its resources and can support its own population with the revenues from its goods and services

entrée salad   a salad larger than an appetizer or side salad and usually including one or more protein items, such as cheese and cold cooked meat or poultry, as well as greens and vegetables

erosion   the removal of soil by the action of wind or water

estuary   a body of water formed where a river meets the sea, and where fresh and saline water mix

ethnic-American cuisines   microcuisines developed by immigrants blending their homeland cuisines with the established regional ingredients and techniques of their new homes

étouffée (eh-too-FAY)   "smothered," in French: a Louisiana dish of food cooked in a thick brown-roux sauce similar in consistency to gravy

fall line   a rocky shelf over which a coastal region's rivers drop in low waterfalls, and above which there is no tidal action

family restaurant   a casual, midlevel restaurant serving American national cuisine dishes; many do not offer alcoholic beverages

farmed game   wild game animals raised in a controlled environment and processed under USDA inspection

fertilization   the process of nourishing the land by replenishing essential nutrients

fiddleheads   the shoot tips of the ostrich fern plant, so named because they are shaped like the scroll of a violin; a wild vegetable seasonal to early spring

filé (FEE-lay) gumbo   Native-American-French type of gumbo in which filé powder replaces okra as the thickener

filé (FEE-lay) powder   ground dried sassafras leaves

filter feeders   oysters and other bivalves that feed by taking in water and extracting nutrients from it

finishing   in meat production, feeding a specific diet to meat animals during the final period before slaughter; finishing regimens include grass-feeding and grain-feeding

first contact   a culture-changing event that occurs when an indigenous group initially meets explorers or settlers arriving in their home territory

first settlers   colonists or pioneers who are the first non-indigenous people to attempt to live in a particular area

flavor layering   when preparing a dish, using the same basic ingredient in two or more forms, often in stages (example: using granulated garlic in the seasoning rub of a meat, braising whole garlic cloves with it, and adding minced garlic to the sauce)

Floribbean cuisine   term used by 1980s food writers to describe Caribbean-influenced South Florida cuisine

foie gras (FWA grah)   the fattened liver of ducks and geese, produced by enhanced feeding

food culture   the ways in which a particular group thinks about food, and how they cook and eat that food

foodways   the various cooking and dining practices of a particular food culture

foreign cuisine   a national or regional cuisine practiced outside its homeland; retains its original ingredients, techniques, and flavors with little or no modification

foundation foods   the most important food products used in a particular cuisine

Four Corners   the point at which the states of New Mexico, Arizona, Colorado, and Utah meet

fresh onion   see knob onion

fried clam bellies   soft-shell clams that are shucked, dipped in a seasoned batter, and deep-fried to golden brown

fried pie   a pastry turnover with sweet or savory filling, fried crisp in vegetable oil or lard

frozen custard   New England term for soft-serve ice cream; technically refers to any ice cream made with egg yolks

fruit cocktail   mixed diced fruits originally served in a martini glass and served as an appetizer

fry bread   puffy, golden discs of deep-fried white wheat flour dough; originally leavened with yeast; modern recipes often substitute baking powder

fusion cuisine   a culinary style blending ingredients and techniques of two individual national or regional cuisines; food historians believe Chef Norman Van Aiken was the first to apply this term to his global style of cooking

gandules (gahn-DOO-lays)   also known as *pigeon peas*, this legume was introduced to Puerto Rico by African slaves

geocultural area an area defined by its settler groups and their cultural characteristics, as well as by topography and boundaries

girdling chopping away a girdle, or wide band, of bark around the trunk of a tree, stopping the flow of water and nutrients from the roots to the leaves, and ultimately killing the tree

gravlax salmon cured with salt and flavored with sugar and dill; the original method involved wrapping the cured fish in leaves or cloth and then burying it underground to keep it cold—hence the name *gravlax*, or "grave fish"

Great Plains the immense area of land stretching from the Mississippi corridor to the Rocky Mountain foothills

grits medium-grind dried whole corn kernels

halal the designation for meats from animals slaughtered according to Islamic dietary law

hamburger steak a round or oval patty formed from chopped or ground beef, usually a tough cut; named after the town of Hamburg, Germany

haole (HOW-lee) "outsider," in Hawai'ian: term for a Caucasian visitor or recently arrived resident

hard cider a fizzy and dry (not sweet) beverage with modest alcohol content produced when sweet apple cider ferments

hard crab *see* hard-shell

hard-shell a crab that has developed a fully calcified, hard exterior carapace, or shell

haute (OAT) ethnic upscale foreign cuisine restaurants that serve their nation's finest dishes in comfortable and evocative settings

hearth the fireplace floor, where most colonial cooking took place

heart of palm the tender core of the sabal palm tree; it is cooked and served hot as a side dish or chilled and served as a salad

high desert arid land at an elevation of more than 4,000 feet that experiences frost and occasional snow

high-status foods valued foods prepared for important guests and utilized as trade goods

hollow a small, horseshoe-shaped mountainside depression with a stream flowing through it

holy trinity Louisiana cuisine's primary aromatic vegetable blend comprising fresh onion or scallion, green bell pepper, and celery; sometimes called *Cajun mirepoix*

hominy dried corn steam processed to soften its starchy endosperm and remove its hull; today sold primarily in canned form

hot-smoke to finish a previously cured product by surrounding it with fragrant smoke at a temperature between 160°F (71°C) and 225°F (107°C); the resulting product has a mild smoke flavor and cooked texture

human seasonal migration the moving of villages and encampments from place to place throughout the year according to necessary activities, most of which involve obtaining food

hybrid cuisine a cooking style that develops organically when an existing food culture and a newly arrived food culture blend ingredients and cooking methods

hydroponics a production method in which edible plants are grown in water enhanced with dissolved nutrients

immigrant dish a dish that results when an immigrant cook prepares an altered version of a homeland cuisine using ingredients available in the new home

immigrant foods items added to the ingredients palette of an established regional cuisine by groups of people who arrive later in the area's history

immigrants settlers who arrive in an area that has already been colonized

imu (EE-moo) traditional Hawai'ian pit oven

indigenous derived from Latin words meaning "inborn" or "original;" an indigenous group comprises the descendants of a land's original inhabitants

indigenous cuisine the cooking style of a region's indigenous people

indigenous dish a dish made primarily with indigenous foods and indigenous cooking techniques

indigenous foods ingredients that are native to a particular place

ingredient staging adding the same ingredient at different stages in the cooking process, resulting in varied textures

Italian-American antipasto a selection of Italian-style cold cuts and cheeses arranged atop a bed of lettuce, usually garnished with olives, tomato wedges, hard-boiled eggs, and pickled vegetables

Japan Current a warm flow of water originating in the Philippine Sea and swirling in a clockwise arc along the northern Pacific Ocean

jerky thin strips of salted, dried meat; derived from the Mexican Spanish word *charqui*

Jewish diaspora successive migrations of Jewish people beginning in the 6th century BCE with exile from Judea and occurring throughout history; in the late 19th century, migration from Eastern Europe brought many Jews to America, with most entering through New York City

jimmy a male hard-shell blue crab

Junipero Serra (hoo-nee-PAY-roh SAY-rah) a Franciscan friar (1713–1784) who left Mexico to establish the first in a string of twenty-one missions from San Diego to Sonoma, California

kama'ainas (kah-mah-ah-EE-nahs) originally, early European settlers of Hawai'i who married into the Hawai'ian aristocracy and were granted high social rank; today the term refers to long-standing Caucasian residents of Hawai'i

kapu in pre-contact Hawai'ian culture, a taboo or restriction

Key lime a small, intensely flavored citrus fruit native to Southeast Asia and eventually cultivated in the Caribbean and the Florida Keys

kippered hot-smoked; refers to fish, usually salmon or herring

knob onion a fully grown onion marketed fresh, before it develops a dry, papery skin

Korean barbeque the most popular style of Korean restaurant cooking; not true barbeque, in this cooking method marinated thin-sliced beef or beef short ribs are grilled at table and served with a spicy sesame-soy dip

kosher foods permissible for consumption by observant Jews

kosher law (*kashrut*) a set of dietary restrictions imposed on Jews by the Old Testament and interpreted by Rabbinical scholars throughout the centuries

lard rendered pork fat

latitude a system of expressing location and discussing climate in numerical degrees ranging from zero degrees at the equator to 90 degrees (north or south) at the poles

leather britches air-dried green beans; in a traditional Appalachian South preservation method, fresh green beans are strung on thread and hung in the rafters to dry; so-called because they resemble leather pants hanging on a line

leaven   to lighten the texture of a baked good by introducing CO_2 gas into its dough or batter; accomplished by chemical ingredients (baking powder or baking soda) or by the action of a living organism (yeast); when the product is baked, the gas expands rapidly, causing the product to rise and resulting in a light, porous crumb

levee   a raised embankment constructed to prevent a river overflowing its banks

living greens   lettuces and herbs sold with intact roots packaged in water

lobster pound   a saltwater tank or pond where freshly caught lobsters are held before they are sold or cooked

local food   term coined in the 1980s to designate Hawai'i's ethnically diverse popular cooking

lo'i (LOW-ee)   pond-fields constructed by early Hawai'ians to raise fish and food plants

lomi-lomi   shredded salt-cured salmon tossed with soy sauce, tomatoes, ginger, and other seasonings; served chilled as an appetizer or side dish; named for the Hawai'ian *lomi-lomi* massage technique used to shred and mix it

long green chile   a large American Southwest chile cultivar harvested when mature but still green; the New Mexico crop is known as *New Mexico green chile*, whereas the California-grown variety is called *Anaheim chile*

Lowcountry   coastal South Carolina: the low, often marshy land between the fall line and the ocean

lu'au (LOO-wow)   (1) Hawai'ian language word for taro leaves; (2) a traditional Hawai'ian dish of taro leaves cooked in coconut milk, usually with octopus (called "squid" in Hawai'i) (3) in Hawai'i, an outdoor celebratory feast featuring traditional Hawai'ian cuisine including foods pit-roasted in an imu

lunchroom   a foodservice operation designed to attract office workers and shoppers as regular midday customers; features low-cost sandwiches, soups, salads, desserts, and nonalcoholic beverages served quickly and efficiently

Maillard (my-YARD) browning   the browning of proteins achieved at 310°F, an effect similar to the caramelization of sugar

Mango Gang   1980s pioneers of the new South Florida style of restaurant cooking: Norman Van Aiken, Allen Susser, Mark Militello, and Doug Rodriguez

maple sugar   a light brown granular sugar made by simmering maple syrup until it crystallizes

marbling   fine veins of fat within the muscle structure of meat that result in succulent mouthfeel

masa   a supple, cohesive dough made by grinding fresh, moist, alkaline-treated dried corn

masa harina   dry, powdered masa flour; literally, "corn dough flour"

Mediterranean climate   a climate defined by warm, wet winters and cool, sunny summers; typified by conditions in Italy and the south of France

melting pot   a vessel in which various metals are heated together to become one cohesive, molten mass; the United States is a figurative melting pot of cultures because it is a nation of many different immigrants

Meso-Americans   the Aztecs, Mayas, and other ancient civilizations of Mexico and central America

microbrewery   a small, independent beer company that specializes in small-batches specialty beers made by traditional methods and, often, with regionally grown ingredients

microcuisine   the unique and sometimes little-known cooking style of a small food culture living and cooking together within the boundaries of a larger culinary region; often sharing an ethnic heritage

microgreens   a food plant's first two true leaves

migrant agricultural worker   a nonresident worker employed primarily to pick crops, typically following a region's harvest cycle by moving from one area to another as crops ripen

mirliton (MEER-leh-ton)   a tropical squash; also known as *chayote* or *christophene*

modular dish   a menu item that can be varied simply by exchanging one component recipe for another

mojito (moh-HEE-toh)   a Cuban cocktail made from fresh sugar cane juice, Key lime juice, rum, and fresh mint

molt   a change that occurs when a crab crawls out of its old shell, a process that takes about two hours and results in a soft-shell crab

monoculture   the practice of specializing in a single cash crop rather than producing a variety of grains, vegetables, and food animals

moonshine   potent corn whiskey produced in homemade stills, primarily in the southern Appalachian Mountains

Mormons   unofficial name for members of The Church of Jesus Christ of Latter-day Saints; members of this church and cultural Mormons are a significant population in Utah

MSG   monosodium glutamate, a food flavor enhancer first isolated in 1907; when ingested, MSG stimulates the taste buds, making bland food taste better

muffaletta   a New Orleans sandwich consisting of Italian-style meats and cheeses and olive salad on a round bread loaf

national cuisine   a unified cooking style common to the majority of a country's population

national restaurant chain   a corporate-owned group of identical foodservice operations strategically placed throughout the country

neck   a low ridge of coastal land located between two rivers

niche market product   in agriculture, a specialty crop grown for a particular target market

nixtamal **(NEES-tah-mal)**   alkaline-processed corn ground into masa and used to make breadlike corn products such as tortillas and tamales

nixtamalization   in industrial food production, the alkaline treatment of dried corn for tortillas and other Mexican and Mexican-American food products

Nor'easter   an Atlantic coast weather pattern in which moisture-laden southeasterly winds move northeast, bringing torrential rain in warm months and heavy snow in winter, dramatically affecting New England

Nuevo Latino cuisine   a fusion of the many similar yet disparate elements of Cuban, Puerto Rican, Dominican, Brazilian, Argentinean, and Mexican cuisines to which innovative chefs added classic European and world cuisines and techniques

Ogallala Aquifer   the nation's largest concentration of underground water, located under the Great Plains near the 100th longitudinal meridian

okra gumbo   a Louisiana soup/stew made by simmering poultry or seafood in a thin, brown roux–thickened sauce; sliced okra adds additional thickening

old sour   a Key West condiment made with Key lime juice, salt, and hot chiles

Old World cuisines   the homeland cooking styles of America's European colonists

Old World dishes   dishes made primarily with colonial domesticates using European cooking technology

oyster dredge   steel rakes dragged behind sailing and motorized vessels, capable of harvesting hundreds of oysters at a time; frowned upon by environmentalists for harming the floors of bays and oceans

Pacific Rim   a circular border of land around the Pacific Ocean comprising the west coasts of North and South America and the east coasts of Australia and Asia

palm heart   *see* heart of palm

panhandle   an elongated section of land belonging to a particular geopolitical state that extends into the territory of one or more other states; example: western Oklahoma

paniolo   Hawai'ian term for cowboy; Mexican cowboys were initially called *Españoles* by Hawai'ians; in the Hawai'ian language the term became *paniolo*

papershell   term for a soft-shell crab that has been out of the water for around 12 hours and whose membrane is beginning to harden, acquiring a leathery, fibrous texture

pareve (pah-REV)   in the Jewish laws of kasruth, term for foods that are considered neutral (neither meat nor dairy): grains, legumes, vegetables, eggs, and fish

paunch   an animal's stomach, used by primitive food cultures as a cooking vessel

pawpaw   a tree fruit indigenous to the Plantation South and southern Appalachian South culinary regions; used in desserts and sweet-savory sauces

peeler   a hard-shell crab whose outer shell has split near the swimming paddles in preparation for molting; also called a *buster* or *shedder*

pellagra   a disease caused by niacin deficiency in people subsisting predominantly on cornbread, corn pone, grits, unprocessed hominy, or other starchy foods without sufficient amounts of the nutrients found in wheat flour, meats, legumes, fruits, and vegetables

Pennsylvania Dutch   descendants of former Rhinelanders who settled in Pennsylvania in the 18th century

pierogi   a plump half-moon of thick noodle dough that may be stuffed with various fillings: savory mashed potatoes, cheese, sauerkraut, chopped meat, and even sweet dessert fillings

piki (PEE-kee) bread   a roll of crisp, wafer-thin flatbread made from a thin batter of ash-alkalized corn flour that is baked on a piki stone

pilot cracker   a hard, crisp cracker inspired by sea biscuits; popular in New England and Hawai'i cuisines

pink singing scallops   small, sweet-tasting bivalves harvested in the Pacific Northwest and sold with shell intact

pioneer cuisine   the hybrid cuisine of U.S. settlers as they moved westward, adding a new set of indigenous ingredients and cooking techniques borrowed from each indigenous group they encountered

pioneer dish   the result of combining previously adopted indigenous ingredients, Old World ingredients, and indigenous ingredients from a new area

pioneer provisions   basic foodstuffs such as flour, salt pork, and dried beans carried west with America's pioneers

pioneers   citizens of a sovereign nation who travel to and create permanent settlements in previously unsettled areas of that nation

piquante **(pee-KAHNT)**   spicy-hot; a tomato-based Creole sauce with fresh or canned green chiles added

pit barbeque   a low, slow, moist and therefore tenderizing cooking method done by suspending tough cuts of meat over the coals of a wood fire built in a hole in the ground; the meat is basted with a "mopping sauce" as it cooks, creating steam and flavor

plains equestrians   Great Plains tribes who made horses and horseback transportation the central aspect of their lives; they reverted to hunter/gatherer status and employed primitive cooking methods

planking   a method of cooking fish on a plank or board, usually alderwood or cedar, that imparts a special flavor when heated along with the fish

plantation   a vast tract of prime land granted to or purchased by by a wealthy merchant or aristocrat and used to produce cash crops

plate lunch   in Hawai'i, an assemblage comprising a local food main course, steamed white rice, and one or more side dishes, all served on a disposable plate

po' boy   a hollowed baguette filled with fried seafood, hot roast beef, meatballs, or Italian cold cuts; a New Orleans specialty sandwich

poi **(POY)**   the staple starch of Hawai'ian cuisine: cooked, pounded taro root, sometimes fermented

poi supper   a formal meal of traditional Hawai'ian cuisine fare; a popular entertainment among Hawai'i's 19th-century *kama'aina* upper class

poke **(POH-kay)**   in Hawai'ian, literally "cut into small pieces"; diced raw fish with seaweed and Asian seasonings; a popular snack or appetizer

poke sallet   the young shoots of the pokeweed plant

posole **(poh-SOH-lay)**   dried corn kernels simmered in alkalized water to remove the hulls, soften the texture, and add flavor and nutrients; the kernels are eaten whole in soups or as a side dish

postcontact cuisine   a hybrid cooking style that develops after an indigenous group makes contact with another culture and adopts some or all of its ingredients and cooking methods

pot liquor   the flavorful, nutritious liquid resulting when collard (and other) greens or string beans are long-cooked in water with seasoning meats

potlatch   a northwestern Native American ceremonial feast, historically held to solidify the power of a particular clan and glorify its leader; modern potlatches are celebrations of generosity and Native American cultural identity

precontact cuisine   the cooking style prevalent before an indigenous group makes first contact with another culture

pueblo   a permanent fortified village often situated on a high mesa top, constructed of adobe bricks and/or stone

Pullman loaf   fine-grained bread baked in a long, retangular, lidded loaf pan; yields a perfectly square slice preferred for sandwiches

pupu (POO-poo)   literally, "small round object"; Hawai'ians used the word *pupu* to describe European canapés; by extension the term *pupu* now refers to all finger foods

pupu (POO-poo) platter   a sampler of Chinese-American and Polynesian-inspired hors d'oeuvres presented with a miniature hibachi grill

quahog (KOH-hog) New England term for hard-shell clam; today often designates large, chowder-size clams

rain shadow area on the leeward slope of a mountain range that receives less/little rainfall because it is blocked from weather systems carrying rain clouds

ramp a wild and particularly odiferous member of the onion family found primarily in the Appalachian mountains

razorback hog feral descendant of swine left behind in the 16th century by the Spanish explorer De Soto's expedition in the American South

recaito (ray-KI-toh) a rough purée of onions, garlic, green peppers, and culantro/recao; used as an aromatic flavor base in Puerto Rican cooking

recao (ray-COW) see culantro

red gravy a thick Italian-American tomato sauce simmered with ham, beef, and/or soup bones; used as a pasta sauce

regional cuisine a unified style of cooking common to the majority of the people living in a culinary region

render to extract pure, fluid fat from solid animal fat; accomplished by heating diced, unsalted fat over low heat; when rendering is complete, the result is a semisolid fat (lard or *schmaltz*) and cracklings

restaurant franchise an ownership system in which an investor purchases a proven restaurant concept and runs the operation using predetermined methods

Rhineland the area bordering the Rhine River as it flows northward from the Swiss Alps along the French/German border through Germany and the Netherlands to the North Sea; Old World homeland of the Pennsylvania Dutch and later German immigrants

rib tips tasty, chewy brisket bones often served as an appetizer

ristra (REE-stra) a braided strand or wreath of dried chile pods; originally crafted to facilitate drying but today primarily decorative

rockfish Chesapeake Bay Shore regional term for the Atlantic striped bass, *Morone saxatilis*

salinity the salt content of a brine or of seawater

salmon bellies the fatty flesh found near a salmon's ventral fins (belly area) that, in Pacific Northwest cuisine, are cured in salt brine and then fried as a breakfast or supper dish accompanied by boiled potatoes

salmon cheeks plump nuggets of tender flesh from the cavities just behind the salmon's gills; sautéed, broiled, or hot-smoked, a Pacific Northwest signature dish

salt pork brine-cured pork belly

salt-rising bread a leavened wheat flour loaf made by a unique natural fermentation process that involves the bacterium *Clostridium perfringens*; popular in New England and northwestern New York state

schnitzel in German-American cuisine, a breaded fried meat cutlet (usually pork or veal)

Scots-Irish in America, colonists originally transplanted from Scotland to Irish Ulster by the British government who later immigrated to the Mid-Atlantic and Appalachian South

scuppernong grapes wild indigenous American grapes native to the Plantation South

seasoning meats in Plantation South and Appalachian South cuisines, cured and smoked meats (typically bacon ends, ham hocks, and pork neck bones) that are simmered in water to make broth for soups and to flavor beans and greens; smoked turkey parts are also used, particularly by African-American Muslims

second settlers settlers who arrive in a land after it has been colonized

Sephardic cooking the traditional cooking of Middle Eastern Jews living throughout the Mediterranean region, including Israel, Italy, Spain, the Middle East, and North Africa

shedder see peeler

shore dinner a New England meal consisting of steamed soft-shell or hard-shell clams, steamed lobster, corn on the cob, coleslaw, and sometimes french fries; often enjoyed outdoors

shortgrass prairie the semiarid flatland west of the 100th longitudinal meridian covered with low-growing shrubs and grasses; used primarily for grazing

sieva (SIV-ee) beans a Carolina Lowcountry variety of lima bean with a distinctive sweet taste

singing scallops a marketing name for small Pacific Northwest pink scallops harvested by divers and sold in-shell

smorgasbord a buffet featuring Scandinavian-style foods

sofrito (soh-FREE-toh) a cooked mixture of onions, garlic, bell peppers, and tomatoes featured in Cuban-American and other Latin-American cuisine dishes

soft-shell clam a bivalve with a loosely hinged oval shell and a protruding neck, or siphon, covered with thick, black skin; often called *steamer clam*

soft-shell crab a crab that has molted its hard shell and is temporarily covered by a soft, skinlike membrane; eaten virtually in its entirety

sook a female hard-shell blue crab

sorghum a grasslike food plant native to Africa; pressed and then boiled in the same manner as maple sap, sorghum sap can be reduced into thick, sweet, golden-colored syrup

soul food this well-known microcuisine is the African-American style of Plantation South cooking

sourdough naturally leavened bread and other baked goods with the tangy flavor of lactic acid produced by the bacteria in its starter; see starter

spit-barbeque cooking method of Native Caribbean origin in which a whole, large carcass or several small fowl or meat cuts are impaled on a long pole that is rotated over the coals of a wood fire

St. Louis–cut ribs a squared-off pork rib section whose brisket bones have been removed

stack cake an Appalachian South signature dessert; a tower of thin, dense pound cake layers filled with cooked fruit purée

starter in bread making, a batter or soft dough containing live yeast that is added to an unleavened batter or dough in order to initiate fermentation; technically, may contain commercial baker's yeast but usually refers to dough masses leavened with ambient wild yeast and bacteria

steak fries thick wedges of skin-on russet potatoes, deep-fried until crisp

steak house a restaurant that serves tender cuts of aged prime beef, originally broiled and later char-grilled, with á la carte accompaniments such as baked potatoes or steak fries and tossed salads

steamers Northeast and Mid-Atlantic term for soft-shell clams

stir-fry a cooking method in which diced or sliced protein food and vegetables are sautéed over high heat and usually bound with a cornstarch-thickened sauce

stone crab claws the claw of the Caribbean Moro crab, so-named because the shells of the claws are so hard that, in order to release the meat, they were bashed with heavy stones; now foodservice operations use hammers and hinged crackers

succotash   a Native American cuisine dish of long-simmered parched corn and dried white or cranberry beans; modern summer succotash is made with fresh sweet corn kernels, fresh lima beans, and often green beans

supermarket   a store that sells a combination of dry grocery products, fresh produce, dairy products, seafood, and meats—in short, everything one needs to prepare meals

super-premium ice cream   rich, dense, high-fat ice cream with high-quality and often unusual flavorings; developed in New England

surimi (soo-REE-mee)   an industrially processed imitation crab product made from fish, primarily pollock

sustainable agriculture   a farming method that uses crop rotation, cover crops, compost, and other natural fertilizers in concert with multiculture planting and animal husbandry to maintain an ecological balance that increases soil fertility and makes chemical pesticides and herbicides unnecessary

swamp cabbage   Florida cracker name for palm heart, a vegetable harvested from the trunk of the Sabal palm tree

swidden agriculture   the cultivation of crops in small forest patches among the standing trunks of trees defoliated by girdling

***table d'hôte* (tah-blah DOTE)**   literally "table of the host"; a restaurant service style in which guests are offered one set menu, typically of several courses, with no choices

tallgrass prairie   temperate flatland extending from the Ohio River Valley to the 100th longitudinal meridian, originally covered with a variety of tall-growing grasses; today most of this area is under crop cultivation

taro   a tropical plant that produces a starchy root vegetable as well as edible leaves

teri   local Hawai'ian slang for *teriyaki*

teriyaki   a Japanese grilling method in which food is both marinated in and basted with a mixture of soy sauce, rice wine, and sugar

terrapin   in America, the diamondback terrapin, a turtle that inhabits semisaline waters; terrapin soup and stew were Mid-Atlantic and Chesapeake Bay Shore signature dishes popular from the 16th through the 19th centuries

***terroir* (tare-WAH)**   French term for the distinctive localized flavor of food grown in naturally fertilized soil; from the phrase *le goût de terroir*: literally "the taste of the soil"

Three Sisters,   The Native American name for the three foundation foods (corn, beans, and squash) of most Native American cuisines

tidewater area   a geographic area comprising land and tidal rivers whose mouths and lower reaches accept a significant inflow of saline bay or seawater at high tide, and that discharge the saline water back into the bay or sea at low tide

tiki (TEE-kee) bar   a restaurant featuring exotic rum-based cocktails and a menu based on Chinese-American food and Polynesian-inspired specialty dishes

tonging   original method of harvesting Chesapeake oysters, in which a person standing in a small, open boat lowers a set of joined iron rakes over the side, then scoops up the oysters lying below on the bay bottom

topography   the location, elevation, physical features, or other geological elements that influence a region's environment

tortilla   (1) in Mexican and Mexican-American cuisines, a thin, round, griddle-baked unleavened bread made from alkaline-processed corn *masa* or wheat flour; (2) in Basque cuisine, a breaded-and-fried custard dessert; (3) in Spanish cuisine, a cake-like omelet similar to an Italian frittata

tossed salad   an American appetizer salad originally made of iceberg lettuce topped with assorted raw and cooked vegetable garnishes and served with the diner's choice of dressing on the side; today romaine lettuce may be used

traditional alkaline processing   soaking and cooking dried corn in alkalized water in order to soften it, remove its hulls, and improve its nutritive qualities

trans-Appalachian flatlands   level and rolling land west of the Appalachian Mountains, including the Ohio River Valley and Great Lakes area

tundra   treeless, flat or rolling land composed of black silt/clay earth spread in a thin layer over permafrost subsoil that remains frozen year round

value-added product   a convenience food product that is partially or completely prepared for eating by an industrial food processor who sells it at a significantly higher price than the commodity from which it is made

victory garden   during World Wars I and II, a backyard or public-space vegetable plot established to free commercial vegetable production for military supply

walleye   a large Great Lakes species of freshwater fish with firm, white, mild-tasting flesh

water ice   Mid-Atlantic term for Italian ice: a coarse-grained, dairy-free frozen dessert usually made from fruit juices

watershed   the land area whose streams, creeks, and rivers flow into a single large body of water

western plateau   the high-elevation flatlands that begin west of the 100th longitudinal meridian and extend to the foothills of the Rocky Mountains

wildings   descendants of abandoned cultivated fruit and nut trees or berry bushes that self-propagated and spread, their seedlings growing without cultivation and appearing to be wild, or indigenous

wild rice   the long, slender, brown seeds of an aquatic grass indigenous to the Great Lakes area; boiled and served as a side dish; a traditional Native American food; available in wild-harvested and less expensive cultivated varieties

Yankee   during colonial times and into the early 1800s, this term referred specifically to New Englanders; in the decades leading to the Civil War, Southerners began using the term to refer to any Northerner

yellow cheese   in the Appalachian South, a firm, aged homemade cheese traditionally colored with egg yolk (later tinted with powdered annatto coloring tablets)

recipe index

Note: **Boldface** type indicates master recipes, *italic* type indicates recipe variations, and roman type indicates component recipes. Master recipes are listed by their full titles.

Aburage Triangles, Flavored, 695
Adobo-Marinated Hen, 697
Ahi Nori Tempura Roll with Shoyu Butter Sauce and Radish Sprouts, 677–679
   var. Ahi Norimaki Sushi, 679
Ahi Poke with Shrimp Chips, 682
All-American Baked Beans with Bacon, Frankfurters, and Cole Slaw, var., 126
All-American Beef Stew, 448
   var. Basque Lamb or Mutton Stew, 448
   var. Great Plains Bison Stew, 448
   var. Hungarian-American Goulash, 448
Allegheny Mountain Apple Dumpling with Vanilla Custard Sauce, 189
   var. Amaretti Peach Dumplings with Vanilla Custard Sauce, 189
   var. Raisin-Walnut Apple Dumplings with Vanilla Custard Sauce, 189
Alligator
   Alligator Fingers al Mojo Criollo, var., 757
   Paneéd Alligator with Mango Aïoli and Tropical Seashell Salad, var., 759
Almond Crunch Filling, 637
Almond-Crusted Goat Cheese Discs, 571
Almond Torte with Raspberry Sauce, var., 349
Amaretti Peach Dumplings with Vanilla Custard Sauce, var., 189
Anchovy Butter, 817
Andouille Sausage and Oyster Jambalaya, var., 285
Annie's Skillet Potatoes, 484
Appalachian-Style Pole Beans, 390
Appalachian-Style Sauerkraut, 394
Appetizers. *See also* Salads; Soups and stews, for soups
   Ahi Norimaki Sushi, var., 679
   Ahi Nori Tempura Roll with Shoyu Butter Sauce and Radish Sprouts, 677–679
   Alligator Fingers al Mojo Criollo, var., 757
   Applewood Smoked Trout with Horseradish Cream and Biscuit Crackers, 382–383
   Armadillo Egg with Fresh Tomato Salsa, 481
   Avocado–Tomato Salsa, var., 331
   Bacon and Cheddar Cheese Potato Chip Mountain for Two, var., 521
   Basque Potato Skins with Peppers and Bacalao, var., 520
   Bay Scallops with Pinot Noir Beurre Rouge and Wilted Baby Spinach, var., 625
   Beer-Battered Soft-Shell Crab Appetizer, var., 221
   Black-Eyed Pea Bollitos with Sofrito Tomato Sauce, var., 764
   Blue Cheese Potato Chip Mountain for Two, 521
   Border-Style Beef Tamal with Red and Green Salsas, 332
   Buckwheat Rolls with Country Ham, Asparagus, and Herbed Fresh Cheese, 379–381
   Cajun Crawfish Rémoulade, 266
   California Roll Sushi with Wasabi-Soy Dip, 578–579
   Cannibal Steak, 482
   Caribbean Seviche, var., 753
   Catfish Fingers al Mojo Criollo, var., 757

Charred Rare Filet Steak, Cannibal Style, var., 482
Chickasaw Bean Cake with Sunflower Salad, 55
Chicken Tamales with Green Salsa, var., 333
Chile Relleno Tamales, var., 333
Chiles Rellenos, Corn-Crumb-Crusted Baked, var., 327
Chilled Avocado Soup with Dungeness Crab and Rosemary Flatbread, 570
Chilled Raw Olympia Oysters with Merlot Mignonette, Grilled "Pemmican" Venison Sausages, and Walla Walla Onion Salad, 626–627
Chorizo Quesadillas with Green Salsa, var., 329
Clams Casino, 814
Clams Oreganata, var., 814
Coconut Shrimp with Spicy Ginger-Soy Dipping Sauce and Shredded Salad, 748–749
Coconut Shrimp with Spicy Mango Dip, var., 749
Corn and Ham Zephyrs, var., 169
Corn Zephyrs with Fresh Tomato Sauce, 169
Crab Imperial Appetizer, var., 215
Crab Louis–Stuffed Artichoke, var., 580
Creole "Barbeque" Shrimp, 268
Creole Shrimp Rémoulade, 265
Deep-Fried Armadillo Eggs, var., 481
Designer Pizzetta with Shredded Duck, Confit Tomatoes, and Mascarpone Cheese, with seven variations, 576–577
Deviled Crab, 215
Dungeness Crab Louis in Avocado Half, 580
Everglades Frog Legs al Mojo Criollo, 756–757
Fried Green Tomatoes with Fresh Tomato Sauce and Bacon, 57
Fried Summer Squash with Fresh Tomato Sauce and Bacon, var., 57
'Gator Sauce Piquante, var., 267
German Potato Latkes with Sour Cream and Applesauce, var., 815
Golden Fried Pierogies, var., 433
Gravlax with Dilled Mustard Sauce and Toast Points, 430–431
Green Chile Quesadilla with Fresh Tomato Salsa, 329
Guacamole Green Sauce, var., 326
Guacamole Shrimp Cocktail, var., 326
Hopi Blue Corn Tamales, var., 333
Huitlacoche Quesadillas with Fresh Tomato Salsa, var., 329
Ida's Chopped Liver with Bagel Crisps, 818
Ida's Potato Latkes with Sour Cream and Scallions, var., 815
Kennett Square Stuffed Mushroom Medley, 165–167
Key West Conch Seviche, 752–753
Key West Scallop Seviche, var., 753
Key West Spanish Mackerel Seviche, var., 753
Lobster, Crab, or Shrimp Tostadas with Guacamole Green Salsa, var., 331
Navajo Tamales, var., 333
Oyster Fritters with Herbed Red Bell Pepper Mayonnaise, 213
Oysters Rockefeller, 269
Oysters Rockefeller au Gratin, var., 269
Passover Chopped Liver with Matzohs, var., 818
Pasta al Autunno, var., 819

Appetizers (Continued)
    Pasta al Estate, var., 819
    Pasta Primavera, 819
    Pau Hana Pupu Platter for Two: Rumaki, Shrimp on Sugarcane,
        Korean Mandoo Dumplings, Chinese Barbeque Baby
        Back Ribs, Poke-Stuffed Mini-Skins, Edamame,
        and Shichimi Wings, 683–687
    Petite Tourtière with Pickled Beets, 113
    Philadelphia Roll Sushi with Ponzu Sauce, var., 579
    Pierogi Medley with Onion Butter Sauce, var., 433
    Pink Singing Scallops with Pinot Noir Beurre Rouge and Wilted
        Baby Spinach, 625
    Potato-Cheddar Pierogies with Onion Butter Sauce, var., 433
    Potato Latke with Smoked Salmon and Caviar, 815
    Russet Potato Skins with Montana Whitefish Caviar and Dilled
        Sour Cream, 520
    Salmon cakes with Homemade Ketchup and Creamy
        Coleslaw, 112
    Salmon Cakes with Ketchup and Pepper Slaw, var., 112
    Salt Cod Cakes with Ketchup and Pepper Slaw, 111–112
    Sauerkraut Pierogies with Onion Butter Sauce, var., 433
    Sausage-Stuffed Mirliton with Creole Tomato Sauce, var., 271
    Seared Foie Gras with Balsamic Onion Marmalade on Straw
        Potato Cake, var., 833
    Shad Roe in Brown Butter with Bacon and Asparagus, 168
    Shredded Pork Tostadas with Roasted Corn and Green Salsa,
        var., 331
    Shrimp and Corn Zephyrs, var., 169
    Shrimp and Tasso-Stuffed Mirliton with Sauce Aurore, 270–271
    Shrimp and Tasso-Stuffed Squash with Creole Tomato Sauce,
        var., 271
    Shrimp 'n' Grits, 54
    Shrimp Sauce Piquante, var., 267
    South Beach Conch Fritters with Spicy Mango Dip, 750–751
    South Beach Shrimp Fritters, var., 751
    Southeast Asian Spring Rolls with Sweet 'n' Hot Dipping Sauce,
        573–575
    Southeast Asian Summer Rolls with Sweet 'n' Hot Dipping
        Sauce, var., 575
    Southern California Crab Cocktail, var., 328
    Southern Sweet Potato Chip Mountain for Two, var., 521
    Southwest Cheese Chile Relleno with Spiced Tomato Sauce, 327
    Southwestern Gravlax on Corn Cakes with Salsa Sour
        Cream, var., 431
    Southwest Grilled Vegetable Tostadas with Roasted Tomato
        Salsa, var., 331
    Spot Prawns and Pacific Littlenecks in Cream, var., 631
    Squash Blossom Quesadillas with Fresh Tomato Salsa, var., 329
    Tartare of Salmon and Striped Bass with Anchovy Croutons,
        816–817
    Tea-Smoked Ahi Tuna with Pickled Vegetable Shreds, var., 583
    Texas "Caviar" with Tortilla Chips, 480
    Texas Gulf Coast Shrimp Cocktail, 328
    Tex-Mex Ground Beef Tostadas with Cheddar and Sour
        Cream, var., 331
    Traditional Baked Creole "Barbeque" Shrimp, var., 268
    Triple Onion Potato Pierogies, 432–433
    Triple Threat Armadillo Eggs, var., 481
    Tuna Tartare with Anchovy Croutons, var., 817
    Twin Tostadas, 330
    Vegetarian Fried Green Tomatoes, var., 57
    Wild Mushroom Quesadillas with Fresh Tomato Salsa, var., 329
    Wisconsin Cheddar Broccoli Rarebit, 429
    Wisconsin Cheddar Woodchuck (Tomato-Bacon Rarebit), var., 429
    Wood-Roasted Olympia Oysters with Merlot Beurre Rouge
        and Crispy Bacon, var., 627
Apple-Rice Pilaf, 631

Apples
    Apple-Cinnamon Upside-Down Cake, var., 454
    Apple Crisp with Vanilla Ice Cream, var., 189
    Apple-Filled Half-Moon Fried Pies with Vanilla
        Ice Cream, var., 401
    Apple Filling for Apple Stack Cake, 397
    Apple-Mushroom Cream Velouté, 181
    Apple Pandowdy with Honey Sour Cream Sauce, 497
        var. Apple-Whiskey-Raisin Pandowdy with Honey Sour
            Cream Sauce, 497
        var. Pawpaw Pandowdy with Honey Sour Cream Sauce, 497
    Apple Stack Cake, 396–397
    Dumplings, 189
    Applewood Smoked Trout with Horseradish Cream and Biscuit
        Crackers, 382–383
        var. Applewood Smoked Trout with Toast Points and Honey
            Mustard Butter, 383
Apricot Sauce, 499
Armadillo Egg with Fresh Tomato Salsa, 481
    var. Deep-Fried Armadillo Eggs, 481
    var. Triple Threat Armadillo Eggs, 481
Asian Aromatics Mix, 587
Aurora Cream Sauce, 166
Avocado
    Avocado–Tomato Salsa, var., 331
    Chilled Avocado Soup, 570
    New Mexico Chilled Avocado Soup, var., 570

Bacon
    Bacon and Cheddar Cheese Potato Chip Mountain
        for Two, var., 521
    Hot Bacon Dressing, 378
Baked Stuffed Shad in Mushroom Cream with Dried Corn
    Pudding and String Beans, 170–171
    var. Baked Stuffed Salmon with Mushroom Cream, Dried Corn
        Pudding, and String Beans, 171
Baked Stuffed Trout with Wild Mushroom Cornbread Dressing
    and Peas 'n' Pearl Onions, 384
    var. Baked Stuffed Trout with Black Walnut–Apple Cornbread
        Dressing, Cider Cream Sauce, and Brussels Sprouts, 384
Balsamic Onion Marmalade, 833
Bananas Foster with Palmier, 289–290
    var. Peaches Foster with Palmier, 290
Banana Spring Rolls with Rum Sauce and Grilled Pineapple
    var. Banana Spring Rolls with Chocolate Sauce and Macadamia
        Nut Ice Cream, 703
Barbeque
    Barbeque Beef Brisket with Cowboy Beans and Ranch-Style
        Slaw, 492–493
        var. Oven Barbequed Beef Brisket with Cowboy Beans
            and Ranch-Style Slaw, 493
    Barbeque Chicken Monterey, var., 339
    Barbeque Chicken Monterey with Cowboy Beans, Green Chile
        Potatoes, and Ranch Salad, var., 339
    Barbeque Pork Shoulder for Pulled or Chopped Pork, var., 71
    Berry Barbeque Sauce, 629
    Chinese Barbeque Baby Back Ribs, 685
    Creole "Barbeque" Shrimp, 268
    DelMarVa Roadside Barbeque Chicken, 224
    Kentucky Barbeque Lamb Shanks, 389
Basmati Pulao, 831
Basque Chicken and Sausage in Spicy Tomato Sauce over
    Pan-Steamed Rice with Three-Pepper Medley, 526–527
    var. Basque-Style Lamb in Spicy Tomato Sauce over
        Pan-Steamed Rice with Three-Pepper Medley, 527
Basque Garbure, var., 519
Basque Potato Skins with Peppers and Bacalao, var., 520

Beans
    All-American Baked Beans with Bacon, Frankfurters, and Cole Slaw, var., 126
    Boston Baked Beans with Salt Pork, 124
    Chickasaw Bean Cake, 55
    Coral Gables Black Bean Soup with Orange, var., 747
    Cowboy Beans, 493
    Creamed Lima Beans, 388
    Cuban Black Beans (side dish), var., 747
    Red Beans 'n' Rice with Grilled Andouille Sausage and Collard Greens, var., 288
    Refried Beans, 330
    Smoked Turkey Red Beans 'n' Rice, var., 288
    Smoky Beef 'n' Bean Soup, 476
    Tidewater Kidney Bean Salad, 225
    U. S. House of Representatives Bean Soup, var., 161
    U. S. Senate Bean Soup, 161
    Ybor City Black Bean Soup, 747
Bear
    Pan-Seared Bear Chop in Cranberry Demi-Glace with Garlic Mashed Potatoes, Root Vegetables, and Wild Mushroom Ragout, var., 532
Beef
    Barbeque Beef Brisket, 492
    Beef Barley Soup with Farmhouse White Bread and Butter, 428
      Beef Noodle Soup, var., 428
      Vegetable Beef Soup, var., 428
    Beef Stew Base, 448
    Beef Tamales, 332–333
    Beer-Braised Beef Short Ribs, 494, 495
    Beer-Braised Beef Short Ribs with Chuck Wagon Macaroni and Wilted Spinach, 494–495
      var. Beer-Braised Beef Short Ribs with Yukon Gold Potatoes and Wilted Spinach, 495
      var. "Goulash," 495
    Cannibal Steak, 482
    Charred Rare Filet Steak, Cannibal Style, var., 482
    Cherokee Beef Stew, var., 392
    Chile con Carne, 347
    Chinese Marinated Beef, 701
    Chopped Beef and Cabbage Jambalaya, var., 285
    Cincinnati Chili, 445
    Fajitas, 343
    Frying Steaks (for chicken-fried steak), 487
    "Goulash," var., 495
    Grilled Filet of Beef with Smoky Steak Sauce, Beer-Batter Onion Rings, Hash Brown Potatoes, and Vegetable Roundup, var., 489
    Jerky, 479
    Mexican Marinated Skirt Steak, 343
    Picadillo with Yellow Rice, Black Beans, Green Papaya Salad, and Tostones, var., 774
    Ropa Vieja, 772
    Smoke-Roasted Prime Rib of Beef, 491
    Smoky Beef 'n' Bean Soup, 476
    Tamales, 332
    Tex-Mex Ground Beef Tostadas with Cheddar and Sour Cream, var., 331
    Trail-Drive Chili, 496
Beer Batter, 489
Beets, Pickled, and Eggs, 434
Beet Soup, Scandinavian, 427
Bento Rice Balls, 691
Berry Barbeque Sauce, 629
Big Island Lemongrass Seafood Soup with Lotus Root Chips, 675–676
    var. Hot and Fragrant Coconut Chicken Soup, 676

Biscotti
    Almond Biscotto, var., 841
    Chocolate-Dipped Burnt-Orange Biscotti, 841
    Chocolate-Dipped Hazelnut Biscotto, var., 841
Biscuit-on-a-Stick, 476
Bison
    Great Plains Bison Stew, var., 448
    Grilled Filet of Bison, 488
Blackberry-Filled Half-Moon Fried Pies with Vanilla Ice Cream, var., 401
Blackened Redfish with Eggplant 'n' Shrimp Pirogue and Maquechoux, 276–278
    var. Blackened Snapper with Eggplant 'n' Shrimp Pirogue and Maquechoux, 278
Black-Eyed Pea Bollitos with Sofrito Tomato Sauce, var., 764
Black Walnut Crisps, 230
Black Walnut Poundcake with Persimmon Sauce, 398–399
    var. Walnut Poundcake with Peach Sauce, 399
"Blind" Tamales (side dish), var., 333
Blood Orange Tart with Marmalade Glaze and Dark Chocolate Drizzle, 591
    var. Orange Tart with Marmalade Glaze and Dark Chocolate Drizzle, 591
Blueberries
    Blueberry Crisp with Vanilla Ice Cream, 133
      var. Apple Crisp with Vanilla Ice Cream, 133
      var. Rhubarb Crisp with Vanilla Ice Cream, 133
      var. Strawberry Crisp with Vanilla Ice Cream, 133
    Blueberry Pie with Whipped Cream, var., 533
    Lattice-Top Blueberry Pie with Buttermilk Ice Cream, var., 449
Blue Cheese Potato Chip Mountain for Two
    var. Bacon and Cheddar Cheese Potato Chip Mountain for Two, 521
    var. Southern Sweet Potato Chip Mountain for Two, 521
Boiled Icing, 79
Border-Style Beef Tamal with Red and Green Salsas, 332
    var. "Blind" Tamales (side dish), 333
    var. Chicken Tamales with Green Salsa, 333
    var. Chile Relleno Tamales, 333
    var. Hopi Blue Corn Tamales, 333
    var. Navajo Tamales, 333
    var. Sweet Dessert Tamales, 333
Borracha Chili, var., 496
Boston Baked Beans with Salt Pork and Fresh Pork, Served with Brown Bread and Piccalilli, 124–126
    var. All-American Baked Beans with Bacon, Frankfurters, and Cole Slaw, 126
Boston Brown Bread, 125
Boston Cream Pie, 131–132
    var. Home-Style Boston Cream Pie, 132
Bourbon Pecan Pie, 77
Braised Brussels Sprouts, 631
Braised Chinese Black Mushrooms, 697
Braised Country Spareribs with Turnips 'n' Turnip Greens, var., 67
Braised Garlic Jus, 491
Brandied Peach Halves, 535
Breaded Pork Chops with Stewed Tomatoes and Baked Macaroni 'n' Cheese, 440–441
    var. Breaded Pork Medallions with Stewed Tomatoes and Macaroni 'n' Cheese, 441
    var. Midwestern Wiener Schnitzel, 441
Bread Stuffing, 122
Broiled Scrod in Lemon Butter Sauce with Parsley Potatoes, Broiled Tomato, and Summer Succotash, 117
    var. Broiled Cod in Lemon Butter Sauce with Parsley Potatoes, Broiled Tomato, and Summer Succotash, 117

Brooklyn Blackout Cake with Chocolate Whipped Cream, 842–843
  var. *Brooklyn Blackout Cake with Vanilla Ice Cream, 843*
Brown Butter, 638
Brownies, Classic, 185
  var. *Cheesecake Brownies, 185*
  var. *Walnut Brownies, 185*
Brunswick Stew, Traditional, var., 386
Brussels Sprouts, Braised, 631
Buckwheat Rolls with Country Ham, Asparagus, and Herbed Fresh Cheese, 379–381
Buckwheat Sourdough Starter, 380
Burnt Sugar Ice Cream, 401
Buttermilk-Marinated Frying Chicken, 62
Buttermilk Velouté for Fish, 525
Butternut Squash Calabashes, 391

Cabbage
  Golabki (Polish-American Stuffed Cabbage), var., 825
  Pepper Slaw, 112
  Ranch-Style Slaw, 493
  Stuffed Savoy Cabbage in Sweet 'n' Sour Sauce with Kasha Varnishkes, 823–825
  Stuffed Savoy Cabbage Rolls, 824
  Toor Dal Cabbage Bundles in Red Curry Broth with Brown Rice and Steamed California Vegetables, var., 585
  Tropical Slaw, 770
Cactus, Grilled, 325
Cactus Cut-Out Cookies, 350
Cajun Cottage Pie with Spicy Tomato Sauce, var., 530
Cakes
  Apple-Cinnamon Upside-Down Cake, var., 454
  Apple Stack Cake, 396–397
  Black Walnut Poundcake with Persimmon Sauce, 398, 399
  Brooklyn Blackout Cake, 842–843
  Carrot Cake with Cream Cheese Frosting
    var. *Carrot Cupcakes, 453*
    var. *Southern-Style Carrot Cake, 453*
  Devil's Food Cake with Vanilla Ice Cream, 450–451
  German-American Black Forest Cake, var., 451
  King's Cake with Queen's Sauce, 294–295
    var. *Large King's Cake with Queen's Sauce, 295*
  Mario's Tres Leches Cake with Lime Marmalade, var., 777
  Sky-High Coconut Cake, 78–79
  Tres Leches Cake with Mandarin Oranges, 776–777
  Walnut Poundcake with Peach Sauce, var., 399
California Roll Sushi with Wasabi-Soy Dip, 578–579
  var. *Philadelphia Roll Sushi with Ponzu Sauce, 579*
Campfire Brook Trout with Corn Relish Tartar Sauce, Annie's Skillet Potatoes, and Grilled Western Vegetables, 483–485
  var. *Campfire Brook Trout with Corn Relish, Cowboy Beans, and Ranch Slaw, 485*
Campfire Fish Dredge, 484
Candied Lime Zest, 775
Candied Orange Zest and Caramelized Orange Zest, 841
Candied Pecans, 56
Cannibal Steak, 482
  var. *Charred Rare Filet Steak, Cannibal Style, 482*
Cannoli
  Cannoli Shells, 839
  Chocolate Chip Cannolo with Mocha Custard Sauce, var., 839
  Mascarpone Cannoli, 839
  Mascarpone Cannoli Filling, 839
Cape Cod Boiled Dinner with Egg Sauce, var., 130
Caribbean Conch Chowder with Yuca Roll, 745
  var. *Caribbean Shrimp Chowder, 745*
  var. *Old Key West Conch Chowder, 745*
Caribbean Seviche, var., 753

Carrots
  Carrot Cake with Cream Cheese Frosting, 452–453
    var. *Carrot Cupcakes, 453*
    var. *Southern-Style Carrot Cake, 453*
  Carrot-Daikon Tangle, 575
  Carrot Purée, 183, 634
  Glazed Baby Carrots, 227
Casino Butter, 814
Cauliflower
  Cauliflower Gratin Discs, 179
  North Indian Braised Cauliflower, 830
Char-Grilled Northwestern Lamb Chops with Pinot Noir Demi-Glace, Porcini Mushrooms, Roasted Potatoes, and Carrot Purée, var., 633
Charleston She-Crab Soup with Buttermilk Biscuit, 52
  var. *Mock She-Crab Soup (using male crabs), 52*
Chayote Wedges, Steamed, 335
Cheese
  Almond-Crusted Goat Cheese Discs, 571
  Baked Macaroni 'n' Cheese, 440
  Cheddar Cheese Sauce, 379
  Cheesecake Brownies, var., 185
  Herbed Fresh Cheese, 381
  Vermont Cheddar Cheese Soup, 110
  Wisconsin Beer and Cheddar Soup, var., 110
  Wisconsin Cheddar Broccoli Rarebit, 429
  Wisconsin Cheddar Woodchuck (Tomato-Bacon Rarebit), var., 429
Cherokee Venison Stew with Shuck Bread, 391–392
  var. *Cherokee Beef Stew with Shuck Bread, 392*
  var. *Cherokee Venison Stew with Corn Pone, 392*
Cherries
  Cherry Vanilla Texmati Rice Pudding with Cherry Sauce, var., 499
  Lattice-Top Cherry Pie, 449
  Reconstituted Cherries, 437
Chesapeake Fried Oysters with Fresh Tomato Cocktail Sauce, 212
  var. *Chesapeake Fried Oysters with Tartar Sauce, 212*
Chesapeake Grill Baste, 223
Chickasaw Bean Cake with Sunflower Salad, 55
  var. *with Kohlrabi Salad, 55*
  var. *with Sprout Salad, 55*
Chicken
  Basque Chicken and Sausage in Spicy Tomato Sauce over Pan-Steamed Rice with Three-Pepper Medley, 526–527
  Bot Boi, 176
  Brunswick Stew, 386
  Buttermilk-Marinated Frying Chicken, 62
  Chicken, Andouille Sausage, and 'Gator Filé Gumbo, var., 281
  Chicken Adobo with Vegetable Pancit
    var. *Filipino Seafood-Vegetable Pancit, 696–697*
    var. *Filipino Vegetable Pancit with Adobo-Grilled Chicken Breast, 696–697*
  Chicken and Sausage Jambalaya, var., 285
  Chicken Chile Verde, var., 338
  Chicken Chop Suey in Crispy Noodle Nest, 586–587
    var. *Sub Gum Chop Suey in Crispy Noodle Nest, 587*
  Chicken Corn Soup, 162
  Chicken Étouffée with Pan-Steamed Rice and Sauté Mirliton, var., 284
  Chicken Fajitas, var., 343
  Chicken-Fried Steak Dredge, 487
  Chicken Hekka with Jasmine Rice, 694–695
  Chicken Monterey with Green Chile Potatoes and Black Bean Pico de Gallo, 339
    var. *Barbeque Chicken Monterey with Cowboy Beans, Green Chile Potatoes, and Ranch Salad, 339*
    var. *Pepper Jack Chicken with Green Chile Potatoes and Black Bean Pico de Gallo, 339*

Chicken Perloo, var., 58
Chicken Pie Filling, 439
Chicken Tamales with Green Salsa, var., 333
Chicken Virginia Roulades, 227
Chicken Virginia Stuffed with Ham and Collards in Creamy
    Mushroom Sauce, Served with Pan-Steamed White Rice
    and Glazed Baby Carrots, 226–227
Chicken with Brunswick Stew and Corn Pone, 385–386
    var. Kentucky Burgoo, 386
    var. Traditional Brunswick Stew, 386
Chinese Marinated Chicken Wings, 684
Country Captain, with variations, 63
Deep-Dish Flaky Pastry Chicken Pie, 438–439
Del MarVa Roadside Barbeque Chicken, 224
Egg-Drop Chicken Corn Soup, var., 163
Grilled Chicken with Pineapple-Avocado Salsa and Boniato
    Fries, var., 765
Gullah Chicken in Spicy Peanut Sauce, var., 53
Hawai'ian Marinated Chicken, 695
Ida's Chopped Liver, 818
Jerk-Marinated Half Hens, 768
Kalua Chicken with Island Fried Rice and Stir-Fry Cabbage,
    var., 698
Maple-Glazed Cornish Hens with Sauerkraut and Hominy,
    var., 394
New Mexico Red Chile Pork or Chicken Enchiladas, var., 337
Pecan-Crusted Chicken Suprêmes, 287
Pennsylvania Dutch Chicken Corn Soup, 162
Pennsylvania Dutch Chicken Pie, var., 177
Southern Fried Chicken, with variations, 61–62
Tilghman Island Chicken Salad with Fried Oysters, 216
Winter Chicken Corn Soup with Rivels, var., 163
Chicory Salad with Beef Jerky, Spiced Pecans, and Smoked
    Tomato Vinaigrette, 478–479
    var. Chicory Salad with Grilled Steak, Spiced Pecans,
        and Smoked Tomato Vinaigrette, 479
Chile con Carne in Tortilla Basket with Olla Beans and Avocado
    Pico de Gallo, 346–347
    var. Venison Chile con Carne, 347
Chile Relleno
    Chile Relleno Tamales, 333
    Corn-Crumb-Crusted Baked, var., 327
    Crumb-Crusted Southwest, var., 327
    Picadillo, var., 327
Chile Verde
    Pork, 338
Chili
    Borracha Chili, var., 496
    Cincinnati, 445
    Cincinnati Chili Bowl, var., 445
    Cincinnati Four-Way Chili, var., 445
    Cincinnati Three-Way Chili, var., 445
    Cincinnati Two-Way Chili, var., 445
    Deep-Dark Secret Chili, var., 496
    Trail-Drive Chili, 496
    Venison Chile con Carne, var., 347
    Venison Chili, var., 496
Chilled Avocado Soup with Tobiko Caviar and Poppy Seed
    Lavash, 570
    var., New Mexico Chilled Avocado Soup, 570
    var. Chilled Avocado Soup with Dungeness Crab and Rosemary
        Flatbread, 570
Chilled Raw Olympia Oysters with Merlot Mignonette,
    Grilled "Pemmican" Venison Sausages, and Walla Walla
    Onion Salad, 626–627
    var. Wood-Roasted Olympia Oysters with Merlot Beurre Rouge
        and Crispy Bacon, 627

Chinese Barbeque Baby Back Ribs, 685
Chinese Marinated Beef, 701
Chinese Marinated Chicken Breast, 587
Chinese Marinated Chicken Wings, 684
Chinese Stir-Fry Sauce for Beef, 701
Chinese-Style Tomato Beef with Sticky Rice, 700–701
    var. Tomato Chicken, 701
Chinese Vegetable Glaze, 583
Chocolate
    Chocolate-Caramel Needles, 293
    Chocolate Chiffon Pie, var., 501
    Chocolate Chip Cannolo with Mocha Custard Sauce,
        var., 839
    Chocolate–Coffee–Macadamia Nut Pie, var., 705
    Chocolate Cream Cheese Hazelnut Tart, 638–639
    Chocolate-Dipped Burnt-Orange Biscotti, 841
    Chocolate-Dipped Hazelnut Biscotto, var., 841
    Chocolate Molasses Glaze, 292
    Chocolate Pots de Crème, var., 640
    Chocolate Voodoo Torte with Raspberry Sauce, 291–293
        var. Chocolate-Pecan Torte with Raspberry Sauce, 293
    Fudge Frosting, 451
    Glaze, 132
    Hot Fudge Sauce, 186
Chorizo Quesadillas with Green Salsa, var., 329
Chuck Wagon Macaroni, 495
Cider Pan Reduction, 633
Cincinnati Five-Way Chili with a Frank, 444–445
    var. Cincinnati Chili Bowl, 445
    var. Cincinnati Four-Way Chili, 445
    var. Cincinnati Three-Way Chili, 445
    var. Cincinnati Two-Way Chili, 445
Cioppino Base, 581
Clams
    Clam Fritters with Herbed Red Bell Pepper Mayonnaise,
        var., 214
    Clams Casino, 814
        var. Clams Oreganata, 814
    New England Clam Chowder, 109
    Portuguese Sausage and Clams with Potatoes and Peppers,
        var., 120
    Summertime Corn and Clam Chowder, var., 109
Classic Cobb Salad
    var. Vegetarian Cobb Salad, 572
Classic Meat Loaf with Mashed Potatoes, Mushroom Gravy,
    and Heartland Vegetable Medley, 446–447
    var. Cottage Pie with Heartland Vegetable Medley, 447
    var. Diner-Style Meat Loaf with French Fries, 447
    var. Hot Meat Loaf Sandwich, 447
Classic Pots de Crème, var., 640
Cobb Salad
    Classic, 572
    Vegetarian, var., 572
Cocoa Sweet Dough Pastry Shell, 639
Coconut
    Buttercream, 79
    Coconut-Breaded Haupia Squares, 706
    Coconut Cake, 77–79
    Coconut Flan, var., 350
    Coconut-Lime Vinaigrette, 759
    Coconut Shrimp with Spicy Ginger-Soy Dipping Sauce
        and Shredded Salad, 748–749
        var. Coconut Shrimp with Spicy Mango Dip, 749
    Coconut Sweet Potatoes, 693
    Coconut Tuile Cups, 778
    Haupia Coconut-Custard Coupe, var., 707
    Hot and Fragrant Coconut Chicken Soup, var., 676

Codfish Cheeks Poached in Hard Cider with Apples
     and Parsnips, Served with Sautéed Kale and Potato
     Croquettes, var., 116
Coffee Flan, var., 350
Coffee Pot de Crème, 640
Collard Greens with Pot Liquor, 72
Conch Fritter Batter, 750
Conch Seviche, 753
Confit Tomatoes, 577
Cookies, Cactus Cut-Out, 350
Coral Gables Black Bean Soup with Orange, var., 747
Corn
     Chicken Corn Soup, 162
     Corn Flour Breading for Seafood, 60
     Corn Relish, 485
     Corn Relish Tartar Sauce, 485
     Corn Zephyrs with Fresh Tomato Sauce, 169
          var. Corn and Ham Zephyrs, 169
          var. Shrimp and Corn Zephyrs, 169
     Creamed, 390
     Creamy Corn and Crab Soup, 210
     Creamy Corn and Green Chile Soup, 324
     Dried Corn Puddings, 171
     Lenape Corn Cakes, 172
     Summertime Corn and Clam Chowder, var., 109
Cornbread
     Cornbread Croutons, 56
     Cornbread Dressing, 74
     Cornbread Dressing, with Wild Mushrooms, 384
Corned Beef. See New England Corned Beef
     Boiled Dinner
Cottage Pie with Heartland Vegetable Medley, var., 447, 530
Country Captain with Pan-Steamed Rice and Fried Okra
     var. with Boneless Chicken, 63
     var. with Fresh Spice Masala, 63
Courtbouillon Sauce, 275
Cowboy Beans, 493
Crab
     Beer-Battered Soft-Shell Crab Appetizer, var., 221
     Crab Cake Salad Appetizer, var., 218
     Crab Imperial, 214, 220
     Crab Imperial Appetizer, var., 215
     Crab Louis–Stuffed Artichoke, var., 580
     Crab-Stuffed Lobster Tails, 762
     Crab-Stuffed Mushrooms, 166
     Crab-Stuffed Mushrooms with Chive Hollandaise, var., 167
     Creamy Corn and Crab Soup, 210
     Creamy Crab, Corn, and Ham Soup, var., 204
     Creamy Crab Soup, var., 204
     Cuban Crab Stuffing, 763
     Deviled Crab, 215
     Dinner-House Crab Cake Platter, var., 218
     Dinner-House Fried Soft-Shell Crab Platter, var., 221
     Dungeness Crab Louis in Avocado Half, 580
     Eastern Shore Crab Cakes, var., 217
     Economy Crab Cakes, var., 217
     Home-Style Seafood-Only Crab Soup, var., 211
     Maryland Crab Cakes, 217
     Sautéed Soft-Shell Crabs, 221
     Wintertime Home-Style Crab Soup, var., 211
Cranberries
     Cranberry-Maple Velouté, 173
     Ice Cream, 137
     Rehydrated, 114
     Sauce, 123
     Sugar-Coated, 135
     Sweet Cranberry Coulis, 188

Crawfish
     Crawfish Bisque with Stuffed Crawfish Heads and Creole
          Baguette, 263–265
          var. Crawfish Bisque with Herbed Crouton and
               Crawfish Tails, 265
     Crawfish Étouffée with Pan-Steamed Rice and Sauté
          Mirliton, 284
          var. Chicken Étouffée with Pan-Steamed Rice and Sauté
               Mirliton, 284
          var. Shrimp Étouffée with Pan-Steamed Rice and Sauté
               Mirliton, 284
     Crawfish Jambalaya, var., 285
Cream Cheese Frosting, 452
Cream Sauce
     Aurora, 166
     Creamy Mushroom Sauce, 227
     Emerald, 167
Creamy Cauliflower Soup with Cracked Hazelnuts and Cougar
     Gold Cheddar Wafers, 622
     var. Creamy Broccoli Soup with Cracked Hazelnuts and Cougar
          Gold Cheddar Wafers, 622
Creamy Corn and Crab Soup with Beaten Biscuit, 210
     var. Creamy Crab, Corn, and Ham Soup, 210
     var. Creamy Crab Soup, 210
Creamy Corn and Green Chile Soup with Flour Tortillas, 324
Crème Brûlée, 837
     var. Ginger Crème Brûlée, 837
     var. Orange Crème Brûlée, 837
Creole "Barbeque" Shrimp, 268
     var. Traditional Baked Creole "Barbeque" Shrimp, 268
Creole Jambalaya with Pepper Medley, 285
     var. Andouille Sausage and Oyster Jambalaya, 285
     var. Chicken and Sausage Jambalaya, 285
     var. Chopped Beef and Cabbage Jambalaya, 285
     var. Crawfish Jambalaya, 285
     var. Quail and Bacon Jambalaya, 285
     var. Shrimp, Crab, and Oyster Jambalaya, 285
     var. Summer Vegetable Jambalaya, 285
Creole Shrimp Rémoulade
     var. Cajun Crawfish Rémoulade, 266
Croutons
     Cornbread, 56
     Onion, 164
     Walnut-Crusted Cheddar, 114
Cuban Black Beans (side dish), var, 747
Cuban Crab-Stuffed Lobster Tails with Florida Watercress
     and Black-Eyed Pea Bollitos, 762–764
     var. Black-Eyed Pea Bollitos with Sofrito Tomato Sauce
          (appetizer), 764
     var. Cuban Crab-Stuffed Shrimp with Florida Watercress
          and Black-Eyed Pea Bollitos, 764
Cuban Sofrito, 764
Cucumber Salad, 225
Custard
     Haupia Coconut-Custard Coupe, var., 707
     Hominy Custard with Glazed Strawberries and Black Walnut
          Crisps, 229–230
     Raisin-Spice Hominy Custard, var., 230
     Strawberry-Topped Hominy Custards, var., 229

Deep-Dish Flaky Pastry Chicken Pie, 438–439
     var. Deep-Dish Flaky Pastry Pheasant Pie, 439
     var. Deep-Dish Flaky Pastry Turkey Pie, 439
DelMarVa Roadside Barbeque Chicken with Tidewater Kidney
     Bean Salad and Cucumber Salad, 224–225
     var. Smoke-Roasted Pork Loin with Tidewater Kidney Bean Salad
          and Cucumber Salad, 225

Delmonico Potato Rounds, 833
Designer Pizzetta with Shredded Duck, Confit Tomatoes, and Mascarpone Cheese, 576–577
  with seven variations, 575
Desserts. *See also* Cakes; Pies
  Allegheny Mountain Apple Dumpling with Vanilla Custard Sauce, 189
  Almond Torte with Raspberry Sauce, var., 349
  Amaretti Peach Dumplings with Vanilla Custard Sauce, var., 189
  Amaretto Plum Galette with Vanilla Custard Sauce, var., 590
  Apple Crisp with Vanilla Ice Cream, var., 189
  Apple Pandowdy with Honey Sour Cream Sauce, 497
  Apple-Whiskey-Raisin Pandowdy with Honey Sour Cream Sauce, var., 497
  Bananas Foster with Palmier, 289–290
  Banana Spring Rolls with Chocolate Sauce and Macadamia Nut Ice, 703
  Banana Spring Rolls with Rum Sauce and Grilled Pineapple, 702–703
  Basque Tostada with Brandied Peach Half, 534
  Black Walnut Crisps, 230
  Blood Orange Tart with Marmalade Glaze and Dark Chocolate Drizzle, 591
  Blueberry Crisp with Vanilla Ice Cream, 133
  Brooklyn Blackout Cake, 842–843
  Brownie Ice Cream Sandwich, var., 186
  Cheesecake Brownies, var., 185
  Cherry Vanilla Texmati Rice Pudding with Cherry Sauce, var., 499
  Chocolate Chip Cannolo with Mocha Custard Sauce, var., 838
  Chocolate–Coffee–Macadamia Nut Pie, 705
  Chocolate-Pecan Torte with Raspberry Sauce, var., 293
  Chocolate Pots de Crème, var., 640
  Chocolate Voodoo Torte with Raspberry Sauce, 291–293
  Classic Brownies, 185
  Classic Pots de Crème, var., 640
  Coconut Flan, var., 350
  Coffee Flan, var., 350
  Cranberry Ice Cream, 137
  Fire and Ice Haupia Custard with Pineapple Compote, 706–707
  Flan with Cactus Cut-Out Cookie, 350
  Fourth of July Shortcake, var., 75
  Frozen Cappuccino Soufflé with Chocolate-Dipped Hazelnut Biscotto, var., 841
  Frozen Chocolate Soufflé with Almond Biscotto, var., 841
  Frozen Soufflé Grand Marnier with Chocolate-Dipped Burnt-Orange Biscotto, 840–841
  Ginger Crème Brûlée with Fortune Cookie, var., 593
  Green Tea Ice Cream with Fortune Cookie, 592–593
  Haupia Coconut-Custard Coupe, var., 705
  Hazelnut Torte with Cherry Sauce, var., 349
  Hershey Brownie Sundae with Philadelphia-Style Ice Cream and Hot Fudge Sauce, 185–186
  Hominy Custard with Glazed Strawberries and Black Walnut Crisps, 228, 229–230
  Italian Plum Galette with Vanilla Custard Sauce, var., 590
  Kona Coffee Choco-Mac Tart with Macadamia Brittle, 704–705
  Lu'au-Style Haupia, var., 707
  Mascarpone Cannolo with Zabaglione Sauce, 838
  Old-Fashioned Biscuit Strawberry Shortcake, 75
  Orange Tart with Marmalade Glaze and Dark Chocolate Drizzle, var., 591
  Pawpaw Pandowdy with Honey Sour Cream Sauce, var., 497
  Peach Shortcake, var., 75
  Pecan Torte with Persimmon Sauce, var., 349
  Pepita Torte with Prickly Pear Sauce, var., 349
  Pink Guava Sorbet, 779

Piñon Pine Nut Torte with Prickly Pear Sauce and Crema, 348–349
  Poached Pear on Frangipane Cake with Almond Crunch Filling and Pinot Noir Syrup, 636–637
  Pumpkin Roll with Cranberry Coulis, 187–188
  Raisin-Spice Hominy Custard, 230
  Raisin-Walnut Apple Dumplings with Vanilla Custard Sauce, var., 189
  Raspberry Frangipane Cakes, var., 637
  Rhubarb Crisp with Vanilla Ice Cream, 133
  Rum-Raisin Texmati Rice Pudding with Apricot Sauce, 498–499
  Santa Rosa Plum Galette with Almond Custard Sauce, 590
  Seattle Coffeehouse Pot de Crème with Chocolate-Dipped Biscotto, 640
  Spice Trade Gingerbread with Cranberry Ice Cream, 136–137
  Spice Trade Gingerbread with Vanilla Custard Sauce, var., 137
  Strawberry Crisp with Vanilla Ice Cream, var., 133
  Sweet Dessert Tamales, var., 333
  Triple-Threat Brownie Ice Cream Sundae, var., 186
  Tropical Fruit Palette with Guava Sorbet in Coconut Tuile, 778–779
  Waffle Ice Cream Sundae, var., 186
  Walnut Brownies, var., 185
  Walnut Torte with Apricot Sauce, var., 349
  Wells Kringle with Lingonberry Sauce, 455
Deviled Crab, 215
  var. Crab Imperial Appetizer, 215
Devil's Food Cake with Vanilla Custard Ice Cream, 450–451
  var. German-American Black Forest Cake, 451
Dilled Lobster Salad in Lobster Shell, var., 115
Dilled Mustard Sauce, 431
Dilled Sour Cream, 520
Dilled Sour Cream Sauce, 119
Diner-Style Meat Loaf with French Fries, var., 447
Dixie Peach Cobbler, 76
  var. Cherry, Blueberry, Apple, or Other Fruit Cobbler, 76
Duck
  Duck, Andouille Sausage, and 'Gator Filé Gumbo, 280–281
    var. Chicken, Andouille Sausage, and 'Gator Filé Gumbo, 281
    var. Duck, Andouille Sausage, and Oyster Filé Gumbo, 281
  Escalopes of Duck with Dried Cherry Demi-Glace and Ojibwa Goose Ragout in Baby Pumpkin, with Braised Kale and Wild Rice, var., 437
  Grilled Rare Duck Breast with Green Peppercorn Demi-Glace, Haricots Verts, and Rutabaga-Mascarpone Purée, var., 827
  Ojibwa Escalopes of Duck with Dried Cherry Demi-Glace, Braised Kale, and Wild Rice, var., 437
  Pan-Seared Breast of Petaluma Duck in Red Wine Roasted Garlic Demi-Glace with Sautéed Flame Grapes, Mashed Potatoes, and Wilted Baby Spinach, var., 589
  Pan-Seared Breast of Petaluma Duck in Zinfandel Demi-Glace with Sautéed Flame Grapes, Roasted Garlic Flan, and Wilted Baby Spinach, 588–589
  Pan-Seared Long Island Duck Breast in Port Wine Demi-Glace, var., 179
  Peachy Duck with Mashed Potatoes and Turnips 'n' Turnip Greens, 67–70
  Port-Glazed Roast Duck Halves, 178
  Roast Duck Leg in Cider Sauce with Pumpkin Gnocchi and Wilted Arugula, var., 633
  Seared Rare Duck Breast with Teriyaki Sauce, Pacific Vegetable Medley, and Bento Rice Balls, var., 691
  Shredded Duck, 576
  Smoke-Roasted Duck Leg in Cider Sauce with Pumpkin Gnocchi and Arugula, 632–633
Dungeness Crab Louis in Avocado Half, 580
  var. Crab Louis–Stuffed Artichoke, 580

Edamame
   Furikake Edamame, 687
Egg-Drop Chicken Corn Soup, var., 163
Eggplant 'n' Shrimp Pirogues, 277
*Eggplant Parmesan with Fresh Tomato Sauce, Potato Gnocchi,
      and Vegetable "Spaghetti," var.*, 836
Emerald Cream Sauce, 167
Enchiladas
   Enchiladas Rancheras, 337
   New Mexico Green Chile Cheese Enchiladas, var., 337
   New Mexico Red Chile Pork or Chicken Enchiladas, var., 337
   Santa Fe Red Chile Cheese Enchiladas, 336–337
   Vegetarian Red Chile Cheese Enchiladas, var., 337
Étouffée, crawfish, 284
Everglades Frog Legs al Mojo Criollo, 756–757
   var. Alligator Fingers al Mojo Criollo, 757
   var. Catfish Fingers al Mojo Criollo, 757

Fajitas, 343
   var. Chicken, 343
   var. Swordfish, 343
Fennel-Yogurt Tomato Sauce, 831
Filipino Seafood-Vegetable Pancit, var., 697
*Filipino Vegetable Pancit with Adobo-Grilled Chicken Breast,
      var.*, 697
Fire and Ice Haupia Custard with Pineapple Compote, 706–707
   var. Haupia Coconut-Custard Coupe, 707
   var. Lu'au-Style Haupia, 707
Fish and seafood. *See also* Clams; Crab; Salmon; Shrimp
   Ahi Norimaki Sushi, var., 679
   Ahi Nori Tempura Roll with Shoyu Butter Sauce and Radish
      Sprouts, 677–679
   Ahi Poke with Shrimp Chips, 682
   Applewood Smoked Trout with Horseradish Cream and Biscuit
      Crackers, 382–383
   Baked Stuffed Shad in Mushroom Cream, 170–171
   Baked Stuffed Trout with Wild Mushroom Cornbread Dressing
      and Peas 'n' Pearl Onions, 384
   Blackened Redfish, 276
   Blackened Snapper, var., 278
   Broiled Cod in Lemon Butter Sauce, var., 117
   Broiled Scrod in Lemon Butter Sauce, 117
   Campfire Brook Trout, 483–485
   *Campfire Brook Trout with Corn Relish, Cowboy Beans,
      and Ranch Slaw, var.*, 485
   Cape Cod Boiled Dinner with Egg Sauce, var., 130
   Caribbean Seviche, var., 753
   Catfish Fingers al Mojo Criollo, var., 757
   Chesapeake Fried Oysters with Fresh Tomato Cocktail
      Sauce, 212
   *Codfish Cheeks Poached in Hard Cider with Apples
      and Parsnips, Served with Sautéed Kale
      and Potato Croquettes, var.*, 116
   Corn Flour Breading for, 60
   *Crawfish Bisque with Herbed Crouton and Crawfish Tails,
      var.*, 265
   Crawfish Bisque with Stuffed Crawfish Heads and Creole
      Baguette, 263–265
   Crawfish Étouffée with Pan-Steamed Rice and Sauté
      Mirliton, 284
   Crawfish Jambalaya, var., 285
   Flounder en Papillote, var., 273
   Grilled Rockfish, 222
   Grilled Whole Baby Snapper, var., 693
   Grilled Whole Baby Snapper Bluefish, var., 174
   Halibut Poached in Hard Cider with Apples and Parsnips, Served
      with Sautéed Kale and Potato Croquettes, 116

Imperial Stuffed Flounder, 220
Key West Conch Seviche, 752–753
Key West Scallop Seviche, var., 753
Key West Spanish Mackerel Seviche, var., 753
Lenape Grilled Fish, var., 173
Lenape Marinated Bluefish Fillets, 173
Lenape Smoke-Roasted Bluefish, 172–173
Mac-Panko-Crusted Mahimahi Fillets, 689
Malanga-Mango-Crusted Red Snapper Fillets, 761
Oyster Fritters with Herbed Red Bell Pepper Mayonnaise, 213
Oyster Pilau, 65
Oysters Rockefeller, 269
Oysters Rockefeller au Gratin, var., 269
Panéed Grouper, 758–759
Panéed Grouper Cheeks, var., 759
Pan-Fried Brook Trout or Ocean Fish, var., 60
Pan-Fried Catfish, 60
   var. Pan-Fried Soft-Shell Crabs, 60
Pan-Seared "Snapper" Bluefish, 174
Peanut-Crusted Mahimahi, var., 689
*Peanut-Crusted Mahimahi with Sticky Rice, Thai Red Curry
      Sauce, and Baby Bok Choy, var.*, 689
Pecan-Crusted Red Snapper, var., 287
Poached Montana Whitefish with Crawfish Tails in Buttermilk
      Velouté with Steamed Mountain Rose Potatoes and Fresh
      Peas, 524–525
*Poached Montana Whitefish with Whitefish Caviar in Dilled
      ButterSauce with Steamed New Potatoes and Fresh Peas,
      var.*, 525
*Poached Steelhead Trout with Crawfish Tails in Buttermilk
      Velouté with Steamed Mountain Rose Potatoes and Fresh
      Peas, var.*, 525
Pompano en Escabeche with Ñame Cake, 766–767
Pompano Papillotes with Champagne Cream, 272–273
*Portuguese Fisherman's Stew with Potatoes and Peppers,
      var.*, 120
Portuguese Mussel Stew with Tomatoes and Peppers, 120
*Portuguese Sausage and Clams with Potatoes and Peppers,
      var.*, 120
Potato-Crusted Bass Fillets, 820
Redfish Courtbouillon, var., 275
Red Snapper *Courtbouillon*, 274–275
Red Snapper Fillet Courtbouillon, var., 275
Salt Cod Cakes, 111
Sautéed Rainbow Trout in Pine Nut Butter Sauce, 522–523
Seafood Okra Gumbo, var., 283, *283*
Seafood Perloo, var., 58
Seared Rare Ahi Tuna, 690–691
Shad Roe in Brown Butter with Bacon and Asparagus, 168
Steelhead Trout and Pacific Littlenecks in Gewürztraminer
      Saffron Cream, 630–631
Swordfish Fajitas, var., 343
Tea-Marinated Tuna Steaks, 583
Tea-Smoked Ahi Tuna, 582–583
*Tea-Smoked Ahi Tuna with Pickled Vegetable Shreds
      (appetizer), var.*, 583
Tilghman Island Seafood Salad with Fried Oysters, var., 216
Tuna Tartare with Anchovy Croutons, var., 817
Yellowtail Snapper Laulaus, 693
Flan with Cactus Cut-Out Cookie, 350
   var. Coconut Flan, 350
   var. Coffee Flan, 350
*Foie Gras, Seared, with Balsamic Onion Marmalade on Straw
      Potato Cake (appetizer), var.*, 833
Fortune Cookies, 593
Fourth of July Shortcake, var., 75
Frangipane Cake Disks, 636

Fried Plantain Strips, 752
Fried tomatoes. *See* Tomatoes
Frog Legs Sauce *Piquante*, 267
  var. 'Gator Sauce Piquante, 267
  var. Shrimp Sauce Piquante, 267
Frozen Soufflé Grand Marnier with Chocolate-Dipped Burnt-
  Orange Biscotto, 840–841
  var. Frozen Cappuccino Soufflé with Chocolate-Dipped Hazelnut
    Biscotto, 841
  var. Frozen Chocolate Soufflé with Almond Biscotto, 841
Fruit. *See particluar types*
Furikake Edamame, 687

Garam Masala, 829
Garden Herb Butter, 377
Garlic
  Braised Garlic Jus, 491
  Garlic "Poi," 689
  Roasted Garlic Flan, 589
'Gator Sauce Piquante, var., 267
Georgia Peanut Soup with Southern Brittle Bread, 53
  var. Gullah Chicken in Spicy Peanut Sauce, 53
Gingerbread, Spice Trade, 136–137
Ginger Crème Brûlée, var., 837
Ginger Crème Brûlée with Fortune Cookie, var., 593
Ginger-Soy Dipping Sauce, 749
Gitksan Planked Salmon with Berry Barbeque Sauce, Roasted
  Fennel–Yukon Gold Potato Purée, and Northwest
  Vegetable Medley, 628–629
  var. Grilled Salmon Steak with Berry Barbeque Sauce, Roasted
    Fennel–Yukon Gold Potato Purée, and Northwest
    Vegetable Medley, 629
Gitskan Baste, 629
Glazed Baby Carrots, 227
Goose
  Escalopes of Goose with Dried Cherry Demi-Glace and Ojibwa
    Goose Ragout in Baby Pumpkin, with Braised Kale and
    Wild Rice, 435–437
    var. Escalopes of Duck with Dried Cherry Demi-Glace and
      Ojibwa GooseRagout in Baby Pumpkin, with Braised
      Kale and Wild Rice, 437
    var. Ojibwa Escalopes of Duck with Dried Cherry Demi-Glace,
      Braised Kale, and Wild Rice, 437
  Ojibwa Goose Ragout, Escalopes of Goose, and Goose
    Reduction, 436
Gravlax with Dilled Mustard Sauce and Toast Points, 430–431
  var. Southwestern Gravlax on Corn Cakes with Salsa Sour
    Cream, 431
Green Beans, Down-Home, 62
Green Chile Quesadilla with Fresh Tomato Salsa
  var. Chorizo Quesadillas with Green Salsa, 329
  var. Huitlacoche Quesadillas with Fresh Tomato Salsa, 329
  var. Squash Blossom Quesadillas with Fresh Tomato Salsa, 329
  var. Wild Mushroom Quesadillas with Fresh Tomato Salsa, 329
Green Chile Sauce, New Mexico, 342
Green Papaya Salad, 774
Green Salsa, 330
Greens Purée, 830
Green Tea Ice Cream with Fortune Cookie, 592–593
  var. Ginger Crème Brûlée with Fortune Cookie, 593
Grill Baste, Chesapeake, 223
Grilled Cactus, 325
Grilled Chicken with Pineapple-Avocado Salsa and Boniato Fries,
  var., 765
Grilled Filet of Bison with Smoky Steak Sauce, Beer-Batter Onion
  Rings, Hash Brown Potatoes, and Vegetable Roundup,
  488–490

  var. Grilled Filet of Beef with Smoky Steak Sauce, Beer-Batter
    Onion Rings, Hash Brown Potatoes, and Vegetable
    Roundup, 489
Grilled Mahimahi with Pineapple-Avocado Salsa and Boniato
  Fries, 765
  var. Grilled Chicken with Pineapple-Avocado Salsa and Boniato
    Fries, 765
  var. Grilled Shrimp and Seashell Salad in Pineapple Boat, 765
Grilled Rare Duck Breast with Green Peppercorn Demi-Glace,
  HaricotsVerts, and Rutabaga-Mascarpone Purée, var., 827
Grilled Rare Squab with Green Peppercorn Demi-Glace, Haricots
  Verts, and Rutabaga-Mascarpone Purée, 826–827
  var. Grilled Rare Duck Breast with Green Peppercorn
    Demi-Glace, Haricots Verts, and Rutabaga-Mascarpone
    Purée, 827
Grilled Rockfish on Grilled Vegetable Ratatouille with Sweet
  Potato Hay, 222–223
Grilled Shrimp and Seashell Salad in Pineapple Boat, var., 765
Grilled Vegetable Ratatouille, 222
Grouse Halves, Seared, and Sawmill Gravy, 395
Guacamole and Chips for Two, 326
  var. Guacamole Green Sauce, 326
  var. Guacamole Shrimp Cocktail, 326
Guava
  Pink Guava Sorbet, 779
Gullah Chicken in Spicy Peanut Sauce, var., 53
Gumbo
  Duck and Andouille Sausage Gumbo Base, 281
  Seafood Gumbo Base, 283
  Shrimp and Crab Okra Gumbo, 282–283

Halibut Poached in Hard Cider with Apples and Parsnips, Served
  with Sautéed Kale and Potato Croquettes, 116
  var. Codfish Cheeks Poached in Hard Cider with Apples
    and Parsnips, Served with Sautéed Kale and Potato
    Croquettes, 116
Haupia Coconut-Custard Coupe, var., 707
Haupia Custard Squares, 707
Hawai'ian Marinated Chicken, 695
Hawai'ian Salted Salmon, 681
Hawai'ian Sashimi Salad, var., 681
Hazelnut Cream Cheese Filling, 639
Hazelnut Torte with Cherry Sauce, var., 349
Hearts of Palm, Ruby Red Marinated, 755
Hekka Sauce, 695
Herb Butter, Mountain, 523
Herbed Fresh Cheese, 381
Herbed Mayonnaise, 130
Herbed Red Bell Pepper Mayonnaise, 214
Herb-Marinated Semiboneless Squabs, 827
Hershey Brownie Sundae with Philadelphia-Style Ice Cream
  and Hot Fudge Sauce, 185–186
  var. Brownie Ice Cream Sandwich, 186
  var. Triple-Threat Brownie Ice Cream Sundae, 186
  var. Waffle Ice Cream Sundae, 186
Home-Style Seafood-Only Crab Soup, var., 211
Hominy
  Home-Style, Buttered, 394
  Hominy Custard with Glazed Strawberries and Black Walnut
    Crisps, 229–230
    var. Raisin-Spice Hominy Custard, 230
  Strawberry-Topped Hominy Custards, 229
Honey Sour Cream Sauce, 497
Hopi Blue Corn Smoked Rabbit Stacked Enchilada Fajitas, 340
  var. Hopi Blue Corn Stacked Enchiladas with Chicken, 342
Hopi Blue Corn Tamales, var., 333
Hoppin' John, Fancy, 72

Horseradish Cream, 130, 382
Hot and Fragrant Coconut Chicken Soup, var., 676
Hot Fudge Sauce, 186
Hot Meat Loaf Sandwich, var., 447
Huckleberry Pie with Whipped Cream, 533
　　var. Blueberry Pie with Whipped Cream, 533
Huitlacoche Quesadillas with Fresh Tomato Salsa, var., 329

Ice cream. *See Desserts*
Ida's Chopped Liver with Bagel Crisps, 818
　　var. Passover Chopped Liver with Matzohs, 818
Imperial Stuffed Flounder with Lemon Butter Sauce, Baby
　　Spinach, and Sweet Potato Pearls, 219–220
　　var. Dinner-House Imperial-Stuffed Flounder Platter, 220
Inside-Out California Rolls, 579
Island Fried Rice, 699

Jamaican-American Jerk Chicken with Rice 'n' Peas, Fried
　　Plantains, and Tropical Slaw, 768–770
Jambalaya Base, 285
Jansson's Temptation, 442
Jerk-Marinated Half Hens, 768
Jerk Paste, 768
Jerk Table Sauce, 769
Jerky, Beef, 479

Kalua Pork Baked in Banana Leaf with Island Fried Rice
　　and Stir-Fry Cabbage, 698–699
　　var. Kalua Chicken with Island Fried Rice and Stir-Fry Cabbage, 698
Kalua Pork Packets and Pork Jus, 699
Kasha, Cooked Whole-Grain, 825
Kennett Square Stuffed Mushroom Medley, 165–167
Kentucky Barbeque Lamb Shank with Creamed Corn, Pole Beans,
　　and Fried Potatoes, 389–390
　　var. Kentucky Barbeque Mutton with "Leather Britches" Beans,
　　　　Creamed Corn, and Fried Potatoes, 390
Kentucky Burgoo, var., 386
Kentucky Limestone Salad with Clemson Blue Cheese, Cornbread
　　Croutons, and Candied Pecans, 56
　　var. with Frizzled Country Ham, Cornbread Croutons, and
　　　　Candied Pecans, 56
Key Lime Pie with Whipped Cream and Candied Lime Zest, 775
　　var. Key Lime Pie with Meringue Topping, 775
Key West Conch Seviche, 752–753
　　var. Caribbean Seviche, 753
　　var. Key West Scallop Seviche, 753
　　var. Key West Spanish Mackerel Seviche, 753
King's Cake with Queen's Sauce, 294–295
　　var. Large King's Cake with Queen's Sauce, 295
Kohlrabi salad, 55
Kona Coffee Choco-Mac Tart with Macadamia Brittle
　　var. Chocolate–Coffee–Macadamia Nut Pie, 705
Korean Mandoo, 686

Lady Baltimore Cake, 228
　　var. Lord Baltimore Cake, 228
Lamb
　　Basque Lamb or Mutton Stew, var., 448
　　*Basque-Style Lamb in Spicy Tomato Sauce over Pan-Steamed
　　　　Rice with Three-Pepper Medley, var.,* 527
　　Char-Grilled Northwestern Lamb Chops, var., 633
　　Lamb Shank, Kentucky Barbeque, 389
　　Lancaster County Roast Lamb, 182–183
　　Navajo Mutton Stew, 345
　　Roast Rack of Northwestern Lamb, 634–635
　　Shepherd's Pie, 528–530
　　Tandoori-Marinated Double Lamb Chops, 829

Lancaster County Roast Lamb in Minted Pan Gravy with Peas 'n'
　　Pearl Onions in Potato Basket and Carrot Purée, 182–183
　　*var., Lancaster County Roast Lamb in Minted Pan Gravy with
　　　　Peas 'n' Pearl Onions in Baked Potato Shell and Carrot
　　　　Puree,* 183
Lattice-Top Cherry Pie with Buttermilk Ice Cream, 449
　　var. Lattice-Top Blueberry Pie with Buttermilk Ice Cream, 449
　　var. Lattice-Top Peach Pie with Buttermilk Ice Cream, 449
Laulau Butter, 693
Leeks, Braised, 821
Lemon Vinaigrette, 813
Lenape Smoke-Roasted Bluefish with Cranberry-Maple Velouté,
　　Corn Cake, and Watercress, 172–173
　　*var. Lenape Grilled Fish with Cranberry-Maple Sauce, Corn Cake
　　　　and Watercress,* 173
Lentils, Green, Ragout of, 821
Lima Beans, Creamed, 388
Lime
　　Candied Lime Zest, 775
　　Coconut-Lime Vinaigrette, 759
　　Key Lime Pie, 775
Lobster
　　Crab-Stuffed Lobster Tails, 762
　　Dilled Lobster Salad in Lobster Shell, var., 115
　　*Lobster, Crab, or Shrimp Tostadas with Guacamole
　　　　Green Salsa, var.,* 331
　　New England Lobster Chowder, var., 109
　　Tarragon Lobster Salad in Lobster Shell, 115
Lomi Lomi Salmon Salad, 680–681
　　var. Hawai'ian Sashimi Salad, 681
Long Island Duckling, Roasted, 178
Lotus Root Chips, 676
Louis Dressing, 580
Lowcountry Shrimp Perloo with Sugar Snap Peas, 58
　　var. Chicken Perloo, 58
　　var. Seafood Perloo, 58
Lu'au-Style Haupia, var., 707

Macadamia Brittle, 705
Macadamia-Crusted Mahimahi with *Liliko'i* Sauce, Garlic
　　"Poi,"and Steamed Baby Bok Choy
　　*var. Peanut-Crusted Mahimahi with Sticky Rice, Thai Red Curry
　　　　Sauce, and Baby Bok Choy,* 689
Macadamia Frangipane, 705
Macadamia Frangipane Sweet Dough Shell, 705
Macaroni 'n' Cheese, Baked, 440
Mac-Panko-Crusted Mahimahi Fillets, 689
Mahimahi Banana Leaf Tamales, 335
Malanga-Mango-Crusted Red Snapper with Fresh Mango Salsa,
　　Black Beans, and Sautéed Chayote, 760–761
Mandoo Dip, 687
Mango
　　Fresh Mango Salsa, 761
　　Mango Aïoli, 759
　　Spicy Mango Dip, 751
Manhattan Clam Chowder with Oyster Crackers, 811
　　var. Quick Manhattan Clam Chowder, 811
Maple Glaze, 128, 393
Maple-Glazed Turkey with Sauerkraut and Hominy, 393–394
　　*var. Maple-Glazed Cornish Hens with Sauerkraut
　　　　and Hominy,* 394
Maple Vinaigrette, 114
Maquechoux, 278
Marinade, New England Salmon, 119
Marinated Skirt Steak, 343
Mario's Tres Leches Cake with Lime Marmalade, var., 777
Marshmallow Topping, 501

Maryland-Style Crab Cakes with Smashed Redskin Potato
    Salad and Summer Garden Diced Vegetable Salad,
    217–218
    var. Crab Cake Salad Appetizer, 218
    var. Dinner-House Crab Cake Platter, 218
    var. Eastern Shore Crab Cakes, 217
    var. Economy Crab Cakes, 217
Masala for Country Captain, 62
Mascarpone Cannolo with Zabaglione Sauce, 838
Mayonnaise
    Herbed, 130
    Herbed Red Bell Pepper, 214
Meat Loaf. *See Classic Meatloaf*
Medallions of Venison in Chokecherry Demi-Glace with Garlic
    Mashed Potatoes, Root Vegetables, and Wild Mushroom
    Ragout, 531–532
    *var. Pan-Seared Bear Chop in Cranberry Demi-Glace with Garlic
        Mashed Potatoes, Root Vegetables, and Wild Mushroom
        Ragout,* 532
Merlot Mignonette, 627
Mexican Marinated Skirt Steak, 343
Mini-Skin Shells, 685
Minnesota Fruit-Stuffed Pork Loin with Jansson's Temptation
    and Watercress, 442–443
    *var. Minnesota Fruit-Stuffed Pork Chop with Jansson's
        Temptation and Watercress,* 443
    *var. Roast Pork Loin with Fruit Sauce, Jansson's Temptation,
        and Watercress,* 443
Mojo Criollo, 757
Mountain Herb Butter, 523
Mushrooms
    Braised Chinese Black Mushrooms, 697
    Crab-Stuffed, 166
    Crab-Stuffed Mushrooms with Chive Hollandaise, var., 167
    Creamy Mushroom Sauce, 227
    Mushroom Cups, 532
    Mushroom Gravy, 447
    Sausage-Stuffed, 166
    Sausage-Stuffed Mushrooms Marinara, var., 167
    Spinach-Stuffed, 165
    *Spinach-Stuffed Mushrooms with Aurora Cream Sauce,
        var.,* 167
    Wild Mushroom Cornbread Dressing, 384
    Wild Mushroom Quesadillas with Fresh Tomato Salsa, var., 329
Mussels
    Portuguese Mussel Stew, 120
Mustard Relish, 130
Mutton Stew, Navajo, 345

Ñame Cakes, 767
Napa Valley Verjus Vinaigrette, 571
Navajo Mutton Stew with Fry Bread and Three Sisters Vegetable
    Medley, 344–345
    var. Navajo Stew with Sweet Potatoes, 345
    var. Navajo Venison Stew, 345
Navajo Tamales, 333
New England Clam Chowder with Pilot Crackers, 109
    var. New England Lobster Chowder, 109
    var. Summertime Corn and Clam Chowder, 109
New England Corned Beef Boiled Dinner with Three Sauces,
    129–130
    var. Cape Cod Boiled Dinner with Egg Sauce, 130
New England Lobster Chowder, var., 109
New England Salmon Marinade, 119
New Mexico Chilled Avocado Soup, var., 570
New Mexico Green Chile Cheese Enchiladas, var., 337
New Mexico Green Chile Sauce, 342

New Mexico Pork *Chile Verde* with Flour Tortillas
    and Pepper-Squash Medley, 338
    var. Chicken Chile Verde, 338
New Mexico Red Chile Pork or Chicken Enchiladas, var., 337
New Mexico Red Chile Sauce, 337
New Orleans Red Beans, 288
Nopal Cactus Salad, 325
    var. Southwestern String Bean Salad, 325
North Indian Braised Cauliflower, 830

Oklahoma Chicken-Fried Steak with Cream Gravy, Mashed
    Potatoes, and Western-Style Greens, 486–487
    *var. Chicken-Fried Turkey with Cream Gravy, Mashed Potatoes,
        and Western-Style Greens,* 487
Okra
    Shrimp and Crab Okra Gumbo, 282–283
    Stewed, 74
Old-Fashioned Biscuit Strawberry Shortcake, 75
    var. Fourth of July Shortcake, 75
    var. Peach Shortcake, 75
Old Key West Conch Chowder, var., 745
Onions
    Onion Croutons, 164
    Onion Potato Pierogies, 432–433
    Stuffed Vidalia Onions, 74
    Walla Walla Onion Salad, 627
Orange Crème Brûlée, var., 837
*Orange Tart with Marmalade Glaze and Dark Chocolate Drizzle,
    var.,* 591
Orange Zest, Candied and Caramelized, 841
*Oven Barbequed Beef Brisket with Cowboy Beans and Ranch-Style
    Slaw, var.,* 493
Oysters
    Chesapeake Fried Oysters with Fresh Tomato Cocktail
        Sauce, 212
        var. Chesapeake Fried Oysters with tartar Sauce, 212
    Oyster Fritters with Herbed Red Bell Pepper
        Mayonnaise, 213
        *var. Clam Fritters with Herbed Red Bell Pepper
            Mayonnaise,* 214
    Oyster Pilau, 65
    Oysters Rockefeller, 269
        var. Oysters Rockefeller au Gratin, 269
    Wood-Roasted Olympia Oysters, var., 627

Palmiers, Miniature, 290
Palouse Valley Brown Lentil Soup with Wheatberry Biscuit, 623
    var. Basque Red Bean Soup with Garlic Crouton, 623
Pancakes
    Sourdough Buckwheat, 380
Panéed Grouper with Mango Aïoli and Tropical Seashell Salad,
    758–759
    *var. Panéed Alligator with Mango Aïoli and Tropical Seashell
        Salad,* 759
    *var. Panéed Grouper Cheeks with Mango Aïoli and Tropical
        Seashell Salad,* 759
    *var. Tropical Seashell Salad with Shrimp (lunch entrée
        or appetizer),* 759
Pan-Roasted Veal Chop in Apple-Mushroom Cream with
    Handmade Noodles and Brussels Sprouts, 180–181
    var. Pan-Roasted Pork Chop, 181
Pan-Seared Breast of Petaluma Duck in Zinfandel Demi-Glace
    with Sautéed Flame Grapes, Roasted Garlic Flan, and
    Wilted Baby Spinach, 588–589
    *var. Pan-Seared Breast of Petaluma Duck in Red Wine Roasted
        Garlic Demi-Glace with Sautéed Flame Grapes, Mashed
        Potatoes, and Wilted Baby Spinach,* 589

Pan-Seared "Snapper" Bluefish on Potato Cake with Jersey Tomato Sauce and Tricolor Peppers, 172–173
  var. Pan-Seared Swordfish on Potato Cake with Jersey Tomato Sauce and Tricolor Peppers, 172–173
Passover Chopped Liver with Matzohs, var., 818
Pasta Primavera, 819
  var. Pasta al Autunno, 819
  var. Pasta al Estate, 819
Pastry Cream Filling, 132
Pau Hana Pupu Platter for Two: Rumaki, Shrimp on Sugarcane, Korean Mandoo Dumplings, Chinese Barbeque Baby Back Ribs, Poke-Stuffed Mini-Skins, Edamame, and Shichimi Wings, 683–687
Pawpaw Pandowdy with Honey Sour Cream Sauce, var., 497
Peaches
  Dixie Peach Cobbler, with variations, 76
  Dried Peach Filling, 401
  Lattice-Top Peach Pie with Buttermilk Ice Cream, var., 449
  Peaches Foster with Palmier, var., 290
  Peach-Filled Half-Moon Fried Pie with Burnt Sugar Ice Cream
    var. Apple-Filled Half-Moon Fried Pies with Vanilla Ice Cream, 401
    var. Blackberry-Filled Half-Moon Fried Pie with Burnt Sugar Ice Cream, 401
  Peach Halves, Brandied, 535
  Peach Shortcake, var., 75
  Peach Upside-Down Cake, var., 454
  Peachy Duck with Mashed Potatoes and Turnips 'n' Turnip Greens, 67–70
    var. Braised Country Spareribs with Turnips 'n' Turnip Greens, 67
  Spiced-Baked, 69
Peanut-Crusted Mahimahi with Sticky Rice, Thai Red Curry Sauce, and Baby Bok Choy, var., 689
Peanut Soup, Georgia, 53
Pears
  Pear Upside-Down Cake, var., 454
  Poached Pear on Frangipane Cake with Almond Crunch Filling and Pinot Noir Syrup, 636–637
  Riesling Poached Pear Slices, 624
Peas
  Rice 'n' Peas, 769
Pecans
  Candied, 56
  Chocolate-Pecan Torte with Raspberry Sauce, var., 293
  Pecan-Crusted Suprême of Chicken with Tasso Cream, Red Rice, and Sautéed Spinach, 286–287
    var. Pecan-Crusted Red Snapper with Tasso Cream, Red Rice, and Sautéed Spinach, 287
  Pecan Pumpkin Pie, var., 135
  Pecan Rice Dressing, var., 65
  Pecan Torte with Persimmon Sauce, var., 349
  Spiced, 479
  Still Master's Pecan Pie, 77
"Pemmican" Venison Sausages, 627
Pennsylvania Dutch Chicken Bot Boi with Saffron Noodles, 175–177
  var. Pennsylvania Dutch Chicken Pie, 177
Pennsylvania Dutch Chicken Corn Soup with Rivels and Cloverleaf Roll, 162–163
  var. Egg-Drop Chicken Corn Soup, 163
  var. Winter Chicken Corn Soup with Rivels, 163
Pennsylvania Dutch Stack Pie, var., 184
Pepita Torte with Prickly Pear Sauce, var., 349
Pepper Jack Chicken with Green Chile Potatoes and Black Bean Pico de Gallo, var., 339
Pepper Slaw, 112

Persimmon Sauce, 399
Petite Tourtière with Pickled Beets, 113
  var. with Homemade Ketchup and Creamy Coleslaw, 113
Pheasant
  Deep-Dish Flaky Pastry Pheasant Pie, var., 439
  Roast Pheasant, var., 395
Philadelphia Roll Sushi with Ponzu Sauce, var., 579
Picadillo Chiles Rellenos, var., 327
Picadillo with Yellow Rice, Black Beans, Green Papaya Salad, and Tostones, var., 774
Piccalilli, 126
Pickled Beets and Eggs, 434
Pickled Vegetable Shreds, 583
Pico de Gallo, var., 331
Pierogi Dough, 432–433
Pierogis. *See also Triple Onion Potato Pierogies*
  Pierogi Dough, 433
Pies
  Apple-Filled Half-Moon Fried Pies with Vanilla Ice Cream, var. (See also p. 401)
  Blackberry-Filled Half-Moon Fried Pies with Vanilla Ice Cream, var., 401
  Blueberry Pie with Whipped Cream, var., 533
  Boston Cream Pie, 131–132
  Chocolate Chiffon Pie, var., 501
  Chocolate–Coffee–Macadamia Nut Pie (See also p. 705)
  Huckleberry Pie with Whipped Cream, 533
  Key Lime Pie with Meringue Topping, var., 775
  Key Lime Pie with Whipped Cream and Candied Lime Zest, 775
  Lattice-Top Blueberry Pie with Buttermilk Ice Cream, var., 449
  Lattice-Top Cherry Pie with Buttermilk Ice Cream, 449
  Lattice-Top Peach Pie with Buttermilk Ice Cream, var., 449
  New England Maple-Walnut Pie, var., 77
  Peach-Filled Half-Moon Fried Pie with Burnt Sugar Ice Cream, 400–401
  Pecan Pumpkin Pie, var., 135
  Pennsylvania Dutch Stack Pie, var., 184
  Pumpkin Pie with Whipped Cream, 134–135
  S'mores Pie, 500
  Still Master's Pecan Pie, 77
  Wet-Bottom Shoofly Pie, var., 184
Pilau-Stuffed Quail, 65
Pineapple
  Pineapple Compote, 707
  Pineapple Salsa, var., 331
  Pineapple Salsa Base, 765
  Pineapple Upside-Down Cake, 454
    var. Apple-Cinnamon Upside-Down Cake, 454
    var. Peach Upside-Down Cake, 454
    var. Pear Upside-Down Cake, 454
Pine Nut Romesco Sauce, 530
Pink Guava Sorbet, 779
Pink Singing Scallops with Pinot Noir Beurre Rouge and Wilted Baby Spinach, 625
  var. Bay Scallops with Pinot Noir Beurre Rouge and Wilted Baby Spinach, 625
Piñon Pine Nut Torte with Prickly Pear Sauce and Crema, 348–349
  var. Almond Torte with Raspberry Sauce, 349
  var. Hazelnut Torte with Cherry Sauce, 349
  var. Pecan Torte with Persimmon Sauce, 349
  var. Pepita Torte with Prickly Pear Sauce, 349
  var. Walnut Torte with Apricot Sauce, 349
Pinot Noir Demi-Glace, 634
Pinot Noir Poached Pears and Pinot Noir Syrup, 637
Pioneer Vegetable Soup with Salt-Rising Bread
  var. Basque Garbure, 519

Pirogues, Eggplant 'n' Shrimp, 277
Plantains
  Fried Plantain Strips, 752
  Tostones, 773
Poached Montana Whitefish with Crawfish Tails in Buttermilk
    Velouté with Steamed Mountain Rose Potatoes and Fresh
    Peas, 524–525
Poached Pear on Frangipane Cake with Almond Crunch Filling
    and Pinot Noir Syrup, 636–637
  var., Raspberry Frangipane Cakes, 637
Pompano en Escabeche with Ñame Cake, 766–767
  var. Pompano en Escabeche Salad (appetizer or lunch
    entrée), 767
Pompano en Papillote with Champagne Cream, Pecan Rice Pilaf,
    Parisienne Carrots, and Haricots Verts, 272–273
  var. Flounder en Papillote, 273
Poppy Seed Dressing, 164
Porcini Bread Pudding Disks, 635
Pork. See also Spareribs
  Barbeque Pork Shoulder for Pulled or Chopped Pork, var., 71
  Breaded Pork Chops, 441
  Breaded Pork Medallions with Stewed Tomatoes and Macaroni
    'n' Cheese, var., 441
  Chinese Barbeque Baby Back Ribs, 685
  Kalua Pork Baked in Banana Leaf with Island Fried Rice
    and Stir-Fry Cabbage, 697–699
  Medallions of Pork in Bourbon Sauce, var., 73
  Minnesota Fruit-Stuffed Pork Chop with Jansson's Temptation
    and Watercress, var., 443
  Minnesota Fruit-Stuffed Pork Loin, 443
  Mustard-Cured Pork Tenderloin, 125
  New Mexico Red Chile Pork or Chicken Enchiladas, var., 337
  Pan-Roasted Pork Chop, var., 181
  Pork Chile Verde, var., 338
  Pork Parmesan with Fresh Tomato Sauce, Potato Gnocchi,
    and Vegetable "Spaghetti," var., 836
  Pork Shoulder, 'Possum-Style, with Sweet Potatoes, 387
  Pork Tenderloin in Bourbon Sauce with Stuffed Vidalia Onion
    and Stewed Okra, 73–74
  Roast Pork Loin with Fruit Sauce, Jansson's Temptation, and
    Watercress, var., 443
  Shredded Pork Tostadas with Roasted Corn and Green Salsa,
    var., 331
  Smoke-Roasted Pork Loin with Tidewater Kidney Bean Salad
    and Cucumber Salad, var., 225
  Wampanoag Maple-Glazed Roast Pork Chop with Winter
    Succotash and Broccoli Florets in Baby Pumpkin, var., 128
Port-Glazed Roast Duck Halves, 178
Portuguese Mussel Stew with Potatoes and Peppers, 120
  var. Portuguese Fisherman's Stew with Potatoes and
    Peppers, 120
  var. Portuguese Sausage and Clams with Potatoes
    and Peppers, 120
'Possum-Style Pork Shoulder with Sweet Potatoes and Creamed
    Lima Beans, 387–388
Potatoes
  Annie's Skillet Potatoes, 484
  Bacon and Cheddar Cheese Potato Chip Mountain
    for Two, var., 521
  Basque Potato Skins with Peppers and Bacalao, var., 520
  Blue Cheese Potato Chip Mountain for Two, 521
  Coconut Sweet Potatoes, 693
  Delmonico Potato Rounds, 833
  Jansson's Temptation, 442
  Mini-Skin Shells, 685
  Potato Baskets, Individual, 183
  Potato Croquettes, 116

Potato Gnocchi, 835
Potato Latke with Smoked Salmon and Caviar
  var. German Potato Latkes with Sour Cream and
    Applesauce, 815
  var. Ida's Potato Latkes with Sour Cream and Scallions, 815
  Wasabi Mashed Potatoes, 583
Potato-Leek Pierogi Filling, 433
Potato Skin Wedges, 520
Roasted Fennel–Yukon Gold Potato Purée, 629
Smashed Redskin Potato Salad, 218
Southern Potato Salad, 60
Southern Sweet Potato Chip Mountain for Two, var., 521
Straw Potato Cakes, 174
Sweet Potato Pearls, 220
Twice-Baked, 491
Pots de Crème, 640
Prickly Pear Sauce, 350
Pumpkin
  Pumpkin Gnocchi, 633
  Pumpkin Pie with Whipped Cream, 134–135
    var. Pecan Pumpkin Pie, 135
  Pumpkin Purée, 66
  Pumpkin Roll with Cranberry Coulis, 187–188
    var. Pumpkin Roll with Whipped Cream, 187
Pu Pu Platter, 683–687

Quail
  Quail and Bacon Jambalaya, var., 285
  Quail with Oyster Pilau Dressing, Pumpkin Purée, and Sautéed
    Spinach, 64–66
    var. with Oyster Pilau Dressing, Winter Squash Purée,
      and Sautéed Spinach, 66
    var. with Pecan Rice Dressing, 65
    var. with Sausage Dressing, 65
  Tandoori Quail with Basmati Pulao, Greens Purée, and Braised
    Cauliflower, var., 831
Queen's Sauce, 295
Quesadilla
  Chorizo Quesadillas with Green Salsa, var., 329
  Green Chile, with Fresh Tomato Salsa, 329
  Huitlacoche Quesadillas with Fresh Tomato Salsa, var., 329
  Squash Blossom Quesadillas with Fresh Tomato Salsa, var., 329
  Wild Mushroom Quesadillas with Fresh Tomato Salsa, var., 329
Quinoa, Black, 523
  var., White Quinoa, 523

Rabbit, Mesquite-Smoked, 341
Ragout of Green Lentils, 821
Raisins, Rummed, 499
Raisin-Spice Hominy Custard, 230
Raisin-Walnut Apple Dumplings with Vanilla Custard
    Sauce, var., 189
Ranch-Style Slaw, 493
Rarebit, Wisconsin Cheddar Broccoli, 429
Raspberry Frangipane Cakes, var., 637
Reconstituted Cherries, 437
Red, White, and Maytag Blue Salad with Pickled Beets
    and Egg, 434
  var. Roasted Beet and Blue Cheese Salad with Quail Eggs, 434
Red and Yellow Bell Pepper Curls, 813
Red Beans 'n' Rice with Andouille Sausage and
    Collard Greens, 288
  var. Red Beans 'n' Rice with Grilled Andouille and Collard
    Greens, 288
  var. Red Beans 'n' Rice with Pork Chop, 288
  var. Smoked Turkey Red Beans 'n' Rice, 288
Red Chile Cheese Enchiladas, 337

Red Chile Salt, 753
Red peppers
    Herbed Red Bell Pepper Mayonnaise, 214
Red Rice, 287
**Red Snapper *Courtbouillon* with Pan-Steamed Rice
    and Smothered Butter Beans, 274–275**
    *var. Redfish Courtbouillon with Pan-Steamed Rice
        and Smothered Butter Beans, 275*
    *var. Red Snapper Courtbouillon with Creole Baguette
        and Green Salad, 275*
    *var. Red Snapper Fillet Courtbouillon with Creole Baguette
        and Green Salad, 275*
Red Wine Demi-Glace For Fish, 822
Red Wine Venison Demi-Glace, 128
Refried Beans, 330
    Refried Black Beans, var., 330
    Vegetarian Refried Beans, var., 330
Relish, Mustard, 130
Rhubarb Crisp with Vanilla Ice Cream, 133
Rice
    Apple-Rice Pilaf, 631
    Basmati Pulao, 831
    Bento Rice Balls, 691
    Island Fried Rice, 699
    Oyster Pilau, 65
    Red Beans 'n' Rice, 288
    Red Rice, 287
    Rice 'n' Peas, 769
    Rum-Raisin Texmati Rice Pudding with Apricot Sauce,
        498–499
    Sushi Rice, 679
    Wild Rice, 437
    Yellow Rice, 773
Riesling Poached Pear Slices, 624
Rivels, 163
Roasted Fennel–Yukon Gold Potato Purée, 629
Roasted Garlic Flan, 589
**Roast Grouse with Sawmill Gravy, Ramp Home Fries, and
    Mountain Vegetable Medley**
    *var. Roast Pheasant with Sawmill Gravy, Ramp Home Fries,
        and MountainVegetable Medley, 395*
**Roast Long Island Duckling in Port Wine Demi-Glace with
    North-Shore Cauliflower Gratin and Arugula, 178–179**
    *var. Pan-Seared Long Island Duck Breast in Port Wine
        Demi-Glace with North-Shore Cauliflower Gratin
        and Arugula, 179*
**Roast Rack of Northwestern Lamb with Pinot Noir Demi-Glace,
    Porcini Bread Pudding, and Baked Walla Walla Onion Filled
    with Carrot Purée, 634–635**
Rockefeller Sauce, 269
**Ropa Vieja with Yellow Rice, Black Beans, Green Papaya Salad,
    and Tostones, 771–774**
    *var. Picadillo with Yellow Rice, Black Beans, Green Papaya
        Salad, and Tostones, 774*
Roulades
    Chicken Virginia, 227
**Ruby Red Grapefruit Salad with Hearts of Palm, Avocado, Moro
    Crab, and Key West Shrimp, 754–755**
    *var. Ruby Red Grapefruit Salad with Hearts of Palm and
        Avocado, 755*
Ruby Red Marinated Hearts of Palm, 755
Ruby Red Vinaigrette for Seafood, 755
Rumaki, 684
Rum-Raisin Texmati Rice Pudding with Apricot Sauce, 498–499
    *var. Cherry Vanilla Texmati Rice Pudding with Cherry
        Sauce, 499*
Rum Sauce, 703

Rum Syrup, 132
**Russet Potato Skins with Montana Whitefish Caviar and Dilled
    Sour Cream**
    var. Basque Potato Skins with Peppers and Bacalao, 520
Rutabaga-Mascarpone Purée, 827

Saffron Bot Boi Noodles, 176
Salad dressings
    Buttermilk Ranch, 477
    Coconut-Lime Vinaigrette, 759
    Hot Bacon Dressing, 378
    Lemon Vinaigrette, 813
    Lomi Lomi Dressing, 681
    Louis Dressing, 580
    Maple Vinaigrette, 114
    Napa Valley Verjus Vinaigrette, 571
    Poppy Seed, 164
    Ruby Red Vinaigrette for Seafood, 755
    Smoked Tomato Vinaigrette, 478
    Southwest-Style Vinaigrette, 325
    Walnut Vinaigrette, 624
Salads, 114
    Chicory, with Beef Jerky, Spiced Pecans, and Smoked Tomato
        Vinaigrette, 478–479
    Classic Cobb Salad, 572
    Crab Cake Salad Appetizer, var., 218
    Cucumber Salad, 225
    Dilled Lobster Salad in Lobster Shell, var., 115
    Fiesta Salad with Ranch Dressing and Salsa, var., 477
    Green Papaya Salad, 774
    Hawai'ian Sashimi Salad, var., 681
    Kentucky Limestone Salad with Clemson Blue Cheese,
        Cornbread Croutons, and Candied Pecans, 56
        *var. with Frizzled Country Ham, Cornbread Croutons,
            and Candied Pecans, 56*
    Kohlrabi Salad, var., 55
    Lomi Lomi Salmon Salad, 680–681
    Nopal Cactus Salad, 325
    Pompano en Escabeche Salad (appetizer or lunch entrée), var., 767
    Ranch-Style Slaw, 493
    Red, White, and Maytag Blue Salad with Pickled Beets
        and Egg, 434
    Roasted Beet and Blue Cheese Salad with Quail Eggs, var., 434
    Ruby Red Grapefruit Salad with Hearts of Palm, Avocado, Moro
        Crab, and Key West Shrimp, 754–755
    *Ruby Red Grapefruit Salad with Hearts of Palm and Avocado,
        var.*, 755
    **Salad of Organic Baby Greens with Almond-Crusted Goat
        Cheese and Napa Valley Verjus Vinaigrette, 571**
    *Salad of Organic Baby Greens with Walnut-Crusted Monterey
        Jack Cheese and Walnut-Verjus Vinaigrette, var.*, 571
    **Salad of Watercress, Pears, Rogue River Blue Cheese, and
        Walnuts in Walnut Vinaigrette, 624**
        *var. Salad of Watercress, Plums, Goat Cheese, and Hazelnuts
            in Hazelnut Vinaigrette, 624*
    Smashed Redskin Potato Salad, 218
    Southern Potato Salad, 60
    Southwestern String Bean Salad, var., 325
    *Spinach, Mushroom, and Bacon Salad with Creamy Blue Cheese
        Dressing, var.*, 164
    Spinach, Mushroom, and Bacon Salad with Poppyseed Dressing, 164
    *Spring Tonic Salad with Hot Bacon Dressing and Hard-Cooked
        Egg, var.*, 378
    Sprout Salad, var., 55
    Summer Garden Diced Vegetable Salad, 218
    Sunflower Salad, 55
    Tall Seafood Salad with Avocado and Tobiko, 812–813

Tarragon Lobster Salad in Lobster Shell, 115
Texas "Caviar" Salad in Tortilla Bowl, var., 480
Tidewater Kidney Bean Salad, 225
Tilghman Island Chicken Salad with Fried Oysters, 216
Tossed, with Buttermilk Dressing, 477
Tropical Seashell Salad, 758
Tropical Seashell Salad with Shrimp, var., 759
Vegetarian Cobb Salad, var., 572
Walla Walla Onion Salad, 627
Watercress and Boston Lettuce Salad with Maple Vinaigrette,
    Cranberries, and Walnut-Crusted Cheddar Crouton, 114
Wilted Salad with Hot Bacon Dressing, 378
Salmon
    Baked Stuffed Salmon, var., 171
    Early-Spring Grilled Salmon with Chervil Sauce, Asparagus,
        and New Potatoes, var., 119
    Fourth-of-July Grilled Salmon, 118–119
    Gitksan Planked Salmon, 628
    Grilled Salmon Steak, var., 629
    Hawai'ian Salted Salmon, 681
    Late-Summer Grilled Salmon, with Dill Sauce, Poached
        Cucumbers, and New Potatoes var., 119
    Lomi Lomi Salmon Salad, 680–681
    Marinated Salmon Pinwheels, 118
    New England Salmon Marinade, 119
    Salmon Cakes with Ketchup and Pepper Slaw, var., 112
    Salmon in Brown Butter with Bacon and Asparagus, var., 168
    Tartare of Salmon and Striped Bass with Anchovy Croutons,
        816–817
Salsa
    Avocado-Tomato, var., 331
    Fresh Tomato, 331
    Green, 331
    Pico de Gallo, var., 331
    Pineapple Salsa, var., 331
Salt Cod Cakes with Ketchup and Pepper Slaw, 111–112
    var. Salmon Cakes with Ketchup and Pepper Slaw, 112
San Francisco Cioppino with North Beach Escarole Salad and
    Sourdough Roll, 581
Santa Fe Red Chile Cheese Enchiladas with Olla Beans and
    Avocado Salad, 336–337
    var. Enchiladas Rancheras, 337
    var. New Mexico Green Chile Cheese Enchiladas, 337
    var. New Mexico Red Chile Pork or Chicken Enchiladas, 337
    var. Vegetarian Red Chile Cheese Enchiladas, 337
Santa Rosa Plum Galette with Almond Custard Sauce, 590
    var. Amaretto Plum Galette with Vanilla Custard Sauce, 590
    var. Italian Plum Galette with Vanilla Custard Sauce, 590
Sauces, butters, dips, glazes
    Anchovy Butter, 817
    Apple-Mushroom Cream Velouté, 181
    Apricot Sauce, 499
    Berry Barbeque Sauce, 629
    Braised Garlic Jus, 491
    Buttermilk Velouté for Fish, 525
    Casino Butter, 814
    Cheddar Cheese Sauce, 379
    Chinese Stir-Fry Sauce for Beef, 701
    Chinese Vegetable Glaze, 583
    Cider Pan Reduction, 633
    Corn Relish Tartar Sauce, 485
    Courtbouillon Sauce, 275
    Cranberry, 123
    Cranberry-Maple Velouté, 173
    Creamy Mushroom Sauce, 227
    Creole Rémoulade Sauce, 266
    Dilled Mustard Sauce, 431

Dilled Sour Cream Sauce, 119
Fennel-Yogurt Tomato Sauce, 831
Fresh Mango Salsa, 761
Fresh Tomato Cocktail Sauce, 212
Garden Herb Butter, 377
Ginger-Soy Dipping Sauce, 749
Gitskan Baste, 629
Guacamole Green Sauce, var., 326
Hekka Sauce, 695
Herbed Mayonnaise, 130
Honey Sour Cream Sauce, 497
Horseradish Cream, 130, 378
Hot Fudge Sauce, 186
Jerk Table Sauce, 769
Laulau Butter, 693
Mandoo Dip, 687
Mango Aïoli, 759
Merlot Mignonette, 627
Mojo Criollo, 757
Persimmon Sauce, 399
Pineapple Salsa Base, 765
Pine Nut Romesco Sauce, 530
Pinot Noir Demi-Glace, 634
Red Wine Demi-Glace For Fish, 822
Rockefeller Sauce, 269
Rum Sauce, 703
Sauce Piquante, 267
Seafood Étouffée Sauce, 284
Seafood Sauce Aurore, 271
Shrimp Creole Sauce, 279
Smoky Steak Sauce, 489
Sofrito Tomato Sauce, 764
Spicy Mango Dip, 751
Stir-Fry Sauce, 587
Strawberry Glaze, 220
Sweet Cranberry Coulis, 188
Sweet 'n' Hot Dipping Sauce, 575
Tartar Sauce, 60
Teriyaki Sauce, 691
Tomato Sauce for Stuffed Cabbage, 824
Wasabi Paste and Wasabi Sauce, 679
Wasabi-Soy Dip, 579
Sauerkraut, Appalachian-Style, 394
Sausage
    Andouille Sausage and Oyster Jambalaya, var., 285
    Chicken and Sausage Jambalaya, var., 285
    Chorizo Quesadillas with Green Salsa, var., 329
    Dressing, var., 65
    Sausage-Stuffed Mirliton with Creole Tomato Sauce, var., 271
    Sausage-Stuffed Mushrooms, 166
    Sausage-Stuffed Mushrooms Marinara, var., 167
Sautéed Rainbow Trout in Pine Nut Butter Sauce with Black
    Quinoa, French-Cut Green Beans, and Herb-Roasted
    Tomato, 522–523
Sautéed Soft-Shell Crabs with Lemon Butter Sauce, Parsley
    Potatoes, and Summer Squash in Tomato Sauce, 221
    var. Beer-Battered Soft-Shell Crab Appetizer, 221
    var. Dinner-House Fried Soft-Shell Crab Platter, 221
Scallops
    Bay Scallops with Pinot Noir Beurre Rouge and Wilted Baby
        Spinach, var., 625
    Pink Singing Scallops with Pinot Noir Beurre Rouge and Wilted
        Baby Spinach, 625
Scandinavian Beet Soup with Knäckebrød, 427
    var. Chilled Scandinavian Beet and Crayfish Soup with
        Knäckebrød, 427
    var. Chilled Scandinavian Beet Soup with Knäckebrød, 427

Scrod, Broiled, in Lemon Butter Sauce, 117
Seafood. *See* Fish and seafood
Seafood Étouffée Sauce, 284
Seared Calf's Liver with Balsamic Onion Marmalade, Delmonico
    Potatoes, and Wilted Baby Spinach, 832–833
    *var. Seared Foie Gras with Balsamic Onion Marmalade on Straw
        Potato Cake (appetizer), 833*
Seared Rare Ahi Tuna with Teriyaki Sauce, Pacific Vegetable
    Medley, and Bento Rice Balls, 690–691
    *var. Seared Rare Duck Breast with Teriyaki Sauce, Pacific
        Vegetable Medley, and Bento Rice Balls, 691*
*Seared Rare Duck Breast with Teriyaki Sauce, Pacific Vegetable
    Medley, and Bento Rice Balls, var., 691*
Seattle Coffeehouse Pot de Crème with Chocolate-Dipped
    Biscotto, 640
Shad
    Baked, Stuffed, in Mushroom Cream, 170–171
Shad Roe in Brown Butter with Bacon and Asparagus, 168
    var. Salmon in Brown Butter with Bacon and Asparagus, 168
Shallots, Frizzled, 827
Shepherd's Pie with Pine Nut Romesco Sauce and Julienne
    Vegetables, 528–530
    var. Cajun Cottage Pie with Spicy Tomato Sauce, 530
    *var. Cottage Pie with Brown Gravy and Heartland Vegetable
        Medley, 530*
Shichimi Coating, 684
Shoofly Pie with Whipped Cream, 184
    var. Pennsylvania Dutch Stack Pie, 184
    var. Wet-Bottom Shoofly Pie, 184
Shrimp
    Coconut Breaded Shrimp, 748
    Creole "Barbeque" Shrimp, 268
        var. Traditional Baked Creole "Barbecue" Shrimp, 268
    Creole Shrimp Rémoulade
        var. Cajun Crawfish Rémoulade, 266
    *Cuban Crab-Stuffed Shrimp with Florida Watercress and Black-
        Eyed Pea Bollitos, var., 764*
    Fried Shrimp Chips, 682
    *Grilled Shrimp and Seashell Salad in Pineapple Boat,
        var., 765*
    Guacamole Shrimp Cocktail, var., 326
    Lowcountry Shrimp Perloo, 58
    Pan-Fried Shrimp, var., 60
    Shrimp, Crab, and Oyster Jambalaya, var., 285
    Shrimp and Crab Okra Gumbo, 282–283
        var. Seafood Okra Gumbo, 283
    Shrimp and Tasso-Stuffed Mirliton with Sauce Aurore, 270–271
        *var. Sausage-Stuffed Mirliton with Creole Tomato
            Sauce, 271*
        *var. Shrimp and Tasso-Stuffed Squash with Sauce
            Aurore, 271*
    Shrimp Creole with Pan-Steamed Rice and Fried Okra
        *var. Seafood Creole with Pan-Steamed Rice and
            Fried Okra, 279*
    *Shrimp Étouffée with Pan-Steamed Rice and Sauté
        Mirliton, var., 284*
    Shrimp 'n' Grits, 54
        var. Shrimp 'n' Grits with Brown Gravy, 54
    Shrimp on Sugarcane, 686
    Shrimp Sauce Piquante, var., 267
    South Beach Shrimp Fritters, var., 751
    Texas Gulf Coast Shrimp Cocktail, 328
Shuck Bread, 392
Sky-High Coconut Cake, 78–79
Slaw
    Pepper Slaw, 112
    Ranch-Style Slaw, 493

Smashed Redskin Potato Salad, 218
Smoked Spareribs with North Carolina Barbeque Sauce, Fancy
    Hoppin' John, and Collard Greens
    var. Barbeque Pork Shoulder for Pulled or Chopped Pork, 71
    var. Grilled Baby Back Ribs, 71
Smoke-Roasted Duck Leg in Cider Sauce with Pumpkin Gnocchi
    and Arugula, 632–633
Smoke-Roasted Duck Leg in Cider Sauce with Pumpkin Gnocchi
    and Arugula
    *var. Char-Grilled Northwestern Lamb Chops with Pinot Noir
        Demi-Glace, Porcini Mushrooms, Roasted Potatoes,
        and Carrot Purée, 633*
    *var. Roast Duck Leg in Cider Sauce with Pumpkin Gnocchi
        and Wilted Arugula, 633*
    *var. Roast Duck Leg in Cider Sauce with Pumpkin Gnocchi
        and Wilted Arugula (omit the marinade)., 633*
Smoke-Roasted Prime Rib of Beef with Twice-Baked Potato
    and Smothered Squash, 490–491
    *var. Roast Prime Rib of Beef with Twice-Baked Potato
        and Vegetable Roundup, 491*
Smoky Beef 'n' Bean Soup, 476
    var. Vaquero Beef 'n' Bean Soup, 476
Smoky Steak Sauce, 489
S'mores Pie, 500
    var. Chocolate Chiffon Pie, 501
Sofrito
    Cuban Sofrito, 764
    Puerto Rican Sofrito, var., 764
    Sofrito for Beans, var., 764
    Sofrito Tomato Sauce, 764
Soft Vanilla Whipped Cream, 75
Sorbet
    Pink Guava Sorbet, 779
Soups and stews
    Basque Garbure, var., 519
    Basque Red Bean Soup with Garlic Crouton, var., 623
    Beef Barley Soup, 428
    Beef Noodle Soup, var., 428
    Big Island Lemongrass Seafood Soup with Lotus Root Chips,
        675–676
    Caribbean Conch Chowder, 745
    Caribbean Shrimp Chowder, var., 745
    Charleston She-Crab Soup, 52
    Cherokee Beef Stew, var., 392
    Chilled Avocado Soup with Tobiko Caviar and Poppy Seed
        Lavash, 570
    *Chilled Scandinavian Beet and Crayfish Soup with Knackebrød,
        var., 427*
    Chilled Scandinavian Beet Soup with Knackebrød, var., 427
    Coral Gables Black Bean Soup with Orange, var., 747
    Crawfish Bisque, 265
    *Crawfish Bisque with Herbed Crouton and Crawfish Tails,
        var., 265*
    Creamy Broccoli Soup, var., 622
    Creamy Cauliflower Soup, 622
    Creamy Corn and Crab Soup, 210
    Creamy Corn and Green Chile Soup, 324
    Creamy Crab, Corn, and Ham Soup, var., 204
    Creamy Crab Soup, var., 204
    Egg-Drop Chicken Corn Soup, var., 163
    Georgia Peanut Soup, 53
    Home-Style Seafood-Only Crab Soup, var., 211
    Hot and Fragrant Coconut Chicken Soup, var., 676
    Lemongrass Seafood Broth, 676
    Manhattan Clam Chowder, 811
    Mock She-Crab Soup (using male crabs), var., 52
    Navajo Mutton Stew, 345

Navajo Stew with Sweet Potatoes, var., 345
Navajo Venison Stew, var., 345
New England Clam Chowder, 109
New England Lobster Chowder, var., 109
Old Key West Conch Chowder, var., 745
Palouse Valley Brown Lentil Soup, 623
Pennsylvania Dutch Chicken Corn Soup, 162–163
Pioneer Vegetable Soup with Salt-Rising Bread, 519
Portuguese Fisherman's Stew with Potatoes and Peppers, var., 120
Portuguese Mussel Stew, 120
Quick Manhattan Clam Chowder, var., 811
San Francisco Cioppino, 581
Scandinavian Beet Soup, 427
Smoky Beef 'n' Bean Soup, 476
Spicy Home-Style Crab Soup, 211
Summer Garden Vegetable Soup, 377
Summertime Corn and Clam Chowder, var., 109
U.S. House of Representatives Bean Soup, var., 161
U.S. Senate Bean Soup, 161
Vaquero Beef 'n' Bean Soup, var., 476
Vegetable Beef Soup, var., 428
Vermont Cheddar Cheese Soup, 110
Winter Chicken Corn Soup, var., 163
Winter Pantry Vegetable Soup, var., 377
Wintertime Home-Style Crab Soup, var., 211
Wisconsin Beer and Cheddar Soup, var., 110
Ybor City Black Bean Soup, 746
Sour Cream, Dilled, 520
Sourdough Buckwheat Cakes, 380
Sourdough Starter, Buckwheat, 380
South Beach Conch Fritters with Spicy Mango Dip
    var. South Beach Shrimp Fritters, 750–751
Southeast Asian Spring Rolls with Sweet 'n' Hot Dipping Sauce, 572–575
    var. Southeast Asian Summer Rolls with Sweet 'n' Hot Dipping Sauce, 575
Southern California Crab Cocktail, var., 328
Southern California Mahimahi Tamal with Jalapeño-Citrus Butter Sauce, Herbed Posole, and Steamed Chayote, 334–335
Southern Fried Chicken with Mashed Potatoes, Cream Gravy, and Down-Home Green Beans
    var. Fried Chicken Salad, 61
    var. Picnic-Style, 61
    var. Spicy, Extra-Crispy, 61
    var. Spicy Fried Chicken Tidbits, 61
    var. with Giblet Gravy, 61
Southern Potato Salad, 60
Southern-Style Carrot Cake, var., 453
Southern Sweet Potato Chip Mountain for Two, var., 521
Southern Turkey Roulade with Cornbread Dressing, Mashed Potatoes, Giblet Gravy, Braised Tender Greens, and Pickled Peach, var., 123
Southwest Cheese Chile Relleno with Spiced Tomato Sauce, 327
    var. Corn-Crumb-Crusted Southwest Chiles Rellenos, 327
    var. Crumb-Crusted Southwest Chiles Rellenos, 327
    var. Picadillo Chiles Rellenos, 327
Southwestern Gravlax on Corn Cakes with Salsa Sour Cream, var., 431
Southwest Grilled Vegetable Tostadas with Roasted Tomato Salsa, var., 331
Spareribs
    Braised Country Spareribs with Turnips 'n' Turnip Greens, var., 67
    Smoked, 71
Spiced Pecans, 479

Spice Trade Gingerbread with Cranberry Ice Cream, 136–137
    var. Spice Trade Gingerbread with Vanilla Custard Sauce, 137
Spicy Home-Style Crab Soup with Sweet Potato Roll, 211
Spicy Mango Dip, 751
Spinach, Mushroom, and Bacon Salad with Poppy Seed Dressing
    var. Spinach, Mushroom, and Bacon Salad with Creamy Blue Cheese Dressing, 164
Spinach-Stuffed Mushrooms, 165
Spinach-Stuffed Mushrooms with Aurora Cream Sauce, var., 167
Spot Prawns and Pacific Littlenecks in Cream, var., 631
Sprout salad, 55
Squab, Herb-Marinated Semiboneless, 827
Squash
    Butternut Squash Calabashes, 391
    Fried Summer Squash with Fresh Tomato Sauce and Bacon, var., 57
    Shrimp and Tasso-Stuffed Squash with Sauce Aurore, var., 271
    Squash Blossom Quesadillas with Fresh Tomato Salsa, var., 321
    Vegetable "Spaghetti," 836
Steelhead Trout and Pacific Littlenecks in Gewürztraminer Saffron Cream with Apple-Rice Pilaf and Braised Brussels Sprouts, 630–631
    var. Spot Prawns and Pacific Littlenecks in Cream (appetizer), 631
Still Master's Pecan Pie, 77
    var. New England Maple-Walnut Pie, 77
Stir-Fry Sauce, 587
Strawberries
    Old-Fashioned Biscuit Strawberry Shortcake, 75
    Strawberry Crisp with Vanilla Ice Cream, var., 133
    Strawberry Glaze, 230
    Strawberry-Topped Hominy Custards, 229
    Sugared Berries, 75
Striped Bass in Potato Crust with Red Wine Sauce, Lentil Ragout, and Leeks, 820–822
    var. Striped Bass in Potato Crust with Roasted Tomato Sauce, Corn Timbale, and Haricots Verts, 822
Stuffed Crawfish Heads, 263
Stuffed Savoy Cabbage in Sweet 'n' Sour Sauce with Kasha Varnishkes, 823–825
    var. Golabki (Polish-American Stuffed Cabbage), 825
Stuffed Vidalia Onions, 74
Sub Gum Chop Suey in Crispy Noodle Nest, var., 587
Succotash
    Summer, 117
    Winter, 128
Sugar-Coated Cranberries, 135
Sugared Berries, 75
Summer Garden Diced Vegetable Salad, 218
Summer Garden Vegetable Soup with Cracklin' Bread, 377
    var. Winter Pantry Vegetable Soup, 377
Summer Succotash, 117
Summer Vegetable Jambalaya, var., 285
Sunflower Salad, 55
    var. Kohlrabi Salad, 55
    var. Sprout Salad, 55
Sushi
    Ahi Norimaki Sushi, var., 679
    California Roll Sushi with Wasabi-Soy Dip, 577–579
    Philadelphia Roll Sushi with Ponzu Sauce, var., 579
    Sushi Rice, 679
Sweet Cranberry Coulis, 188
Sweet Dessert Tamales, var., 333
Sweet 'n' Hot Dipping Sauce, 575
Sweet Potato Pearls, 220
Swordfish Fajitas, var., 343

Tall Seafood Salad with Avocado and Tobiko, 812–813
Tamales
  "Blind" Tamales (side dish), var., 333
  Border-Style Beef Tamal with Red and Green Salsas, 332–333
  Hopi Blue Corn Tamales, var., 333
  Mahimahi Banana Leaf Tamales, 335
  Navajo Tamales, var., 333
  Sweet Dessert Tamales, var., 333
Tandoori Lamb Chops with Basmati Pulao, Greens Purée, and Braised Cauliflower, 828–831
  var. Tandoori Quail with Basmati Pulao, Greens Purée, and Braised Cauliflower, 831
Tartare of Salmon and Striped Bass with Anchovy Croutons, 816–817
  var. Tuna Tartare with Anchovy Croutons, 817
Tartar Sauce, 60
Tea-Smoked Ahi Tuna with Wasabi Mashed Potatoes and Braised Baby Bok Choy, 582–583
  var. Tea-Smoked Ahi Tuna with Pickled Vegetable Shreds (appetizer), 583
Tempura
  Ahi Nori Tempura Roll, 679
  Tempura Batter, 679
Teriyaki Sauce, 691
Texas Butter, 482
Texas "Caviar" with Tortilla Chips, 480
  var. Corny Texas "Caviar," 480
  var. Texas "Caviar" Salad in Tortilla Bowl, 480
Texas Gulf Coast Shrimp Cocktail
  var. Southern California Crab Cocktail, 328
Tex-Mex Ground Beef Tostadas with Cheddar and Sour Cream, var., 331
Tidewater Kidney Bean Salad, 225
Tilghman Island Chicken Salad with Fried Oysters, 216
  var. Tilghman Island Seafood Salad with Fried Oysters, 216
Tomatoes
  Confit Tomatoes, 577
  Fresh Tomato Cocktail Sauce, 212
  Fried Green Tomatoes with Fresh Tomato Sauce and Bacon, 57
    var. Fried Summer Squash with Fresh Tomato Sauce and Bacon, 57
    var. Vegetarian Fried Green Tomatoes, 57
  Stewed, 441
  Tomato Chicken, var., 701
  Tomato Sauce for Stuffed Cabbage, 824
Toor Dal Tofu Bundles in Red Curry Broth with Brown Rice and Steamed California Vegetables, 584–585
  var. Toor Dal Cabbage Bundles in Red Curry Broth with Brown Rice and Steamed California Vegetables, 585
Tossed Salad with Buttermilk Ranch Dressing, 477
  var. Fiesta Salad with Ranch Dressing and Salsa, 477
Tostadas
  Basque Tostada with Brandied Peach Half, 534
  Twin Tostadas, 330–331
    var. Lobster, Crab, or Shrimp Tostadas with Guacamole Green Salsa, 331
    var. Pico de Gallo, 331
    var. Shredded Pork Tostadas with Roasted Corn and Green Salsa, 331
    var. Southwest Grilled Vegetable Tostadas with Roasted Tomato Salsa, 331
    var. Tex-Mex Ground Beef Tostadas with Cheddar and Sour Cream, 331
Tostones, 773

Trail-Drive Chili over Texmati Rice with Cowboy Beans, Longhorn Cheddar, and Sweet Corn Pico de Gallo, 496
  var. Borracha Chili, 496
  var. Deep-Dark Secret Chili, 496
  var. Venison Chili, 496
Tres Leches Cake with Mandarin Oranges, 776–777
Triple Onion Potato Pierogies, 432–433
  var. Golden Fried Pierogies, 433
  var. Pierogi Medley with Onion Butter Sauce, 433
  var. Potato-Cheddar Pierogies with Onion Butter Sauce, 433
  var. Sauerkraut Pierogies with Onion Butter Sauce, 433
Triple-Threat Brownie Ice Cream Sundae, var., 186
Tropical Fruit Palette with Guava Sorbet in Coconut Tuile, 778–779
Tropical Seashell Salad, 758
Tropical Slaw, 770
Turkey
  Chicken-Fried Turkey with Cream Gravy, Mashed Potatoes, and Western-Style Greens, var., 487
  Deep-Dish Flaky Pastry Turkey Pie, var., 439
  Giblet Gravy, 122
  Maple-Glazed Turkey with Sauerkraut and Hominy, 393–394
  Pulled Turkey Leg, 394
  Seasoned Turkey Breast Portions, 393
  Smoked Turkey Red Beans 'n' Rice, Var., 288
  Turkey Roulade with Bread Stuffing, Mashed Potatoes, Giblet Gravy, Brussels Sprouts, and Cranberry Sauce, 121–123
    var. Southern Turkey Roulade with Cornbread Dressing, Mashed Potatoes, Giblet Gravy, Braised Tender Greens, and Pickled Peach, 123
Turnips 'n' Turnip Greens, 69
Twin Tostadas, 330. *See also* Tostadas, for variations

U. S. Senate Bean Soup with Butter Crackers, 161
  var. U. S. House of Representatives Bean Soup, 161

Veal
  Veal Chop, Pan-Roasted, in Apple-Mushroom Cream with Handmade Noodles and Brussels Sprouts, 180–181
  Veal Parmesan with Fresh Tomato Sauce, Potato Gnocchi, and Vegetable "Spaghetti," 834–836
    var. Eggplant Parmesan with Fresh Tomato Sauce, Potato Gnocchi, and Vegetable "Spaghetti," 836
    var. Pork Parmesan with Fresh Tomato Sauce, Potato Gnocchi, and Vegetable "Spaghetti," 836
Vegetables. *See also* Potatoes; Salads; specific vegetables
  Bot Boi, 177
  Corn Relish, 485
  Grilled Vegetable Ratatouille, 222
  Maquechoux, 278
  Pepper Slaw, 112
  Pickled Vegetable Shreds, 583
  Roasted Fennel–Yukon Gold Potato Purée, 629
  Southwest Grilled Vegetable Tostadas with Roasted Tomato Salsa, var., 331
  Summer Garden Vegetable Soup with Cracklin' Bread, 377
  Summer Succotash, 117
  Summer Vegetable Jambalaya, var., 285
  Toor Dal Cabbage Bundles in Red Curry Broth with Brown Rice and Steamed California Vegetables, var., 585
  Vegetable Roundup, 489
  Vegetable "Spaghetti," 836
  Walla Walla Onion Cups, 635
  Western-Style Greens, 487

Vegetarian Cobb Salad, var., 572
Vegetarian Fried Green Tomatoes, var., 57
Vegetarian Red Chile Cheese Enchiladas, var., 337
Velouté, Cranberry-Maple, 173
Venison
    Cherokee Venison Stew, 392
    Medallions of Venison, 531–532
    Navajo Venison Stew, var., 345
    "Pemmican" Venison Sausages, 627
    Red Wine Venison Demi-Glace, 128
    Venison Chile con Carne, var., 347
    Venison Chili, var., 496
    Wampanoag Maple-Glazed Roast Rack of Venison, 127–128
**Vermont Cheddar Cheese Soup with New England Soda
    Bread,** 110
    var. Wisconsin Beer and Cheddar Soup, 110
Vidalia Onions, Stuffed, 74

Waffle Ice Cream Sundae, var., 186
Walla Walla Onion Cups, 635
Walla Walla Onion Salad, 627
Walnut Brownies, var., 185
Walnut-Crusted Cheddar Croutons, 114
Walnut Torte with Apricot Sauce, var., 349
Walnut Vinaigrette, 624
**Wampanoag Maple-Glazed Roast Rack of Venison with Winter
    Succotash and Broccoli Florets in Baby Pumpkin,** 127–128
    *var. Wampanoag Maple-Glazed Roast Pork Chop with Winter
        Succotash and Broccoli Florets in Baby Pumpkin,* 128
Wasabi Mashed Potatoes, 583
Wasabi Paste and Wasabi Sauce, 679
Wasabi-Soy Dip, 579

**Watercress and Boston Lettuce Salad with Maple Vinaigrette,
    Cranberries, and Walnut-Crusted Cheddar Crouton,** 114
    *var. with Mustard Vinaigrette, Grape Tomatoes,
        and Walnut-Crusted Goat Cheese Crouton,* 114
Wells Kringle with Lingonberry Sauce, 455
    var. Wells Kringle with Raspberry Sauce, 455
Western-Style Greens, 487
Wet-Bottom Shoofly Pie, var., 184
Whipped Cream, Soft Vanilla, 75
Wiener Schnitzel, Midwestern, var., 441
Wild Mushroom Cornbread Dressing, 384
Wild Rice, 437
**Wilted Salad with Hot Bacon Dressing and Fried
    Potato Croutons**
    *var. Spring Tonic Salad with Hot Bacon Dressing
        and Hard-Cooked Egg,* 378
Winter Chicken Corn Soup with Rivels, var., 163
Winter Succotash, 128
Wintertime Home-Style Crab Soup, var., 211
Wisconsin Beer and Cheddar Soup, var., 110
Wisconsin Cheddar Broccoli Rarebit, 429
    *var. Wisconsin Cheddar Woodchuck (Tomato-Bacon
        Rarebit),* 429

Ybor City Black Bean Soup with Cuban Bread, 746–747
    var. Coral Gables Black Bean Soup with Orange, 747
    var. Cuban Black Beans (side dish), 747
Yellow Rice, 773
**Yellowtail Snapper Laulau with Coconut Sweet Potatoes
    and Stir-Fry Vegetable Shreds,** 692–693
    *var. Grilled Whole Baby Snapper with Laulau Butter, Coconut
        Sweet Potatoes, and Stir-Fry Vegetable Shreds,* 693

subject index

Note: Page numbers in *italics* indicate inclusive discussions.

Acadian-American cuisine, 20, 107,
   251–252
Acorn meal, 545
Adams, Alto, 728
Adams Ranch, 728
Adobo, 741
African-Americans. *See also* Soul food
   Appalachian South, 367
   and Chesapeake Bay Shore cuisine, 201,
      202, 205
   in Louisiana, 240, 243–252, 255
   and Mid-Atlantic cuisine, 153
   in Midwestern cities, 420, 421
   in New England, 92
   in New York City, 796–797
   in the Plantation South, 41–47, 50
   in South Florida, 725, 732
   in the Western and Central Ranchlands,
      465, 471
African influence, 719, 727, 729, 740–741,
   740–742
Afro-Caribbean influence, 42, 44, 198, 244
Age of Exploration, 88, 306, 611
Age of Immigration, 4, 102
Agribusiness, 414, 552–553
Agriculture
   Alaska, 618
   California, 546, 551–555
   climate change and, 46
   definition of, 11
   desert, 303–307
   Hawai'ian, 652–654
   Louisiana, 238, 245
   Mexican Border, 303
   Mid-Atlantic, 147, 149, 150
   Midwest, 412–416
   Native American, 30–31
   New England, 89, 95, 98, 102
   New York, 791
   Pacific Northwest, 612, 615
   Pennsylvania, 152–153
   Plantation South, 28, 31, 37, 41, 45
   Rocky Mountains, 507, 516
   soil and, 12
   sustainable, 13
   swidden, 30, 38, 87, 366
   topography and climate and, 14
Agutuk, 618
Ais, 723
Aji-li-mojili sauce, 742
Ajolio, 513
Akbar, 804
A la carte, 791
Alaea salt, 656
Alaska
   cooking, 617–619
   gold rush, 613–614

Native Americans, 605–606,
      609–610, 618
   Panhandle, 605
   Russia and, 612
   tundra, 605
Alciatore, Antoine, 255
Alkaline-processed corn, 34, 90, 307, 309
Alligator, 242, 253, 254
Allison, Karen Hubert, 800
Alluvial soil, 237
Altitude, 13
American Bounty restaurant, 156
American buffalo, 462, 465, 466, 472, 510,
      511, 605
American Southwestern cuisine. *See*
   Mexican Border
Anadromous fish, 606, 608
Anaheim chile, 314
An American Place, 799
Anasazi beans, 306
Anglo-Asian California, *538–569*
   Chinese-American microcuisine, 564–565
   contemporary and future cuisine,
      563–564
   cuisine elements, 557, 558
   defining dishes, 565–568
   expansionism and, 547
   modern cuisine, 560–563
   Native Americans and, 545–546
   recipes, 570–593 (*See also* Recipe Index)
   regional ingredients, 594–599
   San Francisco cuisine, 549–551
   seafood, 555–556
   Spanish and Mexican influence, 545–547
   topography and climate, 541–545
   traditional cuisine, 557–560
   wines, 556–557
Anglos, 315
Annatto, 740
Antoine's, 255
Aperitifs, 247
Appalachian Mountains, 27
Appalachian South, *358–376*
   contemporary, 372–373
   cuisine, 366–371
   cuisine elements, 364, 373
   defining dishes, 374–375
   farming, 365–366
   ingredients, 402–403
   Native Americans, 362–364
   Old-World Scots and Scots-Irish, 364
   pioneers in, 364–365
   railroads, industry, and exploitation
      of, 372
   recipes, 359–401 (*See also*
      Recipe Index)
   topography and climate, 361–362

Apple butter, 370
Applejack, 370
Apples, 8, 38, 92–93, 94, 99, 370, 614
Apron (crab undershell), 200
Aquaculture, 615
Aquifers, 13
Archipelago, 649
Arid climate, 303
Arizona 206, 800
Arroz con gandules, 742
Arroz con pollo, 742
Art Deco, 731, 734, 736
Artichokes, 554
Ashkenazi Jewish food, 731
Asian influence, 557–558, 613, 796,
      802–803. *See also* Chinese cuisine;
      Japanese cuisine; Pan
      Asian influence
Asopao, 742
Asparagus, 554
Atlantic oysters, 200–201
Attitudes and beliefs about food
   Appalachian South, 373
   Caribbean, 244
   Central Farmlands and Cities, 418
   Chesapeake Bay Shore, 206
   Chinese cuisine, 557
   Colonial Mexican, 310
   Filipino, 664
   First Hawai'ian, 657
   food culture and, 4, 7–8
   Japanese, 558
   Korean, 664
   Louisiana, 256
   Mexican Border, 317
   Mid-Atlantic, 157
   Native Americans, 17
   New England, 96
   New England Native American, 90
   Old World Basque, 513
   Old World English, 39
   Old World French, 241
   Old World Holland Dutch, 151
   Old-World Scots and Scots-Irish, 364
   Pacific Northwest Native
      American, 610
   Plantation South, 46
   Plantation South Native American, 28
   Portuguese, 662
   Precontact Navajo and Apache, 309
   Precontact Pueblo, 308
   Ranchlands, 467
   South Florida, 736
   West African, 43
Automat, 793
Avocados, 314, 554
Azteca Mills, 316

Bacalao, 513
Back-to-the-land movements, 373
Bacon drippings, 367
Badlands, 461
Baking powder, 41, 45
Baltimore cuisine, 205–206
Barbeque
  Chesapeake Bay Shore, 204
  Hawai'ian, 667
  Korean, 664, 667, 803
  Midwestern, 420
  Plantation South, 44, 45
  Ranchlands, 467, 471
  South Florida, 724–725, 734, 742
Basque immigrant cuisine, 512–514
Bassett's ice cream, 155
Baum, Joe, 798
Bayous, 237–238
Beans, 31, 90–91, 94, 306–307, 467, 510, 513. *See also* Three Sisters crops
Beard, James, 798, 799
Beaten biscuits, 41
Beef
  Farmlands, 416–420
  Hawai'i, 661
  Mexican Border, 312–313, 317
  Midwestern, 416–417
  Puerto Rican, 742
  Ranchlands, 466, 468, 471
  South Florida, 728
Beefalo, 472
Beignets, 255
Beliefs and attitudes. *See* Attitudes and beliefs about food
Ben & Jerry's, 100
Bent's Fort, 511
Beringan land bridge, 28
Bering Strait, 603
Berries, 30, 89, 98–99, 100, 607, 609
Berries (roe), 200
Bertolli, Paul, 562
Biergartens, 794–795
The Big Island, 649
Billfish, 655
Bill of fare, 791
Biscuits, 41
Bison, 462, 465, 466, 472, 510, 511, 605
Bitterroot, 609
Blackened dishes, 245, 255, 256
Black Quinoa, 516
Blubber, 610
Blue crabs, 199–200, 254
Blue Point Oysters, 200
Blue Smoke, 800
Boardinghouse service, 513
Bodegas, 804
Boiled puddings, 94
Bookbinder's, 155, 203
Boomtown cooking, 547–548
Borscht, 618
Boston brown bread, 94
Boston cream pie, 100, 101
Boston scrod, 96
Bottom fish, 655
Boucherie, 252–253
Boudin sausage, 245
Boulangeries, 241

BP oil spill, 256
Breads, 92, 241–242, 245, 417, 469–470, 514, 548
Brewis, 94
Brew pubs, 616
Brine, 93
Brody, Jerome, 793
Brown, Henry C., 512
Brown Derby restaurant, 560
Browning, 252
Brown Palace Hotel, 512
Buffalo chips, 468
Buffalo jump, 463
Burbank, Luther, 551
Burritos, 316
Buster, 199
Buttermilk biscuits, 41
Buttes, 303
Buzzaro, Giuseppe, 550

Cabbages, 93
Cache, 618
Caesar salad, 559
Café au lait, 255
Café des Émigrés, 255
Café du Monde, 255
CAFOs (confined animal feeding operations), 471, 555
Cajun cuisine, 250–253
Cajun napalm, 248
Cajuns, 252
California. *See* Anglo-Asian California; Mexican Border cuisine
California current, 543
California roll, 558
Calousa, 723
Camas, 607, 609
Camino Real, 310, 313
Campbell company, 157
Canadian bacon, 100, 102
Cane syrup, 244
Cannery Row, 555
Canoe plants, 652–653
Cantonese food, 512
Capsicum plant, 307
Caramelization, 252
Cardini, Cesar, 559
Cardozat, Floyd, 805
Caribbean influence, 42, 44, 94, 198, 244, 736
Cascade Mountains, 508, 603
Casseroles, 417, 515
Cast-iron cooking, 39, 241, 469
Castle & Cooke, 660
Cattle barons, 465
Cattle drives, 465
Cattle finishing, 419
Cavelier, René-Robert, 239
Celebrity chefs, 563
Cellar in the Sky, 799
Celts, 365, 370
Central Farmlands and Cities, *404–426*
  cities, 418–421
  cuisine elements, 418
  defining dishes, 423–425
  future cuisine of, 421–422
  ingredients, 456–457

  microcuisines of, 422
  Midwest agriculture, 412–416
  Native Americans, 410–411
  recipes, 427–455 (*See also* Recipe Index)
  topography and climate, 406–410
  traditional cuisine, 416–418
Central plains, 408
Central Valley (California), 541–542, 544
Charcuterie, 252
Charles's Southern Kitchen, 797
Charqui, 464
Chasen's restaurant (California), 560
Chaudières, 242
Chávez, César, 553
Chayote, 244, 733
Cheese, 43, 99, 417, 555, 614
Cheeseburgers, 559–560
Cheese curds, 415
Chenel, Laura, 555
Cherokees, 362–364
Chesapeake Bay Foundation (CBF), 206
Chesapeake Bay Shore, *192–209*
  in the 21st century, 206–207
  cuisine elements, 206
  culture and cuisine, 201–205
  decline and rebirth of, 206
  defining dishes, 207–208
  foundations of cuisine, 198–201
  Native Americans of, 197–198
  recipes, 210–230 (*See also* Recipe Index)
  regional ingredients, 231–232
  restaurant cuisine, 205–206
  topography and climate, 195–197
Chesapeake seasoning (Old Bay), 205
Chèvre, 555
Chez Panisse, 562
Chicago Chop House, 420
Chicago pizza, 421
Chicago steakhouses, 419–420
Chicago stockyards, 419
Chicken-fried steak, 471
Chickies, 725
Chile con carne, 313
Chile con queso, 314, 317, 470
Chile powder *vs.* chili powder, 312, 470
Chile rojo, 313
Chiles, 244, 307, 311–312
Chiles rellenos, 312
Chile verde, 311, 313
Chili Appreciation Society International, 470
Chili *vs* chile, 313, 470
Chimichanga, 316
Chinatown (New York City), 796
Chinatown (San Francisco), 550–551
Chinese cuisine, 557, 613, 662–663, 796
Chinese Exclusion Act, 796
Chinois on Main, 564
Chorizo sausage, 513
Chowder, 98
Choy, Sam, 669
Christophene, 244
Chuck wagon cooking, 466, 468–469
Churchill's, 792
Church of Jesus Christ of Latter Day Saints (LDS), 515
Cider, 93

Cider doughnuts, 100
Cilantro, 740
Cincinnati chili, 421
Cincinnati pork, 419
Cioppino, 550
Citrus, 545, 551, 727, 728, 734
Ciupin, 550
Clabbered cream, 370
Claiborne, Craig, 798
Clambakes, 91, 98, 656
Clams, 97, 201
Clam shacks, 97
Clay pot cooking, 33
Climate. *See* Topography and climate
Coastal plain, 27
Coastal Range, 543
Cocinero, 468
Coconut Grove Lounge, 560
Coconut milk, 736
Cod, 96
Coddies, 97
Codfish cakes, 97
Cold desert, 508
Colonial cuisine, 8, 36–41, 92–94, 791
Colonists, 4
Columbia River, 603
Combination plates, 317
Commander's Palace, 253
Common crackers, 94
Companion planting, 30, 306, 651
Conch (shellfish), 727
Conchs (Florida Keys settlers), 726–727
Confined animal feeding operations
    (CAFOs), 471, 555
Conservative food culture, 7, 8–9, 95
Continental cuisine, 791
Cook, Captain James, 659
Cooked breakfast (Hawai'i), 661
Cookhouses, 468
Cooking media and methods
    Appalachian South, 373
    Caribbean, 244
    Central Farmlands and Cities, 418
    Chesapeake Bay Shore, 206
    Chinese, 557
    Colonial Mexican, 310
    Filipino, 664
    First Hawai'ian, 657
    Japanese, 558
    Korean, 664
    Louisiana, 256
    Mexican Border, 317
    New England, 96
    New England Native American, 90
    Old-Word Scots and Scots-Irish, 364
    Old World English, 39
    Old World French, 241
    Old World Holland, 151
    Mid-Atlantic, 157
    overview, 6, 7
    Pacific Northwest Native American, 610
    Plantation South Native American, 28
    Portuguese, 662
    Precontact Navajo and Apache, 309
    Precontact Pueblo, 308
    Ranchlands, 467
    Old World Basque, 513

South Florida, 736
    West African, 43
    Plantation South, 46
Coontie, 724
Coosie, 468
Cooter, 253
Copeland's restaurant, 797
Copycat cheeses, 415
Corn, 16–17, 31–35, 34, 238, 305–306,
    414. *See also* Three Sisters crops
Cornbread, 35, 41
Corned beef, 93, 102
Corn flour *vs.* cornflour, 35
Cornmeal, 35
Cornmeal mush, 90
Corn pone, 35, 90
Coronado, FranciscoVasquez de, 309
Côte des Allemandes, 245
Counterculture, 560–562
Courtbouillon, 250
Coush-coush, 243
Cover crops, 13
Cowboy slang, 469
Crab cakes, 204
Crab pound, 199–200
Crabs, 199–200, 204, 254
Crackers, 93
Crackers (Florida settlers), 727–728, 732
Cracklings, 40
Cranberries, 98–99
Crawdaddies, 254
Crawfish, 253, 254
Creasy greens, 368
Creek nation, 725
Creole cuisine, 247–250
Crescent City, 239
Crop rotation, 13
Crusted, 736
Cuban influence, 729, 737
Cuisine
    America's national, 21
    culinary regions, 9–10
    development of, 8–9, 10–20
    elements of, 5–8
    foreign, 20–21
    fusion, 561, 564, 735
    history and, 4–5
    hybrid, 4, 19
    microcuisines, 20
    regional, 9
Culantro, 740
Culinary conservative, 7–8
Culinary Institute of America, 156, 798
Culinary liberal, 7–8
Culinary regions, 9
Cultivars, 13
Culture and cuisine, 4–9
Custard, frozen, 100
Cyclical land use, 29

Dairy products, 99–100, 370, 415,
    554–555, 614–615
Darbar, 804
David K's, 805
Dawat, 804
Death Valley, 543, 545
Decré, Fred, 798

Deep South, 27
Defining dishes
    American Southwestern cuisine, 320–323
    Anglo-Asian California, 565–568
    Appalachian South, 374–375
    Central Farmlands, 423–425
    Chesapeake Bay Shore, 207–208
    defined, 9
    Hawai'i, 671–673
    Louisiana, 257–261
    Mid-Atlantic, 158–159
    New England, 103–106
    New York City, 807–809
    Pacific Northwest, 614, 618–620
    Plantation South, 47–49
    Puerto Rico, 742–744
    Rocky Mountains and Great Plains,
        516–517
    South Florida, 737–739
    Western and Central Ranchlands,
        473–474
De Leon, Ponce, 726
DelMarVa Peninsula, 202–203
Delmonico's, 791–792
Delta, 237
Demens, Pete, 729
Desert, 305–307, 508
Desert Land Act of 1877, 465, 466
Designer dishes, 563
De Soto, Hernando, 238
Diamond Jim Brady, 792
Dikon, Roger, 669
Dirty rice, 252
Dodin-Bouffant, 799
Dole, James D., 660
Don the Beachcomber's, 561
Drake, Sir Francis, 610–611
Dressing (stuffing), 252
Drippings, 40
Drive-in restaurants, 559–560
Drowned river, 195
Drying, 464
Dude ranches, 472
Dungeness crab, 556
Dust bowl, 415–416
Dutch influence, 151, 790–791
Dutch oven, 38, 469

Earthquakes, 542–543
Eastern European influence, 413, 418,
    795, 805
Eastern shore, Chesapeake Bay,
    196–197, 413
Economic viability, 19–20, 45
Ellis Island, 794
Ellman, Mark, 669
Entrée salad, 559
Erosion, 12
Escoffier, 247
Escoffier Room, 156
Eskimo, 609–610
Españoles, 661
Estuary, 195
Ethics, 564
Ethnic-American cuisines, 8, 20. *See also*
    Microcuisines
Étouffée, 250

Eulachon fish, 606, 610
Everglades, 722

Fairmont Hotel, 549
Fajitas, 313, 317
Fall line, 27
Family-style service, 513
Faneuil Hall Market, 100
Farming, 11–15. *See also* Agriculture
Farmlands cuisine. *See* Central Farmlands and Cities
Fast food, 559–560
Faults, 542–543
Fertilization, 12–13
Fiddleheads, 89
Filé gumbo, 248
Filé powder, 242–243
Filipino cuisine, in Hawai'i, 664
Finger Lakes, 156
Finishing, 419
Fior d'Italia, 550
Fiorella's Jack Stack Barbecue, 420
First contact, 4
First Hawai'ian cuisine, 656–659
First Hawai'ians, 651–656
First settlers, 4, 18–19
Fish and seafood
    Alaska, 618
    Anglo-Asian California, 555–556
    Chesapeake Bay Shore, 197, 198, 199–207
    Hawai'i, 654–656, 666
    Louisiana, 242
    Mid-Atlantic, 152, 154, 156
    Midwest, 417
    New England, 91, 92, 93, 94, 95, 96–98
    New York City, 792–793
    Pacific Northwest, 606, 607, 615
    Plantation South, 29–30, 37, 43
    Puerto Rico, 742
    Rocky Mountains and Great Plains, 511, 513
    South Florida, 723
Fisher, Carl, 730–731
Fisherman's Wharf, 550, 556
Fiskesuppe, 618
Flagler, Henry, 729
Flan, 313
Flavor layering, 252
Flay, Bobby, 800
Floribbean cuisine, 735
Florida. *See* South Florida and Puerto Rico
Foie gras, 156
Food culture, 5
Food ethics, 564
Food markets, 100, 155, 255, 615–616, 703, 793, 801
Food preservation, 7, 17, 31, 93–94, 371, 464, 658, 660–661, 666
Foodways, 5
Foreign cuisines, 20–21
Forgione, Larry, 800
Foundation foods
    Caribbean, 244
    Central farmlands and cities, 418
    Chesapeake Bay Shore, 206

Chinese, 557
defined, 6
Filipino, 664
First Hawai'ian, 657
Japanese, 558
Korean, 664
Lousiana, 256
Mexican Border cuisine, 317
Mid-Atlantic, 157
New England, 96
New England Native American, 90
Old World Basque cuisine, 513
Old World English, 39
Old World French, 241
Old World Holland Dutch, 151
Old-World Scots and Scots-Irish, 364
Appalachian South, 373
Pacific Northwest Native American, 610
Plantation South Native American, 28
Portuguese, 662
Precontact Navajo and Apache, 309
Precontact Pueblo, 308
Rocky Mountains and Great Basin, 513
South Florida cuisine, 736
West African, 43
Plantation South, 46
Ranchlands, 467
Four Corners, 304, 308
Four Seasons, 798–799
Foxfire series, 373
Franey, Pierre, 798
Fraunce's Tavern, 791
Free persons of color, 240
Free range, 800
French influence, 239–242, 412, 792, 797–800
French Laundry restaurant, 564
French Market, 255
French Pavilion restaurant, 797
Fresh onions, 242
Fried clam bellies, 97
Fried pies, 371
Frozen custard, 100
Fruit
    California, 551–552, 553–554, 559
    Chesapeake Bay Shore, 206
    Louisiana, 241, 244, 256
    Mexican Border cuisine, 317
    Mid-Atlantic, 151, 157
    New England, 90, 96
    Pacific Northwest, 614
    Plantation South, 28, 39, 43, 46
    Southwestern cuisine, 309, 310
Fruit cocktail, 559
Fry bread, 515
Fuerte avocado, 554
Fulton Fish Market, 793
Fusion cuisine, 561, 564, 735

Gadsden Purchase, 547
Gandinga, 742
Gandules, 740
Gannon, Beverly, 669
Garbage salad, 420
Garden Court restaurant, 549
Garlic, 513

Gebhardt, William, 313
Geocultural, 361
Gephardt, William, 471
German influence, 153, 205, 244–245, 314, 370, 413, 417, 422, 471, 794
Ghirardelli Square, 550
Gibson's, 420
Gingerbread, 100
Girdling, 30
Golding, N. S., 615
Gold Rush, 547–549
Goldstein, Joyce, 562
Golubtsy, 618
Gotham Bar and Grill, 800
Goya Foods, 741
Grain-finished beef, 419
Gramercy Tavern, 800
Grand Central Oyster Bar, 203, 793
Grapes, 554. *See also* Wine
Grazing menu, 798
Great American Desert, 508
Great Basin, 508. *See also* Rocky Mountains and Great Basin
Great Lakes, 409, 410
Great Plains, 408
Greek influence, 797
Green, Charlotte, 511
Green corn, 35
Green Goddess dressing, 549, 559
Grilling, 464, 471, 549, 559, 564, 656
Grits, 35
Guacamole, 314, 470
Guest ranches, 472
Gulf finfish, 254
Gulf Oysters, 254
Gulf Shrimp, 254
Gullah cooking, 47, 243
Gumbo, 243, 247–250
Gumbo z'Herbes, 248
Gyro, 797

Haight-Ashbury, 561
Halal meats, 804
Hallacas, 741
Hamburgers, 559–560
Hangtown fry, 548
Haoles, 659, 660, 661
Hard cider, 93
Hard-shell crabs, 199, 200
Harlem, 796
Hass avocado, 554
Haute cuisine, 20
Haute ethnic, 804–805
Hawai'i, 646–674
    characteristics of cuisine, 670
    cuisine elements, 657, 662, 664
    defining dishes, 669, 671–673
    Europeans and Americans in, 659–661
    First Hawai'ian cuisine, 656–659
    First Hawai'ians, 651–656
    future of regional cuisine and local food, 669
    immigrant cuisine, 662–664
    ingredients, 708–716
    local food, 665–668
    local talk, 668

recipes, 675–707 (*See also* Recipe Index)
regional cuisine, 668–669
snacks, 668
traditional cuisine, 661–662
WWII and Postwar development, 664–665
Hawai'ian hot spot, 649
Hearth, 38
Hearts of palm, 724, 733
Heinz ketchup, 157
Hershey's chocolate, 157
High desert, 303–304
High status foods, 31
Hoe cakes, 38
Hofbraus, 794
Holland Dutch influence, 150–154, 156
Hollows, 361
Hollywood, 560
Holy trinity, 241
Homegrown, homemade, 370
Homestead Act of 1862, 412
Homestead area, South Florida, 723
Hominy, 34, 36
Homogeneity, 9
Hooligan oil, 606
Horn & Hardart's Automats, 793
Hornos, 318
Hors d'Oeuverie, 799
Hotdish, 417
Hot smoking, 608
Hot stone griddling, 33
Hubert's, 800
Hudson, Henry, 790
HudsonValley, 156
Human seasonal migration, 29
Hybrid cuisine, 4, 19
Hydroponics, 554

Iceberg lettuce, 553
Ice cream, 99–100, 155, 618
Immigrants
    California, 548, 557
    food and dishes, 8
    Hawai'i, 662–664
    impact of, 19
    Louisiana, 245–247, 256
    Mexican, 315–316
    Mid-Atlantic, 157
    Midwest, 412–413, 421
    New England, 101–102
    New York City, 794–797, 802–805
    Pacific Northwest, 613
Imu, 656–657
Indian corn, 17
Indian cuisine (East Indian), 803–804
Indian pudding, 94, 100
Indian Removal Act, 725
Indigenous cultures, 4, 8, 15–18, 650. *See
    also* First Hawai'ians; Native Americans
Industrial food production, 372, 419
Industrial Revolution, 414
Ingredients
    Anglo-Asian California, 594–599
    Appalachian South, 402–403
    Central Farmlands and Cities, 456–457
    Chesapeake Bay Shore, 231–232

Hawai'i, 708–716
influence on food culture, 5–6
Louisiana, 296–299
Mexican Border, 351–357
Mid-Atlantic region, 190–191
New England, 138–145
New York City, 845–849
Pacific Northwest, 642–645
Plantation South, 80–83
Rocky Mountains and Great Basin, 536–537
South Floida and Puerto Rico, 779–784
Western and Central Ranchlands, 502–503
Ingredient staging, 252
In-N-Out Burger, 560
International Championship Chili Cookoff, 470
Inuit tribe, 609–610
Irish influence, 102, 364–365, 370, 728, 794
Irrigation, 13, 408, 414, 551, 719, 729
Italian-American cuisine, 102, 613, 795, 805–806

Jamaican-American cooking, 734, 804
Jambalaya, 243
James Beard Foundation, 798
Jamestown, Virginia, 36–37
Jams restaurant, 800
Janssen's restaurant, 795
Japan Current, 604
Japanese cuisine, 557–558, 613, 616, 663
Jeaga, 723
Jerk, 734, 804
Jerky, 464
Jet stream, 543
Jewish-American cuisine, 795, 805–806
Jimmy (crab), 200
Joe's Stone Crab restaurant, 732
John Ash & Company restaurant, 564
Josselin, Jean-Marie, 669

Kafka, Barbara, 799
Kama'ainas, 660, 661, 665
Kamano, 660
Kamehameha I, 659
Kapu, 656–657
Katrina, 255–256
Kellogg's, 419
Key lime, 727
Keys, Florida, 726
King's cake, 255
Kippered salmon, 613
Kiva, 305
Knob onions, 242
Kookjies, 151
Korean cuisine, 663–664, 803
Kosher law, 795
Kovi, Paul, 798, 799
K-Paul's, 253
Kraft, James L., 419
Krause, Richard, 564
Krewes, 255
Kulich, 618
Kumin, Albert, 798–799

La Caravelle, 798
La Côte Basque, 798
Lady Baltimore Cake, 205
Lagasse, Emeril, 253
Lagniappe, 245
Lake Okeechobee, 722, 730
Lamacun, 804
Lamb, 513
La Poule d'Or, 549
Lard, 40
La Salle, 239
Latin fusion, 564
Latitude, 13
Laulaus, 662
Layering and staging, 252
Leather britches, 371
Leavening, 470
Lenape tribal group, 790
Le Plaisir, 798
Le Restaurant du Pavillon de France, 797–798
Lewis and Clark expedition, 509, 609, 612
Liberal food culture, 7–8
Liliuokalani, Queen, Hawai'i, 659
Little Italy, New York City, 795
Living greens, 554
Lobster, 97
Lobster palaces, 792
Lobster pound, 97
Local, 370
Local food, Hawai'i, 665–668
Lo'i, 654
Lomi lomi salmon, 661
Longaniza sausage, 513
Long drive, 465
Long green chiles, 311
Long Island cuisine, 152, 156, 791
Los Angeles, 560
Louisiana, *234–262*
    Cajun cuisine, 250–253
    characteristics of cuisine, 253–254
    Creole cuisine, 247–250
    cuisine elements, 241, 244, 256
    defining dishes, 257–261
    French settlement, 239–240
    future of cuisine, 256
    ingredients, 296–299
    Native Americans in, 238–239
    New Orleans food culture and cuisine, 254–256
    recipes, 263–295 (*See also* Recipe Index)
    seven roots of traditional cuisine, 240–247
    topography and climate, 237–238
Lou Malnati's, 421
Lowcountry, 27, 46–47
Lowcountry perloo, 243
Lu'aus, 656, 658–659, 665, 668
Lüchows restaurant, 795
Lunchrooms, 793
Lundy's, 793
Lye, 309

Macadamia nuts, 669
Macondo blowout, 257
Madison, Deborah, 562

Maillard browning, 252
Maize, 16–17
Ma Maison, 563
Mango Gang, 734, 736
Manhattan Island, 790
Manifest Destiny, 547
Manos, 201
Maple sugar, 98
Maple syrup, 89, 90, 94, 98
Marbling, 419
Mardi Gras, 255
Margittai, Tom, 798, 799
Maria Anna Capelli's Highland House, 512
Masa, 309, 316
Masa harina, 316
Mason-Dixon line, 361
Matsuhisa, Nobuyuki, 805
Mavrothalassitis, George, 669
Meat and poultry
   California, 554–555
   Central Farmlands, 416–417, 418–421
   Chesapeake Bay Shore, 206
   Louisiana, 241, 244, 256
   Mexican Border cuisine, 317
   Mid-Atlantic, 151, 157
   New England, 90, 96
   Old World Basque cuisine, 513
   Plantation South, 28, 39, 43, 46
   Southwestern cuisine, 309, 310
   Western Ranchlands, 467
Meat production and packing, 418–419
Mediterranean climate, 543
Melting pot, 4, 8–9, 805
Merriman, Peter, 669
Mesa Grill, 800
Mesas, 303
Meso-Americans, 305–306, 465
Mestizos, 309
Metz, Ferdinand, 798
Mexican Border, *300–323*
   cuisine elements, 308, 309, 310, 317
   defining dishes, 319–322
   ingredients, 351–357
   Mexican-American cuisine, 315–318
   Mexican influence, 315–318, 320–323,
      470–471, 545–547
   Native Americans and, 304–309, 318
   recipes, 324–350 (*See also* Recipe Index)
   Spanish/Mexican influence, 309–312
   topography and climate, 303–304
   traditional and contemporary
      Southwestern cuisine, 312–315
Meyer, Danny, 800
Miami, 729
Miami Beach, 730–731
Miccosukee tribe, 725
Microbreweries, 616
Microclimates, 543, 604
Microcuisines
   Acadian-American, 107, 251
   Central Farmlands, 422
   Chinese-American, 557, 564–565, 613
   Cuban-American, 737
   German-American, 405, 422
   Italian-American, 805–806
   Jewish-American, 805–806
   Lowcountry, 46–47

overview, 20
   Pennsylvania Dutch, 153, 154, 157, 198
   Polish-American, 422
   Scandinavian-American, 422
   Soul Food, 20, 44, 47, 420
   Southwestern Native American, 301,
      305, 318
Microgreens, 554
Mid-Atlantic, *146–160*
   cuisine elements, 151, 157
   defining dishes of, 158–159
   English cooking of, 154–156
   European settlers, 151–152
   industrial food production, 157
   Native Americans, 150–151
   New York, New Jersey, and Pennsylvania,
      152–153
   Pennsylvania Dutch cooking of, 157
   recipes, 161–190 (*See also* Recipe Index)
   regional ingredients, 190–191
   topography and climate, 155
   traditional cuisine of, 153–154
Midwest, 408–409, 412–416. *See also*
   Central Farmlands
Migrant workers, 553
Migration, 4, 29, 88, 91, 150
M & I International Foods, 804
Militello, Mark, 734
Miller, Mark, 562
Mining camp cooking, 547–548
Mirepoix, 241
Mirliton, 244, 733
Mission District (California), 550
Mission system, 310
Mississippi Delta, 237
Mofongo, 741
Mojo criollo, 741
Molasses, 94
Molting, 199
Mondongo, 742
Monoculture system, 414
Monterey Jack cheese, 555
Moonshine, 371
Mormons, 509, 514–515
Morton's of Chicago, 420
Mother-of-pearl, 556
Moussa, 243
Mudbugs, 254
Muffaletta, 255
Muktuk, 610
Mushrooms, 614
Mussels, 98, 206
Mutton, 513

Nachos, 470
National cuisines, 21
Native Americans
   and American Southwestern cuisine,
      304–309
   Appalachian South, 362–364
   California, 545–546
   Central Farmlands, 410–411
   Chesapeake Bay Shore, 197–198
   foundation foods of, 16–17
   influence on modern cuisine, 17–18
   Louisiana, 238–239, 242–243
   Mid-Atlantic, 150–151

New England, 88–91
New York City, 790–791
Pacific Northwest, 605–610
Plantation South, 28–36
Rocky Mountains and Great Basin,
   509, 511
South Florida, 723–726
Southwestern American Native American
   microcuisine, 318
Three Sisters crops, 17, 30–31, 89, 150,
   238, 306–307, 410, 462, 464
western plateau, 462–464
Necks (tidewater), 196
New Amsterdam, 790
New England, *84–108*
   Acadian-American microcuisine, 107
   colonial cuisine, 92–94
   cuisine elements, 90, 96
   defining dishes, 103–106
   dining out in, 100–101
   immigrant cooking in, 101–102
   Native Americans, 88–91
   Pilgrims and Puritans, 91–92
   recipes, 109–137 (*See also* Recipe Index)
   regional ingredients, 138–145
   topography and climate, 87–88
   Yankee culture and traditional cuisine,
      95–100
New England boiled dinner, 93
New Jersey farming and fishing, 152
New Orleans, 239–240, 245, 254–256
New World cuisine, 735
New York City, *786–810*
   American cooking in, 799–800
   defining dishes, 807–809
   food markets, 801
   food products, 152
   and French cooking, 797–798
   haute ethnic, 804–805
   immigrants in, 794–797, 802–805
   ingredients, 845–849
   Italian-American and Jewish-American
      microcuisines, 805–806
   Native Americans and colonists in,
      790–791
   nouvelle cuisine, 799
   recipes, 811–843 (*See also* Recipe Index)
   as a restaurant city, 791–794
   steakhouses, 792
   topography and climate, 789–790
   the World's Fair, 797
New York State. *See* Mid-Atlantic
Niche market products, 156
Ninfa's, 317
9th Street Italian Market, Philadelphia, 155
Nirvana restaurant, 805
Nixtamal/nixtamalization, 309
Nobu, 805
Nor'easter, 88
Nouvelle cuisine, 561, 799
Nouvelle Orleans, 239
Nuevo Latino cuisine, 735, 742
Nuts, 368, 614, 669

Ogallala Aquifer, 408
Ohio River Valley, 409, 410
Okra, 243

Okra gumbo, 248
Old Bay seasoning, 205
Old-growth forests, 605
Old Homestead steakhouse, 792
Old sour, 727
Old World cuisines. *See also* Immigrants
    Basque, 512–514
    defined, 8, 18
    English, 39, 92–93, 369–370
    French, 240–242
    Holland Dutch, 151
    Polish, 422
    Rhineland, 153, 365, 370
    Scots and Scots-Irish, 364
Old World dishes, 8
Olives and olive oil, 554
100th longitudinal meridian, 408
Open-hearth cooking, 38
Open-ocean fish, 655
Oregon Trail, 612
Oscar of the Waldorf, 792
Ota, Amy Ferguson, 669
Oyster dredge, 203
Oysters, 97, 200–201, 203, 254, 512
Oysters Rockefeller, 255

Pacific Northwest, *600–621*
    Alaskan cooking, 617
    cuisine elements, 610
    defining dishes, 618–620
    European and American settlement,
        610–612
    ingredients, 642–645
    modern cuisine, 616–617
    Native Americans, 605–610
    recipes, 622–640 (*See also* Recipe Index)
    topography and climate, 603–605
    traditional cooking, 612–616
Pacific Railway Act, 512
Pacific Rim, 541–545. *See also* Anglo-Asian
    California
Padovani, Philippe, 669
Pad Thai noodles, 803
Pain perdu, 242, 244
Pakistani cuisine, 803–804
Palace Hotel, 549
The Palm, 792
Palm hearts, 724
Palouse Valley, 508
Pan Asian influence, 558
Panhandle, 605
Paniolos, 661
Papershell, 199
Parched corn, 35
Parker, John Palmer, 661
Parker House, 101
Parker House rolls, 101
Pashka, 618
Pasteles, 741
Paunch cooking, 464
Pawpaws, 369
Peeler, 199
Pellagra, 45
Pemmican, 464
Pennsylvania Dutch, 153–154, 157, 205
Pepper Jack cheese, 555
Pequín chile, 307

Perino's, 560
Permafrost, 605
Peroche, 618
Peter Luger steakhouse, 792
Philadelphia cuisine, 154–155
Pho, 803
Piedmont, 27
Pies, 94, 100
Pigeon peas, 740
Pike Place Market, 615–616
Piki bread, 318
Pilgrims and Puritans, 91–92
Pilot crackers, 94
Pineapple cultivation, Hawai'i, 660
Pink singing scallops, 615
Pioneer cooking
    Appalachian South, 364–365
    California, 547–549, 557
    Central Farmlands, 412
    Midwest agriculture and, 412–416
    Pacific Northwest, 610–612
    pioneer cuisine, 8, 18–19
    pioneers defined, 4
    provisions, 364, 467–468
    Rocky Mountains and Great Basin,
        509–511
Piquante (sauce), 250
Pirogue, 245
Pirozhki, 417
Pirozhki pastry turnovers, 804
Pit barbecue, 725
Pit roasting, 33, 656
Pizzeria Uno, 421
Plains equestrians, 463–464
Planking, 609
Plant, Henry, 729
Plantation South, *24–51*
    climate, 27–28
    colonial cuisine of, 36–41
    contemporary cuisine of, 46
    cuisine elements, 28, 39, 43, 46
    defining dishes of, 47–49
    future cuisine of, 46
    influence on Louisiana cuisine, 243
    low country microcuisine, 46–47
    Native Americans of, 28–36
    planter and slave cuisine of, 43–45
    post-Civil War cuisine of, 44–46
    recipes, 52–79 (*See also* Recipe Index)
    regional ingredients, 80–83
    slavery and, 41–44
    Soul Food microcuisine, 20, 44, 47
    topography, 27
Planter cuisine, 43–44
Plate lunch, 667
Ployes, 107
Po'boy sandwich, 255
Poi, 657–658
Poi suppers, 662
Poke, 656, 658, 666
Poke sallet, 368
Polish influence, 422
Polynesian migration, 651–652
Polynesian Triangle, 649
Pompano en Papillote, 255
Ponce de Leon, 726
Pones, 238

Popcorn crawfish, 256
Portale, Alfred, 799
Portuguese cuisine, 101–102, 156, 662
Posole, 309
Postcontact cuisine, 8
Potatoes, 370
Potlatch, 607
Poultry. *See* Meat and poultry
Poutine, 415
Powhatan Confederacy, 31, 36
Prairie, western plateau, 408, 461
Precontact cuisine, 8
Preserved foods. *See* Food preservation
Prohibition, 556, 794
Proteins. *See* Foundation foods
Prudhomme, Paul, 253, 256, 800
Puck, Wolfgang, 563, 564
Pueblo tribes, 305, 308
Puerto Rico, 739–744, 779–784. *See also*
    South Florida and Puerto Rico
Pullman loaf, 417
Pupu platter, 561, 667

Quahogs, 97
Quaker Oats, 316
Quakers, 152–153
Queen Liliuokalani, 659
Quesadillas, 314
Queso fundido, 314
Quick breads, 92
Quinoa, 516

Railroads, 372, 414, 418, 465, 512,
    612, 729
Rain shadow, 303, 461, 507, 605, 650
Ralston, William, 549
Ramps, 368–369
Ramseyer, Charles, 616
Ranching, 464–467. *See also* Western
    and Central Ranchlands
Ranchlands beef, 416–417
Ranchos, 313
Rappahannock River Oysters, 200
Rathskellers, 794
Razorback hog, 238
Reading Terminal Market, 155
Recaito, 741
Recao, 740
Rector's, 792
Red beans 'n' rice, 250
Red flannel hash, 93
Reflector oven, 38
Regional cuisines, 9–21. *See also*
    each region
Religion, 17
Rémoulade sauce, 247
Rendering, 40
Renggli, Seppi, 798, 799
Restaurant Associates, 798
Restaurant cuisine
    Anglo-Asian California, 559–565
    Central Farmlands, 419–420
    Chesapeake Bay Shore, 203–204,
        203–206, 205–206
    Hawai'i, 667, 668
    Louisiana, 250, 253, 255
    Mexican Border, 315, 317–318

Restaurant cuisine (*Continued*)
  Mid-Atlantic, 155
  New England, 100–101
  New York City, 791–794
  Pacific Northwest, 614, 616–617
  Plantation South, 46
  Rocky Mountains, 516
  South Florida, 734–735
Restaurant Leslie, 798
Rhineland, 153, 365
Rhode Island Jonnycakes, 90
Rib tips, 421
Rice, 243–244, 666
Rice flour Teleme, 555
Ristorante Caterina de' Medici, 156
Ristras, 312
Rita (hurricane), 255–256
River Café, Brooklyn, 800
Rockahominie, 34, 35
Rockfish, 201
Rocky Mountain oysters, 513
Rocky Mountains and Great Basin, *504–518*
  Basque immigrant cuisine, 512–514
  cuisine elements, 513
  defining dishes, 516–517
  early Rocky Mountain cooking, 511–512
  ingredients, 536–537
  international dining in Denver, 512
  Mormon cuisine, 514–515
  Native Americans, 509, 511
  pioneer cooking, 509–511
  recipes, 519–535 (*See also* Recipe Index)
  Rocky Mountain rain shadow, 303, 461, 507
  topography and climate, 507–508
  traditional cuisine, 515–516
  wildlife, 508–509
Rodriguez, Doug, 734, 735
Roe, 150
Roemer, Philip, 549
Rogue Creamery, 615
Romanoff's, 560
Root vegetables, 93
Ropa vieja, 742
Rosa Mexicano, 805
Rosenzweig, Ann, 800
Roux, 241, 248–249
Royal Palm Hotel, 729
Rum, 94
Ruminants, 610
Runzas, 417
Russian influence, 611–612, 618, 804
Rye 'n' Injun, 95

Salads, 420, 553–554, 558–559, 736
Salinity, 195, 238
Salmon, 607–609, 608, 615
Salmon bellies, 613
Salmon cheeks, 608, 613
Salsas, 316–317, 736
Salt cod, 96
Salt pork, 93
Salt-rising bread, 514
Samp, 38
Sam's Grill and Seafood Restaurant, 549–550
San Antonio Chilley Stand, 470

Sandwich Islands, 659
San Francisco, 548–549
San Francisco's Greens, 562
Santa Fe Trail, 313, 511
Sashimi, 663, 666
Sauce Piquante, 250
Sausage, 245
Sawgrass, 722
Scablands, 603
Scallops, 97
Scandinavian influence, 413, 422, 618
Schreiber, Cory, 616
Scones, 515
Scots-Irish, 364–365
Scrod, 96
Scuppernong grapes, 368–369
Seabiscuits, 93–94
Seafood. *See* Fish and seafood
Seasoning meats, 40
Seasonings
  Appalachian South, 373
  Caribbean, 244
  Louisiana, 256
  as a category of ingredients, 6
  Central Farmlands and Cities, 418
  Chesapeake Bay Shore, 206
  Chinese, 557
  Colonial Mexican, 310
  Filipino, 664
  Hawai'i, 657
  Japanese, 558
  Korean, 664
  Mexican Border, 317
  New England, 96
  New England Native American, 90
  Old World Basque, 513
  Old World Basque cuisine, 513
  Old World English, 39
  Old World French, 241
  Old World Holland Dutch, 151
  Mid-Atlantic, 157
  Old-World Scots and Scots-Irish, 364
  Pacific Northwest Native American, 610
  Plantation South, 46
  Plantation South Native American, 28
  Portuguese, 662
  Precontact Navajo and Apache, 309, 317
  Precontact Pueblo, 308
  Ranchlands, 467
  South Florida, 736
  West African, 43
Seaweed, 98, 656
Second settlers, 4
Seminoles, 725
Serra, Junipero, 545
Seviche, 727
Seward, William, 612
Shad roe, 150
She-crab soup, 200
Shedder, 199
Sheep ranching, 472
Sheraton, Mimi, 798
Ship's biscuits, 93–94
Shore dinner, 97
Shortgrass prairie, 461
Shrimp, 254
Shuck bread, 35, 238

Shun Lee Dynasty, 804
Sierra Nevadas, 508, 541–542
Sillsalat, 618
Sir Francis Drake Hotel, 549
Slavery, 41–44, 240, 245, 308, 796
Sling bag simmering, 33, 89, 464
Slippery dumplings in gravy, 205
Sloughs, 722–723
Smith, John, 36–37
Smith & Wollensky steakhouse, 792
Smoked meats, 100
Smoke roasting, 33
Smoking, 40
Sod busters, 413
Sofkee, 725
Sofrito, 735
Soft-shell clams, 97
Soft-shell crabs, 199–200
Soil, 12–13
Soltner, André, 798
Sook, 200
Sopaipillas, 313
Sorghum syrup, 371
Soulé, Henri, 798
Soul food, 20, 44, 47, 420, 796–797
Sourdough, 469–470, 510
Sourdough Bread, 548
South Beach, Florida, 731, 734
Southern California, 544
South Florida and Puerto Rico, *718–744*
  American settlers, 727–728
  Cuban influence, 729, 737
  cuisine elements, 737
  defining dishes, Puerto Rico, 742–744
  defining dishes, South Florida, 738–739
  European exploration and settlement, 726–727
  Jamaican-American cooking, 734
  modern South Florida development, 729–731
  new South Florida cuisine, 734–736
  Puerto Rican cuisine, 739–744
  recipes, 745–770 (*See also* Recipe Index)
  regional ingredients, 779–784
  South Florida Native Americans, 723–726
  topography and climate, 721–723
  traditional South Florida cuisine, 732–733
  wildlife, 723
Southwestern American Native American microcuisine, 318
Southwestern cuisine. *See* Mexican Border
Soybeans, 415
Spam (Hormel's), 661, 666
Spanish influence. *See also* Mexican Border
  Appalachian South, 363
  California, 545–546, 554, 555, 556
  Hawai'i, 664
  Louisiana, 238–239, 244–246, 244–247
  Rocky Mountains and Great Basin, 513
  South Florida and Puerto Rico, 726–727, 729, 735, 739–741, 740
  Western and Central Ranchlands, 464–465
Spark's steakhouse, 792
Speakeasies, 794

Spider, 38
Spit barbecue, 724–725, 742
Spit roasting, 33, 656
Spring mix, 553–554
Squash, 17, 31, 90, 307. *See also* Three Sisters crops
Stack cake, 371
Starbucks, 616
Starches. *See* Foundation foods
Starter, 469–470
St. Augustine, 725
Steak fries, 420
Steakhouses, 419–420, 792
Steamed puddings, 100
Steamers, 97, 201
Steppe, 461
St. Louis–cut ribs, 419, 420
Stockli, Albert, 798–799
Stone crab claws, 732
St. Petersburg, Florida, 729
Strehl, Gary, 669
Striped bass (Chesapeake rockfish), 201
Sublimates, 303
Succotash, 91
Sugarcane, 244
Sunchokes, 31
Sunflowers, 31
Super-premium ice creams, 100
Surimi, 618
Surmain, André, 798
Sushi, 557, 663, 666
Susser, Allen, 734
Sustainable agriculture, 13, 562
Sutter, John, 547
Swamp cabbage, 728, 733
Swedish settlement, 151
Swidden agriculture, 30, 38, 87, 366
Sylvia's restaurant, 796–797

21 Club, 794
Tabla, 805
Table d'hôte, 562, 791
Taco Bell, 317
Tacos, 316
Tadich Grill (California), 549
Taíno people, Cuba, 740
Tallgrass prairie, 408
Tangier Oysters, 200
Taro, 654, 670
Tasso, 245
Technology. *See also* Cooking media and methods
  adverse effects of, 415–416
  economic viability of Alaska and, 617–618
  economic viability of the Pacific Northwest and, 612
  horticultural, 414
  industrial food production, 157
  irrigation and well-drilling, 13, 408, 414, 551, 719, 729
  mechanization, 551, 612, 617–618
  New York Automat, 793
  as part of food culture, 5
  rail transportation, 414, 729
  refrigeration and rail shipping, 203
Tectonic plates, 541
Tekesta, 723

Teleme cheese, 555
Tepary beans, 306
Teriyaki, 667
Terracing, 306, 651, 654
Terrapin, 155
Terra restaurant, 564
Terroir, 13
Texas cuisine, 313–314
The Four Seasons, 798–799
Three Sisters crops
  Appalachian South, 153
  Chesapeake Bay Shore, 198
  Louisiana, 239, 242
  Mexican Border, 198
  Native Americans, 17, 30–31, 89, 150, 238, 306–307, 410, 462, 464
  New England, 92
  New York, 791
  Rocky Mountains, 516
  South Florida and Puerto Rico, 725, 740
Tidewater area, 196
Tiki bars, 561
Tillamook cheese, 614
Tobacco, 31, 42
Tonging, 203
Tontine Coffee House, 791
Topography and climate
  Anglo-Asian California, 541–545
  Appalachian South, 361–362
  Central Farmlands, 406–410
  Chesapeake Bay Shore, 195–197
  Hawai'i, 649–651
  importance of, 13–15
  Louisiana, 237–238
  Mexican Border, 303–304
  Mid-Atlantic, 155
  New England, 87
  New York City, 789–790
  Pacific Northwest, 603–605
  Plantation South, 27
  Rocky Mountains and Great Basin, 507–508
  South Florida and Puerto Rico, 721–723
  western plateau, 461–462
Tornado alley, 462
Tortillas, 307, 312, 316
Tossed salad, 420, 559
Tostones, 741
Tower, Jeremiah, 562
Trader Vic's, 561
Traditional alkaline processing, 34
Trans-Appalachian flatlands, 408
Transcontinental Railroad, 465, 511, 512
Triangle of Trade, 94
Tschirky, Oscar, 791, 792
Tubers, 735
Tuna, 655
Tundra, 605
Turkey, 94
Turkish influence, 804
Turtle, 155, 253

Union Square Café, 800
Upwelling, 543

Van Aken, Norman, 734, 735
Vancouver, George, 661

Vaqueros, 313, 317
Vegetables. *See* Foundation foods
Vegetarian, 246, 248, 558, 559, 561, 803–804
Verrazzano, Giovanni da, 790
Volcanoes, 603, 649–650
Vong, 805
Vongerichten, Jean-Georges, 805
Voyageurs, 412

Wagon trains, 511
Wakapapi, 464
Walleye, 417
Wanamaker's department store lunchroom, 155
Wang, T. T., 804
Washington, D.C. cuisine, 156
Washington State University's Creamery, 615
Water, 13, 408, 414, 551, 719, 729
Watermen (Chesapeake), 201–202
Waters, Alice, 562, 564, 734
Watershed, 195
Waxman, Jonathan, 800
West African cuisine, 43
Western and Central Ranchlands, 458–475
  contemporary culture and cuisine, 471–472
  cuisine elements, 467
  defining dishes, 473–474
  ingredients, 502–503
  Native Americanns of, 462–464
  ranching, 464–467
  recipes, 476–501 (*See also* Recipe Index)
  tourism, 472
  traditional cooking, 467–471
  western plateau topography and climate, 408, 461–462
Western shore, Chesapeake Bay, 195–196
West Indian cuisine, 804
Wheat flour and wheat bread, 92, 415. *See also* Foundation foods
Whiteman, Michael, 799
Wildings, 368
Wildlife, 362, 462, 508–509, 515, 607, 618, 723
Wild rice, 410–411
WillametteValley, 612
Wilson, Justin, 253
Windows on the World, 799–800
Wine, 241, 556–557, 616
Women's dining room, 791
Wong, Alan, 669
World's Fair, 1939, 797
World Trade Center, 799–800

Yamaguchi, Roy, 669
Yamamoto, Hidemasa, 564
Yams, 736
Yankee culture, 95–96
Yellow cheese, 370
Young, Brigham, 514
Young, Joseph, 514

Zarela, 805
Zea mais, 17

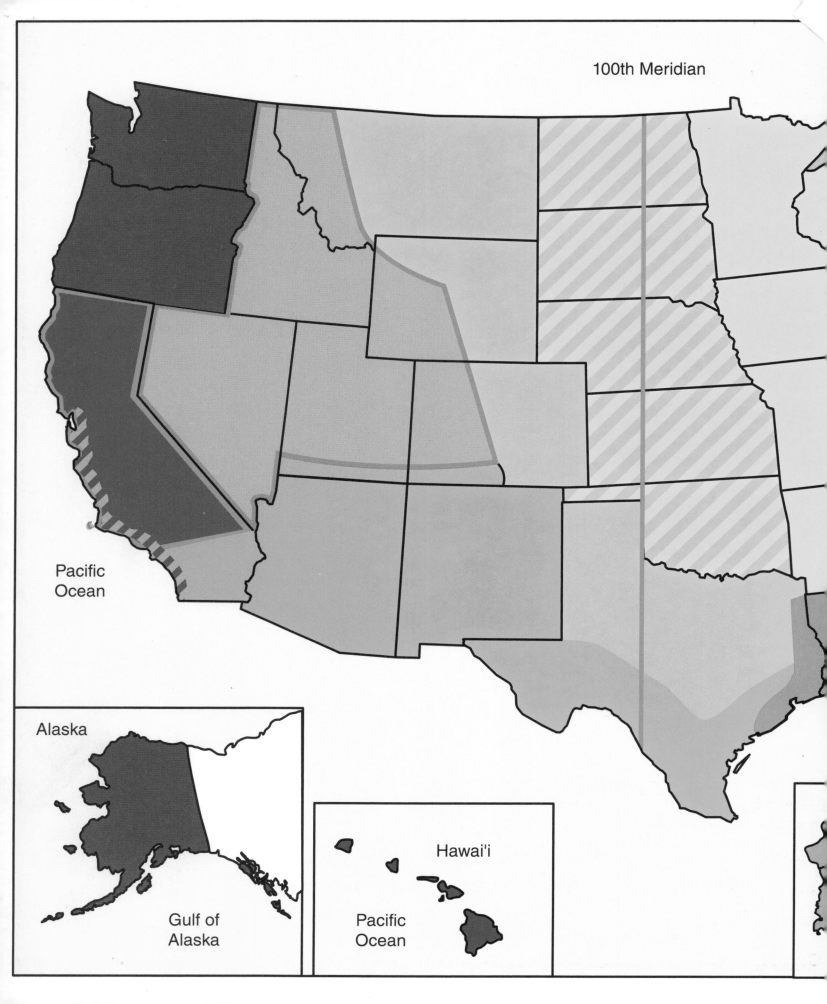

100th Meridian

Pacific
Ocean

Alaska

Gulf of
Alaska

Hawai'i

Pacific
Ocean